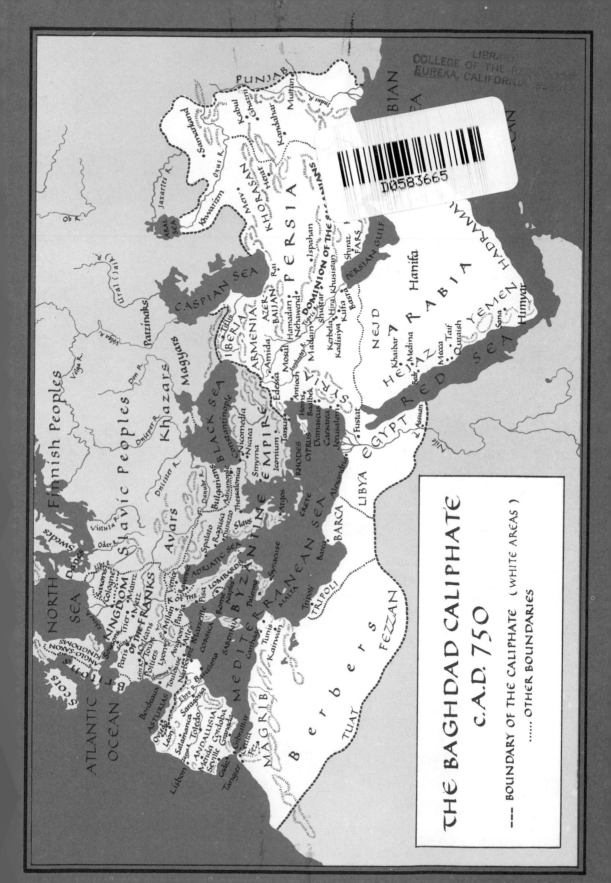

THE BAGHDAD CALIPHATE
c. A.D. 750

--- BOUNDARY OF THE CALIPHATE (WHITE AREAS)
..... OTHER BOUNDARIES

BY WILL DURANT

The Story of Philosophy
Transition
The Pleasures of Philosophy
Adventures in Genius

BY WILL AND ARIEL DURANT
THE STORY OF CIVILIZATION:

The Lessons of History
Interpretations of Life

THE STORY OF CIVILIZATION

THE
AGE OF FAITH

*A History of Medieval Civilization — Christian,
Islamic, and Judaic — from Constantine
to Dante: A.D. 325 – 1300*

By Will Durant

SIMON AND SCHUSTER

NEW YORK : 1950

ISBN 0-671-01200-1
Library of Congress Catalog Card Number 35-10016

MANUFACTURED IN THE UNITED STATES OF AMERICA
BY THE HADDON CRAFTSMEN, INC., SCRANTON, PA.

20   21   22   23   24   25

TO ETHEL, GORDON, AND JIM

To the Reader

THIS book aims to give as full and fair an account of medieval civilization, from A.D. 325 to 1300, as space and prejudice will permit. Its method is integral history—the presentation of all phases of a culture or an age in one total picture and narrative. The obligation to cover the economic, political, legal, military, moral, social, religious, educational, scientific, medical, philosophic, literary, and artistic aspects of four distinct civilizations—Byzantine, Islamic, Judaic, and West European—has made unification and brevity difficult. The meeting and conflict of the four cultures in the Crusades provides a measure of unity; and the tired reader, appalled by the length of the book, may find some consolation in learning that the original manuscript was half again longer than the present text.* Nothing has been retained except what seemed necessary to the proper understanding of the period, or to the life and color of the tale. Nevertheless certain recondite passages, indicated by reduced type, may be omitted by the general reader without mortal injury.

These two volumes constitute Part IV of a history of civilization. Part I, *Our Oriental Heritage* (1935), reviewed the history of Egypt and the Near East to their conquest by Alexander about 330 B.C., and of India, China, and Japan to the present century. Part II, *The Life of Greece* (1939), recorded the career and culture of Hellas and the Near East to the Roman Conquest of Greece in 146 B.C. Part III, *Caesar and Christ* (1944), surveyed the history of Rome and Christianity from their beginnings, and of the Near East from 146 B.C., to the Council of Nicaea in A.D. 325. This book continues the study of the white man's life to the death of Dante in 1321. Part V, *The Renaissance and the Reformation*, covering the period from 1321 to 1648, should appear in 1955; and Part VI, *The Age of Reason*, carrying the story to our own time, should be ready by 1960. This will bring the author so close to senility that he must forgo the privilege of applying the integral method to the two Americas.

Each of these volumes is designed as an independent unit, but readers familiar with *Caesar and Christ* will find it easier to pick up the threads of the present narrative. Chronology compels us to begin with those facets of the quadripartite medieval civilization which are most remote from our normal interest—the Byzantine and the Islamic. The Christian reader will be surprised by the space given to the Moslem culture, and the Moslem scholar will mourn the brevity with which the brilliant civilization of medieval

---

* An occasional hiatus in the numbering of the notes is due to last-minute omissions.

Islam has here been summarized. A persistent effort has been made to be impartial, to see each faith and culture from its own point of view. But prejudice has survived, if only in the selection of material and the allotment of space. The mind, like the body, is imprisoned in its skin.

The manuscript has been written three times, and each rewriting has discovered errors. Many must still remain; the improvement of the part is sacrificed to the completion of the whole. The correction of errors will be welcomed.

Grateful acknowledgment is due to Dr. Ilse Lichtenstadter, of the Asia Institute of New York, for reading the pages on Islamic civilization; to Dr. Bernard Mandelbaum, of the Jewish Theological Seminary of America, for reviewing the pages on medieval Jewry; to Professor Lynn Thorndike, of Columbia University, for the use of his translation of a passage from Alexander Neckham; to the Cambridge University Press for permission to quote translations from Edward G. Browne's *A Literary History of Persia*; to the Public Library of Los Angeles, and specifically to its Hollywood Branch, and to the Library of Congress, for the loan of books; to Miss Rose Mary DeWitte for typing 50,000 notes; to Dr. James L. Whitehead, Dr. C. Edward Hopkin, and Mrs. Will Durant for their learned aid in classifying the material; to Misses Mary and Flora Kaufman for varied assistance; and to Mrs. Edith Digate for her high competence in typing the manuscript.

This book, like all its predecessors, should have been dedicated to my wife, who for thirty-seven years has given me a patient toleration, protection, guidance, and inspiration that not all these volumes could repay. It is at her prompting that these two volumes are dedicated to our daughter, son-in-law, and grandson.

WILL DURANT

November 22, 1949

Table of Contents

BOOK II: ISLAMIC CIVILIZATION: A.D. 569-1258

BOOK V: THE CLIMAX OF CHRISTIANITY:
A.D. 1095-1300

List of Illustrations

Maps of Europe and the Byzantine Empire (A.D. 565), the Caliphate (A.D. 750), and Europe (A.D. 1190) will be found on the inside covers.

All photographs, with the exception of those otherwise marked, were secured through Bettmann Archive.

BOOK I

THE BYZANTINE ZENITH

325-565

CHRONOLOGICAL TABLE

Dates of rulers and popes are of their reigns. All dates are A.D.

226: Ardashir founds Sasanian dynasty
241–72: Shapur I of Persia
251–356: St. Anthony of Egypt
293–373: Athanasius
300–67: Hilary of Poitiers
309–79: Shapur II of Persia
310–400: Ausonius, poet
311–81: Ulfilas, apostle to the Goths
325: Council of Nicaea
325–403: Oribasius, physician
325–91: Ammianus Marcellinus, hist'n
329–79: St. Basil
329–89: Gregory Nazianzen
331: B. of Julian the Apostate
337: Death of Constantine
340–98: St. Ambrose
340–420: St. Jerome
345–407: St. John Chrysostom
345–410: Symmachus, senator
348–410: Prudentius, poet
353–61: Constantius sole emperor
354–430: St. Augustine
359–408: Stilicho, *patricius*
361–3: Julian emperor
363–4: Jovian emperor
364–7: Valentinian I, Western emp.
364–78: Valens Eastern emperor
365–408: Claudian, poet
366–84: Pope Damasus I
372: Huns cross the Volga
375–83: Gratian Western emperor
378: Battle of Hadrianople
379: Theon of Alexandria, math'n
379–95: Theodosius I, emperor
382–92: Affair of Altar of Victory
383–92: Valentinian II, Western emp.
386–404: Jerome's transl. of Bible
387: Baptism of Augustine
389–461: St. Patrick
390: Penance of Theodosius
392–4: Eugenius Western emperor
394: End of the Olympian Games
394–423: Honorius Western emp.
395–408: Arcadius Eastern emp.
395–410: Alaric I King of Visigoths
397: *Confessions* of St. Augustine
c. 400: *Saturnalia* of Macrobius
402: Alaric defeated at Pollentia
403: Ravenna becomes Western capital
404: End of gladiatorial games
407: Roman legions leave Britain
408–50: Theodosius II Eastern emp.
409: Pelagius, theologian
410: Alaric sacks Rome
410–85: Proclus, mathematician
413: Orosius, historian

413–26: Augustine's *City of God*
415: Murder of Hypatia
425: University of Constantinople
425–55: Valentinian III Western emp.
428–31: Nestorius patriarch at C'ple
429: Vandals conquer Africa
431: Council of Ephesus
432–82: Sidonius Apollinaris
432–61: St. Patrick in Ireland
433–54: Aëtius *patricius*
438: Theodosian Code
439: Gaiseric takes Carthage
440–61: Pope Leo I
440: Moses of Chorene, hist'n
449: Anglo-Saxons invade Britain
450–67: Marcian Eastern emp.
450–550: Great age of architecture and
mosaic at Ravenna
451: Attila defeated at Troyes
452: Leo I turns Attila from Rome
453: D. of Attila
454: Valentinian III slays Aëtius
455: Gaiseric sacks Rome
456: Ricimer rules the West
457–61: Majorian Western emp.
466–83: Visigoths conquer Spain
474–91: Zeno Eastern emp.
475–6: Romulus Augustulus
475–526: Theodoric King of Ostrogoths
475–524: Boethius, philosopher
476: End of Western Roman Empire
480–573: Cassiodorus, historian
481: Clovis and the Franks begin
conquest of Gaul
483–531: Kavadh I; Mazdakite communism
490–570: Procopius, historian
491–518: Anastasius I Eastern emp.
493–526: Theodoric rules Italy
525–605: Alexander of Tralles, physician
527–65: Justinian I Eastern emp.
529: Justinian closes schools of Athens;
St. Benedict founds Monte Cassino
530–610: Fortunatus, poet
531–79: Khosru I of Persia
532–7: Cathedral of St. Sophia
533: Belisarius regains Africa
535–53: The "Gothic War" in Italy
538–94: Gregory of Tours, hist'n
546–53: Totila rules Italy
552: Silk culture introduced into Europe
570–636: Isidore of Seville, encyclopedist
577: Anglo-Saxon victory at Deorham
589–628: Khosru II of Persia
616: Persians conquer Egypt
637–42: Arabs conquer Persia
641: End of Sasanian dynasty

CHAPTER I

Julian the Apostate

332-63

I. THE LEGACY OF CONSTANTINE

IN the year 335 the Emperor Constantine, feeling the nearness of death, called his sons and nephews to his side, and divided among them, with the folly of fondness, the government of the immense Empire that he had won. To his eldest son, Constantine II, he assigned the West—Britain, Gaul, and Spain; to his son Constantius, the East—Asia Minor, Syria, and Egypt; to his youngest son, Constans, North Africa, Italy, Illyricum, and Thrace, including the new and old capitals—Constantinople and Rome; and to two nephews Armenia, Macedonia, and Greece. The first Christian Emperor had spent his life, and many another, in restoring the monarchy, and unifying the faith, of the Roman Empire; his death (337) risked all. He had a hard choice: his rule had not acquired the sanctity of time, and could not ensure the peaceable succession of a sole heir; divided government seemed a lesser evil than civil war.

Civil war came none the less, and assassination simplified the scene. The army rejected the authority of any but Constantine's sons; all other male relatives of the dead Emperor were murdered, except his nephews Gallus and Julian; Gallus was ill, and gave promise of an early death; Julian was five, and perhaps the charm of his age softened the heart of Constantius, whom tradition and Ammianus credited with these crimes.[1] Constantius renewed with Persia that ancient war between East and West which had never really ceased since Marathon, and allowed his brothers to eliminate one another in fraternal strife. Left sole Emperor (353), he returned to Constantinople, and governed the reunified realm with dour integrity and devoted incompetence, too suspicious to be happy, too cruel to be loved, too vain to be great.

The city that Constantine had called Nova Roma, but which even in his lifetime had taken his name, had been founded on the Bosporus by Greek colonists about 657 B.C. For almost a thousand years it had been known as Byzantium; and *Byzantine* would persist as a label for its civilization and its art. No site on earth could have surpassed it for a capital; at Tilsit, in 1807, Napoleon would call it the empire of the world, and would refuse to yield it to a Russia fated by the direction of her rivers to long for its control. Here at any moment the ruling power could close a main door between East and West; here the commerce of continents would congregate, and deposit the products of a hundred states; here an army might stand poised to drive back the gentlemen of Persia, the Huns of the East, the Slavs of the North, and the barbarians of the West. The rushing waters provided defense on every side but one, which could be strongly walled; and in the Golden Horn—a quiet inlet of the Bosporus—war fleets and merchantmen might find a haven from attack or storm. The Greeks called the inlet Keras, *horn*, possibly from its shape; *golden* was later added to suggest the wealth brought to this port in fish and grain and trade. Here, amid a population predominantly Christian, and long inured to Oriental monarchy and pomp, the Christian emperor might enjoy the public support withheld by Rome's proud Senate and pagan populace. For a thousand years the Roman Empire would here survive the barbarian floods that were to inundate Rome; Goths, Huns, Vandals, Avars, Persians, Arabs, Bulgarians, Russians would threaten the new capital in turn and fail; only once in that millennium would Constantinople be captured—by Christian Crusaders loving gold a little better than the cross. For eight centuries after Mohammed it would hold back the Moslem tide that would sweep over Asia, Africa, and Spain. Here beyond all expectation Greek civilization would display a saving continuity, tenaciously preserve its ancient treasures, and transmit them at last to Renaissance Italy and the Western world.

In November 324 Constantine the Great led his aides, engineers, and priests from the harbor of Byzantium across the surrounding hills to trace the boundaries of his contemplated capital. Some marveled that he took in so much, but "I shall advance," he said, "till He, the invisible God who marches before me, thinks proper to stop." [2] He left no deed undone, no word unsaid, that could give to his plan, as to his state, a deep support in the religious sentiments of the people and in the loyalty of the Christian Church.

"In obedience to the command of God," [3] he brought in thousands of workmen and artists to raise city walls, fortifications, administrative buildings, palaces, and homes; he adorned the squares and streets with fountains and porticoes, and with famous sculptures conscripted impartially from a hundred cities in his realm; and to divert the turbulence of the populace he provided an ornate and spacious hippodrome where the public passion for games and gambling might vent itself on a scale paralleled only in degenerating Rome. The New Rome was dedicated as capital of the Eastern Empire on May 11, 330—a day that was thereafter annually celebrated with imposing ceremony. Paganism was officially ended; the Middle Ages of triumphant faith were, so to speak, officially begun. The East had won its spiritual battle against the physically victorious West, and would rule the Western soul for a thousand years.

Within two centuries of its establishment as a capital, Constantinople became, and for ten centuries remained, the richest, most beautiful, and most civilized city in the world. In 337 it contained some 50,000 people; in 400 some 100,000; in 500 almost a million.[4] An official document (*c.* 450) lists five imperial palaces, six palaces for the ladies of the court, three for high dignitaries, 4388 mansions, 322 streets, 52 porticoes; add to these a thousand shops, a hundred places of amusement, sumptuous baths, brilliantly ornamented churches, and magnificent squares that were veritable museums of the art of the classic world.[5] On the second of the hills that lifted the city above its encompassing waters lay the Forum of Constantine, an elliptical space entered under a triumphal arch at either end; porticoes and statuary formed its circumference; on the north side stood a stately senate house; at the center rose a famous porphyry pillar, 120 feet high, crowned with the figure of Apollo, and ascribed to Pheidias himself.*

From the Forum a broad Mese or Middle Way, lined with palaces and shops, and shaded with colonnades, led westward through the city to the Augusteum, a plaza a thousand by three hundred feet, named after Constantine's mother Helena as *Augusta*. At the north end of this square rose the first form of St. Sophia—Church of the Holy Wisdom; on the east side was a second senate chamber; on the south stood the main palace of the emperor, and the gigantic public Baths of Zeuxippus, containing hundreds of statues in marble or bronze; at the west end a vaulted monument—the Milion or Milestone—marked the point from which radiated the many magnificent roads (some still functioning) that bound the provinces to the capital. Here, too, on the west of the Augusteum, lay the great Hippodrome. Between this and St. Sophia the imperial or Sacred Palace spread, a complex structure of marble surrounded by 150 acres of gardens and porticoes. Here and there and in the suburbs were the mansions of the aristocracy. In the narrow, crooked, congested·side streets were the shops of the tradesmen, and the homes or tenements of the populace. At its western terminus the Middle Way opened through the "Golden Gate"—in the Wall of Constantine—upon the Sea of Marmora. Palaces lined the three shores, and trembled with reflected glory in the waves.

The population of the city was mainly Roman at the top, and for the rest overwhelmingly Greek. All alike called themselves Roman. While the language of the state was Latin, Greek remained the speech of the people, and, by the seventh century, displaced Latin even in government. Below the great officials and the senators was an aristocracy of landowners dwelling now in the city, now on their country estates. Scorned by these, but rivaling them in wealth, were the merchants who exchanged the goods of Constantinople and its hinterland for those of the world; below these, a swelling bureaucracy of governmental employees; below these the shopkeepers and master work-

---

* Blackened with time and fire, it is now known as the Burnt Pillar.

men of a hundred trades; below these a mass of formally free labor, voteless and riotous, normally disciplined by hunger and police, and bribed to peace by races, games, and a daily dole totaling 80,000 measures of grain or loaves of bread. At the bottom, as everywhere in the Empire, were slaves, less numerous than in Caesar's Rome, and more humanely treated through the legislation of Constantine and the mitigating influence of the Church.[6]

Periodically the free population rose from its toil to crowd the Hippodrome. There, in an amphitheater 560 feet long and 380 wide, seats accommodated from 30,000 to 70,000 spectators;[7] these were protected from the arena by an elliptical moat; and between the games they might walk under a shaded and marble-railed promenade 2766 feet long.[8] Statuary lined the *spina* or backbone of the course—a low wall that ran along the middle length of the arena from goal to goal. At the center of the *spina* stood an obelisk of Thothmes III, brought from Egypt; to the south rose a pillar of three intertwined bronze serpents, originally raised at Delphi to commemorate the victory of Plataea (479 B.C.); these two monuments still stand. The emperor's box, the *Kathisma*, was adorned in the fifth century with four horses in gilded bronze, an ancient work of Lysippus. In this Hippodrome the great national festivals were celebrated with processions, athletic contests, acrobatics, animal hunts and fights, and exhibitions of exotic beasts and birds. Greek tradition and Christian sentiment combined to make the amusements of Constantinople less cruel than those of Rome; we hear of no gladiatorial combats in the new capital. Nevertheless, the twenty-four horse and chariot races that usually dominated the program provided all the excitement that had marked a Roman holiday. Jockeys and charioteers were divided into Blues, Greens, Reds, and Whites, according to their employers and their garb; the spectators—and indeed the whole population of the city—divided likewise; and the principal fashions—the Blues and Greens—fought with throats in the Hippodrome and occasionally with knives in the streets. Only at the games could the populace voice its feelings; there it claimed the right to ask favors of the ruler, to demand reforms, to denounce oppressive officials, sometimes to berate the emperor himself as he sat secure in his exalted seat, from which he had a guarded exit to his palace.

Otherwise the populace was politically impotent. The Constantinian Constitution, continuing Diocletian's, was frankly monarchical. The two senates—at Constantinople and at Rome—could deliberate, legislate, adjudicate; but always subject to the imperial veto; their legislative functions were largely appropriated by the ruler's advisory council, the *sacrum consistorium principis*. The emperor himself could legislate by simple decree, and his will was the supreme law. In the view of the emperors, democracy had failed; it had been destroyed by the Empire that it had helped to win; it could rule a city, perhaps, but not a hundred varied states; it had carried liberty into license, and license into chaos, until its class and civil war had threatened the economic and political life of the entire Mediterranean world. Diocletian and Constantine concluded that order could be restored only by restricting higher offices to an aristocracy of patrician counts (*comites*) and dukes (*duces*), recruited not by birth but through appointment by an emperor who possessed full responsibility and power, and was clothed with all the awesome prestige of ceremonial inaccessibility, Oriental pomp, and ecclesiastical coronation, sanctification, and support. Perhaps the system was warranted by the situation; but it left no check upon the ruler except the advice of complaisant aides and the fear of sudden death. It created a remarkably efficient administrative and judicial organization, and kept the Byzantine Empire in existence for a millennium; but at the cost of political stagnation, public atrophy, court conspiracies, eunuch intrigues, wars of succession, and a score of palace revolutions that gave the throne occasionally to competence, seldom to integrity, too often to an unscrupulous adventurer, an oligarchic cabal, or an imperial fool.

II. CHRISTIANS AND PAGANS

In this Mediterranean world of the fourth century, where the state depended so much on religion, ecclesiastical affairs were in such turmoil that government felt called upon to interfere even in the mysteries of theology. The great debate between Athanasius and Arius had not ended with the Council of Nicaea (325). Many bishops—in the East a majority [9]—still openly or secretly sided with Arius; i.e., they considered Christ the Son of God, but neither consubstantial nor coeternal with the Father. Constantine himself, after accepting the Council's decree, and banishing Arius, invited him to a personal conference (331), could find no heresy in him, and recommended the restoration of Arius and the Arians to their churches, Athanasius protested; a council of Eastern bishops at Tyre deposed him from his Alexandrian see (335); and for two years he lived as an exile in Gaul. Arius again visited Constantine, and professed adherence to the Nicene Creed, with subtle reservations that an emperor could not be expected to understand. Constantine believed him, and bade Alexander, Patriarch of Constantinople, receive him into communion. The ecclesiastical historian Socrates here tells a painful tale:

> It was then Saturday, and Arius was expecting to assemble with the congregation on the day following; but Divine retribution overtook his daring criminality. For going out from the imperial palace . . . and approaching the porphyry pillar in the Forum of Constantine, a terror seized him, accompanied by violent relaxation of his bowels. . . . Together with the evacuations his bowels protruded, followed by a copious hemorrhage, and the descent of the smaller intes-

tine; moreover, portions of his spleen and his liver were eliminated in the effusion of blood, so that he almost immediately died.[10]

Hearing of this timely purge, Constantine began to wonder whether Arius had not been a heretic after all. But when the Emperor himself died, in the following year, he received the rites of baptism from his friend and counselor Eusebius, Bishop of Nicomedia, an Arian.

Constantius took theology more seriously than his father. He made his own inquiry into the paternity of Jesus, adopted the Arian view, and felt a moral obligation to enforce it upon all Christendom. Athanasius, who had returned to his see after Constantine's death, was again expelled (339); church councils, called and dominated by the new Emperor, affirmed merely the likeness, not the consubstantiality, of Christ with the Father; ecclesiastics loyal to the Nicene Creed were removed from their churches, sometimes by the violence of mobs; for half a century it seemed that Christianity would be Unitarian, and abandon the divinity of Christ. In those bitter days Athanasius spoke of himself as *solus contra mundum*; all the powers of the state were opposed to him, and even his Alexandrian congregation turned against him. Five times he fled from his see, often in peril of his life, and wandered in alien lands; through half a century (323–73) he fought with patient diplomacy and eloquent vituperation for the creed as it had been defined under his leadership at Nicaea; he stood firm even when Pope Liberius gave in. To him, above all, the Church owes her doctrine of the Trinity.

Athanasius laid his case before Pope Julius I (340). Julius restored him to his see; but a council of Eastern bishops at Antioch (341) denied the Pope's jurisdiction, and named Gregory, an Arian, as bishop of Alexandria. When Gregory reached the city the rival factions broke into murderous riots, killing many; and Athanasius, to end the bloodshed, withdrew (342).[11] In Constantinople a similar contest raged; when Constantius ordered the replacement of the orthodox patriot Paul by the Arian Macedonius, a crowd of Paul's supporters resisted the soldiery, and three thousand persons lost their lives. Probably more Christians were slaughtered by Christians in these two years (342–3) than by all the persecutions of Christians by pagans in the history of Rome.

Christians divided on almost every point but one—that the pagan temples should be closed, their property confiscated, and the same weapons of the state used against them and their worshipers that had formerly assailed Christianity.[12] Constantine had discouraged, but not forbidden, pagan sacrifices and ceremonies; Constans forbade them on pain of death; Constantius ordered all pagan temples in the Empire closed, and all pagan rituals to cease. Those who disobeyed were to forfeit their property and their lives; and these penalties were extended to provincial governors neglecting to enforce the decree.[13] Nevertheless, pagan isles remained in the spreading Christian sea.

The older cities—Athens, Antioch, Smyrna, Alexandria, Rome—had a large sprinkling of pagans, above all among the aristocracy and in the schools. In Olympia the games continued till Theodosius I (379–95); in Eleusis the Mysteries were celebrated till Alaric destroyed the temple there in 396; and the schools of Athens continued to transmit, with mollifying interpretations, the doctrines of Plato, Aristotle, and Zeno. (Epicurus was outlawed, and became a synonym for atheist.) Constantine and his son continued the salaries of the scholarchs and professors who loosely constituted the University of Athens; lawyers and orators still flocked there to learn the tricks of rhetoric; and pagan sophists—teachers of wisdom—offered their wares to any who could pay. All Athens was fond and proud of Prohaeresius, who had come there as a poor youth, had shared one bed and cloak with another student, had risen to the official chair of rhetoric, and at eighty-seven was still so handsome, vigorous, and eloquent that his pupil Eunapius regarded him as "an ageless and immortal god." [14]

But the leading sophist of the fourth century was Libanius. Born at Antioch (314), he had torn himself away from a fond mother to go and study at Athens; offered a rich heiress as wife if he would stay, he declared that he would decline the hand of a goddess just to see the smoke of Athens.[15] He used his teachers there as stimuli, not oracles; and amid a maze of professors and schools he educated himself. After lecturing for a time at Constantinople and Nicomedia, he returned to Antioch (354), and set up a school that for forty years was the most frequented and renowned in the Empire; his fame (he assures us) was so great that his exordiums were sung in the streets.[16] Ammianus Marcellinus, St. John Chrysostom, and St. Basil were among his pupils. He enjoyed the favor of Christian princes, though he spoke and wrote in defense of paganism and offered sacrifice in the temples. When the bakers of Antioch went on strike he was chosen by both sides as arbitrator; when Antioch revolted against Theodosius I he was named by the chastened city to plead its cause before the Emperor.[17] He survived by almost a generation the assassination of his friend Julian, and the collapse of the pagan revival.

Fourth-century paganism took many forms: Mithraism, Neoplatonism, Stoicism, Cynicism, and the local cults of municipal or rustic gods. Mithraism had lost ground, but Neoplatonism was still a power in religion and philosophy. Those doctrines to which Plotinus had given a shadowy form—of a triune spirit binding all reality, of a Logos or intermediary deity who had done the work of creation, of soul as divine and matter as flesh and evil, of spheres of existence along whose invisible stairs the soul had fallen from God to man and might ascend from man to God—these mystic ideas left their mark on the apostles Paul and John, had many imitators among the Christians, and molded many Christian heresies.[18] In Iamblichus of Syrian Chalcis miracle was added to mystery in Neoplatonic philosophy: the mystic not only saw things unseen by sense, but—by touching God in ecstasy—he acquired divine powers of magic and divination. Iamblichus' disciple, Maximus of Tyre, combined the claim to mystic faculties with a devout and eloquent paganism that conquered Julian. Said Maximus, defending against Christian scorn the use of idols in pagan worship,

> God the father and the fashioner of all that is, older than the sun or sky, greater than time and eternity and all the flow of being, is unnamable by any lawgiver, unutterable by any voice, not to be seen by any eye. But we, being unable to apprehend His essence, use the help of sounds and names and pictures, of beaten gold and ivory and silver, of plants and rivers, torrents and mountain peaks, yearning for the knowledge of Him, and in our weakness naming after His nature all that is beautiful in this world. . . . If a Greek is stirred to the remembrance of God by the art of Pheidias, or an Egyptian by worshiping animals, or another man by a river or a fire, I have no anger for their divergences; only let them note, let them remember, let them love.[19]

It was in part the eloquence of Libanius and Maximus that won Julian from Christianity to paganism. When their pupil reached the throne Maximus rushed to Constantinople, and Libanius raised in Antioch a song of triumph and joy: "Behold us verily restored to life; a breath of happiness passes over all the earth, while a veritable god, under the appearance of a man, governs the world." [20]

III. THE NEW CAESAR

Flavius Claudius Iulianus was born in the purple at Constantinople in 332, nephew of Constantine. His father, his eldest brother, and most of his cousins were slain in the massacre that inaugurated the reign of Constantine's sons. He was sent to Nicomedia to be educated by its Bishop Eusebius; he received an overdose of Christian theology, and gave signs of becoming a saint. At seven he began to study classical literature with Mardonius; the old eunuch's enthusiasm for Homer and Hesiod passed down to his pupil, and Julian entered with wonder and delight into the bright and poetic world of Greek mythology.

In 341, for reasons now unknown, Julian and his brother Gallus were banished to Cappadocia, and were for six years practically imprisoned in the castle of Macellum. Released, Julian was for a time allowed to live in Constantinople; but his youthful vivacity, sincerity, and wit made him too popular for the Emperor's peace of mind. He was again sent to Nicomedia, where he took up the study of philosophy. He wanted to attend the lectures of Libanius there, but was forbidden; however, he arranged to have full notes of the master's discourses brought to him. He was now a handsome and im-

pressionable lad of seventeen, ripe for the dangerous fascination of philosophy. And while philosophy and free speculation came to him in all their
lure, Christianity was presented to him as at once a system of unquestionable
dogma and a Church torn with scandal and schism by the Arian dispute and
the mutual excommunications of East and West.

In 351 Gallus was created Caesar—i.e., heir apparent to the throne—and
took up the task of government at Antioch. Safe for a while from imperial
suspicion, Julian wandered from Nicomedia to Pergamum to Ephesus,
studying philosophy under Edesius, Maximus, and Chrysanthius, who completed his secret conversion to paganism. Suddenly in 354 Constantius summoned both Gallus and Julian to Milan, where he was holding court. Gallus
had overreached his authority, and had ruled the Asiatic provinces with a
despotic cruelty that shocked even Constantius. Tried before the Emperor,
he was convicted of various offenses, and was summarily beheaded. Julian
was kept under guard for several months in Italy; at last he convinced a suspicious monarch that politics had never entered his head, and that his one
interest was in philosophy. Relieved to find that he had only a philosopher
to deal with, Constantius banished him to Athens (355). Having expected
death, Julian easily reconciled himself to an exile that placed him at the fountainhead of pagan learning, religion, and thought.

Six happy months he spent there studying in the groves that had heard
Plato's voice, making friends with Themistius and other immortal and forgotten philosophers, pleasing them with his eagerness to learn, and charming
the citizens with the grace and modesty of his conduct. He compared these
polished pagans, heirs of a millennium of culture, with the grave theologians
who had surrounded him in Nicomedia, or those pious statesmen who had
thought it necessary to kill his father, his brothers, and so many more; and
he concluded that there were no beasts more ferocious than Christians.[21]
He wept when he heard of famous temples overthrown, of pagan priests
proscribed, of their property distributed to eunuchs and partisans.[22] It was
probably at this time that in cautious privacy he accepted initiation into the
Mysteries at Eleusis. The morals of paganism condoned the dissembling of
his apostasy. His friends and teachers, who shared his secret, could hardly
consent to his revealing it; they knew that Constantius would crown him
with inopportune martyrdom, and they looked forward to the time when
their protégé would inherit the throne, and restore their emoluments and
their gods. For ten years Julian conformed in all externals to the Christian
worship, and even read the Scriptures publicly in church.[23]

Amid all this apprehensive concealment a second summons came to present himself before the Emperor at Milan. He hardly dared go; but word was
conveyed to him from the Empress Eusebia that she had promoted his cause
at court, and that he had nothing to fear. To his astonishment Constantius
gave him his sister Helena in marriage, conferred upon him the title of

Caesar, and assigned to him the government of Gaul (355). The shy young celibate, who had come dressed in the cloak of a philosopher, adopted uncomfortably the uniform of a general and the duties of matrimony. It must have further embarrassed him to learn that the Germans, taking advantage of the civil wars that had almost destroyed the military power of the Empire in the West, had invaded the Roman provinces on the Rhine, defeated a Roman army, sacked the old Roman *colonia* of Cologne, taken forty-four other towns, captured all Alsace, and advanced forty miles into Gaul. Faced with this new crisis, Constantius called upon the lad whom he both suspected and despised to metamorphose himself at once into an administrator and a warrior. He gave Julian a guard of 360 men, commissioned him to reorganize the army of Gaul, and sent him over the Alps.

Julian spent the winter at Vienne on the Rhone, training himself with military exercises, and zealously studying the art of war. In the spring of 356 he collected an army at Reims, drove back the German invaders, and recaptured Cologne. Besieged at Sens by the Alemanni—the tribe that gave a name to Germany—he repulsed their attacks for thirty days, managed to secure food for the population and his troops, and outwore the patience of the enemy. Moving south, he met the main army of the Alemanni near Strasbourg, formed his men into a crescent wedge, and with brilliant tactics and personal bravery led them to a decisive victory over forces far outnumbering his own.[24] Gaul breathed more freely; but in the north the Salian Franks still ravaged the valley of the Meuse. Julian marched against them, defeated them, forced them back over the Rhine, and returned in triumph to Paris, the provincial capital. The grateful Gauls hailed the young Caesar as another Julius, and his soldiers already voiced their hopes that he would soon be emperor.

He remained five years in Gaul, repeopling devastated lands, reorganizing the Rhine defenses, checking economic exploitation and political corruption, restoring the prosperity of the province and the solvency of the government, and at the same time reducing taxes. Men marveled that this meditative youth, so lately torn from his books, had transformed himself as if by magic into a general, a statesman, and a just but humane judge.[25] He established the principle that an accused person should be accounted innocent till proved guilty. Numerius, a former governor of Gallia Narbonensis, was charged with embezzlement; he denied the charge, and could not be confuted at any point. The judge Delfidius, exasperated by lack of proofs, cried out: "Can anyone, most mighty Caesar, ever be found guilty if it be enough to deny the charge?" To which Julian replied: "Can anyone be proved innocent if it be enough to have accused him?" "And this," says Ammianus, "was one of many instances of his humanity." [26]

His reforms made him enemies. Officials who feared his scrutiny, or envied his popularity, sent to Constantius secret accusations to the effect that

Julian was planning to seize the imperial throne. Julian countered by writing a fulsome panegyric of the Emperor. Constantius, still suspicious, recalled the Gallic prefect Sallust, who had co-operated loyally with Julian. If we may believe Ammianus, the Empress Eusebia, childless and jealous, bribed attendants to give Julian's wife an abortifacient whenever she was with child; when, nevertheless, Helena bore a son, the midwife cut its navel string so near the body that the child bled to death.[27] Amid all these worries Julian received from Constantius (360) a command to send the best elements of his Gallic army to join in the war against Persia.

Constantius was not unjustified. Shapur II had demanded the return of Mesopotamia and Armenia (358); when Constantius refused, Shapur besieged and captured Amida (now Diyarbekir in Turkish Kurdistan). Constantius took the field against him, and ordered Julian to turn over to the imperial legates, for the campaign in Asia, 300 men from each Gallic regiment. Julian protested that these troops had enlisted on the understanding that they would not be asked to serve beyond the Alps; and he warned that Gaul would not be safe should her army be so depleted. (Six years later the Germans successfully invaded Gaul.) Nevertheless, he ordered his soldiers to obey the legates. The soldiers refused, surrounded Julian's palace, acclaimed him *Augustus*—i.e., Emperor—and begged him to keep them in Gaul. He again counseled obedience; they persisted; Julian, feeling, like an earlier Caesar, that the die was cast, accepted the imperial title, and prepared to fight for the Empire and his life. The army that had refused to leave Gaul now pledged itself to march to Constantinople and seat Julian on the throne.

Constantius was in Cilicia when news reached him of the revolt. For another year he fought Persia, risking his throne to protect his country; then, having signed a truce with Shapur, he marched his legions westward to meet his cousin. Julian advanced with a small force. He stopped for a while at Sirmium (near Belgrade), and there at last proclaimed his paganism to the world. To Maximus he wrote enthusiastically: "We now publicly adore the gods, and all the army that followed me is devoted to their worship."[28] Good fortune rescued him from a precarious position: in November 361 Constantius died of a fever near Tarsus, in the forty-fifth year of his age. A month later Julian entered Constantinople, ascended the throne without opposition, and presided with all the appearance of a loving cousin over Constantius' funeral.

IV. THE PAGAN EMPEROR

Julian was now thirty-one. Ammianus, who saw him often, describes him as

> of medium stature. His hair lay smooth as if it had been combed; and his beard was shaggy and trained to a point; his eyes were bright

and full of fire, bespeaking the keenness of his mind. His eyebrows fine, his nose perfectly straight, his mouth a bit large, with full lower lip; his neck thick and bent, his shoulders large and broad. From his head to his fingertips he was well proportioned, and therefore was strong and a good runner.[29]

His self-portrait is not so flattering:

> Though nature did not make my face any too handsome, nor give it the bloom of youth, I myself out of sheer perversity added to it this long beard. . . . I put up with the lice that scamper about in it as though it were a thicket for wild beasts. . . . My head is disheveled; I seldom cut my hair or my nails, and my fingers are nearly always black with ink.[30]

He prided himself on maintaining the simplicity of a philosopher amid the luxuries of the court. He rid himself at once of the eunuchs, barbers, and spies that had served Constantius. His young wife having died, he resolved not to marry again, and so needed no eunuch; one barber, he felt, could take care of the whole palace staff; as for cooks, he ate only the plainest foods, which anyone could prepare.[31] This pagan lived and dressed like a monk. Apparently he knew no woman carnally after the death of his wife. He slept on a hard pallet in an unheated room;[32] he kept all his chambers unheated throughout the winter "to accustom myself to bear the cold." He had no taste for amusements. He shunned the theater with its libidinous panto-mimes, and offended the populace by staying away from the Hippodrome; on solemn festivals he attended for a while, but finding one race like another, he soon withdrew. At first the people were impressed by his virtues, his as-ceticism, his devotion to the chores and crises of government; they compared him to Trajan as a general, to Antoninus Pius as a saint, to Marcus Aurelius as a philosopher-king.[33] We are surprised to see how readily this young pagan was accepted by a city and an Empire that for a generation had known none but Christian emperors.

He pleased the Byzantine Senate by his modest observance of its traditions and prerogatives. He rose from his seat to greet the consuls, and in general played the Augustan game of holding himself a servant and delegate of the senators and the people. When, inadvertently, he infringed a senatorial privi-lege, he fined himself ten pounds of gold, and declared that he was subject like his fellow citizens to the laws and forms of the republic. From morn till night he toiled at the tasks of government, except for an intermission in the afternoon, which he reserved for study. His light diet, we are told, gave his body and mind a nervous agility that passed swiftly from one business or visitor to another, and exhausted three secretaries every day. He performed with assiduity and interest the functions of a judge; exposed the sophistry of advocates; yielded with grace to the sustained opinions of judges against his own; and impressed everyone with the righteousness of his decisions. He reduced the taxes levied upon the poor, refused the gift of golden crowns traditionally offered by each province to a new emperor, excused Africa from accumulated arrears, and remitted the excessive tribute heretofore exacted from the Jews.[34] He made stricter, and strictly enforced, the requirements for a license to practice medicine. His success as an administrator crowned his triumph as a general; "his fame," says Ammianus, "gradually spread until it filled the whole world." [35]

Amid all these activities of government his ruling passion was philosophy, and his never-forgotten purpose was to restore the ancient cults. He gave orders that the pagan temples should be repaired and opened, that their confiscated property should be restored, and their accustomed revenues renewed. He dispatched letters to the leading philosophers of the day, inviting them to come and live as his guests at his court. When Maximus arrived, Julian interrupted the address he was making to the Senate, ran at full speed to greet his old teacher, and introduced him with grateful praise. Maximus took advantage of the Emperor's enthusiasm, assumed ornate robes and luxurious ways, and was subjected, after Julian's death, to severe scrutiny of the means by which he had acquired so rapidly such unbecoming wealth.[36] Julian took no notice of these contradictions; he loved philosophy too much to be dissuaded from it by the conduct of philosophers. "If anyone," he wrote to Eumenius, "has persuaded you that there is anything more profitable to the human race than to pursue philosophy at one's leisure without interruptions, he is a deluded man trying to delude you." [37]

He loved books, carried a library with him on his campaigns, vastly enlarged the library that Constantine had founded, and established others. "Some men," he wrote, "have a passion for horses, others for birds, others for wild beasts; but I from childhood have been possessed by a passionate longing to acquire books." [38] Proud to be an author as well as a statesman, he sought to justify his policies with dialogues in the manner of Lucian, or orations in the style of Libanius, letters almost as fresh and charming as Cicero's, and formal philosophical treatises. In a "Hymn to a King's Son" he expounded his new paganism; in an essay "Against the Galileans" he gave his reasons for abandoning Christianity. The Gospels, he writes, in a preview of Higher Criticism, contradict one another, and agree chiefly in their incredibility; the Gospel of John differs substantially from the other three in narrative and theology; and the creation story of Genesis assumes a plurality of gods.

> Unless every one of these legends [of Genesis] is a myth, involving, as I indeed believe, some secret interpretation, they are filled with blasphemies against God. In the first place He is represented as ignorant that she who was created to be a helpmate to Adam would be the cause of man's fall. Secondly, to refuse to man a knowledge of

good and evil (which knowledge alone gives coherence to the human mind), and to be jealous lest man should become immortal by partaking of the tree of life—this is to be an exceedingly grudging and envious god. Why is your god so jealous, even avenging the sins of the fathers upon the children? . . . Why is so mighty a god so angry against demons, angels, and men? Compare his behavior with the mildness even of Lycurgus and the Romans towards transgressors. The Old Testament (like paganism) sanctioned and required animal sacrifice. . . . Why do you not accept the Law which God gave the Jews? . . . You assert that the earlier Law . . . was limited in time and place. But I could quote to you from the books of Moses not merely ten but ten thousand passages where he says that the Law is for all time.[39]

When Julian sought to restore paganism he found it not only irreconcilably diverse in practice and creed, but far more permeated with incredible miracle and myth than Christianity; and he realized that no religion can hope to win and move the common soul unless it clothes its moral doctrine in a splendor of marvel, legend, and ritual. He was impressed by the antiquity and universality of myths. "One could no more discover when myth was originally invented . . . than one could find out who was the first man that sneezed." [40] He resigned himself to mythology, and condoned the use of myths to instill morality into unlettered minds.[41] He himself told again the story of Cybele, and how the Great Mother had been carried in the form of a black stone from Phrygia to Rome; and no one could surmise from his narrative that he doubted the divinity of the stone, or the efficacy of its transference. He discovered the need of sensory symbolism to convey spiritual ideas, and adopted the Mithraic worship of the sun as a religious counterpart, among the people, of the philosopher's devotion to reason and light. It was not difficult for this poet-king to pen a hymn to Helios King Sun, source of all life, author of countless blessings to mankind; this, he suggested, was the real Logos, or Divine Word, that had created, and now sustained, the world. To this Supreme Principle and First Cause Julian added the innumerable deities and genii of the old pagan creeds; a tolerant philosopher, he thought, would not strain at swallowing them all.

It would be a mistake to picture Julian as a freethinker replacing myth with reason. He denounced atheism as bestial,[42] and taught doctrines as supernatural as can be found in any creed. Seldom has a man composed such nonsense as in Julian's hymn to the sun. He accepted the Neoplatonist trinity, identified Plato's creative archetypal Ideas with the mind of God, considered them as the intermediary Logos or Wisdom by which all things had been made, and looked upon the world of matter and body as a devilish impediment to the virtue and liberation of the imprisoned soul. Through piety, goodness, and philosophy, the soul might free itself, rise to the contemplation of spiritual realities and laws, and so be absorbed in the Logos, perhaps in the ultimate God Himself. The deities of polytheism were in Julian's belief impersonal forces; he could not accept them in their popular anthropomorphic forms; but he knew that the people would seldom mount to the abstractions of the philosopher, or the mystic visions of the saint. In public and private he practiced the old rituals, and sacrificed so many animals to the gods that even his admirers blushed for his holocausts.[43] During his campaigns against Persia he regularly consulted the omens, after the fashion of Roman generals, and listened carefully to the interpreters of his dreams. He seems to have credited the magic-mongering of Maximus.

Like every reformer, he thought that the world needed a moral renovation; and to this end he designed no mere external legislation but a religious approach to the inner hearts of men. He had been deeply moved by the symbolism of the Mysteries at Eleusis and Ephesus; no ceremony seemed to him better fitted to inspire a new and nobler life; and he hoped that these impressive rites of initiation and consecration might be extended from an aristocratic few to a large proportion of the people. According to Libanius, "he wished rather to be called a priest than an emperor." [44] He envied the ecclesiastical hierarchy of Christianity, its devoted priests and women, the communalism of its worship, the binding persuasiveness of its charity. He was not above imitating the better aspects of a religion which he hoped to supplant and destroy. He called new blood into the pagan priesthood, organized a pagan Church with himself as its head, and importuned his clergy to rival and surpass the Christian ministry in providing instruction to the people, distributing alms to the poor, offering hospitality to strangers, and giving examples of the good life.[45] He established in every town schools for lectures and expositions of the pagan faith. To his pagan priests he wrote like a Francis to fellow monks:

> Act towards me as you think I should act towards you; if you like, let us make this compact, that I am to point out to you what are my views concerning all your affairs, and you in return are to do the same for me concerning my sayings and doings. Nothing in my opinion could be more valuable for us than this reciprocity. . . .[46] We ought to share our money with all men, but more generally with the good and the helpless and the poor. And I will assert, though it will seem paradoxical, that it would be a pious act to share our clothes and food even with the wicked. For it is to the humanity in a man that we give, and not to his moral character.[47]

This pagan was a Christian in everything but creed· and as we read him, and discount his dead mythology, we suspect that he owed many lovable developments of his character to the Christian ethic which had been poured into him in childhood and early youth. How, then, did he behave to the religion in which he had been reared? He allowed Christianity full freedom of preaching, worship, and practice, and recalled the orthodox bishops exiled by Constantius. He withdrew from the Christian Church all state subsidies, and closed to Christians the chairs of rhetoric, philosophy, and literature in the universities, on the ground that these subjects could be taught with sympathy only by pagans.[48] He ended the exemption of the Christian clergy from taxation and burdensome civic duties, and the free use by the bishops of the facilities supplied for the public post. He forbade legacies to churches; made Christians ineligible to governmental offices; [49] ordered the Christians of each community to make full reparation for any damage that they had inflicted upon pagan temples during preceding reigns; and permitted the demolition of Christian churches that had been built upon the illegally seized lands of pagan shrines. When confusion, injustice, and riots resulted from this precipitate logic, Julian sought to protect the Christians, but he refused to change his laws. He was capable of sarcasm hardly becoming a philosopher when he reminded certain Christians who had suffered violence that "their Scriptures exhort them to support their misfortunes with patience." [50] Christians who reacted to these laws with insults or violence were severely punished; pagans who took to violence or insults in dealing with Christians were handled with leniency.[51] In Alexandria the pagan populace had nursed a special hatred for that Arian Bishop George who had taken Athanasius' see; when he provoked them by a public procession satirizing the Mithraic rites they seized him and tore him to pieces; and though few Christians cared to defend him, many Christians were killed or wounded in the attendant disorders (362). Julian wished to punish the rioters, but his advisers prevailed upon him to content himself with a letter of strong protest to the people of Alexandria. Athanasius now came out of hiding, and resumed his episcopal seat; Julian protested that this was done without consulting him, and ordered Athanasius to retire. The old prelate obeyed; but in the following year the Emperor died, and the Patriarch, symbol of the triumphant Galileans, returned to his see. Ten years later, aged eighty, he passed away, rich in honors and scars.

In the end Julian's passionate perseverance defeated his program. Those whom he injured fought him with subtle pertinacity; those whom he favored responded with indifference. Paganism was spiritually dead; it no longer had in it any stimulus to youth, any solace to sorrow, any hope beyond the grave. Some converts came to it, but mostly in expectation of political advancement or imperial gold; some cities restored the official sacrifices, but only in payment for favors; at Pessinus itself, home of Cybele, Julian had to bribe the inhabitants to honor the Great Mother. Many pagans interpreted paganism to mean a good conscience in pleasure. They were disappointed to find Julian more puritan than Christ. This supposed freethinker was the most pious man in the state, and even his friends felt it a nuisance to keep pace with his devotions; or they were skeptics who not too privately smiled at his

outmoded deities and solicitous hecatombs. The custom of sacrificing animals on altars had almost died out in the East, and in the West outside of
Italy; people had come to think of it as a disgrace or a mess. Julian called his
movement Hellenism, but the word repelled the pagans of Italy, who
scorned anything Greek that was not dead. He relied too much on philosophical argument, which never reached to the emotional bases of faith; his
works were intelligible only to the educated, who were too educated to accept them; his creed was an artificial syncretism that struck no roots in the
hopes or fancies of men. Even before he died his failure had become evident;
and the army that loved and mourned him named a Christian to succeed to
his throne.

V. JOURNEY'S END

His last great dream was to rival Alexander and Trajan: to plant the
Roman standards in the Persian capitals, and end once and for all the Persian
threat to the security of the Roman Empire. Eagerly he organized his army,
chose his officers, repaired the frontier fortresses, provisioned the towns that
would mark his route to victory. In the fall of 362 he came to Antioch, and
gathered his troops. The merchants of the city took advantage of the influx
to raise prices; the people complained that "everything is plentiful but everything is dear." Julian called in the economic leaders and pled with them to
restrain their profit seeking; they promised, but did not perform; and at last
he "appointed a fair price for everything, and made it known to all men."
Perhaps to force prices down he had 400,000 *modii* (pecks) of corn brought
in from other cities in Syria and Egypt.[52] The merchants protested that his
prices made profit impossible; they secretly bought up the imported corn,
took it and their goods to other towns, and Antioch found itself with much
money and no food. Soon the populace denounced Julian for his interference. The wits of Antioch made fun of his beard, and of his laborious attendance upon dead gods. He replied to them in a pamphlet, *Misopogon*, or
Hater of Beards, whose wit and brilliance hardly became an emperor. He
sarcastically apologized for his beard, and berated the Antiocheans for their
insolence, frivolity, extravagance, immorality, and indifference to the gods
of Greece. The famous park called Daphne, once a sacred shrine of Apollo,
had been changed into an amusement resort; Julian ordered the amusements
ended and the shrine restored; this had hardly been completed when a fire
consumed it. Suspecting Christian incendiarism, Julian closed the cathedral
of Antioch, and confiscated its wealth; several witnesses were tortured, and
a priest was put to death.[53] The Emperor's one consolation in Antioch was
his "feast of reason" with Libanius.

At last the army was ready, and in March 363 Julian began his campaign.
He led his forces across the Euphrates, then across the Tigris; pursued the re-

treating Persians, but was harassed and almost frustrated by their "scorched earth" policy of burning all crops in their wake; time and again his soldiers were near starvation. In this exhausting campaign the Emperor showed his best qualities; he shared every hardship with his men, ate their scant fare or less, marched on foot through heat and flood, and fought in the front ranks in every battle. Persian women of youth and beauty were among his captives; he never disturbed their privacy, and allowed no one to dishonor them. Under his able generalship his troops advanced to the very gates of Ctesiphon, and laid siege to it; but the inability to get food compelled retreat. Shapur II chose two Persian nobles, cut off their noses, and bade them go to Julian in the guise of men who had deserted because of this cruel indignity, and lead him into a desert. They obeyed; Julian trusted them, and followed them, with his army, for twenty miles into a waterless waste. While he was extricating his men from this snare they were attacked by a force of Persians. The attack was repulsed, and the Persians fled. Julian, careless of his lack of armor, was foremost in their pursuit. A javelin entered his side and pierced his liver. He fell from his horse and was carried to a tent, where his physicians warned him that he had but a few hours to live. Libanius alleged that the weapon came from a Christian hand, and it was noted that no Persian claimed the reward that Shapur had promised for the slaying of the Emperor. Some Christians, like Sozomen, agreed with Libanius' account, and praised the assassin "who for the sake of God and religion had performed so bold a deed." [54] The final scene (June 27, 363) was in the tradition of Socrates and Seneca. Julian, says Ammianus,

> lying in his tent, addressed his disconsolate and sorrowing companions: "Most opportunely, friends, has the time now come for me to leave this life, which I rejoice to restore to Nature at her demand." . . . All present wept, whereupon, even then maintaining his authority, he chided them, saying that it was unbecoming for them to mourn for a prince who was called for a union with heaven and the stars. As this made them all silent, he engaged with the philosophers Maximus and Priscus in an intricate discussion about the nobility of the soul. Suddenly the wound in his side opened wide, the pressure of the blood checked his breath, and after a draught of cold water for which he had asked, he passed quietly away, in the thirty-second year of his age.[55] *

The army, still in peril, required a commander; and its leaders chose Jovian, captain of the imperial guard. The new Emperor made peace with Persia by surrendering four of the five satrapies that Diocletian had seized some seventy years before. Jovian persecuted no one, but he promptly trans-

---

* The story that he died exclaiming, "Thou hast conquered, Galilean," appears first in the Christian historian Theodoret in the fifth century, and is now unanimously rejected as a legend.[56]

ferred state support from the pagan temples to the Church. The Christians of Antioch celebrated with public rejoicings the death of the pagan Emperor.[57] For the most part, however, the victorious Christian leaders preached to their congregations a generous forgetfulness of the injuries that Christianity had borne.[58] Eleven centuries would pass before Hellenism would have another day.

CHAPTER II

The Triumph of the Barbarians

325-476

I. THE THREATENED FRONTIER

PERSIA was but one sector of a 10,000-mile frontier through which, at any point and at any moment, this Roman Empire of a hundred nations might be invaded by tribes unspoiled by civilization and envious of its fruits. The Persians in themselves were an insoluble problem. They were growing stronger, not weaker; soon they would reconquer nearly all that Darius I had held a thousand years before. West of them were the Arabs, mostly penniless Bedouins; the wisest statesman would have smiled at the notion that these somber nomads were destined to capture half the Roman Empire, and all Persia too. South of the Roman provinces in Africa were Ethiopians, Libyans, Berbers, Numidians, and Moors, who waited in fierce patience for the crumbling of imperial defenses or morale. Spain seemed safely Roman behind its forbidding mountains and protecting seas; none surmised that it would become in this fourth century German, and in the eighth Mohammedan. Gaul now surpassed Italy in Roman pride, in order and wealth, in Latin poetry and prose; but in every generation it had to defend itself against Teutons whose women were more fertile than their fields. Only a small imperial garrison could be spared to protect Roman Britain from Scots and Picts on the west and north and from Norse or Saxon pirates on the east or south. Norway's shores were a chain of pirate dens; its people found war less toilsome than tillage, and counted the raiding of alien coasts a noble occupation for hungry stomachs or leisure days. In southern Sweden and its isles the Goths claimed to have had their early home; possibly they were indigenous to the region of the Vistula; in any case they spread as Visigoths southward to the Danube, and as Ostrogoths they settled between the Dniester and the Don. In the heart of Europe—bounded by the Vistula, the Danube, and the Rhine—moved the restless tribes that were to remake the map, and rename the nations, of Europe: Thuringians, Burgundians, Angles, Saxons, Jutes, Frisians, Gepidae, Quadi, Vandals, Alemanni, Suevi, Lombards, Franks. Against these ethnic tides the Empire had no protective wall except in Britain, but merely an occasional fort and garrison along the roads or rivers that marked the frontier limit (*limes*) of the Roman realm. The higher birth rate outside the Empire, and the higher standard of living within it, made immigration or invasion a manifest destiny for the Roman Empire then as for North America today.

Perhaps we should modify the tradition that speaks of these German tribes as barbarians. It is true that in calling them *barbari* the Greeks and Romans meant no compliment. The word was probably brother to the Sanskrit *varvara*, which meant a rough and letterless churl;[1] it appears again in *Berber*. But it was not for nothing that for five centuries the Germans had touched Roman civilization in trade and war. By the fourth century they had long since adopted writing and a government of stable laws. If we except the Merovingian Franks, their sexual morals were superior to those of the Romans and the Greeks.* Though they lacked the civility and graces of a cultured people, they often shamed the Romans by their courage, hospitality, and honesty. They were cruel, but hardly more so than the Romans; they were probably shocked to find that Roman law permitted the torturing of freemen to extort confessions or testimony.[3] They were individualistic to the point of chaos, while the Romans had now been tamed to sociability and peace. In their higher ranks they showed some appreciation of literature and art; Stilicho, Ricimer, and other Germans entered fully into the cultural life of Rome, and wrote a Latin that Symmachus professed to enjoy.[4] In general the invaders—above all, the Goths—were civilized enough to admire Roman civilization as higher than their own, and to aim rather at acquiring it than at destroying it; for two centuries they asked little more than admission to the Empire and its unused lands; and they shared actively in its defense. If we continue to refer to the German tribes of the fourth and fifth centuries as barbarians, it will be in surrender to the convenience of custom, and with these reservations and apologies.

South of the Danube and the Alps the swelling tribes had already entered the Empire by peaceable immigration, even by royal invitation. Augustus ✓ had begun the policy of settling barbarians within the frontier, to replenish vacant areas and legions that the infertile and unmartial Romans no longer filled; and Aurelius, Aurelian, and Probus had adoped the plan. By the end of the fourth century the Balkans and eastern Gaul were predominantly German; so was the Roman army; many high offices, political as well as military, were in Teutonic hands. Once the Empire had Romanized such elements; now the immigrants barbarized the Romans.[5] Romans began to wear fur coats in barbarian style, and to let their hair flow long; some even took to trousers, evoking outraged imperial decrees (397, 416).[6]

The cue for the great invasion came from far-off Mongolian plains. The

---

* Our chief authority here is still the moralistic Tacitus (*Germania*, 18-19); but cf. a letter of Bishop Boniface, *c.* 756: "In old Saxony if a virgin in her father's house, or a married woman under the protection of her husband, should be guilty of adultery, they burn her, strangled by her own hand, and hang her seducer over her grave; or else, cutting off her garments to the waist, modest matrons whip her, and pierce her with knives, till they destroy her"[2]—an extreme device for pegging a price.

Hsiung-nu, or Hiung-nu, or Huns, a division of the Turanian stock, occupied in our third century the region north of Lake Balkash and the Aral Sea.
According to Jordanes, their chief weapon was their physiognomy.

> By the terror of their features they inspired great fear in those
> whom perhaps they did not really surpass in war. They made their
> foes flee in horror because their swarthy aspect was fearful, and they
> had . . . a shapeless lump instead of a head, with pinholes rather than
> eyes. They are cruel to their children on the very day of their birth.
> For they cut the cheeks of the males with a sword, so that before they
> receive the nourishment of milk, they must learn to endure wounds.
> Hence they grow old beardless, and with faces scarred by the sword.
> They are short in stature, quick in bodily movement, alert horsemen,
> ready in the use of bow and arrow, broad-shouldered, and with firm
> set necks always erect in pride.[7]

War was their industry, pasturing cattle was their recreation. "Their
country," said a proverb, "is the back of a horse." [8] Armed with arrows and
knives, equipped with courage and speed, driven by the exhaustion of their
lands and the pressure of their eastern enemies, they advanced into Russia
about 355, overcame and absorbed the Alani, crossed the Volga (372?), and
attacked the almost civilized Ostrogoths in the Ukraine. Ermanaric, the centenarian Ostrogothic King, fought bravely, was defeated, and died, some
said, by his own hand. Part of the Ostrogoths surrendered and joined the
Huns; part fled west into the lands of the Visigoths north of the Danube. A
Visigothic army met the advancing Huns at the Dniester, and was overwhelmed; a remnant of the Visigoths begged permission of the Roman authorities on the Danube to cross the river and settle in Moesia and Thrace.
The Emperor Valens sent word that they should be admitted on condition
that they surrender their arms, and give up their youths as hostages. The
Visigoths crossed, and were shamelessly plundered by imperial officials and
troops; their girls and boys were enslaved by amorous Romans; but after
diligent bribery the immigrants were allowed to keep their arms. Food was
sold them at famine prices, so that hungry Goths gave ten pounds of silver,
or a slave, for a joint of meat or a loaf of bread; at last the Goths were forced
to sell their children into bondage to escape starvation.[9] When they showed
signs of revolt the Roman general invited their leader Fritigern to a banquet,
plotting to kill him. Fritigern escaped, and roused the desperate Goths to
war. They pillaged, burned, and killed until almost all Thrace was laid waste
by their hunger and their rage. Valens hurried up from the East and met the
Goths on the plains of Hadrianople with an inferior force mostly composed
of barbarians in the service of Rome (378). The result, in the words of Ammianus, was "the most disastrous defeat encountered by the Romans since
Cannae" 594 years before.[10] The Gothic cavalry prevailed over the Roman
infantry, and from that day till the fourteenth century the strategy and tac-

tics of cavalry dominated the declining art of war. Two thirds of the Roman army perished, Valens himself was seriously wounded; the Goths set fire to the cottage in which he had taken refuge, and the Emperor and his attendants died in the flames. The victorious horde marched upon Constantinople, but failed to pierce the defenses organized by Valens' widow Dominica. The Visigoths, joined by Ostrogoths and Huns who crossed the unprotected Danube, ravaged the Balkans at will from the Black Sea to the borders of Italy.

II. THE SAVIOR EMPERORS: 364–408

In this crisis the Empire did not cease to produce able rulers. On Jovian's death the army and Senate had passed the crown to Valentinian, a blunt and Greekless soldier recalling Vespasian. With the consent of the Senate he had appointed his younger brother Valens as Augustus and Emperor in the East, while he himself chose the apparently more dangerous West. He refortified the frontiers of Italy and Gaul, built up the army to strength and discipline, and again drove the encroaching Germans back across the Rhine. From his capital at Milan he issued enlightened legislation forbidding infanticide, founding colleges, extending state medicine in Rome, reducing taxes, reforming a debased coinage, checking political corruption, and proclaiming freedom of creed and worship for all. He had his faults and his weaknesses; he was capable of cold cruelties to enemies; and if we may believe the historian Socrates, he legalized bigamy to sanction his marriage with Justina,[11] whose beauty had been too generously described to him by his wife. Nevertheless, it was a tragedy for Rome that he died so soon (375). His son Gratian succeeded to his power in the West, lived up to his father for a year or two, then abandoned himself to amusements and the chase, and left the government to corrupt officials who put every office and judgment up for sale. The general Maximus overthrew him and invaded Italy in an effort to displace Gratian's successor and half brother Valentinian II; but the new Emperor of the East, Theodosius I the Great, marched westward, defeated the usurper, and set the young Valentinian firmly on his Milan throne (388).

Theodosius was a Spaniard. He had distinguished himself as a general in Spain, Britain, and Thrace; he had persuaded the victorious Goths to join his army instead of fighting it; he had ruled the Eastern provinces with every wisdom except tolerance; and half the world looked in awe at his astonishing assemblage of handsome features and majestic presence, ready anger and readier mercy, humane legislation and sternly orthodox theology. While he was wintering at Milan a disturbance characteristic of the times broke out in Thessalonica. The imperial governor there, Botheric, had imprisoned for scandalous immorality a charioteer popular with the citizens. They demanded his release; Botheric refused; the crowd overcame his garrison, killed him and his aides, tore their bodies to pieces, and paraded the streets displaying the severed limbs as emblems of victory. The news of this outburst stirred Theodosius to fury. He sent secret orders that the entire population of Thessalonica should be punished. The people were invited into the hippodrome for games; hidden soldiery fell upon them there, and massacred 7000 men, women, and children (390).[12] Theodosius sent a second order mitigating the first, but it came too late.

The Roman world was shocked by this savage retaliation, and Ambrose, who administered with stoic Christianity the see of Milan, wrote to the Emperor that he, the Bishop, could not again celebrate Mass in the imperial presence until Theodosius should have atoned before all the people for his crime. Though privately remorseful, the Emperor was reluctant to lower the prestige of his office by so public a humiliation. He tried to enter the cathedral, but Ambrose himself barred the way. After weeks of vain efforts Theodosius yielded, stripped himself of all the insignia of empire, entered the cathedral as a humble penitent, and begged heaven to forgive his sins (390). It was an historic triumph and defeat in the war between Church and state.

When Theodosius returned to Constantinople, Valentinian II, a lad of twenty, proved inadequate to the problems that enmeshed him. His aides deceived him, and took power into their venal hands; his master of the militia, the pagan Frank, Arbogast, assumed imperial authority in Gaul; and when Valentinian went to Vienne to assert his sovereignty he was assassinated (392). Arbogast, inaugurating a long line of barbarian kingmakers, raised to the throne of the West a mild and manageable scholar. Eugenius was a Christian, but so intimate with the pagan parties in Italy that Ambrose feared him as another Julian. Theodosius marched westward again, to restore legitimacy and orthodoxy with an army of Goths, Alani, Caucasians, Iberians, and Huns; among its generals were the Goth Gainas who would seize Constantinople, the Vandal Stilicho who would defend Rome, and the Goth Alaric who would sack it. In a two-day battle near Aquileia, Arbogast and Eugenius were defeated (394); Eugenius was surrendered by his soldiers and slain; Arbogast died by his own hand. Theodosius summoned his eleven-year-old son Honorius to be Emperor of the West, and named his eighteen-year-old son Arcadius as co-Emperor of the East. Then, exhausted by his campaigns, he died at Milan (395), in the fiftieth year of his age. The Empire that he had repeatedly united was again divided, and except briefly under Justinian it would never be united again.

Theodosius' sons were effeminate weaklings nursed in an enfeebling security. Though their morals were almost as excellent as their intentions, they were not made to be pilots in a storm; they soon lost hold of affairs, and surrendered administration and policy to their ministers: in the East to the corrupt and avaricious Rufinus, in the West to the able but unscrupulous Stilicho. In 398 this noble Vandal arranged the marriage of his daughter

Maria to Honorius, hoping to be the grandfather as well as the father-in-law of an emperor. But Honorius proved to be as free of passion as of intellect; he spent his time feeding the imperial poultry with tender affection, and Maria died a virgin after having been for ten years a wife.[13]

Theodosius had kept the Goths at peace by employing them in war, and by paying them an annual subsidy as allies. His successor refused to continue this subsidy, and Stilicho dismissed his Gothic troops. The idle warriors craved money and adventure, and their new leader, Alaric, provided both with a skill that outplayed the Romans in diplomacy as well as war. Why, he asked his followers, should the proud and virile Goth submit to be a hireling of effete Romans or Greeks, instead of using his courage and his arms to cut out from the dying Empire a kingdom of his own? In the very year of Theodosius' death, Alaric led almost the whole mass of Thracian Goths into Greece, marched unhindered through the pass of Thermopylae, massacred en route all men of military age, enslaved the women, ravaged the Peloponnesus, destroyed the temple of Demeter at Eleusis, and spared Athens only on receiving a ransom that absorbed most of the city's movable wealth (396). Stilicho went to the rescue, but too late; he maneuvered the Goths into an indefensible position, but made truce with them when a revolution in Africa called him back to the West. Alaric signed an alliance with Arcadius, who allowed him to settle his Goths in Epirus. For four years the Empire was at peace.

It was during those years that Synesius of Cyrene, half Christian bishop and half pagan philosopher, in an address before Arcadius' luxury-loving court at Constantinople, described with clarity and force the alternatives that faced Greece and Rome. How could the Empire survive if its citizens continued to shirk military service, and to entrust its defense to mercenaries recruited from the very nations that threatened it? He proposed an end to luxury and ease and the enlistment or conscription of a citizen army aroused to fight for country and freedom; and he called upon Arcadius and Honorius to rise and smite the insolent barbarian hosts within the Empire, and to drive them back to their lairs behind the Black Sea, the Danube, and the Rhine. The court applauded Synesius' address as an elegant oratorical exercise, and returned to its feasts.[14] Meanwhile Alaric compelled the armorers of Epirus to make for his Goths a full supply of pikes, swords, helmets, and shields.

In 401 he invaded Italy, plundering as he came. Thousands of refugees poured into Milan and Ravenna, and then fled to Rome; farmers took shelter within the walled towns, while the rich gathered whatever of their wealth they could move, and frantically sought passage to Corsica, Sardinia, or Sicily. Stilicho denuded the provinces of their garrisons to raise an army capable of stemming the Gothic flood; and at Pollentia, on Easter morning of 402, he pounced upon the Goths, who had interrupted pillage for prayer. The battle was indecisive; Alaric retreated, but ominously toward unprotected Rome; and only a massive bribe from Honorius persuaded him to leave Italy.

The timid Emperor, on Alaric's approach to Milan, had thought of transferring his capital to Gaul. Now he cast about for some safer place, and found it in Ravenna, whose marshes and lagoons made it impregnable by land, and its shoals by sea. But the new capital trembled like the old when the barbarian Radagaisus led a host of 200,000 Alani, Quadi, Ostrogoths, and Vandals over the Alps, and attacked the growing city of Florentia. Stilicho once more proved his generalship, defeated the motley horde with a relatively small army, and brought Radagaisus to Honorius in chains. Italy breathed again, and the imperial court of patricians, princesses, bishops, eunuchs, poultry, and generals resumed its routine of luxury, corruption, and intrigue.

Olympius, the chancellor, envied and distrusted Stilicho; he resented the great general's apparent connivance at Alaric's repeated escapes, and thought he detected in him the secret sympathy of a German with German invaders. He protested against the bribes that on Stilicho's prompting had been paid or pledged to Alaric. Honorius hesitated to depose the man who for twenty-three years had led Rome's armies to victory and had saved the West; but when Olympius persuaded him that Stilicho was plotting to put his son on the throne, the timid youth consented to his general's death. Olympius at once sent a squad of soldiers to carry out the decree. Stilicho's friends wished to resist; he forbade them, and offered his neck to the sword (408).

A few months later Alaric re-entered Italy.

III. ITALIAN BACKGROUND

The Western Roman Empire, toward the end of the fourth century, presented a complex picture of recovery and decline, of literary activity and sterility, of political pomp and military decay. Gaul prospered, and threatened Italian leadership in every field. Of the approximately 70,000,000 souls in the Empire, 20,000,000 or more were Gauls, hardly 6,000,000 were Italians; [15] the rest were mostly Greek-speaking Orientals; Rome itself since 100 A.D. had been ethnically an Oriental city. Once Rome had lived on the East, as modern Europe lived on its conquests and colonies till the middle of the twentieth century; the legions had sucked the products and precious metals of a dozen provinces into the mansions and coffers of the victors. Now conquest was ended and retreat had begun. Italy was forced to depend upon its own human and material resources; and these had been dangerously reduced by family limitation, famine, epidemics, taxation, waste, and war. Industry had never flourished in the parasitic peninsula; now that its markets were being lost in the East and Gaul, it could no longer support the urban population that had eked out doles by laboring in shops and homes. The *collegia* or guilds suffered from inability to sell their votes in a monarchy where voting was rare. Internal trade fell off, highway brigandage grew; and the once great roads, though still better than any before the nineteenth century, were crumbling into disrepair.

The middle classes had been the mainstay of municipal life in Italy; now they too were weakened by economic decline and fiscal exploitation. Every property owner was subject to rising taxes to support an expanding bureaucracy whose chief function was the collection of taxes. Satirists complained that "those who live at the expense of the public funds are more numerous than those who provide them." [16] Corruption consumed much of the taxes paid; a thousand laws sought to discourage, detect, or punish the malversation of governmental revenue or property. Many collectors overtaxed the simple, and kept the change; in recompense they might ease the tax burdens of the rich for a consideration.[17] The emperors labored to secure an honest collection; Valentinian I appointed in each town a Defender of the City to protect citizens from the chicanery of the *susceptores*; and Honorius remitted the taxes of towns that were in financial straits. Nevertheless, if we may believe Salvian, some citizens fled across the frontier to live under barbarian kings who had not yet learned the full art of taxation; "the agents of the Treasury seemed more terrible than the enemy." [18] Under these conditions the incentives to parentage weakened, and populations fell. Thousands of arable acres were left untilled, creating an economic vacuum that conspired with the surviving wealth of the cities to draw in the land-hungry barbarians. Many peasant proprietors, unable to pay their taxes or to defend their homes against invasion or robbery, turned their holdings over to richer or stronger landlords, and became their *coloni* or cultivators; they bound themselves to give the lord a proportion of their produce, labor, and time in return for guaranteed subsistence, and protection in peace and war. Thus Italy, which would never know full feudalism, was among the first nations to prepare its foundations. A like process was taking form in Egypt, Africa, and Gaul.

Slavery was slowly declining. In a developed civilization nothing can equal the free man's varying wage, salary, or profit as an economic stimulus. Slave labor had paid only when slaves were abundant and cheap. Their cost had risen since the legions had ceased to bring home the human fruits of victory; escape was easy for the slaves now that government was weak; besides, slaves had to be cared for when they ailed or aged. As the cost of slaves mounted, the owner protected his investment in them by more considerate treatment; but the master still had, within limits, the power of life and death over his chattels,[19] could use the law to recapture fugitive slaves, and could have his sexual will with such of them, male or female, as pleased his ambidextrous fancy. Paulinus of Pella complimented himself on the chastity of his youth, when "I restrained my desires . . . never accepted the love of a free woman . . . and contented myself with that of female slaves in my household."[20]

The majority of the rich now lived in their country villas, shunning the turmoil and rabble of the towns. Nevertheless, most of Italy's wealth was still drawn to Rome. The great city was no longer a capital, and seldom saw an emperor, but it remained the social and intellectual focus of the West. And here was the summit of the new Italian aristocracy—not as of old an hereditary caste, but periodically recruited by the emperors on the basis of landed wealth. Though the Senate had lost some of its prestige and much of its power, the senators lived in splendor and display. They filled with competence important administrative posts, and provided public games out of their private funds. Their homes were congested with servants and expensive furniture; one carpet cost $400,000.[21] The letters of Symmachus and Sidonius, the poetry of Claudian, reveal the fairer side of that lordly life, the social and cultural activity, the loyal service of the state, the genial friendliness, the fidelity of mates, the tenderness of parental love.

A priest of Marseille, in the fifth century, painted a less attractive picture of conditions in Italy and Gaul. Salvian's book *On the Government of God* (*c.* 450) addressed itself to the same problem that generated Augustine's *City of God* and Orosius' *History Against the Pagans*—how could the evils of the barbarian invasions be reconciled with a divine and beneficent Providence? These sufferings, Salvian answered, were a just punishment for the economic exploitation, political corruption, and moral debauchery of the Roman world. No such ruthless oppression of poor by rich, he assures us, could be found among the barbarians; the barbarian heart is softer than the Roman's; and if the poor could find vehicles they would migrate en masse to live under barbarian rule.[22] Rich and poor, pagan and Christian within the Empire, says our moralist, are alike sunk in a slough of immorality rarely known in history; adultery and drunkenness are fashionable vices, virtue and temperance are the butts of a thousand jokes, the name of Christ has become a profane expletive among those who call Him God.[23] Contrast with all this, says our second Tacitus, the health and vigor and bravery of the Germans, the simple piety of their Christianity, their lenient treatment of conquered Romans, their mutual loyalty, premarital continence, and marital fidelity. The Vandal chieftain Gaiseric, on capturing Christian Carthage, was shocked to find a brothel at almost every corner; he closed these dens, and gave the prostitutes a choice between marriage and banishment. The Roman world is degenerating physically, has lost all moral valor, and leaves its defense to mercenary foreigners. How should such cowards deserve to survive? The Roman Empire, Salvian concludes, "is either dead, or drawing its last breath," even at the height of its luxury and games. *Moritur et ridet*— it laughs and dies.[24]

It is a terrible picture, obviously exaggerated; eloquence is seldom accurate. Doubtless then, as now, virtue modestly hid its head, and yielded the front page to vice, misfortune, politics, and crime. Augustine paints almost as dark a picture for a like moralizing end; he complains that the churches are often emptied by the competition of dancing girls displaying in the theaters their disencumbered charms.[25] The public games still saw the slaughter of convicts and captives to make a holiday. We surmise the lavish cruelty of such spectacles when Symmachus writes that he spent $900,000 on one celebration, and that the twenty-nine Saxon gladiators who were scheduled to fight in the arena cheated him by strangling one another in compact suicide before the games began.[26] In fourth-century Rome there were 175 holidays in the year; ten with gladiatorial contests; sixty-four with circus performances; the rest with shows in the theaters.[27] The barbarians took advantage of this passion for vicarious battle by attacking Carthage, Antioch, and Trier while the people were absorbed at the amphitheater or the circus.[28] In the year 404 a gladiatorial program celebrated at Rome the dubious victory of Stilicho at Pollentia. Blood had begun to flow when an Oriental monk, Telemachus, leaped from the stands into the arena and demanded that the combats cease. The infuriated spectators stoned him to death; but the Emperor Honorius, moved by the scene, issued an edict abolishing gladiatorial games.* Circus races continued till 549, when they were ended by the exhaustion of the city's wealth in the Gothic wars.

Culturally, Rome had not seen so busy an age since Pliny and Tacitus. Music was the rage; Ammianus [29] complains that it had displaced philosophy, and had "turned the libraries into tombs"; he describes gigantic hydraulic organs, and lyres as large as chariots. Schools were numerous; everyone, says Symmachus, had an opportunity to develop his capacities.[30] The "universities" of professors paid by the state taught grammar, rhetoric, literature, and philosophy to students drawn from all the Western provinces, while the encompassing barbarians patiently studied the arts of war. Every civilization is a fruit from the sturdy tree of barbarism, and falls at the greatest distance from the trunk.

Into this city of a million souls, about the year 365, came a Syrian Greek of noble birth and handsome figure, Ammianus Marcellinus of Antioch. He had been a soldier on the staff of Ursicinus in Mesopotamia as an active participant in the wars of Constantius, Julian, and Jovian; he had lived before he wrote. When peace came in the East he retired to Rome, and undertook to complete Livy and Tacitus by writing the history of the Empire from Nerva to Valens. He wrote a difficult and involved Latin, like a German writing

---

* Our sole authority here is the *Historia Ecclesiastica* (v, 20) of Theodoret of Antioch; the tale may be a pious fraud.

French; he had read too much Tacitus, and had too long spoken Greek. He was a frank pagan, an admirer of Julian, a scorner of the luxury that he ascribed to the bishops of Rome; but for all that he was generally impartial, praised many aspects of Christianity, and condemned Julian's restriction of academic freedom as a fault "to be overwhelmed with eternal silence." [31] He was as well educated as a soldier can find time to be. He believed in demons and theurgy, and quoted in favor of divination its archopponent Cicero.[32] But he was, by and large, a blunt and honest man, just to all factions and men; "no wordy deceit adorns my tale, but untrammeled faithfulness to facts." [33] He hated oppression, extravagance, and display, and spoke his mind about them wherever found. He was the last of the classic historians; after him, in the Latin world, there were only chroniclers.

In that same Rome whose manners seemed to Ammianus snobbish and corrupt, Macrobius found a society of men who graced their wealth with courtesy, culture, and philanthropy. He was primarily a scholar, loving books and a quiet life; in 399, however, we find him serving as *vicarius*, or imperial legate, in Spain. His Commentary on Cicero's *Dream of Scipio* became a popular vehicle of Neoplatonist mysticism and philosophy. His chef-d'oeuvre, quoted by almost every historian these last 1500 years, was the *Saturnalia*, or *Feast of Saturn*, a "Curiosities of Literature" in which the author gathered the heterogeneous harvest of his studious days and bookish nights. He improved upon Aulus Gellius while poaching upon him, by putting his material into the form of an imaginary dialogue among real men—Praetextatus, Symmachus, Flavian, Servius, and others—gathered to celebrate the three-day feast of the Saturnalia with good wine, good food, and learned conversation. Disarius, a physician, is asked some medical questions: Is a simple better than a varied diet?—Why do women rarely, and old men so regularly, get drunk?—"Is the nature of women colder or hotter than that of men?" There is a discourse on the calendar, a long analysis of Virgil's vocabulary, grammar, style, philosophy, and plagiarisms; a collection of *bons mots* from all ages; a treatise on rich banquets and rare foods. In the evenings lighter questions amuse these pundits. Why do we blush with shame and pale with fear?—Why does baldness begin at the top of the head?—Which came first, the chicken or the egg? (*Ovumne prius fuerit an·gallina?*) [34] Here and there in the medley are some noble passages, as when the senator Praetextatus speaks of slavery:

> I shall value men not by their status but by their manners and their morals; these come from our character, that from chance. . . . You must seek for your friends, Evangelus, not only in the Forum or the Senate, but in your own house. Treat your slave with gentleness and goodness, admit him to your conversation, occasionally even into your intimate council. Our ancestors, removing pride from the master and shame from the slave, called the former *pater familias*, the

latter *familiaris* (i.e., one of the family). Your slaves will respect you more readily than they will fear you.[35]

It was some such circle as this that, about 394, welcomed into its number a poet destined to sing the swan song of Rome's magnificence. Claudius Claudianus, like Ammianus, was born in the East, and spoke Greek as a mother tongue; but he must have learned Latin at an early age to write it so fluently well. After a short stay in Rome he went to Milan, found a place on Stilicho's staff, became unofficial poet laureate to the Emperor Honorius, and married a lady of birth and wealth; Claudian had an eye to the main chance, and did not propose to be buried in Potter's Field. He served Stilicho with melodious panegyrics and with savagely vituperative poems against Stilicho's rivals. In 400 he returned to Rome, and was gratefully acclaimed when, in a poem "On the Consulate of Stilicho," he wrote for the Eternal City a eulogy worthy of Virgil himself:

> Consul all but peer of the gods, protector of a city greater than any that on earth the air encompasses, whose amplitude no eye can measure, whose beauty no imagination can picture, whose praise no voice can sound, who raises a golden head under the neighboring stars, and with her seven hills imitates the seven regions of heaven; mother of arms and of law, who extends her sway over all the earth, and was the earliest cradle of justice: this is the city which, sprung from humble beginnings, has stretched to either pole, and from one small place extended its power so as to be coterminous with the light of the sun. . . . 'Tis she alone who has received the conquered into her bosom, and like a mother, not an empress, protected the human race with a common name, summoning those whom she has defeated to share her citizenship, and drawing together distant races with bonds of affection. To her rule of peace we owe it that the world is our home, that we can live where we please, and that to visit Thule and explore its once dreaded wilds is but a sport; thanks to her, all and sundry may drink the waters of the Rhone and quaff Orontes' stream. Thanks to her we are all one people.[36]

The grateful Senate raised a statue to Claudian in Trajan's Forum "as to the most glorious of poets," who had united Virgil's felicity with Homer's power. After further verses in honor of remunerative subjects, Claudian turned his talents to *The Rape of Proserpine*, and told the old tale with haunting pictures of land and sea, and a tender note that recalls the Greek love romances of the time. In 408 he learned that Stilicho had been assassinated, and that many of the general's friends were being arrested and executed. We do not know the remainder of his story.

In Rome, as in Athens and Alexandria, substantial pagan minorities survived, and 700 pagan temples were still standing at the end of the fourth century.[37] Jovian and Valentinian I do not seem to have closed the temples opened by Julian. The Roman priests still (394) met in their sacred colleges, the Lupercalia were celebrated with their old half-savage rites, and the Via Sacra now and then resounded with the prescient bellowing of oxen driven to sacrifice.

The most highly respected of Rome's latter-day pagans was Vettius Praetextatus, leader of the pagan majority in the Senate. All men admitted his virtues—integrity, learning, patriotism, fine family life; some compared him to old Cato and Cincinnatus. Time remembers better his friend Symmachus (345–410), whose letters paint so pleasant a picture of that charming aristocracy which thought itself immortal on the eve of death. Even his family seemed immortal: his grandfather had been consul in 330, his father prefect in 364; he himself was prefect in 384, and consul in 391. His son was a praetor, his grandson would be consul in 446, his great-grandson would be consul in 485, his great-great-grandsons would both be consuls in 522. His wealth was immense; he had three villas near Rome, seven others in Latium, five on the Bay of Naples, others elsewhere in Italy, so that "he could travel up and down the peninsula and be everywhere at home." [38] No one is recorded as having grudged him this wealth, for he spent it generously, and redeemed it with a life of study, public service, blameless morals, and a thousand acts of inconspicuous philanthropy. Christians as well as pagans, barbarians as well as Romans, were among his faithful friends. Perhaps he was a pagan before he was a patriot; he suspected that the culture that he represented and enjoyed was bound up with the old religion, and he feared that the one could not fall without the other. Through fidelity to the ancient rites the citizen would feel himself a link in a chain of marvelous continuity from Romulus to Valentinian, and would learn to love a city and a civilization so bravely built through a thousand years. Not without reason his fellow citizens chose Quintus Aurelius Symmachus as their representative in their last dramatic struggle for their gods.

In 380 the Emperor Gratian, won to a passionate orthodoxy by the eloquent Ambrose, proclaimed the Nicene Creed as compulsory "on all the peoples subject to the governments of our clemency," and denounced as "mad and insane" the followers of other faiths.[39] In 382 he ordered an end to payments by the imperial or municipal treasuries for pagan ceremonies, vestal virgins, or priests; confiscated all lands belonging to temples and priestly colleges; and bade his agents remove from the Senate House in Rome that statue of the goddess Victory which Augustus had placed there in 29 B.C., and before which twelve generations of senators had taken their vows of allegiance to the emperor. A delegation headed by Symmachus was appointed by the Senate to acquaint Gratian with the case for Victoria; Gratian refused to receive them, and ordered Symmachus banished from Rome (382). In 383 Gratian was killed, and the hopeful Senate sent a deputation to his successor. The speech of Symmachus before Valentinian II was acclaimed as a masterpiece of eloquent pleading. It was not expedient, he argued, to end so abruptly religious practices that had through a millennium been associated with the stability of social order and the prestige of the state. After all, "What does it matter by what road each man seeks the truth? By no one road can men come to the understanding of so great a mystery" (*uno itinere non potest perveniri ad tam grande secretum*).[40]

The young Valentinian was moved; Ambrose tells us that even the Christians in the imperial council advised the restoration of the statue of Victory. But Ambrose, who had been absent on a diplomatic mission for the state, overruled the council with an imperious letter to the Emperor. He took up one by one the arguments of Symmachus, and countered them with characteristic force. In effect he threatened to excommunicate the ruler if the plea should be granted. "You may enter the churches, but you will find no priest there to receive you, or you will find them there to forbid you entrance." [41] Valentinian denied the Senate's appeal.

The pagans of Italy made a last effort in 393, risking all on revolution. The half-pagan Emperor Eugenius, refused recognition by Theodosius, and hoping to enlist the pagans of the West in his defense, restored the statue of Victory, and boasted that after defeating Theodosius he would stable his horses in Christian basilicas. Nicomachus Flavianus, son-in-law of Symmachus, led an army to support Eugenius, shared in the defeat, and killed himself. Theodosius marched into Rome, and compelled the Senate to decree the abolition of paganism in all its forms (394). When Alaric sacked Rome the pagans saw in the humiliation of the once lordly city the anger of their neglected gods. The war of the faiths broke the unity and morale of the people, and when the torrent of invasion reached them they could only meet it with mutual curses and divided prayers.

IV. THE BARBARIAN FLOOD

As a postscript to the assassination of Stilicho, Olympius ordered the slaughter of thousands of Stilicho's followers, including the leaders of his barbarian legions. Alaric, who had awaited his opportunity behind the Alps, seized it now. He complained that the 4000 pounds of gold that the Romans had promised him had not been paid; in return for this payment he pledged the noblest Gothic youth as hostages for his future loyalty. When Honorius refused, he marched over the Alps, pillaged Aquileia and Cremona, won to his side 30,000 mercenaries resentful of the slaughter of their leaders, and swept down the Flaminian Way to the very walls of Rome (408). No one resisted him except a solitary monk who denounced him as a robber; Alaric bemused him by declaring that God Himself had commanded the invasion.

The frightened Senate, as in Hannibal's day, was stampeded into barbarism; it suspected Stilicho's widow as an accomplice of Alaric, and put her to death. Alaric responded by cutting off every avenue by which food could enter the capital. Soon the populace began to starve; men killed men, and women their children, to eat them. A delegation was sent to Alaric, asking terms. They warned him that a million Romans were ready to resist; he laughed, and answered, "The thicker the hay, the more easily it is mowed." Relenting, he consented to withdraw on receiving all the gold and silver and valuable movable property in the city. "What will then be left to us?" the envoys asked. "Your lives," was the scornful reply. Rome chose further resistance, but starvation compelled a new offer of surrender. Alaric accepted 5000 pounds of gold, 30,000 pounds of silver, 4000 silk tunics, 3000 skins, 3000 pounds of pepper.

Meanwhile an incalculable number of barbarian slaves, escaping from their Roman masters, entered the service of Alaric. As if in compensation, a Gothic leader, Sarus, deserted Alaric for Honorius, took with him a considerable force of Goths, and attacked the main barbarian army. Alaric, holding this to be a violation of the truce that had been signed, again besieged Rome. A slave opened the gates; the Goths poured in, and for the first time in 800 years the great city was taken by an enemy (410). For three days Rome was subjected to a discriminate pillage that left the churches of St. Peter and St. Paul untouched, and spared the refugees who sought sanctuary in them. But the Huns and slaves in the army of 40,000 men could not be controlled. Hundreds of rich men were slaughtered, their women were raped and killed; it was found almost impossible to bury all the corpses that littered the streets. Thousands of prisoners were taken, among them Honorius' half sister Galla Placidia. Gold and silver were seized wherever found; works of art were melted down for the precious metals they contained; and many masterpieces of sculpture and pottery were joyously destroyed by former slaves who could not forgive the poverty and toil that had generated this beauty and wealth. Alaric restored discipline, and led his troops southward to conquer Sicily; but in that same year he was stricken with fever, and died at Cosenza. Slaves diverted the flow of the river Busento to bare a secure and spacious grave for him; the stream was then brought back to its course; and to conceal the spot the slaves who had performed these labors were slain.[42]

Ataulf (Adolf), Alaric's brother-in-law, was chosen to succeed him as king. He agreed to withdraw his army from Italy on condition that he should be given Placidia in marriage, and that his Visigoths, as *foederati* of Rome, should receive southern Gaul, including Narbonne, Toulouse, and Bordeaux, for their self-governed realm. Honorius refused the marriage; Placidia consented. The Gothic chieftain proclaimed that his ambition was not to destroy the Roman Empire but to preserve and strengthen it. He marched his army out of Italy, and by a judicious mixture of diplomacy and force founded the Visigothic kingdom of Gaul, theoretically subject to the Empire, and with its capital at Toulouse (414). A year later he was assassinated. Placidia, who loved him, wished to remain a perpetual widow, but was awarded by Honorius to the general Constantius. After the death of Constantius (421) and Honorius (423), Placidia became regent for her son Valentinian III, and for twenty-five years ruled the Empire of the West with no discredit to her sex.

Even in Tacitus' days the Vandals were a numerous and powerful nation, possessing the central and eastern portions of modern Prussia. By the time of Constantine they had moved southward into Hungary. Their armies having suffered an overwhelming defeat at the hands of the Visigoths, the remaining Vandals asked permission to cross the Danube and enter the Empire. Constantine consented, and for seventy years they increased and multiplied in Pannonia. The successes of Alaric stirred their imagination; the withdrawal of legions from beyond the Alps to defend Italy left the rich West invitingly open; and in 406 great masses of Vandals, Alani, and Suevi poured over the Rhine and ravaged Gaul. They plundered Mainz, and massacred many of the inhabitants. They moved north into Belgica, and sacked and burned the imperial city of Trier. They bridged the Meuse and the Aisne, and pillaged Reims, Amiens, Arras, and Tournai, almost reaching the English Channel. Turning south, they crossed the Seine and the Loire into Aquitaine and wreaked their vandal fury upon almost all its cities except Toulouse, which was heroically defended by its Bishop Exuperius. They paused at the Pyrenees, then turned east and pillaged Narbonne. Gaul had seldom known so thorough a devastation.

In 409 they entered Spain, 100,000 strong. There, as in Gaul and the East, Roman rule had brought oppressive taxation and orderly administration, wealth concentrated in immense estates, a populace of slaves and serfs and impoverished freemen; and yet, by the mere grace of stability and law, Spain was now among the most prosperous of Roman provinces, and Merida, Cartagena, Cordova, Seville, and Tarragona were among the richest and most cultured cities of the Empire. Into this apparently secure peninsula the Vandals, Suevi, and Alani descended; for two years they plundered Spain from the Pyrenees to the Strait, and extended their conquest even to the African coast. Honorius, unable to defend Roman soil with Roman arms, bribed the Visigoths of southwestern Gaul to recapture Spain for the Empire; their able King Wallia accomplished the task in well-planned campaigns (420); the Suevi retreated into northwest Spain, the Vandals southward into the Andalusia that still bears their name; and Wallia shamed the faithlessness of Roman diplomats by restoring Spain to the imperial power.

Still hungry for conquest and bread, the Vandals crossed over into Africa (429). If we may believe Procopius [43] and Jordanes,[44] they came by the invitation of the Roman governor of Africa, Boniface, who wished their aid against his rival Aëtius, successor to Stilicho; the story is of uncertain authority. In any case the Vandal king was quite capable of originating the plan. Gaiseric was the proud bastard son of a slave, lame but strong, ascetic in regimen, undaunted in conflict, furious in anger, cruel in enmity, but with an unbeaten genius for both negotiation and war. Arrived in Africa, his 80,000 Vandal and Alani warriors, women, and children were joined by the savage Moors, long resentful of Roman domination, and the Donatist heretics, who had been persecuted by the orthodox Christians, and now welcomed a new rule. Out of a population of some 8,000,000 souls in Roman North Africa, Boniface could muster only a negligible number to help his small regular army; overwhelmingly defeated by Gaiseric's horde, he retreated to Hippo, where the aged St. Augustine aroused the population to heroic resistance. For fourteen months the city stood siege (430–1); Gaiseric then withdrew to meet another Roman force, and so overwhelmed it that Valentinian's ambassador signed a truce recognizing the Vandal conquest in Africa. Gaiseric observed the truce until the Romans were off their guard; then he pounced upon rich Carthage and took it without a blow (439). The nobles and the Catholic clergy were dispossessed of their property, and were banished or enserfed; lay and ecclesiastical property was seized wherever found, and torture was not spared to discover its hiding place.[45]

Gaiseric was still young. Though a capable administrator, who reorganized Africa into a lucrative state, he was happiest when engaged in war. Building a great fleet, he ravaged with it the coasts of Spain, Italy, and Greece. No one could tell where his cavalry-laden ships would land next; never in Roman history had such unhindered piracy prevailed in the western Mediterranean. At last the Emperor, as the price of the African corn on which Ravenna as well as Rome lived, made peace with the barbarian king, and even pledged him an imperial daughter in marriage. Rome, soon to be destroyed, continued to laugh and play.

Three quarters of a century had passed since the Huns had precipitated the barbarian invasions by crossing the Volga. Their further movement westward had been a slow migration, less like the conquest of Alaric and Gaiseric than like the spread of colonists across the American continent. Gradually they had settled down in and near Hungary and had brought under their rule many of the German tribes.

About the year 433 the Hun king Rua died, and left his throne to his nephews Bleda and Attila. Bleda was slain—some said by Attila—about 444, and Attila (i.e., in Gothic, "Little Father") ruled divers tribes north of the Danube from the Don to the Rhine. The Gothic historian Jordanes describes him, we do not know how accurately:

He was a man born into the world to shake the nations, the scourge of all lands, who in some way terrified all mankind by the rumors noised abroad concerning him. He was haughty in his walk, rolling his eyes hither and thither, so that the power of his proud spirit appeared in the movement of his body. He was indeed a lover of war, yet restrained in action; mighty in counsel, gracious to suppliants, and lenient to those who were once received under his protection. He was short of stature, with a broad chest and a large head; his eyes were small, his beard was thin and sprinkled with gray. He had a flat nose and a swarthy complexion, revealing his origin.[46]

He differed from the other barbarian conquerors in trusting to cunning more than to force. He ruled by using the heathen superstitions of his people to sanctify his majesty; his victories were prepared by the exaggerated stories of his cruelty which perhaps he had himself originated; at last even his Christian enemies called him the "scourge of God," and were so terrified by his cunning that only the Goths could save them. He could neither read nor write, but this did not detract from his intelligence. He was not a savage; he had a sense of honor and justice, and often proved himself more magnanimous than the Romans. He lived and dressed simply, ate and drank moderately, and left luxury to his inferiors, who loved to display their gold and silver utensils, harness, and swords, and the delicate embroidery that attested the skillful fingers of their wives. Attila had many wives, but scorned that mixture of monogamy and debauchery which was popular in some circles of Ravenna and Rome. His palace was a huge loghouse floored and walled with planed planks, but adorned with elegantly carved or polished wood, and reinforced with carpets and skins to keep out the cold. His capital was a large village probably on the site of the present Buda—a city which until our century was by some Hungarians called Etzelnburg, the City of Attila.

He was now (444) the most powerful man in Europe. Theodosius II of the Eastern Empire, and Valentinian of the Western, both paid him tribute as a bribe to peace, disguising it among their peoples as payments for services rendered by a client king. Able to put into the field an army of 500,000 men, Attila saw no reason why he should not make himself master of all Europe and the Near East. In 441 his generals and troops crossed the Danube, captured Sirmium, Singidunum (Belgrade), Naissus (Nish) and Sardica (Sofia), and threatened Constantinople itself. Theodosius II sent an army against them; it was defeated; and the Eastern Empire won peace only by raising its yearly tribute from 700 to 2100 pounds of gold. In 447 the Huns entered Thrace, Thessaly, and Scythia (southern Russia), sacked seventy towns, and took thousands into slavery. The captured women were added to the wives of the captors, and so began generations of blood mixture that left traces of Mongol features as far west as Bavaria. These Hun raids ruined the Balkans for four centuries. The Danube ceased for a long time to be a main avenue of commerce between East and West, and the cities on its banks decayed.

Having bled the East to his heart's content, Attila turned to the West and found an unusual excuse for war. Honoria, sister of Valentinian III, having been seduced by one of her chamberlains, had been banished to Constantinople. Snatching at any plan for escape, she sent her ring to Attila with an appeal for aid. The subtle King, who had his own brand of humor, chose to interpret the ring as a proposal of marriage; he forthwith laid claim to Honoria and to half the Western Empire as her dowry. Valentinian's ministers protested, and Attila declared war. His real reason was that Marcian, the new Emperor of the East, had refused to continue payment of tribute, and Valentinian had followed his example.

In 451 Attila and half a million men marched to the Rhine, sacked and burned Trier and Metz, and massacred their inhabitants. All Gaul was terrified; here was no civilized warrior like Caesar, no Christian—however Arian—invader like Alaric and Gaiseric; this was the awful and hideous Hun, the *flagellum dei* come to punish Christian and pagan alike for the enormous distance between their professions and their lives. In this crisis Theodoric I, aged King of the Visigoths, came to the rescue of the Empire; he joined the Romans under Aëtius, and the enormous armies met on the Catalaunian Fields, near Troyes, in one of the bloodiest battles of history: 162,000 men are said to have died there, including the heroic Gothic King. The victory of the West was indecisive; Attila retreated in good order, and the victors were too exhausted, or too divided in policy, to pursue him. In the following year he invaded Italy.

The first city to fall in his path was Aquileia; the Huns destroyed it so completely that it never rose again. Verona and Vicenza were more leniently treated; Pavia and Milan bought off the conqueror by surrendering their movable wealth. The road to Rome was now open to Attila; Aëtius had too small an army to offer substantial resistance; but Attila tarried at the Po. Valentinian III fled to Rome, and thence sent to the Hun King a delegation composed of Pope Leo I and two senators. No one knows what happened at the ensuing conference. Leo was an imposing figure, and received most credit for the bloodless victory. History only records that Attila now retreated. Plague had broken out in his army, food was running short, and Marcian was sending reinforcements from the East (452).

Attila marched his horde back over the Alps to his Hungarian capital, threatening to return to Italy in the next spring unless Honoria should be sent him as his bride. Meanwhile he consoled himself by adding to his harem a young lady named Ildico, the frail historic basis of the *Nibelungenlied's* Kriemhild. He celebrated the wedding with an unusual indulgence in food and drink. On the morrow he was found dead in bed beside his young wife;

he had burst a blood vessel, and the blood in his throat had choked him to death (453).[47] His realm was divided among his sons, who proved incompetent to preserve it. Jealousies broke out among them; the subject tribes refused their allegiance to a disordered leadership; and within a few years the empire that had threatened to subdue the Greeks and the Romans, the Germans and the Gauls, and to put the stamp of Asia upon the face and soul of Europe, had broken to pieces and melted away.

V. THE FALL OF ROME

Placidia having died in 450, Valentinian III was free to err in the first person. As Olympius had persuaded Honorius to kill Stilicho who had stopped Alaric at Pollentia, so now Petronius Maximus persuaded Valentinian to kill Aëtius who had stopped Attila at Troyes. Valentinian had no son, and resented the desire of Aëtius to espouse his son to Valentinian's daughter Eudocia. In a mad seizure of alarm the Emperor sent for Aëtius and slew him with his own hand (454). "Sire," said a member of his court, "you have cut off your right hand with your left." A few months later Petronius induced two of Aëtius' followers to kill Valentinian. No one bothered to punish the assassins; murder had long since become the accepted substitute for election. Petronius elected himself to the throne, compelled Eudoxia, Valentinian's widow, to marry him, and forced Eudocia to take as her husband his son Palladius. If we may believe Procopius,[48] Eudoxia appealed to Gaiseric as Honoria had appealed to Attila. Gaiseric had reasons for responding: Rome was rich again despite Alaric, and the Roman army was in no condition to defend Italy. The Vandal King set sail with an invincible armada (455). Only an unarmed Pope, accompanied by his local clergy, barred his way between Ostia and Rome. Leo was not able this time to dissuade the conqueror, but he secured a pledge against massacre, torture, and fire. For four days the city was surrendered to pillage; Christian churches were spared, but all the surviving treasures of the temples were taken to the Vandal galleys; the gold tables, seven-branched candlesticks, and other sacred vessels of Solomon's Temple, brought to Rome by Titus four centuries before, were included in these spoils. All precious metals, ornaments, and furniture in the imperial palace were removed, and whatever remained of value in the homes of the rich. Thousands of captives were enslaved; husbands were separated from wives, parents from children. Gaiseric took the Empress Eudoxia and her two daughters with him to Carthage, married Eudocia to his son Huneric, and sent the Empress and Placidia (the younger) to Constantinople at the request of the Emperor Leo I. All in all, this sack of Rome was no indiscriminate vandalism, but quite in accord with the ancient laws of war. Carthage had leniently revenged the Roman ruthlessness of 146 B.C.

Chaos in Italy was now complete. A half century of invasion, famine, and pestilence had left thousands of farms ruined, thousands of acres untilled, not through exhaustion of the soil but through the exhaustion of man. St. Ambrose (*c.* 420) mourned the devastation and depopulation of Bologna, Modena, Piacenza; Pope Gelasius (*c.* 480) described great regions of northern Italy as almost denuded of the human species; Rome itself had shrunk from 1,500,000 souls to some 300,000 in one century;[49] all the great cities of the Empire were now in the East. The Campagna around Rome, once rich in villas and fertile farms, had been abandoned for the security of walled towns; the towns themselves had been contracted to some forty acres as a means of economically walling them for defense; and in many cases the walls were improvised from the debris of theaters, basilicas, and temples that had once adorned the municipal splendor of Italy. In Rome some wealth still remained even after Gaiseric, and Rome and other Italian cities would recover under Theodoric and the Lombards; but in 470 a general impoverishment of fields and cities, of senators and proletarians, depressed the spirits of a once great race to an epicurean cynicism that doubted all gods but Priapus, a timid childlessness that shunned the responsibilities of life, and an angry cowardice that denounced every surrender and shirked every martial task. Through all this economic and biological decline ran political decay: aristocrats who could administer but could not rule; businessmen too absorbed in personal gain to save the peninsula; generals who won by bribery more than they could win by arms; and a bureaucracy ruinously expensive and irremediably corrupt. The majestic tree had rotted in its trunk, and was ripe for a fall.

The final years were a kaleidoscope of imperial mediocrities. The Goths of Gaul proclaimed one of their generals, Avitus, emperor (455); the Senate refused to confirm him, and he was transformed into a bishop. Majorian (456-61) labored bravely to restore order, but was deposed by his *patricius* or prime minister, the Visigoth Ricimer. Severus (461-5) was an inefficient tool of Ricimer. Anthemius (467-72) was a half-pagan philosopher, unacceptable to the Christian West; Ricimer besieged and captured him and had him killed. Olybrius, by grace of Ricimer, ruled for two months (472), and surprised himself by dying a natural death. Glycerius (473) was soon deposed, and for two years Rome was ruled by Julius Nepos. At this juncture a new conglomeration of barbarians swept down into Italy—Heruli, Sciri, Rugii, and other tribes that had once acknowledged the rule of Attila. At the same time a Pannonian general, Orestes, deposed Nepos, and established his son Romulus (nicknamed Augustulus) on the throne (475). The new invaders demanded from Orestes a third of Italy; when he refused they slew him, and replaced Romulus with their general Odoacer (476). This son of Attila's minister Edecon was not without ability; he convened the cowed Senate, and through it he offered to Zeno, the new Emperor of the

East, sovereignty over all the Empire, provided that Odoacer might as his *patricius* govern Italy. Zeno consented, and the line of Western emperors came to an end.

No one appears to have seen in this event the "fall of Rome"; on the contrary, it seemed to be a blessed unification of the Empire, as formerly under Constantine. The Roman Senate saw the matter so, and raised a statue to Zeno in Rome. The Germanization of the Italian army, government, and peasantry, and the natural multiplication of the Germans in Italy, had proceeded so long that the political consequences seemed to be negligible shifts on the surface of the national scene. Actually, however, Odoacer ruled Italy as a king, with small regard for Zeno. In effect the Germans had conquered Italy as Gaiseric had conquered Africa, as the Visigoths had conquered Spain, as the Angles and Saxons were conquering Britain, as the Franks were conquering Gaul. In the West the great Empire was no more.

The results of the barbarian conquest were endless. Economically it meant reruralization. The barbarians lived by tillage, herding, hunting, and war, and had not yet learned the commercial complexities on which cities thrived; with their victory the municipal character of Western civilization ceased for seven centuries. Ethnically the migrations brought a new mingling of racial elements—a substantial infusion of Germanic blood into Italy, Gaul, and Spain, and of Asiatic blood into Russia, the Balkans, and Hungary. The mixture did not mystically reinvigorate the Italian or Gallic population. What happened was the elimination of weak individuals and strains through war and other forms of competition; the compulsion laid upon everyone to develop strength, stamina, and courage, and the masculine qualities that long security had suppressed; the renewal, by poverty, of healthier and simpler habits of life than those which the doles and luxuries of the cities had bred. Politically the conquest replaced a higher with a lower form of monarchy; it augmented the authority of persons, and reduced the power and protection of laws; individualism and violence increased. Historically, the conquest destroyed the outward form of what had already inwardly decayed; it cleared away with regrettable brutality and thoroughness a system of life which, with all its gifts of order, culture, and law, had worn itself into senile debility, and had lost the powers of regeneration and growth. A new beginning was now possible: the Empire in the West faded, but the states of modern Europe were born. A thousand years before Christ northern invaders had entered Italy, subdued and mingled with its inhabitants, borrowed civilization from them, and with them, through eight centuries, had built a new civilization. Four hundred years after Christ the process was repeated; the wheel of history came full turn; the beginning and the end were the same. But the end was always a beginning.

CHAPTER III

The Progress of Christianity

364-451

THE foster mother of the new civilization was the Church. As the old order faded away in corruption, cowardice, and neglect, a unique army of churchmen rose to defend with energy and skill a regenerated stability and decency of life. The historic function of Christianity was to re-establish the moral basis of character and society by providing supernatural sanctions and support for the uncongenial commandments of social order; to instill into rude barbarians gentler ideals of conduct through a creed spontaneously compounded of myth and miracle, of fear and hope and love. There is an epic grandeur, sullied with superstition and cruelty, in the struggle of the new religion to capture, tame, and inspire the minds of brute or decadent men, to forge a uniting empire of faith that would again hold men together, as they had once been held by the magic of Greece or the majesty of Rome. Institutions and beliefs are the offspring of human needs, and understanding must be in terms of these necessities.

I. THE ORGANIZATION OF THE CHURCH

If art is the organization of materials, the Roman Catholic Church is among the most imposing masterpieces of history. Through nineteen centuries, each heavy with crisis, she has held her faithful together, following them with her ministrations to the ends of the earth, forming their minds, molding their morals, encouraging their fertility, solemnizing their marriages, consoling their bereavements, lifting their momentary lives into eternal drama, harvesting their gifts, surviving every heresy and revolt, and patiently building again every broken support of her power. How did this majestic institution grow?

It began in the spiritual hunger of men and women harassed with poverty, wearied with conflict, awed by mystery, or fearful of death. To millions of souls the Church brought a faith and hope that inspired and canceled death. That faith became their most precious possession, for which they would die or kill; and on that rock of hope the Church was built. It was at first a simple association of believers, an *ecclesia* or gathering. Each *ecclesia* or church chose one or more *presbyteroi*—elders, priests—to lead them, and one or more readers, acolytes, subdeacons, and deacons to assist the priest. As the worshipers grew in number, and their affairs became more complex, the congregations chose a priest or layman in each city to be an *episcopos*—overseer, bishop—to co-ordinate their functioning. As the number of bishops grew, they in turn required supervision and co-ordination; in the fourth century we hear of archbishops, metropolitans, or primates governing the bishops and the churches of a province. Over all these grades of clergy patriarchs held sway at Constantinople, Antioch, Jerusalem, Alexandria, and Rome. At the call of a patriarch or an emperor the bishops and archbishops convened in synods or councils. If a council represented only a province it was called provincial; if it represented only the East or the West it was called plenary; if both, it was general; if its decrees were accepted as binding upon all Christians, it was ecumenical—i.e., applying to the *oikoumene*, or (total Christian) inhabited world. The occasionally resultant unity gave the Church its name of Catholic, or universal.

This organization, whose power rested at last upon belief and prestige, required some regulation of the ecclesiastical life. In the first three centuries of Christianity, celibacy was not required of a priest. He might keep a wife whom he had married before ordination, but he must not marry after taking holy orders; and no man could be ordained who had married two wives, or a widow, a divorcee, or a concubine. Like most societies, the Church was harassed with extremists. In reaction against the sexual license of pagan morals, some Christian enthusiasts concluded from a passage in St. Paul [1] that any commerce between the sexes was sinful; they denounced all marriage, and trembled at the abomination of a married priest. The provincial council of Gengra (*c.* 362) condemned these views as heretical, but the Church increasingly demanded celibacy in her priests. Property was being left in rising amounts to individual churches; now and then a married priest had the bequest written in his name and transmitted it to his children. Clerical marriage sometimes led to adultery or other scandal, and lowered the respect of the people for the priest. A Roman synod of 386 advised the complete continence of the clergy; and a year later Pope Siricius ordered the unfrocking of any priest who married, or continued to live with his wife. Jerome, Ambrose, and Augustine supported this decree with their triple power; and after a generation of sporadic resistance it was enforced with transient success in the West.

The gravest problem of the Church, next to reconciling her ideals with her continuance, was to find a way of living with the state. The rise of an ecclesiastical organization side by side with the officials of the government created a struggle for power in which the accepted subjection of one to the other was the prerequisite of peace. In the East the Church became subordinate to the state; in the West she fought for independence, then for mastery. In either case the union of Church and state involved a profound modification of Christian ethics. Tertullian, Origen, and Lactantius had taught that war is always unlawful; the Church, now protected by the state, resigned herself to such wars as she deemed necessary to protect either the state or the Church. She had not in herself the means of force; but when force seemed desirable she could appeal to the "secular arm" to implement her will. She received from the state, and from individuals, splendid gifts of money, temples, or lands; she grew rich, and needed the state to protect her in all the rights of property. Even when the state fell she kept her wealth; the barbarian conquerors, however heretical, seldom robbed the Church. The authority of the word so soon rivaled the power of the sword.

II. THE HERETICS

The most unpleasant task of ecclesiastical organization was to prevent a fragmentation of the Church through the multiplication of heresies—i.e., doctrines contrary to conciliar definitions of the Christian creed. Once triumphant, the Church ceased to preach toleration; she looked with the same hostile eye upon individualism in belief as the state upon secession or revolt. Neither the Church nor the heretics thought of heresy in purely theological terms. The heresy was in many cases the ideological flag of a rebellious locality seeking liberation from the imperial power; so the Monophysites wished to free Syria and Egypt from Constantinople; the Donatists hoped to free Africa from Rome; and as Church and state were now united, the rebellion was against both. Orthodoxy opposed nationalism, heresy defended it; the Church labored for centralization and unity, the heretics for local independence and liberty.

Arianism, overcome within the Empire, won a peculiar victory among the barbarians. Christianity had been first carried to the Teutonic tribes by Roman captives taken in the Gothic invasions of Asia Minor in the third century. The "apostle" Ulfilas (311?–81) was not quite an apostle. He was the descendant of a Christian captive from Cappadocia, and was born and raised among the Goths who lived north of the Danube. About 341 he was consecrated as their bishop by Eusebius, the Arian prelate of Nicomedia. When the Gothic chieftain Athanaric persecuted the Christians in his dominions, Ulfilas obtained permission from the Arian Constantius to bring the little community of Gothic Christians across the Danube into Thrace. To instruct and multiply his converts he patiently translated, from the Greek into Gothic, all the Bible except the Books of Kings, which he omitted as dangerously martial; and as the Goths had as yet no written language, he composed a Gothic alphabet based upon the Greek. His Bible was the first literary work in any Teutonic tongue. The devoted and virtuous life of Ulfilas generated among the Goths such confidence in his wisdom and integrity that his Arian Christianity was accepted by them without question. As other barbarians received their Christianity in the fourth and fifth centuries from the Goths, nearly all the invaders of the Empire were Arians, and the new kingdoms established by them in the Balkans, Gaul, Spain, Italy, and Africa were officially Arian. Conquerors and conquered differed by only an iota in their faith: the orthodox held Christ to be identical in being (*homoousios*), the Arians considered Him only similar in being (*homoiousios*), with God the Father; but the difference became vital in the politics of the fifth and sixth centuries. By this chance concatenation of events Arianism held its ground till the orthodox Franks overthrew the Visigoths in Gaul, Belisarius conquered Vandal Africa and Gothic Italy, and Recared (589) changed the faith of the Visigoths in Spain.

We cannot interest ourselves today in the many winds of doctrine that agitated the Church in this period—Eunomians, Anomeans, Apollinarians, Macedonians, Sabellians, Massalians, Novatians, Priscillianists; we can only mourn over the absurdities for which men have died, and will. Manicheism was not so much a Christian heresy as a Persian dualism of God and Satan, Good and Evil, Light and Darkness; it thought to reconcile Christianity and Zoroastrianism, and was bitterly buffeted by both. It faced with unusual candor the problem of evil, the strange abundance of apparently unmerited suffering in a world providentially ruled; and felt compelled to postulate an Evil Spirit coeternal with the Good. During the fourth century Manicheism made many converts in East and West. Several of the emperors used ruthless measures against it; Justinian made it a capital crime; gradually it faded out, but it left its influence on such later heretics as the Paulicians, Bogomiles, and Albigensians. In 385 a Spanish bishop, Priscillian, was accused of preaching Manicheism and universal celibacy; he denied the charges; he was tried before the usurping Emperor Maximus at Trier, two bishops being his accusers; he was condemned; and over the protests of St. Ambrose and St. Martin he and several of his companions were burned to death (385).

While meeting all these assailants the Church found herself almost overwhelmed by the Donatist heresy in Africa. Donatus, Bishop of Carthage (315), had denied the efficacy of sacraments administered by priests in a state of sin; the Church, unwilling to risk so much on the virtues of the clergy, wisely repudiated the idea. The heresy nevertheless spread rapidly in North Africa; it enlisted the enthusiasm of the poor, and the theological aberration grew into a social revolt. Emperors fulminated against the movement; heavy fines and confiscations were decreed for persistence in it; the power of buying, selling, or bequeathing property was denied to the Donatists; they were driven from their churches by imperial soldiery, and the churches were turned over to orthodox priests. Bands of revolutionaries, at once Christian and communist, took form under the name of Circumcelliones, or prowlers; they condemned poverty and slavery, canceled debts and liberated slaves, and proposed to restore the mythical equality of primitive man. When they met a carriage drawn by slaves they put the slaves in the carriage and made the master pull it behind him. Usually they contented themselves with robbery; but sometimes, irritated by resistance, they would blind the orthodox or the rich by rubbing lime into their eyes, or would beat them to death with clubs; or so their enemies relate. If they in turn met death they rejoiced, certain of paradise. Fanaticism finally captured them completely; they gave themselves up as heretics, and solicited martyrdom; they stopped wayfarers and asked to be killed; and when even their enemies tired of complying, they leaped into fires, or jumped from precipices, or walked into the sea.[2] Augustine fought Donatism with every means, and for a time seemed to have overcome it; but when the Vandals arrived in Africa the Donatists reappeared in great number, and rejoiced at the expulsion of the orthodox priests. A tradition of fierce sectarian hatred was handed down with pious persistence, and left no united opposition when (670) the Arabs came.

Meanwhile Pelagius was stirring three continents with his attack on the doctrine of original sin, and Nestorius was courting martyrdom by doubts concerning the Mother of God. Nestorius had been a pupil of Theodore of Mopsuestia (350?–?428), who had almost invented the Higher Criticism of the Bible. The Book of Job, said Theodore, was a poem adapted from pagan sources; the Song of Songs was an epithalamium of frankly sensual significance; many of the Old Testament prophecies supposedly referring to Jesus alluded only to pre-Christian events; and Mary was the Mother not of God but only of the human nature in Jesus.[3] Nestorius raised himself to the episcopal see at Constantinople (428), drew crowds with his eloquence, made enemies by his harsh dogmatism, and gave them their opportunity by adopting the ungallant opinion of Theodore about Mary. If Christ was God, then, said most Christians, Mary was *theotokos*, god-bearing, the Mother of God. Nestorius thought the term too strong; Mary, he said, was mother only of the human, not of the divine, nature in Christ. It would be better, he suggested, to call her the Mother of Christ.

Cyril, Archbishop of Alexandria, preached at Easter, 429, a sermon announcing the orthodox doctrine—that Mary is the true mother not of the Godhead itself, but of the incarnate Logos, or Word of God, containing both the divine and the human natures of Christ.[4] Pope Celestine I, stirred by a letter from Cyril, called a council at Rome (430), which demanded that Nestorius be deposed or retract. When Nestorius refused, an ecumenical council at Ephesus (431) not only deposed but excommunicated him. Many bishops protested; but the people of Ephesus broke out into demonstrations of joy that must have awakened memories of Diana-Artemis. Nestorius was

allowed to retire to Antioch; but as he continued to defend himself and demand restoration, the Emperor Theodosius II banished him to an oasis in the
Libyan desert. He survived many years; at last the Byzantine court took pity
on him, and sent him an imperial pardon. The messenger found him dying
(c. 451). His followers withdrew to eastern Syria, built churches, established
a school of learning at Edessa, translated the Bible, Aristotle, and Galen into
Syriac, and played a vital part in acquainting the Moslems with Greek
science, medicine, and philosophy. Persecuted by the Emperor Zeno, they
crossed into Persia, opened an influential school at Nisibis, flourished under
Persian toleration, and founded communities in Balkh and Samarkand, in
India and China. Scattered through Asia, they survive to this day, still denouncing Mariolatry.

The last great heresy of this turbulent period, and the most momentous in
result, was announced by Eutyches, head of a monastery near Constantinople. In Christ, said Eutyches, there were not two natures, human and
divine; there was only the divine. Flavian, the patriarch of Constantinople,
called a local synod which condemned this "Monophysite" heresy, and excommunicated Eutyches. The monk appealed to the bishops of Alexandria
and Rome; Dioscoras, who had succeeded Cyril, persuaded the Emperor
Theodosius to call another council at Ephesus (449). Religion was subordinated to politics; the Alexandrian see continued its war upon the see of Constantinople; Eutyches was exonerated, and Flavian was assailed with such
oratorical violence that he died.[5] The council issued anathemas against any
man who should hold that there were two natures in Christ. Pope Leo I
had not attended the council, but had sent it several letters ("Leo's tome")
supporting Flavian. Shocked by the report of his delegates, Leo branded the
council as the "Robber Synod," and refused to recognize its decrees. A later
council, at Chalcedon in 451, acclaimed Leo's letters, condemned Eutyches,
and reaffirmed the double nature of Christ. But the twenty-eighth canon of
this council affirmed the equal authority of the bishop of Constantinople with
that of Rome. Leo, who had fought for the supremacy of his office as indispensable to the unity and authority of the Church, rejected this canon; and
a long struggle began between the rival sees.

To perfect the confusion, the majority of Christians in Syria and Egypt
refused to accept the doctrines of two natures in the one person of Christ.
The monks of Syria continued to teach the Monophysite heresy, and when
an orthodox bishop was appointed to the see of Alexandria he was torn to
pieces in his church on Good Friday.[6] Thereafter Monophysitism became
the national religion of Christian Egypt and Abyssinia, and by the sixth century predominated in western Syria and Armenia, while Nestorianism grew
in Mesopotamia and eastern Syria. The success of the religious rebellion
strengthened political revolt; and when the conquering Arabs, in the seventh

century, poured into Egypt and the Near East, half the population welcomed them as liberators from the theological, political, and financial tyranny of the Byzantine capital.

III. THE CHRISTIAN WEST

1. Rome

The bishops of Rome, in the fourth century, did not show the Church at her best. Sylvester (314–35) earned the credit for converting Constantine; and pious belief represented him as receiving from the Emperor in the "Donation of Constantine" nearly all of western Europe; but he did not behave as if he owned half the white man's world. Julius I (337–52) strongly affirmed the supreme authority of the Roman see, but Liberius (352–66) submitted, through weakness or age, to the Arian dictates of Constantius. Upon his death Damasus and Ursinus contested the papacy; rival mobs supported them in the most vigorous tradition of Roman democracy; in one day and in one church 137 persons were killed in the dispute.[7] Praetextatus, then pagan prefect of Rome, banished Ursinus, and Damasus ruled for eighteen years with pleasure and skill. He was an archaeologist, and adorned the tombs of the Roman martyrs with beautiful inscriptions; he was also, said the irreverent, an *auriscalpius matronarum*, a scratcher of ladies' ears—i.e., an expert in wheedling gifts for the Church from the rich matrons of Rome.[8]

Leo I, surnamed the Great, held the throne of Peter through a generation of crisis (440–61), and by courage and statesmanship raised the Apostolic See to new heights of power and dignity. When Hilary of Poitiers refused to accept his decision in a dispute with another Gallic bishop, Leo sent him peremptory orders; and the Emperor Valentinian III seconded these with an epoch-making edict imperially confirming the authority of the Roman bishop over all Christian churches. The bishops of the West generally acknowledged, those of the East resisted, this supremacy. The patriarchs of Constantinople, Antioch, Jerusalem, and Alexandria claimed equal authority with the Roman see; and the furious controversies of the Eastern Church proceeded with scant obeisance to the bishop of Rome. Difficulties of communication and travel combined with diversity of language to alienate the Western from the Eastern Church. In the West, however, the popes exercised a growing leadership even in secular affairs. They were subject in nonreligious matters to the Roman state and prefect, and until the seventh century they sought the confirmation of their election from the emperor. But the distance of the Eastern and the weakness of the Western rulers left the popes pre-eminent in Rome; and when, in the face of invasion, both Senate and emperor fled, and civil government collapsed, while the popes stood unawed at their posts, their prestige rapidly rose. The conversion of the

Western barbarians immensely extended the authority and influence of the Roman see.

As rich and aristocratic families abandoned paganism for Christianity, the Roman Church participated more and more in the wealth that came to the Western capital; and Ammianus was surprised to find that the bishop of Rome lived like a prince in the Lateran Palace, and moved through the city with the pomp of an emperor.[9] Splendid churches now (400) adorned the city. A brilliant society took form, in which elegant prelates mingled happily with ornate women, and helped them to make their wills.

While the Christian populace joined the surviving pagans at the theater, the races, and the games, a minority of Christians strove to live a life in harmony with the Gospels. Athanasius had brought to Rome two Egyptian monks; he had written a life of Anthony, and Rufinus had published for the West a history of monasticism in the East. Pious minds were influenced by the reported holiness of Anthony, Schnoudi, and Pachomius; monasteries were established in Rome by Sixtus III (432–440) and Leo I; and several families, while still living in their homes, accepted the monastic rule of chastity and poverty. Roman ladies of wealth, like Marcella, Paula, and three generations of the Melanias, gave most of their funds to charity, founded hospitals and convents, made pilgrimages to the monks of the East, and maintained so ascetic a regimen that some of them died of self-denial. Pagan circles in Rome complained that this kind of Christianity was hostile to family life, the institution of marriage, and the vigor of the state; and polemics fell heavily upon the head of the leading advocate of asceticism—one of the greatest scholars and most brilliant writers ever produced by the Christian Church.

2. St. Jerome

He was born about 340 at Strido, near Aquileia, probably of Dalmatian stock, and was promisingly named Eusebius Hieronymus Sophronius—"the reverend, holy-named sage." He received a good education at Trier and Rome, learned the Latin classics well, and loved them, he thought, to the point of sin. Nevertheless, he was a positive and passionate Christian; he joined with Rufinus and other friends to found an ascetic brotherhood in Aquileia, and preached such counsels of perfection that his bishop reproved him for undue impatience with the natural frailties of man. He replied by calling the bishop ignorant, brutal, wicked, well matched with the worldly flock that he led, the unskillful pilot of a crazy bark.[10] Leaving Aquileia to its sins, Jerome and some fellow devotees went to the Near East and entered a monastery in the Chalcis desert near Antioch (374). The unhealthy climate was too much for them; two died, and Jerome himself was for a time on the verge of death. Undeterred, he left the monastery to live as an anchorite in a desert hermitage, with occasional relapses into Virgil and Cicero. He had brought his library with him, and could not quite turn away from verse and prose whose beauty lured him like some girlish loveliness. His account of the matter reveals the medieval mood. He dreamt that he had died, and was

> dragged before the Judge's judgment seat. I was asked to state my condition, and replied that I was a Christian. But He Who presided said, "Thou liest; thou art a Ciceronian, not a Christian. For where thy treasure is, there will thy heart be also." Straightway I became dumb, and [then I felt] the strokes of the whip—for He had ordered me to be scourged. . . . At last the bystanders fell at the knees of Him Who presided, and prayed Him to pardon my youth and give me opportunity to repent of my error, on the understanding that the extreme of torture should be inflicted upon me if ever I read again the books of Gentile authors. . . . This experience was no sweet or idle dream. . . . I profess that my shoulders were black and blue, and that I felt the bruises long after I awoke. . . . Henceforth I read the books of God with greater zeal than I had ever given before to the books of men.[11]

In 379 he returned to Antioch, and was ordained a priest. In 382 we find him in Rome as secretary to Pope Damasus, and commissioned by him to make an improved Latin translation of the New Testament. He continued to wear the brown robe and the tunic of an anchorite, and lived an ascetic life amid a luxurious papal court. The pious Marcella and Paula received him into their aristocratic homes as their spiritual adviser, and his pagan critics thought he enjoyed the company of women more than became so passionate a praiser of celibacy and virginity. He replied by satirizing the Roman society of the age in ageless terms:

> Those women who paint their cheeks with rouge and their eyes with belladonna, whose faces are covered with powder . . . whom no number of years can convince that they are old; who heap their heads with borrowed tresses . . . and behave like trembling schoolgirls before their grandsons. . . . Gentile widows flaunt silk dresses, deck themselves in gleaming jewelry, and reek of musk. . . . Other women put on men's clothing, cut their hair short . . . blush to be women, and prefer to look like eunuchs. . . . Some unmarried women prevent conception by the help of potions, murdering human beings before they are conceived; others, when they find themselves with child as the result of sin, secure abortion with drugs. . . . Yet there are women who say, "To the pure all things are pure. . . . Why should I refrain from the food which God made for my enjoyment?"[12]

He scolds a Roman lady in terms that suggest an appreciative eye:

> Your vest is slit on purpose. . . . Your breasts are confined in strips of linen, your chest is imprisoned in a tight girdle . . . your shawl

sometimes drops so as to leave your white shoulders bare; and then it hastily hides what it intentionally revealed.[13]

Jerome adds to the moralist's bias the exaggerations of the literary artist molding a period, and of a lawyer inflating a brief. His satires recall those of Juvenal, or of our own time; it is pleasant to know that women have always been as charming as they are today. Like Juvenal, Jerome denounces impartially, fearlessly, and ecumenically. He is shocked to find concubinage even among Christians, and more shocked to find it covered by the pretense of practicing chastity the hard way. "From what source has this plague of 'dearly beloved sisters' found its way into the church? Whence come these unwedded wives? These novel concubines, these one-man harlots? They live in the same house with their male friends; they occupy the same room, often the same bed; yet they call us suspicious if we think that anything is wrong."[14] He attacks the Roman clergy whose support might have raised him to the papacy. He ridicules the curled and scented ecclesiastics who frequent fashionable society, and the legacy-hunting priest who rises before dawn to visit women before they have gotten out of bed.[15] He condemns the marriage of priests and their sexual digressions, and argues powerfully for clerical celibacy; only monks, he thinks, are true Christians, free from property, lust, and pride. With an eloquence that would have enlisted Casanova, Jerome calls upon men to give up all and follow Christ, asks the Christian matrons to dedicate their first-born to the Lord as offerings due under the Law,[16] and advises his lady friends, if they cannot enter a convent, at least to live as virgins in their homes. He comes close to rating marriage as sin. "I praise marriage, but because it produces me virgins";[17] he proposes to "cut down by the ax of virginity the wood of marriage,"[18] and exalts John the celibate apostle over Peter, who had a wife.[19] His most interesting letter (384) is to a girl, Eustochium, on the pleasures of virginity. He is not against marriage, but those who avoid it escape from Sodom, and painful pregnancies, and bawling infants, and household cares, and the tortures of jealousy. He admits that the path of purity is also hard, and that eternal vigilance is the price of virginity.

> Virginity can be lost even by a thought. . . . Let your companions be those who are pale of face and thin with fasting. . . . Let your fasts be of daily occurrence. Wash your bed and water your couch nightly with tears. . . . Let the seclusion of your own chamber ever guard you; ever let the Bridegroom sport with you within. . . . When sleep falls upon you He will come behind the wall, and will put His hand through the door and will touch your belly (*ventrem*). And you will awake and rise up and cry, "I am sick with love." And you will hear Him answer: "A garden enclosed is my sister, my spouse; a spring shut up, a fountain sealed." [20]

The publication of this letter, Jerome tells us, "was greeted with showers of stones"; perhaps some readers sensed a morbid prurience in these strange counsels in a man apparently not yet free from the heat of desire. When, a few months later (384), the young ascetic Blesilla died, many blamed the austerities that had been taught her by Jerome; some pagans proposed to throw him into the Tiber with all the monks of Rome. Unrepentant, he addressed to the hysterically mournful mother a letter of consolation and reproof. In the same year Pope Damasus passed away, and his successor did not renew Jerome's appointment as papal secretary. In 385 he left Rome forever, taking with him Blesilla's mother Paula, and Eustochium her sister. At Bethlehem he built a monastery of which he became head, a convent over which first Paula and then Eustochium presided, a church for the common worship of the monks and nuns, and a hospice for pilgrims to the Holy Land.

He made his own cell in a cave, gathered his books and papers there, gave himself up to study, composition, and administration, and lived there the remaining thirty-four years of his life. He quarreled at pen's point with Chrysostom, Ambrose, Pelagius, and Augustine. He wrote with dogmatic force half a hundred works on questions of casuistry and Biblical interpretation, and his writings were eagerly read even by his enemies. He opened a school in Bethlehem, where he humbly and freely taught children a variety of subjects, including Latin and Greek; now a confirmed saint, he felt that he could read again the classic authors whom he had forsworn in his youth. He resumed the study of Hebrew, which he had begun in his first sojourn in the East; and in eighteen years of patient scholarship he achieved that magnificent and sonorous translation of the Bible into Latin which is known to us as the Vulgate, and remains as the greatest and most influential literary accomplishment of the fourth century. There were errors in the translation as in any work so vast, and some "barbarisms" of common speech which offended the purists; but its Latin formed the language of theology and letters throughout the Middle Ages, poured Hebraic emotion and imagery into Latin molds, and gave to literature a thousand noble phrases of compact eloquence and force.* The Latin world became acquainted with the Bible as never before.

Jerome was a saint only in the sense that he lived an ascetic life devoted to the Church; he was hardly a saint in character or speech. It is sad to find in so great a man so many violent outbursts of hatred, misrepresentation, and controversial ferocity. He calls John, Patriarch of Jerusalem, a Judas, a Satan, for whom hell can never provide adequate punishment;[21] he describes the majestic Ambrose as "a deformed crow";[22] and to make trouble for his old

---

* Jerome's translation was mostly direct, from the original Hebrew or Greek; at times, however, he translated from the Greek versions of Aquila, Symmachus, or Theodotion. His translation, revised in 1592 and 1907, is still the standard Latin text of the Bible for the Roman Catholic world. The "Douai Bible" is the English version of this Vulgate.

friend Rufinus he pursues the dead Origen with such heresy-hunting fury as to force the condemnation of Origen by Pope Anastasius (400). We might rather have pardoned some sins of the flesh than these acerbities of the soul.

His critics punished him without delay. When he taught the Greek and Latin classics they denounced him as a pagan; when he studied Hebrew with a Jew they accused him of being a convert to Judaism; when he dedicated his works to women they described his motives as financial or worse.[23] His old age was not happy. Barbarians came down into the Near East and overran Syria and Palestine (395); "how many monasteries they captured, how many rivers were reddened with blood!" "The Roman world," he concluded sadly, "is falling."[24] While he lived, his beloved Paula, Marcella, and Eustochium died. Almost voiceless and fleshless with austerities, and bent with age, he toiled day after day on work after work; he was writing a commentary on Jeremiah when death came. He was a great, rather than a good, man; a satirist as piercing as Juvenal, a letter writer as eloquent as Seneca, an heroic laborer in scholarship and theology.

3. Christian Soldiers

Jerome and Augustine were only the greatest pair in a remarkable age. Among her "Fathers" the early medieval Church distinguished eight as "Doctors of the Church": in the East Athanasius, Basil, Gregory Nazianzen, John Chrysostom, and John of Damascus; in the West Ambrose, Jerome, Augustine, and Gregory the Great.

The career of Ambrose (340?-398) illustrates the power of Christianity to draw into its service first-rate men who, a generation earlier, would have served the state. Born at Trier, son of the prefect of Gaul, he was by every precedent destined to a political career, and we are not surprised to hear of him next as provincial governor of northern Italy. Residing at Milan, he was in close touch with the emperor of the West, who found in him the old Roman qualities of solid judgment, executive ability, and quiet courage. Learning that rival factions were gathering at the cathedral to choose a bishop, he hurried to the scene, and by his presence and his words quelled an incipient disturbance. When the factions could not agree on a candidate, someone suggested Ambrose; his name brought the people to an enthusiastic unanimity; and the governor, protesting and still unbaptized, was hurriedly christened, ordained to the diaconate, then to the priesthood, then to the episcopacy, all in one week (374).[25]

He filled his new office with the dignity and mastery of a statesman. He abandoned the trappings of political position, and lived in exemplary simplicity. He gave his money and property to the poor, and sold the consecrated plate of his church to ransom captives of war.[26] He was a theologian who powerfully defended the Nicene Creed, an orator whose sermons helped to convert Augustine, a poet who composed some of the Church's earliest and noblest hymns, a judge whose learning and integrity shamed the corruption of secular courts, a diplomat entrusted with difficult missions by both Church and state, a good disciplinarian who upheld but overshadowed the pope, an ecclesiastic who brought the great Theodosius to penance, and dominated the policies of Valentinian III. The young Emperor had an Arian mother, Justina, who tried to secure a church in Milan for an Arian priest. The congregation of Ambrose remained night and day in the beleaguered church in a holy "sit-down strike" against the Empress' orders to surrender the building. "Then it was," says Augustine, "that the custom arose of singing hymns and songs, after the use of the Eastern provinces, to save the people from being utterly worn out by their long and sorrowful vigils."[27] Ambrose fought a famous battle against the Empress, and won a signal victory for intolerance.

At Nola in southern Italy Paulinus (353–431) exemplified a gentler type of Christian saint. Born in an old rich family of Bordeaux, and married to a lady of like high lineage, he studied under the poet Ausonius, entered politics, and rapidly advanced. Suddenly "conversion" came to him in the full sense of a turning away from the world: he sold his property, and gave all to the poor except enough to keep himself in the barest necessities; and his wife Therasia agreed to live with him as his chaste "sister in Christ." The monastic life not yet having established itself in the West, they made their modest home at Nola a private monastery and lived there for thirty-five years, abstaining from meat and wine, fasting many days in every month, and happy to be released from the complexities of wealth. The pagan friends of his youth, above all his old teacher Ausonius, protested against what seemed to them a withdrawal from the obligations of civic life; he answered by inviting them to come and share his bliss. In a century of hatred and violence he kept to the end a spirit of toleration. Pagans and Jews joined Christians at his funeral.

Paulinus wrote charming verse, but only incidentally. The poet who best expressed the Christian view in this age was the Spaniard Aurelius Prudentius Clemens (c. 348–410). While Claudian and Ausonius cluttered their compositions with dead gods, Prudentius sang in the ancient meters the new and living themes: stories of the martyrs (Peri stephanon, or Book of Crowns), hymns for every hour of the day, and an answer in verse to Symmachus' plea for the statue of Victory. It was in this last poem that he made a memorable appeal to Honorius to suppress gladiatorial combats. He did not hate the pagans; he had kind words for Symmachus, and even for Julian; and he begged his fellow Christians not to destroy pagan works of art. He shared Claudian's admiration for Rome, and rejoiced that one might pass through most of the white man's world and be under the same laws, everywhere secure; "wherever we are we live as fellow citizens."[28] In this Christian poet we catch a last echo of the achievement and mastery of Rome.

It was not Rome's least glory that Gaul had now so high a civilization. Corresponding to Ausonius and Sidonius in literature were the great bishops of fourth-century Gaul: Hilary of Poitiers, Remi of Reims, Euphronius of Autun, Martin of Tours. Hilary (d. *c.* 367) was one of the most active defenders of the Nicene Creed, and wrote a treatise in twelve "books" struggling to explain the Trinity. Yet in his modest see at Poitiers we see him living the good life of a devoted churchman—rising early, receiving all callers, hearing complaints, adjusting disputes, saying Mass, preaching, teaching, dictating books and letters, listening to pious readings at his meals, and every day performing some manual labor like cultivating the fields, or weaving garments for the poor.[29] This was the ecclesiastic at his best.

St. Martin left more of a name; 3675 churches and 425 villages in France bear it today. He was born in Pannonia about 316; at twelve he wished to become a monk, but at fifteen his father compelled him to join the army. He was an unusual soldier—giving his pay to the poor, helping the distressed, practicing humility and patience as if he would make a monastery out of the army camp. After five years in military service Martin realized his ambition, and went to live as a monk in a cell, first in Italy, then at Poitiers near the Hilary he loved. In 371 the people of Tours clamored to have him as their bishop, despite his shabby garments and rough hair. He agreed, but insisted on still living like a monk. Two miles from the city, at Marmoutier, he built a monastery, gathered together eighty monks, and lived with them a life of unpretentious austerity. His idea of a bishop was of a man who not only celebrated Mass, preached, administered the sacraments, and raised funds, but also fed the hungry, clothed the naked, visited the sick, and helped the unfortunate. Gaul loved him so that all its parts told stories of his miracles, even of his having raised three men from the dead.[30] France made him one of her patron saints.

The monastery that Martin had founded at Poitiers (362) was the first of many that now sprang up in Gaul. Because the monastic idea had come to Rome through Athanasius' *Life of Anthony*, and Jerome's powerful call to the anchoritic life, the West first took up the most arduous and lonely forms of monasticism, and tried to practice in less genial climates the rigors of monks living under the Egyptian sun. The monk Wulfilaich lived for years, with bare legs and feet, on a column at Trier; in winter the nails fell from his toes, and icicles hung from his beard. St. Senoch, near Tours, enclosed himself so narrowly within four walls that the lower half of his body could not move; in this situation he lived many years, an object of veneration to the populace.[31] St. John Cassian brought the ideas of Pachomius to balance the ecstasy of Anthony; inspired by some sermons of Chrysostom, he established a monastery and convent at Marseille (415), and wrote for it the first Western regimen for the monastic life; before he died (435) some 5000 monks in Provence were living by his rule. Soon after 400 St. Honoratus and St. Caprasius built a monastery on the island of Lérins, facing Cannes. These institutions trained men to cooperative labor, study, and scholarship rather than to solitary devotion; they became schools of theology, and vitally influenced the thought of the West. When the rule of St. Benedict came to Gaul in the next century, it built upon the tradition of Cassian one of the most beneficent religious orders in history.

IV. THE CHRISTIAN EAST

1. The Monks of the East

As the Church ceased to be a set of devotees and became an institution governing millions of men, she tended to adopt a more lenient view of human frailty, and to tolerate, sometimes to share, the pleasures of this world. A minority of Christians held such condescension to be treason to Christ; they resolved to gain heaven by poverty, chastity, and prayer, and retired completely from the world. Possibly Ashoka's missionaries (c. 250 B.C.) had brought to the Near East the monastic forms as well as the theory and ethics of Buddhism; and pre-Christian anchorites like those of Serapis in Egypt, or the Essene communities in Judea, may have transmitted to Anthony and Pachomius the ideals and methods of the strictly religious life. Monasticism was for many souls a refuge from the chaos and war of the barbarian invasions; there were no taxes in the monastery or the desert cell, no military service, no marital strife, no weary toil; ordination to the priesthood was not required of a monk; and after a few years of peace would come eternal bliss.

Egypt, whose climate almost invited monasticism, teemed with anchoritic and cenobitic monks, following the solitary habits of Anthony, or the community life that Pachomius had established at Tabenne. The Nile was banked with monasteries and convents, some containing as many as 3000 monks and nuns. Of the anchorites Anthony (c. 251–356) was by far the most renowned. After wandering from solitude to solitude he fixed his cell on Mount Kolzim, near the Red Sea. Admirers found him out, imitated his devotion, and built their cells as near to his as he would permit; before he died the desert was peopled with his spiritual progeny. He seldom washed, and lived to the age of 105. He declined an invitation from Constantine, but at the age of ninety he journeyed to Alexandria to support Athanasius against the Arians. Only less famous was Pachomius, who (325) founded nine monasteries and one nunnery; sometimes 7000 monks who followed his rule gathered to celebrate some holy day. These cenobites worked as well as prayed; periodically they sailed down the Nile to Alexandria to sell their products, buy their necessities, and join in the ecclesiastical-political fray.

Among the anchorites a keen rivalry arose for the austerity championship. Macarius of Alexandria, says the Abbé Duchesne, "could never hear of any feat of asceticism without at once trying to surpass it." If other monks ate no cooked food in Lent, Macarius ate none for seven years; if some punished themselves with sleeplessness, Macarius could be seen "frantically endeavoring for twenty consecutive nights to keep himself awake." Throughout one Lent he stood upright night and day, and ate nothing except, once a week, a few cabbage leaves; and during this time he continued to work at his basket-weaving trade.[32] For six months he slept in a marsh, and exposed his naked body to poisonous flies.[33] Some monks excelled in feats of solitude; so Serapion inhabited a cave at the bottom of an abyss into which few pilgrims had the hardihood to descend; when Jerome and Paula reached his lair they found a man almost composed of bones, dressed only in a loincloth, face and shoulders covered by uncut hair; his cell was barely large enough for a bed of leaves and a plank; yet this man had lived among the aristocracy of Rome.[34] Some, like Bessarion for forty, Pachomius for fifty, years, never lay down while they slept;[35] some specialized in silence, and went many years without uttering a word; others carried heavy weights wherever they went, or bound their limbs with iron bracelets, greaves, or chains. Many proudly recorded the number of years since they had looked upon a woman's face.[36] Nearly all anchorites lived—some to a great age—on a narrow range of food. Jerome tells of monks who subsisted exclusively on figs or on barley bread. When Macarius was ill someone brought him grapes; unwilling so to indulge himself, he sent them to another hermit, who sent them to another; and so they made the rounds of the desert (Rufinus assures us) until they came back intact to Macarius.[37] The pilgrims who flocked from all quarters of the Christian world to see the monks of the East credited them with miracles as remarkable as those of Christ. They could cure diseases or repel demons by a touch or a word, tame serpents or lions with a look or a prayer, and cross the Nile on the back of a crocodile. The relics of the anchorites became the most precious possession of Christian churches, and are treasured in them to this day.

In the monasteries the abbot required absolute obedience, and tested novices with impossible commands. One abbot (story says) ordered a novice to leap into a raging furnace; the novice obeyed; the flame, we are informed, parted to let him pass. Another monk was told to plant the abbot's walking stick in the earth and water it till it flowered; for years he walked daily to the Nile, two miles away, to draw water to pour upon the stick; in the third year God took pity on him and the stick bloomed.[38] Work was prescribed for the monks, says Jerome,[39] "lest they be led astray by dangerous imaginings." Some tilled fields, some tended gardens, wove mats or baskets, carved wooden shoes, or copied manuscripts; many ancient classics were preserved by their pens. Most Egyptian monks, however, were innocent of letters, and scorned secular knowledge as a futile conceit.[40] Many of them considered cleanliness hostile to godliness; the virgin Silvia refused to wash any part of her body except her fingers; in a convent of 130 nuns none ever bathed, or washed the feet. Towards the end of the fourth century, however, the monks became resigned to water, and the abbot Alexander, scorning this decadence, looked back longingly to the time when monks "never washed the face."[41]

The Near East rivaled Egypt in the number and marvels of its monks and nuns. Jerusalem and Antioch were meshed with monastic communities or cells. The Syrian desert was peopled with anchorites; some of them, like Hindu fakirs, bound themselves with chains to immovable rocks, others disdained so settled a habitation, and roamed over the mountains eating grass.[42] Simeon Stylites (390?–459), we are told, used to go without food through the forty days of Lent; during one Lent he was, at his own insistence, walled up in an enclosure with a little bread and water; on Easter he was unwalled, and the bread and the water were found untouched. At Kalat Seman, in northern Syria, about 422, Simeon built himself a column six feet high and lived on it. Ashamed of his moderation, he built and lived on ever taller columns, until he made his permanent abode on a pillar sixty feet high. Its circumference at the top was little more than three feet; a railing kept the saint from falling to the ground in his sleep. On this perch Simeon lived uninterruptedly for thirty years, exposed to rain and sun and cold. A ladder enabled disciples to take him food and remove his waste. He bound himself to the pillar by a rope; the rope became embedded in his flesh, which putrefied around it, stank, and teemed with worms; Simeon picked up the worms that fell from his sores, and replaced them there, saying to them, "Eat what God has given you." From his high pulpit he preached sermons to the crowds that came to see him, converted barbarians, performed marvelous cures, played ecclesiastical politics, and shamed the moneylenders into reducing their interest charges from twelve to six per cent.[43] His exalted piety created a fashion of pillar hermits, which lasted for twelve centuries, and, in a thoroughly secularized form, persists today.

The Church did not approve of such excesses; perhaps she sensed a fierce pride in these humiliations, a spiritual greed in this self-denial, a secret sensualism in this flight from woman and the world. The records of these ascetics abound in sexual visions and dreams; their cells resounded with their moans as they struggled with imaginary temptations and erotic thoughts; they believed that the air about them was full of demons assailing them; the monks seem to have found it harder to be virtuous in solitude than if they had lived among all the opportunities of the town. It was not unusual for anchorites to go mad. Rufinus tells of a young monk whose cell was entered by a beautiful woman; he succumbed to her charms, after which she disappeared, he thought, into the air; the monk ran out wildly to the nearest village, and leaped into the furnace of a public bath to cool his fire. In another case a young woman begged admission to a monk's cell on the plea that wild beasts were pursuing her; he consented to take her in briefly; but in that hour she happened to touch him, and the flame of desire sprang up in him as if all his years of austerity had left it undimmed. He tried to grasp her, but she vanished from his arms and his sight, and a chorus of demons, we are told, exulted with loud laughter over his fall. This monk, says Rufinus, could no longer bear the monastic life; like Paphnuce in Anatole France's *Thaïs*, he could not exorcise the vision of beauty that he had imagined or seen; he left his cell, plunged into the life of the city, and followed that vision at last into hell.[44]

The organized Church had at first no control over the monks, who rarely took any degree of holy orders; yet she felt responsibility for their excesses, since she shared in the glory of their deeds. She could not afford to agree completely with monastic ideals; she praised celibacy, virginity, and poverty, but could not condemn marriage or parentage or property, as sins; she had now a stake in the continuance of the race. Some monks left their cells or monasteries at will, and troubled the populace with their begging; some went from town to town preaching asceticism, selling real or bogus relics, terror-izing synods, and exciting impressionable people to destroy pagan temples or statuary, or, now and then, to kill an Hypatia. The Church could not tolerate these independent actions. The Council of Chalcedon (451) or-dained that greater circumspection should be used in admitting persons to monastic vows; that such vows should be irrevocable; and that no one should organize a monastery, or leave it, without permission from the bishop of the diocese.

2. The Eastern Bishops

Christianity was now (400) almost completely triumphant in the East. In Egypt the native Christians, or Copts,* were already a majority of the popu-lation, supporting hundreds of churches and monasteries. Ninety Egyptian bishops acknowledged the authority of the patriarch in Alexandria, who almost rivaled the power of the Pharaohs and the Ptolemies. Some of these patriarchs were ecclesiastical politicians of no lovable type, like the Theoph-ilus who burned to the ground the pagan temple and library of Serapis (389). More pleasing is the modest bishop of Ptolemais, Synesius. Born in Cyrene (c. 365), he studied mathematics and philosophy at Alexandria under Hy-patia; to the end of his life he remained her devoted friend, calling her "the true exponent of the true philosophy." He visited Athens and was there confirmed in his paganism; but in 403 he married a Christian lady, and gal-lantly accepted Christianity; he found it a simple courtesy to transform his Neoplatonic trinity of the One, the nous, and the Soul into the Father, Spirit, and the Son.[45] He wrote many delightful letters, and some minor philo-sophical works of which none is of value to anyone today except his essay In Praise of Baldness. In 410 Theophilus offered him the bishopric of Ptole-mais. He was now a country gentleman, with more money than ambition; he protested that he was unfit, that he did not (as the Nicene Creed required) believe in the resurrection of the body, that he was married, and had no in-tention of abandoning his wife. Theophilus, to whom dogmas were instru-ments, winked at these errors, and transformed Synesius into a bishop before

---

* Copt is a Europeanized form of the Arabic Kibt, which is a corruption of the Greek Aigyptos, Egyptian.

the philosopher could make up his mind. It was typical of him that his last letter was to Hypatia, and his last prayer to Christ.[46]

In Syria the pagan temples were disposed of in the manner of Theophilus. Imperial edicts ordered them closed; the surviving pagans resisted the order but resigned themselves to defeat on noting the indifference with which their gods accepted destruction. Asiatic Christianity had saner leaders than those of Egypt.* In a short life of fifty years (329?–379) the great Basil learned rhetoric under Libanius in Constantinople, studied philosophy in Athens, visited the anchorites of Egypt and Syria, and rejected their introverted asceticism; became bishop of Caesarea in Cappadocia, organized Christianity in his country, revised its ritual, introduced self-supporting cenobitic monasticism, and drew up a monastic rule that still governs the monasteries of the Greco-Slavonic world. He advised his followers to avoid the theatrical severities of the Egyptian anchorites, but rather to serve God, health, and sanity by useful work; tilling the fields, he thought, was an excellent prayer. To this day the Christian East acknowledges his pre-eminent influence.

In Constantinople hardly a sign of pagan worship remained. Christianity itself, however, was torn with conflict; Arianism was still powerful, new heresies were always rising, and every man had his own theology. "This city," wrote Basil's brother, Gregory of Nyassa, about 380, "is full of mechanics and slaves who are all of them profound theologians, and preach in the shops and the streets. If you desire a man to change a piece of silver he informs you wherein the Son differs from the Father; if you ask the price of a loaf ... you are told that the Son is inferior to the Father; and if you inquire whether the bath is ready, the answer is, the Son was made out of nothing."[47] In the reign of Theodosius I the Syrian Isaac founded the first monastery in the new capital; similar institutions rapidly multiplied; and by 400 the monks were a power and a terror in the city, playing a noisy role in the conflicts of patriarch with patriarch, and of patriarch with emperor.

Gregory Nazianzen learned the bitterness of sectarian hatred when he accepted a call from the orthodox Christians of Constantinople to be their bishop (379). Valens had just died, but the Arians whom that Emperor had set up were still in ecclesiastical control, and held their services in St. Sophia. Gregory had to house his altar and his congregation in the home of a friend, but he called his modest church by a hopeful name—Anastasia (Resurrection). He was a man of equal piety and learning; he had studied in Athens along with his countryman Basil, and only his second successor would rival his eloquence. His congregation grew and grew till it was larger than those of the official basilicas. On the eve of Easter, 379, a crowd of Ari-

---

* St. Nicholas, in the fourth century, modestly filled the episcopal see of Myra in Lycia, never dreaming that he was to be the patron saint of Russia, of thieves and boys and girls, and at last, in his Dutch name as Santa Claus, to enter into the Christmas mythology of half the Christian world.

ans attacked the Anastasia chapel with a volley of stones. Eighteen months later the orthodox Emperor Theodosius led Gregory in pomp and triumph to his proper throne in St. Sophia. But ecclesiastical politics soon ended his tranquillity; jealous bishops proclaimed his appointment invalid, and ordered him to defend himself before a council. Too proud to fight for his see, Gregory resigned (381) and returned to Cappadocian Nazianzus, to spend the remaining eight years of his life in obscurity and peace.

When his indifferent successor died, the imperial court invited to St. Sophia a priest of Antioch known to history as St. John Chrysostom—of the Golden Mouth. Born (345?) of a noble family, he had imbibed rhetoric from Libanius, and had familiarized himself with pagan literature and philosophy; in general the Eastern prelates were more learned and disputatious than those of the West. John was a man of keen intellect and sharper temper. He disturbed his new congregation by taking Christianity seriously, condemning in plain terms the injustices and immoralities of the age.[48] He denounced the theater as an exhibition of lewd women, and as a school of profanity, seduction, and intrigue. He asked the opulent Christians of the capital why they spent so much of their wealth in loose living, instead of giving most of it to the poor as Christ had commanded. He wondered why some men had twenty mansions, twenty baths, a thousand slaves, doors of ivory, floors of mosaic, walls of marble, ceilings of gold; and threatened the rich with hell for entertaining their guests with Oriental dancing girls.[49] He scolded his clergy for their lazy and luxurious lives,[50] and their suspicious use of women to minister to them in their rectories; he deposed thirteen of the bishops under his jurisdiction for licentiousness or simony; and he reproved the monks of Constantinople for being more frequently in the streets than in their cells. He practiced what he preached: the revenues of his see were spent not in the display that usually marked the Eastern bishoprics, but in the establishment of hospitals and in assistance to the poor. Never had Constantinople heard sermons so powerful, brilliant, and frank. Here were no pious abstractions, but Christian precepts, applied so specifically that they hurt.

> Who could be more oppressive than the landlords? If you look at the way in which they treat their miserable tenants, you will find them more savage than barbarians. They lay intolerable and continual imposts upon men who are weakened with hunger and toil throughout their lives, and they put upon them the burden of oppressive services. . . . They make them work all through the winter in cold and rain, they deprive them of sleep, and send them home with empty hands. . . .
> The tortures and beatings, the exactions and ruthless demands for services, which such men suffer from agents are worse than hunger. Who could recount the ways in which these agents use them for profit and then cheat them? Their labor turns the agent's olive-press;

but they receive not a scrap of the produce which they are compelled illegally to bottle for the agents, and they get only a tiny sum for their work.[51]

Congregations like to be scolded, but not to be reformed. The women persisted in their perfumes, the wealthy in their banquets, the clergy in their female domestics, the theaters in their revelations; and soon every group in the city except the powerless poor was against the man with the golden mouth. The Empress Eudoxia, wife of Arcadius, was leading the gay set of the capital in luxurious living. She interpreted one of John's sermons as alluding to her, and she demanded of her weakling husband that he call a synod to try the patriarch. In 403 a council of Eastern bishops met at Chalcedon. John refused to appear, on the ground that he should not be tried by his enemies. The council deposed him, and he went quietly into exile; but so great a clamor of protest rose from the people that the frightened Emperor recalled him to his see. A few months later he was again denouncing the upper classes, and made some critical comments on a statue of the Empress. Eudoxia once more demanded his expulsion; and Theophilus of Alexandria, always ready to weaken a rival see, reminded Arcadius that the Chalcedon decree of deposition still stood, and could be enforced. Soldiers were sent to seize Chrysostom; he was conveyed across the Bosporus, and banished to a village in Armenia (404). When his faithful followers heard the news they broke out in wild insurrection; and in the tumult St. Sophia and the near-by Senate house were set on fire. From his exile Chrysostom sent letters of appeal to Honorius and the bishop of Rome. Arcadius ordered him removed to the remote desert of Pityus in Pontus. On the way the exhausted prelate died at Comana, in the sixty-second year of his age (407). From that time to this, with brief intermissions, the Eastern Church has remained the servant of the state.

V. ST. AUGUSTINE (354–430)

1. The Sinner

The North Africa in which Augustine was born was a miscellany of breeds and creeds. Punic and Numidian blood mingled with Roman in the population, perhaps in Augustine; so many of the people spoke Punic—the old Phoenician language of Carthage—that Augustine as bishop appointed only priests who could speak it. Donatism challenged orthodoxy, Manicheism challenged both, and apparently the majority of the people were still pagan.[52] Augustine's birthplace was Tagaste in Numidia. His mother, St. Monica, was a devoted Christian, whose life was almost consumed in caring and praying for her wayward son. His father was a man of narrow means and broad principles, whose infidelities were patiently accepted by Monica in the firm belief that they could not last forever.

At twelve the boy was sent to school at Madaura, and at seventeen to higher studies at Carthage. Salvian would soon describe Africa as "the cesspool of the world," and Carthage as "the cesspool of Africa";[53] hence Monica's parting advice to her son:

> She commanded me, and with much earnestness forewarned me, that I should not commit fornication, and especially that I should never defile any man's wife. These seemed to me no better than women's counsels, which it would be a shame for me to follow. . . . I ran headlong with such blindness that I was ashamed among my equals to be guilty of less impudency than they were, whom I heard brag mightily of their naughtiness; yea, and so much the more boasting by how much more they had been beastly; and I took pleasure to do it, not for the pleasure of the act only, but for the praise of it also; . . . and when I lacked opportunity to commit a wickedness that should make me as bad as the lost, I would feign myself to have done what I never did.[54]

He proved an apt pupil in Latin also, and in rhetoric, mathematics, music, and philosophy; "my unquiet mind was altogether intent to seek for learning."[55] He disliked Greek, and never mastered it or learned its literature; but he was so fascinated by Plato that he called him a "demigod,"[56] and did not cease to be a Platonist when he became a Christian. His pagan training in logic and philosophy prepared him to be the most subtle theologian of the Church.

Having graduated, he taught grammar at Tagaste, and then rhetoric at Carthage. Since he was now sixteen "there was much ado to get me a wife"; however, he preferred a concubine—a convenience sanctioned by pagan morals and Roman law; still unbaptized, Augustine could take his morals where he pleased. Concubinage was for him a moral advance; he abandoned promiscuity, and seems to have been faithful to his concubine until their parting in 385. In 382, still a lad of eighteen, he found himself unwillingly the father of a son, whom he called at one time "son of my sin," but more usually Adeodatus—gift of God. He came to love the boy tenderly, and never let him go far from his side.

At twenty-nine he left Carthage for the larger world of Rome. His mother, fearing that he would die unbaptized, begged him not to go, and when he persisted, besought him to take her with him. He pretended to consent; but at the dock he left her at prayer in a chapel, and sailed without her.[57] At Rome he taught rhetoric for a year; but the students cheated him of his fees, and he applied for a professorship at Milan. Symmachus examined him, approved, and sent him to Milan by state post. There his brave mother overtook him, and persuaded him to listen with her to the sermons of Ambrose. He was moved by them, but even more by the hymns the congregation sang. At the same time Monica won him over to the idea of marriage, and in effect betrothed him, now thirty-two, to a girl with more money than years. Augustine agreed to wait two years till she should be twelve. As a preliminary he sent his mistress back to Africa, where she buried her grief in a nunnery. A few weeks of continence unnerved him, and instead of marrying he took another concubine. "Give me chastity," he prayed, "but not yet!" [58]

Amid these diversions he found time for theology. He had begun with his mother's simple faith, but had cast it off proudly at school. For nine years (374–83) he accepted Manichean dualism as the most satisfactory explanation of a world so indifferently compounded of evil and good. For a time he flirted with the skepticism of the later Academy; but he was too emotional to remain long in suspended judgment. At Rome and Milan he studied Plato and Plotinus; Neoplatonism entered deeply into his philosophy, and, through him, dominated Christian theology till Abélard. It became for Augustine the vestibule to Christianity. Ambrose had recommended him to read the Bible in the light of Paul's statement that "the letter killeth but the spirit maketh to live." Augustine found that a symbolic interpretation removed what had seemed to him the puerilities of Genesis. He read Paul's epistles, and felt that here was a man who, like himself, had passed through a thousand doubts. In Paul's final faith there had been no mere abstract Platonic Logos, but a Divine Word that had become man. One day, as Augustine sat in a Milan garden with his friend Alypius, a voice seemed to keep ringing in his ears: "Take up and read; take up and read." He opened Paul again, and read: "Not in rioting and drunkenness, not in chambering and wantonness, not in strife and envying; but put ye on the Lord Jesus Christ, and make not provision for the flesh to fulfill the lusts thereof." The passage completed for Augustine a long evolution of feeling and thought; there was something infinitely warmer and deeper in this strange faith than in all the logic of philosophy. Christianity came to him as a profound emotional satisfaction. Surrendering the skepticism of the intellect, he found, for the first time in his life, moral stimulus and mental peace. His friend Alypius confessed himself ready for a like submission. Monica, receiving their capitulation, melted her heart out in grateful prayer.

On Easter Sunday of 387 Augustine, Alypius, and Adeodatus were baptized by Ambrose, with Monica standing happily by. All four resolved to go to Africa and live a monastic life. At Ostia Monica died, confident of reunion in paradise. Arrived in Africa, Augustine sold his modest patrimony and gave the proceeds to the poor. Then he and Alypius and some friends formed a religious community, and lived at Tagaste in poverty, celibacy, study, and prayer. So was founded (388) the Augustinian order, the oldest monastic fraternity in the West.

2. The Theologian

In 389 Adeodatus passed away, and Augustine mourned him as bitterly as if still uncertain of the eternal bliss awaiting those who died in Christ. Work and writing were his only consolations. In 391 Valerius, Bishop of near-by Hippo (now Bone), asked his aid in administering the diocese, and for this purpose ordained him a priest. Valerius often yielded the pulpit to him, and Augustine's eloquence impressed the congregation even when they could not understand him. Hippo was a seaport of some 40,000 population; the Catholics had one church there, the Donatists another; the remainder of the people were Manicheans or pagans. The Manichean bishop, Fortunatus, had hitherto dominated the theological scene; Donatists joined Catholics in urging Augustine to meet him in debate; he consented; and for two days these novel gladiators crossed words before a crowd that filled the Baths of Sosius. Augustine won; Fortunatus left Hippo, and never returned (392).

Four years later Valerius, alleging his age, asked the congregation to choose his successor. Augustine was unanimously elected; and though he protested and wept, and begged the privilege of returning to his monastery, he was prevailed upon, and for the remaining thirty-four years of his life he was Bishop of Hippo; from this foot of earth he moved the world. He chose one or two deacons, and brought two monks from his monastery to help him; they lived monastically and communistically in the episcopal rectory; Augustine was a bit puzzled to understand how one of his aides, at death, could leave a tidy legacy.[59] All subsisted on a vegetarian diet, reserving meat for guests and the sick. Augustine himself is described as short and thin, and never strong; he complained of a lung disorder, and suffered unduly from the cold. He was a man of sensitive nerves, easily excited, of keen and somewhat morbid imagination, of subtle and flexible intellect. Despite a tenacious dogmatism and some occasional intolerance, he must have had many lovable qualities; several men who came to learn rhetoric from him accepted his lead into Christianity; and Alypius followed him to the end.

He had hardly taken his seat as bishop when he began a lifelong war against the Donatists. He challenged their leaders to public debate, but few cared to accept; he invited them to friendly conferences, but was met first with silence, then with insult, then with violence; several Catholic bishops in North Africa were assaulted, and some attempts seem to have been made upon the life of Augustine himself;[60] however, we do not have the Donatist side of this story. In 411 a council called by the Emperor Honorius met at Carthage to quiet the Donatist dispute; the Donatists sent 279 bishops, the Catholics 286—but *bishop* in Africa meant little more than parish priest. The Emperor's legate, Marcellinus, after hearing both sides, decreed that the Donatists must hold no further meetings, and must hand over all their churches to the Catholics. The Donatists replied with acts of desperate violence, including, we are told, the murder of Restitutus, a priest of Hippo, and the mutilation of another member of Augustine's staff. Augustine urged the government to enforce its decree vigorously;[61] he retracted his earlier view that "no one should be coerced into the unity of Christ ... that we must fight only by arguments, and prevail only by force of reason";[62] he concluded that the Church, being the spiritual father of all, should have a parent's right to chastise an unruly son for his own good;[63] it seemed to him better that a few Donatists should suffer "than that all should be damned for want of coercion."[64] At the same time he pled repeatedly with the state officials not to enforce the death penalty against the heretics.[65]

Aside from this bitter contest, and the cares of his see, Augustine lived in the Country of the Mind, and labored chiefly with his pen. Almost every day he wrote a letter whose influence is still active in Catholic theology. His sermons alone fill volumes; and though some are spoiled by an artificial rhetoric of opposed and balanced clauses, and many deal with local and transient topics in a simple style adapted to his unlettered congregation, many of them rise to a noble eloquence born of mystic passion and profound belief. His busy mind, trained in the logic of the schools, could not be confined within the issues of his parish. In treatise after treatise he labored to reconcile with reason the doctrines of the Church that he had come to revere as the one pillar of order and decency in a ruined and riotous world. He knew that the Trinity was a stumbling block to the intellect; for fifteen years he worked on his most systematic production—*De Trinitate*—struggling to find analogies in human experience for three persons in one God. More puzzling still—filling all Augustine's life with wonder and debate—was the problem of harmonizing the free will of man with the foreknowledge of God. If God is omniscient He sees the future in all details; since God is immutable, this picture that He has of all coming events lays upon them the necessity of occurring as He has foreseen them; they are irrevocably predestined. Then how can man be free? Must he not do what God has foreseen? And if God has foreseen all things, He has known from all eternity the final fate of every soul that He creates; why, then, should He create those that are predestined to be damned?

In his first years as a Christian Augustine had written a treatise *De libero arbitrio* (*On Free Will*). He had sought then to square the existence of evil with the benevolence of an omnipotent God; and his answer was that evil is the result of free will: God could not leave man free without giving him the possibility of doing wrong as well as right. Later, under the influence of Paul's epistles, he argued that Adam's sin had left upon the human race a stain of evil inclination; that no amount of good works, but only the freely given grace of God, could enable the soul to overcome this inclination, erase this stain, and achieve salvation. God offered this grace to all, but many refused it. God knew that they would refuse it; but this possibility of damnation was the price of that moral freedom without which man would not be man. The divine foreknowledge does not destroy this freedom; God merely foresees the choices that man will freely make.[66]

Augustine did not invent the doctrine of original sin; Paul, Tertullian, Cyprian, Ambrose had taught it; but his own experience of sin, and of the "voice" that had converted him, had left in him a somber conviction that the human will is from birth inclined to evil, and can be turned to good only by the gratuitous act of God. He could not explain the evil inclination of the will except as an effect of Eve's sin and Adam's love. Since we are all children of Adam, Augustine argued, we share his guilt, are, indeed, the offspring of his guilt: the original sin was concupiscence. And concupiscence still befouls every act of generation; by the very connection of sex with parentage mankind is a "mass of perdition," and most of us will be damned. Some of us will be saved, but only through the grace of the suffering Son of God, and through the intercession of the Mother who conceived Him sinlessly. "Through a woman we were sent to destruction; through a woman salvation was restored to us." [67]

Writing so much and so hurriedly—often, it appears, by dictation to amanuenses—Augustine fell more than once into exaggerations which later he strove to modify. At times he propounded the Calvinistic doctrine that God arbitrarily chose, from all eternity, the "elect" to whom He would give His saving grace.[68] A crowd of critics rose to plague him for such theories; he conceded nothing, but fought every point to the end. From England came his ablest opponent, the footloose monk Pelagius, with a strong defense of man's freedom, and of the saving power of good works. God indeed helps us, said Pelagius, by giving us His law and commandments, by the example and precepts of His saints, by the cleansing waters of baptism, and the redeeming blood of Christ. But God does not tip the scales against our salvation by making human nature inherently evil. There was no original sin, no fall of man; only he who commits a sin is punished for it; it transmits no guilt to his progeny.[69] God does not predestine man to heaven or hell, does not choose arbitrarily whom He will damn or save; He leaves the choice of our fate to ourselves. The theory of innate human depravity, said Pelagius, was a cowardly shifting to God of the blame for man's sins. Man feels, and therefore is, responsible; "if I ought, I can."

Pelagius came to Rome about 400, lived with pious families, and earned a reputation for virtue. In 409 he fled from Alaric, first to Carthage, then to Palestine. There he dwelt in peace till the Spanish priest Orosius came from Augustine to warn Jerome against him (415). An Eastern synod tried the monk, and declared him orthodox; an African synod, prodded by Augustine, repudiated this finding, and appealed to Pope Innocent I, who declared Pelagius a heretic; whereupon Augustine hopefully announced, "*Causa finita* *est*" (The case is finished).[70] * But Innocent, dying, was succeeded by Zosimus, who pronounced Pelagius guiltless. The African bishops appealed to Honorius; the Emperor was pleased to correct the Pope; Zosimus yielded (418); and the Council of Ephesus (431) condemned as a heresy the Pelagian view that man can be good without the helping grace of God.

Augustine could be caught in contradictions and absurdities, even in morbid cruelties of thought; but he could not be overcome, because in the end his own soul's adventures, and the passion of his nature, not any chain of reasoning, molded his theology. He knew the weakness of the intellect: it was the individual's brief experience sitting in reckless judgment upon the experience of the race; and how could forty years understand forty centuries? "Dispute not by excited argument," he wrote to a friend, "those things which you do not yet comprehend, or those which in the Scriptures appear . . . to be incongruous and contradictory; meekly defer the day of your understanding." [71] Faith must precede understanding. "Seek not to understand that you may believe, but believe that you may understand"—*crede ut intelligas.*[72] "The authority of the Scriptures is higher than all the efforts of the human intelligence." [73] The Bible, however, need not always be taken literally; it was written to be intelligible to simple minds, and had to use corporeal terms for spiritual realities.[74] When interpretations differ we must rest in the decision of the Church councils, in the collective wisdom of her wisest men.[75]

But even faith is not enough for understanding; there must be a clean heart to let in the rays of the divinity that surrounds us. So humbled and cleansed, one may, after many years, rise to the real end and essence of religion, which is "the possession of the living God." "I desire to know God and the soul. Nothing more? Nothing whatever." [76] Oriental Christianity spoke mostly of Christ; Augustine's theology is "of the First Person"; it is of and to God the Father that he speaks and writes. He gives no description of God, for only God can know God fully; [77] probably "the true God has neither sex, age, nor body." [78] But we can know God, in a sense intimately, through creation; everything in the world is an infinite marvel in its organization and functioning, and would be impossible without a creative intelligence; [79] the order, symmetry, and rhythm of living things proclaims a kind of Platonic deity, in whom beauty and wisdom are one.[80]

We need not believe, says Augustine, that the world was created in six "days"; probably God in the beginning created only a nebulous mass (*nebulosa species*); but in this mass lay the seminal order, or productive capacities (*rationes seminales*), from which all things would develop by natural causes.[81] For Augustine, as for Plato, the actual objects and events of this

---

* We cannot find in the extant works or reliable traditions of Augustine the words often attributed to him on this occasion—"*Roma locuta est, causa finita*" (Rome has spoken, the case is finished).

world pre-existed in the mind of God "as the plan of a building is conceived by the architect before it is built"; [82] and creation proceeds in time according to these eternal exemplars in the divine mind.

3. The Philosopher

How shall we do justice so briefly to so powerful a personality, and so fertile a pen? Through 230 treatises he spoke his mind on almost every problem of theology and philosophy, and usually in a style warm with feeling and bright with new-coined phrases from his copious mint. He discussed with diffidence and subtlety the nature of time.[83] He anticipated Descartes' "Cogito, ergo sum": to refute the Academics, who denied that man can be certain of anything, he argued: "Who doubts that he lives and thinks? . . . For if he doubts, he lives." [84] He presaged Bergson's complaint that the intellect, through long dealing with corporeal things, is a constitutional materialist; he proclaimed, like Kant, that the soul is the most directly known of all realities, and clearly stated the idealistic position—that since matter is known only through mind, we cannot logically reduce mind to matter.[85] He suggested the Schopenhauerian thesis that will, not intellect, is fundamental in man; and he agreed with Schopenhauer that the world would be improved if all reproduction should cease.[86]

Two of his works belong to the classics of the world's literature. The *Confessions* (c. 400) is the first and most famous of all autobiographies. It is addressed directly to God, as a 100,000-word act of contrition. It begins with the sins of his youth, tells vividly the story of his conversion, and occasionally bursts into a rhapsody of prayer. All confessions are camouflage, but there was in this one a sincerity that shocked the world. Even as Augustine wrote it—forty-six and a bishop—the old carnal ideas "still live in my memory and rush into my thoughts; . . . in sleep they come upon me not to delight only, but even so far as consent, and most like to the deed";[87] bishops are not always so psychoanalytically frank. His masterpiece is the moving story of how one soul came to faith and peace, and its first lines are its summary: "Thou hast created us for Thyself, and our hearts know no rest until they repose in Thee." His faith is now unquestioning, and rises to a moving theodicy:

> Too late I came to love Thee, O Thou Beauty both so ancient and so fresh. . . . Yea, also the heaven and the earth, and all that is in them, bid me on every side that I should love Thee. . . . What now do I love when I love Thee? . . . I asked the earth, and it answered, I am not it. . . . I asked the sea and the deeps and the creeping things, and they answered: We are not thy God; seek above us. I asked the fleeting winds, and the whole air with its inhabitants answered me: Anaximenes was deceived; I am not God. I asked the heavens, the sun and

moon and stars; nor, said they, are we the God whom Thou seekest. And I replied unto all these: . . . Answer me concerning God; since that you are not He, answer me concerning Him. And they cried out with a loud voice: He made us. . . . They are not well in their wits to whom anything which Thou hast created is displeasing. . . . In Thy gift we rest; . . . in Thy good pleasure lies our peace.* [88]

The *Confessions* is poetry in prose; the *City of God* (413–26) is philosophy in history. When the news of Alaric's sack of Rome reached Africa, followed by thousands of desolate refugees, Augustine was stirred, like Jerome and others, by what seemed an irrational and Satanic calamity. Why should the city whose beauty and power men had built and reverenced through centuries, and now the citadel of Christendom, be surrendered by a benevolent deity to the ravages of barbarians? Pagans everywhere attributed the disaster to Christianity: the ancient gods, plundered, dethroned, and proscribed, had withdrawn their protection from the Rome that under their guidance had grown and prospered for a thousand years. Many Christians were shaken in their faith. Augustine felt the challenge deeply; all his vast temple of theology threatened to collapse if this panic of fear were not allayed. He resolved to devote all the powers of his genius to convincing the Roman world that such catastrophes did not for a moment impugn Christianity. For thirteen years he labored on his book, amid a press of obligations and distractions. He published it in piecemeal installments; the middle of it forgot the beginning and did not foresee the end; inevitably its 1200 pages became a confused concatenation of essays on everything from the First Sin to the Last Judgment; and only the depth of its thought, and the splendor of its style, lifted it out of its chaos to the highest rank in the literature of Christian philosophy.

Augustine's initial answer was that Rome had been punished not for her new religion but for her continued sins. He described the indecency of the pagan stage, and quoted Sallust and Cicero on the corruption of Roman politics. Once Rome had been a nation of stoics, strengthened by Catos and Scipios; she had almost created law, and had given order and peace to half the world; in those heroic days God had made His face to shine upon her. But the seeds of moral decay lay in the very religion of ancient Rome, in gods who encouraged, rather than checked, the sexual nature of man: "the god Virgineus to loose the virgin's girdle, Subigus to place her under the man, Prema to press her down . . . Priapus upon whose huge and beastly member the new bride was commanded by religious order to get up and sit!" [89] Rome was punished because she worshiped, not because she neglected, such deities. The barbarians spared Christian churches and those who

---

* Cf. the theme line of Dante's *Paradiso* (iii, 85): "*La sua voluntate è nostra pace*" (His will is our peace).

fled to them, but showed no mercy to the remnants of pagan shrines; how, then, could the invaders be the agents of a pagan revenge?

Augustine's second answer was a philosophy of history—an attempt to explain the events of recorded time on one universal principle. From Plato's conception of an ideal state existing "somewhere in heaven," from St. Paul's thought of a community of saints living and dead,[90] from the Donatist Tyconius' doctrine of two societies, one of God and one of Satan,[91] Augustine took the basic idea of his book as a tale of two cities: the earthly city of worldly men devoted to earthly affairs and joys; and the divine city of the past, present, and future worshipers of the one true God. Marcus Aurelius had provided a noble phrase: "The poet could say of Athens, Thou lovely city of Cecrops; and shalt not thou say of the world, Thou lovely city of God?"[92]—but Aurelius had meant by this the whole orderly universe. The *civitas Dei*, says Augustine, was founded by the creation of the angels; the *civitas terrena* by the rebellion of Satan. "Mankind is divided into two sorts: such as live according to man, and such as live according to God. These we mystically call the 'two cities' or societies, the one predestined to reign eternally with God, the other condemned to perpetual torment with the Devil."[93] An actual city or empire need not in all aspects be confined within the Earthly City; it may do good things—legislate wisely, judge justly, and aid the Church; and these good actions take place, so to speak, within the City of God. This spiritual city, again, is not identical with the Catholic Church; the Church too may have terrestrial interests, and its members may fall into self-seeking and sin, slipping from one city into the other. Only at the Last Judgment will the two cities be separate and distinct.[94]

By a symbolic extension of her membership to heavenly as well as to earthly souls, to pre-Christian as well as Christian righteous men, the Church may be—and by Augustine occasionally is—identified with the City of God.[95] The Church would later accept this identification as an ideological weapon of politics, and would logically deduce from Augustine's philosophy the doctrine of a theocratic state, in which the secular powers, derived from men, would be subordinate to the spiritual power held by the Church and derived from God. With this book paganism as a philosophy ceased to be, and Christianity as a philosophy began. It was the first definitive formulation of the medieval mind.

4. The Patriarch

The old lion of the faith was still at his post when the Vandals came. To the end he remained in the theological arena, felling new heresies, countering critics, answering objections, resolving difficulties. He considered gravely whether woman will retain her sex in the next world; whether the deformed and the mutilated, the thin and the fat, will be reborn as they were; and how those will be restored who were eaten by others in a famine.[96] But age had come upon him, with sad indignities. Asked about his health he replied: "In spirit I am well . . . in body I am confined to bed. I can neither walk nor stand nor sit down because of swelling piles. . . . Yet even so, since that is the Lord's good pleasure, what should I say but that I am well?" [97]

He had done his best to deter Boniface from rebellion against Rome, and had shared in recalling him to loyalty. As Gaiseric advanced, many bishops and priests asked Augustine should they stay at their posts or flee; he bade them stay, and gave example. When the Vandals laid siege to Hippo, Augustine maintained the morale of the starving people by his sermons and his prayers. In the third month of the siege he died, aged seventy-six. He left no will, having no goods; but he had written his own epitaph: "What maketh the heart of the Christian heavy? The fact that he is a pilgrim, and longs for his own country." [98]

Few men in history have had such influence. Eastern Christianity never took to him, partly because he was thoroughly un-Greek in his limited learning and in his subordination of thought to feeling and will; partly because the Eastern Church had already submitted to the state. But in the West he gave a definitive stamp to Catholic theology. Anticipating and inspiring Gregory VII and Innocent III, he formulated the claim of the Church to supremacy over the mind and the state; and the great battles of popes against emperors and kings were political corollaries of his thought. Until the thirteenth century he dominated Catholic philosophy, giving it a Neoplatonic tinge; and even Aquinas the Aristotelian often followed his lead. Wyclif, Huss, and Luther believed they were returning to Augustine when they left the Church; and Calvin based his ruthless creed upon Augustine's theories of the elect and the damned. At the same time that he stimulated men of intellect, he became an inspiration to those whose Christianity was more of the heart than of the head; mystics tried to retrace his steps in seeking a vision of God; and men and women found food and phrases for their piety in the humility and tenderness of his prayers. It may be the secret of his influence that he united and strengthened both the philosophical and the mystical strains in Christianity, and opened a path not only for Thomas Aquinas but for Thomas à Kempis as well.

His subjective, emotional, anti-intellectual emphasis marked the end of classical, the triumph of medieval, literature. To understand the Middle Ages we must forget our modern rationalism, our proud confidence in reason and science, our restless search after wealth and power and an earthly paradise; we must enter sympathetically into the mood of men disillusioned of these pursuits, standing at the end of a thousand years of rationalism, finding all dreams of utopia shattered by war and poverty and barbarism, seeking consolation in the hope of happiness beyond the grave, inspired and comforted by the story and figure of Christ, throwing themselves upon the mercy and goodness of God, and living in the thought of His eternal presence, His inescapable judgment, and the atoning death of His Son. St. Augustine above all others, and even in the age of Symmachus, Claudian, and Ausonius, reveals and phrases this mood. He is the most authentic, eloquent, and powerful voice of the Age of Faith in Christendom.

VI. THE CHURCH AND THE WORLD

Augustine's argument against paganism was the last rebuttal in the greatest of historic debates. Paganism survived in the moral sense, as a joyous indulgence of natural appetites; as a religion it remained only in the form of ancient rites and customs condoned, or accepted and transformed, by an often indulgent Church. An intimate and trustful worship of saints replaced the cult of the pagan gods, and satisfied the congenial polytheism of simple or poetic minds. Statues of Isis and Horus were renamed Mary and Jesus; the Roman Lupercalia and the feast of the purification of Isis became the Feast of the Nativity;[99] the Saturnalia were replaced by Christmas celebrations, the Floralia by Pentecost, an ancient festival of the dead by All Souls' Day,[100] the resurrection of Attis by the resurrection of Christ.[101] Pagan altars were rededicated to Christian heroes; incense, lights, flowers, processions, vestments, hymns, which had pleased the people in older cults were domesticated and cleansed in the ritual of the Church; and the harsh slaughter of a living victim was sublimated in the spiritual sacrifice of the Mass.

Augustine had protested against the adoration of saints, and in terms that Voltaire might have used in dedicating his chapel at Ferney: "Let us not treat the saints as gods; we do not wish to imitate those pagans who adore the dead. Let us not build them temples, nor raise altars to them; but with their relics let us raise an altar to the one god." [102] The Church, however, wisely accepted the inevitable anthropomorphism of popular theology. She resisted,[103] then used, then abused, the cult of martyrs and relics. She opposed the worship of images and icons, and warned her faithful that these should be reverenced only as symbols; [104] but the ardor of public feeling overcame these cautions, and led to the excesses that aroused the Byzantine iconoclasts. The Church denounced magic, astrology, and divination, but medieval, like ancient, literature, was full of them; soon people and priests would use the sign of the cross as a magic incantation to expel or drive away demons. Exorcisms were pronounced over the candidate for baptism, and total nude immersion was required lest a devil should hide in some clothing or ornament.[105] The dream cures once sought in the temples of Aesculapius could now be obtained in the sanctuary of Sts. Cosmas and Damian in Rome, and would soon be available at a hundred shrines. In such matters it was not the priests who corrupted the people, but the people who persuaded the priests.

The soul of the simple man can be moved only through the senses and the imagination, by ceremony and miracle, by myth and fear and hope; he will reject or transform any religion that does not give him these. It was natural that amid war and desolation, poverty and disease, a frightened people should find refuge and solace in chapels, churches, and cathedrals, in mystic lights and rejoicing bells, in processions, festivals, and colorful ritual.

By yielding to these popular necessities the Church was enabled to inculcate a new morality. Ambrose, always the Roman administrator, had tried to formulate the ethics of Christianity in Stoic terms, converting Cicero to his needs; and in the greater Christians of the Middle Ages, from Augustine to Savonarola, the Stoic ideal of self-control and uncompromising virtue informed the Christian mold. But that masculine morality was not the ideal of the people. They had had Stoics long enough; they had seen the masculine virtues incarnadine half the world; they longed for gentler, quieter ways, by which men might be persuaded to live in stability and peace. For the first time in European history the teachers of mankind preached an ethic of kindliness, obedience, humility, patience, mercy, purity, chastity, and tenderness —virtues perhaps derived from the lowly social origins of the Church, and their popularity among women, but admirably adapted to restore order to a de-moral-ized people, to tame the marauding barbarian, to moderate the violence of a falling world.

The reforms of the Church were greatest in the realm of sex. Paganism had tolerated the prostitute as a necessary mitigation of an arduous monogamy; the Church denounced prostitution without compromise, and demanded a single standard of fidelity for both sexes in marriage. She did not quite succeed; she raised the morals of the home, but prostitution remained, driven into stealth and degradation. Perhaps to counterbalance a sexual instinct that had run wild, the new morality exaggerated chastity into an obsession, and subordinated marriage and parentage to a lifelong virginity or celibacy as an ideal; and it took the Fathers of the Church some time to realize that no society could survive on such sterile principles. But this puritanic reaction can be understood if we recall the licentiousness of the Roman stage, the schools of prostitution in some Greek and Oriental temples, the widespread abortion and infanticide, the obscene paintings on Pompeian walls, the unnatural vice so popular in Greece and Rome, the excesses of the early emperors, the sensuality of the upper classes as revealed in Catullus and Martial, Tacitus and Juvenal. The Church finally reached a healthier view, and indeed came in time to take a lenient attitude to sins of the flesh. Meanwhile some injury was done to the conception of parentage and the family. Too many Christians of these early centuries thought that they could serve God best—or, rather, most easily escape hell—by abandoning their parents, mates, or children, and fleeing from the responsibilities of life in the frightened pursuit of a selfishly individual salvation. In paganism the family had been the social and religious unit; it was a loss that in medieval Christianity this unit became the individual.

Nevertheless the Church strengthened the family by surrounding marriage with solemn ceremony, and exalting it from a contract to a sacrament. By making matrimony indissoluble she raised the security and dignity of the wife, and encouraged the patience that comes from hopelessness. For a time the status of woman was hurt by the doctrine of some Christian Fathers that woman was the origin of sin and the instrument of Satan; but some amends were made by the honors paid to the Mother of God. Having accepted marriage, the Church blessed abundant motherhood, and sternly forbade abortion or infanticide; perhaps it was to discourage these practices that her theologians damned to a limbo of eternal darkness any child that died without baptism. It was through the influence of the Church that Valentinian I, in 374, made infanticide a capital crime.

The Church did not condemn slavery. Orthodox and heretic, Roman and barbarian alike assumed the institution to be natural and indestructible; a few philosophers protested, but they too had slaves. The legislation of the Christian emperors in this matter does not compare favorably with the laws of Antoninus Pius or Marcus Aurelius. Pagan laws condemned to slavery any free woman who married a slave; the laws of Constantine ordered the woman to be executed, and the slave to be burned alive. The Emperor Gratian decreed that a slave who accused his master of any offense except high treason to the state should be burned alive at once, without inquiry into the justice of the charge.[106] But though the Church accepted slavery as part of the law of war, she did more than any other institution of the time to mitigate the evils of servitude. She proclaimed, through the Fathers, the principle that all men are by nature equal—presumably meaning in legal and moral rights; she practiced the principle in so far as she received into her communion all ranks and classes: though no slave could be ordained to the priesthood, the poorest freedman could rise to high places in the ecclesiastical hierarchy. The Church repudiated the distinction made in pagan law between wrongs done to a freeman and those done to a slave. She encouraged manumission, made emancipation of slaves a mode of expiating sins, or of celebrating some good fortune, or of approaching the judgment seat of God. She spent great sums freeing from slavery Christians captured in war.[107] Nevertheless slavery continued throughout the Middle Ages, and died without benefit of clergy.

The outstanding moral distinction of the Church was her extensive provision of charity. The pagan emperors had provided state funds for poor families, and pagan magnates had done something for their "clients" and the poor. But never had the world seen such a dispensation of alms as was now organized by the Church. She encouraged bequests to the poor, to be administered by her; some abuses and malversation crept in, but that the

Church carried out her obligations abundantly is attested by the jealous emulation of Julian. She helped widows, orphans, the sick or infirm, prisoners, victims of natural catastrophes; and she frequently intervened to protect the lower orders from unusual exploitation or excessive taxation.[108] In many cases priests, on attaining the episcopacy, gave all their property to the poor. Christian women like Fabiola, Paula, and Melania devoted fortunes to charitable work. Following the example of pagan *valetudinaria*, the Church or her rich laymen founded public hospitals on a scale never known before. Basil established a famous hospital, and the first asylum for lepers, at Caesarea in Cappadocia. Xenodochia—refuges for wayfarers—rose along pilgrim routes; the Council of Nicaea ordered that one should be provided in every city. Widows were enlisted to distribute charity, and found in this work a new significance for their lonely lives. Pagans admired the steadfastness of Christians in caring for the sick in cities stricken with famine or pestilence.[109]

What did the Church do in these centuries for the minds of men? As Roman schools still existed, she did not feel it her function to promote intellectual development. She exalted feeling above intellect; in this sense Christianity was a "romantic" reaction against the "classic" trust in reason; Rousseau was merely a lesser Augustine. Convinced that survival demanded organization, that organization required agreement on basic principles and beliefs, and that the vast majority of her adherents longed for authoritatively established beliefs, the Church defined her creed in unchangeable dogmas, made doubt a sin, and entered upon an unending conflict with the fluent intellect and changeable ideas of men. She claimed that through divine revelation she had found the answers to the old problems of origin, nature, and destiny; "we who are instructed in the knowledge of truth by the Holy Scriptures," wrote Lactantius (307), "know the beginning of the world and its end." [110] Tertullian had said as much a century before (197), and had suggested a cloture on philosophy.[111] Having displaced the axis of man's concern from this world to the next, Christianity offered supernatural explanations for historical events, and thereby passively discouraged the investigation of natural causes; many of the advances made by Greek science through seven centuries were sacrificed to the cosmology and biology of Genesis.

Did Christianity bring a literary decline? Most of the Fathers were hostile to pagan literature, as permeated with a demonic polytheism and a degrading immorality; but the greatest of the Fathers loved the classics notwithstanding, and Christians like Fortunatus, Prudentius, Jerome, Sidonius, and Ausonius aspired to write verse like Virgil's or prose like Cicero's. Gregory Nazianzen, Chrysostom, Ambrose, Jerome, and Augustine outweigh, even in a literary sense, their pagan contemporaries—Ammianus, Symmachus, Claudian, Julian. But after Augustine prose style decayed; written Latin took over the rough vocabulary and careless syntax of the popular speech; and Latin verse for a time deteriorated into doggerel before molding new forms into majestic hymns.

The basic cause of cultural retrogression was not Christianity but barbarism; not religion but war. The human inundations ruined or impoverished cities, monasteries, libraries, schools, and made impossible the life of the scholar or the scientist. Perhaps the destruction would have been worse had not the Church maintained some measure of order in a crumbling civilization. "Amid the agitations of the world," said Ambrose, "the Church remains unmoved; the waves cannot shake her. While around her everything is in a horrible chaos, she offers to all the shipwrecked a tranquil port where they will find safety." [112] And often it was so.

The Roman Empire had raised science, prosperity, and power to their ancient peaks. The decay of the Empire in the West, the growth of poverty and the spread of violence, necessitated some new ideal and hope to give men consolation in their suffering and courage in their toil: an age of power gave way to an age of faith. Not till wealth and pride should return in the Renaissance would reason reject faith, and abandon heaven for utopia. But if, thereafter, reason should fail, and science should find no answers, but should multiply knowledge and power without improving conscience or purpose; if all utopias should brutally collapse in the changeless abuse of the weak by the strong: then men would understand why once their ancestors, in the barbarism of those early Christian centuries, turned from science, knowledge, power, and pride, and took refuge for a thousand years in humble faith, hope, and charity.

CHAPTER IV

Europe Takes Form

325-529

I. BRITAIN BECOMES ENGLAND: 325–577

UNDER Roman rule every class in Britain flourished except the peasant proprietors. The large estates grew at the expense of small holdings; the free peasant was in many cases bought out, and became a tenant farmer, or a proletarian in the towns. Many peasants supported the Anglo-Saxon invaders against the landed aristocracy.[1] Otherwise, Roman Britain prospered. Cities multiplied and grew, wealth mounted;[2] many homes had central heating and glass windows;[3] many magnates had luxurious villas. British weavers already exported those excellent woolens in which they still lead the world. A few Roman legions, in the third century, sufficed to maintain external security and internal peace.

But in the fourth and fifth centuries security was threatened on every front: on the north by the Picts of Caledonia; on the east and south by Norse and Saxon raiders; on the west by the unsubdued Celts of Wales and the adventurous Gaels and "Scots" of Ireland. In 364–7 "Scot" and Saxon coastal raids increased alarmingly; British and Gallic troops repelled them, but Stilicho had to repeat the process a generation later. In 381 Maximus, in 407 the usurper Constantine, took from Britain, for their personal purposes, legions needed for home defense, and few of these men returned. Invaders began to pour over the frontiers; Britain appealed to Stilicho for help (400), but he was fully occupied in driving Goths and Huns from Italy and Gaul. When a further appeal was made to the Emperor Honorius he answered that the British must help themselves as best they could.[4] "In the year 409," says Bede, "the Romans ceased to rule in Britain." [5]

Faced with a large-scale invasion of Picts, the British leader Vortigern invited some North German tribes to come to his help.[6] Saxons came from the region of the Elbe, Angles from Schleswig, Jutes from Jutland. Tradition —perhaps legend—reports that the Jutes arrived in 449 under the command of two brothers suspiciously named Hengist and Horsa—i.e., stallion and mare. The vigorous Germans drove back the Picts and "Scots," received tracts of land as reward, noted the military weakness of Britain, and sent the joyful word to their fellows at home.[7] Uninvited German hordes landed on Britain's shores; they were resisted with more courage than skill; they alter-

nately advanced and retired through a century of guerrilla war; finally the
Teutons defeated the British at Deorham (577), and made themselves masters
of what would later be called Angle-land—England. Most Britons thereafter
accepted the conquest, and mingled their blood with that of the conquerors;
a hardy minority retreated into the mountains of Wales and fought on; some
others crossed the Channel and gave their name to Brittany. The cities of
Britain were ruined by the long contest; transport was disrupted, industry
decayed; law and order languished, art hibernated, and the incipient Christianity of the island was overwhelmed by the pagan gods and customs of
Germany. Britain and its language became Teutonic; Roman law and institutions disappeared; Roman municipal organization was replaced by village
communities. A Celtic element remained in English blood, physiognomy,
character, literature, and art, but remarkably little in English speech, which
is now a cross between German and French.

If we would feel the fever of those bitter days we must turn from history
to the legends of Arthur and his knights, and their mighty blows to "break
the heathen and uphold the Christ." St. Gildas, a Welsh monk, in a strange
book, half history and half sermon, *On the Destruction of Britain* (546?),
mentions a "siege of Mons Badonicus" in these wars; and Nennius, a later
British historian (*c.* 796), tells of twelve battles that Arthur fought, the last
at Mt. Badon near Bath.[8] Geoffrey of Monmouth (1100?–54) provides
romantic details: how Arthur succeeded his father Uther Pendragon as king
of Britain, opposed the invading Saxons, conquered Ireland, Iceland, Norway, and Gaul, besieged Paris in 505, drove the Romans out of Britain, suppressed at great sacrifice of his men the rebellion of his nephew Modred,
killed him in battle at Winchester, was himself mortally wounded there, and
died "in the 542nd year of Our Lord's incarnation." [9] William of Malmesbury (1090?–1143) informs us that

> when Vortimer [Vortigern's brother] died, the strength of the
> Britons decayed, and they would soon have perished altogether had
> not Ambrosius, the sole survivor of the Romans, . . . quelled the pre-
> sumptuous barbarians with the powerful aid of the warlike Arthur.
> Arthur long upheld the sinking state, and roused the broken spirit
> of his countrymen to war. Finally, at Mt. Badon, relying on an
> image of the Virgin which he had affixed to his armor, he engaged
> 900 of the enemy single-handed, and dispersed them with incredible
> slaughter.[10]

Let us agree that it is incredible. We must be content with accepting Arthur
as in essentials a vague but historical figure of the sixth century, probably
not a saint, probably not a king.[11] The rest we must resign to Chrétien of
Troyes, the delectable Malory, and the chaste Tennyson.

II. IRELAND: 160–529

The Irish believe—and we cannot gainsay them—that their island of "mists and mellow fruitfulness" was first peopled by Greeks and Scythians a thousand or more years before Christ, and that their early chieftains—Cuchalain, Conor, Conall—were sons of God.[12] Himilco, the Phoenician explorer, touched Ireland about 510 B.C., and described it as "populous and fertile." [13] Perhaps in the fifth century before Christ some Celtic adventurers from Gaul or Britain or both crossed into Ireland, and conquered the natives, of whom we know nothing. The Celts apparently brought with them the iron culture of Hallstatt, and a strong kinship organization that made the individual too proud of his clan to let him form a stable state. Clan fought clan, kingdom fought kingdom, for a thousand years; between such wars the members of a clan fought one another; and when they died, good Irishmen, before St. Patrick came, were buried upright ready for battle, with faces turned toward their foes.[14] Most of the kings died in battle, or by assassination.[15] Perhaps out of eugenic obligation, perhaps as vicars of gods who required first fruits, these ancient kings, according to Irish tradition, had the right to deflower every bride before yielding her to her husband. King Conchobar was praised for his especial devotion to this duty.[16] Each clan kept a record of its members and their genealogy, its kings and battles and antiquities, "from the beginning of the world." [17]

The Celts established themselves as a ruling class, and distributed their clans in five kingdoms: Ulster, North Leinster, South Leinster, Munster, Connaught. Each of the five kings was sovereign, but all the clans accepted Tara, in Meath, as the national capital. There each king was crowned; and there, at the outset of his reign, he convened the Feis or convention of the notables of all Ireland to pass legislation binding on all the kingdoms, to correct and record the clan genealogies, and to register these in the national archives. To house this assembly King Cormac mac Airt, in the third century, built a great hall, whose foundations can still be seen. A provincial council—the Aonach, or Fair—met annually or triennially in the capital of each kingdom, legislated for its area, imposed taxes, and served as a district court. Games and contests followed these conventions: music, song, jugglery, farces, story-telling, poetry recitals, and many marriages brightened the occasion, and a large part of the population shared in the festivity. From this distance, which lends enchantment to the view, such a reconciliation of central government and local freedom seems almost ideal. The Feis continued till 560; the Aonach till 1168.

The first character whom we may confidently count as historical is Tuathal, who ruled Leinster and Meath about A.D. 160. King Niall (c. 358) invaded Wales and carried off immense booty, raided Gaul, and was killed (by an Irishman) on the river Loire; from him descended most of the later Irish kings (O'Neills). In the fifth year of the reign of his son Laeghaire (Leary), St. Patrick came to Ireland. Before this time the Irish had developed an alphabet of straight lines in various combinations; they had an extensive literature of poetry and legend, transmitted orally; and they had done good work in pottery, bronze, and gold. Their religion was an animistic polytheism, which worshiped sun and moon and divers natural objects, and peopled a thousand spots in Ireland with fairies, demons, and elves. A priestly clan of white-robed druids practiced divination, ruled sun and winds with magic wands and wheels, caused magic showers and fires, memorized and handed down the chronicles and poetry of the tribe, studied the stars, educated the young, counseled the kings, acted as judges, formulated laws, and sacrificed to the gods from altars in the open air. Among the sacred idols was a gold-covered image called the Crom Cruach; this was the god of all the Irish clans; to him, apparently, sacrifice was offered of the first-born child in every family [18]—perhaps as a check on excessive population. The people believed in reincarnation, but they also dreamed of a heavenly isle across the sea, "where there is no wailing or treachery, nothing rough or harsh, but sweet music striking upon the ear; a beauty of a wondrous land, whose view is a fair country, incomparable in its haze." [19] A story told how Prince Conall, moved by such descriptions, embarked in a boat of pearl and set out to find this happy land.

Christianity had come to Ireland a generation or more before Patrick. An old chronicle, confirmed by Bede, writes, under the year 431: "Palladius is ordained by Pope Celestine, and is sent as their first bishop to the Irish believers in Christ." [20] Palladius, however, died within the year; and the honor of making Ireland unalterably Catholic fell to her patron saint.

He was born in the village of Bonnaventa in western England, of a middle class family, about 389. As the son of a Roman citizen, he was given a Roman name, Patricius. He received only a modest education, and apologized for his *rusticitas*; but he studied the Bible so faithfully that he could quote it from memory to almost any purpose. At sixteen he was captured by "Scot" (Irish) raiders and taken to Ireland, where for six years he served as a herder of pigs.[21] In those lonely hours "conversion" came to him; he passed from religious indifference to intense piety; he describes himself as rising every day before dawn to go out and pray in whatever weather—hail or rain or snow. At last he escaped, found his way to the sea, was picked up, desolate, by sailors, and was carried to Gaul, perhaps to Italy. He worked his way back to England, rejoined his parents, and lived with them a few years. But something called him back to Ireland—perhaps some memory of its rural loveliness, or the hearty kindliness of its people. He interpreted the feeling as a divine message, a call to convert the Irish to Christianity. He went to Lérins and Auxerre, studied for the priesthood, and was ordained. When news reached

Auxerre that Palladius was dead, Patrick was made a bishop, dowered with relics of Peter and Paul, and sent to Ireland (432).

He found there, on the throne of Tara, an enlightened pagan, Laeghaire. Patrick failed to convert the king, but won full freedom for his mission. The Druids opposed him, and showed the people their magic; Patrick met them with the formulas of the exorcists—a minor clerical order—whom he had brought with him to cast out demons. In the *Confessions* that he wrote in his old age Patrick tells of the perils he encountered in his work: twelve times his life was in danger; once he and his companions were seized, held captive a fortnight, and threatened with death; but some friends persuaded the captors to set them free.[22] Pious tradition tells a hundred fascinating stories of his miracles: "he gave sight to the blind and hearing to the deaf," says Nennius,[23] "cleansed the lepers, cast out devils, redeemed captives, raised nine persons from the dead, and wrote 365 books." But probably it was Patrick's character, rather than his wonders, that converted the Irish—the undoubting confidence of his belief, and the passionate persistence of his work. He was not a patient man; he could dispense maledictions and benedictions with equal readiness;[24] but even this proud dogmatism convinced. He ordained priests, built churches, established monasteries and nunneries, and left strong spiritual garrisons to guard his conquests at every turn. He made it seem a supreme adventure to enter the ecclesiastical state; he gathered about him men and women of courage and devotion, who endured every privation to spread the good news that man was redeemed. He did not convert all Ireland; some pockets of paganism and its poetry survived, and leave traces to this day; but when he died (461) it could be said of him, as of no other, that one man had converted a nation.

Only second to him in the affection of the Irish people stands the woman who did most to consolidate his victory. St. Brigid, we are told, was the daughter of a slave and a king; but we know nothing definite of her before 476, when she took the veil. Overcoming countless obstacles, she founded the "Church of the Oak Tree"—Cill-dara—at a spot still so named, Kildare; soon it developed into a monastery, a nunnery, and a school as famous as that which grew at Patrick's Armagh. She died about 525, honored throughout the island; and 10,000 Irish women still bear the name of the "Mary of the Gael." A generation later St. Ruadhan laid a curse upon Tara; after 558, when King Diarmuid died, the ancient halls were abandoned, and Ireland's kings, still pagan in culture, became Christian in creed.

III. PRELUDE TO FRANCE

1. The Last Days of Classic Gaul: 310–480

Gaul, in the fourth and fifth centuries, was materially the most prosperous, intellectually the most advanced, of Roman provinces in the West. The soil was generous, the crafts were skilled, the rivers and the seas bore a teeming trade. State-supported universities flourished at Narbonne, Arles, Bordeaux, Toulouse, Lyons, Marseille, Poitiers, and Trier; teachers and orators, poets and sages enjoyed a status and acclaim usually reserved for politicians and pugilists. With Ausonius and Sidonius, Gaul took over the literary leadership of Europe.

Decimus Magnus Ausonius was the poet and embodiment of this Gallic Silver Age. He was born at Bordeaux about 310, son of its leading physician. He received his education there, and later told the world, in generous hexameters, the virtues of his teachers, remembering their smiles and forgetting their blows.[25] In the even tenor of his years he too became a professor at Bordeaux, taught "grammar" (i.e., literature) and "rhetoric" (i.e., oratory and philosophy) for a generation, and tutored the future Emperor Gratian. The sincere affection with which he writes of his parents, uncles, wife, children, and pupils suggests a home and a life like that of a nineteenth-century university town in the United States. He describes pleasantly the house and fields that he inherited from his father, and where he hopes to spend his declining years. He says to his wife, in the early years of their marriage: "Let us live always as we live now, and let us not abandon the names that we have given each other in our first love. . . . You and I must always remain young, and you shall always be beautiful to me. We must keep no count of the years." [26] Soon, however, they lost the first child that she gave him. Years later he commemorated it lovingly: "I will not leave you unwept, my first-born child, called by my name. Just as you were practicing to change your babbling into the first words of childhood . . . we had to mourn your death. You lie on your great-grandfather's bosom, sharing his grave." [27] His wife died early in their happy marriage, after giving him a daughter and a son. He was so deeply bound to her that he never married again; and in his old age he described with fresh grief the pain of his loss, and the somber silence of the house that had known the care of her hands and the cadence of her feet.

His poems pleased his time by their tender sentiment, their rural pictures, the purity of their Latin, the almost Virgilian smoothness of their verse. Paulinus, the future saint, compared his prose with Cicero's, and Symmachus could not find in Virgil anything lovelier than Ausonius' *Mosella*. The poet had grown fond of that river while with Gratian at Trier; he describes it as running through a very Eden of vineyards, orchards, villas, and prospering farms; for a time he makes us feel the verdure of its banks and the music of its flow; then, with all-embracing bathos, he indites a litany to the amiable fish to be found in the stream. This Whitmanesque passion for cataloguing relatives, teachers, pupils, fish is not redeemed by Whitman's omnivorous feeling and lusty philosophy; Ausonius, after thirty years of grammar, could hardly burn with more than literary passions. His poems are rosaries of friendship, litanies of praise; but those of us who have not known such alluring uncles or seductive professors are rarely exalted by these doxologies.

When Valentinian I died (375), Gratian, now Emperor, called his old tutor to him, and showered him and his with political plums. In quick succession Ausonius was prefect of Illyricum, Italy, Africa, Gaul; finally, at sixty-nine, consul. At his urging, Gratian decreed state aid for education, for poets and physicians, and for the protection of ancient art. Through his influence Symmachus was made prefect of Rome, and Paulinus a provincial governor. Ausonius mourned when Paulinus became a saint; the Empire, threatened everywhere, needed such men. Ausonius too was a Christian, but not too seriously; his tastes, subjects, meters, and mythology were blithely pagan.

At seventy the old poet returned to Bordeaux, to live another twenty years. He was now a grandfather, and could match the filial poems of his youth with the grandparental fondness of age. "Be not afraid," he counsels his grandson, "though the school resound with many a stroke, and the old master wears a scowling face; let no outcry, or sound of stripes, make you quake as the morning hours move on. That he brandishes the cane for a scepter, that he has a full outfit of birches ... is but the outward show to cause idle fears. Your father and mother went through all this in their day, and have lived to soothe my peaceful and serene old age." [28] Fortunate Ausonius, to have lived and died before the barbarian flood!

Apollinaris Sidonius was to Gallic prose in the fifth century what Ausonius had been to Gallic poetry in the fourth. He burst upon the world at Lyons (432), where his father was prefect of Gaul. His grandfather had filled the same office, and his mother was a relative of that Avitus who would become emperor in 455, and whose daughter Sidonius would marry in 452. It would have been difficult to improve upon these arrangements. Papianilla brought him as dowry a luxurious villa near Clermont. His life for some years was a round of visits to and from his aristocratic friends. They were people of culture and refinement, with a flair for gambling and idleness;[29] they lived in their country houses, and seldom soiled their hands with politics; they were quite incapable of protecting their luxurious ease against the invading Goths. They did not care for city life; already French and British wealth was preferring the country to the town. In these sprawling villas—some with 125 rooms—all comforts and elegances were gathered: mosaic floors, columned halls, landscape murals, sculptures in marble and bronze, great fireplaces and baths, gardens and tennis courts,[30] and environing woods in which ladies and gentlemen might hunt with all the glamour of falconry. Nearly every villa had a good library, containing the classics of pagan antiquity and some respectable Christian texts.[31] Several of Sidonius' friends were book collectors; and doubtless there were in Gaul, as in Rome, rich men who valued good bindings above mere contents, and were satisfied with the culture they could get from the covers of their books.

Sidonius illustrates the better side of this genteel life—hospitality, courtesy, good cheer, moral decency, with a touch of chiseled poetry and melodious prose. When Avitus went to Rome to be emperor, Sidonius accompanied him, and was chosen to deliver the welcoming panegyric (456). He returned to Gaul a year later with Avitus deposed; but in 468 we find him in Rome again, holding the high office of prefect of the city amid the last convulsions of the state. Moving comfortably through the chaos, he described the high society of Gaul and Rome in letters modeled upon those of Pliny and Symmachus, and matching them in vanity and grace. Literature now had little to say, and said it with such care that nothing remained but form and charm. At their best there is in these letters that genial tolerance and sympathetic understanding of the educated gentleman which has adorned the literature of France since the days when it was not yet French. Sidonius brought into Gaul the Roman love for gracious *causeries*. From Cicero and Seneca through Pliny, Symmachus, Macrobius, and Sidonius to Montaigne, Montesquieu, Voltaire, Renan, Sainte-Beuve, and Anatole France is one line, almost, by bountiful avatars, one mind.

Lest we misrepresent Sidonius we must add that he was a good Christian and a brave bishop. In 469, unexpectedly and unwillingly, he found himself precipitated from lay status to the episcopacy of Clermont. A bishop in those days had to be a civil administrator as well as a spiritual guide; and men of experience and wealth like Ambrose and Sidonius had qualifications that proved more effective than theological erudition. Having little of such learning, Sidonius had few anathemas to bestow; instead, he gave his silver plate to the poor, and forgave sins with an alarming readiness. From one of his letters we perceive that the prayers of his flock were sometimes interrupted by refreshments.[32] Reality broke into this pleasant life when Euric, King of the Visigoths, decided to annex Auvergne. Each summer, for four years, the Goths laid siege to Clermont, its capital. Sidonius fought them with diplomacy and prayer, but failed; when at last the city fell he was taken captive, and was imprisoned in a fortress near Carcassonne (475). Two years later he was released and restored to his see. How long he survived we do not know; but already at forty-five he wished to be "delivered from the pains and burdens of present life by a holy death." [33] He had lost faith in the

Roman Empire, and now put all his hopes for civilization in the Roman Church. The Church forgave him his half-pagan poetry, and made him a saint.

2. The Franks: 240–511

With the death of Sidonius the night of barbarism closed down upon Gaul. We must not exaggerate that darkness. Men still retained economic skills, traded goods, minted coinage, composed poetry, and practiced art; and under Euric (466–84) and Alaric II (484–507) the Visigothic kingdom in southwestern Gaul was sufficiently orderly, civilized, and progressive to draw praise from Sidonius himself.[34] In 506 Alaric II issued a *Breviarium*, or summary, of laws for his realm; it was a comparatively enlightened code, reducing to rule and reason the relations between the Romano-Gallic population and its conquerors. A like code was enacted (510) by the Burgundian kings who had peaceably established their people and power in southeastern Gaul. Until the revival of Roman law at Bologna in the eleventh century, Latin Europe would be governed by Gothic and Burgundian codes, and the kindred laws of the Franks.

History picks up the Franks in 240, when the Emperor Aurelian defeated them near Mainz. The Ripuarian Franks—"of the bank"—settled early in the fifth century on the west slopes of the Rhine; they captured Cologne (463), made it their capital, and extended their power in the Rhine valley from Aachen to Metz. Some Frank tribes remained on the east side of the river, and gave their name to Franconia. The Salic Franks may have taken their distinguishing name from the river Sala (now Ijssel) in the Netherlands. Thence they moved south and west, and about 356 occupied the region between the Meuse, the ocean, and the Somme. For the most part their spread was by peaceful migration, sometimes by Roman invitation to settle sparsely occupied lands; by these diverse ways northern Gaul had become half Frank by 430. They brought their Germanic language and pagan faith with them; so that during the fifth century Latin ceased to be the speech, and Christianity the religion, of the peoples along the lower Rhine.

The Salic Franks described themselves, in the prologue to their "Salic Law," as "the glorious people, wise in council, noble in body, radiant in health, excelling in beauty, daring, quick, hardened . . . this is the people that shook the cruel yoke of the Romans from its neck."[35] They considered themselves not barbarians but self-liberated freemen; *Frank* meant free, en*franch*ised. They were tall and fair; knotted their long hair in a tuft on the head, and let it fall thence like a horse's tail; wore mustaches but no beards; bound their tunics at the waist with leather belts covered with segments of enameled iron; from this belt hung sword and battle-ax, and articles of toilet like scissors and combs.[36] The men, as well as the women, were fond of jewelry, and wore rings, armlets, and beads. Every able-bodied male was a warrior, taught from youth to run, leap, swim, and throw his lance or ax to its mark. Courage was the supreme virtue, for which murder, rapine, and rape might be readily forgiven. But history, by telescoping one dramatic event into the next, leaves a false impression of the Franks as merely warriors. Their conquests and battles were no more numerous, and far less extensive and destructive, than our own. Their laws show them engaged in agriculture and handicrafts, making northeastern Gaul a prosperous and usually peaceful rural society.

The Salic Law was formulated early in the sixth century, probably in the same generation that saw Justinian's full development of Roman law. We are told that "four venerable chieftains" wrote it, and that it was examined and approved by three successive assemblies of the people.[37] Trial was largely by "compurgation" and ordeal. A sufficient number of qualified witnesses attesting the good character of a defendant cleared him of any charge of which he was not evidently guilty. The number of witnesses required varied with the enormity of the alleged crime: seventy-two could free a supposed murderer, but when the chastity of a queen of France was in question, three hundred nobles were needed to certify the paternity of her child.[38] If the matter at issue still stood in doubt, the law of ordeal was invoked. The accused, bound hand and foot, might be flung into a river, to sink if innocent, to float if guilty (for the water, having been exorcised by religious ceremony, would reject a sinful person);[39] or the accused would be made to walk barefoot through fire or over red-hot irons; or to hold a red-hot iron in his hand for a given time; or to plunge a bare arm into boiling water and pluck out an object from the bottom. Or accuser and accused would stand with arms outstretched in the form of a cross, until one or the other proclaimed his guilt by letting his arm fall with fatigue; or the accused would take the consecrated wafer of the Eucharist and, if guilty, would surely be struck down by God; or trial by combat would decide between two freemen when legal evidence still left a reasonable doubt. Some of these ordeals were old in history: the Avesta indicates that the ordeal of boiling water was used by the ancient Persians; the laws of Manu (before A.D. 100) mention Hindu ordeals by submersion; and ordeals by fire or hot irons appear in Sophocles' *Antigone*.[40] The Semites rejected ordeals as impious, the Romans ignored them as superstitious; the Germans developed them to the full; the Christian Church reluctantly accepted them, and surrounded them with religious ceremony and solemn oath.

Trial by combat was as old as ordeal. Saxo Grammaticus describes it as compulsory in Denmark in the first century A.D.; the laws of the Angles, Saxons, Franks, Burgundians, and Lombards indicate its general use among them; and St. Patrick found it in Ireland. When a Roman Christian complained to the Burgundian King Gundobad that such a trial would decide not guilt but skill, the King replied: "Is it not true that the issue of wars and combats is directed by the judgment of God, and that His Providence awards the victory to the just cause?" [41] The conversion of the barbarians to Christianity merely changed the name of the deity whose judgment was invoked. We cannot judge or understand these customs unless we put ourselves in the place of men who took it for granted that God entered causally into every event, and would not connive at an unjust verdict. With such a dire test to face, accusers uncertain of their case or their evidence would think twice before bothering the courts with their complaints; and guilty defendants would shirk the ordeal, and offer compensation in its place.

For nearly every crime had its price: the accused or convicted man might usually absolve himself by paying a wergild or "man-payment"—one third to the government, two thirds to the victim or his family. The sum varied with the social rank of the victim, and an economical criminal had to take many facts into consideration. If a man immodestly stroked the hand of a woman he was to be fined fifteen denarii ($2.25); * if he so stroked her upper arm, he paid thirty-five denarii ($5.25); if he touched her unwilling bosom he paid forty-five denarii ($6.75).[42] This was a tolerable tariff in comparison with other fines: 2500 denarii ($375) for the assault and robbery of a Frank by a Roman, 1400 for the assault and robbery of a Roman by a Frank, 8000 denarii for killing a Frank, 4000 for killing a Roman: [43] so low had the mighty Roman fallen in the eyes of his conquerors. If, as not seldom happened, satisfactory compensation was not received by the victim or his relatives, they might take their own revenge; in this way vendettas might leave a trail of blood through many generations. Wergild and judicial combat were the best expedients that primitive Germans could devise to wean men from vengeance to law.

The most famous clause in the Salic Law read: "Of Salic land no portion of the inheritance shall go to a woman" (lix, 6); on this basis, in the fourteenth century, France would reject the claim of the English King Edward III to the French throne through his mother Isabelle; whereupon would follow the Hundred Years' War. The clause applied only to realty, which was presumed to require for its protection the military power of a male. In general the Salic Law did no service to women. It exacted a double wergild for their murder,[44] valuing them as the possible mothers of many men. But (like early Roman law) it kept women under the perpetual wardship of father, husband, or son; it made death the penalty for adultery by the wife, but asked no penalty of the adulterous male;[45] and it permitted divorce at the husband's whim.[46] Custom, if not law, allowed polygamy to the Frank kings.

---

* The Salic Law (xiv) equates the denarius as one-fortieth of a solidus, which then contained one sixth of an ounce of gold, or $5.83 in the United States of America in 1946. The medieval scarcity of gold and currency gave to the sums mentioned in the text a much greater purchasing or punishing power than they would have today.

The first Frank king known by name was the Chlodio who attacked Cologne in 431; Aëtius defeated him, but Chlodio succeeded in occupying Gaul as far west as the Somme, and making Tournai his capital. A possibly legendary successor, Merovech ("Son of the Sea"?), gave his name to the Merovingian dynasty, which ruled the Franks till 751. Merovech's son Childeric seduced Basina, wife of a Thuringian king; she went to be his queen, saying she knew no man wiser, stronger, or handsomer. The child of their union was Clovis, who founded France and gave his name to eighteen French kings.*

Clovis inherited the Merovingian throne in 481, aged fifteen. His realm was then a mere corner of Gaul; other Frank tribes ruled the Rhineland, and the Visigothic and Burgundian kingdoms in southern Gaul had been made fully independent by the fall of Rome. Northwest Gaul, still nominally under Roman power, was left defenseless. Clovis invaded it, captured towns and dignitaries, accepted ransoms, sold spoils, bought troops, supplies, and arms, advanced to Soissons, and defeated a "Roman" army (486). During the next ten years he extended his conquests till they touched Brittany and the Loire. He won over the Gallic population by leaving them in possession of their lands, and the orthodox Christian clergy by respecting their creed and their wealth. In 493 he married a Christian, Clothilde, who soon converted him from paganism to Nicene Christianity. Remi, bishop and saint, baptized him at Reims before an audience of prelates and notables judiciously invited from all Gaul; and 3000 soldiers followed Clovis to the font. Perhaps Clovis, longing to reach the Mediterranean, thought France was worth a Mass. The orthodox population in Visigothic and Burgundian Gaul now looked askance at their Arian rulers, and became the secret or open allies of the young Frank king.

Alaric II saw the oncoming tide, and tried to turn it back with fair words. He invited Clovis to a conference; they met at Amboise, and pledged lasting friendship. But Alaric, returning to Toulouse, arrested some orthodox bishops for conspiring with the Franks. Clovis summoned his martial assembly and said: "I take it very hard that these Arians hold part of Gaul. Let us go with God's help and conquer them." [47] Alaric defended himself as well as he could with a divided people; he was defeated at Vouillé, near Poitiers (507), and was slain by Clovis' hand. "After Clovis had spent the winter in Bordeaux," says Gregory of Tours, "and had taken all the treasures of Alaric from Toulouse, he went to besiege Angoulême. And the Lord gave him such grace that the walls fell down of their own accord"; [48] here, so soon, is the characteristic note of the medieval chronicler. Sigebert, the old king of the Ripuarian Franks, had long been an ally of Clovis. To Sigebert's son Clovis now suggested the advantages that would come from Sigebert's death. The

---

* Chlodwig, Ludwig, Clovis, Louis are one name.

son killed his father; Clovis sent professions of friendship to the patricide, and agents to murder him; this having been attended to, Clovis marched to Cologne, and persuaded the Ripuarian chieftains to accept him as their king. "Every day," says Gregory, "God caused his enemies to fall beneath his hand . . . because he walked with a right heart before the Lord, and did the things that were pleasing in His sight." [49]

The conquered Arians were readily converted to the orthodox faith, and their clergy, by omitting an iota, were allowed to retain their clerical rank. Clovis, rich with captives, slaves, spoils, and benedictions, moved his capital to Paris. There, four years later, he died, old at forty-five. Queen Clothilde, having helped to make Gaul France, "came to Tours after the death of her husband, and served there in the church of St. Martin, and dwelt in the place with the greatest chastity and kindness all the days of her life." [50]

3. The Merovingians: 511–614

Clovis, who had longed for sons, had too many at his death. To avoid a war of succession he divided his kingdom among them: Childebert received the region of Paris, Chlodomer that of Orléans, Chlotar that of Soissons, Theodoric that of Metz and Reims. With barbarian energy they continued the policy of unification by conquest. They took Thuringia in 530, Burgundy in 534, Provence in 536, Bavaria and Swabia in 555; and Chlotar I, outliving his brothers and inheriting their kingdoms, governed a Gaul vaster than any later France. Dying (561), he redivided Gaul into three parts: the Reims and Metz region, known as Austrasia (i.e., East), went to his son Sigebert; Burgundy to Gunthram; and to Chilperic the Soissons region, known as Neustria (i.e., Northwest).

From the day of Clovis' marriage the history of France has been bisexual, mingling love and war. Sigebert sent costly presents to Athanagild, Visigothic king of Spain, and asked for his daughter Brunhilda; Athanagild, fearing the Franks even when they bore gifts, consented; and Brunhilda came to grace the halls of Metz and Reims (566). Chilperic was envious; all that he had was a simple wife, Audovera, and a rough concubine, Fredegunda. He asked Athanagild for Brunhilda's sister; Galswintha came to Soissons, and Chilperic loved her, for she had brought great treasures. But she was older than her sister. Chilperic returned to the arms of Fredegunda; Galswintha proposed to go back to Spain; Chilperic had her strangled (567). Sigebert declared war upon Chilperic, and defeated him; but two slaves sent by Fredegunda assassinated Sigebert. Brunhilda was captured, escaped, crowned her young son Childebert II, and ruled ably in his name.

Chilperic is described to us as "the Nero and Herod of our time," ruthless, murderous, lecherous, gluttonous, greedy for gold. Gregory of Tours, our sole authority for this portrait, partly explains it by making him also the Frederick II of his age. Chilperic, he tells us, scoffed at the idea of three persons in one God, and at the conception of God as like a man; held scandalous discussions with Jews; protested against the wealth of the Church and the political activity of the bishops; annulled wills made in favor of churches; sold bishoprics to the highest bidders; and tried to remove Gregory himself from the see of Tours.[51] The poet Fortunatus described the same king as a synthesis of virtues, a just and genial ruler, a Cicero of eloquence; but Chilperic had rewarded Fortunatus' verse.[52]

Chilperic was stabbed to death in 584, possibly by an agent of Brunhilda. He left an infant son, Chlotar II, in whose stead Fredegunda ruled Neustria with as much skill, perfidy, and cruelty as any man of the time. She sent a young cleric to kill Brunhilda; when he returned unsuccessful she had his hands and feet cut off; but these items too are from Gregory.[53] Meanwhile the nobles of Austrasia, encouraged by Chlotar II, raised revolt after revolt against the imperious Brunhilda; she controlled them as well as she could by diplomacy tempered with assassination; finally they deposed her, aged eighty, tortured her for three days, tied her by hair, hand, and foot to the tail of a horse, and lashed the horse to flight (614). Chlotar II inherited all three kingdoms, and the Frank realm was again one.

From this red chronicle we may exaggerate the barbarism that darkened Gaul hardly a century after the urbane and polished Sidonius; men must find some substitute for elections. The unifying work of Clovis was undone by his descendants, as that of Charlemagne would be; but at least government continued, and not all Gauls could afford the polygamy and brutality of their kings. The apparent autocracy of the monarch was limited by the power of jealous nobles; he rewarded their services in administration and war with estates on which they were practically sovereign; and on these great demesnes began the feudalism that would fight the French monarchy for a thousand years. Serfdom grew, and slavery received a new lease of life from new wars. Industry passed from the towns to the manors; the towns shrank in size, and fell under the control of the feudal lords; commerce was still active, but hindered by unstable currencies, highway brigandage, and the rise of feudal tolls. Famine and pestilence fought successfully against the eager reproductiveness of men.

The Frank chieftains intermarried with what remained of the Gallo-Roman senatorial class, and generated the aristocracy of France. It was in these centuries a nobility of force, relishing war, scorning letters, proud of its long beards and silken robes, and almost as polygamous as any Moslem save Mohammed. Seldom has an upper class shown such contempt for morality. Conversion to Christianity had no effect upon them; Christianity seemed to them merely an expensive agency of rule and popular pacification; and in "the triumph of barbarism and religion" barbarism dominated for five centuries. Assassination, patricide, fratricide, torture, mutilation, treachery, adultery, and incest mitigated the boredom of rule. Chilperic, we are told, ordered every joint in Sigila the Goth to be burned with white-hot irons, and each limb to be torn from its socket.[54] Charibert had as mistresses two sisters, one a nun; Dagobert (628–39) had three wives at once. Sexual excesses perhaps accounted for the exceptional sterility of the Merovingian kings: of Clovis' four sons only Chlotar had issue; of Chlotar's four sons only one had a child. The kings married at fifteen, and were exhausted at thirty; many of them died before the age of twenty-eight.[55] By 614 the Merovingian house had spent its energy, and was ready to be replaced.

Amid this chaos education barely survived. By 600 literacy had become a luxury of the clergy. Science was almost extinct. Medicine remained, for we hear of court physicians; but among the people magic and prayer seemed better than drugs. Gregory, Bishop of Tours (538?–94), denounced as sinful the use of medicine instead of religion as a means of curing illness. In his own sickness he sent for a physician, but soon dismissed him as ineffectual; then he drank a glass of water containing dust from St. Martin's tomb, and was completely cured.[56] Gregory himself was the chief prose writer of his time. He knew personally several Merovingian kings, and occasionally served as their emissaries; his *History of the Franks* is a crude, disorderly, prejudiced, superstitious, and vivid firsthand account of the later Merovingian age. His Latin is corrupt, vigorous, direct; he apologizes for his bad grammar, and hopes that sins of grammar will not be punished on Judgment Day.[57] He accepts miracles and prodigies with the trustful imagination of a child or the genial shrewdness of a bishop; "we shall mingle together in our tale the miraculous doings of the saints and the slaughters of the nations." [58] In 587, he assures us, snakes fell from the sky, and a village with all its buildings and inhabitants suddenly disappeared.[59] He denounces everything in anyone guilty of unbelief or of injury to the Church; but he accepts without flinching the barbarities, treacheries, and immoralities of the Church's faithful sons. His prejudices are frank, and can be easily discounted. The final impression is one of engaging simplicity.

After him the literature of Gaul becomes predominantly religious in content, barbarous in language and form—with one shining exception. Venantius Fortunatus (*c.* 530–610) was born in Italy and educated at Ravenna; at thirty-five he moved to Gaul, wrote lauds for its bishops and queens, and developed a platonic affection for Radegunda, wife of the first Chlotar. When she founded a convent Fortunatus became a priest, her chaplain, and finally bishop of Poitiers. He wrote pretty poems in honor of potentates and saints; twenty-nine to Gregory of Tours; a life of St. Martin in heroic verse; above all, some sonorous hymns, of which one, *Pange lingua*, inspired Thomas Aquinas to a similar theme and still higher performance, while another, *Vexilla regis*, became a lasting part of Catholic liturgy. He mingled feeling admirably with poetic skill; reading his fresh and genial lines we discover the existence of kindliness, sincerity, and the tenderest sentiment amid the royal brutalities of the Merovingian age.

IV. VISIGOTHIC SPAIN: 456–711

In 420, as we have seen, the Visigoths of Gaul recaptured Spain from the Vandals, and returned it to Rome. But Rome could not defend it; eighteen years later the Suevi emerged from their hills in the northwest, and overran the peninsula. The Visigoths under Theodoric II (456) and Euric (466) came down again across the Pyrenees, reconquered most of Spain, and this time kept the country as their own. A Visigothic dynasty ruled Spain thereafter till the coming of the Moors.

At Toledo the new monarchy built a splendid capital and gathered an opulent court. Athanagild (564–7) and Leovigild (568–86) were strong rulers, who defeated Frank invaders in the north and Byzantine armies in the south; it was the wealth of Athanagild that won for his daughters the privilege of being murdered as Frank queens. In 589 King Recared changed his faith, and that of most Visigoths in Spain, from Arian to orthodox Christianity; perhaps he had read the history of Alaric II. The bishops now became the chief support of the monarchy, and the chief power in the state; by their superior education and organization they dominated the nobles who sat with them in the ruling councils of Toledo; and though the king's authority was theoretically absolute, and he chose the bishops, these councils elected him, and exacted pledges of policy in advance. Under the guidance of the clergy a system of laws was promulgated (634) which was the most competent and least tolerant of all the barbarian codes. It improved procedure by weighing the evidence of witnesses rather than the character certificates of friends; it applied the same laws to Romans and Visigoths alike, and established the principle of equality before the law.[60] But it rejected freedom of worship, demanded orthodox Christianity of all inhabitants, and sanctioned a long and bitter persecution of the Spanish Jews.

Through the influence of the Church, which retained Latin in her sermons and liturgy, the Visigoths, within a century after their conquest of Spain, forgot their Germanic speech, and corrupted the Latin of the peninsula into the masculine power and feminine beauty of the Spanish tongue. Monastic and episcopal schools provided education, mostly ecclesiastical but partly classical; and academies rose at Vaclara, Toledo, Saragossa, and Seville. Poetry was encouraged, drama was denounced as obscene—which it was. The only name surviving from the literature of Gothic Spain is that of Isidore of Seville (c. 560–636). An edifying legend tells how a Spanish lad, reproved for mental sluggishness, ran away from home, and, tired with wandering, sat down by a well. His eye was caught by the deep furrow in a stone at the edge; a passing maiden explained that the furrow was worn by the attrition of the rope that lowered and raised the bucket. "If," said Isidore to himself, "by daily use the soft rope could penetrate the stone, surely perseverance could overcome the dullness of my brain." He returned to his father's house, and became the learned Bishop of Seville.[61] Actually we know little of his life. Amid the chores of a conscientious cleric he found time to write half a dozen books. Perhaps as an aid to memory he compiled through many years a medley of passages, on all subjects, from pagan and Christian authors; his friend Braulio, Bishop of Saragossa, urged him to publish these excerpts; yielding, he transformed them into one of the most influential books of the Middle Ages—*Etymologiarum sive originum libri xx* (*Twenty Books of Etymologies or Origins*)—now a volume of 900 octavo pages. It is an encyclopedia, but not alphabetically arranged; it deals successively with grammar, rhetoric, and logic as the "trivium"; then with arithmetic, geometry, music, and astronomy as the "quadrivium"; then with medicine, law, chronology, theology, anatomy, physiology, zoology, cosmography, physical geography, architecture, surveying, mineralogy, agriculture, war, sports, ships, costumes, furniture, domestic utensils . . . ; and under each topic it defines, and seeks the origin of, the basic terms. Man, we learn, is called *homo* because God made him from the earth (*humus*); the knees are *genua* because in the foetus they lie opposite the cheeks (*genae*).[62] Isidore was an industrious, if indiscriminate, scholar; he knew considerable Greek, was familiar with Lucretius (rarely mentioned in the Middle Ages), and preserved in extracts many passages of pagan literature that would otherwise have been lost. His work is a farrago of weird etymologies, incredible miracles, fanciful allegorical interpretations of the Scriptures, science and history distorted to prove moral principles, and factual errors that a little observation would have set straight. His book stands as a lasting monument to the ignorance of his time.

Of the arts in Visigothic Spain almost nothing remains. Apparently Toledo, Italica, Cordova, Granada, Merida, and other cities had fine churches, palaces, and public buildings, designed in classic styles but distinguished by Christian symbols and Byzantine ornament.[63] In the palaces and cathedral of Toledo, according to Arab historians, Arab conquerors found twenty-five gold and jeweled crowns; an illuminated Psalter written upon gold leaf with ink made of melted rubies; tissues inwoven, armor inlaid, swords and daggers studded, vases filled, with jewelry; and an emerald table inwrought with silver and gold—one of many costly gifts of the Visigothic rich to their protective Church.

Under the Visigothic regime the exploitation of the simple or unfortunate by the clever or the strong continued as under other governmental forms. Princes and prelates united in a majesty of secular or religious ceremonies,

tabus, and terrors to subdue the passions, and quiet the thoughts, of the populace. Property was concentrated in the hands of a few; the great gulf between
rich and poor, between Christian and Jew, divided the nation into three
states; and when the Arabs came, the poor and the Jews connived at the overthrow of a monarchy and a Church that had ignored their poverty or oppressed their faith.

In 708, on the death of the feeble king Witiza, the aristocracy refused the
throne to his children, but gave it to Roderick. The sons of Witiza fled to
Africa, and asked the aid of Moorish chieftains. The Moors made some tentative raids upon the Spanish coast, found Spain divided and almost defenseless,
and in 711 came over in fuller force. The armies of Tariq and Roderick joined
battle on the shores of Lake Janda in the province of Cadiz; part of the Visigothic forces went over to the Moors; Roderick disappeared. The victorious
Moslems advanced to Seville, Cordova, Toledo; several towns opened their
gates to the invaders. The Arab general Musa established himself in the capital
(713), and announced that Spain now belonged to the prophet Mohammed
and the caliph of Damascus.

V. OSTROGOTHIC ITALY: 493–536

1. Theodoric

When Attila's empire crumbled at his death (453) the Ostrogoths whom
he had subdued regained their independence. The Byzantine emperors paid
them to drive other German barbarians westward, rewarded them with Pannonia, and took Theodoric, the seven-year-old son of their King Theodemir,
to Constantinople as a hostage for Ostrogothic fidelity. In eleven years at
the Byzantine court Theodoric acquired intelligence without education,
absorbed the arts of war and government, but apparently never learned to
write.[64] He won the admiration of the Emperor Leo I; and when Theodemir
died (475), Leo recognized Theodoric as king of the Ostrogoths.

Leo's successor Zeno, fearful that Theodoric might trouble Byzantium,
suggested to him the conquest of Italy. Odoacer had formally acknowledged,
actually ignored, the Eastern emperors; Theodoric, Zeno hoped, might bring
Italy back under Byzantine rule; in any case the two leaders of dangerous
tribes would amuse each other while Zeno studied theology. Theodoric liked
—some say propounded—the idea. As Zeno's *patricius* he led the Ostrogoths,
including 20,000 warriors, across the Alps (488). The orthodox bishops
of Italy, disliking Odoacer's Arianism, supported the Arian invader as representing an almost orthodox emperor. With their help Theodoric broke
Odoacer's sturdy resistance in five years of war, and persuaded him to a
compromise peace. He invited Odoacer and his son to dine with him at

Ravenna, fed them generously, and slew them with his own hand (493). So treacherously began one of the most enlightened reigns in history.

A few campaigns brought under Theodoric's rule the western Balkans, southern Italy, and Sicily. He maintained a formal subordination to Byzantium, struck coins only in the emperor's name, and wrote with due deference to the Senate that still sat in Rome. He took the title of *rex* or king; but this term, once so hateful to Romans, was now generally applied to rulers of regions that acknowledged the sovereignty of Byzantium. He accepted the laws and institutions of the late Western Empire, zealously protected its monuments and forms, and devoted his energy and intelligence to restoring orderly government and economic prosperity among the people whom he had conquered. He confined his Goths to police and military service, and quieted their grumbling with ample pay; administration and the courts remained in Roman hands. Two thirds of the soil of Italy was left to the Roman population, one third was distributed among the Goths; even so not all the arable land was tilled. Theodoric ransomed Roman captives from other nations, and settled them as peasant proprietors in Italy. The Pontine Marshes were drained, and returned to cultivation and health. Believing in a regulated economy, Theodoric issued an "Edict Concerning Prices to be Maintained at Ravenna"; we do not know what prices were decreed; we are told that the cost of food, in Theodoric's reign, was one third lower than before;[65] but this may have been due less to regulation than to peace. He reduced governmental personnel and salaries, ended state subsidies to the Church, and kept taxes low. His revenues nevertheless sufficed to repair much of the damage that invaders had done to Rome and Italy, and to erect at Ravenna a modest palace and the churches of Sant' Apollinare and San Vitale. Verona, Pavia, Naples, Spoleto, and other Italian cities recovered under his rule all the architectural splendor of their brightest days. Though an Arian, Theodoric protected the orthodox Church in her property and worship; and his minister Cassiodorus, a Catholic, phrased in memorable words a policy of religious freedom: "We cannot command religion, for no one can be forced to believe against his will."[66] A Byzantine historian, Procopius, in the following generation, indited an impartial tribute to the "barbarian" king:

> Theodoric was exceedingly careful to observe justice . . . and attained the highest degree of wisdom and manliness. . . . Although in name he was a usurper, yet in fact he was as truly an emperor as any who have distinguished themselves in this office from the beginning of time. Both the Goths and the Romans loved him greatly. . . . When he died he had not only made himself an object of terror to his enemies, but he also left to his subjects a keen sense of bereavement and loss.[67]

2. Boethius

In this environment of security and peace Latin literature in Italy had its final fling. Flavius Magnus Aurelius Cassiodorus (480?–573) served as secretary to both Odoacer and Theodoric. At the latter's suggestion he wrote a *History of the Goths*,[68] which aimed to show supercilious Romans that the Goths, too, had behind them noble ancestors and heroic deeds. Perhaps more objectively Cassiodorus compiled a *Chronicon*, a chronological history of the world from Adam to Theodoric. At the close of his long political career he published as *Variae* a collection of his letters and state papers; some a little absurd, some a bit bombastic, many revealing a high level of morals and statesmanship in the minister and his king. About 540, having seen the ruin and fall of both the governments that he had served, he retired to his estate at Squillace in Calabria, founded two monasteries, and lived there as half monk and half grandee till his death at the age of ninety-three. He taught his fellow monks to copy manuscripts, pagan as well as Christian, and provided a special room—the *scriptorium*—for this work. His example was followed in other religious institutions, and much of our modern treasure of ancient literature is the result of the monastic copying initiated by Cassiodorus. In his last years he composed a textbook—*Institutiones divinarum et humanarum lectionum*—or *Course of Religious and Secular Studies*—which boldly defended the Christian reading of pagan literature, and adopted from Martianus Capella that division of the scholastic curriculum into "trivium" and "quadrivium" which became the usual arrangement in medieval education.

The career of Anicius Manlius Severinus Boethius (475?–524) paralleled that of Cassiodorus, except in longevity. Both were born of rich Roman families, served Theodoric as ministers, labored to build a bridge between paganism and Christianity, and wrote dreary books that were read and treasured for a thousand years. Boethius' father was consul in 483; his father-in-law, Symmachus the Younger, was descended from the Symmachus who had fought for the Altar of Victory. He received the best education that Rome could give, and then spent eighteen years in the schools of Athens. Returning to his Italian villas, he buried himself in study. Resolved to save the elements of a classical culture that was visibly dying, he gave his time—the scholar's most grudging gift—to summarizing in lucid Latin the works of Euclid on geometry, of Nicomachus on arithmetic, of Archimedes on mechanics, of Ptolemy on astronomy.... His translation of Aristotle's *Organon*, or logical treatises, and of Porphyry's *Introduction to the Categories of Aristotle* provided the leading texts and ideas of the next seven centuries in logic, and set the stage for the long dispute between realism and nominalism. Boethius tried his hand also at theology: in an essay on the Trinity he defended the orthodox Christian doctrine, and laid down the principle that where faith and reason conflict, faith should prevail. None of these writings repays reading today, but it would be hard to exaggerate their influence on medieval thought.

Moved by his family's tradition of public service, Boethius dragged himself from these abstruse pursuits into the whirlpool of political life. He rose rapidly; became consul, then *patricius*, then master of the offices—i.e., prime minister (522). He distinguished himself by both his philanthropy and his eloquence; men compared him with Demosthenes and Cicero. But eminence makes enemies. The Gothic officials at the court resented his sympathy with the Roman and the Catholic population, and aroused the suspicions of the King. Theodoric was now sixty-nine, failing in health and mind, wondering how to transmit in stability the rule of an Arian Gothic family over a nation nine tenths Roman and eight tenths Catholic. He had reason to believe that both the aristocracy and the Church were his foes, who impatiently awaited his death. In 523 Justinian, Byzantine regent, issued an edict banishing all Manicheans from the Empire, and barring from civil or military office all pagans and heretics—including all Arians except Goths. Theodoric suspected that the exception was intended to disarm him, but would be withdrawn at the first opportunity; and he judged the decree a poor return for the full liberties that he had accorded to the orthodox creed in the West. Had he not raised to the highest offices that same Boethius who had written an anti-Arian tract on the Trinity? In this very year 523 he had given to the church of St. Peter two magnificent chandeliers of solid silver as a gesture of courtesy to the pope. However, he had offended a great part of the population by protecting the Jews; when mobs destroyed synagogues in Milan, Genoa, and Rome, he had rebuilt the synagogues at public expense.[69]

It was in this conjuncture of events that word reached Theodoric of a senatorial conspiracy to depose him. Its leader, he was told, was Albinus, president of the Senate and friend of Boethius. The generous scholar hastened to Theodoric, guaranteed the innocence of Albinus, and said: "If Albinus is a criminal, I and the whole Senate are equally guilty." Three men of blemished reputation accused Boethius of sharing in the plot, and they adduced a document, bearing Boethius' signature, which invited the Byzantine Empire to reconquer Italy. Boethius denied all charges, and rejected the document as a forgery; later, however, he admitted: "Had there been any hopes of liberty I should have freely indulged them. Had I known of a conspiracy against the King . . . you would not have known of it from me."[70] He was arrested (523).

Theodoric sought some understanding with the Emperor. In words worthy of a philosopher king he wrote to Justin:

> To pretend to dominion over the conscience is to usurp the prerogative of God. By the nature of things the power of sovereigns is confined to political government; they have no right of punishment except over those who disturb the public peace. The most dangerous

heresy is that of a sovereign who separates himself from part of his subjects because they believe not according to his belief.[71]

Justin replied that he had a right to refuse office to men whose loyalty he could not trust, and that the order of society required unity of belief. The Arians of the East appealed to Theodoric to protect them. He asked Pope John I to go to Constantinople and intercede for the dismissed Arians; the Pope protested that this was no mission for one pledged to destroy heresy; but Theodoric insisted. John was received with such honors in Constantinople, and returned with such empty hands, that Theodoric accused him of treason, and flung him into jail, where, a year later, he died.[72]

Meanwhile Albinus and Boethius had been tried before the King, adjudged guilty, and sentenced to death. The frightened Senate passed decrees repudiating them, confiscating their property, and approving the penalty. Symmachus defended his son-in-law, and was himself arrested. Boethius, in prison, now composed one of the most famous of medieval books—De consolatione philosophiae. In its alternation of undistinguished prose and charming verse no tear finds voice; there is only a Stoic resignation to the unaccountable whims of fortune, and an heroic attempt to reconcile the misfortunes of good men with the benevolence, omnipotence, and prescience of God. Boethius reminds himself of all the blessings that life has showered upon him—wealth, and a "noble father-in-law, and a chaste wife," and exemplary children; he recalls his dignities, and the proud moment when he thrilled with his eloquence a Senate whose presiding consuls were both of them his sons. Such bliss, he tells himself, cannot last forever; fortune must balance it now and then with a chastening blow; and so much happiness can forgive so fatal a calamity.[73] And yet such recalled felicity can sharpen affliction: "in all adversity of fortune," says Boethius in a line that Dante made Francesca echo, "it is the most unhappy kind of misfortune to have been happy." [74] He asks Dame Philosophy—whom he personifies in medieval style—where real happiness lies; he discovers that it does not lie in wealth or glory, pleasure or power; and he concludes that there is no true or secure happiness except in union with God; "blessedness is one with divinity." [75] Strangely, there is no suggestion, in this book, of personal immortality, no reference to Christianity or to any specifically Christian doctrine, no line that might not have been written by Zeno, Epictetus, or Aurelius. The last work of pagan philosophy was written by a Christian who, in the hour of death, remembered Athens rather than Golgotha.

On October 23, 524, his executioners came. They tied a cord around his head, and tightened it till his eyes burst from their sockets; then they beat him with clubs till he died. A few months later Symmachus was put to death. According to Procopius,[76] Theodoric wept for the wrong he had done to Boethius and Symmachus. In 526 he followed his victims to the grave.

His kingdom died soon after him. He had nominated his grandson Athalaric to succeed him; but Athalaric being only ten years old, his mother Amalasuntha ruled in his name. She was a woman of considerable education and many accomplishments, a friend and perhaps a pupil of Cassiodorus, who now served her as he had served her father. But she leaned too much toward Roman ways to please her Gothic subjects; and they objected to the classical studies with which, in their views, she was enfeebling the King. She yielded the boy to Gothic tutors; he took to sexual indulgence, and died at eighteen. Amalasuntha associated her cousin Theodahad with her on the throne, having pledged him to let her rule. Presently he deposed and imprisoned her. She appealed to Justinian, now Byzantine Emperor, to come to her aid. Belisarius came.

CHAPTER V

Justinian

527-565

I. THE EMPEROR

IN 408 Arcadius died, and his son Theodosius II, aged seven, became Emperor of the East. Theodosius' sister Pulcheria, having the advantage of him by two years, undertook his education, with such persistent solicitude that he was never fit to govern. He left this task to the praetorian prefect and the Senate, while he copied and illuminated manuscripts; he seems never to have read the Code that preserves his name. In 414 Pulcheria assumed the regency at the age of sixteen, and presided over the Empire for thirty-three years. She and her two sisters vowed themselves to virginity, and appear to have kept their vows. They dressed with ascetic simplicity, fasted, sang hymns and prayed, established hospitals, churches, and monasteries, and loaded them with gifts. The palace was turned into a convent, into which only women and a few priests might enter. Amid all this sanctity Pulcheria, her sister-in-law Eudocia, and their ministers governed so well that in all the forty-two years of Theodosius' vicarious reign the Eastern Empire enjoyed exceptional tranquillity, while the Western was crumbling into chaos. The least forgotten event of this period was the publication of the Theodosian Code (438). In 429 a corps of jurists was commissioned to codify all laws enacted in the Empire since the accession of Constantine. The new code was accepted in both East and West, and remained the law of the Empire until the greater codification under Justinian.

Between Theodosius II and Justinian I the Eastern Empire had many rulers who in their day made great stir, but are now less than memories: the lives of great men all remind us how brief is immortality. Leo I (457-74) sent against Gaiseric (467) the greatest fleet ever assembled by a Roman government; it was defeated and destroyed. His son-in-law Zeno the Isaurian (474-91), anxious to quiet the Monophysites, caused a bitter schism between Greek and Latin Christianity by imperially deciding, in his "unifying" letter, the *Henoticon*, that there was but one nature in Christ. Anastasius (491-518) was a man of ability, courage, and good will; he restored the finances of the state by wise and economical administration, reduced taxes, abolished the contests of men with wild beasts at the games, made Constantinople almost impregnable by building the "Long Walls" for forty miles from the Sea of

Marmora to the Black Sea, expended state funds on many other useful public works, and left in the treasury 320,000 pounds of gold ($134,400,000), which made possible the conquests of Justinian. The populace resented his economies and his Monophysite tendencies; a mob besieged his palace, and killed three of his aides; he appeared to them in all the dignity of his eighty years, and offered to resign if the people could agree on a successor. It was an impossible condition, and the crowd ended by begging him to retain the crown. When presently he died, the throne was usurped by Justin, an illiterate senator (518–27), who so loved his septuagenarian ease that he left the management of the Empire to his brilliant regent and nephew Justinian.

Procopius, his historian and enemy, would have been dissatisfied with Justinian from birth, for the future emperor was born (482) of lowly Illyrian —perhaps Slavic[1]—peasants near the ancient Sardica, the modern Sofia. His uncle Justin brought him to Constantinople, and procured him a good education. Justinian so distinguished himself as an officer in the army, and as for nine years aide and apprentice to Justin, that when the uncle died (527), the nephew succeeded him as emperor.

He was now forty-five, of medium height and build, smooth shaven, ruddy faced, curly haired, with pleasant manners and a ready smile that could cover a multitude of aims. He was as abstemious as an anchorite, eating little and subsisting mostly on a vegetarian regimen;[2] he fasted often, sometimes to exhaustion. Even during these fasts he continued his routine of rising early, devoting himself to state affairs "from early dawn to midday, and far into the night." Frequently when his aides thought he had retired, he was absorbed in study, eager to become a musician and an architect, a poet and a lawyer, a theologian and a philosopher, as well as an emperor; nevertheless he retained most of the superstitions of his time. His mind was constantly active, equally at home in large designs and minute details. He was not physically strong or brave; he wished to abdicate in the early troubles of his reign, and never took the field in his many wars. Perhaps it was a defect of his amiability that he was easily swayed by his friends, and therefore often vacillated in policy; frequently he subordinated his judgment to that of his wife. Procopius, who devoted a volume to Justinian's faults, called him "insincere, crafty, hypocritical, dissembling his anger, double-dealing, clever, a perfect artist in acting out an opinion which he pretended to hold, and even able to produce tears . . . to the need of the moment";[3] but this might be a description of an able diplomat. "He was a fickle friend," continues Procopius, "a truceless enemy, an ardent devotee of assassination and robbery." Apparently he was these at times; but he was also capable of generosity and lenience. A general, Probus, was accused of reviling him, and was tried for treason; when the report of the trial was laid before Justinian he tore it up and sent a message to Probus: "I pardon you for your offense against me; pray that God also may pardon you."[4] He bore frank criticism without resentment. "This tyrant," so unfortunate in his historian, "was the most accessible person in the world. For even men of low estate and altogether obscure had complete freedom not only to come before him but to converse with him."[5]

At the same time he promoted the pomp and ceremony of his court even beyond the precedents of Diocletian and Constantine. Like Napoleon, he keenly missed the support of legitimacy, having succeeded to a usurper; he had no prestige of presence or origin; consequently he resorted to an awe-inspiring ritual and pageantry whenever he appeared in public or before foreign ambassadors. He encouraged the Oriental conception of royalty as divine, applied the term *sacred* to his person and his property, and required those who came into his presence to kneel and kiss the hem of his purple robe, or the toes of his buskined feet.* He had himself anointed and crowned by the patriarch of Constantinople, and wore a diadem of pearls. No government has ever made so much ado as the Byzantine to ensure popular reverence through ceremonial splendor. The policy was reasonably effective; there were many revolutions in Byzantine history, but these were mostly *coups d'état* of the palace personnel; the court was not awed by its own solemnity.

The most significant revolt of the reign came early (532), and nearly cost Justinian his life. The Greens and Blues—the factions into which the people of Constantinople divided according to the dress of their favorite jockeys—had brought their quarrels to the point of open violence; the streets of the capital had become unsafe, and the well-to-do had to dress like paupers to avoid the nocturnal knife. Finally the government pounced down upon both factions, arresting several protagonists. The factions thereupon united in an armed uprising against the government. Probably a number of senators joined in the revolt, and proletarian discontent strove to make it a revolution. Prisons were invaded, and their inmates freed; city police and officials were killed; fires were started that burned down the church of St. Sophia and part of the Emperor's palace. The crowd cried out *"Nika!"* (victory)—and so gave a name to the revolt. Drunk with success, it demanded the dismissal of two unpopular, perhaps oppressive, members of Justinian's council; and he complied. Emboldened, the rebels persuaded Hypatius, of the senatorial class, to accept the throne; against the pleading of his wife he accepted, and went amid the plaudits of the crowd to take the imperial seat at the Hippodrome games. Meanwhile Justinian hid in his palace, and meditated flight; the Empress Theodora dissuaded him, and called for active resistance. Belisarius, leader of the army, took the assignment, assembled a number of Goths from his troops, led them to the Hippodrome, slaughtered 30,000 of the populace, arrested Hypatius, and had him killed in jail. Justinian restored his

---

* A purple cloak had long been the distinguishing garment of the emperor; to "assume the purple" was already a synonym for acquiring the throne.

dismissed officials, pardoned the conspiring senators, and restored to the children of Hypatius their confiscated property.[6] For the next thirty years Justinian was secure, but only one person seems to have loved him.

II. THEODORA

In his book on *Buildings* Procopius described a statue of Justinian's wife: "It is beautiful, but still inferior to the beauty of the Empress; for to express her loveliness in words, or to portray it as a statue, would be altogether impossible for a mere human being."[7] In all his writings except one this greatest of Byzantine historians has nothing but praise for Theodora. But in a book which he left unpublished during his lifetime, and therefore called *Anecdota*—"not given out"—Procopius unfolded so scandalous a tale of the Queen's premarital life that its veracity has been debated for thirteen centuries. This "Secret History" is a brief of candid malice, completely one-sided, devoted to blackening the posthumous reputations of Justinian, Theodora, and Belisarius. Since Procopius is our chief authority for the period, and in his other works is apparently accurate and fair, it is impossible to reject the *Anecdota* as mere fabrication; we may only rate it the angry retaliation of a disappointed courtier. John of Ephesus, who knew the Empress well, and does not otherwise reproach her, calls her simply "Theodora the strumpet."[8] For the rest there is scant corroboration of Procopius' charges in other contemporary historians. Many theologians denounced her heresies, but none of them mentions her depravity—an incredible generosity if her depravity was real. We may reasonably conclude that Theodora began as not quite a lady, and ended as every inch a queen.

She was, Procopius assures us, the daughter of a bear trainer, grew up in the odor of a circus, became an actress and a prostitute, shocked and delighted Constantinople with her lewd pantomimes, practiced abortion with repeated success, but gave birth to an illegitimate child; became the mistress of Hecebolus, a Syrian, was deserted by him, and was lost sight of for a time in Alexandria. She reappeared in Constantinople as a poor but honest woman, earning her living by spinning wool. Justinian fell in love with her, made her his mistress, then his wife, then his queen.[9] We cannot now determine how much truth there is in this proemium; but if such preliminaries did not disturb an emperor, they should not long detain us. Shortly after their marriage Justinian was crowned in St. Sophia; Theodora was crowned Empress at his side; and "not even a priest," says Procopius, "showed himself outraged."[10]

From whatever she had been, Theodora became a matron whose imperial chastity no one impugned. She was avid of money and power, she sometimes gave way to an imperious temper, she occasionally intrigued to achieve ends opposed to Justinian's. She slept much, indulged heartily in food and drink, loved luxury, jewelry, and display, spent many months of the year in her palaces on the shore; nevertheless Justinian remained always enamored of her, and bore with philosophic patience her interferences with his schemes. He had invested her uxoriously with a sovereignty theoretically equal to his own, and could not complain if she exercised her power. She took an active part in diplomacy and in ecclesiastical politics, made and unmade Popes and patriarchs, and deposed her enemies. Sometimes she countermanded her husband's orders, often to the advantage of the state;[11] her intelligence was almost commensurate with her power. Procopius charges her with cruelty to her opponents, with dungeon imprisonments and a few murders; men who seriously offended her were likely to disappear without trace, as in the political morals of our century. But she knew mercy too. She protected for two years, by hiding him in her own apartments, the Patriarch Anthemius, who had been exiled by Justinian for heresy. Perhaps she was too lenient with the adulteries of Belisarius' wife; but to balance this she built a pretty "Convent of Repentance" for reformed prostitutes. Some of the girls repented of their repentance, and threw themselves from the windows, literally bored to death.[12] She took a grandmotherly interest in the marriages of her friends, arranged many matches, and sometimes made marriage a condition of advancement at her court. As might have been expected, she became in old age a stern guardian of public morals.[13]

Finally she interested herself in theology, and debated with her husband the nature of Christ. Justinian labored to reunite the Eastern and the Western Church; unity of religion, he thought, was indispensable to the unity of the Empire. But Theodora could not understand the two natures in Christ, though she raised no difficulties about the three persons in God; she adopted the Monophysite doctrine, perceived that on this point the East would not yield to the West, and judged that the strength and fortune of the Empire lay in the rich provinces of Asia, Syria, and Egypt, rather than in Western provinces ruined by barbarism and war. She softened Justinian's orthodox intolerance, protected heretics, challenged the papacy, secretly encouraged the rise of an independent Monophysite Church in the East; and on these issues she fought tenaciously and ruthlessly against emperor and pope.

III. BELISARIUS

Justinian can be forgiven his passion for unity; it is the eternal temptation of philosophers as well as of statesmen, and generalizations have sometimes cost more than war. To recapture Africa from the Vandals, Italy from the Ostrogoths, Spain from the Visigoths, Gaul from the Franks, Britain from the Saxons; to drive barbarism back to its lairs and restore Roman civilization to all its old expanse; to spread Roman law once more across the white man's world from the Euphrates to Hadrian's Wall: these were no ignoble ambitions, though they were destined to exhaust saviors and saved alike. For these high purposes Justinian ended the schism of the Eastern from the Western Church on papal terms, and dreamed of bringing Arians, Monophysites, and other heretics into one great spiritual fold. Not since Constantine had a European thought in such dimensions.

Justinian was favored with competent generals, and harassed by limited means. His people were unwilling to fight his wars, and unable to pay for them. He soon used up the 320,000 pounds of gold that Justin's predecessors had left in the treasury; thereafter he was forced to taxes that alienated the citizens, and economies that hampered his generals. Universal military service had ceased a century before; now the imperial army was composed almost wholly of barbarian mercenaries from a hundred tribes and states. They lived by plunder, and dreamed of riches and rape; time and again they mutinied in the crisis of battle, or lost a victory by stopping to gather spoils. Nothing united or inspired them except regular pay and able generals.

Belisarius, like Justinian, came of Illyrian peasant stock, recalling those Balkan emperors—Aurelian, Probus, Diocletian—who had saved the Empire in the third century. No general since Caesar ever won so many victories with such limited resources of men and funds; few ever surpassed him in strategy or tactics, in popularity with his men and mercy to his foes; perhaps it merits note that the greatest generals—Alexander, Caesar, Belisarius, Saladin, Napoleon—found clemency a mighty engine of war. There was a strain of sensitivity and tenderness in Belisarius, as in those others, which could turn the soldier into a lover as soon as his bloody tasks were done. And as the Emperor doted on Theodora, so Belisarius adored Antonina, bore with melting fury her infidelities, and, for divers reasons, took her with him on his campaigns.

He won his first honors in war against Persia. After 150 years of peace between the empires, hostilities had been renewed in the old competition for control of the trade routes to Central Asia and India. Amid brilliant victories Belisarius was suddenly recalled to Constantinople; Justinian made peace with Persia (532) by paying Khosru Anushirvan 11,000 pounds of gold; and then sent Belisarius to win back Africa. He had concluded that he could never expect to make permanent conquests in the East: the population there would be hostile, the frontier difficult to defend. But in the West were nations accustomed for centuries to Roman rule, resenting their heretical barbarian masters, and promising co-operation in war as well as taxes in peace. And from Africa added grain would come to quiet the critical mouths of the capital.

Gaiseric had died (477) after a reign of thirty-nine years. Under his successors Vandal Africa had resumed most of its Roman ways. Latin was the official language, and poets wrote in it dead verse to honor forgotten kings. The Roman theater at Carthage was restored, Greek dramas were played again.[14] The monuments of ancient art were respected, and splendid new buildings rose. Procopius pictures the ruling classes as civilized gentlemen touched with occasional barbarism, but mostly neglecting the arts of war, and decaying leisurely under the sun.[15]

In June, 533, five hundred transports and ninety-two warships gathered in the Bosporus, received the commands of the Emperor and the blessings of the patriarch, and sailed for Carthage. Procopius was on Belisarius' staff, and wrote a vivid account of the "Vandal War." Landing in Africa with only 5000 cavalry, Belisarius swept through the improvised defenses of Carthage, and in a few months overthrew the Vandal power. Justinian too hastily recalled him for a triumph at Constantinople; the Moors, pouring down from the hills, attacked the Roman garrison; Belisarius hurried back just in time to quell a mutiny among the troops and lead them to victory. Carthaginian Africa thenceforth remained under Byzantine rule till the Arabs came.

Justinian's crafty diplomacy had arranged an alliance with the Ostrogoths while Belisarius attacked Africa; now he lured the Franks into an alliance while he ordered Belisarius to conquer Ostrogothic Italy. Using Tunisia as a base, Belisarius without much difficulty took Sicily. In 536 he crossed to Italy, and captured Naples by having some of his soldiers creep through the aqueduct into the town. The Ostrogothic forces were meager and divided; the people of Rome hailed Belisarius as a liberator, the clergy welcomed him as a Trinitarian; he entered Rome unopposed. Theodahad had Amalasuntha killed; the Ostrogoths deposed Theodahad, and chose Witigis as king. Witigis raised an army of 150,000 men, and besieged Belisarius in Rome. Forced to economize food and water, and to discontinue their daily baths, the Romans began to grumble against Belisarius, who had only 5000 men in arms. He defended the city with skill and courage, and after a year's effort Witigis returned to Ravenna. For three years Belisarius importuned Justinian for additional troops; they were sent, but under generals hostile to Belisarius. The Ostrogoths in Ravenna, besieged and starving, offered to surrender if Belisarius would become their king. He pretended to consent, took the city, and presented it to Justinian (540).

The Emperor was grateful and suspicious. Belisarius had rewarded himself well out of the spoils of victory; he had won the too-personal loyalty of his troops; he had been offered a kingdom; might he not aspire to seize the throne from the nephew of a usurper? Justinian recalled him, and noticed uneasily the splendor of the general's retinue. The Byzantines, Procopius reports, "took delight in watching Belisarius as he came forth from his home each day. . . . For his progress resembled a crowded festival procession, since he was always escorted by a large number of Vandals, Goths, and Moors. Furthermore, he had a fine figure, and was tall and remarkably handsome. But his conduct was so meek, and his manners so affable, that he seemed like a very poor man, and one of no repute."[16]

The commanders appointed to replace him in Italy neglected the discipline of their troops, quarreled with one another, and earned the contempt of the Ostrogoths. A Goth of energy, judgment, and courage was proclaimed king of the defeated people. Totila gathered desperate recruits from the barbarians wandering homeless in Italy, took Naples (543) and Tibur, and laid siege to Rome. He astonished all by his clemency and good faith; treated captives so well that they enlisted under his banner; kept so honorably the promises by which he had secured the surrender of Naples that men began to wonder who was the barbarian, and who the civilized Greek. The wives of some senators fell into his hands; he treated them with gallant courtesy, and set them free. He condemned one of his soldiers to death for violating a Roman girl. The barbarians in the Emperor's service showed no such delicacy; unpaid by the nearly bankrupt Justinian, they ravaged the country till the population remembered with longing the order and justice of Theodoric's rule.[17]

Belisarius was ordered to the rescue. Reaching Italy, he made his way alone through Totila's lines into beleaguered Rome. He was too late; the Greek garrison was demoralized; its officers were incompetent cowards; traitors opened the gates, and Totila's army, ten thousand strong, entered the capital (546). Belisarius, retreating, sent a message asking him not to destroy the historic city; Totila permitted plunder to his unpaid and hungry troops, but spared the people, and protected the women from soldierly ardor. He made the mistake of leaving Rome to besiege Ravenna; in his absence Belisarius recaptured the city; and when Totila returned, his second siege failed to dislodge the resourceful Greek. Justinian, thinking the West won, declared war on Persia, and called Belisarius to the East. Totila took Rome again (549), and Sicily, Corsica, Sardinia, almost the entire peninsula. At last Justinian gave to his eunuch general Narses "an exceedingly large sum of money," and ordered him to raise a new army and drive the Goths from Italy. Narses accomplished his mission with skill and dispatch; Totila was defeated and was killed in flight; the surviving Goths were permitted to leave Italy safely, and after eighteen years the "Gothic War" came to an end (553).

Those years completed the ruin of Italy. Rome had been five times captured, thrice besieged, starved, looted; its population, once a million, was now reduced to 40,000,[18] of whom nearly half were paupers maintained by papal alms. Milan had been destroyed, and all its inhabitants killed. Hundreds of towns and villages sank into insolvency under the exactions of rulers and the depredations of troops. Regions once tilled were abandoned, and the food supply fell; in Picenum alone, we are told, 50,000 died of starvation during these eighteen years.[19] The aristocracy was shattered; so many of its members had been slain in battle, pillage, or flight that too few survived to continue the Senate of Rome; after 579 we hear of it no more.[20] The great aqueducts that Theodoric had repaired were broken and neglected, and again turned the Campagna into a vast malarial marsh, which remained till our time. The majestic baths, dependent upon the aqueducts, fell into disuse and decay. Hundreds of statues, surviving Alaric and Gaiseric, had been broken or melted down to provide projectiles and machines during siege. Only ruins bore witness to Rome's ancient grandeur as capital of half the world. The Eastern emperor would now for a brief period rule Italy; but it was a costly and empty victory. Rome would not fully recover from that victory till the Renaissance.

IV. THE CODE OF JUSTINIAN

History rightly forgets Justinian's wars, and remembers him for his laws. A century had elapsed since the publication of Theodosius' Code; many of its regulations had been made obsolete by changing conditions; many new laws had been passed which lay in confusion on the statute books; and many contradictions in the laws hampered executives and courts. The influence of Christianity had modified legislation and interpretation. The civil laws of Rome often conflicted with the laws of the nations composing the Empire; many of the old enactments were ill adapted to the Hellenistic traditions of the East. The whole vast body of Roman law had become an empirical accumulation rather than a logical code.

Justinian's unifying passion resented this chaos, as it chafed at the dismemberment of the Empire. In 528 he appointed ten jurists to systematize, clarify, and reform the laws. The most active and influential member of this commission was the quaestor Tribonian, who, despite venality and suspected atheism, remained to his death the chief inspirer, adviser, and executant of Justinian's legislative plans. The first part of the task was accomplished with undue haste, and was issued in 529 as the *Codex Constitutionum*; it was declared to be the law of the Empire, and all preceding legislation was nullified except as re-enacted herein. The proemium struck a pretty note:

> To the youth desirous of studying the law: The Imperial Majesty should be armed with law as well as glorified with arms, that there may be good government in times both of war and of peace; and that the ruler may . . . show himself as scrupulously regardful of justice as triumphant over his foes.[21]

The commissioners then proceeded to the second part of their assignment: to gather into a system those *responsa* or opinions of the great Roman jurists which still seemed worthy to have the force of law. The result was published as the *Digesta* or *Pandectae* (533); the opinions quoted, and the interpretations now given, were henceforth to be binding upon all judges; and all other opinions lost legal authority. Older collections of *responsa* ceased to be copied, and for the most part disappeared. What remains of them suggests that Justinian's redactors omitted opinions favorable to freedom, and by impious fraud transformed some judgments of ancient jurists to better consonance with absolute rule.

While this major work was in process, Tribonian and two associates, finding the *Codex* too laborious a volume for students, issued an official handbook of civil law under the title of *Institutiones* (533). Essentially this reproduced, amended, and brought up to date the *Commentaries* of Gaius, who in the second century had with admirable skill and clarity summarized the civil law of his time. Meanwhile Justinian had been issuing new laws. In 534 Tribonian and four aides embodied these in a revised edition of the *Codex*; the earlier issue was deprived of authority, and was lost to history. After Justinian's death his additional legislation was published as *Novellae* (sc. *constitutiones*) —i.e., new enactments. Whereas the previous publications had been in Latin, this was in Greek, and marked the end of Latin as the language of the law in the Byzantine Empire. All these publications came to be known as the *Corpus iuris civilis*, or Body of Civil Law, and were loosely referred to as the Code of Justinian.

This Code, like the Theodosian, enacted orthodox Christianity into law. It began by declaring for the Trinity, and anathematized Nestorius, Eutyches, and Apollinaris. It acknowledged the ecclesiastical leadership of the Roman Church, and ordered all Christian groups to submit to her authority. But ensuing chapters proclaimed the dominion of the emperor over the Church: all ecclesiastical, like all civil, law, was to emanate from the throne. The Code proceeded to make laws for metropolitans, bishops, abbots, and monks, and specified penalties for clerics who gambled, or attended the theater or the games.[22] Manicheans or relapsed heretics were to be put to death; Donatists, Montanists, Monophysites, and other dissenters were to suffer confiscation of their goods, and were declared incompetent to buy or sell, to inherit or bequeath; they were excluded from public office, forbidden to meet, and disqualified from suing orthodox Christians for debt. A gentler enactment empowered bishops to visit prisons, and to protect prisoners from abuses of the law.

The Code replaced older distinctions of class. Freedmen were no longer treated as a separate group; they enjoyed at once, on their emancipation, all the privileges of freemen; they might rise to be senators or emperors. All freemen were divided into *honestiores*—men of honor or rank—and *humiliores*—commoners. A hierarchy of rank, which had developed among the *honestiores* since Diocletian, was sanctioned by the Code: *patricii, illustres, spectabiles* (hence our *respectable*), *clarissimi*, and *gloriosi*; there were many Oriental elements in this Roman law.

The Code showed some Christian or Stoic influence in its legislation on slavery. The rape of a slave woman, as of a free woman, was to be punished with death.

A slave might marry a free woman if his master consented. Justinian, like the Church, encouraged manumissions; but his law allowed a newborn child to be sold into slavery if its parents were desperate with poverty.[23] Certain passages of the Code legalized serfdom, and prepared for feudalism. A freeman who had cultivated a tract of land for thirty years was required, with his descendants, to remain forever attached to that piece of land; [24] the measure was explained as discouraging the desertion of the soil. A serf who ran away, or became a cleric without his lord's consent, could be reclaimed like a runaway slave.

The status of woman was moderately improved by the Code. Her subjection to lifelong guardianship had been ended in the fourth century, and the old principle that inheritance could pass only through males had become obsolete; the Church, which often received legacies from women, did much to secure these reforms. Justinian sought to enforce the views of the Church on divorce, and forbade it except when one of the parties wished to enter a convent or monastery. But this was too extreme a departure from existing custom and law; large sections of the public protested that it would increase the number of poisonings. The later legislation of the Emperor listed a generous variety of grounds for divorce; and this, with some interruptions, remained the law of the Byzantine Empire till 1453.[25] Penalties imposed by Augustus upon celibacy and childlessness were removed in the Code. Constantine had made adultery a capital crime, though he had rarely enforced the decree; Justinian kept the death penalty for men, but reduced the penalty for the woman to immurement in a nunnery. A husband might with impunity kill the paramour of his wife if, after sending her three witnessed warnings, he found her in his own house, or in a tavern, conversing with the suspected man. Similarly severe penalties were decreed for intercourse with an unmarried woman or a widow, unless she was a concubine or a prostitute. Rape was punished with death and confiscation of property, and the proceeds were given to the injured woman. Justinian not only decreed death for homosexual acts, but often added torture, mutilation, and the public parading of the guilty persons before their execution. In this extreme legislation against sexual irregularities we feel the influence of a Christianity shocked into a ferocious puritanism by the sins of pagan civilization.

Justinian made a decisive change in the law of property. The ancient privilege of agnate relatives—relatives through the male line—to inherit an intestate property was abolished; such inheritance was now to descend to the cognate relatives in direct line—children, grandchildren, etc. Charitable gifts and bequests were encouraged by the Code. The property of the Church, whether in realty or movables, rents, serfs, or slaves, was declared inalienable; no member, and no number of members, of the clergy or the laity could give, sell, or bequeath anything belonging to the Church. These laws of Leo I and Anthemius, confirmed by the Code, became the legal basis of the Church's growing wealth: secular property was dissipated, ecclesiastical property was accumulated, in the course of generations. The Church tried, and failed, to have interest forbidden. Defaulting debtors could be arrested, but were to be released on bail or on their oath to return for trial.

No one could be imprisoned except by order of a high magistrate; and there were strict limits to the time that might elapse between arrest and trial. Lawyers were so numerous that Justinian built for them a basilica whose size may be judged from its library of 150,000 volumes or rolls. Trial was to be held before a magistrate appointed by the emperor; but if both parties so wished, the case could be transferred to the bishop's court. A copy of the Bible was placed before the judge in each trial; the attorneys were required to swear on it that they would do their best to defend their clients honorably, but would resign their case if they found it dishonest; plaintiff and defendant had also to swear on it to the justice of their cause. Penalties, though severe, were seldom mandatory; the judge might mitigate them for women, minors, and drunken offenders. Imprisonment was used as detention for trial, but seldom as a punishment. The Justinian Code retrogressed from the laws of Hadrian and Antoninus Pius by permitting mutilation as a penalty. Tax collectors falsifying returns, and persons copying Monophysite literature, could suffer the loss of a hand, on the theory that the offending member should pay for the crime. Amputation of nose or throat is frequently decreed in the Code; later Byzantine law added blinding, especially as a means for disqualifying heirs or aspirants to the throne. The death penalty was carried out on free persons by beheading, on some slaves by crucifixion. Sorcerers and deserters from the army were burned alive. A condemned citizen might appeal to a higher court, then to the Senate, finally to the emperor.

We can admire the Code of Justinian more readily as a whole than in its parts. It differs most from earlier codes by its rigid orthodoxy, its deeper obscurantism, its vengeful severity. An educated Roman would have found life more civilized under the Antonines than under Justinian. The Emperor could not escape his environment and his time; and in his ambition to unify everything he codified the superstition and barbarity, as well as the justice and charity, of his age. The Code was conservative, like everything Byzantine, and served as a strait jacket for a civilization that seemed destined never to die. It soon ceased to be obeyed except in a narrowing realm. The Eastern nationalist heretics whom it flayed opened their arms to the Moslems, and prospered better under the Koran than under the Code. Italy under the Lombards, Gaul under the Franks, England under the Anglo-Saxons, Spain under the Visigoths, ignored the edicts of Justinian. Nevertheless the Code for some generations gave order and security to a motley assemblage of peoples, and allowed, across the frontiers and along the streets of a dozen nations, freer and safer movement than the same regions enjoy today. It continued to the end the code of the Byzantine Empire; and five centuries after it disappeared in the West it was revived by the jurists of Bologna, accepted by emperors and popes, and entered like a scaffolding of order into the structure of many modern states.

V. THE IMPERIAL THEOLOGIAN

It remained only to unify belief, to weld the Church into a homogeneous instrument of rule. Probably Justinian's piety was sincere, not merely political; he himself, as far as Theodora would permit, lived like a monk in his palace, fasting and praying, poring over theological tomes, and debating doctrinal niceties with professors, patriarchs, and popes. Procopius, with transparent concurrence, quotes a conspirator: "It ill becomes anyone who has even a little spirit in him to refuse to murder Justinian; nor should he entertain any fear of a man who always sits unguarded in some lobby to a late hour of the night, eagerly unrolling the Christian Scriptures in company with priests who are at the extremity of old age." [26] Almost the first use that Justinian had made of his power as regent for Justin was to end the breach that had been widened between the Eastern and the Western Church by the Emperor Zeno's *Henoticon*. By accepting the viewpoint of the papacy, Justinian won the support of the orthodox clergy in Italy against the Goths, and in the East against the Monophysites.

This sect, arguing passionately that there was but one nature in Christ, had become almost as numerous in Egypt as the Catholics. In Alexandria they were so advanced that they in turn could divide into orthodox and heterodox Monophysites; these factions fought in the streets, while their women joined in with missiles from the roofs. When the armed forces of the Emperor installed a Catholic bishop in the see of Athanasius, the congregation greeted his first sermon with a volley of stones, and was slaughtered *in situ* by the imperial soldiery. While Catholicism controlled the Alexandrian episcopacy, heresy spread throughout the countryside; the peasants ignored the decrees of the patriarch and the orders of the Emperor, and Egypt was half lost to the Empire a century before the Arabs came.

In this matter, as in many others, the persistent Theodora overcame the vacillating Justinian. She intrigued with Vigilius, a Roman deacon, to make him pope if he would offer concessions to the Monophysites. Pope Silverius was removed from Rome by Belisarius (537), and was exiled to the island of Palmaria, where he soon died from harsh treatment; and Vigilius was made Pope by the orders of the Emperor. Finally accepting Theodora's view that Monophysitism could not be crushed, Justinian sought to appease its followers in a document of imperial theology known as the Three Chapters. He summoned Vigilius to Constantinople, and urged him to subscribe to this statement. Vigilius reluctantly consented, whereupon the African Catholic clergy excommunicated him (550); he withdrew his consent, was exiled by Justinian to a rock in the Proconnesus, again consented, obtained leave to return to Rome, but died on the way (555). Never had an emperor made so open an attempt to dominate the papacy. Justinian called an ecumenical council to meet at Constantinople (553); hardly any Western bishops attended; the council approved Justinian's formulas, the Western Church rejected them, and Eastern and Western Christianity resumed their schism for a century.

In the end death won all arguments. Theodora's passing in 548 was to Justinian the heaviest of many blows that broke down his courage, clarity, and strength. He was then sixty-five, weakened by asceticism and recurrent crises; he left the government to subordinates, neglected the defenses he had so labored to build, and abandoned himself to theology. A hundred disasters darkened the remaining seventeen years during which he outlived himself. Earthquakes were especially frequent in this reign; a dozen cities were almost wiped out by them; and their rehabilitation drained the Treasury. In 542 plague came; in 556 famine, in 558 plague again. In 559 the Kotrigur Huns crossed the Danube, plundered Moesia and Thrace, took thousands of captives, violated matrons, virgins, and nuns, threw to the dogs the infants born to women captives on the march, and advanced to the walls of Constantinople. The terrified Emperor appealed to the great general who had so often saved him. Belisarius was old and feeble; nevertheless he put on his armor, gathered 300 veterans who had fought with him in Italy, recruited a few hundred untrained men, and went out to meet 7000 Huns. He disposed his forces with his wonted foresight and skill, concealing 200 of his best soldiers in adjoining woods. When the Huns moved forward these men fell upon their flank, while Belisarius met the attack at the head of his little army. The barbarians turned and fled before a single Roman was mortally injured. The populace at the capital complained that Belisarius had not pursued the enemy and brought back the Hun leader as captive. The jealous Emperor listened to envious calumnies against his general, suspected him of conspiracy, and ordered him to dismiss his armed retainers. Belisarius died in 565, and Justinian confiscated half his property.

The Emperor outlived the general by eight months. In his final years his interest in theology had borne strange fruit: the defender of the faith had become a heretic. He announced that the body of Christ was incorruptible, and that Christ's human nature had never been subject to any of the wants and indignities of mortal flesh. The clergy warned him that if he died in this error his soul would "be delivered to the flames, and burn there eternally." [27] He died unrepentant (565), after a life of eighty-three years, and a reign of thirty-eight.

Justinian's death was one more point at which antiquity might be said to end. He was a true Roman emperor, thinking in terms of all the Empire East and West, struggling to keep back the barbarians, and to bring again to the vast realm an orderly government of homogeneous laws. He had accomplished a good measure of this aim: Africa, Dalmatia, Italy, Corsica, Sardinia, Sicily, and part of Spain had been regained; the Persians had been driven out of Syria; the Empire had doubled its extent in his reign. Though his legislation was barbarously severe on heresy and sexual immorality, it represented, by its unity, lucidity, and scope, one of the peaks in the history of law. His administration was sullied with official corruption, extreme taxation, capricious pardons and punishments; but it was also distinguished by a painstaking organization of imperial economy and government; and it created a system of order which, though a stranger to freedom, held civilization together in a corner of Europe while the rest of the continent plunged into the Dark Ages. He left his name upon the history of industry and art; St. Sophia is also his monument. To orthodox contemporaries it must have seemed that once more the Empire had turned back the tide, and won a respite from death.

It was a pitifully brief respite. Justinian had left the treasury empty, as he had found it full; his intolerant laws and thieving taxgatherers had alienated nations as fast as his armies had conquered them; and those armies, decimated, scattered, and ill paid, could not long defend what they had so devastatingly won. Africa was soon abandoned to the Berbers; Syria, Palestine, Egypt, Africa, and Spain to the Arabs; Italy to the Lombards; within a century after Justinian's death the Empire had lost more territory than he had gained. With proud hindsight we may see how much better it would have been to gather the rising nationalities and creeds into a federated union; to offer friendship to the Ostrogoths who had governed Italy comparatively well; and to serve as a protective medium through which the ancient culture might flow unstinted to the newborn states.

We need not accept Procopius' estimate of Justinian; it was refuted by Procopius himself.[28] He was a great ruler, whose very faults sprang from the logic and sincerity of his creed: his persecutions from his certainty, his wars from his Roman spirit, his confiscations from his wars. We mourn the narrow violence of his methods, and applaud the grandeur of his aims. He and Belisarius, not Boniface and Aëtius, were the last of the Romans.

Byzantine Civilization

326-565

I. WORK AND WEALTH

BYZANTINE economy was a modernistic mixture of private enterprise, state regulation, and nationalized industries. Peasant proprietorship was still, under Justinian, the agricultural rule; but estates were expanding, and many farmers were being forced into feudal subjection to great landowners by drought or flood, competition or incompetence, taxation or war. The mineral resources of the soil were owned by the state, but were mostly mined by private agencies on governmental lease. The mines of Greece were exhausted, but old and new veins were worked in Thrace, Pontus, and the Balkans. Most industrial labor was "free"— i.e., compelled only by a distaste for starvation. Direct slavery played a negligible role outside of domestic services and the textile industry; but in Syria, and probably in Egypt and North Africa, forced labor was used by the state to maintain the major irrigation canals.[1] The government produced in its own factories most of the goods required by the army, the bureaucracy, and the court.[2]

About the year 552 some Nestorian monks from Central Asia interested Justinian with an offer to provide the Empire with an independent source of silk. If we recall how many wars Greece and Rome had fought with Persia for control of the trade routes to China and India, and remark the name "silk route" given to the northern passes to the Far East, the name Serica (Silkland) given by the Romans to China, and the name Serindia applied to the region between China and India, we shall understand why Justinian eagerly accepted the proposal. The monks went back to Central Asia and returned with the eggs of silkworms, and probably some seedlings of the mulberry tree.[3] A small silk industry already existed in Greece, but it depended upon wild silkworms, feeding on oak, ash, or cypress leaves. Now silk became a major industry, especially in Syria and Greece; it developed to such an extent in the Peloponnesus as to give that peninsula the new name of Morea— land of the mulberry tree (*morus alba*).

In Constantinople the manufacture of certain silk fabrics and purple dyes was a state monopoly, and was carried on in workshops in or near the imperial palace.[4] Expensive silks and dyed fabrics were permitted only to high officials of the government, and the most costly could be worn only by members of the imperial family. When clandestine private enterprise produced and sold similar stuffs to unprivileged persons, Justinian broke this "black market" by removing most of the restrictions on the use of luxurious silks and dyes; he flooded the shops with state textiles at prices that private competition could not meet; and when the competition had disappeared the government raised the prices.[5] Following Diocletian's example, Justinian sought to extend governmental control to all prices and wages. After the plague of 542 the labor supply fell, wages rose, and prices soared. Like the English Parliament of 1351 after the plague of 1348, Justinian sought to help employers and consumers by a price and wage decree:

> We have learned that since the visitation of God traders, artisans, husbandmen, and sailors have yielded to a spirit of covetousness, and are demanding prices and wages two or three times as great as they formerly received. . . . We forbid all such to demand higher wages or prices than before. We also forbid contractors for buildings, or for agricultural or other work, to pay the workmen more than was customary in old days.[6]

We have no information as to the effect of this decree.

From Constantine to the latter part of Justinian's reign domestic and foreign trade flourished in the Byzantine Empire. Roman roads and bridges were there kept in repair, and the creative lust for gain built maritime fleets that bound the capital with a hundred ports in East and West. From the fifth century to the fifteenth Constantinople remained the greatest market and shipping center in the world. Alexandria, which had held this supremacy from the third century B.C., now ranked in trade below Antioch.[7] All Syria throve with commerce and industry; it lay between Persia and Constantinople, between Constantinople and Egypt; its merchants were shrewd and venturesome, and only the effervescent Greeks could rival them in the extent of their traffic and the subtlety of their ways; their spread throughout the Empire was a factor in that orientalization of manners and arts which marked Byzantine civilization.

As the old trade route from Syria to Central Asia lay through hostile Persia, Justinian sought a new route by establishing friendly relations with the Himyarites of southwestern Arabia and the kings of Ethiopia, who between them controlled the southern gates of the Red Sea. Through those straits and the Indian Ocean Byzantine merchantmen sailed to India; but Persian control of Indian ports wrung the same tolls from this trade as if it had passed through Iran. Defeated on this line, Justinian encouraged the development of harbors on the Black Sea; along these stopping points goods were shipped by water to Colchis, and thence by caravan to Sogdiana, where Chinese and Western merchants could meet and haggle without Persian scrutiny. The rising traffic on this northern route helped to raise Serindia to its medieval peak of wealth and art. Meanwhile Greek commerce maintained its ancient outlets in the West.

This active economy was supported by an imperial currency whose integrity gave it an almost global acceptance. Constantine had minted a new coin to replace Caesar's *aureus*; this *solidus* or "bezant" contained 4.55 grams, or one sixth of a troy ounce of gold, and would be worth $5.83 in the United States of 1946. The metallic and economic deterioration of the *solidus* into the lowly sou illustrates the general rise of prices, and depreciation of currencies, through history, and suggests that thrift is a virtue which, like most others, must be practiced with discrimination. Banking was now highly developed. We may judge the prosperity of the Byzantine Empire at Justinian's accession by his fixing of the maximum interest rate at four per cent on loans to peasants, six per cent on private loans secured by collateral, eight per cent on commercial loans, and twelve per cent on maritime investments.[8] Nowhere else in the world of that time were interest rates so low.

The senatorial aristocracy through land ownership, and the mercantile magnates through far-flung ventures in which the profits were commensurate with the risks, enjoyed such wealth and luxury as only a few had ever known in Rome. The aristocracy of the East had better tastes than that of Rome in the days of Cicero or Juvenal; it did not gorge itself on exotic foods, had a lower rate of divorce, and showed considerable fidelity and industry in serving the state. Its extravagance lay chiefly in ornate dress, in robes of furry hems and dazzling tints, in silken tunics preciously dyed, threaded with gold, and illuminated with scenes from nature or history. Some men were "walking murals"; on the garments of one senator could be found the whole story of Christ.[9] Underneath this social crust of gold was a middle class fretted with taxation, a plodding bureaucracy, a medley of meddlesome monks, a flotsam and jetsam of proletaires exploited by the price system and soothed by the dole.

Morals, sexual and commercial, were not appreciably different from those of other cultures at a like stage of economic development. Chrysostom condemned dancing as exciting passion, but Constantinople danced. The Church continued to refuse baptism to actors, but the Byzantine stage continued to display its suggestive pantomimes; people must be consoled for monogamy and prose. Procopius' *Secret History*, never trustworthy, reports that "practically all women were corrupt" in his time.[10] Contraceptives were a subject of assiduous study and research; Oribasius, the outstanding physician of the fourth century, gave them a chapter in his compendium of medicine; another medical writer, Aëtius, in the sixth century, recommended the use of vinegar or brine, or the practice of continence at the beginning and end of the menstrual period.[11] Justinian and Theodora sought to diminish prostitution by banishing procuresses and brothel keepers from Constantinople, with transient results. In general the status of woman was high; never had women been more unfettered in law and custom, or more influential in government.

II. SCIENCE AND PHILOSOPHY: 364–565

What, in this apparently religious society, was the fate of education, learning, literature, science, and philosophy?

Primary instruction continued in the hands of private teachers paid by the parents per pupil and term. Higher education, till Theodosius II, was provided both by lecturers operating under their own power, and through professors paid by city or state. Libanius complained that these were too poorly paid—that they longed through hunger to go to the baker, but refrained through fear of being asked to pay their debts.[12] However, we read of teachers like Eumenius, who received 600,000 sesterces ($30,000?) a year; [13] in this, as in other fields, the best and the worst received too much, the rest too little. Julian, to propagate paganism, introduced state examinations and appointments for all university teachers.[14] Theodosius II, for opposite reasons, made it a penal offense to give public instruction without a state license; and such licenses were soon confined to conformists with the orthodox creed.

The great universities of the East were at Alexandria, Athens, Constantinople, and Antioch, specializing respectively in medicine, philosophy, literature, and rhetoric. Oribasius of Pergamum (c. 325–403), physician to Julian, compiled a medical encyclopedia of seventy "books." Aëtius of Amida, court physician under Justinian, wrote a similar survey, distinguished by the best ancient analysis of ailments of the eye, ear, nose, mouth, and teeth; with interesting chapters on goiter and hydrophobia, and surgical procedures ranging from tonsillectomy to hemorrhoids. Alexander of Tralles (c. 525–605) was the most original of these medical authors: he named various intestinal parasites, accurately described disorders of the digestive tract, and discussed with unprecedented thoroughness the diagnosis and treatment of pulmonary diseases. His textbook of internal pathology and therapy was translated into Syriac, Arabic, Hebrew, and Latin, and exercised in Christendom an influence only next to that of Hippocrates, Galen, and Soranus.[15] According to Augustine the vivisection of human beings was practiced in the fifth century.[16] Superstition encroached daily on medicine. Most physicians accepted astrology, and some advised different treatments according to the position of the planets.[17] Aëtius recommended, for contraception, that the woman should suspend near her anus the tooth of a child; [18] and Marcellus, in his De medicamentis (395), anticipated modern technique by urging the wearing of a rabbit's foot.[19] Mules fared better than men; the most scientific work of the period was the *Digestorum artis mulomedicinae libri IV* of Flavius Vegetius (383–450); this book almost founded veterinary science, and remained an authority till the Renaissance.

Chemistry and alchemy went hand in hand, with Alexandria as their center. The alchemists were generally sincere investigators; they employed experimental methods more faithfully than any other scientists of antiquity; they substantially advanced the chemistry of metals and alloys; and we cannot be sure that the future will not justify their aims. Astrology too had an honest base; nearly everybody took it for granted that the stars, as well as the sun and moon, affected terrestrial events. But upon these foundations quackery raised a weird ziggurat of magic, divination, and planetary abracadabra. Horoscopes were even more fashionable in medieval cities than in New York or Paris today. St. Augustine tells of two friends who noted carefully the position of the constellations at the birth of their domestic animals.[20] Much of the nonsense of Arabic astrology and alchemy was part of Islam's Greek heritage.

The most interesting figure in the science of this age is that of the pagan mathematician and philosopher Hypatia. Her father Theon is the last man whose name is recorded as a professor at the Alexandrian Museum; he wrote a commentary on Ptolemy's *Syntaxis*, and acknowledged the share of his daughter in its composition. Hypatia, says Suidas, wrote commentaries on Diophantus, on the *Astronomical Canon* of Ptolemy, and on the *Conics* of Apollonius of Perga.[21] None of her works survives. From mathematics she passed to philosophy, built her system on the lines of Plato and Plotinus, and (according to the Christian historian Socrates) "far surpassed all the philosophers of her time." [22] Appointed to the chair of philosophy in the Museum, she drew to her lectures a large audience of varied and distant provenance. Some students fell in love with her, but she seems never to have married; Suidas would have us believe that she married, but remained a virgin nevertheless.[23] Suidas transmits another tale, perhaps invented by her enemies, that when one youth importuned her she impatiently raised her dress, and said to him: "This symbol of unclean generation is what you are in love with, and not anything beautiful." [24] She was so fond of philosophy that she would stop in the streets and explain, to any who asked, difficult points in Plato or Aristotle. "Such was her self-possession and ease of manner," says Socrates, "arising from the refinement and cultivation of her mind, that she not infrequently appeared before the city magistrates without ever losing in an assembly of men that dignified modesty of deportment for which she was conspicuous, and which gained for her universal respect and admiration."

But the admiration was not quite universal. The Christians of Alexandria must have looked upon her askance, for she was not only a seductive unbeliever, but an intimate friend of Orestes, the pagan prefect of the city. When Archbishop Cyril instigated his monastic followers to expel the Jews from Alexandria, Orestes sent to Theodosius II an offensively impartial account of the incident. Some monks stoned the prefect; he had the leader of the mob arrested and tortured to death (415). Cyril's supporters charged Hypatia with being the chief influence upon Orestes; she alone, they argued, prevented a reconciliation between the prefect and the Patriarch. One day a band of fanatics, led by a "reader" or minor clerk on Cyril's staff, pulled her from her carriage, dragged her into a church, stripped her of her garments, battered her to death with tiles, tore her corpse to pieces, and burned the remains in a savage orgy (415).[25] "An act so inhuman," says Socrates, "could not fail to bring the greatest opprobrium not only upon Cyril, but also upon the whole Alexandrian church."[26] However, no personal punishment was exacted; the Emperor Theodosius II merely restricted the freedom of the monks to appear in public (Sept., 416), and excluded pagans from all public office (Dec., 416). Cyril's victory was complete.

Pagan professors of philosophy, after the death of Hypatia, sought security in Athens, where non-Christian teaching was still relatively and innocuously free. Student life was still lively there, and enjoyed most of the consolations of higher education—fraternities, distinctive garbs, hazing, and a general hilarity.[27] The Stoic as well as the Epicurean School had now disappeared, but the Platonic Academy enjoyed a splendid decline under Themistius, Priscus, and Proclus. Themistius (fl. 380) was destined to influence Averroës and other medieval thinkers by his commentaries on Aristotle. Priscus was for a time the friend and adviser of Julian; he was arrested by Valens and Valentinian I on a charge of using magic to give them a fever; he returned to Athens, and taught there till his death at ninety in 395. Proclus (410–85), like a true Platonist, approached philosophy through mathematics. A man of scholastic patience, he collated the ideas of Greek philosophy into one system, and gave it a superficially scientific form. But he felt the mystic mood of Neoplatonism too; by fasting and purification, he thought, one might enter into communion with supernatural beings.[28] The schools of Athens had lost all vitality when Justinian closed them in 529. Their work lay in rehearsing again and again the theories of the ancient masters; they were oppressed and stifled by the magnitude of their heritage; their only deviations were into a mysticism that borrowed from the less orthodox moods of Christianity. Justinian closed the schools of the rhetoricians as well as of the philosophers, confiscated their property, and forbade any pagan to teach. Greek philosophy, after eleven centuries of history, had come to an end.

The passage from philosophy to religion, from Plato to Christ, stands out in certain strange Greek writings confidently ascribed by medieval thinkers to Dionysius "the Areopagite"—one of the Athenians who accepted the teaching of Paul. These works are chiefly four: *On the Celestial Hierarchy*, *On the Ecclesiastical Hierarchy*, *On the Divine Names*, and *On Mystical Theology*. We do not know by whom they were written, or when, or where; their contents indicate an origin between the fourth and sixth centuries; we only know that few books have more deeply influenced Christian theology. John Scotus Erigena translated and built on one of them, Albertus Magnus and Thomas Aquinas reverenced them, a hundred mystics—Jewish and Moslem as well as Christian—fed on them, and medieval art and popular theology accepted them as an infallible guide to celestial beings and ranks. Their general purpose was to combine Neoplatonism with Christian cosmology. God, though incomprehensibly transcendent, is nevertheless immanent in all things as their source and life. Between God and man intervene three triads of supernatural beings: Seraphim, Cherubim, and Thrones; Dominations, Virtues, and Powers; Principalities, Archangels, and Angels. (The reader will recall how Dante ranged these nine groups around the throne of God, and how Milton wove some of their names into a sonorous line.) Creation, in these works, is by emanation: all things flow from God through these mediating angelic ranks; and then, by a reverse process, these nine orders of the celestial hierarchy lead men and all creation back to God.

III. LITERATURE: 364–565

In 425 Theodosius II, or his regents, reorganized higher education in Constantinople, and formally established a university of thirty-one teachers: one for philosophy, two for law, twenty-eight for Latin and Greek "grammar" and "rhetoric." These last included the study of the two literatures; and the large number of teachers assigned to them suggests a lively interest in letters. One such professor, Priscian, composed, about 526, an immense *Grammar* of Latin and Greek, which became one of the most famous textbooks of the Middle Ages. The Eastern Church seems to have raised no objections at this time to the copying of the pagan classics; [29] though a few saints protested, the School of Constantinople transmitted faithfully, to the end of the Byzantine Empire, the masterpieces of antiquity. And, despite the rising cost of parchment, the flow of books was still abundant. About 450 Musaeus, of unknown provenance, composed his famous poem, *Hero and Leander*—how Leander anticipated Byron by swimming the Hellespont to reach his beloved Hero, how he died in the attempt, and how Hero, seeing him flung up dead at the foot of her tower,

> from the sheer crag plunged in hurtling headlong fall
> To find with her dead love a death among the waves.[30]

It was the Christian gentlemen of the Byzantine court who composed, for the final installment of the *Greek Anthology*, graceful love poems in the ancient moods and modes, and in terms of the pagan gods. Here, from Agathias (*c.* 550), is a song that may have helped Ben Jonson to a masterpiece:

> I love not wine; yet if thou'lt make
> A sad man merry, sip first sup,
> And when thou givest I'll take the cup.
> If thy lips touch it, for thy sake

No more may I be stiff and staid
And the luscious jug evade.
The cup conveys thy kiss to me,
And tells the joy it had of thee.[31]

The most important literary work of this age was done by the historians. Eunapius of Sardis composed a lost *Universal History* of the period from 270 to 400, making Justinian his hero, and twenty-three gossipy biographies of the later Sophists and Neoplatonists. Socrates, an orthodox Christian of Constantinople, wrote a *History of the Church* from 309 to 439; it is fairly accurate and generally fair, as we have seen in the case of Hypatia; but this Socrates fills his narrative with superstitions, legends, and miracles, and talks so frequently of himself as if he found it hard to distinguish between himself and the cosmos. He ends with a novel plea for peace among the sects: if peace comes, he thinks, historians will have nothing to write about, and that miserable tribe of tragedy-mongers will cease.[32] Mostly copied from Socrates is the *Ecclesiastical History* of Sozomen, a convert from Palestine, and, like his model, a lawyer at the capital; apparently a legal training was no handicap to superstition. Zosimus of Constantinople composed, about 475, a *History of the Roman Empire*; he was a pagan, but did not yield to his Christian rivals in credulity and nonsense. Toward 525 Dionysius Exiguus—Dennis the Short—suggested a new method of dating events, from the supposed year of Christ's birth. The proposal was not accepted by the Latin Church till the tenth century; and the Byzantines continued to the end to number their years from the creation of the world. It is discouraging to note how many things were known to the youth of our civilization, which are unknown to us today.

The one great historian of the period was Procopius. Born in Palestinian Caesarea (490), he studied law, came to Constantinople, and was appointed secretary and legal adviser to Belisarius. He accompanied the general on the Syrian, African, and Italian campaigns, and returned with him to the capital. In 550 he published his *Books of the Wars*. Knowing at first hand the merits of the general and the parsimony of the ruler, he made Belisarius a brilliant hero, and left Justinian in the shade. The book was received with applause by the public, with silence by the Emperor. Procopius now composed his *Anecdota*, or *Secret History*; but he kept it so successfully from publication or circulation that in 554 he was commissioned by Justinian to write an account of the buildings erected during the reign. Procopius issued *De Aedificiis* in 560, and so loaded it with praise for the Emperor that Justinian might well have suspected it of insincerity or irony. The *Secret History* was not given to the world until after Justinian—and perhaps Procopius—had died. It is a fascinating book, like any denunciation of our neighbors; but there is something unpleasant in literary attacks upon persons who can no longer speak in their own defense. An historian who strains his pen to prove a thesis may be trusted to distort the truth.

Procopius was occasionally inaccurate in matters beyond his own experience; he copied at times the manner and philosophy of Herodotus, at times the speeches and sieges of Thucydides; he shared the superstitions of his age, and darkened his pages with portents, oracles, miracles, and dreams. But where he wrote of what he had seen, his account has stood every test. His industry was courageous, his arrangement of materials is logical, his narrative is absorbing, his Greek is clear and direct, and almost classically pure.

Was he a Christian? Externally, yes; and yet at times he echoes the paganism of his models, the fatalism of the Stoa, the skepticism of the Academy. He speaks of Fortune's

> perverse nature and unaccountable will. But these things, I believe, have never been comprehensible to man, nor will they ever be. Nevertheless there is always much talk on these subjects, and opinions are always being bandied about . . . as each of us seeks comfort for his ignorance. . . . I consider it insane folly to investigate the nature of God. . . . I shall observe a discreet silence concerning these questions, with the sole object that old and venerable beliefs may not be discredited.[33]

IV. BYZANTINE ART: 326–565

1. The Passage from Paganism

The pre-eminent achievements of Byzantine civilization were governmental administration and decorative art: a state that survived eleven centuries, a St. Sophia that stands today.

By Justinian's time pagan art was finished, and half of its works had been mutilated or destroyed. Barbarian ravages, imperial robbery, and pious destruction had began a process of ruination and neglect that continued till Petrarch in the fourteenth century pled, so to speak, for the lives of the survivors. A factor in the devastation was the popular belief that the pagan gods were demons, and that the temples were their resorts; in any case, it was felt, the material could be put to better use in Christian churches or domestic walls. Pagans themselves often joined in the spoliation. Several Christian emperors, notably Honorius and Theodosius II, did their best to protect the old structures,[34] and enlightened clergymen preserved the Parthenon, the temple of Theseus, the Pantheon, and other structures by rededicating them as Christian shrines.

Christianity at first suspected art as a support of paganism, idolatry, and immorality; these nude statues hardly comported with esteem for virginity and celibacy. When the body seemed an instrument of Satan, and the monk replaced the athlete as ideal, the study of anatomy disappeared from art, leaving a sculpture and painting of gloomy faces and shapeless drapery. But when Christianity had triumphed, and great basilicas were needed to house its swelling congregations, the local and national traditions of art reasserted themselves, and architecture lifted itself out of the ruins. Moreover, these spacious edifices cried out for decoration; the worshipers needed statues of Christ and Mary to help the imagination, and pictures to tell to the simple letterless the story of their crucified God. Sculpture, mosaic, and painting were reborn.

In Rome the new art differed little from the old. Strength of construction, simplicity of form, columnar basilican styles, were carried down from paganism to Christianity. Near Nero's Circus on the Vatican hill Constantine's architects had designed the first St. Peter's, with an awesome length of 380 feet and breadth of 212; for twelve centuries this remained the pontifical shrine of Latin Christendom, until Bramante tore it down to raise upon its site the still vaster St. Peter's of today. The church that Constantine built for St. Paul Outside the Walls—San Paolo fuori le mura—on the reputed site of the Apostle's martyrdom, was rebuilt by Valentinian II and Theodosius I on a scale quite as immense—400 by 200 feet.* Santa Costanza, raised by Constantine as a mausoleum for his sister Constantia, remains substantially as erected in 326–30. San Giovanni in Laterano, Santa Maria in Trastevere, San Lorenzo fuori le mura were rebuilt within a century after Constantine began them, and have since been many times repaired. Santa Maria Maggiore was adapted from a pagan temple in 432, and the nave remains essentially as then save for Renaissance decorations.

From that time to our own the basilican plan has been a favorite design for Christian churches; its modest cost, its majestic simplicity, its structural logic and sturdy strength have recommended it in every generation. But it did not lend itself readily to variation and development. European builders began to look about them for new ideas, and found them in the East—even at Spalato, the Adriatic outpost of the Orient. There on the Dalmatian coast Diocletian, at the opening of the fourth century, had given his artists free play to experiment in raising a palace for his retirement; and they accomplished a revolution in European architecture. Arches were there sprung directly from column capitals, with no intervening entablature; so at one stroke were prepared the Byzantine, Romanesque, and Gothic styles. And instead of figured friezes came, in this palace, a strange decoration of zigzag lines, offensive to the classic eye, but long familiar to the Orient. Spalato was the first sign that Europe was to be conquered not only by an Oriental religion, but, at least in the Byzantine world, by Oriental art.

---

* San Paolo fuori le mura was destroyed by fire in 1823, but was restored on the old lines in 1854–70. Its perfect proportions and stately colonnades make it one of the noblest creations of mankind.

2. *The Byzantine Artist*

Whence came to Constantinople that uniquely colorful, somberly brilliant art known as Byzantine? It is a question over which archaeologists have fought with almost the ferocity of Christian soldiers; and by and large the victory has gone to the East. As Syria and Asia Minor grew stronger with industry, and Rome weaker with invasion, the Hellenistic tide that had rushed in with Alexander ebbed back from Asia to Europe. From Sasanian Persia, from Nestorian Syria, from Coptic Egypt, Eastern art influences poured into Byzantium and reached to Italy, even to Gaul; and the Greek art of naturalistic representation gave place to an Oriental art of symbolic decoration. The East preferred color to line, the vault and dome to the timbered roof, rich ornament to stern simplicity, gorgeous silks to shapeless togas. Just as Diocletian and Constantine had adopted the forms of Persian monarchy, so the art of Constantinople looked less and less to the now barbarized West, increasingly to Asia Minor, Armenia, Persia, Syria, and Egypt. Perhaps the victory of Persian arms under Shapur II and Khosru Anushirvan quickened the westward march of Eastern motives and forms. Edessa and Nisibis were in this period flourishing centers of a Mesopotamian culture that mingled Iranian, Armenian, Cappadocian, and Syrian elements,[35] and transmitted them, through merchants, monks and artisans, to Antioch, Alexandria, Ephesus, Constantinople, at last to Ravenna and Rome. The old classic orders —Doric, Ionian, Corinthian—became almost meaningless in an architectural world of arches, vaults, pendentives, and domes.

Byzantine art, so generated, dedicated itself to expounding the doctrines of Christianity, and displaying the glory of the state. It recounted on vestments and tapestries, in mosaics and murals, the life of Christ, the sorrows of Mary, the career of the apostle or martyr whose bones were enshrined in the church. Or it entered the court, decorated the palace of the sovereign, covered his official robes with symbolic emblems or historical designs, dazzled his subjects with flamboyant pageantry, and ended by representing Christ and Mary as an emperor and a queen. The Byzantine artist had small choice of patron, and therefore of subject or style; monarch or patriarch told him what to do, and how. He worked in a group, and seldom left an individual name to history. He achieved miracles of brilliance, he exalted and humbled the people with the splendor of his creations; but his art paid in formalism, narrowness, and stagnation for serving an absolute monarch and a changeless creed.

He commanded abundant materials: marble quarries in the Proconnesus, Attica, Italy; spoliable columns and capitals wherever a pagan temple survived; and bricks almost growing in the sun-dried earth. Usually he worked with mortared brick; it lent itself well to the curved forms imposed upon

him by Oriental styles. Often he contented himself with the cruciform plan
—a basilica crossed with a transept and prolonged to an apse; sometimes he
broke the basilica into an octagon, as in Sts. Sergius and Bacchus' at Constantinople, or in San Vitale's at Ravenna. But his distinctive skill, in which
he surpassed all artists before him or since, lay in raising a circular dome over
a polygonal frame. His favorite means to this end was the pendentive: i.e.,
he built an arch or semicircle of bricks over each side of the polygon, raised
a spherical triangle of bricks upward and inward between each semicircle,
and laid a dome upon the resultant circular ring. The spherical triangles were
the pendentives, "hanging" from the rim of the dome to the top of the polygon. In architectural effect the circle was squared. Thereafter the basilican
style almost disappeared from the East.

Within the edifice the Byzantine builder lavished all the skills of a dozen
arts. He rarely used statuary; he sought not so much to represent figures of
men and women as to create an abstract beauty of symbolic form. Even so
the Byzantine sculptors were artisans of ability, patience, and resource. They
carved the "Theodosian" capital by combining the "ears" of the Ionic with
the leaves of the Corinthian order; and to make profusion more confounded,
they cut into this composite capital a very jungle of animals and plants. Since
the result was not too well adapted to sustain a wall or an arch, they inserted
between these and the capital an impost or "pulvino," square and broad at
the top, round and narrower at the base; and then, in the course of time, they
carved this too with flowers. Here again, as in the domed square, Persia conquered Greece.—But further, painters were assigned to adorn the walls with
edifying or terrifying pictures; mosaicists laid their cubes of brightly colored
stone or glass, in backgrounds of blue or gold, upon the floors or walls, or
over the altar, or in the spandrels of the arches, or wherever an empty surface
challenged the Oriental eye. Jewelers set gems into vestments, altars, columns, walls; metalworkers inserted gold or silver plates; woodworkers
carved the pulpit or chancel rails; weavers hung tapestries, laid rugs, and
covered altar and pulpit with embroidery and silk. Never before had an art
been so rich in color, so subtle in symbolism, so exuberant in decoration, so
well adapted to quiet the intellect and stir the soul.

3. St. Sophia

Not till Justinian did the Greek, Roman, Oriental, and Christian factors
complete their fusion into Byzantine art. The Nika revolt gave him, like another Nero, an opportunity to rebuild his capital. In the ecstasy of a moment's freedom the mob had burned down the Senate House, the Baths of
Zeuxippus, the porticoes of the Augusteum, a wing of the imperial palace,
and St. Sophia, cathedral of the patriarch. Justinian might have rebuilt these

on their old plans, and within a year or two; instead he resolved to spend more time, money, and men, make his capital more beautiful than Rome, and raise a church that would outshine all other edifices on the earth. He began now one of the most ambitious building programs in history: fortresses, palaces, monasteries, churches, porticoes, and gates rose throughout the Empire. In Constantinople he rebuilt the Senate House in white marble, and the Baths of Zeuxippus in polychrome marble; raised a marble portico and promenade in the Augusteum; and brought fresh water to the city in a new aqueduct that rivaled Italy's best. He made his own palace the acme of splendor and luxury: its floors and walls were of marble; its ceilings recounted in mosaic brilliance the triumphs of his reign, and showed the senators "in festal mood, bestowing upon the Emperor honors almost divine." [36] And across the Bosporus, near Chalcedon, he built, as a summer residence for Theodora and her court, the palatial villa of Herion, equipped with its own harbor, forum, church, and baths.

Forty days after the Nika revolt had subsided, he began a new St. Sophia—dedicated not to any saint of that name, but to the *Hagia Sophia*, the Holy Wisdom, or Creative Logos, of God Himself. From Tralles in Asia Minor, and from Ionian Miletus, he summoned Anthemius and Isidore, the most famous of living architects, to plan and superintend the work. Abandoning the traditional basilican form, they conceived a design whose center would be a spacious dome resting not on walls but on massive piers, and buttressed by a half dome at either end. Ten thousand workmen were engaged, 320,000 pounds of gold ($134,000,000) were spent, on the enterprise, quite emptying the treasury. Provincial governors were directed to send to the new shrine the finest relics of ancient monuments; marbles of a dozen kinds and tints were imported from a dozen areas; gold, silver, ivory, and precious stones were poured into the decoration. Justinian himself shared busily in the design and the construction, and took no small part (his scornful adulator tells us) in solving technical problems. Dressed in white linen, with a staff in his hand and a kerchief on his head, he haunted the operation day after day, encouraging the workers to complete their tasks competently and on time. In five years and ten months the edifice was complete; and on December 26, 537, the Emperor and the Patriarch Menas led a solemn inaugural procession to the resplendent cathedral. Justinian walked alone to the pulpit, and lifting up his hands, cried out: "Glory be to God who has thought me worthy to accomplish so great a work! O Solomon! I have vanquished you!"

The ground plan was a Greek cross 250 by 225 feet; each end of the cross was covered by a minor dome; the central dome rose over the square (100 by 100 feet) formed by the intersecting arms; the apex of the dome was 180 feet above the ground; its diameter was 100 feet—32 less than the dome of the Pantheon in Rome. The latter had been poured in concrete in one solid piece; St. Sophia's dome was made of brick in thirty converging panels—a much weaker construction.* The distinction of this dome was not in size but in support: it rested not on a circular structure, as in the Pantheon, but on pendentives and arches that mediated between the circular rim and the square base; never has this architectural problem been more satisfactorily solved. Procopius described the dome as "a work admirable and terrifying . . . seeming not to rest on the masonry below it, but to be suspended by a chain of gold from the height of the sky." [37]

The interior was a panorama of luminous decoration. Marble of many colors—white, green, red, yellow, purple, gold—made the pavement, walls, and two-storied colonnades look like a field of flowers. Delicate stone carvings covered capitals, arches, spandrels, moldings, and cornices with classic leaves of acanthus and vine. Mosaics of unprecedented scope and splendor looked down from walls and vaults. Forty silver chandeliers, hanging from the rim of the dome, helped as many windows to illuminate the church. The sense of spaciousness left by the long nave and aisles, and by the pillarless space under the central dome; the metal lacework of the silver railing before the apse, and of the iron railing in the upper gallery; the pulpit inset with ivory, silver, and precious stones; the solid silver throne of the patriarch; the silk-and-gold curtain that rose over the altar with figures of the Emperor and the Empress receiving the benedictions of Christ and Mary; the golden altar itself, of rare marbles, and bearing sacred vessels of silver and gold: this lavish ornamentation might have warranted Justinian in anticipating the boast of the Mogul shahs—that they built like giants and finished like jewelers.

St. Sophia was at once the inauguration and the culmination of the Byzantine style. Men everywhere spoke of it as "the Great Church," and even the skeptical Procopius wrote of it with awe. "When one enters this building to pray, he feels that it is not the work of human power. . . . The soul, lifting itself to the sky, realizes that here God is close by, and that He takes delight in this, His chosen home." † [38]

4. From Constantinople to Ravenna

St. Sophia was Justinian's supreme achievement, more lasting than his conquests or his laws. But Procopius describes twenty-four other churches built or rebuilt by him in the capital, and remarks: "If you should see one of them by itself you would suppose that the Emperor had built this work only, and had spent the whole time of his reign on this one alone." [39] Throughout the Empire this fury of

---

* In 558 an earthquake caused half the central dome to crash into the church. The dead Isidore's son Isidore rebuilt the dome, strengthening its supports, and raising it twenty-five feet higher than before. Cracks in these supports suggest that the dome now lives a precarious life.

† The Turks, after capturing Constantinople in 1453, covered the mosaics of St. Sophia with plaster, abhorring the "graven images" as idolatry; but in recent years the Turkish government has permitted a corps of workers from the Byzantine Institute of Boston, Massachusetts, to uncover these unsurpassed examples of the mosaic art. The Turkish conquerors almost atoned by adding four graceful minarets, completely harmonious with the domical design.

construction raged till Justinian's death; and that sixth century which marked the beginning of the Dark Ages in the West was in the East one of the richest epochs in architectural history. In Ephesus, Antioch, Gaza, Jerusalem, Alexandria, Salonika, Ravenna, Rome, and from Crimean Kerch to African Sfax, a thousand churches celebrated the triumph both of Christianity over paganism and of the Oriental-Byzantine over the Greco-Roman style. External columns, architraves, pediments, and friezes made way for the vault, the pendentive, and the dome. Syria had a veritable renaissance in the fourth, fifth, and sixth centuries; her schools at Antioch, Berytus (Beirut), Edessa, and Nisibis poured forth orators, lawyers, historians, and heretics; her artisans excelled in mosaics, textiles, and all decorative arts; her architects raised a hundred churches; her sculptors adorned them with lavish reliefs.

Alexandria was the one city in the Empire that never ceased to prosper. Her founder had chosen for her a site that almost forced the Mediterranean world to use her ports and enhance her trade. None of her ancient or early medieval architecture has survived; but the scattered relics of her work in metal, ivory, wood, and portraiture suggest a people as rich in art as in sensuality and bigotry. Coptic architecture, which had begun with the Roman basilica, became under Justinian predominantly Oriental.

The architectural splendor of Ravenna began soon after Honorius made it the seat of the Western Empire in 404. The city prospered in the long regency of Galla Placidia; and the close relations maintained with Constantinople brought Eastern artists and styles to mingle with Italian architects and forms. The typical Oriental plan of a dome placed with pendentives over the transept of a cruciform base appeared there as early as 450 in the Mausoleum where Placidia at last found tranquillity; within it one may still see the famous mosaic of Christ as the Good Shepherd. In 458 Bishop Neon added to the domed baptistery of the Basilica Ursiana a series of mosaics that included remarkably individual portraits of the Apostles. About 500 Theodoric built for his Arian bishop a cathedral named after St. Apollinaris, the reputed founder of the Christian community in Ravenna; here, in world-renowned mosaics, the white-robed saints bear themselves with a stiff solemnity that already suggests the Byzantine style.

The conquest of Ravenna by Belisarius advanced the victory of Byzantine art in Italy. The church of San Vitale was completed (547) under Justinian and Theodora, who financed its decoration, and lent their unseductive features to its adornment. There is every indication that these mosaics are realistic portraits; and emperor and empress must be credited with courage in permitting their likenesses to be transmitted to posterity. The attitudes of these rulers, ecclesiastics, and eunuchs are hard and angular; their stiff frontality is a reversion to preclassical forms; the robes of the women are a mosaic triumph, but we miss here the happy grace of the Parthenon procession, or the *Ara pacis* of Augustus, or the nobility and tenderness of the figures on the portals of Chartres or Reims.

Two years after dedicating San Vitale the Bishop of Ravenna consecrated Sant' Apollinare in Classe—a second church for the city's patron saint, placed in the maritime suburb that had once been the Adriatic base of the Roman fleet (*classis*). Here is the old Roman basilican plan; but on the composite capitals a

Byzantine touch appears in the acanthus leaves unclassically curled and twisted, as if blown by some Eastern wind. The long rows of perfect columns, the colorful (seventh-century) mosaics in the archivolts and spandrels of the colonnades, the lovely stucco plaques in the choir, the cross of gems on a bed of mosaic stars in the apse, make this one of the outstanding shrines of a peninsula that is almost a gallery of art.

5. The Byzantine Arts

Architecture was the masterpiece of the Byzantine artist, but about it or within it were a dozen other arts in which he achieved some memorable excellence. He did not care for sculpture in the round; the mood of the age preferred color to line; yet Procopius lauded the sculptors of his time—presumably the carvers of reliefs—as the equals of Pheidias and Praxiteles; and some stone sarcophagi of the fourth, fifth, and sixth centuries have human figures chiseled with almost Hellenic grace, confused with an Asiatic plethora of ornament. The carving of ivory was a favorite art among the Byzantines; they used it for diptychs, triptychs, book covers, caskets, perfume boxes, statuettes, inlays, and in a hundred decorative ways; in this craft Hellenistic techniques survived unimpaired, and merely turned gods and heroes into Christ and the saints. The ivory chair of Bishop Maximian in the Basilica Ursiana at Ravenna (c. 550) is a major achievement in a minor art.

While the Far East, in the sixth century, was experimenting with oil colors,[40] Byzantine painting adhered to traditional Greek methods: encaustic —colors burnt into panels of wood, canvas, or linen; fresco—colors mixed with lime and applied to wet plaster surfaces; and tempera—colors mixed with size or gum or glue and white of egg, and applied to panels or to plaster already dry. The Byzantine painter knew how to represent distance and depth, but usually shirked the difficulties of perspective by filling in the background with buildings and screens. Portraits were numerous, but few have survived. Church walls were decorated with murals; the fragments that remain show a rough realism, unshapely hands, stunted figures, sallow faces, and incredible coiffures.

The Byzantine artist excelled and reveled in the minute; his extant masterpieces of painting are not murals or panels, but the miniatures with which he literally "illuminated"—made bright with color—the publications of his age.* Books, being costly, were adorned like other precious objects. The miniaturist first sketched his design upon papyrus, parchment, or vellum with a fine brush or pen; laid down a background usually in gold or blue; filled in his colors, and decorated background and borders with graceful and delicate forms. At first he had merely elaborated the initial letter of a chapter or a page; sometimes he essayed a portrait of the author; then he illustrated the

---

* *Miniature* is from *minium*, an Iberian word for the cinnabar that Rome imported from Spain; hence it came to mean vermilion—a favorite color in book illumination.

text with pictures; finally, as his art improved, he almost forgot the text, and spread himself out in luxurious ornament, taking a geometrical or floral motive, or a religious symbol, and repeating it in a maze of variations, until all the page was a glory of color and line, and the text seemed like an intrusion from a coarser world.

The illumination of manuscripts had been practiced in Pharaonic and Ptolemaic Egypt, and had passed thence to Hellenistic Greece and Rome. The Vatican treasures an *Aeneid*, the Ambrosian Library at Milan an *Iliad*, both ascribed to the fourth century, and completely classic in ornament. The transition from pagan to Christian miniatures appears in the *Topographia Christiana* of Cosmas Indicopleustes (*c.* 547), who earned his sobriquet by sailing to India, and his fame by trying to prove that the earth is flat. The oldest extant religious miniature is a fifth-century *Genesis*, now in the Library of Vienna; the text is written in gold and silver letters on twenty-four leaves of purple vellum; the forty-eight miniatures, in white, green, violet, red, and black, picture the story of man from Adam's fall to Jacob's death. Quite as beautiful are the *Joshua Rotulus* (Little Roll of the Book of Joshua) in the Vatican, and the *Book of the Gospels* illuminated by the monk Rabula in Mesopotamia in 586. From Mesopotamia and Syria came the figures and symbols that dominated the iconography, or picture-writing, of the Byzantine world; repeated in a thousand forms in the minor arts, they became stereotyped and conventional, and shared in producing the deadly immutability of Byzantine art.

Loving brilliance and permanence, the Byzantine painter made mosaic his favorite medium. For floors he chose tesserae of colored marble, as Egyptians, Greeks, and Romans had done; for other surfaces he used cubes of glass or enamel in every shade, cut in various sizes, but usually an eighth of an inch square. Precious stones were sometimes mingled with the cubes. Mosaic was often employed in making portable pictures or icons, to be set up in churches or homes, or carried on travels as aids to devotion and safety; preferably, however, the mosaicist sought the larger scope of church or palace walls. In his studio, upon a canvas bearing a colored design, he tentatively laid his cubes; and here his art was strained to produce immediately under his hand the precise gradation and melting of colors to be felt by other eyes from greater distances. Meanwhile a coat of heavy cement, and then a coat of fine cement, were laid upon the surface to be covered; into this matrix the mosaicist, following his canvas model, pressed his cubes, usually with cut edges to the front to catch the light. Curved surfaces like domes, and the conches or shell-like half domes of apses, were favored, since they would catch at different times and angles a variety of softened and shaded light. From this painstaking art Gothic would derive part of its inspiration for stained glass.

Such glass is mentioned in fifth-century texts, but no example remains, and apparently the stain was external, not fused.[41] Glass-cutting and blowing were now a thousand years old, and Syria, their earliest known home, was still a center of the crafts. The art of engraving precious metals or stones had deteriorated since Aurelius; Byzantine gems, coins, and seals are of relatively poor design and workmanship. Jewelers nevertheless sold their products to nearly every class, for ornament was the soul of Byzantium. Goldsmith and silversmith studios were numerous in the capital; gold pyxes, chalices, and reliquaries adorned many altars; and silver plate oppressed the tables of moneyed homes.

Every house, almost every person, carried some textile finery. Egypt led the way here with its delicate, many-colored, figured fabrics—garments, curtains, hangings, and coverings; the Copts were the masters in these fields. Certain Egyptian tapestries of this period are almost identical in technique with the Gobelins.[42] Byzantine weavers made silk brocades, embroideries, even embroidered shrouds—linens realistically painted with the features of the dead. In Constantinople a man was known by the garments he wore; each class prized and defended some distinctive refinement of dress; and a Byzantine assemblage doubtless shone like a peacock's tail.

Among all classes music was popular. It played a rising role in the liturgy of the Church, and helped to fuse emotion into belief. In the fourth century Alypius wrote a *Musical Introduction*, whose extant portions are our chief guide to the musical notation of the Greeks. This representation of notes by letters was replaced, in that century, by abstract signs, *neumes*; Ambrose apparently introduced these to Milan, Hilary to Gaul, Jerome to Rome. About the end of the fifth century Romanus, a Greek monk, composed the words and music of hymns that still form part of the Greek liturgy, and have never been equaled in depth of feeling and power of expression. Boethius wrote an essay *De Musica*, summarizing the theories of Pythagoras, Aristoxenus, and Ptolemy; this little treatise was used as a text in music at Oxford and Cambridge until our times.[43]

One must be an Oriental to understand an Oriental art. To a Western mind the essence of Byzantinism means that the East had become supreme in the heart and head of Greece: in the autocratic government, the hierarchical stability of classes, the stagnation of science and philosophy, the state-dominated Church, the religion-dominated people, the gorgeous vestments and stately ceremonies, the sonorous and scenic ritual, the hypnotic chant of repetitious music, the overwhelming of the senses with brilliance and color, the conquest of naturalism by imagination, the submergence of representative under decorative art. The ancient Greek spirit would have found this alien and unbearable, but Greece herself was now part of the Orient. An Asiatic lassitude fell upon the Greek world precisely when it was to be challenged in its very life by the renewed vitality of Persia and the incredible energy of Islam.

CHAPTER VII

The Persians

224-641

I. SASANIAN SOCIETY

BEYOND the Euphrates or the Tigris, through all the history of Greece and Rome, lay that almost secret empire which for a thousand years had stood off expanding Europe and Asiatic hordes, never forgetting its Achaemenid glory, slowly recuperating from its Parthian wars, and so proudly maintaining its unique and aristocratic culture under its virile Sasanian monarchs, that it would transform the Islamic conquest of Iran into a Persian Renaissance.

Iran meant more, in our third century, than Iran or Persia today. It was by its very name the land of the "Aryans," and included Afghanistan, Baluchistan, Sogdiana, and Balkh, as well as Iraq. "Persia," anciently the name of the modern province of Fars, was but a southeastern fraction of this empire; but the Greeks and Romans, careless about "barbarians," gave the name of a part to the whole. Through the center of Iran, from Himalayan southeast to Caucasian northwest, ran a mountainous dividing barrier; to the east was an arid lofty plateau; to the west lay the green valleys of the twin rivers, whose periodic overflow ran into a labyrinth of canals, and made Western Persia rich in wheat and dates, vines, and fruits. Between or along the rivers, or hiding in the hills, or hugging desert oases, were a myriad villages, a thousand towns, a hundred cities: Ecbatana, Rai, Mosul, Istakhr (once Persepolis), Susa, Seleucia, and magnificent Ctesiphon, seat of the Sasanian kings.

Ammianus describes the Persians of this period as "almost all slender, somewhat dark . . . with not uncomely beards, and long, shaggy hair."[1] The upper classes were not shaggy, nor always slender, often handsome, proud of bearing, and of an easy grace, with a flair for dangerous sports and splendid dress. Men covered their heads with turbans, their legs with baggy trousers, their feet with sandals or laced boots; the rich wore coats or tunics of wool and silk, and girt themselves with belt and sword; the poor resigned themselves to garments of cotton, hair, or skins. The women dressed in boots and breeches, loose shirts and cloaks and flowing robes; curled their black hair into a coil in front, let it hang behind, and brightened it with flowers. All classes loved color and ornament. Priests and zealous Zoroastrians affected white cotton clothing as a symbol of purity; generals preferred red; kings distinguished themselves with red shoes, blue trousers, and a headdress topped with an inflated ball or the head of a beast or a bird. In Persia, as in all civilized societies, clothes made half the man, and slightly more of the woman.

The typical educated Persian was Gallically impulsive, enthusiastic, and mercurial; often indolent, but quickly alert; given to "mad and extravagant talk . . . rather crafty than courageous, and to be feared only at long range" [2] —which was where they kept their enemies. The poor drank beer, but nearly all classes, including the gods, preferred wine; the pious and thrifty Persians poured it out in religious ritual, waited a reasonable time for the gods to come and drink, then drank the sacred beverage themselves.[3] Persian manners, in this Sasanian period, are described as coarser than in the Achaemenid, more refined than in the Parthian;[4] but the narratives of Procopius leave us with the impression that the Persians continued to be better gentlemen than the Greeks.[5] The ceremonies and diplomatic forms of the Persian court were in large measure adopted by the Greek emperors; the rival sovereigns addressed each other as "brother," provided immunity and safe-conducts for foreign diplomats, and exempted them from customs searches and dues.[6] The conventions of European and American diplomacy may be traced to the courts of the Persian kings.

"Most Persians," Ammianus reported, "are extravagantly given to venery,"[7] but he confesses that pederasty and prostitution were less frequent among them than among the Greeks. Rabbi Gamaliel praised the Persians for three qualities: "They are temperate in eating, modest in the privy and in marital relations."[8] Every influence was used to stimulate marriage and the birth rate, in order that man power should suffice in war; in this aspect Mars, not Venus, is the god of love. Religion enjoined marriage, celebrated it with awesome rites, and taught that fertility strengthened Ormuzd, the god of light, in his cosmic conflict with Ahriman, the Satan of the Zoroastrian creed.[9] The head of the household practiced ancestor worship at the family hearth, and sought offspring to ensure his own later cult and care; if no son was born to him he adopted one. Parents generally arranged the marriage of their children, often with the aid of a professional matrimonial agent; but a woman might marry against the wishes of her parents. Dowries and marriage settlements financed early marriage and parentage. Polygamy was allowed, and was recommended where the first wife proved barren. Adultery flourished.[10] The husband might divorce his wife for infidelity, the wife might divorce her husband for desertion and cruelty. Concubines were permitted. Like the ancient Greek hetairai, these concubines were free to move about in public, and to attend the banquets of the men;[11] but legal wives were usually kept in private apartments in the home;[12] this old Persian custom was bequeathed to Islam. Persian women were exceptionally beautiful, and perhaps men had to be guarded from them. In the *Shahnama* of Firdausi it is the women who yearn and take the initiative in courtship and seduction. Feminine charms overcame masculine laws.

Children were reared with the help of religious belief, which seems indispensable to parental authority. They amused themselves with ball games, athletics, and chess,[13] and at an early age joined in their elders' pastimes—archery, horse racing, polo, and the hunt. Every Sasanian found music necessary to the operations of religion, love, and war; "music and the songs of beautiful women," said Firdausi, "accompanied the scene" at royal banquets and receptions;[14] lyre, guitar, flute, pipe, horn, drum, and other instruments abounded; tradition avers that Khosru Parvez' favorite singer, Barbad, composed 360 songs, and sang them to his royal patron, one each night for a year.[15] In education, too, religion played a major part; primary schools were situated on temple grounds, and were taught by priests. Higher education in literature, medicine, science, and philosophy was provided in the celebrated academy at Jund-i-Shapur in Susiana. The sons of feudal chiefs and provincial satraps often lived near the king, and were instructed with the princes of the royal family in a college attached to the court.[16]

Pahlavi, the Indo-European language of Parthian Persia, continued in use. Of its literature in this age only some 600,000 words survive, nearly all dealing with religion. We know that it was extensive;[17] but as the priests were its guardians and transmitters, they allowed most of the secular material to perish. (A like process may have deluded us as to the overwhelmingly religious character of early medieval literature in Christendom.) The Sasanian kings were enlightened patrons of letters and philosophy—Khosru Anushirvan above all: he had Plato and Aristotle translated into Pahlavi, had them taught at Jund-i-Shapur, and even read them himself. During his reign many historical annals were compiled, of which the sole survivor is the *Karnamak-i-Artakhshatr*, or *Deeds of Ardashir*, a mixture of history and romance that served Firdausi as the basis of his *Shahnama*. When Justinian closed the schools of Athens seven of their professors fled to Persia and found refuge at Khosru's court. In time they grew homesick; and in his treaty of 533 with Justinian, the "barbarian" king stipulated that the Greek sages should be allowed to return, and be free from persecution.

Under this enlightened monarch the college of Jund-i-Shapur, which had been founded in the fourth or fifth century, became "the greatest intellectual center of the time."[18] Students and teachers came to it from every quarter of the world. Nestorian Christians were received there, and brought Syriac translations of Greek works in medicine and philosophy. Neoplatonists there planted the seeds of Sufi mysticism; there the medical lore of India, Persia, Syria, and Greece mingled to produce a flourishing school of therapy.[19] In Persian theory disease resulted from contamination and impurity of one or more of the four elements—fire, water, earth, and air; public health, said Persian physicians and priests, required the burning of all putrefying matter, and individual health demanded strict obedience to the Zoroastrian code of cleanliness.[20]

Of Persian astronomy in this period we only know that it maintained an orderly calendar, divided the year into twelve months of thirty days, each month into two seven-day and two eight-day weeks, and added five intercalary days at the end of the year.[21] Astrology and magic were universal; no important step was taken without reference to the status of the constellations; and every earthly career, men believed, was determined by the good and evil stars that fought in the sky—as angels and demons fought in the human soul—the ancient war of Ormuzd and Ahriman.

The Zoroastrian religion was restored to authority and affluence by the Sasanian dynasty; lands and tithes were assigned to the priests; government was founded on religion, as in Europe. An *archimagus*, second only to the king in power, headed an omnipresent hereditary priestly caste of Magi, who controlled nearly all the intellectual life of Persia, frightened sinners and rebels with threats of hell, and kept the Persian mind and masses in bondage for four centuries.[22] Now and then they protected the citizen against the tax-gatherer, and the poor against oppression.[23] The Magian organization was so rich that kings sometimes borrowed great sums from the temple treasuries. Every important town had a fire temple, in which a sacred flame, supposedly inextinguishable, symbolized the god of light. Only a life of virtue and ritual cleanliness could save the soul from Ahriman; in the battle against that devil it was vital to have the aid of the Magi and their *magic*—their divinations, incantations, sorceries, and prayers. So helped, the soul would attain holiness and purity, pass the awful assize of the Last Judgment, and enjoy everlasting happiness in paradise.

Around this official faith other religions found modest room. Mithras, the sun god so popular with the Parthians, received a minor worship as chief helper of Ormuzd. But the Zoroastrian priests, like the Christians, Moslems, and Jews, made persistent apostasy from the national creed a capital crime. When Mani (*c.* 216–76), claiming to be a fourth divine messenger in the line of Buddha, Zoroaster, and Jesus, announced a religion of celibacy, pacifism, and quietism, the militant and nationalistic Magi had him crucified; and Manicheism had to seek its main success abroad. To Judaism and Christianity, however, the Sasanian priests and kings were generally tolerant, much as the popes were more lenient with Jews than with heretics. A large number of Jews found asylum in the western provinces of the Persian Empire. Christianity was already established there when the Sasanians came to power; it was tolerated until it became the official faith of Persia's immemorial enemies, Greece and Rome; it was persecuted after its clergy, as at Nisibis in 338, took an active part in the defense of Byzantine territory against Shapur II,[24] and the Christians in Persia revealed their natural hopes for a Byzantine victory.[25] In 341 Shapur ordered the massacre of all Christians in his Empire; entire villages of Christians were being slaughtered when he restricted the proscription to priests, monks, and nuns; even so 16,000 Christians died in a persecution that lasted till Shapur's death (379). Yezdegird I (399–420) restored religious freedom to the Christians, and helped them rebuild their churches. In 422 a council of Persian bishops made the Persian Christian Church independent of both Greek and Roman Christianity.

Within the framework of religious worship and dispute, governmental edicts and crises, civil and foreign wars, the people impatiently provided the sinews of state and church, tilling the soil, pasturing flocks, practicing handicrafts, arguing trade. Agriculture was made a religious duty: to clear the wilderness, cultivate the earth, eradicate pests and weeds, reclaim waste lands, harness the streams to irrigate the land—these heroic labors, the people were told, ensured the final victory of Ormuzd over Ahriman. Much spiritual solace was needed by the Persian peasant, for usually he toiled as tenant for a feudal lord, and paid from a sixth to a third of his crops in taxes and dues. About 540 the Persians took from India the art of making sugar from the cane; the Greek Emperor Heraclius found a treasury of sugar in the royal palace at Ctesiphon (627); the Arabs, conquering Persia fourteen years later, soon learned to cultivate the plant, and introduced it into Egypt, Sicily, Morocco, and Spain, whence it spread through Europe.[26] Animal husbandry was a Persian forte; Persian horses were second only to Arab steeds in pedigree, spirit, beauty, and speed; every Persian loved a horse as Rustam loved Rakush. The dog was so useful in guarding flocks and homes that the Persians made him a sacred animal; and the Persian cat acquired distinction universally.

Persian industry under the Sasanians developed from domestic to urban forms. Guilds were numerous, and some towns had a revolutionary proletariat.[27] Silk weaving was introduced from China; Sasanian silks were sought for everywhere, and served as models for the textile art in Byzantium, China, and Japan. Chinese merchants came to Iran to sell raw silk and buy rugs, jewels, rouge; Armenians, Syrians, and Jews connected Persia, Byzantium, and Rome in slow exchange. Good roads and bridges, well patrolled, enabled state post and merchant caravans to link Ctesiphon with all provinces; and harbors were built in the Persian Gulf to quicken trade with India. Governmental regulations limited the price of corn, medicines, and other necessaries, and prevented "corners" and monopolies.[28] We may judge the wealth of the upper classes by the story of the baron who, having invited a thousand guests to dinner, and finding that he had only 500 dinner services, was able to borrow 500 more from his neighbors.[29]

The feudal lords, living chiefly on their rural estates, organized the exploitation of land and men, and raised regiments from their tenantry to fight the nation's wars. They trained themselves to battle by following the chase with passion and bravery; they served as gallant cavalry officers, man and animal armored as in later feudal Europe; but they fell short of the Romans in disciplining their troops, or in applying the latest engineering arts of siege and defense. Above them in social caste were the great aristocrats who ruled the provinces as satraps, or headed departments of the government. Administration must have been reasonably competent, for though taxation was less severe than in the Roman Empire of East or West, the Persian treasury was often richer than that of the emperors. Khosru Parvez had $460,000,000 in his coffers in 626, and an annual income of $170,000,000[30]—enormous sums in terms of the purchasing power of medieval silver and gold.

Law was created by the kings, their councilors, and the Magi, on the basis of the old Avestan code; its interpretation and administration were left to the priests. Ammianus, who fought the Persians, reckoned their judges as "upright men of proved experience and legal learning."[31] In general, Persians were known as men of their word. Oaths in court were surrounded with all the aura of religion; violated oaths were punished severely in law, and in hell by an endless shower of arrows, axes, and stones. Ordeals were used to detect guilt: suspects were invited to walk over red-hot substances, or go through fire, or eat poisoned food. Infanticide and abortion were forbidden with heavy penalties; pederasty was punished with death; the detected adulterer was banished; the adulteress lost her nose and ears. Appeal could be made to higher courts, and sentences of death could be carried out only after review and approval by the king.

The king attributed his power to the gods, presented himself as their vicegerent, and emulated their superiority to their own decrees. He called himself, when time permitted, "King of Kings, King of the Aryans and the non-Aryans, Sovereign of the Universe, Descendant of the Gods";[32] Shapur II added "Brother of the Sun and Moon, Companion of the Stars." Theoretically absolute, the Sasanian monarch usually acted with the advice of his ministers, who composed a council of state. Masudi, the Moslem historian, praised the "excellent administration of the" Sasanian "kings, their well-ordered policy, their care for their subjects, and the prosperity of their domains."[33] Said Khosru Anushirvan, according to Ibn Khaldun: "Without army, no king; without revenues, no army; without taxes, no revenue; without agriculture, no taxes; without just government, no agriculture."[34] In normal times the monarchical office was hereditary, but might be transmitted by the king to a younger son; in two instances the supreme power was held by queens. When no direct heir was available, the nobles and prelates chose a ruler, but their choice was restricted to members of the royal family.

The life of the king was an exhausting round of obligations. He was expected to take fearlessly to the hunt; he moved to it in a brocaded pavilion drawn by ten camels royally dressed; seven camels carried his throne, one hundred bore his minstrels. Ten thousand knights might accompany him; but if we may credit the Sasanian rock reliefs he had at last to mount a horse, face in the first person a stag, ibex, antelope, buffalo, tiger, lion, or some other of the animals gathered in the king's park or "paradise." Back in his palace, he confronted the chores of government amid a thousand attendants and in a maze of officious ceremony. He had to dress himself in robes heavy with jewelry, seat himself on a golden throne, and wear a crown so burdensome that it had to be suspended an invisible distance from his immovable head. So he received ambassadors and guests, observed a thousand punctilios of protocol, passed judgment, received appointments and reports. Those who approached him prostrated themselves, kissed the ground, rose only at his bidding, and spoke to him through a handkerchief held to their mouths, lest their breath infect or profane the king. At night he retired to one of his wives or concubines, and eugenically disseminated his superior seed.

II. SASANIAN ROYALTY

Sasan, in Persian tradition, was a priest of Persepolis; his son Papak was a petty prince of Khur; Papak killed Gozihr, ruler of the province of Persis, made himself king of the province, and bequeathed his power to his son Shapur; Shapur died of a timely accident, and was succeeded by his brother Ardashir. Artabanus V, last of the Arsacid or Parthian kings of Persia, refused to recognize this new local dynasty; Ardashir overthrew Artabanus in battle (224), and became King of Kings (226). He replaced the loose feudal rule of the Arsacids with a strong royal power governing through a centralized but spreading bureaucracy; won the support of the priestly caste by restoring the Zoroastrian hierarchy and faith; and roused the pride of the people by announcing that he would destroy Hellenistic influence in Persia, avenge Darius II against the heirs of Alexander, and reconquer all the territory once held by the Achaemenid kings. He almost kept his word. His swift campaigns extended the boundaries of Persia to the Oxus in the northeast, and to the Euphrates in the west. Dying (241), he placed the crown on the head of his son Shapur, and bade him drive the Greeks and Romans into the sea.

Shapur or Sapor I (241–72) inherited all the vigor and craft of his father. The rock reliefs represent him as a man of handsome and noble features; but these reliefs were doubtless stylized compliments. He received a good education, and loved learning; he was so charmed by the conversation of the Sophist Eustathius, the Greek ambassador, that he thought of resigning his throne and becoming a philosopher.[35] Unlike his later namesake, he gave full freedom to all religions, allowed Mani to preach at his court, and declared that "Magi, Manicheans, Jews, Christians, and all men of whatever religion should be left undisturbed" in his Empire.[36] Continuing Ardashir's redaction of the Avesta, he persuaded the priests to include in this Persian Bible secular works on metaphysics, astronomy, and medicine, mostly borrowed from

FIG. 1—*Interior of Santa Maria Maggiore*
Rome

FIG. 2—*Interior of Hagia Sophia*
Constantinople

FIG. 3—*Interior of San Vitale*
Ravenna

FIG. 4—*Detail of Rock Relief*
Taq-I-Bustan
Courtesy of Asia Institute

FIG. 5—*Court of the Great Mosque*
Damascus
Courtesy of Metropolitan Museum of Art

FIG. 6—*Dome of the Rock*
Jerusalem

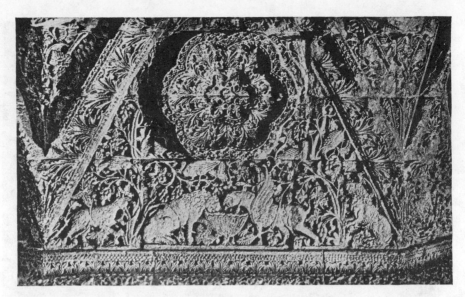

FIG. 7—*Portion of Stone Relief*
Mshatta, Syria

FIG. 8—*Court of El Azhar Mosque*
Cairo

FIG. 9—*Wood Minbar in El Agsa Mosque*
Jerusalem

FIG. 11—*Interior of Mosque*
Cordova

FIG. 10—*Pavilion on Court of Lions, the Alhambra*
Granada

FIG. 12—*Façade of St. Mark's*
Venice

FIG. 13—*Piazza of the Duomo, Showing Baptistry, Cathedral, and Leaning Tower*
Pisa

FIG. 15—*Apse of Cathedral*
Monreale

FIG. 14—*Interior of Capella Palatina*
Palermo

India and Greece. He was a liberal patron of the arts. He was not as great a general as Shapur II or the two Khosrus, but he was the ablest administrator in the long Sasanian line. He built a new capital at Shapur, whose ruins still bear his name; and at Shushtar, on the Karun River, he raised one of the major engineering works of antiquity—a dam of granite blocks, forming a bridge 1710 feet long and 20 feet wide; the course of the stream was temporarily changed to allow the construction; its bed was solidly paved; and great sluice gates regulated the flow. Tradition says that Shapur used Roman engineers and prisoners to design and build this dam, which continued to function to our own century.[37] Turning reluctantly to war, Shapur invaded Syria, reached Antioch, was defeated by a Roman army, and made a peace (244) that restored to Rome all that he had taken. Resenting Armenia's co-operation with Rome, he entered that country and established there a dynasty friendly to Persia (252). His right flank so protected, he resumed the war with Rome, defeated and captured the Emperor Valerian (260), sacked Antioch, and took thousands of prisoners to forced labor in Iran. Odenathus, governor of Palmyra, joined forces with Rome, and compelled Shapur again to resign himself to the Euphrates as the Roman-Persian frontier.

His successors, from 272 to 302, were royal mediocrities. History makes short shrift of Hormizd II (302–9), for he maintained prosperity and peace. He went about repairing public buildings and private dwellings, especially those of the poor, all at state expense. He established a new court of justice devoted to hearing the complaints of the poor against the rich, and often presided himself. We do not know if these strange habits precluded his son from inheriting the throne; in any case, when Hormizd died, the nobles imprisoned his son, and gave the throne to his unborn child, whom they confidently hailed as Shapur II; and to make matters clear they crowned the foetus by suspending the royal diadem over the mother's womb.[38]

With this good start Shapur II entered upon the longest reign in Asiatic history (309–79). From childhood he was trained for war; he hardened his body and will, and at sixteen took the government and the field. Invading eastern Arabia, he laid waste a score of villages, killed thousands of captives, and led others into bondage by cords attached to their wounds. In 337 he renewed the war with Rome for mastery of the trade routes to the Far East, and continued it, with pacific intervals, almost till his death. The conversion of Rome and Armenia to Christianity gave the old struggle a new intensity, as if the gods in Homeric frenzy had joined the fray. Through forty years Shapur fought a long line of Roman emperors. Julian drove him back to Ctesiphon, but retreated ingloriously; Jovian, outmaneuvered, was forced to a peace (363) that yielded to Shapur the Roman provinces on the Tigris, and all Armenia. When Shapur II died Persia was at the height of its power and prestige, and a hundred thousand acres had been improved with human blood.

In the next century war moved to the eastern frontier. About 425 a Turanian people known to the Greeks as Ephthalites, and mistakenly called "White Huns," captured the region between the Oxus and the Jaxartes. The Sasanian King Bahram V (420–38), named Gur—"the wild ass"—because of his reckless hunting feats, fought them successfully; but after his death they spread through fertility and war, and built an empire extending from the Caspian to the Indus, with its capital at Gurgan and its chief city at Balkh. They overcame and slew King Firuz (459–84), and forced King Balas (484–8) to pay them tribute.

So threatened in the east, Persia was at the same time thrown into chaos by the struggle of the monarchy to maintain its authority against the nobles and the priests. Kavadh I (488–531) thought to weaken these enemies by encouraging a communist movement which had made them the chief object of its attack. About 490 Mazdak, a Zoroastrian priest, had proclaimed himself Godsent to preach an old creed: that all men are born equal, that no one has any natural right to possess more than another, that property and marriage are human inventions and miserable mistakes, and that all goods and all women should be the common property of all men. His enemies claimed that he condoned theft, adultery, and incest as natural protests against property and marriage, and as legitimate approximations to utopia. The poor and some others heard him gladly, but Mazdak was probably surprised to receive the approval of a king. His followers began to plunder not only the homes but the harems of the rich, and to carry off for their own uses the most illustrious and costly concubines. The outraged nobles imprisoned Kavadh, and set his brother Djamasp upon the throne. After three years in the "Castle of Oblivion" Kavadh escaped, and fled to the Ephthalites. Eager to have a dependent as the ruler of Persia, they provided him with an army, and helped him to take Ctesiphon. Djamasp abdicated, the nobles fled to their estates, and Kavadh was again King of Kings (499). Having made his power secure, he turned upon the communists, and put Mazdak and thousands of his followers to death.[39] Perhaps the movement had raised the status of labor, for the decrees of the council of state were henceforth signed not only by princes and prelates, but also by the heads of the major guilds.[40] Kavadh ruled for another generation; fought with success against his friends the Ephthalites, inconclusively with Rome; and dying, left the throne to his second son Khosru, the greatest of Sasanian kings.

Khosru I ("Fair Glory," 531–79) was called Chosroes by the Greeks, Kisra by the Arabs; the Persians added the cognomen Anushirvan ("Immortal Soul"). When his older brothers conspired to depose him, he put all his brothers to death, and all their sons but one. His subjects called him "the Just"; and perhaps he merited the title if we separate justice from mercy. Procopius described him as "a past master at feigning piety" and breaking his word;[41] but Procopius was of the enemy. The Persian historian al-Tabari praised Khosru's "penetration, knowledge, intelligence, courage, and prudence," and put into his mouth an inaugural speech well invented if not true.[42] He completely reorganized the government; chose his aides for ability regardless of rank; and raised his son's tutor, Buzurgmihr, to be a celebrated vizier. He replaced untrained feudal levies with a standing army disciplined and competent. He established a more equitable system of taxation, and consolidated Persian law. He built dams and canals to improve the water supply of the cities and the irrigation of farms; he reclaimed waste lands by giving their cultivators cattle, implements, and seed; he promoted commerce by the construction, repair, and protection of bridges and roads; he devoted his great energy zealously to the service of his people and the state. He encouraged —compelled—marriage on the ground that Persia needed more population to man its fields and frontiers. He persuaded bachelors to marry by dowering the wives, and educating their children, with state funds.[43] He maintained and educated orphans and poor children at the public expense. He punished apostasy with death, but tolerated Christianity, even in his harem. He gathered about him philosophers, physicians, and scholars from India and Greece, and delighted to discuss with them the problems of life, government, and death. One discussion turned on the question, "What is the greatest misery?" A Greek philosopher answered, "An impoverished and imbecile old age"; a Hindu replied, "A harassed mind in a diseased body"; Khosru's vizier won the dutiful acclaim of all by saying, "For my part I think the extreme misery is for a man to see the end of life approaching without having practiced virtue."[44] Khosru supported literature, science, and scholarship with substantial subsidies, and financed many translations and histories; in his reign the university at Jund-i-Shapur reached its apogee. He so guarded the safety of foreigners that his court was always crowded with distinguished visitors from abroad.

On his accession he proclaimed his desire for peace with Rome. Justinian, having designs on Africa and Italy, agreed; and in 532 the two "brothers" signed "an eternal peace." When Africa and Italy fell, Khosru humorously asked for a share of the spoils on the ground that Byzantium could not have. won had not Persia made peace; Justinian sent him costly gifts.[45] In 539 Khosru declared war on "Rome," alleging that Justinian had violated the terms of their treaty; Procopius confirms the charge; probably Khosru thought it wise to attack while Justinian's armies were still busy in the West, instead of waiting for a victorious and strengthened Byzantium to turn all its forces against Persia; furthermore, it seemed to Khosru manifest destiny that Persia should have the gold mines of Trebizond and an outlet on the Black Sea. He marched into Syria, besieged Hierapolis, Apamea, and Aleppo, spared them for rich ransoms, and soon stood before Antioch. The reckless population, from the battlements, greeted him not merely with arrows and catapult missiles, but with the obscene sarcasm for which it had earned an international reputation.[46] The enraged monarch took the city by storm, looted its treasures, burned down all its buildings except the cathedral, massacred part of the population, and sent the remainder away to people a new "Antioch" in Persia. Then he bathed with delight in that Mediterranean which had once been Persia's western frontier. Justinian dispatched Belisarius to the rescue, but Khosru leisurely crossed the Euphrates with his spoils, and the cautious general did not pursue him (541). The inconclusiveness of the wars between Persia and Rome was doubtless affected by the difficulty of maintaining an occupation force on the enemy's side of the Syrian desert or the Taurus range; modern improvements in transport and communication have permitted greater wars. In three further invasions of Roman Asia Khosru made rapid marches and sieges, took ransoms and captives, ravaged the countryside, and peaceably retired (542–3). In 545 Justinian paid him 2000 pounds of gold ($840,000) for a five-year truce, and on its expiration 2600 pounds for a five-year extension. Finally (562), after a generation of war, the aging monarchs pledged themselves to peace for fifty years; Justinian agreed to pay Persia annually 30,000 pieces of gold ($7,500,000), and Khosru renounced his claims to disputed territories in the Caucasus and on the Black Sea.

But Khosru was not through with war. About 570, at the request of the Himyarites of southwest Arabia, he sent an army to free them from their Abyssinian conquerors; when the liberation was accomplished the Himyarites found that they were now a Persian province. Justinian had made an alliance with Abyssinia; his successor Justin II considered the Persian expulsion of the Abyssinians from Arabia an unfriendly act; moreover, the Turks on Persia's eastern border secretly agreed to join in an attaack upon Khosru; Justin declared war (572). Despite his age, Khosru took the field in person, and captured the Roman frontier town of Dara; but his health failed him, he suffered his first defeat (578), and retired to Ctesiphon, where he died in 579, at an uncertain age. In forty-eight years of rule he had won all his wars and battles except one; had extended his empire on every side; had made Persia stronger than ever since Darius I; and had given it so competent a system of administration that when the Arabs conquered Persia they adopted that system practically without change. Almost contemporary with Justinian, he was rated by the common consent of their contemporaries as the greater king; and the Persians of every later generation counted him the strongest and ablest monarch in their history.

His son Hormizd IV (579–89) was overthrown by a general, Bahram Cobin, who made himself regent for Hormizd's son Khosru II (589), and a year later made himself king. When Khosru came of age he demanded the throne; Bahram refused; Khosru fled to Hierapolis in Roman Syria; the Greek Emperor Maurice offered to restore him to power if Persia would withdraw from Armenia; Khosru agreed, and Ctesiphon had the rare experience of seeing a Roman army install a Persian king (596).

Khosru Parvez ("Victorious") rose to greater heights of power than any Persian since Xerxes, and prepared his empire's fall. When Phocas murdered and replaced Maurice, Parvez declared war on the usurper (603) as an act of vengeance for his friend; in effect the ancient contest was renewed. Byzantium being torn by sedition and faction, the Persian armies took Dara, Amida, Edessa, Hierapolis, Aleppo, Apamea, Damascus (605–13). Inflamed with success, Parvez proclaimed a holy war against the Christians; 26,000 Jews joined his army; in 614 his combined forces sacked Jerusalem, and massacred 90,000 Christians.[47] Many Christian churches, including that of the Holy Sepulcher, were burned to the ground; and the True Cross, the most cherished of all Christian relics, was carried off to Persia. To Heraclius, the new Emperor, Parvez sent a theological inquiry: "Khosru, greatest of gods and master of the whole earth, to Heraclius, his vile and insensate slave: You say that you trust in your god. Why, then, has he not delivered Jerusalem out of my hands?"[48] In 616 a Persian army captured Alexandria; by 619 all Egypt, as not since Darius II, belonged to the King of Kings. Meanwhile another Persian army overran Asia Minor and captured Chalcedon (617); for ten years the Persians held that city, separated from Constantinople only by the narrow Bosporus. During that decade Parvez demolished churches, transported their art and wealth to Persia, and taxed Western Asia into a destitution that left it resourceless against an Arab conquest now only a generation away.

Khosru turned over the conduct of the war to his generals, retired to his luxurious palace at Dastagird (some sixty miles north of Ctesiphon), and gave himself to art and love. He assembled architects, sculptors, and painters to make his new capital outshine the old, and to carve likenesses of Shirin, the fairest and most loved of his 3000 wives. The Persians complained that she was a Christian; some alleged that she had converted the King; in any case, amid his holy war, he allowed her to build many churches and monasteries. But Persia, prospering with spoils and a replenished slave supply, could forgive its king his self-indulgence, his art, even his toleration. It hailed his victories as the final triumph of Persia over Greece and Rome, of Ormuzd over Christ. Alexander at last was answered, and Marathon, Salamis, Plataea, and Arbela were avenged.

Nothing remained of the Byzantine Empire except a few Asiatic ports, some fragments of Italy, Africa, and Greece, an unbeaten navy, and a besieged capital frenzied with terror and despair. Heraclius took ten years to build a new army and state out of the ruins; then, instead of attempting a costly crossing at Chalcedon, he sailed into the Black Sea, crossed Armenia, and attacked Persia in the rear. As Khosru had desecrated Jerusalem, so now Heraclius destroyed Clorumia, birthplace of Zoroaster, and put out its sacred inextinguishable light (624). Khosru sent army after army against him; they were all defeated; and as the Greeks advanced Khosru fled to Ctesiphon. His generals, smarting under his insults, joined the nobles in deposing him. He was imprisoned, and fed on bread and water; eighteen of his sons were slain before his eyes; finally another son, Sheroye, put him to death (628).

III. SASANIAN ART

Of the wealth and splendor of the Shapurs, the Kavadhs, and the Khosrus nothing survives but the ruins of Sasanian art; enough, however, to heighten our wonder at the persistence and adaptability of Persian art from Darius the Great and Persepolis to Shah Abbas the Great and Isfahan.

Extant Sasanian architecture is entirely secular; the fire temples have disappeared, and only royal palaces remain; and these are "gigantic skeletons," [49] with their ornamental stucco facing long since fallen away. The oldest of these ruins is the so-called palace of Ardashir I at Firuzabad, southeast of Shiraz. No one knows its date; guesses range from 340 B.C to A.D. 460. After fifteen centuries of heat and cold, theft and war, the enormous dome still covers a hall one hundred feet high and fifty-five wide. A portal arch eighty-nine feet high and forty-two wide divided a façade 170 feet long; this façade crumbled in our time. From the rectangular central hall squinch arches led up to a circular dome.* By an unusual and interesting arrangement, the pressure of the dome was borne by a double hollow wall, whose inner and outer frames were spanned by a barrel vault; and to this reinforcement of inner by outer wall were added external buttresses of attached pilasters of heavy stones. Here was an architecture quite different from the classic columnar style of Persepolis—crude and clumsy, but using forms that would come to perfection in the St. Sophia of Justinian.

Not far away, at Sarvistan, stands a similar ruin of like uncertain date: a façade of three arches, a great central hall and side rooms, covered by ovoid domes, barrel vaults, and semicupolas serving as buttresses; from these half domes, by removing all but their sustaining framework, the "flying" or skeletal buttress of Gothic architecture may have evolved.[51] Northwest of Susa another ruined palace, the Ivan-i-Kharka, shows the oldest known example of the transverse vault, formed with diagonal ribs.[52] But the most impressive of Sasanian relics—which frightened the conquering Arabs by its mass—was the royal palace of Ctesiphon, named by the Arabs Taq-i-Kisra, or Arch of Khosru (I). It may be the building described by a Greek historian of A.D. 638, who tells how Justinian "provided Greek marble for Chosroes, and skilled artisans who built for him a palace in the Roman style, not far from Ctesiphon." [53] The north wing collapsed in 1888; the dome is gone; three immense walls rise to a height of one hundred and five feet, with a façade horizontally divided into five tiers of blind arcades. A lofty central arch—the highest (eighty-five feet) and widest (seventy-two feet) elliptical arch known—opened upon a hall one hundred and fifteen by seventy-five

---

* A squinch is a diagonal arch mediating between the upper corner of a polygonal structure and the rim of a superimposed circular or elliptical dome. Creswell thinks this device was invented by the Persians.[50]

feet; the Sasanian kings relished room. These ruined façades imitate the less elegant of Roman front elevations, like the Theater of Marcellus; they are more
impressive than beautiful; but we cannot judge past beauty by present ruins.

The most attractive of Sasanian remains are not the gutted palaces of crumbling
sun-baked brick, but rock reliefs carved into Persia's mountainsides. These gigantic figures are lineal descendants of the Achaemenid cliff reliefs, and are in some
cases juxtaposed with them, as if to emphasize the continuity of Persian power,
and the equality of Sasanian with Achaemenid kings. The oldest of the Sasanian
sculptures shows Ardashir trampling upon a fallen foe—presumably the last of
the Arsacids. Finer are those at Naqsh-i-Rustam, near Persepolis, celebrating
Ardashir, Shapur I, and Bahram II; the kings are drawn as dominating figures,
but, like most kings and men, they find it hard to rival the grace and symmetry
of the animals. Similar reliefs at Naqsh-i-Redjeb and at Shapur present powerful
stone portraits of Shapur I and Bahram I and II. At Taq-i-Bustan—"Arch of the
Garden"—near Kermanshah, two column-supported arches are deeply cut into
the cliff; reliefs on the inner and outer faces of the arches show Shapur II and
Khosru Parvez at the hunt; the stone comes alive with fat elephants and wild pigs;
the foliage is carefully done, and the capitals of the columns are handsomely
carved. There is in these sculptures no Greek grace of movement or smoothness
of line, no keen individualization, no sense of perspective, and little modeling;
but in dignity and majesty, in masculine vitality and power, they bear comparison with most of the arch reliefs of imperial Rome.

Apparently these carvings were colored; so were many features of the palaces;
but only traces of such painting remain. The literature, however, makes it clear
that the art of painting flourished in Sasanian times; the prophet Mani is reported
to have founded a school of painting; Firdausi speaks of Persian magnates adorning their mansions with pictures of Iranian heroes; [54] and the poet al-Buhturi
(d. 897) describes the murals in the palace at Ctesiphon.[55] When a Sasanian
king died, the best painter of the time was called upon to make a portrait of him
for a collection kept in the royal treasury.[56]

Painting, sculpture, pottery, and other forms of decoration shared their designs with Sasanian textile art. Silks, embroideries, brocades, damasks, tapestries,
chair covers, canopies, tents, and rugs were woven with servile patience and
masterly skill, and were dyed in warm tints of yellow, blue, and green. Every
Persian but the peasant and the priest aspired to dress above his class; presents
often took the form of sumptuous garments; and great colorful carpets had been
an appanage of wealth in the East since Assyrian days. The two dozen Sasanian
textiles that escaped the teeth of time are the most highly valued fabrics in
existence.[57] Even in their own day Sasanian textiles were admired and imitated
from Egypt to Japan; and during the Crusades these pagan products were favored
for clothing the relics of Christian saints. When Heraclius captured the palace of
Khosru Parvez at Dastagird, delicate embroideries and an immense rug were
among his most precious spoils.[58] Famous was the "winter carpet" of Khosru
Anushirvan, designed to make him forget winter in its spring and summer scenes:
flowers and fruits made of inwoven rubies and diamonds grew, in this carpet,

beside walks of silver and brooks of pearls traced on a ground of gold.[59] Harun al-Rashid prided himself on a spacious Sasanian rug thickly studded with jewelry.[60] Persians wrote love poems about their rugs.[61]

Of Sasanian pottery little remains except pieces of utilitarian intent. Yet the ceramic art was highly developed in Achaemenid times, and must have had some continuance under the Sasanians to reach such perfection in Mohammedan Iran. Ernest Fenellosa thought that Persia might be the center from which the art of enamel spread even to the Far East; [62] and art historians debate whether Sasanian Persia or Syria or Byzantium originated lusterware and cloisonné.* [63] Sasanian metalworkers made ewers, jugs, bowls, and cups as if for a giant race; turned them on lathes; incised them with graver or chisel, or hammered out a design in *repoussé* from the obverse side; and used gay animal forms, ranging from cock to lion, as handles and spouts. The famous glass "Cup of Khosru" in the Bibliothéque Nationale at Paris has medallions of crystal glass inserted into a network of beaten gold; tradition reckons this among the gifts sent by Harun to Charlemagne. The Goths may have learned this art of inlay from Persia, and may have brought it to the West.[64]

The silversmiths made costly plate, and helped the goldsmiths to adorn lords, ladies, and commoners with jewelry. Several Sasanian silver dishes survive—in the British Museum, the Leningrad Hermitage, the Bibliothéque Nationale, and the Metropolitan Museum of Art; always with kings or nobles at the hunt, and animals more fondly and successfully drawn than men. Sasanian coins sometimes rivaled Rome's in beauty, as in the issues of Shapur I.[65] Even Sasanian books could be works of art; tradition tells how gold and silver trickled from the bindings when Mani's books were publicly burned.[66] Precious materials were also used in Sasanian furniture: Khosru I had a gold table inlaid with costly stones; and Khosru II sent to his savior, the Emperor Maurice, an amber table five feet in diameter, supported on golden feet and encrusted with gems.[67]

All in all, Sasanian art reveals a laborious recovery after four centuries of Parthian decline. If we may diffidently judge from its remains, it does not equal the Achaemenid in nobility or grandeur, nor the Islamic Persian in inventiveness, delicacy, and taste; but it preserved much of the old virility in its reliefs, and foreshadowed something of the later exuberance in its decorative themes. It welcomed new ideas and styles, and Khosru I had the good sense to import Greek artists and engineers while defeating Greek generals. Repaying its debt, Sasanian art exported its forms and motives eastward into India, Turkestan, and China, westward into Syria, Asia Minor, Constantinople, the Balkans, Egypt, and Spain. Probably its influence helped to change the emphasis in Greek art from classic representation to Byzantine ornament, and in Latin Christian art from wooden ceilings to brick or stone vaults and domes and buttressed walls. The great portals and cupolas of Sasanian architecture passed down into Moslem mosques and Mogul palaces and shrines. Nothing is lost in history: sooner or later every creative idea finds opportunity and development, and adds its color to the flame of life.

---

* Ceramic luster is an overglaze of silver, copper, and manganese, fired in a muffle kiln to shield it from direct flame, and simulating the effect of gold or silver on pottery or glass.

IV. THE ARAB CONQUEST

Having killed and succeeded his father, Sheroye—crowned as Kavadh II—made peace with Heraclius; surrendered Egypt, Palestine, Syria, Asia Minor, and western Mesopotamia; returned to their countries the captives taken by Persia; and restored to Jerusalem the remains of the True Cross. Heraclius reasonably rejoiced over so thorough a triumph; he did not observe that on the very day in 629 when he replaced the True Cross in its shrine a band of Arabs attacked a Greek garrison near the River Jordan. In that same year pestilence broke out in Persia; thousands died of it, including the King. His son Ardashir III, aged seven, was proclaimed ruler; a general, Shahr-Baraz, killed the boy and usurped the throne; his own soldiers killed Shahr-Baraz, and dragged his corpse through the streets of Ctesiphon, shouting, "Whoever, not being of royal blood, seats himself upon the throne of Persia, will share this fate"; the populace is always more royalist than the king. Anarchy now swept through a realm exhausted by twenty-six years of war. Social disintegration climaxed a moral decay that had come with the riches of victory.[68] In four years nine rulers contested the throne, and disappeared through assassination, or flight, or an abnormally natural death. Provinces, even cities, declared their independence of a central government no longer able to rule. In 634 the crown was given to Yezdegird III, scion of the house of Sasan, and son of a Negress.[69]

In 632 Mohammed died after founding a new Arab state. His second successor, the Caliph Omar, received in 634 a letter from Muthanna, his general in Syria, informing him that Persia was in chaos and ripe for conquest.[70] Omar assigned the task to his most brilliant commander, Khalid. With an army of Bedouin Arabs inured to conflict and hungry for spoils, Khalid marched along the south shore of the Persian Gulf, and sent a characteristic message to Hormizd, governor of the frontier province: "Accept Islam, and thou art safe; else pay tribute. . . . A people is already upon thee, loving death even as thou lovest life."[71] Hormizd challenged him to single combat; Khalid accepted, and slew him. Overcoming all resistance, the Moslems reached the Euphrates; Khalid was recalled to save an Arab army elsewhere; Muthanna replaced him, and, with reinforcements, crossed the river on a bridge of boats. Yezdegird, still a youth of twenty-two, gave the supreme command to Rustam, governor of Khurasan, and bade him raise a limitless force to save the state. The Persians met the Arabs in the Battle of the Bridge, defeated them, and pursued them recklessly; Muthanna re-formed his columns, and at the Battle of El-Bowayb destroyed the disordered Persian forces almost to a man (624). Moslem losses were heavy; Muthanna died of his wounds; but the Caliph sent an abler general, Saad, and a new army of 30,000 men. Yezdegird replied by arming 120,000 Persians. Rustam led them across the Euphrates to Kadisiya, and there through four bloody days was fought one of the decisive battles of Asiatic history. On the fourth day a sandstorm blew into the faces of the Persians; the Arabs seized the opportunity, and overwhelmed their blinded enemies. Rustam was killed, and his army dispersed (636). Saad led his unresisted troops to the Tigris, crossed it, and entered Ctesiphon.

The simple and hardy Arabs gazed in wonder at the royal palace, its mighty arch and marble hall, its enormous carpets and jeweled throne. For ten days they labored to carry off their spoils. Perhaps because of these impediments, Omar forbade Saad to advance farther east; "Iraq," he said, "is enough."[72] Saad complied, and spent the next three years establishing Arab rule throughout Mesopotamia. Meanwhile Yezdegird, in his northern provinces, raised another army, 150,000 strong; Omar sent against him 30,000 men; at Nahavand superior tactics won the "Victory of Victories" for the Arabs; 100,000 Persians, caught in narrow defiles, were massacred (641). Soon all Persia was in Arab hands. Yezdegird fled to Balkh, begged aid of China and was refused, begged aid of the Turks and was given a small force; but as he started out on his new campaign some Turkish soldiers murdered him for his jewelry (652). Sasanian Persia had come to an end.

BOOK II

ISLAMIC CIVILIZATION

569–1258

CHRONOLOGICAL TABLE FOR BOOK II

CHAPTER VIII

Mohammed

570-632

I. ARABIA *

IN the year 565 Justinian died, master of a great empire. Five years later Mohammed was born into a poor family in a country three quarters desert, sparsely peopled by nomad tribes whose total wealth could hardly have furnished the sanctuary of St. Sophia. No one in those years would have dreamed that within a century these nomads would conquer half of Byzantine Asia, all Persia and Egypt, most of North Africa, and be on their way to Spain. The explosion of the Arabian peninsula into the conquest and conversion of half the Mediterranean world is the most extraordinary phenomenon in medieval history.

Arabia is the largest of all peninsulas: 1400 miles in its greatest length, 1250 in its greatest width. Geologically it is a continuation of the Sahara, part of the sandy belt that runs up through Persia to the Gobi Desert. *Arab* means arid. Physically Arabia is a vast plateau, rising precipitously to 12,000 feet within thirty miles of the Red Sea, and sloping through mountainous wastelands eastward to the Persian Gulf. In the center are some grassy oases and palm-studded villages, where water can be reached by shallow wells; around this nucleus the sands stretch in every direction for hundreds of miles. Snow falls there once in forty years; the nights cool down to 38 degrees Fahrenheit; the daily sun burns the face and boils the blood; and the sand-laden air necessitates long robes and head-bands to guard flesh and hair. The skies are almost always clear, the air "like sparkling wine."[1] Along the coasts an occasional

---

* The rediscovery of Arabia by modern Europeans illustrates the internationalism of science in the nineteenth century. It began in 1761-4, when Carsten Niebuhr traveled through the peninsula under the auspices of the Danish government; his published account (1772) was the first comprehensive description of Arabia. In 1807 Domingo Badia y Leblich, a Spaniard disguised as a Moor, visited Mecca, and gave the first accurate account of the pilgrimage ritual. In 1814-15 Johann Ludwig Burckhardt (1784-1817), a Swiss disguised as a Moslem, spent several months in Mecca and Medina; his learned reports were corroborated by later travelers. In 1853 Richard Burton, an Englishman dressed as an Afghan pilgrim, visited Medina and Mecca, and described his perilous journey in two absorbing volumes. In 1869-70 J. Halévy, a French Jew, explored the sites, and recorded the rock inscriptions, of the ancient Minaean, Sabaean, and Himyarite kingdoms. In 1875 Charles Montagu Doughty, an Englishman, traveled from Damascus in the pilgrimage caravan, and recorded his vicissitudes in *Arabia Deserta* (1888), one of the peaks of English prose. In 1882-8 E. Glaser, an Austrian, in three arduous expeditions, copied 1032 inscriptions, which are now our chief source for the history of pre-Islamic Arabia.

torrent of rain brings the possibility of civilization: most of all on the western littoral, in the Hejaz district with the cities of Mecca and Medina; and southwest in the district of Yemen, the home of the ancient kingdoms of Arabia.

A Babylonian inscription of approximately 2400 B.C. records the defeat of a king of Magan by the Babylonian ruler Naram-Sin. Magan was the capital of a Minaean kingdom in southwest Arabia; twenty-five of its later kings are known from Arabian inscriptions that go back to 800 B.C. An inscription tentatively ascribed to 2300 B.C. mentions another Arabian kingdom, Saba, in Yemen; from Saba or its North Arabian colonies, it is now agreed, the Queen of Sheba "went up" to Solomon about 950 B.C. The Sabaean kings made their capital at Marib, fought the usual wars of "defense," built great irrigation works like the Marib dams (whose ruins are still visible), raised gigantic castles and temples, subsidized religion handsomely, and used it as an instrument of rule.[2] Their inscriptions— probably not older than 900 B.C.—are beautifully carved in an alphabetical script. The Sabaeans produced the frankincense and myrrh that played so prominent a role in Asiatic and Egyptian rituals; they controlled the sea trade between India and Egypt, and the south end of the caravan route that led through Mecca and Medina to Petra and Jerusalem. About 115 B.C. another petty kingdom of southwest Arabia, the Himyarite, conquered Saba, and thereafter controlled Arabian trade for several centuries. In 25 B.C. Augustus, irked by Arabian control of Egyptian-Indian commerce, sent an army under Aelius Gallus to capture Marib; the legions were misled by native guides, were decimated by heat and disease, and failed in their mission; but another Roman army captured the Arab port of Adana (Aden), and gave control of the Egypt-India route to Rome. (Britain repeated this procedure in our time.)

In the second century before Christ some Himyarites crossed the Red Sea, colonized Abyssinia, and gave the indigenous Negro population a Semitic culture and considerable Semitic blood.* The Abyssinians received Christianity, crafts, and arts from Egypt and Byzantium; their merchant vessels sailed as far as India and Ceylon; and seven little kingdoms acknowledged the Negus as their sovereign.† Meanwhile in Arabia many Himyarites followed the lead of their king Dhu-Nuwas and accepted Judaism. With a convert's zeal, Dhu-Nuwas persecuted the Christians of southwest Arabia; they called to their coreligionists to rescue them; the Abyssinians came, conquered the Himyarite kings (A.D. 522), and replaced them with an Abyssinian dynasty. Justinian allied himself with this new state; Persia countered by taking up the cause of the deposed Himyarites, driving out the Abyssinians, and setting up in Yemen (575) a Persian rule that ended some sixty years later with the Moslem conquest of Persia.

* The term *Semitic* is due to the legendary derivation of the peoples so called from Shem, son of Noah (Gen. x, 1). No clear definition of *Semite* can be given. In general the populations of Syria, Palestine, Mesopotamia, and Arabia, and the Arab populations of Africa, may be called Semitic in the sense that they use Semitic languages; the ancient peoples of Asia Minor, Armenia, and the Caucasus, and the peoples of Persia, North India, most of Europe, and all of the Europeanized Americas may be called "Indo-European" as using Indo-Germanic tongues.
† Gibbon, *Decline and Fall of the Roman Empire*, Everyman Library edition, IV, 322. It was one of the major achievements of Gibbon that he recognized the importance of Islam in medieval history, and recorded its political career with remarkable erudition, accuracy, and eloquence.

In the north some minor Arab kingdoms flourished briefly. The sheiks of the Ghassanid tribe ruled northwestern Arabia and Palmyrene Syria from the third to the seventh century as phylarchs, or client kings, of Byzantium. During the same period the Lakhmid kings established at Hira, near Babylon, a semi-Persian court and culture famous for its music and poetry. Long before Mohammed the Arabs had expanded into Syria and Iraq.

Aside from these petty kingdoms of south and north, and to a large extent within them, the political organization of pre-Islamic Arabia was a primitive kinship structure of families united in clans and tribes. Tribes were named from a supposed common ancestor; so the banu-Ghassan thought themselves the "children of Ghassan." Arabia as a political unit, before Mohammed, existed only in the careless nomenclature of the Greeks, who called all the population of the peninsula *Sarakenoi*, Saracens, apparently from the Arabic *sharqiyun*, "Easterners." Difficulties of communication compelled local or tribal self-sufficiency and particularism. The Arab felt no duty or loyalty to any group larger than his tribe, but the intensity of his devotion varied inversely as its extent; for his tribe he would do with a clear conscience what civilized people do only for their country, religion, or "race"—i.e., lie, steal, kill, and die. Each tribe or clan was loosely ruled by a sheik chosen by its leaders from a family traditionally prominent through wealth or wisdom or war.

In the villages men coaxed some grains and vegetables from the unwilling soil, raised a few cattle, and bred some fine horses; but they found it more profitable to cultivate orchards of dates, peaches, apricots, pomegranates, lemons, oranges, bananas, and figs; some nursed aromatic plants like frankincense, thyme, jasmine, and lavender; some pressed *itr* or attar from highland roses; some cupped trees to draw myrrh or balsam from the trunks. Possibly a twelfth of the population lived in cities on or near the west coast. Here was a succession of harbors and markets for Red Sea commerce, while farther inland lay the great caravan routes to Syria. We hear of Arabian trade with Egypt as far back as 2743 B.C.;[3] probably as ancient was the trade with India. Annual fairs called merchants now to one town, now to another; the great annual fair at Ukaz, near Mecca, brought together hundreds of merchants, actors, preachers, gamblers, poets, and prostitutes.

Five sixths of the population were nomad Bedouins, herdsmen who moved with their flocks from one pastureland to another according to season and the winter rains. The Bedouin loved horses, but in the desert the camel was his greatest friend. It pitched and rolled with undulant dignity, and made only eight miles an hour; but it could go without water five days in summer and twenty-five in winter; its udders gave milk, its urine provided hair tonic,* its dung could be burned for fuel; when it died it made tender meat, and its

---

* The nomad women, says Doughty, "wash their babies in camel urine, and think thus to help them from insects; . . . and in this water both men and women comb their long hair."[4]

hair and hide made clothing and tents. With such varied sustenance the Bedouin could face the desert, as patient and enduring as his camel, as sensitive and spirited as his horse. Short and thin, well-knit and strong, he could live day after day on a few dates and a little milk; and from dates he made the wine that raised him out of the dust into romance. He varied the routine of his life with love and feud, and was as quick as a Spaniard (who inherited his blood) to avenge insult and injury, not only for himself but for his clan. A good part of his life was spent in tribal war; and when he conquered Syria, Persia, Egypt, and Spain, it was but an exuberant expansion of his plundering *razzias* or raids. Certain periods in the year he conceded to the "holy truce," for religious pilgrimage or for trade; otherwise, he felt, the desert was his; whoever crossed it, except in that time, or without paying him tribute, was an interloper; to rob such trespassers was an unusually straightforward form of taxation. He despised the city because it meant law and trade; he loved the merciless desert because it left him free. Kindly and murderous, generous and avaricious, dishonest and faithful, cautious and brave, the Bedouin, however poor, fronted the world with dignity and pride, vain of the purity of his inbred blood, and fond of adding his lineage to his name.

On one point above all he brooked no argument, and that was the incomparable beauty of his women. It was a dark, fierce, consuming beauty, worth a million odes, but brief with the tragic hasty fading of hot climes. Before Mohammed—and after him only slightly less so—the career of the Arab woman passed from a moment's idolatry to a lifetime of drudgery. She might be buried at birth if the father so willed;[5] at best he mourned her coming and hid his face from his fellows; somehow his best efforts had failed. Her winsome childhood earned a few years of love; but at seven or eight she was married off to any youth of the clan whose father would offer the purchase price for the bride. Her lover and husband would fight the world to defend her person or honor; some of the seeds and fustian of chivalry went with these passionate lovers to Spain. But the goddess was also a chattel; she formed part of the estate of her father, her husband, or her son, and was bequeathed with it; she was always the servant, rarely the comrade, of the man. He demanded many children of her, or rather many sons; her duty was to produce warriors. She was, in many cases, but one of his many wives. He could dismiss her at any time at will.

Nevertheless her mysterious charms rivaled battle as a theme and stimulus for his verse. The pre-Moslem Arab was usually illiterate, but he loved poetry only next to horses, women, and wine. He had no scientists or historians, but he had a heady passion for eloquence, for fine and correct speech, and intricately patterned verse. His language was closely kin to the Hebrew; complex in inflexions, rich in vocabulary, precise in differentiations, expressing now every nuance of poetry, later every subtlety of philosophy. The Arabs took pride in the antiquity and fullness of their language, loved to roll its mellifluous syllables in oratorical flourishes on tongue or pen, and listened with tense ecstasy to the poets who, in villages and cities, in desert camps or at the fairs, recalled to them, in running meters and endless rhymes, the loves and wars of their heroes, tribes, or kings. The poet was to the Arabs their historian, genealogist, satirist, moralist, newspaper, oracle, call to battle; and when a poet won a prize at one of the many poetry contests, his whole tribe felt honored, and rejoiced. Every year, at the Ukaz fair, the greatest of these contests was held; almost daily for a month the clans competed through their poets; there were no judges but the eagerly or scornfully listening multitudes; the winning poems were written down in brilliantly illuminated characters, were therefore called the Golden Songs, and were preserved like heirlooms in the treasuries of princes and kings. The Arabs called them also *Muallaqat*, or *Suspended*, because legend said that the prize poems, inscribed upon Egyptian silk in letters of gold, were hung on the walls of the Kaaba in Mecca.

Seven such *Muallaqat*, dating from the sixth century, survive from those pre-Islamic days. Their form is the *qasida*, a narrative ode, in elaborately complex meter and rhyme, usually of love or war. In one of them, by the poet Labid, a soldier returns from his campaigns to the village and home where he had left his wife; he finds his cottage empty, his wife gone off with another man; Labid describes the scene with Goldsmith's tenderness, and with greater eloquence and force.[6] In another the Arab women prod their men to battle:

> Courage! courage! defenders of women! Smite with the edge of your swords! . . . We are the daughters of the morning star; soft are the carpets we tread beneath our feet; our necks are adorned with pearls; our tresses are perfumed with musk. The brave who confront the foe we will clasp to our bosoms, but the dastards who flee we will spurn; not for them our embraces! [7]

Unabashedly sensual is an ode by Imru'lqais:

> Fair too was that other, she the veil-hidden one, howdahed how close, how guarded! Yet did she welcome me.
> Passed I twixt her tent-ropes—what though her near-of-kin lay in the dark to slay me, blood-shedders all of them.
> Came I at the mid-night, hour when the Pleiades showed as the links of seed-pearls binding the sky's girdle.
> Stealing in, I stood there. She had cast off from her every robe but one robe, all but her night-garment.
> Tenderly she scolded: What is this stratagem? Speak, on thine oath, thou mad one. Stark is thy lunacy.
> Passed we out together, while she drew after us on our twin track, to hide it, wise, her embroideries,
> Fled beyond the camp-fires. There in security dark in the sand we lay down far from the prying eyes.

By her plaits I wooed her, drew her face near to me, won to her waist
    how frail-lined, hers of the ankle-rings.
Fair-faced she—no redness—noble of countenance, smooth as of glass
    her bosom, bare with its necklaces.
Thus are pearls yet virgin, seen through the dark water, clear in the
    sea-depths gleaming, pure, inaccessible.
Coyly she withdraws her, shows us a cheek, a lip, she a gazelle of
    Wujra; . . . .
Roe-like her throat slender, white as an ariel's, sleek to thy lips up-
    lifted—pearls are its ornament.
On her shoulders fallen thick lie the locks of her, dark as the date-
    clusters hung from the palm-branches. . . .
Slim her waist—a well-cord scarce has its slenderness. Smooth are her
    legs as reed-stems stripped at a water-head.
The morn through she sleepeth, muck-stream in indolence, hardly at
    noon hath risen, girded her day dresses.
Soft her touch—her fingers fluted as water-worms, sleek as the snakes
    of Thobya, tooth-sticks of Ishali.
Lighteneth she night's darkness, ay, as an evening lamp hung for a sign
    of guidance lone on a hermitage.[8]

The pre-Islamic poets sang their compositions to musical accompaniment;
music and poetry were bound into one form. The flute, the lute, the reed
pipe or oboe, and the tambourine were the favored instruments. Singing girls
were often invited to amuse male banqueteers; taverns were equipped with
them; the Ghassanid kings kept a troupe of them to ease the cares of royalty;
and when the Meccans marched against Mohammed in 624 they took with
them a bevy of singing girls to warm their campfires and prod them on to
war. Even in those early "Days of Ignorance," as Moslems would call the
pre-Moslem period, the Arab song was a plaintive cantilena that used few
words, and carried a note so tenaciously along the upper reaches of the scale
that a few verses might provide libretto for an hour.

The desert Arab had his own primitive and yet subtle religion. He feared
and worshiped incalculable deities in stars and moon and the depths of the
earth; occasionally he importuned the mercy of a punitive sky; but for the
most part he was so confused by the swarm of spirits (jinn) about him that
he despaired of appeasing them, accepted a fatalistic resignation, prayed with
masculine brevity, and shrugged his shoulders over the infinite.[9] He seems
to have given scant thought to a life after death; sometimes, however, he had
his camel tied foodless to his grave, so that it might soon follow him to the
other world, and save him from the social disgrace of going on foot in paradise.[10] Now and then he offered human sacrifice; and here and there he
worshiped sacred stones.

The center of this stone worship was Mecca. This holy city owed none of
its growth to climate, for the mountains of bare rock that almost enclosed it

ensured a summer of intolerable heat; the valley was an arid waste; and in all the town, as Mohammed knew it, hardly a garden grew. But its location —halfway down the west coast, forty-eight miles from the Red Sea—made it a convenient stopping point for the mile-long caravans, sometimes of a thousand camels, that carried trade between southern Arabia (and therefore India and Central Africa) and Egypt, Palestine, and Syria. The merchants who controlled this trade formed joint-stock companies, dominated the fairs at Ukaz, and managed the lucrative religious ritual that centered round the Kaaba and its sacred Black Stone.

Kaaba means a square structure, and is one with our word *cube*. In the belief of orthodox Moslems, the Kaaba was built or rebuilt ten times. The first was erected at the dawn of history by angels from heaven; the second by Adam; the third by his son Seth; the fourth by Abraham and his son Ishmael by Hagar . . . the seventh by Qusay, chief of the Quraish tribe; the eighth by the Quraish leaders in Mohammed's lifetime (605); the ninth and tenth by Moslem leaders in 681 and 696; the tenth is substantially the Kaaba of today. It stands near the center of a large porticoed enclosure, the Masjid al-Haram, or Sacred Mosque. It is a rectangular stone edifice forty feet long, thirty-five wide, fifty high. In its southeast corner, five feet from the ground, just right for kissing, is embedded the Black Stone, of dark red material, oval in shape, some seven inches in diameter. Many of its worshipers believe that this stone was sent down from heaven—and perhaps it was a meteorite; most of them believe that it has been a part of the Kaaba since Abraham. Moslem scholars interpret it as symbolizing that part of Abraham's progeny (Ishmael and his offspring) which, rejected by Israel, became, they think, the founders of the Quraish tribe; they apply to it a passage from Psalm cxviii, 22-3: "The stone which the builders rejected is become the head of the corner; this is Yahveh's doing"; and another from Matthew xxi, 42-3, in which Jesus, having quoted these strange words, adds: "Therefore the Kingdom of God shall be taken away from you, and shall be given to a nation bringing forth the fruits thereof"—though the virile Moslems would hardly claim to have fulfilled the ethics of Christ.

Within the Kaaba, in pre-Moslem days, were several idols representing gods. One was called Allah, and was probably the tribal god of the Quraish; three others were Allah's daughters—al-Uzza, al-Lat, and Manah. We may judge the antiquity of this Arab pantheon from the mention of Al-il-Lat (al-Lat) by Herodotus as a major Arabian deity.[11] The Quraish paved the way for monotheism by worshiping Allah as chief god; He was presented to the Meccans as the Lord of their soil, to Whom they must pay a tithe of their crops and the first-born of their herds. The Quraish, as alleged descendants of Abraham and Ishmael, appointed the priests and guardians of the shrine, and managed its revenues. An aristocratic minority of the tribe, as descendants of Qusay, controlled the civil government of Mecca.

At the beginning of the sixth century the Quraish were divided into two factions: one led by the rich merchant and philanthropist Hashim; the other by Hashim's jealous nephew Umayya; this bitter rivalry would determine much history. When Hashim died he was succeeded as one of Mecca's chiefs by his son or younger brother Abd al-Muttalib. In 568 the latter's son Abdallah married Amina, also a descendant of Qusay. Abdallah remained with his bride three days, set out on a mercantile expedition, and died at Medina on the way back. Two months later (569) Amina was delivered of the most important figure in medieval history.

II. MOHAMMED IN MECCA: 569–622 *

His ancestry was distinguished, his patrimony modest: Abdallah had left him five camels, a flock of goats, a house, and a slave who nursed him in his infancy. His name, meaning "highly praised," lent itself well to certain Biblical passages as predicting his advent. His mother died when he was six; he was taken over by his grandfather, then seventy-six, and later by his uncle Abu Talib. They gave him affection and care, but no one seems to have bothered to teach him how to read or write; [12] this feeble accomplishment was held in low repute by the Arabs of the time; only seventeen men of the Quraish tribe condescended to it.[13] Mohammed was never known to write anything himself; he used an amanuensis. His apparent illiteracy did not prevent him from composing the most famous and eloquent book in the Arabic tongue, and from acquiring such understanding of the management of men as seldom comes to highly educated persons.

Of his youth we know almost nothing, though fables about it have filled ten thousand volumes. At the age of twelve, says a tradition, he was taken by Abu Talib on a caravan to Bostra in Syria; perhaps on that journey he picked up some Jewish and Christian lore. Another tradition pictures him, a few years later, as going to Bostra on mercantile business for the rich widow Khadija. Then suddenly we find him, aged twenty-five, marrying her, aged forty and the mother of several children. Until her death twenty-six years later Mohammed lived with Khadija in a monogamous condition highly unusual for a Moslem of means, but perhaps natural in their recipient. She bore him some daughters, of whom the most famous was Fatima, and two sons who died in infancy. He consoled his grief by adopting Ali, the orphan son of Abu Talib. Khadija was a good woman, a good wife, a good merchant; she remained loyal to Mohammed through all his spiritual vicissitudes; and amid all his wives he remembered her as the best.

Ali, who married Fatima, fondly describes his adoptive father at forty-five as

---

* Preferable spellings of *Mohammed* and *Koran* would be *Muhammad* and *Qur'ân*; but it would be pedantry to insist upon them.

> of middle stature, neither tall nor short. His complexion was rosy white; his eyes black; his hair, thick, brilliant, and beautiful, fell to his shoulders. His profuse beard fell to his breast. . . . There was such sweetness in his visage that no one, once in his presence, could leave him. If I hungered, a single look at the Prophet's face dispelled the hunger. Before him all forgot their griefs and pains.[14]

He was a man of dignity, and seldom laughed; he kept his keen sense of humor under control, knowing its hazards for public men. Of a delicate constitution, he was nervous, impressionable, given to melancholy pensiveness. In moments of excitement or anger his facial veins would swell alarmingly; but he knew when to abate his passion, and could readily forgive a disarmed and repentant foe.

There were many Christians in Arabia, some in Mecca; with at least one of these Mohammed became intimate—Khadija's cousin Waraqah ibn Nawfal, "who knew the Scriptures of the Hebrews and the Christians." [15] Mohammed frequently visited Medina, where his father had died; there he may have met some of the Jews who formed a large part of the population. Many a page of the Koran proves that he learned to admire the morals of the Christians, the monotheism of the Jews, and the strong support given to Christianity and Judaism by the possession of Scriptures believed to be a revelation from God. Compared with these faiths the polytheistic idolatry, loose morality, tribal warfare, and political disunity of Arabia may have seemed to him shamefully primitive. He felt the need of a new religion—perhaps of one that would unify all these factious groups into a virile and healthy nation; a religion that would give them a morality not earth-bound to the Bedouin law of violence and revenge, but based upon commandments of divine origin and therefore of indisputable force. Others may have had similar thoughts; we hear of several "prophets" arising in Arabia about the beginning of the seventh century.[16] Many Arabs had been influenced by the Messianic expectations of the Jews; they, too, eagerly awaited a messenger from God. One Arab sect, the Hanifs, already rejected the heathen idolatry of the Kaaba, and preached a universal God, of whom all mankind should be willing slaves.[17] Like every successful preacher, Mohammed gave voice and form to the need and longing of his time.

As he approached forty he became more and more absorbed in religion. During the holy month of Ramadan he would withdraw, sometimes with his family, to a cave at the foot of Mt. Hira, three miles from Mecca, and spend many days and nights in fasting, meditation, and prayer. One night in the year 610, as he was alone in the cave, the pivotal experience of all Mohammedan history came to him. According to a tradition reported by his chief biographer, Muhammad ibn Ishaq, Mohammed related the event as follows:

> Whilst I was asleep, with a coverlet of silk brocade whereon was some writing, the angel Gabriel appeared to me and said, "Read!" I

said, "I do not read." He pressed me with the coverlets so tightly that methought 'twas death. Then he let me go, and said, "Read!" . . . So I read aloud, and he departed from me at last. And I awoke from my sleep, and it was as though these words were written on my heart. I went forth until, when I was midway on the mountain, I heard a voice from heaven saying, "O Mohammed! thou art the messenger of Allah, and I am Gabriel." I raised my head toward heaven to see, and lo, Gabriel in the form of a man, with feet set evenly on the rim of the sky, saying, "O Mohammed! thou art the messenger of Allah, and I am Gabriel." [18]

Returning to Khadija, he informed her of the visions. We are told that she accepted them as a true revelation from heaven, and encouraged him to announce his mission.

Thereafter he had many similar visions. Often, when they came, he fell to the ground in a convulsion or swoon; perspiration covered his brow; even the camel on which he was sitting felt the excitement, and moved fitfully.[19] Mohammed later attributed his gray hairs to these experiences. When pressed to describe the process of revelation, he answered that the entire text of the Koran existed in heaven,[20] and that one fragment at a time was communicated to him, usually by Gabriel.[21] Asked how he could remember these divine discourses, he explained that the archangel made him repeat every word.[22] Others who were near the Prophet at the time neither saw nor heard the angel.[23] Possibly his convulsions were epileptic seizures; they were sometimes accompanied by a sound reported by him as like the ringing of a bell [24]—a frequent occurrence in epileptic fits. But we hear of no tongue-biting, no loss of prehensile strength, such as usually occurs in epilepsy; nor does Mohammed's history show that degeneration of brain power which epilepsy generally brings; on the contrary, he advanced in clarity of thought and in confident leadership and power until his sixtieth year.[25] The evidence is inconclusive; at least it has not sufficed to convince any orthodox Mohammedan.

During the next four years Mohammed more and more openly announced himself as the prophet of Allah, divinely commissioned to lead the Arab people to a new morality and a monotheistic faith. Difficulties were many. New ideas are welcomed only if promising early material advantage; and Mohammed lived in a mercantile, skeptical community, which derived some of its revenues from pilgrims coming to worship the Kaaba's many gods. Against this handicap he made some progress by offering to believers an escape from a threatened hell into a joyous and tangible paradise. He opened his house to all who would hear him—rich and poor and slaves, Arabs and Christians and Jews; and his impassioned eloquence moved a few to belief. His first convert was his aging wife; the second his cousin Ali; the third his servant Zaid, whom he had bought as a slave and had immediately freed; the fourth was his kinsman Abu Bekr, a man of high standing among the Quraish. Abu Bekr brought to the new faith five other Meccan leaders; he and these became the Prophet's six "Companions," whose memories of him would later constitute the most revered traditions of Islam. Mohammed went often to the Kaaba, accosted pilgrims, and preached the one god. The Quraish heard him at first with smiling patience, called him a half-wit, and proposed to send him, at their own expense, to a physician who might cure him of his madness.[26] But when he attacked the Kaaba worship as idolatry they rose to the protection of their income, and would have done him injury had not his uncle Abu Talib shielded him. Abu Talib would have none of the new faith, but his very fidelity to old ways required him to defend any member of his clan.

Fear of a blood feud deterred the Quraish from using violence upon Mohammed or his freemen followers. Upon converted slaves, however, they might employ dissuasive measures without offending tribal law. Several of these were jailed; some were exposed for hours, without head covering or drink, to the glare of the sun. Abu Bekr had by years of commerce saved 40,000 pieces of silver; now he used 35,000 to buy the freedom of as many converted slaves as he could; and Mohammed eased the situation by ruling that recantation under duress was forgivable. The Quraish were more disturbed by Mohammed's welcome to slaves than by his religious creed.[27] Persecution of the poorer converts continued, and with such severity that the Prophet permitted or advised their emigration to Abyssinia. The refugees were well received there by the Christian king (615).

A year later an event occurred which was almost as significant for Mohammedanism as the conversion of Paul had been for Christianity. Omar ibn al-Khattab, hitherto a most violent opponent, was won over to the new creed. He was a man of great physical strength, social power, and moral courage. His allegiance brought timely confidence to the harassed believers, and new adherents to the cause. Instead of hiding their worship in private homes they now preached it boldly in the streets. The defenders of the Kaaba gods formed a league pledged to renounce all intercourse with members of the Hashimite clan who still felt obligated to shield Mohammed. To avert conflict, many Hashimites, including Mohammed and his family, withdrew to a secluded quarter of Mecca, where Abu Talib could provide protection (615). For over two years this separation of the clans continued, until some members of the Quraish, relenting, invited the Hashimites to return to their deserted homes, and pledged them peace.

The little group of converts rejoiced, but the year 619 brought triple misfortune to Mohammed. Khadija, his most loyal supporter, and Abu Talib, his protector, died. Feeling insecure in Mecca, and discouraged by the slow increase of his followers there, Mohammed moved to Taif (620), a pleasant town sixty miles east. But Taif rejected him. Its leaders did not care to offend the merchant aristocracy of Mecca; its populace, horrified by any religious innovation, hooted him through the streets, and pelted him with stones until blood flowed from his legs. Back in Mecca, he married the widow Sauda, and betrothed himself, aged fifty, to Aisha, the pretty and petulant seven-year-old daughter of Abu Bekr.

Meanwhile his visions continued. One night, it seemed to him, he was miraculously transported in his sleep to Jerusalem; there a winged horse, Buraq, awaited him at the Wailing Wall of the Jewish Temple ruins, flew him to heaven, and back again; and by another miracle the Prophet found himself, the next morning, safe in his Mecca bed. The legend of this flight made Jerusalem a third holy city for Islam.

In the year 620 Mohammed preached to merchants who had come from Medina on pilgrimage to the Kaaba; they heard him with some acceptance, for the doctrine of monotheism, a divine messenger, and the Last Judgment were familiar to them from the creed of the Medina Jews. Returning to their city, some of them expounded the new gospel to their friends; several Jews, seeing little difference between Mohammed's teaching and their own, gave it a tentative welcome; and in 622 some seventy-three citizens of Medina came privately to Mohammed and invited him to make Medina his home. He asked would they protect him as faithfully as their own families; they vowed they would, but asked what reward they would receive should they be killed in the process. He answered, paradise.[28]

About this time Abu Sufyan, grandson of Umayya, became the head of the Meccan Quraish. Having been brought up in an odor of hatred for all descendants of Hashim, he renewed the persecution of Mohammed's followers. Possibly he had heard that the Prophet was meditating flight, and feared that Mohammed, once established in Medina, might stir it to war against Mecca and the Kaaba cult. At his urging, the Quraish commissioned some of their number to apprehend Mohammed, perhaps to kill him. Apprised of the plot, Mohammed fled with Abu Bekr to the cave of Thaur, a league distant. The Quraish emissaries sought them for three days, but failed to find them. The children of Abu Bekr brought camels, and the two men rode northward through the night, and through many days for 200 miles, until, on September 24, 622, they arrived at Medina. Two hundred Meccan adherents had preceded them in the guise of departing pilgrims, and stood at the city's gates, with the Medina converts, to welcome the Prophet. Seventeen years later the Caliph Omar designated the first day—July 16, 622 —of the Arabian year in which this Hegira (hijra—flight) took place as the official beginning of the Mohammedan era.

III. MOHAMMED IN MEDINA: 622–30

The city hitherto called Yathrib, later renamed Medinat al-Nabi or "City of the Prophet," was situated on the western edge of the central Arabian plateau. Compared with Mecca it was a climatic Eden, with hundreds of gardens, palm groves, and farms. As Mohammed rode into the town one group after another called to him, "Alight here, O Prophet! ... Abide with us!"—and with Arab persistence some caught the halter of his camel to detain him. His answer was perfect diplomacy: "The choice lies with the camel; let him advance freely"; [29] the advice quieted jealousy, and hallowed his new residence as chosen by God. Where his camel stopped, Mohammed built a mosque and two adjoining homes—one for Sauda, one for Aisha; later he added new apartments as he took new wives.

In leaving Mecca he had snapped many kinship ties; now he tried to replace bonds of blood with those of religious brotherhood in a theocratic state. To mitigate the jealousy already rampant between the Refugees (*Muhajirin*) from Mecca and the Helpers (*Ansar*) or converts in Medina, he coupled each member of the one group with a member of the other in adoptive brotherhood, and called both groups to worship in sacred union in the mosque. In the first ceremony held there he mounted the pulpit and cried in a loud voice, "Allah is most great!" The assembly burst forth in the same proclamation. Then, still standing with his back to the congregation, he bowed in prayer. He descended the pulpit backward, and at its foot he prostrated himself thrice, while continuing to pray. In these prostrations were symbolized that submission of the soul to Allah which gave to the new faith its name *Islam*—"to surrender," "to make peace"—and to its adherents the kindred name of *Muslimin* or Moslems—"the surrendering ones," "those who have made their peace with God." Turning then to the assembly, Mohammed bade it observe this ritual to the end of time; and to this day it is the form of prayer that Moslems follow, whether at the mosque, or traveling in the desert, or mosqueless in alien lands. A sermon completed the ceremony, often announcing, in Mohammed's case, a new revelation, and directing the actions and policies of the week.

For the authority of the Prophet was creating a civic rule for Medina; and more and more he was compelled to address his time and inspirations to the practical problems of social organization, daily morals, even to intertribal diplomacy and war. As in Judaism, no distinction was made between secular and religious affairs; all alike came under religious jurisdiction; he was both Caesar and Christ. But not all Medinites accepted his authority. A majority of the Arabs stood aside as "the Disaffected," viewed the new creed and its ritual skeptically, and wondered whether Mohammed was destroying their traditions and liberties, and involving them in war. Most of the Medina Jews clung to their own faith, and continued to trade with the Meccan Quraish. Mohammed drew up with these Jews a subtle concordat:

> The Jews who attach themselves to our commonwealth shall be protected from all insults and vexations; they shall have an equal right with our own people to our assistance and good offices; they . . .

shall form with the Moslems one composite nation; they shall practice
their religion as freely as the Moslems.... They shall join the Moslems
in defending Yathrib against all enemies. ... All future disputes between those who accept this charter shall be referred, under God, to
the Prophet.[30]

This agreement was soon accepted by all the Jewish tribes of Medina and
the surrounding country: the Banu-Nadhir, the Banu-Kuraiza, the Banu-
Kainuka....

The immigration of two hundred Meccan families created a food shortage
in Medina. Mohammed solved the problem as starving people do—by taking
food where it could be had. In commissioning his lieutenants to raid the caravans that passed Medina, he was adopting the morals of most Arab tribes in
his time. When the raids succeeded, four fifths of the spoils went to the
raiders, one fifth to the Prophet for religious and charitable uses; the share of
a slain raider went to his widow, and he himself at once entered paradise. So
encouraged, raids and raiders multiplied, while the merchants of Mecca,
whose economic life depended on the security of the caravans, plotted revenge. One raid scandalized Medina as well as Mecca, for it took place—and
killed a man—on the last day of Rajab, one of the sacred months when Arab
morality laid a moratorium on violence. In 623 Mohammed himself organized a band of 300 armed men to waylay a rich caravan coming from Syria
to Mecca. Abu Sufyan, who commanded the caravan, got wind of the plan,
changed his route, and sent to Mecca for help. The Quraish came 900 strong.
The miniature armies met at the Wadi * Bedr, twenty miles south of Medina.
If Mohammed had been defeated his career might have ended there and then.
He personally led his men to victory, ascribed it to Allah as a miracle confirming his leadership, and returned to Medina with rich booty and many
prisoners (January, 624). Some of these, who had been especially active in
the persecution at Mecca, were put to death; the rest were freed for lucrative
ransoms.[31] But Abu Sufyan survived, and promised revenge. "Weep not for
your slain," he told mourning relatives in Mecca, "and let no bard bewail
their fate. ... Haply the turn may come, and ye may obtain vengeance. As
for me, I will touch no oil, neither approach my wife, until I shall have gone
forth again to fight Mohammed." [32]

Strengthened by victory, Mohammed used the customary morality of
war. Asma, a Medinese poetess, having attacked him in her rhymes, Omeir,
a blind Moslem, made his way into her room, and plunged his sword so fervently into the sleeping woman's breast that it affixed her to the couch. In the
mosque the next morning Mohammed asked Omeir, "Hast thou slain
Asma?" "Yes," answered Omeir, "is there cause for apprehension?" "None,"
said the Prophet; "a couple of goats will hardly knock their heads together
for it." [33] Afak, a centenarian convert to Judaism, composed a satire on the

---

* A river bed or valley usually dry in summer.

Prophet, and was slain as he slept in his courtyard.[34] A third Medinese poet, Kab ibn al-Ashraf, son of a Jewess, abandoned Islam when Mohammed turned against the Jews; he wrote verses prodding the Quraish to avenge their defeat, and enraged the Moslems by addressing love sonnets to their wives in premature troubadour style. "Who will ease me of this man?" asked Mohammed. That evening the poet's severed head was laid at the Prophet's feet.[35] In the Moslem view these executions were a legitimate defense against treason; Mohammed was the head of a state, and had full authority to condemn.[36]

The Jews of Medina no longer liked this warlike faith, which had once seemed so flatteringly kindred to their own. They laughed at Mohammed's interpretations of their Scriptures, and his claim to be the Messiah promised by their prophets. He retaliated with revelations in which Allah charged the Jews with corrupting the Scriptures, killing the prophets, and rejecting the Messiah. Originally he had made Jerusalem the *qibla*—the point toward which Moslems should turn in prayer; in 624 he changed this to Mecca and the Kaaba. The Jews accused him of returning to idolatry. About this time a Moslem girl visited the market of the Banu-Kainuka Jews in Medina; as she sat in a goldsmith's shop a mischievous Jew pinned her skirt behind her to her upper dress. When she arose she cried out in shame at her exposure. A Moslem slew the offending Jew, whose brothers then slew the Moslem. Mohammed marshaled his followers, blockaded the Banu-Kainuka Jews in their quarter for fifteen days, accepted their surrender, and bade them, 700 in number, depart from Medina, and leave all their possessions behind.

We must admire the restraint of Abu Sufyan, who, after his unnatural vow, waited a year before going forth to battle Mohammed again. Early in 625 he led an army of 3000 men to the hill of Ohod, three miles north of Medina. Fifteen women, including Abu Sufyan's wives, accompanied the army, and stirred it to fervor with wild songs of sorrow and revenge. Mohammed could muster only a thousand warriors. The Moslems were routed; Mohammed fought bravely, received many wounds, and was carried half unconscious from the field. Abu Sufyan's chief wife Hind, whose father, uncle, and brother had been slain at Bedr, chewed the liver of the fallen Hamza— who had slain her father—and made anklets and bracelets for herself from Hamza's skin and nails.[37] Thinking Mohammed safely dead, Abu Sufyan returned in triumph to Mecca. Six months later the Prophet was sufficiently recovered to attack the Banu-Nadhir Jews, charging them with helping the Quraish and plotting against his life. After three weeks' siege they were allowed to emigrate, each family taking with it as much as a camel could carry. Mohammed appropriated some of their rich date orchards for the support of his household, and distributed the remainder among the Refugees.[38] He considered himself at war with Mecca, and felt justified in removing hostile groups from his flanks.

In 626 Abu Sufyan and the Quraish resumed the offensive, this time with 10,000 men, and with material aid from the Banu-Kuraiza Jews. Unable to meet such a force in battle, Mohammed defended Medina by having a trench dug around it. The Quraish laid siege for twenty days; then, disheartened by wind and rain, they returned to their homes. Mohammed at once led 3000 men against the Banu-Kuraiza Jews. On surrendering, they were given a choice of Islam or death. They chose death. Their 600 fighting men were slain and buried in the market place of Medina; their women and children were sold into slavery.

The Prophet had by this time become an able general. During his ten years in Medina he planned sixty-five campaigns and raids, and personally led twenty-seven. But he was also a diplomat, and knew when war should be continued by means of peace. He shared the longings of the Refugees to see their Meccan homes and families, and of both Refugees and Helpers to visit again the Kaaba that had in their youth been the hearth of their piety. As the first apostles thought of Christianity as a form and reform of Judaism, so the Moslems thought of Mohammedanism as a change and development of the ancient Meccan ritual. In 628 Mohammed sent the Quraish an offer of peace, pledging the safety of their caravans in return for permission to fulfill the rites of the annual pilgrimage. The Quraish replied that a year of peace must precede this consent. Mohammed shocked his followers by agreeing; a ten years' truce was signed; and the Prophet consoled his raiders by attacking and plundering the Khaibar Jews in their settlement six days' journey northeast of Medina. The Jews defended themselves as well as they could; ninety-three of them died in the attempt; the rest at last surrendered. They were allowed to remain and cultivate the soil, but on condition of yielding all their property, and half their future produce, to the conqueror. All the survivors were spared except Kinana, their chieftain, and his cousin, who were beheaded for hiding some of their wealth. Safiya, a seventeen-year-old Jewish damsel, betrothed to Kinana, was taken by Mohammed as an added wife.[39]

In 629 the Medina Moslems, to the number of 2000, entered Mecca peacefully; and while the Quraish, to avoid mutual irritations, retired to the hills, Mohammed and his followers made seven circuits of the Kaaba. The Prophet touched the Black Stone reverently with his staff, but led the Moslems in shouting, "There is no god but Allah alone!" Meccans were impressed by the orderly behavior and patriotic piety of the exiles; several influential Quraish, including the future generals Khalid and Amr, adopted the new faith; and some tribes in the neighboring desert offered Mohammed the pledge of their belief for the support of his arms. When he returned to Medina he calculated that he was now strong enough to take Mecca by force.

The ten years' truce had eight years to run; but Mohammed alleged that a tribe allied with the Quraish had attacked a Moslem tribe, and thereby voided the truce (630). He gathered 10,000 men, and marched to Mecca.

Abu Sufyan, perceiving the strength of Mohammed's forces, allowed him to enter unopposed. Mohammed responded handsomely by declaring a general amnesty for all but two or three of his enemies. He destroyed the idols in and around the Kaaba, but spared the Black Stone, and sanctioned the kissing of it. He proclaimed Mecca the Holy City of Islam, and decreed that no unbeliever should ever be allowed to set foot on its sacred soil. The Quraish abandoned direct opposition; and the buffeted preacher who had fled from Mecca eight years before was now master of all its life.

IV. MOHAMMED VICTORIOUS: 630–2

His two remaining years—spent mostly at Medina—were a continuing triumph. After some minor rebellions all Arabia submitted to his authority and creed. The most famous Arabian poet of the time, Kab ibn Zuhair, who had written a diatribe against him, came in person to Medina, surrendered himself to Mohammed, proclaimed himself a convert, received pardon, and composed so eloquent a poem in honor of the Prophet that Mohammed bestowed his mantle upon him.* In return for a moderate tribute the Christians of Arabia were taken under Mohammed's protection, and enjoyed full liberty of worship, but they were forbidden to charge interest on loans.[41] We are told that he sent envoys to the Greek emperor, the Persian king, and the rulers of Hira and Ghassan, inviting them to accept the new faith; apparently there was no reply. He observed with philosophic resignation the mutual destruction in which Persia and Byzantium were engaged; but he does not seem to have entertained any thought of extending his power outside of Arabia.

His days were filled with the chores of government. He gave himself conscientiously to details of legislation, judgment, and civil, religious, and military organization. One of his least inspired acts was his regulation of the calendar. This had consisted among the Arabs, as among the Jews, of twelve lunar months, with an intercalary month every three years to renew concord with the sun. Mohammed ruled that the Moslem year should always consist of twelve lunar months, of alternately thirty and twenty-nine days; as a result the Moslem calendar lost all harmony with the seasons, and gained a year upon the Gregorian calendar every thirty-two and a half years. The Prophet was not a scientific legislator; he drew up no code or digest, had no system; he issued edicts according to the occasion; if contradictions developed he smoothed them with new revelations that sternly superseded the old.[42] Even his most prosaic directives might be presented as revelations from Allah. Harassed by the necessity of adapting this lofty method to mundane affairs, his style lost something of its former eloquence and poetry; but per-

---

* It was later sold to Muawiyah for 40,000 dirhems ($3200), is still preserved by the Ottoman Turks, and is sometimes used as a national standard.[40]

haps he felt that this was small price to pay for having all his legislation bear the awesome stamp of deity. At the same time he could be charmingly modest. More than once he admitted his ignorance. He protested against being taken for more than a fallible and mortal man.[43] He claimed no power to predict the future or to perform miracles. However, he was not above using the method of revelation for very human and personal ends, as when a special message from Allah [44] sanctioned his desire to marry the pretty wife of Zaid, his adopted son.

His ten wives and two concubines have been a source of marvel, merriment, and envy to the Western world. We must continually remind ourselves that the high death rate of the male among the ancient and early medieval Semites lent to polygamy, in Semitic eyes, the aspect of a biological necessity, almost a moral obligation. Mohammed took polygamy for granted, and indulged himself in marriage with a clear conscience and no morbid sensuality. Aisha, in a tradition of uncertain authority, quoted him as saying that the three most precious things in this world are women, fragrant odors, and prayers.[45] Some of his marriages were acts of kindness to the destitute widows of followers or friends, as in the case of Omar's daughter Hafsa; some were diplomatic marriages, as in the case of Hafsa—to bind Omar to him—and the daughter of Abu Sufyan—to win an enemy. Some may have been due to a perpetually frustrated hope for a son. All his wives after Khadija were barren, which subjected the Prophet to much raillery. Of the children borne to him by Khadija only one survived him—Fatima. Mary, a Coptic slave presented to him by the Negus of Abyssinia, rejoiced him, in the last year of his life, with a son; but Ibrahim died after fifteen months.

His crowded harem troubled him with quarrels, jealousies, and demands for pin money.[46] He refused to indulge the extravagance of his wives, but he promised them paradise; and for a time he dutifully spent a night with each of them in rotation; the master of Arabia had no apartment of his own.[47] The alluring and vivacious Aisha, however, won so many attentions out of her turn that the other wives rebelled, until the matter was settled by a special revelation:

> Thou canst defer whom thou wilt of them, and receive of them whom thou wilt; and whomsoever thou desirest of those whom thou hast set aside, it is no sin for thee; that is better, that they may be comforted and not grieve, and may all be pleased with what thou givest them.[48]

Women and power were his only indulgence; for the rest he was a man of unassuming simplicity. The apartments in which he successively dwelt were cottages of unburnt brick, twelve or fourteen feet square, eight feet high, and thatched with palm branches; the door was a screen of goat or camel hair; the furniture was a mattress and pillows spread upon the floor.[49] He was often seen mending his clothes or shoes, kindling the fire, sweeping the floor,

milking the family goat in his yard, or shopping for provisions in the market.[50] He ate with his fingers, and licked them thriftily after each meal.[51] His
staple foods were dates and barley bread; milk and honey were occasional
luxuries; [52] and he obeyed his own interdiction of wine. Courteous to the
great, affable to the humble, dignified to the presumptuous, indulgent to his
aides, kindly to all but his foes—so his friends and followers describe him.[53]
He visited the sick, and joined any funeral procession that he met. He put on
none of the pomp of power, rejected any special mark of reverence, accepted
the invitation of a slave to dinner, and asked no service of a slave that he had
time and strength to do for himself.[54] Despite all the booty and revenue that
came to him, he spent little upon his family, less upon himself, much in
charity.[55]

But, like all men, he was vain. He gave considerable time to his personal
appearance—perfumed his body, painted his eyes, dyed his hair, and wore a
ring inscribed "Mohammed the Messenger of Allah"; [56] perhaps this was for
signing documents. His voice was hypnotically musical. His senses were
painfully keen; he could not bear evil odors, jangling bells, or loud talk. "Be
modest in thy bearing," he taught, "and subdue thy voice. Lo, the harshest of
all voices is that of the ass." [57] He was nervous and restless, subject to occasional melancholy, then suddenly talkative and gay. He had a sly humor.
To Abu Horairah, who visited him with consuming frequency, he suggested: "O Abu Horairah! let me alone every other day, that so affection
may increase." [58] He was an unscrupulous warrior, and a just judge. He
could be cruel and treacherous, but his acts of mercy were numberless. He
stopped many barbarous superstitions, such as blinding part of a herd to pro-
pitiate the evil eye, or tying a dead man's camel to his grave.[59] His friends
loved him to idolatry. His followers collected his spittle, or his cut hair, or
the water in which he had washed his hands, expecting from these objects
magic cures for their infirmities.[60]

His own health and energy had borne up well through all the tasks of love
and war. But at the age of fifty-nine he began to fail. A year previously, he
thought, the people of Khaibar had served him poisonous meat; since then
he had been subject to strange fevers and spells; in the dead of night, Aisha
reported, he would steal from the house, visit a graveyard, ask forgiveness
of the dead, pray aloud for them, and congratulate them on being dead.
Now, in his sixty-third year, these fevers became more exhausting. One night
Aisha complained of a headache. He complained of one also, and asked playfully would she not prefer to die first, and have the advantage of being buried
by the Prophet of Allah—to which she replied, with her customary tartness,
that he would doubtless, on returning from her grave, install a fresh bride in
her place.[61] For fourteen days thereafter the fever came and went. Three
days before his death he rose from his sickbed, walked into the mosque, saw
Abu Bekr leading the prayers in his stead, and humbly sat beside him during

the ceremony. On June 7, 632, after a long agony, he passed away, his head on Aisha's breast.

If we judge greatness by influence, he was one of the giants of history. He undertook to raise the spiritual and moral level of a people harassed into barbarism by heat and foodless wastes, and he succeeded more completely than any other reformer; seldom has any man so fully realized his dream. He accomplished his purpose through religion not only because he himself was religious, but because no other medium could have moved the Arabs of his time; he appealed to their imagination, their fears and hopes, and spoke in terms that they could understand. When he began, Arabia was a desert flotsam of idolatrous tribes; when he died it was a nation. He restrained fanaticism and superstition, but he used them. Upon Judaism, Zoroastrianism, and his native creed he built a religion simple and clear and strong, and a morality of ruthless courage and racial pride, which in a generation marched to a hundred victories, in a century to empire, and remains to this day a virile force through half the world.

CHAPTER IX

The Koran

I. FORM

THE word *qur'ân* means a reading or discourse, and is applied by Moslems to the whole, or to any section, of their sacred scriptures. Like the Jewish-Christian Bible, the Koran is an accumulation, and orthodoxy claims it to be in every syllable inspired by God. Unlike the Bible, it is proximately the work of one man, and is therefore without question the most influential book ever produced by a single hand. At various times in the last twenty-three years of his life Mohammed dictated some fragment of this revelation; each was written upon parchment, leather, palm-leaves, or bones, was read to an assembly, and was deposited in various receptacles with preceding revelations, with no special care to keep them in logical or chronological order. No collection of these fragments was made in the Prophet's lifetime; but several Moslems knew them all by heart, and served as living texts. In the year 633, when many of these *qurra* had died and were not being replaced, the Caliph Abu Bekr ordered Mohammed's chief amanuensis, Zaid ibn Thabit, to "search out the Koran and bring it together." He gathered the fragments, says tradition, "from date leaves and tablets of white stone, and the breasts of men." From Zaid's completed manuscript several copies were made; but as these had no vowels, public readers interpreted some words variously, and diverse texts appeared in different cities of the spreading Moslem realm. To stop this confusion the Caliph Othman commissioned Zaid and three Quraish scholars to revise Zaid's manuscript (651); copies of this official revision were sent to Damascus, Kufa, and Basra; and since then the text has been preserved with unparalleled purity and reverential care.

The nature of the book doomed it to repetition and disorder. Each passage taken separately fulfills an intelligible purpose—states a doctrine, dictates a prayer, announces a law, denounces an enemy, directs a procedure, tells a story, calls to arms, proclaims a victory, formulates a treaty, appeals for funds, regulates ritual, morals, industry, trade, or finance. But we are not sure that Mohammed wanted all these fragments gathered into one book. Many of them were arguments to the man or the moment; they can hardly be understood without the commentary of history and tradition; and none but the Faithful need expect to enjoy them all. The 114 chapters ("suras") are arranged not in the order of their composition, which is unknown, but in the order of their decreasing length. Since the earlier revelations were generally shorter than the later ones, the Koran is history in reverse. The Medina suras, prosaic and practical, appear first; the Mecca suras, poetic and spiritual, appear last. The Koran puts its worst foot forward, and should be begun at the end.

All the suras except the first take the form of discourses by Allah or Gabriel to Mohammed, his followers, or his enemies; this was the plan adopted by the Hebrew prophets, and in many passages of the Pentateuch. Mohammed felt that no moral code would win obedience adequate to the order and vigor of a society unless men believed the code to have come from God. The method lent itself well to a style of impassioned grandeur and eloquence, at times rivaling Isaiah.[1] Mohammed used a mode of utterance half poetry, half prose; rhythm and rhyme are pervasive in it, but irregular; and in the early Meccan suras there is a sonorous cadence and bold sweep of style that are completely felt only by those familiar with the language and sympathetic with the creed. The book is in the purest Arabic, rich in vivid similes, and too florid for Occidental taste. By general consent it is the best, as well as the first, work in the prose literature of Arabia.

II. CREED *

A religion is, among other things, a mode of moral government. The historian does not ask if a theology is true—through what omniscience might he judge? Rather he inquires what social and psychological factors combined to produce the religion; how well it accomplished the purpose of turning beasts into men, savages into citizens, and empty hearts into hopeful courage and minds at peace; how much freedom it still left to the mental development of mankind; and what was its influence in history.

Judaism, Christianity, and Islam assumed that the first necessity for a healthy society is belief in the moral government of the universe—belief that even in the heyday of evil some beneficent intelligence, however unintelligibly, guides the cosmic drama to a just and noble end. The three religions that helped to form the medieval mind agreed that this cosmic intelligence is one supreme God; Christianity added, however, that the one God appears in three distinct persons; Judaism and Islam considered this a disguised polytheism, and proclaimed with passionate emphasis the unity and singleness of God. The Koran devotes a whole sura (cxii) to this theme; the Moslem muezzin chants it daily from a hundred thousand minarets.

Allah is, first of all, the source of life and growth and all the blessings of the earth. Says Mohammed's Allah to Mohammed:

---

* In the following sketch certain passages from the Islamic traditions will be used in elucidation of the Koran, but will be specified as such, usually in the text, always in the notes.

Thou seest the earth barren; but when We send down water thereon, . . . it doth thrill and swell and put forth every lovely kind (xxii, 5). . . . Let man consider his food: how We pour water in showers, then split the earth in clefts, and cause the grain to grow therein, and grapes and green fodder, and olive and palm trees, and garden closes of thick foliage (lxxx, 24-30). . . . Look upon the fruit thereof, and upon its ripening; lo, herein, verily, are portents for a people who believe (vi, 100).

Allah is also a God of power, "Who raised up the heavens without visible support, . . . and ordereth the course of the sun and moon, . . . and spread out the earth, and placed therein firm hills and flowing streams" (xiii, 2-3). Or, in the famous "Throne Verse":

Allah! There is no God save Him, the living, the eternal! Neither slumber nor sleep overtaketh Him. Unto Him belongeth whatsoever is in the earth. Who is he that intercedeth with Him save by His leave? He knoweth that which is in front of them and that which is behind them . . . His throne includeth the heavens and the earth, and He is never weary of preserving them. He is the Sublime, the Tremendous (ii, 255).

But along with His power and justice goes everlasting mercy. Every chapter of the Koran except the ninth, like every orthodox Moslem book, begins with the solemn prelude (called *bismillah* from its first words): "In the name of God the Compassionate, the Merciful"; and though Mohammed stresses the terrors of hell, he never tires of praising the infinite mercy of his God.

Allah is an omniscient deity, and knows our most secret thoughts. "Verily We created man, and We know what his soul whispereth to him, for We are nearer to him than the vein in his neck" (l, 15). Since Allah knows the future as well as the present and the past, all things are predestined; everything has been decreed and fixed from all eternity by the divine will, even to the final fate of every soul. Like Augustine's God, Allah not only knows from eternity who will be saved, but "sendeth whom He will astray, and guideth whom He will" (xxxv, 8; lxxvi, 31). As Yahveh hardened Pharaoh's heart, so Allah says of unbelievers: "We have thrown veils over their hearts lest they should understand the Koran, and into their ears a heaviness; and if thou bid them to the guidance, yet even then they will never be guided" (xviii, 58). This—doubtless intended as a spur to belief—is a hard saying in any religion, but Mohammed thrusts it down with more than Augustinian thoroughness: "Had We pleased," says Allah, "We had certainly given to every soul its guidance. But true shall be the word that has gone forth from Me—I will surely fill hell with jinn [demons] and men together" (xxxii, 13). Once, says a tradition ascribed to Ali, "we were sitting with the Prophet, and he wrote with a stick in the ground, saying: 'There is not one among you whose sitting place is not written by God whether in fire or in paradise.' " [2] This belief in predestination made fatalism a prominent feature in Moslem thought. It was used by Mohammed and other leaders to encourage bravery in battle, since no danger could hasten, nor any caution defer, the predestined hour of each man's death. It gave the Moslem a dignified resignation against the hardships and necessities of life; but it conspired with other factors to produce, in later centuries, a pessimistic inertia in Arab life and thought.

The Koran fills out its supernatural world with angels, jinn, and a devil. The angels serve as Allah's secretaries and messengers, and record the good and wicked deeds of men. The jinn are genii, made out of fire; unlike the angels, they eat, drink, copulate, and die; some are good, and listen to the Koran (lxxii, 8); most are bad, and spend their time getting human beings into mischief. The leader of the evil jinn is Iblis, who was once a great angel, but was condemned for refusing to pay homage to Adam.

The ethic of the Koran, like that of the New Testament, rests on the fear of punishment, and the hope of reward, beyond the grave. "The life of the world is only play, and idle talk, and pageantry" (lvii, 20); only one thing is certain in it, and that is death. Some Arabs thought that death ends all, and laughed at theories of an afterlife as "naught but fables of the men of old" (xxiii, 83); but the Koran vouches for the resurrection of body and soul (lxxv, 3-4). Resurrection will not come at once; the dead will sleep till Judgment Day; but because of their sleep, their awaking will seem to them immediate. Only Allah knows when this general resurrection will take place. But certain signs will herald its coming. In those last days faith in religion will have decayed; morals will be loosened into chaos; there will be tumults and seditions, and great wars, and wise men will wish themselves dead. The final signal will be three trumpet blasts. At the first blast the sun will go out, the stars will fall, the heavens will melt, all buildings and mountains will be leveled with the earth and its plains, and the seas will dry up or burst into flame (xx, 102f). At the second blast all living creatures—angels or jinn or men—will be annihilated, except a few favored of God. Forty years later Israfel, the angel of music, will blow the third blast; then dead bodies will rise from the grave and rejoin their souls. God will come in the clouds, attended by angels bearing the books of all men's deeds, words, and thoughts. The good works will be weighed in a scale against the bad, and each man will so be judged. The inspired prophets will denounce those who rejected their message, and will intercede for those who believed. The good and bad alike will move out upon the bridge al-Sirat, which—finer than a hair and sharper than the edge of a sword—is suspended over the chasms of hell; the wicked and unbelievers will fall from it; the good will pass over it safely into paradise —not through their own merits, but only through the mercy of God. The Koran, like the Fundamentalist forms of Christianity, seems more concerned with right belief than with good conduct; a hundred times it threatens with hell those who reject Mohammed's appeal (iii, 10, 63, 131; iv, 56, 115; vii, 41; viii, 50; ix, 63, etc.). Sins being diverse in degree and kind, there are seven levels in hell, each with punishments adjusted to the offense. There will be burning heat and biting cold; even the most lightly punished will wear shoes of fire. The drink of the damned will be boiling water and filth (lvi, 40f). Perhaps Dante saw some of his visions in the Koran.

Unlike Dante's, Mohammed's picture of heaven is as vivid as his description of hell. Good believers will go there, and those who die for Allah's cause in war; and the poor will enter 500 years before the rich. Paradise is in or above the seventh astronomic heaven; it is one vast garden, watered with pleasant rivers and shaded with spreading trees; the blessed there will be dressed in silk brocades, and be adorned with gems; [3] they will recline on couches, be served by handsome youths, and eat fruit from trees bowing down to fill their hands; there will be rivers of milk, honey, and wine; the saved will drink wine (forbidden on earth) from silver goblets, and will suffer no aftereffects.[4] By the mercy of Allah there will be no speeches at these heavenly banquets (lxxviii, 35); instead there will be virgins "never yet touched by man or jinn, . . . in beauty like the jacinth and coral stone, . . . with swelling bosoms but modest gaze, with eyes as fair and pure as sheltered eggs," [5] and bodies made of musk, and free from the imperfections and indignities of mortal flesh. Each blessed male will have seventy-two of these houris for his reward, and neither age nor weariness nor death shall mar the loveliness of these maidens, or their comrades' bliss (xliv, 56). Since pious and believing women will also enter paradise, some confusion might result, but such difficulties would not be insuperable to men accustomed to polygamy. To these sensual pleasures Mohammed added certain spiritual delights: some of the saved will prefer to recite the Koran; and all of them will experience the supreme ecstasy of beholding Allah's face. "And round about them shall go children, never growing old." [6]

Who could reject such a revelation?

III. ETHICS

In the Koran, as in the Talmud, law and morals are one; the secular is included in the religious, and every commandment is of God. Here are rules not only for manners and hygiene, marriage and divorce, and the treatment of children, slaves, and animals, but also for commerce and politics, interest and debts, contracts and wills, industry and finance, crime and punishment, war and peace.

Mohammed did not disdain commerce—he was its graduate; even in his sovereign Medina days, says a tradition, he bought wholesale, sold retail, and made profit without qualm; sometimes he acted as auctioneer.[7] His language was rich in commercial metaphors; he promised worldly success to good Moslems (ii, 5), and offered heaven as a bargain for a little belief. He threatened hell to lying or cheating merchants; denounced monopolists, and speculators who "keep back grain to sell at a high rate"; [8] and bade the employer "give the laborer his wage before his perspiration dries." [9] He prohibited the taking or giving of interest (ii, 275; iii, 130). No reformer ever more actively taxed the rich to help the poor. Every will was expected to leave something to the poor; if a man died intestate his natural heirs were directed to give a part of their inheritance to charity (iv, 8). Like his religious contemporaries he accepted slavery as a law of nature, but did what he could to mitigate its burdens and its sting.[10]

In like manner he improved the position of woman in Arabia while accepting her legal subjection with equanimity. We find in him the usual quips of the male resenting his enslavement to desire; almost like a Father of the Church he speaks of women as man's supreme calamity, and suspects that most of them will go to hell.[11] He made his own Salic law against women rulers.[12] He allowed women to come to the mosque, but believed that "their homes are better for them"; [13] yet when they came to his services he treated them kindly, even if they brought suckling babes; if, says an amiable tradition, he heard a child cry, he would shorten his sermon lest the mother be inconvenienced.[14] He put an end to the Arab practice of infanticide (xvii, 31). He placed woman on the same footing with man in legal processes and in financial independence; she might follow any legitimate profession, keep her earnings, inherit property, and dispose of her belongings at will (iv, 4, 32). He abolished the Arab custom of transmitting women as property from father to son. Women were to inherit half as much as the male heirs, and were not to be disposed of against their will.[15] A verse in the Koran (xxxiii, 33) seemed to establish purdah: "Stay in your houses, and do not display your finery"; but the emphasis here was on modesty of dress; and a tradition quotes the Prophet as saying to women, "It is permitted you to go out for your needs." [16] With regard to his own wives he asked his followers to speak to them only from behind a curtain.[17] Subject to these restrictions, we find Moslem women moving about freely and unveiled in the Islam of his time, and a century thereafter.

Morals are in part a function of climate: probably the heat of Arabia intensified sexual passion and precocity, and some allowance should be made for men in perpetual heat. Moslem laws were designed to reduce temptation outside of marriage, and increase opportunity within. Premarital continence was strictly enjoined (xxiv, 33), and fasting was recommended as an aid.[18] The consent of both parties was required for marriage; that agreement, duly witnessed, and sealed with a dowry from bridegroom to bride, sufficed for legal marriage, whether the parents consented or not.[19] A Moslem male was allowed to marry a Jewish or Christian woman, but not an idolatress—i.e., a non-Christian polytheist. As in Judaism, celibacy was considered sinful, marriage obligatory and pleasing to God (xxiv, 32). Mohammed accepted polygamy to balance a high death rate in both sexes, the length of maternal nursing, and the early waning of reproductive powers in hot climes; but he limited the number of permitted wives to four, allowing himself a special dispensation. He forbade concubinage (lxx, 29-31), but held it preferable to marriage with an idolatress (ii, 221).

Having allowed the male so many outlets for desire, the Koran punished adultery with a hundred stripes on each sinner (xxiv, 2). But when, on flimsy grounds, Mohammed's favorite wife, Aisha, was suspected of adultery, and gossip persistently besmirched her name, he had a trance and issued a revelation requiring four witnesses to prove adultery; moreover, "those who accuse honorable women, but bring not four witnesses, shall be scourged with eighty stripes, and their testimony shall never again be accepted" (xxiv, 4). Accusations of adultery were thereafter rare.

Divorce was permitted to the male by the Koran, as by the Talmud, on almost any ground; the wife might divorce her husband by returning her dowry to him (ii, 229). While accepting the pre-Islamic liberty of divorce for the male, Mohammed discouraged it, saying that nothing was so displeasing to God; arbiters should be appointed "one from his folk and one from hers," and every effort made at reconciliation (iv, 35). Three successive declarations, at monthly intervals, were required to make a divorce legal; and to compel careful thought about it, the husband was not allowed to remarry his divorced wife until after she had been married and divorced by another man.[20] The husband must not go in to his wife during her periods; she was not to be considered "unclean" at that time, but she must purify herself ritually before resuming cohabitation. Women are "a tilth" to man—a field to be cultivated; it is an obligation of the man to beget children. The wife should recognize the superior intelligence and therefore superior authority of the male; she must obey her husband; if she rebels he should "banish her to a bed apart, and scourge her" (iv, 34). "Every woman who dieth, and her husband is pleased with her, shall enter paradise" (iv, 35).

Here as elsewhere the legal disabilities of women barely matched the power of their eloquence, their tenderness, and their charms. Omar, the future caliph, rebuked his wife for speaking to him in a tone that he considered disrespectful. She assured him that this was the tone in which his daughter Hafsa, and the other wives of Mohammed, spoke to the Prophet of Allah. Omar went at once and remonstrated with Hafsa and another of Mohammed's wives; he was told to mind his business, and he retired in dismay. Hearing of all this, Mohammed laughed heartily.[21] Like other Moslems he quarreled now and then with his wives, but he did not cease to be fond of them, or to speak of women with becoming sentiment. "The most valuable thing in the world," he is reported to have said, "is a virtuous woman."[22]

Twice in the Koran he reminded Moslems that their mothers had carried them with pain, brought them forth with pain, nursed them for twenty-four or thirty months.[23] "Paradise," he said, "is at the foot of the mother."[24]

IV. RELIGION AND THE STATE

The greatest problems of the moralist are first to make co-operation attractive, and then to determine the size of the whole or group with which he will counsel pre-eminent co-operation. A perfect ethic would ask the paramount co-operation of every part with the greatest whole—with the universe itself, or its essential life and order, or God; on that plane religion and morality would be one. But morality is the child of custom and the grandchild of compulsion; it develops co-operation only within aggregates equipped with force. Therefore all actual morality has been group morality.

Mohammed's ethic transcended the limits of the tribe in which he was born, but was imprisoned in the creedal group which he formed. After his victory in Mecca he restricted, but could not quite abolish, the plundering raids of tribe against tribe, and gave to all Arabia, implicitly to all Islam, a new sense of unity, a wider orbit of co-operation and loyalty. "The believers are naught else than brothers" (xlix, 10). Distinction of rank or race, so strong among the tribes, was diminished by similarity of belief. "If a negro slave is appointed to rule you, hear and obey him, though his head be like a dried grape."[25] It was a noble conception that made one people of diverse nations scattered over the continents; this is the glory of both Christianity and Islam.

But to that transcendent love, in both religions, corresponded an astringent antagonism to all who would not believe. "Take not the Jews and the Christians for friends. . . . Choose not your fathers nor your brothers for friends if they take pleasure in disbelief rather than in faith" (v, 51, 55; ix, 23). Mohammed interpreted these principles with some moderation. "Let there be no violence in religion. If they embrace Islam they are surely directed; but if they turn their backs, verily to thee belongs preaching only."[26] "Give a respite to the disbelievers. Deal thou gently with them for a while" (xxxvi, 17). But against Arab unbelievers who did not peaceably submit Mohammed preached the jihad or holy war, a crusade in the name of Allah. After the war with the Quraish had begun, and when the "sacred months" of truce were past, enemy unbelievers were to be killed wherever found (ix, 5). "But if any of the idolaters seeketh thy protection, then protect him that he may hear the word of Allah. . . . If they repent and establish worship" (accept Islam), "then leave their way free" (ix, 5-6). "Kill not the old man who cannot fight, nor young children, nor women."[27] Every able-bodied male in Islam must join in the holy war. "Lo, Allah loveth those who battle for His cause. . . . I swear by Allah . . . that marching about, morning and evening, to fight for religion is better than the world and everything in it; and verily the standing of one of you in the line of battle is better than supererogatory prayers performed in your house for sixty years." [28] This war ethic, however, is no general incitement to war. "Fight in the way of Allah against those who fight against you, but begin not hostilities. Allah loveth not aggressors" (ii, 90). Mohammed accepts the laws of war as practiced by the Christian nations of his time, and wages war against Quraish unbelievers holding Mecca precisely as Urban II would preach a crusade against Moslems holding Jerusalem.

The inevitable gap between theory and practice seems narrower in Islam than in other faiths. The Arabs were sensual, and the Koran accepted polygamy; otherwise the ethic of the Koran is as sternly puritan as Cromwell's; only the uninformed think of Mohammedanism as a morally easy creed. The Arabs were prone to vengeance and retaliation, and the Koran made no pretense at returning good for evil. "And one who attacks you, attack him in like manner. . . . Whoso defendeth himself after he hath suffered wrong, there is no way" (of blame) "against them" (ii, 194; xlii, 41). It is a virile ethic, like that of the Old Testament; it stresses the masculine, as Christianity stressed the feminine, virtues. No other religion in history has so consistently tried to make men strong, or so generally succeeded. "O ye who believe! Endure! Outdo all others in endurance!" (iii, 200). Thus also spake Nietzsche's Zarathustra.

Revered to the edge of idolatry, copied and illuminated with loving skill and care, used as the book from which the Moslem learned to read, and then again as the core and summit of his education, the Koran has for thirteen centuries filled the memory, aroused the imagination, molded the character, and perhaps chilled the intellect, of hundreds of millions of men. It gave to simple souls the simplest, least mystical, least ritualistic, of all creeds, free from idolatry and sacerdotalism. Its message raised the moral and cultural level of its followers, promoted social order and unity, inculcated hygiene, lessened superstition and cruelty, bettered the condition of slaves, lifted the lowly to dignity and pride, and produced among Moslems (barring the revels of some caliphs) a degree of sobriety and temperance unequaled elsewhere in the white man's world. It gave men an uncomplaining acceptance of the hardships and limitations of life, and at the same time stimulated them to the most astonishing expansion in history. And it defined religion in terms that any orthodox Christian or Jew might accept:

> Righteousness is not that ye turn your faces to the East or to the West, but righteousness is this: whosoever believeth in God, and the Last Day, and the angels, and the Book, and the Prophets; and whosoever, for the love of God, giveth of his wealth unto his kindred, unto orphans, and the poor, and the wayfarer, and to the beggar, and for

the release of captives; and whoso observeth prayer . . . and, when
they have covenanted, fulfill their covenant; and who are patient in
adversity and hardship and in the times of violence: these are the
righteous, these are they who believe in the Lord! (ii, 177).

V. THE SOURCES OF THE KORAN

As the style of the Koran is modeled on that of the Hebrew prophets, so
its contents are largely an adaptation of Judaic doctrines, tales, and themes.
The Koran, which excoriates the Jews, is the sincerest flattery they have ever
received. Its basic ideas—monotheism, prophecy, faith, repentance, the Last
Judgment, heaven and hell—seem Jewish in proximate origin, even in form
and dress. It deviated from Judaism chiefly in insisting that the Messiah had
come. Mohammed frankly reports contemporary accusations that his revelations were "nothing but a fraud which he hath fabricated, and other people
have helped him therein, . . . dictating to him morning and evening" (xxv, 5;
xvi, 105). He generously accepts the Hebrew and Christian Scriptures as
divinely revealed (iii, 48). God has given man 104 revelations, of which only
four have been preserved—the Pentateuch to Moses, the Psalms to David, the
Gospel to Jesus, the Koran to Mohammed; whoso rejects any one of these
is, in Mohammed's view, an infidel. But the first three have suffered such
corruption that they can no longer be trusted; and the Koran now replaces
them.[29] There have been many inspired prophets—e.g., Adam, Noah, Abraham, Moses, Enoch, Christ, but last and greatest, Mohammed. From Adam
to Christ Mohammed accepts all the narratives of the Bible, but occasionally
amends them to save the divine honor; so God did not really let Jesus die on
the cross (iv, 157). The Prophet alleges the agreement of the Koran with the
Bible as proof of his divine mission, and interprets various Biblical passages[30]
as predicting his own birth and apostolate.

From the Creation to the Last Judgment he uses Jewish ideas. Allah is
Yahveh; *Allah* is a contraction of *al-Ilah*, an old Kaaba god; a kindred word
was used in various forms in divers Semitic languages to express divinity; so
the Jews used *Elohim*, and Christ on the cross appealed to *Eli*. Both Allah
and Yahveh are gods of compassion, but they are also stern and warlike deities, capable of many human passions, and resolved to have no other god
besides them. The Shema' Yisrael of the Jewish ritual, affirming the unity of
God, is repeated in the first article of Moslem belief—"There is no god but
Allah." The Koranic refrain that Allah is "gracious and compassionate"
echoes the same frequent phrase in the Talmud.[31] The designation of Allah
as *Rahman*, the merciful, recalls the rabbinical use of *Rahmana* for Yahveh
in the Talmudic age.[32] The Talmud loves to say, "The Holy One, Blessed
be He"; Moslem literature follows with the oft-repeated words, "Allah" (or

"Mohammed"), "Blessed be He." Apparently the Jews who acquainted the Prophet with the Bible also gave him snatches of the Talmud; a hundred passages in the Koran echo the Mishna and the Gemaras.[33] The teachings of the Koran about angels, the resurrection, and heaven follow the Talmud rather than the Old Testament. Stories that make up a fourth of the Koran can be traced to haggadic (illustrative) elements in the Talmud.[34] Where the Koran narratives vary from the Biblical accounts (as in the story of Joseph) they usually accord with variations already existing in the haggadic literature of the pre-Moslem Jews.[35]

From the Mishna and halakah—the oral law of the Jews—Mohammed seems to have derived many elements of ritual, even minute details of diet and hygiene.[36] Ceremonial purification before prayer is enjoined, and the hands may be washed with sand if no water can be had—precisely the rabbinical formula. The Jewish institution of the Sabbath pleased Mohammed; he adopted it with a distinction in making Friday a day of prayer for the Moslems. The Koran, like the Mosaic Law, forbids the eating of blood, or the flesh of swine or dogs, or of any animal that has died of itself, or has been killed by another animal, or has been offered to an idol (v, 3; vi, 146); the Koran, however, allows the eating of camel's flesh, which Moses forbade, but which was sometimes the only flesh food available in the desert. The Moslem method of fasting followed the Hebrew model.[37] The Jews were bidden by their rabbis to pray thrice daily, facing toward Jerusalem and the Temple, and to prostrate themselves with forehead to the ground; Mohammed adapted these rules to Islam. The first chapter of the Koran, which is the basic prayer of Islam, is essentially Judaic. The lovely greeting of the Hebrew—*Sholom aleichem*—parallels the noble "Peace be with you" of Islam. Finally, the Talmudic heaven, like the Koranic paradise, is one of frankly physical, as well as ecstatically spiritual, delights.

Some of these elements in creed and practice may have been a common heritage of the Semites; some of them—angels, devils, Satan, heaven, hell, the resurrection, the Last Judgment—had been taken by the Jews from Babylonia or Persia, and may have gone directly from Persia to Islam. In Zoroastrian, as in Mohammedan, eschatology, the resurrected dead must walk upon a perilous bridge over a deep abyss; the wicked fall into hell, the good pass into a paradise where they enjoy, among other dainties, the society of women (houris) whose beauty and ardor will last forever. To Jewish theology, ethics, and ritual, and Persian eschatology, Mohammed added Arab demonology, pilgrimage, and the Kaaba ceremony, and made Islam.

His debt to Christianity was slighter. If we may judge from the Koran, he knew Christianity very imperfectly, its Scriptures only at second hand, its theology chiefly in Persian Nestorian form. His earnest preaching of repentance in fear of the coming Judgment has a Christian tinge. He confuses Mary (Heb. Miriam) the mother of Jesus with Miriam the sister of Moses, and—

misled by the rising worship of Mary in Christendom—thinks that Christians look upon her as a goddess forming a trinity with the Father and Christ (v, 116). He accepts several uncanonical legends about Jesus and the Virgin Birth (iii, 47; xxi, 91). He modestly acknowledges the miracles of Jesus, while making no claim to such powers for himself (iii, 48; v, 110). Like the Docetists, he thinks that God put a phantom in Christ's place on the cross, and drew Him up to heaven unhurt. But Mohammed stopped short of making Jesus the Son of God. "Far is it removed from Allah's transcendent majesty that He should have a son" (iv, 171). He begs "the people of the Scripture" to "come to an agreement between us and you, that we shall worship none but Allah" (iii, 64).

All in all, despite deprecating intimacy with them, Mohammed was well disposed toward Christians. "Consort in the world kindly with Christians" (xxxi, 15). Even after his quarrel with the Jews he counseled toleration toward the "people of the Book"—i.e., the Jews and the Christians.* Mohammedanism, though as fanatic as any faith, concedes that others than Moslems may be saved (v, 73), and requires its followers to honor the "Law" (the Old Testament), the Gospel, and the Koran as all constituting "the Word of God"; here was a refreshing breadth of view. Mohammed adjures the Jews to obey their Law, Christians to obey the Gospel (v, 72); but he invites them to accept also the Koran as God's latest pronouncement. The earlier revelations had been corrupted and abused; now the new one would unite them, cleanse them, and offer all mankind an integrating, invigorating faith.

Three books made and almost filled the Age of Faith: the Bible, the Talmud, the Koran—as if to say that in the rebarbarization of the Roman Empire only a supernatural ethic could restore order to society and the soul. All three books were Semitic, and overwhelmingly Judaic. The drama of medieval history would be the spiritual competition of these Scriptures and the bloody conflict of their creeds.

---

* The term and policy were later extended to the Persians as also having a sacred book, the Avesta.

CHAPTER X

The Sword of Islam

632-1058

I. THE SUCCESSORS: 632-60

MOHAMMED had appointed no successor to his power, but he had chosen Abu Bekr (573-624) to conduct the prayers in the Medina mosque; and after some turmoil and rivalry this mark of preference persuaded the Moslem leaders to elect Abu Bekr the first Caliph of Islam. *Khalifa* ("representative") was at first a designation rather than a title; the official title was *amir al-muminin*, "Commander of the Faithful." Ali, cousin and son-in-law of Mohammed, was disappointed by the choice, and for six months withheld allegiance. Abbas, uncle of both Ali and Mohammed, shared this resentment. From this inaugural disagreement came a dozen wars, an Abbasid dynasty, and a sectarian division that still agitates the Moslem world.

Abu Bekr was now fifty-nine; short, thin, and strong, with scanty hair, and white beard dyed red; simple and abstemious, kindly but resolute; attending personally to details of administration and judgment, and never resting till justice was done; serving without pay till his people overruled his austerity; and then, in his will, returning to the new state the stipends it had paid him. The tribes of Arabia mistook his modest manners for weakness of will; only superficially and reluctantly converted to Islam, they now ignored it, and refused to pay the tithes that Mohammed had laid upon them. When Abu Bekr insisted, they marched upon Medina. The Caliph improvised an army overnight, led it out before dawn, and routed the rebels (632). Khalid ibn al-Walid, the most brilliant and ruthless of Arab generals, was sent out to bring back the turbulent peninsula to orthodoxy, repentance, and tithes.

This internal dissension may have formed one of the many conditions that led to the Arab conquest of western Asia. No thought of so extended an enterprise seems to have occurred to the Moslem leaders at Abu Bekr's accession. Some Arab tribes in Syria rejected Christianity and Byzantium, stood off the imperial armies, and asked for Moslem help. Abu Bekr sent them reinforcements, and encouraged anti-Byzantine sentiment in Arabia; here was an external issue that might weld internal unity. The Bedouins, tired of starvation and used to war, enlisted readily in these apparently limited campaigns; and before they realized it the skeptics of the desert were dying enthusiastically for Islam.

Many causes produced the Arab expansion. There were economic causes: the decline of orderly government in the century before Mohammed had allowed the irrigation system of Arabia to decay; [1] the lowered yield of the soil menaced the growing population; hunger for arable land may have moved the Moslem regiments. [2] Political causes operated: both Byzantium and Persia, exhausted by war and mutual devastation, were in a tempting decline; in their provinces taxation rose while administration lapsed and protection failed. Racial affinities played a part: Syria and Mesopotamia contained Arab tribes that found no difficulty in accepting first the rule, then the faith, of the Arab invaders. Religious considerations entered: Byzantine oppression of Monophysites, Nestorians, and other sects had alienated a large minority of the Syrian and Egyptian population, even some of the imperial garrisons. As the conquest proceeded, the role of religion mounted; the Moslem leaders were passionate disciples of Mohammed, prayed even more than they fought, and in time inspired their followers with a fanaticism that accepted death in a holy war as an open sesame to paradise. Morale factors were involved: Christian ethics and monasticism had reduced in the Near East that readiness for war which characterized Arab custom and Moslem teaching. The Arab troops were more rigorously disciplined and more ably led; they were inured to hardship and rewarded with spoils; they could fight on empty stomachs, and depended upon victory for their meals. But they were not barbarians. "Be just," ran Abu Bekr's proclamation; "be valiant; die rather than yield; be merciful; slay neither old men, nor women, nor children. Destroy no fruit trees, grain, or cattle. Keep your word, even to your enemies. Molest not those religious persons who live retired from the world, but compel the rest of mankind to become Moslems or pay us tribute. If they refuse these terms, slay them." [3] The choice given the enemy was not Islam or the sword; it was Islam or tribute or the sword. Finally, there were military causes of the invasion: as the triumphant Arab armies swelled with hungry or ambitious recruits, the problem arose of giving them new lands to conquer, if only to provide them with food and pay. The advance created its own momentum; each victory required another, until the Arab conquests—more rapid than the Roman, more lasting than the Mongol—summed up to the most amazing feat in military history.

Early in 633 Khalid, having "pacified" Arabia, was invited by a nomad frontier tribe to join it in raiding a neighboring community across the border in Iraq. Restless in idleness or peace, Khalid and 500 of his men accepted the invitation, and in conjunction with 2500 tribesmen invaded Persian soil. We do not know if this adventure had received the consent of Abu Bekr; apparently he accepted the results philosophically. Khalid captured Hira, and sent the Caliph enough booty to elicit from him the famous phrase: "Surely the womb is exhausted. Woman will no more bear a Khalid!" [4] Woman had now become a substantial item in the thought and spoils of the victors. At the siege of Emesa a young Arab leader fired the zeal of his troops by describing the beauty of the Syrian girls. When Hira surrendered, Khalid stipulated that a lady, Kermat, should be given to an Arab soldier who claimed that Mohammed had promised her to him. The lady's family mourned, but Kermat took the matter lightly. "The fool saw me in my youth," she said, "and has forgotten that youth does not last forever." The soldier, seeing her, agreed, and freed her for a little gold.[5]

Before Khalid could enjoy his victory at Hira a message came to him from the Caliph, sending him to the rescue of an Arab force threatened by an over-whelmingly superior Greek army near Damascus. Between Hira and Damascus lay five days' march of waterless desert. Khalid gathered camels, and made them drink plentifully; en route the soldiers drew water from slain camels' bellies, and fed their horses on camels' milk. This commissary was exhausted when Khalid's troops reached the main Arab army on the Yarmuk River sixty miles southwest of Damascus. There, say the Moslem historians, 40,000 (25,000?) Arabs defeated 240,000 (50,000?) Greeks in one of the innumerable decisive battles of history (634). The Emperor Heraclius had risked all Syria on one engagement; henceforth Syria was to be the base of a spreading Moslem empire.

While Khalid was leading his men to victory a dispatch informed him that Abu Bekr had died (634), and that the new caliph, Omar, wished him to yield his command to Abu Obeida; Khalid concealed the message till the battle was won. Omar (Umar Abu Hafsa ibn al-Khattab) (582–644) had been the chief adviser and support of Abu Bekr, and had earned such repute that no one protested when the dying Caliph named him as successor. Yet Omar was the very opposite of his friend: tall, broad-shouldered, and passionate; agreeing with him only in frugal simplicity, bald head, and dyed beard. Time and responsibility had matured him into a rare mixture of hot temper and cool judgment. Having beaten a Bedouin unjustly, he begged the Bedouin—in vain—to inflict an equal number of strokes upon him. He was a severe puritan, demanding strict virtue of every Moslem; he carried about with him a whip wherewith he beat any Mohammedan whom he caught infringing the Koranic code.[6] Tradition reports that he scourged his son to death for repeated drunkenness.[7] Moslem historians tell us that he owned but one shirt and one mantle, patched and repatched; that he lived on barley bread and dates, and drank nothing but water; that he slept on a bed of palm leaves, hardly better than a hair shirt; and that his sole concern was the propagation of the faith by letters and by arms. When a Persian satrap came to pay homage to Omar he found the conqueror of the East asleep among beggars on the steps of the Medina mosque.[8] We cannot vouch for the truth of these tales.

Omar had deposed Khalid because the "Sword of God" had repeatedly tarnished his courage with cruelty. The invincible general took his demotion with something finer than bravery: he put himself unreservedly at the disposal of Abu Obeida, who had the wisdom to follow his advice in strategy and oppose his ferocity in victory. The Arabs, ever skillful horsemen, proved superior to the cavalry, as well as the infantry, of the Persians and the Greeks; nothing in early medieval armament could withstand their weird battle cries, their bewildering maneuvers, their speed; and they took care to choose level battle grounds favorable to the tactical movements of their mounts. In 635 Damascus was taken, in 636 Antioch, in 638 Jerusalem; by 640 all Syria was in Moslem hands; by 641 Persia and Egypt were conquered. The Patriarch Sophronius agreed to surrender Jerusalem if the Caliph would come in person to ratify the terms of capitulation. Omar consented, and traveled from Medina in stately simplicity, armed with a sack of corn, a bag of dates, a gourd of water, and a wooden dish. Khalid, Abu Obeida, and other leaders of the Arab army went out to welcome him. He was displeased by the finery of their raiment and the ornate trappings of their steeds; he flung a handful of gravel upon them, crying: "Begone! Is it thus attired that ye come out to meet me?" He received Sophronius with kindness and courtesy, imposed an easy tribute on the vanquished, and confirmed the Christians in the peaceful possession of all their shrines. Christian historians relate that he accompanied the Patriarch in a tour of Jerusalem. During his ten days' stay he chose the site for the mosque that was to be known by his name. Then, learning that the people of Medina were fretting lest he make Jerusalem the citadel of Islam, he returned to his modest capital.

Once Syria and Persia were securely held, a wave of migration set in from Arabia to north and east, comparable to the migration of Germanic tribes into the conquered provinces of Rome. Women joined in the movement, but not in numbers adequate to Arab zeal; the conquering males rounded out their harems with Christian and Jewish concubines, and reckoned the children of such unions legitimate. By such industry and reckoning the "Arabs" in Syria and Persia were half a million by 644. Omar forbade the conquerors to buy or till land; he hoped that outside of Arabia they would remain a military caste, amply supported by the state, but vigorously preserving their martial qualities. His prohibitions were ignored after his death, and almost nullified by his generosity in life; he divided the spoils of victory eighty per cent to the army, twenty per cent to the nation. The minority of men, having the majority of brains, soon gathered in the majority of goods in this rapidly growing Arab wealth. The Quraish nobles built rich palaces in Mecca and Medina; Zobeir had palaces in several cities, with 1000 horses and 10,000 slaves; Abd-er-Rahman had 1000 camels, 10,000 sheep, 400,000 dinars ($1,912,000). Omar saw with sorrow the decline of his people into luxury.

A Persian slave struck him down while Omar led the prayers in the mosque (644). Unable to persuade Abd-er-Rahman to succeed him, the dying Caliph appointed six men to choose his successor. They named the weakest of their number, perhaps in the hope that they would rule him. Othman ibn

Affan was an old man of kindly intent; he rebuilt and beautified the Medina mosque, and supported the generals who now spread Moslem arms to Herat and Kabul, Balkh and Tiflis, and through Asia Minor to the Black Sea. But it was his misfortune to be a loyal member of that aristocratic Umayyad clan which in early days had been among Mohammed's proudest foes. The Umayyads flocked to Medina to enjoy the fruits of their relationship to the old Caliph. He could not refuse their importunity; soon a dozen lucrative offices warmed the hands of men who scorned the puritanism and simplicity of pious Moslems. Islam, relaxing in victory, divided into ferocious factions: "Refugees" from Mecca vs. "Helpers" from Medina; the ruling cities of Mecca and Medina vs. the fast-growing Moslem cities of Damascus, Kufa, and Basra; the Quraish aristocracy vs. the Bedouin democracy; the Prophet's Hashimite clan led by Ali vs. the Umayyad clan led by Muawiya—son of Mohammed's chief enemy Abu Sufyan, but now governor of Syria. In 654 a converted Jew began to preach a revolutionary doctrine at Basra: that Mohammed would return to life, that Ali was his only legitimate successor, that Othman was a usurper and his appointees a set of godless tyrants. Driven from Basra, the rebel went to Kufa; driven from Kufa, he fled to Egypt, where his preaching found passionate audience. Five hundred Egyptian Moslems made their way to Medina as pilgrims, and demanded Othman's resignation. Refused, they blockaded him in his palace. Finally they stormed into his room and killed him as he sat reading the Koran (656).

The Umayyad leaders fled from Medina, and the Hashimite faction at last raised Ali to the caliphate. He had been in his youth a model of modest piety and energetic loyalty; he was now fifty-five, bald and stout, genial and charitable, meditative and reserved; he shrank from a drama in which religion had been displaced by politics, and devotion by intrigue. He was asked to punish Othman's assassins, but delayed till they escaped. He called for the resignation of Othman's appointees; most of them refused; instead of resigning, Muawiya exhibited in Damascus the bloody garments of Othman, and the fingers that Othman's wife had lost in trying to shield him. The Quraish clan, dominated by the Umayyads, rallied to Muawiya; Zobeir and Talha, "Companions" of the Prophet, revolted against Ali, and laid rival claims to the caliphate. Aisha, proud widow of Mohammed, left Medina for Mecca, and joined in the revolt. When the Moslems of Basra declared for the rebels, Ali appealed to the veterans at Kufa, and promised to make Kufa his capital if they would come to his aid. They came; the two armies met at Khoraiba in southern Iraq in the Battle of the Camel—called so because Aisha commanded her troops from her camel seat. Zobeir and Talha were defeated and killed; Aisha was escorted with all courtesy to her home in Medina; and Ali transferred his government to Kufa, near the ancient Babylon.

But in Damascus Muawiya raised another rebel force. He was a man of the world, who privately put little stock in Mohammed's revelation; religion seemed to him an economical substitute for policemen, but no aristocrat would let it interfere with his enjoyment of the world. In effect his war against Ali sought to restore the Quraish oligarchy to the power and leadership that had been taken from them by Mohammed. Ali's reorganized forces met Muawiya's army at Siffin on the Euphrates (657); Ali was prevailing when Muawiya's general Amr ibn al-As raised copies of the Koran on the points of his soldiers' lances, and demanded arbitration "according to the word of Allah"—presumably by rules laid down in the sacred book. Yielding to the insistence of his troops, Ali agreed; arbitrators were chosen, and were allowed six months to decide the issue, while the armies returned to their homes.

Part of Ali's men now turned against him, and formed a separate army and sect as *Khariji* or Seceders; they argued that the caliph should be elected and removable by the people; some of them were religious anarchists who rejected all government except that of God;[9] all of them denounced the worldliness and luxury of the new ruling classes in Islam. Ali tried to win them back by suasion, but failed; their piety became fanaticism, and issued in acts of disorder and violence; finally Ali declared war upon them and suppressed them. In due time the arbitrators agreed that both Ali and Muawiya should withdraw their claims to the caliphate. Ali's representative announced the deposition of Ali; Amr, however, instead of making a similar withdrawal for Muawiya, proclaimed him Caliph. Amid this chaos a Kharijite came upon Ali near Kufa, and pierced his brain with a poisoned sword (661). The spot where Ali died became a holy place to the Shia sect, which worshiped him as the Wali or vicar of Allah, and made his grave a goal of pilgrimage as sacred as Mecca itself.

The Moslems of Iraq chose Ali's son Hasan to succeed him; Muawiya marched upon Kufa; Hasan submitted, received a pension from Muawiya, retired to Mecca, married a hundred times, and died at forty-five (669), poisoned by the Caliph or a jealous wife. Muawiya received the reluctant allegiance of all Islam; but for his own security, and because Medina was now too far from the center of Moslem population and power, he made Damascus his capital. The Quraish aristocracy, through Abu Sufyan's son, had won their war against Mohammed; the theocratic "republic" of the Successors became a secular hereditary monarchy. Semitic rule replaced the dominance of Persians and Greeks in western Asia, expelled from Asia a European control that had lasted a thousand years, and gave to the Near East, Egypt, and North Africa the form that in essence they would keep for thirteen centuries.

II. THE UMAYYAD CALIPHATE: 661–750

Let us do Muawiya justice. He had won his power first through appointment as governor of Syria by the virtuous Omar; then by leading the reaction against the murder of Othman; then by intrigues so subtle that force had seldom to be used. "I apply not my sword," he said, "where my lash suffices, nor my lash where my tongue is enough. And even if there be one hair binding me to my fellow men I do not let it break; when they pull I loosen, and if they loosen I pull." [10] His path to power was less incarnadined than most of those that have opened new dynasties.

Like other usurpers, he felt the need to hedge his throne with splendor and ceremony. He took as his model the Byzantine emperors, who had taken as their model the Persian King of Kings; the persistence of that monarchical pattern from Cyrus to our time suggests its serviceability in the government and exploitation of an unlettered population. Muawiya felt his methods justified by the prosperity that came under his rule, the quieting of tribal strife, and the consolidation of Arab power from the Oxus to the Nile. Thinking the hereditary principle the sole alternative to chaotic struggles for an elective caliphate, he declared his son Yezid heir apparent, and exacted an oath of fealty to him from all the realm.

Nevertheless, when Muawiya died (680), a war of succession repeated the early history of his reign. The Moslems of Kufa sent word to Husein, son of Ali, that if he would come to them and make their city his capital, they would fight for his elevation to the caliphate. Husein set out from Mecca with his family and seventy devoted followers. Twenty-five miles north of Kufa the caravan was intercepted by a force of Yezid's troops under Obeidallah. Husein offered to submit, but his band chose to fight. Husein's nephew Qasim, ten years old, was struck by one of the first arrows, and died in his uncle's arms; one by one Husein's brothers, sons, cousins, and nephews fell; every man in the group was killed, while the women and children looked on in horror and terror. When Husein's severed head was brought to Obeidallah he carelessly turned it over with his staff. "Gently," one of his officers protested; "he was the grandson of the Prophet. By Allah! I have seen those lips kissed by the blessed mouth of Mohammed!" (680). [11] At Kerbela, where Husein fell, the Shia Moslems built a shrine to his memory; yearly they reenact there the tragedy in a passion play, worshiping the memory of Ali, Hasan, and Husein.

Abdallah, son of Zobeir, continued the revolt. Yezid's Syrian troops defeated him, and besieged him in Mecca; rocks from their catapults fell upon the sacred enclosure and split the Black Stone into three pieces; the Kaaba caught fire, and was burned to the ground (683). Suddenly the siege was lifted; Yezid had died, and the army was needed in Damascus. In two years of royal chaos three caliphs held the throne; finally Abd-al-Malik, son of a cousin of Muawiya, ended the disorder with ruthless courage, and then governed with relative mildness, wisdom, and justice. His general Hajjaj ibn Yusuf subdued the Kufans, and renewed the siege of Mecca. Abdallah, now seventy-two, fought bravely, urged on by his centenarian mother; he was defeated and killed; his head was sent as a certified check to Damascus; his body, after hanging for some time on a gibbet, was presented to his mother (692). During the ensuing peace Abd-al-Malik wrote poetry, patronized letters, attended to eight wives, and reared fifteen sons, of whom four succeeded to his throne; his cognomen meant Father of Kings.

His reign of twenty years paved the way for the accomplishments of his son Walid I (705–15). The march of Arab conquest was now resumed: Balkh was taken in 705, Bokhara in 709, Spain in 711, Samarkand in 712. In the eastern provinces Hajjaj governed with a creative energy that equaled his barbarities: marshes were drained, arid tracts were irrigated, and the canal system was restored and improved; not content with which the general, once a schoolmaster, revolutionized Arabic orthography by introducing diacritical marks. Walid himself was a model king, far more interested in administration than in war. He encouraged industry and trade with new markets and better roads; built schools and hospitals—including the first lazar houses known—and homes for the aged, the crippled, and the blind; enlarged and beautified the mosques of Mecca, Medina, and Jerusalem, and raised at Damascus a still greater one, which still exists. Amid these labors he composed verses, wrote music, played the lute, listened patiently to other poets and musicians, and caroused every second day.[12]

His brother and successor Suleiman (715–17) wasted lives and wealth in a vain attempt upon Constantinople, solaced himself with good food and bad women, and received the praise of posterity only for bequeathing his power to his cousin. Omar II (717–20) was resolved to atone in one reign for all the impiety and liberality of his Umayyad predecessors. The practice and propagation of the faith were the consuming interests of his life. He dressed so simply, wore so many patches, that no stranger took him for a king. He bade his wife surrender to the public treasury the costly jewels that her father had given her, and she obeyed. He informed his harem that the duties of government would absorb him to their neglect, and gave them leave to depart. He ignored the poets, orators, and scholars who had depended on the court, but drew to his counsel and companionship the most devout among the learned in his realm. He made peace with other countries, withdrew the army that had besieged Constantinople, and called in the garrisons that had guarded Moslem cities hostile to Umayyad rule. Whereas his predecessors had discouraged conversions to Islam on the ground that less poll taxes would come to the state, Omar speeded the acceptance of Islam by Christians, Zoroastrians, and Jews; and when his fiscal agents complained that his policy was ruining the treasury, he replied: "Glad would I be, by Allah, to see everybody become Moslem, so that you and I would have to till the soil with our own hands to earn a living."[13] Clever councilors thought to stay the tide of conversions by requiring circumcision; Omar, another Paul, bade them dispense with it. Upon those who still refused conversion he laid severe restrictions, excluded them from governmental employment, and forbade them to build new shrines. After a reign of less than three years he sickened and died.

Another side of Moslem character and custom appears in Yezid II (717–24), last of the royal sons of Abd-al-Malik. Yezid loved a slave girl Habiba as Omar II had loved Islam. While still a youth he had bought her for 4000 pieces of gold; his brother Suleiman, then caliph, had compelled him to return her to the seller; but Yezid had never forgotten her beauty and her tenderness. When he came to power his wife asked him, "Is there, my love, anything in the world left you to desire?" "Yes," he said, "Habiba." The dutiful wife sent for Habiba, presented her to Yezid, and retired into the obscurity of the harem. One day, feasting with Habiba, Yezid playfully threw a grape pit into her mouth; it choked her, and she died in his arms. A week later Yezid died of grief.

Hisham (724–43) governed the realm for nineteen years in justice and peace, improved administration, reduced expenses, and left the treasury full at his death. But the virtues of a saint may be the ruin of a ruler. Hisham's armies were repeatedly defeated, rebellion simmered in the provinces, disaffection spread in a capital that longed for a spendthrift king. His successors disgraced a hitherto competent dynasty by luxurious living and negligent rule. Walid II (743–4) was a skeptic libertine and candid epicurean. He read with delight the news of his uncle Hisham's death; imprisoned Hisham's son, seized the property of the late Caliph's relatives, and emptied the treasury with careless government and extravagant largesse. His enemies reported that he swam in a pool of wine and slaked his thirst as he swam; that he used the Koran as a target for his archery; that he sent his mistresses to preside in his place at the public prayer.[14] Yezid, son of Walid I, slew the wastrel, ruled for six months, and died (744). His brother Ibrahim took the throne but could not defend it; an able general deposed him, and reigned for six tragic years as Merwan II, the last caliph of the Umayyad line.

From a worldly point of view the Umayyad caliphs had done well for Islam. They had extended its political boundaries farther than these would ever reach again; and, barring some illucid intervals, they had given the new empire an orderly and liberal government. But the lottery of hereditary monarchy placed on the throne, in the eighth century, incompetents who exhausted the treasury, surrendered administration to eunuchs, and lost control over that Arab individualism which has nearly always prevented a united Moslem power. The old tribal enmities persisted as political factions; Hashimites and Umayyads hated one another as if they were more closely related than they really were. Arabia, Egypt, and Persia resented the authority of Damascus; and the proud Persians, from contending that they were as good as the Arabs, passed to claiming superiority, and could no longer brook Syrian rule. The descendants of Mohammed were scandalized to see at the head of Islam an Umayyad clan that had included the most unyielding and

last converted of the Prophet's enemies; they were shocked by the easy morals, perhaps by the religious tolerance, of the Umayyad caliphs; they prayed
for the day when Allah would send some savior to redeem them from this
humiliating rule.

All that these hostile forces needed was some initiative personality to give
them unity and voice. Abu al-Abbas, great-great-grandson of an uncle of
Mohammed, provided the leadership from a hiding place in Palestine, organized the revolt in the provinces, and won the ardent support of the Shia
Persian nationalists. In 749 he proclaimed himself caliph at Kufa. Merwan II
met the rebel forces under Abu al-Abbas' uncle Abdallah on the river Zab;
he was defeated; and a year later Damascus yielded to siege. Merwan was
caught and killed, and his head was sent to Abu al-Abbas. The new Caliph
was not satisfied. "Had they quaffed my blood," he said, "it would not have
quenched their thirst; neither is my wrath slaked by this man's blood." He
named himself al-Saffah, the Bloodthirsty, and directed that all princes of
the Umayyad line should be hunted out and slain, to forestall any resurrection
of the fallen dynasty. Abdallah, made governor of Syria, managed the matter
with humor and dispatch. He announced an amnesty to the Umayyads, and
to confirm it he invited eighty of their leaders to dinner. While they ate, his
hidden soldiers, at his signal, put them all to the sword. Carpets were spread
over the fallen men, and the feast was resumed by the Abbasid diners over
the bodies of their foes, and to the music of dying groans. The corpses of
several Umayyad caliphs were exhumed, the almost fleshless skeletons were
scourged, hanged, and burned, and the ashes were scattered to the winds.[15]

III. THE ABBASID CALIPHATE: 750–1058

1. Harun al-Rashid

Abu al-Abbas al-Saffah found himself ruler of an empire extending from
the Indus to the Atlantic: Sind (northwest India), Baluchistan, Afghanistan, Turkestan, Persia, Mesopotamia, Armenia, Syria, Palestine, Cyprus,
Crete, Egypt, and North Africa. Moslem Spain, however, rejected his authority, and in the twelfth year of his reign Sind threw off his rule. Hated
in Damascus, uncomfortable in turbulent Kufa, al-Saffah made Anbar, north
of Kufa, his capital. The men who had helped him to power, and now administered the state, were predominantly Persian in origin or culture; after
al-Saffah had drunk his fill of blood, a certain Iranian refinement and urbanity entered into the manners of the court; and a succession of enlightened
caliphs dignified the growth of wealth by promoting a brilliant flowering of
art and literature, science and philosophy. After a century of humiliation,
Persia conquered her conquerors.

Al-Saffah died of smallpox in 754. His half brother Abu Jafar succeeded him under the name of al-Mansur, "the Victorious." Mansur's mother was a Berber slave; of the thirty-seven Abbasid caliphs, slaves mothered all but three through the institution of concubinage and the legitimation of its progeny; in this way the Moslem aristocracy was perpetually recruited by the democracy of chance and the fortunes of love and war. The new Caliph was forty, tall, slender, bearded, dark, austere; no slave to woman's beauty, no friend of wine or song, but a generous patron of letters, sciences, and arts. A man of great ability and little scruple, by his firm statesmanship he established a dynasty that might else have died at al-Saffah's death. He gave himself sedulously to administration, built a splendid new capital at Baghdad, reorganized the government and the army into their lasting form, kept a keen eye on every department and almost every transaction, periodically forced corrupt officials—including his brother—to disgorge their peculations into the treasury, and dispensed the funds of the state with a conscientious parsimony that won him no friends, but the title of "Father of Farthings." [16] At the outset of his reign he established on a Persian model an institution—the vizierate—which was to play a major role in Abbasid history. As his first vizier he appointed Khalid, son of Barmak; this family of Barmakids was cast for a heavy part in the Abbasid drama. Al-Mansur and Khalid created the order and prosperity whose full fruits were to fall into the lap of Harun al-Rashid.

After a beneficent reign of twenty-two years al-Mansur died on a pilgrimage to Mecca. His son al-Mahdi (775–85) could now afford to be benevolent. He pardoned all but the most dangerous offenders, spent lavishly to beautify the cities, supported music and literature, and administered the empire with reasonable competence. Byzantium having seized the opportunity of the Abbasid revolution to recover Arab-conquered territory in Asia Minor, al-Mahdi sent an army under his son Harun to renew a theft long sanctified by time. Harun drove the Greeks back to Constantinople, and so threatened that capital that the Empress Irene made peace on terms that pledged a yearly payment of 70,000 dinars ($332,500) to the caliphs (784). From that time onward al-Mahdi called the youth Harun al-Rashid—Aaron the Upright. He had previously named another son heir apparent; now, seeing the far superior capacity of Harun, he asked al-Hadi to waive his claim in favor of his younger brother. Al-Hadi, commanding an army in the east, refused, and disobeyed a summons to Baghdad; al-Mahdi and Harun set out to capture him, but al-Mahdi, aged forty-three, died on the way. Harun—so counseled by the Barmakid Yahya, son of Khalid—recognized Hadi as Caliph, and himself as heir apparent. But, as Sa'di was to say, "Ten dervishes can sleep on one rug, but two kings cannot be accommodated in an entire kingdom." [17] Al-Hadi soon set Harun aside, imprisoned Yahya, and proclaimed his own son as successor. Shortly thereafter (786) al-Hadi died; rumor said that his own mother, favoring Harun, had had him smothered with pillows. Harun ascended the throne, made Yahya his vizier, and began the most famous reign in Moslem history.

Legends—above all, the *Thousand and One Nights*—picture Harun as a gay and cultured monarch, occasionally despotic and violent, often generous and humane; so fond of good stories that he had them recorded in state archives, and rewarded a lady raconteur, now and then, by sharing his bed with her.[18] All these qualities appear in history except the gaiety, which perhaps offended the historians. These depict him first of all as a pious and resolutely orthodox Moslem, who severely restricted the liberties of non-Moslems, made the pilgrimage to Mecca every second year, and performed a hundred prostrations with his daily prayers.[19] He drank thirstily, but mostly in the privacy of a few chosen friends.[20] He had seven wives and several concubines; eleven sons and fourteen daughters, all by slave girls except al-Emin, his son by the Princess Zobeida. He was generous with all forms of his wealth. When his son al-Mamun fell in love with one of Harun's palace maids, the Caliph presented her to him, merely asking him in payment to compose some lines of poetry.[21] He enjoyed poetry so intensely that on some occasions he would overwhelm a poet with extravagant gifts, as when he gave the poet Merwan, for one brief but laudatory ode, 5000 pieces of gold ($23,750), a robe of honor, ten Greek slave girls, and a favorite horse.[22] His boon companion was the libertine poet Abu Nuwas; repeatedly angered by the poet's insolence or open immorality, he was repeatedly mollified by exquisite verse. He gathered about him in Baghdad an unparalleled galaxy of poets, jurists, physicians, grammarians, rhetors, musicians, dancers, artists, and wits; judged their work with discriminating taste, rewarded them abundantly, and was repaid by a thousand metrical doxologies. He himself was a poet, a scholar, an impetuous and eloquent orator.[23] No court in history had ever a more brilliant constellation of intellects. Contemporary with the Empress Irene in Constantinople and with Charlemagne in France, and coming a little later than Tsüan Tsung at Chang-an, Harun excelled them all in wealth, power, splendor, and the cultural advancement that adorns a rule.

But he was no dilettante. He shared in the labor of administration, earned repute as a just judge, and—despite unprecedented liberality and display—left 48,000,000 dinars ($228,000,000) in the treasury at his death. He led his armies personally in the field, and maintained all frontiers intact. For the most part, however, he entrusted administration and policy to the wise Yahya. Soon after his accession he summoned Yahya and said: "I invest you with the rule over my subjects. Rule them as you please; depose whom you will, appoint whom you will, conduct all affairs as you see fit"; and in ratification of his words he gave Yahya his ring.[24] It was an act of extreme and imprudent confidence, but Harun, still a youth of twenty-two, judged himself unprepared to rule so wide a realm; it was also an act of gratitude to one who had been his tutor, whom he had come to call father, and who had borne imprisonment for his sake.

Yahya proved to be one of the ablest administrators in history. Affable, generous, judicious, tireless, he brought the government to its highest pitch of efficiency; established order, security, and justice; built roads, bridges, inns, canals; and kept all the provinces prosperous even while taxing them severely to fill his master's purse and his own; for he, too, like the Caliph, played patron to literature and art. His sons al-Fadl and Jafar received high office from him, acquitted themselves well, paid themselves better; they became millionaires, built palaces, kept their own herds of poets, jesters, and philosophers. Harun loved Jafar so well that gossip found scandal in their intimacy; the Caliph had a cloak made with two collars, so that he and Jafar might wear it at the same time, and be two heads with but a single breast; perhaps in this Siamese garb they sampled together the night life of Baghdad.[25]

We do not know the precise causes that so suddenly ended the Barmakids' power. Ibn Khaldun saw the "true cause" in "their assumption of all authority, their jealous disposition of the public revenue, to such degree that al-Rashid was sometimes reduced to asking for a trivial sum without being able to obtain it." [26] As the young ruler grew into middle age, and found no complete expression of his abilities in the pursuit of sensual pleasure and intellectual discourse, he may have regretted the omnipotence with which he had dowered his vizier. When he ordered Jafar to have a rebel executed, Jafar connived at the man's escape; Harun never forgave this amiable negligence. A story worthy of the *Thousand and One Nights* tells how Abbasa, Harun's sister, fell in love with Jafar; now Harun had vowed to keep the Hashimite blood of his sisters as pure as might be of any but high Arabian fluid, and Jafar was Persian. The Caliph permitted them to marry, but on their promise never to meet except in his presence. The lovers soon broke this agreement; Abbasa secretly bore Jafar two sons, who were concealed and reared in Medina. Zobaida, Harun's wife, discovered the situation and revealed it to Harun. The Caliph sent for his chief executioner, Mesrur, bade him kill Abbasa and bury her in the palace, and supervised in person the performance of these commands; then he ordered Mesrur to behead Jafar and bring him the severed head, which was duly done; then he sent to Medina for the children, talked long with the handsome boys, admired them, and had them killed (803). Yahya and al-Fadl were imprisoned; they were allowed to keep their families and servants, but were never released; Yahya died two years after his son, al-Fadl five years after his brother. All the property of the Barmakid family, reputedly amounting to 30,000,000 dinars ($142,500,000), was confiscated.

Harun himself did not long survive. For a while he dulled his sorrow and remorse with work, and welcomed even the toils of war. When Nicephorus

I, Byzantine Emperor, refused to continue the payments pledged by Irene, and boldly demanded the return of the tribute already paid, Harun replied: "In the name of Allah the Merciful, the Compassionate. From Harun, Commander of the Faithful, to Nicephorus, dog of a Roman: I have your letter, O son of an infidel mother. The answer shall be for your eyes to see, not for your ears to hear. Salaam." [27] He took the field at once, and from his new and strategic residence at Raqqa, on the northern frontier, he led into Asia Minor such impetuous expeditions that Nicephorus soon agreed to resume the tribute (806). To Charlemagne—a useful foil to Byzantium—he sent an embassy bearing many presents, including a complicated water clock and an elephant.[28]

Though Harun was now only forty-two, his sons al-Emin and al-Mamun were already competing for the succession, and looking forward to his death. Hoping to mitigate their strife, Harun arranged that al-Mamun should inherit the provinces east of the Tigris, al-Emin the rest, and that on the death of either brother the survivor should rule the whole. The brothers signed this compact, and swore to it before the Kaaba. In that same year 806 a serious rebellion broke out in Khurasan. Harun set out with al-Emin and al-Mamun to suppress it, though he was suffering from severe abdominal pains. At Tus in eastern Iran he could no longer stand. He was in his last agony when Bashin, a rebel leader, was brought before him. Made almost insane by pain and grief, Harun upbraided the captive for causing him to undertake this fatal expedition, ordered Bashin to be cut to pieces limb by limb, and watched the execution of the sentence.[29] On the following day Harun the Upright died (809), aged forty-five.

2. The Decline of the Abbasids

Al-Mamun continued to Merv, and came to an agreement with the rebels. Al-Emin returned to Baghdad, named his infant son heir to his power, demanded of al-Mamun three eastern provinces, was denied them, and declared war. Al-Mamun's general Tahir defeated the armies of al-Emin, besieged and almost destroyed Baghdad, and sent al-Emin's severed head to al-Mamun after a now inviolable custom. Al-Mamun, still remaining in Merv, had himself proclaimed Caliph (813). Syria and Arabia continued to resist him as the son of a Persian slave; and it was not till 818 that he entered Baghdad as the acknowledged ruler of Islam.

Abdallah al-Mamun ranks with al-Mansur and al-Rashid as one of the great caliphs of the Abbasid line. Though capable at times of the fury and cruelty that had disgraced Harun, he was usually a man of mild and lenient temper. In his state council he included representatives of all the major faiths in his realm—Mohammedan, Christian, Jewish, Sabian, Zoroastrian—and guaranteed, until his latest years, full freedom of worship and belief. For a time free thought was *de rigueur* at the Caliph's court. Masudi describes one of al-Mamun's intellectual afternoons:

> Al-Mamun used to hold a salon every Tuesday for the discussion of questions in theology and law. . . . The learned men of diverse sects were shown into a chamber spread with carpets. Tables were brought in laden with food and drink. . . . When the repast was finished, servants fetched braziers of incense, and the guests perfumed themselves; then they were admitted to the Caliph. He would debate with them in a manner as fair and impartial, and as unlike the haughtiness of a monarch, as can be imagined. At sunset a second meal was served, and the guests departed to their homes.[30]

Under al-Mamun the royal support of arts, sciences, letters, and philosophy became more varied and discriminating than under Harun, and left a far more significant result. He sent to Constantinople, Alexandria, Antioch, and elsewhere for the writings of the Greek masters, and paid a corps of translators to render the books into Arabic. He established an academy of science at Baghdad, and observatories there and at Tadmor, the ancient Palmyra. Physicians, jurists, musicians, poets, mathematicians, astronomers enjoyed his bounty; and he himself, like some nineteenth-century mikado, and like every Moslem gentleman, wrote poetry.

He died too young—at forty eight (833)—and yet too late; for in a fever of authoritarian liberalism he disgraced his final years by persecuting orthodox belief. His brother and successor, Abu Ishaq al-Mutassim, shared his good will but not his genius. He surrounded himself with a bodyguard of 4000 Turkish soldiers, as Roman emperors had leaned on a Praetorian Guard; and in Baghdad, as in Rome, the guard became in time and effect the king. The people of the capital complained that al-Mutassim's Turks rode recklessly through the streets and committed unpunished crimes. Fearing popular revolt, the Caliph left Baghdad, and built himself a royal residence some thirty miles north at Samarra. From 836 to 892 eight caliphs * made it their home and sepulcher. For twenty miles along the Tigris they reared great palaces and mosques, and their officials built luxurious mansions with murals, fountains, gardens, and baths. The Caliph al-Mutawakkil affirmed his piety by spending 700,000 dinars ($3,325,000) on a vast congregational mosque, and only a trifle less on a new royal residence, the Jafariya, with a palace called the "Pearl," and a "Hall of Delight," all surrounded with parks and streams. To find money for these structures and their trappings al-Mutawakkil raised taxes and sold public offices to the highest bidders; and to appease Allah he defended orthodoxy with persecution. His son persuaded his Turk-

---

* Mutassim (833–42), Wathiq (842–7), Mutawakkil (847–61), Muntasir (861–2), Mustain (862–6), Mutazz (866–9), Muhtadi (869–70), and Mutamid (870–92), who, shortly before his death, returned the royal seat to Baghdad.

ish guards to kill him, and took the throne as al-Muntasir—"he who triumphs in the Lord."

Internal factors corrupted the caliphate before external force reduced it to subservience. Overindulgence in liquor, lechery, luxury, and sloth watered down the royal blood, and begot a succession of weaklings who fled from the tasks of government to the exhausting delights of the harem. The growth of wealth and ease, of concubinage and pederasty, had like effects among the ruling class, and relaxed the martial qualities of the people. There could not come from such indiscipline the strong hand needed to hold together so scattered and diverse a conglomeration of provinces and tribes. Racial and territorial antipathies festered into repeated revolt; Arabs, Persians, Syrians, Berbers, Christians, Jews, and Turks agreed only in despising one another; and the faith that had once forged unity split into sects that expressed and intensified political or geographical divisions. The Near East lives or dies by irrigation; the canals that nourished the soil needed perpetual protection and care, which no individual or family could provide; when governmental maintenance of the canal system became incompetent or negligent, the food supply lagged behind the birth rate, and starvation had to restore the balance between these basic factors in history. But the impoverishment of the people by famine or epidemic seldom stayed the hand of the tax-gatherer. Peasant, craftsman, and merchant saw their gains absorbed into the expenses and frills of government, and lost the incentive to production, expansion, or enterprise. At last the economy could not support the government; revenues fell; soldiers could not be adequately paid or controlled. Turks took the place of Arabs in the armed forces of the state, as Germans had replaced Romans in the armies of Rome; and from al-Muntasir onward it was Turkish captains that made and unmade, commanded and murdered, the caliphs. A succession of sordid and bloody palace intrigues made the later vicissitudes of the Baghdad caliphate unworthy of remembrance by history.

The weakening of political diligence and military power at the center invited the dismemberment of the realm. Governors ruled the provinces with only formal reference to the capital; they schemed to make their position permanent, at last hereditary. Spain had declared itself independent in 756, Morocco in 788, Tunis in 801, Egypt in 868; nine years later the Egyptian emirs seized Syria, and ruled most of it till 1076. Al-Mamun had rewarded his general Tahir by assigning to him and his descendants the governorship of Khurasan; this Tahirid dynasty (820–72) ruled most of Persia in semisovereignty until replaced by the Saffarids (872–903). In 929–44 a tribe of Shia Moslems, the Hamdanids, captured northern Mesopotamia and Syria, and dignified their power by making Mosul and Aleppo brilliant centers of cultural life; so Sayfu'l-Dawla (944–67), himself a poet, made places at his Aleppo court for the philosopher al-Farabi and the most popular of Arab poets, al-Mutanabbi. The Buwayhids, sons of the Caspian highland chieftain

Buwayh, captured Isfahan and Shiraz, and finally Baghdad (945); for over a century they forced the caliphs to do their bidding; the Commander of the Faithful became little more than the head of orthodox Islam, while the Buwayhid emir, a Shi'ite, assumed direction of the diminishing state. Adud al-Dawla, the greatest of these Buwayhids (949–83), made his capital, Shiraz, one of the fairest cities of Islam, but spent generously also on the other cities of his realm; under him and his successors Baghdad recaptured some of the glory that it had known under Harun.

In 874 the descendants of Saman, a Zoroastrian noble, founded a Samanid dynasty that ruled Transoxiana and Khurasan till 999. We are not wont to think of Transoxiana as important in the history of science and philosophy; yet under the Samanid kings Bokhara and Samarkand rivaled Baghdad as centers of learning and art; there the Persian language was revived, and became the vehicle of a great literature; a Samanid court gave protection, and the use of a rich library, to Avicenna, the greatest of medieval philosophers; and al-Razi, greatest of medieval physicians, dedicated the *al-Mansuri*, his immense summary of medicine, to a Samanid prince. In 990 the Turks captured Bokhara, and in 999 they put an end to the Samanid dynasty. As the Byzantines for three centuries had fought to contain the Arab expansion, so now the Moslems fought to check the westward movement of the Turks; so, later, the Turks would struggle to stay the Mongol flood. Periodically the pressure of a growing population upon the means of subsistence generates the mass migrations that overshadow the other events of history.

In 962 a band of Turkish adventurers from Turkestan invaded Afghanistan under the lead of Alptigin, a former slave, captured Ghazni, and established there a Ghaznevid dynasty. Subuktigin (976–97), first slave, then son-in-law, then successor, of Alptigin, extended his rule over Peshawar and part of Khurasan. His son Mahmud (998–1030) took all Persia from the Gulf to the Oxus, and in seventeen ruthless campaigns added the Punjab to his empire, and much of India's wealth to his coffers. Surfeited with plunder, and fretting over the unemployment caused by demobilization, he spent part of his riches, and some of his men, in building the congregational mosque of Ghazni. Says a Moslem historian:

> It had an immense nave, in which 6000 servants of God might fulfill their duties without inconvenience to one another. And he raised near it a college, and supplied it with a library, and rare volumes. . . . And to those pure walls came students, professors, and divines . . . and from the endowments of the college they received their daily sustenance, and all necessaries, and a yearly or monthly salary.[31]

To this college and his court Mahmud brought many scientists, including al-Biruni, and many poets, including Firdausi, who reluctantly dedicated to him the greatest of Persian poems. During this generation Mahmud stood near the top of the world in more senses than one; but seven years after his death his empire passed into the hands of the Seljuq Turks.

It would be an error to picture the Turks as barbarians. As it was necessary to modify that term as applied to the German conquerors of Rome, so it must be said that the Turks were already passing out of barbarism when they overran Islam. Moving westward from Lake Baikal, the Turks of north central Asia organized themselves in the sixth century under a *khan* or *chagan*. Forging iron found in their mountains, they made weapons as hard as their code, which punished not only treason and murder, but adultery and cowardice, with death. The fertility of their women outran the mortality of their wars. By A.D. 1000 a branch of Turks known by the name of their *beg* or leader Seljuq dominated Transoxiana as well as Turkestan. Mahmud of Ghazni, thinking to halt this rival Turkish power, seized a son of Seljuq, and imprisoned him in India (1029). Undaunted and enraged, the Seljuq Turks under the stern but masterful Tughril Beg took most of Persia, and paved their further advance by sending to the Caliph al-Qaim at Baghdad a deputation announcing their submission to him and Islam. The Caliph hoped that these fearless warriors might free him from his Buwayhid overlords; he invited Tughril Beg to come to his aid. Tughril came (1055), and the Buwayhids fled; al-Qaim married Tughril's niece, and made him "King of the East and the West" (1058). One by one the petty dynasties of Asiatic Islam crumbled before the Seljuqs, and acknowledged again the supremacy of Baghdad. The Seljuq rulers took the title of *sultan*—master—and reduced the caliphs to a merely religious role; but they brought to the government a new vigor and competence, and to Mohammedanism a new fervor of orthodox faith. They did not, like the Mongols two centuries later, destroy what they conquered; they rapidly absorbed the higher civilization, unified into a new empire what had been the scattered members of a dying state, and gave it the strength to endure and survive that long duel, between Christianity and Islam, which we know as the Crusades.

IV. ARMENIA: 325–1060

In the year 1060 the Seljuq Turks extended their conquests to Armenia.

That harassed country has felt the claws of rival imperialisms through many centuries, because its mountains hindered its unity of defense while its valleys provided tempting roads between Mesopotamia and the Black Sea. Greece and Persia fought for those roads as highways of trade and war; Xenophon's Ten Thousand traversed them; Rome and Persia fought for them; Byzantium and Persia, Byzantium and Islam, Russia and Britain. Through all vicissitudes of external pressure or domination, Armenia maintained a practical independence, a vigorous commercial and agricultural economy, a cultural autonomy that produced its own creed, literature, and art. It was the first nation to adopt Christianity as its state religion (303). It took the Monophysite side in the debate about the natures of Christ, refusing to admit that He had shared the infirmities of human flesh. In 491 the Armenian bishops parted from Greek and Roman Christianity and formed an autonomous Armenian Church under its own *katholikos*. Armenian literature used the Greek language until the early fifth century, when Bishop Mesrob invented a national alphabet, and translated the Bible into the Armenian tongue. Since that time Armenia has had an abundant literature, chiefly in religion and history.

From 642 to 1046 the country was nominally subject to the caliphs, but it remained virtually sovereign and zealously Christian. In the ninth century the Bagratuni family established a dynasty under the title of "Prince of Princes," built a capital at Ani, and gave the country several generations of progress and relative peace. Ashot III (952–77) was much loved by his people; he founded many churches, hospitals, convents, and almshouses, and (we are told) never sat down to meals without allowing poor men to join him. Under his son Gagik I (990–1020)—how peculiar our names must seem to the Armenians!—prosperity reached its height: schools were numerous, towns were enriched by trade and adorned by art; and Kars rivaled Ani as a center of literature, theology, and philosophy. Ani had impressive palaces and a famous cathedral (*c.* 980), subtly compounded of Persian and Byzantine styles; here were piers and column clusters, pointed as well as round arches, and other features that later entered into Gothic art. When, in 989, the cupola of St. Sophia in Constantinople was destroyed by an earthquake, the Byzantine emperor assigned the hazardous task of restoring it to Trdat, the architect of the Ani cathedral.[32]

CHAPTER XI

The Islamic Scene

628-1058

I. THE ECONOMY

CIVILIZATION is a union of soil and soul—the resources of the earth transformed by the desire and discipline of men. Behind the façade, and under the burden, of courts and palaces, temples and schools, letters and luxuries and arts, stands the basic man: the hunter bringing game from the woods; the woodman felling the forest; the herdsman pasturing and breeding his flock; the peasant clearing, plowing, sowing, cultivating, reaping, tending the orchard, the vine, the hive, and the brood; the woman absorbed in the hundred crafts and cares of a functioning home; the miner digging in the earth; the builder shaping homes and vehicles and ships; the artisan fashioning products and tools; the pedlar, shopkeeper, and merchant uniting and dividing maker and user; the investor fertilizing industry with his savings; the executive harnessing muscle, materials, and minds for the creation of services and goods. These are the patient yet restless leviathan on whose swaying back civilization precariously rides.

All these were busy in Islam. Men raised cattle, horses, camels, goats, elephants, and dogs; stole the honey of bees and the milk of camels, goats, and cows; and grew a hundred varieties of grains, vegetables, fruits, nuts, and flowers. The orange tree was brought from India to Arabia at some time before the tenth century; the Arabs introduced it to Syria, Asia Minor, Palestine, Egypt, and Spain, from which countries it pervaded southern Europe.[1] The cultivation of sugar cane and the refining of sugar were likewise spread by the Arabs from India through the Near East, and were brought by Crusaders to their European states.[2] Cotton was first cultivated in Europe by the Arabs.[3] These achievements on lands largely arid were made possible by organized irrigation; here the caliphs made an exception to their principle of leaving the economy to free enterprise; the government directed and financed the maintenance of the greater canals. The Euphrates was channeled into Mesopotamia, the Tigris into Persia, and a great canal connected the twin rivers at Baghdad. The early Abbasid caliphs encouraged the draining of marshes, and the rehabilitation of ruined villages and deserted farms. In the tenth century, under the Samanid princes, the region between Bokhara and Samarkand was considered one of the "four earthly paradises"—the others being southern Persia, southern Iraq, and the region around Damascus.

Gold, silver, iron, lead, mercury, antimony, sulphur, asbestos, marble, and precious stones were mined or quarried from the earth. Divers fished for pearls in the Persian Gulf. Some use was made of naphtha and bitumen; an entry in Harun's archives gives the price of "naphtha and reeds" used in burning the corpse of Jafar.[4] Industry was in the handicraft stage, practiced in homes and artisans' shops, and organized in guilds. We find few factories, and no clear advance in technology except the development of the windmill. Masudi, writing in the tenth century, speaks of seeing these in Persia and the Near East; there is no sign of them in Europe before the twelfth century; possibly they were another gift of the Moslem East to its crusading foes.[5] There was much mechanical ingenuity. The water clock sent by Harun al-Rashid to Charlemagne was made of leather and damascened brass; it told the time by metal cavaliers who at each hour opened the door, let fall the proper number of balls on a cymbal, and then, retiring, closed the door.[6] Production was slow, but the worker could express himself in integral work, and made almost every industry an art. Persian, Syrian, and Egyptian textiles were famous for the patient perfection of their technique; Mosul for its cotton *muslin*, Damascus for its *damask* linen, Aden for its wool. Damascus was noted also for its swords of highly tempered steel; Sidon and Tyre for glass of unexcelled thinness and clarity; Baghdad for its glass and pottery; Rayy for pottery, needles, combs; Raqqa for olive oil and soap; Fars for perfume and rugs. Under Moslem rule western Asia attained a pitch of industrial and commercial prosperity unmatched by western Europe before the sixteenth century.[7]

Land transport was chiefly by camels, horses, mules, and men. But the horse was too prized to be chiefly a beast of burden. "Do not call him my horse," said an Arab; "call him my son. He runs more swiftly than the tempest, quicker than a glance. . . . He is so light of foot that he could dance on the breast of your mistress and she would take no hurt." [8] So the camel, "ship of the desert," bore most of the freight of Arab trade; and caravans of 4700 camels swayed across the Moslem world. Great roads radiating from Baghdad led through Rayy, Nishapur, Merv, Bokhara, and Samarkand to Kashgar and the Chinese frontier; through Basra to Shiraz; through Kufa to Medina, Mecca, and Aden; through Mosul or Damascus to the Syrian coast. Caravanserais or inns, hospices and cisterns helped the traveler and his beasts. Much inland traffic was borne on rivers and canals. Harun al-Rashid planned a Suez canal, but Yahya, for unknown reasons, probably financial, discouraged the idea.[9] The Tigris at Baghdad, 750 feet wide, was spanned by three bridges built upon boats.

Over these arteries a busy commerce passed. It was an economic advantage to western Asia that one government united a region formerly divided among four states; customs dues and other trade barriers were removed, and the flow of commodities was further eased by unity of language and faith.

The Arabs did not share the European aristocrat's scorn of the merchant; soon they joined Christians, Jews, and Persians in the business of getting goods from producer to consumer with the least possible profit to either. Cities and towns swelled and hummed with transport, barter, and sale; pedlars cried their wares to latticèd windows; shops dangled their stock and resounded with haggling; fairs, markets, and bazaars gathered merchandise, merchants, buyers, and poets; caravans bound China and India to Persia, Syria, and Egypt; and ports like Baghdad, Basra, Aden, Cairo, and Alexandria sent Arab merchantmen out to sea. Moslem commerce dominated the Mediterranean till the Crusades, plying between Syria and Egypt at one end, Tunis, Sicily, Morocco, and Spain at the other, and touching Greece, Italy, and Gaul; it captured control of the Red Sea from Ethiopia; it reached over the Caspian into Mongolia, and up the Volga from Astrakhan to Novgorod, Finland, Scandinavia, and Germany, where it left thousands of Moslem coins; it answered the Chinese junks that visited Basra by sending Arab dhows out from the Persian Gulf to India and Ceylon, through the Straits and up the Chinese coast to Khanfu (Canton); a colony of Moslem and Jewish merchants was well established there in the eighth century.[10] This vitalizing commercial activity reached its peak in the tenth century, when western Europe was at nadir; and when it subsided it left its mark upon many European languages in such words as *tariff, traffic, magazine, caravan,* and *bazaar.*

The state left industry and commerce free, and aided it with a relatively stable currency. The early caliphs used Byzantine and Persian money, but in 695 Abd-al-Malik struck an Arab coinage of gold dinars and silver dirhems.* Ibn Hawqal (*c.* 975) describes a kind of promissory note for 42,000 dinars addressed to a merchant in Morocco; from the Arabic word *sakk* for this form of credit is derived our word *check*. Investors shared in financing commercial voyages or caravans; and though interest was forbidden, ways were found, as in Europe, of evading the prohibition and repaying capital for its use and risk. Monopolies were illegal, but prospered. Within a century after Omar's death the Arab upper classes had amassed great wealth, and lived on luxurious estates manned by hundreds of slaves.[11] Yahya the Barmakid offered 7,000,000 dirhems ($560,000) for a pearl box made of precious stones, and was refused; the Caliph Muqtafi, if we may believe Moslem figures, left at his death 20,000,000 dinars ($94,500,000) in jewelry and perfumes.[12] When Harun al-Rashid married his son al-Mamun to Buran, her grandmother emptied a shower of pearls upon the groom; and her father scattered among the guests balls of musk, each of which contained a writ en-

---

* The dinar (from the Roman *denarius*) contained 65 grams of gold, or .135 of an ounce, and would be equal to $4.72½ in terms of the price of gold in the United States of America in 1947; we shall roughly reckon it at $4.75. The dirhem (from the Greek *drachma*) contained forty-three grams of silver, worth some eight cents. As the purity of the coinage varied, our equivalents will be only approximate.

titling the possessor to a slave, a horse, an estate, or some other gift.[13] After Muqtadir confiscated 16,000,000 dinars of Ibn al-Jassas' fortune, that famous jeweler remained a wealthy man. Many overseas traders were worth 4,000,-000 dinars; hundreds of merchants had homes costing from 10,000 to 30,000 dinars ($142,500).[14]

At the bottom of the economic structure were the slaves. They were probably more numerous in Islam in proportion to population than in Christendom, where serfdom was replacing slavery. The Caliph Muqtadir, we are told, had 11,000 eunuchs in his household; Musa took 300,000 captives in Africa, 30,000 "virgins" in Spain, and sold them into slavery; Qutayba captured 100,000 in Sogdiana; the figures are Oriental and must be discounted. The Koran recognized the capture of non-Moslems in war, and the birth of children to slave parents, as the sole legitimate sources of slavery; no Moslem (just as in Christendom no Christian) was to be enslaved. Nevertheless a brisk trade developed in slaves captured in raids—Negroes from East and Central Africa, Turks or Chinese from Turkestan, whites from Russia, Italy, and Spain. The Moslem had full rights of life and death over his slaves; usually, however, he handled them with a genial humanity that made their lot no worse—perhaps better, as more secure—than that of a factory worker in nineteenth-century Europe.[15] Slaves did most of the menial work on the farms, most of the unskilled manual work in the towns; they acted as servants in the household, and as concubines or eunuchs in the harem. Most dancers, singers, and actors were slaves. The offspring of a female slave by her master, or of a free woman by her slave, was free from birth. Slaves were allowed to marry; and their children, if talented, might receive an education. It is astonishing how many sons of slaves rose to high place in the intellectual and political world of Islam, how many, like Mahmud and the early Mameluks, became kings.

Exploitation in Asiatic Islam never reached the mercilessness of pagan, Christian, or Moslem Egypt, where the peasant toiled every hour, earned enough to pay for a hut, a loincloth, and food this side of starvation. There was and is much begging in Islam, and much imposture in begging; but the poor Asiatic had a protective skill in working slowly, few men could rival him in manifold adaptation to idleness, alms were frequent, and at the worst a homeless man could sleep in the finest edifice in town—the mosque. Even so, the eternal class war simmered sullenly through the years, and broke out now and then (778, 796, 808, 838) in violent revolt. Usually, since state and church were one, rebellion took a religious garb. Some sects, like the Khurramiyya and the Muhayyida, adopted the communistic ideas of the Persian rebel Mazdak; one group called itself *Surkh Alam*—the "Red Flag." [16] About 772 Hashim al-Muqanna—the "Veiled Prophet" of Khurasan—announced that he was God incarnate, and had come to restore the communism of Mazdak. He gathered various sects about him, defeated many armies, ruled northern Persia for fourteen years, and was finally (786) captured and killed.[17] In 838 Babik al-Khurrani renewed the effort, gathered around him a band known as Muhammira—i.e. "Reds" [18]—seized Azerbaijan, held it for twenty-two years, defeated a succession of armies, and (Tabari would have us believe) killed 255,500 soldiers and captives before he was overcome. The Caliph Mutasim ordered Babik's own executioner to cut off Babik's limbs one by one; the trunk was impaled before the royal palace; and the head was sent on exhibition around the cities of Khurasan [19] as a reminder that all men are born unfree and unequal.

The most famous of these "servile wars" of the East was organized by Ali, an Arab who claimed descent from the Prophet's son-in-law. Near Basra many Negro slaves were employed in digging saltpeter. Ali represented to them how badly they were treated, urged them to follow him in revolt, and promised them freedom, wealth—and slaves. They agreed, seized food and supplies, defeated the troops sent against them, and built themselves independent villages with palaces for their leaders, prisons for their captives, and mosques for their prayers (869). The employers offered Ali five dinars ($23.75) per head if he would persuade the rebels to return to work; he refused. The surrounding country tried to starve them into submission; but when their supplies ran out they attacked the town of Obolla, freed and absorbed its slaves, sacked it, and put it to flames (870). Much encouraged, Ali led his men against other towns, took many of them, and captured control of southern Iran and Iraq to the gates of Baghdad. Commerce halted, and the capital began to starve. In 871 the Negro general Mohallabi, with a large army of rebels, seized Basra; if we may credit the historians, 300,000 persons were massacred, and thousands of white women and children, including the Hashimite aristocracy, became the concubines or slaves of the Negro troops. For ten years the rebellion continued; great armies were sent to suppress it; amnesty and rewards were offered to deserters; many of his men left Ali and joined the government's forces. The remnant was surrounded, besieged, and bombarded with molten lead and "Greek fire"—flaming torches of naphtha. Finally, a government army under the vizier Mowaffaq made its way into the rebel city, overcame resistance, killed Ali, and brought his head to the victor. Mowaffaq and his officers knelt and thanked Allah for His mercies (883).[20] The rebellion had lasted fourteen years, and had threatened the whole economic and political structure of Eastern Islam. Ibn Tulun, governor of Egypt, took advantage of the situation to make the richest of the caliph's provinces an independent state.

II. THE FAITH

Next to bread and woman, in the hierarchy of desire, comes eternal salvation; when the stomach is satisfied, and lust is spent, man spares a little time for God. Despite polygamy, the Moslem found considerable time for Allah, and based his morals, his laws, and his government upon his religion.

Theoretically the Moslem faith was the simplest of all creeds: "There is no god but Allah, and Mohammed is His Prophet." (*La ilaha il-Allah, Muhammad-un Rasulu-llah.*) The simplicity of the formula is only apparent, for its second clause involves the acceptance of the Koran and all its teachings. Consequently the orthodox Moslem also believed in heaven and hell, angels and demons, the resurrection of body and soul, the divine predestination of all events, the Last Judgment, the four duties of Moslem practice— prayer, alms, fasting, and pilgrimage—and the divine inspiration of various prophets who led up to Mohammed. "For every nation," said the Koran, "there is a messenger and prophet" (x, 48); some Moslems reckon such messengers at 224,000; [21] but apparently only Abraham, Moses, and Jesus were considered by Mohammed as having spoken the word of God. Hence the Moslem was required to accept the Old Testament and the Gospels as inspired scriptures; where these contradicted the Koran it was because their divine text had been willfully or unwittingly corrupted by men; in any case the Koran superseded all previous revelations, and Mohammed excelled all the other messengers of God. Moslems proclaimed his mere humanity, but revered him almost as intensely as Christians worshiped Christ. "If I had been alive in his time," said a typical Moslem, "I would not have allowed the Apostle of God to put his blessed foot upon the earth, but would have borne him upon my shoulders wherever he wished to go." [22]

Making their faith still more complex, good Moslems accepted and obeyed, besides the Koran, the traditions (Hadith) preserved by their learned men of their Prophet's customs (Sunna) and conversation. Time brought forward questions of creed, ritual, morals, and law to which the holy book gave no clear answer; sometimes the words of the Koran were obscure, and needed elucidation; it was useful to know what, on such points, the Prophet or his Companions had done or said. Certain Moslems devoted themselves to gathering such traditions. During the first century of their era they refrained from writing them down; they formed schools of Hadith in divers cities, and gave public discourses reciting them; it was not unusual for Moslems to travel from Spain to Persia to hear a Hadith from one who claimed to have it in direct succession from Mohammed. In this way a body of oral teaching grew up alongside the Koran, as the Mishna and Gemara grew up beside the Old Testament. And as Jehuda ha-Nasi gathered the oral law of the Jews into written form in 189, so in 870, al-Bukhari, after researches which led him from Egypt to Turkestan, critically examined 600,-000 Mohammedan traditions, and published 7275 of them in his *Sahih*—"Correct Book." Each chosen tradition was traced through a long chain (*isnad*) of named transmitters to one of the Companions, or to the Prophet himself.

Many of the traditions put a new color upon the Moslem creed. Mohammed had not claimed the power of miracles, but hundreds of pretty traditions told of his wonder-working; how he fed a multitude from food hardly adequate for one man; exorcised demons; drew rain from heaven by one prayer, and stopped it by another; how he touched the udders of dry goats and they gave milk; how the sick were healed by contact with his clothes or his shorn hair. Christian influences seem to have molded many of the traditions; love toward one's enemies was inculcated, though Mohammed had sterner views; the Lord's Prayer was adopted from the Gospels; the parables of the sower, the wedding guests, and the laborers in the vineyard were put into Mohammed's mouth;[23] all in all, he was transformed into an excellent Christian, despite his nine wives. Moslem critics complained that much of the Hadith had been concocted as Umayyad, Abbasid, or other propaganda;[24] Ibn Abi al-Awja, executed at Kufa in 772, confessed to having fabricated 4000 traditions.[25] A few skeptics laughed at the Hadith collections, and composed indecent stories in solemn Hadith form.[26] Nevertheless the acceptance of the Hadith, in one or the other of the approved collections, as binding in faith and morals, became a distinguishing mark of orthodox Moslems, who therefore received the name of Sunni, or traditionalists.

One tradition represented the angel Gabriel as asking Mohammed, "What is Islam?"—and made Mohammed reply: "Islam is to believe in Allah and His Prophet, to recite the prescribed prayers, to give alms, to observe the fast of Ramadan, and to make the pilgrimage to Mecca."[27] Prayer, almsgiving, fasting, and pilgrimage constitute the "Four Duties" of Moslem religion. These, with belief in Allah and Mohammed, are the "Five Pillars of Islam."

Prayer had to be preceded by purification; and as prayer was required of the Moslem five times a day, cleanliness came literally next to godliness. Mohammed, like Moses, used religion as a means to hygiene as well as to morality, on the general principle that the rational can secure popular acceptance only in the form of the mystical. He warned that the prayer of an unclean person would not be heard by God; he even thought of making the brushing of the teeth a prerequisite to prayer; but finally he compromised on the washing of the face, the hands, and the feet (v, 6). A man who had had sexual relations, a woman who had menstruated, or given birth, since the last purification, must bathe before prayer. At dawn, shortly after midday, in late afternoon, at sunset, and at bedtime the muezzin mounted a minaret to sound the *adhan*, or call to prayer:

> Allahu Akbar (God is most great)! Allahu Akbar! Allahu Akbar!
> Allahu Akbar! I bear witness that there is no God but Allah. I bear
> witness that there is no God but Allah. I bear witness that there is no
> God but Allah. I bear witness that Mohammed is the Apostle of Allah.
> I bear witness that Mohammed is the Apostle of Allah. I bear witness
> that Mohammed is the Apostle of Allah. Come to prayer! Come to
> prayer! Come to prayer! Come to success! Come to success! Come to

success! Allahu Akbar! Allahu Akbar! Allahu Akbar! There is no God but Allah!

It is a powerful appeal, a noble summons to rise with the sun, a welcome interruption in the hot work of the day, a solemn message of divine majesty in the stillness of the night; grateful even to alien ears is this strange shrill chant of many muezzins from divers mosques calling the earthbound soul to a moment's communion with the mysterious source of life and mind. On those five occasions all Moslems everywhere must leave off whatever else they may be doing, must cleanse themselves, turn toward Mecca and the Kaaba and recite the same brief prayers, in the same successive postures, in an impressive simultaneity moving with the sun across the earth.

Those who had the time and will would go to the mosque to say their prayers. Usually the mosque was open all day; any Moslem, orthodox or heretic, might enter to make his ablutions, to rest, or to pray. There, too, in the cloistered shade, teachers taught their pupils, judges tried cases, caliphs announced their policies or decrees; people gathered to chat, hear the news, even to negotiate business; the mosque, like the synagogue and the church, was the center of daily life, the home and hearth of the community. Half an hour before Friday noon the muezzin chanted from the minarets the salutation or *salaam*—a blessing on Allah, Mohammed, his family, and the great Companions; and called the congregation to the mosque. The worshipers were expected to have bathed and put on clean clothes, and to have perfumed themselves; or they might perform minor ablutions in the tank or fountain that stood in the courtyard of the mosque. The women usually stayed at home when the men went to the mosque, and vice versa; it was feared that the presence of women, even veiled, would distract the excitable male. The worshipers removed their shoes at the door of the mosque proper, and entered in slippers or stocking feet. There or in the court (if they were numerous) they stood shoulder to shoulder in one or more rows, facing the mihrab or prayer niche in the wall, which indicated the *qibla* or direction of Mecca. An imam or prayer leader read a passage from the Koran and preached a short sermon. Each worshiper recited several prayers, and in the prescribed postures of bowing, kneeling, and prostration; *mosque* meant a place of prostration in prayer.* Then the imam recited a complex series of salutations, benedictions, and orisons, in which the congregation silently joined. There were no hymns, processions, or sacraments; no collections or pew rents; religion, being one with the state, was financed from public funds. The imam was not a priest but a layman, who continued to earn his living by a secular occupation, and was appointed by the mosque warden for a specified period, and a small salary, to lead the congregation in prayer; there was

---

* *Mosque* is from the Arabic *masjid*, from *sajada*, to bow down, adore. In the Near East *masjid* is pronounced *musjid*; in North Africa, *musghid*—whence the French and English forms of the word.

no priesthood in Islam. After the Friday prayers the Moslems were free, if they wished, to engage in work as on any other day; meanwhile, however, they had known a cleansing hour of elevation above economic and social strife, and had unconsciously cemented their community by common ritual.

The second duty of Moslem practice was the giving of alms. Mohammed was almost as critical of the rich as Jesus had been; some have thought that he began as a social reformer revolted by the contrast between the luxury of the merchant nobles and the poverty of the masses; [28] and apparently his early followers were mostly of humble origin. One of his first activities in Medina was to establish an annual tax of two and a half per cent on the movable wealth of all citizens for the relief of the poor. Regular officials collected and distributed this revenue. Part of the proceeds was used to build mosques and defray the expenses of government and war; but war in return brought booty that swelled the gifts to the poor. "Prayer," said Omar II, "carries us halfway to God, fasting brings us to the door of His palace, almsgiving lets us in." [29] The traditions abound in stories of generous Moslems; Hasan, for example, was said to have three times in his life divided his substance with the poor, and twice given away all that he had.

The third duty was fasting. In general the Moslem was commanded to avoid wine, carrion, blood, and the flesh of swine or dogs. But Mohammed was more lenient than Moses; forbidden foods might be eaten in cases of necessity; of a tasty cheese containing some prohibited meat he only asked, with his sly humor, "Mention the name of Allah over it." [30] He frowned on asceticism, and condemned monasticism (vii, 27); Mohammedans were to enjoy the pleasures of life with a good conscience, but in moderation. Nevertheless, Islam, like most religions, required certain fasts, partly as a discipline of the will, partly, we may presume, as hygiene. A few months after settling in Medina he saw the Jews keeping their annual fast of Yom Kippur; he adopted it for his followers, hoping to win the Jews to Islam; when this hope faded he transferred the fast to the month of Ramadan. For twenty-nine days the Moslem was to abstain, during the daylight hours, from eating, drinking, smoking, or contact with the other sex; exceptions were made for the sick, the weary traveler, the very young or old, and women with child or giving suck. When first decreed, the month of fasting fell in winter, when daylight came late and ended soon. But as the lunar calendar of the Moslems made the year shorter than the four seasons, Ramadan, every thirty-three years, fell in midsummer, when the days are long and the Eastern heat makes thirst a torture; yet the good Moslem bore the fast. Each night, however, the fast was broken, and the Moslem might eat, drink, smoke, and make love till the dawn; stores and shops remained open all those nights, inviting the populace to feasting and merriment. The poor worked as usual during the month of fast; the well-to-do could ease their way through it by sleeping during the day. Very pious persons spent the last ten nights of Ramadan in the mosque; on one of those nights, it was believed, Allah began to reveal the Koran to Mohammed; that night was accounted "better than a thousand months"; and simple devotees, uncertain which of the ten was the "Night of the Divine Decree," kept all ten with dire solemnity. On the first day after Ramadan the Moslems celebrated the festival of *Id al-Fitr*, or "Breaking of the Fast." They bathed, put on new clothes, saluted one another with an embrace, gave alms and presents, and visited the graves of their dead.

Pilgrimage to Mecca was the fourth duty of Moslem faith. Pilgrimage to holy places was traditional in the East; the Jew lived in hopes of one day seeing Zion; and pious pagan Arabs, long before Mohammed, had trekked to the Kaaba. Mohammed accepted the old custom because he knew that ritual is less easily changed than belief; and perhaps because he himself hankered after the Black Stone; by yielding to the old rite he opened a wide door to the acceptance of Islam by all Arabia. The Kaaba, purified of its idols, became for all Moslems the house of God; and upon every Mohammedan the obligation was laid (with considerate exceptions for the ailing and the poor) to make the Mecca pilgrimage "as often as he can"—which was soon interpreted as meaning once in a lifetime. As Islam spread to distant lands, only a minority of Moslems performed the pilgrimage; even in Mecca there are Moslems who have never made a ritual visit to the Kaaba.[31]

Doughty has described, beyond all rivalry, the panorama of the pilgrimage caravan moving with fantastic patience across the desert, caught between the hot fury of the sun and the swirling fire of the sands; some 7000 believers, less or more, on foot or horse or donkey or mule or lordly palanquin, but most tossed along between the humps of camels, "bowing at each long stalking pace . . . making fifty prostrations in every minute, whether we would or no, toward Mecca," [32] covering thirty miles in a weary day, sometimes fifty to reach an oasis; many pilgrims sickening and left behind; some dying and abandoned to lurking hyenas or a slower death. At Medina the pilgrims halted to view the tombs of Mohammed, Abu Bekr, and Omar I in the mosque of the Prophet; near those sepulchers, says a popular tradition, a space is reserved for Jesus the son of Miriam.[33]

Sighting Mecca, the caravan pitched its camp outside the walls, for the whole city was *haram*, sacred; the pilgrims bathed, dressed in seamless robes of white, and rode or walked in a line many miles long, over dusty roads, to seek living quarters in the town. During their stay in Mecca they were required to abstain from all disputes, from sexual relations, and from any sinful act.[34] In the months specially ordained for pilgrimage the Holy City became a babbling concourse of tribes and races suddenly doffing nationality and rank in the unanimity of ritual and prayer. Into the great enclosure called the Mosque of Mecca these thousands hurried in tense anticipation of a supreme experience; they hardly noted the elegant minarets of the wall, or the arcades and colonnades of the cloistered interior; but all stopped in awe at the well of Zemzem, whose water, said tradition, had slaked the thirst of Ishmael; every pilgrim drank of it, however bitter its taste, however urgent its effects; some bottled it to take home, to sip its saving sanctity daily, and in the hour of death.[35] At last the worshipers, all eyes and no breath, came, near the center of the enclosure, to the Kaaba itself, a miniature temple illuminated within by silver hanging lamps, its outer wall half draped with a curtain of rich and delicate cloth; and in a corner of it the ineffable Black Stone. Seven times the pilgrims walked around the Kaaba and kissed or touched or bowed to the Stone. (Such circumambulation of a sacred object—a fire, a tree, a maypole, an altar of the Temple at Jerusalem—was an old religious ritual.) Many pilgrims, exhausted and yet sleepless with devotion, passed the night in the enclosure, squatting on their rugs, conversing and praying, and contemplating in wonder and ecstasy the goal of their pilgrimage.

On the second day the pilgrims, to commemorate Hagar's frantic search for water for her son, ran seven times between the hills, Safa and Marwa, that lay outside the city. . . . On the seventh day those who wished to make the "major pilgrimage" streamed out to Mt. Ararat—six hours' journey distant—and heard a three-hour sermon; returning halfway, they spent a night in prayer at the oratory of Muzdalifa; on the eighth day they rushed to the valley of Mina and threw seven stones at three marks or pillars, for so, they believed, Abraham had cast stones at Satan when the Devil interrupted his preparations for slaying his son. . . . On the tenth day they sacrificed a sheep, a camel, and some other horned animal, ate the meat and distributed alms; this ceremony, commemorating similar sacrifices by Mohammed, was the central rite of the pilgrimage; and this "Festival of Sacrifice" was celebrated with like offerings to Allah by Moslems all over the world on the tenth day of the pilgrimage period. The pilgrims now shaved their heads, pared their nails, and buried the cuttings. This completed the Major Pilgrimage; but usually the worshiper paid another visit to the Kaaba before he returned to the caravan camp. There he resumed his profane condition and clothing, and began with proud and comforted spirit the long march back home.

This famous pilgrimage served many purposes. Like that of the Jews to Jerusalem, of the Christians to Jerusalem or Rome, it intensified the worshiper's faith, and bound him by a collective emotional experience to his creed and to his fellow believers. In the pilgrim age a fusing piety brought together poor Bedouins from the desert, rich merchants from the towns, Berbers, African Negroes, Syrians, Persians, Turks, Tatars, Moslem Indians, Chinese—all wearing the same simple garb, reciting the same prayers in the same Arabic tongue; hence, perhaps, the moderation of racial distinctions in Islam. The circling of the Kaaba seems superstitious to the non-Moslem; but the Moslem smiles at similar customs in other faiths, is disturbed by the Christian rite of eating the god, and can understand it only as an external symbol of spiritual communion and sustenance. All religions are superstitions to other faiths.

And all religions, however noble in origin, soon carry an accretion of superstitions rising naturally out of minds harassed and stupefied by the fatigue of the body and the terror of the soul in the struggle for continuance. Most Moslems believed in magic, and rarely doubted the ability of sorcerers to divine the future, to reveal hidden treasures, compel affection, afflict an enemy, cure disease, or ward off the evil eye. Many believed in magic metamorphoses of men into animals or plants, or in miraculous transits through space; this is almost the framework of the *Arabian Nights*. Spirits were everywhere, performing every manner of trick and enchantment upon mortals, and begetting unwanted children upon careless women. Most Moslems, like half the Christian world, wore amulets as protection against evil influences, considered some days lucky, other days unlucky, and believed that dreams might reveal the future, and that God sometimes spoke to man in dreams. Everyone in Islam, as in Christendom, accepted astrology; the skies were charted not only to fix the orientation of mosques and the calendar of religious feasts, but to select a celestially propitious moment for any important enterprise, and to determine the genethlialogy of each individual—i.e., his character and fate as set by the position of the stars at his birth.

Seeming to the outer world so indiscriminately one in ritual and belief, Islam was early divided into sects as numerous and furious as in Christendom. There were the martial, puritanic, democratic Kharijites; Murji'ites who held that no Moslem would be everlastingly damned; Jabrites who denied free will and upheld absolute predestination; Qadarites who defended the freedom of the will; and many others; we pay our respects to their sincerity and omniscience, and pass on. But the Shi'ites belong inescapably to history. They overthrew the Umayyads, captured Persian, Egyptian, and Indian Islam, and deeply affected literature and philosophy. The Shia (i.e., group, sect) had its origin in two murders—the assassination of Ali, and the slaughter of Husein and his family. A large minority of Moslems argued that since Mohammed was the chosen Apostle of Allah, it must have been Allah's intent that the Prophet's descendants, inheriting some measure of his divine spirit and purpose, should inherit his leadership in Islam. All caliphs except Ali seemed to them usurpers. They rejoiced when Ali became caliph, mourned when he was murdered, and were profoundly shocked by Husein's death. Ali and Husein became saints in Shia worship; their shrines were held second in holiness only to the Kaaba and the Prophet's tomb. Perhaps influenced by Persian, Jewish, and Christian ideas of a Messiah, and the Buddhist conception of Bodhisattvas—repeatedly incarnated saints—the Shi'ites considered the descendants of Ali to be Imams ("exemplars"), i.e., infallible incarnations of divine wisdom. The eighth Imam was Riza, whose tomb at Mashhad, in northeastern Persia, is accounted the "Glory of the

Shia World." In 873 the twelfth Imam—Muhammad ibn Hasan—disappeared in the twelfth year of his age; in Shia belief he did not die, but bides his time to reappear and lead the Shia Moslems to universal supremacy and bliss.

As in most religions, the various sects of Islam felt toward one another an animosity more intense than that with which they viewed the "infidels" in their midst. To these *Dhimmi*—Christians, Zoroastrians, Sabaeans, Jews—the Umayyad caliphate offered a degree of toleration hardly equaled in contemporary Christian lands. They were allowed the free practice of their faiths, and the retention of their churches, on condition that they wear a distinctive honey-colored dress, and pay a poll tax of from one to four dinars ($4.75 to $19.00) per year according to their income. This tax fell only upon non-Moslems capable of military service; it was not levied upon monks, women, adolescents, slaves, the old, crippled, blind, or very poor. In return the *Dhimmi* were excused (or excluded) from military service, were exempt from the two and a half per cent tax for community charity, and received the protection of the government. Their testimony was not admitted in Moslem courts, but they were allowed self-government under their own leaders, judges, and laws. The degree of toleration varied with dynasties; the Successors were spasmodically severe, the Umayyads generally lenient, the Abbasids alternately lenient and severe. Omar I ejected all Jews and Christians from Arabia as Islam's Holy Land, and a questionable tradition ascribes to him a "Covenant of Omar" restraining their rights in general; but this edict, if it ever existed, was in practice ignored,[36] and Omar himself continued in Egypt the allowances formerly made to the Christian churches by the Byzantine government.

The Jews of the Near East had welcomed the Arabs as liberators. They suffered now divers disabilities and occasional persecutions; but they stood on equal terms with Christians, were free once more to live and worship in Jerusalem, and prospered under Islam in Asia, Egypt, and Spain as never under Christian rule. Outside of Arabia the Christians of western Asia usually practiced their religion unhindered; Syria remained predominantly Christian until the third Moslem century; in the reign of Mamun (813–33) we hear of 11,000 Christian churches in Islam—as well as hundreds of synagogues and fire temples. Christian festivals were freely and openly celebrated; Christian pilgrims came in safety to visit Christian shrines in Palestine;[37] the Crusaders found large numbers of Christians in the Near East in the twelfth century; and Christian communities have survived there to this day. Christian heretics persecuted by the patriarchs of Constantinople, Jerusalem, Alexandria, or Antioch were now free and safe under a Moslem rule that found their disputes quite unintelligible. In the ninth century the Moslem governor of Antioch appointed a special guard to keep Christian sects from massacring one another at church.[38] Monasteries and nunneries flourished under the skeptical Umayyads; the Arabs admired the work of the monks in agriculture and reclamation, acclaimed the wines of monastic vintage, and enjoyed, in traveling, the shade and hospitality of Christian cloisters. For a time relations between the two religions were so genial that Christians wearing crosses on their breasts conversed in mosques with Moslem friends.[39] The Mohammedan administrative bureaucracy had hundreds of Christian employees; Christians rose so frequently to high office as to provoke Moslem complaints. Sergius, father of St. John of Damascus, was chief finance minister to Abd-al-Malik, and John himself, last of the Greek Fathers of the Church, headed the council that governed Damascus.[40] The Christians of the East in general regarded Islamic rule as a lesser evil than that of the Byzantine government and church.[41]

Despite or because of this policy of tolerance in early Islam, the new faith won over to itself in time most of the Christians, nearly all the Zoroastrians and pagans, and many of the Jews, of Asia, Egypt, and North Africa. It was a fiscal advantage to share the faith of the ruling race; captives in war could escape slavery by accepting Allah, Mohammed, and circumcision. Gradually the non-Moslem populations adopted the Arabic language and dress, the laws and faith of the Koran. Where Hellenism, after a thousand years of mastery, had failed to take root, and Roman arms had left the native gods unconquered, and Byzantine orthodoxy had raised rebellious heresies, Mohammedanism had secured, almost without proselytism, not only belief and worship, but a tenacious fidelity that quite forgot the superseded gods. From China, Indonesia, and India through Persia, Syria, Arabia, and Egypt to Morocco and Spain, the Mohammedan faith touched the hearts and fancies of a hundred peoples, governed their morals and molded their lives, gave them consoling hopes and a strengthening pride, until today it owns the passionate allegiance of 350,000,000 souls, and through all political divisions makes them one.

III. THE PEOPLE

Under the Umayyads the Arabs constituted a ruling aristocracy, and enjoyed a stipend from the state; in return for these privileges, all able-bodied Arab males were subject at any time to military service. As conquerors they were proud of their supposedly unmixed blood and pure speech. With keen genealogical consciousness the Arab added his father's name to his own, as in Abdallah ibn (son of) Zobeir; sometimes he added his tribe and place of origin, and made a biography of a name, as in Abu Bekr Ahmad ibn Jarir al-Azdi. Purity of blood became a myth as the conquerors took conquered women as concubines, and reckoned their offspring as Arabs; but pride of blood and rank remained. The higher class of Arabs moved about on horseback, clothed in white silk and a sword; the commoner walked in baggy trousers, convoluted turban, and pointed shoes; the Bedouin kept his flowing gown, head shawl and band. Long drawers were prohibited by the Prophet, but some Arabs ventured into them. All classes affected jewelry. Women stimulated the male fancy with tight bodices, bright girdles, loose and colorful skirts. They wore their hair in bangs at the front, curls at the side, braids at the back; sometimes they filled it out with black silk threads; often they adorned it with gems or flowers. Increasingly after the year 715, when out of doors, they veiled the face below the eyes; in this way every woman could be romantic, for at any age the eyes of Arab women are perilously beautiful. Women matured at twelve and were old at forty; in the interval they inspired most of Arabic poetry, and maintained the race.

The Moslem had no respect for celibacy, and never dreamed of perpetual continence as an ideal state; most Moslem saints married and had children. Perhaps Islam erred in the opposite direction, and carried marriage to an extreme. It gave the sexual appetite so many outlets within the law that prostitution diminished for a time under Mohammed and the Successors; but exhaustion requires stimulation, and dancing girls soon played a prominent role in the life of even the most married Moslem male. Moslem literature, being intended only for male eyes and ears, was sometimes as loose as male conversation in a Christian land; it contained a superabundance of deliberately erotic books; and Moslem medical works gave much attention to aphrodisiacs.[42] In strict Mohammedan law fornication and pederasty were to be punished with death; but the growth of wealth brought an easier ethic, punished fornication with thirty strokes, and winked at the spread of homosexual love.[43] A class of professional homosexuals (*mukhannath*) arose who imitated the costume and conduct of women, plaited their hair, dyed their nails with henna, and performed obscene dances.[44] The Caliph Suleiman ordered the *mukhannath* of Mecca castrated; and the Caliph al-Hadi, coming upon two women attendants in Lesbian relations, beheaded them on the spot.[45] Despite such discouragement homosexualism made rapid progress; a few years after al-Hadi it was prevalent at Harun's court, and in the songs of his favorite poet Abu Nuwas. The Moslem male, separated from women before marriage by purdah, and surfeited with them after marriage by the harem, fell into irregular relations; and women, secluded from all men but relatives, slipped into similar perversions.

The contact with Persia promoted both pederasty and purdah in Islam. The Arabs had always feared, as well as admired, woman's charms, and had revenged themselves for instinctive subjection to them by the usual male doubts about her virtue and intelligence. "Consult women," said Omar I, "and do the contrary of what they advise."[46] But the Moslems of Mohammed's century had not secluded their women; the two sexes exchanged visits, moved indiscriminately through the streets, and prayed together in the mosque.[47] When Musab ibn al-Zobeir asked his wife Aisha why she never veiled her face, she answered: "Since Allah, may He remain blessed and exalted, hath put upon me the stamp of beauty, it is my wish that the public

should view that beauty, and thereby recognize His grace unto them." [48]
Under Walid II (743–4), however, the harem-and-eunuch system took form,
and purdah developed with it. *Harim*, like *haram*, meant forbidden, sacred;
the seclusion of women was originally due to their being tabu because of
menstruation or childbirth; the harem was a sanctuary. The Moslem husband
knew the passionate temper of the Oriental, felt a need to protect his women,
and saw no escape from their adultery except through their incarceration.
It became reprehensible for women to walk in the streets except for short
distances and veiled; they could visit one another, but usually they traveled
in curtained litters; and they were never to be seen abroad at night. They
were separated from the men in the mosque by a screen or railing or gallery;
finally they were excluded altogether; [49] and religion, which in Latin Christendom has been described as a secondary sexual characteristic of the female,
became in Islam, as public worship, a prerogative of the male. Even more
cruelly, women were forbidden the pleasure of shopping; they sent out for
what they needed; and pedlars, usually women, came to spread their wares
on the harem floor. Rarely, except in the lower classes, did the women sit at
table with their husbands. It was unlawful for a Moslem to see the face of
any woman except his wives, slaves, and near relatives. A physician was
allowed to see only the afflicted part of a woman patient. The man found
the system very convenient; it gave him at home a maximum of opportunity,
and outside the home full freedom from surveillance or surprise. As for the
women themselves, until the nineteenth century, there is no evidence that
they objected to purdah or the veil. They enjoyed the privacy, security, and
comforts of the zenana, or women's quarters; they resented as an insult any
negligence of the husband in maintaining their seclusion; [50] and from their
apparent prison the legal wives still played a lively part in history. Khaizuran,
Harun's mother, and Zobaida, his wife, rivaled in the eighth and ninth centuries the influence and audacity of Aisha in the seventh, and enjoyed a magnificence hardly dreamed of by Mohammed's wives.

The education of girls, in most ranks of the population, seldom went beyond learning their prayers, a few chapters of the Koran, and the arts of the
home. In the upper classes women received considerable instruction, usually
by private tutors, but sometimes in schools and colleges; [51] they learned
poetry, music, and many varieties of needlework; some became scholars,
even teachers. Several were famous for enlightened philanthropy. They were
taught a brand of modesty adapted to their customs; surprised at the bath,
they would cover their faces first; they marveled at the immodesty of European women who bared half their bosoms at a ball and embraced divers men
in a dance; and they admired the forbearance of a God who did not strike
such sinners dead. [52]

As in most civilized countries, marriages were usually arranged by the
parents. The father might marry his daughter to whomever he wished before

she became of age; after that she might choose. Girls were usually married by the age of twelve, and were mothers at thirteen or fourteen; some married at nine or ten; men married as early as fifteen. The betrothal, or marriage contract, pledged the groom to give her a dowry; this remained her property through marriage and divorce. The groom was rarely allowed to see the face of his bride before marriage. The wedding followed eight or ten days after the betrothal; it required no priest, but was accompanied by brief prayers; it involved music, feasting, a "shower" of gifts, and a gay illumination of the bridegroom's street and house. After many ceremonies the husband, in the privacy of the bridal chamber, drew aside the veil of his wife, and said, "In the name of God the Compassionate, the Merciful." [53]

If this belated examination left the groom dissatisfied, he might at once send the wife back to her parents with her dowry. Polygamy in Islam was more often successive than simultaneous; only the rich could afford plural wives. [54] Facility of divorce made it possible for a Moslem to have almost any number of successive mates; Ali had 200; [55] Ibn al-Teiyib, a dyer of Baghdad who lived to be eighty-five, is reported to have married 900 wives. [56] In addition to wives a Moslem might have any number of concubines; Harun contented himself with 200, but al-Mutawakkil, we are told, had 4000, each of whom shared his bed for a night. [57] Some slave merchants trained female slaves in music, song, and sexual seduction, and then sold them as concubines for as much as 100,000 dirhems ($80,000). [58] But we must not think of the usual harem as a private brothel. In most cases the concubines became mothers, and prided themselves on the number and gender of their children; and there were many instances of tender affection between master and concubine. Legal wives accepted concubinage as a matter of course. Zobaida, wife of Harun, presented him with ten concubines. [59] In this way a man's household might contain as many children as an American suburb. A son of Walid I had sixty sons and an unrecorded number of daughters. Eunuchs, forbidden by the Koran, became a necessary appendage to the harem; Christians and Jews participated in importing or manufacturing them; caliphs, viziers, and magnates paid high prices for them; and soon these cunning *castrati* subjected many phases of Moslem government to their narrow competence. In the early centuries after the conquest this harem system prevented the Arabs from being ethnically absorbed by the conquered population, and multiplied them to a number needed to rule their spreading realm. Possibly it had some eugenic effect from the free fertility of the ablest men; but after Mamun polygamy became a source of moral and physical deterioration, and—as mouths grew faster than food—of increasing poverty and discontent.

The position of woman within marriage was one of sacred subjection. She could have only one husband at a time, and could divorce him only at considerable cost. The infidelities of her husband were quite beyond her ken, and were accounted morally negligible; her own infidelity was punishable with death. It is remarkable how many adulteries she managed to commit despite her handicaps. She was reviled and revered, belittled and suppressed, and in most cases was loved with passion and tenderness. "For my wife," said Abu'l Atiyya, "I will gladly renounce all the prizes of life and all the wealth of the world";[60] such professions were frequent, and sometimes sincere. In one matter the Moslem wife was favored as compared with some European women. Whatever property she received was wholly at her disposal, not subject to any claim of her husband or his creditors. Within the security of the zenana she spun, wove, sewed, managed the household and the children, played games, ate sweets, gossiped and intrigued. She was expected to bear many children, as economic assets in an agricultural and patriarchal society; the estimation in which she was held depended chiefly upon her fertility; "a piece of old matting lying in a corner," said Mohammed, "is better than a barren wife."[61] Nevertheless abortion and contraception were widely practiced in the harem. Midwives transmitted ancient techniques, and physicians offered new ones. Al-Razi (d. 924) included in his *Quintessence of Experience* a section "on the means of preventing conception," and listed twenty-four, mechanical or chemical.[62] Ibn Sina (Avicenna, 980–1037), in his famous *Qanun*, gave twenty contraceptive recipes.

In nonsexual morals the Mohammedan did not differ appreciably from the Christian. The Koran more definitely denounced gambling and intoxication (v, 90); but some gambling and much drinking continued in both civilizations. Corruption in government and judiciary flourished in Islam as in Christendom. In general the Moslem seems to have excelled the Christian in commercial morality,[63] fidelity to his word, and loyalty to treaties signed;[64] Saladin was by common consent the best gentleman of the Crusades. The Moslems were honest about lying; they allowed a lie to save a life, to patch up a quarrel, to please a wife, to deceive in war the enemies of the faith.[65] Moslem manners were both formal and genial, and Moslem speech was heavy with compliments and polite hyperbole. Like the Jews, the Moslems greeted one another with a solemn bow and salutation: "Peace [*salaam*] be with you"; and the proper reply of every Moslem was, "On you be peace, and the mercy and blessings of God." Hospitality was universal and generous. Cleanliness was a function of income; the poor were neglected and encrusted, the well-to-do were scrubbed, manicured, and perfumed. Circumcision, though not mentioned in the Koran, was taken for granted as a precaution of hygiene; boys underwent the operation at five or six.[66] Private baths were a luxury of the rich, but public bathhouses were numerous; Baghdad in the tenth century, we are told, had 27,000.[67] Perfumes and incense were popular with men as well as with women. Arabia was famous of old for its frankin cense and myrrh; Persia for its oil of roses or violets or jasmine. Gardens of shrubs, flowers, and fruit trees were attached to many homes; and flowers were loved, above all in Persia, as the very fragrance of life.

How did these people amuse themselves? Largely with feasting, venery in both senses, flirtation, poetry, music, and song; to which the lower orders added cockfights, ropedancers, jugglers, magicians, puppets. . . . We find from Avicenna's *Qanun* that the Moslems of the tenth century had nearly all the sports and physical foibles of our time: boxing, wrestling, running, archery, throwing the javelin, gymnastics, fencing, riding, polo, croquet, weight lifting and ball playing with mallet, hockey stick, or bat.[68] Games of chance being forbidden, cards and dice were not much used; backgammon was popular; chess was allowed, though Mohammed had denounced the carving of the pieces in the likeness of men. Horse racing was popular, and was patronized by the caliphs; in one program, we are informed, 4000 horses took part. Hunting remained the most aristocratic of sports, less violent than in Sasanian times, and often subsiding into falconry. Captured animals were sometimes used as pets; some families had dogs, others monkeys; some caliphs kept lions or tigers to awe subjects and ambassadors.

When the Arabs conquered Syria they were still half-barbarous tribes, recklessly brave, violent, sensual, passionate, superstitious, and skeptical. Islam softened some of these qualities, but most of them survived. Probably the cruelties recorded of the caliphs were no worse in total than those of contemporary Christian kings, Byzantine, Merovingian, or Norse; but they were a disgrace to any civilization. In 717 Suleiman, on pilgrimage to Mecca, invited his courtiers to try their swords on 400 Greeks recently captured in war; the invitation was accepted and the 400 men were beheaded in merry sport as the Caliph looked on.[69] Al-Mutawakkil, enthroned, cast into prison a vizier who had, some years before, treated him with indignity; for weeks the prisoner was kept awake to the point of insanity; then he was allowed to sleep for twenty-four hours; so strengthened, he was placed between boards lined with spikes, which prevented his moving without self-laceration; so he lay in agony for days till he died.[70] Such savagery, of course, was exceptional; normally the Moslem was the soul of courtesy, humanity, and tolerance. He was, if we may describe the mythical average, quick of apprehension and wit; excitable and lazy, easily amused and readily cheerful; finding content in simplicity, bearing misfortune calmly, accepting all events with patience, dignity, and pride. Starting on a long journey, the Moslem took his grave linen with him, prepared at any time to meet the Great Scavenger; overcome in the desert by exhaustion or disease, he would bid the others go on, would perform his final ablutions, hollow out a pit for his grave, wrap himself in his winding sheet, lie down in the trench, and wait for the coming of death, and a natural burial by the wind-blown sands.[71]

IV. THE GOVERNMENT

Theoretically, in the generation after Mohammed, Islam was a democratic republic in the ancient sense: all free adult males were to share in choosing the ruler and determining policy. Actually the Commander of the Faithful was chosen, and policy was decided, by a small group of notables in Medina. This was to be expected; men being by nature unequal in intelligence and scruple, democracy must at best be relative; and in communities with poor communication and limited schooling some form of oligarchy is inevitable. Since war and democracy are enemies, the expansion of Islam promoted one-man rule; unity of command and quickness of decision were required by a martial and imperialist policy. Under the Umayyads the government became frankly monarchical, and the caliphate was transmitted by succession or trial of arms.

Again theoretically, the caliphate was a religious rather than a political office; the caliph was first of all the head of a religious group, Islam; and his primary duty was to defend the faith; in theory the caliphate was a theocracy, a government by God through religion. The caliph, however, was not a pope or a priest, nor could he issue new decrees of the faith. In practice he enjoyed nearly absolute power, limited by no parliament, no hereditary aristocracy, no priesthood, but only by the Koran—which his paid pundits could interpret at his will. Under this despotism there was some democracy of opportunity: any man might rise to high office unless both his parents were slaves.

The Arabs, recognizing that they had conquered decadent but well-organized societies, took over in Syria the Byzantine, in Persia the Sasanian, administrative system; essentially the old order of life in the Near East continued, and even the Hellenic-Oriental culture, overleaping the barrier of language, revived in Moslem science and philosophy. Under the Abbasids a complex system of central, provincial, and local government took form, operated by a bureaucracy that suffered little interruption from royal assassinations and palace revolutions. At the head of the administrative structure was the *hajib* or chamberlain, who in theory merely managed ceremony, but in practice accumulated power by controlling entry to the caliph. Next in rank, but (after Mansur) superior in power, was the vizier, who appointed and supervised the officials of the government, and guided the policy of the state. The leading bureaus were those of taxation, accounts, correspondence, police, post, and a department of grievances, which became a court of appeal from judicial or administrative decisions. Next to the army in the caliph's affections was the bureau of revenue; here all the pervasive pertinacity of the Byzantine tax collectors was emulated, and great sums were sluiced from the nation's economy to maintain the government and the governors. The annual revenue of the caliphate under Harun al-Rashid exceeded 530,000,000 dirhems ($42,400,000) in money, to which were added now incalculable taxes in kind.[72] There was no national debt; on the contrary, the treasury in 786 had a balance of 900,000,000 dirhems.

The public post, as under the Persians and Romans, served only the government and very important persons; its chief use was to transmit intelligence and directives between the provinces and the capital, but it served also as a vehicle of espionage by the vizier upon local officers. The system issued itineraries, available to merchants and pilgrims, giving the names of the various stations, and the distances between them; these itineraries were the basis of Arabic geography. Pigeons were trained and used as letter carriers—the first such use known to history (837). Additional "intelligence" was provided by travelers and merchants, and in Baghdad 1700 "aged women" served as spies. No amount of surveillance, however, could check the Oriental-Occidental appetite for "squeeze" or "graft." The provincial governors, as in Roman days, expected their tenure of office to reimburse them for the expenses of their climb and the tribulations of their descent. The caliphs occasionally forced them to disgorge their accumulations, or sold this right of squeezing to the newly appointed government; so Yusuf ibn Omar extracted 76,000,000 dirhems from his predecessors in the government of Iraq. Judges were well paid, yet they too could be influenced by the generous; and Mohammed (says a tradition) was convinced that out of three judges at least two would go to hell.[73]

The law by which the great realm was ruled claimed to deduce itself from the Koran. In Islam, as in Judaism, law and religion were one; every crime was a sin, every sin a crime; and jurisprudence was a branch of theology. As conquest extended the reach and responsibilities of Mohammed's impromptu legislation, and puzzled it with cases unforeseen in the Koran, the Moslem jurists invented traditions that implicitly or explicitly met their need; hence the Hadith became a second source of Mohammedan law. By strange but repeated coincidence these useful traditions echoed the principles and judgments of Roman and Byzantine law, and still more of the Mishna or Gemara of the Jews.[74] The growing mass and complexity of legal traditions gave sustenance and high status to the legal profession in Islam; the jurists (*faqihs*) who expounded or applied the law acquired by the tenth century almost the power and sanctity of a priestly class. As in twelfth-century France, they allied themselves with the monarchy, supported the absolutism of the Abbasids, and reaped rich rewards.

Four famous schools of law took form in orthodox Islam. Abu Hanifa ibn Thabit (d. 767) revolutionized Koranic law by his principle of analogical interpretation. A law originally enacted for a desert community, he argued, must be interpreted analogously, not literally, when applied to an industrial or urban society; on this basis he sanctioned mortgage loans and interest (forbidden in the Koran), much as Hillel had done in Palestine eight centuries before. "The legal rule," said Hanifa, "is not the same as the rules of grammar and logic. It expresses a general custom, and changes with the circumstances that produced it." [75] Against this liberal philosophy of progressive law the conservatives of Medina put forth a strong defender in Malik ibn Anas (715–95). Basing his system on a study of 1700 juridical Hadith, Malik proposed that since most of these traditions had arisen in Medina, the consensus of opinion in Medina should be the criterion of interpretation of both the Hadith and the Koran. Muhammad al-Shafii (767–820), living in Baghdad and Cairo, thought that infallibility should have a wider base than Medina, and found in the general consensus of the whole Moslem community the final test of legality, orthodoxy, and truth. His pupil Ahmad ibn

Hanbal (780–855) considered this criterion too wide and vague, and founded a fourth school on the principle that law should be determined exclusively by the Koran and the traditions. He denounced the rationalism of the Mutazilites in philosophy, was jailed for orthodoxy by al-Mamun, but held so valiantly to his conservative position that when he died almost the entire population of Baghdad attended his funeral.

Despite this century-long debate, the four schools of law recognized by orthodox Islam agreed in detail as much as they differed in principle. They all assumed the divine origin of the Moslem law, and the necessity of divine origin for any law adequate to control a naturally lawless mankind. They all entered into such minute regulation of conduct and ritual as only Judaism could equal; they prescribed the correct use of toothpicks and matrimonial rights, the proper dress of the sexes, and the moral arrangement of the hair. One legist never ate watermelon because he could not find, in either the Koran or the Hadith, the canonical method for such an operation.[76] The multiplicity of enactments would have stifled human development; but legal fictions and condoned evasions reconciled the rigor of the law with the flow and vigor of life. Even so, and despite the wide acceptance of the liberalizing Hanafite code, Mohammedan law tended to be too conservative, too inflexibly mortised in orthodoxy to allow a free evolution of economy, morals, and thought.

With these provisos we must concede that the early caliphs, from Abu Bekr to al-Mamun, gave successful organization to human life over a wide area, and may be counted among the ablest rulers in history. They might have devastated or confiscated everything, like the Mongols or the Magyars or the raiding Norse; instead they merely taxed. When Omar conquered Egypt he rejected the advice of Zobeir to divide the land among his followers, and the Caliph confirmed his judgment: "Leave it," said Omar, "in the people's hands to nurse and fructify." [77] Under the caliphal government lands were measured, records were systematically kept, roads and canals were multiplied or maintained, rivers were banked to prevent floods; Iraq, now half desert, was again a garden of Eden; Palestine, recently so rich in sand and stones, was fertile, wealthy, and populous.[78] Doubtless the exploitation of simplicity and weakness by cleverness and strength went on under this system as under all governments; but the caliphs gave reasonable protection to life and labor, kept career open to talent, promoted for three to six centuries the prosperity of areas never so prosperous again, and stimulated and supported such a flourishing of education, literature, science, philosophy, and art as made western Asia, for five centuries, the most civilized region in the world.

V. THE CITIES

Before searching out the men and the works that gave meaning and distinction to this civilization we must try to visualize the environment in which they lived. Civilization is rural in base but urban in form; men must gather in cities to provide for one another audiences and stimuli.

Moslem towns were nearly all of modest size, with 10,000 souls or less, cramped into a small and usually walled area for protection against raid or siege, with unlit streets of dust or mud, and little stucco houses hugging their privacy behind a forbidding continuum of external wall; all the glory of the town was concentrated in the mosque. But here and there rose the cities in which Moslem civilization touched its summits of beauty, learning, and happiness.

In Moslem sentiment both Mecca and Medina were holy cities, one as the seat of the ancient Arab shrine and the birthplace of the Prophet, the other as his refuge and home. Walid II rebuilt in splendor the modest mosque at Medina; at Walid's urging, and for 80,000 dinars, the Byzantine emperor sent forty loads of mosaic stones, and eighty craftsmen from Egypt and Greece; the Moslems complained that their Prophet's mosque was being built by Christian infidels. Despite the Kaaba and this mosque, the two cities took on under the Umayyads an aspect of worldly pleasure and luxury that would have shocked the earlier caliphs, and must have gladdened the triumphant Quraish. The spoils of conquest had flowed into Medina, and had been distributed chiefly to its citizens; pilgrims were coming to Mecca in greater number, and with richer offerings than ever before, enormously stimulating trade. The holy cities became centers of wealth, leisure, gaiety, and song; palaces and suburban villas housed an aristocracy surfeited with servants and slaves; concubines accumulated, forbidden wine flowed, singers strummed pleasantly sad melodies, and poets multiplied rhymes of war and love. At Medina the beautiful Suqainah, daughter of the martyred Husein, presided over a salon of poets, jurists, and statesmen. Her wit, charm, and good taste set a standard for all Islam; she could not count her successive husbands on her jeweled fingers; and in some instances she made it a condition of marriage that she should retain full freedom of action.[79] The Umayyad spirit of *joie de vivre* had conquered the abstemious puritanism of Abu Bekr and Omar in the most sacred centers of Islam.

Jerusalem was also a holy city to Islam. Already in the eighth century the Arabs predominated in its population. The Caliph Abd-al-Malik, envying the splendor with which the church of the Holy Sepulcher had been restored after its destruction by Khosru Parvez, lavished the revenues of Egypt to surpass that shrine with a group of structures known to the Moslem world as *Al-Haram al-Sharif* (the venerable sanctuary). At the south end was built (691–4) *Al-Masjid al-Aqsa*—"The Farther Mosque"—so named after a passage in the Koran (xvii, 1). It was ruined by earthquake in 746, restored in 785, and often modified; but the nave goes back to Abd-al-Malik, and most of the columns to Justinian's basilica in Jerusalem. Muqaddasi considered it more beautiful than the Great Mosque at Damascus. Somewhere in the sacred enclosure, it was said, Mohammed had met Abraham, Moses, and Jesus, and had prayed with them; near by he had seen the rock (reckoned by Israel to be the center of the world) where Abraham had thought to sacrifice Isaac, and Moses had received the Ark of the Covenant, and Solomon and Herod had built their temples; from that rock Mohammed had ascended into heaven; if one but had faith he could see in the rock the footprints of the Prophet. In 684, when the rebel Abdallah ibn Zobeir held Mecca and received the revenues of its pilgrims, Abd-al-Malik, anxious to attract some of this sacred revenue, decreed that thereafter this rock should replace the Kaaba as the object of pious pilgrimage. Over that historic stone his artisans (691) raised in Syrian-Byzantine style the famous "Dome of the Rock," which soon ranked as the third of the "four wonders of the Moslem world" (the others were the mosques of Mecca, Medina, and Damascus). It was not a mosque, but a shrine to house the rock; the Crusaders erred twice in calling it the "Mosque of Omar." Upon an octagonal building of squared stones, 528 feet in circuit, rises a dome, 112 feet high, made of wood externally covered with gilded brass. Four elegant portals—their lintels faced by splendid *repoussé* bronze plates—lead into an interior divided into diminishing octagons by concentric colonnades of polished marbles; the magnificent columns were taken from Roman ruins, the capitals were Byzantine. The spandrels of the arches are distinguished by mosaics depicting trees with all the delicacy of a Courbet; even finer are the mosaics of the drum below the dome. Running around the cornice of the outer colonnade, in yellow letters on blue tiles, is an inscription in Kufic—the angular characters favored in Kufa; Saladin had it set up in 1187; it is a lovely example of this unique form of architectural decoration. Within the colonnade is the massive, shapeless rock, 200 feet around. "At dawn," wrote Muqaddasi,

> when the light of the sun first strikes on the cupola, and the drum reflects his rays, then is this edifice a marvelous sight to behold, and such that in all Islam I have never seen the equal; neither have I heard tell of aught built in pagan times that rivals in grace this Dome of the Rock.[80]

Abd-al-Malik's plan to make this monument replace the Kaaba failed; had it succeeded, Jerusalem would have been the center of all the three faiths that competed for the soul of medieval man.

But Jerusalem was not even the capital of the province of Palestine; that honor went to al-Ramlah. Many places that are now poor villages were in Moslem days flourishing towns. "Aqqa" (Acre) "is a large city, spaciously laid out," wrote Muqaddasi in 985; "Sidon is a large city, surrounded by gardens and trees," wrote Idrisi in 1154. "Tyre is a beautiful place," wrote Yaqubi in 891, built on a rock jutting out into the Mediterranean; "its inns are five or six stories high," wrote Nasir-i-Khosru in 1047, "and great is the quantity of wealth exposed in its clean bazaars." [81] Tripoli, to the north, had "a fine harbor, capable of holding a thousand ships." Tiberias was famous for its hot springs and its jasmines. Of Nazareth the Moslem traveler Yaqut wrote in 1224: "Here was born the Messiah Isa, the son of Mariam—peace be upon him! . . . But the people of this place cast dishonor upon her, saying that from all time no virgin has ever borne a child." [82] Baalbek, said Yaqubi, "is one of the finest towns in Syria"; "prosperous and pleasant," added Muqaddasi. Antioch was second only to Damascus among the cities of Syria; the Moslems held it from 635 to 964, the Byzantines then till 1084; the Mohammedan geographers admired its many beautiful Christian churches, its rising terraces of pretty homes, its lush gardens and parks, the running water in every house. Tarsus was a major city; Ibn Hawqal (978) reckoned its male adults at 100,000; the Greek Emperor Nicephorus recaptured it in 965, destroyed all the mosques, and burned all the Korans. Aleppo was enriched by the junction there of two caravan routes: the city "is populous and built of stone," wrote Muqaddasi; "shady streets, with rows of shops, lead to each of the gates of the mosque"; in that shrine was a mihrab famous for the beauty of its carved ivory and wood, and a minbar "most exquisite to behold"; near by were five colleges, a hospital, and six Christian churches. Homs (the ancient Emesa) "is one of the largest cities in Syria," wrote Yaqubi in 891; "nearly all its streets and markets are paved with stones," wrote Istakhri in 950; "the women here," said Muqaddasi, "are beautiful, and famous for their fine skin." [83]

The eastward sweep of the Arab empire favored for its capital a site more central than either Mecca or Jerusalem; and the Umayyads wisely chose Damascus—already heavy with centuries when the Arabs came. Five converging streams made its hinterland the "Garden of the Earth," fed a hundred public fountains, a hundred public baths, and 120,000 gardens,[84] and flowed out westward into a "Valley of Violets" twelve miles long and three miles wide. "Damascus," said Idrisi, "is the most delightful of all God's cities." [85] In the heart of the town, amid a population of some 140,000 souls, rose the palace of the caliphs, built by Muawiya I, gaudy with gold and marble, brilliant with mosaics in floors and walls, cool with ever-flowing fountains and cascades. On the north side stood the Great Mosque, one of 572 mosques in the city, and the sole surviving relic of Umayyad Damascus. In Roman days a temple of Jupiter had adorned the site; on its ruins Theodosius I had built (379) the cathedral of St. John the Baptist. Walid I, about 705, proposed to the Christians that the cathedral should be remodeled and form part of a new mosque, and promised to give them ground and materials for another cathedral anywhere else in the city. They protested, and warned him that "it is written in our books that he who destroys this church will choke to death"; but Walid began the destruction with his own hands. The whole land tax of the empire, we are told, was devoted for seven years to the construction of the mosque; in addition a large sum was given to the Christians to finance a new cathedral. Artists and artisans were brought in from India, Persia, Constantinople, Egypt, Libya, Tunis, and Algeria; all together 12,000 workmen were employed, and the task was completed in eight years. Moslem travelers unanimously describe it as the most magnificent structure in Islam; and the Abbasid caliphs al-Mahdi and al-Mamun—no lovers of the Umayyads or Damascus—ranked it above all other buildings on the earth. A great battle-mented wall, with interior colonnades, enclosed a spacious marble-paved court. On the south side of this enclosure rose the mosque, built of squared stones and guarded by three minarets—one of which is the oldest in Islam. Ground plan and decoration were Byzantine, and were doubtless influenced by St. Sophia. The roof and dome—fifty feet in diameter—were covered with plates of lead. The interior, 429 feet long, was divided into nave and aisles by two tiers of white marble columns, from whose gold-plated Corinthian capitals sprang round or horseshoe arches, the first Moslem examples of this latter form.* The mosaic floor was covered with carpets; the walls were faced with colored marble mosaics and enameled tiles; six beautiful grilles of marble divided the interior; in one wall, facing Mecca, was a mihrab lined with gold, silver, and precious stones. Lighting was effected through seventy-four windows of colored glass, and 12,000 lamps. "If," said a traveler, "a man were to sojourn here a hundred years, and pondered each day on what he saw, he would see something new every day." A Greek ambassador, allowed to enter it, confessed to his associates: "I had told our Senate that the power of the Arabs would soon pass away; but now, seeing here how they have built, I know that of a surety their dominion will endure great length of days." [87] †

Striking northeast from Damascus across the desert, one came to Raqqa on the Euphrates, royal seat of Harun al-Rashid; and then through Hatra and across the Tigris to Mosul; farther northeast lay Tabriz, whose finest age was still to come; then, to the east, Tehran (as yet a minor town), Damghan, and—east of the Caspian—Gurgan. In the tenth century this was a provincial capital noted for its cultured princes; the greatest of them, Shams al-Maali Qabus, was a poet and scholar who sheltered Avicenna at his court, and left behind him, as his tomb, a gigantic tower 167 feet high, the Gunbad-i-Qabus, the only structure standing of a once populous and prosperous city. Along the northern route to the east lay Nishapur, still melodious in Omar Khayyam's verse; Mashhad, the Mecca of Shia Moslems; Merv, capital of a once mighty province; and—usually beyond the reach of the caliph's taxgatherers—Bokhara and Samarkand. Over the mountain ranges to the south lay Ghazni. Poets tell of Mahmud's great palaces there, and of "tall towers that amazed the moon"; still stand the "Triumphal Tower" of

---

* The oldest known form of the horseshoe arch appears in a cave temple at Nasik, India, c. second century B.C.; [86] it was used in a Christian church at Nisibis in Mesopotamia in A.D. 359.

† The Great Mosque of Damascus suffered by fire in 1069, was restored, was burnt almost to the ground by Timur in 1400, was rebuilt, and was severely injured by fire in 1894; since then plaster and whitewash have replaced the medieval decoration. On one wall of the mosque may still be seen the inscription that had overhung the lintel of the Christian church, and which the Moslems never erased: "Thy kingdom, O Christ, is an everlasting kingdom, and Thy dominion endureth forever." [88]

Mahmud, and the more ornate tower of Masud II. Moving back westward, one could find in the eleventh century a dozen prosperous cities in Iran—Herat, Shiraz (with its famous gardens and lovely mosque), Yazd, Isfahan, Kashan, Qasvin, Qum, Hamadan, Kirmanshah, Samana; and in Iraq the populous cities of Basra and Kufa. Everywhere the traveler could see shining domes and sparkling minarets, colleges and libraries, palaces and gardens, hospitals and baths, and the dark and narrow alleys of the eternal poor. And at last Baghdad.

"Blessed be Baghdad!" cried the poet Anwari—

> Blessed be the site of Baghdad, seat of learning and art;
> None can point in the world to a city her equal;
> Her suburbs vie in beauty with the blue vault of the sky;
> Her climate rivals the life-giving breezes of heaven;
> Her stones in their brightness rival diamonds and rubies; . . .
> The banks of the Tigris with their lovely damsels surpass Kullakh;
> The gardens filled with lovely nymphs equal Kashmir;
> And thousands of gondolas on the water
> Dance and sparkle like sunbeams in the air.[89]

It was an old Babylonian city, and not far from ancient Babylon; bricks bearing Nebuchadrezzar's name were found in 1848 under the Tigris there. It throve under the Sasanian kings; after the Moslem conquest it became the seat of several Christian monasteries, mostly Nestorian. From these monks, we are told, the Caliph al-Mansur learned that the site was cool in summer, and free from the mosquitoes that harassed Kufa and Basra. Perhaps the Caliph thought it advisable to put some distance between himself and those unruly cities, already swelling with a revolutionary proletariat; and doubtless he saw strategic advantage in a site safely inland, yet in touch by water, through the Tigris and the major canals, with all the cities on the two rivers, and then through the Gulf with all the ports of the world. So in 762 he transferred his residence from Hashimiya, and the governmental offices from Kufa, to Baghdad, surrounded the site with a threefold circular wall and a moat, changed its official name from Baghdad ("Gift of God") to Medinat-al-Salam ("City of Peace"), and employed 100,000 men to build in four years great brick palaces for himself, his relatives, and the bureaus of the government. At the center of this "Round City of al-Mansur" rose the caliphal palace, called the "Golden Gate" from its gilded entrance, or the "Green Dome" from its gleaming cupola. Outside the walls, and directly on the west bank of the Tigris, al-Mansur built a summer residence, the "Palace of Eternity"; here, for most of his years, Harun al-Rashid made his home. From the windows of these palaces one might see a hundred vessels unloading on the docks the wares of half the earth.

In 768, to provide his son al-Mahdi with independent quarters, al-Mansur built a palace and a mosque on the eastern or Persian side of the river. Around these buildings a suburb grew, Rusafa, connected with the Round City by two bridges resting on boats. As most of the caliphs after Harun made their dwelling in this suburb, it soon outstripped the city of Mansur in size and wealth; after Harun "Baghdad" means Rusafa. From the royal centers, on either side of the Tigris, narrow crooked streets, designed to elude the sun, led out their chasms of noisy shops to the residential districts of the well-to-do. Each craft had its street or mart—perfumers, basket weavers, wire-pullers (in the literal sense), money-changers, silk weavers, booksellers. . . . Over the shops and beyond them were the homes of the people. Almost all dwellings but those of the rich were of unbaked brick, made for a lifetime, but not for much longer. We have no reliable statistics of the population; probably it reached 800,000; some authorities estimate it at 2,000,000;[90] in any case it was in the tenth century the largest city in the world, with the possible exception of Constantinople. There was a crowded Christian quarter, with churches, monasteries, and schools; Nestorians, Monophysites, and orthodox Christians had there their separate conventicles. Harun rebuilt and enlarged an early mosque of al-Mansur, and al-Mutadid rebuilt and enlarged this mosque of Harun. Doubtless several hundred additional mosques served the hopes of the people.

While the poor solaced life with heaven, the rich sought heaven on earth. In or near Baghdad they raised a thousand splendid mansions, villas, palaces—simple without, but "within, nothing but azure and gold." We may imagine this domestic splendor from an incredible passage in Abulfeda, which assures us that the royal palace at Baghdad had on its floors 22,000 carpets, and on its walls 38,000 tapestries, 12,500 of silk.[91] The residences of the caliph and his family, the vizier, and the governmental heads occupied a square mile of the eastern city. Jafar the Barmakid inaugurated an aristocratic migration by building in southeastern Baghdad a mansion whose splendor contributed to his death. He tried to evade Harun's jealousy by presenting the palace to Mamun; Harun accepted it for his son, but Jafar continued to live and frolic in the "Qasr Jafari" till his fall. When the palaces of al-Mansur and Harun began to crumble, new palaces replaced them. Al-Mutadid spent 400,000 dinars ($1,900,000) on his "Palace of the Pleiades" (892); we may judge its extent from the 9000 horses, camels, and mules that were housed in its stables.[92] Al-Muqtafi built next to this his "Palace of the Crown" (902), which, with its gardens, covered nine square miles. Al-Muqtadir raised in his turn the "Hall of the Tree," so named because in its garden pond stood a tree of silver and gold; on the silver leaves and twigs perched silver birds, whose beaks piped mechanical lays. The Buwayhid sultans outspent them all by lavishing 13,000,000 dirhems upon the Muizziyah Palace. When Greek ambassadors were received by al-Muqtadir in 917, they were impressed by the twenty-three palaces of the Caliph and his government, the porticoes of marble columns, the number, size, and beauty of the rugs and tapestries that almost covered floors and walls, the thousand grooms in shining uniforms, the gold and silver saddles and brocaded saddlecloths of the emperor's horses, the variety of tame or wild animals in the spacious parks, and the royal barges, themselves palaces, that rode on the Tigris, waiting the Caliph's whim.

Amid these splendors the upper classes lived a life of luxury, sport, worry, and intrigue. They went to the Maydan or plaza to watch horse races or polo games; drank precious forbidden wine, and ate foods brought from the greatest possible distances at the greatest possible price; robed themselves and their ladies in gorgeous and colorful raiment of silk and gold brocade; perfumed their clothing, hair, and beards; breathed the aroma of burning ambergris or frankincense; and wore jewelry on their heads, ears, necks, wrists, and feminine ankles; "the clinking of thine anklets," sang a poet to a lass, "has bereft me of reason."[93] Usually women were excluded from the social gatherings of the men; poets, musicians, and wits took their place, and doubtless sang or spoke of love; and willowy slave girls danced till the men were their slaves. Politer groups listened to poetic readings, or recitations of the Koran; some formed philosophical clubs like the Brethren of Purity. About 790 we hear of a club of ten members: an orthodox Sunni, a Shi'ite, a Kharijite, a Manichean, an erotic poet, a materialist, a Christian, a Jew, a Sabaean, and a Zoroastrian; their meetings, we are told, were marked by mutual tolerance, good humor, and courteous argument.[94] In general Moslem society was one of excellent manners; from Cyrus to Li Hung Chang the East has surpassed the West in courtesy. It was an ennobling aspect of this Baghdad life that all the permitted arts and sciences found there a discriminating patronage, that schools and colleges were numerous, and the air resounded with poetry.

Of the life of the common people we are told little; we may only assume that they helped to uphold this edifice of grandeur with their services and their toil. While the rich played with literature and art, science and philosophy, the simpler folk listened to street singers, or strummed their own lutes and sang their own songs. Now and then a wedding procession redeemed the din and odor of the streets; and on festive holydays people visited one another, exchanged presents with careful calculation, and ate with keener relish than those who feasted from plates of gold. Even the poor man gloried in the majesty of the caliph and the splendor of the mosque; he shared some dirhems of the dinars that were taxed into Baghdad; he carried himself with the pride and dignity of a capital; and in his secret heart he numbered himself among the rulers of the world.

CHAPTER XII

Thought and Art in Eastern Islam

632-1058

I. SCHOLARSHIP

IF we may believe the traditions, Mohammed, unlike most religious reformers, admired and urged the pursuit of knowledge: "He who leaves
his home in search of knowledge walks in the path of God . . . and the ink
of the scholar is holier than the blood of the martyr";[1] but these traditions
have the ring of pedagogic narcissism. In any case the contact of the Arabs
with Greek culture in Syria awoke in them an eager emulation; and soon the
scholar as well as the poet was honored in Islam.

Education began as soon as the child could speak; it was at once taught to
say, "I testify that there is no God but Allah, and I testify that Mohammed
is His prophet." At the age of six some slave children, some girls, and nearly
all boys except the rich (who had private tutors) entered an elementary
school, usually in a mosque, sometimes near a public fountain in the open
air. Tuition was normally free, or so low as to be within general reach; the
teacher received from the parent some two cents per pupil per week;[2] the
remaining cost was borne by philanthropists. The curriculum was simple:
the necessary prayers of Moslem worship, enough reading to decipher the
Koran, and, for the rest, the Koran itself as theology, history, ethics, and
law. Writing and arithmetic were left to higher education, perhaps because
writing, in the Orient, was an art that required specific training; besides, said
the Moslem, scribes would be available for those who insisted on writing.[3]
Each day a part of the Koran was memorized and recited aloud; the goal set
before every pupil was to learn the entire book by heart. He who succeeded
was called *hafiz*, "holder," and was publicly celebrated. He who also learned
writing, archery, and swimming was called *al-kamil*, "the perfect one." The
method was memory, the discipline was the rod; the usual punishment was
a beating with a palm stick on the soles of the feet. Said Harun to the tutor
of his son Amin: "Be not strict to the extent of stifling his faculties, nor
lenient to the point of . . . accustoming him to idleness. Straighten him as
much as thou canst through kindness and gentleness, but fail not to resort
to force and severity should he not respond." [4]

Elementary education aimed to form character, secondary education to
transmit knowledge. Squatting against a mosque pillar or wall, scholars

offered instruction in Koranic interpretation, Hadith, theology, and law. At an unknown date many of these informal secondary schools were brought under governmental regulation and subsidy as madrasas or colleges. To the basic theological curriculum they added grammar, philology, rhetoric, literature, logic, mathematics, and astronomy. Grammar was emphasized, for Arabic was considered the most nearly perfect of all languages, and its correct use was the chief mark of a gentleman. Tuition in these colleges was free, and in some cases government or philanthropy paid both the salaries of the professors and the expenses of the students.[5] The teacher counted for more than the text, except in the case of the Koran; boys studied men rather than books; and students would travel from one end of the Moslem world to another to meet the mind of a famous teacher. Every scholar who desired a high standing at home had to hear the master scholars of Mecca, Baghdad, Damascus, and Cairo. This international of letters was made easier by the fact that throughout Islam—through whatever diversity of peoples—the language of learning and literature was Arabic; Latin had no wider realm. When a visitor entered a Moslem city he took it for granted that he could hear a scholarly lecture at the principal mosque at almost any hour of the day. In many cases the wandering scholar received not only free instruction at the madrasa, but, for a time, free lodging and food.[6] No degrees were given; what the student sought was a certificate of approval from the individual teacher. The final accolade was the acquirement of *adab*—the manners and tastes, the verbal wit and grace, the lightly carried knowledge, of a gentleman.

When the Moslems captured Samarkand (712) they learned from the Chinese the technique of beating flax and other fibrous plants into a pulp, and drying the pulp in thin sheets. Introduced to the Near East as a substitute for parchment and leather at a time when papyrus was not yet forgotten, the product received the name *papyros*—paper. The first paper-manufacturing plant in Islam was opened at Baghdad in 794 by al-Fadl, son of Harun's vizier. The craft was brought by the Arabs to Sicily and Spain, and thence passed into Italy and France. We find paper in use in China as early as A.D. 105, in Mecca in 707, in Egypt in 800, in Spain in 950, in Constantinople in 1100, in Sicily in 1102, in Italy in 1154, in Germany in 1228, in England in 1309.[7] The invention facilitated the making of books wherever it went. Yaqubi tells us that in his time (891) Baghdad had over a hundred booksellers. Their shops were also centers of copying, calligraphy, and literary gatherings. Many students made a living by copying manuscripts and selling the copies to book dealers. In the tenth century we hear of autograph hunters, and of book collectors who paid great sums for rare manuscripts.[8] Authors received nothing from the sale of their books; they depended on some less speculative mode of subsistence, or upon the patronage of princes or rich men. Literature was written, and art was designed, in Islam, to meet the taste of an aristocracy of money or of blood.

Most mosques had libraries, and some cities had public libraries of considerable content and generous accessibility. About 950 Mosul had a library, established by private philanthropy, where students were supplied with paper as well as books. Ten large catalogues were required to list the volumes in the public library at Rayy. Basra's library gave stipends to scholars working in it. The geographer Yaqut spent three years in the libraries of Merv and Khwarizm, gathering data for his geographical dictionary. When Baghdad was destroyed by the Mongols it had thirty-six public libraries.[9] Private libraries were numberless; it was a fashion among the rich to have an ample collection of books. A physician refused the invitation of the sultan of Bokhara to come and live at his court, on the ground that he would need 400 camels to transport his library.[10] Al-Waqidi, dying, left 600 boxes of books, each box so heavy that two men were needed to carry it;[11] "princes like Sahib ibn Abbas in the tenth century might own as many books as could then be found in all the libraries of Europe combined."[12] Nowhere else in those eighth, ninth, tenth, and eleventh centuries of our era was there so great a passion for books, unless it was in the China of Ming Huang. Islam reached then the summit of its cultural life. In a thousand mosques from Cordova to Samarkand scholars were as numerous as pillars, and made the cloisters tremble with their eloquence; the roads of the realm were disturbed by innumerable geographers, historians, and theologians seeking knowledge and wisdom; the courts of a hundred princes resounded with poetry and philosophical debate; and no man dared be a millionaire without supporting literature or art. The old cultures of the conquered were eagerly absorbed by the quick-witted Arabs; and the conquerors showed such tolerance that of the poets, scientists, and philosophers who now made Arabic the most learned and literary tongue in the world only a small minority were of Arab blood.

The scholars of Islam in this period strengthened the foundations of a distinguished literature by their labors in grammar, which gave the Arabic tongue logic and standards; by their dictionaries, which gathered the word wealth of that language into precision and order; by their anthologies, encyclopedias, and epitomes, which preserved much that was otherwise lost; and by their work in textual, literary, and historical criticism. We gratefully omit their names, and salute their achievement.

Those whom we remember best among the scholars are the historians, for to them we owe our knowledge of a civilization that without them would be as unknown to us as Pharaonic Egypt before Champollion. Muhammad ibn Ishaq (d. 767) wrote a classical *Life of Mohammed*; as revised and enlarged by Ibn Hisham (763) it is—barring the Koran—the oldest significant Arabic prose work

that has reached us. Curious and tireless scholars composed biographical dictionaries of saints, or philosophers, or viziers, or jurists, or physicians, or calligraphers,
or mandarins, or lovers, or scholars. Ibn Qutaiba (828–89) was one of many
Moslems who attempted to write a history of the world; and unlike most historians he had the courage to set his own religion in that modest perspective which
every nation or faith must bear in time's immensity. Muhammad al-Nadim produced in 987 an *Index of the Sciences (Fihrist al-'ulum)*, a bibliography of all
books in Arabic, original or translated, on any branch of knowledge, with a biographical and critical notice of each author, including a list of his virtues and
vices; we may estimate the wealth of Moslem literature in his time by noting that
not one in a thousand of the volumes that he named is known to exist today.[13]

The Livy of Islam [14] was Abu Jafar Muhammad al-Tabari (838–923). Like
so many Moslem writers, he was a Persian, born in Tabaristan, south of the
Caspian Sea. After several years spent as a poor wandering scholar in Arabia,
Syria, and Egypt, he settled down as a jurist in Baghdad. For forty years he devoted himself to composing an enormous universal chronicle—*Annals of the
Apostles and Kings (Kitab akhbar al-Rusul wal-Muluk)*—from the creation to
913. What survives fills fifteen large volumes; we are told that the original was
ten times as long. Like Bossuet, al-Tabari saw the hand of God in every event,
and filled his early chapters with pious nonsense: God "created men to test
them"; [15] God dropped upon the earth a house built of rubies for Adam's dwelling, but when Adam sinned God drew it up again.[16] Al-Tabari followed the
Bible in giving the history of the Jews; accepted the Virgin Birth of Christ (Mary
conceived Jesus because Gabriel blew into her sleeve),[17] and ended Part One with
Jesus' ascension into heaven. Part Two is a far more creditable performance, and
gives a sober, occasionally vivid, history of Sasanian Persia. The method is chronological, describing events year by year, and usually traditional—tracing the
narratives through one or more chains of Hadith to an eyewitness or contemporary of the incident. The method has the virtue of stating sources carefully; but
as al-Tabari makes no attempt to co-ordinate the diverse traditions into a sustained and united narrative his history remains a mountain of industry rather
than a work of art.

Al-Masudi, al-Tabari's greatest successor, ranked him as al-Masudi's greatest
predecessor. Abu-l-Hasan Ali al-Masudi, an Arab of Baghdad, traveled through
Syria, Palestine, Arabia, Zanzibar, Persia, Central Asia, India, and Ceylon; he
claims even to have reached the China Sea. He gathered his gleanings into a
thirty-volume encyclopedia, which proved too long for even the spacious scholars of Islam; he published a compendium, also gigantic; finally (947)—perhaps
realizing that his readers had less time to read than he had to write—he reduced
his work to the form in which it survives, and gave it the fancy title, *Meadows of
Gold and Mines of Precious Stones*. Al-Masudi surveyed omnivorously the geography, biology, history, customs, religion, science, philosophy, and literature of
all lands from China to France; he was the Pliny as well as the Herodotus of the
Moslem world. He did not compress his material to aridity, but wrote at times
with a genial leisureliness that did not shun, now and then, an amusing tale. He
was a bit skeptical in religion, but never forced his doubts upon his audience. In

the last year of his life he summarized his views on science, history, and philosophy in a *Book of Information*, in which he suggested an evolution "from mineral to plant, from plant to animal, and from animal to man." [18] Perhaps these views embroiled him with the conservatives of Baghdad; he was forced, he says, "to leave the city where I was born and grew up." He moved to Cairo, but mourned the separation. "It is the character of our time," he wrote, "to separate and disperse all. . . . God makes a nation prosper through love of the hearth; it is a sign of moral uprightness to be attached to the place of one's birth; it is a mark of noble lineage to dislike separation from the ancestral hearth and home." [19] He died at Cairo in 956, after ten years of exile.

At their best these historians excel in the scope of their enterprise and their interests; they properly combine geography and history, and nothing human is alien to them; and they are far superior to the contemporary historians in Christendom. Even so they lose themselves too long in politics and war and wordy rhetoric; they seldom seek the economic, social, and psychological causes of events; we miss in their vast volumes a sense of orderly synthesis, and find merely a congeries of unco-ordinated parts—nations, episodes, and personalities. They rarely rise to a conscientious scrutiny of sources, and rely too piously upon chains of tradition in which every link is a possible error or deceit; in consequence their narratives sometimes degenerate into childish tales of portent, miracle, and myth. As many Christian historians (always excepting Gibbon) can write medieval histories in which all Islamic civilization is a brief appendage to the Crusades, so many Moslem historians reduced world history before Islam to a halting preparation for Mohammed. But how can a Western mind ever judge an Oriental justly? The beauty of the Arab language fades in translation like a flower cut from its roots; and the topics that fill the pages of Moslem historians, fascinating to their countrymen, seem aridly remote from the natural interests of Occidental readers, who have not realized how the economic interdependence of peoples ominously demands a mutual study and understanding of East and West.

II. SCIENCE [*]

In those lusty centuries of Islamic life the Moslems labored for such an understanding. The caliphs realized the backwardness of the Arabs in science and philosophy, and the wealth of Greek culture surviving in Syria. The Umayyads wisely left unhindered the Christian, Sabaean, or Persian colleges at Alexandria, Beirut, Antioch, Harran, Nisibis, and Jund-i-Shapur; and in those schools the classics of Greek science and philosophy were preserved, often in Syriac translations. Moslems learning Syriac or Greek were intrigued by these treatises; and soon translations were made into Arabic by

---

[*] Every writer on Islamic science must record his debt to George Sarton for his *Introduction to the History of Science*. That monumental work is not only one of the noblest achievements in the history of scholarship; it also performs an inestimable service in revealing the wealth and scope of Moslem culture. Scholars everywhere must hope that every facility will be provided for the completion of this work.

Nestorian Christians or Jews. Umayyad and Abbasid princes stimulated this fruitful borrowing. Al-Mansur, al-Mamun, and al-Mutawakkil dispatched messengers to Constantinople and other Hellenistic cities—sometimes to their traditional enemies the Greek emperors—asking for Greek books, especially in medicine or mathematics; in this way Euclid's *Elements* came to Islam. In 830 al-Mamun established at Baghdad, at a cost of 200,000 dinars ($950,000), a "House of Wisdom" (*Bayt al-Hikmah*) as a scientific academy, an observatory, and a public library; here he installed a corps of translators, and paid them from the public treasury. To the work of this institution, thought Ibn Khaldun,[20] Islam owed that vibrant awakening which in causes—the extension of commerce and the rediscovery of Greece—and results—the flowering of science, literature, and art—resembled the Italian Renaissance.

From 750 to 900 this fertilizing process of translation continued, from Syriac, Greek, Pahlavi, and Sanskrit. At the head of the translators in the House of Wisdom was a Nestorian physician, Hunain ibn Ishaq (809-73)— i.e., John son of Isaac. By his own account he translated a hundred treatises of Galen and the Galenic school into Syriac, and thirty-nine into Arabic; through his renderings some important works of Galen escaped destruction. Further, Hunain translated Aristotle's *Categories*, *Physics*, and *Magna Moralia*; Plato's *Republic*, *Timaeus*, and *Laws*; Hippocrates' *Aphorisms*, Dioscorides' *Materia Medica*, Ptolemy's *Quadripartitum*, and the Old Testament from the Septuagint Greek. Al-Mamun endangered the treasury by paying Hunain in gold the weight of the books he had translated. Al-Mutawakkil made him court physician, but jailed him for a year when Hunain, though threatened with death, refused to concoct a poison for an enemy. His son Ishaq ibn Hunain helped him with his translations, and himself rendered into Arabic the *Metaphysics*, *On the Soul*, and *On the Generation and Corruption of Animals* of Aristotle, and the commentaries of Alexander of Aphrodisias—a work fated to wield great influence on Moslem philosophy.

By 850 most of the classic Greek texts in mathematics, astronomy, and medicine had been translated. It was through its Arabic version that Ptolemy's *Almagest* received its name; and only Arabic versions preserved Books V–VII of the *Conics* of Apollonius of Perga, the *Mechanics* of Hero of Alexandria, and the *Pneumatics* of Philo of Byzantium. Strange to say, the Mohammedans, so addicted to poetry and history, ignored Greek poetry, drama, and historiography; here Islam accepted the lead of Persia instead of Greece. It was the misfortune of Islam and humanity that Plato, and even Aristotle, came into Moslem ken chiefly in Neoplatonic form: Plato in Porphyry's interpretation, and Aristotle discolored by an apocryphal *Theology of Aristotle* written by a Neoplatonist of the fifth or sixth century, and translated into Arabic as a genuine product of the Stagirite. The works of Plato and Aristotle were almost completely translated, though with many inaccuracies; but as the Moslem scholars sought to reconcile Greek philosophy with the Koran, they took more readily to Neoplatonist interpretations of them than to the original books themselves. The real Aristotle reached Islam only in his logic and his science.

The continuity of science and philosophy from Egypt, India, and Babylonia through Greece and Byzantium to Eastern and Spanish Islam, and thence to northern Europe and America, is one of the brightest threads in the skein of history. Greek science, though long since enfeebled by obscurantism, misgovernment, and poverty, was still alive in Syria when the Moslems came; at the very time of the conquest Severus Sebokht, abbot of Ken-nesre on the upper Euphrates, was writing Greek treatises on astronomy, and was making the first known mention of Hindu numerals outside of India (662). The Arabic inheritance of science was overwhelmingly Greek, but Hindu influences ranked next. In 773, at al-Mansur's behest, translations were made of the *Siddhantas*—Indian astronomical treatises dating as far back as 425 B.C.; these versions may have been the vehicle through which the "Arabic" numerals and the zero were brought from India into Islam.[21] In 813 al-Khwarizmi used the Hindu numerals in his astronomical tables; about 825 he issued a treatise known in its Latin form as *Algoritmi de numero Indorum*—"al-Khwarizmi on the Numerals of the Indians"; in time *algorithm* or *algorism* came to mean any arithmetical system based on the decimal notation. In 976 Muhammad ibn Ahmad, in his *Keys of the Sciences*, remarked that if, in a calculation, no number appears in the place of tens, a little circle should be used "to keep the rows." [22] This circle the Moslems called *sifr*, "empty" whence our *cipher*; Latin scholars transformed *sifr* into *zephyrum*, which the Italians shortened into *zero*.

Algebra, which we find in the Greek Diophantes in the third century, owes its name to the Arabs, who extensively developed this detective science. The great figure here—perhaps the greatest in medieval mathematics—was Muhammad ibn Musa (780–850), called al-Khwarizmi from his birthplace Khwarizm (now Khiva), east of the Caspian Sea. Al-Khwarizmi contributed effectively to five sciences: he wrote on the Hindu numerals; compiled astronomical tables which, as revised in Moslem Spain, were for centuries standard among astronomers from Cordova to Chang-an; formulated the oldest trigonometrical tables known; collaborated with sixty-nine other scholars in drawing up for al-Mamun a geographical encyclopedia; and in his *Calculation of Integration and Equation* gave analytical and geometrical solutions of quadratic equations. This work, now lost in its Arabic form, was translated by Gerard of Cremona in the twelfth century, was used as a principal text in European universities until the sixteenth century, and introduced to the West the word *algebra* (*al-jabr*—"restitution," "completion"). Thabit ibn Qurra (826–901), besides making important translations, achieved fame in astronomy and medicine, and became the greatest of

Moslem geometers. Abu Abdallah al-Battani (850–929), a Sabaean of Raqqa known to Europe as Albategnus, advanced trigonometry far beyond its beginnings in Hipparchus and Ptolemy by substituting triangular for Ptolemy's quadrilateral solutions, and the *sine* for Hipparchus' *chord*; he formulated the trigonometrical ratios essentially as we use them today.

The Caliph al-Mamun engaged a staff of astronomers to make observations and records, to test the findings of Ptolemy, and to study the spots on the sun. Taking for granted the sphericity of the earth, they measured a terrestrial degree by simultaneously taking the position of the sun from both Palmyra and the plain of Sinjar; their measurement gave $56\frac{2}{3}$ miles—half a mile more than our present calculation; and from their results they estimated the earth's circumference to approximate 20,000 miles. These astronomers proceeded on completely scientific principles: they accepted nothing as true which was not confirmed by experience or experiment. One of them, Abu'l-Farghani, of Transoxiana, wrote (*c.* 860) an astronomical text which remained in authority in Europe and Western Asia for 700 years. Even more renowned was al-Battani; his astronomical observations, continued for forty-one years, were remarkable for their range and accuracy; he determined many astronomical coefficients with remarkable approximation to modern calculations—the precession of the equinoxes at 54.5″ a year, and the inclination of the ecliptic at 23° 55′.[23] Working under the patronage of the early Buwayhid rulers of Baghdad, Abu'l-Wafa (in the disputed opinion of Sadillot) discovered the third lunar variation 600 years before Tycho Brahe.[24] Costly instruments were built for the Moslem astronomers: not only astrolabes and armillary spheres, known to the Greeks, but quadrants with a radius of thirty feet, and sextants with a radius of eighty. The astrolabe, much improved by the Moslems, reached Europe in the tenth century, and was widely used by mariners till the seventeenth. The Arabs designed and constructed it with aesthetic passion, making it at once an instrument of science and a work of art.

Even more important than the charting of the skies was the mapping of the earth, for Islam lived by tillage and trade. Suleiman al-Tajir—i.e., the merchant—about 840 carried his wares to the Far East; an anonymous author (851) wrote a narrative of Suleiman's journey; this oldest Arabic account of China antedated Marco Polo's *Travels* by 425 years. In the same century Ibn Khordadhbeh wrote a description of India, Ceylon, the East Indies, and China, apparently from direct observation; and Ibn Hauqal described India and Africa. Ahmad al-Yaqubi, of Armenia and Khurasan, wrote in 891 a *Book of the Countries*, giving a reliable account of Islamic provinces and cities, and of many foreign states. Muhammad al-Muqaddasi visited all the lands of Islam except Spain, suffered countless vicissitudes, and in 985 wrote his *Description of the Moslem Empire*—the greatest work of Arabic geography before al-Biruni's *India*.

Abu al-Rayhan Muhammad ibn Ahmad al-Biruni (973–1048) shows the Moslem scholar at his best. Philosopher, historian, traveler, geographer, linguist, mathematician, astronomer, poet, and physicist—and doing major and original work in all these fields—he was at least the Leibniz,[25] almost the Leonardo, of Islam. Born like al-Khwarizmi near the modern Khiva, he signalized again the leadership of the Transcaspian region in this culminating century of medieval science. The princes of Khwarizm and Tabaristan, recognizing his talents, gave him a place at their courts. Hearing of the bevy of poets and philosophers at Khwarizm, Mahmud of Ghazni asked its prince to send him al-Biruni, Ibn Sina, and other savants; the prince felt obliged to comply (1018), and al-Biruni went to live in honor and studious peace with the bellicose ravisher of India. Perhaps it was in Mahmud's train that al-Biruni entered India; in any case he stayed there several years, and learned the language and the antiquities of the country. Returning to Mahmud's court, he became a favorite of that incalculable despot. A visitor from northern Asia offended the king by describing a region, which he claimed to have seen, where for many months the sun never set; Mahmud was about to imprison the man for jesting with royalty when al-Biruni explained the phenomenon to the satisfaction of the king and the great relief of the visitor.[26] Mahmud's son Masud, himself an amateur scientist, showered gifts and money upon al-Biruni, who often returned them to the treasury as much exceeding his needs.

His first major work (*c.* 1000) was a highly technical treatise—*Vestiges of the Past* (*Athar-ul-Baqiya*)—on the calendars and religious festivals of the Persians, Syrians, Greeks, Jews, Christians, Sabaeans, Zoroastrians, and Arabs. It is an unusually impartial study, utterly devoid of religious animosities. As a Moslem al-Biruni inclined to the Shia sect, with an unobtrusive tendency to agnosticism. He retained, however, a degree of Persian patriotism, and condemned the Arabs for destroying the high civilization of the Sasanian regime.[27] Otherwise his attitude was that of the objective scholar, assiduous in research, critical in the scrutiny of traditions and texts (including the Gospels), precise and conscientious in statement, frequently admitting his ignorance, and promising to pursue his inquiries till the truth should emerge. In the preface to the *Vestiges* he wrote like Francis Bacon: "We must clear our minds . . . from all causes that blind people to the truth—old custom, party spirit, personal rivalry or passion, the desire for influence." While his host was devastating India al-Biruni spent many years studying its peoples, languages, faiths, cultures, and castes. In 1030 he published his masterpiece, *History of India* (*Tarikh al-Hind*). At the outset he sharply distinguished between hearsay and eyewitness reports, and classified the varieties of "liars" who have written history.[28] He spent little space on the political history of India, but gave forty-two chapters to Hindu astronomy, and eleven to Hindu religion. He was charmed by the *Bhagavad Gita*. He saw the similarity between the mysticism of the Vedanta, the Sufis, the Neopythagoreans, and the Neoplatonists; he compared excerpts from Indian thinkers with like passages from Greek philosophers, and expressed his preference for the Greeks. "India," he wrote, "has produced no Socrates; no logical method has there expelled fantasy from science." [29] Nevertheless he translated several Sanskrit works of science into Arabic, and, as if to pay a debt, rendered into Sanskrit Euclid's *Elements* and Ptolemy's *Almagest*.

His interest extended to nearly all the sciences. He gave the best medieval account of the Hindu numerals. He wrote treatises on the astrolabe, the planisphere, the armillary sphere; and formulated astronomical tables for Sultan Masud. He took it for granted that the earth is round, noted "the attraction of all things towards the center of the earth," and remarked that astronomic data can be explained as well by supposing that the earth turns daily on its axis and annually around the sun, as by the reverse hypothesis. [30] He speculated on the possibility that the Indus valley had been once the bottom of a sea. [31] He composed an extensive lapidary, describing a great number of stones and metals from the natural, commercial, and medical points of view. He determined the specific gravity of eighteen precious stones, and laid down the principle that the specific gravity of an object corresponds to the volume of water its displaces. [32] He found a method of calculating, without laborious additions, the result of the repeated doubling of a number, as in the Hindu story of the chessboard squares and the grains of sand. He contributed to geometry the solution of theorems that thereafter bore his name. He composed an encyclopedia of astronomy, a treatise on geography, and an epitome of astronomy, astrology, and mathematics. He explained the workings of natural springs and artesian wells by the hydrostatic principle of communicating vessels. [33] He wrote histories of Mahmud's reign, of Subuktigin, and of Khwarizm. Oriental historians call him "the Sheik"—as if to mean "the master of those who know." His multifarious production in the same generation with Ibn Sina, Ibn al-Haitham, and Firdausi, marks the turn of the tenth century into the eleventh as the zenith of Islamic culture, and the climax of medieval thought. [34]

Chemistry as a science was almost created by the Moslems; for in this field, where the Greeks (so far as we know) were confined to industrial experience and vague hypothesis, the Saracens introduced precise observation, controlled experiment, and careful records. They invented and named the *alembic* (*al-anbiq*), chemically analyzed innumerable substances, composed lapidaries, distinguished *alkalis* and acids, investigated their affinities, studied and manufactured hundreds of drugs.* Alchemy, which the Moslems inherited from Egypt, contributed to chemistry by a thousand incidental discov-

---

* Alcohol is an Arabic word, but not an Arabian product. It is first mentioned in an Italian work of the ninth or tenth century. [35] To the Moslems *al-kohl* was a powder for painting the eyebrows.

eries, and by its method, which was the most scientific of all medieval operations. Practically all Moslem scientists believed that all metals were ultimately of the same species, and could therefore be transmuted one into another. The aim of the alchemists was to change "base" metals like iron, copper, lead, or tin into silver or gold; the "philosopher's stone" was a substance—ever sought, never found—which when properly treated would effect this transmutation. Blood, hair, excrement, and other materials were treated with various reagents, and were subjected to calcination, sublimation, sunlight, and fire, to see if they contained this magic *al-iksir* or essence.[36] He who should possess this elixir would be able at will to prolong his life. The most famous of the alchemists was Jabir ibn Hayyan (702–65), known to Europe as Gebir. Son of a Kufa druggist, he practiced as a physician, but spent most of his time with alembic and crucible. The hundred or more works attributed to him were produced by unknown authors, chiefly in the tenth century; many of these anonymous works were translated into Latin, and strongly stimulated the development of European chemistry. After the tenth century the science of chemistry, like other sciences, gave ground to occultism, and did not lift its head again for almost three hundred years.

The remains of Moslem biology in this period are scant. Abu Hanifa al-Dinawari (815–95) wrote a *Book of Plants* based on Dioscorides, but adding many plants to pharmacology. Mohammedan botanists knew how to produce new fruits by grafting; they combined the rose bush and the almond tree to generate rare and lovely flowers.[37] Othman Amr al-Jahiz (d. 869) propounded a theory of evolution like al-Masudi's: life had climbed "from mineral to plant, from plant to animal, from animal to man."[38] The mystic poet Jalal ud-din accepted the theory, and merely added that if this has been achieved in the past, then in the next stage men will become angels, and finally God.[39]

III. MEDICINE

Meanwhile men loved life while maligning it, and spent great sums to stave off death. The Arabs had entered Syria with only primitive medical knowledge and equipment. As wealth came, physicians of better caliber were developed in Syria and Persia, or were brought in from Greece and India. Forbidden by their religion to practice vivisection, or the dissection of human cadavers, Moslem anatomy had to content itself with Galen and the study of wounded men. Arabic medicine was weakest in surgery, strongest in medicaments and therapy. To the ancient pharmacopeia the Saracens added ambergris, camphor, cassia, cloves, mercury, senna, myrrh; and they introduced new pharmaceutical preparations—sirups (Arabic *sharab*), juleps (*golab*), rose water, etc. One of the main features of Italian trade with the Near East was the importation of Arabic drugs. The Moslems established the first apothecary shops and dispensaries, founded the first medieval school of pharmacy, and wrote great treatises on pharmacology. Moslem physicians were enthusiastic advocates of the bath, especially in fevers [40] and in the form of the steam bath. Their directions for the treatment of smallpox and measles could scarcely be bettered today.[41] Anesthesia by inhalation was practiced in some surgical operations; [42] hashish and other drugs were used to induce deep sleep.[43] We know of thirty-four hospitals established in Islam in this period,[44] apparently on the model of the Persian academy and hospital at Jund-i-Shapur; in Baghdad the earliest known to us was set up under Harun al-Rashid, and five others were opened there in the tenth century; in 918 we hear of a director of hospitals in Baghdad.[45] The most famous hospital in Islam was the *bimaristan* founded in Damascus in 706; in 978 it had a staff of twenty-four physicians. Medical instruction was given chiefly at the hospitals. No man could legally practice medicine without passing an examination and receiving a state diploma; druggists, barbers, and orthopedists were likewise subject to state regulation and inspection. The physician-vizier Ali ibn Isa organized a staff of doctors to go from place to place to tend the sick (931); certain physicians made daily visits to jails; there was an especially humane treatment of the insane. But public sanitation was in most places poorly developed; and in four centuries forty epidemics ravaged one or another country of the Moslem East.

In 931 there were 860 licensed physicians in Baghdad.[46] Fees rose with proximity to the court. Jibril ibn Bakhtisha, physician to Harun, al-Mamun, and the Barmakids, amassed a fortune of 88,800,000 dirhems ($7,104,000); we are told that he received 100,000 dirhems for bleeding the caliph twice a year, and a like sum for giving him a semiannual purgative.[47] He successfully treated hysterical paralysis in a slave girl by pretending to disrobe her in public. From Jibril onward there is a succession of famous physicians in Eastern Islam: Yuhanna ibn Masawayh (777–857), who studied anatomy by dissecting apes; Hunain ibn Ishaq, the translator, author of *Ten Treatises on the Eye*—the oldest systematic textbook of ophthalmology; and Ali ibn Isa, greatest of Moslem oculists, whose *Manual for Oculists* was used as a text in Europe till the eighteenth century.

The outstanding figure in this humane dynasty of healers was Abu Bekr Muhammad al-Razi (844–926), famous in Europe as Rhazes. Like most of the leading scientists and poets of his time, he was a Persian writing in Arabic. Born at Rayy near Tehran, he studied chemistry, alchemy, and medicine at Baghdad, and wrote some 131 books, half of them on medicine, most of them lost. His *Kitab al-Hawi* (*Comprehensive Book*) covered in twenty volumes every branch of medicine. Translated into Latin as *Liber continens*, it was probably the most highly respected and frequently used medical textbook in the white world for several centuries; it was one of the nine books that composed the whole library of the medical faculty at the University of Paris in 1395.[48] His *Treatise on Smallpox and Measles* was a masterpiece of direct observation and clinical analysis; it was the first accurate study of infectious diseases, the first effort to distinguish the two ailments. We may judge its influence and repute by the forty English editions printed between 1498 and 1866. The most famous of al-Razi's works was a ten-volume survey of medicine, the *Kitab al-Mansuri* (*Book for al-Mansur*), dedicated to a prince of Khurasan. Gerard of Cremona translated it into Latin; the ninth volume of this translation, the *Nonus Almansoris*, was a popular text in Europe till the sixteenth century. Al-Razi introduced new remedies like mercurial ointment, and the use of animal gut in sutures. He checked the enthusiasm for urinalysis in an age when physicians were prone to diagnose any disease by examining the urine, sometimes without seeing the patient. Some of his shorter works showed a genial side; one was "On the Fact That Even Skillful Physicians Cannot Cure All Diseases"; another was entitled, "Why Ignorant Physicians, Laymen, and Women Have More Success than Learned Medical Men." Al-Razi was by common consent the greatest of Moslem physicians, and the greatest clinician of the Middle Ages.[49] He died in poverty at the age of eighty-two.

In the school of medicine at the University of Paris hang two portraits of Moslem physicians—"Rhazes" and "Avicenna." Islam knew its greatest philosopher and most famous physician as Abu Ali al-Husein ibn Sina (980–1037). His autobiography—one of the few in Arabic literature—shows us how mobile might be, in medieval days, the life of a scholar or sage. Son of a money-changer of Bokhara, Avicenna was educated by private tutors, who gave a Sufi mystic turn to an otherwise scientific mind. "At the age of ten," says Ibn Khallikan, with customary Oriental hyperbole, "he was a perfect master of the Koran and general literature, and had obtained a certain degree of information in theology, arithmetic, and algebra." [50] He studied medicine without a teacher, and while still young began to give gratis treatment. At seventeen he brought back to health the ailing ruler of Bokhara, Nuh ibn Mansur, became an official of the court, and spent eager hours in the Sultan's voluminous library. The breakup of the Samanid power towards the end of the tenth century led Avicenna to take service under al-Mamun, prince of Khwarizm. When Mahmud of Ghazni sent for Avicenna, al-Biruni, and other intellectual lights of al-Mamun's court, Avicenna refused to go. With a fellow scholar, Masihi, he escaped into the desert. There in a dust storm Masihi died; but Avicenna, after many hardships, reached Gurgan, and took service at the court of Qabus. Mahmud circulated throughout Persia a picture of Avicenna, and offered a reward for his capture, but Qabus protected him. When Qabus was murdered, Avicenna was called to treat the emir of Hamadan; he succeeded so well that he was made vizier. But the army did not like his rule; it seized him, pillaged his home, and proposed his death. He escaped, hid himself in the rooms of a druggist, and began in his confinement to write the books that were to make his fame. As he was planning a secret departure from Hamadan he was arrested by the emir's son, and spent several months in jail, where he continued his writing. He again escaped, disguised himself as a Sufi mystic, and after adventures too numerous for our space found refuge and honors at the court of Ala ad-Dawla, the Buwayhid Emir of Isfahan. A circle of scientists and philosophers gathered about him, and held learned conferences over which the emir liked to preside. Some stories suggest that the philosopher enjoyed the pleasures of love as well as of scholarship; on the other hand we get reports of him as absorbed day and night in study, teaching, and public affairs; and Ibn Khallikan quotes from him some unhackneyed counsel: "Take one meal a day. . . . Preserve the seminal fluid with care; it is the water of life, to be poured into the womb." [51] Worn out too soon, he died at fifty-seven on a journey to Hamadan, where to this day pious veneration guards his grave.

Amid these vicissitudes he found time, in office or in jail, in Persian or in Arabic, to write a hundred books, covering nearly every field of science and philosophy. For good measure he composed excellent poems, of which fifteen survive; one of them slipped into the *Rubaiyat* of Omar Khayyam; another, "The Descent of the Soul" (into the body from a higher sphere), is still memorized by young students in the Moslem East. He translated Euclid, made astronomical observations, and devised an instrument like our vernier. He made original studies of motion, force, vacuum, light, heat, and specific gravity. His treatise on minerals was a main source of European geology until the thirteenth century. His remarks on the formation of mountains is a model of clarity:

> Mountains may be due to two different causes. Either they result from upheavals of the earth's crust, such as might occur in violent earthquake; or they are the effect of water, which, cutting for itself a new route, has denuded the valleys. The strata are of different kinds, some soft, some hard; the winds and waters disintegrate the first kind, but leave the other intact. It would require a long period of time for all such changes to be accomplished . . . but that water has been the main cause of these effects is proved by the existence of fossil remains of aquatic animals on many mountains.[52]

Two gigantic productions contain Avicenna's teaching: the *Kitab al-Shifa*, or *Book of Healing* (of the soul), an eighteen-volume encyclopedia of mathematics, physics, metaphysics, theology, economics, politics, and music; and the *Qanun-fi-l-Tibb*, or *Canon of Medicine*, a gigantic survey of physiology, hygiene, therapy, and pharmacology, with sundry excursions into philosophy. The *Qanun* is well organized, and has moments of eloquence; but its scholastic passion for classification and distinction becomes the one disease for which the author has no prescription. He begins with a discouraging admonition: "Every follower of my teachings who wishes to use them profitably should memorize most of this work," [52a] which contains a million words. He conceives medicine as the art of removing an impediment to the normal functioning of nature. He deals first with the major diseases—their symptoms, diagnosis, and treatment; he has chapters on general and individual prophylaxis and hygiene, and on therapy through enemas, bleeding, cautery, baths, and massage. He recommends deep breathing, even occasional shouting, to develop the lungs, chest—and uvula. Book II summarizes Greek and Arabic knowledge of medicinal plants. Book III, on special pathology, contains excellent discussions of pleurisy, empyema, intestinal disorders, sexual diseases, perversions, and nervous ailments, including love. Book IV discusses fevers, surgery, and cosmetics, the care of the hair and the skin. Book V—materia medica—gives detailed directions for concocting 760 drugs. The *Qanun*, translated into Latin in the twelfth century, dethroned al-Razi, and even Galen, as the chief text in European medical schools; it held its place as required reading in the universities of Montpellier and Louvain till the middle of the seventeenth century.

Avicenna was the greatest writer on medicine, al-Razi the greatest physician, al-Biruni the greatest geographer, al-Haitham the greatest optician, Jabir probably the greatest chemist, of the Middle Ages; these five names, so little known in present-day Christendom, are one measure of our provincialism in viewing medieval history. Arabic, like all medieval science, was often sullied with occultism; except in optics it excelled rather in the synthesis of accumulated results than in original findings or systematic research; at the same time, however haltingly, it developed in alchemy that experimental method which is the greatest pride and tool of the modern mind. When Roger Bacon proclaimed that method to Europe, five hundred years after Jabir, he owed his illumination to the Moors of Spain, whose light had come from the Moslem East.

IV. PHILOSOPHY

In philosophy, as in science, Islam borrowed from Christian Syria the legacy of pagan Greece, and returned it through Moslem Spain to Christian Europe. Many influences, of course, ran together to produce the intellectual rebellion of the Mutazilites, and the philosophies of al-Kindi, al-Farabi, Avicenna, and Averroës. Hindu speculations came in through Ghazni and Persia; Zoroastrian and Jewish eschatology played some minor role; and Christian heretics had stirred the air of the Near East with debate on the attributes of God, the nature of Christ and the Logos, predestination and free will, revelation and reason. But the yeast that caused the ferment of thought in Moslem Asia—as in Renaissance Italy—was the rediscovery of Greece. Here, through however imperfect translations of apocryphal texts, a new world appeared: one in which men had reasoned fearlessly about everything, unchecked by sacred scriptures, and had conceived a cosmos not of divine whimsy and incalculable miracle, but of majestic and omnipresent law. Greek logic, fully conveyed through Aristotle's Organon, came like an intoxication to Moslems now gifted with leisure to think; here were the terms and implements they needed for thought; now for three centuries Islam played the new game of logic, drunk like the Athenian youth of Plato's time with the "dear delight" of philosophy. Soon the whole edifice of Mohammedan dogma began to tremble and crack, as Greek orthodoxy had melted under the Sophists' eloquence, as Christian orthodoxy would wince and wilt under the blows of the Encyclopedists and the whips of Voltaire's wit.

What might be called the Moslem Enlightenment had its proximate origin in a strange dispute. Was the Koran eternal or created? Philo's doctrine of the Logos as the timeless Wisdom of God; the Fourth Gospel's identification of Christ with the Logos, the Divine Word or Reason, that was "in the beginning . . . was God," and "without which was not anything made that was made"; [53] the Gnostic and Neoplatonic personification of Divine Wisdom as the agent of creation; the Jewish belief in the eternity of the Torah—all conspired to beget in orthodox Islam a correlative view that the Koran had always existed in the mind of Allah, and that only its revelation to Mohammed was an event in time. The first expression of philosophy in Islam (*c*. 757) was the growth of a school of "Mutazilites"— i.e., Seceders—who denied the eternity of the Koran. They protested their respect for Islam's holy book, but they argued that where it or the Hadith contradicted reason, the Koran or the traditions must be interpreted allegorically; and they gave the name *kalam* or logic to this effort to reconcile reason and faith. It seemed to them absurd to take literally those Koranic passages that ascribed hands and feet, anger and hatred, to Allah; such poetic anthropomorphism, however adapted to the moral and political ends of Mohammed at the time, could hardly be accepted by the educated intellect. The human mind could never know what was the real nature or attributes of God; it could only agree with faith in affirming a spiritual power as the foundation of all reality. Furthermore, to the Mutazilites, it seemed fatal to human morality and enterprise to believe, as orthodoxy did, in the complete predestination of all events by God, and the arbitrary election, from all eternity, of the saved and the damned.

In a hundred variations of these themes, Mutazilite doctrines spread rapidly under the rule of al-Mansur, Harun al-Rashid, and al-Mamun. At first in the privacy of scholars and infidels, then in the soirees of the caliphs, finally in the lecture circles of colleges and mosques, the new rationalism won a voice, even, here and there, ascendancy. Al-Mamun was fascinated by this fledgling flight of reason, defended it, and ended by proclaiming the Mutazilite views as the official faith of the realm. Mingling old habits of Oriental monarchy with the latest ideas of Hellenizing Moslems, al-Mamun in 832

issued a decree requiring all Moslems to admit that the Koran had been created in time; a later decree ruled that no one could be a witness in law, or a
judge, unless he declared his acceptance of the new dogma; further decrees
extended this obligatory acceptance to the doctrines of free will, and the im-
possibility of the soul ever seeing God with a physical eye; at last, refusal to
take these tests and oaths was made a capital crime. Al-Mamun died in 833,
but his successors al-Mutassim and al-Wathiq continued his campaign. The
theologian Ibn Hanbal denounced this inquisition; summoned to take the
tests, he answered all questions by quoting the Koran in favor of the orthodox view. He was scourged to unconsciousness and cast into jail; but his sufferings made him, in the eyes of the people, a martyr and a saint, and prepared
for the reaction that overwhelmed Moslem philosophy.

Meanwhile that philosophy had produced its first major figure. Abu Yusuf
Yaqub ibn Ishaq al-Kindi was born in Kufa about 803, son of the governor
of the city; he studied there and at Baghdad, and won a high reputation at
the courts of al-Mamun and al-Mutassim as translator, scientist, and philosopher. Like so many thinkers in that confident heyday of the Moslem mind,
he was an omnivorous polymath, studying everything, writing 265 treatises
about everything—arithmetic, geometry, astronomy, meteorology, geography, physics, politics, music, medicine, philosophy. . . . He agreed with Plato
that no one could be a philosopher without being first a mathematician, and
he struggled to reduce health, medicine, and music to mathematical relations.
He studied the tides, sought the laws that determine the speed of a falling
body, and investigated the phenomena of light in a book on *Optics* which influenced Roger Bacon. He shocked the Moslem world by writing an
Apology for Christianity.[54] He and an aide translated the apocryphal *Theology of Aristotle*; he was deeply impressed by this forgery, and rejoiced in the
thought that it reconciled Aristotle with Plato—by turning both of them into
Neoplatonists. Al-Kindi's philosophy was Neoplatonism restated: spirit has
three grades—God, the creative World Soul or Logos, and its emanation, the
soul of man; if a man trains his soul to right knowledge he can achieve freedom and deathlessness.[55] Apparently al-Kindi made heroic efforts to be orthodox; yet he took from Aristotle [56] the distinction between the active intellect, which is divine, and the passive intellect of man, which is merely the
capacity for thought; Avicenna would transmit this distinction to Averroës,
who would set the world by the ears with it as an argument against personal
immortality. Al-Kindi associated with Mutazilites; when the reaction came
his library was confiscated, and his deathlessness hung by a thread. He survived the storm, recovered his liberty, and lived till 873.

In a society where government, law, and morality are bound up with a
religious creed, any attack upon that creed is viewed as menacing the foundations of social order itself. All the forces that had been beaten down by the
Arab conquest—Greek philosophy, Gnostic Christianity, Persian national-

ism, Mazdakite communism—were rampantly resurgent; the Koran was questioned and ridiculed; a Persian poet was decapitated for proclaiming the superiority of his verses to the Koran (784);[57] the whole structure of Islam, resting on the Koran, seemed ready to collapse. In this crisis three factors made orthodoxy victorious: a conservative caliph, the rise of the Turkish guard, and the natural loyalty of the people to their inherited beliefs. Al-Mutawakkil, coming to the throne in 847, based his support upon the populace and the Turks; and the Turks, new converts to Mohammedanism, hostile to the Persians, and strangers to Greek thought, gave themselves with a whole heart to a policy of saving the faith by the sword. Al-Mutawakkil annulled and reversed the illiberal liberalism of al-Mamun; Mutazilites and other heretics were expelled from governmental employ and educational positions; any expression of heterodox ideas in literature or philosophy was forbidden; the eternity of the Koran was re-established by law. The Shia sect was proscribed, and the shrine of Husein at Kerbela was destroyed (851). The edict allegedly issued by Omar I against Christians, and extended to the Jews by Harun (807) and soon again ignored, was reissued by al-Mutawakkil (850); Jews and Christians were ordered to wear a distinctive color of dress, put colored patches on the garments of their slaves, ride only on mules and asses, and affix wooden devils to their doors. New churches and synagogues were to be pulled down, and no public elevation of the cross was to be allowed in Christian ceremonies. No Christian or Jew was to receive education in Moslem schools.[58]

In the next generation the reaction took a milder form. Some orthodox theologians, bravely accepting the gage of logic, proposed to prove by reason the truth of the traditional faith. These *mutakallimun* (i.e., logicians) were the Scholastics of Islam; they undertook that same reconciliation of religious dogma with Greek philosophy which Maimonides in the twelfth century would attempt for Judaism, and Thomas Aquinas in the thirteenth for Christianity. Abul-Hasan al-Ashari (873–935) of Basra, after teaching Mutazilite doctrines for a decade, turned against them in his fortieth year, attacked them with the Mutazilite weapon of logic, and poured forth a stream of conservative polemics that shared powerfully in the victory of the old creed. He accepted the predestinarianism of Mohammed without flinching: God has predetermined every act and event, and is their primary cause; He is above all law and morals; He "rules as a sovereign over His creatures, doing what He wills; if He were to send them all to hell there would be no wrong." [59] Not all the orthodox relished this submission of the faith to intellectual debate; many proclaimed the formula *Bila kayf*—"Believe without asking how." [60] The theologians for the most part ceased to discuss basic issues, but lost themselves in the scholastic minutiae of a doctrine whose fundamentals they accepted as axioms.

The ferment of philosophy subsided at Baghdad, only to emerge at minor courts. Sayfu'l-Dawla provided a house at Aleppo for Muhammad Abu Nasr al-Farabi, the first Turk to make a name in philosophy. Born at Farab in Turkestan, he studied logic under Christian teachers at Baghdad and Harran, read Aristotle's *Physics* forty times and the *De Anima* 200 times, was denounced as a heretic at Baghdad, adopted the doctrine and dress of a Sufi, and lived like the swallows of the air. "He was the most indifferent of men to the things of this world," says Ibn Khallikan; "he never gave himself the least trouble to acquire a livelihood or possess a habitation." [61] Sayfu'l-Dawla asked him how much he needed for his maintenance; al-Farabi thought that four dirhems ($2.00) a day would suffice; the prince settled this allowance on him for life.

Thirty-nine works by al-Farabi survive, many of them commentaries on Aristotle. His *Ihsa al-ulum*, or *Encyclopedia of Science*, summarized the knowledge of his time in philology, logic, mathematics, physics, chemistry, economics, and politics. He answered with a straightforward negative the question that would soon agitate the Scholastic philosophers of Christendom: Does the universal (the genus, the species, or the quality) exist apart from the specific individual? Deceived like the rest by the *Theology of Aristotle*, he transformed the hard-headed Stagirite into a mystic, and lived long enough to subside into orthodox belief. Having in his youth professed a theoretical agnosticism,[62] he progressed sufficiently in later life to give a detailed description of the deity.[63] He took over Aristotle's proofs of God's existence very much as Aquinas would do three centuries later: a chain of contingent events requires for its intelligibility an ultimate necessary being; a chain of causes requires a First Cause; a series of motions requires a Prime Mover unmoved; multiplicity requires unity. The ultimate goal of philosophy, never quite attainable, is knowledge of the First Cause; the best approach to such knowledge is purity of soul. Like Aristotle, al-Farabi carefully managed to make himself unintelligible on immortality. He died at Damascus in 950.

One work alone, among his remains, strikes us with its original force: *Al-Medina al-Fadila—The Ideal City*. It opens with a description of the law of nature as one of perpetual struggle of each organism against all the rest— Hobbes' *bellum omnium contra omnes*; every living thing, in the last analysis, sees in all other living things a means to its ends. Some cynics argue from this, says al-Farabi, that in this inescapable competition the wise man is he who best bends others to his will, and most fully achieves his own desires. How did human society emerge from this jungle law? If we may trust al-Farabi's account, there were both Rousseauians and Nietzscheans among the Moslems who took up this question: some thought that society had begun in an agreement, among individuals, that their survival required the acceptance of certain restraints through custom or law; others laughed this "social contract" out of history, and insisted that society, or the state, had begun as the conquest and regimentation of the weak by the strong. States themselves, said these Nietzscheans, are organs of competition; it is natural that states should struggle with one another for ascendancy, security, power, and wealth; war is natural and inevitable; and in that final arbitrament, as in the law of nature, the only right is might. Al-Farabi counters this view with an appeal to his fellow men to build a society not upon envy, power, and strife, but upon reason, devotion, and love.[64] He ends safely by recommending a monarchy based upon strong religious belief.[65]

A pupil of a pupil of al-Farabi established at Baghdad, about 970, an association of savants—known to us only from its founder's place name as the Sidjistani Society—for the discussion of philosophical problems. No questions were asked as to the national origin or religious affiliation of any member. The group seems to have drowned itself in logic and epistemology, but its existence indicates that intellectual appetite survived in the capital. Of greater moment or result was a similar but secret fraternity of scientists and philosophers organized at Basra about 983. These "Brethren of Sincerity" or Purity (*Ikhwan al-Safa*) were alarmed by the weakening of the caliphate, the poverty of the people, and the corruption of morals; they aspired to a moral, spiritual, and political renovation of Islam; and thought that this renewal might be founded upon a blend of Greek philosophy, Christian ethics, Sufi mysticism, Shia politics, and Moslem law. They conceived friendship as a collaboration of abilities and virtues, each party bringing to the union a quality of which the others had lack and need; truth, they thought, comes more readily from a meeting of minds than from individual thought. So they privately met and discussed, with fine freedom, catholicity, and courtesy, all the basic problems of life, and finally issued fifty-one tracts as their considered and co-operative system and epitome of science, religion, and philosophy. A Spanish Moslem, traveling in the Near East about the year 1000, took a fancy to these treatises, collected them, and preserved them.

In these 1134 pages we find scientific explanations of tides, earthquakes, eclipses, sound waves, and many other natural phenomena; a full acceptance of astrology and alchemy; and occasional dallying with magic and numerology. The theology, as in nearly all Moslem thinkers, is Gnostic and Neoplatonic: from the First Cause or God emanates the Active Intelligence (Logos, Reason), from which proceeds the world of bodies and souls. All material things are formed by, and act through, soul. Every soul is restless until it rejoins the Active Intelligence or World Soul. This union demands absolute purity in the soul; ethics is the art of attaining this purity; science, philosophy, and religion are means to such purification. In seeking purity we must try to model ourselves upon the intellectual devotion of Socrates, the universal charity of Christ, and the modest nobility of Ali. When the mind has been emancipated by knowledge it should feel free to reinterpret through allegory, and thereby reconcile with philosophy, "the crude expressions of the Koran, which were adapted to the understanding of an uncivilized desert people" [66]—a sharp Persian retort to Arab pride. All in all, these fifty-one tracts constitute the fullest and most consistent expression that we possess of Moslem thought in the Abbasid age. The orthodox leaders in Baghdad burned them as heresy in 1150, but they continued to circulate, and exercised a pervasive influence upon Moslem and Jewish philosophy—upon al-Ghazali and Averroës, ibn Gabirol and Judah Halevi,[67] the philosophical poet al-Ma'arri, and perhaps upon the man who in his brief life rivaled the scope and depth, and surpassed the rationality, of this co-operative synthesis.

For Ibn Sina—Avicenna—was not content to be a scientist and a world-renowned authority on medicine; doubtless he knew that a scientist completes himself only through philosophy. He tells us that he read Aristotle's *Metaphysics* forty times without understanding it, and that when al-Farabi's commentary enabled him to comprehend the book he was so happy and grateful that he rushed into the street and scattered alms.[68] Aristotle remained to the end his ideal in philosophy; already in the *Qanun* he used of him that phrase, "the philosopher," which was to become in the Latin world a synonym for Aristotle. He detailed his own philosophy in the *Kitab al-Shifa*, and then summarized it in the *Najat*. He had a flair for logic, and insisted on precise definitions. He gave the classic medieval answer to the question whether universals or general ideas (*man, virtue, redness*) exist apart from individual things: they exist (1) *ante res*, "before the things," in the mind of God as Platonic exemplars according to which the things are made; (2) *in rebus*, "in the things" in which they appear or are exemplified; and (3) *post res*, "after the things," as abstract(ed) ideas in the human mind; but universals do not exist in the natural world apart from individual things. Abélard and Aquinas would, after a century of turmoil, give the same reply.

Indeed, Avicenna's metaphysics is almost a summary of what, two centuries after him, the Latin thinkers would syncretize as the Scholastic philosophy. He begins with a laborious restatement of Aristotle and al-Farabi on matter and form, the four causes, the contingent and the necessary, the many and the one, and frets over the puzzle of how the contingent and changeable many—the multiplicity of mortal things—could ever have flowed from the necessary and changeless One. Like Plotinus he thinks to solve the problem by postulating an intermediate Active Intelligence, distributed through the celestial, material, and human world as souls. Finding some difficulty in reconciling God's passage from noncreation to creation with the divine immutability, he proposes to believe, with Aristotle, in the eternity of the material world; but knowing that this will offend the *mutakallimun*, he offers them a compromise by a favorite Scholastic distinction: God is prior to the world not in time but logically, i.e., in rank and essence and cause: the existence of the world depends at every moment upon the existence of its sustaining force, which is God. Avicenna concedes that all entities but God are contingent—i.e., their existence is not inevitable or indispensable. Since such contingent things require a cause for their existence, they cannot be explained except by reverting, in the chain of causes, to a necessary being— one whose essence or meaning involves existence, a being whose existence must be presupposed in order to explain any other existence. God is the only being that exists by its own essence; it is essential that He exist, for without such a First Cause nothing that is could have begun to be. Since all matter is contingent—i.e., its essence does not involve existence—God cannot be material. For like reasons He must be simple and one. Since there is intelligence in created beings, there must be intelligence in their creator. The Supreme Intelligence sees all things—past, present, and future—not in time or sequence but at once; their occurrence is the temporal result of His timeless thought. But God does not directly cause each action or event; things develop by an internal teleology—they have their purposes and destinies written in themselves. Therefore God is not responsible for evil; evil is the price we pay for freedom of will; and the evil of the part may be the good of the whole.[69]

The existence of the soul is attested by our most immediate internal perception. The soul is spiritual for the same reason: we simply perceive it to be so; our ideas are clearly distinct from our organs. The soul is the principle of self-movement and growth in a body; in this sense even the celestial spheres have souls; "the whole cosmos is the manifestation of a universal principle of life." [70] By itself a body can cause nothing; the cause of its every motion is its inherent soul. Each soul or intelligence possesses a measure of freedom and creative power akin to that of the First Cause, for it is an emanation of that Cause. After death the pure soul returns to union with the World Soul; and in this union lies the blessedness of the good.[71]

Avicenna achieved as well as any man the ever-sought reconciliation between the faith of the people and the reasoning of the philosophers. He did not wish, like Lucretius, to destroy religion for the sake of philosophy, nor, like al-Ghazali in the ensuing century, to destroy philosophy for the sake of religion. He treats all questions with reason only, quite independently of the Koran, and gives a naturalistic analysis of inspiration; [72] but he affirms the people's need of prophets who expound to them the laws of morality in forms and parables popularly intelligible and effective; in this sense, as laying or preserving the foundations of social and moral development, the prophet is God's messenger.[73] So Mohammed preached the resurrection of the body, and sometimes described heaven in material terms; the philosopher will doubt the immortality of the body, but he will recognize that if Mohammed had taught a purely spiritual heaven the people would not have listened to him, and would not have united into a disciplined and powerful nation. Those who can worship God in spiritual love, entertaining neither hope nor fear, are the highest of mankind; but they will reveal this attitude only to their maturest students, not to the multitude.[74]

Avicenna's *Shifa* and *Qanun* mark the apex of medieval thought, and constitute one of the major syntheses in the history of the mind. Much of it followed the lead of Aristotle and al-Farabi, as much of Aristotle followed Plato; only lunatics can be completely original. Avicenna occasionally talks what seems to our fallible judgment to be nonsense; but that is also true of Plato and Aristotle; there is nothing so foolish but it may be found in the pages of the philosophers. Avicenna lacked the honest uncertainty, critical spirit, and ever open mind of al-Biruni, and made many more mistakes; synthesis must pay that price as long as life is brief. He surpassed his rivals in the clarity and vivacity of his style, in the ability to relieve and illuminate abstract thought with illustrative anecdote and pardonable poetry, and in the unparalleled scope of his scientific and philosophical range. His influence was immense: it reached out to Spain to mold Averroës and Maimonides, and into Latin Christendom to help the great Scholastics; it is astonishing how much of Albertus Magnus and Thomas Aquinas goes back to Avicenna. Roger Bacon called him "the chief authority in philosophy after Aristotle"; [75] and Aquinas was not merely practicing his customary courtesy in speaking of him with as much respect as of Plato.[76]

Arabic philosophy in the East almost died with Avicenna. Soon after his culminating effort the orthodox emphasis of the Seljuqs, the frightened fideism of the theologians, the victorious mysticism of al-Ghazali put a cloture on speculative thought. It is a pity that we know these three centuries (750–1050) of Arabic efflorescence so imperfectly. Thousands of Arabic manuscripts in science, literature, and philosophy lie hidden in the libraries of the Moslem world: in Constantinople alone there are thirty mosque libraries whose wealth has been merely scratched; in Cairo, Damascus, Mosul, Baghdad, Delhi are great collections not even catalogued; an immense library in the Escorial near Madrid has hardly completed the listing of its Islamic manuscripts in science, literature, jurisprudence, and philosophy.[77] What we know of Moslem thought in those centuries is a fragment of what survives, what survives is a fragment of what was produced; what appears in these pages is a morsel of a fraction of a fragment. When scholarship has surveyed more thoroughly this half-forgotten legacy, we shall probably rank the tenth century in Eastern Islam as one of the golden ages in the history of the mind.

V. MYSTICISM AND HERESY

At their peak philosophy and religion meet in the sense and contemplation of universal unity. The soul untouched by logic, too weak of wing for the metaphysical flight from the many to the one, from incident to law, might reach that vision through a mystic absorption of the separate self in the soul of the world. And where science and philosophy failed, where the brief finite reason of man faltered and turned blind in the presence of infinity, faith might mount to the feet of God by ascetic discipline, unselfish devotion, the unconditional surrender of the part to the whole.

Moslem mysticism had many roots: the asceticism of the Hindu fakirs, the Gnosticism of Egypt and Syria, the Neoplatonist speculations of the later Greeks, and the omnipresent example of ascetic Christian monks. As in Christendom, so in Islam a pious minority protested against any accommodation of religion to the interests and practices of the economic world; they denounced the luxury of caliphs, viziers, and merchants, and proposed to return to the simplicity of Abu Bekr and Omar I. They resented any intermediary between themselves and the deity; even the rigid ritual of the mosque seemed to them an obstacle to that mystic state in which the soul, purified of all earthly concerns, rose not only to the Beatific Vision but to unity with God. The movement flourished most in Persia, perhaps through proximity to India, through Christian influence at Jund-i-Shapur, and through Neoplatonist traditions established by the Greek philosophers who fled from Athens to Persia in 529. Most Moslem mystics called themselves Sufis, from the simple robe of wool (*suf*) that they wore; but within that term were embraced sincere enthusiasts, exalted poets, pantheists, ascetics, charlatans, and men with many wives. Their doctrine varied from time to time, and from street to street. The Sufis, said Averroës, "maintain that the knowledge of God is found in our own hearts, after our detachment from all physical desires, and the concentration of the mind upon the desired object." [78] But many Sufis tried to reach God through external objects too; whatever we see of perfection or loveliness in the world is due to the presence or operation of divinity in them. "O God," said one mystic, "I never listen to the cry of animals, or the quivering of trees, or the murmur of water, or the song of birds, or the rustling wind, or the crashing thunder, without feeling them to be an evidence of Thy unity, and a proof that there is nothing like unto Thee." [79] In reality, the mystic held, these individual things exist only by the divine power in them; their sole reality is this underlying divinity. Therefore God is all; not only is there no god but Allah, there is no being but God. [80] Consequently each soul is God; and the full-blooded mystic shamelessly avers that "God and I are one." "Verily I am God," said Abu Yezid (*c.* 900); "there is no god but me; worship me." [81] "I am He Whom I love," said Husein al-Hallaj; "and He Whom I love is I. . . . I am He Who drowned the people of Noah. . . . I am the Truth." [82] Hallaj was arrested for exaggeration, scourged with a thousand stripes, and burned to death (922). His followers claimed to have seen and talked with him after this interruption, and many Sufis made him their favorite saint.

The Sufi, like the Hindu, believed in a course of discipline as necessary to the mystic revelation of God: purifying exercises of devotion, meditation, and prayer; the full obedience of the novice to a Sufi master or teacher; and the complete abandonment of any personal desire, even the desire for salvation or the mystical union. The perfect Sufi loves God for His own sake, not for any reward; "the Giver," said Abu'l-Qasim, "is better for you than the gift." [83] Usually, however, the Sufi valued his discipline as a means of reaching a true knowledge of things, sometimes as a curriculum leading to a degree of miraculous power over nature, but almost always as a road to union with God. He who had completely forgotten his individual self in such union was called al-insanu-l-Kamil—the Perfect Man.[84] Such a man, the Sufis believed, was above all laws, even above the obligation to pilgrimage. Said a Sufi verse: "All eyes toward the Kaaba turn, but ours to the Beloved's face." [85]

Until the middle of the eleventh century the Sufis continued to live in the world, sometimes with their families and their children; even the Sufis attached small moral worth to celibacy. "The true saint," said Abu Said, "goes in and out amongst the people, eats and sleeps with them, buys and sells in the market, marries and takes part in social intercourse, and never forgets God for a single moment." [86] Such Sufis were distinguished only by their simplicity of life, their piety and quietism, very much like the early Quakers; and occasionally they gathered around some holy teacher or exemplar, or met in groups for prayer and mutual stimulation to devotion; already in the tenth century those strange dervish dances were taking form which were to play so prominent a part in later Sufism. A few became recluses and tormented themselves, but asceticism was in this period discountenanced and rare. Saints, unknown to early Islam, became numerous in Sufism. One of the earliest was a woman, Rabia al-Adawiyya of Basra (717–801). Sold as a slave in youth, she was freed because her master saw a radiance above her head while she prayed. Refusing marriage, she lived a life of self-denial and charity. Asked if she hated Satan, she answered, "My love for God leaves me no room for hating Satan." Tradition ascribes to her a famous Sufi saying: "O God! Give to Thine enemies whatever Thou hast assigned to me of this world's goods, and to Thy friends whatever Thou hast assigned to me in the life to come; for Thou Thyself art sufficient for me." [87]

Let us take, as an example of many Sufis, the saint and poet Abu Said ibn Abi'l-Khayr (967–1049). Born in Mayhana in Khurasan, he knew Avicenna; story has it that he said of the philosopher, "What I see he knows," and that the philosopher said of him, "What I know he sees." [88] In his youth he was fond of profane literature, and claims to have memorized 30,000 verses of pre-Islamic poetry. One day, in his twenty-sixth year, he heard a lecture by Abu Ali, who took as text the ninth verse of the sixth sura of the Koran: "Say Allah! then leave them to amuse themselves in their vain discourse." "At the moment of hearing this word," Abu Said relates, "a door in my breast was opened, and I was rapt from myself." He collected all his books and burned them. "The first step in Sufism," he would say, "is the breaking of inkpots, the tearing up of books, the forgetting of all kinds of knowledge." He retired to a niche in a chapel of his home; "there I sat for seven years, saying continually, 'Allah! Allah! Allah!'"; such repetition of the Holy Name was, with Moslem mystics, a favorite means of realizing *fana*—"passing away from self." He practiced several forms of asceticism: wore the same shirt always, spoke only in dire need, ate nothing till sunset, and then only a piece of bread; never lay down to sleep; made an excavation in the wall of his niche or cell, just high and broad enough to stand in, often closed himself within it, and stuffed his ears to hear no sound. Sometimes at night he would lower himself by a rope into a well, head downward, and recite the entire Koran before emerging—if we were to believe the testimony of his father. He made himself a servant to other Sufis, begged for them, cleaned their cells and privies. "Once, whilst I was seated in the mosque, a woman went up on the roof and bespattered me with filth; and still I heard a voice saying, 'Is not thy Lord enough for thee?'" At forty he "attained to perfect illumination," began to preach, and attracted devoted audiences; some of his hearers, he assures us, smeared their faces with his ass's dung "to gain a blessing." [89] He left his mark on Sufism by founding a monastery of dervishes, and formulating for it a set of rules that became a model for similar institutions in later centuries.

Like Augustine, Abu Said taught that only God's grace, not man's good works, would bring salvation; but he thought of salvation in terms of a spiritual emancipation independent of any heaven. God opens to man one gate after another. First the gate of repentance, then

> the gate of certainty, so that he accepts contumely and endures abasement, and knows for certain by Whom it is brought to pass. . . . Then God opens to him the gate of love; but still he thinks, "I love." . . . Then God opens to him the gate of unity . . . thereupon he perceives that all is He, all is by Him . . . he recognizes that he has not the right to say, "I" or "mine" . . . desires fall away from him, and he becomes free and calm. . . . Thou wilt never escape from thy self until thou slay it. Thy self, which is keeping thee far from God, and saying "So-and-so has treated me ill . . . such a one has done well by me"—all this is polytheism; nothing depends upon the creatures, all upon the Creator. This must thou know; and having said it, thou must stand firm. . . . To stand firm means that when thou hast said "One," thou must never again say "Two." . . . Say "Allah!" and stand firm there. [90]

The same Hindu-Emersonian doctrine appears in one of the many quatrains dubiously ascribed to Abu Said:

> Said I, "To whom belongs Thy beauty?" He
> Replied, "Since I alone exist, to Me;
>   Lover, Beloved, and Love am I in one;
> Beauty, and Mirror, and the eyes that see." [91]

There being no church to canonize such heroes of ecstasy, they received the informal canonization of popular acclaim; and by the twelfth century the Koranic discouragement of the worship of saints as a form of idolatry had been overwhelmed by the natural sentiments of the people. An early saint was Ibrahim ibn Adham (eighth century?), the Abou ben Adhem of Leigh Hunt. Popular imagination attributed miraculous powers to such saints: they knew the secrets of clairvoyance, thought reading, and telepathy; they could swallow fire or glass unhurt, pass through fire unburnt, walk upon water, fly through the air, and transport themselves over great distances in a moment's time. Abu Said reports feats of mind reading as startling as any in current mythography.[92] Day by day the religion that some philosophers supposed to be the product of priests is formed and re-formed by the needs, sentiment, and imagination of the people; and the monotheism of the prophets becomes the polytheism of the populace.

Orthodox Islam accepted Sufism within the Moslem fold, and gave it considerable latitude of expression and belief. But this shrewd policy was refused to heresies that concealed revolutionary politics, or preached an anarchism of morality and law. Of many half-religious half-political revolts the most effective was that of the "Ismaila." In Shia doctrine, it will be recalled, each generation of Ali's descendants, to the twelfth, was headed by a divine incarnation or Imam, and each Imam named his successor. The sixth, Jafar al-Sadiq, appointed his eldest son Ismail to succeed him; Ismail, it is alleged, indulged in wine; Jafar rescinded his nomination, and chose another son, Musa, as seventh Imam (c. 760). Some Shi'ites held the appointment of Ismail to be irrevocable, and honored him or his son Muhammad as seventh and last Imam. For a century these "Ismailites" remained a negligible sect; then Abdallah ibn Qaddah made himself their leader, and sent missionaries to preach the doctrine of the "Seveners" throughout Islam. Before initiation into the sect the convert took an oath of secrecy, and pledged absolute obedience to the Dai-d-Duat, or Grand Master of the order. The teaching was divided into exoteric and esoteric: the convert was told that after passing through nine stages of initiation all veils would be removed, the *Talim* or Secret Doctrine (that God is All) would be revealed to him, and he would then be above every creed and every law. In the eighth degree of initiation the convert was taught that nothing can be known of the Supreme Being, and no worship can be rendered Him.[93] Many survivors of old communistic movements were drawn to the Ismaila by the expectation that a Mahdi or Redeemer would come, who would establish a regime of equality, justice, and brotherly love on the earth. This remarkable confraternity became in time a power in Islam. It won North Africa and Egypt, and founded the Fatimid dynasty; and late in the ninth century it gave birth to a movement that almost brought an end to the Abbasid caliphate.

When Abdallah ibn Qaddah died in 874, an Iraqi peasant named Hamdan ibn al-Ashrath, popularly known as Qarmat, became the leader of the Ismaili sect, and gave it such energy that for a time in Asia it was called, after him, Qaramita, the Carmathians. Planning to overthrow the Arabs and restore the Persian Empire, he secretly enlisted thousands of supporters, and persuaded them to contribute a fifth of their property and income to a common treasury. Again an element of social revolution entered into what was ostensibly a form of mystical religion: the Carmathians advocated a communism of both property and women,[94] organized workmen into guilds, preached universal equality, and adopted an allegorical freethinking interpretation of the Koran. They disregarded the rituals and fasts prescribed by orthodoxy, and laughed at the "asses" who offered worship to shrines and stones.[95] In 899 they established an independent state on the west shore of the Persian Gulf; in 900 they defeated the caliph's army, leaving hardly a man of it alive; in 902 they ravaged Syria to the gates of Damascus; in 924 they sacked Basra, then Kufa; in 930 they plundered Mecca, slew 30,000 Moslems, and carried off rich booty, including the veil of the Kaaba and the Black Stone itself.* The movement exhausted itself in its successes and excesses; citizens united against its threat to property and order; but its doctrines and violent ways were passed on in the next century to the Ismaili of Alamut—the hashish-inspired Assassins.

VI. LITERATURE

In Islam life and religion had drama, but literature had none; it is a form apparently alien to the Semitic mind. And as in other medieval literatures, there was here no novel. Most writing was heard rather than silently read; and those who cared for fiction could not rise to the concentration necessary for a complex and continued narrative. Short stories were as old as Islam or Adam; the simpler Moslems listened to them with the ardor and appetite of children, but the scholars never counted them as literature. The most popular of these stories were the *Fables* of Bidpai and the *Thousand Nights and a Night*. The *Fables* were brought to Persia from India in the sixth century, were translated into Pahlavi, and thence, in the eighth century, into Arabic. The Sanskrit original was lost, the Arabic version survived, and was rendered into forty languages.

Al-Masudi (d. 597) speaks in his *Meadows of Gold*[96] of a Persian book *Hazar Afsana*, or *Thousand Tales*, and of its Arabic translation, *Alf Laylah wa Laylah*; this is the earliest known mention of *The Thousand Nights and a Night*. The plan of the book as described by al-Masudi was that of our *Arabian Nights*; such a framework for a series of stories was already old in India. A great number of these tales circulated in the Oriental world; various collections might differ in their selection, and we are not sure that any story

---

* It was restored to the Kaaba in 951 by order of the Fatimid Caliph al-Mansur.

in our present editions appeared in the texts known to al-Masudi. Shortly after 1700 an incomplete Arabic manuscript, not traceable beyond 1536, was sent from Syria to the French Orientalist Antoine Galland. Fascinated by their whimsical fantasy, their glimpses of intimate Moslem life, perhaps by their occasional obscenity, he issued at Paris in 1704 their first European translation—*Les mille et une nuits*. The book succeeded beyond any expectation; translations were made into every European language; and children of all nations and ages began to talk of Sinbad the Sailor, Aladdin's lamp, and Ali Baba and the Forty Thieves. Next to the Bible (itself Oriental), the *Fables* and the *Nights* are the most widely read books in the world.

Literary prose, in Islam, is a form of poetry. The Arabic temperament was inclined to strong feeling; Persian manners made for ornate speech; and the Arabian language, then common to both peoples, invited rhyme by the similarity of its inflectional endings. So literary prose usually rhymed; preachers and orators and storytellers used rhymed prose; it was in this medium that Badi al-Hamadhani (d. 1008) wrote his famous *Maqamat* (*Assemblies*)— tales told to various gatherings about a wandering rapscallion with less morals than wit. The peoples of the Near East were ear-minded, as were all men before printing; to most Moslems literature was a recited poem or narrative. Poems were written to be read aloud or sung; and everyone in Islam, from peasant to caliph, heard them gladly. Nearly everyone, as in samurai Japan, composed verses; in the educated classes it was a popular game for one person to finish in rhyme a couplet or stanza begun by another, or to compete in forming extempore lyrics or poetic epigrams. Poets rivaled one another in fashioning complex patterns of meter and rhyme; many rhymed the middle as well as the end of a line; a riot of rhyme scurried through Arab verse, and influenced the rise of rhyme in European poetry.

Probably no civilization or period—not even China in the days of Li Po and Tu Fu, nor Weimar when it had "a hundred citizens and ten thousand poets"—ever equaled Abbasid Islam in the number and prosperity of its bards. Abul-Faraj of Isfahan (897–967), toward the end of this age, collected and recorded Arabic poetry in his *Kitab al-Aghani* (*Book of Songs*); its twenty volumes suggest the wealth and variety of Arabic verse. Poets served as propagandists, and were feared as deadly satirists; rich men bought praise by the meter; and caliphs gave high place and fat sums to poets who turned for them a pleasant stanza, or celebrated the glory of their deeds or their tribe. The Caliph Hisham, wishing to recall a poem, sent for the poet Hammad, who luckily remembered it all; Hisham rewarded him with two slave girls and 50,000 dinars ($237,500); [97] no poet will believe the tale. Arabic poetry, which once had sung to Bedouins, now addressed itself to courts and palaces; much of it became artificial, formal, delicately trivial, politely insincere; and a battle of ancients and moderns ensued in which the critics complained that there were great poets only before Mohammed.[98]

Love and war outbid religion as poetic themes. The poetry of the Arabs (this would not be true of the Persians) was seldom mystical; it preferred songs of battle, passion, or sentiment; and as the century of conquest closed, Eve overcame both Mars and Allah as the inspiration of Arab verse. The poets of Islam thrilled with autointoxication in describing the charms of woman—her fragrant hair, jewel eyes, berry lips, and silver limbs. In the deserts and holy cities of Arabia the troubadour motifs took form; poets and philosophers spoke of *adab* as, in one phase, the ethic and etiquette of love; this tradition would pass through Egypt and Africa to Sicily and Spain, and thence to Italy and Provence; and hearts would break in rhyme and rhythm and many tongues.

Hasan ibn Hani won the name of Abu Nuwas—"Father of the Curl"— from his abounding locks. Born in Persia, he found his way to Baghdad, became a favorite of Harun, and may have had with him one or two of the adventures ascribed to them in the *Thousand Nights and a Night*. He loved wine, woman, and his songs; offended the Caliph by too conspicuous toping, agnosticism, and lechery; was often imprisoned and often released; came by leisurely stages to virtue, and ended by carrying beads and the Koran with him everywhere. But the society of the capital liked best the hymns that he had written to wine and sin:

> Come, Suleiman! sing to me,
> And the wine, quick, bring to me! . . .
> While the flask goes twinkling round,
> Pour me a cup that leaves me drowned
> With oblivion—ne'er so nigh
> Let the shrill muezzin cry! [99]

> Accumulate as many sins as thou canst:
>   The Lord is ready to relax His ire.
> When the Day comes, forgiveness thou wilt find
>   Before a mighty King and gracious Sire;
> And gnaw thy fingers, all that joy regretting
>   Which thou didst leave through terror of hell-fire.[100]

The minor courts had their poets too, and Sayfu'l-Dawla provided a place for one who, almost unknown to Europe, is reckoned by the Arabs as their best. His name was Ahmad ibn Husein, but Islam remembers him as al-Mutannabi—"the pretender to prophecy." Born at Kufa in 915, he studied at Damascus, announced himself as a prophet, was arrested and released, and settled down at the Aleppo court. Like Abu Nuwas, he made his own religion, and notoriously neglected to fast or pray or read the Koran; [101] though he denounced life as not quite up to his standards, he enjoyed it too much to think of eternity. He celebrated Sayfu's victories with such zest and verbal artifice that his poems are as popular in Arabic as they are untranslatable into English. One couplet proved mortal to him:

I am known to the horse-troop, the night, and the desert's expanse;
Not more to paper and pen than to sword and the lance.

Attacked by robbers, he wished to flee; his slave inopportunely reminded him of these swashbuckling verses; al-Mutannabi resolved to live up to them, fought, and died of his wounds (965).[102]

Eight years later the strangest of all Arab poets, Abu'l-'Ala al-Ma'arri was born at al-Ma'arratu, near Aleppo. Smallpox left him blind at four; nevertheless he took up the career of a student, learned by heart the manuscripts that he liked in the libraries, traveled widely to hear famous masters, and returned to his village. During the next fifteen years his annual income was thirty dinars, some twelve dollars a month, which he shared with servant and guide; his poems won him fame, but as he refused to write encomiums, he nearly starved. In 1008 he visited Baghdad, was honored by poets and scholars, and perhaps picked up among the freethinkers of the capital some of the skepticism that spices his verse. In 1010 he went back to al-Ma'arratu, became rich, but lived to the end with the simplicity of a sage. He was a vegetarian à l'outrance, avoiding not only flesh and fowl, but milk, eggs, and honey as well; to take any of these from the animal world, he thought, was rank robbery. On the same principle he rejected the use of animal skins, blamed ladies for wearing furs, and recommended wooden shoes.[103] He died at eighty-four; and a pious pupil relates that 180 poets followed his funeral, and eighty-four savants recited eulogies at his grave.[104]

We know him now chiefly through the 1592 short poems called briefly Luzumiyyat (Obligations). Instead of discussing woman and war, like his fellow poets, al-Ma'arri deals boldly with the most basic questions: Should we follow revelation, or reason?—Is life worth living?—Is there a life after death?—Does God exist? . . . Every now and then the poet professes his orthodoxy; he warns us, however, that this is a legitimate precaution against martyrdom, which was not to his taste: "I lift my voice to utter lies absurd; but speaking truth my hushed tones scarce are heard." [105] He deprecates indiscriminate honesty: "Do not acquaint rascals with the essence of your religion, for so you expose yourself to ruin." [106] In simple fact al-Ma'arri is a rationalist agnostic pessimist.

Some hope that an Imam with prophet's gaze
Will rise and all the silent ranks amaze.
   Oh, idle thought! There's no Imam but Reason
To point the morning and the evening ways. . . .

Shall we in these old tales discover truth,
Or are they worthless fables told to youth?
   Our reason swears that they are only lies,
And reason's tree bears verity for truth. . . .

How oft, when young, my friends I would defame,
If our religious faiths were not the same;

But now my soul has traveled high and low;
Now all save Love, to me, is but a name.[107]

He denounces the Moslem divines who "make religion serve the pelf of man," who "fill the mosque with terror when they preach," but conduct themselves no better than "some who drink to a tavern tune." "You have been deceived, honest man, by a cunning knave who preaches to the women."

To his own sordid ends the pulpit he ascends,
    And though he disbelieves in resurrection,
Makes all his hearers quail whilst he unfolds a tale
    Of Last Day scenes that stun the recollection.[108]

The worst scoundrels, he thinks, are those who manage the holy places in Mecca; they will do anything for money. He advises his hearers not to waste their time in pilgrimage,[109] and to be content with one world.

The body nothing feels when soul is flown;
Shall spirit feel, unbodied and alone? . . .[110]

We laugh, but inept is our laughter;
    We should weep, and weep sore,
Who are shattered like glass, and thereafter
    Remolded no more.[111]

And he concludes: "If by God's decree I shall be made into a clay pot that serves for ablutions, I am thankful and content." [112] He believes in a God omnipotent and wise, and "marveled at a physician who denies the Creator after having studied anatomy." [113] But here too he raises difficulties. "Our natures did not become evil by our choice, but by the fates' command. . . ."

Why blame the world? The world is free
    Of sin; the blame is yours and mine.
Grapes, wine, and drinker—these are three;
    But who was at fault, I wonder—he
That pressed the grapes, or he that sipped the wine?

"I perceive," he writes with Voltairean sarcasm, "that men are naturally unjust to one another, but there is no doubt of the justice of Him Who created injustice." [114] And he breaks out into the angry dogmatism of a Diderot:

O fool, awake! The rites ye sacred hold
Are but a cheat contrived by men of old,
Who lusted after wealth, and gained their lust,
And died in baseness—and their law is dust.[115]

Offended by what seemed to him the lies and cruelties of men, al-Ma'arri became a pessimist recluse, the Timon of Islam. Since the evils of society are due to the nature of man, reform is hopeless.[116] The best thing is to live apart, to meet only a friend or two, to vegetate like some placid, half-solitary animal.[117] Better yet is never to be born, for once born we must bear "torment and tribulation" until death yields us peace.

> Life is a malady whose one medicine is death. . . .
> All come to die, alike householder and wanderer.
> The earth seeketh, even as we, its livelihood day by day
> Apportioned; it eats and drinks of human flesh and blood. . . .
> Meseemeth the crescent moon, that shines in the firmament
> Is death's curved spear, its point well sharpened,
> And splendor of breaking day a sabre unsheathed by the Dawn.

We cannot escape these Reapers ourselves; but we can, like good Schopenhauerians, cheat them of the children we might have begotten.

> If ye unto your sons would prove
> By act how dearly them ye love,
> Then every voice of wisdom joins
> To bid you leave them in your loins.[118]

He obeyed his own counsel, and wrote for himself the pithiest, bitterest epitaph:

> My sire brought this on me, but I on none.[119] *

We do not know how many Moslems shared the skepticism of al-Ma-'arri; the revival of orthodoxy after his time served as a conscious or unconscious censor of the literature transmitted to posterity, and, as in Christendom, may mislead us into minimizing medieval doubt. Al-Mutannabi and al-Ma'arri marked the zenith of Arabic poetry; after them the supremacy of theology and the silencing of philosophy drove Arabic verse into the insincerity, artificial passion, and flowering elegance of courtly and trivial lays. But at the same time the resurrection of Persia and its self-liberation from Arab rule were stirring the nation to a veritable renaissance. The Persian tongue had never yielded to Arabic in the speech of the people; gradually, in the tenth century, reflecting the political and cultural independence of the Tabirid, Samanid, and Ghaznevid princes, it reasserted itself as the language of government and letters, and became New or Modern Persian, enriched itself with Arabic words, and adopted the graceful Arabic script. Persia now broke out in magnificent architecture and lordly poetry. To the Arab *qasida* or ode, *qita* or fragment, and *ghazal* or love poem, the poets of Iran added the *mathnawi* or poetic narrative, and the *rubai* (pl. *rubaiyyat*) or quatrain. Everything in Persia—patriotism, passion, philosophy, pederasty, piety—now blossomed into verse.

This efflorescence began with Rudagi (d. 954), who improvised poetry,

---

* The above translations, worthy of Edward FitzGerald, are from three books by R. A. Nicholson, listed in the Bibliography. These volumes, each of them of fascinating interest, have done much to reveal to Western students the variety and beauty of Moslem poetry.

sang ballads, and played the harp at the Samanid court of Bokhara. There, a generation later, Prince Nuh ibn Mansur asked the poet Daqiqi to put into verse the *Khodainama*, or *Book of Kings*, wherein Danishwar (*c.* 651) had gathered the legends of Persia. Daqiqi had written a thousand lines when he was stabbed to death by his favorite slave. Firdausi completed the task, and became the Homer of Persia.

Abu'l-Qasim Mansur (or Hasan) was born at Tus (near Mashhad) about 934. His father held an administrative post at the Samanid court, and bequeathed to his son a comfortable villa at Bazh, near Tus. Spending his leisure in antiquarian research, Abu'l-Qasim became interested in the *Khodainama*, and undertook to transform these prose stories into a national epic. He called his work *Shahnama*—book of the shahs—and, in the fashion of the time, took a pen name, Firdausi (garden), perhaps from the groves of his estate. After twenty-five years of labor he finished the poem in its first form, and set out for Ghazni (999?), hoping to present it to the great and terrible Mahmud.

An early Persian historian assures us that there were then "four hundred poets in constant attendance on Sultan Mahmud." [120] It should have been an unsurpassable barrier, but Firdausi succeeded in interesting the vizier, who brought the immense manuscript to the Sultan's attention. Mahmud (says one account) gave the poet comfortable quarters in the palace, turned over to him reams of historical material, and bade him incorporate these in the epic. All variations of the story agree that Mahmud promised him a gold dinar ($4.70) for each couplet of the revised poem. For an unknown time Firdausi labored; at last (*c.* 1010) the poem reached its final form in 60,000 couplets, and was sent to the Sultan. When Mahmud was about to remit the promised sum, certain courtiers protested that it was too much, and added that Firdausi was a Shi'ite and Mutazilite heretic. Mahmud sent 60,000 silver dirhems ($30,000). The poet, in anger and scorn, divided the money between a bath attendant and a sherbet seller, and fled to Herat. He hid for six months in a bookseller's shop till Mahmud's agents, instructed to arrest him, gave up the search. He found refuge with Shariyar, prince of Shirzad in Tabaristan; there he composed a bitter satire on Mahmud; but Shariyar, fearful of the Sultan, bought the poem for 100,000 dirhems, and destroyed it. If we may believe these figures, and our equivalents, poetry was one of the most lucrative professions in medieval Persia. Firdausi went to Baghdad, and there wrote a long narrative poem, *Yusuf and Zuleika*, a variant of the story of Joseph and Potiphar's wife. Then, an old man of seventy-six, he returned to Tus. Ten years later Mahmud, struck by the vigor of a couplet that he heard quoted, asked the author's name; when he learned that it was by Firdausi he regretted his failure to reward the poet as promised. He despatched to Firdausi a caravan carrying 60,000 gold dinars' worth of indigo, and a letter of apology. As the caravan entered Tus it encountered the poet's funeral (1020?).

The *Shahnama* is one of the major works of the world's literature, if only in size. There is something noble in the picture of a poet putting aside trivial subjects and easy tasks, and giving thirty-five years of his life to telling his country's story in 120,000 lines—far exceeding the length of the *Iliad* and the *Odyssey* combined. Here was an old man mad about Persia, enamored of every detail in its records, whether legend or fact; his epic is half finished before it reaches history. He begins with the mythical figures of the Avesta, tells of Gayamurth, the Zoroastrian Adam, and then of Gayamurth's mighty grandson Jamshid, who "reigned over the land 700 years. . . . The world was happier because of him; death was unknown, neither sorrow nor pain." But after a few centuries "his heart was lifted up with pride, and he forgot whence came his weal. . . . He beheld only himself on the earth, called himself God, and sent forth his image to be worshiped." [121] At last we come to the hero of the epic, Rustam, son of the feudal noble Zal. When Rustam is 500 years old Zal falls in love with a slave girl, and through her gives Rustam a brother. Rustam serves and saves three kings, and retires from military life at the age of 400. His faithful steed Rakhsh ages as leisurely, is almost as great a hero, and receives from Firdausi the affectionate attention bestowed by any Persian upon a fine horse. There are pretty love stories in the *Shahnama*, and something of the troubadour's reverence for woman; there are charming pictures of fair women—one of the Queen Sudaveh, who "was veiled that none might behold her beauty; and she went with the men as the sun marches behind a cloud." [122] But in the case of Rustam the love motif plays a minor part; Firdausi recognizes that the dramas of parental and filial love can be more affecting than those of sexual romance. Amid a distant campaign Rustam has an amour with a Turkish lady, Tahmineh, and then loses track of her; she brings up their son Sohrab in sorrow and pride, telling the youth of his great but vanished father; in a war of Turks against Persians son and sire, neither knowing the other, meet spear to spear. Rustam admires the courage of the handsome lad, and offers to spare him; the boy disdainfully refuses, fights bravely, and is mortally wounded. Dying, he mourns that he has never yet seen his father Rustam; the victor perceives that he has slain his son. Sohrab's horse, riderless, regains the Turkish camp, and the news is brought to Sohrab's mother in one of the finest scenes of the epic.

> The strong emotion choked her panting breath,
> Her veins seemed withered by the cold of death.
> The trembling matrons hastening round her mourned,
> With piercing cries, till fluttering life returned.
> Then gazing up, distraught, she wept again,
> And frantic, seeing 'midst her pitying train

The favorite steed—now more than ever dear,
Its limbs she kissed, and bathed with many a tear;
Clasping the mail Sohrab in battle wore,
With burning lips she kissed it o'er and o'er;
His martial robes she in her arms compressed,
And like an infant strained them to her breast.[123]

It is a vivid narrative, moving rapidly from episode to episode, and finding unity only from the unseen presence of the beloved fatherland in every line. We—who have less leisure than men had before so many labor-saving devices were invented—cannot spare the time to read all these couplets and bury all these kings; but which of us has read every line of the *Iliad*, or the *Aeneid*, or *The Divine Comedy*, or *Paradise Lost*? Only men of epic stomach can digest these epic tales. After 200 pages we tire of Rustam's victories over demons, dragons, magicians, Turks. But we are not Persians; we have not heard the sonorous roll of the original verse; we cannot be moved as Persians are, who in a single province have named 300 villages after Rustam. In 1934 the educated world of Asia, Europe, and the Americas joined in commemorating the millennial anniversary of the poet whose massive book has been for a thousand years the bulwark of the Persian soul.

VII. ART *

When the Arabs invaded Syria their sole art was poetry. Mohammed was believed to have forbidden sculpture and painting as accomplices of idolatry —and music, rich silks, gold and silver ornaments as epicurean degeneracy; and though all these prohibitions were gradually overcome, they almost confined Moslem art in this period to architecture, pottery, and decoration. The Arabs themselves, so recently nomads or merchants, had no mature facility in art; they recognized their limitations, and employed the artists and artisans—adapted the art forms and traditions—of Byzantium, Egypt, Syria, Mesopotamia, Iran, and India. The Dome of the Rock at Jerusalem and the Mosque of Walid II at Damascus were purely Byzantine, even in their decoration. Farther east the old Assyrian and Babylonian tile decoration, and current Armenian and Nestorian church forms, were adopted; and in Persia, after much destruction of Sasanian literature and art, Islam saw the advantages of the column cluster, the pointed arch, the vault, and those styles of floral and geometrical ornament which finally flowered into the arabesque. The result was no mere imitation, but a brilliant synthesis that justified all borrowing. From the Alhambra in Spain to the Taj Mahal

* This section is particularly indebted to the *Survey of Persian Art* edited by Arthur Upham Pope, and especially to the chapters written by himself. His devoted work in this field, like that of James H. Breasted on Egypt, is an enduring monument of meticulous scholarship and discriminating philanthropy.

in India, Islamic art overrode all limits of place and time, laughed at distinctions of race and blood, developed a unique and yet varied character, and expressed the human spirit with a profuse delicacy never surpassed.

Moslem architecture, like most architecture in the Age of Faith, was almost entirely religious; the dwellings of men were designed for brief mortality, but the house of God was to be, at least internally, a thing of beauty forever. Nevertheless, though the remains are scant, we hear of bridges, aqueducts, fountains, reservoirs, public baths, fortresses, and turreted walls built by engineer-architects who in the first centuries after the Arab conquest were in many cases Christian, but in after centuries were predominantly Moslem. The Crusaders found excellent military architecture at Aleppo, Baalbek, and elsewhere in the Islamic East, learned there the uses of machicolated walls, and took from their foes many an idea for their own incomparable castles and forts. The Alcazar at Seville and the Alhambra at Granada were fortresses and palaces combined.

Of Umayyad palaces little survives except a country house at Qusayr Amra in the desert east of the Dead Sea, where the ruins show vaulted baths and frescoed walls. The palace of Adud ad-Dawla at Shiraz, we are assured, had 360 rooms, one for each day in the year, each painted in a unique color combination; one of its largest rooms was a library two stories high, arcaded and vaulted; "there was no book on any subject," says an enthusiastic Moslem, "of which there was not here a copy." [124] Scheherazade's descriptions of Baghdad mansions are fiction, but suggest an ornate magnificence of internal decoration.[125] Rich men had villas in the country as well as homes in the city; even in the city they had formal gardens; but around their villas these gardens became "paradises"—parks with springs, brooks, fountains, tiled pool, rare flowers, shade, fruit, and nut trees, and usually a pavilion for enjoying the open air without the glare of the sun. In Persia there was a religion of flowers; rose festivals were celebrated with sumptuous displays; the roses of Shiraz and Firuzabad were world famous; roses with a hundred petals were gifts grateful to a caliph or a king.[126]

The houses of the poor were then, as they are now, rectangles of sun-dried brick cemented with mud, and roofed with a mixture of mud, stalks, branches, palm leaves, and straw. Better homes had an interior court with a water basin, perhaps a tree; sometimes a wooden colonnade and cloister between court and rooms. Houses rarely faced or opened upon the street; they were citadels of privacy, built for security and peace. Some had secret doors for sudden escape from arrest or attack, or for the inconspicuous entry of a paramour.[127] In all but the poorest houses there were separate quarters for the women, occasionally with their own court. Rich houses had a complicated suite of bathrooms, but most dwellings had no plumbing; water was carried in, waste was carried out. Fashionable homes might have two stories, with a central living room rising to a dome, and a second-story balcony facing the court. All except the poorest houses had at least one window grille (*mashrabiyyah*), a lattice of woodwork to let in light without heat, and allow the occupants to look out unseen; these grilles were often elegantly carved, and served as models for the stone or metal screens that adorned the palace or the mosque. There was no fireplace; heat was provided by charcoal-burning portable braziers. Walls were of plaster, usually painted in many colors. Floors were covered with hand-woven rugs. There might be a chair or two, but the Moslem preferred to squat. Near the wall, on three sides of the room, the floor was raised a foot or so, forming a *diwan*, and was furnished with cushions. There were no specific bedrooms; the bed was a mattress which, during the day, was rolled up and placed in a closet, as in modern Japan. Furniture was simple: some vases, utensils, lamps, and perhaps a niche for books. The Oriental is rich in the simplicity of his needs.

For the poor and pious Moslem it was enough that the mosque itself should be beautiful. It was built with his labor and dirhems; it gathered up his arts and crafts and laid them like a rich carpet at Allah's feet; and that beauty and splendor all men might enjoy. Usually the mosque was situated near the market place, easily accessible. It was not always impressive from without; except for its façade it might be indistinguishable from—even physically attached to—the neighboring structures; and it was rarely built of any more lordly material than stucco-faced brick. Its functions determined its forms: a rectangular court to hold the congregation; a central basin and fountain for ablutions; a surrounding arcaded portico for shelter, shade, and schools; and, on the side of the court facing Mecca, the mosque proper, usually an enclosed section of the portico. It too was rectangular, allowing the worshipers to stand in long lines, again facing Mecca. The edifice might be crowned with a dome, almost always built of bricks, each layer projecting a bit inward beyond the layer beneath, with a surface of plaster to conceal the deviations.[128] As in Sasanian and Byzantine architecture, the transition from rectangular base to circular dome was mediated by pendentives or squinches. More characteristic of mosque architecture was the minaret (*manara*, a lighthouse); probably the Syrian Moslems developed it from the Babylonian ziggurat and the bell tower of Christian churches, the Persian Moslems took the cylindrical form from India, and the African Moslems were influenced in its design by the four-cornered Pharos or lighthouse of Alexandria; [129] perhaps the four corner towers of the old temple area at Damascus influenced the form.[130] In this early period the minaret was simple and mostly unadorned; only in the following centuries would it achieve the lofty slenderness, fragile balconies, decorative arcades, and faïence surfaces that would lead Fergusson to call it "the most graceful form of tower architecture in the world." [131]

The most brilliant and varied decoration was reserved for the interior of the mosque: mosaics and brilliant tiles on floor and mihrab; exquisite shapes and hues of glass in windows and lamps; rich carpets and prayer rugs on the pavement; facings of colored marble for the lower panels of the walls; lovely friezes of Arabic script running round mihrabs or cornices; delicate carvings of wood or ivory, or graceful molding of metal, in doors, ceilings, pulpits, and screens. . . . The pulpit itself, or *minbar*, was of wood carefully carved, and inlaid with ebony or ivory. Near it was the *diqqa*, a reading desk supported by small columns and holding the Koran; the book itself, of course, was a work of calligraphic and miniaturist art. To show the *qibla* or direction of Mecca, a niche was cut into the wall, possibly in imitation of the Christian apse. This mihrab was elaborated until it became almost an altar or chapel, and all the skill of Moslem artists was deployed to make it beautiful with faïence or mosaic, floral or scriptural moldings or reliefs, and colorful patterns in brick, stucco, marble, terra cotta, or tile.

We probably owe this splendor of ornament to the Semitic prohibition of human or animal forms in art: as if in compensation, the Moslem artist invented or adopted an overflowing abundance of non-representational forms. He sought an outlet first in geometrical figures—line, angle, square, cube, polygon, cone, spiral, ellipse, circle, sphere; he repeated these in a hundred combinations, and developed them into swirls, guilloches, reticulations, *entrelacs*, and stars; passing to floral forms, he designed, in many materials, wreaths, vines, or rosettes of lotus, acanthus, or palm tendrils or leaves; in the tenth century he merged all these in the arabesque; and to them all, as a unique and major ornament, he added the Arabic script. Taking usually the Kufic characters, he lifted them vertically, or expanded them laterally, or dressed them in flourishes and points, and turned the alphabet into a work of art. As religious prohibitions slackened, he introduced new motifs of decoration by representing the birds of the air, the beasts of the field, or strange composite animals that dwelt only in his whimsical fantasy. His flair for adornment enriched every form of art—mosaic, miniature, pottery, textiles, rugs; and in nearly every case the design had the disciplined unity of a dominant form or motif developed from center to border, or from beginning to end, as in the elaboration of a musical theme. No material was thought too obdurate for such ornament; wood, metal, brick, stucco, stone, terra cotta, glass, tile, and faïence became the vehicles of such a poetry of abstract forms as no art, not even the Chinese, had ever achieved before.

So illuminated, Islamic architecture raised in Arabia, Palestine, Syria, Mesopotamia, Persia, Transoxiana, India, Egypt, Tunisia, Sicily, Morocco, and Spain an endless chain of mosques in which masculine strength of outward form was always balanced by feminine grace and delicacy of interior ornament. The mosques of Medina, Mecca, Jerusalem, Ramleh, Damascus, Kufa, Basra, Shiraz, Nishapur, and Ardebil; the Mosque of Jafar at Baghdad, the Great Mosque of Samarra, the Zakariyah Mosque of Aleppo, the Mosque of Ibn Tulun and the el-Azhar in old Cairo, the Great Mosque of

Tunis, the Sidi Oqba Mosque of Qairuan, the Blue Mosque of Cordova—
we can do no less, and no more, than name them, for of the hundreds such
that were built in this period only a dozen remain distinguishable; indiscriminate time has leveled the rest through earthquake, negligence, or war.

Persia alone—a fraction of Islam—has yielded to recent research such unsuspected architectural splendor as marks a major event in our rediscovery
of the past.* The revelation was too long delayed; already many masterpieces of Persian architecture had crumbled to earth. Muqaddasi ranked
the mosque of Fasa with that of Medina, and the mosque of Turshiz with the
Great Mosque of Damascus; the mosque of Nishapur, with its marble columns, gold tiles, and richly carved walls, was one of the wonders of the time;
and "no mosque in Khurasan or Sistan equaled in beauty" the mosque of
Herat.[132] We may vaguely judge the exuberance and quality of Persian
architecture in the ninth and tenth centuries from the stucco reliefs and
carved columns and capitals of the mihrab in the Congregational Mosque
at Nayin, now mostly destroyed, and the two lovely minarets that survive at
Damghan. The Friday Mosque at Ardistan (1055) still shows a handsome
mihrab and portal, and many elements that were to appear later in Gothic:
pointed arches, groined pendentives, cross vaults, and ribbed dome.[133] In
these and most Persian mosques and palaces the building material was brick,
as in Sumerian and Mesopotamian antiquity; stone was rare and costly, clay
and heat were plentiful; yet the Persian artist transformed brick layers with
light and shade, novel patterns, and divers attitudes into such variety of
decoration as that modest substance had never known before. Over the
brick, in special places like portals, minbars, and mihrabs, the Persian potter
laid varicolored mosaics and the most brilliant tiles; and in the eleventh century he made bright surfaces more resplendent still with luster-painted
faïence. So every art in Islam humbly and proudly served the mosque.

Sculpture, forbidden to make statues lest idolatry return, devoted itself
to decorative reliefs. Stone was skillfully carved, and stucco, before it hardened, was shaped by hand into a rich diversity of designs. One impressive
sample remains. At Mshatta, in the Syrian desert east of the Jordan, Walid II
began (c. 743), and left unfinished, a winter palace; along the lower surface
of the façade ran a sculptured stone frieze of extraordinary excellence—triangles, rosettes, and borders intricately carved with flowers, fruits, birds,
beasts, and trailing arabesques; this chef-d'oeuvre, transferred to Berlin in
1904, has survived the Second World War. Woodworkers beautified windows, doors, screens, balconies, ceilings, tables, lecterns, pulpits, and
mihrabs with such exquisite carving as may be seen in a panel from Takrit

---

* In 1925 Reza Khan, afterwards Shah of Persia, authorized Arthur Upham Pope to enter
the mosques of Persia, which had been closed to non-Moslems, in order to photograph the
interiors. The result was an epochal revelation of the technical and artistic excellence of Persian
architecture.

in the Metropolitan Museum of Art in New York. Workers in ivory and bone adorned mosques, Korans, furniture, utensils, and persons with carvings and inlays; from this age only one piece has come to us—an elephant rook (in the National Museum at Florence) precariously ascribed to the ninth century and to a chess set allegedly sent by Harun to Charlemagne.[134] The metalworkers of Islam acquired Sasanian techniques, made great bronze, brass, or copper lamps, ewers, bowls, jugs, mugs, cups, basins, and braziers; cast them playfully into the forms of lions, dragons, sphinxes, peacocks, and doves; and sometimes incised them with exquisite patterns, as in a lacelike lamp in the Art Institute of Chicago. Some craftsmen filled incised designs with silver or gold, and made "damascened" metal—an art practiced, but not originated, at Damascus.[135] The swords of Damascus were of highly tempered steel, adorned with reliefs or inlaid with arabesques, scripts, or other patterns in gold or silver threads. The metalworkers of Islam stood at the very top of their art.

When the Moslem conquest settled down to cultural absorption, Mohammedan pottery found itself heir, in Asia, Africa, and Spain, to five ceramic traditions: Egyptian, Greco-Roman, Mesopotamian, Persian, Chinese. Sarre discovered at Samarra some Tang pottery, including porcelain; and early Islamic-Persian wares were frankly copied from Chinese prototypes. Pottery centers developed at Baghdad, Samarra, Rayy, and many other towns. By the tenth century Persian potters were making almost every kind of pottery except porcelain, in every form from hand spittoons to monstrous vases "large enough to hold at least one of the Forty Thieves."[136] At its best Persian pottery showed a subtlety of conception, a splendor of color, a refinement of workmanship, second only to the Chinese and Japanese; for six centuries it had no rival this side of the Pamirs.[137] It was a favorite and congenial art with the Persians; aristocrats collected its masterpieces jealously, and poets like al-Ma'arri and Omar Khayyam found in it many a metaphor for their philosophy. We hear of a ninth-century banquet at which poems were composed and dedicated to the bowls that adorned the board.[138]

In that century the potters of Samarra and Baghdad distinguished themselves by making—perhaps inventing—lustered pottery: the decoration was painted in a metallic oxide upon the glazed coating of the clay, and the vessel was then submitted to a smoky and subdued second firing, which reduced the pigment to a thin layer of metal, and gave the glaze an iridescent glow. Lovely monochromes were produced in this manner, and still lovelier polychromes in gold, green, brown, yellow, and red, in a hundred almost fluid tints. The luster technique was applied also to the ancient Mesopotamian art of decorative tiles. The rich colors of these squares, and their harmonious combinations, gave unique splendor to the portals or mihrabs of a hundred mosques, and to many a palace wall. In the allied art of working glass the

Moslems inherited all the skill of Egypt and Syria. Brilliant lamp shades were made in glass adorned with medallions, inscriptions, or floral designs; and perhaps in this period Syria inaugurated the art of enameled glass, which would reach its peak of excellence in the thirteenth century.

When we recall the exuberant and omnipresent use of painting and sculpture in Catholic cathedrals, and its importance as a vehicle of Christian creed and story, we are struck by the absence of the representative arts in Islam. The Koran had forbidden sculpture (v, 92), but it had said nothing about painting. However, a tradition ascribed to Aisha reported the Prophet as condemning pictures too.[139] Moslem law, Shi'ite as well as Sunnite, enforced the double prohibition. Doubtless Mohammed had been influenced by the Second Commandment and Judaic teaching, and partly by the notion that the artist, in giving form to living things, usurped the function of the Creator. Some theologians relaxed the prohibition, permitting pictures of inanimate things; some winked at the portrayal of animal or human figures on objects intended only for secular use. Certain Umayyad caliphs ignored the prohibitions; about 712 Walid I adorned his summer palace at Qusayr Amra with Hellenistic frescoes depicting hunters, dancing girls, women bathing, and himself on his throne.[140] The Abbasid caliphs professed piety, but had murals in their private chambers; al-Mutasim hired artists, probably Christian, to paint hunting scenes, priests, and naked dancing girls on the walls of his palace at Samarra; and al-Mutawakkil, who persecuted heretics, permitted Byzantine painters to add to these frescoes one that represented Christian monks and a Christian church.[141] Mahmud of Ghazni decorated his palace with pictures of himself, his armies, and his elephants; and his son Masud, shortly before being deposed by the Seljuq Turks, covered the walls of his chambers at Herat with scenes based on Persian or Indian manuals of erotic techniques.[142] A story tells how, at the home of a vizier, two artists vied with each other in realistic representation: Ibn Aziz proposed to paint a dancing girl so that she would seem to be coming out of the wall; al-Qasir undertook a harder task—to paint her so that she would seem to be going into the wall. Each succeeded so well that the vizier gave them robes of honor, and much gold.[143] Many other violations of the interdict could be listed; in Persia particularly we find living things pictured in joyous abundance, and in every form of pictorial art. Nevertheless the prohibition —supported by the people to the point of occasionally mutilating or destroying works of art—delayed the development of Islamic painting, largely restricted it to abstract ornament, almost excluded portraiture (yet we hear of forty portraits of Avicenna), and left the artists completely dependent upon royal or aristocratic patronage.

From this age no Moslem murals survive save those of Qusayr Amra and Samarra; they reveal a strange and barren marriage of Byzantine techniques with Sasanian designs. As if in compensation, Islamic miniatures are among the finest in history. Here fruition came to a varied heritage—Byzantine, Sasanian, and Chinese; and zealous hands carried on an art so intimately beautiful that one almost resents Gutenberg. Like chamber music in modern Europe, so in medieval Islam the illumination of manuscripts with miniature paintings was an art for the aristocratic few; only the rich could maintain an artist in the devoted poverty that produced these patient masterpieces. Here again decoration subordinated representation; perspective and modeling were deliberately ignored; a central motif or form—perhaps a geometrical figure or a single flower—was extended in a hundred variations, until nearly every inch, and even the border, of the page was filled with lines as carefully drawn as if incised. In secular works men, women, and animals might be introduced, in scenes of hunting, humor, or love; but always the ornament was the thing, the fanciful play of delicate line, the liquid flow of harmonious colors, the cool perfection of abstract beauty, intended for a mind at peace. Art is significance rendered with feeling through form; but the feeling must accept discipline, and the form must have structure and meaning, even if the meaning outreach the realm of words. This is the art of illumination, as of the profoundest music.

Calligraphy was an integral part of illumination; one must go as far as China to find again so fraternal a union of writing and design. From Kufa had come the Kufic letters, clumsily angular, crudely sharp; the calligraphers clothed these meager bones with vowel, inflectional, prosodic, diacritical marks, and little floral flourishes; so redeemed, the Kufic script became a frequent feature of architectural decoration. For cursive writing, however, the Naskhi form of the Arabic alphabet proved more attractive; its rounded characters and sinuous horizontal flow were of themselves a decoration; in all the world is no writing or print that equals it in beauty. By the tenth century it had gained the upper hand over Kufic in all but monumental or ceramic lettering; most of the Moslem books that have reached us from the Middle Ages are in Naskhi script. The majority of these surviving volumes are Korans. Merely to copy the holy book was a work of piety sure of divine reward; to illustrate it with pictures was accounted sacrilege; but to lavish beautiful handwriting upon it was deemed the noblest of the arts. Whereas miniaturists were hired artisans poorly paid, calligraphers were sought and honored with royal gifts, and numbered kings and statesmen in their ranks. A scrap of writing by a master's hand was a priceless treasure; already in the tenth century there were bibliophiles who lived and moved and had their being in their collections of fine manuscripts, written on parchment with inks of black, blue, violet, red, and gold. Only a few such volumes have reached us from this age; the oldest is a Koran in the Cairo Library, dated 784. When we add that such works were bound in the softest, strongest leather, tooled or stamped with unexcelled artistry, and the cover itself in many instances adorned with an elegant design, we may without hyperbole rank Islamic books of the ninth to the eighteenth century as the finest ever issued. Which of us can be published in such splendor today?

In the embellishment of Islamic life all the arts mingled like the interlaces of a decorative theme. So the patterns of illumination and calligraphy were woven into textiles, burned into pottery, and mounted on portals and mihrabs. If medieval civilization made little distinction between artist and artisan it was not to belittle the artist but to ennoble the artisan; the goal of every industry was to become an art. The weaver, like the potter, made un-distinguished products for ephemeral use; but sometimes his skill and pa-tience found expression, his dream found form, in robes or hangings, rugs or coverings, embroideries or brocades, woven for many lifetimes, designed with the finesse of a miniature, and dyed in the gorgeous colors so favored of the East. Byzantine, Coptic, Sasanian, Chinese textiles were already fa-mous when the Moslems conquered Syria, Persia, Egypt, and Transoxiana; Islam was quick to learn; and though the Prophet had proscribed silk, Mos-lem factories soon issued the sinful substance in bold abundance for men and women who sought forgiveness for their bodies as well as their souls. A "robe of honor" was the most precious present a caliph could offer his servi-tors. The Moslems became the leading silk merchants of the medieval world. Persian silk *taftah* was bought for European ladies as taffeta. Shiraz was fa-mous for its woolen cloths, Baghdad for its baldachin* hangings and tabby silks; Khuzistan for fabrics of camel's or goat's hair; Khurasan for its sofa (Arabic *suffah*) covers, Tyre for its carpets, Bokhara for its prayer rugs, Herat for its gold brocades. No samples of these products from this period have survived the wear and tear of time; we can only surmise their excellence from later work, and the witness of the writers of their age. An entry in the archives of Harun al-Rashid notes "400,000 pieces of gold, the price of a robe of honor for Jafar, the son of Yahya the Vizier."[144]

VIII. MUSIC

Music, like sculpture, was at first a sin in Islam.[145] It was not forbidden in the Koran; but, if we may believe a dubious tradition, the Prophet, fearful of the songs and dances of promiscuous women, denounced musical instru-ments as the devil's muezzin call to damnation. The theologians, and all the four schools of orthodox law, frowned upon music as raising the winds of passion; but some generously conceded that it was not sinful in itself. The people, always healthier in their conduct than in their creeds, held it as a

---

* From *Baldaq*, the medieval Latin name for Baghdad.

proverb that "wine is as the body, music is as the soul, joy is their off-spring."[146] Music accompanied every stage of Moslem life, and filled a thousand and one Arabian nights with songs of love and war and death. Every palace, and many mansions, engaged minstrels to sing the songs of the poets, or their own. In the startling judgment of an historian fully competent to judge, "the cultivation of music by the Arabs in all its branches reduces to insignificance the recognition of the art in the history of any other country."[147] No Western ear, except after long training, can quite appreciate the quality of Arabian music—its preference of melodic elaboration (arabesques of sound) to harmony and counterpoint, its division of tones not into halves but into thirds, its florid Oriental patterns of structure and rhythm. To us it seems repetitiously simple, monotonously mournful, formlessly weird; to the Arabs European music seems deficient in the number and subtlety of its tones, and vulgarly addicted to useless complexity and monumental noise. The meditative tenderness of Arabian music deeply affects the Moslem soul. Sa'di speaks of a boy "singing such a plaintive melody as would arrest a bird in its flight";[148] al-Ghazali defined ecstasy as "the state that comes from listening to music";[149] one Arabic book gives a chapter to those who fainted or died while listening to Moslem music; and religion, which at first denounced it, later adopted music for the intoxicating dervish ritual.

Moslem music began with ancient Semitic forms and tunes; developed in contact with Greek "modes" that were themselves of Asiatic origin; and felt strong influences from Persia and India. A musical notation, and much musical theory, were taken from the Greeks; al-Kindi, Avicenna, and the Brethren of Sincerity wrote at length on the subject; al-Farabi's *Grand Book on Music* is the outstanding medieval production on the theory of music—"equal, if not superior, to anything that has come down to us from Greek sources."[150] As early as the seventh century the Moslems wrote mensurable music (apparently unknown to Europe before 1190)[151]—their notation indicated the duration, as well as the pitch, of each note.

Among a hundred musical instruments the chief were the lute, lyre, pandore, psaltery, and flute, occasionally reinforced by horn, cymbals, tambourine, castanets, and drum. The lyre was a small harp. The lute was like our mandolin, with a long neck and a curved sounding board made of small glued segments of maple wood; the strings, of catgut, were plucked by the fingers. There were a dozen sizes and varieties of lute. The large lute was called *qitara* from the Greek *kithara*; our words *guitar* and *lute* (Arabic *al-ud*) are from the Arabic. Some string instruments were played with a bow, and the organ was known in both its pneumatic and its hydraulic forms. Certain Moslem cities, like Seville, were celebrated for making fine musical instruments, far superior to anything produced in contemporary Islam.[152] Nearly all instrumental music was intended to accompany or introduce song. Performances were usually confined to four or five instruments at a time, but we also read of large orchestras;[153] and tradition ascribes to the Medina musician Surayj the first use of the baton.[154]

Despite the Moslem madness for music, the status of musicians, except for renowned virtuosos, was low. Few men of the higher classes condescended to study the intoxicating art. The music of a rich household was provided by female slaves; and a school of law held that the testimony of a musician could not be accepted in court.[155] Dancing likewise was almost confined to slaves trained and hired; it was often erotic, often artistic; the Caliph Amin personally directed an all-night ballet in which a large number of girls danced and sang. Contact of the Arabs with Greeks and Persians raised the status of the musician. Umayyad and Abbasid caliphs showered largess upon the great performers of their time. Suleiman I offered prizes as high as 20,000 pieces of silver ($10,000) for a competition among the musicians of Mecca; Walid II held song tournaments, at one of which the first prize was 300,000 pieces of silver ($150,000);[156] these figures are presumably Oriental exaggerations. Mahdi invited to his court the Meccan singer Siyat, "whose soul warmed and chilled more than a hot bath"; and Harun al-Rashid took into his service Siyat's pupil Ibrahim al-Mawsili (i.e., of Mosul), gave him 150,000 dirhems ($75,000), 10,000 more per month, and 100,000 for a single song.[157] Harun so loved music that—against the wont of his class—he encouraged the talent of his young half brother, Ibrahim ibn al-Mahdi, who had a voice of tremendous power and three octaves' range; time seems an impish circle when we hear that he led a kind of Romantic movement in Arabian music against the classical school of Ishaq, son of Ibrahim al-Mawsili.[158] Ishaq was by general consent the greatest musician ever produced by Islam. Al-Mamun used to say of him: "He never sang to me but what I felt that my possessions were increased."[159]

We get a pleasant picture of Moslem society, and of the stir made by music in the Moslem soul, in a story told by Ibrahim al-Mawsili's pupil Mukhariq; we need not believe it to feel its significance:

> After drinking with the Caliph a whole night, I asked his permission to take the air, . . . which he granted. While I was walking I saw a damsel who appeared as if the rising sun beamed from her face. She had a basket, and I followed her. She stopped at a fruiterer's, and bought some fruit; and observing that I was following her, she looked back and abused me several times; but still I followed her until she arrived at a great door. . . . When she had entered, and the door was closed behind her, I sat down opposite to it, deprived of my reason by her beauty. . . . The sun went down upon me while I sat there; and at length there came two handsome young men on asses, and they knocked at the door, and when they were admitted, I entered with them; the master of the house thinking that I was their companion,

and they imagining that I was one of his friends. A repast was brought us, and we ate, and washed our hands, and were perfumed. The master of the house then said to the two young men, "Have ye any desire that I should call such a one?" (mentioning a woman's name). They answered: "If thou wilt grant us the favor, well." So he called for her, and she came, and lo, she was the maiden whom I had seen. . . . A servant maid preceded her, bearing her lute, which she placed in her lap. Wine was then brought, and she sang, while we drank and shook with delight. "Whose air is that?" they asked. She answered, "My master Mukhariq's." She then sang another air, which she said was also mine, while they drank by pints; she looking aside doubtfully at me until I lost my patience, and called out to her to do her best; but in attempting to do so, singing a third air, she overstrained her voice, and I said, "Thou hast made a mistake"; upon which she threw the lute from her lap in anger, saying . . . "Take it thyself, and let us hear thee." I answered, "Well"; and having taken it and tuned it perfectly, I sang the first of the airs which she had sung before me; whereupon all of them sprang to their feet and kissed my head. I then sang the second air, and the third; and their reason almost fled with ecstasy.

The master of the house, after asking his guests and being told by them that they knew me not, came to me, and kissing my hand, said, "By Allah, my master, who art thou?" I answered, "By Allah, I am the singer Mukhariq." "And for what purpose," said he, kissing both my hands, "camest thou hither?" I replied, "As a sponger"—and I related what had happened with respect to the maiden. Thereupon he looked toward his two companions and said to them: "Tell me, by Allah, do ye not know that I gave for that girl 30,000 dirhems ($15,000), and have refused to sell her?" They answered, "It is so." Then, said he, "I take you as witnesses that I have given her to him." "And we," said the two friends, "will pay thee two-thirds of her price." So he put me in possession of the girl; and in the evening, when I departed, he presented me also with rich robes and other gifts, with all of which I went away. And as I passed the places where the maiden had abused me, I said to her, "Repeat thy words to me"; but she would not for shame. Holding the girl's hand, I went with her to the Caliph, whom I found in anger at my long absence; but when I related my story to him he was surprised, and laughed, and ordered that the master of the house and his two friends should be brought before him, that he might requite them; to the former he gave 40,000 dirhems; to each of his two friends 30,000; and to me 100,000; and I kissed his feet and departed.[160]

CHAPTER XIII

Western Islam

641-1086

I. THE CONQUEST OF AFRICA

THE Near East was but a part of the Islamic world. Egypt under the Moslems resurrected her Pharaonic glory; Tunis, Sicily, and Morocco recovered orderly government under Arab leadership, and a passing brilliance illuminated Qairwan, Palermo, and Fez; Moorish Spain was a peak in the history of civilization; and later the Moslem Moguls, ruling India, would "build like giants and finish like jewelers."

While Khalid and other conquerors subdued the East, Amr ibn al-As, only seven years after Mohammed's death, set out from Gaza in Palestine, captured Pelusium and Memphis, and marched upon Alexandria. Egypt had ports and naval bases, and Arab power needed a fleet; Egypt exported corn to Constantinople, and Arabia needed corn. The Byzantine government in Egypt had for centuries used Arab mercenaries as police; these were no hindrance to the conquerors. The Monophysite Christians of Egypt had suffered Byzantine persecution; they received the Moslems with open arms, helped them to take Memphis, guided them into Alexandria. When it fell to Amr after a siege of twenty-three months (641), he wrote to the Caliph Omar: "It is impossible to enumerate the riches of this great city, or to describe its beauty; I shall content myself with observing that it contains 4000 palaces, 400 baths, 400 theaters."[1] Amr prevented pillage, preferring taxation. Unable to understand the theological differences among the Christian sects, he forbade his Monophysite allies to revenge themselves upon their orthodox foes, and upset the custom of centuries by proclaiming freedom of worship for all.

Did Amr destroy the Alexandrian Library? The earliest mention of this story is found in Abd al-Latif (1162–1231), a Moslem scientist;[2] it is more fully given in Bar-Hebraeus (1226–86), a Christianized Jew of eastern Syria, who wrote in Arabic, under the name of Abu-'l-Faraj, an epitome of world history. In his account an Alexandrian grammarian, John Philoponus, asked Amr to give him the manuscripts of the library; Amr wrote to Omar for permission; the Caliph, we are told, replied: "If these writings of the Greeks agree with the Book of God, they are useless, and need not be preserved; if they disagree they are pernicious, and should be destroyed"; legend shortens this probably legendary answer to "Burn the libraries, for they are contained in one book"—the Koran. According to Bar-Hebraeus, Amr distributed the contents of the library among the city's public baths, whose 4000 furnaces were fueled for six months with the papyrus and parchment rolls (642). Against this story it should be noted that (1) a large part of the library had been destroyed by Christian ardor under the Patriarch Theophilus in 392;[3] (2) the remainder had suffered such hostility and neglect that "most of the collection had disappeared by 642";[4] and (3) in the 500 years between the supposed event and its first reporter no Christian historian mentions it, though one of them, Eutychius, Archbishop of Alexandria in 933, described the Arab conquest of Alexandria in great detail.[5] The story is now generally rejected as a fable. In any case the gradual dissolution of the Alexandrian Library was a tragedy of some moment, for it was believed to contain the complete published works of Æschylus, Sophocles, Polybius, Livy, Tacitus, and a hundred others, who have come down to us in mangled form; full texts of the pre-Socratic philosophers, who survive only in snatches; and thousands of volumes of Greek, Egyptian, and Roman history, science, literature, and philosophy.

Amr administered Egypt competently. Part of the oppressive taxation financed the repair of canals and dikes, and the reopening of an eighty-mile canal between the Nile and the Red Sea; ships could now sail from the Mediterranean into the Indian Ocean.[6] (This canal was again choked with sand in 723, and was abandoned.) Amr built a new capital on the site where he had pitched his camp in 641; it was called al-Fustat, apparently from the Arabic for tent; it was the first form of Cairo. There for two centuries (661–868) Moslem governors ruled Egypt for the caliphs of Damascus or Baghdad.

Every conquest creates a new frontier, which, being exposed to danger, suggests further conquest. To protect Moslem Egypt from flank attack by Byzantine Cyrene, an army of 40,000 Moslems advanced through the desert to Barca, took it, and marched to the neighborhood of Carthage. The Moslem general planted his spear in the sand some eighty miles south of the modern Tunis, built a camp, and so founded (670) one of Islam's major cities, Qairwan—"the resting place." Realizing that the capture of Carthage would give the Moslems control of the Mediterranean and an open road to Spain, the Greek emperor sent troops and a fleet; the Berbers, forgetting for a moment their hatred of Rome, joined in defending the city; and it was not till 698 that Carthage was subdued. Soon thereafter Africa was conquered to the Atlantic's shores. The Berbers were persuaded, almost on their own terms, to accept Moslem rule, and presently the Moslem faith. Africa was divided into three provinces: Egypt with its capital at al-Fustat, Ifriqiya with its capital at Qairwan, Maghreb (Morocco) with its capital at Fez.

For a century even these provinces acknowledged the Eastern caliphs as their sovereigns. But the difficulties of communication and transport were increased by the removal of the caliphate to Baghdad; and one by one the

African provinces became independent kingdoms. An Idrisid dynasty (789–974) ruled at Fez, an Aghlabid dynasty (800–909) at Qairwan, and a Tulunid dynasty (869–905) in Egypt. That ancient granary, no longer robbed of its product by foreign masters, entered upon a minor renaissance. Ahmad ibn Tulun (869–84) conquered Syria for Egypt, built a new capital at Qatai (a suburb of al-Fustat), promoted learning and art, raised palaces, public baths, a hospital, and the great mosque that still stands as his monument. His son Khumarawayh (884–95) transmuted this energy into luxury, walled his palace with gold, and taxed his people to provide himself with a pool of quicksilver on which his bed of inflated leather cushions might gently float to win him sleep. Forty years after his death the Tulunids were replaced by another Turkish dynasty, the Ikshidid (935–69). These African monarchies, having no roots in the blood or traditions of the people, had to base their rule on military force and leadership; and when wealth weakened their martial ardor their power melted away.

The greatest of the African dynasties reinforced its military supremacy by associating itself with an almost fanatical religious belief. About 905 Abu Abdallah appeared in Tunisia, preached the Ismaili doctrine of the seven Imams, proclaimed the early coming of the Mahdi or Savior, and won such a following among the Berbers that he was able to overthrow the Aghlabid rule in Qairwan. To meet the expectations he had aroused he summoned from Arabia Obeidallah ibn Muhammad, alleged grandson of the Ismaili prophet Abdallah, hailed him as the Mahdi, made him king (909), and was soon put to death by his king's command. Obeidallah claimed descent from Fatima, and gave her name to his dynasty.

Under the Aghlabids and Fatimids North Africa renewed the prosperity it had known in the heyday of Carthage and under imperial Rome. In the youth of their vigor the Moslem conquerors in the ninth century opened three routes, 1500 to 2000 miles long, across the Sahara to Lake Chad and Timbuctu; northward and westward they established ports at Bône, Oran, Ceuta, and Tangier; a fructifying commerce bound the Sudan with the Mediterranean, and Eastern Islam with Morocco and Spain. Spanish Moslem refugees brought to Morocco the art of leather; Fez flourished as a center of exchange with Spain, and became famous for its dyes, perfumes, and rimless cylindrical red hats.

In 969 the Fatimids wrested Egypt from the Ikshidids, and soon thereafter spread their rule over Arabia and Syria. The Fatimid Caliph Muizz transferred his capital to Qahira (Cairo): as Qatai had been a northeastern extension of Fustat, so Qahira ("the victorious") was a northeastern prolongation of Qatai, and, like its predecessors, began as a military camp. Under Muizz (953–75) and his son Aziz (975–96), the vizier Yaqub ibn Qillis, a Baghdad Jew converted to Islam, reorganized the administration of Egypt, and made the Fatimids the richest rulers of their time. When Muizz' sister

Rashida died she left 2,700,000 dinars ($12,825,000), and 12,000 robes; when his sister Abda died she left 3,000 silver vases, 400 swords damascened in gold, 30,000 pieces of Sicilian textiles, and a hoard of jewelry.[7] But nothing fails like success. The next caliph, al-Hakim (996–1021), went half mad with wealth and power. He arranged the assassination of several viziers, persecuted Christians and Jews, burned many churches and synagogues, and ordered the demolition of the Church of the Holy Sepulcher in Jerusalem; the execution of this order was a contributory cause of the Crusades. As if to repeat the career of Caligula, he proclaimed himself a god, and sent missionaries to establish his cult among the people; when some of these preachers were killed he took Christians and Jews back into favor, and rebuilt their shrines. He was assassinated at the age of thirty-six.

Despite these royal prerogatives Egypt prospered as the commercial link between Europe and Asia. Increasingly the merchants of India and China sailed past the Persian Gulf and up the Red Sea and the Nile into Egypt; the wealth and power of Baghdad declined, those of Cairo grew. Nasir-i-Khosru, visiting the new capital in 1047, described it as having 20,000 houses, mostly of brick, rising to five or six stories, and 20,000 shops "so filled with gold, jewelry, embroideries, and satins that there was no room to sit down."[8] The main streets were protected against the sun, and were lighted at night by lamps. Prices were fixed by the government, and anyone caught charging more was paraded through the city on a camel, ringing a bell and confessing his crime.[9] Millionaires were numerous; one merchant, a Christian, fed the whole population at his own expense during five years of famine caused by the low level of the Nile; and Yaqub ibn Qillis left an estate of some $30,000,000.[10] Such men joined with the Fatimid caliphs in building mosques, libraries, and colleges, and fostering the sciences and the arts. Despite occasional cruelties, wasteful luxuries, the usual exploitation of labor, and the proper number of wars, the rule of the Fatimids was in general beneficent and liberal, and could compare, in prosperity and culture, with any age in Egyptian history.[11]

The wealth of the Fatimids reached its peak in the long reign of Mustansir (1036–94), the son of a Sudanese slave. He built for himself a pleasure pavilion, and lived a life of music, wine, and ease; "this," he said, "is more pleasant than staring at the Black Stone, listening to the muezzin's drone, and drinking impure water" (from Mecca's holy well of Zemzem).[12] In 1067 his Turkish troops rebelled, raided his palace, and carried away, as loot, priceless treasures of art, great quantities of jewelry, and twenty-five camel-loads of manuscripts; some of these served the Turkish officers as fuel to heat their homes, while exquisite leather bindings mended the shoes of their slaves. When Mustansir died the Fatimid empire fell to pieces; its once powerful army broke into quarreling factions of Berbers, Sudanese, and Turks; Ifriqiya and Morocco had already seceded, Palestine revolted, Syria was lost.

When, in 1171, Saladin dethroned the last Fatimid caliph, one more Egyptian dynasty had followed its predecessors through power and pleasure to decay.

II. ISLAMIC CIVILIZATION IN AFRICA: 641–1058

The courts of Cairo, Qairwan, and Fez rivaled one another in the support of architecture, painting, music, poetry, and philosophy. But nearly all the surviving manuscripts of Islamic Africa in this period are hidden in libraries which Western scholarship is just beginning to explore; much of the art has perished, and only the mosques proclaim the vigor and spirit of the age. At Qairwan stands the mosque of Sidi Oqba, originally built in 670, seven times restored, and mostly dating from 838; its cloisters of round arches are upheld by hundreds of Corinthian columns from the ruins of Carthage; its pulpit is a masterpiece of wood carving, its mihrab a splendor of porphyry and faïence; its square and massive minaret—the oldest in the world[13]—set a Syrian style for the minarets of the West. This mosque made Qairwan the fourth holy city of Islam, one of "the four gates to Paradise." Only less sacred and magnificent were the mosques of Fez and Marraqesh, of Tunis and Tripoli.

In Cairo the mosques were many and immense; 300 still adorn that charming capital. The mosque of Amr, begun in 642, was rebuilt in the tenth century; nothing remains of its early constituents except the fine Corinthian columns judiciously rescued from Roman and Byzantine ruins. The mosque of Ibn Tulun (878) precariously preserves its first form and ornament. A high crenellated wall surrounds its roomy court; within are pointed arches older than any others in Egypt except the arch of the Nilometer (865)—a structure built on an island in the Nile to measure the rise of the river; possibly this graceful and convenient form of the arch passed from Egypt through Sicily and the Normans to Gothic Europe.[14] In the zigguratlike minaret, and in the domed tomb of Ibn Tulun, are horseshoe arches—one of the less pleasing features of Moslem art. It is told of Ibn Tulun that he had intended to raise the arches on 300 columns; but when he learned that these could be secured only by dismantling Roman or Christian edifices, he decided, instead, to support the arches with massive piers of brick;[15] here again this mosque may have suggested a characteristic element of the Gothic style. Finally, as if to make the building a steppingstone to Chartres, some of the windows were filled with colored glass, some with grilles of stone in rosette or stellar or other geometrical designs; these, however, are of uncertain date.

In 970–2 Jauhar, the converted Christian slave who had conquered Egypt for the Fatimids, built the mosque of el-Azhar ("the brilliant"); some of the original structure is still in place; here too are pointed arches, rising on 380 columns of marble, granite, or porphyry. The mosque of al-Hakim (990–1012) was built of stone, and most of it survives, though in disuse and decay;

some conception of its medieval splendor may be gathered from its elegant stucco arabesques, and the fine Kufic inscription of the frieze. Once these mosques, now as forbidding as fortresses (and doubtless so designed) were glorified with exquisite carving and lettering, mosaic, and tiled mihrabs, and chandeliers that have become museum rarities. The mosque of Ibn Tulun had 18,000 lamps, many of varicolored enameled glass.[16]

The minor arts were practiced in Islamic Africa with Moslem patience and finesse. Lustered tiles appear in the Qairwan mosque. Nasir-i-Khosru (1050) described Cairene pottery "so delicate and translucent that the hand placed on the outside can be seen from within."[17] Egyptian and Syrian glass continued their ancient excellence. Fatimid rock-crystal wares, preserved intact through a thousand years, are treasured in Venice, Florence, and the Louvre. Wood carvers delighted the eye with their work on mosque doors, pulpit panels, mihrabs, and window lattices. From their Coptic subjects the Egyptian Moslems took the art of decorating boxes, chests, tables, and other objects with inlay or marquetry of wood, ivory, bone, or mother-of-pearl. Jewelry abounded. When Turkish mercenaries raided the chambers of al-Mustansir they came away with thousands of articles in gold—inkstands, chessmen, vases, birds, artificial trees set with precious stones. . . .[18] Among the spoils were curtains of silk brocade worked with gold thread, and bearing the pictures and biographies of famous kings. From the Copts, again, the Moslems learned to stamp and print patterns upon textiles with wooden blocks; this technique was apparently carried from Islamic Egypt to Europe by Crusaders, and may have shared in the development of printing. European merchants rated Fatimid textiles above all others, and told with awe of Cairene and Alexandrian fabrics so fine that a robe could be drawn through a finger ring.[19] We hear of luxurious Fatimid rugs, and of tents made of velvet, satin, damask, silk, and cloth of gold, and decorated with paintings; a tent made for Yazuri, al-Mustansir's vizier, required the labor of 150 men over nine years, cost 30,000 dinars ($142,500), and claimed to picture all the known animal species of the world except *homo lupus*. All that remains of Fatimid paintings is some fragmentary frescoes in the Arab Museum at Cairo. No miniatures survive from Fatimid Egypt, but Maqrizi—who in the fifteenth century wrote a history of painting—tells us that the library of the Fatimid caliphs contained hundreds of richly illuminated manuscripts, including 2400 Korans.

In the days of al-Hakim the caliphal library at Cairo had 100,000 volumes; in al-Mustansir's time, 200,000. We are told that the manuscripts were lent without charge to all responsible students. In 988 the vizier Yaqub ibn Qillis persuaded the Caliph Aziz to provide tuition and maintenance for thirty-five students in the mosque of el-Azhar; thus began the oldest existing university. As this madrasah developed it drew pupils from all the Moslem world, as the University of Paris, a century later, would draw them from all Europe.

Caliphs, viziers, and rich individuals added year by year to the scholarships, until in our time el-Azhar has some 10,000 students and 300 professors.[20] One of the most pleasant sights of world travel is the assemblage of students in the cloisters of this thousand-year-old mosque, each group squatting in a semicircle at the base of a pillar before a seated savant. Famous scholars from all Islam came here to teach grammar, rhetoric, mathematics, poetry, logic, theology, Hadith, Koranic exegesis, and law. The students paid no fees, the teachers received no salaries. Dependent upon governmental subsidy and private philanthropy, the famous university tended to ever more zealous orthodoxy, and its directing ulemas or learned men had a discouraging effect upon Fatimid literature, philosophy, and science. We hear of no great poets under this dynasty.

Al-Hakim set up in Cairo a Dar al-Hikmah ("Hall of Wisdom"); its main function was to teach Ismaili Shi'ite theology; but its curriculum included astronomy and medicine. Al-Hakim financed an observatory, and helped Ali ibn Yunus (d. 1009), perhaps the greatest of Moslem astronomers. After seventeen years of observations Yunus completed the "Hakimite tables" of astral movements and periods, and gave more precise values than before to the inclination of the ecliptic, the precession of the equinoxes, and solar parallax.

The brightest name in Moslem Egyptian science is that of Muhammad ibn al-Haitham, known to medieval Europe as Alhazen. Born at Basra in 965, he won repute there as a mathematician and engineer. Hearing that al-Haitham had a plan for regulating the annual inundation of the Nile, al-Hakim invited him to Cairo. The plan proved impracticable, and al-Haitham had to hide in obscurity from the incalculable Caliph. Fascinated, like all medieval thinkers, by Aristotle's attempt to formulate a rational synthesis of knowledge, he composed several commentaries on the works of the philosopher; none of these commentaries has reached us. We know al-Haitham chiefly by his *Kitab al-Manazir*, or *Book of Optics*; of all medieval productions this is probably the most thoroughly scientific in its method and thought. Al-Haitham studied the refraction of light through transparent mediums like air and water, and came so close to discovering the magnifying lens that Roger Bacon, Witelo, and other Europeans three centuries later based upon his work their own advances toward the microscope and the telescope. He rejected the theory of Euclid and Ptolemy that vision results from a ray leaving the eye and reaching the object; rather "the form of the perceived object passes into the eye, and is transmitted there by the transparent body"—the lens.[21] He remarked the effect of the atmosphere in increasing the apparent size of sun or moon when near the horizon; showed that through atmospheric refraction the light of the sun reaches us even when the sun is as much as nineteen degrees below the horizon; and on this basis he calculated the height of the atmosphere at ten (English) miles. He analyzed the correlation between the weight and the density of the atmosphere, and the effect of atmospheric density upon the weight of objects. He studied with complex mathematical formulas the action of light on spherical or parabolic mirrors, and through the burning glass. He observed the half-moon shape of the sun's image, during eclipses, on the wall opposite a small hole made in the window shutters; this is the first known mention of the *camera obscura*, or dark chamber, on which all photography depends. We could hardly exaggerate the influence of al-Haitham on European science. Without him Roger Bacon might never have been heard of; Bacon quotes him or refers to him at almost every step in that part of the *Opus maius* which deals with optics; and Part VI rests almost entirely on the findings of the Cairene physicist. As late as Kepler and Leonardo European studies of light were based upon al-Haitham's work.

The most striking of all effects produced by the Arab conquest of North Africa was the gradual but almost complete disappearance of Christianity. The Berbers not only accepted Mohammedanism, they became its most fanatical defenders. Doubtless economic considerations entered: non-Moslems paid a head tax, and converts were for a time freed from it. When in 744 the Arab governor of Egypt offered this exemption, 24,000 Christians went over to Islam.[22] Occasional but severe persecutions of Christians may have influenced many to conform to the ruling faith. In Egypt a Coptic minority held out bravely, built their churches like fortresses, maintained their worship in secret, and survive to this day. But the once crowded churches of Alexandria, Cyrene, Carthage, and Hippo were emptied and decayed; the memory of Athanasius, Cyril, and Augustine faded out; and the disputes of Arians, Donatists, and Monophysites gave way to the quarrels of Sunni and Ismaili Mohammedanism. The Fatimids propped up their power by gathering the Ismailites into a Grand Lodge of complex initiations and hierarchical degrees; the members were used for political espionage and intrigue; the forms of the order were transmitted to Jerusalem and Europe, and strongly influenced the organization, ritual, and garb of the Templars, the Illuminati, and the other secret fraternities of the Western world. The American businessman is periodically a zealous Mohammedan, proud of his secret doctrine, his Moroccan fez, and his Moslem shrine.

III. ISLAM IN THE MEDITERRANEAN: 649–1071

Having conquered Syria and Egypt, the Moslem leaders realized that they could not hold the coast without a fleet. Soon their men-of-war seized Cyprus and Rhodes, and defeated the Byzantine navy (652, 655). Corsica was occupied in 809, Sardinia in 810, Crete in 823, Malta in 870. In 827 the old struggle between Greece and Carthage for Sicily was resumed; the Aghlabid caliphs of Qairwan sent expedition after expedition, and the conquest proceeded with leisurely bloodshed and rapine. Palermo fell in 831,

Messina in 843, Syracuse in 878, Taormina in 902. When the Fatimid caliphs succeeded to the Aghlabid power (909) they inherited Sicily as part of their domain. When the Fatimids removed their seat to Cairo their governor of Sicily, Husein al-Kalbi, made himself emir with nearly sovereign authority, and established that Kalbite dynasty under which Moslem civilization in Sicily reached its height.

Fortified by mastery of the Mediterranean, the Saracens now looked appreciatively on the cities of southern Italy. As piracy was quite within the bounds of honored custom at this time, and Christians and Moslems raided Moslem or Christian shores to capture infidels for sale as slaves, Saracen fleets, mostly from Tunisia or Sicily, began in the ninth century to attack Italian ports. In 841 the Moslems took Bari, the main Byzantine base in southeastern Italy. A year later, invited by the Lombard Duke of Benevento to help him against Salerno, they swept across Italy and back, despoiling fields and monasteries as they went. In 846 eleven hundred Moslems landed at Ostia, marched up to the walls of Rome, freely plundered the suburbs and the churches of St. Peter and St. Paul, and leisurely returned to their ships. Seeing that no civil authority could organize Italian defense, Pope Leo IV took charge, bound Amalfi, Naples, Gaeta, and Rome in alliance, and had a chain stretched across the Tiber to halt any enemy. In 849 the Saracens made another attempt to seize the citadel of Western Christianity. The united Italian fleet, blessed by the Pope, gave them battle, and routed them—a scene pictured by Raphael in the Stanze of the Vatican. In 866 the Emperor Louis II came down from Germany, and drove the marauding Moslems of south Italy back upon Bari and Taranto. By 884 they were expelled from the peninsula.

But their raids continued, and central Italy lived through a generation of daily fear. In 876 they pillaged the Campagna; Rome was so endangered that the pope paid the Saracens a yearly bribe of 25,000 *mancusi* (*c.* $25,000) to keep the peace.[23] In 884 they burned the great monastery of Monte Cassino to the ground; in sporadic attacks they ravaged the valley of the Anio; finally the combined forces of the pope, the Greek and German emperors, and the cities of southern and central Italy defeated them on the Garigliano (916), and a tragic century of invasion came to an end. Italy, perhaps Christianity, had had a narrow escape; had Rome fallen, the Saracens would have advanced upon Venice; and Venice taken, Constantinople would have been wedged in between two concentrations of Moslem power. On such chances of battle hung the theology of billions of men.

Meanwhile the polyglot culture of Sicily, yielding with the grace of habit to new conquerors, took on a Moslem veneer. Sicilians, Greeks, Lombards, Jews, Berbers, and Arabs mingled in the streets of the Moslem capital— ancient Panormus, Arabic Balerm, Italian Palermo; all hating one another religiously, but living together with no more than a Sicilian average of passion, poetry, and crime. Here Ibn Hawqal, about 970, found some 300 mosques, and 300 schoolteachers who were highly regarded by the inhabitants "in spite of the fact," says the geographer, "that schoolteachers are notorious for their mental deficiency and light brains."[24] With sunshine and rain co-operating to make a lush vegetation, Sicily was an agricultural paradise; and the clever Arabs reaped the fruits of a well-managed economy. Palermo became a port of exchange between Christian Europe and Moslem Africa; soon it was one of the richest cities in Islam. The Moslem flair for fine dress, brilliant jewelry, and the arts of decoration made for a life of *otium cum dignitate*—leisure without vulgarity. The Sicilian poet Ibn Hamdis (*c.* 1055–1132) describes the vivacious hours of Palermitan youth: the midnight revels, the jolly raid on a convent to buy wine from a surprised but genial nun, the gay mingling of men and women in festival, "when the King of the Revels has outlawed care," and singing girls tease the lute with slender fingers, and dance "like resplendent moons on the stems of willowy trees."[25]

There were thousands of poets in the island, for the Moors loved wit and rhyme, and Sicilian love offered rich themes. There were scholars, for Palermo boasted a university; and great physicians, for Sicilian Moslem medicine influenced the medical school at Salerno.[26] Half the brilliance of Norman Sicily was an Arab echo, an Oriental legacy of crafts and craftsmen to a young culture willing to learn from any race or creed. The Norman conquest of Sicily (1060–91) helped time to efface the vestiges of Islam in the island; Count Roger was proud that he had leveled "Saracen cities, castles, and palaces built with marvelous art."[27] But Moslem style left its mark on the Palace of La Ziza, and on the ceiling of the Capella Palatina; in this chapel of the palace of the Norman kings Moorish ornament serves the shrine of Christ.

IV. SPANISH ISLAM: 711–1086

1. Caliphs and Emirs

It was at first the Moors, not the Arabs, who conquered Spain. Tariq was a Berber, and his army had 7000 Berbers to 300 Arabs. His name is embedded in the rock at whose foot his forces landed; the Moors came to call it Gebel al-Tariq, the Mountain of Tariq, which Europe compressed into Gibraltar. Tariq had been sent to Spain by Musa ibn Nusayr, Arab governor of North Africa. In 712 Musa crossed with 10,000 Arabs and 8000 Moors; besieged and captured Seville and Merida; rebuked Tariq for exceeding orders, struck him with a whip, and cast him into prison. The Caliph Walid recalled Musa and freed Tariq, who resumed his conquests. Musa had appointed his son Abd al-Aziz governor of Seville; Suleiman, Walid's brother, suspected Abd al-Aziz of plotting to make himself independent sovereign of Spain, and despatched assassins to kill him. The head was brought to Suleiman, now caliph, at Damascus; he sent for Musa, who asked: "Grant me his head, that I may close his eyes." Within a year Musa died of grief.[28] We may believe that the story is only a bloody legend.

The victors treated the conquered leniently, confiscated the lands only of those who had actively resisted, exacted no greater tax than had been levied by the Visigothic kings, and gave to religious worship a freedom rare in Spain. Having established their position in the peninsula, the Moslems scaled the Pyrenees and entered Gaul, intent upon making Europe a province of Damascus. Between Tours and Poitiers, a thousand miles north of Gibraltar, they were met by the united forces of Eudes, Duke of Aquitaine, and Charles, Duke of Austrasia. After seven days of fighting, the Moslems were defeated in one of the most crucial battles of history (732); again the faith of countless millions was determined by the chances of war. Thenceforth Charles was Carolus Martellus, or Martel, Charles the Hammer. In 735 the Moslems tried again, and captured Arles; in 737 they took Avignon, and ravaged the valley of the Rhone to Lyons. In 759 Pepin the Short finally expelled them from the south of France; but their forty years of circulation there may have influenced Languedoc's unusual tolerance of diverse faiths, its colorful gaiety, its flair for songs of unpermitted love.

The caliphs of Damascus undervalued Spain; till 756 it was merely "the district of Andalusia," and was governed from Qairwan. But in 755 a romantic figure landed in Spain, armed only with royal blood, and destined to establish a dynasty that would rival in wealth and glory the caliphs of Baghdad. When, in 750, the triumphant Abbasids ordered all princes of the Umayyad family slain, Abd-er-Rahman, grandson of the Caliph Hisham, was the only Umayyad who escaped. Hunted from village to village, he swam the broad Euphrates, crossed into Palestine, Egypt and Africa, and finally reached Morocco. News of the Abbasid revolution had intensified the factional rivalry of Arabs, Syrians, Persians, and Moors in Spain; an Arab group loyal to the Umayyads, fearing that the Abbasid caliph might question their titles to lands given them by Umayyad governors, invited Abd-er-Rahman to join and lead them. He came, and was made emir of Cordova (756). He defeated an army commissioned by the Caliph al-Mansur to unseat him, and sent the head of its general to be hung before a palace in Mecca.

Perhaps it was these events that saved Europe from worshiping Mohammed: Moslem Spain, weakened with civil war and deprived of external aid, ceased to conquer, and withdrew even from northern Spain. From the ninth to the eleventh century the peninsula was divided into Moslem and Christian by a line running from Coimbra through Saragossa and along the Ebro River. The Moslem south, finally pacified by Abd-er-Rahman I and his successors, blossomed into riches, poetry, and art. Abd-er-Rahman II (822–52) enjoyed the fruits of this prosperity. Amid border wars with the Christians, rebellions

among his subjects, and Norman raids on his coasts, he found time to beautify Cordova with palaces and mosques, rewarded poets handsomely, and
forgave offenders with an amiable lenience that may have shared in producing the social disorder that followed his reign.

Abd-er-Rahman III (912–61) is the culminating figure of this Umayyad
dynasty in Spain. Coming to power at twenty-one, he found "Andaluz" torn
by racial faction, religious animosity, sporadic brigandage, and the efforts of
Seville and Toledo to establish their independence of Cordova. Though a
man of refinement, famous for generosity and courtesy, he laid a firm hand
upon the situation, quelled the rebellious cities, and subdued the Arab aristocrats who wished, like their French contemporaries, to enjoy a feudal sovereignty on their rich estates. He invited to his councils men of diverse faiths,
adjusted his alliances to maintain a balance of power among his neighbors and
his enemies, and administered the government with Napoleonic industry and
attention to detail. He planned the campaigns of his generals, often took the
field in person, repulsed the invasions of Sancho of Navarre, captured and
destroyed Sancho's capital, and discouraged further Christian forays during
his reign. In 929, knowing himself as powerful as any ruler of his time, and
realizing that the caliph of Baghdad had become a puppet of Turkish guards,
he assumed the caliphal title—Commander of the Faithful and Defender of
the Faith. When he died he left behind him, in his own handwriting, a modest estimate of human life:

> I have now reigned above fifty [Mohammedan] years in victory or
> peace. . . . Riches and honors, powers and pleasures, have waited on
> my call; nor does any earthly blessing appear to have been wanting to
> my felicity. In this situation I have diligently numbered the days of
> pure and genuine happiness which have fallen to my lot. They amount
> to fourteen. O man! place not thy confidence in this present world! [29]

His son Hakam II (961–76) profited wisely from this half century of unhappy competence. Secure from external danger and internal revolt, he gave
himself to the adornment of Cordova and other cities; built mosques, colleges, hospitals, markets, public baths, and asylums for the poor;[30] made
the University of Cordova the greatest educational institution of his time;
and helped hundreds of poets, artists, and savants. The Moslem historian al-
Maqqari writes:

> The Caliph Hakam surpassed every one of his predecessors in love
> of literature and the sciences, which he himself cultivated and fos-
> tered . . . he converted Andaluz into a great market whereto the liter-
> ary productions of every clime were immediately brought for sale.
> He employed agents to collect books for him in distant countries, and
> remitted to them large sums of money, until the number of books thus
> conveyed to Andaluz exceeded all calculation. He would likewise
> send gifts of money to celebrated authors in the East, to encourage the

publication of works, or to obtain the first copies of them. In this way, knowing that Abu'l Faraj of Isfahan had written a work entitled *Kitab ul-Aghani*, he sent him 1000 dinars of pure gold ($4750), upon which the author forwarded him a copy of this work, even before it had appeared in Iraq.[31]

While the scholar-caliph attended to the amenities of life, he left the administration of the government, even the guidance of national policy, to his able Jewish prime minister Hasdai ibn Shaprut, and the leadership of his armies to a brilliant and unscrupulous general who, under the name of Almanzor, was to provide material for many a Christian drama or romance. His real name was Muhammad ibn Abi Amir. He came of an old Arab family with more genealogy than means; he earned a living by writing petitions for persons who wished to address the caliph; became a clerk in the office of the chief *qadi* or attorney general; and in 967, at the age of twenty-six, was appointed to manage the property of al-Hakam's eldest son, another Abd-er-Rahman. He ingratiated himself with the lad's mother, Queen Subh, charmed her with courtesies and compliments, and impressed her with his tireless ability; soon he was managing her property as well as her son's; and within a year he was named master of the mint. He now became so generous to his friends that rivals accused him of malversation. Al-Hakam summoned him to clear his account; knowing that he could not, Ibn Abi Amir asked a rich friend to advance him the deficit; so armed, he went to the palace, faced his accusers, and carried the matter off so triumphantly that the Caliph appointed him concurrently to several lucrative posts. When Hakam died, Ibn Abi Amir secured the succession to Hakam's son Hisham II (976–1009;–1010–13) by personally directing the murder of a rival claimant. A week later he was made vizier.[32]

Hisham II was a weakling, altogether incapable of rule; from 978 to 1002 Ibn Ali was caliph in all but name. His enemies charged him, quite rightly, with loving philosophy more than the Moslem faith; to silence them he invited the orthodox theologians to weed out from al-Hakam's great library, and burn, all volumes that in any way impugned the Sunni creed; and by this act of dastardly vandalism he earned a useful reputation for piety. At the same time he drew the intellectual classes to his support by secretly protecting the philosophers, welcoming men of letters at his court, and housing there a bevy of poets who drew stipends from the treasury, followed his campaigns, and sang his victories. He built a new town, Zahira, cast of Cordova, for his palace and administrative offices, while the young Caliph, carefully trained to absorption in theology, remained almost a neglected prisoner in the ancient royal residence. To consolidate his position, Ibn Abi Amir reorganized the army mainly with Berber and Christian mercenaries, who, hostile to the Arabs, felt no obligations to the state, but rewarded with personal loyalty his liberality and tact. When the Christian state of Leon aided a domestic rebellion against him, he destroyed the rebels, severely defeated the Leonese, and returned in triumph to his capital; thereafter he assumed the surname of al-Mansur, "the victorious." Plots against him were numerous, but he circumvented them with pervasive espionage and judicious assassination. His son Abdallah joined one of the conspiracies, was detected, and was beheaded. Like Sulla, al-Mansur never left a favor unrewarded, nor an injury unavenged.

The people forgave his crimes because he effectively suppressed other criminals, and secured an impartial provision of justice for rich and poor; never had life or property been so safe in Cordova. Men could not help admire his persistence, intelligence, and courage. One day, while holding court, he felt a pain in his leg; he sent for a physician, who advised cautery; with no interruption to the session, al-Mansur allowed his flesh to be burned without giving any sign of discomfort; "the assembly," says al-Maqqari, "perceived nothing until they smelled the burnt flesh." [33] As a further aid to popularity, he enlarged the mosque of Cordova with the labor of Christian captives, and himself wielded pick and shovel, trowel and saw. Having learned that statesmen who organize successful wars, just or unjust, are exalted by both contemporaries and posterity, he renewed the war with Leon, captured and razed its capital, and massacred the population. Nearly every spring he sallied forth on a new campaign against the infidel north, and never returned without victory. In 997 he took and destroyed the city of Santiago de Compostela, leveled to the ground its famous shrine to St. James, and made Christian captives carry the gates and bells of the church on their shoulders in his triumphal entry into Cordova.[34] (In later years the bells would be returned to Compostela on the backs of Moslem prisoners of war.)

Though sovereign in fact of Moslem Spain, al-Mansur was not content; he longed to be sovereign in name, and to found a dynasty. In 991 he resigned his office to his eighteen-year-old son Abd-al-Malik, added the names *sayid* (lord) and *malik karim* (noble king) to his other titles, and ruled with absolute power. He had wished to die on the battlefield, and, prepared for this consummation, he took his burial shroud with him on his campaigns. In 1002, aged 61, he invaded Castile, captured cities, destroyed monasteries, ravaged fields. On the homeward march he fell ill; refusing medical attendance, he called for his son, and told him that death would come within two days. When Abd-al-Malik wept al-Mansur said: "This is a sign that the Empire will soon decay." [35] A generation later the Cordovan caliphate collapsed.

The history of Moorish Spain after al-Mansur is a chaos of brief reigns, assassinations, racial strife, and class war. The Berbers, scorned and impoverished in the realm that their arms had won, and relegated to the arid plains of Estremadura or the cold mountains of Leon, periodically revolted against the ruling Arab aristocracy. The exploited workers of the towns hated their employers, and changed them spasmodically with murderous insurrection.

All classes united in one hatred—of that Amirid family, the heirs of al-Mansur, which, under his son, almost monopolized the offices of government and the perquisites of power. In 1008 Abd-al-Malik died, and was succeeded as prime minister by his brother Abd-er-Rahman Shandjul. Shandjul drank wine in public, and had a kind word for sin; he preferred to carouse rather than to govern; in 1009 he was deposed by a revolution in which nearly all factions joined. The revolutionary masses got out of hand, plundered the Amirid palaces at Zahira, and burned them to the ground. In 1012 the Berbers captured and pillaged Cordova, slew half the population, exiled the rest, and made Cordova a Berber capital. So briefly does a Christian historian recount the French Revolution of Islamic Spain.

But the ardor that destroys is seldom mated with the patience that builds. Under Berber rule disorder, brigandage, and unemployment mounted; cities subject to Cordova seceded and withheld tribute, and even the owners of great estates made themselves sovereign on their lands. Gradually the surviving Cordovans recovered; in 1023 they expelled the Berbers from the capital, and gave the throne to Abd-er-Rahman V. Seeing no advantage in a return to the old regime, the proletariat of Cordova captured the royal palace, and proclaimed one of their leaders, Muhammad al-Mustakfi, as caliph (1023). Muhammad appointed a weaver as his prime minister. The weaver was assassinated, the proletarian Caliph was poisoned, and in 1027 a union of upper and middle classes elevated Hisham III. Four years later the army took its turn, killed Hisham's prime minister, and demanded Hisham's abdication. A council of leading citizens, perceiving that competition for the throne was making government impossible, abolished the Spanish caliphate, and replaced it with a council of state. Ibn Jahwar was chosen first consul, and ruled the new republic with justice and wisdom.

But it was too late. The political authority and cultural leadership had been irrevocably destroyed. Scholarship and poetry, frightened by civil war, had fled from the "Gem of the World" to the courts of Toledo, Granada, and Seville. Moslem Spain disintegrated into twenty-three *taifas* or city-states, too busy with intrigue and strife to stop the gradual absorption of Mohammedan by Christian Spain. Granada prospered under the able ministry (1038–73) of Rabbi Samuel Halevi, known to the Arabs as Ismail ibn Naghdela. Toledo declared its independence of Cordova in 1035, and fifty years later submitted to Christian rule.

Seville succeeded to the glory of Cordova. Some thought it fairer than that capital; people loved it for its gardens, palm trees, and roses, and a gaiety always ready with music, dance, and song. Anticipating the fall of Cordova, it made itself indepedent in 1023. Its chief justice, Abu'l Qasim Muhammad, found a mat-maker resembling Hisham II, hailed him as Caliph, housed and guided him, and persuaded Valencia, Tortosa, even Cordova, to recognize him; by this simple device the subtle jurist founded the brief Abbadid dynasty. When he died (1042), his son Abbad al-Mutadid succeeded him, ruled Seville with skill and cruelty for twenty-seven years, and extended his power till half of Moslem Spain paid him tribute. His son al-Mutamid (1068–91), at the age of twenty-six, inherited his realm, but neither his ambition nor his cruelty. Al-Mutamid was the greatest poet of Moslem Spain. He preferred the company of poets and musicians to that of politicians and generals, and rewarded his able rivals in poetry with unenvious hand; he thought it not too much to give a thousand ducats ($2,290) for an epigram.[36] He liked Ibn Ammar's poetry, and made him vizier. He heard a girl slave, Rumaykiyya, improvise excellent verses; he bought her, married her, and loved her passionately till his death, while not neglecting the other beauties of his harem. Rumaykiyya filled the palace with her laughter, and drew her lord into a spiral of gaiety; theologians blamed her for her husband's coolness to religion, and the near emptiness of the city's mosques. Nevertheless al-Mutamid could rule as well as love and sing. When Toledo attacked Cordova, and Cordova asked his aid, he sent troops who saved the city from Toledo and made it subject to Seville. The poet-king stood for a precarious generation at the head of a civilization as brilliant as Baghdad's under Harun, as Cordova's under al-Mansur.

2. Civilization in Moorish Spain

"Never was Andalusia so mildly, justly, and wisely governed as by her Arab conquerors." [37] It is the judgment of a great Christian Orientalist, whose enthusiasm may require some discounting of his praise; but after due deductions his verdict stands. The emirs and caliphs of Spain were as cruel as Machiavelli thought necessary to the stability of a government; sometimes they were barbarously and callously cruel, as when Mutadid grew flowers in the skulls of his dead foes, or as when the poetic Mutamid hacked to pieces the lifelong friend who had at last betrayed and insulted him.[38] Against these stray instances al-Maqqari gives a hundred examples of the justice, liberality, and refinement of the Umayyad rulers of Spain.[39] They compare favorably with the Greek emperors of their time; and they were certainly an improvement upon the illiberal Visigothic regime that had preceded them. Their management of public affairs was the most competent in the Western world of that age. Laws were rational and humane, and were administered by a well-organized judiciary. For the most part the conquered, in their internal affairs, were governed by their own laws and their own officials.[40] Towns were well policed; markets, weights and measures were effectively supervised. A regular census recorded population and property. Taxation was reasonable compared with the imposts of Rome or Byzantium. The revenues of the Cordovan caliphate under Abd-er-Rahman III reached 12,045,000 gold dinars ($57,213,750)—probably more than the united governmental revenues of Latin Christendom; [41] but these receipts were due not so much to high taxes as to well-governed and progressive agriculture, industry, and trade.[42]

The Arab conquest was a transient boon to the native peasantry. The overgrown estates of the Visigothic nobles were broken up, and the serfs became proprietors.[43] But the forces that in these centuries were making for feudalism operated in Spain too, though better resisted than in France; the Arab leaders in their turn accumulated large tracts, and farmed them with tenants verging on serfdom. Slaves were slightly better treated by the Moors * than by their former owners; [44] and the slaves of non-Moslems could free themselves merely by professing Islam. The Arabs for the most part left the actual work of agriculture to the conquered; however, they used the latest manuals of agronomy, and under their direction agricultural science developed in Spain far in advance of Christian Europe.[45] The leisurely oxen, hitherto universally used in Spain for plowing or draft, were largely replaced by the mule, the ass, and the horse. Stock breeding of Spanish with Arab strains produced the "noble steed" of the Arab horseman and the Spanish *caballero*. Moslem Spain brought from Asia, and taught to Christian Europe, the culture of rice, buckwheat, sugar cane, pomegranates, cotton, spinach, asparagus, silk, bananas, cherries, oranges, lemons, quinces, grapefruit, peaches, dates, figs, strawberries, ginger, myrrh.[46] The cultivation of the vine was a major industry among the Moors, whose religion forbade wine. Market gardens, olive groves, and fruit orchards made some areas of Spain—notably around Cordova, Granada, and Valencia—"garden spots of the world." The island of Majorca, won by the Moors in the eighth century, became under their husbandry a paradise of fruits and flowers, dominated by the date palm that later gave its name to the capital.

The mines of Spain enriched the Moors with gold, silver, tin, copper, iron, lead, alum, sulphur, mercury. Coral was gathered along Andalusia's shores; pearls were fished along the Catalonian coasts; rubies were mined at Baja and Malaga. Metallurgy was well developed; Murcia was famous for its iron and brass works, Toledo for its swords, Cordova for shields. Handicraft industry flourished. Cordova made "Cordovan" leather for the "cordwainers" (*cordobanes*) of Europe. There were 13,000 weavers in Cordova alone; Moorish carpets, cushions, silk curtains, shawls, divans found eager buyers everywhere. According to al-Maqqari,[48] Ibn Firnas of Cordova, in the ninth century, invented spectacles, complex chronometers, and a flying machine. A merchant fleet of over a thousand ships carried the products of Spain to Africa and Asia; and vessels from a hundred ports crowded the harbors of Barcelona, Almeria, Cartagena, Valencia, Malaga, Cadiz, and Seville. A regu-

---

* By this term we shall mean the Moslem population—partly Arab, mostly Berber—of western North Africa and Spain.

lar postal service was maintained for the government. The official coinage of gold dinars, silver dirhems, and copper *fals* preserved a relative stability in comparison with the currencies of contemporary Latin Christendom; but these Moorish coins, too, gradually deteriorated in weight, purity, and purchasing power.

Economic exploitation proceeded here as elsewhere. Arabs who had extensive estates, and merchants who squeezed producer and consumer alike, absorbed the wealth of the land. For the most part the rich lived in country villas, and left the cities to a proletarian population of Berbers, "Renegades" (Christian converts to Mohammedanism), "Mozarabs" (non-Moslems accepting Moslem ways and Arabic speech), and a sprinkling of palace eunuchs, Slav officers and guardsmen, and household slaves. The Cordovan caliphs, feeling themselves unable to end exploitation without discouraging enterprise, compromised by devoting a quarter of their land income to the relief of the poor.[49]

The desperate faith of the indigent gave a subtle power to the *faqihs* or theologians of the law. Innovations in creed or morals were so abhorred by the populace that heresy and speculation usually hid their heads in obscurity of place or speech; philosophy was silenced, or professed the most respectable conclusions. Apostasy from Islam was punishable with death. Cordovan caliphs themselves were often men of liberal views, but they suspected the Egyptian Fatimid caliphs of using wandering scholars as spies, and occasionally they joined the *faqihs* in persecuting independent thought. On the other hand the Moorish authorities gave freedom of worship to all non-Moslem faiths. The Jews, harshly hounded by the Visigoths, had helped the Moslem conquest of Spain; they lived now—until the twelfth century—in peace with the conquerors, developed wealth and learning, and sometimes rose to high place in the government. Christians faced greater obstacles to political preferment, but many succeeded nevertheless. Christian males, like all males, were subject to compulsory circumcision as a measure of national hygiene; otherwise they were ruled by their own Visigothic-Roman law, administered by magistrates of their own choosing.[50] In return for exemption from military service, free and able Christian males paid a land tax, normally forty-eight dirhems ($24.00) per year for the rich, twenty-four for the middle classes, twelve for manual workers.[51] Christians and Moslems intermarried freely; now and then they joined in celebrating a Christian or Moslem holyday, or used the same building as church and mosque.[52] Some Christians, conforming to the custom of the country, established harems, or practiced pederasty.[53] Clerics and laymen from Christian Europe came in safety and freedom to Cordova, Toledo, or Seville as students, visitors, or travelers. One Christian complained of the results in terms that recall ancient Hebrew criticism of Hellenizing Jews:

My fellow Christians delight in the poems and romances of the Arabs; they study the works of Mohammedan theologians and philosophers, not to refute them, but to acquire a correct and elegant Arabic style.... Alas! the young Christians who are most conspicuous for their talent have no knowledge of any literature or language save the Arabic; they read and study with avidity Arabic books; they amass whole libraries of them at great cost; they everywhere sing the praises of Arabic lore.[54]

We may judge the attractiveness of Islam to Christians from a letter of 1311, which gives the Mohammedan population of Granada at that time as 200,-000, of whom *all but 500* were descendants of Christians converted to Islam.[55] Christians frequently expressed their preference of Moslem to Christian rule.[56]

But there was another side to the picture, and it darkened with time. Though Christians were free, the Church was not. Most of her landed property had been confiscated by a decree affecting all active resisters to the conquest; many churches had been destroyed, and new ones were prohibited.[57] The Moslem emirs inherited from the Visigoth kings the right to appoint and depose bishops, even to summon ecclesiastical councils. The emirs sold bishoprics to the highest bidder, though he might be a skeptic or a libertine. Christian priests were liable to abuse by Moslems in the streets. Moslem theologians commented freely on what seemed to them absurdities in Christian theology, but it was dangerous for Christians to reply in kind.

Under such tense relations a minor incident could lead to a major tragedy. A pretty girl of Cordova, known to us only as Flora, was the child of a mixed marriage. When her Mohammedan father died she resolved to become a Christian. She fled from her brother's guardianship to a Christian home, was caught and beaten by him, persisted in apostasy, and was turned over to a Moslem court. The *qadi*, who might have condemned her to death, ordered her flogged. She escaped again to a Christian home, and there met a young priest, Eulogius, who conceived for her a passionate spiritual attachment. While she hid in a convent another priest, Perfectus, achieved martyrdom by telling some Moslems what he thought of Mohammed; they had promised not to betray him, but the vigor of his exposition so shocked them that they denounced him to the authorities. Perfectus might have saved himself by a retraction; instead he repeated to the judge his conviction that Mohammed was "the servant of Satan." The judge remanded him to jail for some months, hoping for a change of mood; none came; and Perfectus was condemned to death. He marched to the scaffold cursing the Prophet as "an impostor, an adulterer, a child of hell." The Moslems gloated over his decapitation, the Christians of Cordova buried him with pomp as a saint (850).[58]

His death inflamed the theological hatred of both sides. A group of Christian "Zealots" formed, led by Eulogius; they were determined to denounce

Mohammed publicly, and to accept martyrdom joyfully as a promise of para-dise. Isaac, a Cordovan monk, went to the *qadi* and professed a desire for con-version; but when the judge, well pleased, began to expound Mohammedan-ism, the monk interrupted him: "Your Prophet," he said, "has lied and deceived you. May he be accursed, who has dragged so many wretches with him down to hell!" The *qadi* reproved him, and asked had he been drinking; the monk replied: "I am in my right mind. Condemn me to death." The *qadi* had him imprisoned, but asked permission of Abd-er-Rahman II to dismiss him as insane; the Caliph, incensed by the splendor of Perfectus' funeral, or-dered the monk to be executed. Two days later Sancho, a Frank soldier of the palace guard, publicly denounced Mohammed; he was beheaded. On the following Sunday six monks appeared before the *qadi*, cursed Mohammed, and asked for not death only, but "your sharpest tortures"; they were be-headed. A priest, a deacon, and a monk followed their example. The Zealots rejoiced, but many Christians—priests as well as laymen—condemned this lust for martyrdom. "The Sultan," they said to the Zealots, "allows us to ex-ercise our religion, and does not oppress us; why, then, this fanatical zeal?" [59] A council of Christian bishops, summoned by Abd-er-Rahman, reproved the Zealots, and threatened action against them if they continued the agitation. Eulogius denounced the council as cowards.

Meanwhile Flora, her ardor raised by the Zealot movement, left her con-vent, and with another girl, Mary, went before the *qadi*; they both assured him that Mohammed was "an adulterer, an impostor, and a villain," and that Mohammedanism was "an invention of the Devil." The *qadi* committed them to jail. The entreaties of their friends had inclined them to retract when Eulogius prevailed upon them to accept martyrdom. They were beheaded (851), and Eulogius, much encouraged, called for new martyrs. Priests, monks, and women marched to the court, denounced Mohammed, and ob-tained decapitation (852). Eulogius himself earned martyrdom seven years later. After his death the movement subsided. We hear of two cases of mar-tyrdom between 859 and 983, and none thereafter under Moslem rule in Spain.[60]

Among the Moslems religious ardor declined as wealth grew. Despite the rigor of Moslem law, a wave of skepticism rose in the eleventh century. Not only did the mild heresies of the Mutazilites finally enter Spain; a sect arose that declared all religions false, and laughed at commandments, prayer, fast-ing, pilgrimage, and alms. Another group, under the name of "Universal Re-ligion," deprecated all dogmas, and pled for a purely ethical religion. Some were agnostics: the doctrines of religion, they said, "may or may not be true; we neither affirm nor deny them, we simply cannot tell; but our consciences will not allow us to accept doctrines whose truth cannot be demonstrated." [61] The theologians fought back with vigor; when disaster came to Spanish Islam in the eleventh century they pointed to irreligion as its cause; and when for a time Islam prospered again, it was under rulers who once more rooted their power in religious belief, and restricted the controversy between religion and philosophy to the privacy and amusement of their courts.

Despite the philosophers, gleaming cupolas and gilded minarets marked the thousand cities or towns that made Moslem Spain in the tenth century the most urban country in Europe, probably in the world. Cordova under al-Mansur was a civilized city, second only to Baghdad and Constantinople. Here, says al-Maqqari, were 200,077 houses, 60,300 palaces, 600 mosques, and 700 public baths; [62] the statistics are slightly Oriental. Visitors marveled at the wealth of the upper classes, and at what seemed to them an extraordinary general prosperity; every family could afford a donkey; only beggars could not ride. Streets were paved, had raised sidewalks, and were lighted at night; one could travel for ten miles by the light of street lamps, and along an uninterrupted series of buildings. [63] Over the quiet Guadalquivir Arab engineers threw a great stone bridge of seventeen arches, each fifty spans in width. One of the earliest undertakings of Abd-er-Rahman I was an aqueduct that brought to Cordova an abundance of fresh water for homes, gardens, fountains, and baths. The city was famous for its pleasure gardens and promenades.

Abd-er-Rahman I, lonesome for his boyhood haunts, planted in Cordova a great garden like that of the villa in which he had spent his boyhood near Damascus, and built in it his "Palace of the Rissafah." Later caliphs added other structures, to which Moslem fancy gave florid names: Palace of the Flowers . . . of the Lovers . . . of Contentment . . . of the Diadem. Cordova, like later Seville, had its Alcazar (al-qasr, castle, from the Latin castrum), a combination of palace and fortress. Moslem historians describe these mansions as equaling in luxury and beauty those of Nero's Rome: majestic portals, marble columns, mosaic floors, gilded ceilings, and such refined decoration as only Moslem art could give. The palaces of the royal family, the lords and magnates of land and trade, lined for miles the banks of the stately stream. A concubine of Abd-er-Rahman III left him a large fortune; he proposed to spend it ransoming such of his soldiers as had been captured in war; proud searchers claimed they could find none; whereupon the Caliph's favorite wife, Zahra, proposed that he build a suburb and palace to commemorate her name. For twenty-five years (936-61) 10,000 workmen and 1500 beasts toiled to realize her dream. The royal palace of al-Zahra that rose three miles southwest of Cordova was lavishly designed and equipped; 1200 marble columns sustained it; its harem could accommodate 6000 women; its hall of audience had ceiling and walls of marble and gold, eight doors inlaid with ebony, ivory, and precious stones, and a basin of quicksilver whose undulating surface reflected the dancing rays of the sun. Al-Zahra became the residential center of an aristocracy renowned for the grace and polish of its manners, the refinement of its tastes, and the breadth of its intellectual interests. At the opposite end of the city al-Mansur constructed (978) a rival palace, al-Zahira, which also gathered about it a suburb of lords, servants, minstrels, poets, and courtesans. Both suburbs were burned to the ground in the revolution of 1010.

Normally the people forgave the luxury of their princes if these would raise to Allah shrines exceeding their palaces in splendor and scope. The Romans had built in Cordova a temple to Janus; the Christians had replaced it with a cathedral; Abd-er-Rahman I paid the Christians for the site, demolished the church, and replaced it with the Blue Mosque; in 1238 the *reconquista* would turn the mosque into a cathedral; so the good, the true, and the beautiful fluctuate with the fortunes of war. The project became the consolation of Abd-er-Rahman's troubled years; he left his suburban for his city home to superintend the operations, and hoped that he might before his death lead the congregation in grateful prayer in this new and majestic mosque. He died in 788, two years after laying the foundation; his son al-Hisham continued the work; each caliph, for two centuries, added a part, till in al-Mansur's time it covered an area 742 by 472 feet. The exterior showed a battlemented wall of brick and stone, with irregular towers, and a massive minaret that surpassed in size and beauty all the minarets of the time, so that it too was numbered among the innumerable "wonders of the world." [64] Nineteen portals, surmounted by horseshoe arches elegantly carved with floral and geometrical decoration in stone, led into the Court of Ablutions, now the Patio de los Naranjos, or Court of Oranges. In this rectangle, paved with colored tiles, stood four fountains, each cut from a block of solid marble so large that seventy oxen had been needed to haul it from the quarry to the site. The mosque proper was a forest of 1290 columns, dividing the interior into eleven naves and twenty-one aisles. From the column capitals sprang a variety of arches—some semicircular, some pointed, some in horseshoe form, most of them with voussoirs, or wedge stones, alternately red or white. The columns of jasper, porphyry, alabaster, or marble, snatched from the ruins of Roman or Visigothic Spain, gave by their number the impression of limitless and bewildering space. The wooden ceiling was carved into cartouches bearing Koranic and other inscriptions. From it hung 200 chandeliers holding 7000 cups of scented oil, fed from reservoirs of oil in inverted Christian bells also suspended from the roof. Floor and walls were adorned with mosaics; some of these were of enameled glass, baked in rich colors, and often containing silver or gold; after a thousand years of wear these dados still sparkle like jewels in the cathedral walls. One section was marked off as a sanctuary; it was paved with silver and enameled tiles, guarded with ornate doors, decorated with mosaics, roofed with three domes, and marked off with a wooden screen of exquisite design. Within this sanctuary were built the mihrab and *minbar*, upon which the artists lavished their maturest skill. The mihrab itself was an heptagonal recess walled with gold; brilliantly ornamented with enameled mosaics, marble tracery, and gold inscriptions on a ground of crimson and blue; and crowned by a tier of slender columns and trefoil arches as lovely as anything in Gothic art. The pulpit was considered the finest of its kind; it consisted of 37,000 little panels of ivory and precious woods—ebony, citron, aloe, red and yellow sandal, all joined by gold or silver nails, and inlaid with gems. On this *minbar*, in a jeweled box covered with gold-threaded crimson silk, rested a copy of the Koran written by the Caliph Othman and stained with his dying blood. To us, who prefer to adorn our theaters with gilt and brass rather than clothe our cathedrals in jewelry and gold, the decoration of the Blue Mosque seems extravagant; the walls encrusted with the blood of exploited generations, the columns confusingly numerous, the horseshoe arch as structurally weak and aesthetically offensive as obesity on bow legs. Others, however, have judged differently: al-Maqqari (1591–1632) thought this mosque "unequaled in size, or beauty of design, or tasteful arrangement of its ornaments, or boldness of execution"; [65] and even its diminished Christian form is ranked as "by universal consent the most beautiful Moslem temple in the world." [66]

It was a common saying in Moorish Spain that "when a musician dies at Cordova, and his instruments are to be sold, they are sent to Seville; when a rich man dies at Seville, and his library is to be sold, it is sent to Cordova." [67] For Cordova in the tenth century was the focus and summit of Spanish intellectual life, though Toledo, Granada, and Seville shared actively in the mental exhilaration of the time. Moslem historians picture the Moorish cities as beehives of poets, scholars, jurists, physicians, and scientists; al-Maqqari fills sixty pages with their names. [68] Primary schools were numerous, but charged tuition; Hakam II added twenty-seven schools for the free instruction of the poor. Girls as well as boys went to school; several Moorish ladies became prominent in literature or art. [69] Higher education was provided by independent lecturers in the mosques; their courses constituted the loosely organized University of Cordova, which in the tenth and eleventh centuries was second in renown only to similar institutions in Cairo and Baghdad. Colleges were established also at Granada, Toledo, Seville, Murcia, Almeria, Valencia, Cadiz. [70] The technique of paper making was brought in from Baghdad, and books increased and multiplied. Moslem Spain had seventy libraries; rich men displayed their Morocco bindings, and bibliophiles collected rare or beautifully illuminated books. The scholar al-Hadram, at an auction in Cordova, found himself persistently outbid for a book he desired, until the price offered far exceeded the value of the volume. The successful bidder explained that there was a vacant place in his library, into which this book would precisely fit. "I was so vexed," adds al-Hadram, "that I could not help saying to him, 'He gets the nut who has no teeth.' " [71]

Scholars were held in awesome repute in Moslem Spain, and were consulted in simple faith that learning and wisdom are one. Theologians and grammarians could be had by the hundred; rhetoricians, philologists, lexicographers, anthologists, historians, biographers, were legion. Abu Muhammad Ali ibn Hazm (994–1064), besides serving as vizier to the last Umayyads, was a theologian and historian of great erudition. His *Book of Religions and Sects*, discussing Judaism, Zoroastrianism, Christianity, and the principal varieties of Mohammedanism, is one of the world's earliest essays in comparative religion. If we wish to know what an educated Moslem thought of medieval Christianity we need only read one of his paragraphs:

> Human superstition need never excite our astonishment. The most numerous and civilized nations are thralls to it. . . . So great is the multitude of Christians that God alone can number them, and they can boast of sagacious princes and illustrious philosophers. Nevertheless they believe that one is three and three are one; that one of the three is the Father, the other the Son, and the third the Spirit; that the Father is the Son and is not the Son; that a man is God and not God; that the Messiah has existed from all eternity, and yet was created. A sect of theirs, the Monophysites, numbered by hundreds of thousands, believes that the Creator was scourged, buffeted, crucified, and that for three days the universe was without a ruler.[72]

Ibn Hazm, for his part, believed that every word of the Koran was literally true.[73]

Science and philosophy, in Moslem Spain, were largely frustrated by the fear that they would damage the people's faith. Maslama ibn Ahmad (d. 1007), of Madrid and Cordova, adapted the astronomic tables of al-Khwarizmi to Spain. A work doubtfully attributed to him describes one of the many experiments by which alchemy was transmuted into chemistry—the production of mercuric oxide from mercury. Ibrahim al-Zarqali (c. 1029–87) of Toledo made an international name by improving astronomical instruments; Copernicus quoted his treatise on the astrolabe; his astronomical observations were the best of his age, and enabled him to prove for the first time the motion of the solar apogee with reference to the stars; his "Toledan Tables" of planetary movements were used throughout Europe. Abul Qasim al-Zahrawi (936–1013), physician to Abd-er-Rahman III, was honored in Christendom as Abulcasis; he stands at the top of Moslem surgeons; his medical encyclopedia, *al-Tasrif*, included three books on surgery which, translated into Latin, became the standard text of surgery for many centuries. Cordova was in this period the favorite resort of Europeans for surgical operations. Like every civilized city, it had its quota of quacks and money-mad physicians. One Harrani announced a secret specific against intestinal troubles, and sold it at fifty dinars ($237.50) a phial to moneyed fools.[74]

"We forbear," says al-Maqqari, "to mention the poets who flourished under Hisham II and al-Mansur, for they were as numerous as the sands of the ocean." [75] Among them was the princess Wallada (d. 1087); her home at Cordova was a veritable salon of the French Enlightenment; wits, scholars, and poets gathered round her; she made love to a score of them, and wrote about her amours with a freedom that would have shocked Mme. Récamier. Her friend Mugha outdid her in beauty of person and licentiousness of verse. Almost everyone in Andalusia was a poet in those days, and exchanged improvised rhymes at any provocation. The caliphs joined in the sport; and there was seldom a Moorish prince who did not have at his court a poet not only honored but paid. This royal patronge did some injury as well as good; the poetry that has reached us from this age is too often artificial, flowery, lame with laborious similes, and clogged with petty conceits. The theme was love, carnal or Platonic; in Spain, as in the East, the Moslem singers anticipated the methods, moods, and philosophy of the troubadours.[76]

From this dancing galaxy we take one star: Said ibn Judi, son of the prefect of Cordova; an excellent warrior, a constant lover in the plural sense, a master of all the qualities that in Moslem judgment made a perfect gentleman: liberality, courage, skillful horsemanship, good looks, eloquence, poetic talent, strength, and the arts of fencing, wielding the spear, and bending the bow.[77] He was never sure which he loved the more—love or war. Sensitive to the slightest touch of a woman, he suffered a series of infatuations, each of which had every promise of perpetuity. Like a good troubadour, he loved most ardently where he had seen least; his warmest ode was to Jehane, of whom he had seen only a lily hand. He was a candid epicurean, and felt that the burden of proof was always on the moralist. "The sweetest morsel in life," he said, "is when the wine cup goes around; when, after a quarrel, the lovers are reconciled, embrace, and are at peace. I traverse the circle of pleasures as a frenzied war horse that has taken the bit in its teeth. I leave no desire unsatisfied! Steadfast when the angel of death hovers over my head in the day of battle, a pair of bright eyes can sway me as they will." [78] His fellow warriors sometimes resented his seduction of their wives; one officer caught him *in situ*, and killed him (897).

A more heroic end came to a greater poet, al-Mutamid, Emir of Seville. Like other kinglets of disintegrating Spain, he had for several years paid tribute to Alfonso VI of Castile as a bribe to Christian peace. But a bribe always leaves a balance to be paid on demand. With the sinews of war provided by his prey, Alfonso pounced upon Toledo in 1085; and al-Mutamid perceived that Seville might be next. The city-states of Moslem Spain were now too weakened by class and internecine war to offer any adequate resistance. But across the Mediterranean there had arisen a new Moslem dynasty; it was called Almoravid from the *marabout* or patron saint of northwestern Africa; founded on religious fanaticism, it had turned almost every man into a soldier of Allah, and its armies had easily conquered all Morocco. At this juncture the Almoravid king Yusuf ibn Tashfin, a man of courage and cunning, received from the princes of Spain an invitation to rescue them from the Christian dragon of Castile. Yusuf transported his army across the Strait, received reinforcements from Malaga, Granada, and Seville, and met the forces of Alfonso at Zallaka, near Badajoz (1086). Alfonso sent a courtly message to Yusuf: "Tomorrow [Friday] is your holyday, and Sunday is ours; I propose, therefore, that we join battle on Saturday." Yusuf agreed; Alfonso attacked on Friday; al-Mutamid and Yusuf fought well, the Moslems celebrated their holyday with victorious slaughter, and Alfonso barely escaped with 500 men. Yusuf astonished Spain by returning bootyless to Africa.

Four years later he came back. Al-Mutamid had urged him to destroy the power of Alfonso, who was rearming for a fresh assault. Yusuf fought the Christians indecisively, and assumed sovereign power over Moslem Spain. The poor welcomed him, always preferring new masters to old; the intellectual classes opposed him as representing religious reaction; the theologians embraced him. He took Granada without a blow, and delighted the people by abolishing all taxes not prescribed in the Koran (1090). Al-Mutamid and other emirs joined in a league against him, and formed a holy alliance with Alfonso. Yusuf besieged Cordova; its populace delivered it to him. He surrounded Seville; al-Mutamid fought heroically, saw his son killed, broke down in grief, and surrendered. By 1091 all Andalusia except Saragossa was in Yusuf's hands, and Moslem Spain, ruled from Morocco, was again a province of Africa.

Al-Mutamid was sent as a prisoner to Tangier. While there he received from a local poet, Husri, some verses praising him and asking for a gift. The ruined emir had now only thirty-five ducats ($87) in all the world; he sent them to Husri with apologies for the smallness of the gift. Al-Mutamid was transferred to Aghmat, near Morocco, and lived there for some time in chains, always in destitution, still writing poetry, till his death (1095).

One of his poems might have served as his epitaph:

> Woo not the world too rashly, for behold,
> 　　Beneath the painted silk and broidering,
> 　　It is a faithless and inconstant thing.
> Listen to me, Mutamid, growing old.

> And we—that dreamed youth's blade would never rust,
> 　　Hoped wells from the mirage, roses from the sand—
> 　　The riddle of the world shall understand
> And put on wisdom with the robe of dust.[79]

The Grandeur and Decline of Islam

1058-1258

I. THE ISLAMIC EAST: 1058–1250

WHEN Tughril Beg died (1063) he was succeeded as Seljuq sultan by his nephew Alp Arslan, then twenty-six years of age. A well-disposed Moslem historian describes him as

> tall, with mustaches so long that he used to tie up their ends when he wished to shoot; and never did his arrows miss the mark. He wore so lofty a turban that men were wont to say that from its top to the end of his mustaches was a distance of two yards. He was a strong and just ruler, generally magnanimous, swift to punish tyranny or extortion among his officials, and extremely charitable to the poor. He was also devoted to the study of history, listening with great pleasure and interest to chronicles of former kings, and to works that threw light on their characters, institutions, and methods of administration.[1]

Despite these scholarly inclinations, Alp Arslan lived up to his name—"the lion-hearted hero"—by conquering Herat, Armenia, Georgia, and Syria. The Greek Emperor Romanus IV collected 100,000 varied and ill-disciplined troops to meet Arslan's 15,000 experienced warriors. The Seljuq leader offered a reasonable peace; Romanus rejected it scornfully, gave battle at Manzikert in Armenia (1071), fought bravely amid his cowardly troops, was defeated and captured, and was led before the Sultan. "What would have been your behavior," asked Arslan, "had fortune smiled upon your arms?" "I would have inflicted upon thy body many a stripe," answered Romanus. Arslan treated him with all courtesy, released him on the promise of a royal ransom, and dismissed him with rich gifts.[2] A year later Arslan died by an assassin's knife.

His son Malik Shah (1072–92) was the greatest of the Seljuq sultans. While his general Suleiman completed the conquest of Asia Minor, he himself took Transoxiana as far as Bokhara and Kashgar. His able and devoted prime minister, Nizam al-Mulk, brought to this and Arslan's reign much of the brilliance and prosperity that the Barmakids had given to Baghdad in the days of Harun al-Rashid. For thirty years Nizam organized and controlled administration, policy, and finance, encouraged industry and trade, improved roads, bridges, and inns, and made them safe for all wayfarers. He was a generous friend to artists, poets, scientists; raised splendid buildings in Baghdad; founded and endowed a famous college there; and directed and financed the erection of the Great Dome Chamber in the Friday Mosque at Isfahan. It was apparently at his suggestion that Malik Shah summoned Omar Khayyam and other astronomers to reform the Persian calendar. An old tale tells how Nizam, Omar, and Hasan ibn al-Sabbah, when schoolmates, vowed to share with one another any later good fortune; like so many good stories it is probably a legend, for Nizam was born in 1017, while both Omar and Hasan died in 1123–4; and there is no indication that either of these was a centenarian.[3]

At the age of seventy-five Nizam wrote down his philosophy of government in one of the major works of Persian prose—the *Siyasat-nama*, or *Book of the Art of Rule*. He strongly recommended religious orthodoxy in people and king, considered no government secure without a religious base, and deduced from religion the divine right and authority of the sultan. At the same time he did not spare his divine monarch some human advice on the duties of a sovereign. A ruler must avoid excess in wine and levity; must detect and punish official corruption or tyranny; and must, twice a week, hold public audiences at which even the lowliest subject may present petitions or grievances. Nizam was humane but intolerant; he mourned that Christians, Jews, and Shi'ites were employed by the government, and he denounced the Ismailite sect with especial violence as threatening the unity of the state. In 1092 an Ismaili devotee approached him in the guise of a suppliant, and stabbed him to death.

The assassin was a member of the strangest sect in history. About 1090 an Ismaili leader—the same Hasan ibn al-Sabbah whom legend allied with Omar and Nizam—seized the mountain fortress of Alamut ("Eagle's Nest") in northern Persia, and from that stronghold, 10,000 feet above the sea, waged a campaign of terror and murder against the opponents and persecutors of the Ismaili faith. Nizam's book charged the group with being lineally descended from the communistic Mazdakites of Sasanian Persia. It was a secret fraternity, with diverse grades of initiation, and a Grand Master whom the Crusaders called the "Old Man of the Mountain." The lowest degree of the order included the *fidais*, who were required to obey, without hesitation or scruple, any of their leader's commands. According to Marco Polo, who passed by Alamut in 1271, the Master had arranged behind the fortress a garden peopled like the Mohammedan paradise with "ladies and damsels who dallied with the men to their hearts' content." The candidates for admission to the order were given hashish to drink; when stupefied by it, they were brought into the garden; and on recovering their senses they were told that they were in paradise. After four or five days of wine, women, and good food, they were again drugged with hashish, and were carried from the garden. Waking, they asked for the lost paradise, and were told that they would be readmitted to it, and forever, if they should obey the Master faithfully, or be slain in his service.[4] The youths who complied were called *hashshasheen*, drinkers of hashish—whence the word *assassin*. Hasan ruled Alamut for thirty-five years, and made it a center of assassination, education, and art. The organization long survived him; it seized other strongholds, fought the Crusaders, and (it is alleged) killed Conrad of Montferrat at the behest of Richard Coeur de Lion.[5] In 1256 the Mongols under Hulagu captured Alamut and other Assassin centers; thereafter the members of the order were hunted and slain as nihilist enemies of society. Nevertheless it continued as a religious sect, and became in time peaceable and respectable; its zealous adherents in India, Persia, Syria, and Africa acknowledge the Agha Khan as their head, and yearly pay him a tenth of their revenues.[6]

Malik Shah died a month after his vizier. His sons fought a war of succession, and in the ensuing chaos no united Moslem resistance was offered to the Crusades. Sultan Sinjar at Baghdad restored the Seljuq splendor for a reign (1117–57), and literature prospered under his patronage; but after his death the Seljuq realm disintegrated into independent principalities of petty dynasties and warring kings. At Mosul one of Malik Shah's Kurd slaves, Zangi, founded in 1127 the Atabeg ("Father of the Prince") dynasty, which fought the Crusaders zealously, and extended its rule over Mesopotamia. Zangi's son Nur-ud-din Mahmud (1146–73) conquered Syria, made Damascus his capital, ruled with justice and diligence, and plucked Egypt from the dying Fatimids.

The same decadence that had subjected the Abbasids to Buwayhid and Seljuq domination had, two centuries later, debased the caliphs of Cairo to the role of Shia priests in a state actually ruled by their soldier viziers. Immersed in a numerous harem, hedged in by eunuchs and slaves, emasculated by comfort and concubines, the Fatimids allowed their prime ministers to take the title of kings, and to dispense at will the offices and perquisites of government. In 1164 two candidates competed for this royal vizierate. One of them, Shawar, asked the help of Nur-ud-din, who sent him a small force under Shirkuh. Shirkuh slew Shawar, and made himself vizier. When Shirkuh died (1169) he was succeeded by his nephew al-Malik al-Nasir Salah-ed-din Yusuf ibn Ayyub—i.e., the King, the Defender, the Honor of the Faith, Joseph, son of Job—known to us as Saladin.

He was born (1138) at Tekrit on the upper Tigris, of Kurd—non-Semitic —stock. His father Ayyub rose to be governor first of Baalbek under Zangi, then of Damascus under Nur-ud-din. Saladin, brought up in those cities and courts, learned well the arts of statesmanship and war. But with these he combined orthodox piety, a zealous study of theology, and an almost ascetic simplicity of life; the Moslems number him among their greatest saints. His chief garment was a coarse woolen cloth, his only drink was water, and his sexual temperance (after some early indulgence) aroused all but the emulation of his contemporaries. Sent with Shirkuh to Egypt, he gave so good an account of himself as a soldier that he was put in command over Alexandria, which he successfully defended against the Franks (1167). Made vizier at thirty, he devoted himself to restoring orthodox Mohammedanism in Egypt. In 1171 he had the name of the Shia Fatimid caliph replaced in the public prayers by that of the Abbasid caliph—now merely the orthodox pontiff of Baghdad. Al-Adid, last of the Fatimids, was at the time ill in his palace, and did not notice this ecclesiastical revolution; Saladin kept him fully uninformed, so that the wastrel "might die in peace." This the Caliph did presently, and as no successor was appointed, the Fatimid dynasty came to a quiet end. Saladin made himself governor instead of vizier, and acknowledged Nur-ud-din as his sovereign. When he entered the caliphal palace at Cairo he found there 12,000 occupants, all women except the male relatives of the Caliph; and such wealth in jewelry, furniture, ivory, porcelain, glass, and other objects of art as could hardly be rivaled by any other dignitary of that era. Saladin kept nothing of all this for himself, gave the palace to his captains, and continued to live, in the vizier's chambers, a life of fortunate simplicity.

On Nur-ud-din's death (1173) the provincial governors refused to acknowledge his eleven-year-old son as king, and Syria verged again on chaos. Alleging fear that the Crusaders would take the country, Saladin left Egypt with a force of 700 horsemen, and in swift campaigns made himself master of Syria. Returning to Egypt, he took the title of king, and thereby inaugurated the Ayyubid dynasty (1175). Six years later he set out again, made Damascus his capital, and conquered Mesopotamia. There, as at Cairo, he continued to display the stern orthodoxy of his faith. He built several mosques, hospitals, monasteries, and madrasas or theological schools. He encouraged architecture, discountenanced secular science, and shared Plato's disdain for poetry. All wrongs that came to his knowledge were speedily redressed; and taxes were lowered at the same time that public works were extended and the functions of government were carried on with efficiency and zeal. Islam gloried in the integrity and justice of his rule, and Christendom acknowledged in him an infidel gentleman.

We shall not detail the medley of local dynasties that divided Eastern Islam after his death (1193). His sons lacked his ability, and the Ayyubid rule in Syria ended in three generations (1260). In Egypt it flourished till 1250, and reached its zenith under the enlightened Malik al-Kamil (1218–38), friend of Frederick II. In Asia Minor the Seljuqs established (1077–1327) the sultanate of "Rum" (Rome), and for a time made Konya (St. Paul's Iconium) the center of a lettered civilization. Asia Minor, which had been half Greek since Homer, was now de-Hellenized, and became as Turkish as Turkestan; there, today, Turkey holds its precarious seat in a once Hittite capital. An independent tribe of Turks ruled Khwarizm (1077–1231), and extended its power from the Urals to the Persian Gulf. It was in this condition of political atomism that Jenghiz Khan found Asiatic Islam.

Yet even in these declining years Islam led the world in poetry, science, and philosophy, and rivaled the Hohenstaufens in government. The Seljuq sultans—Tughril Beg, Alp Arslan, Malik Shah, Sinjar—were among the ablest monarchs of the Middle Ages; Nizam al-Mulk ranks with the greatest statesmen; Nur-ud-din, Saladin, and al-Kamil were the equals of Richard I, Louis IX, and Frederick II. All these Moslem rulers, and even the minor kings, continued the Abbasid support of literature and art; at their courts we shall find poets like Omar, Nizami, Sa'di, and Jalal ud-din Rumi; and though philosophy faded out under their cautious orthodoxy, architecture flourished more splendidly than before. The Seljuqs and Saladin persecuted Moslem heresy; but they were so lenient to Christians and Jews that Byzantine historians told of Christian communities inviting Seljuq rulers to come and oust oppressive Byzantine governors.[7] Under the leadership of the Seljuqs and Ayyubids Western Asia again prospered in body and mind. Damascus, Aleppo, Mosul, Baghdad, Isfahan, Rayy, Herat, Amida, Nishapur, and Merv were in this period among the best adorned and most cultured cities in the white man's world. It was a brilliant decay.

II. THE ISLAMIC WEST: 1086–1300

In 1249 al-Salih, last Egyptian sultan of the Ayyubid line, passed away. His widow and former slave, Shajar-al-Durr, connived at the murder of her stepson, and proclaimed herself queen. To save their masculine honor, the Moslem leaders of Cairo chose another former slave, Aybak, as her associate. She married him, but continued to rule; and when he attempted a declaration of independence she had him murdered in his bath (1257). She herself was presently battered to death with wooden shoes by Aybak's women slaves.

Aybak had lived long enough to found the Mamluk dynasty. *Mamluk* meant "owned," and was applied to white slaves, usually strong and fearless Turks or Mongols employed as palace guards by the Ayyubid sultans. As in Rome and Baghdad, so in Cairo the guards became the kings. For 267 years (1250–1517) the Mamluks ruled Egypt, and sometimes Syria (1271–1516); they incarnadined their capital with assassinations, and beautified it with art; their courage saved Syria and Egypt—even Europe—when they routed the Mongols at Ain-Jalut (1260). They received less wide acclaim for saving Palestine from the Franks, and driving the last Christian warrior from Asia.

The greatest and least scrupulous of the Mamluk rulers was al-Malik Baibars (1260–77). Born a Turkish slave, his brave resourcefulness raised him to high command in the Egyptian army. It was he who defeated Louis IX at Mansura in 1250; and ten years later he fought with fierce skill under the Sultan Qutuz at Ain-Jalut. He murdered Qutuz on the way back to Cairo, made himself sultan, and accepted with winning grace the triumph that the city had prepared for his victorious victim. He renewed repeatedly the war against the Crusaders, always with success; and for these holy campaigns Moslem tradition honors him next to Harun and Saladin. In peace, says a contemporary Christian chronicler, he was "sober, chaste, just to his people, even kind to his Christian subjects."[8] He organized the government of Egypt so well that no incompetence among his successors availed to unseat the Mamluks till their overthrow by the Ottoman Turks in 1517. He gave Egypt a strong army and navy, cleared its harbors, roads, and canals, and built the mosque that bears his name.

Another Turkish slave deposed Baibars' son, and became Sultan al-Mansur Sayf-al-Din Qalaun (1279–90). History remembers him chiefly for the great hospital that he built at Cairo, and which he endowed with an annuity of a million dirhems ($500,000). His son Nasir (1293–1340) was thrice enthroned but only twice deposed; built aqueducts, public baths, schools, monasteries, and thirty mosques; dug with the forced labor of 100,000 men a canal connecting Alexandria with the Nile; and exemplified Mamluk ways by slaughtering 20,000 animals for the marriage feast of his son. When Nasir traveled through the desert forty camels bore on their backs a garden of rich earth to provide him with fresh vegetables every day.[9] He depleted the treasury, and condemned his successors to a slow decline of the Mamluk power.

These sultans do not impress us as favorably as the Seljuqs or Ayyubids. They undertook great public works, but most of these were accomplished by peasants and *proletaires* exploited to the limit of human tolerance, and for a government completely irresponsible to either the nation or an aristocracy; assassination was the only known form of recall. At the same time these brutal rulers had good taste and a large spirit in literature and art. The Mamluk period is the most brilliant in the history of medieval Egyptian architecture. Cairo was now (1250–1300) the richest city west of the Indus.[10] Markets teeming with all the necessaries and many of the superfluities of life; the great slave mart where one could buy and sell men and maidens; little shops nestling in the walls, and crowded with goods of flexible price; alleys crawling with men and beasts, noisy with pedlars and carts, deliberately narrow for shade and crooked for defense; homes hidden behind stern façades, rooms dark and cool amid the glare and heat and bustle of the streets, and breathing from an inner court or garden close; interiors lushly furnished with hangings, carpets, embroideries, and works of art; men chewing hashish to produce a dreamy intoxication; women gossiping in the zenana, or furtively flirting in a window bay; music strummed from a thousand lutes, and weird concerts in the Citadel; public parks redolent with flowers and picnicking; canals and the great river dotted with cargo barges, passenger vessels, and pleasure boats: this was the Cairo of medieval Islam. One of its poets sang:

> Beside that garden flowed the placid Nile.
> Oft have I steered my *dahabiya* there;
> Oft have I landed to repose awhile,
> And bask and revel in the sunny smile
> Of her whose presence made the place so fair.[11]

Meanwhile in North Africa a succession of dynasties had their day. Zayrids (972–1148) and Hafsids (1228–1534) ruled Tunisia; Hammadids (1007–1152) governed Algeria; Almoravids (1056–1147) and Almohads (1130–1269) held sway in Morocco. In Spain the victorious Almoravids, once the frugal warriors of Africa, rapidly learned the luxurious ways of the Cordovan and Sevillian princes whom they had replaced. The discipline of war gave way to the blandishments of peace; courage yielded to money as the standard of excellence and the goal of desire; women won by their grace and charms a power rivaled only by theologians promising like joys in paradise. Officials became corrupt, and administration, which had been competent under Yusuf ibn Tashfin (1090–1106), was already debased under Ali his son (1106–43). As governmental negligence grew, brigandage spread; roads became unsafe; commerce languished, wealth declined. The kings of Catholic Spain seized their opportunity, and raided Cordova, Seville, and other cities of Moorish Spain. Again the Moslems turned to Africa for deliverance.

There, in 1121, a religious revolution had raised a new sect to power and violence. Abdallah ibn Tumart denounced both the anthropomorphism of the orthodox and the rationalism of the philosophers; he demanded a return to simplicity of life and creed; and ended by proclaiming himself the Mahdi or Messiah promised in the Shia faith. The barbarous tribes of the Atlas range flocked to him, organized themselves under the name of Almohads or Unitarians, overthrew the Almoravid rulers in Morocco, and found it an easy matter to do the like in Spain. Under the Almohad emirs Abd al-Mumin (1145–63) and Abu Yaqub Yusuf (1163–84) order and prosperity returned to Andalusia and Morocco; literature and learning once more raised their heads; and philosophers were protected on the quiet understanding that they would make their works unintelligible. But Abu Yusuf Yaqub (1184–99) yielded to the theologians, forsook philosophy, and ordered all philosophical works to be burned. His son Muhammad al-Nasir (1199–1214) cared for neither philosophy nor religion; he neglected government, specialized in pleasure, and was overwhelmingly defeated by the united armies of Christian Spain at Las Navas de Tolosa in 1212. Almohad Spain broke into small and independent states, which were conquered by the Christians one by one

—Cordova in 1236, Valencia in 1238, Seville in 1248. The harassed Moors retired to Granada, where the Sierra Nevada, or Snowy Ridge, provided some defense; and well-rivered fields flowered into vineyards, olive orchards, and orange groves. A succession of prudent rulers sustained Granada and its dependencies—Xeres, Jaen, Almeria, and Malaga—against repeated Christian assaults; commerce and industry revived, art flourished, the people gained renown for their gay dress and joyous fetes; and the little kingdom survived till 1492 as the last European foothold of a culture that had made Andalusia for many centuries an honor to mankind.

III. GLIMPSES OF ISLAMIC ART: 1058–1250

It was in this age of Berber domination that Moslem Spain raised the Alhambra at Granada and the Alcazar and Giralda at Seville. The new architectural style is often called Morisco, as having entered from Morocco; but its elements came from Syria and Persia, and mark as well the Taj Mahal in India; so wide and rich was the realm of Moslem art. It was a feminine style, aiming no longer at impressive strength as in the mosques of Damascus, Cordova, and Cairo, but at a delicate beauty in which all skill seemed absorbed in decoration, and the sculptor engulfed the architect.

The Almohads were enthusiastic builders. First they built for defense, and surrounded their major cities with mighty walls and towers, like the Torre del Oro, or Tower of Gold, that guarded the Guadalquivir at Seville. The Alcazar there was a union of fortress and palace, and showed a plain, blunt front to the world. Designed by the Toledan architect Jalubi for Abu Yaqub Yusuf (1181), it became after 1248 the favorite domicile of the Christian kings; it was modified, repaired, restored, or enlarged by Pedro I (1353), Charles V (1526) . . . and Isabella (1833); it is now predominantly Christian in origin but predominantly Moorish—or Christian Moorish ("Mudejar")—in workmanship and style.

The same Abu Yaqub Yusuf who began the Alcazar built in 1171 the great mosque of Seville, of which nothing remains. In 1196 the architect Jabir raised the magnificent minaret of the mosque, known to us as the Giralda. The conquering Christians transformed the mosque into a church (1235); in 1401 this was torn down, and on its site—partly with its materials—was erected the vast cathedral of Seville. Of the Giralda the lowest 230 feet are of the original structure, the remaining 82 are a Christian supplement (1568) completely harmonious with the Moorish base. The upper two thirds are richly ornamented with arcaded balconies and lace-like trellises of stucco and stone. At the top is a powerful bronze figure of Faith (1568), which hardly symbolizes the ever-religious mood of Spain by turning with the winds; hence the Spanish name Giralda—that which turns (*gira*). Towers almost as beautiful were raised by the Moors at Marraqesh (1069) and Rabat (1197).

At Granada, in 1248, Muhammad ibn al-Ahmar (1232–73) ordered the erection of Spain's most famous edifice, the Alhambra—i.e., "the red." The chosen site was a mountain crag bounded by deep ravines, and looking down upon two rivers, the Darro and the Genil. The emir found there a fortress, the Alcazaba, dating from the ninth century; he added to it, built the great outer walls of the Alhambra and the earlier of its palaces, and left everywhere his modest motto: "There is no conqueror but Allah." The immense structure has been repeatedly extended and repaired, by Christians as well as Moors. Charles V added his own palace in square Renaissance style, solemn, incongruous, and incomplete. Following the principles of military architecture as developed in Eastern Islam, the unknown architect designed the enclosure first as a fortress capable of holding 40,000 men.[12] The more luxurious taste of the next two centuries gradually transformed this fortress into a congeries of halls and palaces, nearly all distinguished by unsurpassed delicacy of floral or geometrical decoration, carved or stamped in colored stucco, brick, or stone. In the Court of the Myrtles a pool reflects the foliage and the fretted portico. Behind it rises the battlemented Tower of Comares, where the besieged thought to find a last and impregnable redoubt. Within the tower is the ornate Hall of the Ambassadors; here the emirs of Granada sat enthroned, while foreign emissaries marveled at the art and wealth of the tiny kingdom; here Charles V, looking out from a balcony window upon the gardens, groves, and stream below, mused, "How ill-fated the man who lost all this!" [13] In the main courtyard, the Patio de los Leones, a dozen ungainly marble lions guard a majestic alabaster fountain; the slender columns and flowered capitals of the surrounding arcade, the stalactite archivolts, the Kufic lettering, the time-subdued tints of the filigree arabesques, make this the masterpiece of the Morisco style. Perhaps in their enthusiasm and their luxury the Moors here pressed their art beyond elegance to excess; where all is ornament the eye and soul grow weary even of beauty and skill. This delicacy of decoration leaves a sense of frailty, and sacrifices that impression of secure strength which architecture should convey. And yet nearly all this frosting has survived a dozen earthquakes; the ceiling of the Hall of the Ambassadors fell, but the rest remained. In sum this picturesque ensemble of gardens, palaces, fountains, and balconies suggests both the climax and the decay of Moorish art in Spain: a wealth gone to extravagance, a conquering energy relaxed into a flair for ease, a taste for beauty that has subsided from power and grandeur to elegance and grace.

In the twelfth century Moorish art flowed back from Spain into North Africa, and Marraqesh, Fez, Tlemcen, Tunis, Sfax, and Tripoli reached the apogee of their splendor with handsome palaces, dazzling mosques, and labyrinthine slums. In Egypt and the East a new virility was brought into Islamic art by the Seljuqs, the Ayyubids, and the Mamluks. Southeast of Cairo Saladin and his successors, using the forced labor of captured Crusaders, raised the immense Citadel, probably in imitation of the castles built by the Franks in Syria. At Aleppo the Ayyubids reared the Great Mosque and Citadel, and at Damascus the mausoleum of Saladin. Meanwhile an architectural revolution transformed the old courtyard style of mosque into the madrasa or collegiate mosque throughout Eastern Islam. As mosques increased in number, it was no longer necessary to design them with a large central court to hold a numerous congregation; and the rising demand for schools required new educational facilities. From the mosque proper —now almost always crowned with a dominating dome—four wings or transepts spread, each with its own minarets, a richly decorated portal, and a spacious lecture hall. Normally each of the four orthodox schools of theology and law had its own wing; as an honest sultan said, it was desirable to support all four schools, so that at least one would in any case be found to justify the actions of the government. This revolution in design was continued by the Mamluks in mosques and tombs firmly built in stone, guarded with massive doors of damascened bronze, lighted by windows of stained glass, and brilliant with mosaics, carvings in colored stucco, and such enduring tiles as only Islam knew how to make.

Of Seljuq architectural monuments not one in a hundred has survived. In Armenia the mosque of Ani; at Konya the magnificent portal of the mosque of Diwrigi, the immense mosque of Ala-ud-din, the cavernous porch and embroiderylike façade of the Sirtjeli madrasa; in Mesopotamia the Great Mosque of Mosul, and the mosque of Mustansir at Baghdad; in Persia the tower of Tughril Beg at Rayy, the tomb of Sinjar at Merv, the dazzling mihrab of the Alaviyan Mosque at Hamadan, the ribbed vault and unique squinches of the Friday Mosque at Qasvin, and there, too, the great arches and mihrab of the Haydaria Mosque: these are but a few of the structures that remain to prove the skill of Seljuq architects and the taste of Seljuq kings. But more beautiful than any of these—rivaled in Persia only by the later Tomb of Imam Riza at Mashhad—is the masterpiece of the Seljuq age, the Masjid-i-Jami, or Friday Mosque, of Isfahan. Like Chartres or Notre Dame, it bears the labor and stamp or many centuries; begun in 1088, it was several times restored or enlarged, and reached its present form only in 1612. But the larger of the great brick domes carries the inscription of Nizam al-Mulk, and the date 1088. The porch and the sanctuary portals—one eighty feet high—are adorned with mosaic faïence hardly rivaled in all the history of that art. The inner halls are roofed with ribbed vaults, complex squinches, and pointed arches springing from massive piers. The mihrab (1310) has a stucco relief of vine and lotus foliage, and Kufic lettering, unsurpassed in Islam.

Such monuments laugh out of court the notion that the Turks were barbarians. Just as the Seljuq rulers and viziers were among the most capable statesmen in history, so the Seljuq architects were among the most competent and courageous builders of an Age of Faith distinguished by massive and audacious designs. The Persian flair for ornament was checked by the heroic mold of the Seljuq style; and the union of the two moods brought an architectural outburst in Asia Minor, Iraq, and Iran, strangely contemporary with the Gothic flowering in France. Instead of hiding the mosque in a corner of a court, as the Arabs had done, the

Seljuqs gave it a bold and brilliant façade, raised its height, and led it up to a circular or conical dome that brought all the edifice into unity. The pointed arch, the vault, and the dome were now perfectly combined.[14]

All the arts reached their Moslem zenith in this strange age of grandeur and decay. Pottery seemed to the Persians an indispensable amenity of life; and seldom has the ceramic art reached so heterogeneous an excellence.[15] The techniques of luster decoration, of monochrome or polychrome painting over or under glaze, of enamel, tile, faïence, and glass, now perfected their Egyptian, Mesopotamian, Sasanian, and Syrian heritage. Chinese influence entered, especially in the painting of figures, but it did not dominate the Persian style. Porcelain was imported from China; but the scarcity of kaolin in the Near and Middle East discouraged the Moslem manufacture of this translucent ware. Nevertheless, during the twelfth, thirteenth, and fourteenth centuries Persian pottery remained unrivaled —superior in variety of forms, elegance of proportions, brilliance of decoration, grace and delicacy of line.[16]

In general the minor arts in Islam hardly deserved so slighting a name. Aleppo and Damascus in this period produced frail marvels of glass with enamel designs, and Cairo made for mosques and palaces enameled glass lamps which are among the prizes of art collectors today.* The Fatimid treasury dispersed by Saladin contained thousands of crystal or sardonyx vases whose artistry seems beyond our skill today. The old Assyrian art of metalwork reached now an unprecedented height in Syria and Egypt, whence it passed to Venice in the fifteenth century.[18] Copper, bronze, brass, silver, gold were cast or beaten into utensils, weapons, arms, lamps, ewers, basins, bowls, trays, mirrors, astronomical instruments, flower vases, chandeliers, pen boxes, inkstands, braziers, perfume burners, animal figures, Koran cases, andirons, keys, scissors . . . delicately engraved, and in many instances inlaid with precious metals or stones. Brass table tops were incised with superabundant designs, and magnificent metal grilles were made for sanctuaries, doors, or tombs. A silver salver engraved with ibexes, geese, and the name of Alp Arslan, and dated 1066, now in the Boston Museum of Fine Arts, has been judged "the outstanding silver piece of the Islamic period" of Persian art, "and the most important single object surviving from Seljuq times." [19]

Sculpture remained a dependent art, confined to reliefs and carvings of stone or stucco, to ornamental scripts and arabesques; a reckless ruler might have a statue made of himself or his wife or a singing girl, but such figures were secret sins, rarely exposed to public gaze. Wood carving, however, flourished. Doors, pulpits, mihrabs, lecterns, screens, ceilings, tables, lattice windows, cabinets, boxes, combs were cut in lacelike designs, or were laboriously rounded by cross-legged turners revolving their lathes with a bow. A still more incredible patience produced silks, satins, brocades, embroideries, gold-woven velvets, hangings, tents, and rugs of such delicate weave or fascinating design as set the world wonderingly envious. Marco Polo, visiting Asia Minor about 1270, noted there "the most beautiful rugs in the world." [20] John Singer Sargent thought a certain Persian rug "worth all the pictures ever painted"; [21] yet expert opinion judges extant Persian carpets to be imperfect examples of an art in which Persia has for cen-

---

* A little jug of Saracen enameled glass was bought by the Rothschilds for $13,650.[17]

turies led the world. Only tattered fragments remain of Iranian rugs from the Seljuq age, but we may surmise their excellence from their representation in the miniatures of the Mongol period.

Painting in Islam was a major art in miniatures, and an ever less minor art in murals and portraiture. The Fatimid Caliph Amir (1101–30) engaged artists to paint in his rooms at Cairo the portraits of contemporary poets; [22] apparently the old prohibition of "graven images" was weakening. Seljuq painting reached its height in Transoxiana, where Sunnite prejudices against representation was diluted by distance; and Turkish manuscripts picture their heroes abundantly. No certainly Seljuq miniature has reached us, but the heyday of the art in the ensuing Mongol period of Eastern Islam leaves little doubt of its flourishing in Seljuq times. Subtle minds and hands made ever lovelier Korans for Seljuq, Ayyubid, or Mamluk mosques, monasteries, dignitaries, and schools, and engraved upon the leather or lacquer bindings designs as delicate as a spider's web. Rich men spent small fortunes in engaging artists to make the most beautiful books ever known. A corps of papermakers, calligraphers, painters, and bookbinders in some cases worked for seventeen years on one volume. Paper had to be of the best; brushes were put together, we are told, from the white neck hairs of kittens not more than two years old; blue ink was sometimes made from powdered lapis lazuli, and could be worth its weight in gold; and liquid gold was not thought too precious for some lines or letters of design or text. "Imagination," said a Persian poet, "cannot grasp the joy that reason draws from a fine-drawn line." [23]

IV. THE AGE OF OMAR KHAYYAM: 1038–1122

The artists of this age were apparently equaled in number by the poets and savants. Cairo, Alexandria, Jerusalem, Baalbek, Aleppo, Damascus, Mosul, Emesa, Tus, Nishapur, and many other cities boasted colleges; Baghdad alone had thirty in 1064. A year later Nizam al-Mulk added another, the Nizamiya; in 1234 the Caliph Mustansir founded still another, which in size, architecture, and equipment surpassed all the rest; one traveler called it the most beautiful building in the city. It contained four distinct law schools, in which qualified students received free tuition, food, and medical care, and a monthly gold dinar for other expenses; it contained a hospital, a bathhouse, and a library freely open to students and staff. Women probably attended college in some cases, for we hear of a shaikha—a lady professor—whose lectures, like Aspasia's or Hypatia's, drew large audiences (c. 1178).[24] Libraries were now richer and more numerous than ever in Islam; Moslem Spain alone had seventy public libraries. Grammarians, lexicographers, encyclopedists, and historians continued to flourish. Collective biography was a Moslem hobby and forte: Ibn al-Qifti (d. 1248) wrote the lives of 414 philosophers and scientists; Ibn Abi Usaybia (1203–70) performed a like service for 400 physicians; Muhammad Awfi (1228) achieved an encyclopedia of 300 Persian poets without mentioning Omar Khayyam;

and Muhammad ibn Khallikan (1211–82) surpassed all other singlehanded works of this kind in his *Obituaries of Men of Note*, containing brief anecdotal lives of 865 distinguished Mohammedans. It is remarkably accurate for a book covering so wide a field; Ibn Khallikan nevertheless apologized for its imperfections, saying, in its final words, that "God has allowed no book to be faultless except the Koran." Muhammad al-Shahrastani, in a *Book of Religions and Sects* (1128), analyzed the leading faiths and philosophies of the world, and summarized their history; no contemporary Christian could have written so learned and impartial a work.

Moslem fiction never rose above the episodic picaresque proliferation of tales unified only by the persistence of a single character. After the Koran, the *Thousand Nights and a Night*, and the fables of Bidpai, the most popular book in Islam was the *Maqamat* (*Discourses*) of Abu Muhammad al-Hariri (1054–1122) of Basra. Here, in rhymed Arabic prose, are the adventures of the charming scoundrel Abu Zaid, who wins forgiveness for his pranks, crimes, and blasphemies by his genial humor, resourceful cleverness, and tempting philosophy:

> Obey not the fool who forbids thee to pull beauty's rose when in full bloom thou'rt free to possess it; pursue thine end still, though it seem past thy skill; let them say what they will; take thy pleasure and bless it! [25]

Nearly every literate Moslem now wrote poetry, and nearly every ruler encouraged it. If we may take the word of Ibn Khaldun, hundreds of poets could be found at the Almoravid and Almohad courts in Africa and Spain.[26] At a gathering of rival poets in Seville, el-Aama et-Toteli (i.e., the Blind Poet of Tudela) won the prize with lines that sum up half the poetry of the world:

> When she laughs, pearls appear; when she removes her veil, the moon is seen;
> The universe is too narrow to contain her; yet she is enclosed in my heart.[27]

The other poets, we are told, tore up their verses unread. In Cairo Zuheyr sang of love long after his hair was white. In Eastern Islam the breakup of the Empire into small kingdoms increased the number and rivalry of patrons, and helped literature, as in nineteenth-century Germany. Persia was the richest of the nations in her poets. Anwari of Khurasan (fl. 1185) rhymed for a time at the court of Sinjar, whom he praised only next to himself.

> I have a soul ardent as fire, a tongue fluent as water,
> A mind sharpened by intelligence, and verse devoid of flaw.
> Alas! there is no patron worthy of my eulogies!
> Alas! there is no sweetheart worthy of my odes! [28]

Quite as confident was his contemporary Khagani (1106–85), whose arrogance provoked his tutor to a genealogical barb:

My dear Khagani, skillful though you be
In verse, one little hint I give you free:
Mock not with satire any older poet;
Perhaps he's your sire, though you don't know it.[29]

Europe knows Persian poetry chiefly through Omar Khayyam; Persia classes him among her scientists, and considers his quatrains the casual amusement of "one of the greatest mathematicians of medieval times." [30] Abu'l-Fath Umar Khayyami ibn Ibrahim was born at Nishapur in 1038. His cognomen meant tentmaker, but proves nothing about his trade or that of his father Abraham; occupational names, in Omar's time, had lost their literal application, as among the Smiths, Taylors, Bakers, and Porters of our land. History knows little of his life, but records several of his works. His *Algebra*, translated into French in 1857, made significant advances both on al-Khwarizmi and on the Greeks; its partial solution of cubic equations has been judged "perhaps the very highest peak of medieval mathematics." [31] Another of his works on algebra (a manuscript in the Leiden Library) studied critically the postulates and definitions of Euclid. In 1074 the Sultan Malik Shah commissioned him and others to reform the Persian calendar. The outcome was a calendar that required a day's correction every 3770 years—slightly more accurate than ours, which requires a day's correction every 3330 years; [32] we may leave the choice to the next civilization. Mohammedan religion proved stronger than Moslem science, and Omar's calendar failed to win acceptance over Mohammed's. The astronomer's repute is reflected in an anecdote told by Nizami-i-Arudi, who had known him at Nishapur:

> In the winter of A.H. 508 [A.D. 1114–5] the King sent a messenger to Merv bidding its governor tell Umar al-Khayyami to select a favorable time for him to go hunting. . . . Umar looked into the matter for two days, made a careful choice of the desirable time, and himself went to superintend the mounting of the King. When the King had gone a short distance the sky became overcast, a wind rose, and snow and mist supervened. All present fell to laughing, and the King wished to turn back. But Umar said, "Have no anxiety, for this very hour the clouds will clear away, and during these five days there will be no drop of moisture." So the King rode on, and the clouds opened, and during those five days there was no wet, and no cloud was seen.[33]

The *rubaiyah* or quatrain (from *rubai*, composed of four) is in its Persian form a poem of four lines rhyming *aaba*. It is an epigram in the Greek sense, as the expression of a completed thought in terse poetic form. Its origin is unknown, but it long antedated Omar. In Persian literature it is never part of a longer poem, but forms an independent whole, hence Persian collectors

of *rubaiyat* arrange them not by their thought sequence but in the alphabetical order of the final letter of the rhyming syllables.[34] Thousands of
Persian quatrains exist, mostly of uncertain authorship; over 1200 of them
have been attributed to Omar, but often questionably. The oldest Persian
manuscript of the *Rubaiyat* of Omar (in the Bodleian Library at Oxford)
goes back only to 1460, and contains 158 stanzas, alphabetically arranged.[35]
Several of these have been traced to Omar's predecessors —some to Abu
Said, one to Avicenna;[37] it is hardly possible, save in a few cases, to assert
positively that Omar wrote any particular one of the quatrains ascribed
to him.[38]

The German Orientalist Von Hammer, in 1818, was the first European
to call attention to Omar's *rubaiyat*. In 1859 Edward FitzGerald translated
seventy-five of them into English verse of a unique and pithy excellence.
The first edition, though its price was a penny, found few purchasers;
persistent and enlarged reissues, however, succeeded in transforming the
Persian mathematician into one of the most widely read poets in the world.
Of the 110 quatrains translated by FitzGerald forty-nine—in the judgment of
those familiar with the original—are faithful paraphrases of single quatrains
in the Persian text; forty-four are composites, each taking something from
two or more quatrains; two "reflect the whole spirit of the original poem";
six are from quatrains sometimes included in Omar's text, but probably not
his; two were influenced by FitzGerald's reading of Hafiz; three have no
source in any extant text of Omar, were apparently fathered by FitzGerald,
and were suppressed by him in his second edition.[39] Of stanza lxxxi—

> O Thou, who man of baser earth didst make,
> And e'en with Paradise devise the snake,
>   For all the sin wherewith the face of man
> Is blackened, man's forgiveness give—and take!—

no corresponding passage can be found in Omar.[40] For the rest a comparison of FitzGerald's version with a literal translation of the Persian text
indicates that FitzGerald always reflects the spirit of Omar, and is as true
to the original as may reasonably be expected of so poetic a paraphrase.
The Darwinian mood of FitzGerald's time moved him to ignore Omar's
kindly humor, and to deepen the antitheological strain. But Persian authors
only a century later than Omar describe him in terms quite consistent with
FitzGerald's interpretation. Mirsad al-Ibad (1223) called him "an unhappy
philosopher, atheist, and materialist"; al-Qifti's *History of the Philosophers*
(1240) ranked him as "without an equal in astronomy and philosophy," but
termed him an advanced freethinker, constrained by prudence to bridle his
tongue; al-Sharazuri, in the thirteenth century, represented him as an ill-
tempered follower of Avicenna, and listed two works by Omar on philosophy, now lost. Some Sufis sought a mystic allegory in Omar's quatrains,

but the Sufi Najmud-din-Razi denounced him as the arch freethinker of his time.[41]

Influenced perhaps by science, perhaps by the poems of al-Ma'arri, Omar rejected theology with patient scorn, and boasted of stealing prayer rugs from the mosque.[42] He accepted the fatalism of the Moslem creed, and, shorn of hope for an afterlife, fell into a pessimism that sought consolation in study and wine. Stanzas cxxxii-iii of the Bodleian manuscript raise intoxication almost to a world philosophy:

> 'Tis I who have swept with my mustaches the wineshop,
> To what is good and ill of both worlds said good-bye.
> Should both worlds fall like a polo ball into the street,
> You shall seek me out. A-sleeping like a drunkard I shall be. . . .
> From all that is, save wine, to refrain is well. . . .
> To be inebriate, squalid, and vagrant is well.
> One draught of wine is well from Moon to Fish [43]—

that is, from one end of the sky to the other. But when we note how many Persian poets chant similar eulogies to unconsciousness, we wonder is not this Bacchic piety a pose and literary form, like Horace's ambigendrous loves?

Probably such incidental quatrains give a false impression of Omar's life; they doubtless played a minor role in his eighty-five years. We should picture him not as a drunkard sprawling in the street, but as an old savant quietly content with cubic equations, a few constellations and astronomic charts, and an occasional cup with fellow scholars "star-scattered on the grass." He seems to have loved flowers with the passion of a people bound to a parched terrain; and if we trust Nizami-i-Arudi, he was granted his wish to lie where flowers bloomed.

> In the year A.H. 506 [A.D. 1112–3] Umar Khayyami and Muzaffar-i-Isfizari had alighted in the city of Balkh . . . in the house of Emir Abu Sa'd, and I had joined that assembly. In this friendly gathering I heard that Proof of the Truth (Omar) say, "My grave will be in a spot where trees will shed their blossoms on me twice a year." This seemed to me impossible, though I knew that one such as he would not speak idle words.
>
> When I arrived at Nishapur in the year 530 [1135], it being then some thirteen years since that great man had veiled his countenance in the dust . . . I went to visit his grave. . . . His tomb lay at the foot of a garden wall, over which pear trees and peach trees thrust their heads; and on his grave had fallen so many flower petals that his dust was hidden beneath them. Then I remembered his words at Balkh, and I fell to weeping, because on the face of the earth, in all the regions of the habitable globe, I nowhere saw one like unto him.[44]

V. THE AGE OF SA'DI: 1150–1291

Five years after Omar's death a poet far more honored in Persia was born at Gandzha, now Kirovabad, near Tiflis. As if in foil to Omar, Ilyas Abu Muhammad, later known as Nizami, lived a life of genuine piety, rigorously abstained from wine, and devoted himself to parentage and poetry. His *Romance of Layla and Majnun* (1188) is the most popular of all love stories in Persian verse. Qays Majnun (i.e., the Mad) becomes enamored of Layla, whose father compels her to marry another man; Majnun, delirious with disappointment, retires from civilization to the wilderness; only when Layla's name is mentioned does he return to brief sanity. Widowed, she joins him, but dies soon afterward; and Romeo Qays kills himself on her grave. Translation cannot render the melodious intensity of the original.

Even the mystics sang of love, but we have their solemn assurance that the passion they portrayed was but a symbol for the love of God. Muhammad ibn Ibrahim, known to literature as Farid al-Din Attar ("Pearl of Faith, Druggist"), was born near Nishapur (1119), and received his final name from vending perfumes. Feeling a call to religion, he left his shop and entered a Sufi monastery. His forty books, all in Arabic, include 200,000 lines of poetry. His most famous work was the *Mantiq al-Tayr*, or *Discourse of the Birds*. Thirty birds (i.e., Sufis) plan a united search for the king of all birds, Simurgh (Truth). They pass through six valleys: Search, Love, Knowledge, Detachment (from all personal desire), Unification (where they perceive that all things are one), and Bewilderment (from losing all sense of individual existence). Three of the birds reach the seventh valley, Annihilation (of the self), and knock at the door of the hidden king. The royal chamberlain shows each of them a record of its deeds; they are overcome with shame, and collapse into the dust. But from this dust they rise again as forms of light; and now they realize that they and Simurgh (which means thirty birds) are one. They lose themselves henceforth in Simurgh, as shadows vanish in the sun. In other works Attar put his pantheism more directly: reason cannot know God, for it cannot understand itself; but love and ecstasy can reach to God, for He is the essential reality and power in all things, the sole source of every act and motion, the spirit and life of the world. No soul is happy until it loses itself as a part in this spirit as the whole; longing for such union is the only true religion; self-effacement in that union is the only true immortality.[45] The orthodox denounced all this as heresy; a crowd attacked Attar's house and burned it to the ground. However, he was relatively indestructible; tradition claims for him a life of 110 years. Before he died, we are told, he laid his hands in blessing upon the child who would hail him as master, and eclipse his fame.

Jalal-ud-Din Rumi (1201–73) was a native of Balkh, but lived most of his life at Konya. A mysterious Sufi, Shams-i-Tabrizi, came there to preach, and Jalal was so moved by him that he founded the famous order of Mawlawi, or Dancing Dervishes, which still makes Konya its capital. In a comparatively short life Jalal wrote several hundred poems. The shorter ones, collected as his *Divan* or *Book of Odes*, are marked by such depth of feeling, sincerity, and richness, yet naturalness, of imagery as place them at the top of all religious poetry composed since the Psalms. Jalal's main work, the *Mathnawi-i-Ma'nawi* (*Spiritual Couplets*), is a diffuse exposition of Sufism, a religious epic outweighing in bulk all the legacy of "Homer." It has passages of great beauty, but a thing of beauty, laden with words, is not a joy forever. The theme again is universal unity.

> One knocked at the Beloved's door, and a Voice asked from within, "Who is there?"—and he answered, "It is I." Then the Voice said, "This house will not hold Me and Thee," and the door stayed shut. Then went the Lover into the desert, and in solitude fasted and prayed. After a year he returned, and knocked again at the door. And again the Voice asked, "Who is there?" And the Lover said, "It is Thyself!" And the door was opened to him.[46]

> I looked about me to find him. He was not on the Cross. I went to the idol temple, to the ancient pagoda; no trace of Him was visible there. . . . I bent the reins of search to the Kaaba; He was not in that resort of old and young. I questioned Ibn Sina [Avicenna] of His state; He was not in Ibn Sina's range. I gazed into my own heart. There I saw Him. He was nowhere else.

> Every form you see has its archetype in the placeless world;
> If the form perishes, no matter, since its original is everlasting.
> Every fair shape you have seen, every deep saying you have heard—
> Be not cast down that it perished, for that is not so. . . .
> While the fountains flow, the rivers run from it.
> Put grief out of your head, and keep quaffing this river-water;
> Do not think of the water failing, for this water is without end.
> From the moment you came into the world of being
> A ladder was placed before you that you might escape.
> First you were mineral; later you turned to plant;
> Then you became animal; how should this be a secret to you?
> Afterwards you were made man, with knowledge, reason, faith. . . .
> When you have traveled on from now, you will doubtless become an
> angel. . . .
> Pass again from angelhood; enter that ocean,
> That your drop may become a sea. . . .
> Leave aside this "Son"; say ever "One," with all your soul.[48]

And lastly Sa'di. His real name, of course, was much longer—Musharrit ud-Din ibn Muslih ud-Din Abdallah. His father held a post at the court of the

Atabeg Sad ibn Zangi at Shiraz; when the father died the Atabeg adopted the boy, and Sa'di, following Moslem custom, added his patron's name to his own. Scholars debate the dates of his earthly stay—1184–1283,[49] 1184–1291,[50] 1193–1291;[51] in any case he almost spanned a century. "In my youth," he tells us, "I was overmuch religious . . . scrupulously pious and abstinent."[52] After graduating from the Nizamiya College at Baghdad (1226) he began those extraordinary *Wanderjahre* which took him for thirty years through all the Near and Middle East, India, Ethiopia, Egypt, and North Africa. He knew every hardship, and all degrees of poverty; he complained that he had no shoes, until he met a man without feet, "whereupon I thanked Providence for its bounty to myself."[53] In India he exposed the mechanism of a miracle-working idol, and killed the hidden Brahmin who was the god of the machine; in his later rollicking verse he recommended a like summary procedure with all quacks:

> You too, should you chance to discover such trick,
> Make away with the trickster; don't spare him; be quick!
> For if you should suffer the scoundrel to live,
> Be sure that to you he no quarter will give.
> So I finished the rogue, notwithstanding his wails,
> With stones, for dead men, as you know, tell no tales.[54]

He fought against the Crusaders, was captured by the "Infidels," and was ransomed. Gratefully he married the daughter of his ransomer. She turned out to be an intolerable vixen. "The ringlets of the lovely," he wrote, "are a chain on the feet of reason."[55] He divorced her, encountered more ringlets, assumed more chains. He outlived this second wife, retired at fifty to a garden hermitage in Shiraz, and stayed there the last fifty years of his life.

Having lived, he began to write; all his major works, we are told, were composed after this retirement. The *Pandnama* is a *Book of Wisdom*; the *Divan* is a collection of short poems, mostly in Persian, some in Arabic, some pious, some obscene. The *Bustan*, or *Orchard*, expounds in didactic verse Sa'di's general philosophy, relieved by passages of tender sensuality:

> Never had I known moments more delicious. That night I clasped my lady to my breast and gazed into her eyes swimming with sleep. . . . I said to her: "Beloved, my slender cypress tree, now is not the time to sleep. Sing, my nightingale! Let thy mouth open as unfolds the rosebud. Sleep no more, turmoil of my heart! Let thy lips offer me the philter of thy love." And my lady looked upon me and murmured low: "Turmoil of thy heart? Yet dost thou wake me?" . . . Thy lady has repeated all this time that she has never belonged to another. . . . And thou dost smile, for thou knowest that she lies. But what matter? Are her lips less warm beneath thy lips? Are her shoulders less soft beneath thy caress? . . . They say the breeze of May is sweet, as the perfume of the rose, the song of the nightingale, the

green plain, and the blue sky. O thou who knowest not, all these are
sweet only when one's lady is there! [56]

The *Gulistan,* or *Rose Garden* (1258), is a medley of instructive anecdotes
interspersed with delectable poetry.

> An unjust king asked a holy man, "What is more excellent than
> prayer?" The holy man said: "For you to remain asleep till midday,
> that for this one interval you may not afflict mankind." [57] Ten der-
> vishes can sleep on one rug, but two kings cannot be accommodated
> in a whole kingdom.[58] If you court riches, ask not for content-
> ment.[59] The religious man who can be vexed by an injury is as yet a
> shallow brook.[60] Never has anyone acknowledged his own igno-
> rance, except that person who, while another is talking and has not
> yet finished, begins to speak.[61] Had you but one perfection and sev-
> enty faults, your lover would discern only that one perfection.[62]
> Hurry not . . . learn deliberation. The Arab horse makes a few
> stretches at full speed, and breaks down; the camel, at its deliberate
> pace, travels night and day, and gets to the end of its journey.[63] Ac-
> quire knowledge, for no reliance can be placed on riches or posses-
> sions. . . . Were a professional man to lose his fortune, he need not
> feel regret, for his knowledge is of itself a mine of wealth.[64] The se-
> verity of the schoolmaster is more useful than the indulgence of the
> father.[65] Were intellect to be annihilated from the face of the earth,
> nobody could be brought to say, "I am ignorant." * [66] Levity in a nut is
> a sign of its being empty.[67]

Sa'di was a philosopher, but he forfeited the name by writing intelligibly.
His was a healthier philosophy than Omar's; it understood the consolations
of faith, and knew how to heal the sting of knowledge with the simple blessings of a kindly life; Sa'di experienced all the tragedies of the human comedy, and yet insisted on a hundred years. But he was a poet as well as a
philosopher: sensitive to the form and texture of every beauty from a
woman's "cypress limbs" to a star that for a moment possesses by itself all
the evening sky; and capable of expressing wisdom or platitude with brevity, delicacy, and grace. He was never at a loss for an illuminating comparison or an arresting phrase. "To give education to the worthless is like
throwing walnuts upon a dome"; [68] "a friend and I were associating like
two kernels in one almond shell"; [69] "if the orb of the sun had been in the
wallet" of this stingy merchant, "nobody would have seen daylight in the
world till Judgment Day." [70] In the end, despite his wisdom, Sa'di remained
the poet, surrendering his wisdom with a whole heart to the rich slavery
of love.

---

* Cf. the first lines of Descartes' *Discourse on Method:* "Good sense is of all things in the
world the most equally distributed, for everybody thinks himself so abundantly provided with
it, that even those most difficult to please in other matters do not commonly desire more of it
than they already possess."

Fortune suffers me not to clasp my sweetheart to my breast,
Nor lets me forget my exile long in a kiss on her sweet lips pressed.
The noose wherewith she is wont to snare her victims far and wide
I will snatch away, that so one day I may lure her to my side.
Yet I shall not dare caress her hair with a hand that is overbold,
For snared therein, like birds in a gin, are the hearts of lovers untold.
A slave am I to that gracious form, which, as I picture it,
Is clothed in grace with a measuring rod, as tailors a garment fit.
O cypress tree, with silver limbs, this color and scent of thine
Have shamed the scent of the myrtle plant and the bloom of the eglantine.
Judge with thine eyes, and set thy foot in the fair and free,
And tread the jasmine under thy foot, and the flowers of the Judas tree. . . .
O wonder not if in time of spring thou dost rouse such jealousy
That the cloud doth weep while the flowrets smile, and all on account of thee!
If o'er the dead thy feet should tread, those feet so fair and fleet,
No wonder it were if thou shouldst hear a voice from his winding sheet.
Distraction is banned from this our land in the time of our lord the King,
Save that I am distracted with love of thee, and men with the songs I sing.[71]

VI. MOSLEM SCIENCE: 1057–1258

Moslem scholars divided the medieval peoples into two classes—those that cultivated science, and those that did not. In the first class they named the Hindus, Persians, Babylonians, Jews, Greeks, Egyptians, and Arabs. These, in their view, were the elite of the world; the others, of whom the Chinese and the Turks were the best, resembled animals rather than men.[72] The judgment sinned chiefly against the Chinese.

The Moslems continued, in this period, their unchallenged ascendancy in science. In mathematics the most signal advances were made in Morocco and Azerbaijan; we see here again the range of Islamic civilization. In 1229 Hasan al-Marraqushi (i.e., of Marraqesh) published tables of sines for each degree, and tables of versed sines, arc sines, and arc cotangents. A generation later Nasir ud-Din al-Tusi (i.e., of Tus) issued the first treatise in which trigonometry was considered as an independent science rather than an appendage to astronomy; this *Kitab shakl al-qatta* remained without a rival in its field until the *De Triangulis* of Regiomontanus two centuries later. Perhaps Chinese trigonometry, which appears in the second half of the thirteenth century, was of Arabic origin.[73]

The outstanding work of physical science in this age was the *Kitab mizan al-hikmah*, or *Book of the Balance of Wisdom*, written about 1122 by a Greek slave from Asia Minor, Abu'l Fath al-Khuzini. It gave a history of physics, formulated the laws of the lever, compiled tables of specific gravity for many liquids and solids, and proposed a theory of gravitation as a universal force drawing all things towards the center of the earth.[74] Water wheels, known to the Greeks and Romans, were improved by the Moslems; the Crusaders saw such wheels raising water from the Orontes, and introduced them into Germany.[75] Alchemists flourished; they knew, said al-Latif, "300 ways of making dupes." [76] One alchemist drew from Nur-ud-din a substantial loan for alchemical research, and disappeared; a wit, apparently unreproved, published a list of fools in which Nur-ud-din's name led all the rest; and offered, if the alchemist would return, to substitute his name for that of the Sultan.[77]

In 1081 Ibrahim al-Sahdi of Valencia constructed the oldest known celestial globe, a brass sphere 209 millimeters (81.5 inches) in diameter; upon its surface, in forty-seven constellations, were engraved 1015 stars in their respective magnitudes.[78] The Giralda of Seville (1190) was an observatory as well as a minaret; there Jabir ibn Aflah made the observations for his *Islah al-majisti*, or *Correction of the Almagest* (1240). The same reaction against Ptolemaic astronomy marked the works of Abu Ishaq al-Bitruji (Alpetragius) of Cordova, who paved the way for Copernicus by destructively criticizing the theory of epicycles and eccentrics through which Ptolemy had sought to explain the paths and motions of the stars.

The age produced two geographers of universal medieval renown. Abu Abdallah Muhammad al-Idrisi was born at Ceuta (1100), studied at Cordova, and wrote in Palermo, at the behest of King Roger II of Sicily, his *Kitab al-Rujari* (*Roger's Book*). It divided the earth into seven climatic zones, and each zone into ten parts; each of the seventy parts was illustrated by a detailed map; these maps were the crowning achievement of medieval cartography, unprecedented in fullness, accuracy, and scope. Al-Idrisi, like most Moslem scientists, took for granted the sphericity of the earth. Rivaling him for the honor of being the greatest medieval geographer was Abu Abdallah Yaqut (1179–1229). Born a Greek in Asia Minor, he was captured in war and enslaved; but the Baghdad merchant who bought him gave him a good education, and then freed him. He traveled much, first as a merchant, then as a geographer fascinated by places and their diverse populations, dress, and ways. He rejoiced to find ten libraries at Merv, one containing 12,000 volumes; the discriminating curators allowed him to take as many as 200 volumes at a time to his room; those who have loved books as the lifeblood of great men will sense the dusty joy he felt in these treasuries of the mind. He moved on to Khiva and Balkh; there the Mongols almost caught him in their murderous advance; he fled, naked but clutching his manuscripts, across Persia to Mosul. While buttering the bread of poverty as a copyist, he completed his *Mu'jam al-Buldan* (1228)—a vast geographical encyclopedia which summed up nearly all medieval knowledge of the globe. Yaqut included almost everything —astronomy, physics, archaeology, ethnography, history, giving the co-ordinates of the cities and the lives and works of their famous men. Seldom has any man so loved the earth.

Botany, almost forgotten since Theophrastus, revived with the Moslems of this age. Al-Idrisi wrote a herbal, but stressed the botanical rather than merely the medicinal interest of 360 plants. Abu'l Abbas of Seville (1216) earned the surname of al-Nabati, the Botanist, by his studies of plant life from the Atlantic to the Red Sea. Abu Muhammad ibn Baitar of Malaga (1190–1248) gathered all Islamic botany into a vast work of extraordinary erudition, which remained the standard botanical authority till the sixteenth century, and marked him as the greatest botanist and pharmacist of the Middle Ages.[79] Ibn al-Awan of Seville (1190) won a like pre-eminence in agronomy; his *Kitab al-Falaha* (*Book of the Peasant*) analyzed soils and manures, described the cultivation of 585 plants and fifty fruit trees, explained methods of grafting, and discussed the symptoms and cures of plant diseases. This was the most complete treatment of agricultural science in the whole medieval period.[80]

In this as in the preceding age the Moslems produced the leading physicians of Asia, Africa, and Europe. They excelled especially in ophthalmology, perhaps because eye diseases were so prevalent in the Near East; there, as elsewhere, medicine was paid most to cure, least to prevent. Operations for cataract were numerous. Khalifah ibn-abi'l-Mahasin of Aleppo (1256) was so confident of his skill that he operated for cataract on a one-eyed man.[81] Ibn Baitar's *Kitab al-Jami* made medicinal-botanical history; it listed 1400 plants, foods, and drugs, 300 of them new; analyzed their chemical constitution and healing power; and added acute observations on their use in therapy. But the greatest name in this acme of Moslem medicine is Abu Marwan ibn Zuhr (1091–1162) of Seville, known to the European medical world as Avenzoar. He was the third in six generations of famous physicians, all of one family line, and each at the top of his profession. His *Kitab al-Tasir*, or *Book of Simplification on Therapeutics and Diet*, was written at the request of his friend Averroës, who (himself the greatest philosopher of the age) considered him the greatest physician since Galen. Ibn Zuhr's forte was clinical description; he left classical analyses of mediastinal tumors, pericarditis, intestinal tuberculosis, and pharyngeal paralysis.[82] Translations of the *Tasir* into Hebrew and Latin deeply influenced European medicine.

Islam led the world also in the equipment and competence of its hospitals. One founded by Nur-ud-din at Damascus in 1160 gave free treatment and drugs during three centuries; for 267 years, we are told, its fires were never extinguished.[83] Ibn Jubayr, coming to Baghdad in 1184, marveled at the great Bimaristan Adadi, a hospital rising like some royal palace along the banks of the Tigris; here food and drugs were given to the patients without charge.[84] In Cairo, in 1285, Sultan Qalaun began the Maristan al-Mansur, the greatest hospital of the Middle Ages. Within a spacious quadrangular enclosure four buildings rose around a courtyard adorned with arcades and cooled with fountains and brooks. There were separate wards for diverse diseases and for convalescents; laboratories, a dispensary, out-patient clinics, diet kitchens, baths, a library, a chapel, a lecture hall, and particularly pleasant accommodations for the insane. Treatment was given gratis to men and women, rich and poor, slave and free; and a sum of money was disbursed to each convalescent on his departure, so that he need not at once return to work. The sleepless were provided with soft music, professional storytellers, and perhaps books of history.[85] Asylums for the care of the insane existed in all the major cities of Islam.

VII. AL-GHAZALI AND THE RELIGIOUS REVIVAL

Amid these advances of science the old orthodoxy fought to keep the loyalty of the educated classes. The conflict between religion and science led many to skepticism, some to open atheism. Al-Ghazali divided Moslem thinkers into three groups—theists, deists or naturalists, and materialists—and denounced all three groups alike as infidels. The theists accepted God and immortality, but denied creation and the resurrection of the body, and called heaven and hell spiritual conditions only; the deists acknowledged a deity but rejected immortality, and viewed the world as a self-operating machine; the materialists completely rejected the idea of God. A semi-organized movement, the Dahriyya, professed a frank agnosticism; several of these doubting Thomases lost their heads to the executioner. "You torment yourself for nothing," said Isbahan ibn Qara to a pious faster during Ramadan; "man is like a seed of grain that sprouts and grows up and is then mowed down to perish forever. . . . Eat and drink!"[86]

It was in reaction against such skepticism that Mohammedanism produced its greatest theologian, the Augustine and the Kant of Islam. Abu Hamid al-Ghazali was born at Tus in 1058, lost his father early, and was reared by a Sufi friend. He studied law, theology, and philosophy; at thirty-three he was appointed to the chair of law at the Nizamiya College in Baghdad; soon all Islam acclaimed his eloquence, erudition, and dialectical skill. After four years of this glory he was laid low by a mysterious disease. Appetite and digestion failed, paralysis of the tongue occasionally distorted his speech, and his mind began to break down. A wise physician diagnosed his case as mental in origin. In truth, as al-Ghazali later confessed in his remarkable autobiography, he had lost belief in the capacity of reason to sanction the Mohammedan faith; and the hypocrisy of his orthodox teaching had become unbearable. In 1094 he left Baghdad, ostensibly on a pilgrimage to Mecca; actually he went into seclusion, seeking silence, contemplation, and peace. Unable to find in science the support he sought for his crumbling faith, he turned from the outer to the internal world; there, he thought, he found a direct and immaterial reality, which offered a firm basis for belief in a spiritual universe. He subjected sensation—on which materialism seemed to rest—to critical scrutiny; accused the senses of making the stars appear small when, to be so visible from afar, they must be vastly larger than the earth; and concluded from a hundred such examples that sensation by itself could be no certain test of truth. Reason was higher, and corrected one sense with another; but in the end it too rested on sensation. Perhaps there was in man a form of knowledge, a guide to truth, surer than reason? Al-Ghazali felt that he had found this in the introspective meditation of the mystic: the Sufi came closer than the philosopher to the hidden core of reality; the highest knowledge lay in gazing upon the miracle of mind until God appeared within the self, and the self itself disappeared in the vision of an all-absorbing One.[87]

In this mood al-Ghazali wrote his most influential book—*Tahafut al-Filasifa* (*The Destruction of Philosophy*). All the arts of reason were turned against reason. By a "transcendental dialectic" as subtle as Kant's, the Moslem mystic argued that reason leads to universal doubt, intellectual bankruptcy, moral deterioration, and social collapse. Seven centuries before Hume, al-Ghazali reduced reason to the principle of causality, and causality to mere sequence: all that we perceive is that B regularly follows A, not that A causes B. Philosophy, logic, science, cannot prove the existence of God or the immortality of the soul; only direct intuition can assure us of these beliefs, without which no moral order, and therefore no civilization, can survive.[88]

In the end al-Ghazali returned through mysticism to all orthodox views. The old fears and hopes of his youth flowed back upon him, and he professed to feel the eyes and threats of a stern deity close over his head. He proclaimed anew the horrors of the Mohammedan hell, and urged their preaching as necessary to popular morality.[89] He accepted again the Koran and the Hadith. In his *Ihya Ulum al-Din* (*Revival of the Science of Religion*) he expounded and defended his renovated orthodoxy with all the eloquence and fervor of his prime; never in Islam had the skeptics and the philosophers encountered so vigorous a foe. When he died (1111), the tide of unbelief had been effectually turned. All orthodoxy took comfort from him; even Christian theologians were glad to find, in his translated works, such a defense of religion, and such an exposition of piety, as no one had written since Augustine. After him, and despite Averroës, philosophy hid itself in the remote corners of the Moslem world; the pursuit of science waned; and the mind of Islam more and more buried itself in the Hadith and the Koran.

The conversion of al-Ghazali to mysticism was a great victory for Sufism. Orthodoxy now accepted Sufism, which for a time engulfed theology. The mullahs—learned exponents of Moslem doctrine and law—still dominated the official religious and legal world; but the field of religious thought was yielded to Sufi monks and saints. Strangely contemporary with the rise of the Franciscans in Christendom, a new monasticism took form in twelfth-century Islam. Sufi devotees now abandoned family life, lived in religious fraternities under a sheik or master, and called themselves *dervish* or *faqir*—a Persian and an Arabic word for poor man or mendicant. Some by prayer and meditation, some by ascetic self-denial, others in the exhaustion that followed wild dancing, sought to transcend the self and rise to a wonder-working unity with God.

Their doctrine received formulation in the 150 books of Muhyi al-Din ibn al-Arabi (1165–1240)—a Spanish Moslem domiciled in Damascus. The world was never created, said al-Arabi, for it is the external aspect of that which in inward view is God. History is the development of God to self-consciousness, which He achieves at last in man. Hell is temporary; in the end all will be saved. Love is mistaken when it loves a physical and transitory form; it is God Who appears in the beloved, and the true lover will find and love the author of all beauty in any beautiful form. Perhaps recalling some Christians of Jerome's time, al-Arabi taught that "he who loves and remains chaste unto death dies a martyr," and achieves the highest reach of devotion. Many married dervishes professed to live in such chastity with their wives.[90]

Through the gifts of the people some Moslem religious orders became wealthy, and consented to enjoy life. "Formerly," complained a Syrian sheik about 1250, "the Sufis were a fraternity dispersed in the flesh but united in the spirit; now they are a body well clothed carnally, and ragged in divine mystery." [91] The populace smiled tolerantly at these sacred worldlings, but lavished worship upon sincere devotees, ascribed to them miraculous deeds and powers, honored them as saints, celebrated their birthdays, prayed for their intercession with Allah, and made pilgrimages to their tombs. Mohammedanism, like Christianity, was a developing and adjustable religion, which would have startled a reborn Mohammed or Christ.

As orthodoxy triumphed, toleration waned. From Harun al-Rashid on, the so-called "Ordinance of Omar," formerly ignored, was increasingly observed. Theoretically, though not always in practice, non-Moslems were now required to wear distinguishing yellow stripes on their clothing; they were forbidden to ride on horseback, but might use an ass or a mule; they were not to build new churches or synagogues, but might repair old ones; no cross was to be displayed outside a church, no church bell should ring; non-Moslem children were not to be admitted to Moslem schools, but could have schools of their own: this is still the letter of the law—not always enforced—in Islam.[92] Nevertheless there were 45,000 Christians in tenth-century Baghdad; [93] Christian funeral processions passed unharmed through the streets; [94] and Moslem protests continued against the employment of Christians and Jews in high office. Even in the heat and challenge of the Crusades Saladin could be generous to the Christians in his realm.

VIII. AVERROËS

For a time philosophy survived in Moslem Spain by judiciously sprinkling professions of orthodoxy among the timid tentatives of critique; and thought found a precarious freedom in the courts of rulers who enjoyed in private the speculations that they accounted harmful to the populace. So the Almoravid governor of Saragossa chose as his minister and friend Abu Bekr ibn Bajja, who had been born there about 1106. Avempace, as Europe would call him, had reached even in youth an extraordinary proficiency in science, medicine, philosophy, music, and poetry. Ibn Khaldun tells how the governor so admired some verses of the young scholar that he vowed the poet should always walk on gold when entering his presence; whereupon ibn Bajja, lest this vow should abate his welcome, put a gold coin in each of his shoes. When Saragossa fell to the Christians the poet-scientist-minister fled to Fez, where he found himself destitute among Moslems who accused him of atheism. He died at the age of thirty, allegedly by poison. His lost treatise on music was accounted the masterpiece on that subtle subject in the literature of Western Islam. His most famous work, *A Guide to the Solitary*, renewed a basic theme of Arabic philosophy. The human intellect, said Ibn Bajja, is composed of two parts: the "material intellect," which is bound up with the body and dies with it; and the "Active Intellect," or impersonal cosmic mind, which enters into all men, and is alone immortal. Thought is man's highest function; by thought, rather than by mystic ecstasy, man can attain to knowledge of, and union with, the Active Intellect, or God. But thinking is a perilous enterprise, except in silence. The wise man will live in quiet seclusion, shunning doctors, lawyers, and the people; or perhaps a few philosophers will form a community where they may pursue knowledge in tolerant companionship, far from the maddened crowd.[95]

Abu Bekr (Europe's Abubacer) ibn Tufail (1107?–1185) continued the ideas of Ibn Bajja, and almost realized his ideals. He too was scientist, poet, physician, and philosopher. He became the doctor and vizier of the Caliph Abu Yaqub Yusuf at Marraqesh, the Almohad capital in Morocco; he managed to spend most of his waking hours in the royal library, and found time to write, among more technical works, the most remarkable philosophical romance in medieval literature. It took its title from Ibn Sina, and (through Ockley's English translation in 1708) may have suggested *Robinson Crusoe* to Defoe.

Hayy ibn Yaqzan ("Alive, Son of Vigilant"), who gives his name to the tale, was cast in infancy upon an uninhabited island. Nursed by a she-goat, he grew in intelligence and skill, made his shoes and clothes from animal skins, studied the stars, dissected animals alive or dead, and "arrived at the highest degree of knowledge, in this kind, which the most learned naturalists ever attained."[96] He passed from science to philosophy and theology, demonstrated to himself the existence of an all-powerful Creator, practiced asceticism, forswore meat, and achieved an ecstatic union with the Active Intellect.[97] Hayy was now forty-nine, and ripe for an audience. Fortunately a mystic named Asal now had himself deposited on the island, seeking solitude. He met Hayy, who for the first time discovered the existence of mankind; Asal taught him language, and rejoiced to find that Hayy had arrived unaided at a knowledge of God. He confessed to Hayy the coarseness of the popular religion in the land from which he, Asal, had come, and mourned that a modicum of morality had been achieved only by promises of heaven and threats of hell. Hayy resolved to go and convert this benighted people to a higher and more philosophical religion. Arrived, he preached his pantheism in the market place. The populace ignored him, or did not understand him. Hayy concluded that Mohammed was right: that the people can be disciplined to social order only by a religion of myth, miracle, ceremony, and supernatural punishments and rewards. He apologized for his intrusion, returned to his island, and lived there with Asal in daily companionship with placid animals and the Active Intellect; and "thus they continued serving God until they died."

It was with a rare absence of jealousy that Ibn Tufail, about 1153, introduced to the favor of Abu Yakub Yusuf a young lawyer and physician, known to Islam as Abu al-Walid Muhammad ibn Rushd (1126–98), and to medieval Europe as Averroës—the most influential figure in Islamic philosophy. His grandfather and his father had in turn been chief justice of Cordova, and had lavished on him all the education that the old capital could provide. One of his pupils has transmitted what purports to be Averroës' own account of his first interview with the Emir.

> When I was presented to the Prince of Believers I found him alone with Ibn Tufail, who . . . sounded my praises to him with compliments that I did not deserve. . . . The Emir opened the conversation by asking, "What opinion did the philosophers hold about the heavens? Are they eternal, or did they have a beginning?" I was overcome with terror and confusion, and sought some pretext for not answering . . . but the Emir, perceiving my trouble, turned to Ibn Tufail, and began to discourse with him on the question, recalling the opinions of Plato and Aristotle and other philosophers, and the objections that had been made to them by Moslem theologians; all with such fullness of memory as I should not have expected even of professional philosophers. The Emir put me at my ease, and tested my knowledge. When I had retired he sent me a sum of money, a riding horse, and a costly robe of honor.[98]

In 1169 Averroës was appointed chief justice of Seville; in 1172, of Cordova. Ten years later Abu Yaqub called him to Marraqesh to serve as court physician; and he continued in this capacity when (1184) Yaqub was succeeded by Yaqub al-Mansur. In 1194 he was banished to Lucena, near Cordova, to satisfy public resentment of his heresies. He was forgiven and recalled in 1198, but died in that year. His tomb may still be seen at Marraqesh.

His work in medicine has been almost forgotten in his fame as a philosopher; he was, however, "one of the greatest physicians of his time," the first to explain the function of the retina, and to recognize that an attack of smallpox confers subsequent immunity.[99] His encyclopedia of medicine (*Kitab al-Kulliyat fi-l-tibb*), translated into Latin, was widely used as a text in Christian universities. Meanwhile the Emir Abu Yaqub had expressed the

wish that someone would write a clear exposition of Aristotle; and Ibn Tufail recommended the task to Averroës. The suggestion was welcomed, for
Averroës had already concluded that all philosophy was contained in the
Stagirite, who merely needed interpretation to be made contemporary with
any age.* He resolved to prepare for each major work of Aristotle first a
summary, then a brief commentary, then a detailed commentary for advanced students—a mode of progressively complex exposition habitual in
Moslem universities. Unfortunately he knew no Greek, and had to rely on
Arabic translations of Syriac translations of Aristotle; nevertheless his patience, perspicuity, and keen analyses won him throughout Europe the name
of the Commentator, and placed him at once near the head of Moslem philosophy, second only to the great Avicenna himself.

To these writings he added several works of his own on logic, physics,
psychology, metaphysics, theology, law, astronomy, and grammar, and a
reply to al-Ghazali's *Destruction of Philosophy* under the title of *Destruction
of the Destruction* (*Tahafut al-Tahafut*). He argued, as Francis Bacon
would, that though a little philosophy might incline a man to atheism, unhindered study would lead to a better understanding between religion and
philosophy. For though the philosopher cannot accept in their literal sense
the dogmas of "the Koran, the Bible, and other revealed books,"[100] he perceives their necessity in developing a wholesome piety and morality among
the people, who are so harassed with economic importunities that they find
no time for more than incidental, superficial, and dangerous thinking on
first and last things. Hence the mature philosopher will neither utter nor
encourage any word against the established faith.[101] In return the philosopher should be left free to seek the truth; but he should confine his discussions within the circle and comprehension of the educated, and make no
propaganda among the populace.[102] Symbolically interpreted, the doctrines
of religion can be harmonized with the findings of science and philosophy;[103]
such interpretation of sacred texts through symbol and allegory has been
practiced, even by divines, for centuries. Averroës does not explicitly teach,
he merely implies, the doctrine imputed to him by Christian critics—that a
proposition may be true in philosophy (among the educated) and false
(harmful) in religion (and morals).[104] Hence the opinions of Averroës must
be sought not in the minor treatises which he composed for a general audience, but in his more recondite commentaries on Aristotle.

He defines philosophy as "an inquiry into the meaning of existence," with
a view to the improvement of man.[105] The world is eternal; the movements
of the heavens never began, and will never end; creation is a myth.

> The partisans of creation argue that the agent [God] produces a
> [new] being without needing for its production any pre-existing ma-

---

* Santayana, in *The Life of Reason*, adopted the same principle.

terial. . . . It is such imagining that has led the theologians of the three religions existing in our day to say that something can issue from noth.-ing.[106] . . . Motion is eternal and continuous; all motion has its cause in a preceding motion. Without motion there is no time. We cannot conceive of motion having either a beginning or an end.[107]

Nonetheless God is the creator of the world in the sense that it exists at any moment only through His sustaining power, and undergoes, so to speak, a continuous creation through the divine energy.[108] God is the order, force, and mind of the universe.

From this supreme order and intelligence there emanates an order and intelligence in the planets and the stars. From the intelligence in the lowest of the celestial circles (that of the moon) comes the Active or Effective Intellect, which enters into the body and mind of individual men. The human mind is composed of two elements. One is the passive or material intellect —a capacity and possibility of thought, forming a part of the body, and dying with it (the nervous system?). The other is the Active Intellect—a divine influx which activates the passive intellect into actual thought. This Active Intellect has no individuality; it is the same in all men; and it alone is immortal.[109] Averroës compares the operation of the Active Intellect upon the individual or passive intellect with the influence of the sun, whose light makes many objects luminous, but remains everywhere and permanently one.[110] And as fire reaches out to a combustible body, so the individual intellect aspires to be united with the Active Intellect. In this union the human mind becomes like unto God, for it holds all the universe potentially in the grasp of its thought; indeed the world and its contents have no existence for us, and no meaning, except through the mind that apprehends them.[111] Only the perception of truth through reason can lead the mind to that union with God which the Sufis think to reach by ascetic discipline or intoxicating dance. Averroës has no use for mysticism. His notion of paradise is the quiet and kindly wisdom of the sage.[112]

This was Aristotle's conclusion too; and of course the theory of the active and passive intellect (*nous poietikos* and *nous pathetikos*) goes back to Aristotle's *De Anima* (iii, 5) as interpreted by Alexander of Aphrodisias and Themistius of Alexandria, transformed into the emanation theory of the Neoplatonists, and transmitted in philosophic dynasty through al-Farabi, Avicenna, and Ibn Bajja. Here at the end, as in its beginning, Arabic philosophy was Aristotle Neoplatonized. But whereas in most Moslem and Christian philosophers Aristotle's doctrines were retailored to meet the needs of theology, in Averroës Mohammedan dogmas were reduced to a minimum to reconcile them with Aristotle. Hence Averroës had more influence in Christendom than in Islam. His Moslem contemporaries persecuted him, Moslem posterity forgot him, and allowed most of his works to be lost in their Arabic form. Jews preserved many of them in Hebrew translation, and

Maimonides followed in Averroës' steps in seeking to reconcile religion and philosophy. In Christendom the Commentaries, translated into Latin from the Hebrew, fed the heresies of Siger de Brabant, and the rationalism of the School of Padua, and threatened the foundations of Christian belief. St. Thomas Aquinas wrote his *Summae* to stem this Averroistic tide; but he followed Averroës in the method of his Commentaries, in divers interpretations of Aristotle, in choosing matter as the "principle of individuation," in the symbolical explanation of anthropomorphic Scriptural texts, in admitting the possible eternity of the world, in rejecting mysticism as a sufficient basis for theology, and in recognizing that some dogmas of religion are beyond reason, and can be accepted by faith alone.[113] Roger Bacon ranked Averroës next to Aristotle and Avicenna, and added, with characteristic exaggeration, "The philosophy of Averroës today [*c.* 1270] obtains the unanimous suffrage of wise men." [114]

In 1150 the Caliph Mustanjid, at Baghdad, ordered burned all the philosophical works of Avicenna and the Brethren of Sincerity. In 1194 the Emir Abu Yusuf Yaqub al-Mansur, then at Seville, ordered the burning of all works by Averroës except a few on natural science; he forbade his subjects to study philosophy, and urged them to throw into a fire all books of philosophy wherever found. These instructions were eagerly carried out by the people, who resented attacks upon a faith that for most of them was the dearest solace of their harassed lives. About this time Ibn Habib was put to death for studying philosophy.[115] After 1200 Islam shunned speculative thought. As political power declined in the Moslem world, it sought more and more the aid of the theologians and lawyers of orthodoxy. That aid was given, but in return for the suppression of independent thought. Even so, the aid did not suffice to save the state. In Spain the Christians advanced from city to city, until only Granada remained Moslem. In the East the Crusaders captured Jerusalem; and in 1258 the Mongols took and destroyed Baghdad.

IX. THE COMING OF THE MONGOLS: 1219–58

Once again history illustrated the truism that civilized comfort attracts barbarian conquest. The Seljuqs had brought new strength to Eastern Islam; but they too had succumbed to ease, and had allowed the empire of Malik Shah to break down into autonomous kingdoms culturally brilliant and militarily weak. Religious fanaticism and racial antipathies divided the people into bitter sects, and frustrated any united defense against the Crusades.

Meanwhile, on the plains and deserts of northwestern Asia, the Mongols thrived on hardships and primitive fertility. They lived in tents or the open air, followed their herds to fresh pastures, clothed themselves in oxhides, and studied with relish the arts of war. These new Huns, like their kin of eight centuries back, were experts with dagger and sword, and arrows aimed from their flying steeds. If we may believe the Christian missionary Giovanni de Piano Carpini, "they eat anything edible, even lice"; [116] and they had as little repugnance to feeding on rats, cats, dogs, and human blood as our most cultured contemporaries to eating eels and snails. Jenghiz Khan (1167–1227)—i.e., the Great King—disciplined them with severe laws into an irresistible force, and led them to the conquest of Central Asia from the Volga to the Chinese Wall. During the absence of Jenghiz Khan from his capital at Karokorum, a Mongol chieftain rebelled against him, and formed a league with Ala al-Din Muhammad, the Shah of the independent state of Khwarizm. Jenghiz suppressed the rebellion, and sent the Shah an offer of peace. The offer was accepted; but shortly thereafter two Mongol merchants in Transoxiana were executed as spies by Muhammad's governor of Otrar. Jenghiz demanded the extradition of the governor; Muhammad refused, beheaded the chief of the Mongol embassy, and sent its other members back without their beards. Jenghiz declared war, and the Mongol invasion of Islam began (1219).

An army under the Khan's son Juji defeated Muhammad's 400,000 troops at Jand; the Shah fled to Samarkand, leaving 160,000 of his men dead on the field. Another army, under Jenghiz' son Jagatai, captured and sacked Otrar. A third army, under Jenghiz himself, burned Bokhara to the ground, raped thousands of women, and massacred 30,000 men. Samarkand and Balkh surrendered at his coming, but suffered pillage and wholesale slaughter; a full century later Ibn Batuta described these cities as still largely in ruins. Jenghiz' son Tule led 70,000 men through Khurasan, ravaging every town on their march. The Mongols placed captives in their van, and gave them a choice between fighting their fellow men in front, or being cut down from behind. Merv was captured by treachery, and was burned to the ground; its libraries, the glory of Islam, were consumed in the conflagration; its inhabitants were allowed to march out through the gates with their treasures, only to be massacred and robbed in detail; this slaughter (the Moslem historians aver) occupied thirteen days, and took 1,300,000 lives.[117] Nishapur resisted long and bravely, but succumbed (1221); every man, woman, and child there was killed, except 400 artisan-artists who were sent to Mongolia; and the heads of the slain were piled up in a ghastly pyramid. The lovely city of Rayy, with its 3000 mosques and its famous pottery kilns, was laid in ruins, and (a Moslem historian tells us) its entire population was put to death.[118] Muhammad's son Jalal ud-Din collected a new army of Turks, gave Jenghiz battle on the Indus, was defeated, and fled to Delhi. Herat, having rebelled against its Mongol governor, was punished with the slaughter of 60,000 inhabitants. This ferocity was part of the military science of the Mongols; it sought to strike a paralyzing terror into the hearts of later opponents, and to leave no possibility of revolt among the defeated. The policy succeeded.

Jenghiz now returned to Mongolia, enjoyed his 500 wives and concubines, and died in bed. His son and successor Ogotai sent a horde of 300,000 men to capture Jalal ud-Din, who had formed another army at Diarbekr; Jalal was defeated and killed, and the unhindered Mongols ravaged Azerbaijan, northern Mesopotamia, Georgia, and Armenia (1234). Hearing that a rebellion, led by the Assassins, had broken out in Iran, Hulagu, a grandson of Jenghiz, led a Mongol army through Samarkand and Balkh, destroyed the Assassin stronghold at Alamut, and turned toward Baghdad.

Al-Mustasim Billah, last of the Abbasid caliphs of the East, was a learned scholar, a meticulous calligrapher, a man of exemplary gentleness, devoted to religion, books, and charity: this was an enemy to Hulagu's taste. The Mongol accused the Caliph of sheltering rebels, and of withholding promised aid against the Assassins; as penalty he demanded the submission of the Caliph to the Great Khan, and the complete demilitarization of Baghdad. Al-Mustasim returned a boastful refusal. After a month of siege, al-Mustasim sent Hulagu presents and an offer of surrender. Lured by a promise of clemency, he and his two sons gave themselves up to the Mongol. On February 13, 1258, Hulagu and his troops entered Baghdad, and began forty days of pillage and massacre; 800,000 of the inhabitants, we are told, were killed. Thousands of scholars, scientists, and poets fell in the indiscriminate slaughter; libraries and treasures accumulated through centuries were in a week plundered or destroyed; hundreds of thousands of volumes were consumed. Finally the Caliph and his family, after being forced to reveal the hiding place of their secret wealth, were put to death.[119] So ended the Abbasid caliphate in Asia.

Hulagu now returned to Mongolia. His army remained behind, and under other generals it advanced to the conquest of Syria. At Ain Jalut it met an Egyptian army under the Mamluk leaders Qutuz and Baibars, and was destroyed (1260). Everywhere in Islam and Europe men of all faiths rejoiced; the spell of fear was broken. In 1303 a decisive battle near Damascus ended the Mongol threat, and saved Syria for the Mamluks, perhaps Europe for Christianity.

Never in history had a civilization suffered so suddenly so devastating a blow. The barbarian conquest of Rome had been spread over two centuries; between each blow and the next some recovery was possible; and the German conquerors respected, some tried to preserve, the dying Empire which they helped to destroy. But the Mongols came and went within forty years; they came not to conquer and stay, but to kill, pillage, and carry their spoils to Mongolia. When their bloody tide ebbed it left behind it a fatally disrupted economy, canals broken or choked, schools and libraries in ashes, governments too divided, poor, and weak to govern, and a population cut in half and shattered in soul. Epicurean indulgence, physical and mental exhaustion, military incompetence and cowardice, religious sectarianism and obscurantism, political corruption and anarchy, all culminating in piecemeal collapse before external attack—this, and no change of climate, turned Western Asia from world leadership to destitution, from a hundred teeming and cultured cities in Syria, Mesopotamia, Persia, the Caucasus, and Transoxiana into the poverty, disease, and stagnation of modern times.

X. ISLAM AND CHRISTENDOM

The rise and decline of Islamic civilization is one of the major phenomena of history. For five centuries, from 700 to 1200, Islam led the world in power, order, and extent of government, in refinement of manners, in standards of living, in humane legislation and religious toleration, in literature, scholarship, science, medicine, and philosophy. In architecture it yielded the palm, in the twelfth century, to the cathedrals of Europe; and Gothic sculpture found no rival in inhibited Islam. Moslem art exhausted itself in decoration, and suffered from narrowness of range and monotony of style; but within its self-imposed limits it has never been surpassed. In Islam art and culture were more widely shared than in medieval Christendom; kings were calligraphers, and merchants, like physicians, might be philosophers.

In sexual morality during these centuries Christendom probably excelled Islam, though there was not much to choose; Christian monogamy, however evaded in practice, kept the sexual impulse within bounds, and slowly raised the status of woman, while Islam darkened the face of woman with purdah and the veil. The Church succeeded in limiting divorce; and homosexual diversions seem never to have attained, even in Renaissance Italy, the spread and freedom allowed them not in Mohammedan law but in Moslem life. The Moslems seem to have been better gentlemen than their Christian peers; they kept their word more frequently, showed more mercy to the defeated, and were seldom guilty of such brutality as marked the Christian capture of Jerusalem in 1099. Christian law continued to use ordeal by battle, water, or fire while Moslem law was developing an advanced jurisprudence and an enlightened judiciary. The Mohammedan religion, less original than the Hebrew, less embracing in eclecticism than the Christian, kept its creed and ritual simpler and purer, less dramatic and colorful, than the Christian, and made less concession to the natural polytheism of mankind. It resembled Protestantism in scorning the aid and play that Mediterranean religion offered to the imagination and the senses; but it bowed to popular sensualism in its picture of paradise. It kept itself almost free from sacerdotalism, but fell into a narrow and dulling orthodoxy just when Christianity was entering into the most exuberant period of Catholic philosophy.

The influence of Christendom on Islam was almost limited to religion and war. Probably from Christian exemplars came Mohammedan mysticism, monasticism, and the worship of the saints. The figure and story of Jesus touched the Moslem soul, and appeared sympathetically in Moslem poetry and art.[120]

The influence of Islam upon Christendom was varied and immense. From Islam Christian Europe received foods, drinks, drugs, medicaments, armor, heraldry, art motives and tastes, industrial and commercial articles and techniques, maritime codes and ways, and often the words for these things— *orange, lemon, sugar, syrup, sherbet, julep, elixir, jar, azure, arabesque, mattress, sofa, muslin, satin, fustian, bazaar, caravan, check, tariff, traffic, douane, magazine, risk, sloop, barge, cable, admiral*. The game of chess came to Europe from India via Islam, and picked up Persian terms on the way; *checkmate* is from the Persian *shah mat*—"the king is dead." Some of our musical instruments bear in their names evidence of their Semitic origin—*lute, rebeck, guitar, tambourine*. The poetry and music of the troubadours came from Moslem Spain into Provence, and from Moslem Sicily into Italy; and Arabic descriptions of trips to heaven and hell may have shared in forming *The Divine Comedy*. Hindu fables and numerals entered Europe in Arabic dress or form. Moslem science preserved and developed Greek mathematics, physics, chemistry, astronomy, and medicine, and transmitted this Greek heritage, considerably enriched, to Europe; and Arabic scientific terms—*algebra, zero, cipher, azimuth, alembic, zenith, almanac*—still lie imbedded in European speech. Moslem medicine led the world for half a millennium. Moslem philosophy preserved and corrupted Aristotle for Christian Europe. Avicenna and Averroës were lights from the East for the Schoolmen, who cited them as next to the Greeks in authority.

The ribbed vault is older in Islam than in Europe,[121] though we cannot trace the route by which it came into Gothic art. Christian spire and belfry owed much to the minaret,[122] and perhaps Gothic window tracery took a lead from the cusped arcading of the Giralda tower.[123] The rejuvenation of the ceramic art in Italy and France has been attributed to the importation of Moslem potters in the twelfth century, and to the visits of Italian potters to Moslem Spain.[124] Venetian workers in metal and glass, Italian bookbinders, Spanish armorers, learned their techniques from Moslem artisans;[125] and almost everywhere in Europe weavers looked to Islam for models and designs. Even gardens received a Persian influence.

We shall see later by what avenues these influences came: through commerce and the Crusades; through a thousand translations from Arabic into Latin; through the visits of scholars like Gerbert, Michael Scot, and Adelard of Bath to Moslem Spain; through the sending of Christian youths by their Spanish parents to Moslem courts to receive a knightly education [126]—for the Moslem aristocrats were accounted "knights and gentlemen, albeit

Moors"; [127] through the daily contact of Christians with Moslems in Syria, Egypt, Sicily, and Spain. Every advance of the Christians in Spain admitted a wave of Islamic literature, science, philosophy, and art into Christendom. So the capture of Toledo in 1085 immensely furthered Christian knowledge of astronomy, and kept alive the doctrine of the sphericity of the earth. [128]

Behind this borrowing smoldered an undying hate. Nothing, save bread, is so precious to mankind as its religious beliefs; for man lives not by bread alone, but also by the faith that lets him hope. Therefore his deepest hatred greets those who challenge his sustenance or his creed. For three centuries Christianity saw Islam advance, saw it capture and absorb one Christian land and people after another, felt its constricting hand upon Christian trade, and heard it call Christians infidels. At last the potential conflict became actual: the rival civilizations clashed in the Crusades; and the best of the East or West slew the best of the West or East. Back of all medieval history lay this mutual hostility, with a third faith, the Jewish, caught between the main combatants, and cut by both swords. The West lost the Crusades, but won the war of creeds. Every Christian warrior was expelled from the Holy Land of Judaism and Christianity; but Islam, bled by its tardy victory, and ravaged by Mongols, fell in turn into a Dark Age of obscurantism and poverty; while the beaten West, matured by its effort and forgetting its defeat, learned avidly from its enemy, lifted cathedrals into the sky, wandered out on the high seas of reason, transformed its crude new languages into Dante, Chaucer, and Villon, and moved with high spirit into the Renaissance.

The general reader will marvel at the length of this survey of Islamic civilization, and the scholar will mourn its inadequate brevity. Only at the peaks of history has a society produced, in an equal period, so many illustrious men —in government, education, literature, philology, geography, history, mathematics, astronomy, chemistry, philosophy, and medicine—as Islam in the four centuries between Harun al-Rashid and Averroës. Part of this brilliant activity fed on Greek leavings; but much of it, above all in statesmanship, poetry, and art, was original and invaluable. In one sense this zenith of Islam was a recovery of the Near East from Greek domination; it reached back not only to Sasanian and Achaemenid Persia, but to the Judea of Solomon, the Assyria of Ashurbanipal, the Babylonia of Hammurabi, the Akkad of Sargon, the Sumeria of unknown kings. So the continuity of history reasserts itself: despite earthquakes, epidemics, famines, eruptive migrations, and catastrophic wars, the essential processes of civilization are not lost; some younger culture takes them up, snatches them from the conflagration, carries them on imitatively, then creatively, until fresh youth and spirit can enter the race. As men are members of one another, and generations are moments in a family line, so civilizations are units in a larger whole whose name is history; they are stages in the life of man. Civilization is polygenetic—it is the co-operative product of many peoples, ranks, and faiths; and no one who studies its history can be a bigot of race or creed. Therefore the scholar, though he belongs to his country through affectionate kinship, feels himself also a citizen of that Country of the Mind which knows no hatreds and no frontiers; he hardly deserves his name if he carries into his study political prejudices, or racial discriminations, or religious animosities; and he accords his grateful homage to any people that has borne the torch and enriched his heritage.

BOOK III

JUDAIC CIVILIZATION
135–1300

CHRONOLOGICAL TABLE FOR BOOK III

1-220: The Tannaim
189: The Mishna of Jehuda Hanasi
219: Jewish academy at Sura
220: Jewish academy at Pumbeditha
220-500: The Amoraim
280-500: Compilation of the Talmuds
359: Hillel II fixes Jewish calendar
500-650: The Saboraim
658-1040: The Gaonate in Babylonia
815: d. of Mashallah, astronomer
855-955: Isaac Israeli, philosopher
892-942: Saadia Gaon, philosopher
915-70: Hasdai ibn Shaprut, statesman
1000: Monogamy edict of Rabbi
Gershom
1021-70: Ibn Gabirol, poet & philosopher
1038-55: Samuel ibn Naghdela, vizier
1040-1105: Shelomoh ben Yitzhak (Rashi),
Talmudic commentator
1055-66: Joseph ibn Naghdela, vizier
1065-1136: Abraham bar Hiyya,
mathematician
1070-1139: Moses ibn Ezra, poet
1086-1147: Jehuda Halevi, poet
1093-1168: Abraham ibn Ezra, poet
1096: Pogroms of First Crusade
1110-80: Abraham ibn Daud, philosopher
1135-1204: Maimonides
1147: Pogroms of Second Crusade
1160: David Alrui, false messiah
1160-73: Travels of Benjamin of Tudela
1170: The *Mishna Torah* of
Maimonides
1181, 1254, 1306: Jews expelled from France
1190: The *Guide to the Perplexed*
1190: Rise of the Cabala
1190: Pogroms in England
1215: Fourth Council of the Lateran
orders Jewish badge
1234: Books of Maimonides burned at
Montpellier
1242: Burning of Talmud at Paris
1290: Jews expelled from England
c. 1295: The *Sefer ha-Zohar* of Moses of
Leon

CHAPTER XV

The Talmud

I. THE EXILES: 135–565

WITHIN Islam and Christendom a remarkable people maintained through every adversity its own unique culture, consoled and inspired by its own creed, living by its own laws and morality, producing its own poets, scientists, scholars, and philosophers, and serving as the living carriers of fertile seeds between two hostile worlds.

The rebellion of Bar Cocheba (132–5) was not the last effort of the Jews to regain for Judea the freedom that Pompey and Titus had destroyed. Under Antoninus Pius (138–61) they tried again, and failed. Their holy city was forbidden them except on the bitter anniversary of its destruction, when they were allowed, for a consideration, to come and mourn by the walls of their shattered Temple. In Palestine, where 985 towns had been wiped out, and 580,000 men and women had been slain, in Bar Cocheba's revolt, the Jewish population had sunk to half its former volume, and to such an abyss of poverty that cultural life was almost wholly dead. Nevertheless, within a generation after Bar Cocheba, the *Beth Din* or Jewish National Council—a court of seventy-one rabbinical scholars and legists—was established in Tiberias, synagogues and schools were opened, and hope rose again.

The triumph of Christianity brought new difficulties. Before his conversion Constantine had placed the religion of the Jews on a footing of legal equality with those of his other subjects. After his conversion the Jews were oppressed with new restrictions and exactions, and Christians were forbidden to associate with them.[1] Constantius banished the rabbis (337), and made the marriage of a Jew with a Christian woman a capital crime.[2] Julian's brother Gallus taxed the Jews so heavily that many of them sold their children to meet his demands. In 352 they rebelled again, and were again suppressed; Sepphoris was razed to the ground, Tiberias and other cities were partly destroyed, thousands of Jews were killed, thousands were enslaved. The condition of the Palestinian Jews now (359) sank so low, and their communication with other Jewish communities was so difficult, that their patriarch Hillel II resigned their right to determine for all Jews the dates of the Jewish festivals, and issued, for the independent computation of these dates, a calendar that remains in use among the Jews of the world to this day.

From these afflictions the Jews were saved for a moment by the accession of Julian. He reduced their taxes, revoked discriminatory laws, lauded Hebrew charity, and acknowledged Yahveh as "a great god." He asked Jewish leaders why they had abandoned animal sacrifice; when they replied that their law did not permit this except in the Temple at Jerusalem, he ordered that the Temple should be rebuilt with state funds.[3] Jerusalem was again opened to the Jews; they flocked to it from every quarter of Palestine, from every province of the Empire; men, women, and children gave their labor to the rebuilding, their savings and jewelry to the furnishing, of the new Temple;[4] we can imagine the happiness of a people that for three centuries had prayed for this day (361). But as the foundations were being dug, flames burst from the ground, and burnt several workmen to death.[5] The work was patiently resumed, but a repetition of the phenomenon—probably due to the explosion of natural gas—interrupted and discouraged the enterprise. The Christians rejoiced at what seemed a divine prohibition; the Jews marveled and mourned. Then came Julian's sudden death; state funds were withdrawn; the old restrictive laws were re-enacted and made more severe; and the Jews, again excluded from Jerusalem, returned to their villages, their poverty, and their prayers. Soon thereafter Jerome reported the Jewish population of Palestine as "but a tenth part of their previous multitude." [6] In 425 Theodosius II abolished the Palestinian patriarchate. Greek Christian churches replaced the synagogues and schools; and after a brief outburst in 614, Palestine surrendered its leadership of the Jewish world.

The Jews could hardly be blamed if they hoped to fare better in less Christian lands. Some moved east into Mesopotamia and Persia, and reinvigorated that Babylonian Jewry which had never ceased since the Captivity of 597 B.C. In Persia too the Jews were excluded from state office; but as all Persians except the nobility were likewise excluded, there was less offense in the restriction.[7] And there were several persecutions of Jews in Persia. But taxation was less severe, the government was normally co-operative, and the exilarch, or head of the Jewish community, was recognized and honored by the Persian kings. The soil of Iraq was then irrigated and fertile; the Jews there became prosperous farmers as well as clever traders. Some, including famous scholars, grew rich by brewing beer.[8] The Jewish communities in Persia multiplied rapidly, for Persian law permitted, and the Jews practiced, polygamy, for reasons that we have seen under Mohammedan law. The good rabbis Rab and Nahman, when traveling, were accustomed to advertise in each city for temporary wives, to give local youth an exemplar of matrimonial, as against a promiscuous, life.[9] In Nehardea, Sura, and Pumbeditha schools of higher education rose, whose scholarship and rabbinical decisions were honored throughout the Dispersion.

Meanwhile the dispersion of the Jews continued through all the Mediterranean lands. Some went to join old Jewish communities in Syria and Asia

Minor. Some went to Constantinople despite the hostility of Greek emperors and patriarchs. Some turned south from Palestine into Arabia, dwelt in peace and religious freedom with their Arab fellow-Semites, occupied whole regions like Khaibar, almost equaled the Arabs in Yathrib (Medina), made many converts, and prepared the Arab mind for the Judaism of the Koran. Some crossed the Red Sea into Abyssinia, and multiplied so rapidly there that in 315 they were reputed to be half the population.[10] Jews controlled half the shipping of Alexandria, and their prosperity in that excitable city fed the flames of religious animosity.

Jewish communities developed in all the North African cities, and in Sicily and Sardinia. In Italy they were numerous; and though occasionally harassed by the Christian population, they were for the most part protected by pagan emperors, Christian emperors, Theodoric, and the Popes. In Spain there had been Jewish settlements before Caesar, and they had developed there without molestation under the pagan Empire; they prospered under the Arian Visigoths, but suffered disheartening persecutions after King Recared (586–601) adopted the Nicene Creed. We hear of no persecution of Jews in Gaul until the severe enactments of the third and fourth Councils of Orléans (538, 541), a generation after the conquest of Arian Visigothic Gaul by the orthodox Christian Clovis. About 560 the Christians of Orléans burned down a synagogue. The Jews petitioned Gunthram, King of the Franks, to rebuild it at public cost, as Theodoric in like case had done. Gunthram refused. "O King glorious for wonderful wisdom!" exclaimed Bishop Gregory of Tours.[11]

From such tribulations the Jews of the Dispersion always recovered. Patiently they rebuilt their synagogues and their lives; toiled, traded, lent money, prayed and hoped, increased and multiplied. Each settlement was required to maintain at communal expense at least one elementary and one secondary school, both of them usually in the synagogue. Scholars were advised not to live in any town that lacked such schools. The language of worship and instruction was Hebrew; the language of daily speech was Aramaic in the East, Greek in Egypt and Eastern Europe; elsewhere the Jews adopted the language of the surrounding population. The central theme of Jewish education was religion; secular culture was now almost ignored. Dispersed Jewry could maintain itself, in body and soul, only through the Law; and religion was the study and observance of the Law. The faith of their fathers became more precious to the Jews the more it was attacked; and the Talmud and the synagogue were the indispensable support and refuge of an oppressed and bewildered people whose life rested on hope, and their hope on faith in their God.

II. THE MAKERS OF THE TALMUD

In the Temple, the synagogues, and the schools of Palestine and Babylonia the scribes and the rabbis composed those enormous bodies of law and commentary known as the Palestinian and Babylonian Talmuds. Moses, they held, had left to his people not only a written Law in the Pentateuch, but also an oral Law, which had been handed down and expanded from teacher to pupil, from generation to generation. It had been the main point of issue between the Pharisees and the Sadducees of Palestine whether this oral Law was also of divine origin and binding force. As the Sadducees disappeared after the Dispersion of A.D. 70, and the rabbis inherited the tradition of the Pharisees, the oral Law was accepted by all orthodox Jews as God's commandment, and was added to the Pentateuch to constitute the Torah or Law by which they lived, and in which, quite literally, they had their being. The thousand-year-long process by which the oral Law was built up, given form, and put into writing as the Mishna; the eight centuries of debate, judgment, and elucidation that accumulated the two Gemaras as commentaries on the Mishna; the union of the Mishna with the shorter of these Gemaras to make the Palestinian, and with the longer to make the Babylonian, Talmud—this is one of the most complex and astonishing stories in the history of the human mind. The Bible was the literature and religion of the ancient Hebrews; the Torah was the life and blood of the medieval Jews.

Because the Law of the Pentateuch was written, it could not meet all the needs and circumstances of a Jerusalem without freedom, or a Judaism without Jerusalem, or a Jewry without Palestine. It was the function of the Sanhedrin teachers before the Dispersion, and of the rabbis after it, to interpret the legislation of Moses for the use and guidance of a new age or place. Their interpretations and discussions, with majority and minority opinions, were transmitted from one generation of teachers to another. Perhaps to keep this oral tradition flexible, possibly to compel its memorizing, it was not written down. The rabbis who expounded the Law might on occasion call in the help of persons who had accomplished the feat of committing it to memory. In the first six generations after Christ the rabbis were called tannaim—"teachers of the oral Law." As the sole experts in the Law, they were at once the teachers and the judges of their communities in Palestine after the fall of the Temple.

The rabbis of Palestine and of the Dispersion constituted the most unique aristocracy in history. They were no closed or hereditary class; many of them rose from the poorest ranks; most of them earned their living as artisans even after achieving international repute; and until near the end of this period they received no payment for their work as teachers and judges. Rich men sometimes made them silent partners in business enterprises, or took them into their homes, or married their daughters to them to free them from toil. A few of them were spoiled by the high status accorded to them in their communities; some were humanly capable of anger, jealousy, hatred, undue censoriousness, pride; they had frequently to remind themselves that the true scholar is a modest man, if only because wisdom sees the part in the light of the whole. The people loved them for their virtues and their faults, admired them for their learning and their devotion, and told a thousand stories about their judgments and their miracles. To this day no people so honors the student and the scholar as do the Jews.

As rabbinical decisions accumulated, the task of memorizing them became unreasonable. Hillel, Akiba, and Meir attempted various classifications and mnemonic devices, but none of these received general acceptance. Disorder in the transmission of the Law became the order of the day; the number of men who knew the entire oral Law by heart was dangerously reduced, and dispersion was scattering these few to distant lands. About the year 189, at Sepphoris in Palestine, Rabbi Jehuda Hanasi took over and transformed the work of Akiba and Meir, rearranged the whole oral Law, and wrote it down, with some personal additions, as the "Mishna of Rabbi Jehuda." * It was so widely read that it became in time *the* Mishna, the authoritative form of the oral Law of the Jews.

As we have it, the Mishna (i.e., oral teaching) is the result of much editing and interpolation since Jehuda; even so it is a compact summary, designed for memorizing by repetition, and therefore tantalizingly terse and obscure to one who comes to it from any background except that of Jewish life and history. Babylonian and European as well as Palestinian Jews accepted it, but each school placed upon its maxims an individual interpretation. As six "generations" (A.D. 10–220) of rabbinical tannaim had shared in formulating the Mishna, so now six "generations" (220–500) of rabbinical amoraim ("expounders") accumulated those two masses of commentary, the Palestinian and the Babylonian Gemaras. The new teachers did to the Mishna of Jehuda what the tannaim had done to the Old Testament: they debated, analyzed, explained, amended, and illustrated the text to apply it to the new problems and circumstances of their place and time. Towards the end of the fourth century the schools of Palestine co-ordinated their commentaries in the form known as the Palestinian Gemara. About the same time (397) Rab (Rabbi) Ashi, head of the Sura college, began to codify the Babylonian Gemara, and worked on it for a generation; a hundred years later (499) Rabina II bar (son of) Samuel, also at Sura, brought this work to completion. If we note that the Babylonian Gemara is eleven times as long as the Mishna, we shall

---

* A minority of scholars holds that Jehuda did not commit his Mishna to writing, and that it was orally transmitted till the eighth century. For the majority opinion, cf. G. F. Moore, *Judaism in the First Centuries of the Christian Era*, Cambridge, Mass., 1932, Vol. I, p. 151; and W. O. Oesterley and G. H. Box, *Short Survey of the Literature of Rabbinical and Medieval Judaism*, London, 1920, p. 83.

begin to understand why its compilation spanned a century. Through an additional 150 years (500-650) rabbinical saboraim ("reasoners") revised this vast commentary, and gave the finishing touches to the Babylonian Talmud.

The word *talmud* means teaching. Among the amoraim it was applied only to the Mishna; in modern usage it includes both the Mishna and the Gemara. The Mishna is the same in both the Palestinian and the Babylonian Talmuds; the two differ only in the Gemara or commentary, which is four times longer in the Babylonian than in the Palestinian form.* The language of the two Gemaras is Aramaic; that of the Mishna is Neo-Hebraic, with many borrowings from neighbor languages. The Mishna is concise, stating a law in a few lines; the Gemaras are deliberately discursive, giving the diverse opinions of leading rabbis on the Mishna text, describing the circumstances that might require modification of the law, and adding illustrative material. The Mishna is mostly halacha, law; the Gemaras are partly halacha—restating or discussing a law—and partly haggada ("story"). Haggada has been lazily defined as anything in the Talmud that is not halacha. For the most part haggada includes illustrative anecdotes or examples, bits of biography, history, medicine, astronomy, astrology, magic, and theosophy, and exhortations to virtue and obedience to the Law. Often a haggada relieved the minds of the students after some complex and tiring debate. So, we read,

> Rab Ami and Rab Assi were conversing with Rabbi Isaac Napcha, when one of them said to him: "Tell us, sir, some pretty legend"; and the other said: "Pray explain to us, rather, some nice point of law." When he began the legend he displeased the one, and when he began to explain a point of law he offended the other. Whereupon he took up this parable: "I am like the man with the two wives, the one young and the other old. The young one plucked out all his gray hairs, that he might look young; the old wife pulled out all his black hairs, that he might look old; and so between the two he became bald. So it is with me between you." [13]

* The Babylonian Talmud runs to 2947 folio leaves, or some 6000 pages of 400 words each. The Mishna is divided into six *sedarim* (orders), each of these into *masechtoth* (tractates) totaling sixty-three, each of these into *perakim* (chapters), each of these into *mishnayoth* (teachings). Modern editions of the Talmud usually include: (1) the commentary of Rashi (1040-1105), which appears on the interior margins of the text; and (2) *tosaphoth* (additions), discussions of the Talmud by French and German rabbis of the twelfth and thirteenth centuries, which appear on the exterior margins of the text. Many editions add the *Tosefta* or Supplement—remnants of the oral law omitted from the Mishna of Jehuda Hanasi.

This chapter will also quote from the Midrash (exposition), addresses allegedly given by tannaim or amoraim, but assembled and committed to writing between the fourth and the twelfth century, and expounding in popular style various books of the Hebrew Scriptures. Some of the major Midrashim: Genesis Rabbah, on Genesis; Wayyikrah Rabbah, on Leviticus; five Megilloth (scrolls)—on Esther, the Song of Songs, Ruth, Lamentations, and Ecclesiasticus; the Mechilta, on Exodus; the Sifra, on Leviticus; the Sifre, on Numbers and Deuteronomy; the Pesikta, homilies on passages from the Bible.[12]

III. THE LAW

If now, with offensive brevity and ecumenical ignorance, we attempt to sketch some phases of this immense Talmud that entered into every cranny of medieval Hebrew life, let us confess that we are but scratching a mountain, and that our external approach condemns us to error.

1. *Theology*

First, said the rabbis, one must study the Law, written and oral. "Greater is study of Torah than the rebuilding of the Temple." [14] "Every day when a man busies himself with the study of the Law he should say to himself, 'It is as if this day I received it from Sinai.' " [15] No other study is necessary; Greek philosophy, secular science, may be studied only "at that hour which is neither day nor night." [16] Every word of the Hebrew Scriptures is literally the word of God; even the Song of Songs is a hymn inspired by God—to portray allegorically the union of Yahveh with Israel as His chosen bride.* [17] Since without the Law there would be moral chaos, the Law must have existed before the creation of the world, "in the bosom or mind of God";† only its communication to Moses was an event in time. The Talmud, so far as it is halacha, is also God's eternal word; it is the formulation of laws orally communicated to Moses by God, and by Moses to his successors; and its decrees are as binding as anything in the Scriptures.‡ Some rabbis ranked the Mishna above the Scriptures in authority, as being a later and revised form of the Law.[18] Certain rabbinical edicts frankly voided laws of the Pentateuch, or interpreted them into harmlessness.[19] During the Middle Ages (476–1492) the Jews of Germany and France studied the Talmud far more than the Scriptures.

The Talmud, like the Bible, takes for granted the existence of an intelligent and omnipotent God. There were occasional skeptics among the Jews, like the learned Elisha ben Abuyah whom the pious Rabbi Meir befriended; but they were apparently a tiny and hardly vocal minority. The Talmud's God is frankly anthropomorphic: He loves and hates, gets angry,[20] laughs,[21] weeps,[22] feels remorse,[23] wears phylacteries,[24] sits on a throne surrounded

---

* Catholic theologians interpret it as symbolically describing the union of Christ with the Church as His chosen bride.

† Cf. the ancient Chinese belief that the operation and continuance of the universe depends upon the moral law; Heracleitus' comparison of planetary deviations to sins; and Plato's divine archetypal "ideas." The theory goes back to Prov. viii, 22. Jesus accepted the eternity of the Law (Luke xvii, 7; Matt. v, 18). The Moslems, not to be outdone, taught the eternity of the Koran.

‡ No official Jewish council has ever accepted this Talmudic view of the Talmud. Modern Reformed Judaism rejects it.

by a ministering hierarchy of cherubim and seraphim, and studies the Torah three times a day.[25] The rabbis acknowledged that these human attributes were a bit hypothetical; "we borrow terms from His creatures to apply to Him," they said, "in order to assist the understanding";[26] it was not their fault if the commonalty could think only in pictures. They also represented God as the soul of the universe, invisible, pervasive, vitalizing, at once transcendent and immanent, above the world and yet present in every nook and fragment of it. This universal divine presence, the Shekinah (dwelling), is especially real in sacred places, persons, and things, and in moments of study or prayer. Nevertheless this omnipresent God is one. Of all ideas the most distasteful to Judaism is that of a plurality of gods. The unity of God is passionately reiterated against the polytheism of the pagans and the apparent tritheism of the Christian Trinity; it is proclaimed in the most famous and universal of Jewish prayers, the Shema Yisrael: "Hear, O Israel, the Lord is our God, the Lord is one" (*Shema Yisrael adonoi elohenu, adonoi ehad*).[27] No messiah, no prophet, no saint is to have a place beside Him in His temple or worship. The rabbis forbade, except on rare occasions, the utterance of His name, hoping to deter profanity and magic; to avoid the sacred tetragrammaton JHVH they used the word Adonai, Lord, and recommended even for this such substitutions as "The Holy One," "The Merciful One," "The Heavens," and "Our Father which is in heaven." God can and does work miracles, especially through great rabbis; but these marvels are not to be thought of as infractions of nature's laws; there are no laws but the will of God.

Everything created has a divine and beneficent purpose. "God created the snail as a cure for the scab, the fly as a cure for the sting of the wasp, and the gnat as a cure for the bite of the serpent, and the serpent as a cure for a sore."[28] Between God and man there is a continuous relation; every step of man's life is taken in the inescapable sight of God; every deed or thought of man's day honors or dishonors the divine presence. All men are descended from Adam; nevertheless, "man was first created with a tail like an animal";[29] and "up to the generation of Enoch the faces of the people resembled those of monkeys."[30] Man is composed of body and soul; his soul is from God, his body is of the earth. The soul impels him to virtue, the body to sin. Or perhaps his evil impulses come from Satan, and that multitude of malignant spirits which lurks about everywhere.[31] Every evil, however, may be ultimately good; without his earthy desires man might neither toil nor breed; "Come," says a jolly passage, "let us ascribe merit to our ancestors, for if they had not sinned we should not have come into the world."[32]

Sin is natural, but its guilt is not inherited. The rabbis accepted the doctrine of the fall of man, but not of original sin or divine atonement. A man suffers only for his own sins. If he suffers more on earth than his sins seem to warrant, that may be because we do not know the full measure of his sins; or such excess of punishment may be a great blessing, as entitling the sufferer to exceptional rewards in heaven; therefore, said Akiba, a man should rejoice in the multitude of his misfortunes.[33] As for death, it came into the world through sin; a really sinless person would never die.[34] Death is a debt owed by a sinful humanity to the author of all life. A midrash tells a touching story of death and Rabbi Meir:

> While Rabbi Meir was holding his weekly discourse on a Sabbath afternoon, his two beloved sons died suddenly at home. Their mother covered them with a sheet, and forbore to mourn on the sacred day. When Rabbi Meir returned after evening services he asked for his sons, whom he had not seen in the synagogue. She asked him to recite the habdalah [a ceremony marking the close of the Sabbath], and gave him his evening meal. Then she said: "I have a question to ask thee. A friend once gave me jewels to keep for him; now he wishes them again; shall I return them?" "Beyond doubt thou must," said Rabbi Meir. His wife took him by the hand, led him to the bed, and drew back the sheet. Rabbi Meir burst into bitter weeping, and his wife said: "They were entrusted to us for a time; now their Master has taken back His very own." [35]

The Hebrew Scriptures had said little of an immortality of reward and punishment; but that idea now played a major role in rabbinical theology. Hell was pictured at Ge Hinnom or Sheol,* and divided like heaven into seven stories, with graduated degrees of torment. Only the most wicked of the circumcised would enter it,[36] and even confirmed sinners would not be punished forever. "All who go down to hell shall come up again, except these three: he who commits adultery, he who shames another in public, and he who gives another a bad name." [37] Heaven was called Gan Eden, and was represented as a garden of every physical and spiritual delight; the wine there would be of a vintage preserved from the six days of the creation; perfumes would bless the air; and God Himself would join the saved in a banquet whose supreme joy would be the sight of His face. However, some rabbis confessed that no man can say what lies beyond the grave.[38]

The Jews thought of salvation in terms of the nation rather than of the individual. Driven across the earth with apparently irrational ruthlessness, they strengthened themselves with the belief that they were still the chosen and favored people of God. He was their father, and a just God; it could not be that He would break covenant with Israel. Was it not to them that He had given those Scriptures which both the Christians and the Moslems accepted and revered? In the depths of their despair they mounted to such compensatory pride that their rabbis, who had exalted them, had to humble them with

---

* The valley of Hinnom was a rubbish heap outside of Jerusalem, where fires were kept constantly burning to prevent pestilence. Sheol was conceived as a subterranean region of darkness that received all the dead.

reproof. Then, as now, they longed for the land of their nation's birth, and idealized it in loving memory. "He who walks four ells in Palestine is sure of everlasting life," they said; "he who lives in Palestine is without sin"; [39] "even the merest talk of those who dwell in Palestine is Torah." [40] The central part of the daily prayers, the Shemoneh Esreh ("eighteen paragraphs"), included a petition for the coming of the son of David, the Messiah King who would make the Jews a nation again, united, free, worshiping God in their own Temple with the ancient ritual and song.

2. *Ritual*

What distinguished the Jews in this Age of Faith, what kept them one in their scattering, was not theology but ritual, not a creed that Christianity had merely extended and that Islam would substantially adopt, but a ceremonial law of such burdensome complexity that only this proud and high-strung people showed the humility and patience required to obey it. Christianity sought unity through uniform belief, Judaism through uniform ritual. The laws "were given," said Abba Areca, "only for the purpose of disciplining and refining men by their observance." [41]

The ritual was first of all a law of worship. When the synagogue succeeded the Temple, animal sacrifice was replaced by offerings and prayer. But no more in the synagogue than in the Temple was any image of God or man allowed. Every approach to idol worship was shunned; and instrumental music, permitted in the Temple, was forbidden in the synagogue. Here Christianity diverged, Mohammedanism stemmed, from Judaism; the Semites developed a somber piety, the Christians a somber art.

Prayer made every day, almost every hour, a religious experience for the orthodox Jew. Morning prayers were to be said with phylacteries (small cases containing passages from the Scriptures) affixed to the forehead and the arms. No meal was to be eaten without a brief grace before it, and a longer prayer of thanksgiving at its close. But these domestic prayers were not enough; men can be held together only by doing things together; and the rabbis argued, with Oriental hyperbole, that "a man's prayer is heard by God only when offered in a synagogue." [42] The public liturgy consisted mainly of the Shemoneh Esreh, the Shema Yisrael, readings from the Pentateuch, the Prophets, and the Psalms, a homily of Scriptural explanation, the Kaddish (prayers of praise and blessing for the living and the dead), and a concluding benediction. This remains the essential synagogue ritual to the present day.

Far more detailed than these regulations of worship were the rules for cleanliness or ritual purity. Physical hygiene was considered favorable to spiritual health. [43] The rabbis forbade living in a city in which there was no bathhouse, [44] and gave almost medical instructions for the bath. "If one bathes with hot water, and does not follow it with cold water, it is like iron which is inserted into a furnace and not afterward plunged into cold water"; [45] the body, like the iron, must be tempered and steeled. Anointing should follow the bath.[46] Hands were to be washed immediately upon rising, before and after each meal, and before ceremonial prayer or any other ritual observance. Corpses, sexual functions, menstruation, childbirth, vermin, pigs, and leprosy (i.e., various skin diseases) were ritually (i.e., by religious law) unclean. Persons touched or affected by any of these were to go to the synagogue and perform a purification ceremonial. A woman was considered unclean (not to be sexually approached) for forty days after bearing a son, eighty days after bearing a daughter.[47] In accord with the Biblical injunction (Gen. xvii, 9-14), a boy was to be circumcised on his eighth day. This was represented as a sacrifice to, and a covenant with, Yahveh; but the prevalence of the custom among Egyptians, Ethiopians, Phoenicians, Syrians, and Arabs suggests that it was a hygienic measure indicated in a climate more favorable to sexual precocity and excitability than to cleanliness; and this conclusion is reinforced by the rabbinical command that no Jew should keep beyond twelve months an uncircumcised slave.[48]

The Talmud occasionally reads like a manual of home medicine rather than a code of religious laws; it had to be an encyclopedia of advice for its people. The Jews of the fourth and fifth centuries, like most Mediterranean peoples, were slipping back into the medical superstitions and makeshifts of the isolated and the poor; and a good deal of this popular and superstitious medicine entered into the Talmud. Nevertheless we find in the Babylonian Gemara excellent descriptions of the esophagus, larynx, trachea, lungs, meninges, and genitals; tumors of the lungs, cirrhosis of the liver, caseous degeneration, and many other diseases are accurately described; the rabbis note that flies and drinking cups may carry infection; [49] and hemophilia is recognized as an hereditary ailment making circumcision of the offspring inadvisable. Mingled with these ideas are magical formulas for exorcising demons supposed to cause disease.

The rabbis, like all of us, were experts on diet. Dietary wisdom begins with the teeth. These should never be extracted, no matter how they ache,[50] for "if a man chews well with his teeth his feet will find strength." [51] Vegetables and fruits, except the date, are highly recommended. Meat is a luxury, which only the well washed should have.[52] The animal is to be killed in such a way as to minimize its pain, and draw the blood out of the meat; to eat flesh with blood is an abomination. Hence the slaughter of animals for food must be left to trained persons, who will also examine the viscera to make sure that the animal is not diseased. Meat and milk, and dishes prepared with them, must not be eaten at the same meal, or even placed near each other in the kitchen.[53] The flesh of swine is to be abhorred. Eat no eggs, onions, or garlic that have been left overnight without their shell or peel.[54] Eat at stated hours only; "don't peck all day like hens." [55] "More people die from overeating than from undernourishment." [56] "Up to forty eating is beneficial; after that age, drinking is beneficial." [57] Moderation in drinking is better than total abstinence; wine is often a good medicine,[58] and "there is no gladness without it." [59] Pursuing the subject of diet to its end, the rabbis argued that he "who prolongs his stay in a privy lengthens his years," and recommended a prayer of thanksgiving after every answer to nature's call.[60]

They frowned upon asceticism, and counseled their people to enjoy the good things of life where no sin was involved.[61] Fasts were obligatory at certain periods and on some holydays; but perhaps here too religion was used as a prod to health. The wisdom of the race bade the Jews keep festival and make feast now and then, despite the overtones of sorrow and longing that sounded even in their joys. "On a festival a man must make glad his wife and household"; if possible he must outfit them with new clothes.[62] The Sabbath —greatest of Jewish inventions—was apparently a burden in Talmudic days; the pious Jew was then expected to speak as little as possible, light no fire in his home, and spend hours at the synagogue and in prayer. A long tractate discussed with head-splitting hair-splitting just what might and what might not be done on the Sabbath. But the casuistry of the rabbis was directed to mitigating, rather than increasing, the terrors of piety. Their subtlety devised convincing reasons for doing what one had to do on the day of rest. Moreover the good Jew discovered a secret happiness in observing the ancient Sabbath ritual. He began it with a little ceremony of "sanctification" (kiddush). Surrounded by his family and his guests (for this was a favorite day for entertaining friends), he took a full cup of wine, pronounced a benediction over it, drank, and passed the cup along for guests and wife and children to drink. Then he took bread and blessed it, thanking the God "who bringeth forth bread from the earth," and passed portions of it to all who shared his table. No fasting or mourning was permitted on the Sabbath.

Many holydays divided the year, and gave new occasions for pious remembrance or grateful rest. Pesach, beginning on the fourteenth of Nisan (April), commemorated through eight days the escape of the Jews from Egypt. In Biblical times it had been called the Feast of Unleavened Bread, because the Jews had fled with the dough of their bread still unleavened; Talmudic times called it Pesach, i.e., Passover, because Yahveh, smiting the firstborn of the Egyptians, "passed over" those houses whose doorposts had been sprinkled, by the Jewish occupants, with the blood of the lamb.[63] On the first day of the feast the Jews celebrated the Paschal meal (Seder); each father acted as leader of the service for his gathered family, performed with them a ritual recalling those bitter Mosaic days, and passed on, by questions and answers, their treasured story to the young. At Pentecost, seven weeks after Passover, the feast of Shavuot celebrated the wheat harvest, and the revelation on Mt. Sinai. On the first day of Tishri—the seventh month of the ecclesiastical, the first month of the Jewish civil year, corresponding roughly with the autumnal equinox—the Jews celebrated Rosh-ha-Shana, the Feast of the New Year and of the month's new moon, and blew the ram's horn (shofar) to commemorate the revealing of the Torah, to call men to repentance, and to anticipate the happy day when such a blast would summon all the Jews of the world to worship their God in Jerusalem. From the eve of Rosh-ha-Shana to the tenth day of Tishri were penitential days; on all but the ninth of those days pious Jews fasted and prayed; and on the tenth, Yom-ha-Kippurim, the Day of Atonement, from sunset to sunset, they were not to eat or drink or wear shoes or labor or bathe or indulge in love; all day long they attended services in the synagogue, confessed and mourned their sins and those of their people, even from the worship of the Golden Calf. On the fifteenth day of Tishri came Sukkoth, the Feast of Tabernacles; for seven days the Jews were supposed to live in booths, to commemorate the tents in which, it was said, their ancestors had slept during their forty years' sojourn in the wilderness. In the Dispersion a literal fulfillment of this old vintage or harvest festival offered difficulties, and the rabbis showed their good will by redefining *sukka* to mean almost anything that could symbolize a habitation. On the twenty-fifth of the ninth month, Kislev (December), and for seven days thereafter, the festival of Hanukkah, or Dedication, recalled the purification of the Temple by the Maccabees (165 B.C.) after its defilement by Antiochus Epiphanes. And on the fourteenth of Adar (March) the Jews celebrated Purim ("lots"), the deliverance of their people from the wiles of the Persian minister Haman by Esther and Mordecai. Gifts and good wishes were exchanged in a joyful and vinous feast; on that day, said Rab Raba, a man should drink until he could no longer distinguish between "Cursed be Haman!" and "Cursed be Mordecai!" [64]

We must not think of those Talmudic Jews as dour pessimists, sick with the pangs of despised talents, tossed about by the storms of doctrine, and lost in longing for their ravished fatherland. Amid dispersion and oppression, atonement and poverty, they kept their heads erect, relished the tang and strife of life, the brief beauty of their burdened women, and the abiding splendor of earth and sky. "Every day," said Rabbi Meir, "a man should utter a hundred benedictions." [65] And another said, for all of us: "To walk even four ells without bowing the head is an offense to Heaven; for is it not written, 'The whole earth is full of His glory'?" [66]

3. Ethics of the Talmud

The Talmud is not only an encyclopedia of Jewish history, theology, ritual, medicine, and folklore; it is also a treatise on agriculture, gardens, industry, the professions, commerce,[67] finance, taxation, property, slavery, inheritance, theft, legal procedure, and penal law. To do the book justice it would be necessary with polymathic wisdom to survey its judgments in all these fields.

The Talmud is above all a code of ethics, so different from the Christian, and so like the Moslem, that even a running acquaintance with it challenges the view of the Middle Ages as merely the story of medieval Christianity. The three religions agreed in rejecting the practicability of a natural—non-religious—morality; most men, they believed, can be persuaded to tolerable behavior only by the fear of God. All three based their moral code on identical conceptions: the all-seeing eye and all-recording hand of God, the divine authorship of the moral code, and the ultimate equalization of virtue with happiness by post-mortem punishments and rewards. In the two Semitic cultures law, as well as ethics, was inseparable from religion; no distinction was admitted between crime and sin, between civil and ecclesiastical law; every discreditable act is an offense against God, a profanation of His presence and Holy Name.

The three religions agreed further on certain elements of morality: the sanctity of the family and the home, the honor due to parents and the old, the loving care of children, and charity to all. No people has surpassed the Jews in the order of beauty of family life. In Judaism, as in Islam, voluntary celibacy or childlessness was a major sin; [68] to make a home and a family was a religious mandate, [69] the first of the 613 precepts of the Law; "a childless person," says a midrash, [70] "is accounted as dead." Jew, Christian, and Moslem agreed that the adequate continuance of the group is endangered when the religious command to parentage loses its force. Under certain circumstances, however, the rabbis permitted family limitation, preferably by contraception. "There are three classes of women who should employ an absorbent: a minor, lest pregnancy should prove fatal; a pregnant woman, lest abortion should result; and a nursing mother, lest she become pregnant and prematurely wean the child so that it dies." [71]

The Jews, like their contemporaries, were reluctant to have daughters, but rejoiced at the birth of a son; he, not she, could carry on the father's name, family, and property, and tend his grave; the daughter would marry into another, perhaps a distant, household, and be lost to her parents as soon as her rearing was complete. But once children came, they were cherished without favoritism, and with a wise mixture of discipline and love. "If thou must strike a child," said one rabbi, "do it with a shoestring"; [72] "if one refrains from punishing a child," says another, "it will end by becoming utterly depraved." [73] Every sacrifice must be made to give the child an education—i.e., to instruct the mind and train the character by a knowledge of "the Law and the Prophets." "The world is saved," said a Hebrew proverb, "by the breath of school children"; [74] the Shekinah, or divine presence, shines in their faces.

The child in turn must honor and protect the parents, under all conditions, to the end.

Charity was an inescapable obligation. "Greater is he who practices charity than" he who performs "all the sacrifices." [75] Some Jews were niggardly, some were miserly, but by and large no other people has ever given as generously as the Jews. The rabbis had to forbid men to give more than a fifth of their property to charity; yet some were found, at their death, to have given half.[76] "On Abba Umna's face there was always a holy peace. He was a surgeon, but would never accept with his hands any payment for his service. He had a box placed in a corner of his consulting room, so that those who were able to pay could deposit what they wished . . . and those who could not afford to pay would not be shamed." [77] Rab Huna, "when he sat down to a meal, would open the doors and exclaim, 'Let whoever is in need enter and eat.' " [78] Chama ben Ilai gave bread to all who sought it, and kept his hand in his purse when he walked abroad, so that none need hesitate to ask.[79] But the Talmud reproved conspicous giving, and counseled a modest secrecy: "He who dispenses charity in private is greater than Moses." [80]

To the institution of marriage the rabbis addressed all their learning and eloquence; on it and religion rested the whole structure of Jewish life. They did not condemn the sexual appetite, but they feared its force, and labored to control it. Some advised that salt be eaten with bread "to lessen the seminal fluid"; [81] others felt that the only recourse against sexual temptation was hard work combined with study of the Torah. If this availed not, "let him go to a place where he is unknown, put on black clothes, and do what his heart desires; but let him not publicly profane the Name." [82] A man should avoid any situation that may excite his passions; he should not talk much with women; and he "should never walk behind a woman along the road, not even his own wife. . . . A man should walk behind a lion rather than behind a woman." [83] The delightful humor of the rabbis appears again in the story of Reb Kahan. He

> was once selling ladies' baskets when he was exposed to temptation. He pleaded with his tempter to let him off, and promised to return. But instead of returning he went up to the roof of a house and threw himself down. Before he reached the ground Elijah came and caught him, and reproached him with having brought him a distance of 400 miles to save him from self-destruction.[84]

The rabbis apparently felt that virginity is all right in its place, but that perpetual virginity is arrested development; in their view the supreme perfection of a woman is perfect motherhood, as the supreme virtue of man is perfect fatherhood. Every father was urged to save and provide a dowry for each of his daughters, and a marriage settlement for each son, lest their marriage be unhealthily delayed. Early marriage was recommended—at fourteen for the girl, eighteen for the man. A girl might legally marry at twelve years and six months, a man at thirteen. Postponement of marriage was permitted to students engaged in the study of the Law. Some rabbis argued that a man should get his economic footing before marrying—"A man should first build a house, then plant a vineyard, then marry" [85]—but this was a minority opinion, and perhaps involved no contradiction if the parents provided the expected financial aid. The youth was advised to choose his mate not for her beauty but for her prospective qualities as a mother.[86] "Descend a step in choosing a wife, ascend a step in choosing a friend"; [87] to marry a woman above one's rank is to invite contumely.

The Talmud, like the Old Testament and the Koran, allowed polygamy. "A man may marry as many wives as he pleases," said one rabbi; but another passage in the same tractate limited the number to four; and a third required the husband, when taking a second wife, to give a divorce to the first wife if she should ask for it.[88] The institution of the levirate, by which a Jew was required to marry his brother's widow, presumed polygamy, and was probably due not only to kindly sentiment but also to a desire for a high birth rate in a community which, like all ancient and medieval societies, suffered high mortality. Having allowed such freedom of mating for the man, the rabbis made adultery a capital crime. Some of them agreed with Jesus that "one may commit adultery with the eyes"; [89] some went further, saying, "Whoever regards even the little finger of a woman hath already sinned in his heart." [90] But Rab Areca was more humane: "A man will have a demerit in his record on Judgment Day for everything he beheld with his eyes and declined to enjoy." [91]

Divorce by mutual consent was allowed. The husband could be divorced only with his consent; the wife without her consent. To divorce an adulterous wife was mandatory, and divorce was recommended where the wife had remained childless ten years after marriage.[92] The school of Shammai had allowed the husband to put away his wife only for adultery; the school of Hillel allowed it if the husband found in her "anything unseemly." Hillel's view prevailed in the Talmudic period; and Akiba went so far as to say that a husband "may divorce his wife if he finds another woman more beautiful." [93] A man might, without surrendering the marriage settlement, divorce "a woman who transgresses Jewish law, such as going in public with uncovered head, spinning in the street, or conversing with all sorts of men"; or "a loud-voiced woman—i.e., one who talks in her house and her neighbors can hear what she says." [94] Desertion by the husband gave no ground for divorce.[95] Some rabbis permitted the wife to ask the court for divorce from a cruel, impotent, or unwilling husband, or one who did not support her properly,[96] or was maimed, or stank.[97] The rabbis did something to discourage divorce by requiring complex legal formalities, and, in all but a few cases, the forfeiture of both dowry and marriage settlement to the wife. "The very altar sheds tears," said Rabbi Eleazar, "on him who divorces the wife of his youth." [98]

All in all, Talmudic law, like the Mohammedan, was man-made law, and favored the male so strongly as to suggest, in the rabbis, a very terror of woman's power. Like the Christian Fathers, they blamed her for extinguishing the "Soul of the World" through Eve's intelligent curiosity. They considered woman "light-minded," [99] and yet admitted in her an instinctive wisdom missing in man. [100] They deplored the loquacity of women at great length ("Ten measures of speech descended to the world; women took nine, men one" [101]); they condemned their addiction to the occult, [102] to rouge and kohl. [103] They approved of a man spending generously on his wife's raiment, but wished she would beautify herself for her husband rather than for other men. [104] In law, according to one rabbi, "a hundred women are equal to only one witness." [105] Their property rights were as limited in the Talmud as in eighteenth-century England; their earnings, and the income from any property they might own, belonged to their husbands. [106] Woman's place was in the home. In the utopian "Days of the Messiah," said a hopeful rabbi, woman "will bear a child every day." [107] "A man who has a bad wife will never see the face of hell." [108] On the other hand no man is so rich, said Akiba, as one who has a wife noted for her good deeds. [109] "Everything derives from the woman," says a midrash. [110] According to Hebrew proverbs: "All the blessings of a household come through the wife; therefore should her husband honor her. . . . Let men beware of causing women to weep; God counts their tears." [111]

In the most delightful part of the Talmud, the little treatise Pirke Aboth, an unknown editor gathered the maxims of the great rabbis of the last two centuries before, and the first two centuries after, Christ. Many of these apothegms praise wisdom, and some define it.

> Ben Zoma said: Who is wise? He who learns from every man. . . . Who is mighty? He who subdues his (evil) inclination. . . . He that ruleth his spirit is better than he that taketh a city. Who is rich? He who rejoices in his lot. . . . When thou eatest of the labor of thy hands, happy shalt thou be. . . . Who is honored? He who honors his fellow men. [112] . . . Despise not any man, nor anything; for there is no man that has not his hour, and there is nothing that has not its place. [113] . . . All my days I grew up among the sages, and I have found nothing better for a person than silence. . . . [114]
>
> Rabbi Eleazar used to say: One whose wisdom exceeds his deeds may be compared to a tree whereof the branches are many and the roots few, so that when the winds come it is uprooted and turned upon its face. . . . But one whose deeds exceed his wisdom may be

compared to a tree whereof the branches are few and the roots many,
so that even if all the winds in the world blow upon it they move it
not from its place.[115]

IV. LIFE AND THE LAW

The Talmud is not a work of art. The task of reducing the thought of a
thousand years into a coherent system proved too much even for a hundred
patient rabbis. Several tractates are obviously in the wrong *seder* or order;
several chapters are in the wrong tractate; subjects are taken up, dropped,
and lawlessly resumed. It is not the product of deliberation, it is the deliberation itself; all views are recorded, and contradictions are often left unre-
solved; it is as if we had crossed fifteen centuries to eavesdrop on the most
intimate discussions of the schools, and heard Akiba and Meir and Jehuda
Hanasi and Rab in the heat of their debates. Remembering that we are inter-
lopers, that these men and the others have had their casual words snatched
from their mouths and cast into uncalculated contexts and sent hurtling
down the years, we can forgive the casuistry, sophistry, legends, astrology,
demonology, superstition, magic, miracles, numerology, and revelatory
dreams, the Pelion on Ossa of argument crowning a web of fantasy, the con-
solatory vanity forever healing frustrated hope.

If we resent the stringency of these laws, the intrusive minuteness of these
regulations, the Oriental severity of punishment for their violation, we must
not take the matter too much to heart; the Jews made no pretense to keeping
all these commandments, and the rabbis winked on every other page at the
gap between their counsels of perfection and the stealthy frailties of men. "If
Israel should properly observe a single Sabbath," said a cautious rabbi, "the
Son of David would come immediately." [116] The Talmud was not a code of
laws requiring strict obedience; it was a record of rabbinical opinion, gathered for the guidance of leisurely piety. The untutored masses obeyed only
a choice few of the precepts of the Law.

There was in the Talmud a strong emphasis on ritual; but that was in part
the Jew's reaction to the attempts of Church and state to make him abandon
his Law; the ritual was a mark of identity, a bond of unity and continuity, a
badge of defiance to a never-forgiving world. Here and there, in these
twenty volumes, we find words of hatred for Christianity; but they were for
a Christianity that had forgotten the gentleness of Christ; that persecuted the
adherents of the Law that Christ had bidden His followers to fulfill; and that
had, in the view of the rabbis, abandoned the monotheism which was the inalienable essence of the ancient faith. Amid these ceremonial complexities
and controversial barbs we find hundreds of sage counsels and psychological
insights, and occasional passages recalling the majesty of the Old Testament
or the mystical tenderness of the New. The whimsical humor characteristic

of the Jew lightens the burden of the long lesson. So one rabbi tells how Moses entered incognito into Akiba's classroom, sat in the last row, and marveled at the many laws derived by the great teacher from the Mosaic code, and of which its amanuensis had never dreamed.[117]

For 1400 years the Talmud was the core of Jewish education. Seven hours a day, through seven years, the Hebrew youth pored over it, recited it, sank it into his memory by sound and sight; and like the Confucian classics similarly memorized, it formed mind and character by the discipline of its study and the deposit of its lore. The method of teaching was not by mere recitation and repetition; it was also by disputation between master and pupil, between pupil and pupil, and the application of old laws to the circumstances of the new day. The result was a sharpness of intellect, a retentiveness of memory, that gave the Jew an advantage in many spheres requiring clarity, concentration, persistence, and exactitude, while at the same time it tended to narrow the range and freedom of the Jewish mind. The Talmud tamed the excitable nature of the Jew; it checked his individualism, and molded him to fidelity and sobriety in his family and his community. Superior minds may have been hampered by the "yoke of the Law," but the Jews as a whole were saved.

The Talmud can never be understood except in terms of history, as an organ of survival for a people exiled, destitute, oppressed, and in danger of utter disintegration. What the Prophets had done to uphold the Jewish spirit in the Babylonian Captivity, the rabbis did in this wider dispersion. Pride had to be regained, order had to be established, faith and morals maintained, health of body and mind rebuilt after a shattering experience.[118] Through this heroic discipline, this rerooting of the uprooted Jew in his own tradition—stability and unity were restored through continents of wandering and centuries of grief. The Talmud, as Heine said, was a portable Fatherland; wherever Jews were, even as fearful enclaves in alien lands, they could put themselves again into their own world, and live with their Prophets and rabbis, by bathing their minds and hearts in the ocean of the Law. No wonder they loved this book, to us more undulant and diverse than a hundred Montaignes. They preserved even fragments of it with fierce affection, took their turns in reading snatches of the enormous manuscript, paid great sums, in later centuries, to have it printed in all its fullness, wept when kings and popes and parliaments banned or confiscated or burned it, rejoiced to hear Reuchlin and Erasmus defend it, and made it, even to our own time, the most precious possession of their temples and their homes, the refuge, solace, and prison of the Jewish soul.

CHAPTER XVI

The Medieval Jews

565-1300

I. THE ORIENTAL COMMUNITIES

ISRAEL now had a law, but no state; a book, but no home. To 614 Jerusalem was a Christian city; till 629, Persian; till 637, again Christian; then, till 1099, a Moslem provincial capital. In that year the Crusaders besieged Jerusalem; the Jews joined the Moslems in its defense; when it fell, the surviving Jews were driven into a synagogue, and were burned to death.[1] A rapid growth of Palestinian Jewry followed the recapture of Jerusalem by Saladin in 1187; and Saladin's brother, the Sultan al-Adil, welcomed the 300 rabbis who in 1211 fled from England and France. Fifty-two years later, however, Nachmanides found there a mere handful of Jews;[2] the Holy City had become overwhelmingly Mohammedan.

Despite conversions and occasional persecutions, Jews remained numerous in Moslem Syria, Babylonia (Iraq), and Persia, and developed a vigorous economic and cultural life. In their internal affairs they continued, as under the Sasanian kings, to enjoy self-government under their exilarch and the directors of their rabbinical academies. The exilarch was accepted by the caliphs as the head of all the Jews in Babylonia, Armenia, Turkestan, Persia, and Yemen; according to Benjamin of Tudela all subjects of the caliphs were required "to rise in the presence of the Prince of the Captivity and to salute him respectfully."[3] The office of exilarch was hereditary in one famly, which traced its lineage to David; it was a political rather than a spiritual power; and its efforts to control the rabbinate led to its decline and fall. After 762 the directors of the academies elected and dominated the exilarch.

The rabbinical colleges at Sura and Pumbeditha provided religious and intellectual leadership for the Jews of Islam, and in less degree for those of Christendom. In 658 the Caliph Ali freed the academy of Sura from the jurisdiction of the exilarch; thereupon its head, Mar-Isaac, took the title Gaon, or Excellency, and inaugurated the Gaonate, the epoch of the Geonim in Babylonian religion and scholarship.[4] As the college of Pumbeditha rose in revenues and dignity from its proximity to Baghdad, its directors also assumed the title of Gaon. From the seventh to the eleventh century, questions in Talmudic law were addressed to these Geonim from all the Jewish world; and their *responsa* created a new legal literature for Judaism.

The rise of the Geonim coincided with—perhaps in some measure it was necessitated by—a heresy that now shook and divided Oriental Jewry. In 762, when the Exilarch Solomon died, his nephew Anan ben David stood in line for the succession; but the heads of Sura and Pumbeditha, discarding the hereditary principle, installed as exilarch Anan's younger brother Chananya. Anan denounced the two Geonim, fled to Palestine, established his own synagogue, and called upon Jews everywhere to reject the Talmud and obey only the law of the Pentateuch. This was a return to the position of the Sadducees; it corresponded to the repudiation of the "traditions," and exaltation of the Koran, by the Shia sect in Islam, and to the Protestant abandonment of Catholic traditions for a return to the Gospels. Anan went further, and reexamined the Pentateuch in a commentary that marked a bold advance in the critical study of the Biblical text. He protested against the changes that the Talmudic rabbis had made in the Mosaic Law by their adaptive interpretations, and insisted on the strict fulfillment of the Pentateuch decrees; hence his followers received the name of Qaraites *—"adherents of the text." Anan praised Jesus as a holy man who had wished to set aside not the written Law of Moses but only the oral Law of the scribes and the Pharisees; Jesus, in Anan's view, had aimed not to found a new religion but to cleanse and strengthen Judaism.[5] The Qaraites became numerous in Palestine, Egypt, and Spain; they declined in the twelfth century, and only a vanishing remnant survives in Turkey, South Russia, and Arabia. Qaraites of the ninth century, presumably influenced by the Mutazilites of Islam, abandoned Anan's principle of literal interpretation, and proposed that the resurrection of the body, and certain physical descriptions of God in the Bible, should be taken with a metaphorical grain of salt. The orthodox "Rabbanite" Jews, reverting to literalism in their turn, insisted, like orthodox Moslems, that phrases like "God's hand" or "God sitting down" were to be taken literally; some expositors calculated the precise measurements of God's body, members, and beard.[6] A few Jewish freethinkers, like Chivi al-Balchi, rejected even the Pentateuch as a binding law.[7] It was in this environment of economic prosperity, religious freedom, and lively debate that Judaism produced its first famous medieval philosopher.

Saadia ben Joseph al-Fayyumi was born at Dilaz, a village of the Faiyûm, in 892. He grew up in Egypt, and married there. In 915 he migrated to Palestine, then to Babylonia. He must have been an apt student and sound teacher, for at the youthful age of thirty-six he was made Gaon or director of the college at Sura. Perceiving the inroads that Qaraism and skepticism had made upon orthodox Judaism, he set himself the same task that the *mutakallimun* had undertaken in Islam—to demonstrate the full accord of the traditional faith with reason and history. In his brief life of fifty years Saadia produced—mostly in Arabic—a mass of writings rivaled only by those of

---

* From *Qera*, Aramaic for *text*; from *qara*, to read; cf. *Quran*.

Maimonides in the record of medieval Jewish thought. His *Agron*, an Aramaic dictionary of Hebrew, founded Hebrew philology; his *Kitab al-Lugah*, or *Book of Language*, is the oldest known grammar of the Hebrew tongue; his Arabic translation of the Old Testament remained to our time the version used by Arabic-speaking Jews; his several commentaries on books of the Bible rank him as "perhaps the greatest Bible commentator of all time"; [8] his *Kitab al-Amanat*, or *Book of Philosophical Doctrines and Beliefs* (933), is the *Summa contra Gentiles* of Jewish theology.

Saadia accepts both revelation and tradition, the written and the oral Law; but he also accepts reason, and proposes to prove by reason the truth of revelation and tradition. Wherever the Bible clearly contradicts reason, we may assume that the passage is not meant to be taken literally by adult minds. Anthropomorphic descriptions of the deity are to be understood metaphorically; God is not like a man. The order and law of the world indicate an intelligent creator. It is unreasonable to suppose that an intelligent God would fail to reward virtue, but obviously virtue is not always rewarded in this life; consequently there must be another life, which will redeem the apparent injustice of this one. Perhaps the sufferings of the virtuous here are punishments for their occasional sins, so that they may enter paradise at once when they die; and the earthly triumphs of the wicked are rewards for their incidental virtues, so that . . . But even those who achieve the highest virtue, prosperity, and happiness on earth feel in their hearts that there is a better state than this one of indefinite possibilities and limited fulfillments; and how could a God intelligent enough to create so marvelous a world allow such hopes to form in the soul if they were never to be realized? [9] Saadia took a leaf or two from Moslem theologians, and followed their methods of exposition, even, now and then, the details of their argument. In turn his work permeated the Jewish world, and influenced Maimonides. "Were it not for Saadia," said ben Maimon, "the Torah would almost have disappeared." [10]

It must be admitted that Saadia was a man of some acerbity, and that his quarrel with the Exilarch David ben Zakkai injured Babylonian Jewry. In 930 David excommunicated Saadia, and Saadia excommunicated David. In 940 David died, and Saadia appointed a new exilarch; but this appointee was assassinated by Moslems on the ground that he had disparaged Mohammed. Saadia appointed the victim's son to succeed him, whereupon this youth also was slain. The discouraged Jews decided to leave the office unfilled; and in 942 the Babylonian exilarchate closed its career of seven centuries. In that year Saadia died. The disintegration of the Baghdad caliphate, the establishment of Egypt, North Africa, and Spain as independent Moslem states, weakened the bonds between Asiatic, African, and European Jewry. The Babylonian Jews shared in the economic decline of Eastern Islam after the tenth century; the college of Sura closed its doors in 1034, that of Pumbeditha four years later; and in 1040 the Gaonate came to an end. The Crusades further isolated the Babylonian from the Egyptian and European Jews; and after the Mongol sack of Baghdad in 1258 the Babylonian Jewish community almost disappeared from history.

Long before these catastrophes many Oriental Jews had migrated to further Asia, Arabia, Egypt, North Africa, and Europe. Ceylon had 23,000 Hebrews in 1165; [11] several Jewish communities in Arabia survived the hostility of Mohammed; when Amr conquered Egypt in 641 he reported "40,000 tributary" (taxpaying) Jews in Alexandria. As Cairo spread its proliferations, its Jewish population, orthodox and Qaraite, increased. The Egyptian Jews enjoyed self-government in internal affairs under their *nagid*, or prince; they rose to wealth in commerce and to a high place in the administration of the Moslem state.[12] In 960, according to a tradition, four rabbis sailed from Bari in Italy; their vessel was captured by a Spanish Moslem admiral, and they were sold into slavery: Rabbi Moses and his son Chanoch at Cordova, Rabbi Shemaria at Alexandria, Rabbi Hushiel at Qairwan. Each rabbi, we are told, was freed, and founded an academy in the city where he had been sold. It is usually assumed, but not certain, that they were scholars from Sura; in any case they brought the learning of Eastern Jewry to the West, and while Judaism declined in Asia it entered upon its halcyon days in Egypt and Spain.

II. THE EUROPEAN COMMUNITIES

Jews made their way into medieval Russia from Babylonia and Persia through Transoxiana and the Caucasus, and up the Black Sea coast from Asia Minor through Constantinople. In that capital, and in the Byzantine realm, the Jews enjoyed a harassed prosperity from the eighth to the twelfth century. Greece had several substantial Jewish communities, notably at Thebes, where their silk manufactures earned high repute. Up through Thessaly, Thrace, and Macedonia the Jews migrated into the Balkans, and followed the Danube into Hungary. A handful of Hebrew merchants came to Poland from Germany in the tenth century. Jews had been in Germany since pre-Christian times. In the ninth century there were considerable Jewish settlements at Metz, Speyer, Mainz, Worms, Strasbourg, Frankfort, and Cologne. These groups were too busy and mobile with commerce to contribute much to cultural history; however, Gershom ben Jehuda (960–1028) founded a rabbinical academy at Mainz, wrote a Hebrew commentary on the Talmud, and acquired such authority that German Jewry addressed to him, rather than to the Geonim of Babylonia, their questions on Talmudic law.

There were Jews in England in 691.[13] Many more came in with William the Conqueror, and were at first protected by the Norman rulers as providers of capital and collectors of revenue. Their communities in London, Norwich, York, and other English centers were outside the jurisdiction of the local authorities, and were subject only to the king. This legal isolation widened the barrier between Christian and Jew, and played a part in the pogroms of the twelfth century.

Gaul had had Jewish merchants from the time of Caesar. By 600 there were Jewish colonies in all the major cities. The Merovingian kings persecuted them with pious ferocity; Chilperic ordered them all to accept Christianity or have their eyes torn out (581).[14] Charlemagne, while maintaining discriminatory laws against the Jews, protected them as useful and enterprising farmers and craftsmen, merchants, doctors, and financiers, and employed a Jew as his personal physician. In 787, according to a disputed tradition, he brought the Kalonymos family from Lucca to Mainz to encourage Jewish scholarship in the Frank realm. In 797 he sent a Jew as interpreter or as dragoman with an embassy to Harun al-Rashid. Louis the Pious favored the Jews as stimulators of commerce, and appointed a *magister Iudaeorum* to guard their rights. Despite hostile legends, legal disabilities, and occasional minor persecutions, the Jews enjoyed in France in the ninth and tenth centuries a degree of prosperity and peace hardly known again by the Jews of Europe before the French Revolution.[15]

All through Italy there were little Jewish enclaves, from Trani to Venice and Milan. Jews were especially numerous in Padua, and may have influenced the growth of Averroism in the university there. Salerno, home of the first medieval school of scientific medicine in Latin Christendom, contained 600 Jews,[16] several of them noted physicians. The Emperor Frederick II had Jewish scholars at his court in Foggia, and Pope Alexander III (1159–81) had several Jews in high position in his household;[17] but Frederick joined with Pope Gregory IX in oppressive measures against the Jews of Italy.

The Spanish Jews called themselves Sephardim, and traced their origin to the royal tribe of Judah.* After the conversion of King Recared (586–601) to orthodox Christianity the Visigothic government united with the powerful hierarchy of the Spanish Church to make life less attractive to the Jews. They were excluded from public office, and were forbidden to marry Christians or have Christian slaves. King Sisebut ordered all Jews to accept Christianity or emigrate (613); his successor repealed this decree, but the Council of Toledo of 633 ruled that those Jews who had submitted to baptism and then returned to Judaism should be separated from their children and sold into slavery. King Chintila renewed Sisebut's decree (638); and King Egica prohibited Jewish ownership of land, and any business transaction between Christian and Jew (693). When the Moors and Arabs invaded the peninsula (711) the Jews helped them at every turn.

---

* *Sepharad* is the name applied in the Book of Obadiah (i, 20) to a region, presumably Asia Minor, to which some Jews were deported by Nebuchadrezzar (597 B.C.); the word was later applied to Spain. The Jews of Germany were loosely called Ashkenazim through their supposed derivation from Ashkenaz, grandson of Japheth (Gen. x, 3).

The conquerors, to repopulate the land, invited immigration; 50,000 Jews came from Asia and Africa;[18] some towns, like Lucena, were inhabited almost wholly by Jews. Freed from economic disabilities, the Jews of Moslem Spain spread into every field of agriculture, industry, finance, and the professions. They adopted the dress, language, and customs of the Arabs, garbed themselves in turbans and silk robes, rode in carriages, and were hardly distinguishable from their Semitic cousins. Several Jews became court physicians, and one of these was made adviser to the greatest of the caliphs of Cordova.

Hasdai ibn Shaprut (915–70) was to Abd-er-Rahman III what Nizam al-Mulk in the next century would be to Malik Shah. Born in the wealthy and cultured Ibn Ezra family, his father taught him Hebrew, Arabic, and Latin; he studied medicine and other sciences at Cordova, cured the Caliph's ailments, and showed such wide knowledge and good judgment in politics that he was appointed to the diplomatic staff, apparently at the age of twenty-five. He was entrusted with ever larger responsibilities over the financial and commercial life of the state. He had no official title; the Caliph hesitated to arouse resentment by making him officially vizier; but Hasdai performed his many functions with such tact that he won the good will of Arabs, Jews, and Christians alike. He encouraged learning and literature, provided students with scholarships and books, and gathered about him a salon of poets, savants, and philosophers. When he died, Moslems vied with Jews in honoring his memory.

There were similar, if lesser, figures, elsewhere in Moslem Spain. At Seville al-Mutamid invited to his court the scholar and astronomer Isaac ben Baruch, gave him the title of Prince, and made him head rabbi of all the Jewish congregations there.[19] At Granada Samuel Halevi ibn Naghdela rivaled the power and wisdom, and exceeded the learning, of Hasdai ibn Shaprut. Born (993) and reared in Cordova, he combined the study of the Talmud with that of Arabic literature, and both with the selling of spices. When Cordova fell to the Berbers he moved to Malaga, and there added to his modest income by composing letters for petitioners to King Habbus of Granada. Struck with the calligraphy and diction of these letters, the King's vizier visited Samuel, took him to Granada, and installed him in the Alhambra as his secretary. Soon Samuel was also his adviser, and the vizier said that "when Samuel gave counsel the voice of God was heard." Dying, the vizier recommended Samuel as his successor; and in 1027 Samuel became the only Jew openly to hold the office and name of vizier in a Moslem state; this was the more feasible in Granada, where half the population in the eleventh century was Jewish.[20] The Arabs soon applauded the choice, for under Samuel the little state flourished financially, politically, and culturally. He himself was a scholar, poet, astronomer, mathematician, and linguist, knowing seven tongues; he wrote (chiefly in Hebrew) twenty treatises on grammar, several volumes of poetry and philosophy, an introduction to the Talmud, and an anthology of Hebrew literature. He shared his fortune with other poets, came to the rescue of the poet and philosopher Ibn Gabirol, financed young students, and contributed to Jewish communities in three continents. While vizier to the King he was also rabbi to the Jews, and lectured on the Talmud. His grateful people conferred upon him the title of Nagid—Prince (in Israel). When he died (1055) he was succeeded as vizier and Nagid by his son Joseph ibn Naghdela.

Those centuries—the tenth, eleventh, and twelfth—were the golden age of Spanish Jewry, the happiest and most fruitful period in medieval Hebrew history. When Moses ben Chanoch (d. 965), one of the Bari émigrés, was ransomed in Cordova, he organized there, with Hasdai's help, an academy that soon acquired the intellectual leadership of the Jewish world. Similar schools were opened at Lucena, Toledo, Barcelona, Granada . . . ; and whereas the schools of Eastern Jewry had almost confined themselves to religious education, these gave instruction also in literature, music, mathematics, astronomy, medicine, and philosophy.[21] Such education gave to the upper half of the Jewish population in Spain a breadth and depth of culture and refinement at that time equaled only by their Moslem, Byzantine, and Chinese contemporaries. It was then a disgrace for a man of wealth or political position to be unacquainted with history, science, philosophy, and poetry.[22] A Jewish aristocracy took form, graced by beautiful women; perhaps it was too keenly conscious of its superiority, but it redeemed its pride by its sense that good birth and fortune are an obligation to generosity and excellence.

The decline of Spanish Jewry might be dated from the fall of Joseph ibn Naghdela. He served the king almost as ably as his father had done, but not with the modest tact that had reconciled a population half Moorish to be ruled by a Jew. He took all power in his hands, dressed as royally as the king, and laughed at the Koran; gossip called him an atheist. In 1066 the Arabs and Berbers revolted, crucified Joseph, massacred 4000 Jews in Granada, and plundered their homes. The remaining Jews were compelled to sell their lands and emigrate. Twenty years later the Almoravids came from Africa, aflame with orthodoxy; and the long honeymoon of Spanish Moslems and Jews was ended. A Mohammedan theologian announced that the Jews had promised Mohammed to accept Islam at the end of 500 years after the Hegira, if by that time their expected Messiah had not come; the five centuries were up in 1107 by Mohammedan reckoning; the Emir Yusuf demanded the conversion of all the Jews in Spain, but excused them on payment of an enormous sum into his treasury.[23] When the Almohads replaced the Almoravids as rulers of Morocco and Moslem Spain (1148), they gave the Jews and the Christians the same choice that King Sisebut had allowed the Jews 535 years before—apostasy or exile. Many Jews pretended conversion to Islam; many followed the Christians into northern Spain.

There, at first, they found a royal tolerance as magnanimous as that which they had enjoyed for four centuries under Islam. Alfonso VI and VII of Castile treated the Jews well, made Jew and Christian equal before the law, and sternly repressed an anti-Semitic outbreak in Toledo (1107), where there were then 72,000 Jews.[24] A like entente between the mother and daughter religions prevailed for a century in Aragon; indeed King James I invited Jews to settle in Majorca, Catalonia, and Valencia, and in many cases gave Jewish settlers free homes and lands.[25] In Barcelona they dominated commerce in the twelfth century, and owned a third of the soil.[26] The Jews of Christian Spain were severely taxed, but they prospered, and enjoyed internal autonomy. Trade flowed freely between Christian, Jew, and Moor; the three exchanged gifts on holidays; now and then a king contributed to a synagogue building fund.[27] From 1085 even to 1492, Jews could be found in high public office in Spanish Christian states as fiscal agents and diplomats, sometimes as ministers.[28] During the twelfth and thirteenth centuries the Christian clergy joined in this Christian amity.[29]

The first outbreak of intolerance was among the Jews themselves. In 1149 Jehuda ibn Ezra, steward of the palace to Alfonso VII of Leon and Castile, turned the powers of his master's government against the Qaraite Jews of Toledo; the details are unknown, but from that time the once numerous Spanish Qaraites are heard of no more.[30] In 1212 some Christian crusaders entered Spain to help free it from the Moors; for the most part they treated the Jews well; one group attacked the Jews of Toledo and killed many of them; but the Christians of the city rose to the defense of their fellow citizens, and stopped the persecution.[31] Alfonso X of Castile included anti-Judaic legislation in his law code of 1265, but the code was not put into effect till 1348; meanwhile Alfonso employed a Jewish physician and treasurer, presented to the Jews of Seville three mosques to be turned into synagogues,[32] and basked in the splendor that Jewish and Moslem scholarship shed upon his genial reign. In 1276 the military enterprises of Pedro III of Aragon required insufferable taxes; his finance minister and several other officials were Jews; a revolt of nobles and cities against the monarchy compelled the King to dismiss his Jewish aides, and to confirm a resolution of the Cortes (1283) against further employment of Jews in the government. The era of toleration ended when the ecclesiastical Council of Zamora (1313) decreed the imposition of the badge, the segregation of the Jewish from the Christian population, and a ban against the employment of Jewish physicians by Christians, or of Christian servants by Jews.[33]

III. JEWISH LIFE IN CHRISTENDOM

1. Government

Excepting Palermo and a few towns in Spain, the cities of medieval Christendom required no segregation of their Jewish population. Usually, however, the Jews lived in a voluntary isolation for social convenience, physical security, and religious unity. The synagogue was the geographical, social, and economic center of the Jewish quarter, and drew most Jewish dwellings toward it. There was in consequence much overcrowding, to the detriment of public and private sanitation. In Spain the Hebrew sections contained handsome residences as well as hovels and tenements; in the rest of Europe they verged on slums.[34]

Allowing for the universally greater influence of the rich in elections and appointments, the Jewish communities were semidemocratic enclaves in a monarchical world. The taxpaying members of a congregation chose the rabbis and officers of the synagogue. A small group of elected elders sat as a *Beth Din* or communal court; this levied taxes, fixed prices, administered justice, issued ordinances—not always observed—on Jewish diet, dancing, morals, and dress. It was empowered to try Jewish offenders against Jewish law, and had executive officers to carry out its decrees. Penalties ranged from fines to excommunication or banishment. Capital punishment was rarely within the power or custom of the *Beth Din*; in its stead the Jewish court used the *herem* or full excommunication—a majestic and frightening ceremony of charges, curses, and candles extinguished one by one as a symbol of the culprit's spiritual death. The Jews, like the Christians, used excommunication too frequently, so that in both faiths it lost its terror and effectiveness. The rabbis, like the Church, prosecuted heretics, outlawed them, and on rare occasions burned their books.[35]

Normally the Jewish community was not subject to local authority. Its only master was the king; him it paid liberally for a charter protecting its religious and economic rights; later it paid the liberated communes to confirm its autonomy. The Jews, however, were subject to the law of the state, and made it a principle to obey it; "the law of the kingdom is law," said the Talmud.[36] "Pray for the welfare of the government," said another passage, "since but for fear thereof men would swallow one another alive." [37]

The state laid upon the Jews a poll or head tax, property taxes running up to 33%, and taxes on meat, wine, jewelry, imports, and exports; in addition it required "voluntary" contributions from them to help finance a war, a coronation, or a royal "progress" or tour. The English Jews, numbering in the twelfth century one quarter of one per cent of the population, paid eight per cent of the national taxes. They raised a fourth of the levy for the crusade of Richard I, and donated 5000 marks toward his ransom from German captivity—thrice the amount given by the city of London.[38] The Jew was also taxed by his own community, and was periodically dunned for charity, education, and the support of the harassed Jews in Palestine. At any moment, for cause or without, the king might confiscate part or all of the property of "his Jews," for in feudal law they were all his "men." When a king died, his agreement to protect the Jews expired; his successor could be induced to renew it only by a large gift; sometimes this was a third of all Jewish property in the state.[39] In 1463 Albrecht III, Margrave of Brandenburg, declared that every new German king "may, *according to old usage*, either burn all the Jews, or show them his mercy, and, to save their lives, take the third penny" (i.e., one third) "of their property." [40] Bracton, the leading English jurist of the thirteenth century, summed up the matter simply: "A Jew cannot have anything of his own, because whatever he acquires he acquires not for himself but for the king." [41]

2. *Economy*

To these political inconveniences were added economic restrictions. The Jews were not legally or generally prevented from owning land; at one time or another in the Middle Ages they owned considerable tracts in Moslem or Christian Spain, in Sicily, Silesia, Poland, England, and France.[42] But circumstances made such ownership increasingly impractical. Forbidden by Christian law to hire Christian slaves, and by Jewish law to hire Jewish slaves, the Jew had to work his holding with free labor, hard to get and costly to retain. Jewish law forbade the Jew to work on Saturday, Christian law usually forbade him to work on Sunday; such leisure was a hardship. Feudal custom or law made it impossible for a Jew to find a place within the feudal system; any such position required a Christian oath of fealty, and military service; but the laws of nearly all Christian states forbade the Jews to carry arms.[43] In Visigothic Spain King Sisebut revoked all grants of land made to Jews by his predecessors; King Egica "nationalized" all Jewish holdings that had at any time belonged to Christians; and in 1293 the Cortes of Valladolid prohibited the sale of land to Jews. The ever-present possibility of expulsion or attack persuaded the Jews, after the ninth century, to avoid landed property or rural solitude. All these conditions discouraged Jewish agriculture, and inclined the Jew to urban life, to industry, trade, and finance.

In the Near East and in southern Europe the Jews were active in industry; indeed in several cases it was they who brought advanced handicraft techniques from Islam or Byzantium to Western lands. Benjamin of Tudela found hundreds of Jewish glassworkers at Antioch and Tyre; Jews in Egypt and Greece were renowned for the excellence of their dyed and embroidered textiles; and as late as the thirteenth century Frederick II called in Jewish craftsmen to manage the state's silk industry in Sicily. There and elsewhere Jews engaged in the metal trades, especially in goldsmithing and jewelry; they worked the tin mines of Cornwall until 1290.[44] Hebrew artisans in southern Europe were organized in strong guilds, and competed successfully with Christian craftsmen. But in northern Europe the Christian guilds acquired a monopoly in many trades. State after state forbade the Jews to serve Christians as smiths, carpenters, tailors, shoemakers, millers, bakers, or physicians, or to sell wine, flour, butter, or oil in the markets,[45] or to buy a home anywhere except in the Jewish quarter.

So restricted, the Jews took to trade. Rab, the Babylonian Talmudist, had given his people a shrewd motto: "Trade with a hundred florins, and you will afford meat and wine; put the same sum into agriculture, and at most you may have bread and salt." [46] The Jewish pedlar was known in every city and town; the Jewish merchant at every market and fair. International commerce was their specialty, almost their monopoly, before the eleventh century; their packs, caravans, and ships crossed deserts, mountains, and seas; and in most instances they accompanied their goods. They served as commercial links between Christendom and Islam, between Europe and Asia, between the Slavic and the Western states. They handled most of the trade in slaves.[47] They were helped by their skill and patience in learning languages; by the understanding of Hebrew, and the similarity of laws and customs, among widely separated Jewish communities; and by the hospitality of the Jewish quarter in every city to any foreign Jew; so Benjamin of Tudela traveled halfway across the world, and found himself everywhere at home. Ibn Khordadbeh, director of the post for the Baghdad caliphate in 870, told in his *Book of Routes* of Jewish merchants who spoke Persian, Greek, Arabic, Frank, Spanish, and Slavonic; and he described the land and sea routes by which they traveled from Spain and Italy to Egypt, India, and China.[48] These merchants took eunuchs, slaves, brocades, furs, and swords to the Far East, and brought back musk, aloes, camphor, spices, and silks.[49] The capture of Jerusalem by the Crusades, and the conquest of the Mediterranean by the fleets of Venice and Genoa, gave the Italian merchants an advantage over the Jews; and Jewish commercial leadership ended with the eleventh century. Even before the Crusades Venice had forbidden the transport of Jewish merchants on Venetian ships, and soon afterward the Hanseatic League closed its ports on the North Sea and the Baltic to Jewish trade.[50] By the twelfth century Jewish commerce was mostly domestic; and even within that narrow scope it was limited by laws prohibiting the sale of divers goods by Jews.[51]

They turned to finance. In a hostile environment where popular violence might destroy, or royal cupidity confiscate, their immovable goods, the Jews were forced to the conclusion that their savings should be in liquid and mobile form. They took first to the simple business of money-changing, then to receiving money for commercial investment, then to lending money at interest. The Pentateuch [52] and the Talmud [53] had forbidden this among Jews, but not between Jew and non-Jew. As economic life grew more complex, and the need for financing became more acute with the expansion of commerce and industry, the Jews lent one another money through a Christian intermediary,[54] or through silent partnerships in an enterprise and its profits —a device allowed by the rabbis and several Christian theologians.[55] Since both the Koran and the Church forbade the charging of interest, and Christian moneylenders were consequently scarce before the thirteenth century, Moslem and Christian borrowers—including ecclesiastics, churches, and monasteries [56]—applied to Jews for loans; so Aaron of Lincoln financed the building of nine Cistercian monasteries and the great abbey of St. Albans.[57] In the thirteenth century Christian bankers invaded the field, adopted the methods that had been developed by the Jews, and soon surpassed them in wealth and range. "The Christian usurer, although he did not have to safeguard himself to anything like the same extent against the chances of murder and pillage, was no less exacting" than the Jew.[58] Both alike pressed the debtor with Roman severity, and the kings exploited them all.

All moneylenders were subject to high taxation, and, in the case of the Jews, to occasional outright confiscation. The kings made it a principle to allow high interest rates, and periodically to squeeze the profits out of the financiers. The cost of collection was high, and in many cases the creditor had to bribe officials to allow him to capture his due.[59] In 1198 Innocent III commanded all Christian princes, in preparation for the Fourth Crusade, to compel full remission of interest demanded of Christians by Jews.[60] Louis IX, the saintly king of France, "for the salvation of his own soul and those of his ancestors," freed all his subjects from a third of whatever they owed to Jews.[61] English kings on occasion granted letters of release—canceling interest or principle or both—to subjects owing money to Jews; not rarely the kings sold such letters, and noted in their registers the sums they received for their vicarious philanthropy.[62] The British government required a copy of every loan agreement; an Exchequer of the Jews was formed to file and supervise these agreements, and to hear cases concerning them; when a Jewish banker could not meet the taxes or levies laid upon him, the government, checking its record of his loans, confiscated all or part of them, and notified the debtors to pay not the lender but the government.[63] When, in 1187, Henry II levied a special tax upon the people of England, the Jews were compelled to pay one fourth, the Christians one tenth, of their property; nearly half the entire tax was paid by the Jews.[64] At times "the Jews financed the kingdom." [65] In 1210 King John ordered all Jews in England—men, women, and children—to be imprisoned; a "tallage" of 66,000 marks was taken from them;[66] those suspected of concealing the full amount of their hoards were tortured by having a tooth pulled out each day till they confessed.[67] * In 1230 Henry III, charging that the Jews had clipped the coin of the realm (apparently some had), confiscated a third of all the movable property of the English Jews. The operation having proved profitable, it was repeated in 1239; two years later 20,000 silver marks were exacted from the Jews; 60,000 marks—a sum equal to the whole yearly revenue of the Crown—were exacted in 1244. When Henry III borrowed 5000 marks from the Earl of Cornwall, he consigned to him all the Jews of England as security.[68] A series of imposts from 1252 to 1255 drove the Jews to such desperation that they begged permission to leave England *en masse*; permission was refused.[69] In 1275 Edward I strictly prohibited lending at interest. Loans continued nevertheless; and as the risk was greater, interest rates rose. Edward ordered all Jews in England arrested and their goods seized. Many Christian lenders were also arrested, and three of them were hanged. Of the Jews 280 were hanged, drawn, and quartered in London; there were additional executions in the counties; and the property of hundreds of Jews was confiscated to the state.[70]

In the uneasy intervals between confiscations the Jewish bankers prospered, and some became too visibly rich. They not only advanced capital to build castles, cathedrals, and monasteries, but they raised for themselves substantial houses; in England their homes were among the first dwellings built of stone. There were rich and poor among the Jews, despite Rabbi Eleazar's dictum that "all men are equal before God—women and slaves, rich and poor." [71] The rabbis sought to mitigate poverty, and check profiteering wealth, by a variety of economic regulations. They emphasized the responsibility of the group for the welfare of all, and softened the stings of adversity with organized charity. They did not denounce riches, but they succeeded in giving to learning a prestige equal to that of wealth. They branded monopoly and "corners" as sins; [72] they forbade the retailer to profit by more than a sixth of the wholesale price; [73] they watched over weights and measures; they fixed maximum prices and minimum wages.[74] Many of these regulations failed; the rabbis could not isolate the economic life of the Jews from that of their neighbors in Islam or Christendom; and the law of supply and demand of goods and services found a way around all legislation.

3. Morals

The rich tried to atone for their accumulations by abundant charity. They acknowledged the social obligations of wealth, and perhaps they feared the curse or fury of the poor. No Jew is known to have died of hunger while liv-

---

* A mark was half a pound of silver, with a purchasing power probably fifty times as great as that amount today ($5.40).

ing in a Jewish community.[75] Periodically, and as early as the second century after Christ, each member of the congregation, however poor, was assessed by official overseers for a contribution to the *kupah* or "community
chest," which took care of the old, poor, or sick, and the education and marriage of orphans.[76] Hospitality was accorded freely, especially to wandering
scholars; in some communities incoming travelers were billeted in private
homes by officers of the congregation. Jewish philanthropic societies grew
to a great number as the Middle Ages advanced; not only were there many
hospitals, orphanages, poorhouses, and homes for the aged, but there were organizations providing ransoms for prisoners, dowries for poor brides, visits to
the sick, care for destitute widows, and free burial for the dead.[77] Christians
complained of Jewish greed, and tried to stir Christians to charity by citing
the exemplary generosity of the Jews.[78]

Class differences disported themselves in dress, diet, speech, and a hundred
other ways. The simple Jew wore a long-sleeved and girdled robe or caftan,
usually black as if in mourning for his ruined Temple and ravished land; but
in Spain the well-to-do Jews proclaimed their prosperity with silks and furs;
and the rabbis deplored in vain the handle given to hostility and discontent
by such displays. When the king of Castile banned finery in raiment the Jewish males obeyed, but continued to array their wives in splendor; when the
king demanded an explanation they assured him that the royal gallantry
could never have meant the restrictions to apply to women; [79] and the Jews
continued throughout the Middle Ages to robe their ladies well. But they
forbade them to appear in public with uncovered hair; such an offense was
ground for divorce; and the Jew was instructed not to pray in the presence
of a woman whose hair was visible.[80]

The hygienic features of the Law alleviated the effects of congested settlements. Circumcision, the weekly bath, the prohibition of wine or putrid
meat as food, gave the Jews superior protection against diseases rampant in
their Christian vicinities.[81] Leprosy was frequent among the Christian poor,
who ate salted meat or fish, but was rare among the Jews. Perhaps for like
reasons the Jews suffered less than Christians from cholera and kindred ailments.[82] But in the slums of Rome, infested with mosquitoes from the Campagna marshes, Jew and Christian alike shivered with malaria.

The moral life of the medieval Jew reflected his Oriental heritage and his
European disabilities. Discriminated against at every turn, pillaged and
massacred, humiliated and condemned for crimes not his own, the Jew, like
the physically weak everywhere, resorted to cunning in self-defense. The
rabbis repeated again and again that "to cheat a Gentile is even worse than to
cheat a Jew," [83] but some Jews took the chance; [84] and perhaps Christians too
bargained as shrewdly as they knew. Some bankers, Jewish or Christian, were
ruthless in their resolve to be paid; though doubtless there were in the
Middle Ages, as in the eighteenth century, moneylenders as honest and faith-

ful as Meyer Anselm of the *rote Schild*. Certain Jews and Christians clipped coins or received stolen goods.[85] The frequent use of Jews in high financial office suggests that their Christian employers had confidence in their integrity. Of violent crimes—murder, robbery, rape—the Jews were seldom guilty. Drunkenness was rarer among them in Christian than in Moslem lands.

Their sex life, despite a background of polygamy, was remarkably wholesome. They were less given to pederasty than other peoples of Eastern origin. Their women were modest maidens, industrious wives, prolific and conscientious mothers; and early marriage reduced prostitution to a human minimum.[86] Bachelors were rarities. Rabbi Asher ben Yehiel ruled that a bachelor of twenty, unless absorbed in study of the Law, might be compelled to marry by the court.[87] Marriages were arranged by the parents; few girls, says a Jewish document of the eleventh century, were "indelicate or impudent enough to express their own fancies or preference";[88] but no marriage was fully legal without the consent of both parties.[89] The father might give his daughter in marriage in her early years, even at six; but such child marriages were not consummated till maturity, and when the daughter came of age she could annul it if she wished.[90] The betrothal was a formal act, making the girl legally the man's wife; they could not thereafter separate except by a bill of divorce. At the betrothal a contract (ketuba) was signed for the dowry and the marriage settlement. The latter was a sum set aside out of the husband's estate to be paid his wife in case the husband should divorce her or die. Without a marriage settlement of at least 200 zuzas (which could buy a one-family house), no marriage with a virgin bride was valid.

Polygamy was practiced by rich Jews in Islamic lands, but was rare among the Jews of Christendom.[91] Post-Talmudic rabbinical literature refers a thousand times to a man's "wife," never to his "wives." About the year 1000 Rabbi Gershom ben Judah of Mainz decreed the excommunication of any polygamous Jew; and soon thereafter, in all Europe except Spain, polygamy and concubinage became almost extinct among the Jews. Cases continued to occur, however, where a wife barren for ten years after marriage allowed her husband to take a concubine or an additional wife;[92] parentage was vital. The same decree of Gershom abolished the old right of the husband to divorce his wife without her consent or guilt. Divorces were probably less frequent in medieval Jewry than in modern America.

Despite the comparative looseness of the marriage bond in law, the family was the saving center of Jewish life. External danger brought internal unity; and hostile witnesses testify to the "warmth and dignity . . . thoughtfulness, consideration, parental and fraternal affection," that marked and mark the Jewish family.[94] The young husband, merged with his wife in work, joy, and tribulation, developed a profound attachment for her as part of his larger self; he became a father, and the children growing up around him stimulated his reserve energies and engaged his deepest loyalties. He had probably known no woman carnally before marriage, and had, in so small and intimate a community, few chances for infidelity afterward. Almost from their birth he saved to provide a dowry for his daughters and a marriage settlement for his sons; and he took it for granted that he should support them in the early years of their married life; this seemed wiser than to let youth prepare with a decade of promiscuity for the restrictions of monogamy. In many cases the bridegroom came to live with the bride in her father's home—seldom to the increment of happiness. The authority of the oldest father in the home was almost as absolute as in republican Rome. He could excommunicate his children, and might beat his wife within reason; if he seriously injured her the community fined him to the limit of his resources. Usually his authority was exercised with a sternness that never quite concealed a passionate love.

The position of woman was legally low, morally high. Like Plato, the Jew thanked God that he had not been born a woman; and the woman replied humbly, "I thank God that I was made according to His will." [95] In the synagogue the women occupied a separate place in the gallery or behind the men—a clumsy compliment to their distracting charms; and they could not be counted toward making a quorum. Songs in praise of a woman's beauty were considered indecorous, though the Talmud allowed them.[96] Flirtation, if any, was by correspondence; public conversation between the sexes—even between man and wife—was forbidden by the rabbis.[97] Dancing was permitted, but only of woman with woman, of man with man.[98] While the husband was by law the sole heir of his wife, the widow did not inherit from her husband; when he died she received the equivalent of her dowry and the marriage settlement; for the rest her sons, the natural heirs, were relied upon to support her decently. Daughters inherited only in the absence of sons; otherwise they had to depend upon brotherly affection, which seldom failed.[99] Girls were not sent to school; in their case a little knowledge was accounted an especially dangerous thing. However, they were allowed to study privately; we hear of several women who gave public lectures on the Law—though sometimes the lecturer screened herself from her audience.[100] Despite every physical and legal disadvantage, the deserving Jewish woman received after marriage full honor and devotion. Judah ben Moses ibn Tibbon (1170) quoted approvingly a Moslem sage: "None but the honorable honor women, none but the despicable despise them." [101]

The parental relation was more nearly perfect than the marital. The Jew, with the vanity of the commonplace, prided himself on his reproductive ability and his children; his most solemn oath was taken by laying his hand upon the testes of the man receiving the pledge; hence the word *testimony*. Every man was commanded to have at least two children; usually there were more. The child was reverenced as a visitor from heaven, a very angel become flesh. The father was reverenced almost as a vicar of God; the son stood in his father's presence until bidden to be seated, and gave him a solicitous obedience that fully comported with the pride of youth. In the ceremony of circumcision the boy was dedicated to Yahveh by the covenant of Abraham; and every family felt obligated to train one son for the rabbinate. When the boy had completed his thirteenth year he was received into manhood, and into all the obligations of the Law, by a solemn ceremony of confirmation.* Religion cast its awe and sanctity over every stage of development, and eased the tasks of parentage.

4. Religion

In like manner religion stood as a spiritual policeman over every phase of the moral code. Doubtless loopholes were found in the Law, and legal fictions were concocted to restore the freedom of adaptation indispensable to an enterprising people. But apparently the medieval Jew accepted the Law, by and large, as a bulwark saving him not only from eternal damnation but, more visibly, from group disintegration. It harassed him at every turn, but he honored it as the very home and school of his growth, the vital medium of his life.

Every home in Judaism was a church, every school was a temple, every father was a priest. The prayers and ritual of the synagogue had their briefer counterparts in the home. The fasts and festivals of the faith were celebrated there with educative ceremonies that bound the present with the past, the living with the dead and the yet unborn. Every Friday eve of the Sabbath the father called his wife, children, and servants around him, blessed them individually, and led them in prayer, religious readings, and sacred songs. To the doorpost of each major room was attached a tube (mezuzah) containing a parchment roll inscribed with two passages from Deuteronomy (vi, 4-9; xi, 13-21), reminding the Jew that his God is one, and must be loved "with all thy heart and soul and strength." From the age of four the child was brought to the synagogue; and there religion was impressed upon him in his most formative years.

The synagogue was not merely a temple, it was the social center of the Jewish community; *synagoge*, like *ecclesia*, *synod*, and *college*, meant an assemblage, a con-greg-ation. In pre-Christian days it had been essentially a school; it is still called *Schule* by Ashkenazic Jews. In the Dispersion it took on a strange variety of functions. In some synagogues it was the custom to publish, on the Sabbath, the decisions reached by the *Beth Din* during the week; to collect taxes, advertise lost articles, accept complaints of one member against another, and announce the coming sale of property so that any claimant on it might protest the sale. The synagogue dispensed communal

---

* This ceremony of *bar mizvah* ("son of command"—i.e., heir to responsibilities) cannot be traced beyond the fourteenth century,[102] but is probably older.

charity, and, in Asia, served as a lodging for travelers. The building itself was always the finest in the Jewish quarter; sometimes, especially in Spain and Italy, it was an architectural masterpiece, expensively and lovingly adorned. Christian authorities repeatedly forbade the erection of synagogues equaling in height the tallest Christian church in the city; in 1221 Pope Honorius III ordered the destruction of such a synagogue in Bourges.[103] Seville had twenty-three synagogues in the fourteenth century, Toledo and Cordova almost as many; one built in Cordova in 1315 is now maintained as a national monument by the Spanish government.

Every synagogue had a school (*Beth ha-midrash*—House of Study—the Arabic madrasa); in addition there were private schools and personal tutors; probably there was a higher relative literacy among the medieval Jews than among the Christians,[104] though lower than among the Moslems. Teachers were paid by the community or the parents, but all were under communal supervision. Boys went off to school at an early hour—in winter before dawn; some hours later they returned home for breakfast; then they went back to school till eleven, then home for lunch, back to school at noon, a respite between two and three, then more schooling till evening; then at last they were released to their homes for supper, prayers, and bed. Life was a serious matter for the Jewish boy.[105]

Hebrew and the Pentateuch were the primary studies. At the age of ten the student took up the Mishna, at thirteen the major tractates of the Talmud; those who were to be scholars continued the study of Mishna and Gemara from thirteen to twenty or later. Through the diversity of subjects in the Talmud the student received a smattering of a dozen sciences, but almost nothing of non-Jewish history.[106] There was much learning by repetition; the chorus of recitation was so vigorous that some localities excluded schools.[107] Higher education was given in the Yeshibah or academy. The graduate of such an academy was called *talmid hakam*—scholar of the Law; he was usually freed from community taxes; and though he was not necessarily a rabbi, all nonscholars were expected to rise on his coming or going.[108]

The rabbi was teacher, jurist, and priest. He was required to marry. He was paid little or nothing for his religious functions; usually he earned a living in the secular world. He seldom preached; this was left to itinerant preachers (*maggidim*) schooled in sonorous and frightening eloquence. Any member of the congregation might lead it in prayer, read the Scriptures, or preach; usually, however, this honor was granted to some prominent or philanthropic Jew. Prayer was a complex ceremony for the orthodox Hebrew. To be properly performed it required that he should cover his head as a sign of reverence, strap upon his arms and his forehead small cases containing passages from Exodus (xiii, 1-16) and Deuteronomy (vi, 4-9; xi, 13-21), and wear on the borders of his garments fringes inscribed with the basic commandments of the Lord. The rabbis explained these formalities as necessary reminders of the unity, presence, and laws of God; simple Jews came to look upon them as magical amulets possessed of miraculous powers. The culmination of the religious service was a reading from the scroll of the Law, contained in a little ark above the altar.

The Jews of the Dispersion at first frowned upon music in religion as hardly suited to a mood of grief for their lost home. But music and religion are as intimately related as poetry and love; the deepest emotions require for their civilized expression the most emotional of the arts. Music returned to the synagogue through poetry. In the sixth century the *paitanim* or "Neo-Hebraic" poets began to write religious verse, confused with acrostic and alliterative artificialities, but uplifted with the resounding splendor of Hebrew, and filled with that religious ardor which in the Jew now served for both patriotism and piety. The crude but powerful hymns of Eleazar ben Kalir (eighth century) still find a place in some synagogue rituals. Similar poetry appeared among the Jews of Spain, Italy, France, and Germany. One such hymn is sung by many Jews on the Day of Atonement:

> With the coming of Thy Kingdom
>   The hills shall break into song,
> And the islands laugh exultant
>   That they to God belong.
> And all their congregations
>   So loud Thy praise shall sing
> That the farthest peoples, hearing,
>   Shall hail Thee crownéd King.[109]

When such *piutim* or sacred poems were introduced into the synagogue service they were sung by a precentor, and music re-entered the ritual. Furthermore the scriptural readings and the prayers were in many synagogues chanted by a cantor or by the congregation in a "cantillation" whose musical tones were largely improvised, but occasionally followed patterns set in the plain song of the Christian chant.[110] From the singing school of the monastery of St. Gall in Switzerland, at some time before the eleventh century, came the complex chant for the famous Hebrew song *Kol Nidre*—"All Vows." [111]

The synagogue never fully replaced the Temple in the heart of the Jew. The hope that he might some day offer sacrifice to Yahveh before the Holy of Holies on Zion's hill inflamed his imagination, and left him open to repeated deception by false messiahs. About 720 Serene, a Syrian, announced himself to be the expected redeemer, and organized a campaign to recapture Palestine from the Moslems. Jews from Babylonia and Spain abandoned their homes to join his adventure. He was taken prisoner, exposed as a charlatan by the Caliph Yezid II, and was put to death. Some thirty years later Obadiah Abu Isa ben Ishaq of Isfahan led a similar revolt; 10,000 Jews took up the sword and fought bravely under his lead; they were defeated, Abu

Isa was slain in battle, and the Isfahan Jews suffered indiscriminate punishment. When the First Crusade excited Europe, Jewish communities dreamed that the Christians, if victorious, would restore Palestine to the Jews;[112] they awoke from this fantasy to a succession of pogroms. In 1160 David Alrui aroused the Jews of Mesopotamia with the announcement that he was the Messiah, and would restore them to Jerusalem and liberty; his father-in-law, fearing disaster for the Jews from such an insurrection, slew him in his sleep. About 1225 another Messiah appeared in southern Arabia, and stirred the Jews to mass hysteria; Maimonides, in a famous "Letter to the South," exposed the impostor's claims, and reminded the Arabian Jews of the death and destruction that had followed such reckless attempts in the past.[112a] Nevertheless he accepted the Messianic hope as an indispensable support to the Jewish spirit in the Dispersion, and made it one of the thirteen principal tenets of the Jewish faith.[113]

IV. ANTI-SEMITISM: 500–1306

What were the sources of the hostility between non-Jew and Jew?

The main sources have ever been economic, but religious differences have given edge and cover to economic rivalries. The Moslems, living by Mohammed, resented the Jewish rejection of their prophet; the Christians, accepting the divinity of Christ, were shocked to find that His own people would not acknowledge that divinity. Good Christians saw nothing unchristian or inhuman in holding an entire people, through many centuries, responsible for the actions of·a tiny minority of Jerusalem Jews in the last days of Christ. The Gospel of Luke told how "throngs" of Jews welcomed Christ into Jerusalem (xix, 37); how, when He carried His cross to Golgotha, "there followed Him a great company of people, and of women, who also bewailed and lamented Him" (xxiii, 27); and how, after the crucifixion, "all the people that came together to that sight . . . smote their breasts" (xxiii, 48). But these evidences of Jewish sympathy for Jesus were forgotten when, in every Holy Week, the bitter story of the Passion was related from a thousand pulpits; resentment flared in Christian hearts; and on those days the Israelites shut themselves up in their own quarter and in their homes, fearful that the passions of simple souls might be stirred to a pogrom.[114]

Around that central misunderstanding rose a thousand suspicions and animosities. Jewish bankers bore the brunt of the hostility aroused by interest rates that reflected the insecurity of loans. As the economy of Christendom developed, and Christian merchants and bankers invaded fields once dominated by Jews, economic competition fomented hate; and some Christian moneylenders actively promoted anti-Semitism.[115] Jews in official positions, especially in the finance department of governments, were a natural target

for those who disliked both taxes and Jews. Given such economic and religious enmity, everything Jewish became distasteful to some Christians, and
everything Christian to some Jews. The Christian reproached the Jew for
clannish exclusiveness, and did not excuse it as a reaction to discrimination
and occasional physical assault. Jewish features, language, manners, diet,
ritual all seemed to the Christian eye offensively bizarre. The Jews ate when
Christians fasted, fasted when Christians ate; their Sabbath of rest and prayer
had remained Saturday as of old, while that of the Christians had been
changed to Sunday; the Jews celebrated their happy deliverance from Egypt
in a Passover feast that came too close to the Friday on which Christians
mourned the death of Christ. Jews were not allowed by their Law to eat
food cooked, to drink wine pressed, or to use dishes or utensils that had
been touched, by a non-Jew,[116] or to marry any but a Jew; [117] the Christian
interpreted these ancient laws—formulated long before Christianity—as
meaning that to a Jew everything Christian was unclean; and he retorted that
the Israelite himself was not usually distinguished by cleanliness of person
or neatness of dress. Mutual isolation begot absurd and tragic legends on
both sides. Romans had accused Christians of murdering pagan children to
offer their blood in secret sacrifice to the Christian God; Christians of the
twelfth century accused Jews of kidnaping Christian children to sacrifice
them to Yahveh, or to use their blood as medicine or in the making of unleavened bread for the Passover feast. Jews were charged with poisoning the
wells from which Christians drank, and with stealing consecrated wafers to
pierce them and draw from them the blood of Christ.[118] When a few Jewish
merchants flaunted their opulence in costly raiment the Jews as a people
were accused of draining the wealth of Christendom into Jewish hands. Jewish women were suspected as sorceresses; many Jews, it was thought, were
in league with the Devil.[119] The Jews retaliated with like legends about
Christians, and insulting stories about the birth and youth of Christ. The
Talmud counseled the extension of Jewish charity to non-Jews; [120] Bahya
praised Christian monasticism; Maimonides wrote that "the teachings of
Christ and Mohammed tend to lead mankind toward perfection"; [121] but the
average Jew could not understand these courtesies of philosophy, and returned all the hatred that he received.

There were some lucid intervals in this madness. Ignoring state and
Church laws that forbade it, Christians and Jews often mingled in friendship,
sometimes in marriage, above all in Spain and southern France. Christian and
Jewish scholars collaborated—Michael Scot with Anatoli, Dante with Im-
manuel.[122] Christians made gifts to synagogues; and in Worms a Jewish park
was maintained through a legacy from a Christian woman.[123] In Lyons the
market day was changed from Saturday to Sunday for the convenience of
the Jews. Secular governments, finding the Jews an asset in commerce and

finance, gave them a vacillating protection; and in several cases where a state restricted the public movements of Jews, or expelled them from its territory, it was because it could no longer safeguard them from intolerance and violence.[124]

The attitude of the Church in these matters varied with place and time. In Italy she protected the Jews as "guardians of the Law" of the Old Testament, and as living witnesses to the historicity of the Scriptures and to "the wrath of God." But periodically Church councils, often with excellent intentions, and seldom with general authority, added to the tribulations of Jewish life. The Theodosian Code (439), the Council of Clermont (535), and the Council of Toledo (589) forbade the appointment of Jews to positions in which they could impose penalties upon Christians. The Council of Orléans (538) ordered Jews to stay indoors in Holy Week, probably for their protection, and prohibited their employment in any public office. The Third Council of the Lateran (1179) forbade Christian midwives or nurses to minister to Jews; and the Council of Béziers (1246) condemned the employment of Jewish physicians by Christians. The Council of Avignon (1209) retaliated Jewish laws of cleanliness by enjoining "Jews and harlots" from touching bread or fruit exposed for sale; it renewed Church laws against the hiring of Christian servants by Jews; and it warned the faithful not to exchange services with Jews, but to avoid them as a pollution.[125] Several councils declared null the marriage of a Christian with a Jew. In 1222 a deacon was burned at the stake for accepting conversion to Judaism and marrying a Jewess.[126] In 1234 a Jewish widow was refused her dower on the ground that her husband had been converted to Christianity, thereby voiding their marriage.[127] The Fourth Council of the Lateran (1215), arguing that "at times through error Christians have relations with the women of Jews or Saracens, and Jews or Saracens with Christian women," ruled "that Jews and Saracens of both sexes in every Christian province and at all times shall be marked off in the eyes of the public from other people through the character of their dress": after their twelfth year they were to wear a distinctive color—the men on their hats or mantles, the women on their veils. This was in part a retaliation against older and similar laws of Moslems against Christians and Jews. The character of the badge was determined locally by state governments or provincial Church councils; ordinarily it was a wheel or circle of yellow cloth, some three inches in diameter, sewn prominently upon the clothing. The decree was enforced in England in 1218, in France in 1219, in Hungary in 1279; it was only sporadically carried out in Spain, Italy, and Germany before the fifteenth century, when Nicholas of Cusa and San Giovanni da Capistrano campaigned for its full observance. In 1219 the Jews of Castile threatened to leave the country en masse if the decree should be enforced, and the ecclesiastical authorities consented to its revocation. Jewish physicians, scholars, financiers, and travelers were often exempted from the decree. Its observance declined after the sixteenth century, and ended with the French Revolution.

By and large, the popes were the most tolerant prelates in Christendom. Gregory I, though so zealous for the spread of the faith, forbade the compulsory conversion of Jews, and maintained their rights of Roman citizenship in lands under his rule.[128] When bishops in Terracina and Palermo appropriated synagogues for Christian use, Gregory compelled them to make full restitution.[129] To the bishop of Naples he wrote: "Do not allow the Jews to be molested in the performance of their services. Let them have full liberty to observe and keep all their festivals and holydays, as both they and their fathers have done for so long." [130] Gregory VII urged Christian rulers to obey conciliar decrees against the appointment of Jews. When Eugenius III came to Paris in 1145, and went in pomp to the cathedral, which was then in the Jewish quarter, the Jews sent a delegation to present him with the Torah, or scroll of the Law; he blessed them, they went home happy, and the Pope ate a paschal lamb with the king.[131] Alexander III was friendly to Jews, and employed one to manage his finances.[132] Innocent III led the Fourth Lateran Council in its demand for a Jewish badge, and laid down the principle that all Jews were doomed to perpetual servitude because they had crucified Jesus.[133] In a softer mood he reiterated papal injunctions against forcible conversions, and added: "No Christian shall do the Jews any personal injury . . . or deprive them of their possessions . . . or disturb them during the celebration of their festivals . . . or extort money from them by threatening to exhume their dead." [134] Gregory IX, founder of the Inquisition, exempted the Jews from its operation or jurisdiction except when they tried to Judaize Christians, or attacked Christianity, or reverted to Judaism after conversion to Christianity; [135] and in 1235 he issued a bull denouncing mob violence against Jews.[136] Innocent IV (1247) repudiated the legend of the ritual murder of Christian children by Jews:

> Certain of the clergy and princes, nobles and great lords . . . have falsely devised godless plans against the Jews, unjustly depriving them of their property by force, and appropriating it to themselves; they falsely charge them with dividing among them on the Passover the heart of a murdered boy. . . . In fact, in their malice, they ascribe to Jews every murder, wherever it chance to occur. And on the ground of these and other fabrications, they are filled with rage against them, rob them . . . oppress them by starvation, imprisonment, torture, and other sufferings, sometimes even condemning them to death; so that the Jews, though living under Christian princes, are in worse plight than were their ancestors under the Pharaohs. They are driven to leave in despair the land in which their fathers have dwelt since the memory of man. Since it is our pleasure that they shall

not be distressed, we ordain that you behave toward them in a friendly and kind manner. Whenever any unjust attacks upon them come under your notice, redress their injuries, and do not suffer them to be visited in the future by similar tribulations.[137]

This noble appeal was widely ignored. In 1272 Gregory X had to repeat its denunciation of the ritual murder legend; and to give his words force he ruled that thereafter the testimony of a Christian against a Jew should not be accepted unless confirmed by a Jew.[138] The issuance of similar bulls by later popes till 1763 attests both the humanity of the popes and the persistence of the evil. That the popes were sincere is indicated by the comparative security of the Jews, and their relative freedom from persecution, in the Papal States. Expelled from so many countries at one time or another, they were never expelled from Rome or from papal Avignon. "Had it not been for the Catholic Church," writes a learned Jewish historian, "the Jews would not have survived the Middle Ages in Christian Europe." [139]

Before the Crusades the active persecution of Jews in medieval Europe was sporadic. The Byzantine emperors continued for two centuries the oppressive policies of Justinian toward the Jews. Heraclius (628) banished them from Jerusalem in retaliation for their aid to Persia, and did all he could to exterminate them. Leo the Isaurian sought to disprove the rumor that he was Jewish by a decree (723) giving Byzantine Jews a choice between Christianity or banishment. Some submitted; some burned themselves to death in their synagogues rather than yield.[140] Basil I (867–86) resumed the campaign to enforce baptism upon the Jews; and Constantine VII (912–59) required from Jews in Christian courts a humiliating form of oath—*more Judaico*—which continued in use in Europe till the nineteenth century.[141]

When, in 1095, Pope Urban II proclaimed the First Crusade, some Christians thought it desirable to kill the Jews of Europe before proceeding so far to fight Turks in Jerusalem. Godfrey of Bouillon, having accepted the leadership of the crusade, announced that he would avenge the blood of Jesus upon the Jews, and would leave not one of them alive; and his companions proclaimed their intention to kill all Jews who would not accept Christianity. A monk further aroused Christian ardor by declaring that an inscription found on the Holy Sepulcher in Jerusalem made the conversion of all Jews a moral obligation of all Christians.[142] The Crusaders planned to move south along the Rhine, where lay the richest settlements in northern Europe. The German Jews had played a leading part in the development of Rhenish commerce, and had behaved with a restraint and piety that had won the respect of Christian laity and clergy alike. Bishop Rüdiger of Speyer was on cordial terms with the Jews of his district, and gave them a charter guaranteeing their autonomy and security. In 1095 the Emperor Henry IV issued a similar charter for all the Jews of his realm.[143] Upon these peaceful Jewish congregations the news of the crusade, its proposed route, and the threats of its leaders, broke with paralyzing terror. The rabbis proclaimed several days of fasting and prayer.

Arrived at Speyer, the Crusaders dragged eleven Jews into a church, and ordered them to accept baptism; refusing, the eleven were slain (May 3, 1096). Other Jews of the city took refuge with Bishop Johannsen, who not only protected them but caused the execution of certain Crusaders who had shared in the murders at the church. As some Crusaders neared Trier, its Jews appealed to Bishop Egilbert; he offered protection on condition of baptism. Most of the Jews consented; but several women killed their children and threw themselves into the Moselle (June 1, 1096). At Mainz Archbishop Ruthard hid 1300 Jews in his cellars; Crusaders forced their way in, and killed 1014; the Bishop was able to save a few by concealing them in the cathedral (May 27, 1096). Four Mainz Jews accepted baptism, but committed suicide soon afterward. As the Crusaders approached Cologne, the Christians hid the Jews in their homes; the mob burned down the Jewish quarter, and killed the few Jews upon whom they could lay their hands. Bishop Hermann, at great danger to himself, secretly conveyed the Jews from their Christian hiding places to Christian homes in the country; the pilgrims discovered the maneuver, hunted their prey in the villages, and killed every Jew they found (June, 1096). In two of these villages 200 Jews were slain; in four others the Jews, surrounded by the mob, killed one another rather than be baptized. Mothers delivered of infants during these attacks slew them at birth. At Worms Bishop Allebranches received such of the Jews as he could into his palace, and saved them; upon the rest the Crusaders fell with the savagery of anonymity, killing many, and then plundering and burning the homes of the Jews; here many Jews committed suicide rather than repudiate their faith. Seven days later a crowd besieged the episcopal residence; the Bishop told the Jews that he could no longer hold back the mob, and advised them to accept baptism. The Jews asked to be left alone for a while; when the Bishop returned he found that nearly all of them had killed one another. The besiegers broke in and slew the rest; all in all, some 800 Jews died in this pogrom at Worms (August 20, 1096). Similar scenes occurred at Metz, Regensburg, and Prague.[144]

The Second Crusade (1147) threatened to better the example of the First. Peter the Venerable, the saintly Abbot of Cluny, advised Louis VII of France to begin by attacking the French Jews. "I do not require you to put to death these accursed beings . . . God does not wish to annihilate them; but, like Cain the fratricide, they must be made to suffer fearful torments, and be preserved for greater ignominy, for an existence more bitter than death."[145] Abbot Suger of St. Denis protested against this conception of Christianity, and Louis VII contented himself with capital levies on rich Jews. But the German Jews were not let off with mere confiscation. A French monk, Rodolphe, leaving his monastery without permission, preached a pogrom in

Germany. At Cologne Simon "the Pious" was murdered and mutilated; at Speyer a woman was tortured on the rack to persuade her to Christianity. Again the secular prelates did all they could to protect the Jews. Bishop Arnold of Cologne gave them a fortified castle as refuge, and allowed them to arm themselves; the Crusaders refrained from attacking the castle, but killed any unconverted Jew that fell into their clutches. Archbishop Henry at Mainz admitted into his house some Jews pursued by a mob; the mob forced a way in, and killed them before his eyes. The Archbishop appealed to St. Bernard, the most influential Christian of his time; Bernard replied with a strong denunciation of Rodolphe, and demanded an end to violence against the Jews. When Rodolphe continued his campaign Bernard came in person to Germany, and forced the monk to return to his monastery. Shortly thereafter the mutilated body of a Christian was found at Würzburg; Christians charged Jews with the crime, attacked them despite the protests of Bishop Embicho, and killed twenty; many others, wounded, were tended by Christians (1147); and the Bishop buried the dead in his garden.[146] From Germany the idea of beginning the Crusades at home passed back to France, and Jews were massacred at Carentan, Rameru, and Sully. In Bohemia 150 Jews were murdered by Crusaders. After the terror had passed, the local Christian clergy did what it could to help the surviving Jews; and those who had accepted baptism under duress were allowed to return to Judaism without incurring the dire penalties of apostasy.[147]

These pogroms began a long series of violent assaults, which continued till our time. In 1235 an unsolved murder at Baden was laid to the Jews, and a massacre ensued. In 1243 the entire Jewish population of Belitz, near Berlin, was burned alive on the charge that some of them had defiled a consecrated Host.[148] In 1283 the accusation of ritual murder was raised at Mainz, and despite all the efforts of Archbishop Werner, ten Jews were killed, and Jewish homes were pillaged. In 1285 a like rumor excited Munich; 180 Jews fled for refuge to a synagogue; the mob set fire to it, and all 180 were burned to death. A year later forty Jews were killed at Oberwesel on the charge that they had drained the blood of a Christian. In 1298 every Jew in Röttingen was burned to death on the charge of desecrating a sacramental wafer. Rindfleisch, a pious baron, organized and armed a band of Christians sworn to kill all Jews; they completely exterminated the Jewish community at Würzburg, and slew 698 Jews in Nuremberg. The persecution spread, and in half a year 140 Jewish congregations were wiped out.[149] The Jews of Germany, having repeatedly rebuilt their communities after such attacks, lost heart; and in 1286 many Jewish families left Mainz, Worms, Speyer, and other German towns, and migrated to Palestine to live in Islam. As Poland and Lithuania were inviting immigrants, and had not yet experienced pogroms, a slow exodus of Jews from the Rhineland began to the Slavic East.

The Jews of England, excluded from landholding and from the guilds, became merchants and financiers. Some waxed rich through usury, and all were hated for it. Lords and squires equipped themselves for the Crusades with money borrowed from the Jews; in return they pledged the revenues of their lands; and the Christian peasant fumed at the thought of money-lenders fattening on his toil. In 1144 young William of Norwich was found dead; the Jews were accused of having killed him to use his blood; and the Jewish quarter of the city was sacked and fired.[150] King Henry II protected the Jews; Henry III did likewise, but took £422,000 from them in taxes and capital levies in seven years. At the coronation of Richard I in London (1190) a minor altercation, encouraged by nobles seeking escape from their debts to Jews,[151] developed into a pogrom that spread to Lincoln, Stamford, and Linn. In York, in the same year, a mob led by Richard de Malabestia, "who was deeply indebted to the Jews," [152] killed 350 of them; in addition 150 York Jews, led by their Rabbi Yom Tob, slew themselves.[153] In 1211 300 rabbis left England and France to begin life anew in Palestine; seven years later many Jews emigrated when Henry III enforced the edict of the badge. In 1255 rumor spread through Lincoln that a boy named Hugh had been enticed into the Jewish quarter and there had been scourged, crucified, and pierced with a lance, in the presence of a rejoicing Jewish crowd. Armed bands invaded the settlement, seized the rabbi who was supposed to have presided over the ceremony, tied him to the tail of a horse, dragged him through the streets, and hanged him. Ninety-one Jews were arrested, eighteen were hanged; many prisoners were saved by the intercession of courageous Dominican monks.* [154]

During the civil war that disordered England between 1257 and 1267, the populace got out of hand, and pogroms almost wiped out the Jewish communities of London, Canterbury, Northampton, Winchester, Worcester, Lincoln, and Cambridge. Houses were looted and destroyed, deeds and bonds were burned, and the surviving Jews were left almost penniless.[155] The English kings were now borrowing from the Christian bankers of Florence or Cahors; they no longer needed the Jews, and found it troublesome to protect them. In 1290 Edward I ordered the 16,000 remaining Jews of England to leave the country by November 1, abandoning all their immovable realty and all their collectible loans. Many were drowned in crossing the Channel in small boats; some were robbed by the ships' crews; those who reached France were told by the government that they must leave by Lent of 1291.[156]

---

* The Cathedral of Lincoln still shows the relics of a shrine once raised therein to "Little Hugh," and accompanies them with the following notice: "There are many incidents of the story which tend to throw doubt upon it; and the existence of similar stories in England and elsewhere points to their origin in the fanatical hatred of the Jews in the Middle Ages, and the common superstition, now wholly discredited, that ritual murder was a feature of Jewish Paschal rites. Attempts were made as early as the thirteenth century by the Church to protect the Jews against the hatred of the populace, and against these particular accusations."

In France, too, the spiritual climate changed for the Jews with the Crusades against the Turks in Asia and the Albigensian heretics of Languedoc. Bishops preached anti-Semitic sermons that stirred the people; at Béziers an attack upon the Jewish quarter was a regular rite of Holy Week; finally (1160) a Christian prelate forbade such preaching, but required the Jewish community to pay a special tax every Palm Sunday.[157] At Toulouse the Jews were forced to send a representative to the cathedral each Good Friday to receive publicly a box on the ears as a mild reminder of everlasting guilt.[158] In 1171 several Jews were burned at Blois on a charge of using Christian blood in Passover rites.[159] Seeing a chance to turn a pious penny, King Philip Augustus ordered all the Jews in his realm to be imprisoned as poisoners of Christian wells,[160] and then released them on payment of a heavy ransom (1180). A year later he banished them, confiscated all their realty, and gave their synagogues to the Church. In 1190 he had eighty Jews of Orange killed because one of his agents had been hanged by the city authorities for murdering a Jew.[161] In 1198 he recalled the Jews to France, and so regulated their banking business as to secure large profits to himself.[162] In 1236 Christian crusaders invaded the Jewish settlements of Anjou and Poitou—especially those at Bordeaux and Angoulême—and bade all Jews be baptized; when the Jews refused, the crusaders trampled 3000 of them to death under their horses' hoofs.[163] Pope Gregory IX condemned the slaughter, but did not raise the dead. St. Louis advised his people not to discuss religion with Jews; "the layman," he told Joinville, "when he hears any speak ill of the Christian faith, should defend it not with words but with the sword, which he should thrust into the other's belly as far as it will go." [164] In 1254 he banished the Jews from France, confiscating their property and their synagogues; a few years later he readmitted them, and restored their synagogues. They were rebuilding their communities when Philip the Fair (1306) had them all imprisoned, confiscated their credits and all their goods except the clothes they wore, and expelled them, to the number of 100,000, from France, with provisions for one day. The King profited so handsomely from the operation that he presented a synagogue to his coachman.[165]

So crowded a juxtaposition of bloody episodes scattered over two centuries makes a one-sided picture. In Provence, Italy, Sicily, and in the Byzantine Empire after the ninth century there were only minor persecutions of the Jews; and they found means of protecting themselves in Christian Spain. Even in Germany, England, and France the periods of peace were long; and a generation after each tragedy the Jews there were again numerous, and some were prosperous. Nevertheless their traditions carried down the bitter memory of those tragic interludes. The days of peace were made anxious by the ever-present danger of pogroms; and every Jew had to learn by heart the prayer to be recited in the moment of martyrdom.[166] The pursuit of wealth was made more feverish by the harassed insecurity of its gains; the gibes of gamins in the street were ever ready to greet the wearers of the yellow badge; the ignominy of a helpless and secluded minority burned into the soul, broke down individual pride and interracial amity, and left in the eyes of the northern Jew that somber *Judenschmerz*—the sorrow of the Jews—which recalls a thousand insults and injuries.

For that one death on the cross how many crucifixions!

CHAPTER XVII

The Mind and Heart of the Jew

500-1300

I. LETTERS

IN every age the soul of the Jew has been torn between the resolve to make his way in a hostile world, and his hunger for the goods of the mind. A Jewish merchant is a dead scholar; he envies and generously honors the man who, escaping the fever of wealth, pursues in peace the love of learning and the mirage of wisdom. The Jewish traders and bankers who went to the fairs of Troyes stopped on the way to hear the great Rashi expound the Talmud.[1] So, amid commercial cares, or degrading poverty, or mortal contumely, the Jews of the Middle Ages continued to produce grammarians, theologians, mystics, poets, scientists, and philosophers; and for a while (1150–1200) only the Moslems equaled them in widespread literacy and intellectual wealth.[2] They had the advantage of living in contact or communication with Islam; many of them read Arabic; the whole rich world of medieval Moslem culture was open to them; they took from Islam in science, medicine, and philosophy what they had given in religion to Mohammed and the Koran; and by their mediation they aroused the mind of the Christian West with the stimulus of Saracen thought.

Within Islam the Jews used Arabic in daily speech and written prose; their poets kept to Hebrew, but accepted Arabic meters and poetic forms. In Christendom the Jews spoke the language of the people among whom they lived, but wrote their literature, and worshiped Yahveh, in the ancient tongue. After Maimonides the Jews of Spain, fleeing from Almohad persecution, abandoned Arabic for Hebrew as their literary medium. The revival of Hebrew was made possible by the devoted labors of Jewish philologists. The Old Testament text had become difficult to understand through lack of vowels and punctuation; three centuries of scholarship—from the seventh to the tenth—evolved the "Masoretic" (tradition-sanctioned) text by adding vowel points, accent strokes, punctuation marks, verse separations, and marginal notes. Thereafter any literate Jew could read the Scriptures of his people.

Such studies compelled the development of Hebrew grammar and lexicography. The poetry and learning of Menachem ben Saruk (910–70) attracted the attention of Hasdai ben Shaprut; the great minister called him to Cordova, and encouraged him in the task of compiling a dictionary of Biblical Hebrew. Menachem's pupil Jehuda ibn Daud Chayuj (*c.* 1000) put Hebrew grammar upon a scientific basis with three Arabic works on the language of the Bible; Chayuj's pupil Jonah ibn Janaeh (995–1050) of Saragossa surpassed him with an Arabic *Book of Critique* that advanced Hebrew syntax and lexicography; Judah ibn Quraish of Morocco (fl. 900) founded the comparative philology of the Semitic languages by his study of Hebrew, Aramaic, and Arabic; the Qaraite Jew Abraham al-Fasi (i.e., of Fez, c. 980) furthered the matter with a dictionary in which all the words of the Old Testament were reduced to their roots alphabetically arranged. Nathan ben Yechiel of Rome (d. 1106) excelled all other Jewish lexicographers with his dictionary of the Talmud. In Narbonne Joseph Kimchi and his sons Moses and David (1160–1235) labored for generations in these fields; David's *Michlol*, or *Compendium*, became for centuries the authoritative grammar of Hebrew, and was a constant aid to King James' translators of the Bible.[3] These names are chosen from a thousand.

Profiting from this widespread scholarship, Hebrew poetry emancipated itself from Arabic exemplars, developed its own forms and themes, and produced in Spain alone three men quite equal to any triad in the Moslem or Christian literature of their age. Solomon ibn Gabirol, known to the Christian world as the philosopher Avicebron, was prepared by his personal tragedy to voice the feelings of Israel. This "poet among philosophers, and philosopher among poets," as Heine called him,[4] was born at Malaga about 1021. He lost both parents early, and grew up in a poverty that inclined him to morose contemplation. His verses caught the fancy of Yekutiel ibn Hassan, a high official in the Moslem city-state of Saragossa. There for a time Gabirol found protection and happiness, and sang the joy of life. But Yekutiel was assassinated by enemies of the emir, and Gabirol fled. For years he wandered through Moslem Spain, poor and sick, and so thin that "a fly could now bear me up with ease." Samuel ibn Naghdela, himself a poet, gave him refuge at Granada. There Solomon wrote his philosophical works, and pledged his poetry to wisdom:

> How shall I forsake wisdom?
> I have made a covenant with her.
> She is my mother, I am her dearest child;
> She hath clasped her jewels about my neck. . . .
> While life is mine my spirit shall aspire
> Unto her heavenly heights. . . .
> I will not rest until I find her source.[5]

Presumably his impetuous pride caused his quarrel with Samuel. Still a youth in his late twenties, he resumed his wandering poverty; misfortune humbled his spirit, and he turned from philosophy to religion:

> Lord, what is man? A carcass fouled and trodden,
> A noxious creature brimming with deceit,
> A fading flower that shrivels in the heat.[6]

His poetry took at times the somber grandeur of the Psalms:

> Establish peace for us, O Lord,   We wander ever to and fro,
>   In everlasting grace,   Or sit in chains in exile drear;
> Nor let us be of Thee abhorred,   Yet still proclaim, where'er we go,
>   Who art our dwelling place.   The splendor of our Lord is here.[7]

His masterpiece, *Kether Malkuth* (*Royal Crown*), celebrated the greatness of God as his early poems had celebrated his own:

> From Thee to Thee I fly to win   Unto Thy mercy I will cling
> A place of refuge, and within   Until Thou hearken pitying;
> Thy shadow from Thy anger hide,   Nor will I quit my hold of Thee
> Until Thy wrath be turned aside.   Until Thy blessing light on me.[8]

The richness and variety of Jewish culture in Moslem Spain were summed up in the Ibn Ezra family at Granada. Jacob ibn Ezra held an important post in the government of King Habbus under Samuel ibn Naghdela. His home was a salon of literature and philosophy. Of his four sons, reared in this atmosphere of learning, three reached distinction: Joseph rose to high office in the state, and to leadership of the Jewish community; Isaac was a poet, a scientist, and a Talmudist; Moses ibn Ezra (1070–1139) was a scholar, a philosopher, and the greatest Jewish poet of the generation before Halevi. His happy youth ended when he fell in love with a beautiful niece, whose father (his older brother Isaac) married her to his younger brother Abraham. Moses left Granada, wandered through strange lands, and fed his hopeless passion with poetry. "Though thy lips drop honey for others to sip, live on, breathe myrrh for others to inhale. Though thou art false to me, yet shall I be true to thee till the cold earth claims her own. My heart rejoices in the nightingale's song, though the singer soars above me and afar." [9] In the end, like Gabirol, he tuned his harp to piety, and sang psalms of mystic surrender.

Abraham ben Meir ibn Ezra—whom Browning used as a mouthpiece of Victorian philosophy—was a distant relative, but an intimate friend, of Moses ibn Ezra. Born in Toledo in 1093, his youth knew hunger, and thirsted for knowledge in every field. He too wandered from town to town, from occupation to occupation, luckless in all; "were candles my merchandise," he said, with the wry humor of the Jew, "the sun would never set; if I sold burial shrouds, men would live forever." He traveled through Egypt and Iraq to Iran, perhaps to India, back to Italy, then to France and England; at seventy-five he was returning to Spain when he died, still poor, but acclaimed throughout Jewry for both his poetry and his prose. His works were as varied as his domiciles—on mathematics, astronomy, philosophy, religion; his poems ranged through love and friendship, God and nature, anatomy and the seasons, chess and the stars. He gave poetic form to ideas ubiquitous in the Age of Faith, and he anticipated Newman in a Hebrew melody:

> O God of earth and heaven,   And where I fear to stand
>   Spirit and flesh are Thine!   Thy strength brings succor blest.
> Thou hast in wisdom given   Thy mantle hides my sins,
>   Man's inward light divine. . . .   Thy mercies are my sure defense;
> My times are in Thy hand,   And for Thy bounteous providence
>   Thou knowest what is best;   Thou wilt demand no recompense.[10]

His contemporaries valued him chiefly for his Biblical commentaries on every book of the Old Testament. He defended the authenticity and divine inspiration of the Hebrew Scriptures, but interpreted as metaphors the anthropomorphic phrases applied to the Deity. He was the first to suggest that the Book of Isaiah was the work of two prophets, not one. Spinoza considered him a founder of rational Biblical criticism.[11]

The greatest European poet of his age was Jehuda Halevi (1086–1147?). Born at Toledo a year after its capture by Alfonso VI of Castile, he grew up in security under the most enlightened and liberal Christian monarch of the time. One of his early poems pleased Moses ibn Ezra; the older poet invited Jehuda to come and stay with him in Granada; there Moses and Isaac ibn Ezra entertained him for months in their homes. His verses were read, his epigrams were repeated, in every Jewish community in Spain. His poetry reflected his genial character and his fortunate youth; he sang of love with all the skill and artifice of a Moslem or Provençal troubadour, and with the sensuous intensity of the Song of Songs. One poem—"The Garden of His Delight"—put into fervent verse the frankest passages of that erotic masterpiece:

> Come down, her beloved; why tarriest thou
> To feed amid her gardens?
> Turn aside to the couch of love,
> To gather her lilies.
> Secret apples of her breasts
> Give forth their fragrance;
> For thee she hideth in her necklaces
> Precious fruits shining like light. . . .
> She would shame, but for her veil,
> All the stars of heaven.[12]

Leaving the Ibn Ezras' courteous hospitality, Halevi went to Lucena, and studied for several years in the Jewish academy there; he took up medicine, and became an undistinguished practitioner. He founded a Hebrew institute in Toledo, and lectured there on the Scriptures. He married, and had four children. As he grew older he became more conscious of Israel's misfortunes than of his own prosperity; he began to sing of his people, their sorrows, and their faith. Like so many Jews, he longed to end his days in Palestine.

> O City of the World [Jerusalem], beauteous in proud splendor!
> Oh, that I had eagle's wings that I might fly to thee,
> Till I wet thy dust with my tears!
> My heart is in the East, while I tarry in the West.[13]

Comfortable Spanish Jews accepted such verses as a poetical pose, but Halevi was sincere. In 1141, leaving his family in good hands, he began an arduous pilgrimage to Jerusalem. Unfavorable winds drove his ship off course to Alexandria. There the Jewish community feted him, and begged him not to venture into Jerusalem, then in the Crusaders' hands. After some delay he went on to Damietta and Tyre, and thence, for some unknown reason, to Damascus. There he disappeared from history. Legend says that he made his way to Jerusalem, knelt at the first sight of it, kissed the earth, and was trampled to death by an Arab horseman.[14] We do not know if he ever reached the city of his dreams. We do know that at Damascus, perhaps in the last year of his life, he composed an "Ode to Zion" that Goethe ranked among the greatest poems in world literature.[15]

> Art thou not, Zion, fain
> To send forth greetings from thy sacred rock
> Unto thy captive train
> Who greet thee as the remnants of thy flock? . . .
>
> Harsh is my voice when I bewail thy woes;
> But when in fancy's dream
> I see thy freedom, forth its cadence flows,
> Sweet as the harps that hung by Babel's stream. . . .
>
> I would that, where God's Spirit was of yore
> Poured out unto thy holy ones, I might
> There too my soul outpour!
> The house of kings and throne of God wert thou;
> How comes it then that now
> Slaves fill the throne where sat thy kings before?
>
> Oh, who will lead me on
> To seek the posts where, in far distant years,
> The angels in their glory dawned upon
> Thy messengers and seers?
> Oh, who will give me wings
> That I may fly away,
> And there, at rest from all my wanderings,
> The ruins of my heart among thy ruins lay?

I'll bend my face unto thy soil, and hold
Thy stones as precious gold. . . .

Thy air is life unto my soul, thy grains
Of dust are myrrh, thy streams with honey flow;
Naked and barefoot, to thy ruined fanes
How gladly would I go!
To where the ark was treasured, and in dim
Recesses dwelt the holy cherubim. . . .

Perfect in beauty, Zion, how in thee
Do love and grace unite!
The souls of thy companions tenderly
Turn unto thee; thy joy was their delight,
And weeping they lament thy ruin now
In distant exile; for thy sacred height
They long, and toward thy gates in prayer they bow.

The Lord desires thee for His dwelling place
Eternally; and blest
Is he whom God has chosen for the grace
Within thy courts to rest.
Happy is he that watches, drawing near,
Until he sees thy glorious lights arise,
And over whom thy dawn breaks full and clear
Set in the orient skies.
But happiest he who, with exultant eyes
The bliss of thy redeemed ones shall behold,
And see thy youth renewed as in the days of old.[16]

II. THE ADVENTURES OF THE TALMUD

The Jews of that golden age in Spain were too prosperous to be as deeply religious as their poets became in declining years; they produced verses joyous and sensuous and graceful, and expressed a philosophy that confidently reconciled the Holy Scriptures with Greek thought. Even when Almohad fanaticism drove the Jews from Moslem into Christian Spain they continued to prosper; and Jewish academies flourished under Christian tolerance in Toledo, Gerona, and Barcelona in the thirteenth century. But in France and Germany the Jews were not so fortunate. They crowded their narrow quarters timidly, and gave their best minds to the study of the Talmud. They did not bother to justify their faith to the secular world; they never questioned its premises; they consumed themselves in the Law.

The academy founded by Rabbi Gershom at Mainz became one of the most influential schools of its time; hundreds of students gathered there, and shared with Gershom in editing and clarifying, through two generations of labor, the Talmudic text. A similar role was played in France by Rabbi Shelomoh ben Yitzhak (1040–1105), fondly called Rashi from the first letters of his title and his name. Born at Troyes in Champagne, he studied in the Jewish academies of Worms, Mainz, and Speyer; returning to Troyes, he supported his family by selling wine, but gave every leisure hour to the Bible and the Talmud. Though not officially a rabbi, he founded an academy at Troyes, taught there for forty years, and gradually composed commentaries on the Old Testament, the Mishna, and the Gemara. He did not try, as some Spanish scholars had done, to read philosophical ideas into the religious texts; he merely explained these with such lucid learning that his Talmudic commentaries are now printed with the Talmud. The modest purity of his character and his life won him reverence among his people as a saint. Jewish communities everywhere in Europe sent him questions in theology and law, and gave legal authority to his replies. His old age was saddened by the pogroms of the First Crusade. After his death his grandsons Samuel, Jacob, and Isaac ben Meir continued his work. Jacob was the first of the "tosaphists": for five generations after Rashi the French and German Talmudists revised and amended his commentaries with *tosafoth* or "supplements."

The Talmud had hardly been completed when Justinian outlawed the book (553) as "a tissue of puerilities, fables, iniquities, insults, imprecations, heresies, and blasphemies." [17] Thereafter the Church seems to have forgotten the existence of the Talmud; few theologians of the Latin Church could read the Hebrew or Aramaic in which it was written; and for 700 years the Jews were free to study the cherished volumes—so sedulously that they in turn seem almost to have forgotten the Bible. But in 1239 Nicholas Donin, a French Jew converted to Christianity, laid before Pope Gregory IX an indictment of the Talmud as containing shameful insults of Christ and the Virgin, and incitations to dishonesty in dealing with Christians. Some of the charges were true, for the assiduous compilers had so reverenced the tannaim and amoraim as to include in the haggadic or popular portion of the Gemara occasional remarks in which irate rabbis had struck back at Christian critiques of Judaism. [18] But Donin, now more Christian than the Pope, added several charges that could not be substantiated: that the Talmud considered it permissible to deceive, and meritorious to kill, a Christian, no matter how good; that the Jews were allowed by their rabbis to break promises made under oath; and that any Christian who studied the Jewish Law was to be put to death. Gregory ordered all discoverable copies of the Talmud in France, England, and Spain to be turned over to the Dominicans or the Franciscans; bade the monks examine the books carefully; and commanded that the books be burned if the charges proved true. No record has been found of the aftermath of this order. In France Louis IX directed all Jews to surrender their copies of the Talmud on pain of death, and summoned four rabbis to Paris to defend the book in public debate before the King, Queen Blanche, Donin, and two leading Scholastic philosophers—William of Auvergne and Albertus Magnus.[19] After three days' inquiry the King ordered all copies of the Talmud to be burned (1240). Walter Cornutus, Archbishop of Sens, interceded for the Jews, and the King allowed many copies to be restored to their owners. But the Archbishop died soon afterward, and some monks were of opinion that this was the judgment of God on the royal lenience. Convinced by them, Louis ordered the confiscation of all copies of the Talmud; twenty-four cartloads were brought to Paris, and were committed to the flames (1242). The possession of the Talmud was prohibited in France by a papal legate in 1248; and thereafter rabbinical studies and Hebrew literature declined in all of France except Provence.

A similar debate took place in Barcelona in 1263. Raymond of Peñafort, a Dominican monk in charge of the Inquisition in Aragon and Castile, undertook to convert the Jews of these states to Christianity. To equip his preachers he arranged for the teaching of Hebrew in the seminaries of Christian Spain. A converted Jew, Paul the Christian, assisted him, and so impressed Raymond with his knowledge of both Christian and Jewish theology that the monk arranged a disputation between Paul and Rabbi Moses ben Nachman of Gerona before King James I of Aragon. Nachmanides came reluctantly, fearing victory as much as defeat. The debate continued for four days, to the delight of the King; apparently the amenities were reasonably observed. In 1264 an ecclesiastical commission commandeered all copies of the Talmud in Aragon, obliterated the anti-Christian passages, and returned the books to their owners.[20] In an account that Nachmanides wrote of his debate for the Jewish synagogues of Aragon he spoke of Christianity in terms that seemed to Raymond grossly blasphemous.[21] The monk protested to the King, but it was not till 1266 that James, yielding to papal insistence, banished Nachmanides from Spain. A year later the rabbi died in Palestine.

III. SCIENCE AMONG THE JEWS

Jewish science and philosophy in the Middle Ages were almost entirely domiciled in Islam. Isolated and scorned, and yet influenced by their neighbors, the Jews of medieval Christendom took refuge in mysticism, superstition, and Messianic dreams; no situation could have favored science less. Religion, however, encouraged the study of astronomy, for on this depended the correct determination of the holydays. In the sixth century the Jewish astronomers of Babylonia substituted astronomic calculation for direct observation of the heavens; they based the year on the apparent movements of the sun, and the months on the phases of the moon; gave Babylonian names to the months; made some months "full" with thirty days, some "defective" with twenty-nine; and then reconciled the lunar with the solar calendar by inserting a thirteenth month every third, sixth, eighth, eleventh, fourteenth, seventeenth, and nineteenth year in a nineteen-year cycle. In the East the Jews dated events by the Seleucid calendar, which began at 312 B.C.; in Europe, in the ninth century, they adopted the present "Jewish era," *anno mundi*—"year of the world"—beginning with the supposed creation in 3761 B.C. The Jewish calendar is as clumsy and sacred as our own.

One of the earliest astronomers in Islam was the Jewish scholar Mashallah (d. *c.* 815). His *De scientia motus orbis* was translated from Arabic into Latin by Gerard of Cremona, and won wide acclaim in Christendom. His treatise *De mercibus (On Prices)* is the oldest extant scientific work in the Arabic tongue. The foremost mathematical treatise of the age [22] was the *Hibbur ha-meshihah*— on algebra, geometry, and trigonometry—of Abraham ben Hiyya of Barcelona (1065–1136), who also composed a lost encyclopedia of mathematics, astronomy, optics, and music, and the earliest surviving Hebrew treatise on the calendar. Abraham ibn Ezra, in the next generation, found no conflict between writing poetry and advancing combinatorial analysis. These two Abrahams were the first Jews to write scientific works in Hebrew rather than in Arabic. Through such books, and a flood of translations from Arabic into Hebrew, Moslem science and philosophy invaded the Jewish communities of Europe, and broadened their intellectual life beyond purely rabbinical lore.

Profiting in some measure from Islamic science, but also recapturing their own traditions of the healing art, the Jews of this period wrote outstanding treatises on medicine, and became the most esteemed physicians in Christian Europe. Isaac Israeli (*c.* 855–*c.* 955) acquired such fame as an ophthalmologist in Egypt that he was appointed physician to the Aghlabid court at Qairwan. His medical works, translated from Arabic into Hebrew and Latin, were acclaimed as classics throughout Europe; they were used as textbooks at Salerno and Paris, and were quoted, after 700 years of life, in Burton's *Anatomy of Melancholy* (1621). Tradition describes Isaac as indifferent to wealth, an obstinate bachelor, and a centenarian. Probably contemporary with him was Asaf ha-Jehudi, the obscure author of a recently discovered manuscript reckoned to be the oldest extant medical work in Hebrew, and remarkable for its teaching that the blood circulates through the arteries and the veins; had he surmised the function of the heart he would have completely anticipated Harvey.[23]

In Egypt, after the arrival of Maimonides (1165), the medical art was dominated by Jewish practitioners and texts. Abu al-Fada of Cairo wrote the principal ophthalmological treatise of the twelfth century, and al-Kuhin al-Attar composed (*c.* 1275) a pharmacopoeia still used in the Moslem world. The Jewish physicians of southern Italy and Sicily served as one medium through which Arabic medicine entered Salerno. Shabbathai ben Abraham (913–70), called Donnolo, born near Otranto, was captured by Saracens, studied Arabic medicine at Palermo, and then returned to practice in Italy. Benvenutus Grassus, a Jerusalem Jew, studied at Salerno, taught there and at Montpellier, and wrote a *Practica oculorum* (*c.* 1250) which Islam and Christendom alike accepted as the definitive treatise on diseases of the eye; 224 years after its publication it was chosen as the first book to be printed on its theme.

Rabbinical schools, especially in southern France, gave courses in medicine, partly to provide rabbis with a secular income. Jewish physicians trained in the Hebrew academy at Montpellier helped to develop the famous Montpellier school of medicine. The appointment of a Jew as regent of the faculty in 1300 drew upon his people the wrath of the medical authorities in the University of Paris; the Montpellier school was forced to close its doors to Jews (1301), and the Hebrew physicians of the city shared in the banishment of the Jews from France in 1306. By this time, however, Christian medicine had been revolutionized by Jewish and Moslem example and influence. The Semitic practitioners had long since put behind them the theory of sickness as "possession" by demons; and the success of their rational diagnosis and therapy had weakened the belief of the people in the efficacy of relics and other supernatural means of cure.

The monks and secular clergy whose abbeys and churches housed relics and drew pilgrims found it hard to accept this revolution. The Church condemned the intimate reception of Jewish doctors into Christian homes; she suspected that these men had more physic than faith, and she dreaded their influence upon sick minds. In 1246 the Council of Béziers forbade Christians to employ Jewish physicians; in 1267 the Council of Vienna forbade Jewish physicians to treat Christians. Such prohibitions did not prevent some prominent Christians from availing themselves of Jewish medical skill; Pope Boniface VIII, suffering from an eye ailment, called in Isaac ben Mordecai; [24] Raymond Lully complained that every monastery had a Jewish physician; a papal legate was shocked to find that this was also the fate of many nunneries; and Christian kings of Spain enjoyed Jewish medical care down to the reign of Ferdinand and Isabella. Sheshet Benveniste of Barcelona, physician to King James I of Aragon (1213–76), wrote the chief gynecological treatise of his time. The Jews lost their ascendancy in the medical practice of Christendom only when Christian universities, in the thirteenth century, adopted rational medicine.

For so mobile and scattered a people the Jews contributed little to the science of geography. Nevertheless the outstanding travelers of the twelfth century were two Jews—Petachya of Ratisbon and Benjamin of Tudela—who wrote valuable Hebrew narratives of their journeys through Europe and the Near East. Benjamin left Saragossa in 1160, leisurely visited Barcelona, Marseilles, Genoa, Pisa, Rome, Salerno, Brindisi, Otranto, Corfu, Constantinople, the Aegean Isles, Antioch, every important city in Palestine, and Baalbek, Damascus, Baghdad, and Persia. He returned by ship through the Indian Ocean and the Red Sea to Egypt, Sicily, and Italy, and thence overland to Spain; he reached home in 1173, and died soon afterward. His main interest was in the Jewish communities; but he described with fair accuracy and objectivity the geographic and ethnic features of each country on his route. His account is less fascinating, but probably more reliable, than the reports made by Marco Polo a century later. It was translated into nearly all European languages, and remained till our time a favorite book with the Jews.[25]

IV. THE RISE OF JEWISH PHILOSOPHY

The life of the mind is a composition of two forces: the necessity to believe in order to live, and the necessity to reason in order to advance. In ages of poverty and chaos the will to believe is paramount, for courage is the one thing needful; in ages of wealth the intellectual powers come to the fore as offering preferment and progress; consequently a civilization passing from poverty to wealth tends to develop a struggle between reason and faith, a "warfare of science with theology." In this conflict philosophy, dedicated to seeing life whole, usually seeks a reconciliation of opposites, a mediating peace, with the result that it is scorned by science and suspected by theology. In an age of faith, where hardship makes life unbearable without hope, philosophy inclines to religion, uses reason to defend faith, and becomes a disguised theology. Among the three faiths that divided white civilization in the Middle Ages this was least true of Islam, which had most wealth, truer of Christendom, which had less, truest of Judaism, which had least. And Jewish philosophy ventured from faith chiefly in the prosperous Jewry of Moslem Spain.

Medieval Jewish philosophy had two sources: Hebrew religion and Moslem thought. Most Jewish thinkers conceived of religion and philosophy as similar in content and result, differing only in method and form: what religion taught as divinely revealed dogma, philosophy would teach as rationally demonstrated truth. And most Jewish thinkers from Saadia to Maimonides made this attempt in a Moslem milieu, derived their knowledge of Greek philosophy from Arabic translations and Moslem commentaries, and wrote in Arabic for Moslems as well as Jews. Just as Ashari turned against the Mutazilites the weapons of reason, and saved the orthodoxy of Islam, so Saadia, who left Egypt for Babylonia in the very year (915) of Ashari's conversion from skepticism, saved Hebrew theology by his polemic industry and skill; and Saadia followed not only the methods of the Moslem *mutakallimun*, but even the details of their arguments.[26]

Saadia's victory had the same effect in Eastern Judaism as al-Ghazali's in Eastern Islam: it combined with political disorder and economic decline to smother Hebrew philosophy in the Orient. The rest of the story belongs to Africa and Spain. At Qairwan Isaac Israeli found time, amid his medical practice and writing, to compose some influential philosophical works. His *Essay on Definitions* gave several terms to Scholastic logic; his treatise *On the Elements* introduced Aristotle's *Physics* to Hebrew thought; his *Book of Soul and Spirit* replaced the creation story of Genesis with a Neoplatonist scheme of progressive emanations ("splendors") from God to the material world; here was one source of the Cabala.

Ibn Gabirol had more influence as a philosopher than as a poet. It is one of the *jeux d'esprit* of history that the Scholastics quoted him with respect as Avicebron, and thought him a Moslem or a Christian; not till 1846 did Salomon Munk discover that Ibn Gabirol and Avicebron were one.[27] The misunderstanding had almost been prepared by Gabirol's attempt to write philosophy in terms fully independent of Judaism. His anthology of proverbs —*Choice of Pearls*—took nearly all its quotations from non-Jewish sources, though Hebrew folklore is peculiarly rich in pointed and pithy apothegms. One pearl is quite Confucian: "How shall one take vengeance on an enemy? By increasing one's good qualities." [28] This is practically a summary of the treatise *On the Improvement of the Moral Qualities*, which Gabirol seems to have composed at twenty-four, when philosophy is unbecoming. By an artificial schematism the young poet derived all virtues and vices from the five senses, with platitudinous results; but the book had the distinction of seeking to construct, in the Age of Faith, a moral code unsupported by religious belief.[29]

With like audacity Gabirol's chef-d'oeuvre—*Mekor Hayim*—refrained from quoting either the Bible, the Talmud, or the Koran. It was this unusual supernationalism that made the book so offensive to the rabbis and, when translated into Latin as *Fons vitae* (*The Fountain of Life*), so influential in Christendom. Gabirol accepted the Neoplatonism that permeated all Arabic philosophy, but he imposed upon it a voluntarism that stressed the action of the will in God and man. We must, said Gabirol, assume the existence of God as first substance, first essence, or primary will, in order to understand the existence or motion of anything at all; but we cannot know the attributes of God. The universe was not created in time, but flows in continuous and graduated emanations from God. Everything in the universe except God is composed of matter and form; these always appear together, and can be separated only in thought.[30] The rabbis repudiated this Avicennian cosmology as a disguised materialism; but Alexander of Hales, St. Bonaventure, and Duns Scotus accepted the universality of matter under God, and the primacy of will. William of Auvergne nominated Gabirol as "the noblest of all philosophers," and thought him a good Christian.

Jehuda Halevi rejected all speculation as vain intellectualism; like al-Ghazali he feared that philosophy was undermining religion—not merely by questioning dogma, or ignoring it, or interpreting the Bible metaphorically, but even more by substituting argument for devotion. Against the invasion of Judaism by Plato and Aristotle, and the seduction of Jews by Mohammedanism, and the continuing attacks of Qaraite Jews upon the Talmud, the poet wrote one of the most interesting books of medieval philosophy—the *Al-Khazari* (*c.* 1140). He presented his ideas in a dramatic *mise-en-scène*— the conversion of the Khazar king to the Jewish faith. Luckily for Halevi the book, though written in the Arabic language, used the Hebrew alphabet, which confined its audience to educated Jews. For the story, bringing a bishop, a mullah, and a rabbi before the curious king, makes short work of both Mohammedanism and Christianity. When the Christian and the Moslem quote the Hebrew Scriptures as the word of God, the king dismisses them and keeps the rabbi; and most of the book is the conversation of the rabbi instructing a docile and circumcised king in Judaic theology and ritual. Says the royal pupil to his teacher: "There has been nothing new since your religion was promulgated, except certain details concerning paradise and hell." [31] So encouraged, the rabbi explains that Hebrew is the language of God, that God spoke directly only to the Jews, and that only the Jewish prophets were divinely inspired. Halevi smiles at philosophers who proclaim the supremacy of reason, and subject God and the heavens to their syllogisms and categories, while obviously the human mind is merely a fragile and infinitesimal fraction of a vast and complex creation. The wise man (who is not necessarily learned) will recognize the weakness of reason in transmundane affairs; he will keep to the faith given him in the Scriptures; and he will believe and pray as simply as a child.[32]

Despite Halevi, the fascination of reason survived, and the Aristotelian invasion continued. Abraham ibn Daud (1110–80) was as deeply Jewish as Halevi; he defended the Talmud against the Qaraites, and proudly narrated the *History of the Jewish Kings in the Second Commonwealth*. But along with countless Christians, Moslems, and Jews of the twelfth and thirteenth centuries, he aspired to prove his faith with philosophy. Like Halevi, he was born in Toledo, and made his living as a physician. His Arabic *Kitab al-aqidah al-rafiah* (*Book of the Sublime Faith*) gave the same answer to Halevi that Aquinas would give to the Christian enemies of philosophy: the peaceful defense of a religion against nonbelievers requires reasoning, and cannot rest upon simple faith. A few years before Averroës (1126–98), a generation before Maimonides (1135–1204), a century before St. Thomas Aquinas (1224–74), Ibn Daud labored to reconcile the faith of his fathers with the philosophy of Aristotle. The Greek would have been amused to find himself the recipient of such a triple compliment, or to learn that the Jewish philosophers knew him only in the summaries of al-Farabi and Avicenna, who knew him through imperfect translations and a Neoplatonist forgery. Truer than St. Thomas to their common Aristotelian source, Ibn Daud, like Averroës, claimed immortality only for the universal psyche, not for the individual soul; [33] here, Halevi might have complained, Aristotle triumphed over the Talmud as well as the Koran. Jewish philosophy, like medieval philosophy in general, had begun with Neoplatonism and piety, and was culminating in Aristotle and doubt. Maimonides would take his start from this Aristotelian stand of Ibn Daud, and would face with courage and skill all the problems of reason in conflict with faith.

V. MAIMONIDES: 1135–1204

The greatest of medieval Jews was born in Cordova, son of the distinguished scholar, physician, and judge Maimon ben Joseph. The boy received the name of Moses, and it became an adage among Jews that "from Moses to Moses there arose none like Moses." His people knew him as Moses ben Maimon, or, more briefly, Maimuni; when he became a famous rabbi the initials of his title and his name were combined into the fond appellation Rambam; and the Christian world expressed his parentage by terming him Maimonides. A probably legendary story tells how the boy showed a distaste for study, and how the disappointed father, calling him "the butcher's son," packed him off to live with the father's former teacher, Rabbi Joseph ibn Migas.[34] From this poor beginning the second Moses became adept in Biblical and rabbinical literature, in medicine, mathematics, astronomy, and philosophy; he was one of the two most learned men of his time. His only rival was Averroës. Strange to say, these outstanding thinkers, born in the same city only nine years apart, seem never to have met; and apparently Maimonides read Averroës only in old age, after his own books had been written.[35]

In 1148 Berber fanatics captured Cordova, destroyed churches and synagogues, and gave Christians and Jews a choice between Islam and exile. In 1159 Maimonides, with his wife and children, left Spain; for nine years they lived in Fez, pretending to be Moslems; [36] for there, too, no Jews or Christians were allowed. Maimonides justified superficial adherence to Islam among endangered Jews in Morocco by arguing that "we are not asked to render active homage to heathenism, but only to recite an empty formula; the Moslems themselves know that we utter it insincerely in order to circumvent bigots." [37] The head rabbi of Fez did not agree with him, and suffered martyrdom in 1165. Fearing the same fate, Maimonides left for Palestine; thence he moved to Alexandria (1165) and old Cairo, where he lived till his death. Soon recognized as one of the ablest practitioners of his time, he became personal physician to Saladin's eldest son, Nur-ud-Din Ali, and to Saladin's vizier al-Qadi al-Fadil al-Baisani. He used his favor at court to secure protection for the Jews of Egypt; and when Saladin conquered Palestine Maimonides persuaded him to let the Jews settle there again.[38] In 1177 Maimonides was made *Nagid* or head of the Jewish community in Cairo. A Moslem jurist indicted him (1187) as an apostate from Islam, and demanded the usual death penalty; Maimonides was saved by the vizier, who ruled that a man converted to Mohammedanism by force could not rightly be considered a Moslem.[39]

During these busy years in Cairo he composed most of his books. Ten medical works in Arabic transmitted the ideas of Hippocrates, Galen, Dioscorides, al-Razi, and Avicenna. *Medical Aphorisms* reduced Galen to 1500 short statements covering every branch of medicine; it was translated into Hebrew and Latin, and was frequently quoted in Europe under the formula *Dixit Rabbi Moyses*. For Saladin's son he wrote a treatise on diet; and for Saladin's nephew al-Muzaffar I, Sultan of Hamah, he composed an *Essay on Intercourse (Maqala fi-l-jima)*—on sexual hygiene, impotence, priapism, aphrodisiacs. . . . The introduction to this work struck an unhackneyed note:

> Our Lord His Majesty [al-Muzaffar]—may God prolong his power!—ordered me to compose a treatise that would help him increase his sexual powers, as he . . . had some hardship in this way. . . . He does not wish to depart from his customs concerning sexual intercourse, is alarmed by the abatement of his flesh, and desires an augmentation [of his virility] on account of the increasing number of his female slaves.[40]

To these writings Maimonides added several monographs—on poisons, asthma, hemorrhoids, and hypochondria—and a learned *Glossary of Drugs*. Like all books, these medical works contain several items not in accord with the passing infallibilities of our time—e.g., if the right testis is larger than the left, the first child will be male; [41] but they are marked by an earnest desire to help the sick, by a courteous consideration of contrary opinions, and by wisdom and moderation of prescription and advice. Maimonides never prescribed drugs where diet could serve.[42] He warned against overeating: "The stomach must not be made to swell like a tumor." [43] He thought that wine was healthful in moderation.[44] He recommended philosophy as a training in the mental and moral balance and calm conducive to health and longevity.[45]

At the age of twenty-three Maimonides began a commentary on the Mishna, and labored on it for a decade amid commerce, medicine, and perilous journeys by land and sea. Published at Cairo (1158) as *Kitab al-siraj*, or *Book of the Lamp*, its clarity, erudition, and good judgment at once placed Maimonides, still a youth of thirty-three, next to Rashi as a commentator on the Talmud. Twelve years later he issued his greatest work, written in Neo-Hebraic, and provocatively called *Mishna Torah*. Here, in logical order and lucid brevity, were arranged all the laws of the Pentateuch, and nearly all those of the Mishna and the Gemaras. "I have entitled this work *Mishna Torah [Repetition of the Law]*," said the introduction, "for the reason that a person who first reads the written Law [the Pentateuch] and then this compilation, will know the whole oral Law, without needing to consult any other book." [46] He omitted some Talmudic regulations concerning omens, amulets, and astrology; he was among the few medieval thinkers who rejected astrology.[47] He classified the 613 precepts of the Law under fourteen heads, devoted a "book" to each head, and undertook not only to explain each law, but to show its logical or historical necessity. Only one of the fourteen books has been translated into English; it forms a substantial volume; we may judge the immensity of the original.

It is clear from this work, and from the later *Guide to the Perplexed*, that Maimonides was not openly a freethinker. He endeavored as far as he could to reduce Scriptural miracles to natural causes, but he taught the divine inspiration of every word in the Pentateuch, and the orthodox rabbinical doctrine that the whole oral Law had been transmitted by Moses to the elders of Israel.[48] Perhaps he felt that the Jews could not claim less for their Scriptures than the Christians and Moslems claimed for them; perhaps he, too, considered social order impossible without belief in the divine origin of the moral code. He was a stern and dictatorial patriot: "All Israelites are bound to follow everything in the Babylonian Talmud, and we should force the Jews of every land to adhere to the customs established by the Talmudic sages." [49] A bit more liberal than most Moslems and Christians of the time, he thought that a virtuous and monotheistic non-Jew would go to heaven, but he was as severe as Deuteronomy or Torquemada on heretics within the Hebrew pale; any Jew who repudiated the Jewish Law should be put to death; and "according to my opinion, all members of an Israelite community which has insolently and presumptuously transgressed any of the divine precepts must be put to death." [50] He anticipated Aquinas in defending death for heresy on the ground that "cruelty against those who mislead the people to seek vanity is real clemency to the world"; [51] and he accepted without trouble the Scriptural penalty of death for witchcraft, murder, incest, idolatry, violent robbery, kidnaping, filial disobedience, and breaking the Sabbath.[52] The condition of the Jews migrating from ancient Egypt and trying to form a state out of a destitute and homeless horde may have warranted these laws; the precarious status of the Jews in Christian Europe or Moslem Africa, always subject to attack, conversion, or demoralization, required a hard code to forge order and unity; but in these matters (and before the Inquisition) Christian theory, and probably Jewish practice, were more humane than Jewish law. A better side of this stern spirit shows in Maimonides' advice to the Jews of his age: "If heathens should say to Israelites, 'Surrender one of your number to us that we may put him to death,' they should all suffer death rather than surrender a single Israelite to them." [53]

Pleasanter is his picture of the scholar growing into a sage. He approved the rabbinical saying that "a bastard who is a scholar [of the Law] takes precedence of an ignorant high priest." [54] He advised the scholar to give three hours daily to earning a living, nine hours to studying the Torah. Believing environment more influential than heredity, he counseled the student to seek association with good and wise men. The scholar should not marry until he has reached the maturity of his learning, has acquired a trade, and has bought a home.[55] He may marry four wives, but should cohabit with each of them only once a month.

Although connubial intercourse with one's wife is always permitted, this relation too should be invested by the scholar with sanctity. He should not be always with his spouse, like a rooster, but should fulfill his marital obligation on Friday nights. . . . When cohabiting, neither husband nor wife should be in a state of intoxication, lethargy, or melancholy. The wife should not be asleep at the time.[56]

And so at last is produced the sage. He

cultivates extreme modesty. He will not bare his head or his body. . . . When speaking he will not raise his voice unduly. His speech with all men will be gentle. . . . He will avoid exaggeration or affected speech. He will judge everyone favorably; he will dwell on the merits of others, and never speak disparagingly of anybody.[57]

He will avoid restaurants except in extreme emergency; "the wise man will eat nowhere except at home and at his own table." [58] He will study the Torah every day until his death. He will beware of false Messiahs, but will never lose his faith that some day the real Messiah will come, and restore Israel to Zion, and bring all the world to the true faith, and to abundance, brotherhood, and peace. "The other nations vanish, but the Jews last forever." [59]

The *Mishna Torah* irritated the rabbis; few could forgive the presumption of aiming to displace the Talmud; and many Jews were scandalized by the reported assertion of Maimonides [60] that he who studies the Law is higher than he who obeys it. Nevertheless the book made its author the leading Jew of the time. All Eastern Israel accepted him as its counselor, and sent him questions and problems; it seemed for a generation that the Gaonate had been revived. But Maimonides, not pausing to enjoy his renown, began work at once on his next book. Having codified and clarified the Law for orthodox Jews, he turned to the task of restoring to the Jewish fold those who had been seduced by philosophy or lured into the Qaraite communities of heretical Jews in Egypt, Palestine, or North Africa. After another decade of labor he issued to the Jewish world his most famous work, the *Guide to the Perplexed* (1190). Written in Arabic with Hebrew characters, it was soon translated into Hebrew as *Moreh Nebuchim*, and into Latin, and aroused one of the bitterest intellectual tempests of the thirteenth century.

"My primary object," says the introduction, "is to explain certain words occurring in the Prophetic books"—i.e., the Old Testament. Many Biblical terms and passages have several meanings; literal, metaphorical, or symbolical. Taken literally, some of them are a stumbling block to persons sincerely religious but also respectful of reason as man's highest faculty. Such persons must not be forced to choose between religion without reason or reason without religion. Since reason was implanted in man by God, it cannot be contrary to God's revelation. Where such contradictions occur, Maimonides suggests, it is because we take literally expressions adapted to the imaginative and pictorial mentality of the simple, unlettered people to whom the Bible was addressed.

> Our sages have said, It is impossible to give a full account of the creation to man. . . . It has been treated in metaphors in order that the uneducated may comprehend it according to the measure of their faculties and the feebleness of their apprehension, while educated persons may take it in a different sense.[61]

From this starting point Maimonides advances to a discussion of deity. That some supreme intelligence rules the universe he deduces from the evidences of design in nature; but he ridicules the notion that all things have been made for the sake of man.[62] Things exist only because God, their source and life, exists; "if it could be supposed that He does not exist, it would follow that nothing else could possibly exist." Since in this way it is essential that God exist, His existence is identical with His essence. Now "a thing which has in itself the necessity of existence, cannot have for its existence any cause whatever." * [63] Since God is intelligent, He must be incorporeal; therefore all Biblical passages implying physical organs or attributes in God must be interpreted figuratively. In truth, says Maimonides (probably following the Mutazilites), we cannot know anything of God except that He exists. Even the nonphysical terms that we use of Him—intelligence, omnipotence, mercy, affection, unity, will—are homonyms; i.e., they have different meanings when applied to God than as used of man. Just what their meaning is in God's case we shall never know; we can never define Him; we must not ascribe to Him any positive attributes, qualities, or predicates whatever. When the Bible tells how God or an angel "spoke" to the Prophets, we must not imagine a voice or sound. "Prophecy consists in the most perfect development of the imaginative faculty"; it is "an emanation from the Divine Being" through dream or ecstatic vision; what the Prophets relate took place not in actuality, but only in such vision or dream, and must in many cases be interpreted allegorically.[64] "Some of our sages clearly stated that Job never existed, and that he is a poetic fiction . . . revealing the most important truths." [65] Any man, if he develops his faculties to their height, is capable of such prophetic revelations; for human reason is a continuing revelation, not basically different from the vivid insight of the prophet.

Did God create the world in time, or is the universe of matter and motion, as Aristotle thought, eternal? Here, says Maimonides, reason is baffled; we can prove neither the eternity nor the creation of the world; let us therefore hold to our fathers' faith in its creation.[66] He proceeds to interpret the creation story of Genesis allegorically: Adam is active form or spirit; Eve

---

* These propositions, formulated by Avicenna, were adopted by St. Thomas Aquinas, and were adapted by Spinoza to the idea of a self-existing substance.

is passive matter, which is the root of all evil; the serpent is imagination.[67] But evil is no positive entity; it is merely the negation of good. Most of our misfortunes are due to our own fault; other evils are evil only from a human or limited standpoint; a cosmic view might discover in every evil the good or need of the whole.[68] God permits to man the free will that lets him be a man; man sometimes chooses evil; God has foreseen the choice, but does not determine it.

Is man immortal? Here Maimonides applies to the full his capacity for mystifying his readers. In the *Guide* he avoids the question, except to say that "the soul that remains after death is not the soul that lives in a man when he is born"; [69] the latter—the "potential intellect"—is a function of the body and dies with it; what survives is the "acquired" or "active intellect," which existed before the body and is never a function of it.[70] This Aristotelian-Averroist view apparently denied individual immortality. In the *Mishna Torah* Maimonides rejected the resurrection of the body, ridiculed the Moslem notion of a physically epicurean paradise, and represented this, in Islam and Judaism alike, as a concession to the imagination and the moral needs of the populace.[71] In the *Guide* he added that "incorporeal entities can only be numbered when they are forces situated in a body"; [72] * which seemed to imply that the incorporeal spirit which survived the body had no individual consciousness. As physical resurrection had become a central doctrine of both Judaism and Mohammedanism, many protests were aroused by these skeptical intimations. Transliterated into Arabic, the *Guide* made a stir in the Moslem world; a Mohammedan scholar, Abd al-Latif, denounced it as "undermining the principles of all faiths by the very means with which it appears to buttress them." [73] Saladin was at this time engaged in a life-and-death struggle with the Crusaders; always orthodox, he now more than ever resented heresy as threatening Moslem morale in the heat of a holy war; in 1191 he ordered the execution of Surawardi, a mystic heretic. In the same month Maimonides issued a *Maqala*, or discourse, "On the Resurrection of the Dead"; he again expressed his doubts about corporeal immortality, but announced that he accepted it as an article of faith.

The storm subsided for a time, and he busied himself in his work as a physician, and in writing *responsa* to doctrinal and ethical inquiries from the Jewish world. When (1199) Samuel ben Judah ibn Tibbon, who was translating the *Guide* into Hebrew, proposed to visit him, he warned him not to expect

> to confer with me on any scientific subject for even one hour, either by day or by night; for the following is my daily occupation. I dwell in Fustat, and the Sultan resides at Cairo two Sabbath days' journey [a mile and a half] distant. My duties to the regent [Saladin's son] are very heavy. I am obligated to visit him every day, early in the

---

* A source for Aquinas' doctrine of matter as the "principle of individuation"?

morning; and when he or any of his children, or any inmate of his harem, is indisposed, I dare not quit Cairo, but must stay during the greater part of the day in the palace. . . . I do not return to Fustat until the afternoon. . . . Then I am almost dying with hunger. I find the antechambers filled with people, theologians, bailiffs, friends, and foes. . . . I dismount from my animal, wash my hands, and beg my patients to bear with me while I partake of some refreshments—the only meal I take in twenty-four hours. Then I attend my patients . . . until nightfall, sometimes until two hours in the night, or even later. I prescribe while lying on my back from fatigue; and when night falls I am so exhausted I can scarcely speak. In consequence of this, no Israelite can have any private interview with me except on the Sabbath. On that day the whole congregation, or at least a majority, come to me after the morning service, when I instruct them. . . . We study together till noon, when they depart.[74]

He was prematurely worn out. Richard I of England sought him as personal physician, but Maimonides could not accept the invitation. Saladin's vizier, seeing his exhaustion, pensioned him. He died in 1204, aged sixty-nine. His remains were conveyed to Palestine, where his tomb may still be seen in Tiberias.

VI. THE MAIMONIDEAN WAR

Maimonides' influence was felt in Islam and Christendom as well as in the Jewish world. Mohammedan pundits studied the *Guide* under the direction of Jewish teachers; Latin translations of it were used at the universities of Montpellier and Padua; and it was frequently quoted at Paris by Alexander of Hales and William of Auvergne. Albertus Magnus followed the lead of Maimonides on many points; and St. Thomas often considered the views of Rabbi Moyses, if only to reject them. Spinoza, with perhaps some lack of historical understanding, criticized Maimonides' allegorical interpretation of the Scriptures as a disingenuous attempt to preserve the authority of the Bible; but he hailed the great rabbi as "the first who openly declared that Scripture must be accommodated to reason"; [75] and he took from Maimonides some ideas on prophecy, miracles, and the attributes of God.[76]

In Judaism itself Maimonides' influence was revolutionary. His own posterity carried on his work as scholars and Jews: his son Abraham ben Moses succeeded him as *Nagid* and court physician in 1205; his grandson David ben Abraham and his great-grandson Solomon ben Abraham also succeeded to the leadership of the Egyptian Jews; and all three continued the Maimonidean tradition in philosophy. For a while it became fashionable to Aristotelize the Bible through allegorical legerdemain, and to reject the historicity of its narratives; Abraham and Sarah, for example, were merely a legend representing matter and form; and Jewish ritual laws had only a symbolical purpose and truth.[77] The whole structure of Judaic theology seemed about to fall upon the heads of the rabbis. Some of them fought back vigorously: Samuel ben Ali of Palestine, Abraham ben David of Posquières, Meïr ben Todros Halevi Abulafia of Toledo, Don Astruc of Lunel, Solomon ben Abraham of Montpellier, Jonah ben Abraham Gerundi of Spain, and many more. They protested against "selling the Scriptures to the Greeks," denounced the attempt to replace the Talmud with philosophy, deplored Maimonides' doubts on immortality, and rejected his unknowable God as a metaphorical abstraction that would never stir a soul to piety or prayer. The followers of the mystic Cabala joined in the attack, and desecrated Maimonides' tomb.[78]

The Maimonidean war divided the Jewish communities of southern France precisely when orthodox Christianity was waging there a war of extermination against the Albigensian heresy. And as Christian orthodoxy defended itself against rationalism by banning the books of Aristotle and Averroës from the universities, so Rabbi Solomon ben Abraham of Montpellier—perhaps to forestall Christian attacks upon Jewish congregations as harboring rationalists—took the unusual step of anathematizing the philosophical works of Maimonides, and excommunicating all Jews who should study profane science or literature, or who should treat the Bible allegorically. The supporters of Maimonides, led by David Kimchi and Jacob ben Machir Tibbon, retaliated by persuading the congregations of Lunel, Béziers, and Narbonne in Provence, and those of Saragossa and Lerida in Spain, to excommunicate Solomon and his followers. Solomon now took a still more startling step: he denounced the books of Maimonides to the Dominican Inquisition at Montpellier as containing heresies dangerous to Christianity as well as Judaism. The monks accommodated him, and all procurable publications of the philosopher were burned in public ceremonies at Montpellier in 1234, and at Paris in 1242. Forty days later the Talmud itself was burned at Paris.

These events drove the supporters of Maimonides to bitter fury. They arrested the leading adherents of Solomon at Montpellier, convicted them of informing against fellow Jews, and condemned them to have their tongues cut out; apparently Solomon was put to death.[79] Rabbi Jonah, regretting his share in the burning of Maimonides' books, came to Montpellier, did public penance in the synagogue, and undertook a pilgrimage of repentance to Moses ben Maimon's grave. But Don Astruc resumed the war by proposing a rabbinical ban on any study of the profane sciences. Nachmanides and Asher ben Yehiel supported him; and in 1305 Solomon ben Abraham ben Adret, the revered and powerful leader of the Barcelona congregations, issued a decree of excommunication against any Jew who should teach, or should before the age of twenty-five dare to study, any secular science except medicine, or any non-Jewish philosophy. The liberals of Montpellier replied by excommunicating any Jew who debarred his son from the study of science.[80] Neither ban had any wide effect; Jewish youths, here and there, continued to study philosophy. But the great influence of Adret and Asher in Spain, and the growth of persecution and fear throughout a Europe now subject to the Inquisition, drove the Jewish communities back into intellectual as well as ethnic isolation. The study of science declined among them; purely rabbinical studies ruled the Hebrew schools. After its escapade with reason the Jewish soul, haunted with theological terrors and an encompassing enmity, buried itself in mysticism and piety.

VII. THE CABALA

The isles of science and philosophy are everywhere washed by mystic seas. Intellect narrows hope, and only the fortunate can bear it gladly. The medieval Jews, like the Moslems and the Christians, covered reality with a thousand superstitions, dramatized history with miracles and portents, crowded the air with angels and demons, practiced magical incantations and charms, frightened their children and themselves with talk of witches and ghouls, lightened the mystery of sleep with interpretations of dreams, and read esoteric secrets into ancient tomes.

Jewish mysticism is as old as the Jews. It received influences from the Zoroastrian dualism of darkness and light, from the Neoplatonist substitution of emanations for creation, from the Neopythagorean mysticism of number, from Gnostic theosophies of Syria and Egypt, from the apocrypha of early Christianity, from the poets and mystics of India, Islam, and the medieval Church. But its basic sources were in the Jewish mentality and tradition themselves. Even before Christ there had circulated among the Jews secret interpretations of the creation story in Genesis and of Chapters I and X of Ezekiel; in the Mishna it was forbidden to expound these mysteries except privately to a single and trustworthy scholar. Imagination was free to conceive accounts of what had preceded the creation or Adam, or what would follow the destruction of the world. Philo's theory of the Logos or Divine Wisdom as the creative agency of God was a lofty sample of these speculations. The Essenes had secret writings which were zealously guarded from disclosure, and Hebrew apocrypha like the Book of Jubilees expounded a mystic cosmogony. A mystery was made of the Ineffable Name of Yahveh: its four letters—the "Tetragrammaton"—were whispered to hold a hidden meaning and miraculous efficacy, to be transmitted only to the mature and discreet. Akiba suggested that God's instrument in creating the world was the Torah or Pentateuch, and that every word or letter of these holy books had an occult significance and power. Some Babylonian Geonim ascribed such occult powers to the letters of the Hebrew alphabet, and to the names of the angels; he who knew those names could control all the forces of nature. Learned men played with white or black magic—marvelous capacities obtainable through alliance of the soul with angels or demons. Necromancy, bibliomancy, exorcism, amulets, incantations, divination, and casting of lots played their part in Jewish as in Christian life. All the wonders of astrology were included; the stars were letters, a mysterious sky-writing that only the initiate could read.[81]

Sometime in the first century A.D. there appeared in Babylonia an esoteric book called *Sefer Yezira—The Book of Creation*. Mystic devotees, including Jehuda Halevi, attributed its composition to Abraham and God. Creation, it taught, had been effected through the mediation of ten *sefiroth*—numbers or principles: the spirit of God, three emanations therefrom—air, water, and fire, three spatial dimensions to the left, and three dimensions to the right. These principles determined the content, while the twenty-two letters of the Hebrew alphabet determined the forms through which creation could be understood by the human mind. The book elicited learned commentaries, from Saadia to the nineteenth century.

About 840 a Babylonian rabbi brought these mystic doctrines to the Jews of Italy, whence they spread to Germany, Provence, and Spain. Ibn Gabirol was probably influenced by them in his theory of the intermediate beings between God and the world. Abraham ben David of Posquières used the "secret tradition" as a means of drawing Jews away from the rationalism of Maimonides. His son Isaac the Blind and his pupil Azriel were probably the authors (*c.* 1190) of the *Sefer-ha-Bahir*, or *Book of Light*, a mystical commentary on the first chapter of Genesis; here the demiurgic emanations of the *Sefer Yezira* were changed into Light, Wisdom, and Reason; and this triplication of the Logos was offered as a Jewish Trinity.[82] Eleazar of Worms (1176–1238) and Abraham ben Samuel Abulafia (1240–91) offered the Secret Doctrine as a more profound and rewarding study than the Talmud. Like Islamic and German mystics, they applied the sensuous language of love and marriage to the relation between the soul and God.

By the thirteenth century the word *qabala*, tradition, had come into general use to describe the Secret Doctrine in all its phases and products. About 1295 Moses ben Shem Tob of Leon published the third Cabalistic classic, the *Sefer ha-Zohar*, or *Book of Splendor*. He ascribed its composition to Simon ben Yohai, a tanna of the second century; Simon, said Moses, had been inspired by the angels and the ten *sefiroth* to reveal to his esoteric readers secrets formerly reserved for the days of the coming Messiah. All the elements of the Cabala were brought together in the Zohar: the all-inclusiveness of a God knowable only through love, the Tetragrammaton, the creative demiurges and emanations, the Platonic analogy of macrocosm and microcosm, the date and mode of the Messiah's coming, the pre-existence and transmigration of the soul, the mystical meaning of ritual acts, numbers, letters, points, and strokes, the use of ciphers, acrostics, and the backward reading of words, the symbolical interpretation of Biblical texts, and the conception of woman as sin and yet as also the embodiment of the mystery of creation. Moses of Leon marred his performance by making Simon ben Yohai refer to an eclipse of 1264 in Rome, and use several ideas apparently unknown before the thirteenth century. He deceived many, but not his wife; she confessed that her Moses thought Simon an excellent financial device.[83] The success of the book inspired similiar forgeries, and some later Cabalists paid Moses in his own counterfeit by publishing their speculations under his name.

The influence of the Cabala was far-reaching. For a time the Zohar rivaled the Talmud as the favorite study of the Jews; some Cabalists attacked the Talmud as antiquated, literalistic logic-chopping; and some Talmudists, including the learned Nachmanides, were strongly influenced by the Cabalistic school. Belief in the authenticity and divine inspiration of the Cabala was widespread among European Jews.[84] Their work in science and philosophy suffered correspondingly, and the Golden Age of Maimonides ended in the brilliant nonsense of the Zohar. Even upon Christian thinkers the Cabala exercised some fascination. Raymond Lully (1235?–1315) adapted from it the number and letter mysticism of his *Ars magna*; Pico della Mirandola (1463–94) thought that he had found in the Cabala final proofs for the divinity of Christ.[85] Paracelsus, Cornelius Agrippa, Robert Fludd, Henry More, and other Christian mystics fed on its speculations; Johannes Reuchlin (1455–1522) confessed to poaching upon the Cabala for his theology; and perhaps Cabalistic ideas infected Jakob Böhme (1575–1624). If a greater proportion of Jews than of Moslems or Christians sought consolation in mystic revelations, it was because this world turned its worst face to them, and forced them, for life's sake, to cloak reality in a web of imagination and desire. It is the unfortunate who must believe that God has chosen them for His own.

VIII. RELEASE

From mystic exaltation, Messianic disillusionment, periodic persecution, and the hard routine of economic life, the medieval Jews found refuge in the obscurity of their congregations and the consolations of their ritual and creed. They celebrated with piety the festivals that recalled their history, their tribulations, and their ancient glory, and patiently adjusted to their urban existence the ceremonies that once had divided the agricultural year. The vanishing Qaraites kept the Sabbath in darkness and cold, lest they violate the Law by kindling fires or lighting lamps; but most Jews, while the rabbis winked, brought in Christian friends or servitors to keep the fires burning and tend the lights. Every chance for a banquet was seized with generosity and pomp: the family gave a feast on the circumcision or confirmation of a son, the betrothal or marriage of a son or daughter, the visit of a noted scholar or relative, the occurrence of some religious festival. Sumptuary regulations of the rabbis forbade the providers of such banquets to invite more than twenty men, ten women, five girls, and all relatives up to the third generation. A wedding feast sometimes lasted a week, and not even the Sabbath was allowed to interrupt it. The bridal pair were crowned with roses, myrtle, and olive branches; their path was strewn with nuts and wheat; barley grains were thrown over them as a hint to fertility; songs and quips accompanied every stage of the event; and in later medieval days a professional jester was engaged to ensure full merriment. Sometimes his jests were mercilessly truthful; but almost always he accepted Hillel's genial decree, that "every bride is beautiful." [86]

So the passing generation celebrated its own replacement, rejoiced in its children's children, and subsided into a harassed but kindly old age. We see the faces of such old Jews in Rembrandt's portraits: features bearing the history of the people and the individual, beards breathing wisdom, eyes haunted with sad memories but softened with indulgent love. Nothing in Moslem or Christian morals could surpass the mutual affection of young and old in Judaism, the love that overlooks all faults, the quiet guidance of immaturity by experience, and the dignity with which the life fully lived accepts the naturalness of death.

When he made his will the Jew left not only worldly goods to his offspring, but spiritual counsel. "Be one of the first in synagogue," reads the will of Eleazar of Mainz (c. 1337); "do not speak during prayers; repeat the responses; and after the service do acts of kindness." And then the final instruction:

> Wash me clean, comb my hair, trim my nails, as I was wont to do in my lifetime, so that I may go clean to my eternal resting place, just as I used to go on every Sabbath to the synagogue. Put me in the ground at the right hand of my father; if the space be a little narrow, I am sure that he loves me well enough to make room for me by his side.[87]

When the last breath was drawn, the eyes and mouth of the dead were closed by the eldest son or the most distinguished son or relative; the body was bathed and anointed with aromatic unguents, and wrapped in spotless linen. Almost everyone belonged to a burial society, which now took the corpse, watched over it, gave it the last religious rites, and accompanied it to the grave. In the funeral the pallbearers walked with bare feet; the women preceded the bier, chanted a dirge, and beat a drum. Any stranger who encountered the procession was expected to fall in with it and accompany it to the grave. Usually the coffin was placed near those of dead relatives; to be buried was for a man "to lie with his fathers," "to be gathered unto his people." The mourners did not despair. They knew that though the individual might die, Israel would carry on.

BOOK IV

THE DARK AGES

566–1095

CHRONOLOGICAL TABLE FOR BOOK IV

c. 850: The Book of Kells; Leo of Salonika, math'n
852–88: Boris Bulgarian khan & saint
857–91: Photius patriarch at C'ple
858–67: Pope Nicholas I
859: Rurik Grand Prince of Russia
860–933: Harald Haarfager first King of Norway
862: The Variagi at Novgorod
863: Mission of Cyril and Methodius to Moravians
867–86: Basil I founds Macedonian dynasty
871–901: Alfred the Great
872: Norsemen colonize Iceland
875–7: Charles the Bald, Western emp.
886: Norse besiege Paris
886–912: Leo VI the Wise, Eastern emp.
887f: Anglo-Saxon Chronicle
888: Odo King of France
893–927: Simeon Bulgar emperor
899–943: Magyars ravage Europe
905: Sancho I founds Kingdom of Navarre
910: Abbey of Cluny founded
911: Conrad I King of Germany; Rollo Duke of Normandy
912–50: Constantine VII Porphyrogenitus
c. 917: The Greek Anthology
919–36: Henry I the Fowler King of Germany
925–88: St. Dunstan
928–35: Venceslas I King of Bohemia
930: Icelandic Althing est'd
934–60: Haakon the Good King of Norway
936–73: Otto I King of Germany
950: Zenith of medieval Irish literature
955: Otto defeats Magyars on the Lechfeld
961: Convent of St. Lavra on Mt. Athos
962: Otto I Western Roman emperor
963: Otto deposes Pope John XII
963–9: Nicephorus Phocas Eastern emp.
965–95: Haakon the "Great Earl" King of Norway
968: Hroswitha, dramatist
973–83: Otto II of Germany
975–1035: Sancho the Great King of Navarre
976: Suidas' *Lexicon*
976–1014: Brian Borumha King of Munster
976–1026: Basil II Eastern emperor
976–1071: St. Mark's at Venice
980–1015: Vladimir I Prince of Kiev
983–1002: Otto III of Germany
987–96: Hugh Capet founds Capetian dynasty of French kings

989: Russia converted to Christianity
992–1025: Boleslav I first King of Poland
994f: Cluny monastic reform
997–1038: St. Stephen King of Hungary
999–1003: Pope Sylvester II (Gerbert)
1000: Leif Ericsson in "Vinland"
1002–24: Henry II of Germany
1007–28: Fulbert Bishop of Chartres
1009–1200: German Romanesque
1013: Sweyn of Denmark conquers England
1014: Brian Borumha defeats Norse at Clontarf
1015–30: St. Olaf King of Norway
1016–35: Cnut King of England
1018–80: Michael Psellus, historian
1022–87: Constantine the African, translator
1024–39: Conrad II of Germany
1028–50: Zoë and Theodora rule Eastern Empire
1033–1109: St. Anselm
1034–40: Duncan I King of Scotland
1035–47: Magnus the Good King of Norway
1039–56: Henry III of Germany
1040–52: Macbeth usurper King of Scotland
1040–99: Rodrigo Diaz el Cid
1043–66: Edward the Confessor King of England
1046–71: Church of St. Ambrose at Milan
1048f: Abbey of Jumièges
1049–54: Pope Leo IX
1052: d. of Earl Godwin, statesman
1054: Schism of Greek from Roman Church
1055–6: Theodora Eastern empress
1056–1106: Henry IV of Germany
1057–9: Isaac Comnenus Eastern emp.
1057–72: Peter Damian Bishop of Ostia
1058: Malcolm III of Scotland deposes Macbeth
1059–61: Pope Nicholas II; College of Cardinals established
1060: Robert Guiscard Duke of Apulia
1061–91: Norman Conquest of Sicily
1063: Prince Harold conquers Wales
1063f: Cathedral of Pisa
1066: Harold King of England; Battle of Hastings; Norman Conquest of England
1073–85: Pope Gregory VII Hildebrand
1075: Decree against lay investiture; excommunication of Henry IV
1077: Henry IV at Canossa
1081–1118: Alexius I Eastern emp.
1085: Sack of Rome by Robert Guiscard

CHAPTER XVIII

The Byzantine World

565-1095

I. HERACLIUS

IF now we turn from the Oriental side of the endless duel between East and West, we are soon moved with sympathy for a great empire harassed at once with internal discord and, on every side, external attack. Avars and Slavs were crossing the Danube and taking possession of imperial lands and towns; Persians were preparing to overrun Western Asia; Spain was lost to the Visigoths; and the Lombards, three years after Justinian's death, conquered half of Italy (568). Plague swept the Empire in 542 and again in 566; famine in 569; poverty, barbarism, and war broke down communications, discouraged commerce, stifled literature and art.

Justinian's successors were men of ability, but only a century of Napoleons could have coped with their problems. Justin II (565–78) fought vigorously against an expanding Persia. Tiberius II (578–82), favored by the gods with almost every virtue, was taken by them after a brief and just reign. Maurice (582–602) attacked the invading Avars with courage and skill, but received little support from the nation; thousands entered monasteries to escape military service; and when Maurice forbade the monasteries to receive new members until the danger was over, the monks clamored for his fall.[1] The centurion Phocas led a revolution of the army and the populace against the aristocracy and the government (602); the five sons of Maurice were butchered before his eyes; the old Emperor refused to let the nurse of his youngest child save it by substituting for it her own; he himself was beheaded; the six heads were hung up as a spectacle for the people, and the bodies were cast into the sea. The Empress Constantina and her three daughters, and many of the aristocracy, were slain, usually with torture, with or without trial; eyes were pierced, tongues were torn out, limbs were amputated;[2] once more the scenes of the French Revolution were rehearsed.

Khosru II took advantage of the disorder, and renewed the old war of Persia against Greece. Phocas made peace with the Arabs, and transported the entire Byzantine army into Asia; he was everywhere defeated by the Persians, while the Avars, unresisted, seized nearly all the agricultural hinterland of Constantinople. The aristocracy of the capital appealed to Heraclius, the Greek governor of Africa, to come to the rescue of the Empire and their property. He excused himself on the ground of age, but sent them his son. The younger Heraclius fitted out a fleet, sailed into the Bosporus, overthrew Phocas, exhibited the mutilated corpse of the usurper to the populace, and was hailed as emperor (610).

Heraclius deserved his title and his name. With almost the energy of Heracles he set himself to reorganize the shattered state. He spent ten years in rebuilding the morale of the people, the strength of the army, and the resources of the treasury. He gave land to peasants on condition that the eldest son in each family should render military service. Meanwhile the Persians captured Jerusalem (614), and advanced to Chalcedon (615); only the Byzantine navy, still controlling the waters, saved the capital and Europe. Soon afterward the Avar hordes marched up to the Golden Horn, raided the suburbs, and took thousands of Greeks into slavery. The loss of the hinterland and of Egypt cut off the city's supply of grain, and compelled abolition of the dole (618). Heraclius, desperate, thought of transporting his army to Carthage and thence attempting to retake Egypt; the people and the clergy refused to let him go, and the Patriarch Sergius agreed to lend him the wealth of the Greek Church, at interest, to finance a holy war for the recapture of Jerusalem.[3] Heraclius made peace with the Avars, and at last (622) set out against the Persians.

The campaigns that followed were masterpieces of conception and execution. For six years Heraclius carried the war to the enemy, and repeatedly defeated Khosru. In his absence a Persian army and a host of Avars, Bulgars, and Slavs laid siege to Constantinople (626); an army despatched by Heraclius defeated the Persians at Chalcedon, and the garrison and populace of the capital, roused by the Patriarch, scattered the barbarian horde. Heraclius marched to the gates of Ctesiphon; Khosru II fell; Persia pled for peace, and surrendered all that Khosru had taken from the Greek Empire. After seven years' absence, Heraclius returned in triumph to Constantinople.

He hardly deserved the fate that shamed his old age. Weakened by disease, he was devoting his last energies to strengthening the civil administration when suddenly wild Arab tribes poured into Syria (634), defeated an exhausted Greek army, and captured Jerusalem (638); and even as the Emperor lay on his deathbed Egypt fell (641). Persia and Byzantium had fought each other to a common ruin. Under Constans II (642–68) the Arab victories continued; thinking the Empire beyond saving, Constans spent his last years in the West, and was killed in Syracuse. His son Constantine IV Pogonatus was abler or luckier. When through five crucial years (673–8) the Moslems made another effort to take Constantinople, "Greek fire," now mentioned for the first time, saved Europe. The new weapon, allegedly invented by Callinicus of Syria, was akin to our flame throwers, an incendiary mixture of naphtha, quicklime, sulphur, and pitch; it was thrown against enemy ships or troops on flaming arrows, or blown against them through tubes, or shot on iron balls bearing flax and tow soaked in oil; or it was loaded and fired on small boats which were set adrift against the foe. The composition of the mixture was a secret successfully guarded for two centuries by the Byzantine government; to reveal any knowledge of it was treason and sacrilege. The Saracens finally discovered the formula, and used "Saracen fire" against the Crusaders. Until the invention of gunpowder it was the most talked-of weapon in the medieval world.

The Moslems made another assault upon the Greek capital in 717. An army of 80,000 Arabs and Persians under Moslema crossed the Hellespont at Abydos, and besieged Constantinople from the rear. At the same time the Arabs fitted out a fleet of 1800 vessels, presumably small; this armada entered the Bosporus, overshadowing the straits, said a chronicler, like a moving forest. It was the good fortune of the Greeks that in this crisis an able general, Leo "the Isaurian," replaced the incompetent Theodosius III on the throne, and assumed the organization of defense. He disposed the small Byzantine navy with tactical skill, and saw to it that every ship was well supplied with Greek fire. In a little while the Arab vessels were aflame, and nearly every ship in the great fleet was destroyed. The Greek army made a sortie upon the besiegers, and won so decisive a victory that Moslema withdrew to Syria.

II. THE ICONOCLASTS: 717–802

Leo III derived his cognomen from the district of Isauria in Cilicia; according to Theophanes he was born there of Armenian parentage. His father moved thence to Thrace, raised sheep, and sent 500 of them, with his son Leo in the bargain, as a present to the Emperor Justinian II. Leo became a guardsman of the palace, then commander of the Anatolian legions, finally, by the convincing suffrage of the army, emperor. He was a man of ambition, strong will, and patient perseverance; a general who repeatedly defeated Moslem forces greatly superior to his own; a statesman who gave the Empire the stability of just laws justly enforced, reformed taxation, reduced serfdom, extended peasant proprietorship, distributed lands, repopulated deserted regions, and constructively revised the laws. His only fault was autocracy.

Perhaps in his Asiatic youth he had imbibed from Moslems, Jews, Manicheans, Monophysites, and Paulicians a Stoic-Puritan conception of religion that condemned the addiction of popular Christianity to image worship, ceremonialism, and superstition. The Old Testament (Deut. iv, 15) had explicitly forbidden any "graven image of any figure, male or female, the likeness of any beast that is on the earth." The early Church had frowned upon images as relics of paganism, and had looked with horror upon pagan sculptures purporting to represent the gods. But the triumph of Christianity under Constantine, and the influence of Greek surroundings, traditions, and statuary in Constantinople and the Hellenistic East, had softened this opposition. As the number of worshiped saints multiplied, a need arose for identifying and remembering them; pictures of them and of Mary were produced in great number; and in the case of Christ not only His imagined form but His cross became objects of reverence—even, for simple minds, magic talismans. A natural freedom of fancy among the people turned the holy relics, pictures, and statues into objects of adoration; people prostrated themselves before them, kissed them, burned candles and incense before them, crowned them with flowers, and sought miracles from their occult influence. In Greek Christianity especially, sacred images were everywhere—in churches, monasteries, houses and shops, even on furniture, trinkets, and clothes. Cities in danger from epidemic, famine, or war tended to rely upon the power of the relics they harbored, or on their patron saint, rather than on human enterprise. Fathers and councils of the Church repeatedly explained that the images were not deities, but only reminders thereof;[4] the people did not care to make such distinctions.

Leo III was offended by these excesses of popular faith; it seemed to him that paganism was in this manner reconquering Christianity; and he felt keenly the satire directed by Moslems, Jews, and Christian sects against the superstitions of the orthodox multitude. To weaken the power of the monks over the people and the government, and win the support of Nestorians and Monophysites, he assembled a great council of bishops and senators, and with their consent he promulgated in 726 an edict requiring the complete removal of icons from the churches; representations of Christ and the Virgin were forbidden; and church murals were to be covered with plaster. Some of the higher clergy supported the edict; the lower clergy and the monks protested, the people revolted. Soldiers trying to enforce the law were attacked by worshipers horrified and infuriated by this desecration of the dearest symbols of their faith. In Greece and the Cyclades rebel forces proclaimed a rival emperor, and sent a fleet to capture the capital. Leo destroyed the fleet, and imprisoned the leaders of the opposition. In Italy, where pagan forms of worship had never died, the people were almost unanimous against the edict; Venice, Ravenna, and Rome drove out the Imperial officers; and a council of Western bishops summoned by Pope Gregory II anathematized the Iconoclasts—image breakers—without naming the Emperor. The patriarch of Constantinople joined the revolt, and sought by it to restore the independence of the Eastern Church from the state. Leo deposed him (730), but did him no violence; and the edict was so mildly enforced that when Leo died (741), most of the churches retained their frescoes and mosaics unharmed.

His son Constantine V (741–75) continued his policy, and received from hostile historians the genial epithet of Copronymus—"named from dung." A council of Eastern bishops, called by him at Constantinople (754), condemned image worship as "abominable," charged that through such worship

"Satan had re-introduced idolatry," denounced "the ignorant artist who with his unclean hands gives form to that which should be believed only by the heart," [5] and decreed that all images in the churches should be erased or destroyed. Constantine executed the decree without moderation or tact; imprisoned and tortured resisting monks; again eyes or tongues were torn out, noses were cut off; the patriarch was tortured and beheaded (767). Like Henry VIII, Constantine V closed monasteries and convents, confiscated their property, turned the buildings to secular uses, and bestowed monastic lands upon his favorites. At Ephesus the imperial governor, with the approval of the Emperor, assembled the monks and nuns of the province, and forced them to marry one another as an alternative to death.[6] The persecution continued for five years (765–71).

Constantine exacted from his son Leo IV (775–80) an oath to continue the Iconoclastic policy; Leo did what he could despite his weak constitution. Dying, he named his ten-year-old son Constantine VI as emperor (780–97), and nominated his widow, the Empress Irene, as regent during the youth's minority. She ruled with ability and without scruple. Sympathizing with the religious feelings of the people and her sex, she quietly ended the enforcement of the Iconoclast edicts; permitted the monks to return to their monasteries and their pulpits, and convened the prelates of Christendom in the Second Council of Nicaea (787), where 350 bishops, under the lead of papal legates, restored the veneration—not the worship—of sacred images as a legitimate expression of Christian piety and faith.

In 790 Constantine VI came of age. Finding his mother reluctant to surrender her power, he deposed and exiled her. Soon the amiable youth relented; he brought her back to court, and associated her with him in the imperial power (792). In 797 she had him imprisoned and blinded, and thereafter reigned under the title of emperor—not *basilissa* but *basileus*. For five years she administered the Empire with wisdom and finesse: lowered taxes, scattered largess among the poor, founded charitable institutions, and beautified the capital. The people applauded and loved her, but the army fretted at being ruled by a woman more capable than most men. In 802 the Iconoclasts revolted, deposed her, and made her treasurer Nicephorus emperor. She yielded quietly, and asked of him only a decent and safe retreat; he promised it, but banished her to Lesbos, and left her to earn a scanty living as a seamstress. Nine months later she died, with hardly a penny or a friend. The theologians forgave her crimes because of her piety, and the Church canonized her as a saint.

III. IMPERIAL KALEIDOSCOPE: 802–1057

A full perspective of Byzantine civilization would require at this point a record of many emperors and some empresses—not of their intrigues, palace revolutions, and assassinations, but of their policy and legislation, and their age-long effort to protect the diminishing Empire from Moslems on the south and Slavs and Bulgars on the north. In some respects it is an heroic picture: through all the fluent shifts of appearing and disappearing figures the Greek heritage was in good measure preserved; economic order and continuity were maintained; civilization continued, as if by some enduring impetus from the ancient labors of Pericles and Augustus, Diocletian and Constantine. In other aspects it is a sorry spectacle of generals climbing over slain rivals to imperial power, to be slain in their turn; of pomp and luxury, eye-gouging and nose-cutting, incense and piety and treachery; of emperor and patriarch unscrupulously struggling to determine whether the empire should be ruled by might or myth, by sword or word. So we pass by Nicephorus I (802–11) and his wars with Harun al-Rashid; Michael I (811–13), dethroned and tonsured into monkhood because of his defeat by the Bulgars; Leo V the Armenian (813–20), who again forbade the worship of images, and was assassinated while singing an anthem in church; Michael II (820–9) the illiterate "Stammerer," who fell in love with a nun, and persuaded the Senate to entreat him to marry her;[7] Theophilus (829–42), a legislative reformer, royal builder, and conscientious administrator, who revived the Iconoclastic persecution, and died of dysentery; his widow Theodora, who as an able regent (842–56) ended the persecution; Michael III "the Drunkard" (842–67), whose amiable incompetence left the government first to his mother and, after her death, to his cultured and capable uncle Caesar Bardas. Then suddenly a unique and unexpected figure appeared on the scene, overthrew every precedent except violence, and founded the powerful Macedonian dynasty.

Basil the Macedonian was born (812?) near Hadrianople of an Armenian peasant family. As a child he was captured by Bulgars, and lived his youth among them beyond the Danube, in what was then called Macedonia. Escaping in his twenty-fifth year, he made his way to Constantinople, and was hired as groom by a diplomat who admired his physical strength and massive head. He accompanied his master on a mission to Greece, and there attracted the attention, and some of the wealth, of the widow Danielis. Back in the capital, he tamed a spirited horse for Michael III, was taken into the Emperor's service, and, though quite illiterate, rose to the position of lord chamberlain. Basil was ever convenient and competent; when Michael sought a husband for his mistress, Basil divorced his peasant wife, sent her to Thrace with a comforting dowry, and married Eudocia, who continued her services to the Emperor.[8] Michael supplied Basil with a mistress, but the Macedonian thought he deserved the throne as reward. He persuaded Michael that Bardas was plotting to depose him, and then killed Bardas with his own enormous hands (866). Long accustomed to reign without ruling, Michael made Basil coemperor and left him all the tasks of government. When Michael threatened to dismiss him, Basil arranged and supervised his assassination, and became sole emperor (867): so, even under hereditary monarchy, career was open to talent. With such servility and crime the letterless son of a peasant established the longest of all Byzantine dynasties, and began a nineteen-year reign of excellent administration, legislating wisely, judging justly, replenishing the treasury, and building new churches and palaces for the city that he had captured. No one dared oppose him; and when he died by a hunting accident the throne passed with unwonted quiet to his son.

Leo VI (886–912) was the complement of his father: learned, bookish, sedentary, mild; gossip concluded that he was Michael's, not Basil's, son, and perhaps Eudocia was not sure. He earned his cognomen of "the Wise" not by his poetry, nor by his treatises on theology, administration, and war, but by his reorganization of provincial and ecclesiastical government, his new formulations of Byzantine law, and his meticulous regulation of industry. Though an admiring pupil of the scholarly patriarch Photius, and himself devoted to piety, he shocked the clergy, and amused the people, by four marriages. His first two wives died without bearing him a son; Leo insisted on a son as the only alternative to a war of succession; the moral theology of the Church forbade a third marriage; Leo persisted, and his fourth wife, Zoë, crowned his resolution with a boy.

Constantine VII (912–58) was called Porphyrogenitus—"born in the purple"—i.e., in the porphyry-lined apartment reserved for the use of expecting empresses. He inherited his father's literary tastes, not his administrative capacity. He composed for his son two books on the art of government: one on the "themes" or provinces of the Empire, and a *Book of Ceremonies* describing the ritual and etiquette required of the emperor. He supervised the compilation of works on agriculture, medicine, veterinary medicine, and zoology, and formed an "historians' history of the world" by selecting extracts from historians and chroniclers. Under his patronage Byzantine literature flourished in its polished and anemic way.

Perhaps Romanus II (958–63) was like other children, and did not read his father's books. He married a Greek girl, Theophano; she was suspected of poisoning her father-in-law and hastening Romanus' death; and before her twenty-four-year-old husband was dead she seduced into her arms the ascetic general Nicephorus II Phocas, who with her connivance seized the throne. Nicephorus had already driven the Moslems from Aleppo and Crete (961); in 965 he drove them from Cyprus, in 968 from Antioch; it was these victories that shattered the Abbasid caliphate. Nicephorus pled with the patriarch to promise all the rewards and honors of martyrdom to soldiers who should fall in battle against the Moslems; the patriarch refused on the ground that all soldiers were temporarily polluted by the blood that they shed; had he consented, the Crusades might have begun a century earlier. Nicephorus lost ambition, and retired into the palace to live like an anchorite. Bored with this monastic existence, Theophano became the mistress of the general John

Tzimisces. With her connivance he killed Nicephorus (969) and seized the throne; remorseful, he repudiated and exiled her, and went off to atone for his crimes by transient victories against the Moslems and the Slavs.

His successor was one of the most powerful personalities in Byzantine history. Basil II, born to Romanus and Theophano (958), had served as co-emperor with Nicephorus Phocas and Tzimisces; now (976) he began at the age of eighteen an undivided rule that lasted half a century. Troubles encompassed him: his chief minister plotted to displace him; the feudal barons, whom he proposed to tax, financed conspiracies against him; Bardas Sclerus, general of the eastern army, rebelled, and was suppressed by Bardas Phocas, who then had himself proclaimed emperor by his troops; the Moslems were recovering nearly all that Tzimisces had won from them in Syria; the Bulgars were at their zenith, encroaching upon the Empire in east and west. Basil suppressed the revolt, reclaimed Armenia from the Saracens, and in a ruthless thirty years' war destroyed the Bulgarian power. After his victory in 1014 he blinded 15,000 prisoners, leaving one eye in every hundredth man to lead the tragic host back to Samuel, the Bulgarian tsar; perhaps in terror rather than in admiration the Greeks called him Bulgaroctonus, Killer of Bulgars. Amid these campaigns he found time to war against "those who enriched themselves at the expense of the poor." By his laws of 996 he sought to break up some of the large estates, and to encourage the spread of a free peasantry. He was about to lead an armada against the Saracens in Sicily when death surprised him in his sixty-eighth year. Not since Heraclius had the Empire been so extensive, nor since Justinian so strong.

The Byzantine decline was resumed under his aged brother Constantine VIII (1025–8). Having no offspring but three daughters, Constantine persuaded Romanus Argyrus to marry the eldest, Zoë, who was nearing fifty. As regent, and with the help of her sister Theodora, Zoë governed the state through the reigns of Romanus III (1028–34), Michael IV (1034–42), Michael V (1042), and Constantine IX (1042–55); and seldom had the Empire been better ruled. The imperial sisters attacked corruption in state and Church, and forced officials to disgorge their embezzled hoards; one who had been chief minister surrendered 5300 pounds of gold ($2,226,000) which he had secreted in a cistern; and when the Patriarch Alexis died, a cache of 100,000 pounds of silver ($27,000,000) was discovered in his rooms.[9] For a brief interlude the sale of offices was stopped. Zoë and Theodora sat as judges on the highest tribunal, and dispensed stern justice. Nothing could rival Zoë's impartiality. Having at sixty-two married Constantine IX, and knowing that her cosmetic skill had preserved barely the surface of her charms, she allowed her new husband to bring his mistress Sclerena to live in the royal palace; he chose quarters between their apartments, and Zoë never visited him without making sure that he was disengaged.[10] When Zoë died (1050), Theodora retired to a convent, and Constantine IX ruled for five years with wisdom and taste; he chose men of competence and culture for his aides, rebeautified St. Sophia, built hospitals and refuges for the poor, and supported literature and art. At his death (1055) the supporters of the Macedonian dynasty led a popular revolt that brought the virgin Theodora out of her conventual retreat, and, much against her will, crowned her empress. Despite her seventy-four years she and her ministers governed efficiently; but in 1056 she died so suddenly that chaos ensued. The palace aristocracy named Michael VI emperor; the army preferred the general Isaac Comnenus. One battle decided the issue; Michael became a monk, and Comnenus entered the capital in 1057 as emperor. The Macedonian dynasty had come to an end after 190 years of violence, war, adultery, piety, and excellent administration.

Isaac Comnenus resigned after two years, named Constantine Ducas, the president of the Senate, as his successor, and entered a monastery. When Constantine died (1067) his widow Eudocia acted as regent for four years; but the demands of war required a sterner leader, and she married and crowned Romanus IV. Romanus was defeated by the Turks at Manzikert (1071), returned to Constantinople in disgrace, was deposed, imprisoned, and blinded, and was allowed to die of his untended wounds. When Alexius Comnenus I, nephew of Isaac Comnenus, came to the throne (1081), the Byzantine Empire seemed near its fall. The Turks had taken Jerusalem (1076), and were advancing through Asia Minor; the Patzinak and Cuman tribes were approaching Constantinople from the north; the Normans were attacking the Byzantine outposts in the Adriatic; the government and the army were crippled with treason, incompetence, corruption, and cowardice. Alexius met the situation with subtlety and courage. He sent agents to foment revolution in Norman Italy; gave Venice commercial privileges in return for the aid of its navy against the Normans; confiscated Church treasures to rebuild his army; took the field in person, and won victories by strategy rather than by blood. Amid these foreign cares he found time to reorganize the government and its defenses, and gave the tottering Empire another century of life. In 1095, in a far-reaching stroke of diplomacy, he appealed to the West to come to the aid of the Christian East; at the Council of Piacenza he offered a reunion of the Greek with the Latin Church in return for the unity of Europe against Islam. His appeal conspired with other factors to unleash the first of those dramatic Crusades that were to save, and then destroy, Byzantium.

IV. BYZANTINE LIFE: 566–1095

At the beginning of the eleventh century the Greek Empire, through the arms and statesmanship of the Isaurian and Macedonian dynasties, had reached again the power, wealth, and culture of its zenith under Justinian. Asia Minor, northern Syria, Cyprus, Rhodes, the Cyclades, and Crete had

been wrested from the Moslems; southern Italy was once more Magna
Grecia, ruled by Constantinople; the Balkans had been recaptured from
Bulgars and Slavs; Byzantine industry and commerce again dominated the
Mediterranean; Greek Christianity had triumphed in the Balkans and Russia;
and Greek art and literature were enjoying a Macedonian renaissance. The
revenue of the state in the eleventh century reached the present equivalent of
$2,400,000,000.[11]

Constantinople was at the crest of its curve, surpassing ancient Rome and
Alexandria, contemporary Baghdad and Cordova, in trade, wealth, luxury,
beauty, refinement, and art. Its population of nearly a million [12] was now predominantly Asiatic or Slav—Armenians, Cappadocians, Syrians, Jews, Bulgars, and half-Slav Greeks, with a colorful infusion of merchants and soldiers
from Scandinavia, Russia, Italy, and Islam; and at the top a thinning layer
of Greek aristocrats. A thousand varieties of homes—gabled, terraced, or
domed—with balconies, loggias, gardens, or pergolas; full markets reeking
with the products of all the world; a thousand narrow muddy streets of
tenements and shops; splendid thoroughfares bordered with stately mansions
and shady porticoes, peopled with statuary, spanned with arches of triumph,
and leading out to the countryside through guarded gates in the fortress
walls; complex royal palaces—the Triconchus of Theophilus, the New Palace
of Basil I, the Bucoleon of Nicephorus Phocas, descending by marble stairs
to a sculptured colonnaded wharf on the Sea of Marmora; churches "as
many as there are days in the year" (said a traveler), and several of them
architectural jewels; altars enshrining the most revered and precious relics in
Christendom; monasteries unashamedly magnificent without, and turbulent
with proud saints within; St. Sophia ever newly adorned, glowing with candles and lamps, heavy with incense, solemn with pageantry, sonorous with
convincing chants: this was the frame, half gold and half mud, of teeming life
in the Byzantine capital.

Within the city palaces of the aristocracy and the great merchants, and in
the villas of seaside and hinterland, every luxury available to that age could
be found, and decoration uninhibited by Semitic tabus: marbles of every
grain and hue, murals and mosaics, sculptures and fine pottery, curtains slid-
ing on silver rods, tapestries and carpets and silks, doors inlaid with silver or
ivory, furniture exquisitely carved, table services of silver or gold. Here
moved the world of Byzantine society: men and women of fine face and
figure, dressed in colored silks and lace and furs, and rivaling the graces,
amours, and intrigues of Bourbon Paris and Versailles. Never were ladies
better powdered and scented, jeweled and coiffured; in the imperial palaces
fires were kept burning all the year long to brew the perfumes required to
deodorize queens and princesses.[13] Never before had life been so ornate and
ceremonious, so colorful with processions, receptions, spectacles and games,
so minutely ordained by protocol and etiquette. At the Hippodrome as well

as in the court the firmly established aristocracy flaunted its finest raiment and ornament; on the highways its stately equipages passed, so reckless as to earn the hatred of the pedestrian poor, and so rich as to bring down the anathemas of prelates who served God in vessels, and on altars, of marble, alabaster, silver, and gold. Constantinople, said Robert of Clari,[14] contained "two thirds of the world's wealth"; even the common "Greek inhabitants," reported Benjamin of Tudela, "seem all to be the children of kings." [15]

"If Constantinople," said a twelfth-century writer, "surpasses all other cities in wealth, it also surpasses them in vice." [16] All the sins of a great city found room here, impartially in rich and poor. Brutality and piety took turns in the same imperial souls; and among the people intensity of religious need could be adjusted to the corruption or violence of politics and war. The castration of children to serve as eunuchs in harems and administration, the assassination or blinding of present or potential rivals for the throne, continued through divers dynasties and the monotonous kaleidoscope of changeless change. The populace, disordered and manipulated by divisions of race, class, or creed, was fickle, bloodthirsty, periodically turbulent; bribed by the state with doles of bread, oil, and wine; diverted by horse races, beast baitings, rope dancing, indecent pantomimes in the theater, and by imperial or ecclesiastical pageantry in the streets. Gambling halls and saloons were everywhere; houses of prostitution could be found on almost every street, sometimes "at the very church doors." [17] The women of Byzantium were famous for their licentiousness and their religious devotion, the men for their quick intelligence and unscrupulous ambition. All classes believed in magic, astrology, divination, sorcery, witchcraft, and miraculous amulets. The Roman virtues had disappeared even before the Latin tongue; Roman and Greek qualities had been overwhelmed by a flood of uprooted Orientals who had lost their own morality and had taken on no other except in words. Yet even in this highly theological and sensual society the great majority of men and women were decent citizens and parents, who settled down after youthful frolics to the joys and sorrows of family life, and grudgingly performed the work of the world. The same emperors who blinded their rivals poured out charity to hospitals, orphanages, homes for the aged, free hostels for travelers.[18] And in that aristocracy where luxury and ease seemed the order of every day, there were hundreds of men who gave themselves, with a zeal tempered by venality, to the tasks of administration and statesmanship, and somehow managed, despite all overturns and intrigues, to save the realm from every disaster, and to maintain the most prosperous economy in the medieval Christian world.

The bureaucracy that Diocletian and Constantine had established had become in seven centuries an effective engine of administration, reaching every region of the realm. Heraclius had replaced the old division of the Empire into provinces by a division into "themes," or military units ruled by a *strategos* or military governor; this was one of a hundred ways in which the Islamic threat modified Byzantine institutions. The themes retained considerable self-government, and prospered under this centralized rule; they received a continuity of order without bearing the direct force of the struggles and violence that disturbed the capital. Constantinople was ruled by the emperor, the patriach, and the mob; the themes were governed by Byzantine law. While Islam confused law with theology, and Western Europe floundered through the chaos of a dozen barbarian codes, the Byzantine world cherished and extended the legacy of Justinian. The "novels" or new laws of Justin II and Heraclius, the *Ecloga*, or selected laws, issued by Leo III, the *Basilica*, or royal edicts, promulgated by Leo VI, and the "novels" of the same Leo, adjusted the Pandects of Justinian to the changing needs of five centuries; codes of military, ecclesiastical, maritime, mercantile, and rural law gave order and dependability to legal judgments in army and clergy, in markets and ports, on the farm and the sea; and in the eleventh century the school of law at Constantinople was the intellectual center of secular Christendom. So the Byzantines preserved Rome's greatest gift—Roman law— through a millennium of peril and change, until its revival at Bologna in the twelfth century revolutionized the civil law of Latin Europe and the canon law of the Roman Church. The Byzantine Maritime Code of Leo III, developed from the nautical regulations of ancient Rhodes, was the first body of commercial law in medieval Christendom; it became in the eleventh century the source of similar codes for the Italian republics of Trani and Amalfi; and by that lineage entered into the legal heritage of the modern world.

The Rural Code was a creditable attempt to check feudalism and establish a free peasantry. Small holdings were given to retired soldiers; larger tracts belonging to the state were cultivated by soldiers as a form of military service; and great areas were colonized by heretical sects transported from Asia into Thrace and Greece. Still vaster regions were settled, under governmental compulsion or protection, by barbarian groups who were judged less dangerous within the Empire than outside; so Goths were received into Thrace and Illyria, Lombards into Pannonia, Slavs into Thrace, Macedonia, and Greece; by the tenth century the Peloponnesus was predominantly Slav, and Slavs were numerous in Attica and Thessaly. State and Church co-operated to diminish slavery; imperial legislation forbade the sale of slaves, or the enslavement of a freeman, and automatically emancipated slaves who entered the army or the clergy, or married a free person. In Constantinople slavery was in effect limited to domestic service, but it flourished there.

Nevertheless it is almost a Newtonian law of history that large agricultural holdings, in proportion to their mass and nearness, attract smaller holdings, and, by purchase or otherwise, periodically gather the land into great estates; in time the concentration becomes explosive, the soil is redivided by taxation or revolution, and concentration is resumed. By the tenth century most of the soil of the Byzantine East was owned in extensive domains by rich land-lords (*dynatoi*, "powerful men"), or by churches, monasteries, or hospitals endowed with supporting terrain by pious legacy. Such tracts were worked by serfs, or by *coloni* legally free but economically chained. The owners, equipped with retinues of clients, guards, and domestic slaves, led lives of refined luxury in their villas or their city palaces. We see the good and bad of these great lords in the story of Basil I's benefactress, the lady Danielis. When she visited him in Constantinople 300 slaves took turns supporting the litter, or covered couch, in which she traveled from Patras. She brought to her imperial protégé richer presents than any sovereign had ever sent to a Byzantine emperor; 400 youths, 100 eunuchs, and 100 maidens were but a part of her gift; there were also 400 pieces of art-woven textiles, 100 pieces of cambric (each so fine that it could be enclosed in the joint of a reed), and a dinner service in silver and gold. During her lifetime she gave away much of her wealth; at her death she willed the rest to Basil's son. Leo VI found himself suddenly dowered with eighty villas and farms, masses of coin and jewelry and plate, costly furniture, rich stuffs, numberless cattle, thousands of slaves.[19]

Such Greek gifts were not altogether pleasing to the emperors. The wealth so gleaned from the flesh and sweat of millions of men gave the owners a power collectively dangerous to any sovereign. Out of self-interest as well as humanity, the emperors sought to halt this process of concentration. The severe winter of 927–8 ended in famine and plague; starving peasants sold their holdings to great landowners at desperately low prices, or merely in exchange for subsistence. In 934 the regent Romanus issued a "novel" that denounced the landlords as having "shown themselves more merciless than famine and plague"; it required the restoration of properties bought for less than half a "fair price"; and permitted any seller, within three years, to re-purchase the land he had sold, and at the price he had received. The edict had only a negligible effect; concentration continued; moreover, many free farm-ers, complaining of high taxes, sold their lands and moved to the towns—if possible, to Constantinople and the dole. Basil II renewed the struggle of emperors against nobles. His decree of 996 permitted the seller at any time to redeem his land at the price of its sale; voided titles to lands acquired in contravention of the law of 934, and demanded the immediate return of such lands to their former owners, without cost. These laws were in large measure evaded, and a modified feudalism was sporadically established by the eleventh century in the Byzantine East. But the effort of the emperors was not lost; the surviving free peasantry, under the stimulus of ownership, covered the land with farms, orchards, vineyards, beehives, and ranches; the large pro-prietors developed scientific agriculture to its medieval zenith; and from the eighth to the eleventh century Byzantine agriculture kept pace with the pros-perity of Byzantine industry.

The Eastern Empire in this period acquired an urban and semi-industrial character quite different from the ruralism of Latin Europe north of the Alps. Miners and metallurgists actively explored and developed the lead, iron, copper, and gold in the soil. Not only Constantinople but a hundred other Byzantine cities—Smyrna, Tarsus, Ephesus, Durazzo, Ragusa, Patras, Corinth, Thebes, Salonika, Hadrianople, Heraclea, Selymbria—throbbed and resounded with tanners, cobblers, saddlers, armorers, goldsmiths, jewelers, metalworkers, carpenters, wood carvers, wheelwrights, bakers, dyers, weavers, potters, mosaicists, painters. . . . As caldrons and caverns of manufacturing and exchange, Constantinople, Baghdad, and Cordova in the ninth century almost rivaled the bustle and bedlam of a modern metropolis. Despite Persian competition the Greek capital still led the white world in the production of fine tissues and silks; only second to it in this regard were Argos, Corinth, and Thebes. The textile industry was highly organized, and used much slave labor; most other workers were free artisans. The proletarian population of Constantinople and Salonika were class-conscious, and staged many unsuccessful revolts. Their employers formed a considerable middle class, acquisitive, charitable, industrious, intelligent, and fiercely conservative. The major industries, including their workers, artists, managers, merchants, lawyers, and financiers, were organized into *systemata*, or corporation guilds, lineally descended from the ancient *collegia* and *artes*, and akin to the large economic units of a modern "corporative" state. Each corporation had a monopoly in its line, but was strictly regulated by legislation in its purchases, prices, methods of manufacture, and conditions of sale; governmental examiners kept surveillance over operations and accounts; and at times maximum wages were fixed by law. Minor industries, however, were left to free workers and individual enterprise. The arrangement gave order, prosperity, and continuity to Byzantine industry, but it checked initiative and invention, and tended to an Oriental fixity of status and life.[20]

Commerce was encouraged by state maintenance or supervision of docks and ports, governmentally regulated insurance and loans on bottomry, a vigorous war on piracy, and the most stable currency in Europe. Over all commerce the Byzantine government exercised a pervasive control—prohibited certain exports, monopolized the trade in corn and silk, charged export and import duties, and taxed sales.[21] It almost invited its early replacement as commercial mistress of the Aegean and Black Seas by allowing foreign merchants—Armenians, Syrians, Egyptians, Amalfians, Pisans, Venetians, Genoese, Jews, Russians, and Catalans—to carry most of its trade, and to set up semi-independent "factories" or agencies in or near the capital. Interest charges were permitted, but were limited by law to twelve, ten, eight per cent, or even less. Bankers were numerous; and perhaps it was the moneylenders of Constantinople, rather than those of Italy, who developed the bill of exchange,[22] and organized the most extensive credit system in Christendom before the thirteenth century.

V. THE BYZANTINE RENAISSANCE

From the labor and skill of the people and the superfluities of the rich there came in the ninth and tenth centuries a remarkable revival of letters and arts. Although the Empire to its dying day called itself Roman, nearly all Latin elements had disappeared from it except Roman law. Since Heraclius, Greek had been the language of government, literature, and liturgy, as well as of daily speech, in the Byzantine East. Education was now completely Greek. Nearly every free male, many women, even many slaves, received some education. The University of Constantinople, which, like letters in general, had been allowed to decay in the crises of the Heraclian age, was restored by Caesar Bardas (863), and attained high repute for its courses in philology, philosophy, theology, astronomy, mathematics, biology, music, and literature; even the pagan Libanius and the godless Lucian were read. Tuition was largely free to qualified students, and the teachers were paid by the state. Libraries, public and private, were numerous, and still preserved those classic masterpieces which had been forgotten in the disordered West.

This ample transmission of the Greek heritage was at once stimulating and restrictive. It sharpened and widened thought, and lured it from its old round of homiletical eloquence and theological debate. But its very wealth discouraged originality; it is easier for the ignorant than for the learned to be original. Byzantine literature was intended chiefly for cultured and leisurely ladies and gentlemen; polished and polite, artistic and artificial, Hellenistic but not Hellenic, it played on the surface, and spared the heart, of human life. Though the churchmen of the period were remarkably tolerant, thought of its own accord, through habits formed in youth, stayed within the circle of orthodoxy, and the iconoclasts were more pious than the priests.

It was another Alexandrian age of scholarship. Pundits analyzed language and prosody, wrote epitomes, "outlines," and universal histories, compiled dictionaries, encyclopedias, anthologies. Now (917) Constantine Cephalas collected *The Greek Anthology*; now (976) Suidas accumulated his encyclopedic lexicon. Theophanes (*c.* 814) and Leo the Deacon (b. 950) wrote valuable histories of their own or recent times. Paul of Ægina (615–90) composed an encyclopedia of medicine that combined Moslem theory and practice with the legacy of Galen and Oribasius; it discussed in almost modern terms operations for cancer of the breast, hemorrhoids, catheterization of the bladder, lithotomy, castration; eunuchs were manufactured, says Paul, by crushing the testicles of children in a hot bath.[23]

The outstanding Byzantine scientist of these centuries was an obscure and impoverished teacher, Leo of Salonika (c. 850), of whose existence Constantinople took no notice until a caliph invited him to Baghdad. One of his pupils, captured in war, became the slave of a Moslem dignitary, who soon marveled at the youth's knowledge of geometry. Al-Mamun, learning of it, induced him to join in a discussion of geometrical problems at the royal palace, was impressed by his performance, heard with eager curiosity his account of his teacher, and at once sent Leo an invitation to Baghdad and affluence. Leo consulted a Byzantine official, who consulted the Emperor Theophilus, who hastened to secure Leo with a state professorship. Leo was a polymath, and taught and wrote on mathematics, astronomy, astrology, medicine, and philosophy. Al-Mamun submitted to him several problems in geometry and astronomy, and was so pleased with the replies that he offered Theophilus eternal peace and 2000 pounds of gold if the Emperor would lend him Leo for a while. Theophilus refused, and made Leo Archbishop of Salonika to keep him out of al-Mamun's reach.[24]

Leo, Photius, and Psellus were the stellar luminaries of this age. Photius (820?–91), the most learned man of his time, was in six days graduated from layman to patriarch, and belongs to religious history. Michael Psellus (1018?–80) was a man of the world and the court, an adviser of kings and queens, a genial and orthodox Voltaire who could be brilliant on every subject, but landed on terra firma after every theological argument or palace revolution. He did not let his love of books dull his love of life. He taught philosophy at the University of Constantinople, and received the title of Prince of Philosophers. He entered a monastery, found the monastic career too peaceful, returned to the world, served as prime minister from 1071 to 1078, and had time to write on politics, science, medicine, grammar, theology, jurisprudence, music, and history. His *Chronographia* recorded the intrigues and scandals of a century (976–1078) with candor, verve, and vanity (he describes Constantine IX as "hanging on Psellus' tongue" [25]). Here, as a sample, is a paragraph from his description of the revolt that restored Theodora to the throne in 1055:

> Each [soldier in the crowd] was armed: one grasped a hatchet, another a battle-ax, one a bow, another a lance; some of the populace carried heavy stones; and all ran in great disorder . . . to the apartments of Theodora. . . . But she, taking refuge in a chapel, remained deaf to all their cries. Abandoning persuasion, the crowd used force upon her; some, drawing their daggers, threw themselves upon Theodora as if to kill her. Boldly they snatched her from the sanctuary, clothed her in sumptuous robes, seated her on a horse, and, circling about her, led her to the church of St. Sophia. Now all the population, highborn as well as low, joined in paying her homage, and all proclaimed her queen.[26]

The personal letters of Psellus were almost as charming and revealing as Cicero's; his speeches, verses, and pamphlets were the talk of the day; his malicious humor and lethal wit were an exciting stimulus amid the ponderous erudition of his contemporaries. Compared with him and Photius and Theophanes, the Alcuins, Rabani, and Gerberts of the contemporary West were timid emigrants from barbarism into the Country of the Mind.

The most conspicuous side of this Byzantine renaissance was its art. From 726 to 842 the Iconoclastic movement prohibited the sculptural or (with less strictness) pictorial representation of sacred beings; but in compensation it freed the artist from a monotonous confinement within ecclesiastical themes, and turned him to the observation, portrayal, and decoration of secular life. The gods were replaced as subjects by the imperial family, aristocratic patrons, historical events, the animals of the forest, the plants and fruits of the field, the fond *trivia* of domestic life. Basil I built in his palace the Nea, or New Church, "all adorned," says a contemporary, "with fine pearls, gold, shining silver, mosaics, silks, and marble in a thousand varieties." [27] Much of the decoration recently uncovered in St. Sophia was the work of the ninth century. The central dome was rebuilt in 975 after an earthquake, and then received its great mosaic of Christ seated on a rainbow; additional mosaics were set up in 1028; the massive cathedral, like a living organism, achieved continued life by the death and renewal of its parts. The bronze doors installed in 838 were so renowned for excellence that similar doors were ordered from Constantinople for the monastery of Monte Cassino, the cathedral of Amalfi, and the basilica of San Paolo outside the walls of Rome; the last pair, made in Constantinople in 1070, still survives as a testimony to Byzantine art.

The royal or "Sacred Palace," of which the Nea formed the chapel, was a growing congeries of chambers, reception halls, churches, baths, pavilions, gardens, peristyles, and courts; almost every emperor added something to it. Theophilus gave the group a new Oriental touch with a throne room known as Triconchos, from the shell-like apses that formed three of its sides—a plan imported from Syria. North of this he built the Hall of the Pearl; south of it several *heliaka* or sunrooms, and the Kamilas, an apartment with roof of gold, columns of green marble, and an exceptionally fine mosaic representing on a gold ground men and women gathering fruit. Even this mosaic was surpassed in an adjoining structure, on whose walls green mosaic trees stood out against a golden mosaic sky; and by the floor of the Hall of Harmony, whose marble tesserae gave the effect of a meadow in full flower. Theophilus carried his taste for bizarre splendor *à outrance* in his palace of Magnaura: in its audience chamber a golden plane tree overhung the throne; golden birds sat on the branches and the throne; golden griffins lay on either side of the royal seat, and golden lions at its foot; when a foreign ambassador was presented, the mechanical griffins rose, the mechanical lions stood up, swished their tails and roared, and the birds broke into mechanical song.[28] All this was a frank copy of like absurdities in the palace of Harun al-Rashid at Baghdad.

Constantinople was beautified with the taxes of commerce and the "themes," but enough remained to add some lesser splendors to the provincial capitals. The monasteries, rich again, rose in stately mass: in the tenth century the Lavra and Iviron at Athos; in the eleventh, St. Luke's in Phocis, the Nea Moni in Chios, the convent of Daphni near Eleusis—whose almost classic mosaics are the finest examples of the mid-Byzantine style. Georgia, Armenia, and Asia Minor shared in the movement, and became outposts of Byzantine art. The public buildings of Antioch drew Moslem eulogies. In Jerusalem the church of the Holy Sepulcher was rebuilt soon after Heraclius' victories. In Egypt, before and after the Arab conquest, the Coptic Christians raised domed churches modest in size, but adorned with such artistry in metal, ivory, wood and textiles that all the skills of Pharaonic, Ptolemaic, Roman, Byzantine, and Mohammedan Egypt seemed to have reached them as an unimpaired legacy. The Iconoclastic persecutions drove thousands of monks from Syria, Asia Minor, and Constantinople to southern Italy, where they were protected by the popes; through these refugees, and through Oriental merchants, Byzantine styles of architecture and decoration flourished in Bari, Otranto, Benevento, Naples, even Rome. Ravenna continued to be Greek in art, and produced in the seventh century the magnificent mosaics of St. Apollinaris in Classe. Salonika remained Byzantine, and adorned its own St. Sophia with somber mosaic apostles as gaunt as El Greco's saints.

In all these lands and cities, as in the capital, the Byzantine renaissance poured forth masterpieces of mosaic, miniature, pottery, enamel, glass, wood, ivory, bronze, iron, gems, and textiles woven, dyed, and decorated with a skill that all the world honored. Byzantine artists made cups of blue glass decorated under the surface with golden foliage, birds, and human figures; glass vessels with a necking of enameled arabesques and flowers; and other forms of glass so exquisite that they were the favorite gifts of Byzantine emperors to foreign potentates. Even more valued as presents were the costly robes, shawls, copes, and dalmatics that displayed Byzantine textile art; such were "Charlemagne's cloak" in the cathedral of Metz, and the delicate silks found at Aachen in the coffin of that king. Half the majesty that hedged in the Greek emperor, much of the awe that exalted the patriarch, some of the splendor that clothed the Redeemer, the Virgin, and the martyrs in the ritual of the Church, came from gorgeous vestments that embodied the lives of a dozen artisans, the technique of centuries, and the richest dyes of land and sea. The Byzantine goldsmiths and gem cutters were at the top of their line until the thirteenth century; the treasury of St. Mark's at Venice is rich with the spoils of their craft. To this age belong the astonishingly realistic mosaic of St. Luke, now in the Collège des Hautes Études at Paris; the glowing head of Christ in the "Deesis" mosaic in St. Sophia's; and the immense mosaic, covering forty square yards, unearthed in Istanbul in 1935 from the ruins of the palace of the Macedonian emperors.[29] When Iconoclasm subsided, or where it did not reach, the churches fed piety with icons painted in tempera upon wood, and sometimes cased in enameled or jeweled frames. No miniatures in all the history of illumination surpass the "Vision of Ezekiel" in the ninth-century volume of Gregory Nazianzen's sermons in the Bibliothèque Nationale at Paris; [30] or the 400 illustrations of the "Menologus" manuscript in the Vatican (*c.* 1000); or the pictures of David in the Paris Psalter (*c.* 900). We shall find in them no perspective, no modeling of forms through light and shade; but, as ample recompense, a rich and sensuous coloring, a lively play of imagination, a new knowledge of human and animal anatomy, a happy riot of beasts and birds, of plants and flowers, among saints and deities, fountains, arcades, and porticoes—birds pecking at fruit, bears dancing, stags and bulls locking their horns in battle, and a leopard lifting an impious leg to make a flowing initial for a pious phrase.[31]

Byzantine potters had long known the art of enameling—i.e., applying to a terra-cotta or metal base a metallic oxide which, when fired, fused with the base and gave it both protection and brilliance. The art had come from the Orient to ancient Greece, had disappeared in the third century B.C., and had reappeared in the third century A.D. This mid-Byzantine period was rich in enamels—portrait medallions, icons, crosses, reliquaries, cups, chalices, book covers, and ornaments for harness and other equipage. As early as the sixth century Byzantium received from Sasanian Persia the art of cloisonné enamel: the colored paste was poured into surface areas confined by thin wires or metal strips; these *cloisons*, soldered to a metal base, constituted the decorative design. A famous example of Byzantine cloisonné is a reliquary made (*c.* 948) for Constantine Porphyrogenitus, and now in Limburg; it is characteristically Byzantine in its minute and conscientious execution, its ornate and luxurious ornament.

No other art has been so overwhelmingly religious as the Byzantine. A church council of 787 laid down the law: "It is for painters to execute; it is for the clergy to ordain the subjects and govern the procedure." [32] Hence the somber seriousness of this art, its narrow scope of theme, its monotony of method and style, the rarity of its ventures into realism, humor, and common life; ornate and brilliant beyond rival, it never reached the lusty variety and scandalous secularity of mature Gothic art. So much the more must we marvel at its victories and influence. All Christendom from Kiev to Cadiz acknowledged its leadership and flattered it with imitation; even China bowed to it now and then. In its Syrian forms it shared with Persia in molding the architecture, mosaics, and decorative motives of Islamic art. Venice modeled itself on Constantinople, and St. Mark's on the Church of the Apostles there; Byzantine architecture appeared in France, and mounted as far north as Aachen. Illuminated manuscripts everywhere in the West confessed Byzantine influence. The Bulgars took over Byzantine faith and ornament; and the conversion of Vladimir to Greek Christianity opened a dozen avenues by which Byzantine art entered into Russian life.

From the fifth to the twelfth century Byzantine civilization led Christian Europe in administration, diplomacy, revenue, manners, culture, and art. Probably never before had there been a society so splendidly adorned, or a religion so sensuously colorful. Like every other civilization, it rested on the backs of serfs or slaves, and the gold and marble of its shrines and palaces were the transmuted sweat of workers toiling on or in the earth. Like every other culture of its time, it was cruel; the same man who knelt before the image of the Virgin could slaughter the children of Maurice before their father's eyes. There was something shallow about it, a veneer of aristocratic refinement covering a mass of popular superstition, fanaticism, and literate ignorance; * and half the culture was devoted to perpetuating that ignorance. No science, no philosophy, was allowed to develop in conflict with that ignorance; and for a thousand years no addition was made by a Greek civilization to man's knowledge of the world. No work of Byzantine literature has caught the imagination of mankind, or won the suffrages of time. Oppressed by the fullness of its heritage, imprisoned in the theological labyrinths in which dying Greece had lost the Christianity of Christ, the medieval Greek mind could not rise to a mature and realistic view of man and the world; it broke Christianity in half over a vowel, and again over a word, and shattered the Eastern Roman Empire by seeing treason in every heresy.

The marvel remains that this civilization lasted so long. What hidden resources, or inner vitality, enabled it to survive the victories of Persia in Syria, the loss of Syria, Egypt, Sicily, and Spain to the Moslems? Perhaps the same religious faith that weakened defense by relying upon relics and miracles gave some order and discipline to a people perennially patient, however periodically turbulent, and surrounded emperor and state with an aura of sanctity that frightened change. The bureaucracy, collectively immortal, gave continuity and stability through all wars and revolutions, kept internal peace, regulated the economy, and gathered in the taxes that permitted the Empire to expand again almost to its Justinian amplitude. Though the possessions of the caliphs were vaster than the Byzantine, their revenues were probably less; and the looseness of Moslem government, the inadequacy of its communications and its administrative machinery, allowed the Abbasid dominion to disintegrate in three centuries, while the Byzantine Empire endured through a millennium.

Byzantine civilization performed three vital functions. For a thousand years it stood as a bulwark of Europe against Persia and Eastern Islam. It

---

* In 669 the army of the Orient "theme" demanded that the Empire should have three simultaneous emperors, to accord with the Trinity.[33]

faithfully cherished and fully transmitted—until plundered by the Crusaders in 1204—the recopied texts that handed down the literature, science, and philosophy of ancient Greece. Monks fleeing Iconoclast emperors brought Greek manuscripts to South Italy, and restored there a knowledge of Greek letters; Greek professors, shunning Moslem and Crusader alike, left Constantinople, sometimes settled in Italy, and served as carriers of the classic germ; so year by year Italy rediscovered Greece, until men drank themselves drunk at the fountain of intellectual freedom. And finally, it was Byzantium that won Bulgars and Slavs from barbarism to Christianity, and brought the immeasurable force of the Slavic body and soul into the life and destiny of Europe.

VI. THE BALKANS: 558–1057

For only a few hundred miles north of Constantinople were troubled oceans of men disdainful of letters and half in love with war. The Hun tide had hardly ebbed when a new people of kindred blood, the Avars, moved from Turkestan through southern Russia (558), enslaved masses of Slavs, raided Germany to the Elbe (562), drove the Lombards into Italy (568), and so ravaged the Balkans that the Latin-speaking population there was almost wiped out. For a time the power of the Avars reached from the Baltic to the Black Sea. In 626 they besieged and almost captured Constantinople; their failure began their decline; in 805 they were conquered by Charlemagne; and gradually they were absorbed by the Bulgars and the Slavs.

The Bulgars, originally a mixture of Hun, Ugrian, and Turkish blood, had formed part of the Hun empire in Russia. After Attila's death one branch established a kingdom—"Old Bulgaria"—along the Volga around the modern Kazan; their capital, Bolgar, was enriched by the river trade, and prospered till it was destroyed by the Tatars in the thirteenth century. In the fifth century another branch migrated southwest to the valley of the Don; one tribe of these, the Utigurs, crossed the Danube (679), founded a second Bulgarian kingdom in the ancient Moesia, enslaved the Slavs there, adopted their language and institutions, and were ultimately absorbed into the Slavic stock. The new state reached its zenith under the Khagan or Khan (Chief) Krum (802), a man of barbarian courage and civilized cunning. He invaded Macedonia—a province of the Eastern Empire—captured 1100 pounds of gold, and burned the town of Sardica, now, as Sofia, Bulgaria's capital.

The Emperor Nicephorus bettered the instruction by burning Pliska, Krum's capital (811), but Krum trapped and destroyed the Greek army in a mountain pass, slew Nicephorus, and made the imperial skull his drinking cup. In 813 he besieged Constantinople, fired its suburbs, and devastated Thrace, rehearsing the events of 1913. He was preparing another attack when he burst a blood vessel and died. His son Omurtag made peace with the Greeks, who yielded to him half of Thrace. Under Khan Boris (852–88) Bulgaria adopted Christianity. Boris himself, after a long reign, entered a monastery; emerged four years later to depose his elder son Vladimir and enthrone his younger son Simeon; lived till 907, and was canonized as the first of Bulgaria's national saints. Simeon (893–927) became one of the great kings of his time; he extended his rule to Serbia and the Adriatic, called himself "Emperor and Autocrat of All the Bulgars and Greeks," and repeatedly made war against Byzantium; but he tried to civilize his people with translated Greek literature, and to beautify his Danubian capital with Greek art. A contemporary describes Preslav as "a marvel to behold," full of "high palaces and churches" richly adorned; in the thirteenth century it was the largest city in the Balkans; some scanty ruins remain. After Simeon's death Bulgaria was weakened with civil strife. Bogomil heretics converted half the peasantry to pacifism and communism; Serbia recovered its independence in 931; the Emperor John Tzimisces reconquered eastern Bulgaria for the Greek Empire in 972; Basil II conquered western Bulgaria in 1014; and Bulgaria became again (1018–1186) a province of Byzantium.

Meanwhile that harassed Empire had received a visit (934–42) from a new barbarian horde. The Magyars, like the Bulgars, were probably derived from those tribes, loosely named Ugri or Igurs (whence *ogre*), who wandered on the western confines of China; they too had, through long association, a strong infusion of Hun and Turkish blood; they spoke a tongue closely related to those of the Finns and the Samoyeds. In the ninth century they migrated from the Ural-Caspian steppes to the lands adjoining the Don, the Dnieper, and the Black Sea. There they lived by tilling the soil in summer, fishing in winter, and at all seasons capturing and selling Slavs as slaves to the Greeks. After some sixty years in the Ukraine they again moved westward. Europe was then at nadir; no strong government existed west of Constantinople; no united army stood in the way. In 889 the Magyars overran Bessarabia and Moldavia; in 895, under their chieftain Arpad, they began their permanent conquest of Hungary; in 899 they poured over the Alps into Italy, burned Pavia and all its forty-three churches, massacred the inhabitants, and for an entire year ravaged the peninsula. They conquered Pannonia, raided Bavaria (900–7), devastated Carinthia (901), took Moravia (906), plundered Saxony, Thuringia, Swabia (913), southern Germany, and Alsace (917), and overwhelmed the Germans on the Lech, a tributary of the Danube (924). All Europe trembled and prayed, for these invaders were still pagan, and all Christendom seemed doomed. But in 933 the Magyars were defeated at Gotha, and their advance was stayed. In 943 they again invaded Italy; in 955 they pillaged Burgundy. At last in that year the united armies of Germany, under Otto I, won a decisive victory on the Lechfeld, or valley of the Lech, near Augsburg; and Europe, having in one terrible century (841–955) fought the Normans in the north, the Moslems in the south, and the Magyars in the east, could breathe among its ruins.

The Magyars, subdued, made Europe more secure by accepting Christianity (975). Prince Geza feared the absorption of Hungary into the re-expanding Byzantine Empire; he chose Latin Christianity to win peace in the West, and married his son Stephen to Gisela, daughter of Henry II, Duke of Bavaria. Stephen I (997–1038) became Hungary's patron saint and greatest king; he organized the Magyars on the lines of German feudalism, and accentuated the religious basis of the new society by accepting the kingdom and crown of Hungary from Pope Sylvester II (1000). Benedictine monks flocked in, built monasteries and villages, and introduced Western techniques of agriculture and industry. So, after a century of war, Hungary passed from barbarism to civilization; and when Queen Gisela presented a cross to a German friend it was already a masterpiece of the goldsmith's art.

The earliest known home of the Slavs was a marshy region of Russia enclosed by Kiev, Mohilev, and Brest-Litovsk. They were of Indo-European stock, and spoke languages related to German and Persian. Periodically overrun by nomad hordes, often enslaved, always oppressed and poor, they grew patient and strong through endless hardships; and the fertility of their women overcame the high mortality born of famine, disease, and chronic war. They lived in caves or mud huts; hunted, herded, fished, and tended bees; sold honey, wax, and skins; and slowly resigned themselves to settled tillage. Themselves hunted even into hardly accessible marshes and forests, brutally captured and callously sold, they adopted the morals of their time, and bartered men for goods. Inhabiting a cold and damp terrain, they warmed themselves with strong liquor; they found Christianity preferable to Mohammedanism, which forbade alcoholic drinks.[34] Drunkenness, uncleanliness, cruelty, and a passion for pillage were their outstanding faults; thrift, caution, and imagination hovered in them between virtue and vice; but also they were good-natured, hospitable, sociable, and loved games, dances, music, and song. The chieftains were polygamous, the poor monogamous, the women—bought or captured for marriage—were anomalously faithful and obedient.[35] The patriarchal families were loosely organized in clans, and these in tribes. The clans may have owned property in common in their early pastoral stage;[36] but the growth of agriculture—in which different degrees of energy and ability, on diverse soils, produced unequal results—generated private or family property. Frequently divided by migration and fraternal war, the Slavs developed a variety of Slavonic languages: Polish, Wendish, Czech, and Slovak in the west; Slovene, Serbo-Croat, and Bulgarian in the south; Great Russian, White Russian, and Little Russian (Ruthenian and Ukrainian) in the east; nearly all of these, however, have remained intelligible to the speakers of any one of them. Pan-Slavism of speech and customs, along with space, resources, and a vitality born of hard conditions, rigorous selection, and simple food, made the spreading power of the Slavs.

As the German tribes moved south and west in their migrations into Italy and Gaul, an area of low population pressure was left behind them in north and central Germany; drawn into this vacuum, and prodded by the invading Huns, the Slavs expanded westward across the Vistula even to the Elbe; in these lands they became the Wends, Poles, Czechs, Vlachs, and Slovaks of later history. Towards the end of the sixth century a torrent of Slav immigration flooded rural Greece. The cities closed their gates against it, but a strong Slavonic infusion entered the Hellenic blood. About 640 two kindred Slav tribes, the Srbi and the Chrobati, repeopled Pannonia and Illyricum. The Serbs accepted Greek, the Croats Roman, Christianity; this religious division, crossing ethnic and linguistic unity, weakened the nation against its neighbors, and Serbia fluctuated between independence and subjection to Byzantium or Bulgaria. In 989 the Bulgarian Tsar Samuel, having defeated and captured the Serbian John Vladimir, gave him his daughter Kossara in marriage, and allowed him to return to Zita, his capital, as a vassal prince; this is the theme of the oldest Serb novel, *Vladimir and Kossara*, written in the thirteenth century. The coastal cities of the ancient Dalmatia—Zara, Spalato, Ragusa —retained their Latin language and culture; the remainder of Serbia became Slav. Prince Voislav freed Serbia in 1042; but in the twelfth century it again acknowledged the suzerainty of Byzantium.

When, at the end of the eighth century, this amazing migration of the Slavs was complete, all central Europe, the Balkans, and Russia were a Slavic sea beating upon the borders of Constantinople, Greece, and Germany.

VII. THE BIRTH OF RUSSIA: 509–1054

The Slavs were but the latest of many peoples who rejoiced in the rich soil, spacious steppes, and many navigable rivers of Russia, and mourned the miasmic marshes and forbidding forests, and the absence of natural barriers to hostile invasion, summer's heat, or winter's cold. On its least inhospitable coasts—the western and northern fringes of the Black Sea—the Greeks had founded a score of towns—Olbia, Tanais, Theodosia, Panticapeum (Kerch) . . .—as early as the seventh century B.C.; and had engaged in trade and war with the Scythians of the hinterland. These natives, probably of Iranian origin, imbibed some civilization from the Persians and the Greeks, and even produced a philosopher—Anacharsis (600 B.C.)—who came to Athens and argued with Solon.

During the second century B.C. another Iranian tribe, the Sarmatians, conquered and displaced the Scythians; and amid this turmoil the Greek colonies decayed. In the second century A.D. the Goths entered from the west, and established the Ostrogothic kingdom; about 375 this was overthrown by the Huns; and thereafter, for centuries, the southern plains of Russia saw hardly any civilization, but rather a succession of nomad hordes—Bulgars, Avars, Slavs, Khazars, Magyars, Patzinaks, Cumans, and Mongols. The Khazars were of Turkish origin; in the seventh century they expanded through the Caucasus into south Russia, established an orderly dominion from the Dnieper to the Caspian Sea, and built a capital, Itil, at a mouth of the Volga near the present Astrakhan. Their kings and upper classes accepted the Jewish religion; hemmed in between a Moslem and a Christian empire,

they probably preferred to displease both equally rather than one dangerously; at the same time they gave full freedom to the varied creeds of the
people. Seven courts administered justice—two for Moslems, two for Christians, two for Jews, one for heathens; an appeal was allowed from the last five
to the Moslem courts, whose administration of justice was at that time considered best.[37] Encouraged by this enlightened policy, merchants of various
faiths gathered in the Khazar towns; a lively trade developed there between
the Baltic and the Caspian Seas, and Itil, in the eighth century, was one of the
great commercial cities of the world. In the ninth century Khazaria was overrun by Turkish nomads; the government could no longer protect its trade
channels from brigandage and piracy; and in the tenth century the Khazar
kingdom melted away into the ethnic chaos from which it had taken form.

Into that motley multitude of south and central Russia in the sixth century
came a migration of Slavic tribes from the Carpathian Mountains. They
settled the valleys of the Dnieper and the Don, and reached out more thinly
to Lake Ilmen in the north. For centuries they multiplied, year by year clearing the forests, draining the swamps, eliminating wild beasts, creating the
Ukraine. They spread over the plains in a movement of human fertility
rivaled only by the Hindus and the Chinese. All through known history they
have been on the march—into the Caucasus and Turkestan, into the Urals and
Siberia; this process of colonization goes on today, and the Slav ocean every
year enters new ethnic bays.

Early in the ninth century an apparently negligible attack came upon Slavdom from the northwest. The Scandinavian Vikings could spare men and energy from their assaults upon Scotland, Iceland, Ireland, England, Germany,
France, and Spain to send into northern Russia bands of one or two hundred
men to prey upon the communities of Balts, Finns, and Slavs, and then return
with their booty. To protect their robberies with law and order, these Vae-
ringjar or Varangians ("followers"—of a chieftain) established fortified posts
on their routes, and gradually they settled down as a ruling Scandinavian
minority of armed merchants among a subject peasantry. Some towns hired
them as guardians of social order and security; apparently the guardians converted their wages into tribute, and became the masters of their employers.[38]
By the middle of the ninth century they governed Novgorod ("new fort")
and had extended their rule as far south as Kiev. The routes and settlements
they controlled were loosely bound into a commercial and political empire
called Ros or Rus, a term of much disputed derivation. The great rivers that
traversed the land connected—through canals and short overland hauls—the
Baltic and Black Seas, and invited a southward expansion of Varangian trade
and power; soon these fearless merchant-warriors were selling their goods or
services in Constantinople itself. Conversely, as commerce grew more regular on the Dnieper, the Volkhov, and the Western Dvina, Moslem merchants came up from Baghdad and Byzantium and traded spices, wines, silks,

and gems for furs, amber, honey, wax, and slaves; hence the great number of Islamic and Byzantine coins found along these rivers, and even in Scandinavia. As Moslem control of the eastern Mediterranean blocked the flow of European products through French and Italian outlets to Levantine ports, Marseille, Genoa, and Pisa declined in the ninth and tenth centuries, while in Russia towns like Novgorod, Smolensk, Chernigov, Kiev, and Rostov flourished through Scandinavian, Slavic, Moslem, and Byzantine trade.

The Ancient Chronicle of Russia (twelfth century) gave personality to this Scandinavian infiltration by its tale of "three princes": the Finnish and Slavic population of Novgorod and its vicinity, having driven out their Varangian overlords, fell to so much quarreling among themselves that they invited the Varangians to send them a ruler or general (862). Three brothers came, says the story—Rurik, Sineus, and Truvor—and established the Russian state. The story may be true, despite latter-day skepticism; or it may be a patriotic gloss on a Scandinavian conquest of Novgorod. The *Chronicle* further relates that Rurik sent two of his aides, Askold and Dir, to take Constantinople; that these Vikings stopped en route to capture Kiev, and then declared themselves independent of both Rurik and the Khazars. In 860 Kiev was strong enough to send a fleet of 200 vessels to attack Constantinople; the expedition failed, but Kiev remained the commercial and political focus of Russia. It gathered under its power an extensive hinterland; and its earliest rulers—Askold, Oleg, and Igor—rather than Rurik at Novgorod, might justly be called the founders of the Russian state. Oleg, Igor and the able Princess Olga (Igor's widow), and her warrior son Sviatoslav (962–72) widened the Kievan realm until it embraced nearly all the eastern Slavonic tribes, and the towns of Polotsk, Smolensk, Chernigov, and Rostov. Between 860 and 1043 the young principality made six attempts to take Constantinople; so old is the Russian drive to the Bosporus, the Russian hunger for secure access to the Mediterranean.

With Vladimir (972–1015), fifth "Grand Duke of Kiev," Rus, as the new principality called itself, became Christian (989). Vladimir married the sister of the Emperor Basil II, and thereafter, till 1917, Russia, in religion, alphabet, coinage, and art, was a daughter of Byzantium. Greek priests explained to Vladimir the divine origin and right of kings, and the usefulness of this doctrine in promoting social order and monarchical stability.[39] Under Vladimir's son Yaroslav (1036–54) the Kievan state reached its zenith. Its authority was loosely acknowledged, and taxes were received by it, from Lake Ladoga and the Baltic to the Caspian, the Caucasus, and the Black Sea. The Scandinavian invaders were absorbed, and Slav blood and speech prevailed. Social organization was frankly aristocratic; the prince entrusted administration and defense to a higher nobility of boyars, and a lesser nobility of *dietski* or *otroki*—pages or retainers; below these came the merchants, the townspeople, the semiservile peasantry, and the slaves. A code of laws—*Russkaya Pravda*, or

Russian Right—sanctioned private revenge, the judicial duel, and the compurgative oath, but established trial by a jury of twelve citizens.[40] Vladimir founded a school for boys at Kiev, Yaroslav another at Novgorod. Kiev, the meeting point of boats from the Volkhov, the Dvina, and the lower Dnieper, took toll of all passing merchandise. Soon it was rich enough to build 400 churches and a great cathedral—another St. Sophia—in the Byzantine style. Greek artists were imported to decorate these buildings with mosaics, frescoes, and other Byzantine ornament; and Greek music entered to prepare for the triumphs of Russian choral song. Slowly Russia lifted itself out of its dirt and dust, built palaces for its princes, raised cupolas above huts of mud, and out of the patient strength of its people reared little isles of civilization in a still barbarous sea.

CHAPTER XIX

The Decline of the West

566-1066

WHILE Islam was on the march, and Byzantium was recovering from seemingly fatal blows, Europe fought its way up through the "Dark Ages." This is a loose term, which any man may define to his prejudice; we shall arbitrarily confine it to non-Byzantine Europe between the death of Boethius in 524 and the birth of Abélard in 1079. Byzantine civilization continued to flourish during this period, despite severe losses of territory and prestige. But Western Europe in the sixth century was a chaos of conquest, disintegration, and rebarbarization. Much of the classic culture survived, for the most part silent and hidden in a few monasteries and families. But the physical and psychological foundations of social order had been so disturbed that centuries would be needed to restore them. Love of letters, devotion to art, the unity and continuity of culture, the cross-fertilization of communicating minds, fell before the convulsions of war, the perils of transport, the economies of poverty, the rise of vernaculars, the disappearance of Latin from the East and of Greek from the West. In the ninth and tenth centuries the Moslem control of the Mediterranean, the raiding of European coasts and towns by Normans, Magyars, and Saracens accelerated this localism of life and defense, this primitivism of thought and speech. Germany and Eastern Europe were a maelstrom of migrations, Scandinavia was a pirates' lair, Britain was overrun by Angles, Saxons, Jutes, and Danes; Gaul by Franks, Normans, Burgundians, and Goths; Spain was torn between Visigoths and Moors; Italy had been shattered by the long war between the Goths and Byzantium, and the land that had given order to half the world suffered for five centuries a disintegration of morals, economy, and government.

And yet during that long darkness Charlemagne, Alfred, and Otto I gave intervals of order and stimulus to France, England, and Germany; Erigena resurrected philosophy, Alcuin and others restored education, Gerbert imported Moslem science into Christendom, Leo IX and Gregory VII reformed and strengthened the Church, architecture developed the Romanesque style; and Europe began in the eleventh century its slow ascent to the twelfth and thirteenth, the greatest of medieval centuries.

I. ITALY: 566–1095

1. The Lombards: 568–774

Three years after the death of Justinian, Byzantine rule was extinguished in northern Italy by the Lombard invasion.

Paul the Deacon, who was one of them, thought that the Lombards or *Longobardi* owed their name to their long beards.[1] They themselves believed that their original home had been Scandinavia,[2] and so Dante, their descendant,[3] apostrophized them.[4] We find them on the lower Elbe in the first century, on the Danube in the sixth, used by Narses in his Italian campaign of 552, sent back to Pannonia after his victory, but never forgetting the fruitful loveliness of northern Italy. In 568, pressed on north and east by Avars, 130,-000 Lombards—men, women, children, and baggage—moved laboriously across the Alps into "Lombardy," the lush plains of the Po. Narses, who might have stopped them, had been deposed and disgraced a year before; Byzantium was busy with Avars and Persians; Italy itself, exhausted by the Gothic War, had no stomach for fighting, no money to pay for vicarious heroism. By 573 the Lombards held Verona, Milan, Florence, and Pavia—which became their capital; in 601, they captured Padua, in 603 Cremona and Mantua, in 640 Genoa. Their mightiest king, Liutprand (712–44), took Ravenna in eastern Italy, Spoleto in the center, Benevento in the south, and aspired to unite all Italy under his rule. Pope Gregory III could not allow the papacy to become a Lombard bishopric; he called in the unsubdued Venetians, who retook Ravenna for Byzantium. Liutprand had to content himself with giving northern and central Italy the best government they had had since Theodoric the Goth. Like Theodoric, he could not read.[5]

The Lombards developed a progressive civilization. The king was elected and advised by a council of notables, and usually submitted his legislation to a popular assembly of all free males of military age. King Rathari (643) published a code of laws at once primitive and advanced: it allowed money compensation for murder, proposed to protect the poor against the rich, ridiculed the belief in witchcraft, and gave freedom of worship to Catholic, Arian, and pagan alike.[6] Intermarriage absorbed the Germanic invaders into the Italian blood and won them to the Latin tongue; the Lombards left their signature here and there in blue eyes, blond hair, and a few Teutonic words in Italian speech. As the conquest subsided into law, the commerce natural to the valley of the Po was resumed; by the end of the Lombard period the cities of northern Italy were rich and strong, ready for the arts and wars of their medieval peak. Literature faltered; from this age and realm time has preserved only one book of significance—Paul the Deacon's *History of the Lombards (c.*

748); it is dull, poorly arranged, and without a grain of philosophic salt. But Lombardy left its name on architecture and finance. The building trades had retained some of their old Roman organization and skill; one group, the *magistri Comacini*, or masters of Como, took the lead in compounding a "Lombard" style of architecture that would later ripen into Romanesque.

Within a generation after Liutprand the Lombard kingdom broke against the rock of the papacy. King Aistulf seized Ravenna in 751, and ended the Byzantine exarchate. As the *ducatus Romanus* or duchy of Rome had been legally under the exarch, Aistulf claimed Rome as part of his widened realm. Pope Stephen II called upon Constantine Copronymus for aid; the Greek emperor sent a harmless note to Aistulf; Stephen, in a move of endless results, appealed to Pepin the Short, King of the Franks. Scenting empire, Pepin crossed the Alps, overwhelmed Aistulf, made Lombardy a Frank fief, and gave all central Italy to the papacy. The popes continued to acknowledge the formal suzerainty of the Eastern emperors, but Byzantine authority was now ended in northern Italy. The Lombard vassal King Desiderius tried to restore the independence and conquests of Lombardy; Pope Hadrian I summoned a new Frank; Charlemagne swept down upon Pavia, consigned Desiderius to a monastery, ended the Lombard kingdom, and made it a province of the Franks (774).

2. *The Normans in Italy: 1036–85*

Italy was now abandoned to a thousand years of divided and alien rule, whose details we shall not chronicle. In 1036 the Normans began the conquest of southern Italy from the Byzantine power. The lords of Normandy were wont to transmit land to all sons equally, as in modern France; but whereas in France the law resulted in small families, in medieval Normandy it resulted in small holdings. With no taste for peaceful poverty, and with a zest for adventure and rapine still warm in their Viking memories, some lusty Normans hired themselves out to the rival dukes of southern Italy, fought valiantly for and against Benevento, Salerno, Naples, and Capua, and were given the town of Aversa as their reward. Other Norman young bloods, hearing of lands to be won for a blow or two, left Normandy for Italy. Soon the Normans there numbered enough to fight for themselves; and by 1053 the boldest of them, Robert Guiscard (i.e., the Wise or Wily), had carved out a Norman kingdom in southern Italy. He was such stuff as myths are made of: taller than any of his soldiers, strong of arm and will, fair of features, blond of hair and beard, splendid in dress, greedy and liberal of gold, occasionally cruel, always brave.

Recognizing no law but force and guile, Robert overran Calabria, took Benevento almost over the dead body of Pope Leo IX (1054), struck alliance with Nicholas II, pledged him tribute and vassalage, and received from him title to Calabria, Apulia, and Sicily (1059). Leaving his younger brother Roger to conquer Sicily, he himself captured Bari (1071), and drove the Byzantines from Apulia. Fretting at the Adriatic barrier, he dreamed of crossing it, taking Constantinople, and making himself the mightiest monarch in Europe. He improvised a fleet, and defeated the Byzantine navy off Durazzo (1081). Byzantium appealed to Venice; Venice responded, for she could not be less than queen of the Adriatic; and in 1082 her skillful galleys routed Guiscard's ships not far from the site of his recent victory. But in the following year Robert, with Caesarean energy, transported his army to Durazzo, defeated there the forces of Alexius I, the Greek Emperor, and marched across Epirus and Thessaly almost to Salonika. Then, on the verge of realizing his dream, he received a desperate appeal from Pope Gregory VII to come and save him from the Emperor Henry IV. Leaving his army in Thessaly, Robert hurried back to Italy, raised a new force of Normans, Italians, and Saracens, rescued the Pope, captured Rome from the Germans, suppressed an uprising of the people against his army, and allowed his angry soldiers to burn and sack the city so thoroughly that not even the Vandals of 451 could equal this destructiveness (1084). Meanwhile his son Bohemond returned to confess that his army in Greece had been destroyed by Alexius. The old buccaneer built a third fleet, defeated the Venetian navy off Corfu (1084), took the Ionian isle of Cephalonia, and died there, of infection or poison, at the age of seventy (1085). He was the first and greatest of the *condottieri*, the robber captains of Italy.

3. *Venice: 451–1095*

Meanwhile, at the northern end of the peninsula, a new state had been born, destined to grow in power and splendor while most of Italy withered in anarchy. In the barbarian invasions of the fifth and sixth centuries—above all during the Lombard invasion of 568—the populations of Aquileia, Padua, Belluno, Feltre, and other towns fled for safety to join the fisher folk who dwelt in the little islands formed by the Piave and Adige Rivers at the head of the Adriatic Sea. Some refugees remained after the crises passed, and founded the communities of Heraclea, Melamocco, Grado, Lido . . . and Rivo Alto (Deep River)—which, as Rialto, became the seat of their united government (811). A tribe of Veneti had occupied northeastern Italy long before Caesar; in the thirteenth century the name Venezia was applied to the unique city that had grown from the refugee settlements.

Life was hard there at first. Fresh water was difficult to secure, and was valued like wine. Forced to market on the mainland, in exchange for wheat and other commodities, the fish and salt that they drew from the sea, the

Venetians became a people of boats and trade. Gradually the commerce of northern and central Europe with the Near East flowed through Venetian ports. The new federation, to protect itself from Germans and Lombards, acknowledged Byzantium as its overlord; but the inaccessibility of the islands, in their shallow waters, to attack by land or sea, the industry and fortitude of the citizens, the mounting wealth of their spreading trade, gave the little state an unbroken sovereignty through a thousand years.

Twelve tribunes—apparently one for each of the twelve principal islands— managed the government till 697, when the communities, feeling the need of a united authority, chose their first *dux* or doge—leader or duke—to serve until death or revolution should depose him. Doge Agnello Badoer (809–27) so skillfully defended the city against the Franks that the doges were chosen from his descendants till 942. Under Orseolo II (991–1008) Venice revenged herself against the raids of Dalmatian pirates by storming their lairs, absorb- ing Dalmatia, and establishing her control over the Adriatic. In 998 the Venetians began to celebrate, on every Ascension Day, this maritime victory and mastery by the symbolic ceremony of the *sposalizia*: the doge, from a gaily decorated galley, flung into the open waters a consecrated ring, and cried in Latin: "We marry you, the sea, in sign of our true and perpetual dominion." [7] Byzantium was glad to accept Venice as an independent ally, and rewarded her useful friendship with such commercial privileges at Con- stantinople and elsewhere that Venetian trade reached out to the Black Sea and even to the ports of Islam.

In 1033 an aristocracy of commerce ended the hereditary transmission of the ducal power, returned to the principle of election by an assembly of citi- zens, and compelled the doge henceforth to govern in collaboration with a senate. By this time Venice was already called "the golden" (*Venetia aurea*), and her people were famous for their luxurious dress, their wide- spread literacy, and their civic devotion and pride. They were a restlessly acquisitive tribe, clever and subtle, courageous and quarrelsome, pious and unscrupulous; they sold Christian slaves to the Saracens,[8] and with part of the profit they built shrines to the saints. The Rialto shops had able craftsmen who inherited the industrial skills of Roman Italy; a busy local trade moved along the canals, silently but for the terse cries of the gondoliers; the island quays were picturesque with adventurous galleys laden with the products of Europe and the East. Mercantile voyages were financed by capitalist loans, paying normally twenty per cent.[9] The gap between rich (*maggiori*) and poor (*minori*) widened as the rich became vastly richer, the poor only slightly less poor. No mercy was shown to simplicity. The race went to the swift, the battle to the strong. The *minori* walked on bare ground, and the refuse of their houses ran along the streets and into the canals; the *maggiori* built splendid palaces, and sought to appease God and the people with the most ornate cathedral in the Latin world. The Palace of the Doges, first raised in 814, burnt in 976, bore many changes of face and figure before finding its graceful blend of Moorish ornament and Renaissance form.

In 828 some Venetian merchants stole from an Alexandrian church what purported to be the relics of St. Mark. Venice made the apostle her patron saint, and ravaged half the world to enshrine his bones. The first St. Mark's, begun in 830, was so damaged by fire in 976 that Peter Orseolo II began a new and larger edifice. Byzantine artisans were summoned, who modeled it on Justinian's church of the Holy Apostles in Constantinople—with five domes over a cruciform plan. For nearly a century the work proceeded; the main structure was finished in substantially its present form in 1071, and was consecrated in 1095. The relics of St. Mark having been lost in the fire of 976, and their absence threatening the sanctity of the cathedral, it was arranged that on the day of consecration the worshipers should gather in the church and pray that the relics might be found. According to a tradition dear to good Venetians, a pillar succumbed to their orisons, fell to the ground, and revealed the evangelical bones.[10] The building was repeatedly damaged and repaired; hardly a decade but saw some alteration or embellishment; the St. Mark's that we know is of no one date or period, but is a stone and jewel record of a millennium. Marble facings were added to the brick walls in the twelfth century; columns of every variety were imported from a dozen cities; Byzantine artists naturalized in Venice executed mosaics for the cathedral in the twelfth and thirteenth centuries; four bronze horses were appropriated from conquered Constantinople in 1204, and were placed over the main portal; Gothic artists in the fourteenth century added pinnacles, window tracery, and a sanctuary screen; and in the seventeenth century Renaissance painters covered half the mosaics with indifferent murals. Through all these changes and centuries the strange edifice kept its character and unity—always Byzantine and Arabic, ornate and bizarre: the exterior overwhelmingly brilliant with arches, buttresses, spires, pillars, portals, pinnacles, encrusted polychrome marble, carved cornices, and stately bulbous domes; the interior with its dark wilderness of colored columns, carved or painted spandrels, somber frescoes, 5000 square yards of mosaic, floor inlaid with jasper, porphyry, agate, and other precious stones; and the *Pala d'oro*, or golden reredos, made of costly metals and cloisonné enamel in Constantinople in 976, overloaded with 2400 gems, and set up behind the main altar in 1105. In St. Mark's, as in St. Sophia's, the Byzantine passion for decoration outran itself. God was to be honored with marble and jewelry; man was to be terrified, disciplined, encouraged, and consoled by a hundred scenes from the Christian epic, from the creation to the destruction of the world. St. Mark's was the supreme and characteristic expression of a Latin people exuberantly won to an Oriental art.

4. Italian Civilization: 566–1095

While eastern and southern Italy remained Byzantine in culture, the rest of the peninsula evolved a new civilization—a new language, religion, and art—from its Roman heritage. For even amid invasion, chaos, and poverty, that heritage was never wholly lost. The Italian language was the rude Latin of the ancient populace, transforming itself slowly into the most melodious of all tongues. Italian Christianity was a romantic and colorful paganism, an affectionate polytheism of local and protective saints, a frank mythology of legend and miracle. Italian art suspected Gothic as barbarous, clung to the basilican style, and finally, in the Renaissance, returned to Augustan forms. Feudalism never prospered in Italy; the cities never lost their ascendancy over the countryside; industry and commerce, not agriculture, paved the roads to wealth.

Rome, never a commercial city, continued to decline. Its senate had perished in the Gothic War; its ancient municipal institutions, after 700, were empty tools and rebel dreams. The motley populace, living in a squalor alleviated by sexual license and papal alms, could express its political emotions only by frequent uprisings against foreign masters or disfavored popes. The old aristocratic families spent their time competing with one another for control of the papacy, or with the papacy for control of Rome. Where consuls, tribunes, and senators had once forged laws with rods and axes, social order was now barely sustained by the decrees of ecclesiastical councils, the sermons and agents of bishops, and the dubious example of thousands of monks, of every nationality, not seldom idle and not always celibate. The Church had denounced the promiscuity of the public baths; the great halls and pools of the thermae were deserted, and the pagan art of cleanliness was in decay. The imperial aqueducts having been ruined by neglect or war, the people drank the waters of the Tiber.[11] The Circus Maximus and the Colosseum, of bloody memory, were no longer used; the Forum began in the seventh century to revert to the cow pasture from which it had been formed; the Capitol was paved with mire; old temples and public buildings were dismembered to provide material for Christian churches and palaces. Rome suffered more from Romans than from Vandals and Goths.[12] The Rome of Caesar was dead, and the Rome of Leo X had yet to be born.

The old libraries were scattered or destroyed, and intellectual life was almost confined to the Church. Science succumbed to the superstition that gives romance to poverty. Only medicine kept its head up, clinging with monastic hands to the Galenic heritage. Perhaps out of a Benedictine monastery at Salerno, in the ninth century, a lay medical school took form which bridged the gap between ancient and medieval medicine, as Hellenized south Italy bridged the gap between Greek and medieval culture. Salerno had been a health resort for over a thousand years. Local tradition described its *collegium Hippocraticum* as composed of ten physician instructors, of whom one was a Greek, one a Saracen, one a Jew.[13] About the year 1060 Constantine "the African," a Roman citizen who had studied medicine in the Moslem schools of Africa and Baghdad, brought to Monte Cassino (where he became a monk) and to nearby Salerno an exciting cargo of Islamic medical lore. His translations of Greek and Arabic works in medicine and other fields shared in the resurrection of science in Italy. At his death (*c.* 1087) the school of Salerno stood at the head of medical knowledge in the Christian West.

The distinctive achievement of art in this age was the establishment of the Romanesque architectural style (774–1200). Inheriting the Roman tradition of solidity and permanence, the Italian builders thickened the walls of the basilica, crossed the nave with a transept, added towers or attached pillars as buttresses, and supported with columns or clustered piers the arches that upheld the roof. The characteristic Romanesque arch was a simple semicircle, a form of noble dignity, better fitted to span a space than to bear a weight. In early Romanesque the aisles—in later Romanesque the nave and aisles—were vaulted, i.e., roofed with arched masonry. The exterior was usually plain, and of unfaced brick. The interior, though moderately adorned with mosaics, frescoes, and carvings, shunned the luxurious decoration of the Byzantine style. Romanesque was Roman; it sought stability and power rather than Gothic elevation and grace; it aimed to subdue the soul to a quieting humility rather than lift it to a heaven-storming ecstasy.

Italy produced in this period two masterpieces of Romanesque: the modest church of Sant' Ambrogio at Milan, and the immense *duomo* of Pisa. The building from whose doors Ambrose had barred an emperor was rebuilt by Benedictines in 789, and again decayed. From 1046 to 1071 Archbishop Guido had it completely remodeled from a colonnaded basilica into a vaulted church. Nave and aisles, formerly roofed with wood, now sustained—by round arches springing from compound piers—a vaulted ceiling of brick and stone. The groins or ridges formed in the vault by the intersecting masonry arches were reinforced with "ribs" of brick; this is the oldest "ribbed vault" in Europe.

The simple front of Sant' Ambrogio seems all the world apart from the complex façade of the cathedral of Pisa, but the elements of style are the same. After the decisive victory of the Pisan over the Saracen fleet near Palermo (1063), the city commissioned the architects Buschetto (a Greek?) and Rinaldo to commemorate the battle, and offer part of the spoils to the Virgin, by erecting a shrine that should make all Italy envious. Nearly the entire massive edifice was made of marble. Above the west portals—later (1606) equipped with superb bronze doors—four tiers of open arcades spanned the façade in immoderate iteration. Within, a profusion of elegant columns—booty of varied provenance—divided the church into nave and double aisles; and over the crossing of transept and nave rose an unpleasantly elliptical dome. This was the first of the great cathedrals of Italy; and it remains one of the most impressive works of medieval man.

II. CHRISTIAN SPAIN: 711–1095

The history of Christian Spain in this period is that of one long crusade—the rising resolve to expel the Moors. These were rich and strong; they held the most fertile terrain, and had the best government; the Christians were poor and weak, their soil was difficult, their mountain barriers shut them off from the rest of Europe, divided them into petty kingdoms, and encouraged provincial chauvinism and fraternal strife. In this passionate peninsula more Christian blood was shed by Christians than by Moors.

The Moslem invasion of 711 drove the unconquered Goths, Suevi, Christianized Berbers, and Iberian Celts into the Cantabrian Mountains of northwestern Spain. The Moors pursued them, but were defeated at Covadonga (718) by a small force under the Goth Pelayo, who thereupon made himself King of Asturias, and so founded the Spanish monarchy. The repulse of the Moors at Tours allowed Alfonso I (739–57) to extend the Asturian frontiers into Galicia, Lusitania, and Viscaya. His grandson Alfonso II (791–842) annexed the province of Leon, and made Oviedo his capital.

In this reign occurred one of the pivotal events of Spanish history. A shepherd, allegedly guided by a star, found in the mountains a marble coffin whose contents were believed by many to be the remains of the Apostle James, "brother of the Lord." A chapel was built on the site, and later a splendid cathedral; Santiago de Compostela—"St. James of the Field of the Star"—became a goal of Christian pilgrimage only less sought than Jerusalem and Rome; and the sacred bones proved invaluable in stirring morale, and raising funds, for the wars against the Moors. St. James was made the patron saint of Spain, and spread the name Santiago over three continents. Beliefs make history, especially when they are wrong; it is for errors that men have most nobly died.

East of Asturias, and just south of the Pyrenees, lay Navarre. Its inhabitants were mostly of Basque stock—probably of mixed Celtic Spanish and African Berber blood. Helped by their mountains they successfully defended their independence against Moslems, Franks, and Spaniards; and in 905 Sancho I García founded the kingdom of Navarre, with Pamplona as his capital. Sancho "the Great" (994–1035) won his title by absorbing Leon, Castile, and Aragon; for a time Christian Spain verged on unity; but at his death Sancho undid his life's work by dividing his realm among his four sons. The kingdom of Aragon dates its existence from this division. By pressing back the Moslems in the south, and peacefully incorporating Navarre in the north (1076), it came by 1095 to include a large part of north-central Spain. Catalonia—northeastern Spain around Barcelona—was conquered by Charlemagne in 788, and was ruled by French counts who made the region a semi-independent "Spanish March"; its language, Catalan, was an interesting compromise between Provençal French and Castilian. Leon, in the northwest, entered history with Sancho the Fat, who was so heavy that he could walk only by leaning upon an attendant. Deposed by the nobles, he went to Cordova, where the famous Jewish physician and statesman Hasdai ben Shaprut cured him of obesity. Now as lithe as Don Quixote, Sancho returned to Leon and reconquered his throne (959).[14] Castile, in central Spain, was named from its castles; it fronted Moslem Spain, and lived in continual readiness for war. In 930 its knights refused any longer to obey the kings of Asturias or Leon, and set up an independent state, with its capital at Burgos. Fernando I (1035–65) united Leon and Galicia to Castile, compelled the emirs of Toledo and Seville to pay him yearly tribute, and, like Sancho the Great, canceled his labors with his death by dividing his realm among his three sons, who zealously continued the tradition of internecine war among the Christian Spanish kings.

Agricultural poverty and political disunity kept Christian Spain far behind its Moslem rival in the south and its Frank rival in the north in the amenities and arts of civilization. Even within each little kingdom unity was an interlude; the nobles almost ignored the kings except in war, and ruled their serfs and slaves in feudal sovereignty. The ecclesiastical hierarchy formed a second nobility; bishops, too, owned land, serfs, and slaves, led their own troops in war, usually ignored the popes, and ruled Spanish Christianity as a well-nigh independent church. In 1020 at Leon, nobles and bishops joined in national councils, and legislated as a parliament for the kingdom of Leon. The Council of Leon granted to that city a charter of self-government, making it the first autonomous commune in medieval Europe; similar charters were granted to other Spanish cities, probably to enlist their ardor and funds in the war against the Moors; and a limited urban democracy rose amid the feudalism, and under the monarchies, of Spain.

The career of Rodrigo (Ruy) Diaz illustrates the bravery, chivalry, and chaos of Christian Spain in the eleventh century. He has come down to us rather under the title the Moors gave him of El Cid (Arabic *sayid*)—noble or lord—than under his Christian sobriquet of El Campeador—the Challenger or Champion. Born at Bivar near Burgos about 1040, he grew up as a *caballero* or military adventurer, fighting anywhere for any paying cause; by the age of thirty he was admired throughout Castile for his daring skill in combat, and distrusted for his apparently equal readiness to fight Moors for Christians, or Christians for Moors. Sent by Alfonso VI of Castile to collect tribute due from al-Mutamid, the poet emir of Seville, he was accused, on his return, of keeping part of the tribute, and was banished from Castile (1081). He became a freebooter, organized a small army of soldiers of fortune, and sold his services to Christian or Moslem rulers indifferently. For

eight years he served the emir of Saragossa, and extended the Moorish dominion at the expense of Aragon. In 1089, leading 7000 men, mostly Moslems, he captured Valencia, and exacted from it a monthly tribute of 10,000
gold dinars. In 1090 he seized the count of Barcelona, and held him for a
ransom of 80,000 dinars. Finding Valencia closed to him on his return from
this expedition, he besieged it for a year; when it surrendered (1094) he
violated all the conditions on which it had laid down its arms, burned its
chief justice alive, divided the possessions of the citizens among his followers, and would have burned the judge's wife and daughters too had not the
city and his own soldiers raised a cry of protest.[15] In this and other ways
the Cid behaved in the fashion of his times. He atoned for his sins by governing Valencia with ability and justice, and making it a saving rampart
against the Almoravid Moors. When he died (1099) his wife Jimena held
the city for three years. An admiring posterity transformed him by legend
into a knight moved only by a holy zeal to restore Spain to Christ; and his
bones at Burgos are revered as those of a saint.[16]

So divided against itself, Christian Spain achieved its slow *reconquista* only
because Moslem Spain finally surpassed it in fragmèntation and anarchy.
The fall of the Cordovan caliphate in 1036 offered an opportunity brilliantly
used by Alfonso VI of Castile. With the help of al-Mutamid of Seville he
captured Toledo (1085) and made it his capital. He treated the conquered
Moslems with Moslem decency, and encouraged the absorption of Moorish culture into Christian Spain.

III FRANCE: 614–1060

1. The Coming of the Carolingians: 614–768

When Clotaire II became king of the Franks, the Merovingian dynasty seemed
secure; never before had a monarch of that family ruled so large and united a
realm. But Clotaire was indebted for his rise to the nobles of Austrasia and Burgundy; he rewarded them with increased independence and enlarged domains,
and chose one of them, Pepin I the Elder, as his "Mayor of the Palace." The *major
domus*—"head of the house"—had been originally the superintendent of the royal
household and overseer of the royal estates; his administrative functions grew as
the Merovingian kings concentrated on debauchery and intrigue; step by step
he took control of the courts, the army, the finances. Clotaire's son King Dagobert (628–39) checked for a time the power of the *major domus* and the grandees.
"He rendered justice to rich and poor alike," says the chronicler Fredegar; "he
took little sleep or food, and cared only so to act that all men should leave his
presence full of joy and admiration";[17] however, Fredegar adds, "he had three
queens and a host of concubines," and was "a slave to incontinence."[18] Under
his negligent successors—the *rois fainéants* or do-nothing kings—power passed

again to the mayor of the palace. Pepin II the Younger defeated his rivals at the battle of Testry (687), expanded his title from *major domus* to *dux et princeps Francorum*, and ruled all Gaul except Aquitaine. His illegitimate son Charles Martel (the Hammer), nominally as mayor of the palace and Duke of Austrasia, ruled all Gaul under Clotaire IV (717-19). He resolutely repelled invasions of Gaul by Frisians and Saxons, and saved Europe for Christianity by turning back the Moslems at Tours. He supported Boniface and other missionaries in the conversion of Germany, but in the critical financial needs of his career he confiscated church lands, sold bishoprics to generals, quartered his troops on monasteries, beheaded a protesting monk,[19] and was condemned to hell in a hundred sermons and tracts.

In 751 his son Pepin III, as *major domus* to Childeric III, sent an embassy to Pope Zacharias to ask would it be sinful to depose the Merovingian puppet and make himself king in fact as well as name. Zacharias, who needed Frank support against the ambitious Lombards, answered with a comforting negative. Pepin called an assembly of nobles and prelates at Soissons; he was there unanimously chosen king of the Franks (751); and the last of the do-nothing kings was tonsured and sent to a monastery. In 754 Pope Stephen II came to the abbey of St. Denis outside of Paris, and anointed Pepin *rex Dei gratia*, "king by the grace of God." So ended the Merovingian dynasty (486-751), so began the Carolingian (751-987).

Pepin III "the Short" was a patient and far-seeing ruler, pious and practical, loving peace and invincible in war, and moral beyond any royal precedent in the Gaul of those centuries. All that Charlemagne accomplished was prepared by Pepin; in their two reigns of sixty-three years (751–814) Gaul was at last transformed into France. Pepin recognized the difficulty of governing without the aid of religion; he restored the property, privileges, and immunities of the Church; brought sacred relics to France, and bore them on his shoulders in impressive pageantry; rescued the papacy from the Lombard kings, and gave it a spacious temporal power in the "Donation of Pepin" (756). He was content to receive in return the title of *patricius Romanus*, and a papal injunction to the Franks never to choose a king except from his progeny. He died in the fullness of his power in 768, after bequeathing the realm of the Franks jointly to his sons Carloman II and the Charles who was to be Charlemagne.

2. *Charlemagne: 768–814.*

The greatest of medieval kings was born in 742, at a place unknown. He was of German blood and speech, and shared some characteristics of his people—strength of body, courage of spirit, pride of race, and a crude simplicity many centuries apart from the urbane polish of the modern French. He had little book learning; read only a few books—but good ones; tried in his old age to learn writing, but never quite succeeded; yet he could speak old Teutonic and literary Latin, and understood Greek.[20]

In 771 Carloman II died, and Charles at twenty-nine became sole king.

Two years later he received from Pope Hadrian II an urgent appeal for aid against the Lombard Desiderius, who was invading the papal states. Charlemagne besieged and took Pavia, assumed the crown of Lombardy, confirmed the Donation of Pepin, and accepted the role of protector of the Church in all her temporal powers. Returning to his capital at Aachen, he began a series of fifty-three campaigns—nearly all led in person—designed to round out his empire by conquering and Christianizing Bavaria and Saxony, destroying the troublesome Avars, shielding Italy from the raiding Saracens, and strengthening the defenses of *Francia* against the expanding Moors of Spain. The Saxons on his eastern frontier were pagans; they had burned down a Christian church, and made occasional incursions into Gaul; these reasons sufficed Charlemagne for eighteen campaigns (772–804), waged with untiring ferocity on both sides. Charles gave the conquered Saxons a choice between baptism and death, and had 4500 Saxon rebels beheaded in one day;[21] after which he proceeded to Thionville to celebrate the nativity of Christ.

At Paderborn in 777 Ibn al-Arabi, the Moslem governor of Barcelona, had asked the aid of the Christian king against the caliph of Cordova. Charles led an army across the Pyrenees, besieged and captured the Christian city of Pamplona, treated the Christian but incalculable Basques of northern Spain as enemies, and advanced even to Saragossa. But the Moslem uprisings that al-Arabi had promised as part of the strategy against the caliph failed to appear; Charlemagne saw that his unaided forces could not challenge Cordova; news came that the conquered Saxons were in wild revolt and were marching in fury upon Cologne; and with the better part of valor he led his army back, in long and narrow file, through the passes of the Pyrenees. In one such pass, at Roncesvalles in Navarre, a force of Basques pounced down upon the rear guard of the Franks, and slaughtered nearly every man in it (778); there the noble Hruodland died, who would become three centuries later the hero of France's most famous poem, the *Chanson de Roland*. In 795 Charlemagne sent another army across the Pyrenees; the Spanish March—a strip of northeast Spain—became part of Francia, Barcelona capitulated, and Navarre and Asturias acknowledged the Frankish sovereignty (806). Meanwhile Charlemagne had subdued the Saxons (785), had driven back the advancing Slavs (789), had defeated and dispersed the Avars (790–805), and had, in the thirty-fourth year of his reign and the sixty-third of his age, resigned himself to peace.

In truth he had always loved administration more than war, and had taken to the field to force some unity of government and faith upon a Western Europe torn for centuries past by conflicts of tribe and creed. He had now brought under his rule all the peoples between the Vistula and the Atlantic, between the Baltic and the Pyrenees, with nearly all of Italy and much of the Balkans. How could one man competently govern so vast and varied a realm? He was strong enough in body and nerves to bear a thousand re-sponsibilities, perils, and crises, even to his sons' plotting to kill him. He had in him the blood or teaching of the wise and cautious Pepin III, and of the ruthless Charles Martel, and was something of a hammer himself. He ex-tended their power, guarded it with firm military organization, propped it with religious sanction and ritual. He could vision large purposes, and could will the means as well as wish the ends. He could lead an army, persuade an assembly, humor the nobility, dominate the clergy, rule a harem.

He made military service a condition of owning more than a pittance of property, and thereby founded martial morale on the defense and extension of one's land. Every freeman, at the call to arms, had to report in full equip-ment to the local count, and every noble was responsible for the military fitness of his constituents. The structure of the state rested on this organ-ized force, supported by every available psychological factor in the sanctity of anointed majesty, the ceremonial splendor of the imperial presence, and the tradition of obedience to established rule. Around the king gathered a court of administrative nobles and clergymen—the seneschal or head of the palace, the "count palatine" or chief justice, the "palsgraves" or judges of the palace court, and a hundred scholars, servants, and clerks. The sense of public participation in the government was furthered by semiannual as-semblies of armed property owners, gathered, as military or other conven-ience might dictate, at Worms, Valenciennes, Aachen, Geneva, Paderborn . . . usually in the open air. At such assemblies the king submitted to smaller groups of nobles or bishops his proposals for legislation; they considered them, and returned them to him with suggestions; he formulated the *capitula*, or chapters of legislation, and presented these to the multitude for their shouted approval; rarely the assembly voiced disapproval with a collective grunt or moan. Hincmar, Archbishop of Reims, has transmitted an intimate picture of Charles at one of these gatherings, "saluting the men of most note, conversing with those whom he seldom saw, showing a tender interest to-ward the elders, and disporting himself with the young." At these meetings each provincial bishop and administrator was required to report to the King any significant event in his locality since the previous convocation. "The King wished to know," says Hincmar, "whether in any part or corner of the Kingdom the people were restless, and the cause thereof." [22] Sometimes (continuing the old Roman institution of *inquisitio*) the representatives of the King would summon leading citizens to inquire and give under oath a "true statement" (*veredictum*) as to the taxable wealth, the state of public order, the existence of crimes or criminals, in the district visited. In the ninth century, in Frank lands, this verdict of a *jurata*, or sworn group of inquir-ers, was used to decide many local issues of land ownership or criminal guilt. Out of the *jurata*, through Norman and English developments, would come the jury system of modern times. [23]

The empire was divided into counties, each governed in spiritual matters by a bishop or archbishop, and in secular affairs by a *comes* (companion— of the king) or count. A local assembly of landholders convened twice or thrice a year in each provincial capital to pass upon the government of the region, and serve as a provincial court of appeals. The dangerous frontier counties, or marches, had special governors—*graf*, *margrave*, or *markherzog*; Roland of Roncesvalles, for example, was governor of the Breton march. All local administration was subject to *missi dominici*—"emissaries of the master" —sent by Charlemagne to convey his wishes to local officials, to review their actions, judgments, and accounts; to check bribery, extortion, nepotism, and exploitation, to receive complaints and remedy wrongs, to protect "the Church, the poor, and wards and widows, and the whole people" from malfeasance or tyranny, and to report to the King the condition of the realm; the *Capitulare missorum* establishing these emissaries was a Magna Carta for the people, four centuries before England's Magna Carta for the aristocracy. That this capitulary meant what it said appears from the case of the duke of Istria, who, being accused by the *missi* of divers injustices and extortions, was forced by the King to restore his thievings, compensate every wronged man, publicly confess his crimes, and give security against their repetition. Barring his wars, Charlemagne's was the most just and enlightened government that Europe had known since Theodoric the Goth.

The sixty-five capitularies that remain of Charlemagne's legislation are among the most interesting bodies of medieval law. They were not an organized system, but rather the extension and application of previous "barbarian" codes to new occasion or need. In some particulars they were less enlightened than the laws of King Liutprand of Lombardy: they kept the old wergild, ordeals, trial by combat, and punishment by mutilation;[24] and decreed death for relapse into paganism, or for eating meat in Lent—though here the priest was allowed to soften the penalty.[25] Nor were all these capitularies laws; some were answers to inquiries, some were questions addressed by Charlemagne to officials, some were moral counsels. "It is necessary," said one article, "that every man should seek to the best of his strength and ability to serve God and walk in the way of His precepts; for the Lord Emperor cannot watch over every man in personal discipline."[26] Several articles struggled to bring more order into the sexual and marital relations of the people. Not all these counsels were obeyed; but there runs through the capitularies a conscientious effort to transform barbarism into civilization.

Charlemagne legislated for agriculture, industry, finance, education, and religion as well as for government and morals. His reign fell into a period when the economy of southern France and Italy was at low ebb through the control of the Mediterranean by the Saracens. "The Christians," said Ibn Khaldun, "could no longer float a plank upon the sea."[27] The whole structure of commercial relations between Western Europe and Africa and the Levant was disturbed; only the Jews—whom Charlemagne sedulously protected for this reason—connected the now hostile halves of what under Rome had been a united economic world. Commerce survived in Slavic and Byzantine Europe, and in the Teutonic north. The English Channel and the North Sea were alive with trade; but this too would be disordered, even before Charlemagne's death, by Norse piracy and raids. Vikings on the north and Moslems on the south almost closed the ports of France, and made her an inland and agricultural state. The mercantile middle class declined, leaving no group to compete with the rural aristocracy; French feudalism was promoted by Charlemagne's land grants and by the triumphs of Islam.

Charlemagne struggled to protect a free peasantry against spreading serfdom, but the power of the nobles, and the force of circumstance, frustrated him. Even slavery grew for a time, as a result of the Carolingian wars against pagan tribes. The King's own estates, periodically extended by confiscations, gifts, intestate reversions, and reclamation, were the chief source of the royal revenue. For the care of these lands he issued a *Capitulare de villis* astonishingly detailed, and revealing his careful scrutiny of all state income and expense. Forests, wastelands, highways, ports, and all mineral subsoil resources were the property of the state.[28] Every encouragement was given to such commerce as survived; the fairs were protected, weights and measures and prices were regulated, tolls were moderated, speculation in futures was checked, roads and bridges were built or repaired, a great span was thrown across the Rhine at Mainz, waterways were kept open, and a canal was planned to connect the Rhine and the Danube, and thereby the North with the Black Sea. A stable currency was maintained; but the scarcity of gold in France and the decline of trade led to the replacement of Constantine's gold *solidus* with the silver pound.

The energy and solicitude of the King reached into every sphere of life. He gave to the four winds the names they bear today. He established a system of poor relief, taxed the nobles and the clergy to pay its costs, and then made mendicancy a crime.[29] Appalled by the illiteracy of his time, when hardly any but ecclesiastics could read, and by the lack of education among the lower clergy, he called in foreign scholars to restore the schools of France. Paul the Deacon was lured from Monte Cassino, and Alcuin from York (782), to teach the school that Charlemagne organized in the royal palace at Aachen. Alcuin (735–804) was a Saxon, born near York, and educated in the cathedral school that Bishop Egbert had founded there; in the eighth century Britain and Ireland were culturally ahead of France. When King Offa of Mercia sent Alcuin on a mission to Charlemagne, the latter begged the scholar to remain; Alcuin, glad to be out of England when the Danes were "laying it desolate, and dishonoring the monasteries with adultery,"[30] consented to stay. He sent to England and elsewhere for books and teachers, and soon the palace school was an active center of study, of the revision and copying of manuscripts, and of an educational reform that spread throughout the realm. Among the pupils were Charlemagne, his wife Liutgard, his sons, his daughter Gisela, his secretary Eginhard, a nun, and many more. Charlemagne was the most eager of all; he seized upon learning as he had absorbed states; he studied rhetoric, dialectic, astronomy; he made heroic efforts to write, says Eginhard, "and used to keep tablets under his pillow in order that at leisure hours he might accustom his hand to form the letters; but as he began these efforts so late in life, they met with ill success."[31] He studied Latin furiously, but continued to speak German at his court; he compiled a German grammar, and collected specimens of early German poetry.

When Alcuin, after eight years in the palace school, pled for a less exciting environment, Charlemagne reluctantly made him Abbot of Tours (796). There Alcuin spurred the monks to make fairer and more accurate copies of the Vulgate of Jerome, the Latin Fathers, and the Latin classics; and other monasteries imitated the example. Many of our best classical texts have come down to us from these monastic *scriptoria* of the ninth century; practically all extant Latin poetry except Catullus, Tibullus, and Propertius, and nearly all extant Latin prose except Varro, Tacitus, and Apuleius, were preserved for us by the monks of the Carolingian age.[32] Many of the Caroline manuscripts were handsomely illuminated by the patient art of the monks; to this "Palace School" of illumination belonged the "Vienna" Gospels on which the later German emperors took their coronation oath.

In 787 Charlemagne issued to all the bishops and abbots of Francia an historic *Capitulare de litteris colendis*, or directive on the study of letters. It reproached ecclesiastics for "uncouth language" and "unlettered tongues," and exhorted every cathedral and monastery to establish schools where clergy and laity alike might learn to read and write. A further capitulary of 789 urged the directors of these schools to "take care to make no difference between the sons of serfs and of freemen, so that they might come and sit on the same benches to study grammar, music, and arithmetic." A capitulary of 805 provided for medical education, and another condemned medical superstitions. That his appeals were not fruitless appears from the many cathedral or monastic schools that now sprang up in France and western Germany. Theodulf, Bishop of Orléans, organized schools in every parish of his diocese, welcomed all children to them, and forbade the priest instructors to take any fees;[33] this is the first instance in history of free and general education. Important schools, nearly all attached to monasteries, rose in the ninth century at Tours, Auxerre, Pavia, St. Gall, Fulda, Ghent, and elsewhere. To meet the demand for teachers Charlemagne imported scholars from Ireland, Britain, and Italy. Out of these schools were to come the universities of Europe.

We must not overestimate the intellectual quality of the age; this scholastic resurrection was the awakening of children rather than the maturity of such cultures as then existed in Constantinople, Baghdad, and Cordova. It did not produce any great writers. The formal compositions of Alcuin are stiflingly dull; only his letters and occasional verses show him as no pompous pedant but a kindly soul who could reconcile happiness with piety. Many men wrote poetry in this short-lived renaissance, and the poems of Theodulf are pleasant enough in their minor way. But the only lasting composition of that Gallic age was the brief and simple biography of Charlemagne by Eginhard. It follows the plan of Suetonius' *Lives of the Caesars*, and even snatches passages therefrom to apply to Charlemagne; but all is forgiven to an author who modestly describes himself as "a barbarian, very little versed in the Roman tongue." [34] He must have been a man of talent nevertheless, for Charlemagne made him royal steward and treasurer and intimate friend, and chose him to supervise, perhaps to design, much of the architecture of this creative reign.

Palaces were built for the Emperor at Ingelheim and Nijmegen; and at Aachen, his favorite capital, he raised the famous palace and chapel that survived a thousand dangers to crumble under the shells and bombs of the Second World War. The unknown architects modeled its plan on the church of San Vitale at Ravenna, which owed its form to Byzantine and Syrian exemplars; the result was an Oriental cathedral stranded in the West. The octagonal structure was surmounted by a circular dome; the interior was divided by a circular two-storied colonnade, and was "adorned with gold and silver and lamps, railings and doors of solid bronze, columns and crucibles brought from Rome and Ravenna," [35] and a famous mosaic in the dome.

Charlemagne was profusely generous to the Church; at the same time he made himself her master, and used her doctrines and personnel as instruments of education and government. Much of his correspondence was about religion; he hurled scriptural quotations at corrupt officials or worldly clerics; and the intensity of his utterance forbids suspicion that his piety was a political pose. He sent money to distressed Christians in foreign lands, and in his negotiations with Moslem rulers he insisted on fair treatment of their Christian population. [36] Bishops played a leading part in his councils, assemblies, and administration; but he looked upon them, however reverently, as his agents under God; and he did not hesitate to command them, even in matters of doctrine or morals. He denounced image worship while the popes were defending it; required from every priest a written description of how baptism was administered in his parish, sent the popes directives as numerous as his gifts, suppressed insubordination in monasteries, and ordered a strict watch on convents to prevent "whoring, drunkenness, and covetousness" among the nuns. [37] In a capitulary of 811 he asked the clergy what they meant by professing to renounce the world, when "we see" some of them "laboring day by day, by all sorts of means, to augment their possessions; now making use, for this purpose, of menaces of eternal flames, now of promises of eternal beatitude; despoiling simple-minded people of their property in the name of God or some saint, to the infinite prejudice of their lawful heirs." Nevertheless he allowed the clergy their own courts, decreed that a tithe or tenth of all produce of the land should be turned over to the Church, gave the clergy control of marriages and wills, and himself bequeathed two thirds of his estates to the bishoprics of his realm.[38] But he required the bishops now and then to make substantial "gifts" to help meet the expenses of the government.

Out of this intimate co-operation of Church and state came one of the most brilliant ideas in the history of statesmanship: the transformation of Charlemagne's realm into a Holy Roman Empire that should have behind it all the prestige, sanctity, and stability of both Imperial and papal Rome. The popes had long resented their territorial subordination to a Byzantium that gave them no protection and no security; they saw the increasing subjection of the patriarch to the emperor at Constantinople, and feared for their own freedom. We do not know who conceived or arranged the plan of a papal coronation of Charlemagne as Roman emperor; Alcuin, Theodulf, and others close to him had discussed its possibility; perhaps the initiative lay with them, perhaps with the councilors of the popes. There were great difficulties in the way: the Greek monarch already had the title of Roman emperor, and full historic right to that title; the Church had no recognized authority to convey or transfer the title; to give it to a rival of Byzantium might precipitate a gigantic war of Christian East against Christian West, leaving a ruined Europe to a conquering Islam. It was of some help that Irene had seized the Greek throne (797); now, some said, there was no Greek emperor, and the field was open to any claimant. If the bold scheme could be carried through there would again be a Roman emperor in the West, Latin Christianity would stand strong and unified against schismatic Byzantium and threatening Saracens, and, by the awe and magic of the imperial name, barbarized Europe might reach back across centuries of darkness, and inherit and Christianize the civilization and culture of the ancient world.

On December 26, 795, Leo III was chosen Pope. The Roman populace did not like him; it accused him of various misdeeds; and on April 25, 799, it attacked him, maltreated him, and imprisoned him in a monastery. He escaped, and fled for protection to Charlemagne at Paderborn. The King received him kindly, and sent him back to Rome under armed escort, and ordered the Pope and his accusers to appear before him there in the following year. On November 24, 800, Charlemagne entered the ancient capital in state; on December 1 an assembly of Franks and Romans agreed to drop the charges against Leo if he would deny them on solemn oath; he did; and the way was cleared for a magnificent celebration of the Nativity. On

Christmas Day, as Charlemagne, in the chlamys and sandals of a *patricius Romanus*, knelt before St. Peter's altar in prayer, Leo suddenly produced a jeweled crown, and set it upon the King's head. The congregation, perhaps instructed beforehand to act according to ancient ritual as the *senatus populusque Romanus* confirming a coronation, thrice cried out: "Hail to Charles the Augustus, crowned by God the great and peace-bringing Emperor of the Romans!" The royal head was anointed with holy oil, the Pope saluted Charlemagne as Emperor and Augustus, and offered him the act of homage reserved since 476 for the Eastern emperor.

If we may believe Eginhard, Charlemagne told him that had he known Leo's intention to crown him he would not have entered the church. Perhaps he had learned of the general plan, but regretted the haste and circumstances of its execution; it may not have pleased him to receive the crown from a pope, opening the door to centuries of dispute as to the relative dignity and power of donor and recipient; and presumably he anticipated difficulties with Byzantium. He now sent frequent embassies and letters to Constantinople, seeking to heal the breach; and for a long time he made no use of his new title. In 802 he offered marriage to Irene as a means of mutually legitimizing their dubious titles;[39] but Irene's fall from power shattered this elegant plan. To discourage any martial attack by Byzantium he arranged an entente with Harun al-Rashid, who sealed their understanding by sending him some elephants and the keys to the Christian holy places in Jerusalem. The Eastern emperor, in retaliation, encouraged the emir of Cordova to renounce allegiance to Baghdad. Finally, in 812, the Greek *basileus* recognized Charlemagne as coemperor, in return for Charlemagne's acknowledgment of Venice and southern Italy as belonging to Byzantium.

The coronation had results for a thousand years. It strengthened the papacy and the bishops by making civil authority derive from ecclesiastical conferment; Gregory VII and Innocent III would build a mightier Church on the events of 800 in Rome. It strengthened Charlemagne against baronial and other disaffection by making him a very vicar of God; it vastly advanced the theory of the divine right of kings. It contributed to the schism of Greek from Latin Christianity; the Greek Church did not relish subordination to a Roman Church allied with an empire rival to Byzantium. The fact that Charlemagne (as the Pope desired) continued to make Aachen, not Rome, his capital, underlined the passage of political power from the Mediterranean to northern Europe, from the Latin peoples to the Teutons. Above all, the coronation established the Holy Roman Empire in fact, though not in theory. Charlemagne and his advisers conceived of his new authority as a revival of the old imperial power; only with Otto I was the distinctively new character of the regime recognized; and it became "holy" only when Frederick Barbarossa introduced the word *sacrum* into his title in 1155. All in all, despite its threat to the liberty of the mind and the citizen, the Holy

Roman Empire was a noble conception, a dream of security and peace, order and civilization restored in a world heroically won from barbarism, violence, and ignorance.

Imperial formalities now hedged in the Emperor on occasions of state. Then he had to wear embroidered robes, a golden buckle, jeweled shoes, and a crown of gold and gems, and visitors prostrated themselves to kiss his foot or knee; so much had Charlemagne learned from Byzantium, and Byzantium from Ctesiphon. But in other days, Eginhard assures us, his dress varied little from the common garb of the Franks—linen shirt and breeches next to the skin, and over these a woolen tunic perhaps fringed with silk; hose fastened by bands covered his legs, leather shoes his feet; in winter he added a close-fitting coat of otter or marten skins; and always a sword at his side. He was six feet four inches tall, and built to scale. He had blond hair, animated eyes, a powerful nose, a mustache but no beard, a presence "always stately and dignified." [40] He was temperate in eating and drinking, abominated drunkenness, and kept in good health despite every exposure and hardship. He often hunted, or took vigorous exercise on horseback. He was a good swimmer, and liked to bathe in the warm springs of Aachen. He rarely entertained, preferring to hear music or the reading of a book while he ate. Like every great man he valued time; he gave audiences and heard cases in the morning while dressing and putting on his shoes.

Behind his poise and majesty were passion and energy, but harnessed to his aims by a clairvoyant intelligence. His vital force was not consumed by half a hundred campaigns; he gave himself also, with never aging enthusiasm, to science, law, literature, and theology; he fretted at leaving any part of the earth, or any section of knowledge, unmastered or unexplored. In some ways he was mentally ingenuous; he scorned superstition and proscribed diviners and soothsayers, but he accepted many mythical marvels, and exaggerated the power of legislation to induce goodness or intelligence. This simplicity of soul had its fair side: there was in his thought and speech a directness and honesty seldom permitted to statesmanship.

He could be ruthless when policy required, and was especially cruel in his efforts to spread Christianity. Yet he was a man of great kindness, many charities, warm friendships, and varied loves. He wept at the death of his sons, his daughter, and Pope Hadrian. In a poem *Ad Carolum regem* Theodulf draws a pleasant picture of the Emperor at home. On his arrival from labors his children gather about him; son Charles takes off the father's cloak, son Louis his sword; his six daughters embrace him, bring him bread, wine, apples, flowers; the bishop comes in to bless the King's food; Alcuin is near to discuss letters with him; the diminutive Eginhard runs to and fro like an ant, bringing in enormous books.[41] He was so fond of his daughters that he dissuaded them from marriage, saying that he could not bear to be without them. They consoled themselves with unlicensed amours, and bore several illegitimate children.[42] Charlemagne accepted these accidents with good humor, since he himself, following the custom of his predecessors, had four successive wives and five mistresses or concubines. His abounding vitality made him extremely sensitive to feminine charms; and his women preferred a share in him to the monopoly of any other man. His harem bore him some eighteen children, of whom eight were legitimate.[43] The ecclesiastics of the court and of Rome winked leniently at the Moslem morals of so Christian a king.

He was now head of an empire far greater than the Byzantine, surpassed, in the white man's world, only by the realm of the Abbasid caliphate. But every extended frontier of empire or knowledge opens up new problems. Western Europe had tried to protect itself from the Germans by taking them into its civilization; but now Germany had to be protected against the Norse and the Slavs. The Vikings had by 800 established a kingdom in Jutland, and were raiding the Frisian coast. Charles hastened up from Rome, built fleets and forts on shores and rivers, and stationed garrisons at danger points. In 810 the king of Jutland invaded Frisia and was repulsed; but shortly thereafter, if we may follow the chronicle of the Monk of St. Gall, Charlemagne, from his palace at Narbonne, was shocked to see Danish pirate vessels in the Gulf of Lyons.

Perhaps because he foresaw, like Diocletian, that his overreaching empire needed quick defense at many points at once, he divided it in 806 among his three sons—Pepin, Louis, and Charles. But Pepin died in 810, Charles in 811; only Louis remained, so absorbed in piety as to seem unfit to govern a rough and treacherous world. Nevertheless, in 813, at a solemn ceremony, Louis was elevated from the rank of king to that of emperor, and the old monarch uttered his *nunc dimittis*: "Blessed be Thou, O Lord God, Who hast granted me the grace to see with my own eyes my son seated on my throne!"[44] Four months later, wintering at Aachen, he was seized with a high fever, and developed pleurisy. He tried to cure himself by taking only liquids; but after an illness of seven days he died, in the forty-seventh year of his reign and the seventy-second year of his life (814). He was buried under the dome of the cathedral at Aachen, dressed in his imperial robes. Soon all the world called him Carolus Magnus, Karl der Grosse, Charlemagne; and in 1165, when time had washed away all memory of his mistresses, the Church which he had served so well enrolled him among the blessed.

3. The Carolingian Decline

The Carolingian renaissance was one of several heroic interludes in the Dark Ages. It might have ended the darkness three centuries before Abélard had it not been for the quarrels and incompetence of Charlemagne's successors, the feudal anarchy of the barons, the disruptive struggle between Church and state, and the Norman, Magyar, and Saracen invasions invited by these ineptitudes. One man, one lifetime, had not availed to establish a new civilization. The short-lived revival was too narrowly clerical; the common citizen had no part in it; few of the nobles cared a fig for it, few of them even bothered to learn how to read. Charles himself must bear some blame for the collapse of his empire. He had so enriched the clergy that the power of the bishops, now that his strong hand was lifted, outweighed that of the emperor; and he had been compelled, for military and administrative reasons, to yield a dangerous degree of independence to the courts and barons in the provinces. He had left the finances of an imperially burdened government dependent upon the loyalty and integrity of these rude aristocrats, and upon the modest income of his own lands and mines. He had not been able, like the Byzantine emperors, to build up a bureaucracy of civil servants responsible only to the central power, or capable of carrying on the government through all vicissitudes of imperial personnel. Within a generation after his death the *missi dominici*, who had spread his authority through the counties, were disbanded or ignored, and the local lords slipped out of central control. Charlemagne's reign was a feat of genius; it represented political advancement in an age and region of economic decline.

The cognomens given to his successors by their contemporaries tell the story: Louis the Pious, Charles the Bald, Louis the Stammerer, Charles the Fat, Charles the Simple. Louis the "Pious"* (814–40) was as tall and handsome as his father; modest, gentle, and gracious, and as incorrigibly lenient as Caesar. Brought up by priests, he took to heart the moral precepts that Charlemagne had practiced with such moderation. He had one wife, and no concubines; he expelled from the court his father's mistresses and his sisters' paramours, and when the sisters protested, he immured them in nunneries. He took the priests at their word, and bade the monks live up to their Benedictine rule. Wherever he found injustice or exploitation he tried to stop it, and to right what wrong had been done. The people marveled to find him always taking the side of the weak or poor.

Feeling bound by Frank custom, he divided his empire into kingdoms ruled by his sons—Pepin, Lothaire, and Louis "the German" (whom we shall call Ludwig). By his second wife, Judith, Louis had a fourth son, known to history as Charles the Bald; Louis loved him with almost grandparental infatuation, and wished to give him a share of the empire, annulling the division of 817; the three older sons objected, and began eight years of civil war against their father. The majority of the nobles and the clergy supported the rebellion; the few who seemed loyal deserted Louis in a crisis at Rothfeld (near Colmar), which thereafter was known as the *Lügenfeld*, the Field

---

* A time-ingrown mistranslation of *pius*, which means reverent, faithful, kind, gentle, and much besides.

of Lies. Louis bade his remaining supporters leave him for their own protection, and surrendered to his sons (833). They jailed and tonsured Judith,
confined young Charles in a convent, and ordered their father to abdicate
and do public penance. In a church at Soissons Louis, surrounded by thirty
bishops, and in the presence of his son and successor Lothaire, was compelled
to bare himself to the waist, prostrate himself upon a haircloth, and read
aloud a confession of crime. He took the gray garb of a penitent, and for
a year was imprisoned in a monastery. From this moment a united episcopate ruled France amid the disintegration of the Carolingian house.

Popular sentiment revolted against Lothaire's treatment of Louis. Many
nobles and some prelates responded to the appeals of Judith to annul the
deposition; a quarrel among the sons ensued; Pepin and Ludwig released
their father, restored him to his throne, and returned Judith and Charles to
his arms (834). Louis took no revenge, but forgave all. When Pepin died
(838) a new partition was made; Ludwig did not like it, and invaded Saxony.
The old Emperor again took the field, and repelled the invasion; but he fell
ill of exposure on the way back, and died near Ingelheim (840). Among his
last words were a message of forgiveness to Ludwig, and an appeal to Lothaire, now Emperor, to protect Judith and Charles.

Lothaire tried to reduce Charles and Ludwig to the rank of vassals; they
defeated him at Fonteney (841), and took at Strasbourg an oath of mutual
loyalty famous as our oldest document in French. In 843, however, they
signed with Lothaire the Treaty of Verdun, and partitioned the empire of
Charlemagne into approximately the modern states of Italy, Germany, and
France. Ludwig received the lands between the Rhine and the Elbe, Charles
received most of France and the Spanish March. Lothaire received Italy, and
the lands between the Rhine on the east and the Scheldt, Saône, and Rhone
on the west; this heterogeneous terrain, stretching from Holland to Provence, took his name as *Lothari regnum*, Lotharingia, Lothringar, Lorraine.
It had no ethnic or linguistic unity, and inevitably became the battleground
between Germany and France, repeatedly changing masters in the bloody
fluctuations of victory and defeat.

During these costly civil wars, weakening the government, man power,
wealth, and morale of Western Europe, the expanding tribes of Scandinavia
invaded France in a barbarian wave that resumed and completed the havoc
and terror of the German migrations of four centuries before. While the
Swedes were infiltrating Russia, and the Norwegians were getting a foothold
in Ireland, and the Danes were conquering England, a mixture of Scandinavians whom we may call Norse or Northmen raided the coastal and river
cities of France. After the death of Louis the Pious these raids became great
expeditions, with fleets of over a hundred vessels fully manned with oarsmen-
warriors. In the ninth and tenth centuries France endured forty-seven Norse
attacks. In 840 the raiders sacked Rouen, beginning a century of assaults

upon Normandy; in 843 they entered Nantes and slew the bishop at his altar; in 844 they sailed up the Garonne to Toulouse; in 845 they mounted the Seine to Paris, but spared the city on receiving a tribute of 7000 pounds of silver. In 846—while the Saracens were attacking Rome—the Northmen conquered Frisia, burned Dordrecht, and sacked Limoges. In 847 they besieged Bordeaux, but were repulsed; in 848 they tried again, captured it, plundered it, massacred its population, and burned it to the ground. In the following years they dealt a like fate to Beauvais, Bayeux, St.-Lô, Meaux, Évreux, Tours; we may surmise something of the terror by noting that Tours was pillaged in 853, 856, 862, 872, 886, 903, and 919.[45] Paris was pillaged in 856, again in 861, and burned in 865. At Orléans and Chartres the bishops organized armies and drove back the invaders (855); but in 856 Danish pirates sacked Orléans. In 859 a Norse fleet sailed through Gibraltar into the Mediterranean; raided towns along the Rhone as far north as Valence; crossed the Gulf of Genoa, and plundered Pisa and other Italian cities. Baffled here and there by the fortified castles of the nobles, the invaders rifled or destroyed the treasures of the unprotected churches and monasteries, often burning them and their libraries, and sometimes killing the priests and monks. In the litanies of those dark days men prayed, *Libera nos a furore Normanorum*—"Deliver us from the Norse fury!" [46] As if in a conspiracy with the Northmen, the Saracens took Corsica and Sardinia in 810, ravaged the French Riviera in 820, sacked Arles in 842, and held most of the French Mediterranean coast till 972.

What were the kings and barons doing in all this half century of destruction? The barons, themselves harassed, were loath to go to the aid of other regions, and responded weakly to appeals for united action. The kings were busy with their wars for territory or the Imperial throne, and sometimes encouraged the Norse to raid a rival's shores. In 859 Archbishop Hincmar of Reims directly accused Charles the Bald of negligence in the defense of France. Charles was succeeded (877–88) by worse weaklings—Louis II the Stammerer, Louis III, Carloman, and Charles the Fat. By the accidents of time and death all the realm of Charlemagne was again united under Charles the Fat, and the dying empire had another chance to fight for its life. But in 880 the Norse captured and burned Nijmegen, and turned Courtrai and Ghent into Norman strongholds; in 881 they burned Liége, Cologne, Bonn, Prüm, and Aachen; in 882 they captured Trier, killing the archbishop who led its defense; in the same year they took Reims, forcing Hincmar to flight and death. In 883 they seized Amiens, but retired on receiving 12,000 pounds of silver from King Carloman. In 885 they took Rouen, and sailed up to Paris in 700 ships with 30,000 men. The governor of the city, Count Odo or Eudes, and its Bishop Gozlin led a valiant resistance; for thirteen months Paris stood siege, and made a dozen sorties; finally Charles the Fat, instead of coming to the rescue, paid the Northmen 700 pounds of silver, and gave them permission to go up the Seine and winter in Burgundy, which they pillaged to their hearts' content. Charles was deposed, and died in 888. Odo was chosen king of France, and Paris, its strategic value now proved, became the seat of government.

Odo's successor, Charles the Simple (898–923), protected the region of the Seine and the Saône, but raised no hand against Norse depredations in the rest of France. In 911 he conceded to Rolf or Rollo, a Norman chieftain, the districts of Rouen, Lisieux, and Évreux, which the Normans already held; they consented to do feudal homage for them to the king, but laughed in his face as they performed the ceremony. Rollo agreed to baptism; his people followed him to the font, and slowly subsided into agriculture and civilization. So Normandy began, as a Norse conquest in France.

The simple king had found a solution for Paris at least; now the Normans themselves would block invaders entering the Seine. But elsewhere the Norse raids continued. Chartres was pillaged in 911, Angers in 919; Aquitaine and Auvergne were plundered in 923; Artois and the Beauvais region in 924. Almost at the same time the Magyars, having ravaged southern Germany, entered Burgundy in 917, crossed and recrossed the French frontier unhindered, robbed and burned the monasteries near Reims and Sens (937), passed like consuming locusts through Aquitaine (951), burned the suburbs of Cambrai, Laon, and Reims (954), and leisurely looted Burgundy. Under these repeated blows of Norse and Hun the fabric of social order in France verged upon total collapse. Cried an ecclesiastical synod at Trosle in 909:

> The cities are depopulated, the monasteries ruined and burned, the country reduced to solitude. . . . As the first men lived without law . . . so now every man does what seems good in his own eyes, despising laws human and divine. . . . The strong oppress the weak; the world is full of violence against the poor, and of the plunder of ecclesiastical goods. . . . Men devour one another like the fishes in the sea.[47]

The last Carolingian kings—Louis IV, Lothaire IV, Louis V—were well-meaning men, but they had not in their blood the iron needed to forge a living order out of the universal desolation. When Louis V died without issue (987), the nobles and prelates of France sought leadership in some other line than the Carolingian. They found it in the descendants of a marquess of Neustria significantly named Robert the Strong (d. 866). The Odo who had saved Paris was his son; a grandson, Hugh the Great (d. 956), had acquired by purchase or war almost all the region between Normandy, the Seine, and the Loire as his feudal realm, and had wielded more wealth and power than the kings. Now Hugh's son, called Hugh Capet, had inherited this wealth and power, and apparently the ability that had won them. Archbishop Adalbero, guided by the subtle scholar Gerbert, proposed Hugh Capet as king of France. He was unanimously elected (987), and that Capetian dynasty began which, in direct or collateral line, would rule France until the Revolution.

4. Letters and Arts: 814–1066

Perhaps we exaggerate the damage done by the Norse and Magyar raids; to crowd them into a page for brevity's sake darkens unduly the picture of a life in which there were doubtless intervals of security and peace. Monasteries continued to be built throughout this terrible ninth century, and were often the centers of busy industry. Rouen, despite raids and fires, grew stronger from trade with Britain; Cologne and Mainz dominated commerce on the Rhine; and in Flanders thriving centers of industry and trade developed at Ghent, Ypres, Lille, Douai, Arras, Tournai, Dinant, Cambrai, Liége, and Valenciennes.

The monastic libraries suffered tragic losses of classic treasures during the raids, and doubtless many churches were then destroyed which had opened schools on the lines of Charlemagne's decree. Libraries survived at the monasteries or churches of Fulda, Lorsch, Reichenau, Mainz, Trier, Cologne, Liége, Laon, Reims, Corbie, Fleury, St. Denis, Tours, Bobbio, Monte Cassino, St. Gall. . . . The Benedictine monastery at St. Gall was acclaimed for its writers as well as for its school and its books. Here Notker Balbulus—the Stammerer—(840–912) wrote excellent hymns and the *Chronicle of the Monk of St. Gall*; here Notker Labeo—the Thick-lipped—(950–1022) translated Boethius, Aristotle, and other classics into German; these translations, among the first productions of German prose, helped to fix the forms and syntax of the new tongue.

Even in harassed France the monastic schools were lighting up these Dark Ages. Remy of Auxerre opened a public school at Paris in 900; and in the tenth century schools were established at Auxerre, Corbie, Reims, and Liége. At Chartres, about 1006, Bishop Fulbert (960–1028) founded a school that became the most renowned in France before Abélard; there the *venerabilis Socrates*, as his pupils called him, organized the teaching of science, medicine, and classical literature as well as theology, Scripture, and liturgy. Fulbert was a man of noble devotion, saintly patience, and endless charity. To his school, before the end of the eleventh century, would come such scholars as John of Salisbury, William of Conches, Berengar of Tours, and Gilbert de la Porrée. Meanwhile, now at Compiègne, now at Laon, the Palace School established by Charlemagne reached the height of its glory under the encouragement and protection of Charles the Bald.

To this Palace School, in 845, Charles invited divers Irish and English scholars. Among them was one of the most original and audacious minds of the Middle Ages, a man whose existence casts doubt upon the advisability of retaining the phrase "Dark Ages" even for the ninth century. His name doubly revealed his origin. Johannes Scotus Eriugena—"John the Irishman, born in Erin"; we shall call him simply Erigena. Though apparently not an ecclesiastic, he was a man of wide learning, a master of Greek, a lover of Plato and the classics, and something of a wit. A story that has all the earmarks of literary invention tells how Charles the Bald, dining with him, asked him *Quid distat inter sottum et Scotum*—"What distinguishes" (literally, what separates) "a fool from an Irishman?"—to which John is said to have answered, "The table." [48] Nevertheless Charles was fond of him, attended his lectures, and probably enjoyed his heresies. John's book on the Eucharist interpreted the sacrament as symbolical, and by implication questioned the Real Presence of Christ in the consecrated bread or wine. When Gottschalk, a German monk, preached absolute predestinarianism, and therefore denied free will in man, Archbishop Hincmar asked Erigena to write a reply. The resultant treatise *De divina praedestinatione* (*c.* 851) began with a startling exaltation of philosophy: "In earnestly investigating and attempting to discover the reason of all things, every means of attaining to a pious and perfect doctrine lies in that science and discipline which the Greeks call philosophy." In effect the book denied predestination; the will is free in both God and man; God does not know evil, for if He knew it, He would be the cause of it. The answer was more heretical than Gottschalk's, and was condemned by two church councils in 855 and 859. Gottschalk was confined in a monastery till his death, but the King protected Erigena.

In 824 the Byzantine Emperor Michael the Stammerer had sent to Louis the Pious the Greek manuscript of a book, *The Celestial Hierarchy*, believed by Christian orthodoxy to have been composed by Dionysius "the Areopagite." Louis the Pious turned the manuscript over to the monastery of St. Denis, but nobody there could translate its Greek. Erigena, at the King's request, now undertook the task. The translation deeply influenced Erigena, and re-established in unofficial Christian theology the Neoplatonist picture of a universe evolving or emanating out of God through different stages or degrees of diminishing perfection, and slowly returning through different degrees back into the deity.

This became the central idea of John's own masterpiece, *De divisione naturae* (867). Here, amid much nonsense, and two centuries before Abélard, is a bold subjection of theology and revelation to reason, and an attempt to reconcile Christianity with Greek philosophy. John accepts the authority of the Bible; but since its sense is often obscure, it must be interpreted by reason —usually by symbolism or allegory. "Authority," says Erigena, "sometimes proceeds from reason, but reason never from authority. For all authority that is not approved by true reason seems weak. But true reason, since it rests on its own strength, needs no reinforcement by any authority." [49] "We should not allege the opinions of the holy Fathers . . . unless it be necessary thereby to strengthen arguments in the eyes of men who, unskillful in reasoning, yield rather to authority than to reason." [50] Here is the Age of Reason moving in the womb of the Age of Faith.

John defines Nature as "the general name for all things that are and that are not"—i.e., all objects, processes, principles, causes, and thoughts. He divides Nature into four kinds of being: (1) that which creates but is not created—viz., God; (2) that which is created and creates—viz., the prime causes, principles, prototypes, Platonic Ideas, Logos, by whose operation the world of particular things is made; (3) that which is created and does not create— viz., the said world of particular things; and (4) that which neither creates nor is created—i.e., God as the final and absorbing end of all things. "God is everything that truly is, since He makes all things and is made in all things." There was no creation in time, for this would imply a change in God. "When we hear that God made everything, we ought to understand nothing other than that God is in all things—i.e., subsists as the essence of all things." [51] "God Himself is comprehended by no intellect; neither is the secret essence of anything created by Him comprehensible. We perceive only accidents, not essences" [52]—phenomena, not noumena, as Kant would say. The sensible qualities of things are not inherent in the things themselves, but are produced by our forms of perception. "When we hear that God wishes, loves, chooses, sees, hears . . . we should think nothing else than that His ineffable essence and power are being expressed by meanings co-natural with us" (congenial to our nature) "lest the true and pious Christian be silenced concerning the Creator, and dare say nothing of Him for the instruction of simple souls." [53] Only for a like purpose may we speak of God as masculine or feminine; "He" is neither.[54] If we take "Father" as meaning the creative substance or essence of all things, and "Son" as the divine Wisdom according to which all things are made or governed, and "Spirit" as the life or vitality of creation, we may think of God as a Trinity. Heaven and hell are not places, but conditions of soul; hell is the misery of sin, heaven is the happiness of virtue and the ecstasy of the divine vision (the perception of divinity) revealed in all things to the soul that is pure.[55] The Garden of Eden was such a state of soul, not a place on the earth.[56] All things are immortal: animals too, like men, have souls that pass back, after death, into the God or creative spirit from whom they emanated.[57] All history is a vast outward flow of creation by emanation, and an irresistible inward tide that finally draws all things back into God.

There have been worse philosophies than this, and in ages of illumination. But the Church properly suspected it as reeking with heresy. In 865 Pope Nicholas I demanded of Charles the Bald that he should either send John to Rome for trial, or dismiss him from the Palace School, "that he may no longer give poison to those who seek for bread." [58] We do not know the outcome. William of Malmesbury [59] relates that "Johannes Scotus came to England and our monastery, as report says; was pierced with the iron pens of the boys whom he instructed," and died from the results; probably the tale was a schoolboy's wishful dream. Philosophers like Gerbert, Abélard, and Gilbert de la Porrée were secretly influenced by Erigena, but for the most part he was forgotten in the chaos and darkness of the age. When in the thirteenth century his book was exhumed from oblivion it was condemned by the Council of Sens (1225), and Pope Honorius III ordered that all copies should be sent to Rome and there be burned.

In these disturbed centuries French art marked time. Despite Charlemagne's example, the French continued to build their churches on the basilican plan. About 996 William of Volpiano, an Italian monk and architect, became head of the Norman abbey of Fécamp. He brought with him many of the devices of the Lombard and Romanesque style; and apparently it was his pupils who built the great Romanesque abbey church of Jumièges (1045-67). In 1042 another Italian, Lanfranc, entered the Norman monastery at Bec, and soon made it a vibrant intellectual center. Students flocked to it in such number that new buildings had to be provided; Lanfranc designed them, perhaps with some more expert help. Not a stone remains of his structures; but the Abbaye aux Hommes at Caen (1077-81) survives as a testimony to the powerful Romanesque style developed in Normandy by Lanfranc and his fellows.

All over France and Flanders in the eleventh century new churches were built, and artists adorned them with murals, mosaics, and statuary. Charlemagne had directed that church interiors should be painted for the instruction of the faithful; the palaces at Aachen and Ingelheim were decorated with frescoes; and doubtless many churches followed these examples. The last fragments of the Aachen frescoes were destroyed in 1944; but similar murals survive in the church of St. Germain at Auxerre. These differ only in scale from the style and figures in the manuscript illumination of the time. At Tours, in the reign of Charles the Bald, a great Bible was written and painted by the monks, and presented to the King; it is now No. 1 of the Latin codices in the Bibliothèque Nationale at Paris. Still more beautiful is the "Lothaire" Gospel also made at this time by the monks of Tours. The monks of Reims, in the same ninth century, produced the famous "Utrecht" Psalter —108 vellum leaves containing the Psalms and the Apostles' Creed, exuberantly illustrated with a veritable menagerie of animals and a museum of tools and occupations. In these lively pictures a lusty realism transforms the once stiff and conventional figures of miniature art.

5. The Rise of the Dukes: 987-1066

The France that Hugh Capet ruled (987-996) now stood out as a separate nation, no longer acknowledging the suzerainty of the Holy Roman Empire;

the unification of western continental Europe achieved by Charlemagne was never restored, except momentarily by Napoleon and Hitler. But Hugh's France was not our France; Aquitaine and Burgundy were virtually independent duchies, and Lorraine would for seven centuries attach itself to Germany. It was a France heterogeneous in race and speech: northeastern France was more Flemish than French, and had a large German element in its blood; Normandy was Norse; Brittany was Celtic and aloof, dominated by refugees from Britain; Provence was still in stock and speech a Roman-Gallic "province"; France near the Pyrenees was Gothic; Catalonia, technically under the French monarchy, was Goth-alonia. The Loire divided France into two regions of diverse cultures and tongues. The task of the French monarchy was to unify this diversity, and make a nation from a dozen peoples. The task would take 800 years.

To improve the chances of an orderly succession, Hugh, in the first year of his reign, had had his son Robert crowned co-king. Robert the Pious (996–1031) is accounted a "mediocre king," [60] perhaps because he shunned the glory of war. Having some dispute over boundaries with the Emperor Henry II of Germany, he arranged a meeting with him, exchanged presents, and reached a peaceable agreement. Like Louis IX, Henry IV, and Louis XVI, Robert had a kindly feeling for the weak and the poor, and protected them as well as he could from the unscrupulous strong. He offended the Church by marrying his cousin Bertha (998), bore excommunication patiently therefor and the taunts of those who thought her a witch; finally he separated from her and lived unhappily forever afterward. At his death, we are told, "There was great mourning and intolerable grief." [61] A war of succession followed between his sons; the elder, Henry I (1031–60), won, but only by the help of Robert, Duke of Normandy. When that long conflict (1031–9) ended, the monarchy was so impoverished in money and men that it could no longer prevent the dismemberment of France by powerful and independent lords.

About the year 1000, through the gradual appropriation of surrounding territory by great landowners, France was divided into seven main principalities ruled by counts or dukes: Aquitaine, Toulouse, Burgundy, Anjou, Champagne, Flanders, and Normandy. These dukes or counts were in nearly all cases the heirs of chieftains or generals to whom estates had been granted, for military or administrative services, by the Merovingian or Carolingian kings. The king had become dependent upon these magnates for mobilizing troops and protecting frontier provinces; after 888 he no longer legislated for the whole realm, or gathered taxes from it; the dukes and counts passed laws, levied taxes, waged war, judged and punished, as practically sovereign powers on their estates, and merely offered the king a formal homage and limited military service. The authority of the king in law, justice, and finance was narrowed to his own royal domain, later called the Île de France—the region of the Saône and middle Seine from Orléans to Beauvais and from Chartres to Reims.

Of all the relatively independent duchies, Normandy grew most rapidly in authority and power. Within a century after its cession to the Northmen, it had become—perhaps through proximity to the sea and its position between England and Paris—the most enterprising and adventurous province in France. The Norse were now enthusiastic Christians, had great monasteries and abbey schools, and reproduced with a recklessness that would soon drive Norman youth to carve new kingdoms out of old states. The progeny of the Vikings made strong governors, not too finicky about their morals, nor palsied with scruples, but able to rule with a firm hand a turbulent population of Gauls, Franks, and Norse. Robert I (1028–35) was not yet duke of Normandy when in 1026 his eye was caught by Harlette, daughter of a tanner in Falaise. She became his cherished mistress according to an old Danish custom, and soon presented him with a son known to his contemporaries as William the Bastard, to us as William the Conqueror. Weighed down by his sins, Robert in 1035 left Normandy on a penitential pilgrimage to Jerusalem. Before going he called his chief barons and prelates to him and said to them:

> By my faith, I will not leave ye lordless. I have a young bastard who will grow, please God, and of whose good qualities I have great hope. Take him, I pray you, for lord. That he was not born in wedlock matters little to you; he will be none the less able in battle . . . or to render justice. I make him my heir, and I hold him seized, from this present, of the whole duchy of Normandy.[62]

Robert died en route; for a time nobles ruled for his son; but soon William began to issue orders in the first person. A rebellion tried to unseat him, but he put it down with dignified ferocity. He was a man of craft and courage and farseeing plans, a god to his friends, a devil to his foes. He bore with good humor many quips about his birth, and signed himself, now and then, *Gulielmus Nothus*—William the Bastard; but when he besieged Alençon, and the besieged hung hides over their walls in allusion to his grandfather's trade, he cut off the hands and feet, and gouged out the eyes, of his prisoners, and shot these members from his catapults into the town. Normandy admired his brutality and iron rule, and prospered. William moderated the exploitation of the peasantry by the nobles, and appeased these with fiefs; he dominated and presided over the clergy, and appeased them with gifts. He attended devoutly to his religious duties, and shamed his father by unprecedented marital fidelity. He fell in love with the beautiful Matilda, daughter of Baldwin, Count of Flanders; he was not disconcerted by her two children and her living but separated husband; she sent William away with insults, saying that she "would rather be a veiled nun than marry a bastard"; [63] he persevered, won her, and married her despite the denunciations of the clergy.

He deposed Bishop Malger and Abbot Lanfranc for condemning the marriage, and burned down part of the abbey of Bec in his rage. Lanfranc persuaded Pope Nicholas II to validate the union; and William, in atonement, built at Caen the famous Norman Abbaye aux Hommes. By this marriage William allied himself with the Count of Flanders; in 1048 he had already signed an entente with the king of France. Having so guarded and garnished his flanks, he proceeded, at the age of thirty-nine, to conquer England.

CHAPTER XX

The Rise of the North

566-1066

I. ENGLAND: 577–1066

1. Alfred and the Danes: 577–1016

AFTER the battle of Deorham (577) the Anglo-Saxon-Jute conquest of England met with only minor resistance; and soon the invaders divided the country. The Jutes organized a kingdom in Kent; the Angles formed three kingdoms—Mercia, Northumberland, and East Anglia; the Saxons another three in Wessex, Essex, and Sussex—i.e., West, East, and South Saxony. These seven little kingdoms, and others smaller still, provided the "history of England" until King Egbert of Wessex, by arms or subtlety, united most of them under his rule (829).

But even before this new Angle-land was molded by the Saxon king, those Danish invasions had begun which were to rack the island from sea to sea, and threaten its nascent Christianity with a wild and letterless paganism. "In the year 787," says the Anglo-Saxon Chronicle, "came three ships to the West Saxon shores . . . and they slew folk. These were the first ships of Danish men that sought land of Engle folk." In 793 another Danish expedition raided Northumberland, sacked the famous monastery of Lindisfarne, and murdered its monks. In 794 the Danes entered the Wear and pillaged Wearmouth and Jarrow, where the learned Bede had labored half a century before. In 838 the raids attacked East Anglia and Kent; in 839 a pirate fleet of 350 vessels moored in the Thames, while their crews pillaged Canterbury and London. In 867 Northumberland was conquered by a force of Danes and Swedes; thousands of "English" men were slain, monasteries were sacked, libraries were scattered or destroyed. York and its neighborhood, whose school had given Alcuin to Charlemagne, were reduced to destitution and ignorance. By 871 most of England north of the Thames was subject to the invaders. In that year a Danish army under Guthrum marched southward to attack Reading, the Wessex capital; Ethelred the king and his young brother Alfred met the Danes at Ashdown and won; but in a second engagement at Merton Ethelred was mortally wounded, and the English fled.

Alfred mounted the throne of West Saxony at the age of twenty-two (871). Asser describes him as then *illiteratus*, which could mean either illiterate or Latinless.[1] He was apparently epileptic, and suffered a seizure at his wedding feast; but he is pictured as a vigorous hunter, handsome and graceful, and surpassing his brothers in wisdom and martial skill. A month after his accession he led his little army against the Danes at Wilton, and was so badly defeated that to save his throne he had to buy peace from the foe; but in 878 he won a decisive victory at Ethandun (Edington). Half the Danish host crossed the Channel to raid weakened France; the rest, by the Peace of Wedmore, agreed to confine themselves to northeastern England in what came to be called the Danelaw.

Alfred, says the not quite reliable Asser, led his army into East Anglia "for the sake of plunder," conquered the land, and—perhaps to unify England against the Danes—made himself king of East Anglia and Mercia as well as of Wessex. Then, like a lesser Charlemagne, he turned to the work of restoration and government. He reorganized the army, built a navy, established a common law for his three kingdoms, reformed the administration of justice, provided legal protection for the poor, built or rebuilt cities and towns, and erected "royal halls and chambers with stone and wood" for his growing governmental staff.[2] An eighth of his revenue was devoted to relief of the poor; another eighth to education. At Reading, his capital, he established a palace school, and gave abundantly to the educational and religious work of churches and monasteries. He recalled sadly how in his boyhood "the churches stood filled with treasures and books . . . before they had all been ravaged and burned" by the Danes; now "so clean was learning decayed among English folk that very few there were . . . that could understand their rituals in English, or translate aught out of Latin." [3] He sent abroad for scholars—for Bishop Asser from Wales, for Erigena from France, and for many others—to come and instruct his people and himself. He mourned that he had had so little time for reading, and he now gave himself like a monk to pious and learned studies. He still found reading difficult; but "night and day he commanded men to read to him." Recognizing, almost before any other European, the rising importance of the vernacular tongues, he arranged to have certain basic books rendered into English; and he himself laboriously translated Boethius' *Consolation of Philosophy*, Gregory's *Pastoral Care*, Orosius' *Universal History*, and Bede's *Ecclesiastical History of England*. Again like Charlemagne, he gathered the songs of his people, taught them to his children, and joined the minstrels of his court in singing them.

In 894 a fresh invasion of Danes reached Kent; the Danes of the Danelaw sent them reinforcements; and the Welsh—Celtic patriots still unconquered by the Anglo-Saxons—signed an alliance with the Danes. Alfred's son Edward fell upon the pirate camp and destroyed it, and Alfred's new navy dispersed the Danish fleet (899). Two years later the King died, having lived only fifty-two years, and reigned for twenty-eight. We cannot compare him with a giant like Charlemagne, for the area of his enterprise was small; but in his moral qualities—his piety, unassuming rectitude, temperance, patience, courtesy, devotion to his people, anxiety to further education—he offered to the English nation a model and stimulus that it gratefully received and soon forgot. Voltaire admired him perhaps immoderately: "I do not think that there ever was in the world a man more worthy of the regard of posterity than Alfred the Great." [4]

Toward the end of the tenth century the Scandinavian attack on England was resumed. In 991 a force of Norwegian Vikings under Olaf Tryggvesson raided the English coast, plundered Ipswich, and defeated the English at Maldon. Unable to resist further, the English under King Ethelred (978– 1013, called the Redeless—counselless—because he refused the advice of his nobles) bought off the Danes with successive gifts of 10,000, 16,000, 24,000, 36,000, and 48,000 pounds of silver, which were raised by the first general taxes levied in England—the shameful and ruinous Danegeld. Ethelred, seeking foreign aid, negotiated an alliance with Normandy, and married Emma, daughter of the Norman Duke Richard I; from that union would spring much history. Believing or pretending that the Danes of England were plotting to kill him and the nation's Witenagemot or parliament, Ethelred secretly ordered a general massacre of the Danes everywhere in the island (1002). We do not know how thoroughly the order was carried out; probably all male Danes of arms-bearing age in England were slaughtered, and some women; among these was the sister of King Sweyn of Denmark. Swearing revenge, Sweyn invaded England in 1003, and again in 1013, this time with all his forces. Ethelred's nobles deserted him, he fled to Normandy, and Sweyn was master and king of England. When Sweyn died (1014) Ethelred renewed the struggle; the nobles again deserted him, and made their peace with Sweyn's son Cnut (1015). Ethelred died in besieged London; his son Edmund "Ironside" fought bravely, but was overwhelmed by Cnut at Assandun (1016). Cnut was now accepted by all England as its king, and the Danish Conquest was complete.

2. Anglo-Saxon Civilization: 577–1066

The Conquest was only political; Anglo-Saxon institutions, speech, and ways had in six centuries sunk such roots that to this day neither the government nor the character nor the language of the English can be understood without them. In the newless intervals between war and war, crime and crime, there had been a reorganization of tillage and trade, a resurrection of literature, a slow formation of order and law.

History gives no ground for the delusion that Anglo-Saxon England was a paradise of free peasants living in democratic village communities. The leaders of the Anglo-Saxon hosts appropriated the land; by the seventh century a few families owned two thirds of the soil of England;[5] by the eleventh century most towns were included in the property of a thane (noble), a bishop, or the king. During the Danish invasions many peasants exchanged ownership for protection; by 1000 the bulk of them paid rent in produce or labor to some lord.[6] There were *tun-moots* or town meetings, and *folk-moots* or *hundred-moots* that served as assemblies and courts for a shire; but only landowners were allowed to attend these gatherings; and after the eighth century they declined in authority and frequency, and were largely replaced by the manorial courts of the lords. The government of England lay essentially in the national Witenagemot ("meeting of the wise")—a relatively small assemblage of thanes, bishops, and the leading ministers of the Crown. Without the consent of this incipient Parliament no English king could be chosen or sustained, or add a rood to the personal estates from which he derived his regular revenues; without it he could not legislate or tax or judge or wage war or make peace.[7] The only resource of the monarchy against this aristocracy lay in an informal alliance of throne and Church. The English state before and after the Norman Conquest depended upon the clergy for public education, social order, national unity, even for political administration. St. Dunstan, Abbot of Glastonbury, became chief counselor under kings Edmund (940–6) and Edred (946–55). He defended the middle and lower classes against the nobles, boldly criticized monarchs and princes, was exiled by King Edwig (955–9), was recalled by Edgar (959–75), and secured the crown for Edward the Martyr (975–8). He built St. Peter's Church at Glastonbury, encouraged education and art, died (988) as Archbishop of Canterbury, and was revered as England's greatest saint before Thomas à Becket.

In this centrifugal government national law developed slowly, and the old Germanic law, modified in phrase and circumstance, sufficed. Compurgation, wergild, and ordeal survived, but trial by combat was unknown. The wergild varied instructively in Anglian law: the fine or composition-money for killing a king was 30,000 thrimsas ($13,000); a bishop, 15,000; a thane or a priest, 2,000; a ceorl or free peasant, 266. By Saxon law a man paid one or two shillings for inflicting a wound an inch long, thirty shillings for slicing off an ear; it should be added, however, that a shilling could buy a sheep. By the laws of Ethelbert an adulterer was obliged to pay the husband a fine and buy him another wife.[8] Any person who resisted a court order was declared an "out-law"; his goods were forfeited to the king, and anyone might kill him with impunity. In some cases wergild was not admitted, and severe punishments were inflicted: enslavement, flogging, castration, amputation—of hands, feet, upper lip, nose, or ear—and death by hanging, beheading, burning, stoning, drowning, or precipitation into an abyss.[9]

The economy, like the law, was primitive, and far less developed than in Roman Britain. Much work had been done in clearance and drainage, but England in the ninth century was still half forest, heath, or fen; and wild beasts—bears, boars, wolves—still lurked in the woods. The farms were tilled mostly by bondmen or slaves. Men might fall into slavery through debt or crime; wives and children could be sold into slavery by husbands or fathers in need; and all the children of a slave, even if begotten by freemen, were slaves. The owner might kill his slave at will. He might make a female slave pregnant, and then sell her. The slave could not enter a suit at court. If a stranger slew him, the modest wergild went to his master. If he fled and was caught he might be flogged to death.[10] The main commerce of Bristol was in slaves. Nearly all the population was rural; towns were hamlets, and cities were towns.* London, Exeter, York, Chester, Bristol, Gloucester, Oxford, Norwich, Worcester, Winchester were small, but grew rapidly after Alfred's time. When Bishop Mellitus came to preach in London in 601 he found only "a scanty and heathen population" [11] in what had been a metropolis in Roman days. In the eighth century the city grew again as a strategic point commanding the Thames; under Canute it became the national capital.

Industry usually worked for a local market; weaving and embroidery, however, were more advanced, and exported their products to the Continent. Transport was difficult and dangerous; foreign commerce was slight. The use of cattle as a medium of exchange survived till the eighth century, but in that century several kings issued a silver coinage of shillings and pounds. In tenth-century England four shillings could buy a cow, six an ox.[12] Wages were commensurately low. The poor lived in wooden thatched huts on a vegetarian diet; wheat bread and meat were for the well-to-do, or a Sunday feast. The rich adorned their rude castles with figured hangings, warmed themselves with furs, made their garments gay with embroidery, and brightened their persons with gems.

Manners and morals were not as prim or refined as in some later periods of English history. We hear much about rudeness, coarseness, brutality, lying, treachery, theft, and other hardy perennials; the buccaneering Normans of 1066, including some bastards, professed to be amazed at the low moral and cultural level of their victims. The moist climate persuaded the Anglo-Saxons to heavy eating and hard drinking, and the "ale feast" was their notion—like ours—of a convention or a holiday. St. Boniface, with picturesque exaggeration, described the eighth-century English, "both Christians and pagans, as refusing to have legitimate wives, and continuing to live in lechery and adultery after the manner of neighing horses and braying asses"; [13] and in 756 he wrote to King Ethelbald:

> Your contempt for lawful matrimony, were it for chastity's sake, would be laudable; but since you wallow in luxury, and even in adultery with nuns, it is disgraceful and damnable. . . . We have heard that almost all the nobles of Mercia follow your example, desert their lawful wives, and live in guilty intercourse with adulteresses and nuns. . . . Give heed to this: if the nation of the Angles, . . . despising lawful matrimony, gives free indulgence to adultery, a race ignoble and scorning God must necessarily issue from such unions, and will destroy the country by their abandoned manners.[14]

In the earlier centuries of Anglo-Saxon rule the husband could divorce his wife at will, and remarry. The Synod of Hertford (673) denounced this custom, and gradually the influence of the Church promoted the stability of unions. Women were held in high honor, though this did not preclude their occasional

---

* Many English towns have kept Anglo-Saxon suffixes—*tun* (town), *ham* (home), *wick* (house or creek), *thorp* (village), *burh* (borough, burg).

enslavement. They received little book education, but found this no handicap in attracting and influencing men. Kings patiently wooed proud women, and consulted their wives on public policy.[15] Alfred's daughter Ethelfled, as regent and queen, gave Mercia for a generation effective and conscientious government. She built cities, planned military campaigns, and captured Derby, Leicester, and York from the Danes. "From the difficulties experienced in her first labor," says William of Malmesbury, "she ever afterward refused the embraces of her husband, protesting that it was unbecoming the daughter of a king to give way to a delight which, after a time, produced such unpleasant consequences." [16] It was in this period (*c.* 1040) that there lived in Mercia, as wife of its ruling Earl Leofric, the lady Godgifa, who, as Godiva, played an attractive role in legend, and earned a statue in Coventry.*

Education, like everything else, suffered from the Anglo-Saxon Conquest, and slowly recovered after the conversion of the conquerors. Benedict Biscop opened a monastic school at Wearmouth about 660; Bede was one of its graduates. Archbishop Egbert established at York (735) a cathedral school and library that became the chief seat of secondary education in England. These and other schools made England in the second half of the eighth century the leader of European learning north of the Alps.

The fine devotion of the monastic educators shines out in the greatest scholar of his time, the Venerable Bede (673–735). He summed up his life with modest brevity:

> Bede, the servant of Christ, a priest of the monastery of the blessed apostles Peter and Paul, which is at Wearmouth and Jarrow. Who, being born in the territory of that monastery, was delivered up by my kinsfolk, when I was seven years of age, to be brought up by the most reverend abbot Benedict [Biscop]; and from that time spending all the days of my life in the same monastery, I have applied all my diligence to the study of the Scriptures; and observing the regular discipline, and keeping the daily service of singing in the church, I have taken delight always either to learn, or to teach, or to write. . . . In the nineteenth year of my life I was made deacon; in my thirtieth I became a priest . . . and from that time until the fifty-ninth year of my age I have employed myself upon Holy Scripture, and in these following works . . .[17]

—all in Latin. They included Biblical commentaries, homilies, a chronology of world history, treatises on grammar, mathematics, science, and theology, and above all, the *Historia ecclesiastica gentis Anglorum,* or *Church History of the English Nation* (731). Unlike most monastic histories, this is no dry chronicle. Perhaps, towards the end, it is too heavy with miracles, and always it is innocently credulous, as befitted a mind immured from the age of seven; nevertheless it is a clear and captivating narrative, rising now and then to a simple eloquence, as in the description of the Anglo-Saxon Conquest.[18] Bede had an intellectual

---

* Leofric, in the legend, agreed to relieve the town of a burdensome tax if she would ride naked through the streets. All the world knows the rest of the story.

conscience; he took great pains with chronology, and is generally accurate; he specified his sources, sought firsthand evidence, and quoted pertinent and available documents. "I would not," he said, "that my children should read a lie" [19]— meaning, we hope, the 600 pupils whom he taught. He died four years after penning the above autobiography; and all the tenderness and faith of medieval piety are in its concluding lines:

> And I beseech Thee, merciful Jesus, that to whom Thou hast of Thy goodness given sweetly to drink in the words of the knowledge of Thee, Thou wilt also vouchsafe, in Thy loving kindness, that he may one day come to Thee, the fountain of all wisdom, and stand forever before Thy face.

Bede notes that five languages were spoken in his England: English, British (Celtic), Irish, Pict (Scotch), and Latin. "English" was the language of the Angles, but it differed little from Saxon, and was intelligible to Franks, Norwegians, and Danes; these five peoples spoke varieties of German, and English grew out of German speech. As early as the seventh century there was a considerable Anglo-Saxon literature. We must judge it largely from fragments, for most of it perished when Christianity brought in the Latin script (replacing the runic characters of Anglo-Saxon writing), when the Danish Conquest destroyed so many libraries, and when the Norman Conquest almost swamped the English language with French words. Moreover, many of these Anglo-Saxon poems were pagan, and had been transmitted orally through generations of "gleemen" or minstrels who were a bit loose in life and speech, and whom monks and priests were forbidden to hear. It was probably an eighth-century monk, however, who wrote one of the oldest extant Anglo-Saxon fragments—a verse paraphrase of Genesis, not quite as inspired as the original. Interpolated into the poem is the translation of a German narrative of the Fall; here the verse comes to life, largely because Satan is represented as a defiant and passionate rebel; perhaps Milton found here a hint for his Lucifer. Some of the Anglo-Saxon poems are elegies; so "The Wanderer" tells of happy days gone by in the baronial hall; now the lord is dead, "all this firm-set earth becomes empty," and "sorrow's crown of sorrow is remembering happier things"; [20] not even Dante improved the expression of this idea. Usually these old poems sing blithely and lustily of war; the "Lay of the Battle of Maldon" (c. 1000) sees only heroism in the English defeat; and the old warrior Byrhtwold, standing over his slain lord, "taught courage" to the overwhelmed Saxons in words presaging Malory:

> Thought shall be the harder, heart the keener, mood shall be the more, as our might lessens. Here our prince lies low, they have hewn him to death! Grief and sorrow forever on the man that leaves this war-play! I am old of years, but hence I will not go; I think to lay me down by the side of my lord, by the side of the man I cherished. [21]

The longest and noblest of the Anglo-Saxon poems, *Beowulf*, was composed, presumably in England, in the seventh or eighth century, and is preserved in a British Museum manuscript dating back to 1000. Its 3183 lines are apparently the complete work. The verse is rhymeless but alliterative antistrophic rhythm, in a West Saxon dialect quite unintelligible to us today. The story seems childish: Beowulf, prince of the Geats (Goths?) in southern Sweden, crosses the sea to free the Danish King Hrothgar from the dragon Grendel; he overcomes Grendel, and even Grendel's mother; sails back to Geatland, and reigns justly for fifty years. A third dragon, a firedrake, now appears, and ravages the land of the Geats; Beowulf attacks it, and is seriously wounded, his comrade Wiglaf comes to his aid, and together they kill the beast. Beowulf dies of his wound, and is burned on a funeral pyre. The tale is not so naïve as this sounds; the dragons of medieval literature represent the wild beasts that lurked in the woods about the towns of Europe; the terrified imagination of the people might be forgiven for conceiving them fantastically; and it gratefully wove legends about the men who conquered such animals, and made the hamlets safe.

Certain passages of the poem are incongruously Christian, as if some kindly monkish editor had sought to preserve a heathen masterpiece by inserting here and there a pious line. But the tone and incidents are purely pagan. It was life and love and battle on the earth that interested these "fair women and brave men," not some strifeless' paradise beyond the grave. At the outset, when the Danish king Scyld is buried in the Viking style, in a boat pushed crewless out to sea, the author adds: "Men cannot tell for a truth who received that burden." But it was not a gay paganism. A somber tone pervades the poem, and enters even into the feasting in Hrothgar's hall. Through the lilt and sigh of the flowing lines we catch the plaint of the gleeman's harp.

> Then Beowulf sat down on a seat by the wall . . . he talked of his wound, of the hurt sore unto death; he knew well that he had ended his days. . . . Then men bold in battle rode about the burial mound; They were minded to utter their grief, to lament the King, to make a chant and speak of the man; they exalted his heroic life, and praised his valorous deeds with all their strength. . . . They said that among the kings of the world he was the mildest of men and most kindly, most gentle to his people, and most eager for praise. . . . Thus it is fitting that a man should extol his friendly lord . . . and should love him heartily, when he must needs depart from his body and pass away.[22]

Beowulf is probably the oldest extant poem in the literature of Britain; but Caedmon's (d. 680) is the oldest name. We know him only through a pretty passage in Bede. In the monastery of Whitby, says the *Ecclesiastical History*,[23] was a simple brother who found it so hard to sing that whenever his turn came to chant he fled to some hiding place. One night as he lay asleep in his stable lair, it seemed to him that an angel appeared and said: "Caedmon, sing me something!" The monk protested that he could not; the angel commanded; Caedmon tried, and was startled at his success. In the morning he recalled the song, and sang it; thereafter he lisped in numbers, and turned Genesis, Exodus, and the Gospels into verse "put together," says Bede, "with very great sweetness and pricking of the heart." Nothing remains of them except a few lines translated into Latin by Bede. A year later Cynewulf (b. *o.* 750), minstrel at a Northum-

brian court, tried to realize the story by versifying divers religious narratives—
"Christ," "Andreas," "Juliana"; but these works, contemporary with *Beowulf*,
are by comparison dead with rhetoric and artifice.

Literary prose comes later than poetry in all literatures, as intellect matures
long after fancy blooms; men talk prose for centuries "without knowing it,"
before they have leisure or vanity to mold it into art. Alfred is the first clear
figure in the prose literature of England; his translations and prefaces were eloquent through simple sincerity; and it was he who, by dint of editing and adding,
transformed the "Bishop's Roll," kept by the clerks of Winchester cathedral,
into the most vigorous and vivid sections of the *Anglo-Saxon Chronicle*—the
first substantial work of English prose. His teacher Asser may have written most
of the *Life of Alfred*; perhaps it is a later compilation (*c.* 974); [24] in any event
it is an early instance of the readiness with which Englishmen used English instead
of Latin for works of history or theology, while the Continent still blushed to
write such dignities in the "vulgar" speech.

Even amid poetry and war men and women found time and spirit to give
form to significance, and beauty to things of use. Alfred established a school of
art at Athelney, brought to it from all quarters monks skilled in arts and crafts,
and "continued, during his frequent wars," says Asser, "to teach his workers in
gold, and his artificers of all kinds." [25] Dunstan, not content with being both a
statesman and a saint, worked cleverly in metal and gold, was a good musician,
and built a pipe organ for his cathedral at Glastonbury. Art work in wood, metal,
and cloisonné enamel was carried on; gem-cutters joined with carvers to make
the jeweled and sculptured crosses of Ruthwell and Bewcastle (*c.* 700); a famous
equestrian statue of King Cadwallo (d. 677) was cast in brass near Ludgate;
women made coverlets and tapestries and embroideries "of a most delicate
thread"; [26] the monks of Winchester illuminated with radiant color a tenth-
century benedictional. Winchester itself and York built stone cathedrals as early
as 635; Benedict Biscop brought the Lombard style to England from the church
that he built at Wearmouth in 674; and Canterbury rebuilt in 950 the cathedral
that had survived from Roman times. We know from Bede that Benedict Biscop's
church was adorned with paintings made in Italy, "so that all who entered, even
if ignorant of letters, whichever way they turned, should either contemplate the
ever-lovely aspect of Christ and His saints ... or, having the Last Judgment before
their eyes, might remember to examine themselves more strictly." [27] In general
the seventh century saw an exuberance of construction in Britain; the Anglo-
Saxon Conquest was complete, the Danish had not begun; and architects, who
had heretofore built in wood, now had the resources and spirit to raise great
shrines in stone. Yet it must be confessed that Benedict imported his architects,
glassmakers, and goldsmiths from Gaul; Bishop Wilfrid brought sculptors and
painters from Italy to decorate his seventh-century church at Hexham; and the
beautifully illuminated Gospel Book of Lindisfarne (*c.* 730) was the work of
Irish monks transplanted by the eremitical or missionary zeal to that bleak isle off
the Northumberland coast. The coming of the Danes ended this brief renascence;
and not until the sound establishment of Cnut's power did English architecture
resume its climb to majesty.

3. Between Conquests: 1016–1066

Cnut was more than a conqueror; he was a statesman. His early reign was tarnished with cruelty: he banished the children of Edmund Ironsides, and had Edmund's brother murdered to forestall an Anglo-Saxon restoration. But then, noting that the widow and sons of King Ethelred were alive at Rouen, he cut many knots by offering Emma his hand in marriage (1017). She was thirty-three, he twenty-three. She consented, and at one stroke Cnut secured a wife, an alliance with Emma's brother the Duke of Normandy, and a safe throne. From that moment his reign became a blessing for England. He brought under discipline the disorderly nobles who had broken the unity and spirit of England. He protected the island from further invasion, and gave it twelve years of peace. He accepted Christianity, built many churches, raised a shrine at Assandun to commemorate the Anglo-Saxons, as well as the Danes, who had fought there, and himself made a pilgrimage to Edmund's tomb. He promised to follow the existing laws and institutions of England, and kept his word with two exceptions: he insisted that county government, which had been debased by autocratic nobles, should be under his own appointees; and he replaced the archbishop with a lay minister as chief counselor to the Crown. He developed an administrative staff and civil service that gave unprecedented continuity to the government. After the insecure early years of his rule, nearly all his appointees were Englishmen. He labored constantly in the tasks of state, and repeatedly visited every part of his kingdom to supervise the administration of justice and the execution of the laws. He came in as a Dane, and died as a Englishman. He was King of Denmark as well as of England, and in 1028 he became also King of Norway; but it was from Winchester that he ruled this triple realm.

The Danish Conquest continued that long process of foreign invasion and racial mixture which culminated in the Norman Conquest and finally produced the English people. Celt and Gaul, Angle and Saxon and Jute, Dane and Norman, mingled their blood, in marriage or otherwise, to transform the undistinguished and uninitiative Briton of Roman days into the vocal buccaneers of Elizabeth's time, and the silent world conquerors of later centuries. The Danes, like the Germans and the Norse, brought into England an almost mystic love of the sea, a willingness to accept its treacherous invitation to adventure and trade in distant lands. Culturally, the Danish invasions were a blight. Architecture marked time; the art of illumination decayed from 750 to 950; and the intellectual progress so promoted by Alfred was checked, even as in Gaul Norse raids were canceling the labors of Charlemagne.

Cnut might have repaired more of the damage his people had wrought had he been granted a longer life. But men wear out rapidly in war or government. Cnut died in 1035, aged forty. Norway at once threw off the Danish yoke; Harthacnut, Cnut's son and appointed heir, had all he could do to protect Denmark against Norwegian invasion; another son, Harald Harefoot, ruled England for five years, then died; Harthacnut ruled it for two years, and passed away (1042). Before his death he summoned from Normandy the surviving son of Ethelred and Emma, and recognized this Anglo-Saxon stepbrother as heir to the English throne.

But Edward the Confessor (1042–66) was as much of a foreigner as any Dane. Carried to Normandy by his father at the age of ten, he had passed thirty years at the Norman court, brought up by Norman nobles and priests, and trained to a guileless piety. He brought to England his French speech, customs, and friends. These friends became high officials and prelates of the state, received royal grants, built Norman castles in England, showed their scorn for English language and ways, and began the Norman Conquest a generation before the Conqueror.

Only one Englishman could compete with them in influencing the mild and malleable King. Earl Godwin, governor of Wessex, and first counselor of the realm under Cnut, Harald, and Harthacnut, was a man of both wealth and wisdom, a master of patient diplomacy, of convincing eloquence and administrative skill; the first great lay statesman in English history. His experience in the government gave him an ascendancy over the King. His daughter Edith became Edward's wife, and might have made Godwin grandfather to a king; but Edward begot no children. When Godwin's son Tostig married Judith, daughter of the count of Flanders, and Godwin's nephew Sweyn became ruler of Denmark, the Earl had forged by marriages a triple alliance that made him the strongest man in northern Europe, far more powerful than his King. Edward's Norman friends roused him to jealousy; he deposed Godwin; the Earl fled to Flanders, while his son Harold went to Ireland and raised an army against the Confessor (1051). The English nobles, resenting the Norman ascendancy, invited Godwin to return, and pledged him the support of their arms. Harold invaded England, defeated the King's troops, ravaged and plundered the southwest coast, and joined his father in an advance up the Thames. The populace of London rose to acclaim them; the Norman officials and prelates fled; a Witenagemot of English nobles and bishops gave Godwin a triumphant reception; and Godwin resumed his confiscated property and his political power (1052). A year later, exhausted with tribulation and victory, he died.

Harold was appointed Earl of Wessex, and succeeded in some measure to his father's power. He was now thirty-one, tall, handsome, strong, gallant, reckless; merciless in war, generous in peace. In a whirlwind of bold campaigns he conquered Wales for England, and presented the head of the Welsh chieftain Gruffydd to the pleased and horrified King (1063). In a gentler phase of his impetuous career he poured out funds to build the abbey church at Waltham (1060), and to support the college that grew out of the cathedral school. All England beamed upon the romantic youth.

The great architectural event of Edward's reign was the beginning (1055) of Westminster Abbey. While living in Rouen he had become familiar with the Norman style; now, in commissioning the abbey that was to be the shrine and tomb of England's genius, he bade or let it be designed in Norman Romanesque, on the same lines as the magnificent abbey church which had been started only five years before at Jumièges; here again was a Norman conquest before William. Westminster Abbey was the beginning of an architectural efflorescence that would give England the finest Romanesque buildings in Europe.

In that abbey Edward was laid to rest early in the fateful year 1066. On January 6 the assembled Witenagemot elected Harold king. He had hardly been crowned when news came that William, Duke of Normandy, claimed the throne and was preparing war. Edward, said William, had in 1051 promised to bequeath him the English crown in gratitude for thirty years of protection in Normandy. Apparently the promise had been made,[28] but Edward, regretting or forgetting it, had, shortly before his death, recommended Harold as his successor; in any case such a promise had no validity unless approved by the Witan. But, said William, Harold, on a visit to him at Rouen (date now unknown), had accepted knighthood from him, had become William's "man," owed him submission according to feudal law, and had promised to recognize and support him as heir to Edward's throne. Harold admitted this pledge.[29] But again no oath of his could bind the English nation; the representatives of that nation had freely chosen him for its king; and Harold now resolved to defend that choice. William appealed to the Pope; Alexander II, counseled by Hildebrand, condemned Harold as a usurper, excommunicated him and his adherents, and declared William the lawful claimant of the English throne; he blessed William's proposed invasion, and sent him a consecrated banner and a ring containing, within a diamond, a hair of St. Peter's head.[30] Hildebrand was glad to set a precedent for the papal disposition of thrones and deposition of kings; ten years later he would apply the precedent to Henry IV of Germany; and it would come in handy in 1213 with King John. Lanfranc, Abbot of Bec, joined William in calling the people of Normandy—indeed of all countries—to a holy war against the excommunicated king.

The sins of Harold's wild youth were now visited upon his benevolent maturity. His brother Tostig, long since exiled by the Witan, had not been recalled by Harold come to power. Tostig now allied himself with William, raised an army in the north, and persuaded King Harald Hardrada of Norway to join him by promising him the English throne. In September, 1066, as William's armada of 1400 vessels sailed from Normandy, Tostig and

Hardrada invaded Northumberland. York surrendered to them, and Hardrada was there crowned King of England. Harold rushed up with what troops he had, and defeated the northern invaders at Stamford Bridge (September 25); in that battle Tostig and Hardrada died. Harold moved south with a diminished force far too small to pit against William's host, and every adviser bade him wait. But William was burning and harrowing southern England, and Harold felt bound to defend the soil that he once had ravaged but now loved. At Senlac, near Hastings, the two armies met (October 14), and fought for nine hours. Harold, his eye pierced by an arrow, fell blinded with blood, and was dismembered by Norman knights: one cut off his head, another a leg, another scattered Harold's entrails over the field. When the English saw their captain fallen they fled. So great were the butchery and chaos that the monks who were later commissioned to find Harold's body could not discover him until they led to the scene Edith Swansneck, who had been his mistress. She identified her lover's mutilated body, and the fragments were buried in the church at Waltham that he had built. On Christmas Day, 1066, William I was crowned King of England.

II. WALES: 325–1066

Wales had been won for Rome by Frontinus and Agricola A.D. 78. When the Romans retired from Britain, Wales resumed its freedom, and suffered its own kings. In the fifth century western Wales was occupied by Irish settlers; later Wales received thousands of Britons fleeing from the Anglo-Saxon conquerors of their island. The Anglo-Saxons stopped at the Welsh barrier, and called the unsubdued people Wealhas—"foreigners." The Irish and the Britons found in Wales a kindred Celtic stock, and soon the three groups mingled as Cymri—"fellow countrymen"; this became their national name, and Cymru their name for their land. Like most Celtic peoples— Bretons, Cornish, Irish, the Gaels of northern Scotland—they based their social order almost wholly on the family and the clan, and so jealously that they resented the state, and looked with unappeasable distrust upon any individual or people of alien blood. Their clan spirit was balanced by uncalculating hospitality, their indiscipline by bravery, their hard life and climate by music and song and loyal friendship, their poverty by an imaginative sentiment that made every girl a princess, and every second man a king.

Only next to kings stood the bards. They were the soothsayers, historians, and royal counselors, as well as the poets, of their people. Two among them left enduring names—Taliesin and Aneurin, both of the sixth century; there were hundreds more; and the tales they spun crossed the Channel to Brittany to reach polished form in France. The bards constituted a poetic clerical caste; no one was admitted to their order except after strict training in the lore of their race. The candidate for admission was called a *mabinog*; the material he studied was *mabinogi*; hence the name *Mabinogion* for such of their tales as have survived.[31] In their present form they are not older than the fourteenth century, but probably they go back to this period, when Christianity had not taken Wales. They are primitively simple, paganly animistic, and weird with strange animals and marvelous events; overcast with a somber certainty of exile, defeat, and death, yet in a mood of gentleness all the world away from the lust and violence of Icelandic *Eddas*, Norse sagas, and the *Nibelungenlied*. In the loneliness of Welsh mountains there grew a romantic literature of devotion to the nation, to woman, and, later, to Mary and Jesus, that shared in begetting chivalry, and those wondrous tales of Arthur and his valorous-amorous knights sworn to "break the heathen and uphold the Christ."

Christianity came to Wales in the sixth century, and soon thereafter opened schools in the monasteries and cathedrals. The learned Bishop Asser, who served King Alfred as secretary and biographer, came from the town and cathedral of St. David's in Pembrokeshire. These Christian shrines and settlements bore the brunt of pirate attacks from Normandy, until King Rhodri the Great (844–78) drove them off and gave the island a vigorous dynasty. King Hywel the Good (910–50) united all Wales, and provided it with a uniform code of laws. Gruffydd ap Llywelyn (1039–63) was too successful; when he defeated Mercia, the nearest of the English counties, Harold, the future king of England, proclaimed a war of preventive defense, and conquered Wales for Britain (1063).

III. IRISH CIVILIZATION: 461–1066

At the death of St. Patrick, and until the eleventh century, Ireland was divided into seven kingdoms: three in Ulster, the others Connaught, Leinster, Munster, Meath. Normally these kingdoms fought among themselves, for lack of transport to wider spheres of strife; but from the third century onward we hear of Irish raids and settlements on west British coasts. The chroniclers call these raiders Scots—apparently a Celtic word for wanderers; throughout this period "Scot" means Irishman. War was endemic: till 590 the women, till 804 the monks and priests, were required to fight alongside more ordinary warriors.[32] A code of laws essentially similar to the "barbarian" codes of the Continent was administered by *brehons*—highly trained lawyer-judges who, as early as the fourth century, taught law schools and wrote legal treatises in the Gaelic tongue.[33] Ireland, like Scotland, missed conquest by Rome, and therefore missed the boon of Roman law and orderly government; law never quite succeeded in replacing vengeance with judgment, or passion with discipline. Government remained basically tribal, and only at moments achieved a national unity and scope.

The unit of society and economy was the family. Several families made a sept, several septs a clan, several clans a tribe. All members of a tribe were supposedly descended from a common ancestor. In the tenth century many families prefixed *Ui* or *O'* (grandson) to a tribal name to indicate their descent; so the O'Neills claimed descent from Niall Glundubh, King of Ireland in 916. Many others assumed their father's name, merely prefixing *Mac* —i.e., son. Most of the land in the seventh century was owned in common by clans or septs; [34] private property was limited to household goods; [35] but by the tenth century individual ownership had spread. Soon there was a small aristocracy holding large estates, a numerous class of free peasants, a small class of renters, a still smaller class of slaves.[36] Materially and politically the Irish in the three centuries after the coming of Christianity (461–750) were more backward than the English; culturally they were probably the most advanced of all the peoples north of the Pyrenees and the Alps.

This strange imbalance had many sources: the influx of Gallic and British scholars fleeing from the Germanic invasions of the fifth century, the growth of commercial contacts with Britain and Gaul, and the exemption of Ireland, before the ninth century, from foreign attack. Monks and priests and nuns opened schools of every scope and degree; one at Clonard, established in 520, had 3000 students (if we may believe patriotic historians); [37] there were others at Clonmacnois (544), Clonfert (550), and Bangor (560). Several gave a twelve-year course leading to the doctorate in philosophy, and including Biblical studies, theology, the Latin and Greek classics, Gaelic grammar and literature, mathematics and astronomy, history and music, medicine and law.[38] Poor scholars whose parents could not support them were maintained by public funds, for most students were preparing for the priesthood, and the Irish made every sacrifice to further that vocation. These schools continued the study of Greek long after knowledge of that language had almost disappeared from the other countries of Western Europe. Alcuin studied at Clonmacnois; in Ireland John Scotus Erigena learned the Greek that made him the marvel of the court of Charles the Bald in France.

The mood and literature of the age favored legend and romance. Here and there some minds turned to science, like the astronomer Dungal, or the geometer Fergil, who taught the sphericity of the earth. About 825 the geographer Dicuil reported the discovery of Iceland by Irish monks in 795, and exemplified the midnight day of the Irish summer by noting that one could then find light enough to pick the fleas from his shirt.[39] Grammarians were numerous, if only because Irish prosody was the most complicated of its time. Poets abounded, and held high state in society; usually they combined the functions of teacher, lawyer, poet, and historian. Grouped in bardic schools around some leading poet, they inherited many of the powers and prerogatives of the pre-Christian Druid priests. Such bardic schools flourished without a break from the sixth to the seventeenth century, usually supported by grants of land from Church or state.[40] The tenth century had four nationally known poets: Flann MacLonain, Kenneth O'Hartigan, Eochaid O'Flainn, and that MacLiag whom King Brian Boru made archollamh, or poet laureate.

In this age the sagas of Ireland took literary form. Much of their material antedated Patrick, but had been transmitted orally; now it was put into a running mixture of rhythmic prose and ballad verse; and though it has reached us only in manuscripts later than the eleventh century, it is the poets of this period who made it literature. One cycle of sagas commemorated the mythical ancestors of the Irish people. A "Fenian" or "Ossianic" cycle recounted in stirring stanzas the adventures of the legendary hero Finn Mac-Cumhail and his descendants the Fianna or Fenians. Most of these poems were ascribed by tradition to Finn's son Ossian, who, we are informed, lived 300 years, and died in St. Patrick's time after giving the saint a piece of his pagan mind. An "Heroic" cycle centered around the old Irish king Cuchulain, who encounters war and love in a hundred lusty scenes. The finest saga of this series told the story of Deirdre, daughter of Felim, King Conor's leading bard. At her birth a Druid priest prophesies that she will bring many sorrows to her land of Ulster; the people cry out "Let her be slain," but King Conor protects her, rears her, and plans to marry her. Day by day she grows in loveliness. One morning she sees the handsome Naoise playing ball with other youths; she retrieves a misthrown ball and hands it to him, and "he pressed my hand joyously." The incident touches off her ripe emotions, and she begs her handmaid, "O gentle nurse, if you wish me to live, take a message to him, and tell him to come and talk with me secretly tonight." Naoise comes, and drinks in her beauty to intoxication. On the following night he and his two brothers, Ainnle and Ardan, take the willing Deirdre out of the palace and across the sea to Scotland. A Scotch king falls in love with her, and the brothers hide her in the highlands. After some time King Conor sends a message: he will forgive them if they will come back to Erin. Naoise, longing for his native soil and youthful haunts, consents, though Deirdre warns him and foretells treachery. After reaching Ireland they are attacked by Conor's soldiers; the brothers fight bravely, but are all killed; and Deirdre, insane with grief, flings herself upon the ground, drinks the blood of her dead lover, and sings a strange dirge:

> On a day that the nobles of Alba [Scotland] were feasting...
> To the daughter of the lord of Duntrone
> Naoise gave a secret kiss.
> He sent her a frisky doe,
> A deer of the forest with a faun at its foot,
> And he went aside to her on a visit
> While returning from the host of Inverness.
> But when I heard that,

My head filled with jealousy,
I launched my little skiff upon the waves;
I did not care whether I died or lived.
They followed me, swimming,
Ainnle and Ardan, who never uttered falsehood,
And they turned me in to land again,
Two who would subdue a hundred.
Naoise pledged me his word of truth,
And he swore in presence of his weapons, three times,
That he would never cloud my countenance again
Till he should go from me to the army of the dead.
Alas! if she were to hear this night
That Naoise was under cover in the clay,
She would weep most certainly,
And I, I would weep with her sevenfold.

The oldest version of "Deirdre of the Sorrows" ends with a powerful simplicity: "There was a large rock near. She hurled her head at the stone, so that she broke her skull and was dead." [41]

Poetry and music were near allied in Ireland, as elsewhere in medieval life. Girls sang as they wove or spun or milked the cow; men sang as they plowed the field or marched to war; missionaries strummed the harp to muster an audience. The favorite instruments were the harp, usually of thirty strings, plucked with the finger tips; the *timpan*, an eight-string violin played with plectrum or bow; and the bagpipe, slung from the shoulder and inflated by the breath. Giraldus Cambrensis (1185) judged the Irish harpers the best he had ever heard—a high tribute from music-loving Wales.

The finest product of Irish art in this period was not the famous Ardagh chalice (*c.* 1000)—an astonishing union of 354 pieces of bronze, silver, gold, amber, crystal, cloisonné enamel, and glass; it was the "Book of Kells"— the Four Gospels in vellum, done by Irish monks at Kells in Meath, or on the isle of Iona, in the ninth century, and now the prize possession of Trinity College, Dublin. Through the slow intercommunication of monks across frontiers, Byzantine and Islamic styles of illumination entered Ireland, and for a moment reached perfection there. Here, as in Moslem miniatures, human or animal figures played an insignificant role; none was worth half an initial. The spirit of this art lay in taking a letter, or a single ornamental motive, out of a background of blue or gold, and drawing it out with fanciful humor and delight till it almost covered the page with its labyrinthine web. Nothing in Christian illuminated manuscripts surpasses the Book of Kells. Gerald of Wales, though always jealous of Ireland, called it the work of angels masquerading as men. [42]

As this golden age of Ireland had been made possible by freedom from the Germanic invasions that threw the rest of Latin Europe back by many centuries, so it was ended by such Norse raids as in the ninth and tenth centuries annulled in France and England the progress so laboriously made by Charlemagne and Alfred. Perhaps the news had reached Norway and Denmark— both still pagan—that the Irish monasteries were rich in gold, silver, and jewelry, and that the political fragmentation of Ireland forestalled united resistance. An experimental raid came in 795, did little damage, but confirmed the rumor of this unguarded prey. In 823 greater invasions plundered Cork and Cloyne, destroyed the monasteries of Bangor and Moville, and massacred the clergy. Thereafter raids came almost every year. Sometimes brave little armies drove them back, but they returned, and sacked monasteries everywhere. Bands of Norse invaders settled near the coast, founded Dublin, Limerick, and Waterford, and levied tribute from the northern half of the island. Their King Thorgest made St. Patrick's Armagh his pagan capital, and enthroned his heathen wife on the altar of St. Kieran's Church at Clonmacnois.[43] The Irish kings fought the invaders separately, but at the same time they fought one another. Malachi, King of Meath, captured Thorgest and drowned him (845); but in 851 Olaf the White, a Norwegian prince, established the kingdom of Dublin, which remained Norse till the twelfth century. An age of learning and poetry gave way to an era of ruthless war, in which Christian as well as pagan soldiers pillaged and fired monasteries, destroyed ancient manuscripts, and scattered the art of centuries. "Neither bard nor philosopher nor musician," says an old Irish historian, "pursued his wonted profession in the land." [44]

At last a man appeared strong enough to unite the kingdoms into an Irish nation. Brian Borumha or Boru (941–1014) was brother to King Mahon of Munster, and headed the Dalgas clan. The brothers fought a Danish army near Tipperary (968) and destroyed them, giving no quarter; then they captured Limerick, and despatched every Northman they could find. But two kinglets—Molloy of Desmond and Donovan of Hy Carbery—fearing that the marching brothers would absorb their realms, entered into a league with the immigrant Danes, kidnaped Mahon, and slew him (976). Brian, now king, again defeated the Danes, and killed Molloy. Resolved to unify all Ireland, and rejecting no means to this end, Brian allied himself with the Danes of Dublin, overthrew with their aid the king of Meath, and was acknowledged monarch of all Ireland (1013). Enjoying peace after forty years of war, he rebuilt churches and monasteries, repaired bridges and roads, founded schools and colleges, established order and repressed crime; an imaginative posterity illustrated the security of this "King's peace" by the story —often occurring elsewhere—how a lovely lass, richly jeweled, traveled across the country alone and unharmed. Meanwhile the Norse in Ireland raised another army, and marched against the aging king. He met them at Clontarf, near Dublin, on Good Friday, April 23, 1014, and defeated them; but his son Murrogh was killed in the battle, and Brian himself was slain in his tent.

For a time the harassed country recovered the luxuries of peace. In the eleventh century art and literature revived; the Book of Leinster and the Book of Hymns almost equaled the Book of Kells in splendor of illumination; historians and scholars flourished in the monastic schools. But the Irish spirit had not yet been tamed. The nation again divided into hostile kingdoms, and spent its strength in civil war. In 1172 a handful of adventurers from Wales and England found it a simple matter to conquer—another matter to rule—the "Island of Doctors and Saints."

IV. SCOTLAND: 325–1066

Late in the fifth century a tribe of Gaelic *Scotti* from the north of Ireland migrated to southwestern Scotland, and gave their name first to a part, then to all, of the picturesque peninsula north of the Tweed. Three other peoples contested the possession of this ancient "Caledonia": the Picts, a Celtic tribe, established above the Firth of Forth; the Britons, refugees from the Anglo-Saxon invasion of Britain, settled between the River Derwent and the Firth of Clyde; and the Angles or English between the River Tyne and the Firth of Forth. From all these the Scottish nation was formed: English in speech, Christian in religion, as fiery as the Irish, as practical as the English, as subtle and imaginative as any Celt.

Like the Irish, the Scotch were loath to relinquish their kinship organization, to replace the clan by the state. The intensity of their class conflicts was rivaled only by their proud loyalty to their clan, and their tenacious resistance to foreign foes. Rome failed to conquer them; on the contrary, neither Hadrian's Wall between the Solway and the Tyne (A.D. 120), nor that of Antoninus Pius, sixty miles farther north between the firths of Forth and Clyde (140), nor the campaigns of Septimius Severus (208) or Theodosius (368) availed to end the periodical invasion of Britain by the hungry Picts. In 617 the Saxons under Edwin, King of Northumbria, captured the hill stronghold of the Picts, and named it Ed(w)inburgh. In 844 Kenneth Mac-Alpin united the Picts and Scots under his crown; in 954 the tribes recaptured Edinburgh, and made it their capital; in 1018 Malcolm II conquered Lothian (the region north of the Tweed), and merged it with the realm of the Picts and Scots. Celtic supremacy seemed assured; but the Danish invasions of England drove thousands of "English" into south Scotland, and poured a strong Anglo-Saxon element into the Scottish blood.

Duncan I (1034–40) gathered all four peoples—Picts, Scots, Celtic British, and Anglo-Saxons—into one kingdom of Scotland. Duncan's defeat by the English at Durham gave an opening to his general Macbeth, who claimed the throne because his wife Gruoch was granddaughter of Kenneth III. Macbeth murdered Duncan (1040), reigned for seventeen years, and was murdered by Duncan's son Malcolm III. Of seventeen kings who ruled Scotland from 844 to 1057, twelve died by assassination. It was a violent age of bitter struggle for food and water, freedom and power. In those dour years Scotland had little time for the frills and graces of civilization; three centuries were to pass before Scottish literature would begin. Norse raiders captured the Orkney Islands, the Faroes, the Shetlands, and the Hebrides; and Scotland lived ever under the threat of conquest by those fearless Vikings who were spreading their power and seed over the Western world.

V. THE NORTHMEN: 800–1066

1. *The Kings' Saga*

Apparently the Northmen were Teutons whose ancestors had moved up through Denmark and across the Skaggerak and Kattegat into Sweden and Norway, displacing a Celtic population that had displaced a Mongolian people akin to the Laplanders and Eskimos.[45] An early chieftain, Dan Mikillati, gave his name to Denmark—Dan's march or province; the ancient tribe of Suiones, described by Tacitus as dominating the great peninsula, left their name in Sweden (Sverige), and in many kings called Sweyn; Norway (Norge) was simply the northern way. *Skane*, the name given to Sweden by the elder Pliny, became in Latin *Scandia*, and begot the *Scandinavia* that now covers three nations of kindred blood and mutually intelligible speech. In all three countries the fertility of women, or the imagination of men, outran the fertility of the soil; the young or discontent took to their boats and prowled about the coasts for food, slaves, wives, or gold; and their hunger acknowledged no laws and no frontiers. The Norwegians overflowed into Scotland, Ireland, Iceland, and Greenland; the Swedes into Russia; the Danes into England and France.

Life's brevity forbids the enumeration of gods or kings. Gorm (860–935) gave Denmark unity; his son Harald Bluetooth (945–85) gave it Christianity; Sweyn Forkbeard (985–1014) conquered England, and made Denmark for a generation one of the great powers of Europe. King Olaf Skottkonung (994–1022) made Sweden Christian, and Uppsala his capital. In 800 Norway was a conglomeration of thirty-one principalities, separated by mountains, rivers, or fjords, and each ruled by a warrior chief. About 850 one such leader, Halfdan the Black, from his capital at Trondheim, subdued most of the others, and became Norway's first king. His son Harald Haarfager (860–933) was challenged by rebellious chieftains; the Gyda whom he wooed refused to marry him until he should conquer all Norway; he vowed never to clip or comb his hair till it was done; he accomplished it in ten years, married Gyda and nine other women, cut his hair, and received his distinguishing name—the Fair-haired.[46] One of his many sons, Haakon the Good (935–61), ruled Norway well for twenty-seven years; "peace lasted so long," complained a Viking warrior, "that I was afraid I might come to die of old age, within doors on a bed." [47] Another Haakon—"the Great Earl"—governed Norway ably for thirty years (965–95); but in his old age he offended the "bonders," or free peasants, by taking their daughters as concubines, and sending them home after a week or two. The bonders called in Olaf Tryggvesson, and made him king.

Olaf, son of Tryggve, was a great grandson of Harald of the Fair Hair. He was "a very merry frolicsome man," said Snorri of Iceland, "gay and social, very generous, and finical in his dress . . . stout and strong, the handsomest of men, excelling in bodily exercises every Northman that ever was heard of." [48] He could run across the oars outside his ship while men were rowing; could juggle three sharp-pointed daggers, could cast two spears at once, and "could cut equally well with either hand." [49] Many a quarrel he had, and many an adventure. While in the British Isles he was converted to Christianity, and became its merciless advocate. When he was made King of Norway (995) he destroyed pagan temples, built Christian churches, and continued to live in polygamy. The bonders opposed the new religion fiercely, and demanded that Olaf should make sacrifice to Thor as in the ancient ritual; he agreed, but proposed to offer Thor the most acceptable sacrifice—the leading bonders themselves; whereupon they became Christians. When one of them, Rand, persisted in paganism, Olaf had him bound, and forced a serpent down his throat by burning the serpent's tail; the viper made its way through Rand's stomach and side, and Rand died.[50] Olaf proposed marriage to Sigrid, Queen of Sweden; she accepted, but refused to abandon her pagan faith; Olaf struck her in the face with his glove, saying, "Why should I care to have thee, an old faded woman, a heathen jade?" "This may some day be thy death," said Sigrid. Two years later the kings of Sweden and Denmark, and Earl Eric of Norway, made war against Olaf; he was defeated in a great naval battle near Rügen; he leaped full-armed into the sea, and never rose again (1000). Norway was divided among the victors.

Another Olaf, called the Saint, reunited Norway (1016), restored order, gave righteous judgment, and completed the conversion of the land to Christianity. "He was a good and very gentle man," says Snorri, "of little speech, and openhanded, but greedy of money," and slightly addicted to concubines.[51] One bonder who preferred paganism had his tongue cut out, another his eyes.[52] The bonders conspired with King Cnut of Denmark and England, who came with fifty ships and drove Olaf from Norway (1028); Olaf returned with an army and fought for his throne at Stiklestad; he was defeated, and died of his wounds (1030); on the site posterity dedicated a cathedral to him as Norway's patron saint. His son Magnus the Good (1035–47) recaptured the kingdom, and gave it good laws and government; his grandson

Harald the Stern (1047–66) ruled Norway with merciless justice until the year when William of Normandy took England.

About 860 a band of Northmen from Norway or Denmark rediscovered Iceland, and were not quite displeased to find it so similar to their own land in mists and fjords. Norwegians fretting under the new absolutism of Harald Haarfager migrated to the island in 874; and by 934 it was as thickly settled as it would ever be before the Second World War. Each of the four provinces had its *thing*, or assembly; in 930 an *allthing*, or united parliament, was established—one of the earliest institutions in the history of representative government, making Iceland then the only fully free republic in the world. But the same vigor and independence of spirit that motivated the migration and molded this parliament limited the effectiveness of the common government and laws; powerful individuals, rooted on their great estates, became the law of their lands, and soon revived in Iceland the feuds that had made Norway so difficult for her kings. In the year 1000 the *allthing* formally adopted Christianity; but King Olaf the Saint was scandalized to hear that the Icelanders continued to eat horseflesh and practice infanticide. Perhaps because the winter nights were long and cold, a literature of myths and sagas grew up that apparently excelled in quantity and quality the like tales told in the homelands of the Norse.

Sixteen years after the rediscovery of Iceland, a Norwegian skipper, Gunnbjörn Ulfsson, sighted Greenland. About 985 Thorwald and his son Eric the Red established a Norwegian colony there. In 986 Bjerne Herjulfsson discovered Labrador; and in the year 1000 Leif, son of Eric the Red, landed on the American continent; we do not know whether it was Labrador or Newfoundland or Cape Cod. Leif Ericsson wintered in "Vinland" (wine land), and then returned to Greenland. In 1002 his brother Thorwald, with thirty men, spent a year in Vinland. An interpolation, not later than 1395, in the "Saga of Olaf Tryggvesson," by Snorri Sturluson (1179-1241), tells of five separate expeditions by Norsemen to continental America between 985 and 1011. In 1477 Christopher Columbus, by his own account, sailed to Iceland, and studied its traditions of the new world.[53]

2. Viking Civilization *

Social order among the Norse, as elsewhere, was based upon family discipline, economic co-operation, and religious belief. "In him who well considers," says a passage in *Beowulf*, "nothing can stifle kinship." [54] Un-

---

* *Viking* is from Old Norse *vik*, a creek or fjord; *vik* appears in this sense in Narvik, Schleswig, Reykjavik, Berwick, Wicklow, etc. *Vikingr* meant one who raided the country adjoining the fjords. "Viking civilization" will here be used as meaning the culture of the Scandinavian peoples in the "Viking Age"—A.D. 700–1100.

wanted children were exposed to die; but once accepted, the child received a judicious compound of discipline and love. There were no family names; each son merely added his father's name to his own: Olaf Haraldsson, Magnus Olafsson, Haakon Magnusson. Long before Christianity came to them, the Scandinavians, in naming a child, poured water over him as a symbol of admission into the family.

Education was practical: girls learned the arts of the home, including the brewing of ale; boys learned to swim, ski, work wood and metal, wrestle, row, skate, play hockey (from Danish *hoek*, hook), hunt, and fight with bow and arrow, sword or spear. Jumping was a favorite exercise. Some Norwegians, fully armed and armored, could jump above their own height, or swim for miles; some could run faster than the fleetest horse.[55] Many children learned to read and write; some were trained in medicine or law. Both sexes sang lustily; a few in either sex played musical instruments, usually the harp; we read in the *Elder Edda* how King Gunnar could play the harp with his toes, and charm snakes with its tones.

Polygamy was practiced by the rich till the thirteenth century. Marriages were arranged by the parents, often through purchase; the free woman could veto such an arrangement,[56] but if she married against the will of her parents her husband was declared an outlaw, and might legally be slain by her relatives. A man could divorce his wife at will; but unless he gave good reason he too was subject to assassination by her family. Either mate might divorce the other for dressing like the opposite sex—as when the wife wore breeches, or the man wore a shirt open at the breast. A husband might kill with impunity— i.e., without provoking a blood feud—any man whom he caught in illicit relations with his wife.[57] Women worked hard, but they remained sufficiently delectable to stir men on to kill one another for their sakes; and men dominant in public life were, as everywhere, recessive at home. In general the position of woman was higher in pagan than in later Christian Scandinavia;[58] she was the mother not of sin but of strong brave men; she had one-third—after twenty years of marriage one-half—right in all wealth acquired by her husband; she was consulted by him in his business arrangements, and mingled freely with men in her home.

Work was held in honor, and all classes shared in it. Fishing was a major industry, and hunting was a necessity rather than a sport. Picture the power of will and toil that cleared the forests of Sweden, and tamed to tillage the frozen slopes of Norway's hills; the wheat fields of Minnesota are the offspring of American soil crossed with Norwegian character. Large estates were few; Scandinavia has excelled in the wide distribution of land among a free peasantry. An unwritten insurance softened disaster: if a farmer's house burned down, his neighbors joined him in rebuilding it; if his cattle were destroyed by disease or an "act of God," they contributed to his flocks a number of animals equal to half his loss. Nearly every Northman was a craftsman, especially skilled in wood. The Norse were backward in using iron, which came to them only in the eighth century; but then they made a variety of strong and handsome tools, weapons, and ornaments of bronze, silver, and gold;[59] shields, damascened swords, rings, pins, harness were often objects of beauty and pride. Norse shipwrights built boats and warships not larger, but apparently sturdier, than those of antiquity; flat-bottomed for steadiness, sharp in the bow to ram the enemy; four to six feet deep, sixty to one hundred and eighty feet long; propelled partly by a sail, mostly by oars—ten, sixteen or sixty to a side; these simple vessels carried Norse explorers, traders, pirates, and warriors down the rivers of Russia to the Caspian and Black Seas, and over the Atlantic to Iceland and Labrador.

The Vikings divided themselves into *jarls* or earls, *bondi* or peasant proprietors, and thralls or slaves; and (like the guardians in Plato's *Republic*) they sternly taught their children that each man's class was a decree of the gods, which only the faithless would dare to change.[60] Kings were chosen from royal blood, the provincial governors from the *jarls*. Along with this frank acceptance of monarchy and aristocracy as natural concomitants of war and agriculture, went a remarkable democracy by which the landowners acted as legislators and judges in a local *hus-thing* or meeting of householders, a village *mot*, a provincial *thing* or assembly, and a national *allthing* or parliament. It was a government of laws and not merely of men; violence was the exception, judgment the rule. Feud revenge incarnadined the sagas, but even in that Viking Age of blood and iron the wergild was replacing private vengeance, and only the sea-rovers were men with no law but victory or defeat. Harsh punishments were used to persuade to order and peace men hardened by the struggle with nature; adulterers were hanged, or trodden to death by horses; incendiaries were burned at the stake; parricides were suspended by the heels next to a live wolf similarly hung; rebels against the government were torn asunder by horses driven apart, or were dragged to death behind a wild bull;[61] perhaps in these barbarities the law had not yet replaced, but only socialized, revenge. Even piracy at last gave way to law; the robbers subsided into traders, and substituted wits for force. Much of the sea law of Europe is Norse in origin, transmitted through the Hanseatic League.[62] Under Magnus the Good (1035–47) the laws of Norway were inscribed on a parchment called from its color the "Grey Goose"; this still survives, and reveals enlightened edicts for the control of weights and measures, the policing of markets and ports, the state succor of the sick and the poor.[63]

Religion helped law and the family to turn the animal into a citizen. The gods of the Teutonic pantheon were not mythology to the Norse, but actual divinities feared or loved, and intimately connected with mankind by a thousand miracles and amours. In the wonder and terror of primitive souls all the forces and major embodiments of nature had become personal deities; and the more powerful of these required a sedulous propitiation that did not stop short of human sacrifice. It was a crowded Valhalla: twelve gods and twelve goddesses; divers giants (Jotuns), fates (Norns), and Valkyries—messengers and ale-bearers of the gods; and a sprinkling of witches, elves, and trolls. The gods were magnified mortals, subject to birth, hunger, sleep, sickness, passion, sorrow, death; they excelled men only in size, longevity, and power. Odin (German Woden), the father of all the gods, had lived near the Sea of Azov in Caesar's time; there he had built Asgard, or the Garden of the Gods, for his family and his counselors. Suffering from land hunger, he conquered north Europe. He was not unchallenged nor omnipotent; Loki scolded him like a fishwife,[64] and Thor quite ignored him. He wandered over the earth seeking wisdom, and bartered an eye for a drink at wisdom's well; then he invented letters, taught his people writing, poetry, and the arts, and gave them laws. Anticipating the end of his earthly life, he called an assembly of Swedes and Goths, wounded himself in nine places, died, and returned to Asgard to live as a god.

In Iceland Thor was greater than Odin. He was the god of thunder, war, labor, and law; the black clouds were his frowning brows, the thunder was his voice, the lightning was his hammer flung from the skies. The Norse poets, perhaps already as skeptical as Homer, had much fun with him, like the Greeks with Hephaestus or Heracles; they represented him in all sorts of predicaments and toils; nevertheless he was so loved that nearly every fifth Icelander usurped his name—Thorolf, Thorwald, Thorstein. . . .

Great in legend, minor in worship, was Odin's son Baldur, "dazzling in form and feature . . . mildest, wisest, and most eloquent" of the gods;[65] the early missionaries were tempted to identify him with Christ. He had a terrible dream of his impending death, and told the gods of it; the goddess Frigga exacted an oath from all minerals, animals, and plants that none would injure him; his glorious body thereafter repelled all hurtful objects, so that the gods amused themselves by hurling at him stones and darts, axes and swords; all weapons were turned away, and left him scatheless. But Frigga had neglected to pry an oath of innocuousness from "a little shrub called mistletoe," as being too feeble to hurt any man; Loki, the irreverent mischief-maker among the gods, cut off a twig of it, and persuaded a blind deity to throw it at Baldur; pierced with it, Baldur expired. His wife Nep died of a broken heart, and was burned on the same pyre with Baldur and his gorgeously caparisoned horse.[66]

The Valkyries—"Choosers of the Slain"—were empowered to decree the death date of each soul. Those men who died basely were thrust down into the realms of Hel, the goddess of the dead; those who died in battle were led by the Valkyries to Valhalla—"Hall of the Chosen"; there, as favorite sons of Odin, they were reincarnated in strength and beauty to spend their days in manly battle and their nights in drinking ale. But (says late Norse mythology) the time came when the Jotuns—monstrous demons of disorder and destruction—declared war upon the gods, and fought with them to mutual extinction. In this Twilight of the Gods all the universe fell to ruin: not merely sun and planets and stars, but, at the last, Valhalla itself, and all its warriors and deities; only Hope survived—that in the movement of slow time a new earth would form, a new heaven, a better justice, and a higher god than Odin or Thor. Perhaps that mighty fable symbolized the victory of Christianity, and the hardy blows that two Olafs struck for Christ. Or had the Viking poets come to doubt—and bury—their gods?

It was a marvelous mythology, second only to the Greek in fascination. The oldest form in which it has come down to us is in those strange poems to which error has given the name of *Edda*.* In 1643 a bishop discovered in the Royal Library of Copenhagen a manuscript containing some old Icelandic poems; by a double mistake he called them the *Edda* of Saemund the Wise (*c.* 1056–1133), an Icelandic scholar-priest. It is now generally agreed that the poems were composed in Norway, Iceland, and Greenland by unknown authors at unknown dates between the eighth and twelfth centuries, that Saemund may have collected, but did not write, them, and that *Edda* was not their name. But time sanctions error as well as theft, and compromises by calling the poems the *Poetic* or *Elder Edda*. Most of them are narrative ballads of the old Scandinavian or Germanic heroes or gods. Here for the first time we meet with Sigurd the Volsung and other heroes, heroines, and villains destined to take more definite form in the *Volsungasaga* and the *Nibelungenlied*. The most powerful of the *Edda* poems is the *Voluspa*, wherein the prophetess Völva describes with somber and majestic imagery the creation of the world, its coming destruction, and its ultimate regeneration. In quite different style is "The High One's Lay," in which Odin, after meeting all sorts of conditions and men, formulates his maxims of wisdom, not always like a god:

> Much too early I came to many places, or too late; the beer was not yet ready, or was already drunk.[67] . . . The best drunkenness is when everyone after it regains his reason.[68] . . . In a maiden's words none should place faith, nor in a woman's; for guile has been laid in their breasts;[69] . . . this I experienced when I strove to seduce that discreet maiden; . . . nor of that damsel gained I aught.[70] . . . At eve the day is to be praised, a sword after it is tested, a woman after she is cremated.[71] . . . Of the words that a man speaks to another he often pays the penalty [72] . . . the tongue is the bane of the head.[73] Even in three words quarrel not with a worse man; often the better man yields, when the worse strikes.[74] . . . He should rise early who covets another's property or wife.[75] . . . Moderately wise should a man be,

---

* The word first occurs in a tenth-century fragment, where it means a great-grandmother; by some prank of time it came to mean the technical laws of Norwegian prosody, and was so used by Snorri Sturluson when (1222) he wrote under that title a treatise on Norse mythology and the poetic art; this we know as the Prose or Younger Edda.

not over-wise. . . . Let no man know his destiny beforehand; thus
will his mind be most free from care. . . . A wise man's heart is seldom
glad.[76] . . . One's home is best, small though it be [77] . . . best is one's
hearth, and the sight of the sun.[78]

Probably the poems of the *Elder Edda* were preserved by word of mouth
until the twelfth century, when they were put into writing. In the Viking
Age letters were runes, as in north Germany and Anglo-Saxon England;
these twenty-four symbols (literally, "mysteries") constituted an alphabet
roughly formed on Greek and Latin cursive scripts. Literature, however,
could in that age dispense with letters; minstrel skalds composed, memorized,
recited, and orally transmitted their lays of the Teutonic gods, and of that
"Heroic Age" (from the fourth to the sixth century) when the Germanic
peoples spread their power over Europe. Sturluson and others preserved
some fragments of the lays, and the names of many skalds. The most famous
of these was Sigvat Thordarsson, who served St. Olaf as court poet and
candid counselor. Another, Egil Skallagrimsson (900–83), was the leading
figure of his time in Iceland—a mighty warrior, an individualistic baron, a
passionate poet. In his old age he lost his youngest son by drowning, and was
about to kill himself with grief when his daughter persuaded him to write a
poem instead. His *Sonartorrek* ("The Loss of the Son") is a defiant denunciation of the god, whom he blames for the death; he regrets that he cannot
find Odin and fight him as he has fought other enemies. Then a softer mood
comes, as he reflects that the gods have given him not only sorrow but the
gift of poesy; reconciled, he resolves to live, and resumes his high seat in the
councils of his country.[79]

The literature of Scandinavia in this period doubtless exaggerates the violence of Viking society, as journalism and history, luring the reader with the
exceptional, miss the normal flow of human life. Nevertheless the hard conditions of early Scandinavia compelled a struggle for existence in which only
men of the toughest fiber could survive; and a Nietzschean ethic of unscrupulous courage rose out of ancient customs of feud and revenge and the lawless
piracy of ungoverned seas. "Tell me what faith you are of," one Viking asked
of another. "I believe in my own strength," was the reply.[80] Gold Harald
wanted the throne of Norway, and proposed to get it by force. His friend
Haakon advised him: "Consider with thyself what thou art man enough to
undertake; for to accomplish such a purpose requires a man bold and firm,
who will stick at neither good nor evil to accomplish what is intended." [81]
Some of these men found such pleasure in battle as almost anesthetized their
wounds; some went into a battle frenzy known as *berserksgangr*—"the ber-
serk's way"; the *berserkers*—"bear-shirters"—were champions who rushed
into combat without shirts of mail, and fought and howled like animals, bit
their shields in fury, and then, the battle over, fell into a coma of exhaustion.[82]

Only the brave would enter Valhalla; and all sins would be forgiven to him who died for his group in war.

So trained in hardship and wild games, the "men of the fjords" rowed out and conquered kingdoms for themselves in Russia, Pomerania, Frisia, Normandy, England, Ireland, Iceland, Greenland, Italy, and Sicily. These ventures were not invasions by masses of soldiery like the Moslem hijad or the Magyar flood; they were the reckless sallies of mere handfuls of men, who thought all weakness criminal and all strength good, who hungered for land, women, wealth, and power, and felt a divine right to share in the fruits of the earth. They began like pirates and ended like statesmen; Rollo gave a creative order to Normandy, William the Conqueror to England, Roger II to Sicily; they mingled their fresh blood of the north, like an energizing hormone, with that of peoples made torpid by rural routine. History seldom destroys that which does not deserve to die; and the burning of the tares makes for the next sowing a richer soil.

VI. GERMANY: 566–1106

1. The Organization of Power

The Norse irruptions were the final phase of those barbarian invasions that had stemmed from Germany five centuries before, and had shattered the Roman Empire into the nations of Western Europe. What had become of the Germans who had remained in Germany?

The exodus of great tribes—Goths, Vandals, Burgundians, Franks, Lombards—left Germany underpopulated for a time; the Slavic Wends moved westward from the Baltic states to fill the vacuum; and by the sixth century the Elbe was the ethnic, as it is at present the political, frontier between the Slavic and the Western world. West of the Elbe and the Saale were the surviving German tribes: Saxons in north central Germany, East Franks along the lower Rhine, Thuringians between them, Bavarians (once Marcomanni) along the middle Danube, and Swabians (once Suevi) along and between the upper Rhine and upper Danube, and along the eastern Jura and the northern Alps. There was no Germany, only German tribes. Charlemagne for a time gave them the unity of conquest, and the essentials of a common order; but the collapse of the Carolingian Empire loosened these bonds; and until Bismarck tribal consciousness and local particularism fought every centralizing influence, and weakened a people uncomfortably shut in by enemies, the Alps, and the sea.

The Treaty of Verdun (843) had in effect made Louis or Ludwig the German, grandson of Charlemagne, the first king of Germany. The Treaty of Mersen (870) gave him additional territory, and defined Germany as the land between the Rhine and the Elbe, plus part of Lorraine, and the bishoprics of Mainz, Worms, and Speyer. Louis was a statesman of the first order, but he had three sons; and on his death (876) his realm was divided among them. After a decade of chaos, during which the Northmen raided the Rhine cities, Arnulf, illegitimate offspring of Louis' son Carloman, was elected king of "East Francia" (887), and drove back the invaders. But his successor, Louis "the Child" (899–911), proved too young and weak to hold back the Magyars, who ravaged Bavaria (900), Carinthia (901), Saxony (906), Thuringia (908), and Alemannia (909). The central government failed to protect these provinces; each had to provide its own defense; the provincial dukes organized armies by giving lands in fief to retainers who paid in military service. The forces so raised gave the dukes virtual independence of the crown, and established a feudal Germany. On the death of Louis the nobles and prelates, successfully claiming the right of choosing the king, gave the throne to Conrad I, Duke of Franconia (911–18). Conrad spent himself in strife with Duke Henry of Saxony, but had the wit to recommend Henry as his successor. Henry I, called "the Fowler" because of his love of hunting, drove back the Slavic Wends to the Oder, fortified Germany against the Magyars, defeated them in 933, and prepared, by his patient labors, for the achievements of his son.

Otto I the Great (936–73) was the Charlemagne of Germany. He was twenty-four at his accession, but was already a king in bearing and ability. Sensing the value of ceremony and symbolism, he persuaded the dukes of Lorraine, Franconia, Swabia, and Bavaria to act as his attendants in his solemn coronation at Aachen by Archbishop Hildebert. Later the dukes rebelled against his growing power, and induced his younger brother Henry to join in a plot to depose him; Otto discovered and suppressed the conspiracy, and forgave Henry, who conspired again and was again forgiven. The subtle King gave new duchies to his friends and relatives, and gradually subordinated the dukes; later monarchs would not inherit his resolution and skill, and much of medieval Germany was consumed in conflicts between feudalism and royalty. In this contest the German prelates sided with the King, and became his administrative aides and counselors, sometimes his generals. The King appointed bishops and archbishops as he named other officials of the government; and the German Church became a national institution, only loosely attached to the papacy. Using Christianity as a unifying force, Otto fused the German tribes into a powerful state.

On the urging of his bishops, Otto attacked the Wends, and sought to convert them to Christianity by the sword. He compelled the king of Denmark and the dukes of Poland and Bohemia to accept him as their feudal suzerain. Aspiring to the throne of the Holy Roman Empire, he welcomed the invitation of Adelaide, the pretty widow of King Lothaire of Italy, to rescue her from the indignities to which she had been subjected by the new King Berengar II. Otto combined politics deftly with romance: he invaded Italy, married Adelaide, and allowed Berengar to retain his kingdom only as a fief of the German crown (951). The Roman aristocracy refused to acknowledge a German as emperor and therefore as master of Italy; now began a contest that would last for three centuries. The rebellion of his son Ludolf and his son-in-law Conrad called Otto back to Germany, lest in trying to become emperor he should cease to be king. When the Magyars again invaded Germany (954), Ludolf and Conrad welcomed them, and supplied them with guides. Otto put down the rebellion, forgave Ludolf, reorganized his army, and so decisively defeated the Magyars at the Lechfeld, near Augsburg (955), that Germany won a long period of security and peace. Otto now devoted himself to internal affairs—restored order, suppressed crime, and for a time created a united Germany, the most prosperous state of its time.

Imperial opportunity returned when Pope John XII appealed for his aid against Berengar (959). Otto invaded Italy with a strong force, entered Rome peaceably, and was crowned Roman Emperor of the West by John XII in 962. The Pope, regretting this action, complained that Otto had not fulfilled a promise to restore the Ravenna exarchate to the papacy. Otto took the extreme step of marching into Rome, summoning a synod of Italian bishops, and persuading it to depose John and make a layman Pope as Leo VIII (963). The papal territory was now confined to the duchy of Rome and the Sabine region; the rest of central and northern Italy was absorbed into a Holy Roman Empire that became an appanage of the German crown. From these events German kings would conclude that Italy was part of their inheritance; and the popes would conclude that no man could become Roman emperor of the West except by papal coronation.

Otto, nearing death, forestalled disorder by having his son Otto II crowned coemperor by Pope John XIII (967); and he secured as his son's wife Theophano, daughter of Romanus II the Byzantine Emperor (972); Charlemagne's dream of a marital union of the two empires was transiently made real. Then, old in deeds but still only sixty years of age, Otto passed away (973), and all Germany mourned him as its greatest king. Otto II (973–83) spent himself in efforts to add southern Italy to his realm, and died prematurely in the attempt. Otto III (983–1002) was then a boy of three; his mother Theophano and his grandmother Adelaide ruled as regents for eight years. Theophano, in her eighteen years of influence, brought something of Byzantine refinement to the German court, and stimulated the Ottonian renaissance in letters and arts.

At the age of sixteen (996) Otto III began to rule in his own name. Influenced by Gerbert and other churchmen, he proposed to make Rome his capital, and unite all Christendom under a restored Roman Empire, ruled jointly by emperor and pope. The nobles and populace of Rome and Lombardy interpreted the plan as a conspiracy to establish a German-Byzantine rule over Italy; they resisted Otto, and established a "Roman Republic"; Otto suppressed it, and executed its leader Crescentius. In 999 he made Gerbert Pope; but the twenty-two years of Otto's life, and the four years of Gerbert's papacy, proved too brief for the implementation of his policy. Half a saint but in some measure a man, Otto fell in love with Stephania, widow of Crescentius; she consented to be his mistress and poisoner; the young king, feeling death in his veins, became a weeping penitent, and died at Viterbo at the age of twenty-two.[83]

Henry II (1002–24), last of the Saxon line of German kings, labored to restore the power of the monarch in Italy and Germany, where the reigns of two boys had strengthened the dukes and emboldened neighboring states. Conrad II (1024–39), beginning the Franconian or Salian line of emperors, pacified Italy, and added to Germany the kingdom of Burgundy or Arles. Needing funds, he sold bishoprics for sums so large that his conscience irked him; he swore never again to take money for an ecclesiastical appointment, and "almost succeeded in keeping his oath." [84] His son Henry III (1039–56) brought the new empire to its zenith. On the "Day of Indulgence," at Constance in 1043, he offered pardon to all those who had injured him, and exhorted his subjects to renounce all vengeance and hatred. For a decade his preaching and example—perhaps also his power—reduced the feuds of the dukes, and co-operated with the contemporary "Truce of God" to bring a brief golden age to Central Europe. He patronized learning, founded schools, and completed the cathedrals of Speyer, Mainz, and Worms. But he was no saint pledged to eternal peace. He warred with Hungary till it recognized him as its feudal suzerain. He deposed three rival claimants to the papacy, and appointed two successive popes. In all Europe no other power equaled his. In the end he pushed his authority to an extreme that aroused opposition among both the prelates and the dukes, but he died before the storm, and bequeathed to Henry IV a hostile papacy and a troubled realm.

Henry was four when crowned king at Aachen, six at his father's death. His mother and two archbishops served as regents till 1065; then the fifteen-year-old boy was declared of age, and found himself vested with an imperial power that must have turned any youthful head. He came naturally to believe in absolute monarchy, and sought to rule accordingly; soon he was at odds or war with one or another of the great nobles who had in his helplessness almost dismembered his realm. The Saxons resented the taxes laid upon them, and refused to restore the crown lands that he claimed; for fifteen years (1072–88) he fought an intermittent war with them; when he defeated them in 1075 he compelled their whole force, including its proudest nobles and its martial bishops, to walk disarmed and barefoot between the files of his army, and lay their act of surrender at his feet. In that same year Pope Gregory VII issued a decree against lay investiture—the appointment of bishops or abbots by laymen. Henry, standing on the precedents of a century, never doubted his right to make such appointments; he fought Gregory for ten years in diplomacy and war, and literally to the death, in one of the bitterest conflicts in medieval history. The rebellious nobles of Germany took advantage of the quarrel to strengthen their feudal power, and the humiliated Saxons renewed their revolt. Henry's sons joined the opposition; and in 1098 the Diet of Mainz declared Henry V king. The son took the father prisoner, and compelled him to abdicate (1105); the father escaped, and was forming a new army when he died at Liége, in the fifty-seventh year of his age (1106). Pope Paschal II could not grant Christian burial to an unrepentant excommunicate; but the people of Liége, defying Pope and King, gave Henry IV a royal funeral, and buried him in their cathedral.

2. German Civilization: 566–1106

Through these five centuries the labor of men and women tilling the soil and rearing children conquered Germany for civilization. The forests were fearfully immense, harbored wild animals, impeded communication and unity; nameless heroes of the woodland felled the trees—perhaps too recklessly. In Saxony the struggle against the self-regenerating forest and the infectious marsh went on for a thousand years, and only the thirteenth century gave man the victory. Generation after generation the hardy, hearty peasants pushed back the beasts and the wilderness, tamed the land with mattock and plow, planted fruit trees, herded flocks, tended vines, and consoled their loneliness with love and prayer, flowers and music and beer. Miners dug salt, iron, copper, lead, and silver from the earth; manorial, monastic, and domestic handicraft wedded Roman to German skills; trade flowed ever more busily over the rivers and into the North and Baltic Seas. At last the great campaign was won; barbarism still lurked in the laws and the blood; but the gap had been spanned between the tribal chaos of the fifth century and the Ottonian renaissance of the tenth. From 955 to 1075 Germany was the most prosperous country in Europe, rivaled only by that northern Italy which had received law and order from German kings. Old Roman towns like Trier, Mainz, and Cologne carried on; new cities grew around the episcopal seats at Speyer, Magdeburg, and Worms. About 1050 we begin to hear of Nuremberg.

The Church was the educator, as well as the administrator, of Germany in this age. Monastic schools—really colleges—were opened at Fulda, Tegernsee, Reichenau, Gandersheim, Hildesheim, and Lorsch. Rabanus Maurus (776?–856), after studying under Alcuin at Tours, became abbot of the great monastery at Fulda in Prussia, and made its school famous throughout Europe as the mother of scholars and of twenty-two affiliated institutions. He extended the curriculum to include many sciences, and reproved the superstitions that ascribed natural events to occult powers.[85] The library at Fulda grew to be one of the largest in Europe; to it we owe Suetonius, Tacitus, and Ammianus Marcellinus. An uncertain tradition attributes to Rabanus the majestic hymn, *Veni Creator Spiritus*, which is sung at the consecration of popes, bishops, or kings.[86] St. Bruno, who was both the Duke of Lorraine and the Archbishop of Cologne, and became imperial chancellor under Otto the Great, opened a school in the royal palace to train an administrative class; he brought scholars and books from Byzantium and Italy, and himself taught Greek and philosophy.

The German language had as yet no literature; nearly all writing was done by clerics, and in Latin. The greatest German poet of the age was Walafrid Strabo (809–49), a Swabian monk at Reichenau. For a time he was tutor to Charles the Bald in the palace of Louis the Pious at Aachen; he found an enlightened patron in Louis' wife, the beautiful and ambitious Judith. Returning to Reichenau as its abbot, he gave himself to religion, poetry, and gardening; and in a delightful poem *De cultura hortorum—On the Care of Gardens*—he described one by one the herbs and flowers that he tended so fondly.

His greatest rival in the literature of Germany in these centuries was a nun. Hroswitha was only one of many German women who in this age were distinguished for culture and refinement. Born about 935, she entered the Benedictine convent at Gandersheim. The standard of instruction must have been higher than we should have expected, for Hroswitha became familiar with the poets of pagan Rome, and learned to write Latin fluently. She composed some lives of saints in Latin hexameters, and a minor epic about Otto the Great. But the works that make her memorable are six Latin prose comedies in the manner of Terence. Her purpose, she tells us, was "to make the small talent vouchsafed her by Heaven give forth, under the hammer of devotion, a faint sound to the praise of God." [87] She mourns the pagan indecency of Latin comedy, and proposes to offer a Christian substitute; but even her plays turn on a profane love that hardly conceals a warm undercurrent of physical desire. In the best of her brief dramas, *Abraham*, a Christian anchorite leaves his hermitage to care for an orphaned niece. She elopes with a seducer, is soon deserted, and becomes a prostitute. Abraham traces her, disguises himself, and enters her chamber. When she kisses him she recognizes him, and recoils in shame. In a tender and poetic colloquy he persuades her to abandon her life of sin, and return to their home. We do not know whether these dramatic sketches were ever performed. The modern drama developed not out of such echoes of Terence, but out of the ceremonies and "mysteries" of the Church, crossed with the farces of wandering mimes.

As the Church gave a home to poetry, drama, and historiography, so she provided subjects and funds for art. German monks, stirred by Byzantine and Carolingian examples, and helped by the patronage of German princesses, produced in this age a hundred illuminated manuscripts of high excellence. Bernewald, Bishop of Hildesheim from 993 to 1022, was almost a summary of the culture of his age: a painter, a calligrapher, a metalworker, a mosaicist, an administrator, a saint. He made his city an art center by assembling artists of diverse provenance and skills; with their help, but also with his own hands, he fashioned jeweled crosses, gold and silver candlesticks chased with animal and floral forms, and a chalice set with antique gems, one of which represented the three Graces in their wonted nudity.[88] The famous bronze doors which his artists made for his cathedral were the first historiated metal doors of the Middle Ages to be solidly cast instead of being composed of flat panels affixed to wood. Domestic architecture showed no signs yet of the lovely forms that would grace German cities in the Renaissance; but church architecture now graduated from wood to stone, imported from Lombardy Romanesque ideas of transept, choir, apse, and towers, and began the cathedrals of Hildesheim, Lorsch, Worms, Mainz, Trier, Speyer, and Cologne. Foreign critics complained of flat timbered ceilings and excessive external decoration in this "Rhenish Romanesque"; but these churches well expressed the solid strength of the German character, and the spirit of an age laboriously struggling up to civilization.

CHAPTER XXI

Christianity in Conflict

529-1085

I. ST. BENEDICT: *c.* 480-543

THE year 529, which saw the closing of the Athenian schools of philosophy, saw also the opening of Monte Cassino, the most famous monastery in Latin Christendom. Its founder, Benedict of Nursia, was born at
Spoleto, apparently of the dying Roman aristocracy. Sent to Rome for an
education, he was scandalized by the sexual license there, or, some say, he
loved and lost.[1] At the age of fifteen he fled to a remote spot five miles from
Subiaco, in the Sabine hills; made his cell in a cave at the foot of a precipice;
and lived there for some years as a solitary monk. The *Dialogues* of Pope
Gregory I tell how Benedict fought valiantly to forget the woman

> the memory of whom the wicked spirit put into his mind, and by that
> memory so mightily inflamed with concupiscence the soul of God's
> servant . . . that, almost overcome with pleasure, he was of a mind to
> forsake the wilderness. But suddenly, assisted by God's grace, he came
> to himself; and seeing many thick briers and nettle bushes growing
> hard by, off he cast his apparel, and threw himself into the midst of
> them, and there wallowed so long that when he rose up all his flesh
> was pitifully torn; and so by the wounds of his body he cured the
> wounds of his soul.[2]

After he had lived there for some years, and his steadfastness had won him
fame, he was importuned by the monks of a nearby monastery to be their
abbot. He warned them that his rule would be severe; they persisted, and he
went with them; after a few months of his stern regimen they put poison in
his wine. He resumed his solitary life; but young devotees came to live near
him and solicit his guidance; fathers brought their sons, even from Rome, to
be taught by him; by 520 twelve little monasteries, each with twelve monks,
had risen round his cave. When of even these monks many found his rule too
strict, he removed with the most ardent of his followers to Monte Cassino, a
hill 1715 feet above sea level, overlooking the ancient town of Casinum, forty
miles northwest of Capua. There he demolished a pagan temple, founded (*c.*
529) a monastery, and formulated that Benedictine Rule which was to guide
most monasteries in the West.

The monks of Italy and France had erred in imitating the solitary asceticism of the East; both the climate and the active spirit of Western Europe
made such a regimen discouragingly difficult, and led to many relapses.
Benedict did not criticize the anchorites, nor condemn asceticism, but he
thought it wiser to make asceticism communal, not individual; there should
be no show or rivalry in it; at every step it was to be under an abbot's control,
and stop short of injury to health or mind.

Hitherto, in the West, no vows had been demanded of those who entered
the monastic life. Benedict felt that the aspirant should serve a novitiate, and
learn by experience the austerities to be required of him; only after such a
trial might he take the vows. Then, if he still wished, he was to pledge himself, in writing, to "the perpetuity of his stay, the reformation of his manners,
and obedience"; and this vow, signed and witnessed, was to be laid upon the
altar by the novice himself in a solemn ritual. Thereafter the monk must not
leave the monastery without the abbot's permission. The abbot was to be
chosen by the monks, and was to consult them on all matters of importance;
but the final decision was to rest with him, and they were to obey him in
silence and humility. They were to speak only when necessary; they were
not to jest or laugh loudly; they were to walk with their eyes on the ground.
They were to own nothing, "neither a book, nor tablets, nor a pen—nothing
at all. . . . All things shall be held in common."[3] Conditions of previous wealth
or slavery were to be ignored and forgotten. The abbot

> shall make no distinction of persons in the monastery. . . . A freeborn
> man shall not be preferred to one coming from servitude, unless there
> be some other and reasonable cause. For whether we are bond or free,
> we are all one in Christ. . . . God is no respecter of persons.[4]

Alms and hospitality were to be given within the means of the monastery, to
all who asked for it. "All guests who come shall be received as though they
were Christ."[5]

Every monk must work—in the fields or shops of the monastery, in the
kitchen, about the house, copying manuscripts. . . . Nothing was to be eaten
till noon, and in Lent not till sundown. From mid-September to Easter there
was to be but one meal a day; in the summer months, two, for then the days
were long. Wine was allowed, but no flesh of any four-footed beast. Work
or sleep was to be frequently interrupted with communal prayer. Influenced
by Eastern exemplars, Benedict divided the day into "canonical hours"—
hours of prayer as established by canon or rule. The monks were to rise at
two A.M., repair to the chapel, and recite or sing "nocturns"—scriptural
readings, prayers, and psalms; at dawn they gathered for "matins" or
"lauds"; at six for "prime"—the first hour; at nine for "tierce"—the third; at
noon for "sext"—the sixth; at three for "none"—the ninth; at sunset for vespers—the evening hour; at bedtime for "compline"—the completion. Bedtime

was nightfall; the monks almost dispensed with artificial light. They slept in their clothes, and seldom bathed.[6]

To these specific regulations Benedict added some general counsels of Christian perfection:

> 1. In the first place, to love the Lord God with the whole heart, the whole soul, the whole strength. 2. Then one's neighbor as oneself. 3. Then not to kill . . . nor commit adultery . . . nor steal . . . nor covet . . . nor bear false witness. . . . 8. To honor all men. . . . 11. To chasten the body. . . . 13. To love fasting. 14. To relieve the poor. 15. To clothe the naked. 16. To visit the sick. . . . 30. Not to do injuries, and to bear them patiently. . . . 31. To love one's enemies. . . . 53. Not to be fond of much talking. . . . 61. Not to desire to be called a saint . . . but to be one. . . . 71. After a disagreement to be reconciled before the going down of the sun. 72. And never to despair of the mercy of God.[7]

In an age of war and chaos, of doubt and wandering, the Benedictine monastery was a healing refuge. It took dispossessed or ruined peasants, students longing for some quiet retreat, men weary of the strife and tumult of the world, and said to them: "Give up your pride and freedom, and find here security and peace." No wonder a hundred similar Benedictine monasteries rose throughout Europe, each independent of the rest, all subject only to the pope, serving as communistic isles in a raging individualistic sea. The Benedictine Rule and order proved to be among the most enduring creations of medieval man. Monte Cassino itself is a symbol of that permanence. Lombard barbarians sacked it in 589; the Lombards retired; the monks returned. The Saracens destroyed it in 884; the monks rebuilt it; earthquake ruined it in 1349; the monks restored it; French soldiery pillaged it in 1799; the shells and bombs of the Second World War leveled it to the ground in 1944. Today (1948) the monks of St. Benedict, with their own hands, are building it once more. *Succisa virescit*: cut down, it blooms again.

II. GREGORY THE GREAT: 540?–604

While Benedict and his monks peacefully worked and prayed at Monte Cassino, the Gothic War (536–53) passed up and down Italy like a withering flame, leaving disorder and poverty in its wake. Urban economy was in chaos. Political institutions lay in ruins; in Rome no secular authority survived except that of imperial legates weakly supported by unpaid and distant troops. In this collapse of worldly powers the survival of ecclesiastical organization appeared even to the emperors as the salvation of the state. In 554 Justinian promulgated a decree requiring that "fit and proper persons, able to administer the local government, be chosen as governors of the provinces *by the bishops and chief persons* of each province." [8] But Justinian's corpse was hardly cold when the Lombard invasion (568) subjected northern Italy again to barbarism and Arianism, and threatened the whole structure and leadership of the Church in Italy. The crisis called forth a man, and history once more testified to the influence of genius.

Gregory was born at Rome three years before Benedict's death. He came of an ancient senatorial family, and his youth was spent in a handsome palace on the Caelian Hill. On the death of his father he fell heir to a large fortune. He rose rapidly in the *ordo honorum*, or sequence of political plums; at thirty-three he was prefect—as we should say, mayor—of Rome. But he had no taste for politics. Having finished his year of office, and apparently convinced by the condition of Italy that the ever-heralded end of the world was at hand,[9] he used the greater part of his fortune to found seven monasteries, distributed the rest in alms to the poor, laid aside all vestiges of his rank, turned his palace into the monastery of St. Andrew, and became its first monk. He subjected himself to extreme asceticism, lived for the most part on raw vegetables and fruits, and fasted so often that when Holy Saturday came, on which fasting was pre-eminently enjoined, it seemed that another day of abstinence would kill him. Yet the three years that he spent in the monastery were always recalled by him as the happiest of his life.

Out of this peace he was drawn to serve Pope Benedict I as "seventh deacon"; and in 579 he was sent by Pope Pelagius II as ambassador to the imperial court at Constantinople. Amid the wiles of diplomacy and the pomp of palaces he continued to live like a monk in habit, diet, and prayer; [10] nevertheless he gained some helpful experience of the world and its chicanery. In 586 he was recalled to Rome, and became Abbot of St. Andrew's. In 590 a terrible bubonic plague decimated the population of Rome; Pelagius himself was a victim; and at once the clergy and people of the city chose Gregory to succeed him. Gregory was loath to leave his monastery, and wrote to the Greek emperor asking him to refuse confirmation of the election; the city prefect intercepted the letter; and as Gregory was preparing flight he was seized and brought by force to St. Peter's, and there was consecrated Pope; or so we are told by another Gregory.[11]

He was now fifty, and already bald, with large head, dark complexion, aquiline nose, sparse and tawny beard; a man of strong feeling and gentle speech, of imperial purposes and simple sentiment. Austerities and responsibilities had ruined his health; he suffered from indigestion, slow fever, and gout. In the papal palace he lived as he had in the monastery—dressed in a monk's coarse robe, eating the cheapest foods, sharing a common life with the monks and priests who aided him.[12] Usually absorbed in problems of religion and the state, he could unbend into words and deeds of paternal affection. A wandering minstrel appeared at the gate of the palace with organ and monkey; Gregory bade the man enter, and gave him food and drink.[13] Instead of spending the revenues of the Church in building new edifices, he used them in charity, in gifts to religious institutions throughout Christendom, and in redeeming captives of war. To every poor family in Rome he distributed monthly a portion of corn, wine, cheese, vegetables, oil, fish, meat, clothing, and money; and every day his agents brought cooked provisions to the sick or infirm. His letters, stern to negligent ecclesiastics or to political potentates, are jewels of sympathy to persons in distress: to a peasant exploited on Church lands, to a slave girl wishing to take the veil, to a noble lady worried about her sins. In his conception the priest was literally a pastor, a shepherd caring for his flock, and the good Pope had every right to compose his *Liber pastoralis curae* (590), a manual of advice to bishops, which became a Christian classic. Though always ailing and prematurely old, he spent himself in ecclesiastical administration, papal politics, agricultural management, military strategy, theological treatises, mystic ecstasies, and a solicitous concern with a thousand details of human life. He chastened the pride of his office with the humility of his creed; he called himself, in the first of his extant epistles, *servus servorum Dei*, "servant of the servants of God"; and the greatest popes have accepted the noble phrase.

His administration of the Church was marked by economic wisdom and stern reform. He struggled to suppress simony and concubinage in the clergy. He restored discipline in the Latin monasteries, and regulated their relations with the secular clergy and the pope. He improved the canon of the Mass, and perhaps contributed to the development of "Gregorian" chant. He checked exploitation on the papal estates, advanced money to tenant farmers, and charged no interest. But he collected due revenues promptly, slyly offered rent reductions to converted Jews, and received, for the Church, legacies of land from barons frightened by his sermons on the approaching end of the world.[14]

Meanwhile he met the ablest rulers of his day in political duels, won often, sometimes lost, but in the end left the power and prestige of the papacy, and the "Patrimony of Peter" (i.e., the Papal States in central Italy) immensely extended and enhanced. He formally acknowledged, but in practice largely ignored, the sovereignty of the Eastern emperor. When the duke of Spoleto, at war with the Imperial exarch of Ravenna, threatened Rome, Gregory signed a peace with the duke without consulting the exarch or the emperor. When the Lombards besieged Rome Gregory shared in organizing defense.

He mourned every minute given to earthly concerns, and apologized to his congregation for his inability to preach comforting sermons amid the worldly cares that troubled his mind. In the few years of peace allowed him he turned happily to the task of spreading the Gospel through Europe. He brought the rebellious bishops of Lombardy to submission, restored orthodox Catholicism in Africa, received the conversion of Arian Spain, and won England with forty monks. While Abbot of St. Andrew's he had seen some

English captives exposed for sale in a slave market at Rome; he was struck, says the patriotic Bede, by their

> white skin and comely countenance and hair of excellent beauty. And beholding them awhile he demanded, as they say, out of what region or land they had been brought. And it was answered that they came from Britain, where such was the appearance of the inhabitants. Again, he asked whether the people of that island were Christian men . . . and answer was made that they were paynims. Then this good man . . . "alas," quoth he, "it is a piteous case that the author of darkness possesseth such bright beautied people, and that men of such gracious outward sheen do bear a mind void of inward grace." Again, therefore, he enquired what was the name of that people. Answer was given that they were called Angles. Whereon he said, "Well are they so called, for they have an angel's face, and it is meet that such men were inheritors with the angels in heaven." [15]

The story—too pretty to be credible—goes on to say that Gregory asked and received of Pope Pelagius II permission to lead some missionaries to England; that Gregory started out, but was halted by a locust dropping upon the page of Scripture that he was reading; "*locusta!*" he cried; "that means *loco sta*"— stay in your place.[16] Impressed soon afterward into the papacy, he did not forget England. In 596 he sent thither a mission under Augustine, Prior of St. Andrew's. Arrived in Gaul, the monks were turned back by Frank stories of Saxon savagery; those "angels," they were informed, "were wild beasts who preferred killing to eating, thirsted for human blood, and liked Christian blood best of all. Augustine returned to Rome with these reports, but Gregory reproved and encouraged him, and sent him back to accomplish peaceably in two years what Rome had transiently achieved by ninety years of war.

Gregory was not a philosopher-theologian like the great Augustine, nor a master of style like the brilliant Jerome; but his writings so deeply influenced and expressed the medieval mind that beside him Augustine and Jerome seem classical. He left behind him books of popular theology so rich in nonsense that one wonders whether the great administrator believed what he wrote, or merely wrote what he thought it well for simple and sinful souls to believe. His biography of Benedict is the most pleasing of these books—a charming idyl of reverence, with no pretense to critical sifting of legend from fact. His 800 letters are his best literary legacy; here this varied man reveals himself in a hundred phases, and gives unconsciously an intimate picture of his mind and times. His *Dialogues* were loved by the people because they offered as history the most amazing tales of the visions, prophecies, and miracles of Italy's holy men. Here the reader learned of massive boulders moved by prayer, of a saint who could make himself invisible, of poisons rendered harmless by the sign of the cross, of provisions miraculously supplied and increased, of the sick made whole and the dead restored to life. The power of relics ran through these dialogues, but none more marvelous than the chains that were believed to have bound Peter and Paul; Gregory cherished these with adoration; he sent filings from them as presents to his friends; and with one such offering he wrote to a sufferer from ailing eyesight: "Let these be continually applied to your eyes, for many miracles have been wrought by this same gift." [17] The Christianity of the masses had captured the mind or pen of the great Pope.

His deeper venture into theology took the form of the *Magna moralia*—a six-volume commentary on the Book of Job. He takes the drama as literal history in every line; but also he seeks in every line an allegorical or symbolical significance, and ends by finding in Job the full Augustinian theology. The Bible is in every sense the word of God; it is a complete system of wisdom and beauty in itself; and no man should waste his time and debase his morals by reading the pagan classics. However, the Bible is occasionally obscure, and is often couched in popular or pictorial language; it needs careful interpretation by trained minds; and the Church, as custodian of sacred tradition, is the only proper interpreter. Individual reason is a weak and divisive instrument, not designed to deal with supersensual realities; and "when the intellect seeks to understand beyond its powers, it loses even that which it understood." [18] God is beyond our understanding; we can only say what He is not, not what He is; "almost everything that is said of God is unworthy, for the very reason that it is capable of being said." [19] Hence Gregory makes no formal attempt to prove the existence of God. But, he argues, we can adumbrate Him by considering the human soul: is it not the living force and guide of the body? "Many of our time," says Gregory, ". . . have often seen souls departing from the body." [20] The tragedy of man is that by original sin his nature is corrupt, and inclines him to wickedness; and this basic spiritual malformation is transmitted from parent to child through sexual procreation. Left to himself, man would heap sin upon sin, and richly deserve everlasting damnation. Hell is no mere phrase; it is a dark and bottomless subterranean abyss created from the beginning of the world; it is an inextinguishable fire, corporeal and yet able to sear soul as well as flesh; it is eternal, and yet it never destroys the damned, or lessens their sensitivity to pain. And to each moment of pain is added the terror of expected pain, the horror of witnessing the tortures of loved ones also damned, the despair of ever being released, or allowed the blessing of annihilation.[21] In a softer mood Gregory developed Augustine's doctrine of a purgatory in which the dead would complete their atonement for forgiven sins. And like Augustine, Gregory comforted those whom he had terrified by reminding them of the gift of God's grace, the intercession of the saints, the fruits of Christ's sacrifice, the mysterious saving effect of sacraments available to all Christian penitents.

Perhaps Gregory's theology reflected his health as well as the frightening chaos of his time. "In eleven months," he wrote in 599, "I have rarely been able to leave my bed. I am so tormented with gout and painful anxieties that . . . every day I look for the relief of death." And in 600: "For nearly two years I have been confined to my couch, so afflicted with pain that even on festivals I can hardly get up for three hours to celebrate Mass. I am daily at the point of death, and daily being driven back from it." And in 601: "It is long since I have been able to leave my couch. I look longingly for death." [22] It came in 604.

He dominated the end of the sixth century as Justinian had dominated its beginning; and his effect on religion was exceeded in this epoch only by that of Mohammed. He was not a learned man, nor a profound theologian; but because of his simplicity he influenced the people more deeply than the Augustine whose lead he followed with engaging humility. In mind he was the first completely medieval man.[23] While his hand managed a scattered empire, his thought dwelt on the corruption of human nature, the temptations of ubiquitous devils, and the approaching end of the world. He preached with power that religion of terror which was to darken men's minds for centuries; he accepted all the miracles of popular legend, all the magical efficacy of relics, images, and formulas; he lived in a world haunted with angels, demons, wizards, and ghosts. All sense of a rational order in the universe had departed from him; it was a world in which science was impossible, and only a fearful faith remained. The next seven centuries would accept this theology; the great Scholastics would toil to give it the form of reason; it would constitute the tragic background of *The Divine Comedy*.

But this same man, superstitious and credulous, physically shattered with a terrified piety, was in will and action a Roman of the ancient cast, tenacious of purpose, stern of judgment, prudent and practical, in love with discipline and law. He gave a law to monasticism, as Benedict had given it a rule; he built the temporal power of the papacy, freed it from imperial domination, and administered it with such wisdom and integrity that men would look to the papacy as a rock of refuge through tempestuous centuries. His grateful successors canonized him, and an admiring posterity called him Gregory the Great.

III. PAPAL POLITICS: 604-867

His early successors found it hard to live up to his height of virtue or power. For the most part they accepted domination by exarch or emperor, and were repeatedly humiliated in their efforts to resist. The Emperor Heraclius, anxious to unify his rescued realm, sought to reconcile the Monophysite East—which held that there was but one nature in Christ—with the orthodox West, which distinguished two; his manifesto, *Ekthesis* (638), proposed an agreement through the doctrine of monothelism—that there was but one will in Christ. Pope Honorius I agreed, adding that the question of one or two wills was "a point which I leave to grammarians as a matter of very little importance"; [24] but the theologians of the West denounced his compliance. When the Emperor Constans II issued a proclamation (648) favoring monothelism, Pope Martin I rejected it. Constans ordered the exarch of Ravenna to arrest him and bring him to Constantinople; refusing to yield, the Pope was banished to the Crimea, where he died (655). The Sixth Ecumenical Council, meeting at Constantinople in 680, repudiated monothelism, and condemned Pope Honorius, *post mortem*, as "a favorer of heretics." [25] The Eastern Church, chastened by the loss of Monophysite Syria and Egypt to the Moslems, concurred in the decision, and theological peace hovered for a moment over East and West.

But the repeated humiliations of the papacy by the Eastern emperors, the weakening of Byzantium by Moslem expansion in Asia, Africa, and Spain, by Moslem control of the Mediterranean, and by the inability of Constantinople or Ravenna to protect the papal estates in Italy from Lombard assaults, drove the popes to turn from the declining Empire and seek aid from the rising Franks. Pope Stephen II (752–7), fearful that a Lombard capture of Rome would reduce the papacy to a local bishopric dominated by Lombard kings, appealed to the Emperor Constantine V; no help came thence; and the Pope, in a move fraught with political consequences, turned to the Franks. Pepin the Short came, subdued the Lombards, and enriched the papacy with the "Donation of Pepin," giving it all central Italy (756); so was established the temporal power of the popes. This brilliant papal diplomacy culminated in the coronation of Charlemagne by Leo III (800); thereafter no man could be an accepted emperor in the West without anointment by a pope. The harassed bishopric of Gregory I had become one of the greatest powers in Europe. When Charlemagne died (814), the domination of the Church by the Frank state was reversed; step by step the clergy of France subordinated its kings; and while the empire of Charlemagne collapsed, the authority and influence of the Church increased.

At first it was the episcopacy that profited most from the weakness and quarrels of the French and German kings. In Germany the archbishops, allied with the kings, enjoyed over property, bishops, and priests a feudal power that paid only lip service to the popes. Apparently it was the resentment of the German bishops, irked by this archiepiscopal autocracy, that generated the "False Decretals"; this collection, which would later fortify the papacy, aimed first of all to establish the right of bishops to appeal from their metropolitans to the popes. We do not know the date or provenance of these Decretals; probably they were put together at Metz about 842. The author was a French cleric who called himself Isidorus Mercator. It was an ingenious compilation. Along with a mass of authentic decrees by councils or popes, it included decrees and letters that it attributed to pontiffs from Clement I (91–100) to Melchiades (311–14). These early documents were designed to show that by the oldest traditions and practice of the Church no bishop might be deposed, no Church council might be convened, and no major issue might be decided, without the consent of the pope. Even the early pontiffs, by these evidences, had claimed absolute and universal authority as vicars of Christ on earth. Pope Sylvester I (314–35) was represented as having received, in the "Donation of Constantine," full secular as well as religious authority over all western Europe; consequently the "Donation of Pepin" was but a halting restoration of stolen property; and the repudiation of Byzantine suzerainty by the pope in crowning Charlemagne appeared as the long-delayed reassertion of a right derived from the founder of the Eastern Empire himself. Unfortunately, many of the unauthentic documents quoted Scripture in the translation of St. Jerome, who was born twenty-six years after the death of Melchiades. The forgery would have been evident to any good scholar, but scholarship was at low ebb in the ninth and tenth centuries. The fact that most of the claims ascribed by the Decretals to the early bishops of Rome had been made by one or another of the later pontiffs disarmed criticism; and for eight centuries the popes assumed the authenticity of these documents, and used them to prop their policies.*

By a happy coincidence the "False Decretals" appeared shortly before the election of one of the most commanding figures in papal history. Nicholas I (858–67) had received an exceptionally thorough education in the law and traditions of the Church, and had been apprenticed to his high office by being a favored aide of several popes. He equaled the great Gregorys (I and VII) in strength of will, and surpassed them in the extent and success of his claims. Starting from premises then accepted by all Christians—that the Son of God had founded the Church by making Peter her first head, and that the bishops of Rome inherited their power from Peter in direct line—Nicholas reasonably concluded that the pope, as God's representative on earth, should enjoy a suzerain authority over all Christians—rulers as well as subjects—at least in matters of faith and morals. Nicholas eloquently expounded this simple argument, and no one in Latin Christendom dared contradict it. Kings and archbishops could only hope that he would not take it too seriously.

They were disappointed. When Lothaire II, King of Lorraine, wished to divorce his Queen Theutberga and marry his mistress Waldrada, the chief prelates of his kingdom granted his wish (862). Theutberga appealed to Nicholas, who sent legates to Metz to examine the matter; Lothaire bribed the legates to confirm the divorce; the archbishops of Trier and Cologne brought this decision to the Pope; Nicholas discovered the fraud, excommunicated the archbishops, and ordered Lothaire to dismiss his mistress and take back his wife. Lothaire refused, and marched with an army against Rome. Nicholas remained for forty-eight hours in St. Peter's in fasting and prayer; Lothaire lost courage, and submitted to the Pope's commands.

Hincmar, Archbishop of Reims, and the greatest prelate in Latin Europe after the Pope himself, dismissed a bishop, Ratherad, who appealed to Nicholas (863). Having reviewed the case, Nicholas ordered Ratherad reinstated; when Hincmar hesitated, the Pope threatened to lay an interdict—a suspension of all church services—upon his province; Hincmar fumed and yielded. To kings as well as prelates Nicholas wrote as one having supreme authority, and only Photius of Constantinople dared gainsay him. In nearly every case later developments showed the

---

* Lorenzo Valla, in 1440, so definitely exposed the frauds in the "False Decretals" that all parties now agree that the disputed documents are forgeries.[26]

Pope to have been on the side of justice; and his stern defense of morality was a lamp and tower in a decadent age. When he died, the power of the papacy was acknowledged more widely than ever before.

IV. THE GREEK CHURCH: 566–898

The patriarchs of the Eastern Church could not admit the overriding jurisdiction of the bishop of Rome for a simple reason: they had long since been subordinated to the Greek emperors, and these would not till 871 abandon their claim to sovereignty over Rome and its popes. The patriarchs occasionally criticized, disobeyed, even denounced, the emperors; but they were appointed and deposed by the emperors, who called ecclesiastical councils, regulated church affairs by state law, and published their theological opinions and directives to the ecclesiastical world. The only checks on the religious autocracy of the emperor in Eastern Christendom were the power of the monks, the tongue of the patriarch, and the vow taken by the emperor, at his coronation by the patriarch, that he would introduce no novelty into the Church.

Constantinople—indeed all the Greek East—was now dotted with monasteries and nunneries in far greater number than in the West. The monastic passion captured some of the Byzantine emperors themselves: they lived like ascetics amid the luxury of the palace, heard Mass daily, ate abstemiously, and bemoaned their sins as sedulously as they committed them. The piety of emperors and of the moribund rich enlarged and multiplied the monasteries with gifts and legacies; men and women of high rank, frightened by omens of death, sought admission to monasteries, and brought with them an ingratiating wealth that would no longer be subject to taxation; others deeded some of their property to a monastery, which then paid them an annuity. Many monasteries claimed to possess relics of revered saints; people credited the monks with control of the wonder-working power of these relics, and offered their coins in the hope of making an unreasonable profit on their investments. A minority of the monks disgraced their faith with idleness, venery, faction, and greed; the majority were reconciled to virtue and peace; altogether the monks enjoyed a popular veneration, a material wealth, and even a political influence that no emperor could ignore. Theodore (759–826), Abbot of the monastery of Studion in Constantinople, was an exemplar of monastic piety and power. Dedicated to the Church by his mother in his childhood, he accepted the Christian mood so thoroughly that in his mother's last illness he complimented her on her approaching death and glory. He drew up for his monks a code of labor, prayer, chastity, and intellectual development that could stand comparison with that of Benedict in the West. He defended the use of religious images, and boldly denied, before the Emperor Leo V, that the secular power had any jurisdiction over ecclesiastical affairs. Four times he was banished for this intransigeance; but from his exile he continued to resist the Iconoclasts till his death.

Differences of language, liturgy, and doctrine during these centuries drove Latin and Greek Christianity further and further apart, like a biological species divided in space and diversified in time. Greek liturgy, ecclesiastical vestments, vessels, and ornaments were more complex, ornate, and artistically wrought than those of the West; the Greek cross had equal arms; the Greeks prayed standing, the Latins kneeling; the Greeks baptized by immersion, the Latins by aspersion; marriage was forbidden to Latin, permitted to Greek, priests; Latin priests shaved, Greek priests had contemplative beards. The Latin clergy specialized in politics, the Greek in theology; heresy almost always rose in an East that had inherited the Greek passion for defining the infinite. From the old Gnostic heresies of Bardesanes in Syria, and perhaps from the westward movement of Manichean ideas, there arose in Armenia, about 660, a sect of Paulicians that took its name from St. Paul, rejected the Old Testament, the sacraments, the reverence paid to images, the symbolism of the cross. Like some advancing pullulation these groups and theories spread through the Near East into the Balkans, Italy, and France. They bore heroically the most merciless persecutions, and still survive as remnants in the Molokhani, the Khlysti, and the Dukhobors.

The monothelite controversy was more agitated by the emperors than by the people. And doubtless the people were not responsible for the *filioque* that so tragically advanced the schism of Greek from Latin Christianity. The Nicene Creed had spoken of "the Holy Ghost, who proceedeth from the Father"—*ex patre procedit*; for 250 years this sufficed; but in 589 a church council at Toledo made the statement read *ex patre filioque procedit*—"proceedeth from the Father and the Son"; this addition was accepted in Gaul, and zealously adopted by Charlemagne. The Greek theologians protested that the Holy Ghost proceeded not from but through the Son. The popes held the balance patiently for a time, and not until the eleventh century was the *filioque* officially entered into the Latin creed.

Meanwhile a struggle of wills was added to the conflict of ideas. Among the monks who had fled from Iconoclastic oppression was Ignatius, son of the Emperor Michael I. In 840 the Empress Theodora recalled the monk, and made him patriarch. He was a man of piety and courage; he denounced the prime minister Caesar Bardas, who had divorced his wife and lived with the widow of his son; and when Bardas persisted in incest Ignatius excluded him from the Church. Bardas banished Ignatius, and raised to the patriarchate the most accomplished scholar of the age (858). Photius (820?–91) was a master of philology, oratory, science, and philosophy; his lectures at the University of Constantinople had drawn to him a group of devoted students, to whom he opened his library and his home. Shortly before his promotion to the patriarchal see he had completed an encyclopedic *Myriobiblion* in 280 chapters, each of which reviewed and sampled an important book; through this vast compilation many passages of classic literature were preserved. His broad culture raised Photius above the fanaticism of the populace, which could not understand why he remained on such good terms with the emir of Crete. His sudden elevation from layman to patriarch offended the clergy of Constantinople; Ignatius refused to resign, and appealed to the bishop of Rome. Nicholas I sent legates to Constantinople to inquire into the case; and in letters to the Emperor Michael III and Photius he laid down the principle that no ecclesiastical matter of grave moment should be decided anywhere in Christendom without the consent of the pope. The Emperor called a church council, which ratified the appointment of Photius, and the Pope's legates joined in the confirmation. When they returned to Rome Nicholas repudiated them as having exceeded their instructions; he ordered the Emperor to reinstate Ignatius; and when his command was ignored he excommunicated Photius (863). Bardas threatened to send an army to depose Nicholas; the Pope, in an eloquent reply, scornfully pointed to the Emperor's submission to the marauding Slavs and Saracens.

> *We* have not invaded Crete; *we* have not depopulated Sicily; *we* have not subdued Greece; *we* have not burned the churches in the very suburbs of Constantinople; yet while these pagans with impunity conquer, burn, and lay waste [your territories], we, Catholic Christians, are menaced with the vain terror of your arms. Ye release Barabbas, and kill Christ.[27]

Photius and the Emperor called another church council, which excommunicated the Pope (867), and denounced the "heresies" of the Roman Church—among them the procession of the Holy Ghost from the Father *and* the Son, the shaving of priestly beards, and the enforced celibacy of the clergy; "from this usage," said Photius, "we see in the West so many children who do not know their fathers."

While Greek messengers were bearing these pleasantries to Rome, the situation was suddenly changed (867) by the accession of Basil I, who had murdered Caesar Bardas and had superintended the assassination of Michael III. Photius denounced the new Emperor as a murderer, and refused him the sacraments. Basil called a church council, which obediently deposed, insulted, and banished Photius, and restored Ignatius. But when Ignatius soon thereafter died, Basil recalled Photius; a council reinstated him as patriarch; and (Nicholas I having died) Pope John VIII approved. The schism of East and West was for a moment postponed by the death of the protagonists.

V. THE CHRISTIAN CONQUEST OF EUROPE: 529–1054

The most momentous event in the religious history of these centuries was not the quarrel of the Greek with the Latin Church, but the rise of Islam as a challenge to Christianity in both East and West. The religion of Christ had hardly consolidated its victories over the pagan Empire and the heresies when suddenly its most fervid provinces were torn from it, and with alarming ease, by a faith that scorned both the theology and the ethics of Christianity. Patriarchs still sat, by Moslem tolerance, in the sees of Antioch, Jerusalem, and Alexandria; but the Christian glory was departed from those regions; and what Christianity remained in them was heretical and nationalist. Armenia, Syria, and Egypt had set up church hierarchies quite independent of either Constantinople or Rome. Greece was saved to Christianity; there the monks triumphed over the philosophers, and the great monastery of the Holy Lavra, established on Mt. Athos in 961, rivaled the majesty of the Parthenon, which had become a Christian church. Africa still had many Christians in the ninth century, but they were rapidly diminishing under the handicaps of Moslem rule. In 711 most of Spain was lost to Islam. Defeated in Asia and Africa, Christianity turned north, and resumed the conquest of Europe.

Italy, bravely but narrowly saved from the Saracens, was divided between the Greek and Latin forms of Christianity. Almost on the dividing line was Monte Cassino. Under the long rule (1058–87) of Abbot Desiderius the monastery reached the zenith of its fame. From Constantinople he brought not only two magnificent bronze doors, but craftsmen who adorned the interiors with mosaics, enamels, and artistry in metal, ivory, and wood. The monastery became almost a university, with courses in grammar, classical as well as Christian literature, theology, medicine, and law. Following Byzantine models, the monks executed exceptionally fine illuminated manuscripts, and copied in a beautiful book hand the classics of pagan Rome; some classics were only thus preserved. In Rome the Church, under Pope Boniface IV and his successors, instead of permitting the further disintegration of pagan temples, reconsecrated them to Christian use and care: the Pantheon was dedicated to the Virgin Mary and All Martyrs (609), the temple of Janus became the church of St. Dionysius, the temple of Saturn became the church of the Saviour. Leo IV (847–55) renewed and embellished St. Peter's; and through the growth of the papacy and the coming of pilgrims, a polyglot suburb grew around that group of ecclesiastical buildings which took its name from the ancient Vatican Hill.

France was now the richest possession of the Latin Church. The Merovingian kings, confident of buying heaven after enjoying polygamy and murder, showered the bishoprics with lands and revenues. Here, as elsewhere, the Church received legacies from penitent magnates and devout heiresses; Chilperic's prohibition of such bequests was soon canceled by Gunthram. By one of the many pleasantries of history, the Gallic clergy were almost wholly recruited from the Gallo-Roman population; the converted Franks knelt at the feet of those whom they had conquered, and gave back in pious donations what they had stolen in war.[28] The clergy were the ablest, best educated, and least immoral element in Gaul; they almost monopolized literacy; and though a small minority led scandalous lives, most of them labored faithfully to give schooling and morals to a population suffering from the greed and wars of their lords and kings. The bishops were the chief secular as well as religious authorities in their dioceses; and their tribunals were the favorite resort of litigants even in non-ecclesiastical concerns. Everywhere they took under their protection orphans and widows, paupers and slaves. In many dioceses the Church provided hospitals; one such *hôtel-Dieu*—"inn of God"—was opened in Paris in 651. St. Germain, Bishop of Paris in the second half of the sixth century, was known throughout Europe for his work in raising funds— and spending his own—to emancipate slaves. Bishop Sidonius of Mainz banked the Rhine; Bishop Felix of Nantes straightened the course of the Loire; Bishop Didier of Cahors constructed aqueducts. St. Agobard (779– 840), Archbishop of Lyons, was a model of religion and a foe of superstition; he condemned trial by duel or ordeal, the worship of images, the magical explanation of storms, and the fallacies involved in the prosecutions for witchcraft; he was "the clearest head of his time." [29] Hincmar, the aristocratic primate of Reims (845–82), presided over a score of church councils, wrote sixty-six books, served as prime minister to Charles the Bald, and almost established a theocracy in France.

In each country Christianity took on the qualities of the national temperament. In Ireland it became mystic, sentimental, individualistic, passionate; it adopted the fairies, the poetry, the wild and tender imagination of the Celt; the priests inherited the magic powers of the Druids and the myths of the bards; and the tribal organization favored a centrifugal looseness in the structure of the Church—almost every locality had an independent "bishop." More numerous and influential than the bishops and priests were the monks who, in groups seldom numbering more than twelve, formed half-isolated and mostly autonomous monasteries throughout the island, recognizing the pope as head of the Church, but submitting to no external control. The earlier monks lived in separate cells, practicing a somber asceticism and meeting only for prayer; a later generation—the "Second Order of Irish Saints"—diverged from this Egyptian tradition, studied together, learned Greek, copied manuscripts, and established schools for clerics and laity. From the Irish schools in the sixth and seventh centuries a succession of renowned and redoubtable saints passed over into Scotland, England, Gaul, Germany, and Italy to revitalize and educate a darkened Christianity. "Almost all Ireland," wrote a Frank about 850, "comes flocking to our shores with a troop of philosophers." [30] As Germanic invasions of Gaul and Britain had driven scholars from those lands to Ireland, so now the wave returned, the debt was paid; Irish missionaries flung themselves upon the victorious pagan Angles, Saxons, Norwegians, and Danes in England, and upon the illiterate and half-barbarous Christians of Gaul and Germany, with the Bible in one hand and classic manuscripts in the other; and for a time it seemed that the Celts would win back through Christianity the lands they had lost to force. It was in the Dark Ages that the Irish spirit shone with its strongest light.

The greatest of these missionaries was St. Columba. We know him well through the biography written (*c.* 679) by Adamnan, one of his successors at Iona. Columba was born at Donegal in 521, of royal stock; like Buddha he was a saint who could have been a king. At school in Moville he showed such devotion that his schoolmaster named him Columbkille—Column of the Church. From the age of twenty-five he founded a number of churches and monasteries, of which the most famous were at Derry, Durrow, and Kells. But he was a fighter as well as a saint, "a man of powerful frame and mighty voice";[31] his hot temper drew him into many quarrels, at last into war with King Diarmuid; a battle was fought in which, we are told, 5000 men were killed; Columba, though victorious, fled from Ireland (563), resolved to convert as many souls as had fallen in that engagement at Cooldrevna. He now founded on the island of Iona, off the west coast of Scotland, one of the most illustrious of medieval monasteries. Thence he and his disciples brought the Gospel to the Hebrides, Scotland, and northern England. And there, after converting thousands of pagans and illuminating 300 "noble books," he died, in prayer at the altar, in his seventy-eighth year.

Kindred to him in spirit and name was St. Columban. Born in Leinster about 543, he does not enter history till we find him, aged thirty-two, establishing monasteries in the wilds of the Vosges Mountains of France. At Luxeuil he instructed his novices:

> You must fast every day, pray every day, work every day, read every day. A monk must live under the rule of one father, and in the society of many brethren, that he may learn humility from one, patience from another, silence from a third, gentleness from a fourth. . . . He must go to bed so tired that he will fall asleep on the way.[32]

Punishments were severe, usually by flogging: six stripes for coughing when beginning a psalm, or neglecting to manicure the nails before saying Mass, or smiling during services, or striking the teeth on the chalice at communion; twelve for omitting grace at meal; fifty for being late at prayers, one hundred for engaging in a dispute, two hundred for speaking familiarly with a woman.[33] Despite this reign of terror there was no lack of novices; Luxeuil had sixty monks, many from rich families. They lived on bread, vegetables, and water, cleared forests, plowed fields, planted and reaped, fasted and prayed. Here Columban established the *laus perennis*, or unending praise: all day and night, through relays of monks, litanies were to rise to Jesus, Mary, and the Saints.[34] A thousand monasteries like Luxeuil are a pervasive element in the medieval scene.

The stern temper that framed this rule allowed no compromise with other views; and Columban, who banned disputes, found himself in repeated quarrels with the bishops—whose authority he ignored—with secular officials—whose interferences he repelled—and even with the popes. For the Irish celebrated Easter according to a reckoning practiced by the early Church but abandoned by her in 343. In a consequent conflict with the Gallic clergy these appealed to Gregory the Great; Columban rejected the Pope's instructions, saying, "The Irish are better astronomers than you Romans," and bade Gregory accept the Irish mode of calculation or be "looked upon as a heretic and repudiated with scorn by the churches of the West." [35] The rebellious Irishman was expelled from Gaul (609) for denouncing the wickedness of Queen Brunhild; he was put by force on a vessel bound for Ireland; the ship was driven back to France; Columban crossed the forbidden land and preached to the pagans of Bavaria. He could hardly have been as terrible a man as his rule and career picture him, for we are told that squirrels perched confidently on his shoulders and ran in and out of his cowl.[36] Leaving a fellow Irishman to found (613) the monastery of St. Gall on Lake Constance, he painfully crossed the St. Gotthard Pass, and established the monastery of Bobbio in Lombardy in 613. There, two years later, in the austerity of his solitary cell, he died.

Tertullian mentions Christians in Britain in 208; Bede speaks of St. Alban as dying in the persecution by Diocletian; British bishops attended the Council of Sardica (347). Germanus, Bishop of Auxerre, went to Britain in 429 to suppress the Pelagian heresy.[37] William of Malmesbury avers that the Bishop, presumably on a later visit, routed an army of Saxons by having his British converts shout "Hallelujah!" at them.[38] From this vigorous condition British Christianity pined and almost died in the Anglo-Saxon invasions; we hear nothing of it again until, at the end of the sixth century, the disciples of Columba entered Northumberland, and Augustine, with seven other monks, reached England from Rome. Doubtless Pope Gregory had learned that Ethelbert, the pagan King of Kent, had married Bertha, a Christian Merovingian princess. Ethelbert listened courteously to Augustine, remained unconvinced, but gave him freedom to preach, and provided food and lodging for him and his fellow monks in Canterbury. At last (599) the Queen prevailed upon the King to accept the new faith; and many subjects followed their example. In 601 Gregory sent the pallium to Augustine, who became the first in an impressive line of distinguished archbishops of Canterbury. Gregory was lenient to the lingering paganism of England; he allowed the

old temples to be christened into churches, and permitted the custom of sacrificing oxen to the gods to be gently transformed into "killing them to the
refreshing of themselves to the praise of God"; [39] so that the English merely
changed from eating beef when they praised God to praising God when they
ate beef.

Another Italian missionary, Paulinus, carried Christianity to Northumberland (627). Oswald, King of Northumberland, invited the monks of Iona
to come and preach to his people; and to help their work he gave them the
island of Lindisfarne off the east coast. There St. Aidan (634) founded a
monastery that glorified its name by missionary devotion and the splendor
of its illuminated manuscripts. There and at Melrose Abbey St. Cuthbert
(635?–87) left behind him loving memories of his patience, piety, good
humor, and good sense. The holiness of such men, and perhaps the peace
and security they enjoyed amid recurrent wars, brought many neophytes
to the monasteries and nunneries that now arose in England. Despite occasional lapses into the ways of common men, the monks gave dignity to work
by their labor in woods and fields; here too, as in France and Germany, they
led the advance of civilization against marsh and jungle as well as against
illiteracy, violence, lechery, drunkenness, and greed. Bede thought that too
many Englishmen were entering monasteries; that too many monasteries
were being founded by nobles to put their property beyond taxation; and
that the tax-exempt lands of the Church were absorbing too much of England's soil; too few soldiers were left, he warned, to preserve England from
invasion.[40] Soon the Danes, then the Normans, would prove the worldly wisdom of the monk.

Strife found its way even into monastic peace when the Benedictine monks
of southern England, following the Roman ritual and calendar, came into
contact and conflict with the Irish monks and calendar and liturgy in the
north. At the Synod of Whitby (664) St. Wilfrid's eloquence decided the
issue—technically, the proper day for Easter—in favor of Rome. The Irish
missionaries pugnaciously resigned themselves to the decision. The British
Church, unified and endowed, became an economic and political power, and
took a leading role in civilizing the people and governing the state.

Christianity came to Germany as the gift of Irish and English monks. In
690 the Northumbrian monk Willibrord, who had been educated in Ireland,
crossed the North Sea with twelve adventurous aides, fixed his episcopal seat
at Utrecht, and labored for forty years to convert the Frisians. But these
realistic lowlanders saw in Willibrord the hand of his protector Pepin the
Young, and feared that their conversion would subject them to the Franks;
moreover, they were not pleased to be told that all their unbaptized forebears
were in hell. A Frisian king, having learned this as he stood on the brink

of baptism, turned away, saying that he preferred to spend eternity with his ancestors.[41]

A stronger man than Willibrord renewed the campaign in 716. Winfrid (680?–754), an English noble and Benedictine monk, won the name of Boniface from Pope Gregory II, and the title of "Apostle of Germany" from a pious posterity. Near Fritzlar in Hesse he found an oak tree worshiped by the people as the home of a god; he felled it; and the populace, amazed at his survival, flocked to be baptized. Great monasteries were set up at Reichenau (724), Fulda (744), and Lorsch (763). In 748 Boniface was made Archbishop of Mainz; he appointed bishops, and organized the German Church into a powerful engine of moral, economic, and political order. Having accomplished his mission in Hesse and Thuringia, and seeking to crown his career with a martyr's death, Boniface gave up his proud episcopate, and entered Frisia resolved to complete the work of Willibrord. He had labored there a year when he was attacked by the pagans and slain. A generation later Charlemagne brought Christianity to the Saxons with fire and sword; the obstinate Frisians thought it time to yield; and the conquest of Rome's conquerors by Roman Christianity was complete.

The final triumph of the faith in Europe was the conversion of the Slavs. In 861 Prince Rostislav of Moravia, noting the entrance into his realm of a Latin Christianity that ignored the vernacular in its liturgy, applied to Byzantium for missionaries who would preach and pray in the vulgar tongue. The emperor sent him two brothers, Methodius and Cyril, who, having been reared in Salonika, spoke Slavonic with ease. They were welcomed, but found that the Slavs had as yet no alphabet to fully express their language in writing; the few Slavs who wrote used Greek and Latin characters to represent their speech. Cyril thereupon invented the Slavonic alphabet and script by adopting the Greek alphabet with the values that Greek usage had given it by the ninth century—B sounded as V, H as I (English E), Chi as the Scotch ch; and he devised original letters for Slavonic sounds not expressible by Greek characters. With this alphabet Cyril translated into Slavonic the Septuagint Greek version of the Old Testament, and the Greek liturgical texts, thereby inaugurating a new written language and a new literature.

A struggle now ensued between Greek and Latin Christianity to see which should capture the Slavs. Pope Nicholas I invited Cyril and Methodius to Rome, where Cyril took monastic vows, fell ill, and died (869); Methodius returned to Moravia as an archbishop consecrated by the Pope. Pope John VIII allowed the use of the Slavonic liturgy, Stephen V forbade it. Moravia, Bohemia, and Slovakia (these constituting the Czechoslovakia of today), and later Hungary and Poland, were won to the Latin Church and rite; while Bulgaria, Serbia, and Russia accepted the Slavonic liturgy and alphabet, gave their allegiance to the Greek Church, and took their culture from Byzantium.

Political calculations influenced these religious transformations. The conversion of the Germans aimed to incorporate them firmly into the realm of the Franks. King Harald Bluetooth imposed Christianity upon Denmark (974) as part of the price that the Emperor Otto II demanded for peace; Boris of Bulgaria, after flirting with the papacy, went over to the Greek Church (864) to win protection against an expanding Germany; and Vladimir I made Russia Christian (988) to win the hand of Anna, sister of the Greek Emperor Basil II, and to obtain part of the Crimea as her dowry.[42] For two centuries the Russian Church acknowledged the patriarch of Constantinople; in the thirteenth century it declared its independence; and after the fall of the Eastern Empire (1453) the Russian Church became the dominant factor in the Greek Orthodox world.

The victorious soldiers in this Christian conquest of Europe were the monks, and the nurses in this war were the nuns. The monks helped the peasant pioneers to bring the wilderness under cultivation, to clear the forest and the brush, to drain the swamps and bridge the creeks and cut the roads; they organized industrial centers, schools, and charity; copied manuscripts and collected modest libraries; gave moral order, courage, and comfort to bewildered men uprooted from their traditional customs, cults, or homes. Benedict of Aniane labored, dug, and reaped amid his monks; and the monk Theodulf, near Reims, drove the plow so faithfully for twenty-two years that after his death it was kept as an object of veneration.

Periodically, after superhuman exaltations of virtue, devotion, and energy, monks and nuns relapsed into human nature, and in almost every century a campaign of monastic reform was needed to lift the monks again to the unnatural heights of their rule. Some monks enlisted in passing moods of piety and self-surrender, and were maladapted to the discipline after their ecstasy waned. Some were oblates, who had been brought to the monasteries and vowed to the monastic life by their parents when they were children of seven or more years of age, sometimes when they were infants in the cradle; and these vicarious vows were held irrevocable until, in 1179, papal decrees allowed their annulment at the age of fourteen.[43] In 817 Louis the Pious, shocked by the lax discipline of French monasteries, called a national assembly of abbots and monks at Aachen, and commissioned Benedict of Aniane to re-establish the Rule of St. Benedict of Nursia in all the monasteries of the realm. The new Benedict labored sedulously; but he died in 821, the wars of the kings soon disordered the Frank Empire, and Norman, Magyar, and Saracen raids despoiled hundreds of monasteries. Monks wandered homeless into the secular world; and those who returned after the wave of devastation had receded brought with them worldly ways. Feudal lords seized monasteries, appointed their abbots, appropriated their revenues. By

900 the monasteries of the West, like almost every institution in Latin Europe, had sunk to the lowest point in their medieval history. Some clergy, secular and regular, said St. Odo of Cluny (d. 942), "do so set to naught the Virgin's Son that they commit fornication in His very courts, nay in those very inns which the devotion of the faithful hath built in order that chastity may be kept safely within their fenced precincts; they so overflow with lust that Mary hath no room wherein to lay the child Jesus." [44] It was from Cluny that the great reform of the monasteries came.

About 910 twelve monks had established a monastery there in the hills of Burgundy, almost on the German-French frontier. In 927 Abbot Odo revised its rule towards a moral rigor combined with physical lenience: asceticism was rejected, baths were recommended, diet was generous, beer and wine were allowed; but the old vows of poverty, obedience, and chastity were to be unremittingly enforced. Similar institutions were opened elsewhere in France; but whereas each monastery had heretofore been a lawless law unto itself, or had been loosely subject to local bishop or lord, the new Benedictine monasteries allied with Cluny were ruled by priors subject both to the abbots of Cluny and to the popes. Under Cluny's abbots Mayeul (954–94), Odilo (994–1049), and Hugh (1049–1109) the movement for monastic affiliation spread from France to England, Germany, Poland, Hungary, Italy, and Spain; many old monasteries joined the "Cluniac Congregation"; by 1100 some 2000 "priories" acknowledged Cluny as their mother and ruler. The power so organized, free from state interference and episcopal supervision, gave the papacy a new weapon with which to control the secular hierarchy of the Church. At the same time it made possible a courageous reform of monasticism by the monks themselves. Disorder, idleness, luxury, immorality, simony were brought under firm rule; and Italy beheld the strange sight of a French monk, Odo, invited to Italy to reform Monte Cassino itself. [45]

VI. THE NADIR OF THE PAPACY: 867–1049

Reform reached Rome last of all. The populace of the city had always been unmanageable, even when the Imperial eagle had wielded legions in its claws; now the pontiffs, armed only with a weak militia, the majesty of their office, and the terror of their creed, found themselves the prisoners of a jealous aristocracy, and of a citizenry whose piety suffered from nearness to Peter's throne. The Romans were too proud to be impressed by kings, and too familiar to be awed by popes; they saw in the Vicars of Christ men subject like themselves to sickness, error, sin, and defeat; and they came to view the papacy not as a fortress of order and a tower of salvation, but as a collection agency whereby the pence of Europe might provide the dole of Rome. By the tradition of the Church no pope could be elected without

the consent of the Roman clergy, nobles, and populace. The rulers of Spoleto, Benevento, Naples, and Tuscany, and the aristocracy of Rome divided
into factions as of old; and whichever faction prevailed in the city intrigued
to choose and sway the pope. Between them they dragged the papacy, in
the tenth century, to the lowest level in its history.

In 878 Duke Lambert of Spoleto entered Rome with his army, seized Pope
John VIII, and tried to starve him into favoring Carloman for the Imperial
throne. In 897 Pope Stephen VI had the corpse of Pope Formosus (891–6)
exhumed, dressed it in purple robes, and tried before an ecclesiastic council
on the charge of violating certain Church laws; the corpse was condemned,
stripped, mutilated, and plunged into the Tiber.[46] In the same year a political revolution in Rome overthrew Stephen, who was strangled in jail.[47] For
several years thereafter the papal chair was filled by bribery, murder, or the
favor of women of high rank and low morality. For half a century the family of Theophylact, a chief official of the papal palace, made and unmade
popes at will. His daughter Marozia secured the election of her lover as Pope
Sergius III (904–11);[48] his wife Theodora procured the election of Pope
John X (914–28). John has been accused of being Theodora's paramour,
but on inadequate evidence;[49] certainly he was an excellent secular leader,
for it was he who organized the coalition that in 916 repulsed the Saracens
from Rome. Marozia, after having enjoyed a succession of lovers, married
Guido, Duke of Tuscany; they conspired to unseat John; they had his
brother Peter killed before his face; the Pope was thrown into prison, and
died there a few months later from causes unknown. In 931 Marozia raised
to the papacy John XI (931–5), commonly reputed to be her bastard son
by Sergius III.[50] In 932 her son Alberic imprisoned John in the Castle of
Sant' Angelo, but allowed him to exercise from jail the spiritual functions
of the papacy. For twenty-two years Alberic ruled Rome as the dictatorial
head of a "Roman Republic." At his death he bequeathed his power to his
son Octavian, and made the clergy and people promise to choose Octavian
pope when Agapetus II should die. It was done as he ordered; in 955 Marozia's grandson became John XII, and distinguished his pontificate by orgies
of debauchery in the Lateran palace.[51]

Otto I of Germany, crowned Emperor by John XII in 962, learned the
degradation of the papacy at first hand. In 963, with the support of the Transalpine clergy, Otto returned to Rome, and summoned John to trial before
an ecclesiastical council. Cardinals charged that John had taken bribes for
consecrating bishops, had made a boy of ten a bishop, had committed adultery with his father's concubine and incest with his father's widow and her
niece, and had made the papal palace a very brothel. John refused to attend
the council or to answer the charges; instead he went out hunting. The council deposed him and unanimously chose Otto's candidate, a layman, as Pope
Leo VIII (963–5). After Otto had returned to Germany John seized and

mutilated the leaders of the Imperial party in Rome, and had himself restored by an obedient council to the papacy (964).[52] When John died (964)
the Romans elected Benedict V, ignoring Leo. Otto came down from Germany, deposed Benedict, and restored Leo, who thereupon officially recognized the right of Otto and his Imperial successors to veto the election of
any future pope.* On Leo's death Otto secured the election of John XIII
(965–72). Benedict VI (973–4) was imprisoned and strangled by a Roman
noble, Bonifazio Francone, who made himself pope for a month, then fled
to Constantinople with as much papal treasury as he could carry. Nine years
later he returned, killed Pope John XIV (983–4), again appropriated the
papal office, and died peaceably in bed (985). The Roman Republic again
raised its head, assumed authority, and chose Crescentius as consul. Otto III
descended upon Rome with an irresistible army, and a commission from
the German prelates to end the chaos by making his chaplain Pope Gregory
V (996–9). The young Emperor put down the Republic, pardoned Crescentius, and went back to Germany. Crescentius at once re-established the
Republic, and deposed Gregory (997). Gregory excommunicated him, but
Crescentius laughed, and arranged the election of John XVI as pope. Otto
returned, deposed John, gouged out his eyes, cut off his tongue and nose,
and paraded him through the streets of Rome on an ass, with his face to the
tail. Crescentius and twelve Republican leaders were beheaded, and their
bodies were hung from the battlements of Sant' Angelo (998).[53] Gregory
resumed the papacy, and died, probably of poison, in 999. Otto replaced
him with one of the most brilliant of all the popes.

Gerbert was born of lowly parentage near Aurillac in Auvergne (c. 940),
and at an early age entered a monastery there. At the abbot's suggestion, he
went to Spain to study mathematics; and in 970 Count Borel of Barcelona
took him to Rome. Pope John XIII was impressed by the monk's learning,
and recommended him to Otto I. For a year Gerbert taught in Italy, and
at that time or later had Otto II among his pupils. Then he went to Reims
to study logic in the cathedral school; and presently we find him head of
the school (972–82). He taught an unusual variety of subjects, including
the classic poets; he wrote an excellent Latin, and letters sometimes rivaling
those of Sidonius. Wherever he went he collected books, and spent his funds
recklessly to have copies made of manuscripts in other libraries; perhaps we
owe to him the preservation of Cicero's orations.[54] He led the Christian
world in mathematics, introduced an early form of the "Arabic" numerals,
wrote on the abacus and the astrolabe, and composed a treatise on geometry;
he invented a mechanical clock, and an organ operated by steam.[55] So many
were his scientific accomplishments that after his death he was reputed to
have possessed magical powers.[56]

---

* The Roman Catholic Church regards Leo VIII as antipope, and attributes no validity to
his actions or decrees.

When Adalbero died (988), Gerbert sought to succeed him as archbishop of Reims; but Hugh Capet appointed instead Arnulf, a bastard son of the dying Carolingian house. Arnulf plotted against Hugh, an ecclesiastical council deposed him despite papal protests, and chose Gerbert archbishop (991). Four years later a papal legate persuaded a synod at Moisson to unseat Gerbert. The humiliated scholar went to the court of Otto III in Germany, received every honor there, and molded the mind of the young king to the idea of restoring a Roman Empire with its capital at Rome. Otto made him archbishop of Ravenna, and, in 999, pope. Gerbert took the name of Sylvester II, as if to say that he would be a second Sylvester to a second world-unifying Constantine. Had he and Otto lived another decade they might have realized their dream, for Otto was the son of a Byzantine princess, and Gerbert might have become a philosopher-king. But in the fourth year of his papacy Gerbert died, poisoned, said Roman rumor, by the same Stephania who had poisoned Otto.

Their aspirations, and the busy politics of the world around them, show how few were the Christians who took seriously the notion that the world would end in the year 1000. At the beginning of the tenth century a Church council had announced that the final century of history had begun;[57] at its close a small minority of men so believed, and prepared themselves for the Last Judgment. The great majority went on their wonted ways, working, playing, sinning, praying, and trying to outlive senility. There is no evidence of any panic of fear in the year 1000, nor even of any rise in gifts to the Church.[58]

After the death of Gerbert the decay of the papacy was resumed. The counts of Tusculum, in league with the German emperors, bought bishops and sold the papacy with hardly an effort at concealment. Their nominee Benedict VIII (1012–24) was a man of vigor and intelligence; but Benedict IX (1032–45), made pope at the age of twelve, led so shameful and riotous a life[59] that the people rose and drove him out of Rome. Through Tusculan aid he was restored; but tiring of the papacy he sold it to Gregory VI (1045–6) for one (or two) thousand pounds of gold.[60] Gregory astonished Rome by being almost a model pope; apparently he had bought the papacy in a sincere desire to reform it and liberate it from its overlords. The Tusculan house could not favor such a reform; it made Benedict IX pope again, while a third faction set up Sylvester III. The Italian clergy appealed to the Emperor Henry III to end this disgrace; he came to Sutri, near Rome, and convened an ecclesiastical council; it imprisoned Sylvester, accepted Benedict's resignation, and deposed Gregory for admittedly buying the papacy. Henry persuaded the council that only a foreign pope, protected by the emperor, could terminate the debasement of the Church. The Bishop of Bamberg was elected as Clement II (1046–7); he died a year later; and Damasus II (1047–8) also succumbed to the malaria that now regularly came out of the undrained Campagna. At last in Leo IX (1049–54) the papacy found a man who could face its problems with courage, learning, integrity, and a piety long rare in Rome.

VII. THE REFORM OF THE CHURCH: 1049–54

Three internal problems agitated the Church at this time: simony in the papacy and the episcopacy, marriage or concubinage in the secular clergy, and sporadic incontinence among the monks.

Simony—the sale of church offices or services—was the ecclesiastical correlate of contemporary corruption in politics. Good people were one source of simony; so the mother of Guibert of Nogent, anxious to devote him to the Church, paid ecclesiastical authorities to make him a cathedral canon at eleven; a church council at Rome in 1099 mourned the frequency of such cases. As bishops in England, Germany, France, and Italy administered profane as well as ecclesiastical affairs, and were feudally endowed with lands or villages or even cities to supply their necessary revenues, ambitious men paid secular powers great sums for such appointments, and greedy potentates overrode all decencies to earn these bribes. In Narbonne a boy of ten was made archbishop on paying 100,000 solidi (1016).[61] Philip I of France consoled an unsuccessful applicant for an episcopal see with blithe counsel: "Let me make my profit out of your rival; then you can try to get him degraded for simony; and afterward we can see about satisfying you."[62] The French kings, following a tradition established by Charlemagne, regularly appointed the bishops of Sens, Reims, Lyons, Tours, and Bourges; elsewhere in France the bishops were appointed by dukes or counts.[63] Many bishoprics became in the eleventh century the hereditary patrimony of noble families, and were used as provision for bastards or younger sons; in Germany one baron possessed and transmitted eight bishoprics.[64] A German cardinal alleged (c. 1048) that the simoniacal buyers of sees and benefices had sold the marble facings of churches, even the tiles from their roofs, to reimburse themselves for the cost of their appointments.[65] Such appointees were men of the world; many lived in luxury, engaged in war, allowed bribery in episcopal courts,[66] named relatives to ecclesiastical posts, and worshiped Mammon with undivided loyalty; Pope Innocent III would say of an archbishop of Narbonne that he had a purse where his heart should have been.[67] The purchase of sees became so usual that practical men accepted it as normal; but reformers cried out that Simon Magus had captured the Church.[68]

Among the general clergy the moral problem hovered between marriage and concubinage. In the ninth and tenth centuries the marriage of priests was customary in England, Gaul, and north Italy. Pope Hadrian II (867–72) himself had been a married man;[69] and Bishop Ratherius of Verona (tenth century) reported that practically all priests in his diocese were married. By the beginning of the eleventh century celibacy in the secular clergy was exceptional.[70] It would be a mistake to consider clerical marriage immoral; though often contrary to the canons and ideals of the Church, it was quite in accord with the customs and moral judgments of the times. At Milan a married priest stood higher in public repute than one unmarried;[71] the latter was suspected of concubinage. Even concubinage—the regular cohabitation of an unmarried man with an unmarried woman—was condoned by public opinion. The great majority of the European clergy led apparently decent moral lives; and all through the Middle Ages we hear of priests and bishops living in saintly devotion to their flocks. Here and there, however, there were scandalous exceptions. In 742 Bishop Boniface complained to Pope Zachary that bishoprics were being given to "greedy laymen and adulterous clerics,"[72] and that some deacons "kept four or five concubines";[73] and the Venerable Bede, in the same century, condemned "some bishops" of England for "laughter, jesting, tales, revelings, drunkenness, and . . . dissolute living."[74] Towards the end of the first millennium such charges became more numerous. Ralph Glaber described the clergy of that period as sharing in the general immorality of the age. An Italian monk, Peter Damian (1007–72), presented to the Pope a book ominously entitled *Liber Gomorrhianus*, in which he described, with the exaggerations to be expected from his sanctity, the vices of the clergy; one chapter was "On the Diversity of Sins Against Nature." Damian strongly urged the prohibition of clerical marriage.

The Church had long since opposed clerical marriage on the ground that a married priest, consciously or not, would put his loyalty to wife and children above his devotion to the Church; that for their sake he would be tempted to accumulate money or property; that he would try to transmit his see or benefice to one of his offspring; that an hereditary ecclesiastical caste might in this way develop in Europe as in India; and that the combined economic power of such a propertied priesthood would be too great for the papacy to control. The priest should be totally devoted to God, the Church, and his fellow men; his moral standard must be higher than that of the people, and must confer upon him the prestige necessary to public confidence and reverence. Several councils had demanded celibacy of the clergy; one—at Pavia in 1018—had decreed a status of perpetual slavery, and disbarment from inheritance, for all children of priests.[75] But clerical marriage continued.

Leo IX found the see of Peter impoverished by clerical bequests of Church benefices to clerical offspring, by baronial seizures of Church estates, and by the highway robbery of pilgrims bringing prayers, petitions, and offerings to Rome. He organized protection for the pilgrims, recaptured alienated ecclesiastical property, and set himself to the heavy task of ending simony and clerical marriage. Turning over the domestic and administrative cares of the papacy to the shrewd and devoted monk who was to become Gregory VII,

Leo left Rome in 1049, resolved to examine at first hand the morals of the clergy, and the functioning of the Church, in the major cities of Europe. The dignity of his bearing, the unaffected austerity of his life, at once revived the respect that men had held for the highest official of the Church; vice hid its head as he approached; and Godfrey of Lorraine, who had plundered churches and defied kings, trembled under papal excommunication, submitted to be publicly scourged before the altar of the church that he had ruined in Verdun, undertook to repair the church, and labored in the work with his own hands. At Cologne Leo held papal court, and received every honor from a German clergy proud of a German pope. Passing into France, he presided over a tribunal at Reims, and conducted an inquiry into lay and clerical morals, the sale of ecclesiastical offices, the spoliation of church property, the relaxation of monastic rules, and the rise of heresy. Every bishop present was ordered to confess his sins. One after another, including archbishops, accused himself. Leo sternly reproved them, deposed some, forgave some, excommunicated four, summoned others to Rome and public penance. He commanded the clergy to dismiss their wives and concubines, and to forgo the use of arms. The Council of Reims further decreed that bishops and abbots were to be elected by the clergy and the people, prohibited the sale of ecclesiastical offices, and forbade the clergy to receive fees for administering the eucharist, attending the sick, or burying the dead. A council in Mainz (1049), under Leo's urging, enacted similar reforms for Germany. In 1050 he returned to Italy, presided at the Council of Vercelli, and condemned the heresy of Berengar of Tours.

With his long and arduous visitation of the North Leo had restored the prestige of the papacy, replaced the German emperor as the head of the German Church, brought the French and Spanish episcopates to acknowledge the authority of the pope, and made some progress toward cleansing the clergy of venality and venery. In 1051 and 1052 he made further campaigns in Germany and France; presided over a great ecclesiastical assembly at Worms, and another at Mantua. Returning at last to Rome, he took on the uncongenial task of defending the Papal States by military means. The Emperor Henry III had given him the duchy of Benevento; Duke Pandulf of Capua refused to recognize the grant, and, with the help of Robert Guiscard's Normans, took and held the duchy. Leo asked for a German army to help him oust Pandulf; he received only 700 men; to these he added some untrained Italians; and at their head he marched against the Normans, whose cavalry alone numbered 3000 buccaneers skilled in war. The Normans overwhelmed Leo's forces, captured him, and then knelt to ask his pardon for having killed 500 of his men. They took him to Benevento, and there, with all courtesy, kept him prisoner for nine months. Heartbroken, and penitent for having taken the sword, Leo wore nothing but sackcloth, slept on a carpet and a stone, and passed nearly all the day in prayer. The Normans saw

that he was dying, and released him. He entered Rome amid universal rejoicing, absolved all whom he had excommunicated, ordered a coffin placed in
St. Peter's, sat beside it for a day, and died at the altar. The lame, the dumb,
and the lepers came from all parts of Italy to touch his corpse.

VIII. THE GREAT EASTERN SCHISM: 1054

It was in St. Leo's pontificate that Greek and Latin Christianity were finally divorced. While Western Europe was shrouded in the darkness, misery,
and ignorance of the ninth and tenth centuries, the Eastern Empire, under
the Macedonian emperors (867–1057), recovered some of the territory it
had lost to the Arabs, reasserted its leadership in south Italy, and experienced
a new flowering of literature and art. The Greek Church drew strength and
pride from the revived wealth and power of the Byzantine state, won Russia,
Bulgaria, and Serbia to the Eastern observance, and resented more sharply
than ever the claims of a debased and impoverished papacy to the ecclesiastical monarchy of the Christian world. To the Greeks of this age the Germans,
Franks, and Anglo-Saxons of the contemporary West seemed crude barbarians, an illiterate and violent laity led by a worldly and corrupt episcopate.
The papal rejection of the Byzantine emperor for the king of the Franks, the
papal appropriation of the exarchate of Ravenna, the papal coronation of a
rival Roman emperor, the papal drive into Greek Italy—these galling political
events, and not the slight diversities of creed, severed Christendom into East
and West.

In 1043 Michael Cerularius was appointed Patriarch of Constantinople. He
was a man of noble birth, wide culture, keen intellect, and resolute will.
Though a monk, he had risen through a political rather than an ecclesiastical
career; he had been a high minister of the Empire, and would hardly have accepted the patriarchate if it had involved submission to Rome. In 1053 he circulated a Latin treatise by a Greek monk, which strongly criticized the
Roman Church for enforcing clerical celibacy contrary to apostolic example
and ecclesiastical tradition, for using unleavened bread in the Eucharist, and
for adding *filioque* to the Nicene Creed. In that same year Cerularius closed
all those churches in Constantinople that observed the Latin ritual, and excommunicated all clergy who should persist in its use. Leo, then at the height
of his pontificate, despatched a letter to Cerularius demanding that the Patriarch should recognize the supremacy of the popes, and branding any church
that refused such recognition as "an assembly of heretics, a conventicle of
schismatics, a synagogue of Satan." [76] In a milder mood Leo sent legates to
Constantinople to discuss with the emperor and the Patriarch the differences
that kept the two branches of Christianity apart. The emperor received the
legates cordially, but Cerularius denied their competence to deal with the

issues. Leo died in April, 1054, and the papacy remained vacant for a year. In July the legates, taking matters into their own hands, deposited on the altar of St. Sophia a bull excommunicating Cerularius. Michael convened a council representing all Eastern Christianity; it recapitulated the grievances of the Greek against the Roman Church, including the shaving of the beard; it formally condemned the bull of the legates, and "all who had helped in drawing it up, whether by their advice or even by their prayers." [77] The schism was now complete.

IX. GREGORY VII HILDEBRAND: 1073–85

It was a great misfortune for Christianity that an interval of chaos and weakness separated the pontificate of Leo IX from that of one of the strongest popes in the history of the Church.

Hildebrand is a German name, and suggests a German lineage; Gregory's contemporaries interpreted it to mean *Hellbrand*, pure flame. He was born of lowly parentage in the hamlet of Sovano in the marshes of Tuscany (1023?). He was educated in the convent of St. Mary on the Aventine at Rome, and entered the Benedictine order. When Pope Gregory VI was deposed and banished to Germany in 1046 Hildebrand accompanied him as chaplain; during that year in Cologne he learned much about Germany that helped him in his later struggle with Henry IV. Soon after his return to Rome he was made a cardinal subdeacon by Leo IX, and was appointed administrator of the Papal States and at the same time legate to France; we may judge from this remarkable elevation of a youth of twenty-five the reputation that he had so soon acquired for political and diplomatic ability. Popes Victor II (1055–7) and Stephen IX (1057–8) continued to employ him in high capacities. In 1059 Nicholas II became Pope largely through Hildebrand's influence; and the indispensable monk, not yet a priest, was made papal chancellor.

It was at his urging that Nicholas and the Lateran Council of 1057 issued an edict transferring the election of the pope to the College of Cardinals; by that one stroke Hildebrand proposed to rescue the papacy from Roman nobles and German emperors. Already the young ecclesiastical statesman had formulated a far-reaching policy. To secure the papacy from German domination he closed his eyes to the swashbuckling raids of the Normans in southern Italy, recognized their expropriations, and approved their ambitions, in return for a pledge of military protection. In 1073, after serving eight popes for twenty-five years, Hildebrand himself was raised to the papacy. He resisted, preferring to rule behind the throne; but cardinals, clergy, and people cried out, "St. Peter wills Hildebrand to be Pope!" He was ordained priest, was consecrated Pope, and took the honored name of Gregory.

He was small of stature, homely of feature, keen of eye, proud of spirit, strong of will, sure of the truth, and confident of victory. Four purposes inspired him: to complete Leo's reform of clerical morals, to end lay investiture, to unify all Europe in one church and one republic headed by the papacy, and to lead a Christian army to the East to reclaim the Holy Land from the Turks. Early in 1074 he wrote to the counts of Burgundy and Savoy, and to the Emperor Henry IV, begging them to raise funds and troops for a crusade which he proposed to lead in person. The counts were not moved, and Henry was too insecure on his throne to think of a crusade.

The Lateran Council of 1059, under Nicholas II and Hildebrand, had excommunicated any priest who kept a wife or a concubine, and had forbidden Christians to attend the Mass of a priest known to keep a woman in his house. Reluctant to break up the families of their clergy, many bishops in Lombardy refused to promulgate these decrees, and prominent clerics in Tuscany defended clerical marriage as both moral and canonical. The legislation could not be enforced, and the idea that clergymen living in "sin" could not administer valid sacraments was so enthusiastically taken up by heretical preachers that the papal appeal to the congregations was withdrawn.[78] When Hildebrand became Gregory VII (1073) he attacked the problem with uncompromising determination. A synod in 1074 renewed the decrees of 1059; Gregory sent these to all the bishops of Europe with a stern command to promulgate and enforce them; and absolved the laity from obedience to priests who disregarded them. The reaction was again violent. Many priests declared that they would abandon their calling rather than their wives; others deprecated the decrees as making unreasonable demands on human nature, and predicted that their enforcement would promote secret promiscuity. Bishop Otto of Constance openly favored and protected his married clergy. Gregory excommunicated him, and absolved his flock from obedience to him. In 1075 Gregory took the further step of commanding the dukes of Swabia and Carinthia, and other princes, to use force, if necessary, in keeping recalcitrant clergy from performing priestly functions. Several German princes obeyed him; and many priests unwilling to dismiss their wives were deprived of their parishes.[79] Gregory was to die without victory; but Urban II, Paschal II, and Calixtus II reaffirmed and executed his decrees. The Council of the Lateran in 1215 under Innocent III issued a final condemnation, and clerical marriage slowly disappeared.

The problem of investiture seemed simpler than that of clerical marriage. Assuming, as kings and popes agreed, that Christ had established the Church, it seemed clear that her bishops and abbots should be chosen by churchmen rather than by laymen; and surely it was scandalous that a king should not only appoint bishops, but (as in Germany) invest them with the episcopal staff and ring—sacred symbols of spiritual power. But to the kings an opposite conclusion was equally evident. Admitting, as most German bishops and abbots would have done, that they had been invested by the king with lands, revenues, and secular responsibilities, it seemed meet and just, by feudal law, that these prelates—at least the bishops—should owe their appointment and temporal allegiance to the king, as they had done without demurrer under Constantine and Charlemagne. If they were released from such subordination and loyalty half the land of Germany—which had by this time been granted to bishoprics and monasteries [80]—would escape control by the state, and their due and wonted service to it. The German bishops, and many Lombard bishops of German origin and appointment, suspected that Gregory was seeking to end their relative ecclesiastical autonomy, and subordinate them completely to the Roman see. Gregory was willing that the bishops should continue their feudal obligations to the king,[81] but unwilling that they should surrender the lands they had received by royal grant; [82] by the law of the Church the property of the Church was inalienable. Gregory complained that lay appointment had begotten most of the simony, worldliness, and immorality that had appeared in the German and French episcopates. He felt that the bishops must be brought under the papal authority, or else the Western, like the Eastern, Church would become a subservient appendage to the state.

Behind this historic conflict lay the question of papacy versus empire: which should unify and govern Europe? The German emperors claimed that their power was also divine, as being a necessity of social order; had not St. Paul said that "the powers that be are ordained by God"? Were they not, according to the popes themselves, the heirs of the Empire of Rome? They stood for the freedom of the part as Gregory stood for the unity and order of the whole. Privately they resented—so long before the Reformation—the flow of gold in fees and Peter's pence from Germany to Italy; [83] and they saw in the papal policy an effort of Latin Rome to renew its ancient control over what Italy scorned as the barbarian Teutonic North. They freely admitted the supremacy of the Church in spiritual matters, but asserted a like supremacy for the state in temporal or earthly affairs. To Gregory this seemed a disorderly dualism; spiritual considerations, he felt, should dominate material concerns, as the sun dominates the moon; [84] the state should be subordinate to the Church—the City of Man to the City of God—in all matters involving doctrine, education, morals, justice, or ecclesiastical organization. Had not the kings of France and the emperors of the Holy Roman Empire implicitly admitted that the spiritual was the source and sovereign of the temporal power by accepting archiepiscopal or papal anointment or consecration? The Church, as a divine institution, merited universal authority; the pope, as the vicegerent of God, had the right and duty to depose bad kings, and to confirm or reject the choice made of rulers by men or circumstance.[85] "Who," asked Gregory, in a passionate epistle to Bishop Hermann of Metz, "is ignorant that kings and princes had their origin in those who, ignorant of God, and covering themselves with pride, violence, and perfidy, in fact nearly every crime . . . claimed to rule over their peers—i.e., men—in blind lust and intolerable arrogance?" [86] Looking upon the political division, chaos, and wars of Europe, it seemed to Gregory that the only escape from that age-old misery was a world order in which these states should surrender something of their jealous sovereignty, and acknowledge the pope as their feudal suzerain, the majestic head of a universal, or at least a European, Christian Republic.

The first step toward this end was the liberation of the papacy from German control. The second was to bring all bishops under the authority of the papal see, at least to this degree, that the bishop should be chosen by the clergy and people of the diocese under the auspices of a bishop nominated by the pope or the metropolitan, and that the election should be valid only when confirmed by the archbishop or the pope.[87] Gregory began with a letter (1073) to the bishop of Châlons, in which he threatened to excommunicate King Philip Augustus of France for selling bishoprics. In 1074 he sent a general letter to the French episcopate calling upon them to denounce the crimes of the King to his face, and to discontinue all religious services in France should Philip refuse to reform.[88] Lay investiture continued there nevertheless, but the French bishops proceeded with caution, and left the issue to be fought out in Germany.

In February, 1075, a synod of Italian bishops at Rome, under the lead of Gregory, issued decrees against simony, clerical marriage, and lay investiture. With strange precipitance, Gregory at once excommunicated for simony five bishops who were councilors of Henry IV; he suspended the bishops of Pavia and Turin, deposed the bishop of Piacenza, and ordered Bishop Hermann of Bamberg to come to Rome to clear himself from charges of simony. When Hermann tried to bribe the papal tribunal Gregory unceremoniously deposed him. He politely asked Henry to nominate a fit successor for the Bamberg see; Henry not only nominated a court favorite, but invested him with episcopal ring and staff without waiting for papal approval— a procedure accordant with custom, but openly defiant of the Roman synod's decree. As if to make still clearer his rejection of Gregory's demands, Henry appointed bishops to the sees of Milan, Fermo, and Spoleto—almost under the nose of the Pope—and kept in his favor the excommunicated councilors.

In December, 1075, Gregory sent Henry a letter of remonstrance, and commissioned the bearers to add an oral message threatening to excommunicate the King should he continue to ignore the Roman synod's decrees. Henry summoned a council of German bishops to Worms (January 24, 1076); twenty-four came, some stayed away. Before this assembly Hugh, a Roman cardinal, accused Gregory of licentiousness, cruelty, and witchcraft, and of obtaining the papacy by bribery and violence; and he reminded the bishops that the custom of centuries required, for the election of any pope, the consent of the German emperor—which Gregory had not asked. The Emperor, emboldened by his recent suppression of a Saxon revolt, proposed the deposition of the Pope; all bishops present signed the decree; a council of Lombard bishops at Piacenza approved it; and Henry sent it to Gregory with a choice superscription: "Henry, King not by usurpation but by God's ordinance, to Hildebrand, not Pope but false monk." [89] The message was delivered to Gregory at a synod in Rome (February 21, 1076); the 110 bishops there present, all from Italy and Gaul, wished to kill the messenger, but Gregory protected him. The synod excommunicated the bishops who had signed the Worms decree; and the Pope launched upon the Emperor a triple sentence of excommunication, anathema, and deposition, and released Henry's subjects from their oaths of obedience (February 22, 1076). Henry countered by persuading the bishop of Utrecht to anathematize Gregory— "the perjured monk"—from the pulpit of the cathedral. All Europe was shocked by the papal deposition of an emperor, and still more by the imperial deposition, and episcopal cursing, of a pope. The religious sentiment proved stronger than the national, and public support rapidly deserted the Emperor. Saxony resumed its revolt; and when Henry summoned the bishops and nobles of his realm to councils at Worms and Mainz his call was almost universally ignored. On the contrary the German aristocracy, seeing in the situation a chance to strengthen their feudal power against the King, met at Tribur (October 16, 1076), approved the excommunication of the Emperor, and declared that should he not obtain absolution from the Pope by February 22, 1077, they would name a successor to his throne. It was arranged between the nobles and the papal legates at Tribur that a diet should be held at Augsburg on February 2, 1077, under the presidency of the Pope, to settle the affairs of the Church and the kingdom.

Henry retired to Speyer, defeated and almost entirely deserted. Believing that the proposed diet would confirm his deposition, he sent messengers to Rome, offering to come there and ask for absolution. Gregory replied that as he would soon leave for Augsburg he could not receive Henry at Rome. En route north, the Pope was entertained at Mantua by his friend and supporter Matilda, Countess of Tuscany. Here he learned that Henry had entered Italy. Fearing that the King would raise an army among the antipapal population of Lombardy, Gregory took refuge in Matilda's fortified castle at Canossa, high in the Apennines near Reggio Emilia. There on January 25, 1077, at the height of one of the severest winters that Italy could recall, Henry, says Gregory's report to the German princes,

> came in person to Canossa . . . bringing with him only a small retinue.
> . . . He presented himself at the gate of the castle, barefoot and clad
> only in wretched woolen garments, beseeching us with fears to grant
> him absolution and forgiveness. This he continued to do for three
> days, while all those about us were moved to compassion at his plight,

and interceded for him with tears and prayers. . . . At length we removed the excommunication from him, and received him again into the bosom of Holy Mother Church.[90]

Gregory hesitated so long through no hardness of heart. He had agreed to make no peace with Henry without consulting the German princes; and he knew that if Henry, forgiven, should rebel again, a second excommunication would have diminished effect, and might receive less support from the nobility; on the other hand the Christian world would have found it hard to understand why the Vicar of Christ should refuse forgiveness to so humble a penitent. The event was a spiritual triumph for Gregory, but a subtle diplomatic victory for Henry, who now automatically regained his throne. Gregory returned to Rome, and devoted himself for the next two years to ecclesiastical legislation chiefly aimed to enforce clerical celibacy. The German princes, however, proclaimed Rudolf of Swabia King of Germany (1077), and Henry's strategy seemed to have failed. But now that he had freed himself from the papal ban he found fresh sympathy from a people not enamored of the nobility; a new army was recruited to defend him; and for two years the rival kings ravaged Germany in civil war. Gregory, after long vacillation, gave his support to Rudolf, excommunicated Henry a second time, forbade Christians to serve him, and offered absolution from their sins to all who should enlist under Rudolf's flag (March, 1080).[91]

Henry acted precisely as before. He called a council of favorable nobles and bishops at Mainz; the council deposed Gregory; a council of bishops from Germany and northern Italy at Brixen confirmed the deposition, declared Archbishop Guibert of Ravenna Pope, and commissioned Henry to execute its decrees. The rival armies met on the banks of the Saale in Saxony (October 15, 1080); Henry was defeated, but Rudolf was killed. While the rebel nobles divided on the question of a successor to Rudolf, Henry entered Italy, marched unresisted through Lombardy, recruiting another army as he went, and laid siege to Rome. Gregory appealed to Robert Guiscard for help, but Robert was far away. The Pope appealed to William I, whose conquest of England he had sanctioned and helped, but William was not sure that he wanted Henry to lose this royal argument. The people of Rome defended the Pontiff bravely, but Henry was able to seize a large part of Rome, including St. Peter's, and Gregory fled to the Castello Sant' Angelo. A synod in the Lateran palace, at Henry's command, deposed and excommunicated Gregory, and consecrated Guibert as Pope Clement III (March 24, 1084); and a week later Clement crowned Henry Emperor. For a year Henry was master of Rome.

But in 1085 Robert Guiscard, leaving his campaign against Byzantium, approached Rome at the head of 36,000 men. Henry had no army to resist such a force; he fled to Germany, Robert entered the capital, freed Gregory, sacked Rome, left half of it in ruins, and took Gregory to Monte Cassino; the populace of Rome was so infuriated against the Normans that the Pope, their ally, could not remain there in safety. Clement returned to Rome as apparent Pope. Gregory went on to Salerno, held another synod, excommunicated Henry again, and then broke down in body and spirit. "I have loved right- eousness," he said, "and hated iniquity; therefore I die in exile." He was only sixty-two; but the nervous strain of his bitter controversies had worn him out; and his apparent defeat by the man whom he had forgiven at Canossa left him no will to live. There at Salerno, May 25, 1085, he died.

Perhaps he had loved righteousness too imperiously, and had hated iniquity too passionately; it is reserved to the philosopher, and forbidden to the man of action, to see elements of justice in the position of his enemy. Innocent III, a century later, would realize a large part of Gregory's dream of a world united under the Vicar of Christ; but he would win in a more temperate spirit and with wiser diplomacy. And yet Innocent's victory was made pos- sible by Gregory's defeat. Hildebrand had grasped higher than his reach, but he had for a decade raised the papacy to the greatest height and power that it had yet known. His uncompromising war against clerical marriage suc- ceeded, and prepared for his successors a clergy whose undivided loyalty immeasurably strengthened the Church. His campaign against simony and lay investiture would win a tardy victory, but in the end his view would pre- vail, and the bishops of the Church would become the willing servitors of the papacy. His use of papal legates was destined to extend the power of the popes into every parish in Christendom. Through his initiative papal elec- tions were now free from royal domination. They would soon give the Church an amazing succession of strong men; and ten years after Gregory's death the kings and nobles of the world would acknowledge Urban II as the head of Europe in that synthesis of Christianity, feudalism, chivalry, and im- perialism which we know as the Crusades.

CHAPTER XXII

Feudalism and Chivalry

600-1200

I. FEUDAL ORIGINS

IN the six centuries that followed the death of Justinian, a remarkable collaboration of circumstances slowly effected a basic transformation of economic life in the West European world.

Certain conditions already noted came together to prepare for feudalism. As the cities of Italy and Gaul became unsafe during the German invasions, aristocrats moved out to their rural villas, and surrounded themselves with agricultural dependents, "client" families, and military aides. Monasteries whose monks tilled the soil and practiced handicrafts accentuated the centrifugal movement toward half-isolated economic units in the countryside. Roads injured by war, neglected by poverty, and endangered by highwaymen, could no longer maintain adequate communication and exchange. State revenues declined as commerce contracted and industry fell; impoverished governments could no longer provide protection for life, property, and trade. The obstruction of commerce compelled the villas to seek economic self-sufficiency; many manufactured articles formerly bought from the cities were—from the third century onward—produced on the great estates. In the fifth century the letters of Sidonius Apollinaris show us rural lords living in luxury on spacious holdings tilled by a semiservile tenantry; they are already a feudal aristocracy, possessing their own judiciary [1] and soldiery,[2] and differing from the later barons chiefly in knowing how to read.

The same factors that paved the way for feudalism between the third century and the sixth established it between the sixth and the ninth. Merovingian and Carolingian kings paid their generals and administrators with grants of land; in the ninth century these fiefs became hereditary and semi-independent through the weakness of the Carolingian kings. The Saracen, Norse, and Magyar invasions of the eighth, ninth, and tenth centuries repeated and cemented the results of the German invasions six centuries before: central protection failed, the local baron or bishop organized a localized order and defense, and remained possessed of his own force and court. Since the invaders were often mounted, defenders who could afford a horse were in demand; cavalry became more important than infantry; and just as in early Rome a class of *equites*—men on horseback—had taken form between patrician and plebs, so in France, Norman England, and Christian Spain a class of mounted knights grew up between the duke or baron and the peasantry. The people did not resent these developments; in an atmosphere of terror, when attack might come at any time, they craved military organization; they built their homes as near to the baronial castle or fortified monastery as they could; and they readily gave allegiance and service to a lord—i.e., a law-ward—or to a duke—i.e., one who could lead; we must imagine their terror to understand their subjection. Freemen who could no longer protect themselves offered their land or labor to some strong man in return for shelter and support; in such cases of "commendation" the baron usually assigned to "his man" a tract to be held as a "precarium," on a lease revocable by the donor at any time; this precarious tenure became the usual form of serf possession of land. Feudalism was the economic subjection and military allegiance of a man to a superior in return for economic organization and military protection.

It cannot be rigidly defined, for it had a hundred variations in time and place. Its origins lay in Italy and Germany, but its most characteristic development came in France. In Britain it may have begun as the enserfment of Britons by Anglo-Saxon conquerors,[3] but for the most part it was there a Gallic importation from Normandy. It never matured in northern Italy or Christian Spain; and in the Eastern Empire the great landowners never developed military or judicial independence, nor that hierarchy of fealties which seemed in the West essential to feudalism. Large sectors of Europe's peasantry remained unfeudalized: the shepherds and ranchers of the Balkans, eastern Italy, Spain; the vine growers of western Germany and southern France; the sturdy farmers of Sweden and Norway; the Teutonic pioneers beyond the Elbe; the mountaineers of the Carpathians, the Alps, the Apennines, and the Pyrenees. It was not to be expected that a continent so physically and climatically diverse should have a uniform economy. Even within feudalism conditions of contract and status varied from nation to nation, from manor to manor, from time to time. Our analysis will apply chiefly to the France and England of the eleventh and twelfth centuries.

II. FEUDAL ORGANIZATION

1. The Slave

In those lands and times society consisted of freemen, serfs, and slaves. Freemen included nobles, clerics, professional soldiers, practitioners of the professions, most merchants and artisans, and peasants who owned their land with little or no obligation to any feudal lord, or leased it from a lord for a money rent. Such peasant proprietors constituted some four per cent of the farming population of England in the eleventh century; they were more numerous in western Germany, northern Italy, and southern France; they probably constituted a quarter of the total peasant population in Western Europe.[4]

Slavery diminished as serfdom increased. In twelfth-century England it was mostly confined to household service; in France north of the Loire it was negligible; in Germany it rose in the tenth century, when no compunction was felt in capturing pagan Slavs for menial tasks on German estates, or for sale in Moslem or Byzantine lands. Conversely, Moslems and Greeks were kidnaped by slave traders along the shores of the Black Sea, western Asia, or northern Africa for sale as farm hands, domestic servants, eunuchs, concubines, or prostitutes in Islam or Christendom.[5] The slave trade flourished especially in Italy, probably due to the nearness of Moslem countries, which could be preyed upon with a good conscience; it seemed a fair revenge for Saracen raids.

An institution that had lasted throughout known history appeared inevitable and eternal, even to honest moralists. It is true that Pope Gregory I freed two of his slaves with admirable words about the natural liberty of all men;[6] but he continued to use hundreds of slaves on the papal estates,[7] and approved laws forbidding slaves to become clerics or marry free Christians.[8] The Church denounced the sale of Christian captives to Moslems, but permitted the enslavement of Moslems and of Europeans not yet converted to Christianity. Thousands of captured Slavs and Saracens were distributed among monasteries as slaves; and slavery on church lands and papal estates continued till the eleventh century.[9] Canon law sometimes estimated the wealth of church lands in slaves rather than in money; like secular law, it considered the slave as a chattel; it forbade church slaves to make wills, and decreed that any *peculium* or savings of which they died possessed should belong to the Church.[10] The archbishop of Narbonne, in his will of 1149, left his Saracen slaves to the bishop of Béziers.[11] St. Thomas Aquinas interpreted slavery as one consequence of Adam's sin, and as economically expedient in a world where some must toil in order that others may be free to defend them.[12] Such views were in the tradition of Aristotle, and in the spirit of the times. The rule of the Church, that her property should never be alienated except at its full market value,[13] was unfortunate for her slaves and serfs; emancipation sometimes proved more difficult on ecclesiastical than on secular properties.[14] Nevertheless the Church progressively restricted the slave traffic by forbidding the enslavement of Christians at a time when Christianity was spreading rapidly.

The decline of slavery was due not to moral progress but to economic change. Production under direct physical compulsion proved less profitable or convenient than production under the stimulus of acquisitive desire. Servitude continued, and the word *servus* served for both slave and serf; but in time it became the word *serf*, as *villein* became *villain*, and *Slav* became *slave*. It was the serf, not the slave, who made the bread of the medieval world.

2. *The Serf*

Typically the serf tilled a plot of land owned by a lord or baron who gave him a life tenure and military protection as long as he paid an annual rent in products, labor, or money. He could be evicted at the owner's will; [15] and at his death the land passed to his children only by consent and satisfaction of the lord. In France he could be sold independently of the land, for some forty shillings ($400.00?); sometimes he (i.e., his labor) was sold by his owner in part to one person, in part to another. In France he could abjure the feudal contract by surrendering the land and all his possessions to the seigneur. In England he was denied this right of migration, and fugitive medieval serfs were recaptured as zealously as fugitive modern slaves.

The feudal dues of the serf to the owner of his land were numerous and diverse; some intelligence must have been required even to remember them. (1) He paid annually three taxes in money: (a) a small head tax, to the government but through the baron; (b) a small rent (*cens*); (c) an arbitrary charge (*taille*) levied by the owner yearly or oftener. (2) He annually gave the lord a share—usually a *dîme* or tenth—of his crops and livestock. (3) He owed his lord many days of unpaid labor (*corvée*); this was an inheritance from older economies, in which tasks like clearing woods, draining marshes, digging canals, raising dykes, were performed by the peasants collectively as an obligation to the community or king. Some lords required three days weekly through most of the year, four or five days a week in plowing or harvest time; additional labor days, paid only by meals, might be exacted in emergencies. This obligation of *corvée* lay upon only one male in each household. (4) The serf was obliged to grind his corn, bake his bread, brew his beer, press his grapes, at the lord's mill, oven, vat, or press, and pay a small fee for each such use. (5) He paid a fee for the right to fish, hunt, or pasture his animals, on the lord's domain. (6) His actions at law had to be brought before the baronial court, and cost him a fee varying with the gravity of the case. (7) He had to serve at call in the baron's regiment in war. (8) If the baron was captured, the serf was expected to contribute to the ransom. (9) He contributed also to the substantial gift due to the lord's son on being made a knight. (10) He paid the baron a tax on all products that he took for sale to market or fair. (11) He could not sell his beer or wine until the lord had had two weeks' prior time to sell the lord's beer or wine. (12) In many cases he was obliged to buy a prescribed quantity of wine yearly from his lord; if he did not buy in time, says one customal (a collection of the laws of a manor), "then the lord shall pour a four-gallon measure over the man's roof; if the wine runs down, the tenant must pay for it; if it runs upward, he shall pay nothing." [16] (13) He paid a fine if he sent a son to higher education or gave him to the Church, for thereby the manor lost a hand. (14) He paid a tax, and required the lord's consent, in case he or his children married a person not belonging to his manor, for then the lord would lose some or all of the offspring; on many estates permission and fee were required for any marriage at all. (15) In scattered instances [17] we hear of the *ius primae noctis* or *droit du seigneur*, whereby the lord might claim the "right of the first night" with the serf's bride; but in almost all cases the serf was allowed to "redeem" his bride by paying a fee to the lord; [18] in this form the *ius primae noctis* survived in Bavaria till the eighteenth century.[19] On some English estates the lord fined the peasant whose daughter had sinned; on some Spanish estates a peasant wife convicted of adultery forfeited part or all of her belongings to the lord.[20] (16) If the peasant died without issue residing with him, the house and land reverted to the lord by escheat. If his heir was an unmarried daughter, she could retain the holding only by marrying a man living on the same manor. In any event, as a kind of inheritance tax, the lord, on the death of a serf tenant, was entitled to take an animal, or an article of furniture or clothing, from the holding; in some cases the parish priest took a similar *mortuarium*; [21] in France these death dues were exacted only when the serf died without a codomiciled heir. (17) On some—especially on ecclesiastical—manors he paid an annual and an inheritance tax to the *Vogt* who provided military defense for the estate. To the Church the peasant paid an annual tithe or tenth of his produce.

From so varied an assortment of dues—never all exacted from one family—it is impossible to calculate the total of a serf's obligations. For late medieval Germany it has been reckoned at two thirds of his produce.[21a] The power of custom, pre-eminent in agricultural regimes, favored the serf: usually his dues in money and kind tended to remain the same through centuries,[22] despite rising production and depreciated currencies. Many disabilities or obligations that lay on the serf in theory or law were softened or annulled by baronial indulgence, effective resistance, or the erosion of time.[23] Perhaps in general the misery of the medieval serf has been exaggerated; the dues exacted of him were largely in lieu of a money rent to the owner, and taxes to the community, to maintain public services and public works; probably they bore a smaller proportion to his income than our federal, state, county, and school taxes bear to our income today.[24] The average peasant of the twelfth century was at least as well off as some sharecroppers in modern states, and better off than a Roman *proletaire* in Augustus' reign. [25] The baron did not consider himself an exploiter; he functioned actively on the manor, and seldom enjoyed great wealth. The peasants, till the thirteenth century, looked up to him with admiration, often with affection; if the lord became a childless widower they sent deputations to him to urge remarriage, lest the estate be left without a regular heir, and be despoiled in a war of succession.[26] Like most economic and political systems in history, feudalism was what it had to be to meet the necessities of place and time and the nature of man.

The peasant's cottage was of fragile wood, usually thatched with straw and turf, occasionally with shingles. We hear of no fire-fighting organization before 1250; when one of these cottages took fire it was usually a total loss. As often as not the house had only one room, at most two; a wood-burning fireplace, an oven, a kneading trough, table and benches, cupboard and dishes, utensils and andirons, caldron and pothanger, and near the oven, on the earthen floor, an immense mattress of feathers or straw, on which the peasant, his wife and children, and his overnight guest all slept in promiscuous and mutual warmth. Pigs and fowl had the run of the house. The women kept the place as clean as circumstances would permit, but the busy peasants found cleanliness a nuisance, and stories told how Satan excluded serfs from hell because he could not bear their smell.[27] Near the cottage was a barn with horse and cows, perhaps a beehive and a hennery. Near the barn was a dunghill to which all animal or human members of the household contributed. Roundabout were the tools of agriculture and domestic industry. A cat controlled the mice, and a dog watched over all.

Dressed in a blouse of cloth or skins, a jacket of leather or wool, belt and trousers, high shoes or boots, the peasant must have made a sturdy figure, not much different from the peasant of France today; we must picture him not as an oppressed and beaten man, but as a strong and patient hero of the plow, sustained, as every man is, by some secret, however irrational, pride. His wife worked as hard as himself, from dawn to dark. In addition she supplied him with children; and since children were assets on the farm, she bore them abundantly; nevertheless we read in the Franciscan Pelagius (c. 1330) how some peasants "often abstain from their wives, lest children be born, fearing, under pretext of poverty, that they cannot bring up so many." [28]

The food of the peasant was substantial and wholesome—dairy products, eggs, vegetables, and meat; but genteel historians mourn that he had to eat black—i.e., whole grain—bread.[29] He shared in the social life of the village, but had no cultural interests. He could not read; a literate serf would have been an offense to his illiterate lord. He was ignorant of everything but farming, and not too skilled in that. His manners were rough and hearty, perhaps gross; in this turmoil of European history he had to survive by being a good animal, and he managed it. He was greedy because poor, cruel because fearful, violent because repressed, churlish because treated as a churl. He was the mainstay of the Church, but he had more superstition than religion. Pelagius charged him with cheating the Church of her tithes, and neglecting to observe the holydays and the fasts; Gautier de Coincy (thirteenth century) complained that the serf "has no more fear of God than a sheep, does not give a button for the laws of Holy Church." [30] He had his moments of heavy, earthy humor, but in the fields and in his home he was a man of spare speech, straitened vocabulary, and solemn mood, too consumed by toil and chores to waste his energy on words or dreams. Despite his superstitions he was a realist; he knew the merciless whims of the sky, and the certainty of death; one season of drouth could bring him and his brood to starvation. Sixty times between 970 and 1100 famine mowed men down in France; no British peasant could forget the famines of 1086 and 1125 in Merrie England; and the bishop of Trier in the twelfth century was shocked to see starving peasants kill and eat his horse.[31] Flood and plague and earthquake entered the play, and made every comedy a tragedy at last.

3. *The Village Community*

Around the baronial villa some fifty to five hundred peasants—serfs, half free, or free—built their village, living not in isolated homesteads but, for safety's sake, close together within the walls of the settlement. Usually the village was part of one or more manors; most of its officials were appointed by the baron, and were responsible only to him; but the peasants chose a reeve or provost to mediate between them and the lord, and to co-ordinate their agricultural activity. In the market place they gathered periodically to barter goods in the residuum of trade that survived the economic self-containment of the manor. The village rural household raised its own vegetables and some of its meat, spun its wool or linen, made most of its clothing. The village blacksmith hammered out iron tools, the tanner made leather goods, the carpenter built cottages and furniture, the wheelwright made carts; fullers, dyers, masons, saddlers, cobblers, soapmakers . . . lived in the village or came there transiently to ply their crafts on demand; and a public butcher or baker competed with the peasant and the housewife in preparing meat and bread.

Nine tenths of the feudal economy were agricultural. Normally, in eleventh-century France and England, the cultivated land of the manor was yearly divided into three fields; one was planted to wheat or rye, one to barley or oats, one was left fallow. Each field was subdivided into acre or half-acre strips, separated by "balks" of unplowed turf. The village officials assigned to each peasant a variable number of strips in each field, and bound him to rotate his crops in accord with a plan fixed by the community. The whole field was plowed, harrowed, planted, cultivated, and harvested by the joint labor of all. The scattering of one man's strips among three or more fields may have aimed to give him a fair share of unequally productive lands; and the co-operative tillage may have been a survival from a primitive communism of which scant trace remains. In addition to these strips each peasant fulfilling his feudal dues had the right to cut timber, pasture his cattle, and gather hay in the manorial woods, common, or "green." And usually he had enough land around his cottage for a garden and flowers.

Agricultural science in feudal Christendom could hardly compare with that of Columella's Romans, or of Moslem Mesopotamia or Spain. Stubble and other refuse were burned on the fields to fertilize the soil and rid it of insects and weeds; marl or other limy earths provided a crude manure; there were no artificial fertilizers, and the costs of transport limited the use of animal dung; the archbishop of Rouen emptied the offal of his stables into the Seine instead of carting it to his fields in nearby Deville. Peasants pooled their pence to buy a plow or harrow for their common use. Till the eleventh century the ox was the draft animal; he ate less expensively, and in old age could be eaten more profitably than the horse. But about 1000 the harness makers invented the stiff collar that would allow a horse to draw a load without choking; so dressed, the horse could plow three or four times as much in a day as the ox; in wet temperate climates speed of plowing was important; so during the eleventh century the horse more and more replaced the ox, and lost his high status as reserved for travel, hunting, and war.[32] Water mills, long known to the Moslem East, entered Western Europe toward the end of the twelfth century.[33]

The Church eased the toil of the peasant with Sundays and holydays, on which it was a sin to do "servile work." "Our oxen," said the peasants, "know when Sunday comes, and will not work on that day." [34] On such days, after Mass, the peasant sang and danced, and forgot in hearty rustic laughter the dour burden of sermon and farm. Ale was cheap, speech was free and profane, and loose tales of womankind mingled with awesome legends of the saints. Rough games of football, hockey, wrestling, and weight throwing pitted man against man, village against village. Cockfighting and bullbaiting flourished; and hilarity reached its height when, within a closed circle, two blindfolded men, armed with cudgels, tried to kill a goose or a pig. Sometimes, of an evening, peasants visited one another, played indoor games, and drank; usually, however, they stayed at home, for no streets were lit; and at home, since candles were dear, they went to bed soon after dark. In the long nights of the winter the family welcomed the cattle into the cottage, thankful for their heat.

So, by hard labor and mute courage, rather than by the initiatives and skills that proper incentives breed, the peasants of Europe fed themselves and their masters, their soldiers and clergy and kings. They drained marshes, raised dykes, cleared woods and canals, cut roads, built homes, advanced the frontier of cultivation, and won the battle between jungle and man. Modern Europe is their creation. Looking now at these neat hedges and ordered fields, we cannot see the centuries of toil and tribulation, breaking back and heart, that beat the raw materials of reluctantly bountiful nature into the economic foundations of our life. Women, too, were soldiers in that war; it was their patient fertility that conquered the earth. Monks fought for a time as bravely as any; planted their monasteries as outposts in the wilds, forged an economy out of chaos, and begot villages in the wilderness. At the beginning of the Middle Ages the greater part of Europe's soil was untilled and unpeopled forest and waste; at their end the Continent had been won for civilization. Perhaps, in proper perspective, this was the greatest campaign, the noblest victory, the most vital achievement, of the Age of Faith.

4. The Lord

Under every system of economy men who can manage men manage men who can only manage things. In feudal Europe the manager of men was the baron—in Latin *dominus*, in French *seigneur* (the Roman *senior*), in German *Herr* (master), in English *lord*. His functions were threefold: to give military protection to his lands and their inhabitants; to organize agriculture, industry, and trade on these lands; to serve his liege lord or his king in war. In an economy reduced to elementals and fragments by centuries of migration, invasion, rapine, and war, society could survive only by the local independence and sufficiency of food supply and soldiery. Those who could organize defense and tillage became the natural lords of the land. Ownership and management of land became the source of wealth and power; and an age of landed aristocracy began that would last till the Industrial Revolution.

The basic principle of feudalism was mutual fealty: the economic and military obligation of serf or vassal to the lord, of lord to suzerain or superior lord, of suzerain to king, of king to suzerain, of suzerain to lord, of lord to vassal and serf. In return for the services of his serfs, the lord gave them land on a life tenure verging on ownership; he allowed them, for a modest fee, the use of his ovens, presses, mills, waters, woods, and fields; he commuted many labor dues for small money payments, and let others lapse in the oblivion of time. He did not dispossess the serf—usually he took care of him—in helpless sickness or old age.[35] On feast days he might open his gates to the poor, and feed all who came. He organized the maintenance of bridges, roads, canals, and trade; he found markets for the manor's surplus products, "hands" for its operations, money for its purchases. He brought in good stock for breeding purposes, and allowed his serfs to service their flocks with his selected males. He could strike—in some localities or circumstances he could kill—a serf with impunity; but his sense of economy controlled his brutality. He exercised judicial as well as military powers over his domain, and profited unduly from fines levied in the manorial court; but this court, though often intimidated by his bailiff, was mostly manned by serfs themselves; and that the rude justice there decreed was not too oppressive appears from the readiness of the serf to buy indemnity from service in these judicial assemblies. Any serf who cared and dared could speak his mind in the manorial court; some dared; and in their piecemeal and unintended way these tribunals helped to forge the liberties that ended serfdom.

A feudal lord could own more than one manor or estate. In such case he appointed a "seneschal" to supervise his "domain"—i.e., all his manors—and a steward or bailiff for each; and he would move from manor to manor with his household to consume their products on the spot. He might have a castle on each of his estates. Descended from the walled camp (*castrum, castellum*) of the Roman legions, from the fortified villa of the Roman noble, or from the fortress or *burg* of the German chieftain, the feudal castle or château was built less for comfort than for security. Its outermost protection was a wide, deep fosse or moat; the earth thrown up and inward from the moat formed a mound into which were sunk square posts bound together to form a continuous stockade. Across the moat a cleated drawbridge led up to an iron gate or portcullis, which protected a massive door in the castle wall. Within this wall were stables, kitchen, storehouses, outhouses, bakery, laundry, chapel, and servants' lodgings, usually all of wood. In war the tenants of the manor crowded with their cattle and movables into this enclosure. At its center rose the donjon, the house of the master; in most cases it was a large square tower, also of wood; by the twelfth century it was built of stone and took a rounded form as easier for defense. The lowest story of the donjon was a storehouse and dungeon; above this dwelt the lord and his family. From these donjons, in the eleventh and twelfth centuries, developed the castles and châteaux of England, Germany, and France, whose impregnable stones were the military basis of the lord's power against his tenants and the king.

The interior of the donjon was dark and confined. Windows were few and small, and seldom glazed; usually canvas, oiled paper, shutters, or lattices kept out most rain and much light; artificial light was provided by candles or torches. In most cases there was but one room to each of the three stories. Ladders and trap doors, or winding stairs, connected the floors. On the second story was the main hall, serving as the baron's court of justice, and as dining room, living room, and bedroom for most of his household. At one end there might be a raised platform or dais, on which the lord, his family, and his guest ate their meals; others ate from removable tables placed before benches in the aisles. At retiring time mattresses were laid upon the floor or upon low wooden bedsteads in the aisles; all the household slept in this one room, with screens providing privacy. The walls were whitewashed or painted; they were adorned with banners, weapons, and armor, and the room might be protected from drafts by hangings or tapestries. The floor, paved with tile or stone, was covered with rushes and boughs. In the middle of the room a kind of central heating was generated by a wood fire in a hearth. Till the later Middle Ages there was no chimney; smoke escaped through a louver or "lantern" in the roof. Behind the dais a door opened into a "solar," where the lord, his family, and his guest might take their ease and the sun; furniture was more comfortable there, with a carpet, a fireplace, and a luxurious bed.

The lord of the manor dressed himself in a tunic, usually of colored silk, adorned with some geometrical or floral design; a cape covering the shoulders, and loose enough to be raised over the head; short drawers and breeches; stockings that reached up the thighs; and long shoes with toes curled up like prows. At his belt swung a scabbard and sword; from his neck usually hung some pendant like a cross. To distinguish one helmeted and armored knight from another in the First Crusade,[36] European nobles adopted the Islamic practice[37] of marking their garments, livery, standards, armor, and equipage with heraldic devices or coats of arms; henceforth heraldry developed an esoteric jargon intelligible only to heralds and knights.* Despite all adornments the lord was no parasitic idler. He rose at dawn, mounted his tower to detect any approaching peril, hastily breakfasted, perhaps attended Mass, had "dinner" at 9 A.M., supervised the multifarious operations of the manor, shared actively in some of them, gave orders of the day to steward, butler, groom, and other servitors, received wayfarers and visitors, had "supper" with them and his family at five, and usually retired at nine. On some days the routine was broken by hunting, more rarely by tournaments, now and then by war. He entertained frequently, and exchanged presents lavishly with his guests.

His wife was almost as busy as himself. She bore and reared many children. She directed the many servants (with an occasional box on the ear), kept an eye on bakery, kitchen, and laundry, superintended the making of butter and cheese, the brewing of beer, the salting down of meat for the winter, and that major household industry of knitting, sewing, spinning, weaving, and embroidery, which made most of the family's clothing. If her husband went to war she took over the military and economic management of the estate, and was expected to supply his financial needs as he campaigned; if he was taken prisoner she had to squeeze a ransom for him out of the toil of his serfs or from the sale of her finery and gems. If her husband died sonless she might inherit the seigneury, and become its *domina, dame*; but she was expected to remarry soon to provide the estate and her suzerain with military protection or service; and the suzerain limited her choice to a few candidates capable of meeting these obligations. In the privacy of the castle she could be an amazon or a termagant, and give her husband blow for blow. In her leisure hours she dressed her vigorous body in flowing fur-hemmed robes of silk, dainty headgear and footwear, and gleaming jewelry—an ensemble fit to send a troubadour into amorous or literary ecstasy.

Her children received an education quite different from that of the universities. The sons of the aristocracy were rarely sent to public schooling;

---

* Yellow, white, blue, red, green, black, and violet received respectively the names of or (gold), argent (silver), azure, gules, vert, sable, and purpure. Azure blue was a color adopted from the East, hence one of its names, ultramarine; gules were trimmings of fur—usually dyed red—worn by Crusaders around the wrists and neck (Latin *gula*, throat). In the thirteenth century these heraldic emblems or blazons (i.e., shields) were used by abbeys, towns, and nations as well as by families. Over their heraldic emblems or banners old families usually placed a laconic motto—*En bonne foi, Ni plus ni moins*, etc.[38]

in many cases no effort was made to teach them how to read. Literacy was left to clerks or scribes who could be hired for a pittance. Intellectual knowledge was scorned by most feudal knights; du Guesclin, one of the most honored figures of chivalry, trained himself in all the arts of war, and learned to face all weathers stoutly, but never bothered to learn how to read; only in Italy and Byzantium did the nobles carry on a literary tradition. Instead of going to a school, the boy of knightly family was sent, about the age of seven, to serve as page in another aristocratic household. There he learned obedience, discipline, manners, dress, the knightly code of honor, and the skills of joust and war; perhaps the local priest added some training in letters and reckoning. Girls were taught a hundred useful or pretty arts by merely seeing and doing. They took care of guests, and of the knight returning from battle or tournament; they unbuckled his armor, prepared his bath, laid out clean linen and raiment and perfumes for him, and waited on him at table with modest courtesy and tutored grace. They, rather than the boys, learned to read and write; they provided most of the audience for troubadours, trouvères, and jongleurs, and for the romantic prose and poetry of the time.

The baron's household often included some vassals or retainers. The vassal was a man who, in return for his military service, personal attendance, or political support, received from the lord some substantial boon or privilege —usually a tract of land with its serfs; in such cases usufruct belonged to the vassal, ownership remained with the lord. A man too proud or strong to be a serf, yet too limited to provide his own military security, performed an act of "homage" to a feudal baron: knelt bareheaded and weaponless before him, placed his hands in the hands of the seigneur, declared himself that lord's *homme* or man (while retaining his rights as a freeman), and by an oath on sacred relics or the Bible pledged the lord eternal fealty. The seigneur raised him, kissed him, invested him with a fief,* and gave him, in symbol thereof, a straw, stick, lance, or glove. Thenceforward the seigneur owed his vassal protection, friendship, fidelity, and economic and legal aid; he must not, says a medieval lawyer, insult his vassal, or seduce his vassal's wife or daughter;[39] if he does, the vassal may "throw down the glove" as a de-fy—i.e., as a release from fealty—and yet keep his fief.

The vassal might "subinfeudate" part of his land to a lesser vassal, who would then bear the same relation and responsibility to him that he bore to his lord. A man might hold fiefs from several lords, and owe them "simple homage" and limited service; but to one "liege" lord he pledged "liege homage"—full allegiance and service in peace and war. The lord himself, however great, might be vassal to another lord by holding property or privilege in fief from him; he might even be vassal to—hold a fief from—the vassal of another lord. All lords were vassals of the king. In these intricate relationships the

---

* *Fief*, Latin *feudum*, is from the old German or Gothic *faihu*, cattle; it is kin to the Latin *pecus*, and, like it, acquired the secondary meaning of goods or money.

prime bond was not economic but military; a man gave or owed military service and personal fealty to a lord; property was merely his reward. In theory feudalism was a magnificent system of moral reciprocity, binding the men of an endangered society to one another in a complex web of mutual obligation, protection, and fidelity.

5. The Feudal Church

Sometimes the lord of the manor was a bishop or an abbot. Though many monks labored with their hands, and many monasteries and cathedrals shared in parish tithes, additional support was necessary for great ecclesiastical establishments; and this came mostly from kings and nobles in gifts of land, or shares in feudal revenues. As these gifts accumulated, the Church became the largest landholder in Europe, the greatest of feudal suzerains. The monastery of Fulda owned 15,000 small villas, that of St. Gall had 2000 serfs;[40] Alcuin at Tours was lord of 20,000 serfs.[41] Archbishops, bishops, and abbots received investiture from the king, pledged their fealty to him like other feudatories, carried such titles as duke and count, minted coin, presided over episcopal or abbey courts, and took on the feudal tasks of military service and agricultural management. Bishops or abbots accoutered with armor and lance became a frequent sight in Germany and France; Richard of Cornwall, in 1257, mourned that England had no such "warlike and mettlesome bishops." [42] So enmeshed in the feudal web, the Church found herself a political, economic, and military, as well as a religious, institution; her "temporalities" or material possessions, her "feudalities" or feudal rights and obligations, became a scandal to strict Christians, a talking point for heretics, a source of consuming controversy between emperors and popes. Feudalism feudalized the Church.

6. The King

Just as the Church was in the twelfth century a feudal and hierarchical structure of mutual protection, service, and fealty, sanctioned by benefices and topped by a suzerain pope, so the secular feudal regime demanded for its completion a lord of all vassals, a suzerain of all secular suzerains, a king. Theoretically the king was the vassal of God, and governed by divine right in the sense that God permitted, and thereby authorized, his rule. Practically, however, the king had been elevated by election, inheritance, or war. Men like Charlemagne, Otto I, William the Conqueror, Philip Augustus, Louis IX, Frederick II, and Louis the Fair enlarged their inherited power by force of character or arms; but normally the kings of feudal Europe were not so much the rulers of their peoples as the delegates of their vassals. They were chosen or accepted by the great barons and ecclesiastics; their direct power was limited to their own feudal domain or manors; elsewhere in their kingdom the serf and vassal swore fealty to the lord who protected them, rarely to the king whose small and distant forces could not reach out to guard the scattered outposts of the realm. The state, in feudalism, was merely the king's estate.

In Gaul this atomization of rule proceeded furthest because the Carolingian princes weakened themselves by dividing the empire, because the bishops subdued them to ecclesiastical subservience, and because the Norse attacks broke most violently upon France. In this perfected feudalism the king was *primus inter pares*; he stood an inch or two above the princes, dukes, marquises, and counts; but in practice he was, like these "peers of the realm," a feudal baron limited for revenue to his own lands, forced to move from one royal manor to another for sustenance, and dependent in war and peace upon the military aid or diplomatic service of rich vassals who seldom pledged him more than forty days of armed attendance in the year, and spent half their time plotting to unseat him. To win or reward support, the crown had granted estate after estate to powerful men; in the tenth and eleventh centuries too small a domain remained to the French king to give him secure ascendancy over his vassal lords. When they made their estates hereditary, established their own police and courts, and minted their own coinage, he lacked the force to prevent them. He could not interfere with the jurisdiction of these vassals over their own lands except in the capital cases that appealed to him; he could not send his officers or tax collectors into their domains; he could not stop them from making independent treaties or waging independent war. In feudal theory the French king owned all the lands of the lords who called him their sovereign; in reality he was merely a great landlord, not necessarily the greatest; and never did his holdings equal those of the Church.

But as the inability of the kings to protect their realm had generated feudalism, so the inability of feudal lords to maintain order among themselves, or to provide a uniform government for an expanding commercial economy, weakened the barons and strengthened the kings. The zeal for martial contests absorbed the aristocracies of feudal Europe in private and public wars; the Crusades, the Hundred Years' War, the Wars of the Roses, and finally the wars of religion drank up their blood. Some of them, impoverished and recognizing no law, became robber barons who pillaged and murdered at will; and the excesses of liberty called for a unified power that would maintain order throughout the realm. Commerce and industry generated a growing and wealthy class outside the feudal bond; merchants resented feudal tolls and the insecurity of transport through feudal domains; and they demanded that private law should be superseded by a central government. The king allied himself with their class and the rising towns; they provided the finances for the assertion and extension of his authority; and all who felt oppressed or injured by the lords looked to the king for rescue and redress. The ecclesiastical barons were usually vassal and loyal to the king; the popes, however often at odds with royalty, found it easier to deal with a monarch than with a scattered and half-lawless nobility. Upheld by these diverse forces, the French and English kings made their power hereditary, instead of elective, by crowning a son or brother before their own death; and men accepted hereditary monarchy as the alternative to feudal anarchy. The improvement of communication and the increased circulation of money made regular taxation possible; the mounting royal revenue financed larger royal armies; the rising class of jurists attached themselves to the throne, and strengthened it by the centralizing influence of revived Roman law. By the year 1250 the jurists asserted the royal jurisdiction over all persons in the realm; and by that time the oath of allegiance was taken by all Frenchmen not to their lord but to their king. At the end of the thirteenth century Philip the Fair was strong enough to subdue not only his barons, but the papacy itself.

The French kings softened the transition for the aristocracy by replacing the rights of private coinage, judgment, and war with titles and privileges at the royal court. The greater vassals formed the *curia regis*, or king's court; they became courtiers instead of potentates; and the ritual of the baronial castle graduated into a ceremonious attendance upon the audiences, the table, and the bedchamber of the king. The sons and daughters of the nobility were sent to serve the king and queen as pages or maids of honor, and learned the courtesies of the court; the royal household became the school of the aristocracy of France. The culminating ceremony was the coronation of the French king at Reims, of the German emperor at Aachen or Frankfort; then all the elite of the land gathered in awesome raiment and equipage; the Church extended all the mystery and majesty of her rites to solemnize the accession of the new ruler; his power became thereby a divine authority, which no man could gainsay except through brazen blasphemy. The feudal lords crowded to the court of the monarchy that had subdued them, and the Church conferred divine right upon the kings who would destroy her European leadership and power.

III. FEUDAL LAW

In the feudal regime, where the judges and executors of civil law were usually illiterate, custom and law were largely one. When question rose as to law or penalty, the oldest members of the community were asked what had been the custom thereon in their youth. The community itself was therefore the chief source of law. The baron or king might give commands, but these were not laws; and if he exacted more than custom sanctioned he would be frustrated by universal resistance, vocal or dumb.[43] Southern France had a written law as a Roman heritage; northern France, more feudal, preserved for the most part the laws of the Franks; and when in the thirteenth century these laws too were put into writing, they became even harder to change than before, and a hundred legal fictions rose to reconcile them with reality.

The feudal law of property was complex and unique. It recognized three forms of land possession: (1) the allod, unconditional ownership; (2) the fief—land whose usufruct, but not ownership, was ceded to a vassal on condition of noble service; and (3) tenure—where the usufruct was ceded to a serf or tenant on condition of feudal dues. In feudal theory only the king enjoyed absolute ownership; even the loftiest noble was a tenant, whose possession was conditional on service. Nor was the lord's possession completely individual; every son had a birthright in the ancestral lands, and could obstruct their sale.[44] Usually the whole estate was bequeathed to the eldest son. This custom of primogeniture, unknown to Roman or barbarian law,[45] became advisable under feudal conditions because it put the military protection and economic management of the estate under one head, presumably the most mature. Younger sons were encouraged to venture forth and carve out new estates in other lands. Despite its limitations on ownership, feudal law yielded to no other in reverence for property, and in severity of punishments for violating property rights. A German code held that if a man removed the bark from one of the willow trees that held a dyke, "his belly shall be ripped up, and his bowels shall be taken out and wound around the harm he has done"; and as late as 1454 a Westphalian ordinance held that a man who had criminally removed his neighbor's landmark should be buried in the earth with his head sticking out, and the land should then be plowed by oxen and men who had never plowed before; "and the buried man may help himself as best he can." [46]

Procedure in feudal law largely followed the barbarian codes, and extended their efforts to substitute public penalties for private revenge. Churches, market places, "towns of refuge" were endowed with the right of sanctuary; by such restrictions vengeance might be stayed till the law could supervene. Manorial courts tried cases between tenant and tenant, or between tenant and lord; contests between lord and vassal, or lord and lord, were submitted to a jury of "peers of the barony"—men of at least equal standing, and of the same fief,[47] with the complainant, and sitting in some baronial hall; episcopal or abbey courts tried cases involving persons in orders; while the highest appeals were heard by a royal court composed of peers of the realm, and sometimes presided over by the king. In the manorial courts plaintiff as well as defendant was imprisoned till judgment was pronounced. In all courts the plaintiff who lost was subject to the same penalty that would have been visited upon the defendant if guilty. Bribery was popular in all courts.[48]

Trial by ordeal continued throughout the feudal period. About the year 1215 some heretics at Cambrai were subjected to the hot iron test; suffering burns, they were led to the stake; but, we are told, one was spared when, upon confessing his errors, his hand immediately healed, leaving no trace of the burn. The growth of philosophy through the twelfth century, and the renewed study of Roman law, begot a distaste for these "ordeals of God." Pope Innocent III secured their complete prohibition by the Fourth Lateran Council in 1216; Henry III adopted this prohibition into English law (1219), Frederick II into the Neapolitan Code

(1231). In Germany the old tests persisted into the fourteenth century; Savonarola underwent the ordeal by fire at Florence in 1498; it was revived in the trial of witches in the sixteenth century.[49]

Feudalism encouraged the old Germanic trial by combat, partly as a mode of proof, partly in lieu of private revenge. The Normans re-established it in Britain after its disuse by the Anglo-Saxons, and it remained on the English statute book till the nineteenth century.[50] In 1127 a knight named Guy was accused by another named Hermann of complicity in the assassination of Charles the Good of Flanders; on Guy denying it, Hermann challenged him to a judicial duel; they fought for hours, till they were both unhorsed and weaponless; they passed from fencing to wrestling, and Hermann demonstrated the justice of his charge by tearing Guy's testicles from his body; whereupon Guy expired.[51] Perhaps ashamed of such barbarities, feudal custom accumulated restrictions on the right to challenge. The accuser, to acquire such a right, was required to make out a probable case; the defendant might refuse to fight if he had proved an alibi; a serf could not challenge a freeman, nor a leper a sound man, nor a bastard a man of legitimate birth; in general one might challenge only a person of equal rank with himself. The laws of several communities gave the court the right to forbid any judicial duel at its discretion. Women, ecclesiastics, and persons suffering physical disability were exempt from challenge, but they might choose "champions"—professionally skilled duelists—to represent them. As early as the tenth century we find paid champions used as substitutes even by able-bodied males; since God would decide the issue according to the justice of the accusation, the identity of the combatants seemed irrelevant. Otto I submitted to duel by champions the question of his daughter's chastity, and the disputed succession to certain estates;[52] and in the thirteenth century King Alfonso X of Castile had recourse to such a duel to decide whether he should introduce Roman law into his kingdom.[53] Embassies were sometimes supplied with champions in case diplomatic quarrels should admit of resolution by duels. Until 1821 such a champion figured in the coronation ceremony of English kings; he was by that date a picturesque relic; but in the Middle Ages he was supposed to fling his gauntlet upon the ground and loudly proclaim his readiness to defend in duel against any man the divine right of the new monarch to the crown.[54]

The use of champions cast discredit upon trial by combat; the rising *bourgeoisie* outlawed it in communal legislation; Roman law replaced it in southern Europe in the thirteenth century. The Church repeatedly denounced it, and Innocent III made the prohibition absolute (1215). Frederick II excluded it from his Neapolitan dominions; Louis IX abolished it in the regions directly subject to his rule (1260); and Philip the Fair (1303) forbade it anywhere in France. The duel derives not so much from judicial combat as from the ancient right of private revenge.

Feudal penalties were barbarously severe. Fines were innumerable. Imprisonment was used as a detention for trial, rather than as a punishment; but it could be a torture in itself when the cell was infested with vermin, rats, or snakes.[55] Men and women might be condemned to the public pillory or stocks, and be a target for public ridicule, decayed food, or stones. The ducking stool was used for minor crimes, and as a discouragement to gossips and shrews; the condemned person was strapped to a chair which was fastened to a long lever and was thereby submerged in a stream or a pond. Tougher convicts could be sentenced to serve as galley slaves: half naked and poorly fed, they were chained to the benches and compelled, on penalty of the severest flogging, to row to exhaustion. Flogging with lash or rod was a common punishment. Flesh—sometimes the face—might be branded with a letter symbolizing the crime; perjury and blasphemy could be punished by piercing the tongue with a hot iron. Mutilation was common; hands or feet, ears or nose, were cut off, eyes were gouged out; and William the Conqueror, to deter crime, decreed "that no one shall be killed or hanged for any misdeeds, but rather that his eyes be plucked out, and his hands, feet, and testicles cut off, so that whatever part of his body remains will be a living sign to all of his crime and iniquity." [56] Torture was little used in feudalism; Roman and ecclesiastical law revived it in the thirteenth century. Theft or murder was punished sometimes with exile, more often with beheading or hanging; women murderers were buried alive.[57] An animal that had killed a human being might also be buried alive or hanged. Christianity preached mercy, but ecclesiastical courts decreed the same penalties as lay courts for similar crimes. The abbey court of St. Geneviève buried seven women alive for theft.[58] Perhaps in a rude age barbarous punishments were needed to deter lawless men. But these barbarities continued till the eighteenth century; and the worst tortures were practiced not upon murderers by barons but upon pious heretics by Christian monks.

IV. FEUDAL WAR

Feudalism arose as the military organization of a harassed agricultural society; its virtues were martial rather than economic; its vassals and lords were expected to train themselves for war, and be ready at any moment to leave the plowshare for the sword.

The feudal army was the feudal hierarchy organized by ties of feudal allegiance, and strictly stratified according to grades of nobility. Princes, dukes, marquises, counts, and archbishops were generals; barons, seigneurs, bishops, and abbots were captains; knights or chevaliers were cavalrymen; squires were servitors to barons or knights; "men-at-arms"—the militia of communes or villages—fought as infantry. Behind the feudal army, as we see it in the Crusades, a crowd of "varlets" followed on foot, without officers or discipline; they helped to despoil the conquered, and eased the suffering of fallen and wounded enemies by despatching them with battle-axes or clubs.[59] But essentially the feudal army was the man on horseback multiplied. Infantry, insufficiently mobile, had lost its pre-eminence since Hadrianople (378), and would not regain it till the fourteenth century. Cavalry was the battle arm of chivalry; they and the cavalier, the chevalier, and the *caballero* took their names from the horse.

The feudal warrior used lance and sword or bow and arrow. The knight enlarged his ego to include his sword, and gave it an affectionate name; though doubtless it was the trouvères who called Charlemagne's sword *Joyeuse*, Roland's *Durandel*, and Arthur's *Excalibur*. The bow had many forms: it might be a simple short bow, drawn at the breast; or a longbow aimed from the eye and ear; or a crossbow, in which the cord, drawn taut in the groove of a stock, was suddenly released, sometimes by a trigger, and propelled a missile of iron or stone. The crossbow was old; the longbow was first prominently used by Edward I (1272–1307) in his wars with the Welsh. In England archery was the main element in military training, and a leading element in sport. The development of the bow began the military debacle of feudalism; the knight scorned to fight on foot, but the archers killed his horse, and forced him to uncongenial ground. The final blow to feudal military power would come in the fourteenth century with gunpowder and cannon, which, from a safe distance, killed the armored knight and shattered his castle.

Having a horse to carry him, the feudal warrior could afford to burden himself with armor. In the twelfth century the fully accoutered knight covered his body from neck to knees with a hauberk—a coat of chain mail with sleeves for the arms—and an iron hood that covered all the head except eyes, nose, and mouth; his legs and feet were housed in greaves of mail. In combat he further capped himself with a steel helmet whose "nasal"—a projecting iron blade—guarded the nose. The visored casque and armor of metal plates appeared in the fourteenth century as defense against the long- or crossbow, and continued till the seventeenth; then nearly all armor was abandoned for the advantages of mobility. As a shield the knight suspended from his neck, and grasped by inner straps with his left hand, a buckler made of wood, leather, and iron bands, and adorned at the center with a buckle of gilded iron. The medieval knight was a mobile fort.

Fortification was the chief and usually adequate defense in feudal war. An army defeated in the field might find refuge within manor walls, and a last stand could be made in the donjon tower. The science of siege declined in the Middle Ages; the complex organization and equipment for battering down enemy walls proved too costly or laborious for dignified knights; but the art of the sapper or military miner held its own. Navies, too, were reduced in a world whose will to war outran its means. War galleys remained like those of the ancients—armed with battle towers on the decks, and propelled by freemen or galley slaves. What was lacking in power was made up in ornament, on the ship as on the man. Over a coat of pitch that preserved the wood of the vessel from water and air, medieval shipwrights and artists painted brilliant colors mixed with wax—white, vermilion, ultramarine blue; they gilded the prow and rails, and sculptured figures of men, beasts, and gods on prow and stern. Sails were gaily tinted, some in purple, some in gold; and a seigneur's ship was emblazoned with his coat of arms.

Feudal war differed from both ancient and modern war in greater frequency and less mortality and cost. Every baron claimed the right of private war against any man not bound to him by feudal ties, and every king was free to embark at any time upon honorable robbery of another ruler's lands. When king or baron went to war, all his vassals and relatives to the seventh degree were pledged to follow and fight for him for forty days. There was scarce a day in the twelfth century when some part of what is now France was not at war. To be a good warrior was the crown of a knight's development; he was expected to give or take hard blows with relish or fortitude; his last ambition was a warrior's death on "the field of honor," not a "cow's death" in bed.[60] Berthold of Ratisbon complained that "so few great lords reach their right age or die a right death"; [61] but Berthold was a monk.

The game was not too dangerous. Ordericus Vitalis, describing the battle of Brémule (1119), reports that "of the 900 knights who fought, only three were killed." [62] At the battle of Tinchebrai (1106), where Henry I of England won all Normandy, 400 knights were captured, but not one of Henry's knights was slain. At Bouvines (1214), one of the most bloody and decisive battles of the Middle Ages, 170 of 1500 knights engaged lost their lives.[63] Armor and fortress gave advantage to the defense; a fully armored man could hardly be killed except by cutting his throat as he lay on the ground; and this was discountenanced by chivalry. Moreover it was wiser to capture a knight and accept ransom for him than to slay him and invite feud revenge. Froissart mourned the slaughter, at one battle, of "as many good prisoners as would well have brought 400,000 francs." [64] Knightly rules and reciprocal prudence counseled courtesy to prisoners, and moderation in ransoms asked. Usually a prisoner was released on his word of honor to return with his ransom by a given date, and rare was the knight who broke such a pledge.[65] It was the peasantry that suffered most from feudal wars. In France, Germany, and Italy each army raided the lands and pillaged the houses of the vassals and serfs of the enemy, and captured or killed all cattle not gathered within defensive walls. After such a war many peasants drew their own plows, and many starved to death for lack of grain.

Kings and princes strove to maintain some interludes of internal peace. The Norman dukes succeeded in Normandy, England, and Sicily; the count of Flanders in his realm, the count of Barcelona in Catalonia, Henry III for a generation in Germany. For the rest it was the Church that led in limiting war. From 989 to 1050 various Church councils in France decreed a *Pax Dei*, or Peace of God, and promised excommunication to all who should use violence upon noncombatants in war. The French Church organized a peace movement in various centers, and persuaded many nobles not only to forgo private war but to join in outlawing it. Bishop Fulbert of Chartres (960?–1028), in a famous hymn, gave thanks to God for the unaccustomed peace. The movement was enthusiastically acclaimed by the common people, and good souls prophesied that within five years the peace program would be

accepted by all Christendom.[66] French Church councils, from 1027 on, proclaimed the *Treuga Dei*, or Truce of God, perhaps recalling the Moslem
prohibition of war in time of pilgrimage: all were to abstain from violence
during Lent, in season of harvest or vintage (August 15 to November 11), on
specified holydays, and for a part of each week—usually from Wednesday
evening to Monday morning; in its final form the Truce allowed eighty days
in the year for private or feudal war. These appeals and fulminations helped;
private war was gradually ended by the co-operation of the Church, the
growing strength of the monarchies, the rise of the towns and *bourgeoisie*,
and the absorption of martial energies in the Crusades. In the twelfth century
the Truce of God became part of civil, as well as of canon, law in western
Europe. The Second Lateran Council (1139) forbade the use of military
engines against men.[67] In 1190 Gerhoh of Reichersburg proposed that the
pope should forbid all wars among Christians, and that all disputes among
Christian rulers should be submitted to papal arbitration.[68] The kings thought
this a bit too advanced; they waged international wars more abundantly as
private wars decreased; and in the thirteenth century the popes themselves,
playing the royal game of power with human pawns, used war as an instrument of policy.

V. CHIVALRY

Out of old Germanic customs of military initiation, crossed with Saracen
influences from Persia, Syria, and Spain, and Christian ideas of devotion and
sacrament, flowered the imperfect but generous reality of chivalry.

A knight was a person of aristocratic birth—i.e., of titled and landowning
family—who had been formally received into the order of knighthood. Not
all "gentle" men (i.e., men distinguished by their *gens* or ancestry) were
eligible to knighthood or title; younger sons, except of royal blood, were
normally confined to modest properties that precluded the expensive appur-
tenances of chivalry; such men remained squires unless they carved out new
lands and titles of their own.

The youth who aimed at knighthood submitted to long and arduous discipline. At seven or eight he entered as a page, at twelve or fourteen as a
squire, into the service of a lord; waited upon him at table, in the bedchamber,
on the manor, in joust or battle; fortified his own flesh and spirit with dangerous exercises and sports; learned by imitation and trial to handle the weapons
of feudal war. When his apprenticeship was finished he was received into the
knightly order by a ritual of sacramental awe. The candidate began with a
bath as a symbol of spiritual, perhaps as a guarantee of physical, purification;
hence he could be called a "knight of the bath," as distinguished from those
"knights of the sword" who had received their accolade on some battlefield
as immediate reward for bravery. He was clothed in white tunic, red robe,

and black coat, representing respectively the hoped-for purity of his morals, the blood he might shed for honor or God, and the death he must be prepared to meet unflinchingly. For a day he fasted; he passed a night at church in prayer, confessed his sins to a priest, attended Mass, received communion, heard a sermon on the moral, religious, social, and military duties of a knight, and solemnly promised to fulfill them. He then advanced to the altar with a sword hanging from his neck; the priest removed the sword, blessed it, and replaced it upon his neck. The candidate turned to the seated lord from whom he sought knighthood, and was met with a stern question: "For what purpose do you desire to enter the order? If to be rich, to take your ease, and be held in honor without doing honor to knighthood, you are unworthy of it, and would be to the order of knighthood what the simoniacal clerk is to the prelacy." The candidate was prepared with a reassuring reply. Knights or ladies then clothed him in knightly array of hauberk, cuirass or breastplate, armlets, gauntlets (armored gloves), sword, and spurs.* The lord, rising, gave him the accolade (i.e., on the neck)—three blows with the flat of the sword upon the neck or shoulder, and sometimes a slap on the cheek, as symbols of the last affronts that he might accept without redress; and "dubbed" him with the formula, "In the name of God, St. Michael, and St. George I make thee knight." The new knight received a lance, a helmet, and a horse; he adjusted his helmet, leaped upon his horse, brandished his lance, flourished his sword, rode out from the church, distributed gifts to his attendants, and gave a feast for his friends.

He was now privileged to risk his life in tournaments that would train him still further in skill, endurance, and bravery. Begun in the tenth century, the tournament flourished above all in France, and sublimated some part of the passions and energies that disordered feudal life. It might be proclaimed through a herald, by a king or a great lord, to celebrate the ordination of a knight, the visit of a sovereign, or the marriage of royal blood. The knights who offered to take part came to the appointed town, hung their armorial bearings from the windows of their rooms, and affixed their coats of arms to castles, monasteries, and other public places. Spectators examined these, and were free to lodge complaint of wrong done by any intending participant; tournament officials would hear the case, and disqualify the guilty; there was then a "blot on his 'scutcheon," or shield. To the excited gathering came horse dealers to equip the knight, haberdashers to clothe him and his horse in fit array, moneylenders to ransom the fallen, fortunetellers, acrobats, mimes, troubadours and trouvères, wandering scholars, women of loose morals, and ladies of high degree. The whole occasion was a colorful festival of song and dance, trysts and brawls, and wild betting on the contests.

A tournament might last almost a week, or but a day. At a tournament

---

* Gold spurs were the sign of a knight, silver spurs of a squire; to "win his spurs" (of gold) meant to attain to knighthood.

in 1285 Sunday was a day of assembly and fete; Monday and Tuesday were given to jousts; Wednesday was a day of rest; Thursday saw the tourney that gave its name to the tournament. The lists, or field of battle, were a town square or an outlying open space, partly enclosed by stands and balconies from which the richer gentry, clothed in all the splendor of medieval costume, watched the fray; commoners stood on foot around the field. The stands were decorated with tapestries, drapes, pennants, and coats of arms. Musicians prefaced the engagement with music, and celebrated with flourishes the most brilliant strokes of the game. Between contests the noble lords and ladies scattered coins among the pedestrian crowd, who received them with cries of "*Largesse!*" and "*Noël!*"

Before the first contest the knights entered the lists by marching on to the field in brilliant equipage and stately steps, followed by their mounted squires, and sometimes led in gold or silver chains by the ladies for whose glory they were to fight. Usually each knight carried on his shield, helmet, or lance a scarf, veil, mantle, bracelet, or ribbon that his chosen lady had taken from her dress.

The joust or tilt was a single combat of rival knights; they rode against each other "at full tilt," and launched their lances of steel. If either contestant was unhorsed the rules required the other to dismount; and the fight was continued on foot till one or the other cried quits, or was *hors de combat* through fatigue or wounds or death, or until judges or king called a halt. The victor then appeared before the judges, and solemnly received a prize from them or from some fair lady. Several such tilts might fill a day. The climax of the festival came with the tourney; the enlisted knights ranged themselves in opposed groups, and fought an actual battle, though usually with blunted arms; in the tourney at Neuss (1240) some sixty knights were killed. In such tourneys prisoners were taken, and ransom exacted, as in war; the horses and armor of the captives belonged to the victors; the knights loved money even more than war. The *fabliaux* tell of a knight who protested the Church's condemnation of tournaments on the ground that if effective it would end his only means of livelihood.[69] When all the contests were over the survivors and the noble spectators joined in an evening of feasting, song, and dance. The winning knights enjoyed the privilege of kissing the loveliest women, and heard poems and songs composed in commemoration of their victories.

Theoretically the knight was required to be a hero, a gentleman, and a saint. The Church, anxious to tame the savage breast, surrounded the institution of knighthood with religious forms and vows. The knight pledged himself always to speak the truth, defend the Church, protect the poor, make peace in his province, and pursue the infidels. To his liege lord he owed a loyalty more binding than filial love; to all women he was to be a guardian, saving their chastity; to all knights he was to be a brother in mutual courtesy and aid. In war he might fight other knights; but if he took any of them prisoner he must treat them as his guests; so the French knights captured at Crécy and Poitiers lived, till ransomed, in freedom and comfort on the estates of their English captors, sharing in feasts and sports with their hosts.[70] Above the conscience of the commons feudalism exalted the aristocratic honor and *noblesse oblige* of the knight—a pledge of martial valor and feudal fidelity, of unstinting service to all knights, all women, all weak or poor. So *virtus*, manliness, was restored to its Roman masculine sense after a thousand years of Christian emphasis on feminine virtues. Chivalry, despite its religious aura, represented a victory of Germanic, pagan, and Arab conceptions over Christianity; a Europe attacked on every side needed the martial virtues again.

All this, however, was chivalric theory. A few knights lived up to it, as a few Christians rose to the arduous heights of Christian selflessness. But human nature, born of jungle and beast, sullied the one ideal like the other. The same hero who one day fought bravely in tournament or battle might on another be a faithless murderer; he might carry his honor as proudly as his plume, and, like Lancelot, Tristram, and realer knights, break up fine families with adultery. He might prate of protecting the weak, and strike unarmed peasants down with a sword; he treated with scorn the manual worker on whose labor rested his citadel of gallantry, and with frequent coarseness and occasional brutality the wife whom he had sworn to cherish and protect.[71] He could hear Mass in the morning, rob a church in the afternoon, and drink himself into obscenity at night; so Gildas, who lived among them, described the British knights of that sixth century in which some poets placed Arthur and "the great order of the Table Round."[72] He talked of loyalty and justice, and filled the pages of Froissart with treachery and violence. While German poets sang of chivalry, German knights engaged in fisticuffs, incendiarism, and the highway robbery of innocent travelers.[73] The Saracens were astonished by the crudeness and cruelty of the Crusaders; even the great Bohemund, to show his contempt of the Greek emperor, sent him a cargo of sliced off noses and thumbs.[74] Such men were exceptional, but they were plentiful. It would of course be absurd to expect soldiers to be saints; good killing requires its own unique virtues. These rough knights drove the Moors into Granada, the Slavs from the Oder, the Magyars from Italy and Germany; they tamed the Norse into Normans, and brought French civilization into England on the points of their swords. They were what they had to be.

Two influences moderated the barbarism of chivalry: woman and Christianity. The Church partly succeeded in diverting feudal pugnacity into the Crusades. Perhaps she was helped by the rising adoration of Mary the Virgin Mother; once more the feminine virtues were exalted to check the bloody ardor of vigorous men. But it may be that living women, appealing to sense as well as soul, had even more influence in transforming the warrior into a

gentleman. The Church repeatedly forbade tournaments, and was gaily ignored by the knights; the ladies attended tournaments, and were not ignored.
The Church frowned upon the role of women in tournaments and in poetry;
a conflict arose between the morals of noble ladies and the ethics of the
Church; and in the feudal world the ladies and the poets won.

Romantic love—i.e., love that idealizes its object—has probably occurred
in every age, in degree loosely corresponding with the delay and obstacles
between desire and fulfillment. Until our own age it was rarely the cause of
marriage; and if we find it quite apart from marriage when knighthood was
in flower, we must view that condition as more normal than our own. In most
ages, and above all in feudalism, women married men for their property, and
admired other men for their charm. Poets, having no property, had to marry
at low level or love at long range, and they aimed their fairest songs at in-
accessible dames. The distance between lover and beloved was usually so
great that even the most passionate poetry was taken as only a pretty compliment, and a well-mannered lord rewarded poets for inditing amorous
verses to his wife. So the viscount of Vaux continued his hospitality and
favors to the troubadour Peire Vidal after Peire addressed love poems to
the viscountess—even after Peire had tried to seduce her [75]—though this was
a degree of amiability not usually to be presumed upon. The troubadour
argued that marriage, combining a maximum of opportunity with a minimum
of temptation, could hardly engender or sustain romantic love; even the pious
Dante seems never to have dreamed of addressing love poems to his wife, or
to have found any unseemliness in addressing them to another woman, single
or married. The knight agreed with the poet that knightly love had to be for
some other lady than his own wife, usually for the wife of another knight.[76]
Most knights, though we must not often suspect them of marital fidelity,
laughed at "courtly love," resigned themselves in time to their mates, and
consoled themselves with war. We hear of knights turning cold ears to ladies
offering romance.[77] Roland, in the *Chanson*, died with scarce a thought of his
affianced bride Aude, who would die of grief on hearing of his death.
Women, too, were not all romantic; but from the twelfth century it became
a convention with many of them that a lady should have a lover, Platonic or
Byronic, added to her husband. If we may believe the medieval romances, the
knight was pledged to the *devoir* or service of the lady who had given him
her colors to wear; she could impose dangerous exploits to test or distance
him; and if he served her well she was expected to reward him with an
embrace or better; this is the "guerdon" that he claimed. To her he dedicated
all his feats of arms; it was her name that he invoked in the crises of combat
or the breath of death. Here again feudalism was not a part of Christianity
but its opposite and rival. Women, theologically so stinted in love, asserted
their freedom and molded their own moral code; the worship of woman in
the flesh competed with the adoration of the Virgin. Love proclaimed itself

an independent principle of worth, and offered ideals of service, norms of conduct, scandalously ignoring religion even when borrowing its terms and forms.[78]

So complicated a severance of love and marriage raised many problems of morals and etiquette; and, as in Ovid's days, authors dealt with these questions with all the nicety of casuists. Some time between 1174 and 1182 one Andreas Capellanus—Andrew the Chaplain—composed a *Tractatus de amore et de amoris remedio* (*Treatise on Love and Its Cure*), in which, among other matters, he laid down the code and principles of "courtly love." Andrew limits such love to the aristocracy; he unblushingly assumes that it is the illicit passion of a knight for another knight's wife, but considers its distinguishing characteristic as the homage, vassalage, and service of the man to the woman. This book is the chief authority for the existence of medieval "courts of love," in which titled ladies answered queries and handed down decisions about *l'amour courtois*. In Andrew's time, if we may credit his account, the leading lady in this procedure was the princess poetess Marie, Countess of Champagne; a generation earlier it had been her mother, the most fascinating woman in feudal society, Eleanor, Duchess of Aquitaine, sometime Queen of France, and later of England. Occasionally, according to the *Tractatus*, mother and daughter presided together as judges in the court of love at Poitiers.[79] Andrew knew Marie well, served her as chaplain, and apparently wrote his book to publish her theories and judgments of love. "Love," he says, "teaches everyone to abound in good manners"; under Marie's tutelage, we are assured, the rough aristocracy of Poitiers became a society of generous women and gallant men.

The poems of the troubadours contain several references to such courts of love, maintained by high ladies—the viscountess of Narbonne, the countess of Flanders, and others—at Pierrefeu, Avignon, and elsewhere in France;[80] ten, fourteen, sixty women, we are told, sat in judgment on cases submitted to them mostly by women, sometimes by men; disputes were settled, lovers' quarrels healed, penalties laid upon violators of the code. So (according to Andrew) Marie of Champagne, on April 27, 1174, issued a *responsum* to the inquiry, "Can real love exist between married people?" She replied in the negative on the ground that "lovers grant everything gratuitously, without being constrained by any motive of necessity; married people are compelled as a duty to submit to one another's wishes." [81] All the courts, says our merry Andrew, agreed on thirty-one "Laws of Love": (1) Marriage cannot be pleaded as an excuse for refusing to love.... (3) No one can really love two people at the same time. (4) Love never stands still; it always increases or diminishes. (5) Favors unwillingly yielded are tasteless. . . . (11) It is not becoming to love those ladies who only love with a view to marriage. . . . (14) Too easy possession renders love contemptible; possession that is attended with difficulties makes love ... of great price.... (19) If

love once begins to diminish, it quickly fades away, and rarely recovers. . . .
(21) Love invariably increases under the influence of jealousy. . . . (23) A
person who is the prey of love eats little and sleeps little. . . . (26) Love can
deny nothing to love.[82]

These courts of love, if they ever existed, were parts of a kind of parlor
game played by the ladies of the aristocracy; busy barons took no known
notice of them, and amorous knights made their own rules. But there can be
no doubt that increasing wealth and idleness generated a romance and etiquette of love that filled the poetry of the troubadours and the early Renaissance. "In June, 1283," writes the Florentine historian Villani (1280?–1348),

> at the festival of St. John, when the city of Florence was happy, quiet,
> and at peace . . . a social union was formed, composed of a thousand
> people who, all clad in white, called themselves the Servants of Love.
> They arranged a succession of sports, merrymakings, and dances with
> ladies; nobles and bourgeois marched to the sound of trumpets and
> music, and held festive banquets at midday and at night. This Court
> of Love lasted nearly two months, and it was the finest and most fa-
> mous that had ever been in Tuscany.[83]

Chivalry, beginning in the tenth century, reached its height in the thirteenth, suffered from the brutality of the Hundred Years' War, shriveled
in the merciless hate that divided the English aristocracy in the Wars of the
Roses, and died in the theological fury of the religious wars of the sixteenth
century. But it left its decisive mark upon the society, education, manners,
literature, art, and vocabulary of medieval and modern Europe. The orders
of knighthood—of the Garter, the Bath, the Golden Fleece—multiplied to
the number of 234 in Britain, France, Germany, Italy, Spain; and schools like
Eton, Harrow, and Winchester combined the chivalric ideal with "liberal"
education in the most effective training of mind and will and character in
pedagogical history. As the knight learned manners and gallantry at the
court of noble or king, so he transmitted something of this *courtoisie* to those
below him in the social scale; modern politeness is a dilution of medieval
chivalry. The literature of Europe flourished, from the *Chanson de Roland*
to *Don Quixote*, by treating knightly characters and themes; and the rediscovery of chivalry was one of the exciting elements in the Romantic movement of literature in the eighteenth and nineteenth centuries. Whatever its
excesses and absurdities in literature, however far chivalry in fact fell short
of its ideals, it remains one of the major achievements of the human spirit,
an art of life more splendid than any art.

In this perspective the feudal picture is not merely one of serfdom, illiteracy, exploitation, and violence, but as truly a scene of lusty peasants clearing
the wilderness; of men colorful and vigorous in language, love, and war; of
knights pledged to honor and service, seeking adventure and fame rather
than comfort and security, and scorning danger, death, and hell; of women

patiently toiling and breeding in peasant cottages, and titled ladies mingling the tenderest prayers to the Virgin with the bold freedom of a sensuous poetry and courtly love—perhaps feudalism did more than Christianity to raise the status of woman. The great task of feudalism was to restore political and economic order to Europe after a century of disruptive invasions and calamities. It succeeded; and when it decayed, modern civilization rose upon its ruins and its legacy.

The Dark Ages are not a period upon which the scholar can look with superior scorn. He no longer denounces their ignorance and superstition, their political disintegration, their economic and cultural poverty; he marvels, rather, that Europe ever recovered from the successive blows of Goths, Huns, Vandals, Moslems, Magyars, and Norse, and preserved through the turmoil and tragedy so much of ancient letters and techniques. He can feel only admiration for the Charlemagnes, Alfreds, Olafs, and Ottos who forced an order upon this chaos; for the Benedicts, Gregorys, Bonifaces, Columbas, Alcuins, Brunos, who so patiently resurrected morals and letters out of the wilderness of their times; for the prelates and artisans that could raise cathedrals, and the nameless poets that could sing, between one war or terror and the next. State and Church had to begin again at the bottom, as Romulus and Numa had done a thousand years before; and the courage required to build cities out of jungles, and citizens out of savages, was greater than that which would raise Chartres, Amiens, and Reims, or cool Dante's vengeful fever into measured verse.

BOOK V

THE CLIMAX OF CHRISTIANITY
1095–1300

750–1100: The Elder Edda
842: Strasbourg Oath uses vernaculars
c. 1000: Rise of polyphonic music
1020: First communal charter (to Leon)
1040: Guido of Arezzo's musical staff
1050–1122: Roscelin, philosopher
1056–1114: Nestor & the Russian Chronicle
1056–1133: Hildebert of Tours, poet
1066–87: William I King of England
1066–1200: Norman architecture in England
1076–1185: Gilbert de la Porrée, phil'r
1079–1142: Abélard, philosopher
1080: Consuls in Lucca; rise of self-governing cities in Italy
1080–1154: William of Conches, phil'r
1081–1151: Abbot Suger of St. Denis
1083–1148: Anna Comnena, historian
1085: English Domesday Book
1086–1127: William X, Duke of Aquitaine, first known troubadour
1088f: Irnerius & Roman law at Bologna
1088–99: Pope Urban II
1089–1131: Abbey of Cluny
1090–1153: St. Bernard
1093–1109: Anselm Archb'p of Canterbury
1093–1175: Durham Cathedral
c. 1095: *Chanson de Roland*
1095: Proclamation of First Crusade
1095–1164: Roger II of Sicily
1098: Cistercian Order founded
1098–1125: Henry V King of Germany
1099: Crusaders take Jerusalem
1099–1118: Pope Paschal II
1099–1143: Latin Kingdom of Jerusalem
1099–1179: St. Hildegarde
c. 1100: Arabic numerals in Europe; paper manufactured in Constantinople
1100–35: Henry I King of England
1100–55: Arnold of Brescia, reformer
1104–94: Transition style in architecture
1105: Adelard's *Quaestiones naturales*
1110: University of Paris takes form
1113: Prince Monomakh quiets revolution in Kiev
1114–58: Otto of Freising, historian
1114–87: Gerard of Cremona, translator
1117: Abélard teaches Héloïse
1117–80: John of Salisbury, phil'r
c. 1120: Est't of the Hospitalers

1121: Abélard condemned at Soissons
1122: Concordat of Worms
1122–1204: Eleanor of Aquitaine
1123: First Lateran Council
1124–53: David I King of Scotland
1127: Est't of Knights Templar
1133f: Abbey of St. Denis rebuilt in Gothic
1135–54: Stephen King of England
1137: The first Cortes; Geoffrey of Monmouth's *Historia Britonum*
1137–96: Walter Map(es), satirist
1138: Conrad III begins Hohenstaufen line
1139–85: Alfonso I Enriquez, first king of Portugal
1140: Abélard condemned at Sens
1140–91: Chrétien de Troyes
1140–1227: The Goliardic poets
1142: Rise of Guelf & Ghibelline factions
1142: *Decretum* of Gratian
1145–1202: Joachim of Flora
1146–7: Revolt of Arnold of Brescia
1147–1223: Giraldus Cambrensis, geographer
c. 1150: The *Nibelungenlied*
1150: *Sententiae* of Peter Lombard; sculptures of Moissac; flying buttress used at Noyon
1150–1250: Heyday of French troubadours
1152–90: Frederick I Barbarossa emperor of Holy Roman Empire
1154–9: Pope Hadrian IV
1154–89: Henry II begins Plantagenet line
1154–1256: York Minster
1156: Moscow founded
1157: Bank of Venice issues gov't bonds
1157–82: Valdemar I King of Denmark
1157–1217: Alexander Neckham, naturalist
1159–81: Pope Alexander III
c. 1160: The *Cid*
1160–1213: Geoffrey de Villehardouin, hist'n
1163–1235: Notre Dame de Paris
1165–1220: Wolfram von Eschenbach, poet
c. 1165–1228: Walther von der Vogelweide, poet
1167: Lombard League formed; beginning of Oxford University

1167–1215: Peire Vidal, troubadour
1170: Murder of Thomas à Becket; "Strongbow" begins conquest of Ireland; Peter Waldo at Lyons
1170–1221: St. Dominic
1170–1245: Alexander of Hales, phil'r
1172f: Palace of the Doges
1174–1242: Wells Cathedral
1175–1234: Michael Scot
1175–1280: Early English Gothic
1175f: Canterbury Cathedral
1176: Carthusian Order est'd; Frederick Barbarossa defeated at Legnano
1178f: Albigensian heresy; Peterborough Cathedral
1178–1241: Snorri Sturluson, hist'n
1179: Third Lateran Council
c. 1180: University of Montpellier est'd; Marie de France, poetess
1180–1225: Philip II Augustus of France
1180–1250: Leonardo de Fibonacci, math'n
c. 1180–1253: Robert Grosseteste, scientist
1182–1216: St. Francis of Assisi
1185–1219: Lesser Armenia fl. under Leo III
1185–1237: Bamberg Cathedral
1189–92: Third Crusade
1189–99: Richard I Coeur de Lion
1190: Teutonic Order founded
1190–7: Henry VI of Germany
1192–1230: Ottakar I King of Bohemia
1192–1280: Lincoln Minster
1193–1205: Enrico Dandolo Doge of Venice
1193–1280: Albertus Magnus
1194–1240: Llywelyn the Great of Wales
1194–1250: Frederick II of Sicily
1195–1231: St. Anthony of Padua
1195–1390: Bourges Cathedral
1198–1216: Pope Innocent III
1199–1216: King John of England
c. 1200: David of Dinant, phil'r
1200–1304: Cloth Hall of Ypres
1200–59: Matthew Paris, hist'n
1200–64: Vincent of Beauvais, encyclop't
1201: Germans conquer Livonia
1201–1500: Cathedral of Rouen
1202–4: Fourth Crusade
1202–5: Philip II of France takes Normandy, Anjou, Maine, and Brittany from England
1202–41: Valdemar II King of Denmark
1204–29: Albigensian Crusades
1204–50: La Merveille of Mont St. Michel
1204–61: Latin Kingdom of Constant'ple
1205: Oldest Christian reference to magnetic compass; Hartman von Aue's *Der arme Heinrich*

1205–1303: Cathedral of Leon
1206–22: Theodore Lascaris Eastern emp.
1207–28: Stephen Langton Archb'p of Cant'y
1208: St. Francis founds Friars Minor; Innocent III lays interdict on Engl'd
1209: Cambridge University founded
1210: Aristotle forbidden at Paris; Gottfried of Strasbourg's *Tristan*
1211–1427: Reims Cathedral
1212: Children's Crusade; Santa Clara founds Poor Clares
1213–76: James I King of Aragon
1214: Philip II wins at Bouvines
1214–92: Roger Bacon
1215: Magna Carta; Fourth Lateran Council; Dominican Order founded
1216–27: Pope Honorius III
1216–72: Henry III King of England
1217: Fifth Crusade
1217–52: Ferdinand III of Castile
1217–62: Haakon IV of Norway
1220–45: Salisbury Cathedral
1220–88: Amiens Cathedral
1221–74: St. Bonaventure
1221–1567: Cathedral of Burgos
1224: University of Naples est'd
1224–1317: Jean de Joinville, hist'n
1225: Laws of the *Sachsenspiegel*
1225–74: St. Thomas Aquinas, phil'r
1225–78: Niccolò Pisano, sculptor
1226–35: Regency of Blanche of Castile
1226–70: Louis IX of France
1227: University of Salamanca est'd; beginning of papal Inquisition
1227–41: Pope Gregory IX
1227–1493: Cathedral of Toledo
1227–1552: Cathedral of Beauvais
1228f: Church of San Francesco at Assisi
1228: Sixth Crusade; Frederick II recovers Jerusalem
1229–1348: Cathedral of Siena
1230f: Cathedral of Strasbourg
1230–75: Guido Guinizelli
1232–1300: Arnolfo di Cambio, artist
1232–1315: Raymond Lully, phil'r
1235–81: Siger of Brabant, phil'r
1235–1311: Arnold of Villanova, physician
1237: Mongols invade Russia; William of Lorris' *Roman de la Rose*
1240: Victory of Alexander Nevsky on Neva
c. 1240: *Aucassin et Nicolette*

1240–1302: Cimabue
1240–1320: Giovanni Pisano, artist
1241: Mongols defeat Germans at Liegnitz, take Cracow, and ravage Hungary
1243–54: Pope Innocent IV
1244: Moslems capture Jerusalem
1245: First Council of Lyons deposes Frederick II
1245: Giovanni de Piano Carpini visits Mongolia
1245–8: Ste. Chapelle
1245–72: Westminster Abbey
1248: St. Louis leads Seventh Crusade
1248–1354: The Alhambra
1248–1880: Cathedral of Cologne
1250: St. Louis captured; Frederick II d.; Bracton's *De legibus et consuetudinibus Angliae*
1252–62: Formation of Hanseatic League
1252–82: Alfonso X the Wise of Castile
1253–78: Ottokar II of Bohemia
1254–61: Pope Alexander IV
1255–1319: Duccio of Siena, painter
1258: Haakon IV of Norway conquers Iceland
1258–66: Manfred King of Sicily
1258–1300: Guido Cavalcanti
c. 1260: Flagellants
1260–1320: Henri de Mondeville, surgeon
1261: Michael VIII Palaeologus restores Eastern Empire at Constantinople
1265: Simon de Montfort's Parliament
1265–1308: Duns Scotus, phil'r
1265–1321: Dante
1266: *Opus maius* of Roger Bacon
1266–85: Charles of Anjou King of Sicily
1266–1337: Giotto
1268: Defeat of Conradin; end of Hohenstaufen line
1269: Baibars takes Jaffa and Antioch
1270: Louis IX leads Eighth Crusade
1271–95: Marco Polo in Asia

1272–1307: Edward I King of England
1273–91: Rudolf of Hapsburg Emperor of Holy Roman Empire
1274: Second Council of Lyons
1279–1325: Diniz King of Portugal
1280–1380: English Decorated Gothic
1282: Sicilian Vespers; Pedro III of Aragon takes Sicily
1283: Edward I reconquers Wales
1284: Belfry of Bruges
1285–1314: Philip IV the Fair of France
c. 1290: *Golden Legend* of Iacopo de Voragine; Jean de Meung's *Roman de la Rose*
1290–1330: Cathedral of Orvieto
1291: Mamluks take Acre; end of Crusades; League of the Swiss cantons
1292–1315: John Balliol King of Scotland
1294: Lanfranchi founds French surgery
1294: Church of Santa Croce at Florence
1294–1303: Pope Boniface VIII
1294–1436: Cathedral of Santa Maria de Fiore at Florence
1295: Edward I's "Model Parliament"
1296: Boniface's bull *Clericis laicos*
1298: Wallace defeated at Falkirk; Palazzo Vecchio and Baptistery at Florence
1298f: Cathedral of Barcelona
1302: Flemish defeat the French at Courtrai; Boniface's bull *Unam sanctam*; Philip IV calls States General
1305–16: Pope Clement V
1308–13: Henry VII Western Emperor
1309: Clement removes papacy to Avignon
1310–12: Suppression of Templars in France
1314: Scotland wins independence at Bannockburn
1315: Swiss defeat Hapsburg army at Morgarten and establish the Swiss Confederacy

CHAPTER XXIII

The Crusades

1095-1291

I. CAUSES

THE Crusades were the culminating act of the medieval drama, and perhaps the most picturesque event in the history of Europe and the Near East. Now at last, after centuries of argument, the two great faiths, Christianity and Mohammedanism, resorted to man's ultimate arbitrament— the supreme court of war. All medieval development, all the expansion of commerce and Christendom, all the fervor of religious belief, all the power of feudalism and glamor of chivalry came to a climax in a Two Hundred Years' War for the soul of man and the profits of trade.

The first proximate cause of the Crusades* was the advance of the Seljuq Turks. The world had adjusted itself to Moslem control of the Near East; the Fatimids of Egypt had ruled mildly in Palestine; and barring some exceptions, the Christian sects there had enjoyed a wide liberty of worship. Al-Hakim, the mad caliph of Cairo, had destroyed the church of the Holy Sepulcher (1010), but the Mohammedans themselves had contributed substantially to its restoration.[1] In 1047 the Moslem traveler Nasir-i-Khosru described it as "a most spacious building, capable of holding 8000 persons, and built with the utmost skill. Inside, the church is everywhere adorned with Byzantine brocade, worked in gold. . . . And they have portrayed Jesus— peace be upon Him!—riding upon an ass."[2] This was but one of many Christian churches in Jerusalem. Christian pilgrims had free access to the holy places; a pilgrimage to Palestine had long been a form of devotion or penance; everywhere in Europe one met "palmers" who, as a sign of pilgrimage accomplished, wore crossed palm leaves from Palestine; such men, said Piers Plowman, "had leave to lie all their lives thereafter."[3] But in 1070 the Turks took Jerusalem from the Fatimids, and pilgrims began to bring home accounts of oppression and desecration. An old story, not verifiable, relates that one wayfarer, Peter the Hermit, brought to Pope Urban II, from Simeon, Patriarch of Jerusalem, a letter detailing the persecution of Christians there, and imploring papal aid (1088).

The second proximate cause of the Crusades was the dangerous weakening of the Byzantine Empire. For seven centuries it had stood at the crossroads

---

* From the Spanish *cruzada*—"marked with the cross."

of Europe and Asia, holding back the armies of Asia and the hordes of the steppes. Now its internal discords, its disruptive heresies, its isolation from the West by the schism of 1054, left it too feeble to fulfill its historic task. While the Bulgars, Patzinaks, Cumans, and Russians assaulted its European gates, the Turks were dismembering its Asiatic provinces. In 1071 the Byzantine army was almost annihilated at Manzikert; the Seljuqs captured Edessa, Antioch (1085), Tarsus, even Nicaea, and gazed across the Bosporus at Constantinople itself. The Emperor Alexius I (1081–1118) saved a part of Asia Minor by signing a humiliating peace, but he had no military means of resisting further attack. If Constantinople should fall, all Eastern Europe would lie open to the Turks, and the victory of Tours (732) would be undone. Forgetting theological pride, Alexius sent delegates to Urban II and the Council of Piacenza, urging Latin Europe to help him drive back the Turks; it would be wiser, he argued, to fight the infidels on Asiatic soil than wait for them to swarm through the Balkans to the Western capitals.

The third proximate cause of the Crusades was the ambition of the Italian cities—Pisa, Genoa, Venice, Amalfi—to extend their rising commercial power. When the Normans captured Sicily from the Moslems (1060–91), and Christian arms reduced Moslem rule in Spain (1085f), the western Mediterranean was freed for Christian trade; the Italian cities, as ports of exit for domestic and transalpine products, grew rich and strong, and planned to end Moslem ascendancy in the eastern Mediterranean, and open the markets of the Near East to West European goods. We do not know how close these Italian merchants were to the ear of the Pope.

The final decision came from Urban himself. Other popes had entertained the idea. Gerbert, as Sylvester II, had appealed to Christendom to rescue Jerusalem, and an abortive expedition had landed in Syria (c. 1001). Gregory VII, amid his consuming strife with Henry IV, had exclaimed, "I would rather expose my life in delivering the holy places than reign over the universe." [4] That quarrel was still hot when Urban presided over the Council of Piacenza in March of 1095. He supported the plea of Alexius' legates there, but counseled delay till a more widely representative assembly might consider a war against Islam. He was too well informed to picture victory as certain in so distant an enterprise; he doubtless foresaw that failure would seriously damage the prestige of Christianity and the Church. Probably he longed to channel the disorderly pugnacity of feudal barons and Norman buccaneers into a holy war to save Europe and Byzantium from Islam; he dreamed of bringing the Eastern Church again under papal rule, and visioned a mighty Christendom united under the theocracy of the popes, with Rome once more the capital of the world. It was a conception of the highest order of statesmanship.

From March to October of 1095 he toured northern Italy and southern France, sounding out leaders and ensuring support. At Clermont in Auvergne the historic council met; and though it was a cold November, thousands of people came from a hundred comn. .ities, pitched their tents in the open fields, gathered in a vast assemblage that no hall could hold, and throbbed with emotion as their fellow Frenchman Urban, raised on a platform in their midst, addressed to them in French the most influential speech in medieval history.

> O race of Franks! race beloved and chosen by God! . . . From the confines of Jerusalem and from Constantinople a grievous report has gone forth that an accursed race, wholly alienated from God, has violently invaded the lands of these Christians, and has depopulated them by pillage and fire. They have led away a part of the captives into their own country, and a part they have killed by cruel tortures. They destroy the altars, after having defiled them with their uncleanliness. The kingdom of the Greeks is now dismembered by them, and has been deprived of territory so vast in extent that it could not be traversed in two months' time.
>
> On whom, then, rests the labor of avenging these wrongs, and of recovering this territory, if not upon you—you upon whom, above all others, God has conferred remarkable glory in arms, great bravery, and strength to humble the heads of those who resist you? Let the deeds of your ancestors encourage you—the glory and grandeur of Charlemagne and your other monarchs. Let the Holy Sepulcher of Our Lord and Saviour, now held by unclean nations, arouse you, and the holy places that are now stained with pollution. . . . Let none of your possessions keep you back, nor anxiety for your family affairs. For this land which you now inhabit, shut in on all sides by the sea and the mountain peaks, is too narrow for your large population; it scarcely furnishes food enough for its cultivators. Hence it is that you murder and devour one another, that you wage wars, and that many among you perish in civil strife.
>
> Let hatred, therefore, depart from among you; let your quarrels end. Enter upon the road to the Holy Sepulcher; wrest that land from a wicked race, and subject it to yourselves. Jerusalem is a land fruitful above all others, a paradise of delights. That royal city, situated at the center of the earth, implores you to come to her aid. Undertake this journey eagerly for the remission of your sins, and be assured of the reward of imperishable glory in the Kingdom of Heaven.[5]

Through the crowd an excited exclamation rose: *Dieu li volt*—"God wills it!" Urban took it up, and called upon them to make it their battle cry. He bade those who undertook the crusade to wear a cross upon brow or breast. "At once," says William of Malmesbury, "some of the nobility, falling down at the knees of the Pope, consecrated themselves and their property to the service of God." [6] Thousands of the commonalty pledged themselves likewise; monks and hermits left their retreats to become in no metaphysical sense soldiers of Christ. The energetic Pope passed to other cities—Tours, Bordeaux, Toulouse, Montpellier, Nîmes . . . and for nine months preached the crusade. When he reached Rome after two years' absence, he was enthusiastically acclaimed by the least pious city in Christendom. He assumed, with no serious opposition, the authority to release Crusaders from commitments hindering the crusade; he freed the serf and the vassal, for the duration of the war, from fealty to their lord; he conferred upon all Crusaders the privilege of being tried by ecclesiastical instead of manorial courts, and guaranteed them, during their absence, the episcopal protection of their property; he commanded—though he could not quite enforce—a truce to all wars of Christians against Christians; he established a new principle of obedience above the code of feudal loyalty. Now, more than ever, Europe was made one. Urban found himself the accepted master, at least in theory, of Europe's kings. All Christendom was moved as never before as it feverishly prepared for the holy war.

II. THE FIRST CRUSADE: 1095–99

Extraordinary inducements brought multitudes to the standard. A plenary indulgence remitting all punishments due to sin was offered to those who should fall in the war. Serfs were allowed to leave the soil to which they had been bound; citizens were exempted from taxes; debtors enjoyed a moratorium on interest; prisoners were freed, and sentences of death were commuted, by a bold extension of papal authority, to life service in Palestine. Thousands of vagrants joined in the sacred tramp. Men tired of hopeless poverty, adventurers ready for brave enterprise, younger sons hoping to carve out fiefs for themselves in the East, merchants seeking new markets for their goods, knights whose enlisting serfs had left them laborless, timid spirits shunning taunts of cowardice, joined with sincerely religious souls to rescue the land of Christ's birth and death. Propaganda of the kind customary in war stressed the disabilities of Christians in Palestine, the atrocities of Moslems, the blasphemies of the Mohammedan creed; Moslems were described as worshiping a statue of Mohammed,[7] and pious gossip related how the Prophet, fallen in an epileptic fit, had been eaten alive by hogs.[8] Fabulous tales were told of Oriental wealth, and of dark beauties waiting to be taken by brave men.[9]

Such a variety of motives could hardly assemble a homogeneous mass capable of military organization. In many cases women and children insisted upon accompanying their husbands or parents, perhaps with reason, for prostitutes soon enlisted to serve the warriors. Urban had appointed the month of August, 1096, as the time of departure, but the impatient peasants who were the first recruits could not wait. One such host, numbering some 12,000 persons (of whom only eight were knights), set out from France in March under Peter the Hermit and Walter the Penniless (Gautier sans-Avoir); another, perhaps 5000 strong, started from Germany under the priest Gott-schalk; a third advanced from the Rhineland under Count Emico of Leinin-gen. It was chiefly these disorderly bands that attacked the Jews of Germany and Bohemia, rejected the appeals of the local clergy and citizenry, and de-generated for a time into brutes phrasing their blood lust in piety. The re-cruits had brought modest funds and little food, and their inexperienced leaders had made scant provision for feeding them. Many of the marchers had underestimated the distance; and as they advanced along the Rhine and the Danube the children asked impatiently, at each turn, was not this Jerusa-lem? [10] When their funds ran out, and they began to starve, they were forced to pillage the fields and homes on their route; and soon they added rape to rapine.[11] The population resisted violently; some towns closed their gates against them, and others bade them Godspeed with no delay. Arriving at last before Constantinople quite penniless, and decimated by famine, plague, leprosy, fever, and battles on the way, they were welcomed by Alexius, but not satisfactorily fed; they broke into the suburbs, and plundered churches, houses, and palaces. To deliver his capital from these praying locusts, Alexius provided them with vessels to cross the Bosporus, sent them supplies, and bade them wait until better armed detachments could arrive. Whether through hunger or restlessness, the Crusaders ignored these instructions, and advanced upon Nicaea. A disciplined force of Turks, all skilled bowmen, marched out from the city and almost annihilated this first division of the First Crusade. Walter the Penniless was among the slain; Peter the Hermit, disgusted with his uncontrollable host, had returned before the battle to Constantinople, and lived safely till 1115.

Meanwhile the feudal leaders who had taken the cross had assembled each his own force in his own place. No king was among them; indeed Philip I of France, William II of England, and Henry IV of Germany were all under sentence of excommunication when Urban preached the crusade. But many counts and dukes enlisted, nearly all of them French or Frank; the First Cru-sade was largely a French enterprise, and to this day the Near East speaks of West Europeans as Franks. Duke Godfrey, Seigneur of Bouillon (a small estate in Belgium), combined the qualities of soldier and monk—brave and competent in war and government, and pious to the point of fanaticism. Count Bohemund of Taranto was Robert Guiscard's son; he had all the cour-age and skill of his father, and dreamed of slicing a kingdom for himself and his Norman troops out of the former Byzantine possessions in the Near East. With him was his nephew Tancred of Hauteville, destined to be the hero of Tasso's *Jerusalem Delivered*: handsome, fearless, gallant, generous, loving glory and wealth, and universally admired as the ideal of a Christian knight. Raymond, Count of Toulouse, had already fought Islam in Spain; now, in old age, he dedicated himself and his vast fortune to the larger war; but a haughty temper spoiled his nobility, and avarice stained his piety.

By diverse routes these hosts made their way to Constantinople. Bohemund proposed to Godfrey that they seize the city; Godfrey refused, saying that he had come only to fight infidels; [12] but the idea did not die. The masculine, half-barbarous knights of the West despised these subtle and cultured gentlemen of the East as heretics lost in effeminate luxury; they looked with astonishment and envy upon the riches laid up in the churches, palaces, and markets of the Byzantine capital, and thought that fortune should belong to the brave. Alexius may have gotten wind of these notions among his saviors; and his experience with the peasant horde (for whose defeat the West had censured him) inclined him to caution, perhaps to duplicity. He had asked for assistance against the Turks, but he had not bargained upon the united strength of Europe gathering at his gates; he could never be sure whether these warriors aspired to Jerusalem so much as to Constantinople, nor whether they would restore to his Empire any formerly Byzantine territory that they might take from the Turks. He offered the Crusaders provisions, subsidies, transport, military aid, and, for the leaders, handsome bribes; [13] in return he asked that the nobles should swear allegiance to him as their feudal sovereign; any lands taken by them were to be held in fealty to him. The nobles, softened with silver, swore.

Early in 1097 the armies, totaling some 30,000 men, still under divided leadership, crossed the straits. Luckily, the Moslems were even more divided than the Christians. Not only was Moslem power in Spain spent, and in northern Africa rent with religious faction, but in the East the Fatimid caliphs of Egypt held southern Syria, while their foes, the Seljuq Turks, held northern Syria and most of Asia Minor. Armenia rebelled against its Seljuq conquerors, and allied itself with the "Franks." So helped, the arms of Europe advanced to the siege of Nicaea. On Alexius' pledge that their lives would be spared, the Turkish garrison surrendered (June 19, 1097). The Greek Emperor raised the Imperial flag over the citadel, protected the city from indiscriminate pillage, and appeased the feudal leaders with substantial gifts; but the Christian soldiery complained that Alexius was in league with the Turks. After a week's rest, the Crusaders set out for Antioch. They met a Turkish army under Qilij Arslan near Dorylaeum, won a bloody battle (July 1, 1097), and marched through Asia Minor with no other enemies than a shortage of water and food, and a degree of heat for which the Western blood was unprepared. Men, women, horses, and dogs died of thirst on that bitter march of 500 miles. Crossing the Taurus, some nobles separated their forces from the main army to make private conquests—Raymond, Bohemund, and Godfrey in Armenia, Tancred and Baldwin (brother of Godfrey) in Edessa; there Baldwin, by strategy and treachery,[14] founded the first Latin principality in the East (1098). The mass of the Crusaders complained ominously at these delays; the nobles returned, and the advance to Antioch was resumed.

Antioch, described by the chronicler of the *Gesta Francorum* as a "city extremely beautiful, distinguished, and delightful,"[15] resisted siege for eight months. Many Crusaders died from exposure to the cold winter rains, or from hunger; some found a novel nourishment by chewing "the sweet reeds called *zucra*" (Arabic *sukkar*); now for the first time the "Franks" tasted sugar, and learned how it was pressed from cultivated herbs.[16] Prostitutes provided more dangerous sweets; an amiable archdeacon was slain by the Turks as he reclined in an orchard with his Syrian concubine.[17] In May, 1098, word came that a great Moslem army was approaching under Karbogha, Prince of Mosul; Antioch fell (June 3, 1098) a few days before this army arrived; many of the Crusaders, fearing that Karbogha could not be withstood, boarded ships on the Orontes, and fled. Alexius, advancing with a Greek force, was misled by deserters into believing that the Christians had already been defeated; he turned back to protect Asia Minor, and was never forgiven. To restore courage to the Crusaders, Peter Bartholomew, a priest from Marseille, pretended to have found the spear that had pierced the side of Christ; when the Christians marched out to battle the lance was carried aloft as a sacred standard; and three knights, robed in white, issued from the hills at the call of the papal legate Adhemar, who proclaimed them to be the martyrs St. Maurice, St. Theodore, and St. George. So inspired, and under the united command of Bohemund, the Crusaders achieved a decisive victory. Bartholomew, accused of a pious fraud, offered to undergo the ordeal of fire as a test of his veracity. He ran through a gauntlet of burning faggots, and emerged apparently safe; but he died of burns or an overstrained heart on the following day; and the holy lance was withdrawn from the standards of the host.[18]

Bohemund became by grateful consent Prince of Antioch. Formally he held the region in fief to Alexius; actually he ruled it as an independent sovereign; the chieftains claimed that Alexius' failure to come to their aid released them from their vows of allegiance. After spending six months in refreshing and reorganizing their weakened forces, they led their armies toward Jerusalem. At last, on June 7, 1099, after a campaign of three years, the Crusaders, reduced to 12,000 combatants, stood in exaltation and fatigue before the walls of Jerusalem. By the humor of history, the Turks whom they had come to fight had been expelled from the city by the Fatimids a year before. The caliph offered peace on terms of guaranteed safety for Christian pilgrims and worshipers in Jerusalem, but Bohemund and Godfrey demanded unconditional surrender. The Fatimid garrison of 1000 men resisted for forty days. On July 15 Godfrey and Tancred led their followers over the walls, and the Crusaders knew the ecstasy of a high purpose accomplished after heroic suffering. Then, reports the priestly eyewitness Raymond of Agiles,

wonderful things were to be seen. Numbers of the Saracens were beheaded . . . others were shot with arrows, or forced to jump from the
towers; others were tortured for several days and then burned in
flames. In the streets were seen piles of heads and hands and feet. One
rode about everywhere amid the corpses of men and horses.[19]

Other contemporaries contribute details: women were stabbed to death,
suckling babes were snatched by the leg from their mothers' breasts and
flung over the walls, or had their necks broken by being dashed against
posts; [20] and 70,000 Moslems remaining in the city were slaughtered. The
surviving Jews were herded into a synagogue and burned alive. The victors
flocked to the church of the Holy Sepulcher, whose grotto, they believed,
had once held the crucified Christ. There, embracing one another, they wept
with joy and release, and thanked the God of Mercies for their victory.

III. THE LATIN KINGDOM OF JERUSALEM: 1099–1143

Godfrey of Bouillon, whose exceptional integrity had finally won recognition, was chosen to rule Jerusalem and its environs under the modest title
of Defender of the Holy Sepulcher. Here, where Byzantine rule had ceased
465 years before, no pretense was made of subordination to Alexius; the
Latin kingdom of Jerusalem became at once a sovereign state. The Greek
Church was disestablished, its patriarch fled to Cyprus, and the parishes of
the new kingdom accepted the Latin liturgy, an Italian primate, and papal
rule.

The price of sovereignty is the capacity for self-defense. Two weeks after
the great liberation, an Egyptian army came up to Ascalon to reliberate a
city holy for too many faiths. Godfrey defeated it, but a year later he died
(1100). His less able brother, Baldwin I (1100–18), took the loftier title of
king. Under King Fulk, Count of Anjou (1131–43), the new state included
most of Palestine and Syria; but the Moslems still held Aleppo, Damascus,
and Emesa. The kingdom was divided into four feudal principalities, centering respectively at Jerusalem, Antioch, Edessa, and Tripolis. Each of the
four was parceled into practically independent fiefs, whose jealous lords
made war, coined money, and otherwise aped sovereignty. The king was
elected by the barons, and was checked by an ecclesiastical hierarchy subject only to the pope. He was further weakened by ceding the control of
several ports—Jaffa, Tyre, Acre, Beirut, Ascalon—to Venice, Pisa, or Genoa
as the price of naval aid and seaborne supplies. The structure and law of the
kingdom were formulated in the Assizes of Jerusalem—one of the most logical and ruthless codifications of feudal government. The barons assumed all
ownership of land, reduced the former owners—Christian or Moslem—to the
condition of serfs, and laid upon them feudal obligations severer than any

in contemporary Europe. The native Christian population looked back to Moslem rule as a golden age.[21]

The young kingdom had many elements of weakness, but it had a unique support in new orders of military monks. As far back as 1048 the merchants of Amalfi had obtained Moslem permission to build a hospital at Jerusalem for poor or ailing pilgrims. About 1120 the staff of this institution was reorganized by Raymond du Puy as a religious order vowed to chastity, poverty, obedience, and the military protection of Christians in Palestine; and these Hospitalers, or Knights of the Hospital of St. John, became one of the noblest charitable bodies in the Christian world. About the same time (1119) Hugh de Payens and eight other crusader knights solemnly dedicated themselves to monastic discipline and the martial service of Christianity. They obtained from Baldwin II a residence near the site of Solomon's Temple, and were soon called Knights Templar. St. Bernard drew up a stern rule for them, which was not long obeyed; he praised them for being "most learned in the art of war," and bade them "wash seldom," and closely crop their hair.[22] "The Christian who slays the unbeliever in the Holy War," wrote Bernard to the Templars, in a passage worthy of Mohammed, "is sure of his reward; more sure if he himself is slain. The Christian glories in the death of the pagan, because Christ is thereby glorified"; [23] men must learn to kill with a good conscience if they are to fight successful wars. A Hospitaler wore a black robe with a white cross on the left sleeve; a Templar a white robe with a red cross on the mantle. Each hated the other religiously. From protecting and nursing pilgrims the Hospitalers and Templars passed to active attacks upon Saracen strongholds; though the Templars numbered but 300, and the Hospitalers some 600, in 1180,[24] they played a prominent part in the battles of the Crusades, and earned great repute as warriors. Both orders campaigned for financial support, and received it from Church and state, from rich and poor; in the thirteenth century each owned great estates in Europe, including abbeys, villages, and towns. Both astonished Christians and Saracens by building vast fortresses in Syria, where, dedicated individually to poverty, they enjoyed collective luxury amid the toils of war.[25] In 1190 the Germans in Palestine, aided by a few at home, founded the Teutonic Knights, and established a hospital near Acre.

Most of the Crusaders returned to Europe after freeing Jerusalem, leaving the man power of the harassed government perilously low. Many pilgrims came, but few remained to fight. On the north the Greeks watched for a chance to recover Antioch, Edessa, and other cities which they claimed as Byzantine; to the east, the Saracens were being aroused and unified by Moslem appeals and Christian raids. Mohammedan refugees from Jerusalem told in bitter detail the fall of that city to the Christians; they stormed the Great Mosque of Baghdad, and demanded that Moslem arms should liberate Jerusalem, and the sacred Dome of the Rock, from unclean infidel hands.[26] The caliph was powerless to heed their pleas, but Zangi, the young slave-born Prince of Mosul, responded. In 1144 his small well-led army took from the Christians their eastern outpost al-Ruah; and a few months later he recaptured Edessa for Islam. Zangi was assassinated, but he was succeeded by a son, Nur-ud-din, of equal courage and greater ability. It was the news of these events that stirred Europe to the Second Crusade.

IV. THE SECOND CRUSADE: 1146–8

St. Bernard appealed to Pope Eugenius III to sound another call to arms. Eugenius, enmeshed in conflict with the infidels of Rome, begged Bernard to undertake the task himself. It was a wise suggestion, for the saint was a greater man than he whom he had made Pope. When he left his cell at Clairvaux to preach the crusade to the French, the skepticism that hides in the heart of faith was silenced, and the fears spread by narratives of the First Crusade were stilled. Bernard went directly to King Louis VII, and persuaded him to take the cross. With the King at his side he spoke to a multitude at Vézelay (1146); when he had finished, the crowd enlisted en masse; the crosses prepared proved too few, and Bernard tore his robe to pieces to provide additional emblems. "Cities and castles are emptied," he wrote to the Pope; "there is not left one man to seven women, and everywhere there are widows to still living husbands." Having won France he passed to Germany, where his fervent eloquence induced the Emperor Conrad III to accept the crusade as the one cause that could unify the Guelf and Hohenstaufen factions then rending the realm. Many nobles followed Conrad's lead; among them the young Frederick of Swabia who would become Barbarossa, and would die in the Third Crusade.

At Easter of 1147 Conrad and the Germans set out; at Pentecost Louis and the French followed at a cautious distance, uncertain whether the Germans or the Turks were their most hated foes. The Germans felt a like hesitation between Turks and Greeks; and so many Byzantine towns were pillaged on the way that many closed their gates, and dispensed a scanty ration by baskets let down from the walls. Manuel Comnenus, now Eastern Emperor, gently suggested that the noble hosts should cross the Hellespont at Sestos, instead of going through Constantinople; but Conrad and Louis refused. A party in Louis' council urged him to take Constantinople for France; he refrained; but again the Greeks may have learned of his temptation. They were frightened by the stature and armor of the Western knights, and amused by their feminine entourage. His troublesome Eleanor accompanied Louis, and troubadours accompanied the Queen; the counts of Flanders and Toulouse were escorted by their countesses, and the baggage train of the French was heavy with trunks and boxes of apparel and cosmetics designed to ensure the beauty of these ladies against all the vicissitudes of climate, war, and time. Manuel hastened to transport the two armies across the Bosporus, and supplied the Greeks with debased coinage for dealings with the Crusaders. In Asia a dearth of provisions, and the high prices demanded by the Greeks, led to many conflicts between saviors and saved; and Frederick of the Red Beard mourned that his sword had to shed Christian blood for the privilege of encountering infidels.

Conrad insisted, against Manuel's advice, on taking the route followed by the First Crusade. Despite or because of their Greek guides, the Germans fell into a succession of foodless wastes and Moslem snares; and their loss of life was disheartening. At Dorylaeum, where the First Crusade had defeated Qilij Arslan, Conrad's army met the main Moslem force, and was so badly beaten that hardly one Christian in ten survived. The French army, far behind, was deceived by false news of a German victory; it advanced recklessly, and was decimated by starvation and Moslem raids. Reaching Attalia, Louis bargained with Greek ship captains to transport his army by sea to Christian Tarsus or Antioch; the captains demanded an impossible fee per passenger; Louis and several nobles, Eleanor and several ladies, took passage to Antioch, leaving the French army in Attalia. Mohammedan forces swept down upon the city, and slaughtered nearly every Frenchman in it (1148).

Louis reached Jerusalem with ladies but no army, Conrad with a pitiful remnant of the force with which he had left Ratisbon. From these survivors, and soldiers already in the capital, an army was improvised, and marched against Damascus under the divided command of Conrad, Louis, and Baldwin III (1143–62). During the siege disputes arose among the nobles as to which should rule Damascus when it fell. Moslem agents found their way into the Christian army, and bribed certain leaders to a policy of inaction or retreat.[27] When word came that the emirs of Aleppo and Mosul were advancing with a large force to relieve Damascus, the advocates of retreat prevailed; the Christian army broke into fragments, and fled to Antioch, Acre, or Jerusalem. Conrad, defeated and diseased, returned in disgrace to Germany. Eleanor and most of the French knights returned to France. Louis remained another year in Palestine, making pilgrimages to sacred shrines.

Europe was stunned by the collapse of the Second Crusade. Men began to ask how it was that the Almighty allowed His defenders to be so humiliated; critics assailed St. Bernard as a reckless visionary who had sent men to their death; and here and there emboldened skeptics called in question the most basic tenets of the Christian faith. Bernard replied that the ways of the Almighty are beyond human understanding, and that the disaster must have been a punishment for Christian sins. But from this time the philosophic doubts that Abélard (d. 1142) had scattered found expression even among the people. Enthusiasm for the Crusades rapidly waned; and the Age of Faith prepared to defend itself by fire and sword against the inroads of alien beliefs, or no belief at all.

V. SALADIN

Meanwhile a strange new civilization had developed in Christian Syria and Palestine. The Europeans who had settled there since 1099 gradually adopted the Near Eastern garb of wound headdress and flowing robe as suited to a climate of sun and sand. As they became more familiar with the Moslems living in the kingdom, mutual unfamiliarity and hostility decreased. Moslem merchants freely entered Christian settlements and sold their wares; Moslem and Jewish physicians were preferred by Christian patients;[28] Moslem worship in mosques was permitted by the Christian clergy; and the Koran was taught in Moslem schools in Christian Antioch and Tripolis. Safe conducts for travelers and traders were exchanged between Christian and Moslem states. As only a few Christian wives had come with the Crusaders, many Christian settlers married Syrian women; soon their mixed offspring constituted a large element of the population. Arabic became the daily speech of all commoners. Christian princes made alliances with Moslem emirs against Christian rivals, and Moslem emirs sometimes asked the aid of the "polytheists" in diplomacy or war. Personal friendships developed between Christians and Mohammedans. Ibn Jubair, who toured Christian Syria in 1183, described his fellow Moslems there as prosperous, and as well treated by the Franks. He mourned to see Acre "swarming with pigs and crosses," and odorous with a vile European smell, but he had some hopes that the infidels would gradually be civilized by the superior civilization to which they had come.[29]

In the forty years of peace that followed the Second Crusade, the Latin kingdom of Jerusalem continued to be torn with internal strife, while its Moslem enemies moved toward unity. Nur-ud-din spread his power from Aleppo to Damascus (1164); when he died, Saladin brought Egypt and Moslem Syria under one rule (1175). Genoese, Venetian, and Pisan merchants disordered the Eastern ports with their mortal rivalry. Knights quarreled for the royal power in Jerusalem; and when Guy de Lusignan maneuvered his way to the throne (1186), disaffection spread among the aristocracy; "if this Guy is a king," said his brother Geoffrey, "I am worthy to be a god." Reginald of Châtillon made himself sovereign in the great castle of Karak beyond the Jordan, near the Arabian frontier, and repeatedly violated the truce arranged between the Latin king and Saladin. He announced his intention to invade Arabia, destroy the tomb of "the accursed camel driver" at Medina, and smash the Kaaba at Mecca in fragments to the ground.[30] His small force of knightly adventurers sailed down the Red Sea, landed at el-Haura, and marched to Medina; they were surprised by an

Egyptian detachment, and all were cut down except a few who escaped with Reginald, and some prisoners who were taken to Mecca and slaughtered instead of goats at the annual pilgrimage sacrifice (1183).

Saladin had heretofore contented himself with minor forays against Palestine; now, offended to the depths of his piety, he re-formed the army that had won him Damascus, and met the forces of the Latin kingdom in an indecisive battle on the historic plain of Esdraelon (1183). A few months later he attacked Reginald at Karak, but failed to enter the citadel. In 1185 he signed a four-year truce with the Latin kingdom. But in 1186 Reginald, bored with peace, waylaid a Moslem caravan, and took rich booty and several prisoners, including Saladin's sister. "Since they trusted in Mohammed," said Reginald, "let Mohammed come and save them." Mohammed did not come; but Saladin, infuriated, sounded the call for a holy war against the Christians, and swore to kill Reginald with his own hand.

The crucial engagement of the Crusades was fought at Hittin, near Tiberias, on July 4, 1187. Saladin, familiar with the terrain, took up positions controlling all the wells; the heavily armored Christians, having marched across the plain in midsummer heat, entered battle gasping with thirst. Taking advantage of the wind, the Saracens started a brush fire whose smoke further harassed the Crusaders. In the blind confusion the Frank footmen were separated from the cavalry, and were cut down; the knights, fighting with desperation against weapons, smoke, and thirst, at last fell exhausted to the ground, and were captured or slain. Apparently by Saladin's orders, no mercy was shown to Templars or Hospitalers. He directed that King Guy and Duke Reginald be brought before him; to the King he gave drink as a pledge of pardon; to Reginald he gave the choice of death or acknowledging Mohammed as a prophet of God; when Reginald refused, Saladin slew him. Part of the booty taken by the victors was the True Cross, which had been borne as a battle standard by a priest; Saladin sent it to the caliph at Baghdad. Seeing that no army remained to challenge him, he proceeded to capture Acre, where he freed 4000 Moslem prisoners, and paid his troops with the wealth of the busy port. For a few months nearly all Palestine was in his hands.

As he approached Jerusalem the leading citizens came out to bid for peace. "I believe," he told them, "that Jerusalem is the home of God, as you also believe; and I will not willingly lay siege to it, or put it to assault." He offered it freedom to fortify itself, and to cultivate unhindered the land for fifteen miles around, and promised to supply all deficiencies of money and food, until Pentecost; if, when that day came, they saw hope of being rescued, they might keep the city and honorably resist him; if no such prospect appeared, they were to yield peaceably, and he would spare the lives and property of the Christian inhabitants. The delegates refused the offer, saying that they would never surrender the city where the Saviour had died for mankind.[31] The siege lasted only twelve days. When the city capitulated, Saladin required a ransom of ten gold pieces ($47.50?) for each man, five for each woman, one for each child; the poorest 7000 were to be freed on the surrender of the 30,000 gold bezants (c. $270,000) which had been sent to the Hospitalers by Henry II of England. These terms were accepted, says a Christian chronicler, "with gratitude and lamentation"; perhaps some learned Christians compared these events of 1187 with those of 1099. Saladin's brother al-Adil asked for the gift of a thousand slaves from the still unransomed poor; it was granted, and he freed them. Balian, leader of the Christian resistance, asked a like boon, received it, and freed another thousand; the Christian primate asked and received and did likewise. Then Saladin said: "My brother has made his alms, and the patriarch and Balian have made theirs; now I would make mine"; and he freed all the old who could not pay. Apparently some 15,000 of the 60,000 captured Christians remained unransomed, and became slaves. Among the ransomed were the wives and daughters of the nobles who had been killed or captured at Hittin. Softened by their tears, Saladin released to them such husbands and fathers (including King Guy) as could be found in Moslem captivity, and (relates Ernoul, squire to Balian) to "the dames and damsels whose lords were dead he distributed from his own treasure so much that they gave praise to God, and published abroad the kindness and honor that Saladin had done them."[32]

The freed King and nobles took an oath never to bear arms against him again. Safe in Christian Tripolis and Antioch, they were "released by the sentence of the clergy from the enormity of their promise," and laid plans of vengeance against Saladin.[33] The Sultan allowed the Jews to dwell again in Jerusalem, and gave Christians the right to enter, but unarmed; he assisted their pilgrimage, and protected their security.[34] The Dome of the Rock, which had been converted into a church, was purified from Christian taint by sprinkling with rose water, and the golden cross that had surmounted the cupola was cast down amid Moslem cheers and Christian groans. Saladin led his wearied troops to the siege of Tyre, found it impregnable, dismissed most of his army, and retired ill and worn to Damascus (1188), in the fiftieth year of his age.

VI. THE THIRD CRUSADE: 1189–92

The retention of Tyre, Antioch, and Tripolis left the Christians some strands of hope. Italian fleets still controlled the Mediterranean, and stood ready to carry fresh Crusaders for a price. William, Archbishop of Tyre, returned to Europe, and recounted to assemblies in Italy, France, and Germany the fall of Jerusalem. At Mainz his appeal so moved Frederick Barbarossa that the great Emperor, sixty-seven years old, set out almost at once with his army (1189), and all Christendom applauded him as the second Moses who would open a way to the Promised Land. Crossing the Hellespont at Gallipoli, the new host, on a new route, repeated the errors and tragedies of the First Crusade. Turkish bands harassed its march and cut off its supplies; hundreds starved to death; Frederick was drowned ignominiously in the little river of Salef in Cilicia (1190); and only a fraction of his army survived to join in the siege of Acre.

Richard I of the Lion Heart, recently crowned King of England at the age of thirty-one, resolved to try his hand on the Moslems. Fearing French encroachment, in his absence, upon English possessions in France, he insisted that Philip Augustus should accompany him; the French king—a lad of twenty-three—agreed; and the two youthful monarchs received the cross from William of Tyre in a moving ceremony at Vézelay. Richard's army of Normans (for few Englishmen took part in the Crusades) sailed from Marseille, Philip's army from Genoa, for a rendezvous in Sicily (1190). There the kings quarreled and otherwise amused themselves for half a year. Tancred, King of Sicily, offended Richard, who seized Messina "quicker than a priest could chant matins," and restored it for 40,000 ounces of gold. So solvent, he embarked his army for Palestine. Some of his ships were wrecked on the coast of Cyprus; the crews were imprisoned by the Greek governor; Richard paused for a moment, conquered Cyprus, and gave it to Guy de Lusignan, the homeless king of Jerusalem. He reached Acre in June of 1191, a year after leaving Vézelay. Philip had preceded him; the siege of Acre by the Christians had already lasted nineteen months, and had cost thousands of lives. A few weeks after Richard's arrival the Saracens surrendered. The victors asked, and were promised, 200,000 gold pieces ($950,000), 1600 selected prisoners, and the restoration of the True Cross. Saladin confirmed the agreement, and the Moslem population of Acre, excepting the 1600, were allowed to depart with such provisions as they could carry. Philip Augustus, ill with fever, returned to France, leaving behind him a French force of 10,500 men. Richard became sole leader of the Third Crusade.

Now began a confused and unique campaign in which blows and battles alternated with compliments and courtesies, while the English King and the Kurd Sultan illustrated some of the finest qualities of their civilizations and creeds. Neither was a saint: Saladin could dispense death with vigor when military purposes seemed to him to require it; and the romantic Richard permitted some interruptions in his career as a gentleman. When the leaders of besieged Acre delayed in carrying out the agreed terms of surrender, Richard had 2500 Moslem prisoners beheaded before the walls as a hint to hurry.[35] When Saladin learned of this he ordered the execution of all prisoners thereafter taken in battle with the English King. Changing his tune, Richard proposed to end the Crusades by marrying his sister Joan to Saladin's brother al-Adil. The Church denounced the scheme, and it was dropped.

Knowing that Saladin would not stay quiet in defeat, Richard reorganized his forces and prepared to march sixty miles southward along the coast to relieve Jaffa, which, again in Christian hands, was under Moslem siege. Many nobles refused to go with him, preferring to stay behind in Acre and intrigue for the kingship of the Jerusalem which they trusted Richard would take. The German troops returned to Germany, and the French army repeatedly disobeyed the orders, and frustrated the strategy, of the British King. Nor were the rank and file ready for renewed effort. After the long siege, says the Christian chronicler of Richard's crusade, the victorious Christians,

> given up to sloth and luxury, were loath to leave a city so rich in comforts—to wit, the choicest of wines and the fairest of damsels. Many, by a too intimate acquaintance with these pleasures, became dissolute, till the city was polluted by their luxury, and their gluttony and wantonness put wise men to the blush.[36]

Richard made matters more difficult by ordering that no women should accompany the army except washerwomen, who could not be an occasion of sin. He atoned for the defects of his troops by the excellence of his generalship, the skill of his engineering, and his inspiring valor on the field; in these respects he excelled Saladin, as well as all other Christian leaders of the Crusades.

His army met Saladin's at Arsuf, and won an indecisive victory (1191). Saladin offered to renew battle, but Richard withdrew his men within Jaffa's walls. Saladin sent him an offer of peace. During the negotiations Conrad, Marquis of Montferrat, who held Tyre, entered into separate correspondence with Saladin, proposing to become his ally, and retake Acre for the Moslems, if Saladin would agree to his appropriating Sidon and Beirut. Despite this offer, Saladin authorized his brother to sign with Richard a peace yielding to the Christians all the coastal cities that they then held, and half of Jerusalem. Richard was so pleased that he ceremoniously conferred knighthood upon the son of the Moslem ambassador (1192). A while later, hearing that Saladin was faced with revolt in the East, he rejected Saladin's terms, besieged and took Darum, and advanced to within twelve miles of Jerusalem. Saladin, who had dismissed his troops for the winter, called them back to arms. Meanwhile dissension broke out in the Christian camp, scouts reported that the wells on the road to Jerusalem had been poisoned, and the army would have nothing to drink. A council was held to decide strategy; it voted to abandon Jerusalem and march upon Cairo, 250 miles away. Richard, sick, disgusted, and despondent, retired to Acre, and thought of returning to England.

But when he heard that Saladin had again attacked Jaffa, and had taken it in two days, Richard's pride revived him. With such troops as he could muster he sailed at once for Jaffa. Arrived in the harbor, he cried, "Perish the hindmost!" and leaped to his waist into the sea. Swinging his famous Danish ax, he beat down all who resisted him, led his men into the city, and cleared it of Moslem soldiery almost before Saladin could learn what had occurred (1192). The sultan summoned his main army to his rescue. It far outnumbered Richard's 3000, but the reckless courage of the King carried the day. Seeing Richard unmounted, Saladin sent him a charger, calling it a shame that so gallant a warrior should have to fight on foot. Saladin's soldiers soon had enough; they reproached him for having spared the Jaffa garrison, which was now fighting again. Finally, if we may believe the Christian account, Richard rode along the Saracen front, lance at rest, and none dared attack him.[37]

On the next day fortune changed. Reinforcements reached Saladin; and Richard, sick again, and unsupported by the knights at Acre and Tyre, once more sued for peace. In his fever he cried out for fruit and a cooling drink; Saladin sent him pears and peaches and snow, and his own physician. On September 2, 1192, the two heroes signed a peace for three years, and partitioned Palestine: Richard was to keep all the coastal cities he had conquered, from Acre to Jaffa; Moslems and Christians were to pass freely into and from each other's territory, and pilgrims would be protected in Jerusalem; but that city was to remain in Moslem hands. (Perhaps the Italian merchants, interested chiefly in controlling the ports, had persuaded Richard to yield the Holy City in return for the coastal area.) The peace was celebrated with feasts and tournaments; "God alone," says Richard's chronicler, "knoweth the measureless delight of both peoples";[38] for a moment men ceased to hate. Boarding his ship for England, Richard sent a last defiant note to Saladin, promising to return in three years and take Jerusalem. Saladin replied that if he must lose his land he had liefer lose it to Richard than to any other man alive.[39]

Saladin's moderation, patience, and justice had defeated Richard's brilliance, courage, and military art; the relative unity and fidelity of the Moslem leaders had triumphed over the divisions and disloyalties of the feudal chiefs; and a short line of supplies behind the Saracens proved of greater advantage than Christian control of the seas. The Christian virtues and faults were better exemplified in the Moslem sultan than in the Christian king. Saladin was religious to the point of persecution, and allowed himself to be unreasonably bitter against the Templars and Hospitalers. Usually, however, he was gentle to the weak, merciful to the vanquished, and so superior to his enemies in faithfulness to his word that Christian chroniclers wondered how so wrong a theology could produce so fine a man. He treated his servants with gentleness, and himself heard all petitions. He "esteemed money as little as dust," and left only one dinar in his personal treasury.[40] Not long before his death he gave his son ez-Zahir instructions that no Christian philosopher could surpass:

> My son, I commend thee to the most high God. . . . Do His will, for that way lies peace. Abstain from shedding blood . . . for blood that is spilt never sleeps. Seek to win the hearts of thy people, and watch over their prosperity; for it is to secure their happiness that thou art appointed by God and me. Try to gain the hearts of thy ministers, nobles, and emirs. If I have become great it is because I have won men's hearts by kindness and gentleness.[41]

He died in 1193, aged only fifty-five.

VII. THE FOURTH CRUSADE: 1202–4

The Third Crusade had freed Acre, but had left Jerusalem unredeemed; it was a discouragingly small result from the participation of Europe's greatest kings. The drowning of Barbarossa, the flight of Philip Augustus, the brilliant failure of Richard, the unscrupulous intrigues of Christian knights in the Holy Land, the conflicts between Templars and Hospitalers, and the renewal of war between England and France broke the pride of Europe and further weakened the theological assurance of Christendom. But the early death of Saladin, and the breakup of his empire, released new hopes. Innocent III (1198–1216), at the very outset of his pontificate, demanded another effort; and Fulk de Neuilly, a simple priest, preached the Fourth Crusade to commoners and kings. The results were disheartening. The Emperor Frederick II was a boy of four; Philip Augustus thought one crusade enough for a lifetime; and Richard I, forgetting his last word to Saladin, laughed at Fulk's exhortations. "You advise me," he said, "to dismiss my three daughters—pride, avarice, and incontinence. I bequeath them to the most deserving: my pride to the Templars, my avarice to the monks of Cîteaux, my incontinence to the prelates." [42] But Innocent persisted. He suggested that a campaign against Egypt could succeed through Italian control of the Mediterranean, and would offer a means of approaching Jerusalem from rich and fertile Egypt as a base. After much haggling Venice agreed, in return for 85,000 marks of silver ($8,500,000), to furnish shipping for 4500 knights and horses, 9000 squires, 20,000 infantry, and supplies for nine months; it would also provide fifty war galleys; but on condition that half the spoils of conquest should go to the Venetian Republic.[43] The Venetians, however, had no intention of attacking Egypt; they made millions annually by exporting timber, iron, and arms to Egypt, and importing slaves; they did not propose to jeopardize this trade with war, or to share it with Pisa and Genoa. While negotiating with the Crusaders' committee, they made a secret treaty with the sultan of Egypt, guaranteeing that country against invasion (1201).[44] Ernoul, a contemporary chronicler, alleges that Venice received a huge bribe to divert the crusade from Palestine.[45]

In the summer of 1202 the new hosts gathered in Venice. There were Marquis Boniface of Montferrat, Count Louis of Blois, Count Baldwin of Flanders, Simon de Montfort of Albigensian fame, and, among many other notables, Geoffroi de Villehardouin (1160–1213), Marshal of Champagne, who would not only play a leading part in the diplomacy and campaigns of the crusade, but would enshrine its scandalous history in face-saving memoirs that marked the beginning of French prose literature. France, as usual, supplied most of the Crusaders. Every man had been instructed to bring a sum of money, proportionate to his means, to raise the 85,000 marks payable to Venice for her outlay. The total fell short by 34,000 marks. Thereupon Enrico Dandolo, the almost blind doge "of the great heart," with all the sanctity of his ninety-four years, proposed that the unpaid balance should be forgiven if the Crusaders would help Venice capture Zara. This was now the most important Adriatic port after Venice itself; it had been conquered by Venice in 998, had often revolted and been subdued; it now belonged to Hungary, and was that country's only outlet to the sea; its wealth and power were growing, and Venice feared its competition for the Adriatic trade. Innocent III denounced the proposal as villainous, and threatened to excommunicate all participants. But the greatest and most powerful of the popes could not make his voice heard above the clamor of gold. The combined fleets attacked Zara, took it in five days, and divided the spoils. Then the Crusaders sent an embassy to the Pope begging his absolution; he gave it, but demanded the restoration of the booty; they thanked him for the absolution, and kept the booty. The Venetians ignored the excommunications, and proceeded to the second part of their plan—the conquest of Constantinople.

The Byzantine monarchy had learned nothing from the Crusades. It gave little help, and derived much profit; it regained most of Asia Minor, and looked with equanimity upon the mutual weakening of Islam and the West in the struggle for Palestine. The Emperor Manuel had arrested thousands of Venetians in Constantinople, and had for a time ended Venetian commercial privileges there (1171).[46] Isaac II Angelus (1185–95) had not scrupled to ally himself with the Saracens.[47] In 1195 Isaac was deposed, imprisoned, and blinded by his brother Alexius III. Isaac's son, another Alexius, fled to Germany; in 1202 he went to Venice, asked the Venetian Senate and the Crusaders to rescue and restore his father, and promised in return all that Byzantium could supply for their attack upon Islam. Dandolo and the French barons drove a hard bargain with the youth: he was persuaded to pledge the Crusaders 200,000 marks of silver, equip an army of 10,000 men for service in Palestine, and submit the Greek Orthodox Church to the

Roman Pope.[48] Despite this subtle sop, Innocent III forbade the Crusaders, on pain of excommunication, to attack Byzantium. Some nobles refused to share in the expedition; a part of the army considered itself absolved from the Crusade, and went home. But the prospect of capturing the richest city in Europe proved irresistible. On October 1, 1202, the great fleet of 480 vessels sailed amid much rejoicing, while priests on the war-castles of the ships sang *Veni Creator Spiritus.*[49]

After divers delays the armada arrived before Constantinople on June 24, 1203. "You may be assured," says Villehardouin,

> that those who had never seen Constantinople opened wide eyes now; for they could not believe that so rich a city could be in the whole world, when they saw her lofty walls and her stately towers wherewith she was encompassed, and these stately palaces and lofty churches, so many in number as no man might believe who had not seen them, and the length and breadth of this town which was sovereign over all others. And know that there was no man among us so bold but that his flesh crept at the sight; and therein was no marvel; for never did any men undertake so great a business as this assault of ours, since the beginning of the world.[50]

An ultimatum was delivered to Alexius III: he must restore the Empire to his blinded brother or to the young Alexius, who accompanied the fleet. When he refused, the Crusaders landed, against weak opposition, before the walls of the city; and the aged Dandolo was the first to touch the shore. Alexius III fled to Thrace; the Greek nobles escorted Isaac Angelus from his dungeon to the throne, and in his name a message was sent to the Latin chieftains that he was waiting to welcome his son. After drawing from Isaac a promise to abide by the commitments that his son had made with them, Dandolo and the barons entered the city, and the young Alexius IV was crowned coemperor. But when the Greeks learned of the price at which he had bought his victory they turned against him in anger and scorn. The people reckoned the taxes that would be needed to raise the subsidies promised to his saviors; the nobility resented the presence of an alien aristocracy and force; the clergy rejected with fury the proposal that they should bow to Rome. Meanwhile some Latin soldiers, horrified to find Moslems worshiping in a mosque in a Christian city, set fire to the mosque, and slew the worshipers. The fire raged for eight days, spread through three miles, and laid a considerable section of Constantinople in ashes. A prince of royal blood led a popular revolt, killed Alexius IV, reimprisoned Isaac Angelus, took the throne as Alexius V Ducas, and began to organize an army to drive the Latins from their camp at Galata. But the Greeks had been too long secure within their walls to have kept the virtues of their Roman name. After a month of siege they surrendered; Alexius V fled, and the victorious Latins passed like consuming locusts through the capital (1204).

So long kept from their promised prey, they now—in Easter week—subjected the rich city to such spoliation as Rome had never suffered from Vandals or Goths. Not many Greeks were killed—perhaps 2000; but pillage was unconfined. The nobles divided the palaces among them, and appropriated the treasures they found there; the soldiers entered homes, churches, shops, and took whatever caught their fancy. Churches were rifled not only of the gold, silver, and jewels accumulated by them through a millennium, but of sacred relics that would later be peddled in Western Europe at good prices. St. Sophia suffered more damage than the Turks would inflict upon it in 1453; [51] the great altar was torn to pieces to distribute its silver and gold.[52] The Venetians, familiar with the city that had once welcomed them as merchants, knew where the greatest treasures lay, and stole with superior intelligence; statues and textiles, slaves and gems, fell discriminately into their hands; the four bronze horses that had surveyed the Greek city would now romp over the Piazza di San Marco; nine tenths of the collections of art and jewelry that would later distinguish the Treasury of St. Mark's came from this well-managed theft.[53] Some attempt was made to limit rape; many of the soldiers modestly contented themselves with prostitutes; but Innocent III complained that the pent-up lust of the Latins spared neither age nor sex nor religious profession, and that Greek nuns had to bear the embraces of French or Venetian peasants or grooms.[54] Amid the pillage libraries were ransacked, and precious manuscripts were ruined or lost; two further fires consumed libraries and museums as well as churches and homes; of the plays of Sophocles and Euripides, till then completely preserved, only a minority survived. Thousands of art masterpieces were stolen, mutilated, or destroyed.

When the riot of rapine had subsided, the Latin nobles chose Baldwin of Flanders to head the Latin kingdom of Constantinople (1204), and made French its official language. The Byzantine Empire was divided into feudal dominions, each ruled by a Latin noble. Venice, eager to control the routes of trade, secured Hadrianople, Epirus, Acarnania, the Ionian Isles, part of the Peloponnesus, Euboea, the Aegean Isles, Gallipoli, and three eighths of Constantinople; the Genoese were dispossessed of their Byzantine "factories" and outposts; and Dandolo, now limping in imperial buskins, took the title of "Doge of Venice, Lord of One Fourth and One Eighth of the Roman Empire"; [55] soon afterward he died, in the fullness of his unscrupulous success. The Greek clergy were mostly replaced by Latins, in some cases precipitated into holy orders for the occasion; and Innocent III, still protesting against the attack, accepted with grace the formal reunion of the Greek with the Latin Church. Most of the Crusaders returned home with their spoils; some settled in the new dominions; only a handful reached Palestine, and without effect. Perhaps the Crusaders thought that Constantinople, in their hands, would be a stronger base against the Turks than Byzantium had been. But generations of strife between the Latins and the Greeks now absorbed

the vitality of the Greek world; the Byzantine Empire never recovered from
the blow; and the capture of Constantinople by the Latins prepared, across
two centuries, its capture by the Turks.

VIII. THE COLLAPSE OF THE CRUSADES: 1212–91

The scandal of the Fourth Crusade, added in a decade to the failure of the
Third, gave no comfort to a Christian faith soon to be faced with the rediscovery of Aristotle and the subtle rationalism of Averroës. Thinkers were
much exercised to explain why God had allowed the defeat of His defenders
in so holy a cause, and had granted success only to Venetian villainy. Amid
these doubts it occurred to simple souls that only innocence could regain the
citadel of Christ. In 1212 a German youth vaguely known to history as
Nicholas announced that God had commissioned him to lead a crusade of
children to the Holy Land. Priests as well as laity condemned him, but the
idea spread readily in an age even more subject than most to waves of emotional enthusiasm. Parents struggled to deter their children, but thousands of
boys (and some girls in boys' clothing), averaging twelve years, slipped
away and followed Nicholas, perhaps glad to escape from the monarchy of
the home to the freedom of the road. The swarm of 30,000 children, leaving
mostly from Cologne, passed down the Rhine and over the Alps. Many died
of hunger; some stragglers were eaten by wolves; thieves mingled with the
marchers and stole their clothing and food. The survivors reached Genoa,
where the earthy Italians laughed them into doubt; no ships would carry
them to Palestine; and when they appealed to Innocent III he gently told
them to go home. Some marched disconsolately back over the Alps; many
settled in Genoa and learned the ways of a commercial world.

In France, in this same year, a twelve-year-old shepherd named Stephen
came to Philip Augustus, and announced that Christ, appearing to him while
he tended his flock, had bidden him lead a children's crusade to Palestine.
The king ordered him to return to his muttons; nevertheless 20,000 young-
sters gathered to follow Stephen's lead. They made their way across France
to Marseille, where, Stephen had promised them, the ocean would divide to
let them reach Palestine dryshod. It failed them; but two shipowners offered
to take them to their destination without charge. They crowded into seven
ships, and sailed forth singing hymns of victory. Two of the ships were
wrecked off Sardinia, with the loss of all on board; the other children were
brought to Tunisia or Egypt, where they were sold as slaves. The shipowners
were hanged by order of Frederick II.[56]

Three years later Innocent III, at the Fourth Lateran Council, again appealed to Europe to recover the land of Christ, and returned to the plan that
Venice had frustrated—an attack upon Egypt. In 1217 the Fifth Crusade left

Germany, Austria, and Hungary under the Hungarian King Andrew, and safely reached Damietta, at the easternmost mouth of the Nile. The city fell after a year's siege; and Malik al-Kamil, the new Sultan of Egypt and Syria, offered terms of peace—the surrender of most of Jerusalem, the liberation of Christian prisoners, the return of the True Cross. The Crusaders demanded an indemnity as well, which al-Kamil refused. The war was resumed, but went badly; expected reinforcements did not come; finally an eight-year truce was signed that gave the Crusaders the True Cross, but restored Damietta to the Moslems, and required the evacuation of all Christian troops from Egyptian soil.

The Crusaders blamed their tragedy upon Frederick II, the young Emperor of Germany and Italy. He had taken the crusader's vow in 1215, and had promised to join the besiegers at Damietta; but political complications in Italy, and perhaps an inadequate faith, detained him. In 1228, while excommunicate for his delays, Frederick set out on the Sixth Crusade. Arrived in Palestine, he received no help from the good Christians there, who shunned an outlaw from the Church. He sent emissaries to al-Kamil, who was now leading the Saracen army at Nablus. Al-Kamil replied courteously; and the Sultan's ambassador, Fakhru'd Din, was impressed by Frederick's knowledge of the Arabic language, literature, science, and philosophy. The two rulers entered into a friendly exchange of compliments and ideas; and to the astonishment of both Christendom and Islam they signed a treaty (1229) by which al-Kamil ceded to Frederick Acre, Jaffa, Sidon, Nazareth, Bethlehem, and all of Jerusalem except the enclosure—sacred to Islam—containing the Dome of the Rock. Christian pilgrims were to be admitted to this enclosure to perform their prayers on the site of Solomon's Temple; and similar rights were to be enjoyed by Mohammedans in Bethlehem. All prisoners on either side were to be released; and for ten years and ten months each side pledged itself to peace.[57] The excommunicate Emperor had succeeded where for a century Christendom had failed; the two cultures, brought together for a moment in mutual understanding and respect, had found it possible to be friends. The Christians of the Holy Land rejoiced, but Pope Gregory IX denounced the pact as an insult to Christendom, and refused to ratify it. After Frederick's departure the Christian nobility of Palestine took control of Jerusalem, and allied the Christian power in Asia with the Moslem ruler of Damascus against the Egyptian Sultan (1244). The latter called to his aid the Khwarazmian Turks, who captured Jerusalem, plundered it, and massacred a large number of its inhabitants. Two months later Baibars defeated the Christians at Gaza, and Jerusalem once more fell to Islam (October, 1244).

While Innocent IV preached a crusade against Frederick II, and offered to all who would war against the Emperor in Italy the same indulgences and privileges granted to those who served in the Holy Land, the saintly Louis

IX of France organized the Seventh Crusade. Shortly after the fall of Jerusalem he took the cross, and persuaded his nobles to do likewise; to certain
reluctant ones, at Christmas, he presented costly garments bearing an inwoven cross. He labored to reconcile Innocent with Frederick, so that a
united Europe might support the Crusade. Innocent refused; instead, he sent
a friar—Giovanni de Piano Carpini—to the Great Khan, suggesting a union
of Mongols and Christians against the Turks; the Khan replied by inviting
the submission of Christendom to the Mongol power. At last, in 1248, Louis
set out with his French knights, including Jean Sieur de Joinville, who would
narrate the exploits of his King in a famous chronicle. The expedition
reached Damietta, and soon captured it; but the annual inundation of the
Nile, which had been forgotten in planning the campaign, began as the Crusaders arrived, and so flooded the country that they were confined to Damietta for half a year. They did not altogether regret it; "the barons," says
Joinville, "took to giving great feasts . . . and the common people took to
consorting with lewd women." [58] When the army resumed its march it was
depleted by hunger, disease, and desertion, and weakened with indiscipline.
At Mansura, despite brave fighting, it was defeated, and fled in wild rout;
10,000 Christians were captured, including Louis himself, fainting with dysentery (1250). An Arab physician cured him; after a month of tribulation
he was released, but only in return for the surrender of Damietta, and a ransom of 500,000 *livres* ($3,800,000). When Louis agreed to this enormous
ransom, the sultan reduced it by a fifth, and trusted the King for an unpaid
half.[59] Louis led the remnant of his army to Acre, and stayed there four years,
vainly calling upon Europe to cease its wars and join him in a new campaign.
He dispatched the monk William of Rubruquis to the Mongol Khan renew-
ing the invitation of Innocent—with similar results. In 1254 he returned to
France.

His years in the East had quieted the factionalism of the Christians there;
his departure released it. From 1256 to 1260 a civil war of the Venetians
against the Genoese in the Syrian ports dragged every faction into it, and
exhausted the Christian forces in Palestine. Seizing the opportunity, Baibars, the slave Sultan of Egypt, marched up the coast and took one Christian
town after another: Caesarea (1265), Safad (1266), Jaffa (1267), Antioch
(1268). The captured Christians were slaughtered or enslaved, and Antioch
was so devastated with plunder and fire that it never recovered.

Roused to new fervor in his old age, Louis IX took the cross a second time
(1267). His three sons followed his example; but the French nobility rejected his plans as quixotic, and refused to join; even Joinville, who loved
him, would have none of this Eighth Crusade. This time the King, wise in
government and foolish in war, landed his inadequate forces in Tunisia, hoping to convert its bey to Christianity, and to attack Egypt from the west. He
had hardly touched African soil when he "fell sick of a flux in the stom-

ach," [60] and died with the word "Jerusalem" on his lips (1270). A year later Prince Edward of England landed at Acre, bravely led some futile sallies, and hurried back to accept the English crown.

The final disaster came when some Christian adventurers robbed a Moslem caravan in Syria, hanged nineteen Moslem merchants, and sacked several Moslem towns. Sultan Khalil demanded satisfaction; receiving none, he marched against Acre, the strongest Christian outpost in Palestine; taking it after a siege of forty-three days, he allowed his men to massacre or enslave 60,000 prisoners (1291). Tyre, Sidon, Haifa, and Beirut fell soon afterward. The Latin kingdom of Jerusalem maintained a ghostly existence for a time in the titles of vain potentates, and for two centuries a few adventurers or enthusiasts embarked upon sporadic and futile efforts to resume the "Great Debate"; but Europe knew that the Crusades had come to an end.

IX. THE RESULTS OF THE CRUSADES

Of their direct and professed purposes the Crusades had failed. After two centuries of war, Jerusalem was in the hands of the ferocious Mamluks, and Christian pilgrims came fewer and more fearful than before. The Moslem powers, once tolerant of religious diversity, had been made intolerant by attack. The Palestinian and Syrian ports that had been captured for Italian trade were without exception lost. Moslem civilization had proved itself superior to the Christian in refinement, comfort, education, and war. The magnificent effort of the popes to give Europe peace through a common purpose had been shattered by nationalistic ambitions and the "crusades" of popes against emperors.

Feudalism recovered with difficulty from its failure in the Crusades. Suited to individualistic adventure and heroism within a narrow range, it had not known how to adjust its methods to Oriental climates and distant campaigns. It had bungled inexcusably the problem of supplies along a lengthening line of communications. It had exhausted its equipment, and blunted its spirit, by conquering not Moslem Jerusalem but Christian Byzantium. To finance their expeditions to the East, many knights had sold or mortgaged their properties to lord, moneylender, Church, or king; for a price they had resigned their rights over many towns in their domains; to many peasants they had sold remission of future feudal dues. Serfs by the thousands had used the crusader's privilege to leave the land, and thousands had never returned to their manors. While feudal wealth and arms were diverted to the East, the power and wealth of the French monarchy rose as one of the major results of the Crusades. At the same time both the Roman Empires were weakened: the Western emperors lost prestige by their failures in the Holy Land, and by their conflicts with a papacy exalted by the Crusades; and the Eastern Empire, though reborn in 1261, never regained its former power or repute. The Crusades, however, had this measure of success, that without them the Turks would have taken Constantinople long before 1453. For Islam, too, was weakened by the Crusades, and fell more easily before the Mongol flood.

Some of the military orders suffered tragic fates. Those Hospitalers who survived the massacre at Acre fled to Cyprus. In 1310 they captured Rhodes from the Moslems, changed their name to the Knights of Rhodes, and ruled the island till 1522; expelled then by the Turks, they removed to Malta, became the Knights of Malta, and continued to exist there till their disbandment in 1799. The Teutonic Knights, after the fall of Acre, transferred their headquarters to Marienburg in the Prussia they had conquered for Germany from the Slavs. The Templars, driven from Asia, reorganized in France. Possessed of rich holdings throughout Europe, they settled down to enjoy their revenues. Free from taxation, they lent money at lower interest rates than the Lombards and the Jews, and reaped lush profits. Unlike the Hospitalers, they maintained no hospitals, established no schools, succored no poor. At last their hoarded wealth, their armed state within the state, their insubordination to the royal power, aroused the envy, fear, and wrath of King Philip IV the Fair. On October 12, 1310, by his order, and without warning, all Templars in France were arrested, and the royal seal was set on all their goods. Philip accused them of indulging homosexual lusts, of having lost their Christian faith through long contact with Islam, of denying Christ and spitting upon the cross, of worshiping idols, of being in secret league with the Moslems, and of having repeatedly betrayed the Christian cause. A tribunal of prelates and monks loyal to the King examined the prisoners; they denied the royal charges, and were put to the torture to induce them to confess. Some, suspended by the wrists, were repeatedly drawn up and suddenly let down; some had their bare feet held over flames; some had sharp splinters driven under their fingernails; some had a tooth wrenched out day after day; some had heavy weights hung from their genitals; some were slowly starved. In many cases all these devices were used, so that most of the prisoners, when examined again, were weak to the point of death. One showed the bones that had fallen from his roasted feet. Many of them confessed to all the charges of the King; some told how life and liberty had been promised them, under the royal seal, if they would admit the allegations of the government. Several of them died in jail; some killed themselves; fifty-nine were burned at the stake (1310), protesting their innocence to the end. Du Molay, the Grand Master of the order, confessed under torture; led to the stake, he withdrew his confession; and the inquisitors proposed to try him again. Philip denounced the delay, and ordered him to be burned at once; and the royal presence graced the execution. All the property of the Templars in France was confiscated by the state. Pope Clement V protested against these procedures; the French clergy supported the King; the Pope, a virtual prisoner at Avignon, ceased resistance, and abolished the order at Philip's behest (1312). Edward II, also needing money, confiscated the property of the Templars in England. Some of the wealth so appropriated by Philip and Edward was surrendered to the Church; some of it was granted by the kings to favorites, who by these means founded great manors, and supported the kings against the older feudal nobility.

Possibly some of the Crusaders had learned in the East a new tolerance for sexual perversions; this, and the reintroduction of public baths and private latrines in the West may be included among the results of the Crusades. Probably through contact with the Moslem East, the Europeans returned to the old Roman custom of shaving the beard.[61] A thousand Arabic words now came into the European languages. Oriental romances flowed into Europe, and found new dress in the nascent vernaculars. Crusaders impressed by the enameled glass of the Saracens may have brought from the East the technical secrets that led to the improved stained glass of the developed Gothic cathedrals.[62] The compass, gunpowder, and printing were known in the East before the Crusades ended, and may have come to Europe in the backwash of that tidal wave. Apparently the Crusaders were too unlettered to care for "Arabic" poetry, science, or philosophy; Moslem influences in such fields came rather through Spain and Sicily than through the contacts of these wars. Greek cultural influences were felt by the West after the capture of Constantinople; so William of Moerbeke, Flemish Archbishop of Corinth, furnished Thomas Aquinas with translations of Aristotle made directly from the original. In general the discovery, by the Crusaders, that the followers of another faith could be as civilized, humane, and trustworthy as themselves, if not more so, must have set some minds adrift, and contributed to the weakening of orthodox belief in the thirteenth and fourteenth centuries. Historians like William, Archbishop of Tyre, spoke of Moslem civilization with a respect, sometimes with an admiration, that would have shocked the rude warriors of the First Crusade.[63]

The power and prestige of the Roman Church were immensely enhanced by the First Crusade, and progressively damaged by the rest. The sight of diverse peoples, of lordly barons and proud knights, sometimes of emperors and kings, uniting in a religious cause led by the Church raised the status of the papacy. Papal legates entered every country and diocese to stir recruiting and gather funds for the Crusades; their authority encroached upon, often superseded, that of the hierarchy; and through them the faithful became almost directly tributary to the pope. The collections so made became customary, and were soon applied to many purposes besides the Crusades; the pope acquired, to the active dissatisfaction of the kings, the power to tax their subjects, and divert to Rome great sums that might have gone to royal coffers or local needs. The distribution of indulgences for forty days' service in Palestine was a legitimate application of military science; the granting of

similar indulgences to those who paid the expenses of a Crusader seemed forgivable; the extension of like indulgences to those who contributed to funds
managed by the popes, or who fought papal wars in Europe against Frederick, Manfred, or Conrad, became an added source of irritation to the kings,
and of humor to the satirists. In 1241 Gregory IX directed his legate in Hungary to commute for a money payment the vows of persons pledged to a
crusade, and used the proceeds to help finance his life-and-death struggle
with Frederick II.[64] Provençal troubadours criticized the Church for diverting aid from Palestine by offering equal indulgences for a crusade against the
Albigensian heretics in France.[65] "The faithful wondered," says Matthew
Paris, "that the same plenary remission of sins was promised for shedding
Christian, as for shedding infidel, blood." [66] Many landowners, to finance
their crusade, sold or mortgaged their property to churches or monasteries
to raise liquid funds; some monasteries in this way acquired vast estates; when
the failure of the Crusades lowered the prestige of the Church, her wealth
became a ready target of royal envy, popular resentment, and critical rebuke.
Some attributed the disasters of Louis IX in 1250 to the simultaneous campaign of Innocent IV against Frederick II. Emboldened skeptics argued that
the failure of the Crusades refuted the claims of the pope to be God's vicar
or representative on earth. When, after 1250, monks solicited funds for further crusades, some of their hearers, in humor or bitterness, summoned beggars and gave them alms in the name of Mohammed; for Mohammed, they
said, had shown himself stronger than Christ.[67]

Next to the weakening of Christian belief, the chief effect of the Crusades
was to stimulate the secular life of Europe by acquaintance with Moslem
commerce and industry. War does one good—it teaches people geography.
The Italian merchants who throve on the Crusades learned to make good
charts of the Mediterranean; the monkish chroniclers who accompanied the
knights received and transmitted a new conception of the vastness and variety of Asia. The zest for exploration and travel was stirred; and Baedekers
appeared to guide pilgrims to and through the Holy Land. Christian physicians learned from Jewish and Moslem practitioners, and surgery profited
from the Crusades.

Trade followed the cross, and perhaps the cross was guided by trade. The
knights lost Palestine, but the Italian merchant fleets won control of the
Mediterranean not only from Islam but from Byzantium as well. Venice,
Genoa, Pisa, Amalfi, Marseille, Barcelona had already traded with the Moslem East, the Bosporus, and the Black Sea; but this traffic was immensely enlarged by the Crusades. The Venetian conquest of Constantinople, the transport of pilgrims and warriors to Palestine, the purveyance of supplies to
Christians and others in the East, the importation of Oriental products into
Europe—all these supported a degree of commerce and maritime transport
unknown since the most flourishing days of Imperial Rome. Silks, sugar,

spices—pepper, ginger, cloves, cinnamon—rare luxuries in eleventh-century Europe—came to it now in delightful abundance. Plants, crops, and trees already known to Europe from Moslem Spain were now more widely transplanted from Orient to Occident—maize, rice, sesame, carob, lemons, melons, peaches, apricots, cherries, dates . . . shallot and scallion were named from the port, Ascalon, that shipped them from the East to the West; and apricots were long known as "Damascus plums."[68] Damasks, muslins, satins, velvets, tapestries, rugs, dyes, powders, scents, and gems came from Islam to adorn or sweeten feudal and bourgeois homes and flesh.[69] Mirrors of glass plated with metallic film now replaced those of polished bronze or steel. Europe learned from the East to refine sugar, and make "Venetian" glass.

New markets in the East developed Italian and Flemish industry, and promoted the growth of towns and the middle class. Better techniques of banking were introduced from Byzantium and Islam; new forms and instruments of credit appeared; more money circulated, more ideas, more men. The Crusades had begun with an agricultural feudalism inspired by German barbarism crossed with religious sentiment; they ended with the rise of industry, and the expansion of commerce, in an economic revolution that heralded and financed the Renaissance.

CHAPTER XXIV

The Economic Revolution

1066-1300

I. THE REVIVAL OF COMMERCE

EVERY cultural flowering finds root and nourishment in an expansion
of commerce and industry. Moslem seizure of eastern and southern
Mediterranean ports and trade, Moslem, Viking, and Magyar raids, political
disorder under the successors of Charlemagne, had driven European economic and mental life to nadir in the ninth and tenth centuries. The feudal
protection and reorganization of agriculture, the taming of Norse pirates
into Norman peasants and merchants, the repulse and conversion of the
Huns, the recapture of the Mediterranean by Italian trade, the reopening of
the Levant by the Crusades, and the awakening contact of the West with
the more advanced civilizations of Islam and Byzantium, provided in the
twelfth century the opportunity and stimulus for the recovery of Europe,
and supplied the material means for the cultural blossoming of the twelfth
century and the medieval meridian of the thirteenth. For society, as well as
for an individual, *primum est edere, deinde philosophari*—eating must come
before philosophy, wealth before art.

The first step in the economic revival was the removal of restraints on internal trade. Shortsighted governments had levied a hundred charges upon the
transport and sale of goods—for entering ports, crossing bridges, using roads
or rivers or canals, offering goods for purchase at markets or fairs. Feudal
barons felt justified in exacting tolls on wares passing through their domains,
as states do now; and some of them gave real protection and service to merchants by armed escorts and convenient hospitality.* But the result of state
and feudal interference was sixty-two toll stations on the Rhine, seventy-
four on the Loire, thirty-five on the Elbe, seventy-seven on the Danube . . . ; a
merchant paid sixty per cent of his cargo to carry it along the Rhine.[1] Feudal
wars, undisciplined soldiery, robber barons, and pirates on rivers and seas,
made roads and waterways a martial risk to merchants and travelers. The
Truce and Peace of God helped land commerce by proclaiming relatively
safe periods for travel; and the growing power of the kings diminished rob-

---

* Some feudal mansions hung their shields, or displayed their coats of arms, above their
portals as a sign of readiness to provide hospitality; hence such later roadhouse signs as "The
Red Eagle," "The Golden Lion," "The Gray Bear."

bery, established uniform measures and weights, limited and regulated tolls, and removed tolls altogether from certain roads and markets in the time of the great fairs.

Fairs were the life of medieval trade. Pedlars, of course, carried small wares from door to door, artisans sold their products in their shops, market days gathered sellers and buyers in the towns; barons sheltered markets near their castles, churches allowed them in their yards, kings housed them in *halles* or stores in the capitals. But wholesale and international trade centered in the regional fairs periodically held at London and Stourbridge in England, at Paris, Lyons, Reims, and the Champagne in France, at Lille, Ypres, Douai, and Bruges in Flanders, at Cologne, Frankfort, Leipzig, and Lübeck in Germany, at Geneva in Switzerland, at Novgorod in Russia. . . . The most famous and popular of these fairs took place in the county of Champagne at Lagny in January, at Bar-sur-Aube in Lent, at Provins in May and September, at Troyes in September and November. Each of these six fairs lasted six or seven weeks, so that in sequence they provided an international market through most of the year; they were conveniently located to bring the products and merchants of France, the Lowlands, and the Rhine Valley into contact with those of Provence, Spain, Italy, Africa, and the East; altogether they constituted a major source of French wealth and power in the twelfth century. Originating as early as the fifth century in Troyes, they declined when Philip IV (1285–1314), having taken Champagne from its enlightened counts, taxed and regulated the fairs into penury. In the thirteenth century they gave place to maritime commerce and ports.

Shipbuilding and navigation had slowly improved since Roman days. Hundreds of coastal cities had good lighthouses; many—like Constantinople, Venice, Genoa, Marseille, Barcelona—had commodious docks. Vessels were usually small, with half a deck or none, and carrying some thirty tons; so limited, they could ascend rivers far inland; hence towns like Narbonne, Bordeaux, Nantes, Rouen, Bruges, Bremen, though some distance from the sea, were accessible to ocean-going ships, and became flourishing ports. Some Mediterranean vessels were larger, carrying 600 tons and 1500 passengers; [2] Venice gave Louis IX a ship 108 feet long, manned by 110 men. The ancient galley was still the regular type, with high ornamental poop, one or two masts and sails, and a low hull for two or three banks of oars—which might total 200. Most oarsmen were free enlisted men; galley slaves were rare in the Middle Ages.[3] The art of tacking before the wind, known in the sixth century, developed leisurely until the twelfth, when—mostly on Italian ships —fore and aft rigs were added to the old square sail; [4] but the chief motive power still remained in the oars. The compass, of doubtful origin,* appeared in Christian navigation about 1200; Sicilian mariners made it available in

---

* It may have originated in Europe; cf. *Speculum*, April, 1940, p. 146.

rough waters by resting the magnetic needle on a movable pivot; [5] even so another century passed before mariners (the Norse excepted) dared leave sight of land and steer a straight course across open sea. From November 11 to February 22 ocean voyages were exceptional; they were forbidden to ships of the Hanseatic League; and most Mediterranean or Black Sea shipping halted in that period. Sea travel was as slow as in antiquity; from Marseille to Acre took fifteen days. Voyages were not recommended for health; piracies and shipwrecks were numerous, and the sturdiest stomachs were upset. Froissart tells how Sir Hervé de Léon took fifteen days tossing between Southampton and Harfleur, and "was so troubled that he had never health afterward." [6] As poor compensation, fares were low; sixpence paid for a Channel crossing in the fourteenth century; and proportionate costs for freight and long voyages gave water transport an advantage that in the thirteenth century transformed the political map of Europe.

The Christian reconquest of Sardinia (1022), Sicily (1090), and Corsica (1091) from the Saracens opened the Straits of Messina and the central Mediterranean to European shipping; and the victories of the First Crusade regained all but the southern ports of that sea. So unshackled, commerce bound Europe into a widening web of trade routes, and connected it not only with Christians in Asia, but with Islamic Africa and Asia, even with India and the Far East. Goods from China or India came through Turkestan, Persia, and Syria to Syrian or Palestinian ports; or through Mongolia to the Caspian and the Volga; or by boat to the Persian Gulf, up the Tigris or Euphrates, and over mountains and deserts to the Black Sea, or the Caspian, or the Mediterranean; or by the Red Sea through canals or caravans to Cairo and Alexandria. From the Moslem ports of Africa trade—mostly Christian in the thirteenth century—fanned outward to Asia Minor and Byzantium; to Cyprus, Rhodes, and Crete; to Salonika, the Piraeus, Corinth, and Patras; to Sicily, Italy, France, and Spain. Constantinople added her luxury products to the stream of goods, and fed the traffic up the Danube and the Dnieper to Central Europe, Russia, and the Baltic states. Venice, Pisa, and Genoa captured the westward Byzantine trade, and fought like savages for the Christian mastery of the sea.

Strategically placed between the East and West athwart the Mediterranean, with ports facing in three directions upon that sea, and with northern cities commanding the passes of the Alps, Italy was geographically bound to profit most from the trade of Europe with Byzantium, Palestine, and Islam. On the Adriatic stood Venice, Ravenna, Rimini, Ancona, Bari, Brindisi, Taranto; on the south, Crotone; along her west coast Reggio, Salerno, Amalfi, Naples, Ostia, Pisa, and Lucca carried a rich commerce, and Florence, the banker, pulled the financial strings; the Arno and the Po took some of the trade inland to Padua, Ferrara, Cremona, Piacenza, and Pavia; Rome drew the tithes and fees of European piety to her shrines; Siena and Bologna stood at the generative crossing of great interior roads; Milan, Como, Brescia, Verona, and Venice gathered into their laps the fruits of the trade that moved over the Alps to and from the Danube and the Rhine. Genoa dominated the Tyrrhenian Sea as Venice ruled the Adriatic; her merchant fleet numbered 200 vessels manned by 20,000 men; her trading ports reached from Corsica to Trebizond. Like Venice and Pisa, Genoa traded freely with Islam: Venice with Egypt, Pisa with Tunisia, Genoa with Moorish Africa and Spain. Many of them sold arms to the Saracens during the Crusades. Powerful popes like Innocent III denounced all traffic with the Moslems, but gold ran thicker than faith or blood, and the "blasphemous trade" went on.[7]

Her wars with Venice weakened Genoa, and the ports of southern France and western Spain reached out for a share of Mediterranean commerce. Marseille, stagnant during the Moslem ascendancy, recaptured for a time her old pre-eminence; but nearby Montpellier, stimulated by her polyglot population and culture of Gauls, Moslems, and Jews, rivaled Marseille in the twelfth century as a southern gateway of France. Barcelona profited from the old Jewish mercantile families that remained after its reconquest from Islam; there and at Valencia Christian Spain, blocked by the Pyrenees, found contact with the Mediterranean world. Cadiz, Bordeaux, La Rochelle, and Nantes sent their ships along the Atlantic coasts to Rouen, London, and Bruges; Genoa in the thirteenth century, Venice in 1317, sent vessels through Gibraltar to all these Atlantic ports; by 1300 trade over the Alps diminished, and Atlantic commerce began to lift the Atlantic nations to that leadership which Columbus would ensure.

France grew rich on her rivers, liquid strands of unifying trade; the Rhone, Garonne, Loire, Saône, Seine, Oise, and Moselle fructified her commerce as well as her fields. Britain could not yet rival her; but the Cinque (Five) Ports on the Channel welcomed foreign ships and goods; and the Thames at London was already in the twelfth century bordered with a continuous line of docks, where exports of cloth, wool, and tin paid for spices from Arabia, silks from China, furs from Russia, and wines from France. Busier still—busier than any other northern port—was Bruges, commercial capital and outlet of a Flanders rich in both agriculture and industry. There, as in Venice and Genoa, the east-west crossed the north-south axis of European trade. Situated near the North Sea coast opposite England, it imported English wool to be woven by Flemish or French looms; sufficiently inland to give safe harbor, it attracted the fleets of Genoa, Venice, and western France, and allowed them to reallocate their wares along a hundred routes to minor ports. As ocean transport became safer and cheaper, overland commerce declined, and Bruges succeeded to the Champagne fairs as the northern focus of European trade. Heavy river traffic on the Meuse, the Scheldt, and the Rhine brought to Bruges the goods of western Germany and eastern France for export to Russia, Scandinavia, England, and Spain. Other towns were nourished by that river trade: Valenciennes, Cambrai, Tournai, Ghent, and Antwerp on the Scheldt; Dinant, Liége, and Maestricht on the Meuse.

Bruges was the chief western member of the Hanseatic League. To promote international co-operation against external competition, to arrange congenial association for merchants stationed away from home, to protect themselves from pirates, highwaymen, fluctuating currencies, defaulting debtors, tax collectors, and feudal tolls, the commercial towns of northern Europe formed in the twelfth century various alliances, which the Germans called *hanses*—i.e., unions or guilds. London, Bruges, Ypres, Troyes, and twenty other cities formed the "London Hanse." Lübeck, which had been founded in 1158 as an outpost of German war and trade with Scandinavia, entered into a similar union with Hamburg (1210) and Bruges (1252).* Gradually other cities joined—Danzig, Bremen, Novgorod, Dorpat, Magdeburg, Thorn, Berlin, Visby, Stockholm, Bergen, London; at its height in the fourteenth century the League bound fifty-two towns. It held the mouths of all the great rivers—Rhine, Weser, Elbe, Oder, Vistula—that brought the products of Central Europe to the North or Baltic Sea; it controlled the trade of northern Europe from Rouen to Novgorod. For a long time it monopolized the herring fisheries of the Baltic, and the trade of the Continent with England. It established courts for the settlement of disputes among its members, defended its members against lawsuits from without, and at times waged war as an independent power. It made laws regulating the commercial operations, even the moral conduct, of its member cities and men; it protected its merchants from arbitrary legislation, taxes, and fines; it enforced boycotts against offending cities; it punished default, dishonesty, or the purchase of stolen goods. It established a "factory" or trading post in each member city, kept its merchants under its own German laws wherever they went, and forbade them to marry foreigners.

The Hanseatic League was for a century an agency of civilization. It cleared the Baltic and North Seas of pirates, dredged and straightened waterways, charted currents and tides, marked off channels, built lighthouses, ports, and canals, established and codified maritime law, and in general substituted order for chaos in northern European trade. By organizing the mercantile class into powerful associations, it protected the *bourgeoisie* against the barons, and promoted the liberation of cities from feudal control. It sued the king of France for League goods ruined by his troops, and forced the king of England to pay for Masses to redeem from purgatory the souls of Hanseatic merchants drowned by Englishmen.[8] It spread German commerce, language, and culture eastward into Prussia, Livonia, and Estonia, and made great cities of Königsberg, Libau, Memel, and Riga. It controlled the prices and qualities of goods traded in by its members, and established such a reputa-

---

* This may be taken as the birth date of the Hanseatic League, though that name was not used till 1370.

tion for integrity that the name *Easterlings* (Men from the East), which the English gave them, was adopted by the English as meaning *sterling* worth, and was in this form attached to *silver* or *pound* as meaning trustworthy or real.

But in time the Hanse became an oppressor as well as a defender. It limited too tyrannically the independence of its constituents; forced cities into memberships by boycotts or violence; fought its competitors by fair means or foul; it was not above hiring pirates to injure a rival's trade. It organized its own armies, and set itself up as a state within many states. It did what it could to oppress and suppress the artisan class from which it derived its wares; all laborers, and many others, came to fear and hate it as the most powerful of all monopolies ever engaged in the restraint of trade. When the workers of England revolted in 1381, they pursued all the Hanseatics even into church sanctuaries, and murdered all those who could not say "bread and cheese" with a pure English accent.[9]

About 1160 the Hanse seized the Swedish island of Gotland, and developed Visby as a base and bastion for the Baltic trade. Decade by decade it extended its control over the commerce and politics of Denmark, Poland, Norway, Sweden, Finland, and Russia. In thirteenth-century Russia, reported Adam of Bremen, Hanseatic merchants "are as plentiful as dung . . . and strive as hard to get a marten skin as if it were everlasting salvation."[10] They fixed their seat at Novgorod on the Volkhov, lived there as an armed merchant garrison, used St. Peter's Church as a warehouse, stacked wine casks around its altar, guarded these stores like ferocious dogs, and fulfilled all the outward observances of religious piety.[11]

Not content, the League turned its thoughts to controlling the trade of the Rhine. Cologne, which had formed a *hanse* of its own, was forced into subordination. But farther south the Hanseatic was stopped by the Rhenish League, formed in 1254 by Cologne, Mainz, Speyer, Worms, Strasbourg, and Basel. Still farther south Augsburg, Ulm, and Nuremberg handled the trade that came up from Italy; to this day one may see in Venice the Fondaco de' Tedeschi, their depot on the Grand Canal. Regensburg and Vienna stood at the western end of the great Danube artery that took the products of inland Germany through Salonika into the Aegean, or through the Black Sea to Constantinople, Russia, Islam, and the East. So European trade came full circle, and the web of medieval commerce was complete.

What sort of men were the merchants who sent their goods along these routes amid the suspicious faces, strange tongues, and jealous creeds of a dozen lands? They came from many peoples and countries, but a great number of them were Syrians, Jews, Armenians, or Greeks. They were seldom such businessmen as we know today, safe and sedentary behind a desk in their own city. Usually they moved with their goods; often they traveled great distances to buy cheaply where the products they wanted abounded, and returned to sell dear where their goods were rare. Normally they sold, as well as bought, wholesale—*en gros*, said the French. The English translated *en gros* into *grosser*, and used this first form of the word *grocer* to mean one who sold spices in bulk.[12] Merchants were adventurers, explorers, knights of the caravan, armed with daggers and bribes, ready for highwaymen, pirates, and a thousand tribulations.

The variety of laws and the multiplicity of jurisdictions were perhaps the worst of their harassments, and the progressive formulation of an international law of commerce and navigation was one of their major achievements. If a merchant traveled by land he was subject to a new court, and perhaps different laws, at every feudal domain; if his wares were spilled upon the road, the local lord could claim them. If his ship was stranded it belonged by the "law of wreck" to the landlord upon whose shores it fell; a Breton lord boasted that a dangerous rock on his coast was the most precious stone in his crown.[13] For centuries the merchants fought this abuse; in the twelfth they began to secure its abrogation. Meanwhile the international Jewish traders had accumulated for their own use a code of mercantile law; these regulations became the foundation of the law merchant of the eleventh century.[14] This *ius mercatorum* grew year by year through the ordinances issued by lords or kings for the protection of merchants or visitors from foreign states. Special courts were established to administer the law merchant; and significantly these courts disregarded such old forms of evidence or trial as torture, duel, or ordeal.

As early as the sixth century in the laws of the Visigoths, foreign merchants had received the right, in disputes affecting only themselves, to be judged by delegates from their own countries; so began that consular system by which a trading nation maintained abroad "consuls," counselors, to protect and aid their nationals. Genoa established such a consulate at Acre in 1180; French cities followed suit in the twelfth century. Agreements among nations—even between Christian and Moslem states—for such consular rights were among the best medieval contributions to international law.

A measure of maritime law had survived from antiquity; it never ceased among the enlightened merchants of Rhodes; and one of the oldest maritime codes was the *Code des Rhodiens* of 1167. The *Lois d'Oléron* were issued at the end of the twelfth century by an island off Bordeaux to govern the wine trade, and were adopted by France, Flanders, and England. The Hanseatic League published a detailed code of maritime regulations for its members: precautions to be taken for the safety of passengers and cargo, obligations of rescuer and rescued, duties and wages of captains and crews, and conditions under which a merchant vessel might or should become a man-of-war. Penalties in these codes were severe, but apparently severity was necessary to establish traditions and habits of nautical discipline and reliability. The Middle Ages disciplined men for ten centuries in order that modern men might for four centuries be free.

II. THE PROGRESS OF INDUSTRY

The development of industry kept pace with the expansion of commerce; wider markets stimulated production, and mounting production nourished trade.

Transport progressed least. Most medieval highways were avenues of dirt and dust or mud; no crown or culverts carried water from the road; holes and pools abounded; fords were many, bridges few. Burdens were carried on pack mules or horses rather than in carts, which could not so well avoid the holes. Carriages were large and clumsy, rode on iron tires, and had no springs;[15] they were so uncomfortable, however ornate, that most men and women preferred to travel on horseback—both sexes astride. Until the twelfth century the maintenance of roads depended upon the owner of the adjoining property, who wondered why he should spend to mend what chiefly transients used. In the thirteenth century Frederick II, inspired by Moslem and Byzantine examples, ordered the repair of roads in Sicily and southern Italy; and about the same time the first "royal highways" were built in France—by laying stone cubes in a loose bed of earth or sand. In the same century the cities began to pave their central streets. Florence, Paris, London, and the Flemish towns built excellent bridges. In the twelfth century the Church organized religious fraternities for the repair or construction of bridges, and offered indulgences to those who shared in the work; such *frères pontifs* built the bridge at Avignon, which still preserves four arches from their hands. Some monastic orders, pre-eminently the Cistercians, toiled to keep roads and bridges functioning. From 1176 to 1209 king, clergy, and citizens contributed funds or labor to raising London Bridge; houses and a chapel rose over it, and twenty stone arches carried it across the Thames. Early in the thirteenth century the first known suspension bridge was thrown over a gorge in the St. Gotthard Pass of the Alps.

Roads being painful, waterways were popular, and played the leading role in the transport of goods. One boat could carry as much as 500 animals, and far more cheaply. From the Tagus to the Volga the rivers of Europe were its main highways, and their direction and outlets determined the spread of population, the growth of towns, and often national military policy. Canals were innumerable, though locks were unknown.

Whether by boat or by land, travel was arduous and slow. A bishop took twenty-nine days to go from Canterbury to Rome. Couriers with fresh relays of horses could make a hundred miles a day; but private couriers were costly, and the post (re-established in Italy in the twelfth century) was normally confined to government affairs. Here and there—as between London and Oxford or Winchester—a regular stagecoach service was available. News, like men, traveled slowly; intelligence of Barbarossa's death in Cilicia took four months to reach Germany.[16] Medieval man could eat his breakfast without being disturbed by the industriously collected calamities of the world; or those that came to his ken were fortunately too old for remedy.

Some advances were made in the harnessing of natural power. The Domesday Book recorded 5000 water mills in England in 1086; and a drawing of 1169 pictures a water wheel whose leisurely revolutions were multiplied to high speed by a succession of diminishing gears.[17] With such acceleration the water wheel became a basic instrument of industry; a water-driven sawmill appears in Germany in 1245;[18] one water mill at Douai (1313) was used in making edged tools. The windmill, first reported in western Europe in 1105, spread rapidly after Christian notice of its wide use in Islam; [19] Ypres alone had 120 in the thirteenth century.

Improved tools and expanding needs encouraged an outburst of mining. The commercial demand for a reliable gold coinage, and the increasing ability of people to satisfy the passion for jewelry, led to renewed washing of gold grains from rivers, and the mining of gold in Italy, France, England, Hungary, and above all in Germany. Toward 1175 rich veins of copper, silver, and gold were found in the Erz Gebirge (i.e., ore mountains); Freiberg, Goslar, and Annaberg became the centers of a medieval "gold rush"; and from the little town of Joachimsthal came the word *joachimsthaler*—meaning coins mined there—and, by inevitable shortening, the German and English words *thaler* and *dollar*.[20] Germany became the chief provider of precious metal for Europe, and its mines formed the foundation—its commerce the framework—of its political power. Iron was mined in the Harz Mountains and in Westphalia, in the Lowlands, England, France, Spain, and Sicily, and once more in ancient Elba. Derbyshire mined lead, Devon, Cornwall, and Bohemia tin, Spain mercury and silver, Italy sulphur and alum, and Salzburg took its name from its great deposits of salt. Coal, used in Roman England but apparently neglected in the Saxon period, was mined again in the twelfth century. In 1237 Queen Eleanor abandoned Nottingham Castle because of fumes from the coal burned in the town below; and in 1301 London forbade the use of coal because smoke was poisoning the city—medieval instances of a supposedly modern woe.[21] Nevertheless by the end of the thirteenth century coal was actively mined at Newcastle and Durham, and elsewhere in England, Belgium, and France.

The ownership of mineral deposits became a confusion of laws. When feudal tenure was strong the lord claimed all mineral rights in his land, and mined the deposits with his serfs. Ecclesiastical properties made similar claims, and used serfs or hired miners to exhume valuable deposits from their land. Frederick Barbarossa decreed that the sovereign was sole proprietor of all minerals in the soil, and that these could be worked only by firms under state control.[22] This reassumption of the "regalian right" usual under the Roman emperors became the law of medieval Germany. In England the crown claimed all silver and gold deposits; baser metals could be mined by the land-owner on payment of a "royal-ty" to the king.[23]

Smelting was by charcoal, and used up much wood in still primitive fur-naces. Even so the coppersmiths of Dinant produced fine brass wares; the ironworkers of Liége, Nuremberg, Milan, Barcelona, and Toledo made excel-lent arms and tools; and Seville was renowned for its steel. Toward the end of the thirteenth century cast iron (fused at 1535 degrees C.) began to replace wrought iron (softened by 800 degrees C.); nearly all previous ironworking had been by hammering—the *smiting* from which the smith derived his Saxon name. Bell founding was an important industry, for cathedrals and town bel-fries rivaled one another in the weight, sonority, and timbre of their bells. Coppersmiths made curfews (*couvre-feus*) to cover hearth fires when cur-few rang. Saxony was famous for its bronze founders, England for its pewter —a mixture of copper, bismuth, antimony, and tin. Wrought iron made ele-gant window gratings, majestic grilles for cathedral choirs, and mighty hinges that spread in varied forms over doors for strength and ornament. Goldsmiths and silversmiths were numerous, for gold or silver plate served not only to display or disguise one's worth, but also to hedge a man against deflated currencies, and to give him, in emergency, a form of wealth con-vertible into food or goods.

In the thirteenth century the textile industry in Flanders and Italy assumed a large-scale, semicapitalist structure, in which thousands of workers pro-duced goods for the general market, and earned profits for investors whom they seldom saw. In Florence the *Arte della Lana*, or Wool Guild, had great factories (*fondachi*) where washers, fullers, sorters, spinners, weavers, in-spectors, and clerks worked under one roof, with materials, tools, and looms over which they had no ownership or control.[24] Wholesale cloth merchants organized factories, provided equipment, secured labor and capital, fixed wages and prices, arranged distribution and sale, took the risks of enterprise, bore the losses of failure, and reaped the profits of success.[25] Other employers preferred to farm out the raw material to individual workers or families who, with their own equipment, would turn it into finished products at home, and would deliver these to the merchant for a wage or price; in this manner thou-sands of men and women in Italy, Flanders, and France were brought into industrial occupations.[26] Amiens, Beauvais, Lille, Laon, St. Quentin, Provins, Reims, Troyes, Cambrai, Tournai, Liége, Louvain—above all, Ghent, Bruges, Ypres, and Douai—became whirlpools of such commission industry, famous for their artistry and their revolts. Laon gave its name to *lawn* (a linen), Cambrai to cambric, and the diaper pattern took its name from d'Ypres.[27] At Ghent 2300 weavers worked at looms; Provins had 3200 in the thirteenth century.[28] A dozen Italian cities had their own textile industries. At Florence in the twelfth century the *Arte della Lana* specialized in the production of dyed woolen goods; early in the thirteenth century the *Arte di Calimala*, or Cloth Guild, organized an extensive business in the import of wool and the export of finished fabrics. By 1306 Florence had 300 textile factories, and by 1336, 30,000 textile workers.[29] Genoa made fine velvets and gold-threaded silks. Toward the end of the thirteenth century Vienna imported Flemish weavers, and soon had a flourishing textile industry of her own. England had almost a monopoly in northern Europe's production of wool; it sent most of its products to Flanders, and thereby bound that country to it in policy and war. The town of Worstead, in Norfolk, gave its name to a variety of woolen cloth. Spain also turned out fine wool; her merino sheep were a main source of her national income.

The Arabs had brought the culture and manufacture of silk to Spain in the eighth century, and to Sicily in the ninth; and Valencia, Cartagena, Seville, Lisbon, and Palermo continued the arts after becoming Christian. Roger II imported Greek and Jewish silk weavers from Corinth and Thebes into Palermo in 1147, and housed them in a palace; through these men and their children sericulture spread through Italy. Lucca organized the manufacture of silk on a capitalistic scale, rivaled by Florence, Milan, Genoa, Modena, Bologna, and Venice. The art crossed the Alps, and developed skilled practitioners in Zurich, Paris, and Cologne.

A hundred other crafts rounded out the scope of medieval industry. Potters glazed earthenware vessels by powdering their moistened surface with lead and baking them in a gentle heat, adding copper or bronze to the lead if they wished a green instead of a yellow glaze. As buildings and fires became more costly in the growing cities of the thirteenth century, tiles replaced thatched roofs; London made the change mandatory in 1212. The building trades must have been competent, for some of the sturdiest structures existing in Europe date from this period. Industrial glass was made for mirrors, windows, and vessels, but on a relatively small scale. Cathedrals had the finest glass ever produced, but many houses had none. Glass blowing was practiced in western Europe from at least the eleventh century; probably the art had never ceased in Italy from its heyday under the Roman Empire. Paper, till the twelfth century, was imported from the Moslem East or Spain; but in 1190 a paper mill was opened at Ravensburg in Germany, and in the thirteenth century Europe began to make paper from linen. Hides were among the leading articles of international commerce, and tanning was universal; glovers, saddlers, purse makers, shoemakers, and cobblers were jealously distinct. Furs were brought in from north and east, and were dressed for royalty, nobility, and *bourgeoisie*. Wine and beer served instead of central heating, and many towns profited by a municipal monopoly of brewing. The Germans already led the world in this ancient art; and Hamburg, with 500 breweries in the fourteenth century, owed most of its prosperity to its ale.

Aside from textiles, industry remained in the handicraft stage. Workers serving a local market—bakers, cobblers, blacksmiths, carpenters, etc.—controlled their own equipment and product, and remained individually free. Most industry was still carried on in the homes of the workers, or in shops attached to their homes; and most families performed for themselves many of the tasks now delegated to shops or factories—baked their bread, wove their clothing, mended their shoes. In this domestic industry progress was slow; tools were simple, machines few; motives of competition and profit did not stimulate men to invention, or the replacement of human skill with mechanical power. And yet this may have been the most wholesome form of industrial organization in history. Its productivity was low, its degree of contentment was probably and relatively high. The worker remained near his family; he determined the hours and (in some measure) the price of his work; his pride in his skill gave him character and confidence; he was an artist as well as an artisan; and he had the artist's satisfaction of seeing an integral product taking form under his hands.

III. MONEY

The commercial and industrial expansion revolutionized finance. Commerce could not advance by barter; it required a stable standard of value, a convenient medium of exchange, and ready access to investment funds.

Under Continental feudalism the great lords and prelates exercised the right of mintage, and European economy suffered from a bedlam of currencies worse than today's. Counterfeiters and coin clippers multiplied the chaos. The kings ordered such gentry to be dismembered, or emasculated, or boiled alive;[30] but they themselves repeatedly debased their currencies.* Gold became scarce after the barbarian invasions, and disappeared from the coinages of Western Europe after the Moslem conquest of the East; between the eighth and the thirteenth centuries all such coinages were in silver or baser metals. Gold and civilization wax and wane together.

In the Byzantine Empire, however, gold was coined throughout the Middle Ages. As contact between West and East grew, Byzantine gold coins, called bezants in the West, began to circulate through Europe as the most honored money in Christendom. In 1228 Frederick II, having observed the beneficent effect of a stable gold currency in the Near East, minted in Italy the first gold coins of western Europe. He called them *augustales* in frank emulation of Augustan coins and prestige; they deserved the name, for though imitative, they were of noble design, and reached at once the highest level of medieval

---

* "In this year," says the Anglo-Saxon Chronicle for 1125, "King Henry bade that all the mint-men" (counterfeiters) "in England ... should lose each of them the right hand, and their testicles beneath." [31]

numismatic art. In 1252 both Genoa and Florence issued gold coins; the Florentine florin, equaling in value a pound of silver, was the more beautiful and viable, and was accepted throughout Europe. By 1284 all the major nations of Europe except England had a trustworthy gold coinage—an achievement sacrificed in the turmoil of the twentieth century.

By the end of the thirteenth century the kings of France had bought up or confiscated nearly all seignorial rights to the coining of money. The French monetary system kept till 1789 the terms, though hardly the values, established by Charlemagne: the *livre* or pound of silver; the *sou* or twentieth part of a *livre*; and the *denier* or twelfth part of a *sou*. This system was brought to England by the Norman invasion; there, too, the "pound sterling" was divided into twenty parts—shillings—and each of these into twelve parts —pence. The English took the words pound, shilling, and penny from the German *Pfund, Schilling, and Pfennig*; but took the signs for them from the Latin: £ from *libra*, s. from *solidus*, d. from *denarius*. England did not arrive at a gold currency till 1343; her silver currency, however, as established by Henry II (1154–89), remained the most stable in Europe. In Germany the silver mark was coined in the tenth century, at half the value of the French or British pound.

Despite these developments, medieval currencies suffered from fluctuations of value, the unsteady ratio of silver to gold, the power of the kings and cities—sometimes of nobles and ecclesiastics—to call in all coins at any time, charge a fee for reminting, and issue new coins debased with more alloy. Through the dishonesty of the mints, through the more rapid increase of gold than of goods, through the convenience of redeeming national debts in depreciated money, an irregular deterioration affected all European currencies through medieval and modern times. In France the *livre* had in 1789 only 1.2 per cent of its value under Charlemagne.[32] We may judge the fall of money from some typical prices: at Ravenna in 1268 a dozen eggs cost "a penny"; at London in 1328 a pig cost four shillings, an ox fifteen;[33] in thirteenth-century France three francs bought a sheep, six a pig.[34] History is inflationary.*

Where did the money come from that financed and expanded commerce and industry? The greatest single provider was the Church. She had an unparalleled organization for raising funds, and had always a liquid capital available for any purpose; she was the greatest financial power in Christendom. Moreover, many individuals deposited private funds for safekeeping with churches or monasteries. From her wealth the Church lent money to persons or institutions in difficulty. Loans were made chiefly to villagers

---

* Coulton, the leading English medievalist, reckoned English currency in 1200 as worth forty times its value in 1930.[35] Ignoring fluctuations during the Middle Ages, this volume calculates medieval monetary values at approximately fifty times the values of corresponding units of currency or precious metal in 1948.

seeking to improve their farms; they acted as land banks and played a beneficent role in promoting a free peasantry.[36] As early as 1070 they lent money
to neighboring lords in exchange for a share in the revenues of the lords'
property;[37] through these mortgage loans the monasteries became the first
banking corporations of the Middle Ages. The abbey of St. André in France
did so flourishing a banking business that it hired Jewish moneylenders to
manage its financial operations.[38] The Knights Templar lent money on interest to kings and princes, lords and knights, churches and prelates; their mortgage business was probably the largest in the world in the thirteenth century.

But these loans by church bodies were usually for consumption or for
political use, seldom for financing industry or trade. Commercial credit
began when an individual or a family, by what Latin Christendom called
commenda, commended or entrusted money to a merchant for a specific
voyage or enterprise, and received a share of the profits. Such a silent or
"sleeping" partnership was an ancient Roman device, probably relearned by
the Christian West from the Byzantine East. So useful a way of sharing in
profits without directly contravening the ecclesiastical prohibition of interest
was bound to spread; and the "company" (*com-panis*, bread-sharer) or family investment became a *societas*, a partnership in which several persons, not
necessarily kin, financed a group or series of ventures rather than one. Such
financial organizations appeared in Genoa and Venice toward the end of the
tenth century, reached a high development in the twelfth, and largely accounted for the rapid growth of Italian trade. These investment groups often
distributed their risk by buying "parts" in several ships or ventures at a time.
When, in fourteenth-century Genoa, such shares (*partes*) were made transferable, the joint-stock company was born.

The greatest single source of *finance* capital—i.e., funds to meet the pre-
income costs of an undertaking—was the professional financier. He had
begun in antiquity as a money-changer, and had long since developed into a
moneylender, investing his own and other people's money in enterprises, or
in loans to churches, monasteries, nobles, or kings. The role of the Jews as
moneylenders has been exaggerated; they were powerful in Spain, and for
a time in Britain, weak in Germany, outdone in Italy and France by Christian
financiers.[39] The chief lender to the kings of England was William Cade; the
chief lenders in thirteenth-century France and Flanders were the Louchard
and Crespin families of Arras; [40] William the Breton described Arras at that
time as "glutted with usurers." [41] Another center of northern finance was the
bourse (*bursa*, purse) or money market of Bruges. A still more powerful
group of Christian moneylenders originated in Cahors, a town of southern
France. Matthew Paris writes:

> In these days (1235) the abominable plague of Cahorsians raged so
> fiercely that there was scarcely any man in all England, especially
> among the prelates, who was not entangled in their nets. The king

was indebted to them for an incalculable account. They circumvented the indigent in their necessities, cloaking their usury under the
pretense of trade.[42]

The papacy for a time entrusted its financial affairs in England to the Cahors-
ian bankers; but their ruthlessness so offended the English that one of their
number was murdered at Oxford, Bishop Roger of London pronounced an
anathema upon them, and Henry III banished them from England. Robert
Grosseteste, Bishop of Lincoln, lamented on his deathbed the extortions of
"the merchants and exchangers of our lord the Pope," who "are harder than
the Jews." [43]

It was the Italians who developed banking to unprecedented heights in the
thirteenth century. Great banking families rose to supply the sinews of far-
reaching Italian trade: the Buonsignori and Gallerani in Siena, the Frescobaldi, Bardi, and Peruzzi in Florence, the Pisani and Tiepoli in Venice. . . .
They extended their operations beyond the Alps, and lent great sums to the
ever-needy kings of England and France, to barons, bishops, abbots, and
towns. Popes and kings employed them to collect revenues, manage mints
and finances, advise on policy. They bought wool, spices, jewelry, and silk
wholesale, and owned ships and hotels from one end of Europe to the other.[44]
By the middle of the thirteenth century these "Lombards," as the North
called all Italian bankers, were the most active and powerful financiers in the
world. They were hated at home and abroad for their exactions, and were
envied for their wealth; every generation borrows, and denounces those who
lend. Their rise dealt a heavy blow to Jewish international banking, and they
were not above recommending the banishment of these patient competitors.[45]
The strongest of the "Lombards" were the Florentine banking firms, of
whom eighty are recorded between 1260 and 1347.[46] They financed the political and military campaigns of the papacy, and reaped rich rewards; and
their position as papal bankers provided a useful cover in operations that
were hardly in harmony with the views of the Church on interest. They made
profits worthy of modern times; the Peruzzi, for example, paid a forty per
cent dividend in 1308.[47] But these Italian firms almost atoned for their greed
by their vitalizing services to commerce and industry. When their tide ebbed
they left some of their terms—*banco, credito, debito, cassa* (money box,
cash), *conto, disconto, conto corrente, netto, bilanza, banca rotta* (bank
broken, bankruptcy)—in almost all European languages.[48]

As these words suggest, the great money firms of Venice, Florence, and
Genoa, in or before the thirteenth century, developed nearly all the functions
of a modern bank. They accepted deposits, and carried current accounts—
between parties having an unfinished series of money transactions. As early
as 1171 the Bank of Venice arranged exchanges of accounts among its clients
by mere bookkeeping operations.[49] They made loans, and as security they
accepted jewelry, costly armor, government bonds, or the right to collect

taxes or manage the public revenue. They received goods in bond for transfer to other countries. Through their international connections they were able to issue letters of credit by which a deposit made in one country would be returned to the depositor, or his appointee, in another country—a device long known to the Jews, the Moslems, and the Templars.[50] Conversely, they wrote bills of exchange: a merchant, in return for goods or a loan, gave a promissory note to pay the creditor at one of the great fairs or international banks by a stated time; these notes were balanced against one another at fair or bank, and only the final balance was paid in money; hundreds of transactions could now take place without the nuisance of carrying or exchanging great sums and weights of coin. As the banking centers became clearing houses, the bankers avoided the long journey to the fairs. Merchants throughout Europe and the Levant could draw on their accounts in the banks of Italy, and have their balances settled by interbank bookkeeping.[51] In effect the utility and circulation of money were increased tenfold. This "credit system"—made possible by mutual trust—was not the least important or honorable aspect of the economic revolution.

Insurance too had its beginnings in the thirteenth century. The merchant guilds gave their members insurance against fire, shipwreck, and other misfortunes or injuries, even against lawsuits incurred for crimes—whether the members were guilty or innocent.[52] Many monasteries offered a life annuity: in return for a sum of money paid down, they promised to provide the donor with food and drink, sometimes also with clothes and lodging, for the rest of his life.[53] As early as the twelfth century a Bruges banking house offered insurance on goods; and a chartered insurance company was apparently established there in 1310.[54] The Bardi of Florence, in 1318, accepted insurance risks on overland assignments of cloth.

The first government bonds were issued by Venice in 1157. The needs of war led the republic to exact forced loans from the citizens; and a special department (*Camera degli Impresidi*) was set up to receive the loans, and give the subscribers interest-bearing certificates as state guarantees of repayment. After 1206 these government bonds were made negotiable and transferable; they could be bought or sold, or used as security for loans. Similar certificates of municipal indebtedness were accepted at Como in 1250 as equivalent to metal currency. Since paper money is merely a governmental promise to pay, these negotiable gold certificates marked the beginning of paper money in Europe.[55]

The complicated operations of the bankers, the papacy, and the monarchies required a careful system of bookkeeping. Archives and account books swelled with records of rents, taxes, receipts, expenditures, credits, and debts. The accounting methods of imperial Rome, lost in western Europe in the seventh century, continued in Constantinople, were adopted by the Arabs, and were revived in Italy during the Crusades. A fully developed system of double-entry bookkeeping appears in the communal accounts of Genoa in 1340; the loss of Genoese records for the years from 1278 to 1340 leaves open the probability that this advance was also an achievement of the thirteenth century.[56]

IV. INTEREST

The greatest obstacle to the development of banking was the ecclesiastical doctrine of interest. This had three sources: Aristotle's condemnation of interest as an unnatural breeding of money by money,[57] Christ's condemnation of interest,[58] and the reaction of the Fathers of the Church against commercialism and usury in Rome. Roman law had legalized interest, and "honorable men" like Brutus had charged merciless rates. Ambrose had denounced the theory that one may do what he likes with his own:

> "My own," say you? What is your own? When you came from your mother's womb, what wealth did you bring with you? That which is taken by you, beyond what suffices you, is taken by violence. Is it that God is unjust in not distributing the means of life to us equally, so that you should have abundance while others are in want? Or is it not rather that He wished to confer upon you marks of His kindness, while He crowned your fellow man with the virtue of patience? You, then, who have received the gift of God, think you that you commit no injustice by keeping to yourself alone what would be the means of life to many? It is the bread of the hungry you cling to, it is the clothing of the naked you lock up; the money you bury is the redemption of the poor.[59]

Other Church Fathers had verged upon communism. "The use of all that is in the world," said Clement of Alexandria, "ought to be common to all men. But by injustice one man has called this his own, another that; and so has come division among men." [60] Jerome held all profit unjust; Augustine considered all "business" an evil, as "turning men from seeking true rest, which is God." [61] Pope Leo I had rejected these extreme doctrines; but the mood of the Church continued unsympathetic to commerce, suspicious of all speculation and profit, hostile to all "engrossing," "forestalling," and "usury"—by which last term the Middle Ages meant any interest charge whatever. "Usury," said Ambrose, "is whatever is added to the capital"; [62] and Gratian embodied this blunt definition in the canon law of the Church.

The councils of Nicaea (325), Orléans (538), Mâcon (585), and Clichy (626) had forbidden the clergy to lend money for gain. The capitularies of Charlemagne for 789, and the Church councils of the ninth century, extended the prohibition to laymen. The revival of Roman law in the twelfth century emboldened Irnerius and the "glossators" of Bologna to defend interest, and they were able to quote Justinian's Code in its behalf. But the Third Council of the Lateran (1179) renewed the prohibition, and decreed "that manifest usurers shall not be admitted to communion, nor, if they die in sin, to Christian burial; and no priest shall accept their alms." [63] Innocent III must have taken a more lenient view, for in 1206 he advised that in certain cases a dowry "should be committed to some merchant," so that an income might be derived from it "by honest gain." [64] Gregory IX, however, returned to the conception of usury as any receipt of any profit on a loan;[65] and this remained the law of the Roman Church till 1917.

The wealth of the Church was in land, not in trade; she scorned merchants as the feudal baron scorned them; land and labor (including management) seemed to her the only true creators of wealth and value. She resented the rising power and opulence of a mercantile class not too well disposed to feudal landowners or to the Church; she had for centuries thought of all moneylenders as Jews; and she felt justified in rebuking the hard terms exacted by moneylenders from needy ecclesiastical institutions. By and large, the effort of the Church to control the profit motive was an heroic assertion of Christian morality; it formed a wholesome contrast to the imprisonment or enslavement of debtors that had disgraced Greek, Roman, and barbarian life and law. We cannot be sure that men are happier today than they would have been had the view of the Church prevailed.

For a long time the legislation of governments supported the position of the Church; and the prohibition of interest was enforced in the secular courts.[66] But commercial necessity proved stronger than fear of prison or hell. The expansion of trade and industry demanded the use of idle money by active enterprise; states at war or in other emergencies found it easier to borrow than to tax; guilds both lent and borrowed at interest; landowners extending their property, or leaving for crusades, welcomed the moneylender; churches themselves, and monasteries, survived their crises or rising costs or needs by recourse to the Lombards, the Cahorsians, or the Jews.

The wits of men found many subterfuges from the law. A borrower would sell land cheap to the lender, leave him the usufruct as interest, and later repurchase the land. Or the landowner sold to the lender some or all of the annual rents or revenues of his land; if, for example, A sold to B for $100 the rents of a parcel yielding $10.00 a year, B was in effect lending A $100 at ten per cent. Many monasteries invested their funds by buying such "rent charges"—above all in Germany, where the word for interest, *Zins*, grew out of the medieval Latin for rents, *census*.[67] Towns borrowed money by deeding to the lender a share in their revenues.[68] Individuals and institutions, including monasteries, lent money in return for secret gifts or fictitious sales.[69] Pope Alexander III complained in 1163 that "many of the clergy" (chiefly monastic) "while they shrink from common usury as from a thing too plainly condemned, do notwithstanding lend money to others who are in need, take their possessions in pledge, and receive the fruits therefrom accruing beyond the principal lent." [70] Some borrowers pledged themselves to pay "damages" increasing for every day or month of delay in repaying a loan; and the date of payment was placed so early as to make such concealed interest inevitable;[71] on this basis the Cahorsians lent money to certain monasteries on terms equivalent to sixty per cent per year.[72] Many banking firms openly lent at interest, and claimed immunity on the theory that the law applied only to individuals. The cities of Italy made no excuses for paying interest on their government bonds. In 1208 Innocent III remarked that if all usurers were excluded from the Church as canon law demanded, all churches might as well be closed.[73]

The Church reluctantly adjusted herself to realities. St. Thomas Aquinas, about 1250, courageously formulated a new ecclesiastical doctrine of interest: the investor in a business enterprise might legitimately share in the gain if he actually shared in the risk or the loss; [74] and loss was interpreted to include any delay in the repayment of the loan beyond a stipulated date.[75] St. Bonaventura and Pope Innocent IV accepted the principle, and widened it to legitimize a payment made to a lender in return for the temporary loss of the use of his capital.[76] Some fifteenth-century canonists admitted the right of states to issue interest-bearing bonds; Pope Martin V in 1425 legalized the sale of rent charges; after 1400 most European states repealed their laws against interest; and the Church prohibition survived as a dead letter which all agreed to ignore. The Church tried to find a solution by encouraging St. Bernardino of Feltre and other ecclesiastics in establishing, from 1251 on, *montes pietatis*—"hills of love"—where trustworthy persons in need, by depositing some article as a pledge, might obtain loans without interest. But these precursors of our pawnbrokers' shops touched only a small sector of the problem; the needs of commerce and industry remained, and capital rose to meet them.

The professional moneylenders exacted high rates of interest not so much because they were conscienceless devils as because they ran great risks of loss and head. They could not always enforce their contracts through appeals to the law; their accumulations were subject to requisition by kings or emperors; they could at any moment be banished, and were at all times damned. Many loans were never repaid; many borrowers died bankrupt; some went on crusades, were excused from paying interest, and never returned. When borrowers defaulted, the lenders could only make up the loss by raising rates on other loans; the good loan had to pay for the bad one, as the price of commodities bought must include the cost of commodities spoiled before sale. In twelfth-century France and England the interest rate ranged between 33⅓% and 43⅓%;[77] sometimes it rose to 86%; in prosperous Italy it sank to 12½% to 20%;[78] Frederick II, about 1240, tried to lower the rate to 10%, but soon paid more than that to Christian moneylenders. As late as 1409 the government of Naples allowed 40% as the legal maximum.[79] The interest rate fell as the security of loans rose, and as the competition of lenders increased. Gradually, through a thousand experiments and errors, men learned to use the new financial tools of a progressive economy, and the Age of Money began in the Age of Faith.

V. THE GUILDS

In ancient Rome there were countless *collegia, scholae, sodalitates, artes*—associations of artisans, merchants, contractors, political clubs, secret fraternities, religious brotherhoods. Did any of these survive to beget the medieval guilds?

Two letters of Gregory I (590–604) refer to a corporation of soap makers at Naples, and to another of bakers at Otranto. In the law code of the Lombard King Rotharis (636–52) we read of *magistri Comacini*—apparently master masons from Como, who speak of one another as *collegantes*—colleagues of the same *collegium*.[80] Associations of transport workers are mentioned in seventh-century Rome and in tenth-century Worms.[81] The ancient guilds continued in the Byzantine Empire. In Ravenna we find references to many *scholae* or economic associations—in the sixth century to bakers, in the ninth to notaries and merchants, in the tenth to fishermen, in the eleventh to victualers. We hear of artisan *ministeria* in ninth-century Venice, and of a gardeners' *schola* in eleventh-century Rome.[82] Doubtless most of the ancient guilds in the West succumbed to the barbarian invasions, and the resulting reruralization and poverty; but some seem to have survived in Lombardy. When commerce and industry recovered in the eleventh century the conditions that had begotten the *collegia* regenerated the guilds.

Consequently these were strongest in Italy, where the old Roman institutions were best preserved. In Florence, in the twelfth century, we find *arti*—"arts," craft unions—of notaries, clothiers, wool merchants, bankers, physicians and druggists, mercers or silk dealers, furriers, tanners, armorers, innkeepers. . . .[83] These guilds were apparently modeled on those of Constantinople.[84] North of the Alps the destruction of the ancient *collegia* was presumably more complete than in Italy; yet we find them mentioned in the laws of Dagobert I (630), the capitularies of Charlemagne (779, 789), and the ordinances of Archbishop Hincmar of Reims (852). In the eleventh century the guilds reappear in France and Flanders, and multiply rapidly as *charités, frairies* (brotherhoods), or *compagnies*. In Germany the guilds (*hanse*) stemmed from old *Markgenossenschaften*—local associations for mutual aid, religious observances, and holiday hilarity. By the twelfth century many of these had become trade or craft unions; and by the thirteenth century these were so strong that they contested political as well as economic authority with the municipal councils.[85] The Hanseatic League was such a guild. The first mention of English guilds is in the laws of King Ine (688–726), which speak of *gegildan*—associates who helped one another to pay any wergild assessed against them. The Anglo-Saxon word *gild* (cf. the German *Geld*, the English *gold* and *yield*) meant a contribution to a common fund, and later the society that administered the fund. The oldest reference to English trade guilds is dated 1093.[86] By the thirteenth century nearly every important town in England had one or more guilds, and a kind of municipal "guild socialism" held sway in England and Germany.

Nearly all the guilds of the eleventh century were merchant guilds: they included only independent merchants and master workmen; they excluded all persons dependent upon others. They were frankly institutions in restraint of trade. They usually persuaded their towns to keep out, by a high protective tariff or elsewise, goods competitive with their own; such alien goods, if allowed to enter the town, were sold at prices fixed by the affected guild. In many cases a merchant guild obtained from commune or king a local or national monopoly in its line or field. The Paris Company for the Transit of Merchandise by Water almost owned the Seine. By city ordinance or economic pressure the guild usually compelled craftsmen to work only for the guild or with its consent, and to sell its products only to or through the guild.

The greater guilds became powerful corporations; they dealt in a variety of goods, purchased raw materials wholesale, provided insurance against losses, organized the food supply and sewage disposals of their towns, paved streets, built roads and docks, deepened harbors, policed highways, supervised markets, regulated wages, hours, conditions of labor, terms of apprenticeship, methods of production and sale, prices of materials and wares.[87] Four or five times a year they fixed a "just price" that in their judgment gave fair stimulus and reward to all parties concerned. They weighed, tested, counted all products bought or sold in their trade and area, and did their best to keep inferior or dishonest goods from the market.[88] They banded together to resist robbers, feudal lords and tolls, refractory workmen, tax-levying governments. They took a leading part in politics, dominated many municipal councils, effectively supported the communes in their struggles against barons, bishops, and kings, and themselves evolved into an oppressive oligarchy of merchants and financiers.

Usually each guild had its own guild hall, which in the later Middle Ages might be architecturally ornate. It had a complex personnel of presiding aldermen, recorders, treasurers, bailiffs, sergeants. . . . It had its own courts to try its members, and required its members to submit their disputes to the guild court before resorting to state law. It obligated its members to help a fellow guildsman in sickness or distress, to rescue or ransom him if attacked or jailed.[89] It supervised the morals, manners, and dress of its members, and fixed a penalty for coming to meeting stockingless. When two members of the Leicester Merchants' Guild engaged in fisticuffs at Boston Fair, their fellows fined them a barrel of beer, to be co-operatively drunk by the guild.[90] Each guild had an annual feast for its patron saint, when a brief prelude of prayer sanctioned a day of moist exuberance. It shared in financing and adorning the city's churches or cathedral, and in preparing and performing those miracle plays which mothered the modern drama; and in municipal parades its dignitaries marched in gorgeous liveries, displaying the banners of their trade in colorful pageantry. It provided for its members insurance against fire, flood, theft, imprisonment, disability, and old age.[91] It built hospitals, almshouses, orphanages and schools. It paid for the funerals of its dead, and for the Masses that would rescue their souls from purgatory. Its prosperous decedents seldom failed to remember it in their wills.

Normally excluded from these merchant guilds, and yet subject to their economic regulations and political power, the craftsmen in each industry began in the twelfth century to form in each town their own craft guilds. In 1099 we find guilds of weavers in London, Lincoln, and Oxford, and, soon afterward, of fullers, tanners, butchers, goldsmiths. . . . Under the names of *arti*, *Zunfte*, *métiers*, "companies," "mysteries," they spread throughout Europe in the thirteenth century; Venice had fifty-eight, Genoa thirty-three, Florence twenty-one, Cologne twenty-six, Paris one hundred. About 1254 Étienne Boileau, "provost of merchants"—secretary of commerce—under Louis IX, issued an official *Livre des Métiers*, or *Book of Trades*, giving the rules and regulations of 101 Paris guilds. The division of labor in this list is astonishing: in the leather industry, for example, there were separate unions for skinners, tanners, cobblers, harness makers, saddlers, and makers of fine leather goods; in carpentry there were distinct unions of chest makers, cabinetmakers, boatbuilders, wheelwrights, coopers, twiners. Each guild jealously guarded its craft secrets, fenced in its field of work against outsiders, and engaged in lively jurisdictional disputes.[92]

In the spirit of the times the craft guild took a religious form and a patron saint, and aspired to monopoly. Ordinarily no one might follow a craft unless he belonged to its guild.[93] The guild leaders were annually elected by full assemblies of their craft, but were often chosen by seniority and wealth. Guild regulations determined—as far as merchant guilds, municipal ordinances, and economic law would allow—the conditions under which the members worked, the wages they received, the prices they charged. Guild rules limited the number of masters in an area, and of apprentices to a master; forbade the industrial employment of women except the master's wife, or of men after six P.M.; and punished members for unjust charges, dishonest dealing, and shoddy goods. In many cases the guild proudly stamped its products with its "trademark" or "[guild]hallmark," certifying their quality;[94] the cloth guild of Bruges expelled from the city a member who had forged the

Bruges hallmark on inferior goods.[95] Competition among masters in quantity of production or price of product was discouraged, lest the cleverest or hardest masters become too rich at the expense of the rest; but competition in quality of product was encouraged among both masters and towns. Craft, like merchant, guilds, built hospitals and schools, provided diverse insurance, succored poor members, dowered their daughters, buried the dead, cared for widows, gave labor as well as funds to building cathedrals and churches, and pictured their craft operations and insignia in cathedral glass.

The fraternal spirit among the masters did not prevent a sharp gradation of membership and powers in the craft guilds. At the bottom was the apprentice, ten to twelve years old, bound by his parents, for a period of from three to twelve years, to live with a master workman, and serve him in shop and home. In return he received food, clothing, shelter, and instruction in the trade; in the later years of his service, wages and tools; at the end of his term, a gift of money to start him on his own. If he ran away he was to be returned to his master and punished; if he continued to abscond he was forever debarred from the craft. On completing his service he became a journeyman (*serviteur, garçon, compagnon,* varlet), passing from one master to another as a day (*journée*) laborer. After two or three years the journeyman, if he had enough capital to open his own shop, was examined for technical ability by a board of his guild; if he passed he was made a master. Sometimes—but only in the later Middle Ages—the candidate was required to submit to the governors of the guild a "masterpiece"—a satisfactory sample of his craft.

The graduate craftsman, or master, owned his tools, and usually produced goods directly on order of the consumer, who in some cases provided the materials, and might at any time come in and watch the work. The middleman, in this system, did not control the avenues between the maker and the user of goods. The scale of the craftsman's operations was limited by the market for which he produced, which was usually his town; but he was not dependent upon the fluctuations of a general market, or the mood of distant investors or purchasers; he did not know the economic paranoia of alternating exaltations and depressions. His hours were long—eight to thirteen hours a day; but he chose them himself, worked in a wisely leisurely way, and enjoyed many a religious holiday. He ate nourishing food, bought sturdy furniture, wore simple but durable clothing, and had at least as wide a cultural life as the master workman of today. He did not read much, and was spared much stupefying trash; but he shared actively in the song and dance, the drama and ritual, of his community.

Throughout the thirteenth century the craft guilds waxed in number and power, and provided a democratic check on the oligarchic merchant guilds. But the craft guilds in turn became an aristocracy of labor. They tended to restrict mastership to masters' sons; they underpaid their journeymen, who in the fourteenth century weakened them with repeated revolt; and they raised ever higher barriers against entry into their membership or their towns.[96] They were excellent organizations for an industrial age when difficulties of transportation often narrowed the market to local buyers, and capital accumulations were not yet sufficiently rich and fluid to finance large-scale undertakings. When such funds appeared the guilds—merchant or craft —lost control of the market, and therefore of the conditions of work. The Industrial Revolution destroyed them in England by the slow fatality of economic change; and the French Revolution abruptly disbanded them as hostile to that freedom and dignity of work that for a bright moment they had once sustained.

VI. THE COMMUNES

The economic revolution of the twelfth and thirteenth centuries, like those of the eighteenth and the twentieth, caused a revolution in society and government. New classes rose to economic and political power, and gave to the medieval city that virile and pugnacious independence which culminated in the Renaissance.

The question of heredity versus environment affects the cities, as well as the guilds, of Europe; were they the lineal descendants of Roman municipalities, or new concretions deposited by the stream of economic change? Many Roman cities maintained their continuity through centuries of chaos, poverty, and decay; but only a few in Italy and southeastern France kept the old Roman institutions, and fewer still the old Roman law. North of the Alps, barbarian laws had overlaid the Roman heritage; and in some measure the political customs of the German tribe or village had seeped even into ancient municipalities. Most transalpine towns belonged to feudal domains, and were ruled by the will and appointees of their feudal lords. Municipal institutions were alien, feudal institutions natural, to the Teutonic conquerors. Outside of Italy, the medieval city rose through the formation of new commercial centers, classes, and powers.

The feudal town had grown up, usually on elevations, at the junction of roads, or along vital waterways, or on frontiers. Around the walls of the feudal castle or fortified monastery the modest industry and trade of the townsmen or burgesses had slowly developed. When Norse and Magyar raids subsided, this extramural activity expanded, shops multiplied, and merchants and craftsmen, once transient, became settled residents of the town. In war, however, insecurity returned; and the extramural population built a second wall, of wider circumference than the feudal moat, to protect itself, its shops, and its goods. The feudal baron or bishop still owned and ruled this enlarged town as part of his domain; but its growing population was increasingly commercial and secular, fretted under feudal tolls and controls, and plotted to win municipal liberty.

Out of old political traditions and new administrative needs an assembly of citizens and a corps of officials took form; and more and more this "commune"—the body politic—regulated the affairs of the city—the body geographical. Towards the end of the eleventh century the merchant leaders began to demand from the feudal overlords charters of communal freedom for the towns. With characteristic shrewdness they played one overlord against the other—baron against bishop, knight against baron, king against any of them or all. The townsmen used diverse means to achieve municipal freedom: they took a solemn oath to refuse and resist baronial or episcopal tolls or taxes; they offered the lord a flat sum, or an annuity, for a charter; on the royal domain they won autonomy by money grants, or services in war; sometimes they bluntly announced their independence, and fought a violent revolution. Tours fought twelve times before its liberty was won. Lords in need or debt, especially in preparing for a crusade, sold charters of self-government to the towns that they held in fief; many English cities in this way won their local autonomy from Richard I. Some lords, above all in Flanders, granted charters of incomplete freedom to cities whose commercial development enhanced baronial revenues. The abbots and bishops resisted longest, for their consecration oath bound them not to lower the income of their abbeys or sees—by which their many ministrations were financed; hence the struggle of the towns against their ecclesiastical owners was most bitter and prolonged.

The Spanish kings favored the communes as foils to a troublesome nobility, and the royal charters were many and liberal. Leon received its charter from the king of Castile in 1020, Burgos in 1073, Najera in 1076, Toledo in 1085; and Compostela, Cadiz, Valencia, Barcelona soon followed. In Germany feudalism, in Italy the cities, profited from the mutual exhaustion of Empire and papacy in the war of investitures and other conflicts between Church and state. In northern Italy the cities attained a political vigor hardly known before or since. As the Alpine streams fed the great rivers of Lombardy and Tuscany, and these accommodated commerce and fertilized the plains, so the commerce of transalpine Europe and western Asia, meeting in northern Italy, generated there a mercantile *bourgeoisie* whose wealth rebuilt old cities, raised up new ones, financed literature and art, and proudly cast off feudal bonds. The nobility from their castles in the countryside fought a losing war against the communal movement; yielding, they took up residence in the city, and swore loyalty to the commune. The bishops, who for centuries had been the real and able governors of the Lombard towns, were subdued with the help of the popes, whose authority they had long ignored. In 1080 we hear of "consuls" governing Lucca; in 1084 we find them at Pisa, in 1098 at Arezzo, in 1099 at Genoa, in 1105 at Pavia, in 1138 at Florence. The cities of northern Italy continued till the fifteenth century to acknowledge the formal sovereignty of the Empire, and indited their state papers in its name;[97] but in practice and effect they were free; and the ancient regime of city-state was revived, with all its chaos and stimulus.

In France the enfranchisement of the cities involved a long and often violent struggle. At Le Mans (1069), Cambrai (1076), and Reims (1139) the ruling bishops, by excommunication or force, succeeded in suppressing the communes set up by the citizens; at Noyon, however, the bishop of his own accord gave a charter to the town (1108). St. Quentin freed itself in 1080, Beauvais in 1099, Marseille in 1100, Amiens in 1113. At Laon in 1115 the citizens took advantage of their corrupt bishop's absence to establish a commune; on his return he was bribed to take oath to protect it; a year later he induced King Louis VI to suppress it. In the monk Guibert of Nogent's account of what followed we sample the intensity of the communal revolution:

> On the fifth day of Easter week . . . there arose a disorderly noise throughout the city, men shouting "Commune!" . . . Citizens now entered the bishop's court with swords, battle-axes, bows, hatchets, clubs, and spears, a very great company. . . . The nobles rallied from all sides to the bishop. . . . He, with some helpers, fought them off with stones and arrows. . . . He hid himself in a cask . . . and piteously implored them, promising that he would cease to be their bishop, would give them unlimited riches, and would leave the country. And as they with hardened hearts jeered at him, one named Bernard, lifting his battle-ax, brutally dashed out the brains of that sacred, though sinner's, head; and he, slipping between the hands of those who held him, was dead before he reached the ground, stricken by another blow under the eye-sockets and across the nose. There brought to his end, his legs were cut off, and many another wound inflicted. Thibaut, seeing a ring on the Bishop's finger, and not being able to draw it off, cut off the finger.[98]

The cathedral was fired, and was razed to the ground. Thinking to take two steps at once, the pillagers began to sack and burn the mansions of the aristocracy. A royal army stormed the city, and joined nobles and clergy in massacring the population. The commune was suppressed. Fourteen years later it was restored; and the citizens labored with pious enthusiasm to rebuild the cathedral that they or their fathers had destroyed.

The struggle continued for a century. At Vézelay (1106) the people killed Abbot Arnaud and set up a commune. Orléans rose in 1137, but failed. Louis VII granted Sens a charter in 1146, but revoked it three years later on petition of the abbot within whose domains the city lay; the populace killed the abbot and his nephew, but failed to re-establish the commune. The bishop of Tournai fought a civil war for six years (1190–6) to overthrow the commune; the pope excommunicated all the citizens. On Easter Sunday of 1194 the people of Rouen sacked the houses of the cathedral canons; in 1207 the city was put under a papal interdict. In 1235 at Reims the stones brought into the city to rebuild the cathedral were seized by the populace and were used for missiles and barricades in a revolt against the highest ecclesiastic in Gaul; he and his canons fled, and did not return until two years later, when the pope induced Louis VII to abolish the commune. Many cities of France never succeeded, till the Revolution, in establishing their freedom; but in north France most of the cities were freed between 1080 and 1200, and, under the stimulus of liberty, entered upon their greatest age. It was the communes that built the Gothic cathedrals.

In England the kings won the support of the cities against the nobility by granting them charters of limited self-government. William the Conqueror gave such a charter to London; similar charters were yielded by Henry II to Lincoln, Durham, Carlisle, Bristol, Oxford, Salisbury, and Southampton; and in 1201 Cambridge bought its communal rights from King John. In Flanders the ruling counts made substantial concessions to Ghent, Bruges, Douai, Tournai, Lille . . . but overcame all attempts at complete municipal independence. Leyden, Haarlem, Rotterdam, Dordrecht, Delft, and other Dutch cities obtained charters of local autonomy in the thirteenth century. In Germany the liberation was long drawn out, and mostly peaceful; the bishops, who had for centuries ruled the cities as feudatories of the emperors, yielded to Cologne, Trier, Metz, Mainz, Speyer, Strasbourg, Worms, and other cities the right to select their own magistrates and make their own laws.

By the end of the twelfth century the communal revolution was won in western Europe. The cities, though seldom completely free, had thrown off their feudal masters, ended or reduced feudal tolls, and severely limited ecclesiastical rights. The Flemish cities forbade the establishment of new monasteries, and the bequest of land to churches; they restricted the right of the clergy to be tried by episcopal courts, and contested clerical control of primary schools.[99] The mercantile *bourgeoisie* now dominated municipal and economic life. In nearly all the communes the merchant guilds were recognized as self-governing bodies; in some cases the commune and the merchant guild were identical organizations; usually the two were distinct, but the commune rarely contravened the interests of the guilds. The lord mayor of London was chosen by the city guilds. Now, for the first time in a thousand years, the possession of money became again a greater power than the possession of land; nobility and clergy were challenged by a rising plutocracy. Even more than in antiquity the mercantile *bourgeoisie* turned its wealth, energy, and ability to political advantage. In most cities it eliminated the poor from assemblies or offices. It oppressed the manual worker and the peasant, monopolized the profits of commerce, taxed the community heavily, and spent much of the revenue in internal strife, or in external wars to capture markets and destroy competitors. It tried to suppress artisan associations, and refused them the right to strike, under penalty of exile or death. Its regulation of prices and wages aimed at its own good, to the serious detriment of the working class.[100] As in the French Revolution, the defeat of the feudal lords was a victory chiefly for the business class.

Nevertheless the communes were a magnificent reassertion of human liberty. At the call of the bell from the town campanile, the citizens flocked to assemble, and chose their municipal officers. The cities formed their own communal militia, defended themselves lustily, defeated the trained troops of the German emperor at Legnano (1176), and fought one another to mutual exhaustion. Though the administrative councils soon narrowed their membership to a mercantile aristocracy, the municipal assemblies were the first representative government since Tiberius; they, rather than Magna Carta, were the chief parent of modern democracy.[101] The atavistic relics of feudal or tribal law—compurgations, duels, ordeals—were replaced by the legal and orderly examination of witnesses; the wergild or blood price gave way to fines, imprisonment, or corporal punishment; the law's delays were reduced, legal contracts replaced feudal status and loyalties, and a whole new body of business law created a new order in European life.

The young democracy leaped at once to a semisocialistic state-managed economy. The commune minted its own currency, ordered and supervised public works, built roads, bridges, and canals, paved some city streets, organized the food supply, forbade forestalling, engrossing, or regrading, brought seller and buyer into direct contact at markets and fairs, examined weights and measures, inspected commodities, punished adulteration, controlled exports and imports, stored grain for lean years, provided grain at fair prices in emergencies, and regulated the prices of essential foods and beer. When it found that a price set too low discouraged the production of a desirable commodity, it allowed certain wholesale prices to seek their own level through competition, but established courts or "assizes" of bread and ale to keep the retail price of these necessities in constant relation with the cost of wheat or barley.[102] Periodically it published a list of fair prices. It assumed that for every commodity there must be a "just price," combining costs of materials and labor; the theory ignored supply and demand, and fluctuations in the value of currency. Some communes, like Basel or Genoa, assumed a monopoly of the trade in salt; others, like Nuremberg, brewed their own beer, or stored corn in municipal granaries.[103] The flow of goods was impeded by municipal protective tariffs;[104] and in some cases by requiring transient merchants to expose their goods for sale in the town before passing through.[105] As in our century, these regulations were often circumvented by the subtlety of refractory citizens; "black markets" were numerous.[106] Many of these restrictive ordinances brought more harm than good, and soon ceased to be enforced.

But all in all, the work of the medieval communes did credit to the skill and courage of the businessmen who managed them. Under their leadership Europe experienced in the twelfth and thirteenth centuries such prosperity

as it had not known since the fall of Rome. Despite epidemics, famines, and
wars, the population of Europe swelled under the communal system as not
for a thousand years before. The population of Europe had begun to decline in the second century, and had probably reached nadir in the ninth
century. From the eleventh century to the Black Death (1349) it rose again
with the resurrection of commerce and industry. In the region between the
Moselle and the Rhine it probably multiplied tenfold; in France it may have
reached 20,000,000—hardly less than in the eighteenth century.[107] The
economic revolution involved a migration from country to city almost as
definite as in recent times. Constantinople with 800,000, Cordova and Palermo with half a million each, had long been populous; but before 1100
only a few cities north of the Alps had more than 3000 souls.[108] By 1200 Paris
had some 100,000; Douai, Lille, Ypres, Ghent, Bruges, approximately 50,000
each; London 20,000. By 1300 Paris had 150,000, Venice, Milan, Florence
100,000,[109] Siena and Modena 30,000,[110] Lübeck, Nuremberg, and Cologne
20,000, Frankfort, Basel, Hamburg, Norwich, York 10,000. Of course all
these figures are loose and hazardous estimates.

The growth of population was both a result and a cause of the economic
development: it came from improved protection of life and property, better
exploitation of natural resources through industry, and the wider spread of
food and goods through rising wealth and trade; conversely it offered an
expanding market to commerce and industry, to literature, drama, music,
and art. The competitive pride of the communes turned their wealth into
cathedrals, city halls, bell towers, fountains, schools, and universities. Civilization crossed seas and mountains in the wake of trade; from Islam and
Byzantium it swept over Italy and Spain, and marched over the Alps into
Germany, France, Flanders, and Britain. The Dark Ages became a memory, and Europe was alive again with lusty youth.

We must not idealize the medieval town. It was picturesque (to the modern eye) with castle-crowned hill and towered wall, with thatched or tiled
houses, cottages, and shops crowding gregariously around cathedral, castle
or public square. But for the most part its streets were narrow and tortuous
alleys (ideal for defense and shade), where men and beasts moved to the
clatter of hoofs and words and wooden shoes, and with the leisureliness of
an age that had no machines to spare its muscle and wear its nerves. Around
many of the city dwellings were gardens, chicken coops, pig pens, cow pastures, dunghills. London was finicky and decreed that "he who will nourish
a pig, let him keep it in his own house"; elsewhere the swine rooted freely
among the open garbage piles.[111] Every now and then heavy rains swelled
the rivers and flooded fields and cities, so that men rowed boats into Westminster Palace.[112] After rain the streets would be muddy for days; men wore
boots then, and fine ladies were borne in carriages or chairs, undulating from

hole to hole. In the thirteenth century some cities paved their main streets with cobblestones; in most cities, however, the streets were unpaved, unsafe for foot or nose. Monasteries and castles had good drainage systems;[113] cottages usually had none. Here and there were grassy or sandy squares, with a pump from which people might drink, and a trough for passing animals.

North of the Alps houses were nearly all of wood; only the richest nobles and merchants built of brick or stone. Fires were frequent, and often swept unchecked through a town. In 1188 Rouen, Beauvais, Arras, Troyes, Provins, Poitiers, and Moissac were all destroyed by fire; Rouen was burned down six times between 1200 and 1225.[114] Tile roofs became the custom only in the fourteenth century. Fire fighting was by bucket brigades, heroic and incompetent. Watchmen were provided with a long hook to pull down a burning house if it threatened other buildings. Since all wished to live near the castle for security, buildings rose to several stories, sometimes six; and the upper floors projected charmingly and alarmingly over the street. Towns issued ordinances limiting the height of buildings.

Despite these difficulties—hardly felt because felt by nearly all—life could be interesting in the medieval city. Markets were crowded, talk was plentiful, dress and goods were colorful, pedlars cried their wares, craftsmen plied their trades. Strolling players might be performing a miracle or mystery play in the square; a religious procession might pass down the street, with proud merchants and sturdy workers marching, and gaudy floats and solemn vestments and stirring song; some glorious church might be a-building; some pretty lass might lean from a balcony; the town belfry might summon the citizens to meeting or to arms. At sunset curfew rang, and bade all people hasten home, for there were no lights in the streets except candles in windows, and here and there a lamp before a shrine. A nocturnal burgher would have his servants precede him with torches or lanterns and arms, for police were rare. The wise citizen retired early, shunning the tedium of illiterate evenings, and knowing that at dawn the noisy cocks would crow, and work would clamor to be done.

VII. THE AGRICULTURAL REVOLUTION

The growth of industry and commerce, the spread of a money economy, and the rising demand for labor in the towns transformed the agricultural regime. The municipalities, eager to get new "hands," announced that any person living in a town for 366 days without being claimed, identified, and taken as a serf, became automatically free, and would enjoy the protection of the commune's laws and power. In 1106 Florence invited all the peasants of the surrounding villages to come and live there as freemen. Bologna and other towns paid feudal lords to let their serfs move into the city. A large number of serfs escaped, or were invited, to open new lands east of the Elbe, where they became automatically free.

Those who remained on the manor showed a troublesome resistance to feudal dues long sanctioned by time. Emulating the town guilds, many serfs formed rural associations—*confrèries, conjurations*—and bound themselves by oath to act together in refusing feudal dues. They stole or destroyed seignorial charters that recorded their bondage or obligations; they burned down the castles of obstinate seigneurs; they threatened to abandon the domain if their demands were not met. In 1100 the villeins of St. Michel-de-Beauvais announced that they would thereafter marry any woman they pleased, and would give their daughters to any man who pleased them. In 1102 the serfs of St. Arnoul-de-Crépy refused their abbot lord the traditional heriot, or death due, or to pay a fine for letting their daughters marry outside the domain. Similar rebellions broke out in a dozen towns from Flanders to Spain. The feudal lords found it increasingly difficult to make a profit out of serf labor; rising resistance required costly superintendence at every turn; villein labor in manorial shops proved more expensive, and less competent, than the free labor that produced like goods in the towns.

To keep the peasants on the land, and make their labor profitable to himself, the baron commuted the old feudal dues for money payments, sold freedom to serfs who could pay for it with their savings, leased more and more of the demesne to free peasants for a money rental, and hired free labor for the workshops on his estate. Year by year, following the lead of the Moslem and Byzantine East, western Europe, from the eleventh to the thirteenth century, passed from payments predominantly in kind to payments predominantly in currency. Feudal landlords, desiring the manufactured products that commerce laid before their eyes, craved money with which to purchase them; going off to the Crusades, they wanted money rather than food and goods; governments demanded taxes in money, not in kind; the landlords yielded to the course of events, and sold their products for cash instead of consuming them by laborious migration from villa to villa. The change to a money economy proved costly for the feudal landlords; the commutations and rents they received acquired the fixity of medieval custom, and could not be raised as rapidly as the value of money fell. Many of the aristocracy had to sell their land—usually to the rising *bourgeoisie*; some nobles, as early as 1250, died landless or destitute.[115] Early in the fourteenth century King Philip the Fair of France freed the serfs on the royal domain, and in 1315 his son Louis X ordered the liberation of all serfs "on fair and suitable conditions." [116] Gradually, from the twelfth to the sixteenth century, at different times in divers countries west of the Elbe, serfdom gave place to peasant proprietorship; the feudal manor broke up into small estates, and the peasantry rose in the thirteenth century to a degree of freedom and prosperity that it had not known for a thousand years. The seignorial courts lost their jurisdiction over the peasants, and the village community elected its own officers, who swore allegiance not to the local lord but only to the crown. The emancipation in western Europe was not quite complete till 1789; many feudal lords still claimed the old rights in law, and would try, in the fourteenth century, to restore them in fact; but the movement toward free and mobile labor could not be stopped so long as commerce and industry grew.

The new stimulus of freedom co-operated with an immense widening of the agricultural market to improve the methods, tools, and products of tillage. The rising population of the towns, the increase of wealth, the new facilities of finance and trade expanded and enriched the rural economy. New industries created a demand for industrial crops—sugar cane, aniseed, cumin, hemp, flax, vegetable oils, and dyes. The nearness of populous towns promoted cattle raising, dairy farming, and market gardening. From thousands of vineyards in the valleys of the Tiber, the Arno, the Po, the Guadalquivir, the Tagus, the Ebro, the Rhone, the Gironde, the Garonne, the Loire, the Seine, the Moselle, the Meuse, the Rhine, and the Danube wine flowed along the rivers and over land and sea to console the toilers of Europe's fields, workshops, and counting rooms; even England, from the eleventh to the sixteenth century, made wine. To feed the hungry towns, where fast days were numerous and meat was costly, great fleets went out into the Baltic and North Seas to bring in herring and other fish; Yarmouth owed its life to the herring trade; the merchants of Lübeck acknowledged their debt to it by carving herrings on their pews; [117] and honest Dutchmen admitted that they had "built upon herrings" the proud city of Amsterdam.[118]

Agricultural technique slowly improved. The Christians learned from the Arabs in Spain, Sicily, and the East; and the Benedictine and Cistercian monks brought old Roman and new Italian tricks of farming, breeding, and soil preservation to the countries north of the Alps. The strip system was abandoned in laying out new farms, and each farmer was left to his own initiative and enterprise. In Flanders fields reclaimed from swamps the peasants of the thirteenth century practiced a three-field rotation of crops, in which the soil was used each year, but was triennially replenished by fodder or leguminous plants. Powerful teams of oxen drew iron plowshares more deeply into the soil than before. Most plows, however, were still (1300) of wood; only a few regions knew the use of manure; and wagon wheels were seldom shod with iron tires. Cattle raising was difficult because of prolonged droughts; but the thirteenth century saw the first experiments in the crossing and acclimatization of breeds. Dairy farming was unprogressive; the average cow in the thirteenth century gave little milk, and hardly a pound of butter per week. (A well-bred cow now yields ten to thirty pounds of butter per week.)

While their masters fought one another, the peasants of Europe fought the greater battle, more heroic and unsung, of man against nature. Between the eleventh and the thirteenth century the sea had thirty-five times swept over barriers and across the Lowlands, creating new gulfs and bays where once there had been land, and drowning 100,000 persons in a century. From the eleventh to the fourteenth century the peasants of these regions, under their princes and abbots, transported blocks of stone from Scandinavia and Germany, and built the "Golden Wall" behind which the Belgians and the Dutch have developed two of the most civilized states in history. Thousands of acres were rescued from the sea, and by the thirteenth century the Lowlands were latticed with canals. From 1179 to 1257 the Italians cut the famous Naviglio Grande, or Great Canal, between Lake Maggiore and the Po, fertilizing 86,485 acres of land. Between the Elbe and the Oder patient immigrants from Flanders, Frisia, Saxony, and the Rhineland turned the marshy *Mooren* into rich fields. The superabundant forests of France were progressively cleared, and became the farms that through centuries of political turmoil have kept France fed. Perhaps it was this mass heroism of clearance, drainage, irrigation, and cultivation, rather than any victories of war or trade, that provided the foundation on which, in final analysis, rest all the triumphs of European civilization in the last 700 years.

VIII. THE CLASS WAR

In the early Middle Ages there had been only two classes in western Europe: German conquerors and native conquered; by and large the later aristocracies in England, France, Germany and northern Italy were descendants of the conquerors, and remained conscious of this blood relationship even amid their wars. In the eleventh century there were three classes: the nobles, who fought; the clergy, who prayed; and the peasants, who worked. The division became so traditional that most men thought it ordained by God; and most peasants, like most nobles, assumed that a man should patiently continue in the class into which he had been born.

The economic revolution of the twelfth century added a new class—the burgesses or *bourgeoisie*—the bakers, merchants, and master craftsmen of the towns. It did not yet include the professions. In France the classes were called *états*—estates or states—and the *bourgeoisie* was reckoned as the *tiers état*, or "third estate." It controlled municipal affairs, and won entry into the English Parliament, the German Diet, the Spanish Cortes, and the States-General—the rarely convened national parliament of France; but it had, before the eighteenth century, little influence on national policy. The nobles continued to rule and administer the state, though they were now a minor force in the cities. They lived in the country (except in Italy), scorned city

dwellers and commerce, ostracized any of their class who married a bourgeois, and were certain that an aristocracy of birth is the only alternative
to a plutocracy of business, or a theocracy of myths, or a despotism of arms.
Nevertheless the wealth that came from commerce and industry began now
to compete—and in the eighteenth century would surpass—the wealth that
came from the ownership of land.

The rich merchants fretted over aristocratic airs, and scorned and exploited the craftsman class. They lived in ornate mansions, bought fine
furniture, ate exotic foods, and garbed themselves in costly dress. Their
wives covered expanding forms with silks and furs, velvets and jewelry; and
Jeanne of Navarre, Queen of France, was piqued to find herself welcomed
into Bruges by 600 bourgeois ladies as gorgeously robed as herself. The
nobles complained, and demanded sumptuary laws to check this insolent
display; such laws were periodically passed; but as the kings needed bourgeois support and funds, these laws were only spasmodically enforced.

The rapid growth of urban population favored the bourgeois owners of
city realty; and the consequent unemployment made it easier to manage
the manual working class. The proletariat of servants, apprentices, and journeymen had little education and no political power, and lived in a poverty
sometimes more dismal than the serf's. A thirteenth-century day laborer in
England received some two pence per day—roughly equivalent, in purchasing power, to two dollars in the United States of America in 1948. A carpenter received four and one eighth pence ($4.12) per day; a mason three
and one eighth, an architect twelve pence plus traveling expenses and occasional gifts.[119] Prices, however, were commensurately low: in England in
1300 a pound of beef cost a farthing (twenty-one cents); a fowl one penny
(eighty-four cents); a quarter of wheat five shillings nine and one half
pence ($57.90).[120] The work day began at dawn and ended at dusk—sooner
on the eve of Sunday or a feast day. There were some thirty feast days in
the year, but in England probably not more than six exempted the people
from toil. The hours were a bit longer, the real wages no worse—some would
say higher[121]—than in eighteenth- or nineteenth-century England.

Toward the end of the thirteenth century the class struggle became class
war. Every generation saw some revolt of the peasantry, particularly in
France. In 1251 the oppressed peasantry of France and Flanders rose against
their secular and ecclesiastical landlords. Calling themselves *Pastoureux*
(Shepherds), they formed a kind of revolutionary crusade under the lead of
an unlicensed preacher known as "the Master of Hungary." They marched
from Flanders through Amiens to Paris; discontented peasants and *proletaires* joined them en route, until they numbered over a hundred thousand
men. They bore religious banners, and proclaimed devotion to King Louis
IX, then a prisoner of the Moslems in Egypt; but they were ominously armed
with clubs, daggers, axes, pikes, and swords. They denounced the corrup-

tion of government, the tyranny of the rich over the poor, the covetous hypocrisy of priests and monks; and the populace cheered their denunciations. They assumed the ecclesiastical rights of preaching, granting absolution, and performing marriages, and slew some priests who opposed them. Passing on to Orléans, they massacred scores of clergy and university students. But there and at Bordeaux the police overcame them; their leaders were captured and executed; and the wretched survivors of the futile march were hunted like dogs and dispersed into divers haunts of misery. Some escaped to England, and raised a minor peasant uprising, which was in turn suppressed.[122]

In the industrial towns of France the craft guilds rose in repeated strikes or armed insurrection against the political and economic monopoly and dictation of the merchant class. In Beauvais the mayor and some bankers were manhandled by 1500 rioters (1233). At Rouen the textile workers rebelled against the merchant drapers, and killed the mayor who intervened (1281). At Paris King Philip the Fair dissolved the workers' unions on the ground that they were plotting revolution (1295, 1307). Nevertheless the craft guilds won admission to the municipal assemblies and magistracies at Marseille (1213), Avignon, Arles (1225), Amiens, Montpellier, Nîmes. . . . Sometimes a member of the clergy would side with the rebels, and give them slogans. "All riches," said a thirteenth-century bishop, "come from theft; every rich man is a thief or the heir of a thief."[123] Similar revolts disordered the Flanders towns. Despite the penalty of death or banishment for strike leaders, the coppersmiths of Dinant rose in 1255, the weavers of Tournai in 1281, of all Ghent in 1274, of Hainault in 1292. The workers of Ypres, Douai, Ghent, Lille, and Bruges joined in revolt in 1302, defeated a French army at Courtrai, won the admission of their representatives to communal councils and offices, and revoked the oppressive legislation with which the mercantile oligarchy had harassed the crafts. Acquiring power for a time, the weavers sought to fix—even to reduce—the wages of the fullers, who then allied themselves with the merchant rich.[124]

In 1191 the merchant guilds won control of London; soon afterward they offered King John an annual payment if he would suppress the weavers' guild; John complied (1200).[125] In 1194 one William Fitzobert or Longbeard preached to the poor of London the need of a revolution. Thousands listened to him eagerly. Two burgesses sought to kill him; he fled into a church, was forced out by smoke, and committed hara-kiri almost by the Japanese ritual. His followers worshiped him as a martyr, and kept as sacred the soil that had received his blood.[126] The popularity of Robin Hood, who robbed great lords and prelates but was kind to the poor, suggests the class feeling in twelfth-century Britain.

The bitterest conflicts took place in Italy. At first the workers joined with the merchant guilds in a series of bloody insurrections against the nobles; by the end of the thirteenth century this struggle was won. For a time the industrial population shared in the government of Florence. Soon, however, the great merchants and entrepreneurs secured ascendancy in the city council, and imposed such arduous and arbitrary rules upon their employees that the struggle entered, in the fourteenth century, its second phase —sporadic and intermittent war between the rich industrialists and the workers in the factories. It was amid these scenes of civil strife that St. Francis preached the gospel of poverty, and reminded the *nouveaux riches* that Christ had never had any private property.[127]

The communes, like the guilds, declined in the fourteenth century through the expansion of a municipal into a national economy and market, in which their rules and monopolies obstructed the development of invention, industry, and trade. They suffered further through their chaotic internal strife, their ruthless exploitation of the surrounding countryside, their narrow municipal patriotism, their conflicting policies and currencies, their petty wars upon one another in Flanders and Italy, and their inability to organize themselves into an autonomous confederation that might have survived the growth of the royal power. After 1300 several French communes petitioned the king to assume their governance.

Even so the economic revolution of the thirteenth century was the making of modern Europe. It eventually destroyed a feudalism that had completed the function of agricultural protection and organization, and had become an obstacle to the expansion of enterprise. It transformed the immobile wealth of feudalism into the fluent resources of a world-wide economy. It provided the machinery for a progressive development of business and industry, which substantially increased the power, comforts, and knowledge of European man. It brought a prosperity that in two centuries could build a hundred cathedrals, any one of which presumes an amazing abundance and variety of means and skills. Its production for an extending market made possible the national economic systems that underlay the growth of the modern states. Even the class war that it let loose may have been an added stimulant to the minds and energies of men. When the storm of the transition had subsided, the economic and political structure of Europe had been transformed. A flowing tide of industry and commerce washed away deep-rooted impediments to human development, and carried men onward from the scattered glory of the cathedrals to the universal frenzy of the Renaissance.

CHAPTER XXV

The Recovery of Europe

1095-1300

I. BYZANTIUM

ALEXIUS I COMNENUS, after guiding the Eastern Empire successfully through Turkish and Norman wars and the First Crusade, ended
his long reign (1081–1118) amid a characteristically Byzantine intrigue.
His eldest daughter, Anna Comnena, was a paragon of learning, a compendium of philosophy, a poet of parts, a politician of subtlety, an historian of
accomplished mendacity. Betrothed to the son of the Emperor Michael VII,
she felt herself marked for empire by her birth, her beauty, and her brains;
and she could never forgive her brother John for being born and succeed-
ing to the throne. She conspired to assassinate him, was detected and forgiven, retired to a convent, and chronicled her father's career in a prose
Alexiad. John Comnenus (1118–43) astonished Europe by a reign of private
virtue, administrative competence, and victorious campaigns against pagan,
Moslem, and Christian foes; for a time it seemed that he would restore the
Empire to its former scope and glory; but a scratch from a poisoned arrow
in his own quiver ended his life and his dream.

His son Manuel I (1143–80) was an incarnate Mars, dedicated to war and
delighting in it, ever in the van of his troops, welcoming single combat,
and winning every battle but the last. Stoic in the field, he was an epicurean
in his palace, luxurious in food and dress, and happy in the incestuous love
of his niece. Under his indulgent patronage literature and scholarship flourished again; the ladies of the court encouraged authors, and themselves condescended to write poetry; and Zonaras now compiled his immense *Epitome
of History*. Manuel built for himself a new palace, the Blachernae, on the seashore at the end of the Golden Horn; Odom of Deuil thought it "the fairest building in the world; its pillars and walls were half covered with gold,
and encrusted with jewels that shone even in the obscurity of the night."[1]
Constantinople in the twelfth century rehearsed the Italian Renaissance.

This splendor of the capital, and the many wars that the aging empire
waged to ward off death, required heavy taxation, which the enjoyers of
luxuries passed on to the producers of necessaries. The peasants grew poorer,
and surrendered to serfdom; the manual workers of the cities lived in noi-
some slums, whose dark filth harbored uncounted crimes. Vague semicom-

munistic movements of revolt agitated the proletarian flux,[2] but have been forgotten in the careless repetitiousness of time. Meanwhile the capture of Palestine by the Crusaders had opened Syrian ports to Latin commerce, and Constantinople lost to the rising cities of Italy a third of its maritime trade. Christian and Moslem alike aspired to capture this treasury of a millennium's wealth. A good Moslem, visiting the city in Manuel's heyday, prayed: "May God in His generosity and grace deign to make Constantinople the capital of Islam!"[3] And Venice, daughter of Byzantium, invited the chivalry of Europe to join her in raping the Queen of the Bosporus.

The Latin kingdom of Constantinople, established by the Fourth Crusade, endured but fifty-seven years (1204–61). Rootless in the race, faith, or customs of the people—hated by a Greek Church forcibly subjected to Rome —weakened by its division into feudal principalities each aping sovereignty— lacking the experience required to organize and regulate an industrial and commercial economy—attacked by Byzantine armies without and conspiracies within—and unable to draw from a hostile population the revenues needed for military defense, the new kingdom stood only as long as Byzantine revenge lacked unity and arms.

The conquerors fared best in Greece. Frank, Venetian, and other Italian nobles hastened to carve the historic land into feudal baronies, built picturesque castles on dominating sites, and ruled with dash and competence a supine and industrious population. Prelates of the Latin Church replaced the exiled bishops of the Orthodox faith; and monks from the West crowned the ancient hills with monasteries that were monuments and treasuries of medieval art. A proud Frank took the title of duke of Athens, which Shakespeare, by a venial error of 2000 years, would un-Baconianly apply to Theseus. But the same martial spirit that had reared these little kingdoms destroyed them with fraternal strife; rival factions fought suicidal wars in the hills of the Morea and on the plains of Boeotia; and when the "Grand Catalan Company" of military adventurers from Catalonia invaded Greece (1311), the flower of Frank chivalry there was slaughtered in battle near the Cephisus River, and helpless Hellas became the plaything of Spanish buccaneers.

Two years after the fall of Constantinople, Theodore Lascaris, son-in-law of Alexius III, set up a Byzantine government in exile at Nicaea. All Anatolia, with the rich cities of Prusa, Philadelphia, Smyrna, and Ephesus, welcomed his rule; and his just and able administration brought new prosperity to these regions, new life to Greek letters, and new hope to Greek patriots. Farther east, at Trebizond, Alexius Comnenus, son of Manuel, established another Byzantine kingdom; and a third took form in Epirus under Michael Angelus. Lascaris' son-in-law and successor, John Vatatzes (1222–54), added part of Epirus to the Nicaean kingdom, recaptured Salonika from the Franks (1246), and might have regained Constantinople itself had he not been called back to Asia Minor by learning that Pope Innocent IV had invited the advancing Mongols to attack him from the East (1248). The Mongols rejected the papal plan on the ironical pretense that they were loath to encourage "the mutual hatred of Christians."[4] John's long reign was one of the most creditable in history. Despite expensive campaigns to restore Byzantine unity, he lowered taxes, encouraged agriculture, built schools, libraries, churches, monasteries, hospitals, and homes for the old or the poor.[5] Literature and art prospered under him, and Nicaea became one of the richest, fairest cities of the thirteenth century.

His son Theodore Lascaris II (1254–8) was an ailing scholar, learned and bemused; he died after a brief reign, and Michael Paleologus, leader of the discontented aristocracy, usurped the throne (1259–82). If we may believe the historians, Michael had every fault—"selfish, hypocritical . . . an inborn liar, vain, cruel, and rapacious";[6] but he was a subtle strategist and a triumphant diplomat. By one battle he made his power in Epirus secure; by an alliance with Genoa he won ardent aid against the Venetians and the Franks in Constantinople. He instructed his general Strategopulus to feint an attack upon the capital from the West; Strategopulus approached the city with only a thousand men; finding it weakly guarded, he entered and took it without a blow. King Baldwin II fled with his retinue, and the Latin clergy of the city came after him in righteous panic. Michael, hardly believing the news, crossed the Bosporus, and was crowned emperor (1261). The Byzantine Empire, which the world had thought dead, awoke to a post-mortem life; the Greek Church resumed its independence; and the Byzantine state, corrupt and competent, stood for two centuries more as a treasury and vehicle of ancient letters, and a frail but precious bulwark against Islam.

II. THE ARMENIANS: 1060–1300

About 1080 many Armenian families, resenting Seljuq domination, left their country, crossed the Taurus Mountains, and established the kingdom of Lesser Armenia in Cilicia. While Turks, Kurds, and Mongols ruled Armenia proper, the new state maintained its independence for three centuries. In a reign of thirty-four years (1185–1219) Leo II repelled the attacks of the sultans of Aleppo and Damascus, took Isauria, built his capital at Sis (now in Turkey), made alliances with the Crusaders, adopted European laws, encouraged industry and commerce, gave privileges to Venetian and Genoese merchants, founded orphanages, hospitals, and schools, raised his people to unparalleled prosperity, earned the name of Magnificent, and was altogether one of the wisest and most beneficent monarchs in medieval history. His son-in-law Hethum I (1226–70), finding the Christians unreliable, allied himself with the Mongols, and rejoiced at the expulsion of the Seljuqs from

Armenia (1240). But the Mongols became converts to Mohammedanism, warred on Lesser Armenia, and reduced it to ruins (1303f.). In 1335 Armenia was conquered by the Mamluks, and the country was divided among feudal lords. Through all this turbulence the Armenians continued to show an inventive skill in architecture, a high excellence in miniature painting, and a resolutely independent form of Catholicism which turned back all attempts at domination by either Constantinople or Rome.

III. RUSSIA AND THE MONGOLS: 1054–1315

In the eleventh century southern Russia was held by semibarbarous tribes—Cumans, Bulgars, Khazars, Polovtsi, Patzinaks. . . . The remainder of European Russia was divided into sixty-four principalities—chiefly Kiev, Volhynia, Novgorod, Suzdalia, Smolensk, Ryazan, Chernigov, and Pereyaslavl. Most of the principalities acknowledged the suzerainty of Kiev. When Yaroslav, Grand Prince of Kiev, died (1054), he distributed the principalities, according to their importance, among his sons in order of their seniority. The eldest received Kiev; and by a unique *rota* system it was arranged that at any princely death each princely survivor should move up from a lesser to a greater province. In the thirteenth century several principalities were further split into "appanages"—regions assigned by the princes to their sons. In the course of time these appanages became hereditary, and formed the basis of that modified feudalism which would later share with the Mongol invasion the blame for keeping Russia medieval while western Europe advanced. In this period, however, the Russian towns had a busy handicraft industry, and a richer trade than they would have in many later centuries.

The power of each prince, though usually inherited, was limited by a popular *veche* or assembly, and by a senate of nobles (*boyarskaya duma*). Administration and law were mostly left to the clergy; these, with a few nobles, merchants, and moneylenders, almost monopolized literacy; with Byzantine texts or models before them, they gave Russia letters and laws, religion and art. Through their labors the *Russkaya Pravda*, Russian Right or Law, first formulated under Yaroslav, received emendation and definitive codification (*c.* 1160). The Russian Church was given full jurisdiction over religion and the clergy, marriage, morals, and wills; and she had unchecked authority over the slaves and other personnel on her extensive properties. Her efforts moderately raised the legal status of the slave in Russia, but the traffic in slaves continued, and reached its height in the twelfth century.[7]

That same century saw the decline and fall of the Kievan realm. The feudal anarchy of the West had its rival in the tribal and princely anarchy of the East. Between 1054 and 1224 there were eighty-three civil wars in Russia, forty-six invasions of Russia, sixteen wars by Russian states upon non-

Russian peoples, and 293 princes disputing the throne of sixty-four princi-palities.[8] In 1113 the impoverishment of the Kievan population by war, high interest charges, exploitation, and unemployment aroused revolutionary rioting; the infuriated populace attacked and plundered the homes of the employers and moneylenders, and occupied the offices of the government for a moment's mastery. The municipal assembly invited Prince Monomakh of Pereyaslavl to become Grand Prince of Kiev. He came reluctantly, and played a role like Solon's in the Athens of 594 B.C. He lowered the rate of interest on loans, restricted the self-sale of bankrupt debtors into slavery, limited the authority of employers over employees, and by these and other measures—denounced as confiscatory by the rich and as inadequate by the poor—averted revolution and reorganized peace.[9] He labored to end the feuds and wars of the princes, and to give Russia political unity; but the task was too great for his twelve years of rule.

After his death the strife of princes and classes was resumed. Meanwhile the continued possession of the lower Dniester, Dnieper, and Don by alien tribes, and the growth of Italian commerce at Constantinople, in the Black Sea, and in the ports of Syria, diverted to Mediterranean channels much of the trade that formerly had passed from Islam and Byzantium up the rivers of Russia to the Baltic states. The wealth of Kiev declined, and its martial means or spirit failed. As early as 1096 its barbarian neighbors began to raid its hinterland and suburbs, plundering monasteries and selling captured peas-ants as slaves. Population ebbed from Kiev as a danger spot, and man power further fell. In 1169 the army of Andrey Bogolyubski sacked Kiev so thor-oughly, and enslaved so many thousands of its inhabitants, that for three cen-turies the "mother of Russian cities" almost dropped out of history. The seizure of Constantinople and its trade by Venetians and Franks in 1204, and the Mongol invasions of 1229-40, completed the ruin of Kiev.

In the second half of the twelfth century the leadership of Russia passed from the "Little Russians" of the Ukraine to the rougher, hardier "Great Russians" of the region around Moscow and along the upper Volga. Founded in 1156, Moscow was in this age a small village serving Suzdalia (which ran northeast from Moscow) as a frontier post on the route from the cities of Vladimir and Suzdal to Kiev. Andrey Bogolyubski (1157-74) fought to make his principality of Suzdalia supreme over all Russia; but he died by the hand of an assassin while campaigning to bring Novgorod, like Kiev, under his sway.

The city of Novgorod was situated in northwestern Russia, on both sides of the Volkhov, near the exit of that river from Lake Ilmen. As the Volkhov emptied into Lake Ladoga in the north, and other rivers left Lake Ilmen to the south and west, and the Baltic, via Lake Ladoga, was neither too close for safety nor too far for trade, Novgorod developed a vigorous internal and foreign commerce, and became the eastern pivot of the Hanseatic

League. It traded through the Dnieper with Kiev and Byzantium, and through the Volga with Islam. It almost monopolized the traffic in Russian furs, for its control reached from Pskov in the west to the Arctic on the north, and almost to the Urals on the east. After 1196 the vigorous merchant-aristocrats of Novgorod dominated the assembly that ruled the principality through its elected prince. The city-state was a free republic, and called itself "My Lord Novgorod the Great." If a prince proved unsatisfactory, the burgesses would "make a reverence and show him the way to leave" town; if he resisted they clapped him into jail. When Sviatopolk, Grand Prince of Kiev, wished to force his son upon them as prince (1015), the Novgorodians said, "Send him here if he has a spare head." [10] But the republic was not a democracy; the workers and small traders had no voice in the government, and could influence policy only by repeated revolts.

Novgorod reached its zenith under Prince Alexander Nevsky (1238–63). Pope Gregory IX, anxious to win Russia from Greek to Latin Christianity, preached a crusade against Novgorod; a Swedish army appeared on the Neva; Alexander defeated it near the present Leningrad (1240), and won his surname from the river. His victory made him too great for a republic, and won him exile; but when the Germans took up the crusade, captured Pskov, and advanced to within seventeen miles of Novgorod, the frightened assembly begged Alexander to return. He came, recaptured Pskov, and defeated the Livonian Knights on the ice of Lake Peipus (1242). In his last years he had the humiliation of leading his people under the Mongol yoke.

For the Mongols entered Russia in overwhelming force. They came from Turkestan through the Caucasus, crushed a Georgian army there, and pillaged the Crimea. The Cumans, who had for centuries warred against Kiev, begged for Russian aid, saying, "Today they have seized our land, tomorrow they will take yours." [11] Some Russian princes saw the point, and led several divisions to join the Cuman defense. The Mongols sent envoys to propose a Russian alliance against the Cumans; the Russians killed the envoys. In a battle on the banks of the Kalka River, near the Sea of Azov, the Mongols defeated the Russian-Cuman army, captured several Russian leaders by treachery, bound them, and covered them with a platform on which the Mongol chieftains ate a victory banquet while their aristocratic prisoners died of suffocation (1223).

The Mongols retired to Mongolia, and busied themselves with the conquest of China, while the Russian princes resumed their fraternal wars. In 1237 the Mongols returned under Batu, a great-nephew of Jenghiz Khan; they were 500,000 strong, and nearly all mounted; they came around the northern end of the Caspian, put the Volga Bulgars to the sword, and destroyed Bolgar, their capital. Batu sent a message to the Prince of Ryazan: "If you want peace, give us the tenth of your goods"; he answered, "When we are dead you may have the whole." [12] Ryazan asked the principalities for help; they refused it; it fought bravely, and lost the whole of its goods. The irresistible Mongols sacked and razed all the towns of Ryazan, swept into Suzdalia, routed its army, burned Moscow, and besieged Vladimir. The nobles had themselves tonsured, and hid in the cathedral as monks; they died when the cathedral and all the city were given to the flames. Suzdal, Rostov, and a multitude of villages in the principality were burned to the ground (1238). The Mongols moved on toward Novgorod; turned back by thick forests and swollen streams, they ravaged Chernigov and Pereyaslavl, and reached Kiev. They sent envoys asking for surrender; the Kievans killed the envoys. The Mongols crossed the Dnieper, overrode a weak resistance, sacked the city, and killed many thousands; when Giovanni de Piano Carpini saw Kiev six years later, he described it as a town of 200 cottages, and the surrounding terrain as dotted with skulls. The Russian upper and middle classes had never dared to arm the peasants or the city populace; when the Mongols came the people were helpless to defend themselves, and were massacred or enslaved at the convenience of the conquerors.

The Mongols advanced into Central Europe, won and lost battles, returned through Russia ravaging, and on a branch of the Volga built a city, Sarai, as the capital of an independent community known as the Golden Horde. Thence Batu and his successors kept most of Russia under domination for 240 years. The Russian princes were allowed to hold their lands, but on condition of annual tribute—and an occasional visit of homage over great distances—to the khan of the Horde, or even to the Great Khan in Mongolian Karakorum. The tribute was collected by the princes as a head tax that fell with cruel equality upon rich and poor, and those who could not pay were sold as slaves. The princes resigned themselves to Mongol mastery, for it protected them from social revolt. They joined the Mongols in attacking other peoples, even Russian principalities. Many Russians married Mongols, and certain features of Mongolian physiognomy and character may have entered the Russian stock.[13] Some Russians adopted Mongol ways of speech and dress. Made a dependency of an Asiatic power, Russia was largely severed from European civilization. The absolutism of the khan united with that of the Byzantine emperors to beget the "Autocrat of All the Russias" in later Muscovy.

Recognizing that they could not keep Russia quiet by force alone, the Mongol chieftains made peace with the Russian Church, protected her possessions and personnel, exempted them from taxation, and punished sacrilege with death. Grateful or compelled, the Church recommended Russian submission to the Mongol masters, and publicly prayed for their safety.[14] To find security amid alarms, thousands of Russians became monks; gifts were showered upon religious organizations, and the Russian Church became immensely rich amid the general poverty. A spirit of submissiveness was developed in the people, and opened a road to centuries of despotism. Nevertheless it was Russia, bending under the Mongol whirlwind, that stood as a vast moat and trench protecting most of Europe from Asiatic conquest. All the fury of that human tempest spent itself upon the Slavs—Russians, Bohemians, Moravians, Poles—and the Magyars; Western Europe trembled, but was hardly touched. Perhaps the rest of Europe could go forth toward political and mental freedom, toward wealth, luxury, and art, because for over two centuries Russia remained beaten, humbled, stagnant, and poor.

IV. THE BALKAN FLUX

At an alien distance the Balkans are a mountainous mess of political instability and intrigue, of picturesque subtlety and commercial craft, of wars, assassinations, and pogroms. But to the native Bulgar, Rumanian, Hungarian, or Yugoslav his nation is the product of a thousand years' struggle to win independence from encompassing empires, to maintain a unique and colorful culture, to express the national character unhindered in architecture, dress, poetry, music, and song.

For 168 years Bulgaria, once so powerful under Krum and Simeon, remained subject to Byzantium. In 1186 the discontent of the Bulgar and Vlach (Wallachian) population found expression in two brothers, John and Peter Asen, who possessed that mixture of shrewdness and courage which the situation and their countrymen required. Summoning the people of Trnovo to the church of St. Demetrius, they persuaded them that the saint had left Greek Salonika to make Trnovo his home, and that under his banner Bulgaria could regain liberty. They succeeded, and amiably divided the new empire between them, John ruling at Trnovo, Peter at Preslav. The greatest monarch of their line, and in all Bulgarian history, was John Asen II (1218–41). He not only absorbed Thrace, Macedonia, Epirus, and Albania; he governed with such justice that even his Greek subjects loved him; he pleased the popes with allegiance and monastic foundations; he supported commerce, literature, and art with enlightened laws and patronage; he made Trnovo one of the best adorned cities of Europe, and raised Bulgaria, in civilization and culture, to a level with most of the nations of his time. His successors did not inherit his wisdom; Mongol invasions disordered and weakened the state (1292–5), and in the fourteenth century it succumbed first to Serbia and then to the Turks.

In 1159 the Zhupan (Chieftain) Stephen Nemanya brought the various Serb clans and districts under one rule, and in effect founded the Serb kingdom, which his dynasty governed for 200 years. His son Sava served the nation as archbishop and statesman, and became one of its most revered saints. The country was still poor, and even the royal palaces were of wood; it had a flourishing port, Ragusa (now Dubrovnik), but this was an independent city-state, which in 1221 became a Venetian protectorate. During these centuries Serbian art, Byzantine in origin, achieved a style and excellence of its own. In the monastery church of St. Panteleimon at Nerez (c. 1164) the murals reveal a dramatic realism unusual in Byzantine painting, and anticipate by a century some methods of treatment once thought original to Duccio and Giotto. Amid these and other Serbian murals of the twelfth or thirteenth century appear royal portraits individualized beyond any known Byzantine precedent.[15] Medieval Serbia was moving toward a high civilization when heresy and persecution destroyed the national unity that might have withstood the Turkish advance. Bosnia, too, after its medieval zenith under the Ban (King) Kulin (1180–1204), was weakened by religious disputes; and in 1254 it fell subject to Hungary.

After the death of Stephen I (1038) Hungary was disturbed by pagan Magyar revolts against the Catholic kings, and by the efforts of Henry III to annex Hungary to Germany. Andrew I defeated Henry; and when the Emperor Henry IV renewed the attempt King Geza I frustrated it by giving Hungary to Pope Gregory VII and receiving it back as a papal fief (1076). During the twelfth century rivals for the kingship nurtured feudalism by large grants of land to nobles in return for support; and in 1222 the nobility was strong enough to draw from Andrew II a "Golden Bull" remarkably like the Magna Carta that King John of England had signed in 1215. It denied the heritability of feudal fiefs, but promised to summon a diet every year, to imprison no noble without a trial before the "count palatine" (i.e., a count of the imperial palace), and to levy no taxes upon noble or ecclesiastical estates. This royal edict, named from its golden case or seal, constituted for seven centuries a charter of liberty for the Hungarian aristocracy, and enfeebled the Hungarian monarchy precisely at a time when the Mongols were preparing for Europe one of the greatest crises in its history.

We may judge the extent of the Mongol reach and grasp when we note that in 1235 Ogadai, the Great Khan, sent out three armies—against Korea, China, and Europe. The third army, under Batu, crossed the Volga in 1237, 300,000 strong— no undisciplined horde but a force rigorously trained, ably led, and equipped not only with powerful siege engines but with novel firearms whose use the Mongols had learned from the Chinese. In three years these warriors laid waste nearly all southern Russia. Then Batu, as if unable to conceive of defeat, divided them into two armies: one marched into Poland, took Cracow and Lublin, crossed the Oder, and defeated the Germans at Liegnitz (1241); the other, under Batu, surmounted the Carpathians, invaded Hungary, met the united forces of Hungary and Austria at Mohi, and so overwhelmed them that medieval chroniclers, never moderate with figures, estimated the Christian dead at 100,000, and the Emperor Frederick II reckoned the Hungarian casualties as "almost the whole military force of the kingdom." [16] Here, by the inexorable irony of history, defeated and victors were of one blood; the fallen nobility of Hungary were descendants of the Mongol Magyars who had ravaged the land three centuries before. Batu took Pesth and Esztergom (1241), while a body of Mongols crossed the Danube and pursued the Hungarian King Bela IV to the Adriatic shore, burning and destroying wildly on the way. Frederick II vainly called upon Europe to unite against the menace of conquest by Asia; Innocent IV vainly tried to woo the Mongols to Christianity and peace. What saved Christianity and Europe was simply the death of Ogadai, and the return of Batu to Karakorum to participate in the election of a new khan. Never in history had there been so extensive a devastation—from the Pacific Ocean to the Adriatic and the Baltic Seas.

Bela IV returned to ruined Pesth, repeopled it with Germans, moved his capital across the Danube to Buda (1247), and slowly restored his country's shattered economy. A newborn nobility organized again the great ranches and farms on which servile herdsmen and tillers produced food for the nation. German miners moved down from the Erz Gebirge, and extracted the rich ores of Transylvania. Life and manners were still rude, tools were primitive, houses were wattled huts. Amid the confusion of races and tongues, across the hostile divisions of classes and creeds, men sought their daily bread and gain, and restored that economic continuity which is the soil of civilization.

V. THE BORDER STATES

As, in a limitless universe, any point may be taken as center, so, in the pageant of civilizations and states, each nation, like each soul, interprets the drama of history or life in terms of its own role and character. North of the Balkans lay another medley of peoples—Bohemians, Poles, Lithuanians, Livonians, Finns; and each, with life-giving pride, hung the world upon its own national history.

In the earlier Middle Ages the Finns, distant relatives of the Magyars and the Huns, dwelt along the upper Volga and Oka. By the eighth century they had migrated into the hardy, scenic land known to outsiders as Finland, and to Finns as Suomi, the Land of Marsh. Their raids upon the Scandinavian coasts induced the Swedish King Eric IX to conquer them in 1157. At Uppsala Eric left a bishop with them as a germ of civilization; the Finns killed Bishop Henry, and then made him their patron saint. With quiet heroism they cleared the forests, drained the marshes, channeled their "10,000 lakes," [17] gathered furs, and fought the snow.

South of the Gulf of Finland the same ax- and spadework was accomplished by tribes akin to the Finns—Borussians (Prussians), Esths (Estonians), Livs (Livonians), Litva (Lithuanians), and Latvians or Letts. They hunted, fished, kept bees, tilled the soil, and left letters and arts to the less vigorous posterity for whom they toiled. All but the Estonians remained pagan till the twelfth century, when the Germans brought Christianity and civilization to them with fire and sword. Finding that Christianity was being used by the Germans as a means of infiltration and domination, the Livonians killed the missionaries, plunged into the Dvina to wash off the stain of baptism, and returned to their native gods. Innocent III preached a crusade against them; Bishop Albert entered the Dvina with twenty-three men-of-war, built Riga as his capital, and subjected Livonia to German rule (1201). Two religious-military orders, the Livonian Knights and the Teutonic Knights, completed the conquest of the Baltic states for Germany, carved out vast holdings for themselves, converted the natives to Christianity, and reduced them to serfdom.[18] Heartened by this success, the Teutonic Knights advanced into Russia, hoping to win at least its western provinces for Germany and Latin Christianity; but they were defeated on Lake Peipus (1242) in one of the innumerable decisive battles of history.

Around these Baltic states surged an ocean of Slavs. One group called itself Polanie—"people of the fields"—and tilled the valleys of the Warthe and the Oder; another, the Mazurs, dwelt along the Vistula; a third, the Pomorzanie ("by the sea"), gave its name to Pomerania. In 963 the Polish prince Mieszko I, to avoid conquest by Germany, confided Poland to the protection of the popes; thenceforth Poland, turning its back upon the semi-Byzantine Slavdom of the East, cast in its lot with western Europe and Roman Christianity. Mieszko's son Boleslav I (992–1025) conquered Pomerania, annexed Breslau and Cracow, and made himself the first King of Poland. Boleslav III (1102–39) divided the kingdom among his four sons; the monarchy was weakened; the aristocracy parceled the land into feudal principalities, and Poland fluctuated between freedom and subjection to Germany or Bohemia. In 1241 the Mongol avalanche came down upon the land, took Cracow, the capital, and leveled it to the ground. As the Asiatic flood receded a wave of German immigration swept into western Poland, leaving there a strong admixture of German language, laws, and blood. At the same time (1246) Boleslav V welcomed Jews fleeing from pogroms in Germany, and encouraged them to develop commerce and finance. In 1310 King Wenceslas II of Bohemia was elected King of Poland, and united the two nations under one crown.

Bohemia and Moravia had been settled by Slavs in the fifth and sixth centuries. In 623 a Slavic chieftain, Samo, freed Bohemia from the Avars, and established a monarchy that died with him in 658. Charlemagne invaded the land in 805, and for an unknown period Bohemia and Moravia were parts of the Carolingian Empire. In 894 the Přemysl family brought both lands under their enduring dynasty; but the Magyars ruled Moravia for half a century (907–57), and in 928 Henry I made Bohemia subject to Germany. Duke Wenceslas I (928–35) brought prosperity to Bohemia despite this intermittent dependency. He had been given a thoroughly Christian upbringing by his mother, St. Ludmilla; and he did not cease to be a Christian when he became a ruler. He fed and clothed the poor, protected orphans and widows, gave hospitality to strangers, and bought freedom for slaves. His brother tried to assassinate him as lacking the vices desirable in a king; Wenceslas struck him down with his own hand, and forgave him; but other members of the conspiracy murdered the King on his way to Mass on September 25, 935. The day is annually celebrated as the feast of Wenceslas, Bohemia's tutelary saint.

Warlike dukes succeeded him. From their strategic castle and capital at Prague, Boleslav I (939–67) and II (967–99) and Bratislav I (1037–55) conquered Moravia, Silesia, and Poland; but Henry III forced Bratislav to evacuate Poland and resume the payment of tribute to Germany. Ottokar I (1197–1230) freed Bohemia, and became its first king. Ottokar II (1253–78) subjected Austria, Styria, and Carinthia. Eager to develop industry and a middle class as counterweights to a rebellious nobility, Ottokar II encouraged German immigration, until nearly all the towns of Bohemia and Moravia were predominantly German.[19] The silver mines of Kutna Hora became the ground of Bohemia's prosperity, and the goal of her many invaders. In 1274 Germany declared war against Ottokar; his nobles refused to support him; he surrendered his conquests, and kept his throne only as a German fief. But when the Emperor Rudolf of Hapsburg interfered in the internal affairs of Bohemia, Ottokar raised a new army and fought the Germans at Dürnkrut; again deserted by the nobles, he plunged into the thickest ranks of the enemy and died in desperate combat.

Wenceslas II (1278–1305) won peace by renewed vassalage, and laboriously restored order and prosperity. With his death the Přemyslid dynasty came to an end after a rule of 500 years. The Bohemians, the Moravians, and the Poles were the only survivors of the Slav migration that had once filled eastern Germany to the Elbe; and they were now subject to the German power.

VI. GERMANY

The victor in the historic contest over lay investiture was the aristocracy of Germany—the dukes, lords, bishops, and abbots, who, after the defeat of Henry IV, controlled a weakened monarchy, and developed a centrifugal feudalism that in the thirteenth century deposed Germany from the leadership of Europe.

Henry V (1106–1125), having overthrown his father, continued his father's struggle against barons and popes. When Paschal II refused to crown him emperor except on surrender of the right to lay investiture, he imprisoned Pope and cardinals. When he died the nobility overthrew the principle of hereditary monarchy, ended the Franconian dynasty, and made Lothair III of Saxony king. Thirteen years later Conrad III of Swabia began the Hohenstaufen dynasty, the most powerful line of kings in German history.

Duke Henry of Bavaria rejected the electors' choice, and was supported by his uncle Welf, or Guelf; now flared up that strife between "Guelf" and "Ghibelline" which was to have so many forms and issues in the twelfth and thirteenth centuries.* The Hohenstaufen army besieged the Bavarian rebels in the town and fortress of Weinsberg; there, says an old tradition, the rival cries "Hi Welf!" and "Hi Weibling!" established the names of the warring groups; and there (says a pretty legend), when the victorious Swabians accepted the surrender of the town on the understanding that the women alone were to be spared, and were to be allowed to depart with whatever they could carry, the sturdy housewives marched forth with their husbands on their backs.[20] A truce was called in 1142, when Conrad went on crusade; but Conrad failed and returned in disgrace. The House of Hohenstaufen seemed stamped with disgrace when its first outstanding figure reached the throne.

Friedrich ("Lord of Peace") or Frederick I (1152–90) was thirty when chosen king. He was not imposing—a small, fair-skinned man with yellow hair, and a red beard that won him in Italy the name of Barbarossa. But his head was clear and his will was strong; his life was spent in labors for the state; and though he suffered many defeats, he brought Germany again to the leadership of the Christian world. Carrying in his veins the blood of both the Hohenstaufens and the Welfs, he proclaimed a *Landfried*, or Peace

---

* "Ghibelline" was a variant of Waiblingen, a village owned by the Hohenstaufens. This family took its name—"High Staufen"—from a mountain castle and village in Swabia.

of the Land, conciliated his enemies, quieted his friends, and sternly suppressed feuds, disorder, and crime. His contemporaries described him as genial, and ever ready with a winning smile; but he was a "terror to evildoers," and the barbarism of his penal laws advanced civilization in Germany. His private life was justly praised for decency; however, he divorced his first wife on grounds of consanguinity, and married the heiress of the count of Burgundy, winning a kingdom with his bride.

Anxious for papal coronation as emperor, he promised Pope Eugenius III aid against the rebellious Romans and the troublesome Normans in return for the imperial ointment. Arrived at Nepi, near Rome, the proud young king met the new pontiff, Hadrian IV, and omitted the customary rite by which the secular ruler held the pope's bridle and stirrup and helped him to dismount. Hadrian reached the ground unaided, and refused Frederick the "kiss of peace," and the crown of empire, until the traditional ritual should be performed. For two days the aides of Pope and King disputed the point, hanging empire on protocol; Frederick yielded; the Pope retired and made a second entry on horseback; Frederick held the papal bridle and stirrup, and thereafter spoke of the *Holy* Roman Empire in the hope that the world would consider the emperor, as well as the pope, the vicegerent of God.

His imperial title made him also King of Lombardy. No German ruler since Henry IV had taken this title literally; but Frederick now sent to each of the northern Italian cities a podesta to govern it in his name. Some cities accepted, some rejected, these alien masters. Loving order more than liberty, and perhaps anxious to control the Italian outlets of German trade with the East, Frederick set out in 1158 to subdue the rebellious towns, which loved liberty more than order. He summoned to his court at Roncaglia the learned legists who were reviving Roman law at Bologna; he was pleased to learn from them that by that law the emperor held absolute authority over all parts of the Empire, owned all property in it, and might modify or abrogate private rights whenever he thought it desirable for the state. Pope Alexander III, fearing for the temporal rights of the papacy, and citing the donations of Pepin and Charlemagne, repudiated these claims, and, when Frederick insisted on them, excommunicated him (1160). The cries of Guelf and Ghibelline now passed into Italy to denote respectively the supporters of the Pope and those of the Emperor. For two years Frederick besieged obdurate Milan; capturing it at last he burned it to the ground (1162). Angered by this ruthlessness, and galled by the exactions of the German podestas, Verona, Vicenza, Padua, Treviso, Ferrara, Mantua, Brescia, Bergamo, Cremona, Piacenza, Parma, Modena, Bologna, and Milan formed the Lombard League (1167). At Legnano, in 1176, the troops of the League defeated Frederick's German army, and forced him to a six years' truce. A year later Emperor and Pope were reconciled; and at Constance Frederick signed (1183) a treaty restoring self-government to the Italian cities. These in return recognized the formal suzerainty of the Empire and magnanimously agreed to provision Frederick and his retinue on his visits to Lombardy.

Defeated in Italy, Frederick triumphed everywhere else. He successfully asserted the imperial authority over Poland, Bohemia, and Hungary. He reasserted over the German clergy, in practice if not in words, all the rights of appointment that Henry IV had claimed, and won the support of that clergy even against the popes.[21] Germany, glad to woo him from Italy, basked in the splendor of his power, and gloried in the knightly pageantry of his coronations, his marriages, and his festivals. In 1189 the old Emperor led 100,000 men on the Third Crusade, perhaps hoping to unite East and West in a Roman Empire restored to its ancient scope. A year later he was drowned in Cilicia.

Like Charlemagne he had drunk too deeply of the Roman tradition; he had exhausted himself in the effort to revive a dead past. Admirers of monarchy mourned his defeats as victories for chaos; devotees of democracy celebrate them as stages in the development of freedom. Within the limits of his vision he was justified; Germany and Italy were sinking into a licentious disorder; only a strong imperial authority could put an end to feudal feuds and municipal wars; order had to pave the way before a rational liberty could grow. In the later weakness of Germany, loving legends formed about Frederick I; what the thirteenth century imagined of his grandson was in time applied to Barbarossa: he was not really dead, he was only sleeping in the Kyffhauser Mountain in Thuringia; his long beard could be seen growing through the marble that covered him; some day he would wake up, shrug the earth from his shoulders, and make Germany again orderly and strong. When Bismarck forged a united Germany a proud people saw in him Barbarossa risen triumphantly from the tomb.[22]

Henry VI (1190–7) almost realized his father's dream. In 1194, with the help of Genoa and Pisa, he conquered southern Italy and Sicily from the Normans; all Italy but the Papal States submitted to him; Provence, Dauphiné, Burgundy, Alsace, Lorraine, Switzerland, Holland, Germany, Austria, Bohemia, Moravia, and Poland were united under Henry's rule; England acknowledged itself his vassal; the Almohad Moors of Africa sent him tribute; Antioch, Cilicia, and Cyprus asked to be included in the Empire. Henry eyed France and Spain with unsated appetite, and planned to conquer Byzantium. The first detachments of his army had already embarked for the East when Henry, aged thirty-three, succumbed to dysentery in Sicily.

He had made no provision for so ignominious a revenge by the climate of his conquest. His only son was a lad of three; a decade of disorder ensued while would-be emperors fought for the throne. When Frederick II came of age the war of empire and papacy was resumed; it was fought in Italy by a German-Norman monarch become Italian, and will be better viewed from the Italian scene. Another generation of turmoil followed the death of Frederick II (1250)—that *herrenlose, schreckliche Zeit* (Schiller called it), that "masterless, frightful age" in which the electoral princes sold the throne of Germany to any weakling who would leave them free to consolidate their independent power. When the chaos cleared the Hohenstaufen dynasty had ended; and in 1273 Rudolf of Hapsburg, making Vienna his capital, began a new line of kings. To win the imperial crown Rudolf signed in 1279 a declaration recognizing the complete subordination of the royal to the papal power, and renouncing all claims to southern Italy and Sicily. Rudolf never became emperor; but his courage, devotion, and energy restored order and prosperity to Germany, and firmly established a dynasty that ruled Austria and Hungary till 1918.

Henry VII (1308–13) made a final effort to unite Germany and Italy. With scant support from the nobles of Germany, and a small following of Walloon knights, he crossed the Alps (1310), and was welcomed by many Lombard cities tired of class war and interurban strife, and anxious to throw off the political authority of the Church. Dante hailed the invader with a treatise *On Monarchy* boldly proclaiming the freedom of the secular from the spiritual power, and appealed to Henry to save Italy from papal domination. But the Florentine Guelfs won the upper hand, the turbulent cities withdrew their support, and Henry, surrounded with enemies, died of the malarial fever with which Italy now and then repays her importunate lovers.

Turned back in the south by natural barriers of topography, race, and speech, Germany found outlet and recompense in the east. German and Dutch migration, conquest, and colonization reclaimed three fifths of Germany from the Slavs; fertile Germans expanded along the Danube into Hungary and Rumania; German merchants organized fairs and outlets at Frankfort on the Oder, Breslau, Prague, Cracow, Danzig, Riga, Dorpat, and Reval, and trading centers everywhere from the North Sea and the Baltic to the Alps and the Black Sea. The conquest was brutal, the results were an immense advance in the economic and cultural life of the border.

Meanwhile the absorption of the emperors in Italian affairs, the recurrent need of enlisting or rewarding the support of lords and knights with grants of land or power, and the weakening of the German monarchy by papal opposition and Lombard revolts, had left the nobility free to engross the countryside and reduce the peasantry to serfdom; and feudalism triumphed in thirteenth-century Germany at the very time when it was succumbing to the royal power in France. The bishops, whom the earlier emperors had favored as a foil to the barons, had become a second nobility, as rich, powerful and independent as the secular lords. By 1263 seven nobles—the archbishops of Mainz, Trier, and Cologne, the dukes of Saxony and Bavaria, the count palatine, and the margrave of Brandenburg—had been entrusted by the feudality with the authority to choose the king; and these electors hedged in the powers of the ruler, usurped royal prerogatives, and seized crown lands. They might have acted as a central government and given the nation unity; they did not; between elections they went their several ways. No German nation existed yet; there were only Saxons, Swabians, Bavarians, Franks. . . . There was as yet no national parliament, but only territorial diets, *Landtage*; a *Reichstag*, or Diet of the Commonwealth, established in 1247, languished feebly in the Interregnum, and acquired prominence only in 1338. A corps of *ministeriales*—serfs or freedmen appointed by the king—provided a loose bureaucracy and continuity of government. No one capital centered the country's loyalty and interest; no one system of laws governed the realm. Despite the efforts of Barbarossa to impose Roman law upon all Germany, each region kept its own customs and code. In 1225 the laws of the Saxons were formulated in the *Sachsenspiegel*, or Saxon Mirror; in 1275 the *Schwabenspiegel* codified the laws and customs of Swabia. These codes asserted the ancient right of the people to choose their king, and of the peasants to keep their freedom and their land; serfdom and slavery, said the *Sachsenspiegel*, are contrary to nature and the will of God, and owe their origin to force or fraud.[23] But serfdom grew.

The age of the Hohenstaufens (1138–1254) was the greatest age of Germany before Bismarck. The manners of the people were still crude, their laws chaotic, their morals half Christian, half pagan, and their Christianity half a cover for territorial robbery. Their wealth and comforts could not compare, city for city, with those of Flanders or Italy. But their peasantry was industrious and fertile, their merchants enterprising and adventurous, their aristocracy the most cultured and powerful in Europe, their kings the secular heads of the Western world, ruling a realm from the Rhine to the Vistula, from the Rhone to the Balkans, from the Baltic to the Danube, from the North Sea to Sicily. Out of a virile commercial life a hundred cities had taken form; many of them had charters of self-government; decade by decade they grew in wealth and art, until in the Renaissance they would be the pride and glory of Germany, and be mourned in our day as a beauty that has passed from the earth.

VII. SCANDINAVIA

After a century of happy obscurity Denmark re-entered world history with Waldemar I (1157–82). Helped by his minister Absalon, Archbishop of Lund, he organized a strong government, cleared his seas of pirates, and enriched Denmark by protecting and encouraging trade. In 1167 Absalon founded Copenhagen as a "market haven"—Kjoebenhavn. Waldemar II (1202–41) replied to German aggression by conquering Holstein, Hamburg, and Germany northeast of the Elbe. "For the honor of the Blessed Virgin" he undertook three "crusades" against the Baltic Slavs, captured northern Estonia, and founded Reval. In one of these campaigns he was attacked in his camp, and escaped death, we are told, partly by his own valor, partly through the timely descent, from heaven, of a red banner bearing a white cross; this *Dannebrog*, or Dane's Cloth, became thereafter the battle standard of the Danes. In 1223 he was taken prisoner by Count Henry of Schwerin, and was released, after two and a half years, only on his surrendering to the Germans all his Germanic and Slav conquests except Rügen. He devoted the remainder of his remarkable life to internal reforms and the codification of Danish law. At his death Denmark was double its present area, included southern Sweden, and had a population equal to that of Sweden (300,000) and Norway (200,000) combined. The power of the kings declined after Waldemar II, and in 1282 the nobles secured from Eric Glipping a charter recognizing their assembly, the *Danehof*, as a national parliament.

Only the imaginative empathy of a great novelist could make us visualize the achievement of Scandinavia in these early centuries—the heroic conquest, day by day, foot by foot, of a difficult and dangerous peninsula. Life was still primitive; hunting and fishing, as well as agriculture, were primary sources of sustenance; vast forests had to be cleared, wild animals had to be brought under control, waters had to be channeled to productive courses, harbors had to be built, men had to harden themselves to cope with a nature that seemed to resent the intrusion of man. Cistercian monks played a noble role in this agelong war, cutting timber, tilling the soil, and teaching the peasants improved methods of agriculture. One of the many heroes of the war was Earl Birger, who served Sweden as prime minister from 1248 to 1266, abolished serfdom, established the reign of law, founded Stockholm (*c.* 1255), and inaugurated the Folkung dynasty (1250–1365) by putting his son Waldemar on the throne. Bergen grew rich as the outlet of Norway's trade, and Visby, on the island of Gotland, became the center of contact between Sweden and the Hanseatic League. Excellent churches were built, cathedral and monastic schools multiplied, poets strummed their lays; and Iceland, far off in the Arctic mists, became in the thirteenth century the most active literary center in the Scandinavian world.

VIII. ENGLAND

1. William the Conqueror

William the Conqueror ruled England with a masterly mixture of force, legality, piety, subtlety, and fraud. Elevated to the throne by a cowed Witan, he swore to observe existing English law. Some thanes in the west and north took advantage of his absence in Normandy to try revolt (1067); he returned, and passed like a flame of revenge through the land, and "harried the north" with such judicious killing and destruction of homes, barns, crops, and cattle that northern England did not fully recover till the nineteenth century.[24] He distributed the choicest lands of the kingdom in great estates among his Norman aides, and encouraged these to build castles as fortresses of defense against a hostile population.* He kept large tracts as crown lands; one parcel, thirty miles long, was set aside as a royal hunting preserve; all houses, churches, and schools therein were leveled to the ground to clear the way for horses and hounds; and any man who slew a hart or hind in this New Forest was to lose his eyes.[25]

So was founded the new nobility of England, whose progeny still bear, now and then, French names; and the feudalism that before had been relatively weak covered the land, and reduced most of the conquered people to serfdom. All the soil belonged to the king; but Englishmen who could show that they had not resisted the Conquest were allowed to repurchase their lands from the state. To list and know his spoils, William sent agents in 1085 to record the ownership, condition, and contents of every parcel of land in England; and "so narrowly did he commission them," says the old Chronicle, "that there was not a yard of land, nay . . . not even an ox, nor a cow, nor a swine, that was not set down in his writ." [26] The result was the Domesday Book, ominously so named as the final "doom" or judgment in all disputes of realty. To assure himself military support, and limit the power of his great vassals, William summoned all important landowners of England—60,000 of them—to a concourse at Salisbury (1086), and made every man pledge his paramount fealty to the king. It was a wise precaution against the individualistic feudalism that was at that time dismembering France.

One must expect a strong government after a conquest. William set up or deposed knights and earls, bishops and archbishops and abbots; he did not hesitate to jail great lords, and to assert his right over ecclesiastical appointments against the same powerful Gregory VII who was in these years bringing the Emperor Henry IV to Canossa. To prevent fires he ordered a curfew —i.e., a covering or extinction of hearth fires, and therefore in winter retirement to bed—by eight P.M. for the people of England.[27] To finance his spreading government and conquests he laid heavy taxes upon all sales, imports, exports, and the use of bridges and roads; he restored the Danegeld, which Edward the Confessor had abolished; and when he learned that some Englishmen, to elude his fingers, had placed their money in monastic vaults, he had all monasteries searched and all such hoards removed to his own treasury. His royal court readily accepted bribes, and honestly recorded them in the public register.[28] It was frankly a government of conquerors resolved that the profits of their enterprise should be commensurate with its risks.

---

* Robin Hood, famous in legend but obscure in history, may have been one of the Anglo-Saxons who continued for over a century a guerrilla resistance against the Norman conquerors. The English poor celebrated his memory as an unbeaten rebel who lived in Sherwood Forest, acknowledged no Norman law, robbed the lords, helped the serfs, and worshiped the saints.

The Norman clergy shared in the victory. The able and pliant Lanfranc was brought in from Caen and was made Archbishop of Canterbury and first minister to the King. He found the Anglo-Saxon clergy addicted to hunting, dicing, and marriage,[29] and replaced them with Norman priests, bishops, and abbots; he drew up a new monastic constitution, the Customs of Canterbury, and raised the mental and moral level of the English clergy. Probably at his suggestion William decreed the separation of ecclesiastical from secular courts, ordered all spiritual matters to be submitted to the canon law of the Church, and pledged the state to enforce the penalties fixed by ecclesiastical tribunals. Tithes were levied upon the people for the support of the Church. But William required that no papal bull or letter should be given currency or force in England without his approval, and that no papal legate should enter England without the royal consent. The national assembly of the bishops of England, which had been part of the Witan, was hereafter to be a distinct body, and its decrees were to have no validity except when confirmed by the King.[30]

Like most great men, William found it easier to rule a kingdom than his family. The last eleven years of his life were clouded by quarrels with his Queen Matilda. His son Robert demanded full authority in Normandy; denied this, he rebelled; William fought him indecisively, and made peace by promising to bequeath the duchy to Robert. The King grew so stout that he could hardly mount a horse. He warred with Philip I of France over boundaries; when he tarried at Rouen, almost immovable with corpulence, Philip jested (it was said) that the King of England was "lying in," and there would be a grand display of candles at his churching. William swore that he would indeed light many candles. He ordered his army to burn down Mantes and all its neighborhood, and to destroy all crops and fruits; and it was done. Riding happily amid the ruins, William was thrown against the iron pommel of his saddle by a stumble of his horse. He was carried to the priory of St. Gervase near Rouen. He confessed his sins in gross, and made his will; distributed his treasure penitently among the poor and to the Church, and provided for the rebuilding of Mantes. All his sons except Henry deserted his deathbed to fight for the succession; his officers and servants fled with what spoils they could take. A rustic vassal bore his remains to the Abbaye aux Hommes at Caen (1087). The coffin made for him proved too small for his corpse; when the attendants tried to force the enormous bulk into the narrow space the body burst, and filled the church with a royal stench.[31]

The results of the Norman Conquest were limitless. A new people and class were imposed upon the Danes who had displaced the Anglo-Saxons who had conquered the Roman Britons who had mastered the Celts . . .; and centuries would elapse before the Anglo-Saxon and Celtic elements would reassert themselves in British blood and speech. The Normans were akin to the Danes, but in the century since Rollo they had become Frenchmen; and with their coming the customs and speech of official England became for three centuries French. Feudalism was imported from France into England with its trappings, chivalry, heraldry, and vocabulary. Serfdom was more deeply and mercilessly imposed than ever in England before.[32] The Jewish moneylenders who came in with William gave a new stimulus to English trade and industry. The closer connection with the Continent brought to England many ideas in literature and art; Norman architecture achieved its greatest triumphs in Britain. The new nobility brought new manners, fresh vitality, a better organization of agriculture; and the Norman lords and bishops improved the administration of the state. The government was centralized. Though it was through despotism, the country was unified; life and property were made more secure, and England entered upon a long period of internal peace. She was never successfully invaded again.

2. *Thomas à Becket*

It is an adage in England that between two strong kings a weak king intervenes; but there is no limit to the number of intermediate middlings. After the Conqueror's death his eldest son Robert received Normandy as a separate kingdom. A younger son, William Rufus (the Red, 1087–1100), was crowned King of England on promising good behavior to his anointer and minister Lanfranc. He ruled as a tyrant till 1093, fell sick, promised good behavior, recovered, and ruled as a tyrant till he was shot to death, while hunting, by an unknown hand. The saintly Anselm, who succeeded Lanfranc as Archbishop of Canterbury, withstood him patiently, and was sent back to France.

A third son of the Conqueror, Henry I (1100–35), recalled Anselm. The prelate-philosopher demanded an end to the royal election of bishops; Henry refused; after a tedious quarrel it was agreed that English bishops and abbots were to be chosen by cathedral chapters or the monks in the presence of the king, and should do homage to him for their feudal possessions and powers. Henry loved money and hated waste; he taxed heavily but governed providently and justly; he kept England in order and at peace, except that with one battle—at Tinchebrai in 1106—he restored Normandy to the British crown. He bade the nobles "restrain themselves in dealing with the wives, sons, and daughters of their men";[33] he himself had many illegitimate sons and daughters by various mistresses,[34] but he had the grace and wisdom to marry Maud, scion of both the Scottish and pre-Norman English kings, thereby bringing old royal blood into the new royal line.

In his last days Henry made the barons and bishops swear fealty to his daughter Matilda and her young son, the future Henry II. But on the King's death Stephen of Blois, grandson of the Conqueror, seized the throne, and England suffered fourteen years of death and taxes in a civil war marked by the most horrible cruelties.[35] Meanwhile Henry II grew up, married Eleanor of Aquitaine and her duchy, invaded England, forced Stephen to recognize him as heir to the throne, and, on Stephen's death, became king (1154); so ended the Norman, and began the Plantagenet, dynasty.* Henry was a man of strong temper, eager ambition, and proud intellect, half inclined to atheism.[36] Nominally master of a realm that reached from Scotland to the Pyrenees, including half of France, he found himself apparently helpless in a feudal society where the great lords, armed with mercenaries and fortified in castles, had pulverized the state into baronies. With awesome energy the youthful king gathered money and men, fought and subdued one lord after another, destroyed the feudal castles, and established order, security, justice, and peace. With a masterly economy of cost and force he brought under English rule an Ireland conquered and despoiled by Welsh buccaneers. But this strong man, one of the greatest kings in England's history, was shattered and humbled by encountering in Thomas à Becket a will as inflexible as his own, and in religion a power then mightier than any state.

Thomas was born in London about 1118, of middle-class Norman parentage. His precocious brilliance of mind caught the eye of Theobald, Archbishop of Canterbury, who sent him to Bologna and Auxerre to study civil and canon law. Returning to England he entered orders, and soon rose to be Archdeacon of Canterbury. But, like so many churchmen of those centuries, he was a man of affairs rather than a clergyman; his interest and skill lay in administration and diplomacy; and he showed such ability in these fields that at the age of thirty-seven he was made secretary of state. For a time he and Henry accorded well; the handsome chancellor shared the intimacy and knightly sports, almost the wealth and power, of the King. His table was the most sumptuous in England; and his charity to the poor was equaled by his hospitality to his friends. In war he led in person 700 knights, fought single combats, planned campaigns. When he was sent on a mission to Paris his luxurious equipage of eight chariots, forty horses, and 200 attendants alarmed the French, who wondered how rich must be the king of so opulent a minister.

In 1162 he was appointed Archbishop of Canterbury. As if by some magic incantation, he now changed his ways abruptly and thoroughly. He gave up his stately palace, his royal raiment, his noble friends. He sent in his resignation as chancellor. He put on coarse garb, wore a haircloth next to his skin, lived on vegetables, grains, and water, and every night washed the feet of thirteen beggars. He became now an unyielding defender of all the rights,

---

* Geoffrey of Anjou, father of Henry II, had worn a sprig (*planta*) of the broom plant (Fr. *genêt*) in his hat.

privileges, and temporalities of the Church. Among these rights was the exemption of the clergy from trial by civil courts. Henry, who aspired to spread his rule over all classes, raged to find that crimes by the clergy often went unpunished by ecclesiastical courts. Assemblying the knights and bishops of England at Clarendon (1164), he persuaded them to sign the Constitutions of Clarendon, which ended many clerical immunities; but Becket refused to put his archiepiscopal seal upon the documents. Henry promulgated the new laws nevertheless, and summoned the ailing prelate to trial at the royal court. Becket came, and quietly withstood his own bishops, who joined in declaring him guilty of feudal disobedience to his suzerain the King. The court ordered his arrest; he announced that he would appeal the case to the Pope; and in his archiepiscopal robes, which none dared touch, he walked unharmed from the room. That evening he fed a great number of the poor in his London home. During the night he fled in disguise, by devious routes, to the Channel; crossed the turbulent strait in a frail vessel, and found haven in a monastery at St. Omer in the realm of the king of France. He submitted his resignation as archbishop to Pope Alexander III, who defended his stand, reinvested him with his see, but sent him for a time to live as a simple Cistercian monk in the abbey of Pontigny.

Henry banished from England all of Becket's relatives, of any age or sex. When Henry came to Normandy Thomas left his cell, and from a pulpit at Vézelay pronounced excommunication upon those English clergymen who upheld the Constitutions of Clarendon (1166). Henry threatened to confiscate the property of all priories, in England, Normandy, Anjou, and Aquitaine, affiliated with the abbey of Pontigny if its abbot continued to harbor Becket; the frightened abbot begged Thomas to leave, and the ailing rebel lived for a time on alms in a dingy inn at Sens. Alexander III, prodded by Louis VII of France, commanded Henry to restore the Archbishop to his see or face an interdict of all religious services in the territories under English rule. Henry yielded. He came to Avranches, met Becket, promised to remedy all his complaints, and held the Archbishop's stirrup as the triumphant prelate mounted to return to England (1169). Back in Canterbury, Thomas repeated his excommunication of the bishops who had opposed him. Some of these went to Henry in Normandy and roused him to fury with perhaps exaggerated accounts of Becket's behavior. "What!" exclaimed Henry, "shall a man who has eaten my bread . . . insult the King and all the kingdom, and not one of the lazy servants whom I nourish at my table does me right for such an affront?" Four knights who heard him went to England, apparently without the knowledge of the King. On December 30, 1170, they found the Archbishop at the altar of the cathedral in Canterbury; and there they cut him down with their swords.

All Christendom rose in horror against Henry, branding him with a spontaneous and universal excommunication. After secluding himself in his cham-

bers and refusing food for three days, the King issued orders for the apprehension of the assassins, sent emissaries to the Pope to declare his innocence,
and promised to perform any penance that Alexander might require. He rescinded the Constitutions of Clarendon, and restored all the previous rights
and property of the Church in his realm. Meanwhile the people canonized
Becket, and proclaimed that many miracles were worked at his tomb; the
Church officially pronounced him a saint (1172); and soon thousands were
making pilgrimage to his shrine. Finally Henry, too, came to Canterbury as
a penitent pilgrim; all the last three miles he walked with bare and bleeding
feet on the flinty road; he prostrated himself before the tomb of his dead foe,
begged the monks to scourge him, and submitted to their blows. His strong
will broke under the weight of general obloquy and mounting troubles in
his realm. His wife Eleanor, banished and imprisoned by the adulterous King,
plotted with her sons to depose him. His eldest son Henry led feudal rebellions against him in 1173 and 1183, and died in revolt. In 1189 his sons Richard and John, impatiently awaiting his death, allied themselves with Philip
Augustus of France in war upon their father. Driven from Le Mans, he denounced the God who had taken from him this town of his birth and love;
and dying at Chinon (1189), he cursed with his last breath the sons who had
betrayed him, and the life that had given him power and glory, riches and
mistresses, enemies, contumely, treacheries, and defeat.

He had not quite failed. He had surrendered to Becket dead what he had
refused to Becket living; yet in that bitter dispute it was Henry's contention
that won the accolade of time: from reign to reign, after him, the secular
courts spread their jurisdiction over clerical, as well as lay, subjects of the
king.[37] He liberated English law from feudal and ecclesiastical limitations,
and set it upon the path of development that has made it one of the supreme
legal achievements since imperial Rome. Like his great-grandfather the Conqueror he strengthened and unified the government of England by reducing
to discipline and order a rebellious and anarchic nobility. There he succeeded
too well: the central government became strong to the verge of irresponsible
and incalculable despotism; and the next round in the historic alternation
between order and liberty belonged to the aristocracy and freedom.

3. Magna Carta

Richard I the Lion-Hearted succeeded without challenge to his father's
throne. Son of the adventurous, impulsive, irrepressible Eleanor, he followed
in her steps rather than in those of the somber and competent Henry. Born
in Oxford in 1157, he was delegated by his mother to administer her dominions in Aquitaine. There he imbibed the skeptical culture of Provence, the
"gay science" of the troubadours, and was never afterward an Englishman.

He loved adventure and song more than politics and administration; he crowded a century of romance into his forty-two years, and gave to the poets of his time the compliment of imitation as well as the encouragement of patronage. The first five months of his reign were spent in gathering funds for a crusade; he appropriated for the purpose the full treasury left by Henry II; he removed thousands of officials, and reappointed them for a consideration; he sold charters of freedom to cities that could pay, and acknowledged Scotland's independence for 15,000 marks—not that he loved money less, but adventure more. Within half a year of his accession he was off to Palestine. He cared as little for his own safety as for others' rights; he taxed his realm to the utmost, and squandered revenue in luxury, feasting, and display; but he galloped through the final decade of the twelfth century with such bravado and bravery that his fellow poets ranked him above Alexander, Arthur, and Charlemagne.

He fought and loved Saladin, failed and swore to conquer him, turned homeward, and was captured on the way (1192) by Duke Leopold of Austria, whom he had offended in Asia. Early in 1193 Leopold surrendered him to the Emperor Henry VI, who held a grudge against Henry II and Richard; despite the law, generally recognized in Europe, against the detention of a Crusader, Henry VI kept the King of England prisoner in a castle at Dürnstein on the Danube, and demanded for him from England a ransom of 150,000 marks ($15,000,000)—double the whole annual revenue of the British crown. In the meantime Richard's brother John tried to seize the throne; resisted, he fled to France, and joined Philip Augustus in attacking England. Philip, violating a pledge of peace, attacked and seized English possessions in France, and offered great bribes to Henry VI to keep Richard prisoner. Richard fretted in comfortable durance, and wrote an excellent ballad [38] appealing to his country for ransom. Through this turmoil Eleanor governed successfully as regent, with the wise counsel of her justiciar Hubert Walter, Archbishop of Canterbury; but they found it hard to raise the ransom. Finally released (1194), Richard hurried to England, levied taxes and troops, and led an army across the Channel to avenge himself and Britain against Philip. Tradition holds that he refused the sacraments for years lest he be required to forgive his faithless enemy. He recovered all the territory that Philip had captured, and resigned himself to a peace that allowed Philip to live. In the interlude he quarreled with a vassal, Adhemar, Viscount of Limoges, who had found a cache of gold on his land. Adhemar offered Richard a part, Richard demanded all, and besieged him. An arrow from Adhemar's castle struck the King, and Richard Coeur de Lion died in his forty-third year in a dispute over a mess of gold.

His brother John (1199–1216)* succeeded him after some opposition and

---

* Nicknamed Lackland because, unlike his elder brothers, he had not received from his father any appanage on the Continent.

distrust; and Archbishop Walter made him swear a coronation oath that his throne was held by the election of the nation (i.e., the nobles and prelates) and the grace of God. But John, having been false to his father, his brother, and his wife, was not sorely hampered by one more vow. Like Henry II and Richard I he gave little evidence of religious belief. It was said that he had never taken the Eucharist since coming of age, not even on his coronation day.[39] The monks charged him with atheism, and told how, having caught a fat stag, he had remarked: "How plump and well fed is this animal! and yet, I dare swear, he never heard Mass"—which the monks resented as an allusion to their corpulence.[40] He was a man of much intellect and little scruple; an excellent administrator; "no great friend to the clergy," and therefore, said Holinshed, a bit maligned by monastic chroniclers;[41] not always in the wrong, but often alienating men by his sharp temper and wit, his scandalous humor, his proud absolutism, and the tax exactions to which he felt driven in defending Continental England against Philip Augustus.

In 1199 John secured permission from Pope Innocent III to divorce Isabel of Gloucester on grounds of consanguinity, and soon thereafter he married Isabella of Angoulême, despite her betrothal to the count of Lusignan. The nobility of both countries took offense, and the count appealed to Philip for redress. About the same time the barons of Anjou, Touraine, Poitou, and Maine protested to Philip that John was oppressing their provinces. By feudal fealties going back to the cession of Normandy to Rollo, the territorial lords of France, even in provinces owned by England, acknowledged the French king as their feudal suzerain; and by feudal law John, as Duke of Normandy, was vassal to the king of France. Philip summoned his royal vassal to come to Paris and defend himself against divers charges and appeals. John refused. The French feudal court declared his possessions in France forfeited, and awarded Normandy, Anjou, and Poitou to Arthur, Count of Brittany, a grandson of Henry II. Arthur laid claim to the throne of England, raised an army, and besieged at Mirabeau Queen Eleanor, who, though eighty, led a force in defense of her unruly son. John rescued her, captured Arthur, and apparently ordered his death. Philip invaded Normandy. John was too busy honeymooning at Rouen to lead his troops; they were defeated; John fled to England; and Normandy, Maine, Anjou, and Touraine passed to the French crown.

Pope Innocent III, at odds with Philip, had done what he could to help John; John now quarreled with Innocent. On the death of Hubert Walter (1205) the King persuaded the older monks of Canterbury to elect John de Gray, Bishop of Norwich, to the vacant see. A group of younger monks chose Reginald, their subprior, as archbishop. The rival candidates hurried to Rome, seeking papal confirmation; Innocent rejected them both, and appointed to the see Stephen Langton, an English prelate who for the past twenty-five years had lived in Paris, and was now a professor of theology in the university there. John protested that Langton had no preparation for the office of primate of England, a position involving political as well as ecclesiastical functions. Ignoring John's demurrers, Innocent, at Viterbo in Italy, consecrated Stephen archbishop of Canterbury (1207). John defied Langton to set foot on English soil; threatened to burn the cloisters over the heads of the rebellious Canterbury monks; and swore "by the teeth of God" that if the Pope laid an interdict on England he would banish every Catholic clergyman from the land, and would put out the eyes and cut off the nose of some of them for good measure. The interdict was pronounced (1208); all religious services of the clergy in England were suspended except baptism and extreme unction; churches were closed by the clergy, church bells were silenced, and the dead were buried in unconsecrated ground. John confiscated all episcopal or monastic properties, and gave them to laymen. Innocent excommunicated the King; John ignored the decree, and waged successful campaigns in Ireland, Scotland, and Wales. The people trembled under the interdict, but the nobles acquiesced in the spoliation of Church property as transiently diverting the royal appetite from their own wealth.

Proud of his apparent victory, John offended many by his excesses. He neglected his second wife to beget illegitimate children upon careless mistresses; jailed Jews to milk their money from them; allowed some imprisoned prelates to die of hardships; alienated nobles by adding insults to taxes; and strictly enforced the unpopular forestry laws. In 1213 Innocent used his last resort: he promulgated a decree of deposition against the English King, released John's subjects from their oath of allegiance, and declared the King's possessions to be now the lawful spoil of whoever could wrest them from his sacrilegious hands. Philip Augustus accepted the invitation, assembled an impressive army, and marched to the Channel coast. John prepared to resist invasion; but now he discovered that the nobles would not support him in a war against a Pope armed with physical as well as spiritual force. Furious against them, and seeing the imminence of defeat, he struck a bargain with Pandulf, the papal legate: if Innocent would withdraw his decrees of excommunication, interdict, and deposition, and would change from foe to friend, John pledged himself to return all confiscated ecclesiastical property, and to submit his crown and his kingdom to the Pope in feudal vassalage. It was so agreed; John surrendered all England to the Pope, and received it back, after five days, as a papal fief subject to perpetual tribute and fealty (1213).

John embarked for Poitou to attack Philip, and commanded the barons of England to follow him with arms and men. They refused. The victory of Philip at Bouvines deprived John of German and other allies to whom he had looked for aid against an expanding France. He returned to England to face an embittered aristocracy. The nobles resented his inordinate taxation for disastrous wars, his violations of precedent and law, his bartering of England for Innocent's forgiveness and support. To force the issue, John required of them a scutage—a money payment in lieu of military service. They sent him instead a deputation demanding a return to the laws of Henry I, which had protected the rights of the nobles and limited the powers of the king. Receiving no satisfactory answer, the nobles collected their armed forces at Stamford; and while John dallied at Oxford they sent emissaries to London, who won the support of the commune and the court. At Runnymede on the Thames, near Windsor, the forces of the aristocracy encamped opposite the few supporters of the King. There John made his second great surrender, and signed (1215) Magna Carta, the most famous document in English history.

> John, by the grace of God King of England . . . to his archbishops, bishops, abbots, earls, barons . . . and all his faithful subjects, greeting. Know ye that we . . . have by this our present Charter confirmed, for us and our heirs forever:
>
> 1. That the Church of England shall be free, and have her whole rights and liberties inviolable. . . .
>
> 2. We grant to all the freemen of our kingdom, for us and for our heirs forever, all the below-written liberties. . . .
>
> 12. No scutage or aid shall be imposed . . . unless by the general council of our kingdom. . . .
>
> 14. For holding the general council concerning the assessment of aids and scutage . . . we shall cause to be summoned the archbishops, bishops, abbots, earls, and greater barons of the realm * . . . and all others who hold of us in chief. . . .
>
> 15. We will not in future grant to anyone that he may take aid of his own free [non-slave] tenants, except to ransom his body, and to make his eldest son a knight, and once to marry his eldest daughter; and for this there shall be only a reasonable aid. . . .
>
> 17. Common pleas shall not follow our court, but shall be held in some fixed place. . . .
>
> 36. Nothing henceforth shall be given or taken for a writ of inquisition . . . but it shall be granted freely [i.e., no man shall be long imprisoned without trial]. . . .
>
> 39. No freeman shall be taken, or imprisoned, or disseised [dispossessed], or outlawed, or banished, or in any way destroyed . . . unless by the lawful judgment of his peers [his equals in rank], or by the law of the land.
>
> 40. We will sell to no man, we will not deny to any man, either justice or right.
>
> 41. All merchants shall have safe and secure conduct to go out of, and to come into, England, and to stay there, and to pass as well by land as by water, for buying or selling . . . without any unjust tolls. . . .
>
> 60. All the aforesaid customs and liberties . . . all people of our king-

---

* The five groups here named became later the House of Lords.

dom, as well clergy as laity, shall observe, as far as they are concerned, towards their dependents. . . .

Given under our hand, in the presence of witnesses, in the meadow called Runnymede, the 15th day of June, in the 17th year of our reign.[42]

The Great Charter deserves its fame as the foundation of the liberties today enjoyed by the English-speaking world. It was indeed limited; it defined the rights of the nobles and the clergy far more than of the whole people; no arrangements were made to implement the pious gesture of Article 60; the Charter was a victory for feudalism rather than for democracy. But it defined and safeguarded basic rights; it established habeas corpus and trial by jury; it gave to an incipient Parliament a power of the purse that would later arm the nation against tyranny; it transformed absolute into limited and constitutional monarchy.

John, however, had no idea that he had immortalized himself by surrendering his despotic powers or claims. He signed under duress; and on the morrow he plotted to annul the Charter. He appealed to the Pope; and Innocent III, whose policy now required the support of England against France, came to the defense of his humiliated vassal by proclaiming the Charter void, and forbidding John to obey, or the nobles to enforce, its terms. The barons ignored the decree. Innocent excommunicated them and the citizens of London and the Five Ports; but Stephen Langton, who had led in formulating the Charter, refused to publish the edict. Papal legates in England suspended Langton, promulgated the decree, raised an army of mercenaries in Flanders and France, and with it ravaged the English nobility with fire and sword, plunder, murder, and rape. Apparently the nobles had no dependable public support; instead of resisting with their own feudal levies they invited Louis, son of the French King, to invade England, defend them, and take the English throne as his reward; had the plan succeeded, England might have become part of France. Papal legates forbade Louis to cross the Channel, and excommunicated him and all his followers when he persisted. Louis, arriving in London, received the homage and fealty of the barons. Everywhere outside of mercantile London John was victorious, and merciless. Then, amid the energy and fury of his triumph, he was struck down by dysentery, made his way painfully to a monastery, died at Newark in the forty-ninth year of his age.

A papal legate crowned John's six-year-old son as Henry III (1216–72); a regency was formed with the earl of Pembroke at its head; encouraged by this elevation of one of their number, the nobles went over to Henry, and sent Louis back to France. Henry grew into an artist-king, a connoisseur of beauty, the inspiration and financier for the building of Westminster Abbey. He thought the Charter a disintegrating force, and tried to abrogate it, but failed. He taxed the nobles within an inch of revolution, always swearing that the latest levy would be the last. The popes needed money, too, and, with the

King's consent, drew tithes from English parishes to support the wars of the papacy against Frederick II. The memory of these exactions prepared the revolts of Wycliffe and Henry VIII.

Edward I (1272–1307) was less a scholar than his father, and more a king; ambitious, strong of will, tenacious in war, subtle in policy, rich in stratagems and spoils, yet capable of moderation and caution, and of farseeing purposes that made his reign one of the most successful in English history. He reorganized the army, trained a large force of archers in the use of the longbow, and established a national militia by ordering every able-bodied Englishman to possess, and learn the use of, arms; unwittingly, he created a military basis for democracy. So strengthened, he conquered Wales, won and lost Scotland, refused to pay the tribute that John had promised the popes, and abolished the papal suzerainty over England. But the greatest event of his reign was the development of Parliament. Perhaps without willing it, Edward became the central figure in England's finest achievement—the reconciliation, in government and character, of liberty and law.

4. The Growth of the Law

It was in this period—from the Norman Conquest to Edward II—that the law and government of England took the forms which they maintained till the nineteenth century. Through the superimposition of Norman feudal upon Anglo-Saxon local law, English law for the first time became national— no longer the law of Essex or Mercia or the Danelaw, but "the law and custom of the realm"; we can hardly realize now what a legal revolution was implied when Ranulf de Glanville (d. 1190) used this phrase.[43] Under the stimulus of Henry II, and the guidance of his justiciar Glanville, English law and courts acquired such repute for expedition and equity (tempered with corruption) that rival kings in Spain submitted their dispute to the royal court of England.[44] Glanville may have been the author of a *Treatise on Laws* (*Tractatus de legibus*) traditionally ascribed to him; in any case it is our oldest textbook of English law. Half a century later (1250–6) Henry de Bracton achieved the first systematic digest in his five-volume classic *On the Laws and Customs of England* (*De legibus et consuetudinibus Angliae*).

The King's rising need for money and troops forced the expansion of the Anglo-Saxon Witenagemot into the English Parliament. Impatient to raise more funds than the lords would vote him, Henry III summoned two knights from each county to join the barons and prelates in the Great Council of 1254. When Simon de Montfort, son of a famous Albigensian crusader, led a revolt of the nobles against Henry III in 1264, he tried to win the middle classes to his cause by asking not only two knights from each county, but also two leading citizens from each borough or town, to join the barons in a national assembly. The towns were growing, the merchants had money; it was worth while consulting these men if they would pay as well as talk. Edward I profited from Simon's example. Caught in the toils of simultaneous wars with Scotland, Wales, and France, he was constrained to seek the support and funds of all ranks. In 1295 he summoned the "Model Parliament," the first complete Parliament in English history. "What touches all," his writ of summons read, "should be approved by all, and . . . common dangers should be met by measures agreed upon in common." [45] So Edward invited two burgesses "from every city, borough, and leading town" to attend the Great Council at Westminster. These men were chosen by the more substantial citizens in each locality; no one dreamed of universal suffrage in a society where only a minority could read. In the "Model Parliament" itself the "commons" did not at once hold equal powers with the aristocracy. There was as yet no annual Parliament, meeting at its own will as the sole source of law. But by 1295 the principle was accepted that no statute passed by Parliament could be abrogated except by Parliament; and in 1297 it was further agreed that no taxes were to be levied without Parliament's consent. Such were the modest beginnings from which grew the most democratic government in history.

The clergy only reluctantly attended this enlarged Parliament. They sat apart, and refused to vote supplies except in their provincial assemblies. Ecclesiastical courts continued to try all cases involving canon law, and most cases involving any member of the clergy. Clerics accused of felonies might be tried by secular authorities; but those convicted of crimes short of high treason were, through "benefit of clergy," handed over to an ecclesiastical court, which alone could punish them. Moreover, most judges in secular tribunals were ecclesiastics, for education in law was largely confined to the clergy. Under Edward I the secular courts became more secular. When the clergy refused to join in voting supplies, Edward I, arguing that those who were protected by the state should share its burdens, directed his courts to hear no cause in which a churchman was plaintiff, but to try every suit in which a cleric was defendant.[46] In further retaliation Edward's Council of 1279, by the Statute of Mortmain, forbade the grant of lands to ecclesiastical bodies without the royal consent.

Despite this divided jurisdiction, English law developed rapidly under William I, Henry II, John, and Edward I. It was a thoroughly feudal law, and bore down heavily on the serf; crimes of freemen against serfs were usually amerced by fines. The law allowed women to own, inherit, or bequeath property, make contracts, sue and be sued, and gave the wife a dower right of one third in her husband's real property; but all the movable property that she brought to her marriage, or acquired during it, belonged to her husband.[47] Legally all land belonged to the king, and was held from him in fief. Normally the whole estate of a feudal lord was bequeathed to the eldest son, not only to keep the property intact, but to protect the feudal suzerain from a division of vassal responsibility in dues and war. Among the free peasantry no such rule of primogeniture obtained.

In so feudal a code the law of contract remained immature. An Assize of Measures (1197) standardized weights, measures, and coins, and provided state supervision of their use. Enlightened commercial legislation in England began with the Statute of Merchants (1283) and the Merchants' Charter (*Carta mercatoria*, 1303)—two more achievements of Edward I's creative reign.

Legal procedure slowly improved. To enforce the laws every ward had a "watch," every borough a constable, every shire a shire-reeve, or sheriff. All men were bound to raise a "hue and cry" on perceiving a violation of the law, and to join in pursuing the offender. Bail was admitted. It is a major credit to English law that torture was not used in examining suspects or witnesses. When Edward II was induced by Philip IV of France to arrest the English Templars, he could find no evidence by which to convict them. Thereupon Pope Clement V, doubtless constrained by Philip, wrote to Edward: "We hear that you forbid torture as contrary to the laws of your land. But no state law can override canon law, our law. Therefore I command you at once to submit those men to torture." [48] Edward yielded; but torture was not again used in English legal procedure till the reign of "Bloody" Mary (1553–8).

The Normans brought to England the old Frank system of *inquisitio*, or judicial inquiry by a *jurata* or sworn group of local citizens, into the fiscal and legal affairs of a district. The Assize of Clarendon (*c.* 1166) developed this "jury" plan by permitting litigants to submit the question of their veracity not to trial by combat but to "the country"—i.e., to a jury of twelve knights chosen from the local citizenry, in the presence of the court, by four knights named by the sheriff. This was the grand assize, or major sitting; in the petty assize, or minor session for the trial of ordinary cases, the sheriff himself chose twelve freemen from the neighborhood. Men shunned jury service then as now, and had no notion that the system would be one of the foundations of democracy. By the end of the thirteenth century verdict by a jury had almost everywhere in England replaced the old tests of barbarian law.

5. The English Scene

England in 1300 was ninety per cent rural, with a hundred towns whose modern successors would rank them as villages, and one city, London, boasting of 40,000 population [49]—four times more than any other town in England, but far inferior in wealth or beauty to Paris, Bruges, Venice, or Milan, not to speak of Constantinople, Palermo, or Rome. Houses were of wood, two or three stories high, with gabled roofs; often the upper story projected beyond the one beneath. City law forbade emptying the end products of kitchen, bedroom, or bath through the windows, but the tenants of upper stories often yielded to the convenience. Most of the slops from the houses found their way into the current of rain water that ran along the curbs. It was forbidden to cast feces, permissible to empty urinals, into this gutter stream.[50] The municipal council did what it could to improve sanitation—ordered citizens to clean the streets before their homes, levied fines for negligence, and hired "rakers" to gather garbage and filth and cart these to dung boats on the Thames. Horses, cattle, pigs, and poultry were kept by many citizens; but this was no great evil, since there were many open spaces, and nearly every house had a garden. Here and there rose a structure of stone like the Temple Church, Westminster Abbey, or the Tower of London, which William the Conqueror had built to guard his capital and shelter distinguished prisoners. Londoners were already proud of their city; soon Froissart would say that "they are of more weight than all the rest of England, for they are the most mighty in wealth and men"; and the monk Thomas of Walsingham would describe them as "of all people almost the most proud, arrogant, and greedy, disbelieving in ancient customs, disbelieving in God." [51]

Through these centuries the amalgamation of Norman, Anglo-Saxon, Danish, and Celtic stocks, speech, and ways produced the English nation, language, and character. As Normandy fell away from England, the Norman families in Britain forgot Normandy and learned to love their new land. The mystic and poetic qualities of the Celt remained, especially in the lower classes, but were tempered by Norman vigor and earthiness. Amid the strife of nations and classes, and the blows of famine and plague, the resultant Briton could still make what Henry of Huntingdon (1084?–1155) called *Anglia plena iocis*—Merry England—a nation of abounding energy, rude jests, boisterous games, good fellowship, a love of dancing, minstrelsy, and ale. From those virile loins and generations would come the hearty sensuality of Chaucer's pilgrims, and the magnificent bombast of the cultured swash-bucklers of the Elizabethan age.

IX. IRELAND—SCOTLAND—WALES: 1066–1318

In the year 1154 Henry II became King of England, and an Englishman, Nicholas Breakspear, became Pope Hadrian IV. A year later Henry sent John of Salisbury to Rome with a subtle message: Ireland was in a state of political chaos, literary decline, moral debasement, religious independence and decay; would not the Pope permit Henry to take possession of the individualistic isle and restore it to social order and papal obedience? If we may believe Giraldus Cambrensis, the Pope agreed, and by the bull *Laudabiliter* granted Ireland to Henry on condition of restoring orderly government there, bringing the

Irish clergy into better co-operation with Rome, and arranging that a penny (83¢) should be paid yearly to the See of Peter for every house in Ireland.[52] Henry was too busy at the time to take advantage of this *nihil obstat*; but he remained in a receptive mood.

In 1166 Dermot MacMurrough, King of Leinster, was defeated in war by Tiernan O'Rourke, King of Brefni, whose wife he had seduced. Expelled by his subjects, he fled with his beautiful daughter Eva to England and France, and secured from Henry II a letter assuring royal good will to any of his subjects who should help Dermot to regain the Leinster throne. At Bristol Dermot received from Richard FitzGilbert, Earl of Pembroke in Wales, known as "Strongbow," a pledge of military support in return for Eva's hand in marriage, and the succession to Dermot's kingdom. In 1169 Richard led a small force of Welshmen into Ireland, restored Dermot with the help of the Leinster clergy, and, on Dermot's death (1171), inherited the kingdom. Rory O'Connor, then High King of Ireland, led an army against the Welsh invaders, and bottled them up in Dublin. The besieged made an heroic sortie, and the ill-trained and poorly equipped Irish fled. Summoned by Henry II, Strongbow crossed to Wales, met the King, and agreed to surrender to him Dublin and other Irish ports, and to hold the rest of Leinster in fief from the English crown. Henry landed near Waterford (1171) with 4000 men, won the support of the Irish clergy, and received the allegiance of all Ireland except Connaught and Ulster; the Welsh conquest was turned into a Norman-English conquest without a battle. A synod of Irish prelates declared their full submission to the Pope, and decreed that thereafter the ritual of the Irish Church should conform to that of England and Rome. Most of the Irish kings were allowed to keep their thrones, on condition of feudal fealty and annual tribute to the king of England.

Henry had accomplished his purpose with economy and skill, but he erred in thinking that the forces which he left behind him could sustain order and peace. His appointees fought one another for the spoils, and their aides and troops plundered the country with a minimum of restraint. The conquerors did their best to reduce the Irish to serfdom. The Irish resisted with guerrilla warfare, and the result was a century of turmoil and destruction. In 1315 some Irish chieftains offered Ireland to Scotland, where Robert Bruce had just defeated the English at Bannockburn. Robert's brother Edward landed in Ireland with 6000 men; Pope John XXII pronounced excommunication upon all who should aid the Scots; but nearly all Irishmen rose at Edward's call, and in 1316 they crowned him King. Two years later he was defeated and slain near Dundalk, and the revolt collapsed in poverty and despair.

The Scots, said Ranulf Higden, a fourteenth-century Briton, "be light of heart, strong and wild enough; but by mixing with Englishmen, they be much amended. They be cruel upon their enemies, and hate bondage most of anything, and hold it foul sloth if any man dieth in bed, and great worship if he die in the field." [53]

Ireland remained Irish but lost its liberty; Scotland became British, but remained free. Angles, Saxons, and Normans multiplied in the lowlands, and reorganized agricultural life on a feudal plan. Malcolm III (1058–93) was a warrior who repeatedly invaded England; but his Queen Margaret was an Anglo-Saxon princess who converted the Scottish court to the English language, brought in English-speaking clergy, and reared her sons in English ways. The last and strongest of them, David I (1124–53), made the Church his chosen instrument of rule, founded English-speaking monasteries at Kelso, Dryburgh, Melrose, and Holyrood, levied tithes (for the first time in Scotland) for the support of the Church, and gave so lavishly to bishops and abbots that people mistook him for a saint. Under David I Scotland, in all but its highlands, became an English state.[54]

But it was not the less independent. The English immigrants were transformed into patriotic Scots; from their number came the Stuarts and the Bruces. David I invaded and captured Northumberland; Malcolm IV (1153–65) lost it; William the Lion (1165–1214), trying to regain it, was taken prisoner by Henry II, and was freed only on pledging homage to the king of England for the Scottish crown (1174). Fifteen years later he bought release from this pledge by helping to finance Richard I in the Third Crusade, but the English kings continued to claim feudal suzerainty over Scotland. Alexander III (1249–86) recovered the Hebrides from Norway, maintained friendly relations with England, and gave Scotland a golden age of prosperity and peace.

At Alexander's death Robert Bruce and John Balliol, descendants of David I, contested the succession. Edward I of England seized the opportunity; by his support Balliol was made King, but acknowledged the overlordship of England (1292). When, however, Edward ordered Balliol to raise troops to fight for England in France, the Scotch nobles and bishops rebelled, and bade Balliol make alliance with France against England (1295). Edward defeated the Scots at Dunbar (1296), received the submission of the aristocracy, dethroned Balliol, appointed three Englishmen to rule Scotland for him, and returned to England.

Many Scotch nobles owned land in England, and were thereby mortgaged to obedience. But the older Gaelic Scots strongly resented the surrender. One of them, Sir William Wallace, organized an "army of the commons of Scotland," routed the English garrison, and for a year ruled Scotland as regent for Balliol. Edward returned, and defeated Wallace at Falkirk (1298). In 1305 he captured Wallace and had him disemboweled and quartered according to the English law of treason.

A year later another defender was forced into the field. Robert Bruce, grandson of the Bruce who had claimed the throne in 1286, quarreled with John Comyn, a leading representative of Edward I in Scotland, and killed him. Thereby committed to rebellion, Bruce had himself crowned King, though only a small group of nobles supported him, and the pope excommunicated him for his crime. Edward once more marched north, but died on the way (1307). Edward II's incompetence was a blessing for Bruce; the nobles and clergy of Scotland rallied to the outlaw's banner; his reinforced armies, bravely led by his brother Edward and Sir James Douglas, captured Edinburgh, invaded Northumberland, and seized Durham. In 1314 Edward II led into Scotland the largest army that the land had ever seen, and met the Scots at Bannockburn. Bruce had had his men dig and conceal pits before his position; many of the English, charging, fell into the morass, and the English army was almost totally destroyed. In 1328 the regents for Edward III, involved in war with France, signed the Treaty of Northampton, making Scotland once more free.

Meanwhile a like struggle had come to other issue in Wales. William I claimed suzerainty over it as part of the realm of the defeated Harold. He had no time to add it to his conquests, but he set up three earldoms on its eastern frontier, and encouraged their lords to expand them into Wales. South Wales was meanwhile overrun by Norman buccaneers, who left the prefix Fitz (*fils*, son) on some Welsh names. In 1094 Cadwgan ap Bledyn subdued these Normans; in 1165 the Welsh defeated the English at Corwen; and Henry II, busy with Becket, acknowledged the independence of South Wales under its enlightened King Rhys ap Gruffydd (1171). Llywelyn the Great, by his ability in both war and statesmanship, extended his rule over nearly all the country. His sons quarreled and disordered the land, but his grandson Llywelyn ap Gruffydd (d. 1282) restored unity, made peace with Henry III, and created for himself the title of Prince of Wales. Edward I, intent on uniting Wales and Scotland with England, invaded Wales with an immense army and fleet (1282); Llywelyn died in a chance encounter with a small border force; his brother David was captured by Edward, and his severed head, with Llywelyn's, was suspended from the Tower of London and left to bleach in the sun, wind, and rain. Wales was made a part of England (1284), and Edward in 1301 gave the title of Prince of Wales to the heir to the English throne.

Through these exaltations and depressions the Welsh kept their own language and their old customs, tilled their rough soil with obstinate courage, and solaced their days and nights with legend, poetry, music, and song. Their bards now gave form to the tales of the *Mabinogion*, enriching literature with a mystic melodious tenderness uniquely Welsh. Annually the bards and minstrels assembled in a national eisteddfod (from *eistedd*, to sit), which can be traced back to 1176; contests were held in oratory, poetry, singing, and the playing of musical instruments. The Welsh could fight bravely, but not long; they were soon eager to return and protect at first hand their women, children, and homes; and one of their proverbs wished that "every ray of the sun were a poniard to pierce the friends of war." [55]

X. THE RHINELANDS: 1066–1315

The countries huddled about the lower Rhine and its many mouths were among the richest in the medieval world. South of the Rhine lay the county of Flanders, running from Calais through modern Belgium to the Scheldt. Formally it was a fief held from the French king; actually it was ruled by a dynasty of enlightened counts, checked only by the proud autonomy of the towns. Near the Rhine the people were Flemish, of Low German origin, and spoke a German dialect; west of the Lys River they were Walloons—a mixture of Germans and French on a Celtic base—and spoke a dialect of French. Commerce and industry fattened and disturbed Ghent, Audenaarde, Courtrai, Ypres, and Kassel in the Flemish northeast, and Bruges, Lille, and Douai in the Walloon southwest; in these cities population was denser than anywhere else in Europe north of the Alps. In 1300 the cities dominated the counts; the magistrates of the larger communities formed a supreme court for the county, and negotiated on their own authority with foreign cities and governments.[56] Usually the counts co-operated with the cities, encouraged manufactures and trade, maintained a stable currency, and as early as 1100 —two centuries before England—established uniform measures and weights for all the towns.

The class war ultimately destroyed the freedom of both the cities and the counts. As the proletariat rose in number, resentment, and power, and the counts sided with them as an offset to the bumptious *bourgeoisie*, the merchants sought support from Philip Augustus of France, who promised it in the hope of bringing Flanders effectively under the French crown. England, anxious to keep the chief market for her wool out of the control of the French king, allied herself with the counts of Flanders and Hainault, the duke of Brabant, and Otto IV of Germany. Philip defeated this coalition at Bouvines (1214), subdued the counts, and protected the merchants in their oligarchic regime. The conflict of powers and classes continued. In 1297 Count Guy de Dampierre again allied Flanders with England; Philip the Fair invaded Flanders, imprisoned Guy, and forced him to cede the country to France. But when the French army moved to occupy Bruges the commons rose, overcame the troops, massacred rich merchants, and gained possession of the town. Philip sent a large army to avenge this affront; the workers of the towns formed themselves into an impromptu army, and defeated the knights and mercenaries of France in the battle of Courtrai (1302). The aged Guy de Dampierre was released and restored, and the strange alliance of feudal counts and revolutionary *proletaires* enjoyed a decade of victory.

What we now know as Holland was, from the third to the ninth century, part of the Frank kingdom. In 843 it became the northernmost portion of the buffer state of Lorraine created by the Treaty of Verdun. In the ninth and tenth centuries it was divided into feudal fiefs for better resistance to Norse raids. The Germans who cleared and settled the heavily wooded district north of the Rhine called it Holtland, i.e., Woodland. Most of the people were serfs, absorbed in the struggle to wrest a living from a land that had always to be diked or drained; half of Holland exists by the taming of the sea. But there were cities, too, not quite as rich and turbulent as the Flemish towns, but soundly based on steady industry and orderly trade. Dordrecht was the most prosperous; Utrecht was a center of learning; Haarlem was the seat of the Count of Holland; Delft became the capital for a time; then, toward 1250, The Hague.* Amsterdam made its debut in 1204, when a feudal lord built a fortress château at the mouth of the Amstel River; the sheltered site on the Zuider Zee, and the pervasive canals, invited commerce; in 1297 the city was made a free port, where goods could be received and reshipped free of customs duties; and thenceforth little Holland played a large part in the economic world. There as elsewhere commerce nourished culture; in the thirteenth century we find a Dutch poet, Maerlant, who vigorously satirized the luxurious life of the clergy; and in the monasteries Dutch art, in sculpture, pottery, painting, and illumination, was beginning its unique and extraordinary career.

South of Holland lay the duchy of Brabant, which then contained the cities of Antwerp, Brussels, and Louvain. Liége was ruled independently by its bishops, who allowed it a large measure of autonomy. Still farther south were the counties of Hainault, Namur, Limburg, and Luxembourg; the duchy of Lorraine, with the cities of Trier, Nancy, and Metz; and several other principalities, nominally subject to the German emperor, but left for the most part to their ruling counts. Each of these districts had a vibrant history of politics, love, and war; we salute them and move on. South and west of them lay Burgundy, in what is now east central France; its varying boundaries discourage definition; its political fortunes would fill vain tomes. In 888 Rudolf I made it an independent kingdom; in 1032 Rudolf III bequeathed it to Germany; but in that year part of it was united, as a duchy, to France. The dukes of Burgundy, like its early kings, governed with intelligence, and for

---

* The counts had previously used the place as a hunting rendezvous; hence its name, *'s Graven Haag,* the Count's Lodge, now den Haag.

the most part cherished peace. Their great age would come in the fifteenth century.

In classical times Switzerland was the home of diverse tribes—Helvetii, Raeti, Lepontii—of mixed Celtic, Teutonic, and Italic origin. In the third century the Alemanni occupied and Germanized the northern plateau. After the collapse of the Carolingian Empire the land was divided into feudal fiefs subject to the Holy Roman Empire. But it is difficult to enslave mountaineers; and the Swiss, while acknowledging some feudal dues, soon liberated themselves from serfdom. The villages in democratic assemblies chose their own officials, and ruled themselves by the ancient Germanic laws of the Alemanni and Burgundians. For mutual protection the peasants neighboring Lake Lucerne formed themselves into "Forest Cantons" (*Waldstätte*)—Uri, Nidwalden, and Schwyz, which later gave its name to the state. The sturdy burghers of the towns that had grown along the Alpine passes—Geneva, Constance, Fribourg, Berne, and Basel—elected their own officials, and administered their own laws. Their feudal overlords raised no objection to this so long as basic feudal taxes were paid.[57]

The Hapsburg counts who, from 1173, held the northern districts, proved an exception to this rule, and earned the hatred of the men of Schwyz by attempting to apply feudal dues in full severity. In 1291 the three Forest Cantons formed an "Everlasting League," and swore a *confederatio* to give one another aid against external aggression or internal disturbance, to arbitrate all differences, and to recognize no judge who was not a native of the valley, or had bought his office. Lucerne, Zurich, and Constance soon joined the League. In 1315 the Hapsburg dukes sent two armies into Switzerland to enforce all feudal dues. In the pass of Morgarten the infantry of Schwyz and Uri, armed with halberds, defeated the Austrian cavalry in "the Marathon of Switzerland." The Austrian forces withdrew; the three cantons renewed their oath of mutual support (December 9, 1315), and created the Swiss Confederacy. It was not yet an independent state; the free citizens acknowledged certain feudal obligations, and the suzerainty of the Holy Roman Emperor. But feudal lords and holy emperors had learned to respect the arms and liberties of the Swiss cantons and towns; and the victory of Morgarten had opened the way to the most stable and sensible democracy in history.*

---

* There appears to be no historical warrant for the existence of William Tell.[58]

XI. FRANCE: 1060–1328

1. *Philip Augustus*

At the accession of Philip II Augustus (1180) France was a minor and harassed state, hardly promising any grandeur to come. England held Normandy, Brittany, Anjou, Touraine, and Aquitaine—a domain thrice the size of that directly controlled by the French king. Most of Burgundy adhered to Germany, and the flourishing county of Flanders was in effect an independent principality. So were the counties of Lyons, Savoy, and Chambéry. So was Provence—southeastern France—rich in wine, oil, fruit, poets, and the cities of Arles and Avignon, Aix and Marseille. The Dauphiné, centering about Vienne, had been bequeathed to Germany as part of Burgundy; it was now independently ruled by a *dauphin* who took his title from the dolphin that was an emblem of his family.

France proper was divided into duchies, counties, seignories, seneschalties, and *bailliages* (bailiwicks) governed—in order of increasing dependence upon the king—by dukes, counts, seigneurs, seneschals (royal stewards), and bailiffs. This loose aggregation, already called Francia in the ninth century, was in diverse degrees, and with many limitations, subject to the French king. Paris, his capital, was in 1180 a city of wooden buildings and muddy streets; its Roman name, Lutetia, had meant the town of mud. Philip Augustus, shocked by the smell of the thoroughfares that ran beside the Seine, ordered that all the streets of Paris should be paved with solid stone.[59]

He was the first of three powerful rulers who in this age raised France to the intellectual, moral, and political leadership of Europe. But there had been strong men before him. Philip I (1060–1108) made a secure niche for himself in history by divorcing his wife at forty and persuading Count Fulk of Anjou to cede to him the Countess Bertrade. A priest was found to solemnize the adultery as marriage, but Pope Urban II, coming to France to preach the First Crusade, excommunicated the King. Philip persisted in sin for twelve years; at last he sent Bertrade away and was shriven; but a while later he repented his repentance, and resumed his Queen. She traveled with him to Anjou, taught her two husbands amity, and seems to have served both of them to the best of her charms.[60]

Having grown fat at forty-five, Philip handed over the major affairs of state to his son Louis VI (1108–37), himself known as Louis the Fat. He deserved a better name. For twenty-four years he fought, finally with success, the robber barons who plundered travelers on the roads; he strengthened the monarchy by organizing a competent army; he did what he could to protect the peasants, the artisans, and the communes; and he had the good sense to make the Abbot Suger his chief minister and friend. Suger of St.

Denis (1081–1151) was the Richelieu of the twelfth century. He managed the affairs of France with wisdom, justice, and farsight; he encouraged and improved agriculture; he designed and built one of the earliest and finest masterpieces of the Gothic style; and he wrote an illuminating account of his ministry and work. He was the most valuable bequest left by Louis the Fat to his son, whom Suger served till death.

Louis VII (1137–80) was the man of whom Eleanor of Aquitaine said that she had married a king only to find him a monk. He labored conscientiously at his royal tasks, but his virtues ruined him. His devotion to government appeared to Eleanor as marital neglect; his patience with her amours added insult to negligence; she divorced him, and gave her hand and her duchy of Aquitaine to Henry II of England. Disillusioned with life, Louis turned to piety, and left to his son the task of building a strong France.

Philip II Augustus, like a later Philippe, was a *bourgeois gentilhomme* on the throne: a master of practical intelligence softened with sentiment, a patron of learning with no taste for it, a man of shrewd caution and prudent courage, of quick temper and ready amnesty, of unscrupulous but controlled acquisitiveness, of a moderated piety that could be generous to the Church without allowing religion to countermand his politics, and of a patient perseverance that won what bold adventurousness might never have attained. Such a man, at once prosaic and *auguste*,* amiably inflexible and ruthlessly wise, was what his country needed at a time when, between Henry II's England and Barbarossa's Germany, France might have ceased to be.

His marriages disturbed Europe. His first wife, Isabella, died in 1189; and four years later he married Ingeborg, a princess of Denmark. These marriages were political, and brought more property than romance. Ingeborg was not to Philip's taste; he ignored her after a day; and within the year he persuaded a council of French bishops to grant him a divorce. Pope Celestine III refused to confirm the decree. In 1196, defying the Pope, he married Agnes of Meran. Celestine excommunicated him, but Philip remained obstinate; "I had rather lose half my domains," he said in a moment of tenderness, "than separate from Agnes." Innocent III commanded him to take back Ingeborg; when Philip refused, the invincible Pope interdicted religious services in Philip's domain. Philip, in a rage, deposed all bishops who obeyed the interdict. "Happy Saladin!" he mourned, "who had no pope above him"; and he threatened to turn Mohammedan.[61] After four years of this spiritual war the people began to grumble with fear of hell. Philip dismissed his beloved Agnes (1202), but kept Ingeborg confined at Étampes till 1213, when he recalled her to his bed.

Amid these joys and tribulations Philip reconquered Normandy from England (1204), and in the next two years annexed Brittany, Anjou, Maine,

---

* This title, applied to him by his chaplain, found no medieval currency, but was applied to him by modern French historians.

Touraine, and Poitou to his directly ruled terrain. He was now strong enough to dominate all the dukes, counts, and seigneurs of his realm; his *baillis* and seneschals supervised local government; his kingdom had become an international power, not a strip of land along the Seine. John of England, so shorn, was not resigned; he persuaded Otto IV of Germany and the counts of Boulogne and Flanders to join him against this swelling France; John would attack through Aquitaine (still England's), the others from the northeast. Instead of dividing his forces to meet these separate assaults, Philip led his main army against John's allies, and defeated them at Bouvines, near Lille (1214). That battle decided many issues. It deposed Otto, secured the German throne to Frederick II, ended German hegemony, and hastened the decline of the Holy Roman Empire. It reduced the counts of Flanders to French obedience, added Amiens, Douai, Lille, and St. Quentin to the French crown, and in effect extended northeastern France to the Rhine. It left John helpless against his barons, and forced him to sign Magna Carta. It weakened monarchy and strengthened feudalism in England and Germany, while it strengthened monarchy and weakened feudalism in France. And it favored the growth of the French communes and middle classes, which had vigorously supported Philip in peace and war.

Having trebled the royal domain, Philip governed it with devotion and skill. Half the time at odds with the Church, he replaced ecclesiastics in council and administration with men from the rising lawyer class. He gave charters of autonomy to many cities, encouraged trade by privileges to merchants, alternately protected and plundered the Jews, and fattened his exchequer by commuting feudal services into money payments; the royal revenue was doubled from 600 to 1200 livres ($240,000) a day. In his reign the façade of Notre Dame was completed, and the Louvre was built as a fortress to guard the Seine.[62] When Philip died (1223) the France of today had been born.

2. St. Louis

His son Louis VIII (1223–6) ruled too briefly to accomplish much; history remembers him chiefly for having married the admirable Blanche of Castile, and begetting by her the one man in medieval history who, like Ashoka in ancient India, succeeded in being at once and in fact a saint and a king. Louis IX was twelve, his mother was thirty-eight, when Louis VIII died. Daughter of Alfonso IX of Castile, granddaughter of Henry II and Eleanor of Aquitaine, Blanche lived up to her royal blood. She was a woman of beauty and charm, energy, character, and skill; at the same time she impressed her age by her untarnished virtue as wife and widow, and her devotion as the mother of eleven children; France honored her not only as *Blanche la bonne reine*, but equally as *Blanche la bonne mère*. She freed many serfs on the royal estates, spent great sums on charity, and provided dowries for girls whose poverty discouraged love. She helped to finance the building of Chartres Cathedral, and it was through her influence that its stained glass showed Mary not as virgin but as queen.[63] She loved her son Louis too jealously, and was ungenerous to his wife. She trained him sedulously to Christian virtue, and told him that she would rather see him dead than have him commit a mortal sin;[64] but it was not her doing that he became a devotee. She herself rarely sacrificed policy to sentiment; she joined in the cruel Albigensian Crusade to extend the power of the crown in southern France. For nine years (1226–35), while Louis grew up, she governed the realm; and seldom has France been better ruled. At the outset of her regency the barons revolted, thinking to recapture from a woman the powers they had lost to Philip II; she overcame them with wise and patient diplomacy. She resisted England ably, and then signed a truce on just terms. When Louis IX came of age and assumed the government, he inherited a kingdom powerful, prosperous, and at peace.

He was a handsome lad, taller by a head than most of his knights, with finely cut features, clear skin, and rich blond hair; elegant in tastes, fond of luxurious furniture and colorful clothes; no bookworm, but given to hunting and falconry, amusements and athletic games; not yet a saint, for a monk complained to Blanche of the royal flirtations; she found him a wife, and he settled down. He became a model of conjugal fidelity and parental energy; he had eleven children, and took an intimate share in their education. Gradually he abandoned luxury, lived more and more simply, and consumed himself in government, charity, and piety. He had a kingly conception of monarchy as an organ of national unity and continuity, and as a protection of the poor and weak against the superior or fortunate few.

He respected the rights of the nobles, encouraged them to fulfill their obligations to serfs and vassals and suzerain, but would brook no feudal infringements of the new royal power. He interfered resolutely to repress injustices of lord to man, and in several cases severely punished barons who had executed men without due trial. When Enguerrand de Coucy hanged three Flemish students for killing some rabbits on his estate, Louis had him locked up in the tower of the Louvre, threatened to hang him, and released him on condition that he build three chapels where Masses were to be said daily for his victims; that he give the forest where the young scholars had hunted to the abbey of St. Nicholas; that he lose on his estates the rights of jurisdiction and hunting; that he serve three years in Palestine; and pay the King a fine of 12,500 pounds.[65] Louis forbade feud vengeance and private feudal war, and condemned the judicial duel. As trial by evidence replaced trial by combat, the baronial courts were progressively superseded by the royal courts organized in each locality by the bailiffs of the King; the right of appeal from baronial judges to the central royal court was established; and in France, as in England, the thirteenth century saw feudal law give way to a common law of the realm. Never since Roman days had France enjoyed such security and prosperity; in this reign the wealth of France sufficed to bring Gothic architecture to its greatest abundance and perfection.

He believed and proved that a government could be just and generous in its foreign relations without losing prestige and power. He avoided war as long as possible; but when aggression threatened he organized his armies efficiently, planned his campaigns, and—in Europe—carried them through with energy and skill to an honorable peace that left no passion for revenge. As soon as the safety of France was assured, he adopted a policy of conciliation which accepted the compromise of opposed rights while rejecting the appeasement of unjust claims. He restored to England and Spain territory that his predecessors had seized; his councilors mourned, but peace endured, and France remained free from attack even during the long absences of Louis on crusades. "Men feared him," said William of Chartres, "because they knew that he was just." [66] From 1243 to 1270 France waged no war against a Christian foe. When her neighbors fought one another Louis labored to reconcile them, scorning the suggestion of his council that such strife should be fomented to weaken potential enemies.[67] Foreign kings submitted their disputes to his arbitration. People marveled that so good a man should be so good a king.

He was not "that perfect monster whom the world ne'er knew"—the completely faultless man. He was occasionally irritable, perhaps through ill health. The simplicity of his soul sometimes verged upon culpable ignorance or credulity, as in the ill-conceived crusades and maladroit campaigns in Egypt and Tunisia, where he lost many lives besides his own; and though he was honest with his Moslem enemies he could not apply to them the same generous understanding that had succeeded so well with his Christian foes. His childlike certitude of belief led him to a religious intolerance that helped to establish the Inquisition in France, and it quieted his natural pity for the victims of the Albigensian Crusade. His treasury was swelled by confiscating the goods of condemned heretics,[68] and his usual good humor failed him toward the French Jews.

But with these deductions he came nobly close to the Christian ideal. "On no day of my life," reports Joinville, "did I ever hear him speak evil of anyone." [69] When his Moslem captors accepted by mistake a sum 10,000 livres ($2,000,000) short of the ransom promised for his release, Louis, restored safely to freedom, sent to the Saracens the additional payment in full, to the disgust of his councilors.[70] Before leaving on his first crusade he bade his officials, throughout his realm, to "receive in writing, and to examine, the grievances that may be brought against us or our ancestors, as also allegations of injustices or exactions of ·which our bailiffs, provosts, foresters, sergeants, or their subordinates may have been guilty." [71] "Ofttimes," says Joinville, "he would go, after Mass, and seat himself against a tree in the wood of Vincennes, and make us sit around him. And all those who had any cause in hand came and spoke to him without hindrance or usher." He would settle some cases himself, and turn others over to the councilors seated about him, but he gave each pleader the right of appeal to the king.[72] He founded and endowed hospitals, asylums, monasteries, hospices, a home for the blind, and another (the Filles-Dieu) for redeemed prostitutes. He ordered his agents in each province to search out the old and poor and provide for them at the public expense. Wherever he went he made it a principle to feed, every day, 120 poor people; he had three of them join him for dinner, served them himself, and washed their feet.[73] Like Henry III of England, he waited on lepers, and fed them with his own hands. When famine struck Normandy he spent an enormous sum getting food to the needy there. He gave alms daily to the sick, the poor, widows, women in confinement, prostitutes, disabled workingmen, "so that hardly it would be possible to number his alms." [74] Nor were these acts of charity spoiled by publicity. The poor whose feet he washed were chosen from the blind; the act was done in private, and the recipients were not told that their attendant was the king. His ascetic self-lacerations were unknown to others until revealed on his flesh after his death.[75]

In the campaign of 1242 he contracted malaria in the marshy regions of Saintonge; it brought on pernicious anemia, and in 1244 he was near death. Perhaps such experiences turned him more and more to religion; indeed, it was on recovering from that illness that he took the oath to crusade. He weakened himself with ascetic self-mortification. When he returned from his first crusade, aged only thirty-eight, he was already bent and bald, and nothing remained of his youthful beauty except the radiant grace of his simple faith and good will. He wore a hair shirt under a monk's brown robe, and had himself scourged with little iron chains. He loved the new monastic orders, Franciscans and Dominicans, gave to them without stint, and was with difficulty dissuaded from himself becoming a Franciscan. He heard two Masses daily, recited the canonical prayers of tierce, sext, none, vespers, and compline, said fifty Ave Marias before retiring, and rose at midnight to join the priests at matins in the chapel.[76] He abstained from marital inter-course in Advent and Lent. Most of his subjects smiled at his devotions, and called him "Brother Louis." One bold woman told him: "It would be better that another should be king in your place, for you are only king of the Franciscans and the Dominicans. . . . It is an outrage that you should be king of France. It is a great marvel that they don't put you out." Louis replied: "You tell the truth . . . I am not worthy to be king, and if it had pleased our Saviour, another would have been in my place, who would have known better how to govern the kingdom." [77]

He shared with enthusiasm in the superstitions of his time. The abbey of St. Denis claimed to have a nail from the True Cross; one day the nail was mislaid after its ceremonial exhibition to the people; a great furore arose; the nail was found, and the King was much relieved; "I had rather," he said, "that the best city in my kingdom had been swallowed up." [78] In 1236 Baldwin II of Constantinople, appealing for funds to rescue his ailing state, sold to Louis for 11,000 livres ($2,200,000) the crown of thorns worn by Jesus during His Passion. Five years later Louis bought from the same auctioneer a piece of the True Cross. Possibly these purchases were intended as grants in aid to a Christian kingdom in distress. To receive the relics Louis commissioned Peter of Montreuil to build Sainte Chapelle.

With all his deep piety Louis was no tool of the clergy. He recognized their human shortcomings, and chastised them with good example and open rebuke. [79] He restricted the powers of ecclesiastical courts, and asserted the authority of the law over all citizens, lay or clerical. In 1268 he issued the first Pragmatic Sanction, limiting the power of the papacy in ecclesiastical appointments and taxation in France: "We will that no one may raise or collect in any manner exactions or assessments of money, which have been imposed by the court of Rome . . . unless the cause be reasonable, pious, most urgent . . . and recognized by our express and spontaneous consent, and by that of the Church of our realm." *

Despite his monastic propensities Louis always remained the king, and preserved the royal majesty even when, as Fra Salimbene describes him, "spare and slender, having the face of an angel, and a countenance full of grace," [81] he appeared on foot, in pilgrim's habit and with pilgrim's staff, to begin his first crusade (1248). Queen Blanche, whom he left, despite her sixty years, as regent with the fullest powers, wept as they parted: "Most sweet fair son, fair tender son, I shall never see you more." [82] He was captured in Egypt, and was held for a ransom that Blanche with great difficulty raised and paid; but when, defeated and humbled, he returned to France (1252), he found his mother dead. In 1270, weak with illness, he set out again, this time for Tunisia. It was not so quixotic an enterprise as its failure made it out to be. Louis had allowed his brother, Charles of Anjou, to lead a French army into Italy not only to check German domination there, but also in the hope that Sicily might be made a base for a French invasion of Tunisia. Shortly after reaching Tunisia the great crusader, older in body than in years, died of dysentery. Twenty-seven years later the Church canonized him. Generations and centuries looked back to his reign as the Golden Age of France, and wondered why an inscrutable Providence would not send them his like again. He was a Christian king.

---

* Milman, *History of Latin Christianity*, VI, 119. The edict is generally accepted as genuine; [80] but it may have been forged by the lawyers of Philip IV as a weapon against Boniface VIII; cf. *The Catholic Encyclopedia*, s.v. Louis IX.

3. *Philip the Fair*

France was strengthened by the Crusades, in which she took a leading part. The long reigns of Philip Augustus and Louis IX gave her government continuity and stability, while England suffered the negligent Richard I, the reckless John, and the incompetent Henry III, and while Germany disintegrated in the wars between the emperors and the popes. By 1300 France was the strongest power in Europe.

Philip IV (1285–1314) was called *le Bel* for his handsome figure and face, not for his subtle statecraft and pitiless audacity. His aims were vast: to bring all classes—nobles and clergy as well as townsmen and serfs—under the direct law and control of the king; to base French growth on commerce and industry rather than on agriculture; and to extend the boundaries of France to the Atlantic, the Pyrenees, the Mediterranean, the Alps, and the Rhine. He chose his aides and councilors not from the great ecclesiastics and barons who had served French kings for four centuries past, but from the lawyer class that came to him impregnate with the imperial ideas of Roman law. Pierre Flotte and Guillaume de Nogaret were brilliant intellects careless of morals and precedents; under their guidance Philip rebuilt the legal structure of France, replaced feudal with royal law, overcame his foes by shrewd diplomacy, and in the end broke the power of the papacy, and made the pope in effect a prisoner of France. He tried to detach Guienne from England, but found Edward I too strong for him. He won Champagne, Brie, and Navarre by marriage, and bought with hard cash Chartres, Franche-Comté, the Lyonnais, and part of Lorraine.

Always needing money, he spent half his wits and time inventing taxes and raising funds. He commuted for money the military obligations of the barons to the crown. He repeatedly debased the coinage, and insisted on taxes being paid in bullion or in honest coin. He exiled the Jews and the Lombards, and destroyed the Templars, to confiscate their wealth. He forbade the export of precious metal from his realm. He laid heavy taxes upon exports, imports, and sales, and a war tax of a penny upon every livre of private wealth in France. Finally, without consulting the pope, he taxed the wealth of the Church, which now owned a quarter of the land of France. The results belong to the story of Boniface VIII. When the old Pope, broken by the struggle, died, Philip's agents and money secured the election of a Frenchman as Clement V, and the removal of the papacy to Avignon. Never had any layman won so great a victory over the Church. Henceforth, in France, the lawyers ruled the priests.

The grand master of the Templars, as he went to the stake, predicted that Philip would follow him within a year. It so befell; and not only Philip but Clement too died in 1314—the triumphant King aged only forty-six. The

French people had admired his tenacity and courage, and had upheld him against Boniface; but they cursed his memory as the most grasping monarch in their history. France was almost broken by his victory. His debased currency disordered the national economy, high rents and prices impoverished the people, taxation retarded industry, and the banishment of the Lombards and the Jews crippled the sinews of commerce and ruined the great fairs. The prosperity that had mounted under Louis the Saint declined under the master of every trick of law and diplomatic craft.[83]

Three sons of Philip mounted the throne and descended into the grave within fourteen years of his death. None of them left sons to inherit his power. Charles IV (d. 1328) left daughters, but the old Salic law was invoked to refuse them the crown. The nearest male heir of the royal family was Philip of Valois, nephew of Philip the Fair. With his accession the direct line of the Capetian kings ended, and the rule of the House of Valois began.

A *coup d'oeil* of France in this period shows remarkable advances in economy, law, education, literature, and art. Serfdom was rapidly disappearing as the growth of urban industry lured men from the farms. Paris in 1314 had some 200,000 inhabitants, France some 22,000,000.[84] Brunetto Latini, fleeing from the political violence of Florence, marveled at the peace and security that reigned in the streets of Paris under Louis IX, the busy handicrafts and commerce of the towns, the fruitful fields and vineyards of the pleasant countryside around the capital.[85]

The rise of the business and professional classes, almost rivaling the nobility in wealth, compelled their representation in the *États généraux*, or States-General, which Philip IV summoned to Paris in 1302 to give him moral and financial support in his conflict with Boniface. Such general assemblies of the three estates or classes—nobles, clergy, commons—were called only in emergencies (1302, 1308, 1314 . . .), and were cleverly guided by the lawyers who served the king as a *conseil d'état* or Council of State. The Parlement of Paris, which took form under Louis IX, was not a representative assembly, but a group of some ninety-four lawyers and clerics apppointed by the king, and meeting once or twice a year to serve as a supreme court. Its *ordonnances* built up a body of national law based upon Roman rather than Frank codes, and giving the monarchy the full support of the classical legal tradition.

The intellectual excitement of the age of Philip IV is preserved for us in the political treatises of one of his supporters—Pierre Dubois (1255–1312), a lawyer who represented Coutances in the States-General of 1302. In a *Supplication du peuple de France au roi contre le pape Boniface* (1304)— An Appeal of the People of France to the King against Pope Boniface—and in a tract *On the Recovery of the Holy Land* (1306), Dubois threw out suggestions that reveal the sharp division that now separated the legal from the ecclesiastical mind in France. The Church, said Dubois, should be disendowed, should no longer receive financial support from the state; the French Church should be separated from Rome; the papacy should be divorced from all temporal power; and the authority of the state should be supreme. Philip should be made emperor of a united Europe, with Constantinople as his capital. An international court should be set up to adjudicate the quarrels of nations, and an economic boycott should be declared against any Christian nation that warred upon another. A school of Oriental studies should be established at Rome. Women should have the same educational opportunities and political rights as men.[86]

It was the age of the troubadours in Provence, of the trouvères in the north, of the *Chanson de Roland* and other *chansons de geste*, of *Aucassin et Nicolette* and the *Roman de la Rose*, of the first outstanding French historians—Villardhouin and Joinville. In this period great universities were organized in Paris, Orléans, Angers, Toulouse, and Montpellier. It began with Roscelin and Abélard, and culminated in the zenith of the Scholastic philosophy. It was the age of the Gothic ecstasy—of the majestic cathedrals of St. Denis, Chartres, Notre Dame, Amiens, and Reims, and of Gothic sculpture in its most spiritual perfection. Frenchmen were forgivably proud of their country, their capital, and their culture; a national unifying patriotism was replacing the provincialism of the feudal era; already, as in the *Chanson de Roland*, men spoke lovingly of *la douce France*, "sweet France." It was in France, as in Italy, the climax of Christian civilization.

XII. SPAIN: 1096–1285

The Christian reconquest of Spain proceeded as rapidly as the fraternal chaos of the Spanish kings would permit. The popes gave the name and privileges of crusaders to Christians who would help drive back the Moors in Spain; some Templars came from France to help the cause; and three Spanish military religious orders—the Knights of Calatrava, of Santiago, of Alcantara—were formed in the twelfth century. In 1118 Alfonso I of Aragon captured Saragossa; in 1195 the Christians were defeated at Alarcos; but in 1212 they almost wiped out the main Almohad army at Las Navas de Tolosa. The victory was decisive; Moorish resistance broke down, and one by one the Moslem citadels fell: Cordova (1236), Valencia (1238), Seville (1248), Cadiz (1250). Thereafter the *reconquista* halted for two centuries, to allow time for the wars of the kings.

When Alfonso VIII of Castile was defeated at Alarcos the kings of Leon and Navarre, who had promised to go to his help, invaded his kingdom, and Alfonso had to make peace with the infidels to protect himself against the infidelity of the Christians.[87] Fernando III (1217-52) reunited Leon and

Castile, pushed the Catholic frontier to Granada, made Seville his capital, the great mosque his cathedral, the Alcazar his residence; the Church considered him a bastard at his birth, and made him a saint after his death. His son Alfonso X (1252–84) was an excellent scholar and an irresolute king. Attracted by the Moorish learning that he found in Seville, Alfonso *el Sabio*, the Wise, braved the bigots by hiring Arab and Jewish, as well as Christian, scholars to translate Moslem works into Latin for the instruction of Europe. He established a school of astronomy, whose "Alfonsine Tables" of heavenly bodies and movements became standard for Christian astronomers. He organized a corps of historians who wrote under his name a history of Spain and a vast and general history of the world. He composed some 450 poems, some in Castilian, some in Galician-Portuguese; many were set to music, and survive as one of the most substantial monuments of medieval song. His literary passion overflowed in books written or commissioned by him on draughts, chess, dice, stones, music, navigation, alchemy, and philosophy. Apparently he ordered a translation of the Bible to be made directly from the Hebrew into Castilian. With him the Castilian language assumed the pre-eminence from which it has since ruled the literary life of Spain. He was in effect the founder of Spanish and Portuguese literature, of Spanish historiography, of Spanish scientific terminology. He tarnished a brilliant career by intriguing to secure the throne of the Holy Roman Empire; he spent much Spanish treasure in the attempt; he sought to replenish his coffers by raising taxes and debasing the coinage; he was deposed in favor of his son, survived his downfall by two years, and died a broken man.

Aragon rose to prominence through the marriage of its Queen Petronilla to Count Ramon Berenguer of Barcelona (1137); Aragon thereby acquired Catalonia, including the greatest of Spanish ports. Pedro II (1196–1213) brought the new kingdom to prosperity by protecting with vigorously enforced law the security of harbors, markets, and roads; he made his court at Barcelona the gay and amorous center of Spanish chivalry and troubadours, and saved his soul—and insured his title—by presenting Aragon to Innocent III as a feudal fief. His son Jaime or James I (1213–76) was five when Pedro died in battle; the Aragonese nobles seized the opportunity to renew their feudal independence; but James took the reins at ten, and soon brought the nobles under royal discipline. Still a youth of twenty, he captured the commercially strategic Balearic Islands from the Moors (1229–35), and regained from them Valencia and Alicante. In 1265, in a chivalric gesture of Spanish unity, he conquered Murcia from the Moors and presented it to the king of Castile. Wiser than Alfonso the Wise, he made himself the most powerful Spanish monarch of his century, the rival of Frederick II and Louis IX. His shrewd intelligence and unscrupulous courage likened him to Frederick; but his loose morality, his many divorces, his ruthless wars and occasional brutality discourage comparison with St. Louis. He conspired to seize southwestern France, but the patient Louis outplayed him, though yielding to him Montpellier. In his old age James plotted to conquer Sicily as a bastion of strategy and a haven of commerce, and to make the western Mediterranean a Spanish sea; but the realization of this dream was left to his son. Pedro III (1276–85) married a daughter of Frederick's son Manfred, King of Sicily, and felt entitled to that island when Charles of Anjou seized it with the blessing of the pope. Pedro renounced the papal suzerainty over Aragon, accepted excommunication, and sailed off to fight for Sicily.

As in England and France, this period saw in Spain both the rise and the decline of feudalism. The nobles began by almost ignoring the central power; they and the clergy were exempt from taxation, which fell the more heavily upon cities and trade; but they ended by submitting to kings armed with their own troops, supported by the revenues and militia of the towns, and endowed with the prestige of a reviving Roman law that assumed absolute monarchy as an axiom of government. At the beginning of the period there was no Spanish law; there were separate law codes for each state, and for each class in each state. Fernando III began, Alfonso X completed, a new system of Castilian law, which from its seven divisions came to be known as the *Siete Partidas*, or (Laws of) the Seven Parts (1260–5)—one of the most complete and important codes in legal history. Based on the laws of the Spanish Visigoths, but remodeled to accord with Justinian's *Institutes*, the *Siete Partidas* proved too advanced for their age; for seventy years they were largely ignored; but in 1338 they became the actual law of Castile, and in 1492 of all Spain. A like code was introduced into Aragon by James I. In 1283 Aragon promulgated an influential code of commercial and maritime law, and established at Valencia, and later at Barcelona and in Majorca, courts of the Consulate of the Sea.

Spain led the medieval world in developing free cities and representative institutions. Seeking the support of the cities against the nobles, the kings gave charters of self-government to many towns. Municipal independence became a passion in Spain; little towns demanded their liberty from larger ones, or from the nobles, the Church, the king; when they succeeded they raised their own gallows in the market place as a symbol of their freedom. Barcelona in 1258 was ruled by a council of 200 members, of whom a majority represented industry or trade.[88] For a time the towns were sovereign to the point of independently waging wars against the Moors or one another. But also they formed *hermandades*—brotherhoods—for mutual action or security. In 1295, when the nobles tried to subdue the communes, thirty-four towns formed the *Hermandad de Castilla*, pledged themselves to a common defense, and raised a joint army. This Brotherhood, having overcome the nobles, supervised and checked the officials of the king, and passed laws for the common observance of the member towns, which sometimes numbered a hundred.

It had long been the custom of Spanish kings to call, on occasion, an assembly of nobles and clergy; one such gathering, meeting in 1137, received for the first time the name *Cortes*, courts. In 1188, at the Cortes of Leon, businessmen from the towns were included—probably the earliest instance of representative political institutions in Christian Europe. In this historic congress the king promised not to make war or peace, or issue any decree, without the consent of the Cortes.[89] In Castile the first such Cortes of nobles, clergy, and *bourgeoisie* met in 1250—forty-five years before the "Model Parliament" of Edward I. The Cortes did not directly legislate, but it formulated "petitions" to the king; and its power of the purse often persuaded his assent. A decree of the Cortes of Catalonia in 1283, accepted by the king of Aragon, ruled that thereafter no national legislation should be issued without the consent of the citizens (*cives*); another provision required the king to summon the Cortes annually; these enactments anticipated by over a quarter of a century similar pronouncements (1311, 1322) of the English Parliament. Furthermore, the Cortes appointed members from each social class to a *Junta*, or Union, to keep watch, in the intervals between the sessions of the Cortes, over the administration of the laws and funds that it had voted.[90]

The problem of government in Spain was complicated by divisive mountains impeding the wide enforcement of a common law. The uneven terrain, the dry plateaus, and the periodic devastations of war discouraged agriculture, and made Spain largely a grazing land for cattle and sheep. The fine sheep herds fed thousands of looms in the towns, and Spain maintained its ancient high reputation for the quality of its wool. Internal trade was harassed by difficulties of transport and diversities of weights, measures, and currencies; but foreign trade grew in the ports of Barcelona, Tarragona, Valencia, Seville, and Cadiz; Catalan merchants were everywhere; and in 1282 the merchants of Castile held a position in Bruges rivaled only by the Hanseatic League.[91] Merchants and manufacturers became the chief financial support of the crown. The urban proletariat organized itself into guilds (*gremios*), but these were strictly controlled by the kings, and the working classes suffered economic exploitation without political representation.

Most of the industrial workers were either Jews or *Mudejares*—Moslems in Christian Spain. The Jews prospered in Aragon and Castile; they shared actively in the intellectual life of the two kingdoms; many of them were rich merchants; but at the end of this period they were subjected to increasing restrictions. The Mudejares were allowed freedom of worship, and considerable self-government; they too included many rich merchants; and a few found entry to the royal courts. Their craftsmen strongly influenced Spanish architecture, woodwork, and metalwork to the Mudejar style—the use of Moorish forms and themes in Christian art. Alfonso VI, in a catholic moment, called himself *Emperador de los Dos Cultos*—Emperor of the Two Faiths.[92] But the Mudejares in general had to wear a distinctive garb, live in a separate section of each city, and bear especially heavy taxation. Ultimately the wealth aggregated by their industrial and commercial skill excited the envy of the majority race; in 1247 James I ordered their expulsion from Aragon; over 100,000 of them left, taking their technical skills with them; and Aragonese industry thereafter declined.

The partial absorption of Moslem culture into Spanish civilization, the stimulus of victory over an ancient enemy, the growth of industry and wealth, and of manners and tastes, stirred the mental life of Spain. The thirteenth century saw the establishment of six universities in Spain. Alfonso II of Aragon (1162–96) was the first Spanish troubadour; soon there were hundreds; and they not only wrote poetry, they developed the ceremonies of the Church into secular plays, opening a path to the triumphs of Lope de Vega and Calderon. To this period belongs the *Cid*, the national epic of Spain. Better than all these were the music, songs, and dances that flowed from the hearts of the people in their homes and streets, and graduated into the splendor and pageantry of the royal courts. The first recorded bullfight in the modern style was given at Ávila in 1107 to adorn a wedding feast; by 1300 it was a common sport in the cities of Spain. At the same time the French knights who came to help against the Moors brought the ideas and tournaments of chivalry. Respect for women, or for a man's exclusive property in a woman, was made a point of honor as vital as a man's pride in his courage and integrity; the duel of honor became a part of Spanish life. The mixture of European and Afro-Semitic blood, of Occidental and Oriental culture, of Syrian and Persian motives with Gothic art, of Roman hardness with Eastern sentiment, generated the Spanish character, and made Spanish civilization, in the thirteenth century, a unique and colorful element in the European scene.

XIII. PORTUGAL: 1095

In the year 1095 Count Henry of Burgundy, a crusading knight in Spain, so pleased Alfonso VI of Castile and Leon that the King gave him a daughter, Theresa, in marriage, and included in her dowry, as a fief, a county of Leon named Portugal.* The territory had been won from Moslem Spain only thirty-one years before; and south of the Mondego River the Moors still ruled. Count Henry felt uncomfortable as anything less than a king; from their marriage he and his wife plotted to make their fief an independent state. When Henry died (1112), Theresa continued to labor for independence. She taught her nobles and vassals to think in terms of national liberty; she encouraged her cities to fortify themselves and study the arts of war. She led her soldiers in person on campaign after campaign, and between wars she surrounded herself with musicians, poets, and lovers.[93] She was defeated,

---

* From the seaport town called Portus Cale by the Romans, and Oporto ("the port") today.

captured, released, and restored to her fief; she lavished funds upon an illicit love, was deposed, went into exile with her lover, and died in poverty (1130).

It was through her inspiration and preparations that her son, Affonso I Henriques (1128–85), achieved her aims. Alfonso VII of Castile promised to recognize him as sovereign ruler of any land that he might conquer from the Moors below the Douro River. With all the reckless bravery of his father and the spirit and pertinacity of his mother, Affonso Henriques attacked the Moors, defeated them at Ourique (1139), and proclaimed himself King of Portugal. The hierarchy persuaded the two kings to submit the matter to Pope Innocent II, who decided in favor of Castile. Affonso Henriques reversed this decision by offering his new kingdom to the papacy as a fief. Alexander III accepted it, and recognized him as King of Portugal (1143) on condition of annual tribute to the See of Rome.[94] Affonso Henriques resumed his wars with the Moors, captured Santarem and Lisbon, and extended his rule to the Tagus. Under Affonso III (1248–79) Portugal reached its present mainland limits, and Lisbon, strategically placed at the mouth of the Tagus, became its port and capital (1263). An old legend said that Ulysses-Odysseus had founded the city and given it its ancient name Ulyssipo, which the carelessness of tongues transformed into Olisipo and Lisboa.

The last years of Affonso II were embittered by civil war with his son Diniz, who wondered why his father took so long to die. From this dubious beginning Diniz moved into a long and beneficent reign (1279–1325). Peace with Leon and Castile was achieved by a marital alliance; strife with another heir to the throne was averted by the mediation of Isabel, Diniz' saintly queen. Renouncing the glories of war, Diniz devoted himself to the economic and cultural development of his kingdom. He founded schools of agriculture, taught his people improved methods of husbandry, planted trees to check erosion, helped commerce, built ships and cities, organized a Portuguese navy, and negotiated a commercial treaty with England; so he earned the title fondly given him by his subjects—*Re Lavrador*, the Worker King. He was an industrious administrator, and a just judge. He supported poets and scholars, and himself wrote the best poetry of his nation and time; through him Portuguese ceased to be a Galician dialect and became a literary language. In his *pastorellas* he gave literary form to the songs of the people; and at his court troubadours were encouraged to sing the joys and pains of love. Diniz himself was a connoisseur in women, and preferred his bastards to his one legitimate son. When this son rebelled and raised an army to unseat his father, St. Isabel, who had lived apart from the merry court of the King, rode between the hostile forces, proposed to be the first victim of their violence, and shamed her husband and her son to peace (1323).

CHAPTER XXVI

Pre-Renaissance Italy

1057-1308

I. NORMAN SICILY: 1090-1194

IT is remarkable to how many different environments, from Scotland to Sicily, the Normans adapted themselves; with what violent energy they aroused sleeping regions and peoples; and how completely, in a few centuries, they were absorbed by their subjects, and disappeared from history.

For a turbulent century they ruled southern Italy as successors to the Byzantine power, and Sicily as heirs to the Saracens. In 1060 Roger Guiscard, with a tiny band of buccaneers, began the invasion of the island; by 1091 its conquest was complete; in 1085 Norman Italy accepted Roger as its ruler; and when he died (1101) the "two Sicilies"—the island and southern Italy—were already a power in the politics of Europe. Control of the Straits of Messina, and of the fifty miles between Sicily and Africa, gave the Normans a decisive commercial and military advantage. Amalfi, Salerno, and Palermo became the foci of an active trade with all Mediterranean ports, including Moslem centers in Tunisia and Spain. Sicily, now a papal fief, replaced Mohammedan mosques with resplendent Christian churches, and in southern Italy Greek prelates gave way to Roman Catholic priests.

Roger II (1101-54) made Palermo his capital, extended his rule in Italy to Naples and Capua, and in 1130 expanded his title from Count to King. He had all the ambition and courage, resourcefulness and subtlety of his uncle Robert Guiscard; so alert in thought and industrious in action that Idrisi, his Moslem biographer, said of him that he accomplished more asleep than other men awake.[1] Opposed by the popes, who feared his encroachment upon the Papal States; by the German emperors, who resented his annexation of the Abruzzi; by the Byzantines, who dreamed of regaining southern Italy; and by the Moslems of Africa, who longed to recapture Sicily, he fought them all, sometimes several of them at once, and emerged with his kingdom greater than before, and with new acquisitions in Tunis, Sfax, Bône, and Tripoli. He made use of the intelligent Saracens, Greeks and Jews of Sicily to organize a better civil service and administrative bureaucracy than any other nation in Europe had at the time. He allowed the feudal organization of agriculture in Sicily, but kept his barons in check with a royal court whose law covered every class. He enriched the economy of Sicily by bringing in silk weavers from Greece, and furthered commerce by competent protection of life, travel, and property. He allowed religious freedom and cultural autonomy to Moslems, Jews, and Greek Catholics, opened career to all talent, himself wore Moslem garb, liked Moslem morals, and lived as a Latin king in an Oriental court. His kingdom was for a generation "the richest and most civilized state in Europe," [2] and he was "the most enlightened ruler of his age." [3] Without him Frederick II, a still greater king, would have been impossible.

The *King Roger's Book* of Idrisi suggests the prosperity of Norman Sicily. A hardy busy peasantry covered the rich soil with crops, and kept the cities fed. They lived in hovels, and suffered the usual exploitation of the useful by the clever, but their life was dignified with a colorful piety, and brightened with festivals and song. Every season of the agricultural year had its dances and chants; and vintage time brought bacchanalian feasts that bound ancient Saturnalia with modern Carnival. Even to the poorest there remained love, and folk songs ranging from license and satire to lyrics of purest tenderness. In the town of San Marco, said Idrisi, "the air is perfumed by the violets growing everywhere." Messina, Catania, Syracuse flourished again as in Carthaginian, Greek, or Roman days. Palermo seemed to Idrisi the finest city in the world: "It turns the heads of all who see it . . . it has buildings of such beauty that travelers flock to it, drawn by the fame of the marvels of architecture, the exquisite workmanship, the admirable conceptions of art." The central street was a panorama of "towering palaces, high and superb hostels, churches . . . baths, shops of great merchants. . . . All travelers say outright that there are nowhere buildings more marvelous than those of Palermo, nor any sight more exquisite than her pleasure gardens." And the Moslem traveler Ibn Jubair, seeing Palermo in 1184, exclaimed: "A stupendous city! . . . The palaces of the king encircle it as a necklace clasps the throat of a maiden with well-filled bosom." [4] Visitors were struck by the variety of languages spoken in Palermo, the peaceful mingling of races and faiths, the neighborly confusion of churches, synagogues, and mosques, the elegantly dressed citizens, the busy streets, the quiet gardens, the comfortable homes.

In those homes and palaces the arts of the East served the conquerors from the West. The looms of Palermo wove gorgeous stuffs in silk and cloth of gold; the ivory workers made little caskets shaped and carved in delicate or whimsical designs; the mosaicists covered floors, walls, and ceilings with Oriental themes. Greek and Saracen architects and artisans raised churches, monasteries, and palaces whose plan and ornament, showing no trace of Norman styles, gathered up a thousand years of Byzantine or Arabic influence. In 1143 Greek artists built for Greek nuns, with funds provided by Roger's Admiral George, a convent dedicated to Santa Maria dell' Ammiraglio, but now known as the Martorana from its founder. It has been so often restored that little remains of its twelfth-century elements. Typically an Arabic inscription from a Greek Christian hymn runs round the inner dome. The floor is of gleaming varicolored marble; eight columns of dark porphyry frame three apses, their capitals are most gracefully carved; walls and spandrels and vaults glitter with golden mosaics, including a famous *Christos Pantocrater*—the Universal King—in the sanctuary cupola. Finer still is the Capella Palatina, the chapel of the palace begun by Roger II in 1132. Here everything is exquisite: the simple design of the marble pavement, the perfection of the slender columns and their diverse capitals, the 282 mosaics filling every tempting space, above the altar the solemn figure of Christ in one of the sovereign mosaics of the world, and, over all, a massive timber ceiling in honeycomb design, carved, gilded, or painted with Oriental figures of elephants, antelopes, gazelles, and "angels" that were probably houris from a Mohammedan's dream of paradise. In all medieval or modern art there is no royal chapel that can compare with this jewel of Norman Sicily.

Roger died in 1154, aged fifty-nine. His son William I (1154–66) earned the title of "the Bad," partly because his life was written by his enemies, partly because he let others govern while he lived amid eunuchs and concubines in Oriental ease. In his reign the Moslems of Tunisia rose against the Christians, and ended Norman power in Africa. William II (1166–89) lived much the same sort of life as "the Bad," but was called "the Good" by amiable biographers if only to avoid a confusion of names. He asked pardon for his lax morals by financing in 1176 the monastery and cathedral of Monreale—a "mount royal" five miles outside of Palermo. The exterior is a disagreeable confusion of shafts and interlacing columns; the cloisters are a work of majestic strength and beauty; the mosaics of the interior are renowned but crude; the capitals, however, are richly carved with realistic life—Noah drunk and sleeping, a swineherd tending a pig, an acrobat standing on his head.

Perhaps the Oriental morals of the Norman Sicilian kings weakened their constitutions and shortened their line. Forty years after the death of Roger II his dynasty ingloriously died. William II left no children, and Tancred, illegitimate son of a son of Roger II, was chosen king (1189). Meanwhile the German emperor Henry VI had married Constance, an aunt of William II; eager to unite all Italy under the imperial crown, he claimed the throne of the Sicilies; he secured the active alliance of Pisa and Genoa, whose commerce was irked by Norman control of the central Mediterranean; in 1194 he appeared before Palermo with irresistible force, persuaded it to open its gates to him, and was there crowned King of Sicily. When he died (1197) he left his thrones to his three-year-old son Frederick, who was to become the most powerful and enlightened monarch of a thirteenth century rich in puissant kings.

II. THE PAPAL STATES

North of Norman Italy lay the city-state of Benevento, ruled by dukes of Lombard origin. Beyond this were the lands under the immediate temporal power of the popes—the "Patrimony of Peter"—including Anagni, Tivoli, Rome, and thence to Perugia.

Rome was the center, but hardly the model, of Latin Christianity. No city in Christendom had less respect for religion, except as a vested interest. Italy took only a modest part in the Crusades; Venice shared in the Fourth only to capture Constantinople; the Italian cities thought of them chiefly as opportunities to establish ports, markets, and trade in the Near East; Frederick II postponed his crusade as long as he could, and embarked upon it with a minimum of religious belief. There were religious souls in Rome, gentle spirits who aided pilgrims to maintain the shrines; but their voices were seldom heard above the din of politics.

Aside from the papacy, Rome was in this period a poor city. The Norman sack of 1084 had capped six centuries of destruction and neglect. The population had shrunk to some 40,000 from its ancient million. It was not a hub of commerce or industry. While cities of northern Italy led the economic revolution, the Papal States tarried in a simple agrarian regime. Market gardens, vineyards, and cattle paddocks mingled with homes and ruins within the walls of Aurelia. The lower classes of the capital lived half by handicraft, half by ecclesiastical charity; the middle classes were a medley of merchants, lawyers, teachers, bankers, students, and resident or visiting priests; the upper classes were the higher clergy and the landed nobility. The old Roman custom of owning in the country and living in the city still prevailed. Long since shorn of any general patriotism that would have united them for national defense, the Roman nobles divided into factions led by rich and powerful families—Frangipani, Orsini, Colonna, Pierleoni, Caetani, Savelli, Corsi, Conti, Annibaldi. . . . Each family made its Roman residence a castle-fortress, armed its members and retainers, and frequently indulged in street brawls, occasionally in civil wars. The popes, having only spiritual weapons little feared in Rome, struggled in vain to keep order in the city; they were repeatedly subjected to insult there, sometimes to violence; and many of them, for peace or safety, fled to Anagni, Viterbo, or Perugia, even to Lyons, at last to Avignon.

The popes had dreamed of a theocracy in which the Word of God, interpreted by the Church, would suffice as law; they found themselves crushed amid the autocracy of the emperors, the oligarchy of the nobles, and the democracy of the citizens. The relics of the Forum and the Capitol kept alive, among the Romans, the memory of their ancient republic; and periodically an effort was made to restore the old autonomy and forms. The leading nobles were still called senators, though the Senate had disappeared; consuls were chosen or appointed, though they wielded no power; and some old manuscripts preserved the half-forgotten edicts of Roman law. Inspired by the rise of free cities in northern Italy, the people of Rome, in the twelfth century, began to demand a return to secular self-government. In 1143 they elected a Senate of fifty-six members, and for some years thereafter elected new senators annually.

The mood of the time called for a voice, and found it in Arnold of Brescia. Tradition reports that he had studied under Abélard in France. He returned to Brescia as a monk, practicing such austerities that Bernard described him as a man who "neither eats nor drinks." He was substantially orthodox in doctrine, but denied the validity of sacraments administered by priests in a state of sin. He held it immoral for a priest to own property, demanded a return of the clergy to apostolic poverty, and advised the Church to surrender all her material possessions and political power to the state. At the Council of the Lateran in 1139 Innocent II condemned him and commanded him to silence; but Pope Eugenius III absolved him on condition of a pilgrimage to various churches in Rome. It was a kindly error; the sight of the old republican landmarks fired the imagination of Arnold; standing amid the ruins, he called upon the Romans to reject clerical rule, and to restore the Roman Republic (1145). Fascinated by his fervor, the people chose consuls and tribunes to be actual governors, and established an equestrian order to serve as leaders in a new militia of defense. Intoxicated with the ease of this glorious revolution, the followers of Arnold renounced not only the temporal power of the popes, but the authority, in Italy, of the German emperors of the Holy Roman Empire; indeed, they argued, it was the Roman Republic that should rule not Italy alone, but, as of old, the "world." [5] They rebuilt and fortified the Capitol, seized St. Peter's, turned it into a castle, took possession of the Vatican, and levied taxes upon pilgrims. Eugenius III fled to Viterbo and Pisa (1146), while St. Bernard, from Clairvaux, hurled denunciations against the people of Rome, and reminded them that their subsistence depended on the presence of the papacy. For ten years the *Comune di Roma* ruled the city of the Caesars and the popes.

Plucking up his courage, Eugenius III returned to Rome in 1148. He confined himself for a time to spiritual functions, distributed charity, and won the affection of the populace. His second successor, Hadrian IV, shocked by the killing of a cardinal in a public tumult, laid an interdict upon the capital (1155). Fearful of a profounder revolution than the aristocracy could digest, the Senate abrogated the Republic and surrendered to the Pope. Arnold, excommunicated, hid himself in the Campagna. When Frederick Barbarossa approached Rome Hadrian asked him to arrest the rebel. Arnold was found and apprehended; he was turned over by the Emperor to the papal prefect of Rome, and was by him hanged (1155). The corpse was burned, and the ashes were thrown into the Tiber "for fear," said a contemporary, "that the people would gather them up and honor them as the ashes of a martyr." [6] His ideas outlived him, and reappeared in the Paterine and Waldensian heretics of Lombardy, in the Albigensians of France, in Marsilius of Padua, and in the leaders of the Reformation. The Senate continued to exist till 1216, when Innocent III succeeded in replacing it with one or two senators congenial to the papal cause. The temporal power of the popes survived till 1870.

At different times the Papal States included Umbria, with Spoleto and Perugia; the "March," or frontier land, of Ancona on the Adriatic; and the Romagna, or Rome-ruled region, with the cities of Rimini, Imola, Ravenna, Bologna, and Ferrara. Ravenna continued to decline in this period, while Ferrara rose to prominence under the wise leadership of the house of Este. Under the lead of the great lawyers produced by its university, Bologna developed a virile communal life. It was among the first cities to choose a podesta to govern the internal affairs of the commune, and a *capitano* to lead it in its external relations. Peculiar requirements ruled the choice of the podesta or man of power: he must be a noble, a foreigner to the city, and over thirty-six years of age; he must own no property within the commune, and must have no relative among the electors; he must not be kin to, or come from the same place as, the preceding podesta. These strange rules, adopted to secure impartial administration, prevailed in many Italian communes. The "captain of the people" was chosen not by the communal council but by the popular party, dominated by the merchant guilds; he represented not the poor but the business class. In later centuries he would extend his power at the expense of the podesta, as the *bourgeoisie* would come to surpass the nobility in wealth and influence.

III. VENICE TRIUMPHANT: 1096–1311

North of Ferrara and the Po lay the district of Veneto, proud of the cities of Venice, Treviso, Padua, Vicenza, and Verona.

It was in this period that Venice matured her power. Her alliance with Byzantium gave her entry to Aegean and Black Sea ports. At Constantinople, in the twelfth century, her nationals are said to have numbered over 100,000, and to have held a section of the city in terror by their insolence and their brawls. Suddenly the Greek Emperor Manuel, prodded by the jealous Genoese, turned against the Venetians in his capital, arrested a great number of them, and ordered a wholesale confiscation of their goods (1171). Venice declared war; her people labored night and day to build a fleet; and in 1171 the Doge Vitale Michieli II led 130 ships against Euboea as a first goal of strategy against the Straits. But on Euboea's shores his troops fell sick

with a disease said to have been caused by Greeks poisoning the water supply; so many thousands died that the ships could not be manned for war; the
Doge led his armada back to Venice, where the plague infected and decimated the inhabitants; and at a meeting of the assembly the Doge, blamed
for these misfortunes, was stabbed to death (1172).[7] It is against the background of these events that we must view the Fourth Crusade, and the oligarchic revolution that transformed the constitution of Venice.

The great merchants, fearing the collapse of their commercial empire if
such defeats continued, resolved to take the election of the doge, and the
determination of public policy, from the general assembly, and establish a
more select council, which should be better fitted to consider and transact
affairs of state, and might serve as a check upon both the passions of the people and the autocracy of the doge. The three highest judges of the Republic
were persuaded to appoint a commission to draw up a new constitution. Its
report recommended that each of the six wards of the city-state should
choose two leading men, each of whom should choose forty able men; the
480 deputies so chosen were to form the *Maggior Consiglio*, or Greater
Council, as the general legislature of the nation. The Greater Council in turn
was to choose sixty of its members as a Senate to govern commerce, finance,
and foreign relations. The *arrengo* or popular assembly was to meet only to
ratify or reject proposals of war or peace. A Privy Council of six men, elected
severally from the six wards, was to govern the state in any interregnum, and
its sanction was to be required to legalize any governmental action of a
doge. The first Greater Council elected by this procedure chose thirty-four
of its members, who chose eleven of their number, who then, in public deliberation in the cathedral of San Marco, chose the doge (1173). A cry of
protest arose from the people at losing their right of naming the head of the
state; but the new doge diverted the disturbance by scattering coin among
the crowd.[8] In 1192, on the election of Enrico Dandolo, the Greater Council
required the Doge to swear, in his coronation oath, to obey all the laws of
the state. The mercantile oligarchy was now supreme.

Dandolo, already eighty-four, proved to be one of the strongest leaders
in Venetian history. Through his Machiavellian diplomacy and personal
heroism Venice avenged the disaster of 1171 by capturing and despoiling
Constantinople in 1204; thereby Venice became the dominant power in the
Eastern Mediterranean and the Black Sea, and the commercial leadership of
Europe passed from Byzantium to Italy. In 1261 the Genoese aided the
Greeks to regain Constantinople, and were rewarded with commercial preference there; but three years later the Venetian fleet defeated the Genoese
near Sicily, and the Greek emperor was forced to restore the favored po-
sition of Venice in his capital.

The triumphant oligarchy capped these external victories with another
constitutional stroke. In 1297 the Doge Pietro Gradenigo pushed through

the Council a proposal that only those citizens—and their male posterity—should be eligible to the Council who had sat in it since 1293.[9] The great majority of the people were excluded from office by this "Closing of the Council." A closed caste was created; a *Libro d'oro*, or Golden Book, of marriages and births within this patrician caste was kept to ensure purity of blood and monopoly of power; the mercantile oligarchy decreed itself an aristocracy of birth. When the people planned a revolt against the new constitution their leaders were admitted into the hall of the Council, and were immediately hanged (1300).

It must be admitted that this frank and ruthless oligarchy governed well. Public order was better maintained, public policy more shrewdly guided, laws more stable and effective, than in the other communities of medieval Italy. Venetian laws for the regulation of physicians and apothecaries preceded similar statutes of Florence by half a century. In 1301 laws forbade unhealthy industries in residential quarters, and excluded from Venice industries that poured injurious fumes into the air. Navigation laws were rigorous and detailed. All imports and exports were subject to state supervision and control. Diplomatic reports covered trade more than politics, and economic statistics were here for the first time made a part of government.[10]

Agriculture was almost unknown in Venice, but handicrafts were highly developed, for Venice had imported from the old cities of the Eastern Mediterranean arts and crafts half submerged by political upheavals in the West. Venetian products in iron, brass, glass, gold cloth, and silk were renowned in three continents. The building of boats for pleasure, commerce, or war was probably the greatest of Venetian industries; it reached a capitalistic stage of mass labor and corporate finance, and almost a socialistic stage through control by its chief client, the state. Picturesque galleys with lofty prows, painted sails, and as many as 180 oars bound Venice with Constantinople, Tyre, Alexandria, Lisbon, London, and a score of other cities in a golden chain of ports and trade. Goods from the valley of the Po came to Venice to be reshipped; the products of the Rhine cities came over the Alps to spread out from her quays to the Mediterranean world; the Rialto became the busiest thoroughfare in Europe, crowded with merchants, sailors, and bankers from a hundred lands. The wealth of the North could not compare with the opulence of a city where everything was geared to commerce and finance, and where one ship sent to Alexandria and back brought 1000 per cent on the investment—if it encountered no enemy, pirate, or destructive storm.[11] In the thirteenth century Venice was the richest city in Europe, equaled perhaps only by those Chinese cities that her Marco Polo incredibly described.

Faith declines as wealth increases. The Venetians made much use of religion in government, and consoled the voteless with processions and paradise; but the ruling classes rarely allowed Christianity, or excommunication, to interfere with business or war. *Siamo Veneziani, poi Cristiani*, ran their motto: "We are Venetians; after that we are Christians."[12] Ecclesiastics were excluded from any share in the government.[13] Venetian merchants sold arms and slaves, and sometimes gave military intelligence, to Moslems at war with Christians.[14] A certain liberality went with this broad-minded venality: Moslems might come safely to Venice; and the Jews—especially in the Giudecca on the island of Spinalunga—might worship peacefully in their synagogues.

Dante denounced the "unbridled lasciviousness" of the Venetians,[15] but we must not trust the strictures of one who cursed so ecumenically. More significant are the severe penalties prescribed in Venetian law for parents who prostituted their children, or the vainly repeated laws to check electoral corruption.[16] The impression we get is of a hard and brilliant aristocracy stoically resigned to the poverty of the masses, and a populace solacing poverty with the uncornered joys of love. As early as 1094 we hear of the Carnival; in 1228 the first mention of masks; in 1296 the Senate made the last day before Lent (the French *mardi gras*) a public holiday. On such occasions both sexes flaunted their most expensive finery. Rich ladies crowned themselves with jeweled tiaras or hoods, or turbans woven with cloth of gold; their eyes gleamed through veils of gold or silver web; their necks held strings of pearls; their hands were gloved with chamois or silk; their feet were shod with sandals or shoes of leather, wood, or cork, embroidered in red and gold; their gowns were of fine linen, silk, or brocade, sprinkled with gems, and cut low in the neck to the scandal and fascination of their times. They wore false hair, they painted and powdered, they laced and fasted to be slim.[17] They moved freely in public at any time, joined with shy allure in pleasure parties and gondola escapades, and listened willingly to troubadours importing Provence modes of song for the eternal themes of love.

The Venetians did not, in this period, go in for culture. They had a good public library, but seem to have made little use of it. No contributions to learning, no lasting poetry, appeared amid this unrivaled wealth. Schools were numerous in the thirteenth century, and we hear of private and state scholarships for poor students; but as late as the fourteenth century there were Venetian judges who could not read.[18] Music was held in high esteem. Art was not yet the superb coloratura of later days; but wealth was bringing to Venice the art of many lands, taste was growing, the foundation was being laid, and old Roman skills survived, above all in glass.

We must not picture the Venice of that age as quite so lovely as Wagner or Nietzsche found it in the nineteenth century. Houses were of wood, and streets were simple earth; the Piazza di San Marco, however, was paved with brick in 1172, and the pigeons were there as early as 1256. Pretty bridges began to curve over the canals, and over the Grand Canal the *traghetti* already ferried many passengers. The side canals were probably less malodor-

ous then than now, for time is needed for any full ripening. But no faults of
street or stream could close the soul to the grandeur of a city lifting itself up,
century by century, out of the marshes and mists of the lagoons; or the wonder of a people rising out of desolation and isolation to cover the sea with its
ships, and levy tribute of wealth and beauty upon half the world.

Between Venice and the Alps lay the city and March of Treviso, of which
we shall note only that its people so loved life that it won the name of *Marca
amorosa* or *gioiosa*. In 1214, we are told, the city celebrated the festival of the
Castello d'amore: a wooden castle was set up, and hung with carpets, drapes,
and garlands; pretty Trevisan women held it, armed with scented water,
fruit, and flowers; youthful cavaliers from Venice competed with gay blades
from Padua in besieging the ladies, bombarding them with like weapons; the
Venetians, they say, won the day by mingling ducats with their flowers; in
any case the castle and its fair defenders fell.[19]

IV. FROM MANTUA TO GENOA

West of the Veneto the famous cities of Lombardy ruled the plains between the Po and the Alps: Mantua, Cremona, Brescia, Bergamo, Como,
Milan, Pavia. South of the Po, in what is now Emilia, were Modena, Reggio,
Parma, Piacenza; lovers of Italy will not resent these sonorous litanies. Between Lombardy and France the province of Piedmont enclosed Vercelli
and Turin; and south of these Liguria bent around the gulf and city of
Genoa. The wealth of the region was the gift of the Po, which crossed the
peninsula from west to east, carrying the commerce, filling the canals, water-
ing the fields. The growth of industry and trade gave these cities the wealth
and pride that enabled them generally to ignore their nominal sovereign, the
German emperor, and to subdue the semifeudal lords of their hinterland.

Usually a cathedral stood at the center of these Italian towns, to brighten
life with the drama of devotion and the spur of hope; near it a baptistery to
mark the entry of the child into the privileges and responsibilities of Christian citizenship, and a campanile to sound the call to worship, assembly, or
arms. In the neighboring piazza or public square peasants and craftsmen offered their products, actors, acrobats, and minstrels performed, heralds cried
their proclamations, citizens chatted after Sunday Mass, and youths or
knights engaged in sports or tournaments. A town hall, some shops, some
houses or tenements helped to form a guard of brick around the square. From
this center ran the crooked, winding, climbing streets, so narrow that when
a cart or horseman passed, the pedestrians dodged into a doorway or flattened themselves against a wall. As the thirteenth century progressed and
wealth grew, the stucco houses were roofed with red tiles, making a pic-

turesque pattern for those who could forget the odors and the mud. Only a few streets, and the central square, were paved. Around the city ran a towered and battlemented wall, for war was frequent, and a man had to know how to fight if he cared to be other than a monk.

The greatest of these cities were Genoa and Milan. Genoa—*la superba,* its lovers called it—was perfectly placed for business and pleasure, rising on a hill before a sea that invited commerce, and sharing in the warm climate of a Riviera that reached out to Rapallo on the east and San Remo on the west. Already a busy port in Roman days, Genoa developed a population of merchants, manufacturers, bankers, shipwrights, sailors, soldiers, and politicians. Genoese engineers brought in clear water from the Ligurian Alps by an aqueduct worthy of ancient Rome, and raised a gigantic mole out in the bay to give her great harbor security in storm and war. Like the Venetians of this epoch, the Genoese cared little for letters or art; they spent themselves in conquering competitors and exploring new avenues for gain. The Bank of Genoa was almost the state; it lent money to the city on condition of collecting the municipal revenue; through this power it dominated the government, and every party that came into office had to pledge loyalty to the Bank.[20] But the Genoese were as brave as they were acquisitive. They cooperated with Pisa to sweep the Saracens from the Western Mediterranean (1015–1113), and then fought Pisa intermittently until they shattered their rival's power in the naval battle of Meloria (1284). For that last conflict Pisa called all men between the ages of twenty and sixty, Genoa all between eighteen and seventy; we may judge from this the spirit and passion of the age. "As there is a natural loathing between men and serpents," wrote the monk Salimbene, "so is there between the Pisans and the Genoese, between the Pisans and the men of Lucca." [21] In that engagement off the coast of Corsica the men fought hand to hand until half the combatants were dead; "and there was such wailing in Genoa and Pisa as was never heard in those cities from their foundation to our times." [22] Learning of this disaster to Pisa, the good men of Lucca and Florence thought it an excellent time to send an expedition against that unfortunate city; but Pope Martin IV commanded them to stay their hands. Meanwhile the Genoese pushed into the East, and came into competition with the Venetians; and between these two rose the bitterest hatred of all. In 1255 they contested the possession of Acre; the Hospitalers fought on the side of Genoa, the Templars for Venice; in that battle alone 20,000 men fell; [23] it destroyed Christian unity in Syria, and perhaps decided the failure of the Crusades. The struggle between Genoa and Venice continued till 1379, when the Genoese suffered at Chioggia the same culminating defeat that they had inflicted upon the Pisans a century before.

Of the Lombard cities Milan was the richest and most powerful. Once a Roman capital, she was proud of her age and her traditions; the consuls of her republic defied the emperors, her bishops defied the popes, her people shared or sheltered heresies that challenged Christianity itself. In the thirteenth century she had 200,000 inhabitants, 13,000 houses, 1000 taverns.[24] Herself loving liberty, she did not willingly concede it to others; she patrolled the roads with her troops to force caravans, withersoever bound, to go to Milan first; she ruined Como and Lodi, and struggled to subjugate Pisa, Cremona, and Pavia; she could not rest until she controlled all the commerce of the Po.[25] At the Diet of Constance in 1154 two citizens of Lodi appeared before Frederick Barbarossa and implored his protection for their town; the Emperor warned Milan to desist from her attempts upon Lodi; his message was rejected with scorn and trampled under foot; Frederick, eager to subdue Lombardy to imperial obedience, seized the opportunity to destroy Milan (1162). Five years later her survivors and friends had rebuilt the city, and all Lombardy rejoiced in her resurrection as a symbol of Italy's resolve never to be ruled by a German king. Frederick yielded. But before he died he married his son Henry VI to Constance, daughter of Roger II of Sicily. In Henry's son the Lombard League would find a more terrible Frederick.

V. FREDERICK II: 1194–1250

1. The Excommunicate Crusader

Constance was thirty when she married Henry, forty-two when she gave birth to her only child. Fearing doubts of her pregnancy and of her child's legitimacy, she had a tent erected in the market place of Iesi (near Ancona); and there, in the sight of all, she was delivered of the boy who was to become the most fascinating figure of the culminating medieval century. In his veins the blood of the Norman kings of Italy merged with the blood of the Hohenstaufen emperors of Germany.

He was four when, at Palermo, he was crowned King of Sicily (1198). His father had died a year earlier, his mother died a year afterward. Her will besought Pope Innocent III to undertake the guardianship, education, and political protection of her son, and offered him in return a handsome stipend, and the regency and renewed suzerainty of Sicily. He accepted gladly, and used his position to end that union of Sicily with Germany which Frederick's father had just achieved; the popes reasonably dreaded an empire that should encompass the Papal States on every side and in effect imprison and dominate the papacy. Innocent provided for Frederick's education, but supported Otto IV for the German throne. Frederick grew up in neglect, sometimes in poverty, so that compassionate citizens of Palermo had on occasion to bring the royal gamin food.[26] He was allowed to run free in the streets and markets of the polyglot capital, and to pick his associates wherever he pleased. He received no systematic education, but his avid mind learned from all that he heard or saw; the world would later marvel at the scope and detail of his knowledge. In those days and ways he acquired Arabic and Greek, and some of the lore of the Jews. He grew familiar with different peoples, garbs, customs, and faiths, and never quite lost his youthful habit of tolerance. He read many volumes of history. He became a good rider and fencer, and a lover of horses and hunting. He was short but strong, with "a fair and gracious countenance," [27] and long, red, curly hair; clever, positive, and proud. At twelve he dismissed Innocent's deputy regent and took over the government; at fourteen he came of age; at fifteen he married Constance of Aragon, and set out to reclaim the imperial crown.

Fortune favored him, for a price. Otto IV had violated his agreement to respect the sovereignty of the Pope in the Papal States; Innocent excommunicated him, and ordered the barons and bishops of the Empire to elect as Emperor his young ward Frederick, "as old in wisdom as he is young in years." [28] But Innocent, so suddenly turning toward Frederick, did not veer from his purpose of protecting the papacy. As the price of his support he required from Frederick (1212) a pledge to continue tribute and fealty from Sicily to the popes; to guard the inviolability of the Papal States; to keep the "Two Sicilies"—Norman southern Italy and the island—perpetually separated from the Empire; to reside in Germany as Emperor and leave the Sicilies to his infant son Henry as King of Sicily under a regent to be appointed by Innocent; furthermore, Frederick bound himself to maintain all the powers of the clergy in his realm, to punish heretics, and to take the cross as a crusader. Financing his trip and retinue with money provided by the Pope, Frederick entered a Germany still held by Otto's armies. But Otto was defeated by Philip Augustus at Bouvines; his resistance collapsed; and Frederick was crowned emperor in a splendid ceremony at Aachen (1215). There he solemnly renewed his pledge to undertake a crusade; and in the full enthusiasm of triumphant youth he won many princes to make the same vow. For a moment he seemed to Germany a God-sent David who would free David's Jerusalem from the heirs of Saladin.

But delays ensued. Otto's brother Henry raised an army to depose Frederick, and the new Pope, Honorius III, agreed that the young Emperor must defend his throne. Frederick overcame Henry, but meanwhile he became involved in imperial politics. Apparently he already longed for his native Italy; the heat and blood of the South were in his temperament, and Germany irked him; of his fifty-six years only eight were spent there. He granted large feudal powers to the barons, gave charters of self-government to several cities, and entrusted the government of Germany to Archbishop Engelbert of Cologne and Herman of Salza, the able Grand Master of the Teutonic Knights. Despite Frederick's apparent negligence Germany enjoyed prosperity and peace during the thirty-five years of his reign. The barons and bishops were so satisfied with their absentee landlord that to please him they crowned his seven-year-old son Henry "King of the Romans"—i.e., heir to the imperial throne (1220). At the same time Frederick appointed himself regent of Sicily for Henry, who remained in Germany. This rather inverted the plans of Innocent, but Innocent was dead. Honorius yielded, and even crowned Frederick emperor at Rome, for he was anxious that Frederick should embark at once to rescue the Crusaders in Egypt. However, the barons in South Italy and the Saracens in Sicily staged a revolt; Frederick argued that he must restore order in his Italian realm before venturing on a long absence. Meanwhile (1222) his wife died. Hoping to prod him to fulfill his vow, Honorius persuaded him to marry Isabella, heiress to the lost kingdom of Jerusalem. Frederick complied (1225), and added the title of King of Jerusalem to those of King of Sicily and Emperor of the Holy Roman Empire. Trouble with the Lombard cities again delayed him. In 1227 Honorius died, and the stern Gregory IX ascended the papal throne. Frederick now prepared in earnest, built a great fleet, and gathered 40,000 crusaders at Brindisi. There a terrible plague broke out in his army. Thousands died, more thousands deserted. The Emperor himself, and his chief lieutenant, Louis of Thuringia, caught the infection. Nevertheless Frederick gave the order to sail. Louis died, and Frederick grew worse. His doctors, and the higher clergy who were with him, advised him to return to Italy. He did, and sought a cure at Pozzuoli. Pope Gregory, his patience exhausted, refused to hear the explanations of Frederick's emissaries, and announced to the world the excommunication of the Emperor.

Seven months later, still excommunicate, Frederick set sail for Palestine (1228). On learning of his arrival in Syria, Gregory absolved the subjects of Frederick and his son Henry from their oaths of allegiance, and began negotiations to depose the Emperor. Taking these actions as a declaration of war, Frederick's regent in Italy invaded the Papal States. Gregory retaliated by sending an army to invade Sicily; monks spread a rumor that Frederick was dead; and soon a large part of Sicily and southern Italy were in papal hands. Two Franciscan delegates of the Pope reached Acre soon after Frederick, and forbade any man in the Christian ranks to obey the excommunicate. The Saracen commander, al-Kamil, astonished to find a European ruler who understood Arabic and appreciated Arabic literature, science, and philosophy, made a favorable peace with Frederick, who now entered Jerusalem as a bloodless conqueror. As no clergyman would crown him King of Jerusalem, he crowned himself in the church of the Holy Sepulcher. The bishop of Caesarea, calling the shrine and city desecrated by Frederick's presence, laid an interdict upon religious services in Jerusalem and Acre. Some Knights Templar, learning that Frederick planned to visit the reputed site of Christ's baptism in the Jordan, sent secret word to al-Kamil, suggesting that here was a chance for the Sultan to capture the Emperor. The Moslem commander sent the letter to Frederick. To free Jerusalem from its interdict, the Emperor left it on the third day, and went to Acre. There, as he walked to his ship, the Christian populace bombarded him with filth.[29]

Arrived at Brindisi, Frederick organized an impromptu army, and advanced to recapture the towns that had yielded to the Pope. The papal army fled, the cities opened their gates; only Sora resisted, and stood siege; it was captured and reduced to ashes. At the frontier of the Papal States Frederick stopped, and sent the Pope a plea for peace. The Pope agreed; the Treaty of San Germano was signed (1230); the excommunication was withdrawn. For a moment there was peace.

2. The Wonder of the World

Frederick turned to administration, and from his court at Foggia, in Apulia, wrestled with the problems of too wide a realm. He visited Germany in 1231, and confirmed, in a "Statute in Favor of Princes," the powers and privileges that he and his son had extended to the barons; he was willing to surrender Germany to feudalism if that would leave him at peace to develop his ideas in Italy. Perhaps he recognized that the battle of Bouvines had ended German hegemony in Europe, and that the thirteenth century belonged to France and Italy. He paid for his neglect of Germany in the rebellion and suicide of his son.

Out of the polyglot passions of Sicily his despotic hand forged an order and prosperity recalling the brilliance of Roger II's reign. The rebellious Saracens of the hills were captured, were transported to Italy, were trained as mercenaries, and became the most reliable soldiers in Frederick's army; we may imagine the wrath of the popes at the sight of Moslem warriors led by a Christian emperor against papal troops. Palermo remained in law the capital of the *Regno*, as the Two Sicilies were briefly called; but the real capital was Foggia. Frederick loved Italy more ardently than most Italians; he marveled that Yahveh had made so much of Palestine when Italy existed; he called his southern kingdom the apple of his eye, "a haven amidst the floods, a pleasure garden amidst a wilderness of thorns." [30] In 1223 he began to build at Foggia the rambling castle-palace of which only a gateway remains today. Soon a city of palaces rose about his own to house his aides. He invited the nobles of his Italian realm to serve as pages at his court; there they rose through widening functions to administer the government. Head of them all was Piero delle Vigne, a graduate of the school of law at Bologna; Frederick made him logothete or secretary of state, and loved him as a brother or a son. At Foggia, as at Paris seventy years later, lawyers replaced the clergy in administration; here, in the state nearest to the See of Peter, the secularization of government was complete.

Reared in an age of chaos, and learned in Oriental ideas, Frederick never dreamed that the order called a state could be maintained except by monarchical force. He seems honestly to have believed that without a strong central power men would destroy, or repeatedly impoverish, themselves through crime, ignorance, and war. Like Barbarossa he valued social order more highly than popular liberty, and felt that the ruler who competently maintains order earns all the luxuries of his keep. He allowed some measure of public representation in his government: twice a year, at five points in the *Regno*, assemblies met to deal with local problems, complaints, and crimes; to these assemblies he summoned not only the nobles and prelates of the district, but four deputies from each major city, and two from each town. For the rest Frederick was an absolute monarch; he accepted as axiomatic the basic principle of Roman civil law—that the citizens had handed over to the emperor the sole right to legislate. At Melfi in 1231 he issued for the *Regno*— chiefly through the legal skill and counsel of Piero delle Vigne—the *Liber Augustalis*, the first scientifically codified system of laws since Justinian, and one of the most complete bodies of jurisprudence in legal history. It was in some ways a reactionary code: it accepted all the class distinctions of feudalism, and maintained old rights of the lord over the serf. In many ways it was a progressive code: it deprived the nobles of legislative, judicial, and minting powers, centering these in the state; it abolished trial by combat or ordeal; it provided for state prosecutors to pursue crimes that heretofore had gone unpunished if no citizen brought in a complaint. It condemned the law's delays, advised judges to cut down the perorations of advocates, and required the state courts to sit daily except on holidays.

Like most medieval rulers, Frederick carefully regulated the national economy. A "just price" was established for various services and goods. The state nationalized the production of salt, iron, steel, hemp, tar, dyed fabrics, and silks; [31] it operated textile factories with Saracen slave women workers and eunuch foremen; [32] it owned and operated slaughter houses and public baths; it created model farms, fostered the cultivation of cotton and sugar cane, cleared woods and fields of injurious animals, built roads and bridges, and sank wells to augment the water supply.[33] Foreign trade was largely managed by the state, and was carried in vessels owned by the government; one of these had a crew of 300 men.[34] Internal traffic tolls were reduced to a minimum, but tariffs on exports and imports provided the chief revenues of the state. There were many other taxes, for this government, like all others, could always find uses for money. To Frederick's credit must be put a sound and conscientious currency.

To make this monolithic state majestic and holy without relying upon a Christianity normally hostile to him, Frederick strove to restore in his own person all the awe and splendor that had hedged a Roman emperor. His exquisite coins were stamped with no Christian word or symbol, but with the circular legend *IMP/ROM/Cesar/Aug*; and on the reverse was the Roman eagle encircled with the name *Fridericus*. The people were taught that the Emperor was in a sense the Son of God; his laws were the divine justice codified, and were referred to as *Iustitia*—almost the third person of a new trinity. Anxious to place himself beside the old Roman emperors in the history and galleries of art, Frederick commissioned sculptors to carve his likeness in stone. A bridgehead at the Volturno, a gate at Capua were adorned with reliefs, in ancient style, of himself and his aides; nothing remains of these works except a female head of great beauty.[35] This pre-Renaissance attempt to revive classic art failed, washed away by the Gothic wave.

Despite his near-divinity and royal industry, Frederick found it possible to enjoy life at all levels in his Foggia court. An army of slaves, many of them Saracens, ministered to his wants and managed the bureaucracy. In 1235, his second wife having died, he married again; but Isabella of England could not understand his mind or morals, and retired into the background while Frederick consorted with mistresses and begot an illegitimate son. His enemies charged him with maintaining a harem, and Gregory IX accused him of sodomy.[36] Frederick explained that all these white or black ladies or lads were used only for their skill in song, dance, acrobatics, or other entertainment traditional in royal courts. In addition to these he kept a menagerie of wild beasts; and sometimes he traveled with a retinue of leopards, lynxes, lions, panthers, apes, and bears, led on a chain by Saracen slaves. Frederick loved hunting and hawking, collected strange birds, and wrote for his son Manfred an admirable and scientific treatise on falconry.

Next to hunting, he took delight in educated and graceful conversation—*delicato parlare*. He preferred the meeting of true minds to the joust of arms. He himself was the most cultured *causeur* of his time, and was noted for his wit and repartee; this Frederick was his own Voltaire.[37] He spoke nine languages and wrote seven. He corresponded in Arabic with al-Kamil, whom he called his dearest friend after his own sons; in Greek with his son-in-law, the Greek Emperor John Vatatzes; and in Latin with the Western world. His associates—especially Piero delle Vigne—formed their admirable Latin style on the classics of Rome; they keenly felt and emulated the classic spirit, and almost anticipated the humanists of the Renaissance. Frederick himself was a poet, whose Italian verses won Dante's praise. The love poetry of Provence and Islam entered his court, and was taken up by the young nobles who served there; and the Emperor, like some Baghdad potentate, loved to relax, after a day of administration or hunting or war, with pretty women around him, and poets to sing his glory and their charms.

As he grew older Frederick turned more and more to science and philosophy. Here above all he was stirred by the Moslem heritage of Sicily. He read many Arabic masterpieces himself, brought Moslem and Jewish scientists and philosophers to his court, and paid scholars to translate into Latin the scientific classics of Greece and Islam. He was so fond of mathematics that he persuaded the Sultan of Egypt to send him a famous mathematician, al-Hanifi; and he was intimate with Leonardo Fibonacci, the greatest Christian mathematician of the age. He shared some of the superstitions of his time, and delved into astrology and alchemy. He lured to his court the polymath Michael Scot, and studied occult science with him, and chemistry, metallurgy, and philosophy. His curiosity was universal. He sent questions in science and philosophy to scholars at his court, and as far abroad as Egypt, Arabia, Syria, and Iraq. He kept a zoological garden for study rather than for amusement, and organized experiments in the breeding of poultry, pigeons, horses, camels, and dogs; his laws establishing closed seasons for hunting were based on careful records of pairing and breeding seasons—for which the animals of Apulia were said to have written him a vote of thanks. His legislation included an enlightened regulation of medical practice, operations, and the sale of drugs. He favored the dissection of cadavers; Moslem physicians marveled at his knowledge of anatomy. The extent of his learning in philosophy appears in his request to some Moslem savants to resolve certain discrepancies between the views of Aristotle and Alexander of Aphrodisias on the eternity of the world. "O fortunate emperor!" exclaimed Michael Scot, "I verily believe that if ever a man could escape death by his learning it would be you." [38]

Lest the learning of the scholars whom he had assembled should die with their deaths, Frederick founded in 1224 the University of Naples—a rare example of a medieval university established without ecclesiastical sanction. He called to its faculty scholars in all arts and sciences, and paid them high salaries; and he assigned subsidies to enable poor but qualified students to attend. He forbade the youths of his *Regno* to go outside of it for their higher education. Naples, he hoped, would soon rival Bologna as a school of law, and would train men for public administration.

Was Frederick an atheist? He had been pious in his youth, and perhaps retained the basic tenets of Christianity till his crusade. Intimate intercourse with Moslem leaders and thinkers seems to have ended his Christian faith. He was attracted by Moslem learning, and considered it far superior to the Christian thought and knowledge of his day. At the Diet of German princes in Friuli (1232) he cordially received a Moslem deputation, and later, in the sight of bishops and princes, joined these Saracens in a banquet celebrating a Mohammedan religious feast.[39] "It was said by his rivals," reports Matthew Paris, "that the Emperor agreed and believed in the law of Mohammed more than that of Jesus Christ . . . and was more a friend to the Saracens than to the Christians." [40] A rumor credited by Gregory IX charged him with saying that "three conjurors so craftily led away their contemporaries as to gain the mastery of the world—Moses, Jesus and Mohammed";[41] all Europe buzzed with this blasphemy. Frederick denied the charge, but it helped to

turn public opinion against him in the final crisis of his life. He was unquestionably something of a freethinker. He had his doubts about the creation
of the world in time, personal immortality, the virgin birth, and other doctrines of the Christian faith.[42] In rejecting trial by ordeal he asked: "How
could a man believe that the natural heat of glowing iron will turn cool
without an adequate cause, or that, because of a seared conscience, the element of water will refuse to accept [submerge] the accused?"[43] In all his
reign he built one Christian church.

Within limits he gave freedom of worship to the diverse faiths in his kingdom. Greek Catholics, Mohammedans, and Jews were allowed to practice
their religions unmolested, but (with one exception) they could not teach
in the university, or rise to official position in the state. All Moslems and
Hebrews were required to wear a dress that would distinguish them from
Christians; and the poll tax that Moslem rulers levied on Christians and Jews
in Islam was here levied upon Jews and Saracens as a substitute for military
service. Conversion from Christianity to Judaism or Islam was severely punished in Frederick's laws. But when, in 1235, the Jews of Fulda were accused
of "ritual murder"—the killing of a Christian child to use its blood at the
Passover festival—Frederick came to their rescue, and denounced the story
as a cruel legend. He had several Jewish scholars at his court.[44]

The great anomaly of this rationalist's reign was the persecution of heresy. Frederick did not allow liberty of thought and speech, even to the
professors in his university; it was a privilege confined to himself and his associates. Like most rulers, he recognized the necessity of religion for social
order, and could not allow it to be undermined by his savants; besides, the
suppression of heresy facilitated an intermittent peace with the popes. While
some other monarchs of the thirteenth century hesitated to co-operate with
the Inquisition, Frederick gave it his full support. The popes and their greatest enemy agreed in this alone.

3. Empire vs. Papacy

As Frederick's rule at Foggia developed, his far-reaching aims became ever
clearer: to establish his rule throughout Italy, to unify Italy and Germany
in a restored Roman Empire, and perhaps to make Rome again the political
as well as the religious capital of the Western world. When in 1226 he invited the nobles and cities of Italy to a diet at Cremona he showed his hand
by including in his invitation the duchy of Spoleto, then a papal state, and by
marching his troops through the lands of the popes. The Pope forbade the
nobles of Spoleto to attend. The Lombard cities, suspecting that Frederick
planned to subject them to a real, instead of nominal, submission to the Empire, refused to send delegates; instead they formed the second Lombard

League, in which Milan, Turin, Bergamo, Brescia, Mantua, Bologna, Vicenza, Verona, Padua, and Treviso pledged themselves to a defensive and offensive alliance for twenty-five years. The diet was never held.

In 1234 his son Henry revolted against his father and allied himself with the Lombard League. Frederick rode up from southern Italy to Worms, without an army but with plenty of cash; the rebellion collapsed at the news of his coming or the touch of his gold; Henry was put into prison, languished there for seven years, and then, while being transferred to another place of confinement, rode his horse over a cliff to death. Frederick went on to Mainz, presided over a diet there, and persuaded many of the assembled nobles to join him in a campaign for the restoration of imperial power in Lombardy. So aided, he defeated the army of the League at Cortenuova (1237); all the cities surrendered but Milan and Brescia; Gregory IX offered to mediate, but Frederick's dream of unity could not be reconciled with the Italian love of liberty.

At this juncture Gregory, though ninety and ailing, decided to throw in his lot with the League, and risk the whole temporal power of the popes on the issue of war. He had no fondness for the Lombard towns; he too, like Frederick, considered their liberty a license to chaotic strife; and he knew that they harbored heretics openly hostile to the wealth and temporal power of the Church; at this very time the heretics of besieged Milan were defiling altars and turning crucifixes upside down.[45] But if Frederick overcame these cities the Papal States would be engulfed within a united Italy and a united Empire dominated by a foe of Christianity and the Church. In 1238 Gregory persuaded Venice and Genoa to join him and the League in war against Frederick; in a powerful encyclical he charged the Emperor with atheism, blasphemy, and despotism, and a desire to destroy the authority of the Church; in 1239 he excommunicated him, ordered every Roman Catholic prelate to proclaim him an outlaw, and absolved his subjects from their oath of allegiance. Frederick replied in a circular letter to the kings of Europe, repudiating the charge of heresy, and accusing the Pope of wishing to destroy the Empire and to reduce all kings to subservience to the papacy. The final struggle between empire and papacy was on.

The kings of Europe sympathized with Frederick, but paid small heed to his appeal for help. The nobility in Germany and Italy sided with him, hoping to restore the cities to feudal obedience. In the cities themselves the middle and lower classes were generally for the Pope; and the old German terms Waibling and Welf, in the form of Ghibelline and Guelf, were revived to signify respectively the adherents of the empire and the defenders of the papacy. Even in Rome this division held, and Frederick had many supporters there. As he approached Rome with a small army one city after another opened its gates to him as to a second Caesar. Gregory anticipated capture, and led a mournful procession of priests through the capital. The courage and frailty of the old Pope touched the hearts of the Romans, and many took up arms to protect him. Unwilling to force the issue, Frederick by-passed Rome, and wintered at Foggia.

He had persuaded the German princes to crown his son Conrad King of the Romans (1237); he had placed his son-in-law, the able but brutal Ezzelino da Romano, over Vicenza, Padua, and Treviso; and had set over the other surrendered cities his favorite son Enzio, "in face and figure our very image," handsome, proud, and gay, brave in battle and accomplished in poetry. In the spring of 1240 the Emperor captured Ravenna and Faenza, and in 1241 he destroyed Benevento, the center of the papal forces. His fleet intercepted a Genoese convoy carrying toward Rome a group of French, Spanish, and Italian cardinals, bishops, abbots, and priests; Frederick confined them in Apulia as hostages to bargain with. He soon released the French; but his long detention of the rest, and the death of several in his prisons, shocked a Europe accustomed to consider the clergy inviolable; and many now believed that Frederick was the Antichrist predicted some years before by the mystic Joachim of Flora. Frederick offered to release the prelates if Gregory would make peace, but the old Pope remained firm even to death (1241).

Innocent IV was more conciliatory. At the urging of St. Louis he agreed on terms of peace (1244). But the Lombard cities refused to ratify this agreement, and reminded Innocent that Gregory had pledged the papacy against a separate peace. Innocent left Rome secretly, and fled to Lyons. Frederick resumed the war, and no force seemed now capable of preventing his conquest and absorption of the Papal States, and the establishment of his power in Rome. Innocent summoned the prelates of the Church to the Council of Lyons; the Council renewed the excommunication of the Emperor, and deposed him as an immoral, impious, and unfaithful vassal of his acknowledged suzerain the Pope (1245). At the Pope's urging a group of German nobles and bishops chose Henry Raspe as anti-Emperor; and when he died they named William of Holland to succeed him. Excommunication was pronounced against all supporters of Frederick, and religious services were interdicted in all regions loyal to him; a crusade was proclaimed against him and Enzio, and those who had taken the cross for the redemption of Palestine were granted all the privileges of crusaders if they joined the war against the infidel Emperor.

Surrendering to a fury of hatred and revenge, Frederick now burned all bridges behind him. He issued a "Reform Manifesto," denouncing the clergy as "slaves to the world, drunk with self-indulgence; the increasing stream of their wealth has stifled their piety." [46] In the *Regno* he confiscated the treasures of the Church to finance his war. When a town in Apulia led a conspiracy to capture him he had the ringleaders blinded, then mutilated, then killed. Receiving a call for help from his son Conrad, he set out for

Germany; at Turin he learned that Parma had overthrown his garrison, that Enzio was in peril, and that all northern Italy, and even Sicily, were in revolt. He put down rebellion after rebellion in town after town; took hostages from each of them, and slew these men when their towns rebelled. Prisoners found to be messengers of the Pope had their hands and feet cut off; and Saracen soldiers, immune to Christian tears and threats, were used as executioners.[47]

During the siege of Parma Frederick, impatient of inaction, went off with Enzio and fifty knights to hunt waterfowl in the neighboring marshes. While they were away the men and women of Parma came out in a desperate sortie, overwhelmed the disordered and leaderless forces of the Emperor, captured the Emperor's treasury, his "harem," and his menagerie. He levied heavy taxes, raised a new army, and resumed the struggle. Evidence was brought to him that his trusted premier, Piero delle Vigne, was conspiring to betray him; Frederick had him arrested and blinded; whereupon Piero beat his head against the wall of his jail till he died (1249). In that same year news came that Enzio had been captured by the Bolognese in battle at La Fossalta. About the same time Frederick's doctor tried to poison him. The quick succession of these blows broke the spirit of the Emperor; he retired to Apulia, and took no further part in the war. In 1250 his generals won many successes, and the tide seemed to have turned. St. Louis, captured by Moslems in Egypt, demanded of Innocent IV an end to the war, so that Frederick might come to the Crusaders' aid. But even as hope revived, the body failed. Dysentery, the humbling nemesis of medieval kings, struck the proud Emperor down. He asked for absolution, and received it; the freethinker donned the garb of a Cistercian monk, and died at Fiorentino on December 13, 1250. People whispered that his soul had been borne off by devils through the pit of Mt. Etna into hell.

His influence was not apparent; his empire soon collapsed, and a greater chaos ruled it than when he came. The unity for which he fought disappeared, even in Germany; and the Italian cities followed liberty, and its creative stimulus, through disorder to the piecemeal tyranny of dukes and *condottieri* who, hardly knowing it, inherited the unmorality of Frederick, his intellectual freedom, and his patronage of letters and arts. The *virtù*, or masculine unscrupulous intelligence, of the Renaissance despots was an echo of Frederick's character and mind, without his grace and charm. The replacement of the Bible with the classics, of faith with reason, of God with Nature, of Providence with Necessity, appeared in the thought and court of Frederick, and, after an orthodox interlude, captured the humanists and philosophers of the Renaissance; Frederick was the "man of the Renaissance" a century before its time. Machiavelli's *Prince* had Caesar Borgia in mind, but it was Frederick who had prepared its philosophy. Nietzsche had

Bismarck and Napoleon in mind, but he acknowledged the influence of Frederick—"the first of Europeans according to my taste." [48] Posterity, shocked by his morals, fascinated by his mind, and vaguely appreciating the grandeur of his imperial vision, applied to him again and again the epithets coined by Matthew Paris: *stupor mundi et immutator mirabilis*—"the marvelous transformer and wonder of the world."

VI. THE DISMEMBERMENT OF ITALY

Frederick's will left the Empire to his son Conrad IV, and appointed his illegitimate son Manfred regent of Italy. Revolts against Manfred broke out almost everywhere in Italy. Naples, Spoleto, Ancona, Florence submitted to papal legates; "let the heavens rejoice and the earth be glad!" exclaimed Innocent IV. The victorious Pope returned to Italy, made Naples his military headquarters, moved to annex the *Regno* to the Papal States, and planned a less direct suzerainty over the northern Italian towns. But these cities, while joining the Pope in his *Te Deum*, were resolved to defend their independence against pontiffs as well as emperors. Meanwhile Ezzelino and Uberto Pallavicino held several of the cities in fealty to Conrad; neither of these men had any respect for religion; heresy flourished under their rule; there was danger that all northern Italy would be lost to the Church. Suddenly young Conrad, with a fresh army of Germans, came down over the Alps, reconquered disaffected towns, and entered the *Regno* in triumph— only to die of malaria (May, 1254). Manfred assumed charge of the imperial forces, and routed a papal army near Foggia (December 2). Innocent was on his deathbed when the news of this defeat reached him; he died in despair (December 7), murmuring, "Lord, because of his iniquity Thou hast corrupted man."

The rest of the tale is a brilliant chaos. Pope Alexander IV (1254–6) organized a crusade against Ezzelino; the tyrant was wounded and captured; he refused doctors, priests, and food, and died of self-starvation, impenitent and unshrived (1259). His brother Alberigo, likewise guilty of brutalities and crimes, was also captured, and was made to witness the torture of his family; then his flesh was torn from his body with pincers, and while he was still alive he was tied to a horse and dragged to death.[49] Christians and atheists alike now ran to savagery, except for the gay and charming bastard Manfred. Having defeated the papal troops again at Montaperto (1260), he remained for the next six years master of South Italy; he had time to hunt and sing and write poetry, and "had not his like in the world," said Dante, "for playing of stringed instruments." [50] Pope Urban IV (1261–4), despairing of finding in Italy a corrective for Manfred, and perceiving that the papacy must henceforth rely on France for protection, appealed to Louis IX to accept the Two Sicilies as a fief. Louis refused, but allowed his brother, Charles of Anjou, to receive from Urban the "kingdom of Naples and Sicily" (1264). Charles marched through Italy with 30,000 French troops, and routed Manfred's lesser force; Manfred leaped amid the enemy and died a nobler death than his sire's. In the following year a lad of fifteen, Conradin, son of Conrad, came down from Germany to challenge Charles; he was defeated at Tagliacozzo, and was publicly beheaded in the market square of Naples in 1268. With him, and the death of the long-imprisoned Enzio four years later, the House of Hohenstaufen reached a pitiful end; the Holy Roman Empire became a ceremonious ghost, and the leadership of Europe passed to France.

Charles made Naples his capital, established in the Two Sicilies a French nobility and bureaucracy, French soldiery, monks and priests, and ruled and taxed with a scornful absolutism that made the region long for a resurrected Frederick, and inclined Pope Clement IV to mourn the papal victory. On Easter Monday of 1282, as Charles was preparing to lead his fleet to conquer Constantinople, the populace of Palermo, their hatred unleashed by the insulting familiarity of a French gendarme with a Sicilian bride, rose in violent revolt and killed every Frenchman in the city. The accumulated bitterness may be judged from the savagery with which Sicilian men ripped open with their swords the wombs of Sicilian women made pregnant by French soldiers or officials, and trampled the alien embryos to death under their feet.[51] Other cities followed Palermo's lead, and over 3000 Frenchmen in Sicily were slaughtered in a massacre known as the "Sicilian Vespers" because it began at the hour of evening prayer. French ecclesiastics in the island were not spared; churches and convents were invaded by the normally pious Sicilians, and monks and priests were slain without benefit of clergy. Charles of Anjou swore "a thousand years" of revenge, and promised to leave Sicily "a blasted, barren, uninhabited rock"; [52] Pope Martin IV excommunicated the rebels, and proclaimed a crusade against Sicily. Unable to defend themselves, the Sicilians offered their island to Pedro III of Aragon. Pedro came with an army and a fleet, and established the House of Aragon as kings of Sicily (1282). Charles made futile efforts to recapture the island; his fleet was destroyed; he died of exhaustion and chagrin at Foggia (1285); and his successors, after seventeen years of vain struggle, contented themselves with the kingdom of Naples.

North of Rome the Italian cities played Empire against papacy and maintained a heady liberty. At Milan the Della Torre family ruled to the general satisfaction for twenty years; a coalition of nobles under Otto Visconti captured office in 1277, and the Visconti, as *capitani* or *duci*, gave Milan competent oligarchic government for 170 years. Tuscany—including Arezzo, Florence, Siena, Pisa, and Lucca—had been bequeathed to the papacy by the Countess Matilda (1107), but this theoretical papal tenure seldom interfered with the right of the cities to rule themselves, or to find their own despots.

Siena, like so many Tuscan towns, had a proud past, going back to Etruscan days. Ruined in the barbarian invasions, it revived in the eighth century as a midway stop on the road of pilgrimage and commerce between Florence and Rome. We hear of merchant guilds there in 1192, then of craft guilds, then of bankers. The House of Buonsignori, founded in 1209, became one of the leading mercantile and financial institutions in Europe; its agents were everywhere; its loans to merchants, cities, kings, and popes totaled an enormous sum. Florence and Siena contested the control of the Via Francesa that connected them; the two commercial cities fought exhausting wars with each other intermittently from 1207 to 1270; and as Florence supported the popes in the struggles between Empire and papacy, Siena supported the emperors. The victory of Manfred at Montaperto (1260) was chiefly a victory of Siena over Florence. The Sienese, though fighting against the pope, ascribed their success in that battle to their patron saint, the Virgin Mother of God. They gave Siena to Mary as a fief, placed the proud legend *Civitas Virginis* on their coins, and laid the keys of the city at the feet of the Virgin in the great cathedral which they had dedicated to her name. Every year they celebrated the feast of her Assumption into heaven with a solemn and stirring ceremony. On the eve of the festival all the citizens, from the age of eighteen to seventy, each holding a lighted candle, formed in procession, according to their parishes, behind their priests and their magistrates, marched to the *duomo*, and renewed their vows of fealty to the Virgin. On the feast day itself another procession came—of representatives from conquered or dependent cities, villages, and monasteries; these delegates too marched to the cathedral, brought gifts, and repeated their oath of allegiance, to the commune of Siena and its Queen. In the city square, Il Campo, a great fair was held on this day; goods from a hundred cities could be bought there; acrobats, singers, and musicians performed; and the booth provided for gambling was second in attendance only to Mary's shrine.

The century from 1260 to 1360 saw the apogee of Siena. In those hundred years it built the cathedral (1245–1339), the massive *Palazzo pubblico* (1310–20), and the lovely campanile (1325–44). Niccolò Pisano carved a lordly fountain for the *duomo* in 1266; and by 1311 Duccio di Buoninsegna was adorning Sienese churches with some of the earliest masterpieces of Renaissance painting. But the proud city undertook more than it could finance. The victory of Montaperto was fatal to Siena; the defeated Pope laid an interdict upon the town, forbidding the entry of goods or the payment of debts; and many Sienese banks failed. In 1270 Charles of Anjou incorporated the chastened city into the Guelf (or Papal) League. Thereafter Siena was dominated and outshone by her ruthless rival in the north.

VII. THE RISE OF FLORENCE: 1095–1308

Florentia, named for its flowers, had begun some two centuries before Christ as a trading post on the Arno where it received the Mugnone. Ruined by the barbarian invasions, it recovered in the eighth century as a crossroads on the Via Francesa between France and Rome. Ready access to the Mediterranean encouraged maritime trade. Florence acquired a large mercantile fleet, which brought in dyes and silk from Asia, wool from England and Spain, and exported finished textiles to half the world. A zealously guarded trade secret enabled Florentine dyers to color silks and woolens in shades of beauty unsurpassed even in the long-skilled East. The great wool guilds—the *Arte della Lana* and the *Arte de' Calimala* *—imported their own materials, and made lush profits in transforming them into finished goods. Most of the work was done in small factories, some of it in city or rural homes. The merchants provided the materials, collected the marketable product, and paid by the piece. The competition of home workers—chiefly women—kept factory wages low; the weavers were not allowed to take united action to raise their wages or better their working conditions; and they were forbidden to emigrate. To further promote discipline, the employers persuaded the bishops to issue pastoral letters, to be read from all pulpits four times a year, threatening with ecclesiastical censure, even excommunication, the worker who repeatedly wasted wool.[53]

This industry and trade needed ready supplies of investment capital; and soon the bankers contested with the merchants the control of Florentine life. They acquired large estates through foreclosures; they became indispensable to the pope through financial control of ecclesiastical properties mortgaged to them; and in the thirteenth century they had almost a monopoly of papal finance in Italy.[54] The general alliance of Florence with the popes in their struggle against the emperors was motivated partly by this financial nexus, partly by fear of imperial and aristocratic encroachments upon municipal and mercantile liberties. The bankers were therefore the chief supporters of the papal party in Florence. It was they who financed the invasion of Italy by Charles of Anjou through a loan of 148,000 livres ($29,600,000) to Pope Urban IV. When Charles seized Naples the Florentine bankers, to secure repayment, were allowed to mint the coin and collect the taxes of the new kingdom, to monopolize the trade in armor, silk, wax, oil, and grain, and the supply of arms and provisions to the troops.[55] These Florentine bankers, if we may believe Dante, were not the polished manipulators of our age, but coarse and greedy buccaneers of lucre, who made fortunes by foreclosures and charged unconscionable interest on loans

---

* So called from its display center, a "Wicked Lane" formerly devoted to courtesans.

—like that Folco Portinari who fathered Dante's Beatrice.[56] They spread their operations over a wide region. About 1277 we find two Florentine banking firms—the Brunelleschi and the Medici—controlling finance in Nîmes. The Florentine House of Franzesi financed the wars and intrigues of Philip IV; and from his reign Italian bankers dominated French finance till the seventeenth century. Edward I of England borrowed 200,000 gold florins ($2,160,000) from the Frescobaldi of Florence in 1295. Such loans were risky, and subjected the economic life of Florence to distant and apparently irrelevant events. A multiplication of political investments and governmental defaults, capped by the fall of Boniface VIII and the removal of the papacy to Avignon (1307), brought a series of bank failures to Italy, a general depression, and intensified class war.

Three classes divided the secular life of Florence: the *popolo minuto* or "little people"—shopkeepers and artisans; the *popolo grasso* or "fat people"— employers or businessmen; and the *grandi* or nobles. The artisans, grouped in *arti minori* or lesser guilds, were largely manipulated in politics by the masters, merchants, and financiers who filled the *arti maggiori* or major guilds. In the competition to control the government the "little" and the "fat" people united for a time as *popolani* against the nobles, who claimed ancient feudal dues from the city, and supported first the emperors and then the popes against municipal liberties. The *popolani* organized a militia in which every able-bodied resident of the city had to serve and to learn the arts of war; so prepared, they captured and demolished the castles of the nobles in the countryside, and forced the nobles to come and dwell within the city walls under municipal law. The nobles, still rich with rural rents, built palace-castles in the town, divided into factions, fought one another in the streets, and competed to see which faction should overthrow the limited democracy of Florence and set up an aristocratic constitution. In 1247 the Uberti faction led a Ghibelline revolt to establish in Florence a government favorable to Frederick; the *popolani* resisted bravely, but a detachment of German knights routed them, and the Florentine democracy fell. The leading Guelfs fled from the city; their homes were torn down in unforgetting revenge for their destruction of feudal castles a century before; thereafter each fluctuation of victory in the war of the classes and factions was celebrated by the exile of the defeated leaders and the confiscation or destruction of their property.[57] For three years the Ghibelline aristocracy, backed by a garrison of German soldiers, ruled the city; then, as an aftermath of Frederick's death, a Guelf revolt of the middle and lower classes captured the government (1250), and appointed a *capitano del popolo* to check the podesta, as the ancient tribunes of the people had checked the consuls of Rome. The exiled Guelfs were recalled, and the triumphant *bourgeoisie* cemented its domestic success with wars against Pisa and Siena to control the road of Florentine commerce to the sea and to Rome. The richer merchants became a new nobility, and sought to confine state offices to their class.

The defeat of Florence at Montaperto by Siena and Manfred entailed a second flight of the Guelf leaders; and for six years Florence was ruled by Manfred's delegates. The collapse of the imperial cause in 1268 brought the Guelfs back to power, nominally subject to Charles of Anjou. To control the podesta, who was an appointee of Charles, they established a body of twelve *anziani* ("ancients" or elders) to "advise" that official, and a Council of One Hundred "without whose sanction no important measure, nor any expenditure, is to be undertaken." [58] Taking advantage of Charles's pre-occupation with the Sicilian Vespers, the *bourgeoisie* in 1282 put through a constitutional change by which a "Priory of the Arts," composed of six *priori* (foremen) chosen from the greater guilds, became in effect the ruling body in the city government. Through all these mutations the office of po-desta survived, but shorn of power; the merchants and the bankers were supreme.

The vanquished party of the old nobility reorganized itself under the hand-some and haughty Corso Donati, and, for unknown reasons, received the name of *Neri*, the Blacks. The new nobility of bankers and merchants, led by the Cerchi family, took the name of *Bianchi*, the Whites. Hopeless of aid from the shattered Empire, the old nobility turned to the Pope for succor from the triumphant *bourgeoisie*. Through the Spini, his Florentine agents in Rome, Donati planned with Boniface VIII to capture control of Florence. The Tuscan factions had infected the Papal States, and Boniface despaired of restoring order there unless he should secure a decisive voice in the mu-nicipal governments of Tuscany. [59] A Florentine attorney learned of these negotiations, and accused three Spini agents in Rome of treason to Florence. The *priori* condemned the three men (April, 1300), whereupon the Pope threatened to excommunicate the accusers. A group of armed nobles of the Donati faction assaulted certain officers of the guilds. The Priory, of which Dante was now a member, exiled several nobles, in defiance of the Pope (June, 1300). Boniface appealed to Charles of Valois to enter Italy, subdue Florence, and recapture Sicily from Aragon.

Charles reached Florence in November, 1301, and announced that he had come only to establish order and peace. But soon thereafter Corso Donati entered the city with an armed band, sacked the houses of the priors who had banished him, threw open the prisons, and released not only his friends but all who cared to escape. Riot ran loose; nobles and criminals joined in robbing, kidnaping, killing; warehouses were plundered; heiresses were forced to marry impromptu suitors, and the fathers were compelled to sign rich settlements. Finally Corso turned out the priors and the podesta; the Blacks chose a new Priory, which submitted all its proposed measures to the Black leaders; for seven years Corso was the dashing dictator of Florence. The deposed priors were tried, condemned, and banished, including Dante

(1302); 359 Whites were sentenced to death, but most of them were allowed to escape into exile. Charles of Valois accepted these events gracefully, and 24,000 florins ($4,800,000) for his trouble, and departed south. In 1304 the unchecked Blacks set fire to the homes of their enemies; 1400 houses were destroyed, leaving the center of Florence in ashes. The Blacks then divided into new factions, and in one of a hundred acts of violence Corso Donati was stabbed to death (1308).

We must remind ourselves again that the historian, like the journalist, is forever tempted to sacrifice the normal to the dramatic, and never quite conveys an adequate picture of any age. During these conflicts of popes and emperors, Guelfs and Ghibellines, Blacks and Whites, Italy was sustained by a hard-working peasantry; perhaps then, as now, Italian fields were cultivated with art as well as industry, and were divided and arranged to please the eye as well as feed the flesh. Hills and crags and mountains were carved and terraced to hold grapevines, fruit and nut orchards, and olive trees; and gardens were laboriously walled to check erosion and hold the precious rain. In the cities a hundred industries absorbed the great majority of men, and left little time for the strife of speeches, votes, knives, and swords. Merchants and bankers were not all merciless ghouls; they too, if only by their acquisitive fever, made the cities hum and grow. Nobles like Corso Donati, Guido Cavalcanti, Can Grande della Scala could be men of culture even if, now and then, they used their swords to make a point. Women moved with vibrant freedom in this high-spirited society; love was for them no wordy sham of troubadours, nor the grim fusion of sweating peasants, nor yet the service of a knight to a parsimonious goddess; it was a gallant and ardent amorousness leading with reckless despatch to a full-bodied abandonment and unpremeditated motherhood. Here and there, in this ferment, teachers maneuvered with desperate patience to insert instruction into reluctant youth; prostitutes eased the tumescence of imaginative men; poets distilled their foiled desire into compensatory verse; artists hungered while seeking perfection; priests played politics and consoled the bereaved and the poor; and philosophers struggled through a labyrinth of myths toward the bright mirage of truth. There was a stimulus in this society, an excitement and competition, that sharpened men's wits and tongues, brought forth their reserve and unsuspected powers, and lured them, even if by their own destruction, to clear the way and set the stage for the Renaissance. Through many pains, and the shedding of blood, would come the great Rebirth.

CHAPTER XXVII

The Roman Catholic Church

1095-1294

I. THE FAITH OF THE PEOPLE

IN many aspects religion is the most interesting of man's ways, for it is his ultimate commentary on life and his only defense against death. Nothing is more moving, in medieval history, than the omnipresence, almost at times the omnipotence, of religion. It is difficult for those who today live in comfort and plenty to go down in spirit into the chaos and penury that molded medieval faiths. But we must think of the superstitions, apocalypses, idolatry, and credulity of medieval Christians, Moslems, and Jews with the same sympathy with which we should think of their hardships, their poverty, and their griefs. The flight of thousands of men and women from "the world, the flesh, and the Devil" into monasteries and nunneries suggests not so much their cowardice as the extreme disorder, insecurity, and violence of medieval life. It seemed obvious that the savage impulses of men could be controlled only by a supernaturally sanctioned moral code. Then, above all, the world needed a creed that would balance tribulation with hope, soften bereavement with solace, redeem the prose of toil with the poetry of belief, cancel life's brevity with continuance, and give an inspiring and ennobling significance to a cosmic drama that might else be a meaningless and intolerable procession of souls, species, and stars stumbling one by one into an inescapable extinction.

Christianity sought to meet these needs with a tremendous and epic conception of creation and human sin, of the Virgin Mother and the suffering God, of the immortal soul destined to face a Last Judgment, to be damned to everlasting hell, or to be saved for eternal bliss by a Church administering through her sacraments the divine grace earned by the Redeemer's death. It was within this encompassing vision that most Christian lives moved and found their meaning. The greatest gift of medieval faith was the upholding confidence that right would win in the end, and that every seeming victory of evil would at last be sublimated in the universal triumph of the good.

The Last Judgment was the pivot of the Christian, as of the Jewish and the Moslem, faith. The belief in the Second Advent of Christ, and the end of the world, as preludes to the Judgment, had survived the disappointments of the apostles, the passing of the year 1000, and the fears and hopes of forty generations; it had become less vivid and general, but it had not died; "wise men," said Roger Bacon in 1271, considered the end of the world to be near.[1] Every great epidemic or disaster, every earthquake or comet or other extraordinary event was looked upon as heralding the end of the world. But even if the world continued, the souls and bodies of the dead would be resurrected at once * to face their Judge.

Men hoped vaguely for heaven, but vividly feared hell. There was much tenderness in medieval Christianity, probably more than in any other religion in history, but the Catholic, like the early Protestant, theology and preaching, felt called upon to stress the terror of hell.† Christ was to this age no "gentle Jesus meek and mild," but the stern avenger of every mortal sin. Nearly all churches showed some representation of Christ the Judge; many had pictures of the Last Judgment, and these portrayed the tortures of the damned more prominently than the bliss of the saved. St. Methodius, we are told, converted King Boris of Bulgaria by painting a picture of hell on the wall of the royal palace.[4] Many mystics claimed to have had visions of hell, and described its geography and terror.[5] The monk Tundale, in the twelfth century, reported exquisite details. In the center of hell, he said, the Devil was bound to a burning gridiron by red-hot chains; his screams of agony never ended; his hands were free, and reached out and seized the damned; his teeth crushed them like grapes; his fiery breath drew them down his burning throat. Assistant demons with hooks of iron plunged the bodies of the damned alternately into fire or icy water, or hung them up by the tongue, or sliced them with a saw, or beat them flat on an anvil, or boiled them or strained them through a cloth. Sulphur was mixed with the fire in order that a vile stench might be added to the discomforts of the damned; but the fire gave no light, so that a horrible darkness shrouded the incalculable diversity of pains.[6] The Church herself gave no official location or description of hell; but she frowned upon men who, like Origen, doubted the reality of its material fires.[7] The purpose of the doctrine would have been frustrated by its mitigation. St. Thomas Aquinas held that "the fire which will torment the bodies of the damned is corporeal," and located hell in "the lowest part of the earth." [8]

To common medieval imagination, and to such men as Gregory the Great, the Devil was no figure of speech but a life and blood reality, prowling about everywhere, suggesting temptations and creating all kinds of evil; he could usually be sent packing by a dash of holy water or the sign of the cross; but he left an awful odor of burning sulphur behind him. He was a great ad-

---

* The early Christian theory that all judgment of the dead would be postponed till the "doomsday" of the end of the world had been replaced by the doctrine that every person would be judged immediately after his death.[2]

† Cf. General William Booth (1829–1912) on the methods of his Salvation Army preachers: "Nothing moves the people like the terrific. They must have hell-fire flashed before their faces, or they will not move." [3]

mirer of women, used their smiles and charms as bait to lure his victims, and occasionally won their favors—if the ladies themselves might be believed. So a woman of Toulouse admitted that she had frequently slept with Satan, and had, at the age of fifty-three, given birth, through his services, to a monster with a wolf's head and a serpent's tail.[9] The Devil had an immense cohort of assistant demons, who hovered around every soul and persistently maneuvered to lead it into sin. They, too, liked to lie as "incubi" with careless or lonely or holy women.[10] The monk Richalm described them as "filling the whole world; the whole air is but a thick mass of devils, always and everywhere in wait for us . . . it is marvelous that any one of us should be alive; were it not for God's grace, no one of us could escape." [11] Practically everybody, including the philosophers, believed in this multitude of demons; but a saving sense of humor tempered this demonology, and most healthy males looked upon the little devils rather as poltergeist mischief-makers than as objects of terror. Such demons, it was believed, intruded audibly but invisibly into conversations, cut holes in people's garments, and threw dirt at passersby. One tired demon sat on a head of lettuce, and was inadvertently eaten by a nun.[12]

More alarming was the doctrine that "many are called but few are chosen" (Matt. xxii, 14). Orthodox theologians—Mohammedan as well as Christian —held that the vast majority of the human race would go to hell.[13] Most Christian theologians took literally the statement ascribed to Christ: "He that believeth and is baptized shall be saved; but he that believeth not shall be damned" (Mark xvi, 16). St. Augustine reluctantly concluded that infants dying before being baptized went to hell.[14] St. Anselm thought that the damnation of unbaptized infants (vicariously guilty through the sin of Adam and Eve) was no more unreasonable than the slave status of children born to slaves—which he considered reasonable.[15] The Church softened the doctrine by teaching that unbaptized infants went not to hell but to limbo— *Infernus puerorum*—where their only suffering was the pain of the loss of paradise.[16] Most Christians believed that all Moslems—and most Moslems (Mohammed excepted) believed that all Christians—would go to hell; and it was generally accepted that all "heathen" were damned.[17] The Fourth Lateran Council (1215) declared that no man could be saved outside the Universal Church.[18] Pope Gregory IX condemned as heresy Raymond Lully's hope that "God hath such love for His people that almost all men will be saved, since, if more were damned than saved, Christ's mercy would be without great love." [19] No other prominent churchman allowed himself to believe—or say—that the saved would outnumber the damned.[20] Berthold of Regensburg, one of the most famous and popular preachers of the thirteenth century, reckoned the proportion of the damned to the saved as a hundred thousand to one.[21] St. Thomas Aquinas thought that "in this also doth God's mercy chiefly appear, that He raiseth a few to that salvation wherefrom very many fail." [22] Volcanoes were supposed by many to be the mouths of hell; their rumbling was a faint echo of the moans of the damned; [23] and Gregory the Great argued that the crater of Etna was daily widening to receive the enormous number of souls that were fated to be damned. [24] The congested bowels of the earth held in their hot embrace the great majority of all the human beings that had ever been born. From that hell there would be no respite nor escape through all eternity. Said Berthold: Count the sands of the seashore, or the hairs that have grown on man or beast since Adam; reckon a year of torment for each grain or hair, and that span of time would hardly represent the beginning of the agony of the condemned. [25] The last moment of a man's life was decisive for all eternity; and the fear that that final moment might find one sinful and unshrived lay heavy on men's souls.

These terrors were in some careful measure mitigated by the doctrine of purgatory. Prayers for the dead were a custom as old as the Church; penances undergone, and Masses said, to aid the dead, can be traced as far back as 250. [26] Augustine had discussed the possibility of a place of purging punishment for sins forgiven but not fully atoned for before death. Gregory I had approved the idea, and had suggested that the pains of souls in purgatory might be shortened and softened by the prayers of their living friends. [27] The theory did not fully capture popular belief till Peter Damian, about 1070, gave it the afflatus of his fevered eloquence. In the twelfth century it was advanced by the spread of a legend that St. Patrick, to convince some doubters, had allowed a pit to be dug in Ireland, into which several monks descended; some returned, said the tale, and described purgatory and hell with discouraging vividness. The Irish knight Owen claimed to have gone down through that pit into hell in 1153; and his account of his nether experiences had a prodigious success. [28] Tourists came from afar to visit this pit; financial abuses developed; and Pope Alexander VI, in 1497, ordered it closed as an imposture. [29]

What proportion of the people in medieval Christendom accepted the doctrines of Christianity? We hear of many heretics, but most of these admitted the basic tenets of the Christian creed. At Orléans in 1017 two men, "among the worthiest in lineage and learning," denied creation, the Trinity, heaven, and hell as "mere ravings." [30] John of Salisbury, in the twelfth century, tells of hearing many persons talk "otherwise than faith may hold"; [31] in that century, says Villani, there were at Florence epicureans who scoffed at God and the saints, and lived "according to the flesh." [32] Giraldus Cambrensis (1146?–1220) tells of an unnamed priest who, reproved by another for careless celebration of the Mass, asked whether his critic really believed in transubstantiation, the Incarnation, the Virgin Birth, and resurrection— adding that all this had been invented by cunning ancients to hold men in terror and restraint, and was now carried on by hypocrites. [33] The same Gerald of Wales quotes the scholar Simon of Tournai (*c.* 1201) as crying out, one day, "Almighty God! how long will this superstitious sect of Christians, and this upstart invention endure?"[34] Of this Simon the story is told that in a lecture he proved by ingenious arguments the doctrine of the Trinity, and then, elated by the applause of his audience, boasted that he could disprove the doctrine with yet stronger arguments; whereupon, we are told, he was immediately stricken with paralysis and idiocy.[35] About 1200 Peter, Prior of Holy Trinity in Aldgate, London, wrote: "There are some who believe that there is no God, and that the world is ruled by chance. . . . There are many who believe neither in good or evil angels, nor in life after death, nor in any other spiritual and invisible thing."[36] Vincent of Beauvais (1200?-64) mourned that many "derided visions and stories" (of the saints) "as vulgar fables or lying inventions," and added, "We need not wonder if such tales get no credence from men who believe not in hell."[37]

The doctrine of hell stuck in many throats. Some simple souls asked "why God had created the Devil if He foresaw Satan's sin and fall?"[38] Skeptics argued that God could not be so cruel as to punish finite sin with infinite pain; to which the theologians answered that a mortal sin was an offense against God, and therefore involved infinite guilt. A weaver of Toulouse, in 1247, remained unconvinced. "If," he said, "I could lay hold on that god who, out of a thousand men whom he has made, saves one and damns all the rest, I would tear and rend him tooth and nail as a traitor, and would spit in his face."[39] Other skeptics argued more genially that hell-fire must in time calcine the soul and body to insensitivity, so that "he who is used to hell is as comfortable there as anywhere else."[40] The old joke about hell having more interesting company than heaven appears in the French idyl of *Aucassin et Nicolette* (*c.* 1230).[41] Priests complained that most people put off thought of hell to their deathbed, confident that however sinful their lives, "three words" (*ego te absolvo*) "will save me."[42]

Apparently there were village atheists then as now. But village atheists leave few memorials behind them; and the literature that has come down from the Middle Ages was largely composed by churchmen, or was largely screened by ecclesiastical selection. We shall find "wandering scholars" composing irreverent poetry, rough burghers swearing the most blasphemous oaths; people sleeping and snoring,[43] even dancing[44] and whoring,[45] in church; and "more lechery, gluttony, murder, and robbery in the Sunday" (said a friar) "than reigned all the week before."[46] Such items, suggesting a lack of real faith, might be multiplied by heaping up instances from a hundred countries and a thousand years on one page; they serve to warn us against exaggerating medieval piety; but the Middle Ages still convey to the student a pervasive atmosphere of religious practices and beliefs. Every European state took Christianity under its protection, and enforced submission to the Church by law. Nearly every king loaded the Church with gifts.

Nearly every event in history was interpreted in religious terms. Every incident in the Old Testament prefigured something in the New; *in vetere testamento*, said Augustine, *novum latet, in novo vetus patet*; e.g., said the great Bishop, David watching Bathsheba bathing symbolized Christ beholding His Church cleansing herself from the pollution of the world.[47] Everything natural was a supernatural sign. Every part of a church, said Guillaume Durand (1237?-96), Bishop of Mende, has a religious meaning: the portal is Christ, through whom we enter heaven; the pillars are the bishops and doctors who uphold the Church; the sacristy, where the priest puts on his vestments, is the womb of Mary, where Christ put on human flesh.[48] Every beast, to this mood, had a theological significance. "When a lioness gives birth to a cub," says a typical medieval bestiary, "she brings it forth dead, and watches over it three days, until the father, coming on the third day, breathes upon its face and brings it to life. So the Father Almighty raised His Son Our Lord Jesus Christ from the dead." [49]

The people welcomed, and for the most part generated, a hundred thousand tales of supernatural events, powers, and cures. An English urchin tried to steal some pigeon fledglings from a nest; his hand miraculously adhered to the stone upon which he leaned; only three days of prayer by the community released him.[50] A child offered bread to the sculptured Infant of a Nativity shrine; the Christ Babe thanked it, and invited it to paradise; three days later the child died.[51] A "certain lecherous priest wooed a woman. Unable to win her consent, he kept the most pure Body of the Lord in his mouth after Mass, hoping that if he thus kissed her she would be bent to his desire by the force of the Sacrament. . . . But when he would fain have gone forth from the church he seemed to himself to grow so huge that he struck his head against the ceiling." He buried the wafer in a corner of the church; later he confessed to another priest; they dug up the wafer, and found it had turned into the blood-stained figure of a crucified man.[52] A woman kept the sacred wafer in her mouth from church to home, and placed it in a hive to reduce mortality among the bees; these built "for their most sweet Guest, out of their sweetest honeycombs, a tiny chapel of marvelous workmanship."[53] Pope Gregory I filled his works with stories of this kind. Perhaps the people, or the literate among them, took such tales with a grain of salt, or as pleasant fiction no worse than the wondrous narratives wherewith our presidents and kings relax their burdened brains; credulity may have changed its field rather than its scope. There is a touching faith in many of these medieval legends: so, when the beloved Pope Leo IX returned to Italy from his tour of reform in France and Germany, the river Aniene divided like the Red Sea to let him pass.[54]

The power of Christianity lay in its offering to the people faith rather than knowledge, art rather than science, beauty rather than truth. Men preferred it so. They suspected that no one could answer their questions; it was prudent, they felt, to take on faith the replies given with such quieting authoritativeness by the Church; they would have lost confidence in her had she ever admitted her fallibility. Perhaps they distrusted knowledge as the bitter fruit of a wisely forbidden tree, a mirage that would lure man from the Eden of simplicity and an undoubting life. So the medieval mind, for the most part, surrendered itself to faith, trusted in God and the Church, as modern man trusts in science and the state. "You cannot perish," said Philip Augustus to his sailors in a midnight storm, "for at this moment thousands of monks are rising from their beds, and will soon be praying for us." [55] Men believed that they were in the hands of a power greater than any human knowledge could give. In Christendom, as in Islam, they surrendered to God; and even amid profanity, violence, and lechery, they sought Him and salvation. It was a God-intoxicated age.

II. THE SACRAMENTS

Next to the determination of the faith, the greatest power of the Church lay in the administration of the sacraments—ceremonies symbolizing the conferment of divine grace. "In no religion," said St. Augustine, "can men be held together unless they are united in some sort of fellowship through visible symbols or sacraments." [56] *Sacramentum* was applied in the fourth century to almost anything sacred—to baptism, the cross, prayer; in the fifth century Augustine applied it to the celebration of Easter; in the seventh century Isidore of Seville restricted it to baptism, confirmation, and the Eucharist. In the twelfth century the sacraments were finally fixed at seven: baptism, confirmation, penance, the Eucharist, matrimony, holy orders, and extreme unction. Minor ceremonies conferring divine grace—like sprinkling with holy water, or the sign of the cross—were distinguished as "sacramentals."

The most vital sacrament was baptism. It had two functions: to remove the stain of original sin, and, by this new birth, to formally receive the individual into the Christian fold. At this ceremony the parents were expected to give the child the name of a saint who was to be its patron, model, and protector; this was its "Christian name." By the ninth century the early Christian method of baptism by total immersion had been gradually replaced by aspersion—sprinkling—as less dangerous to health in northern climes. Any priest—or, in emergency, any Christian—could confer baptism. The old custom of deferring baptism to the later years of life had now been replaced by infant baptism. In some congregations, especially in Italy, a special chapel, the baptistery, was constructed for this sacrament.

In the Eastern Church the sacraments of confirmation and Eucharist were conferred immediately after baptism; in the Western Church the age of confirmation was gradually postponed to the seventh year, in order that the child might learn the essentials of the Christian faith. It was administered only by a bishop, with a "laying on of hands," a prayer that the Holy Ghost would enter the candidate, an anointing of the forehead with chrism, and a slight blow on the cheek; so, as in the dubbing of a knight, the young Christian was confirmed in his faith, and was sworn by implication into all the rights and duties of a Christian.

More important was the sacrament of penance. If the doctrines of the Church inculcated a sense of sin, she offered means of periodically cleansing the soul by confessing one's sins to a priest and performing the assigned penances. According to the Gospel (Matt. xvi, 19; xviii, 18), Christ had forgiven sins, and had endowed the apostles with a similar power to "bind and loose." This power, said the Church, had descended by apostolic succession from the apostles to the early bishops, from Peter to the popes; and in the twelfth century the "power of the keys" was extended by bishops to the priests. The public confession practiced in primitive Christianity had been replaced in the fourth century by private confession, to spare embarrassment to dignitaries, but public confession survived in some heretical sects, and a public penance might be imposed for such monstrous crimes as the massacre of Thessalonica or the murder of Becket. The Fourth Council of the Lateran (1215) made annual confession and communion a solemn obligation, whose neglect was to exclude the offender from church services and Christian burial. To encourage and protect the penitent a "seal" was placed upon every private confession: no priest was allowed to reveal what had been so confessed. From the eighth century onward "Penitentials" were published, prescribing canonical (ecclesiastically authorized) penances for each sin— prayers, fasts, pilgrimage, almsgiving, or other works of piety or charity.

"This wondrous institution," as Leibniz called the sacrament of penance,[57] had many good effects. It gave the penitent relief from secret and neurotic broodings of remorse; it allowed the priest to improve by counsel and warnings the moral and physical health of his flock; it comforted the sinner with the hope of reform; it served, said the skeptical Voltaire, as a restraint upon crime;[58] "auricular confession," said Goethe, "should never have been taken from mankind."[59] There were some bad effects. Sometimes the institution was used for political purposes, as when priests refused absolution to those who sided with the emperors against the popes;[60] occasionally it was used as a means of inquisition, as when St. Charles Borromeo (1538–84), Archbishop of Milan, instructed his priests to demand of penitents the names of any heretics or suspects known to them;[61] and some simple souls mistook absolution as license to sin again. As the fervor of faith cooled, the severe canonical penances tempted penitents to lie, and priests were permitted to substitute lighter penalties, usually some charitable contribution to a cause approved by the Church. From these "commutations" grew indulgences.

An indulgence was not a license to commit sin, but a partial or plenary exemption, granted by the Church, from some or all of the purgatorial punishment merited by earthly sin. Absolution in confession removed from sin the guilt that would have condemned the sinner to hell, but it did not absolve him from the "temporal" punishment due to his sin. Only a small minority of Christians completely atoned on earth for their sins; the balance of atonement would be exacted in purgatory. The Church claimed the right to remit such punishments by transmitting to any Christian penitent who performed stipulated works of piety or charity a fraction of the rich treasury of grace earned by Christ's sufferings and death, and by saints whose merits outweighed their sins. Indulgences had been granted as far back as the ninth century; some were given in the eleventh century to pilgrims visiting sacred shrines; the first plenary indulgence was that which Urban II offered in 1095 to those who would join the First Crusade. From these uses the custom arose of giving indulgences for repeating certain prayers, attending special religious services, building bridges, roads, churches, or hospitals, clearing forests or draining swamps, contributing to a crusade, to an ecclesiastical institution, to a Church jubilee, to a Christian war. . . . The system was put to many good uses, but it opened doors to human cupidity. The Church commissioned certain ecclesiastics, usually friars, as *quaestiarii* to raise funds by offering indulgences in return for gifts, repentance, and prayer. These solicitors—whom the English called "pardoners"—developed a competitive zeal that scandalized many Christians; they exhibited real or false relics to stimulate contributions; and they kept for themselves a due or undue part of their receipts. The Church made several efforts to reduce these abuses. The Fourth Lateran Council ordered bishops to warn the faithful against false relics and forged credentials; it ended the right of abbots, and limited that of bishops, to issue indulgences; and it called upon all ecclesiastics to exercise moderation in their zeal for the new device. In 1261 the Council of Mainz denounced many *quaestiarii* as wicked liars, who displayed the stray bones of men or beasts as those of saints, trained themselves to weep on order, and offered purgatorial bargains for a maximum of coin and a minimum of prayer.[62] Similar condemnations were issued by church councils at Vienne (1311) and Ravenna (1317).[63] The abuses continued.

Next to baptism the most vital sacrament was the Eucharist, or Holy Communion. The Church took literally the words ascribed to Christ at the Last Supper: of the bread, "this is my body"; and of the wine, "this is my blood." The main feature of the Mass was the "transubstantiation" of wafers of bread and a chalice of wine into the body and blood of Christ by the miraculous power of the priest; and the original purpose of the Mass was to allow the faithful to partake of the "body and blood, soul and divinity," of the Second Person of the Triune God by eating the consecrated Host and drinking the consecrated wine. As the drinking of the transubstantiated wine risked spill-

ing the blood of Christ, the custom arose in the twelfth century of communicating through taking only the Host; and when some conservatives
(whose views were later adopted by the Hussites of Bohemia) demanded
communion in both forms to make sure that they received the blood as well
as the body of the Lord, theologians explained that the blood of Christ was
"concomitant" with His body in the bread, and His body was "concomitant" with His blood in the wine.[64] A thousand marvels were told of the
power of the consecrated Host to cast out devils, cure disease, stop fires, and
detect perjury by choking liars.[65] Every Christian was required to communicate at least once a year; and the First Communion of the young Christian
was made an occasion of solemn pageantry and happy celebration.

The doctrine of the Real Presence developed slowly; its first official formulation was by the Council of Nicaea in 787. In 855 a French Benedictine
monk, Ratramnus, taught that the consecrated bread and wine were only
spiritually, not carnally, the body and blood of Christ. About 1045 Berengar,
Archdeacon of Tours, questioned the reality of transubstantiation; he was
excommunicated; and Lanfranc, Abbot of Bec, wrote a reply to him (1063),
stating the orthodox doctrine:

> We believe that the earthly substance . . . is, by the ineffable, in-
> comprehensible . . . operation of heavenly power, converted into the
> essence of the Lord's body, while the appearance, and certain other
> qualities, of the same realities remain behind, in order that men should
> be spared the shock of perceiving raw and bloody things, and that
> believers should receive the fuller rewards of faith. Yet at the same
> time the same body of the Lord is in heaven . . . inviolate, entire, with-
> out contamination or injury.[66]

The doctrine was proclaimed as an essential dogma of the Church by the
Lateran Council of 1215; and the Council of Trent in 1560 added that every
particle of the consecrated wafer, no matter how broken, contains the whole
body, blood, and soul of Jesus Christ. Thus one of the oldest ceremonies of
primitive religion—the eating of the god—is widely practiced and revered in
European and American civilization today.

By making matrimony a sacrament, a sacred vow, the Church immensely
raised the dignity and permanence of the marriage bond. In the sacrament
of holy orders the bishop conferred upon the new priest some of the spiritual
powers inherited from the apostles and presumably given to these by God
Himself in the person of Christ. And in the final sacrament—extreme unction
—the priest heard the confession of the dying Christian, gave him the absolution that saved him from hell, and anointed his members so that they might
be cleansed of sin and fit for resurrection before his Judge. His survivors
gave him Christian burial instead of pagan cremation, because the Church
held that the body too would rise from the dead. They wrapped him in his

shroud, placed a coin in his coffin as if for Charon's ferriage,[66a] and bore him to his grave with solemn and costly ceremony. Mourners might be hired to weep and wail; the relatives put on black garments for a year; and no one could tell, from grief so long sustained, that a contrite heart and a ministering priest had won for the departed the pledge of paradise.

III. PRAYER

In every great religion ritual is as necessary as creed. It instructs, nourishes, and often begets, belief; it brings the believer into comforting contact with his god; it charms the senses and the soul with drama, poetry, and art; it binds individuals into fellowship and a community by persuading them to share in the same rites, the same songs, the same prayers, at last the same thoughts.

The oldest Christian prayers were the *Pater noster* and the *Credo*; toward the end of the twelfth century the tender and intimate *Ave Maria* began to take form; and there were poetic litanies of praise and supplication. Some medieval prayers verged on magic incantations to elicit miracles; some ran to an importunate iteration that desperately overruled Christ's ban on "vain repetitions." [67] Monks and nuns, and later the laity, from an Oriental custom brought in by Crusaders,[68] gradually developed the rosary. As this was made popular by Dominican monks, so the Franciscans popularized the *Via Crucis*, or Way or Stations of the Cross, by which the worshiper recited prayers before each of fourteen pictures or tableaux representing stages in the Passion of Christ. Priests, monks, nuns, and some laymen sang or recited the "canonical hours"—prayers, readings, psalms, and hymns formulated by Benedict and others, and gathered into a *breviarium* by Alcuin and Gregory VII. Every day and night, at intervals of some three hours, and from a million chapels and hearths, these conspiring prayers besieged the sky. Pleasant must have been their music to homes within their hearing; *dulcis cantilena divini cultus*, said Ordericus Vitalis, *quae corda fidelium mitigat ac laetificat*—"sweet is the song of the divine worship, which comforts the hearts of the faithful, and makes them glad." [69]

The official prayers of the Church were often addressed to God the Father; a few appealed to the Holy Ghost; but the prayers of the people were addressed mostly to Jesus, Mary, and the saints. The Almighty was feared; He still carried, in popular conception, much of the severity that had come down from Yahveh; how could a simple sinner dare to take his prayer to so awful and distant a throne? Jesus was closer, but He too was God, and one hardly ventured to speak to Him face to face after so thoroughly ignoring His Beatitudes. It seemed wiser to lay one's prayer before a saint certified by canonization to be in heaven, and to beg his or her intercession with Christ. All the poetic and popular polytheism of antiquity rose from the never dead past, and filled Christian worship with a heartening communion of spirits, a brotherly nearness of earth to heaven, redeeming the faith of its darker elements. Every nation, city, abbey, church, craft, soul, and crisis of life had its patron saint, as in pagan Rome it had had a god. England had St. George, France had St. Denis. St. Bartholomew was the protector of the tanners because he had been flayed alive; St. John was invoked by candlemakers because he had been plunged into a caldron of burning oil; St. Christopher was the patron of porters because he had carried Christ on his shoulders; Mary Magdalen received the petitions of perfumers because she had poured aromatic oils upon the Saviour's feet. For every emergency or ill men had a friend in the skies. St. Sebastian and St. Roch were mighty in time of pestilence. St. Apollinia, whose jaw had been broken by the executioner, healed the toothache; St. Blaise cured sore throat. St. Corneille protected oxen, St. Gall chickens, St. Anthony pigs. St. Médard was for France the saint most frequently solicited for rain; if he failed to pour, his impatient worshipers, now and then, threw his statue into the water, perhaps as suggestive magic.[70]

The Church arranged an ecclesiastical calendar in which every day celebrated a saint; but the year did not find room for the 25,000 saints that had been canonized by the tenth century. The calendar of saints was so familiar to the people that the almanac divided the agricultural year by their names. In France the feast of St. George was the day for sowing. In England St. Valentine's Day marked the winter's end; on that happy day birds (they said) coupled fervently in the woods, and youths put flowers on the window sills of the girls they loved. Many saints received canonization through the insistent worship of their memory by the people or the locality, sometimes against ecclesiastical resistance. Images of the saints were set up in churches and public squares, on buildings and roads, and received a spontaneous worship that scandalized some philosophers and Iconoclasts. Bishop Claudius of Turin complained that many folk "worship images of saints; . . . they have not abandoned idols, but only changed their names." [71] In this matter, at least, the will and need of the people created the form of the cult.

With so many saints there had to be many relics—their bones, hair, clothing, and anything that they had used. Every altar was expected to cover one or more such sacred memorials. The basilica of St. Peter boasted the bodies of Peter and Paul, which made Rome the chief goal of European pilgrimage. A church in St. Omer claimed to have bits of the True Cross, of the lance that had pierced Christ, of His cradle and His tomb, of the manna that had rained from heaven, of Aaron's rod, of the altar on which St. Peter had said Mass, of the hair, cowl, hair shirt, and tonsure shavings of Thomas à Becket, and of the original stone tablets upon which the Ten Commandments had been traced by the very finger of God.[72] The cathedral of Amiens enshrined the head of St. John the Baptist in a silver cup.[73] The abbey of St. Denis housed the crown of thorns and the body of Dionysius the Areopagite. Each of three scattered churches in France professed to have a complete corpse of Mary Magdalen; [74] and five churches in France vowed that they held the one authentic relic of Christ's circumcision. [75] Exeter Cathedral showed parts of the candle that the angel of the Lord used to light the tomb of Jesus, and fragments of the bush from which God spoke to Moses. [76] Westminster Abbey had some of Christ's blood, and a piece of marble bearing the imprint of His foot. [77] A monastery at Durham displayed one of St. Lawrence's joints, the coals that had burned him, the charger on which the head of the Baptist had been presented to Herod, the Virgin's shirt, and a rock marked with drops of her milk. [78] The churches of Constantinople, before 1204, were especially rich in relics; they had the lance that had pierced Christ and was still red with His blood, the rod that had scourged Him, many pieces of the True Cross enshrined in gold, the "sop of bread" given to Judas at the Last Supper, some hairs of the Lord's beard, the left arm of John the Baptist. . . . [79] In the sack of Constantinople many of these relics were stolen, some were bought, and they were peddled in the West from church to church to find the highest bidder. All relics were credited with supernatural powers, and a hundred thousand tales were told of their miracles. Men and women eagerly sought even the slightest relic, or relic of a relic, to wear as a magic talisman—a thread from a saint's robe, some dust from a reliquary, a drop of oil from a sanctuary lamp in the shrine. Monasteries vied and disputed with one another in gathering relics and exhibiting them to generous worshipers, for the possession of famous relics made the fortune of an abbey or a church. The "translation" of the bones of Thomas à Becket to a new chapel in the cathedral of Canterbury (1220) drew from the attending worshipers a collection valued at $300,000 today. [80] So profitable a business enlisted many practitioners; thousands of spurious relics were sold to churches and individuals; and monasteries were tempted to "discover" new relics when in need of funds. The culmination of abuse was the dismemberment of dead saints so that several places might enjoy their patronage and power. [81]

It is to the credit of the secular clergy, and of most monasteries, that while fully accepting the miraculous efficacy of genuine saintly relics, they discountenanced, and often denounced, the excesses of this popular fetishism. Some monks, seeking privacy for their devotions, resented the miracles wrought by their relics; at Grammont the abbot appealed to the remains of St. Stephen to stop his wonder-working, which was luring noisy crowds; "otherwise," he threatened, "we will throw your bones into the river." [82] It was the people, not the Church, that took the lead in creating or swelling the legends of relic miracles; and the Church in many cases warned the public to discredit the tales. [83] In 386 an imperial decree presumably requested by the Church forbade the "carrying about or sale of" the remains of "martyrs"; St. Augustine complained of "hypocrites in the garb of monks" who "trade in members of martyrs, if martyrs they be"; and Justinian repeated the edict of 386.[84] About 1119 Abbot Guibert of Nogent wrote a treatise *On the Relics of Saints*, calling a halt to the relic craze. Many of the relics, he says, are of "saints celebrated in worthless records"; some "abbots, enticed by the multitude of gifts brought in, suffered the fabrication of false miracles." "Old wives and herds of base wenches chant the lying legends of patron saints at their looms . . . and if a man refute their words they will attack him . . . with their distaffs." The clergy, he notes, have rarely the heart or courage to protest; and he confesses that he too held his peace when relic-mongers offered to eager believers "some of that very bread which Our Lord pressed with His own teeth"; for "I should rightly be condemned for a madman if I should dispute with madmen." [85] He observes that several churches have complete heads of St. John the Baptist, and marvels at the hydra heads of that undecapitable saint.[86] Pope Alexander III (1179) forbade monasteries to carry their relics about seeking contributions; the Lateran Council of 1215 prohibited the display of relics outside their shrines; [87] and the Second Council of Lyons (1274) condemned the "debasement" of relics and images.[88]

In general the Church did not so much encourage superstitions as inherit them from the imagination of the people or the traditions of the Mediterranean world. The belief in miracle-working objects, talismans, amulets, and formulas was as dear to Islam as to Christianity, and both religions had received these beliefs from pagan antiquity. Ancient forms of phallic worship lingered far into the Middle Ages, but were gradually abolished by the Church.[89] The worship of God as Lord of Hosts and King of Kings inherited Semitic and Roman ways of approach, veneration, and address; the incense burnt before altar or clergy recalled the old burnt offerings; aspersion with holy water was an ancient form of exorcism; processions and lustrations continued immemorial rites; the vestments of the clergy and the papal title of *pontifex maximus* were legacies from pagan Rome. The Church found that rural converts still revered certain springs, wells, trees, and stones; she thought it wiser to bless these to Christian use than to break too sharply the customs of sentiment. So a dolmen at Plouaret was consecrated as the chapel of the Seven Saints, and the worship of the oak was sterilized by hanging images of Christian saints upon the trees.[90] Pagan festivals dear to the people, or necessary as cathartic moratoriums on morality, reappeared as Christian feasts, and pagan vegetation rites were transformed into Christian liturgy. The people continued to light midsummer fires on St. John's Eve, and the celebration of Christ's resurrection took the pagan name of Eostre, the old Teutonic goddess of the spring. The Christian calendar of the saints replaced the Roman *fasti*; ancient divinities dear to the people were allowed to revive under the names of Christian saints; the Dea Victoria of the Basses-Alpes became St. Victoire, and Castor and Pollux were reborn as Sts. Cosmas and Damian.

The finest triumph of this tolerant spirit of adaptation was the sublimation of the pagan mother-goddess cults in the worship of Mary. Here too the people took the initiative. In 431 Cyril, Archbishop of Alexandria, in a famous sermon at Ephesus, applied to Mary many of the terms fondly ascribed by the pagans of Ephesus to their "great goddess" Artemis-Diana; and the Council of Ephesus in that year, over the protests of Nestorius, sanctioned for Mary the title "Mother of God." Gradually the tenderest features of Astarte, Cybele, Artemis, Diana, and Isis were gathered together in the worship of Mary. In the sixth century the Church established the Feast of the Assumption of the Virgin into heaven, and assigned it to August 13, the date of ancient festivals of Isis and Artemis.[91] Mary became the patron saint of Constantinople and the imperial family; her picture was carried at the head of every great procession, and was (and is) hung in every church and home in Greek Christendom. Probably it was the Crusades that brought from the East to the West a more intimate and colorful worship of the Virgin.[92]

The Church herself did not encourage Mariolatry. The Fathers had recommended Mary as an antidote to Eve; but their general hostility to woman as "the weaker vessel" and the source of most temptations to sin; the timid flight of monks from women; the tirades of preachers against the charms and foibles of the sex—these could hardly have led to the intense and ecumenical adoration of Mary. It was the people who created the fairest flower of the medieval spirit, and made Mary the most beloved figure in history. The population of a recovering Europe could no longer accept the stern picture of a god damning the majority of his creatures to hell; and of their own accord the people softened the terrors of the theologians with the pity of the Mother of Christ. They would approach Jesus—still too sublime and just—through her who refused no one, and whom her Son could not refuse. A youth, says Caesarius of Heisterbach (1230), was persuaded by Satan, on the promise of great wealth, to deny Christ, but could not be induced to deny Mary; when he repented, the Virgin persuaded Christ to forgive him. The same monk tells of a Cistercian lay brother who was heard to pray to Christ: "Lord, if Thou free me not from this temptation, I will complain of Thee to Thy mother." [93] Men prayed so much to the Virgin that popular fancy pictured Jesus as jealous; to one who had deluged heaven with Ave Marias He appeared (says a pretty legend), and gently reproached him: "My mother thanks you much for all the salutations you make to her, but still you should not forget to salute me too." [94] Just as the sternness of Yahveh had necessitated Christ, so the justice of Christ needed Mary's mercy to temper it. In effect the Mother—the oldest figure in religious worship—became, as Mohammed had prophetically misconceived her, the third person of a new Trinity. Everyone joined in her love and praise: rebels like Abélard bowed to her; satirists like Rutebeuf, roistering skeptics like the wandering scholars, never ventured one irreverent word about her; knights vowed themselves to her service, and cities gave her their keys; the rising *bourgeoisie* saw in her the sanctifying symbol of motherhood and the family; the rough men of the guilds—even the blaspheming heroes of barracks and battlefields—vied with peasant maidens and bereaved mothers in bringing their prayers and gifts to her feet.[95] The most passionate poetry of the Middle Ages was the litany that in mounting fervor proclaimed her glory and besought her aid. Images of her rose everywhere, even at street corners, at crossroads, and in the fields. Finally, in the twelfth and thirteenth centuries, in the noblest birth of religious feeling in history, the poor and the rich, the humble and the great, the clergy and the laity, the artists and the artisans devoted their savings and their skills to honor her in a thousand cathedrals nearly all dedicated to her name, or having as their chief splendor some Lady Chapel set aside as her shrine.

A new religion had been created, and perhaps Catholicism survived by absorbing it. A Gospel of Mary took form, uncanonical, incredible, and indescribably charming. The people begot the legends, the monks wrote them down. So *The Golden Legend* told how a widow surrendered her only son to her country's call; the youth was captured by the enemy; the widow prayed daily to the Virgin to redeem and restore her son; when many weeks passed without response, the woman stole the sculptured Child from the Virgin's arms and hid Him in her home; whereupon the Virgin opened the prison, released the youth, and bade him: "Tell your mother, my child, to return me my Son now that I have returned hers." [96] About 1230 a French prior, Gaultier de Coincy, gathered the Mary legends into a tremendous poem of 30,000 lines. Therein we find the Virgin curing a sick monk by having him suck milk from her *douce mamelle*; a robber who always prayed to her before embarking on his thefts, was caught and hanged, but was supported by her unseen hands until, her protection of him being perceived, he was released; and a nun who left her convent to lead a life of sin, returned years later in broken repentance, and found that the Virgin—to whom she had never omitted a daily prayer—had all the time filled her place as sacristan, so that none had noted her absence.[97] The Church could not approve of all these stories, but she made great festivals of the events in Mary's life—the Annunciation, the Visitation, the Purification (Candlemas), the Assumption; and finally, yielding to the appeals of generations of the laity and of Franciscan monks, she allowed the faithful to believe, and in 1854 bade them believe, in the Immaculate Conception—that Mary had been conceived free of that taint of original sin which, in the Christian theology, lay upon every child born of man and woman since Adam and Eve.

The worship of Mary transformed Catholicism from a religion of terror— perhaps necessary in the Dark Ages—into a religion of mercy and love. Half the beauty of Catholic worship, much of the splendor of Catholic art and song, are the creation of this gallant faith in the devotion and gentleness, even the physical loveliness and grace, of woman. The daughters of Eve have entered the temple and have transformed its spirit. Partly because of that new Catholicism feudalism was chastened into chivalry, and the status of woman was moderately raised in a man-made world; because of it medieval and Renaissance sculpture and painting gave to art a depth and tenderness rarely known to the Greeks. One can forgive much to a religion and an age that created Mary and her cathedrals.

IV. RITUAL

In art and hymns and liturgy the Church wisely made place for the worship of the Virgin; but in the older elements of her practice and ritual she insisted on the sterner and more solemn aspects of the faith. Following ancient customs, and perhaps for reasons of health, she prescribed periodical fasts: all Fridays were to be meatless; throughout the forty days of Lent no meat, eggs, or cheese might be eaten, and the fast was not to be broken till the hour of none (three P.M.); furthermore, there were to be in that period no weddings, no rejoicing, no hunting, no trials in court, no sexual intercourse.[98] These were counsels of perfection, seldom fully observed or enforced, but they helped to strengthen the will and to tame the excessive appetites of an omnivorous and carnal population.

The liturgy of the Church was another ancient inheritance, remolded into lofty and moving forms of religious drama, music, and art. The Psalms of the Old Testament, the prayers and homilies of the Jerusalem Temple, readings from the New Testament, and the administration of the Eucharist, constituted the earliest elements of the Christian service. The division of the Church into Eastern and Western resulted in divergent rites; and the inability of the early popes to extend their full authority beyond Central Italy resulted in a diversity of ceremony even in the Latin Church. A ritual established at Milan spread to Spain, Gaul, Ireland, and North Britain, and was not overcome by the Roman form till 664. Pope Hadrian I, probably completing labors begun by Gregory I, reformed the liturgy in a "Sacramentary" sent to Charlemagne toward the end of the eighth century. Guillaume Durand wrote the medieval classic on the Roman liturgy in his *Rationale divinorum officiorum*, or *Rational Exposition of the Divine Offices* (1286); we may judge its wide acceptance from the fact that it was the first book printed after the Bible.

The center and summit of the Christian worship was the Mass. In the first four centuries this ceremony was called the Eucharist or thanksgiving; and that sacramental commemoration of the Last Supper remained the essence of the service. Around it there gathered in the course of twelve centuries a complicated succession of prayers and songs, varying with the day and season of the year and the purpose of the individual Mass, and inscribed for the convenience of the priest in the missal, or Book of the Mass. In the Greek rite, and sometimes in the Latin, the two sexes were separated in the congregation. There were no chairs; all stood, or, at the most solemn moments, knelt. Exceptions were made for old or weak people; and for monks or canons, who had to stand through long services, little ledges were built into the choir stalls to support the base of the spine; these *misericordiae* (mercies) became a favorite recipient of the wood carver's skill. The officiating priest entered in a toga covered by alb, chasuble, maniple, and stole—colorful garments bearing symbolical decorations; the most prominent symbols were usually the letters IHS—i.e., *Iesos Huios Soter*, "Jesus Son [of God], Saviour." The Mass itself was begun at the foot of the altar with a humble Introit: "I shall go in to the altar of God," to which the acolyte added, "To God Who giveth joy to my youth." The priest ascended the altar, and kissed it as the sacred repository of saintly relics. He intoned the *Kyrie eleison* ("Lord have mercy upon us")—a Greek survival in the Latin Mass; and recited the *Gloria* ("Glory to God in the highest") and the *Credo*. He consecrated little wafers of bread and a chalice of wine into the body and blood of Christ with the words *Hoc est corpus meum* * and *Hic est sanguinis meus*; and offered these transubstantiated elements—namely His Son—as a propitiatory sacrifice to God in commemoration of the sacrifice on the cross, and in lieu of the ancient sacrifice of living things. Turning to the worshipers, he bade them lift up their hearts to God: *sursum corda*; to which the acolyte, representing the congregation, answered, *Habemus ad Dominum*: "We hold them up to the Lord." The priest then recited the triple *Sanctus*, the *Agnus Dei*, and the *Pater noster*; himself partook of the consecrated bread and wine, and administered the Eucharist to communicants. After some additional prayers he pronounced the closing formula—*Ite, missa est*—"Depart, it is dismissal"—from which the Mass (*missa*) probably derived its name.[99] In late forms there still followed a blessing of the congregation by the priest, and another Gospel reading—usually the Neoplatonic exordium of the Gospel of St. John. Normally there was no sermon except when a bishop officiated, or when, after the twelfth century, a friar came to preach.

At first all Masses were sung, and the congregation joined in the singing; from the fourth century onward the vocal participation of the worshipers declined, and "canonical choristers" provided the musical response to the celebrant's chant.† The hymns sung in the various services of the Church are among the most moving products of medieval sentiment and art. The known history of the Latin hymn begins with Bishop Hilary of Poitiers (d. 367). Returning to Gaul from exile in Syria, he brought home some Greco-Oriental hymns, translated them into Latin, and composed some of his own; all of these are lost. Ambrose at Milan made a new beginning; eighteen sur-

---

* From these words cynics formed the phrase "hocus-pocus."
† For the music of the Mass, see below, Chapter XXXIII.

vive of his sonorous hymns, whose restrained fervor so affected Augustine. The noble hymn of faith and thanksgiving, *Te Deum laudamus*, formerly ascribed to Ambrose, was probably written by the Romanian Bishop Nicetas of Remisiana toward the end of the fourth century. In later centuries the Latin hymns may have assumed a new delicacy of feeling and form under the influence of Moslem and Provençal love poetry.[100] Some of the hymns (like some Arabic poems) verged on jingling doggerel, tipsy with excess of rhyme; but the better hymns of the medieval flowering—the twelfth and thirteenth centuries—developed a subtle turn of compact phrase, a melodiousness of frequent rhyme, a grace and tenderness of thought, that rank them with the greatest lyrics in literature.

To the famous monastery of St. Victor, outside of Paris, there came about 1130 a Breton youth known to us only as Adam of St. Victor. He lived there in quiet content his remaining sixty years, imbibed the spirit of the famous mystics Hugo and Richard, and expressed it humbly, beautifully, and powerfully in hymns mostly designed as sequences for the Mass. A century after him a Franciscan monk, Jacopone da Todi (1228?–1306), composed the supreme medieval lyric, the *Stabat Mater*. Jacopone was a successful lawyer in Todi, near Perugia; his wife was renowned for both goodness and loveliness; she was crushed to death by the fall of a platform at a festival; Jacopone became insane with grief, roamed the Umbrian roads as a wild vagrant crying out his sins and sorrows; smeared himself with tar and feathers, and walked on all fours; joined the Franciscan tertiaries, and wrote the poem that sums up the tender piety of his time:

Stabat mater dolorosa	Stood the mother broken-hearted
iuxta crucem lacrimosa,	All in tears before the cross
dum pendebat filius;	While her Son hung dying;
cuius animan gementem	Through her spirit heavy laden,
contristantem et dolentem	Mourning for Him and in pain,
pertransivit gladius.	Pierced a sword of grief.
O quam tristis et afflicta	Oh, how sad and deep-afflicted
fuit illa benedicta	Was that mother, all so blessed,
mater unigeniti!	Of the only Son!
Quae maerebat et dolebat,	Wailed she then and sore lamented,
et tremebat, cum videbat	Trembled when she saw the torture
nati poenas incliti.	Of her noble Son.
Quis est homo qui non fleret	Who is he that would not sorrow
matrem Christi si videret	If he saw our Saviour's mother
in tanto supplicio?	In such agony?
Quis not posset contristari,	Who could help but share her sadness,
piam matrem contemplari,	Seeing her, the loving mother,
dolentem cum filio? . . .	Grieving with her Son? . . .

Eia, mater, fons amoris,	Come, my mother, fount of loving,
me sentire vim doloris	Make me feel your fullest anguish,
fac, ut tecum lugeam;	Let me mourn with you;
fac ut ardeat cor meum	Let my heart be fired with ardor
in amando Christum deum	Loving Christ our God and Saviour,
ut sibi complaceam.	Let me please Him so!
Sancta mater, illud agas,	Holy mother, do this for me:
crucifixi fige plagas	Plant the blows of Him so martyred
cordi meo valide;	Deeply in my heart;
tui nati vulnerati,	Of your offspring sorely wounded,
tam dignati pro me pati,	Bearing ignominy for me,
poenas mecum divide.	Let me share the pains!
Fac me vere tecum flere	Let me truly weep beside you,
crucifixo condolere,	Mourn with you the Crucified,
donec ego vixero.	All my living years.
Iuxta crucem tecum stare,	Standing by the cross together
te libenter sociare	Would that I might e'er be with you,
in planctu desidero.	Gladly bound in grief.
Fac me cruce custodiri	Let me by the cross be guarded,
morte Christi praemuniri	Saved by Christ's redeeming Passion,
confoveri gratia;	Cherished by His grace;
quando corpus morietur,	When my body shall have perished,
fac ut animae donetur	Let my soul in heaven's glory
paradisi gloria.	See Him face to face.

Only two poems rival this among medieval Christian hymns. One is the *Pange lingua* that St. Thomas Aquinas composed for the Corpus Christi feast. The other is the terrible *Dies irae*, or "Day of Wrath," written about 1250 by Thomas of Celano, and still sung in the Mass for the Dead; here the horror of the Last Judgment inspires a poem as dark and perfect as any of Dante's tormented dreams.[101]

To the moving ritual of her prayers, hymns, and Mass the Church added the imposing ceremonies and processions of religious festivals. In northern countries the Feast of the Nativity took over the pleasant rites wherewith the pagan Teutons had celebrated the victory of the sun, at the winter solstice, over the advancing night; hence the "Yule" logs that burned in German, North French, English, Scandinavian homes, and the Yule trees laden with gifts, and the merry feasting that tried strong stomachs till the Twelfth Night thereafter. There were countless other feasts or holydays—Epiphany, Circumcision, Palm Sunday, Easter, Ascension, Pentecost. . . . Such days—and only in less degree all Sundays—were exciting events in the life of medieval man. For Easter he confessed such of his sins as he cared to remember, bathed, cut his beard or hair, dressed in his best and most uncomfortable clothes, received God in the Eucharist, and felt more profoundly than ever the momentous Christian drama of which he was made a part. In many towns, on the last three days of Holy Week, the events of the Passion were represented in the churches by a religious play, with dialogue and plain chant; and several other occasions of the ecclesiastical year were signalized with such "mysteries." About 1240 Juliana, prioress of a convent near Liége, reported to her village priest that a supernatural vision had urged upon her the need of honoring with a solemn festival the body of Christ as transubstantiated in the Eucharist; in 1262 Pope Urban IV sanctioned such a celebration, and entrusted to St. Thomas Aquinas the composition of an "office" for it—appropriate hymns and prayers; the philosopher acquitted himself wonderfully well in this assignment; and in 1311 the Feast of Corpus Christi was finally established and was celebrated on the first Thursday after Pentecost, with the most impressive procession of the Christian year. Such ceremonies drew immense crowds, and glorified numerous participants; they opened the way to the medieval secular drama; and they helped the pageantry of the guilds, the tournaments and knightly initiations, and the coronation of kings, to occupy with pious flurry and sublimating spectacle the occasional leisure of men not natively inclined to order and peace. The Church based her technique of moralization through faith not on arguments to reason but on appeals to the senses through drama, music, painting, sculpture, architecture, fiction, and poetry; and it must be confessed that such appeals to universal sensibilities are more successful—for evil as well as for good—than challenges to the changeful and individualistic intellect. Through such appeals the Church created medieval art.

The culminating pageants were at the goals of pilgrimage. Medieval men and women went on pilgrimage to fulfill a penance or a vow, or to seek a miraculous cure, or to earn an indulgence, and doubtless, like modern tourists, to see strange lands and sights, and find adventure on the way as a relief from the routine of a narrow life. At the end of the thirteenth century there were some 10,000 sanctioned goals of Christian pilgrimage. The bravest pilgrims fared to distant Palestine, sometimes barefoot or clothed only in a shirt, and usually armed with cross, staff, and purse all given by a priest. In 1054 Bishop Liedbert of Cambrai led 3000 pilgrims to Jerusalem; in 1064 the archbishops of Cologne and Mainz, and the bishops of Speyer, Bamberg, and Utrecht started for Jerusalem with 10,000 Christians in their wake; 3000 of them perished on the way; only 2000 returned safely to their native lands. Other pilgrims crossed the Pyrenees, or risked themselves on the Atlantic, to visit the reputed bones of the apostle James at Compostela in Spain. In England pilgrims sought the tomb of St. Cuthbert at Durham, the grave of Edward the Confessor in Westminster, or that of St. Edmund at Bury, the church supposedly founded by Joseph of Arimathea at Glastonbury, and above all, the shrine of Thomas à Becket at Canterbury. France drew pilgrims to St. Martin's at Tours, to Notre Dame at Chartres, Notre Dame at Le-Puy-en-Velay. Italy had the church and bones of St. Francis at Assisi, and the Santa Casa, or Holy House, at Loreto, which the pious believed to be the very dwelling in which Mary had lived with Jesus at Nazareth; when the Turks drove the last Crusader from Palestine this cottage was carried by angels through the air and deposited in Dalmatia (1291), then flown across the Adriatic to the Ancona woods (*lauretum*) from which the honored village took its name.

Finally, all the roads of Christendom led pilgrims to Rome, to see the tombs of Peter and Paul, to earn indulgences by visiting the Stations or famous churches of the city, or to celebrate some jubilee, or joyous anniversary, in Christian history. In 1299 Pope Boniface VIII declared a jubilee for 1300, and offered a plenary indulgence to those who should come and worship in St. Peter's in that year. It was estimated that on no day in those twelve months had Rome less than 200,000 strangers within her gates; and a total of 2,000,000 visitors, each with a modest offering, deposited such treasure before St. Peter's tomb that two priests, with rakes in their hands, were kept busy night and day collecting the coins.[102] Guidebooks taught the pilgrims by what roads to travel, and what points to visit at their goal or on the way. We may weakly imagine the exaltation of the tired and dusty pilgrims when at last they sighted the Eternal City, and burst into the Pilgrims' Chorus of joy and praise:

> O Roma nobilis, orbis et domina,
> cunctarum urbium excellentissima,
> roseo martyrum sanguine rubea,
> albis et virginum liliis candida;
> salutem dicimus tibi per omnia;
> te benedicimus; salve per saecula!

"O noble Rome, of all this world the queen, of all the cities the most excellent! O ruby red with martyrs' rosy blood, yet white with lilies pure of virgin maids; we give thee salutation through all years; we bless thee; through all generations hail!"

To these varied religious services the Church added social services. She taught the dignity of labor, and practiced it through the agriculture and industry of her monks. She sanctified the organization of labor in the guilds, and organized religious guilds to perform works of charity.[103] Every church was a sanctuary with right of asylum in which hunted men might find some breathless refuge till the passions of their pursuers could yield to the processes of law; to drag men from such a sanctuary was a sacrilege entailing excommunication. The church or cathedral was the social as well as the religious center of the village or town. Sometimes the sacred precinct, or even the church itself, was used, with genial clerical consent, to store grain or hay or wine, to grind corn or brew beer.[104] There most of the villagers had been baptized, there most of them would be buried. There the older folk would gather of a Sunday for gossip or discussion, and the young men and women to see and be seen. There the beggars assembled, and the alms of the Church were dispensed. There nearly all the art that the village knew was brought together to beautify the House of God; and the poverty of a thousand homes was brightened by the glory of that temple which the people had built with their coins and hands, and which they considered their own, their collective and spiritual home. In the church belfry the bells rang the hours of the day or the call to services and prayer; and the music of those bells was sweeter than any other except the hymns that bound voices and hearts into one, or warmed a cooling faith with the canticles of the Mass. From Novgorod to Cadiz, from Jerusalem to the Hebrides, steeples and spires raised themselves precariously into the sky because men cannot live without hope, and will not consent to die.

V. CANON LAW

Side by side with this complex and colorful liturgy there developed the even more complex body of ecclesiastical legislation that regulated the conduct and decisions of a Church governing a wider and more varied realm than any empire of the time. Canon law—the "law of the rule" of the Church —was a slow accretion of old religious customs, scriptural passages, opinions of the Fathers, laws of Rome or the barbarians, the decrees of Church councils, and the decisions and opinions of the popes. Some parts of the Justinian Code were adapted to govern the conduct of the clergy; other parts were recast to accord with the views of the Church on marriage, divorce, and wills. Collections of ecclesiastical legislation were made in the sixth and eighth centuries in the West, and periodically by Byzantine emperors in the East. The laws of the Roman Church received their definitive medieval formulation by Gratian about 1148.

As a monk of Bologna, Gratian may have studied under Irnerius in the university there; certainly his digest shows a wide acquaintance with both Roman law and medieval philosophy. He called his book *Concordia discordantium canonum*—reconciliation of discordant regulations; later generations called it his *Decretum*. It drew into order and sequence the laws and customs, the conciliar and papal decrees, of the Church down to 1139 on her doctrine, ritual, organization, and administration, the maintenance of ecclesiastical property, the procedure and precedents of ecclesiastical courts, the regulation of monastic life, the contract of marriage, and the rules of bequest. The method of exposition may have stemmed from Abélard's *Sic et non*, and had in turn some influence on Scholastic method after Gratian: it began with an authoritative proposition, quoted statements or precedents contradicting it, sought to resolve the contradiction, and added a commentary. Though the book was not accepted by the medieval Church as a final authority, it became, for the period it covered, the indispensable and almost sacred text. Gregory IX (1234), Boniface VIII (1294), and Clement V (1313) added supplements; these and some minor additions were published with Gratian's *Concordia* in 1582 as *Corpus iuris canonici*, a body of canonical—Church-regulating—law comparable with the *Corpus iuris civilis* of Justinian.*

Indeed, the field covered by canon law was larger than that covered by any contemporary civil code. It embraced not merely the structure, dogmas, and operation of the Church, but rules for dealing with non-Christians in Christian lands; procedure in the investigation and suppression of heresy; the organization of crusades; the laws of marriage, legitimacy, dower, adultery, divorce, wills, burial, widows, and orphans; laws of oath, perjury, sacrilege, blasphemy, simony, libel, usury, and just price; regulations for schools and universities; the Truce of God and other means of limiting war and organizing peace; the conduct of episcopal and papal courts; the use of excommunication, anathema, and interdict; the administration of ecclesiastical penalties; the relations between civil and ecclesiastical courts, between state and Church. This vast body of legislation was held by the Church to be binding on all Christians, and she reserved the right to punish any infraction of it with a variety of physical or spiritual penalties, except that no ecclesiastical court was to pronounce a "judgment of blood"—i.e., condemn to capital punishment.

Usually, before the Inquisition, the Church relied on spiritual terrors. Minor excommunication excluded a Christian from the sacraments and ritual of the Church; any priest could pronounce this penalty; and to believers it meant everlasting hell if death should reach the offender before absolution came. A major excommunication (the only kind now used by the Church) could be pronounced only by councils or by prelates higher than a priest, and only upon persons within their jurisdiction. It removed the victim from all legal or spiritual association with the Christian community: he could not sue or inherit or do any valid act in law, but he could be sued; and no Christian was to eat or talk with him on pain of minor excommunication. When King Robert of France was excommunicated (998) for marrying his cousin he was abandoned by all his courtiers and nearly all his servants; two domestics who remained threw into the fire the victuals left by him at his meals, lest they be contaminated by them. In extreme cases the Church added to excommunication anathema—a curse armed and detailed with all the careful pleonasm of legal phraseology. As a last resort the pope could lay an interdict upon any part of Christendom—i.e., suspend all or most religious services. A people feeling the need of the sacraments, and fearful of death supervening upon

---

* On May 20, 1918, the revised *Corpus iuris canonici* became the official law of the Church.

unforgiven sins, sooner or later compelled the excommunicated individual to make his peace with the Church. Such interdicts were laid upon France in 998, Germany in 1102, England in 1208, Rome itself in 1155.

The excessive use of excommunication and interdict weakened their effectiveness after the eleventh century.[105] Popes employed interdict, now and then, for political purposes, as when Innocent II threatened Pisa with interdict if it did not join the Tuscan League.[106] Wholesale excommunications—e.g., for false returns of tithes due the Church—were so numerous that large sections of the Christian community were outlawed at once or without knowing it; and many who knew it ignored the curse or laughed it off.[107] Milan, Bologna, and Florence thrice received wholesale excommunications in the thirteenth and fourteenth centuries; Milan ignored the third edict for twenty-two years. Said Bishop Guillaume le Maire in 1311: "I have sometimes seen with my own eyes three or four hundred excommunicates in a single parish, and even seven hundred . . . who despised the Power of the Keys, and uttered blasphemous and scandalous words against the Church and her ministers." [108] Philip Augustus and Philip the Fair paid little attention to the decrees that excommunicated them.

Such occasional indifference marked the beginning of a decline in the authority of canon law over the laity of Europe. As the Church had taken so wide an area of human life under her rule when, in the first Christian millennium, secular powers had broken down, so in the thirteenth and fourteenth centuries, as secular government grew stronger, one phase after another of human affairs was recaptured by civil from canon law. The Church properly won in the matter of ecclesiastical appointments; in most other fields her authority began to decline—in education, marriage, morals, economy, and war. The states that had grown up under the protection, and by the permission, of the social order that she had created declared themselves of age, and began that long process of secularization which culminates today. But the work of the canonists, like most creative activity, was not lost. It prepared and trained the Church's greatest statesmen; it shared in transmitting Roman law to the modern world; it raised the legal rights of widows and children, and established the principle of dower in the civil law of Western Europe;[109] and it helped to shape the form and terms of Scholastic philosophy. Canon law was among the major achievements of the medieval mind.

VI. THE CLERGY

Medieval parlance divided all persons into two classes: those who lived under a religious rule, and those who lived "in the world." A monk was "a religious"; so was a nun. Some monks were also priests, and constituted the "regular clergy"—i.e., clergy following a monastic rule (*regula*). All other clergy were called "secular," as living in the "world" (*saeculum*). All ranks of clergy were distinguished by the tonsure—a shaven crown of the head—and wore a long robe, of any single color but red or green, buttoned from head to foot. The term *clergy* included not only those in "minor orders"—i.e., church doorkeepers, readers, exorcists, and acolytes—but all university students, all teachers, and all who, having taken the tonsure as students, later became physicians, lawyers, artists, authors, or served as accountants or literary aides; hence the later narrowing of the terms *clerical* and *clerk*. Clerics who had not taken major orders were allowed to marry, and to take up any respectable profession, and they were under no obligation to continue the tonsure.

The three "major" or "holy orders"—subdeacon, deacon, priest—were irrevocable, and generally closed the door to marriage after the eleventh century. Instances of marriage or concubinage in the Latin priesthood after Gregory VII are recorded,[110] but they become more and more exceptional.* The parish priest had to content himself with spiritual joys. As the parish was normally coterminous with a manor or a village, he was usually appointed by the lord of the manor [111] in collusion with the bishop. He was seldom a man of much schooling, for a university education was costly and books were rare; it was enough if he could read the breviary and the missal, administer the sacraments, and organize the parish for worship and charity. In many cases he was only a *vicarius*, a vicar or substitute, hired by a rector to do the religious work of the parish for a fourth of the revenues of the "benefice"; in this way one rector might hold four or five benefices while the parish priest lived in humble poverty,[112] eking out his income with "altar fees" for baptisms, marriages, burials, and Masses for the dead. Sometimes, in the class war, he sided with the poor, like John Ball.[113] His morals could not compare with those of the modern priest, who has been put on his best behavior by religious competition; but by and large he did his work with patience, conscience, and kindliness. He visited the sick, comforted the bereaved, taught the young, mumbled his breviary, and brought some moral and civilizing leaven to a rough and lusty population. Many parish priests, said their cruelest critic, "were the salt of the earth." [114] "No other body of men," said the freethinking Lecky, "have ever exhibited a more single-minded and unworldly zeal,

---

* The general celibacy of monks, priests, and nuns after 1215 presents a problem in genetics. It may be that Europe suffered some biological loss by the abstention of so many able persons from parentage, but we do not know to what extent superior ability is inherited. Less theoretical were the effects of the numerical disbalance caused between the sexes in the lay population by the withdrawal of monks and priests from marriage. As commercial and other travel, war and Crusades, feuds and other hazards raised the death rate of men above that of women, a substantial percentage of the female sex was left to spinsterhood or promiscuity. The Church welcomed into nunneries such qualified women as cared to enter, but monks and priests combined far outnumbered nuns. The unmarried daughters of the nobility were often dowered to a convent; but in other classes surplus women resigned themselves to the spinning wheel, or lived as tolerated aunts with their relatives, or devoted themselves, in shame and terror, to satisfying the demands of respectable men.

refracted by no personal interests, sacrificing to duty the dearest of earthly objects, and confronting with dauntless heroism every form of hardship, of suffering, and of death." [115]

Priesthood and episcopate constituted the *sacerdotium*, or sacerdotal order. The bishop was a priest selected to co-ordinate several parishes and priests into one diocese. Originally and theoretically he was chosen by priests and people; usually, before Gregory VII, he was named by the baron or king; after 1215 he was elected by the cathedral chapter in co-operation with the pope. To his care were committed many secular as well as ecclesiastical affairs, and his episcopal court tried some civil cases as well as all those involving clergy of any rank. He had the power to appoint and depose priests; but his authority over the abbots and monasteries in his diocese diminished in this period, as the popes, fearing the power of the bishops, brought the monastic orders under direct papal control. His revenues came partly from his parishes, mostly from the estates attached to his see; sometimes he gave more to a parish than he received from it. Candidates for a bishopric usually agreed to pay—at first to the king, later to the pope—a fee for their nomination; and as secular rulers they sometimes yielded to the amiable weakness of appointing relatives to lucrative posts; Pope Alexander III complained that "when God deprived bishops of sons the Devil gave them nephews." [116] Many bishops lived in luxury, as became feudal lords; but many were consumed in devotion to their spiritual and administrative tasks. After the reform of the episcopate by Leo IX the bishops of Europe were, in mind and morals, the finest body of men in medieval history.

Above the bishops of a province stood the archbishop or metropolitan. He alone could call, or preside over, a provincial council of the Church. Some archbishops, by their character or their wealth, ruled nearly all the life of their provinces. In Germany the archbishops of Hamburg, Bremen, Cologne, Trier, Mainz, Magdeburg, and Salzburg were powerful feudal lords, who were in several instances chosen by the emperors to administer the Empire, or to serve as ambassadors or royal councilors; the archbishops of Reims, Rouen, and Canterbury played a similar role in France, Normandy, and England. Certain archbishops—of Toledo, Lyons, Narbonne, Reims, Cologne, Canterbury—were made "primates," and exercised a debated authority over all the ecclesiastics of their region.

The bishops gathered in council constituted, periodically, a representative government for the Church. In later centuries these councils would lay claim to powers superior to those of the pope; but in this, the age of the greatest pontiffs, no one in Western Europe questioned the supreme ecclesiastical and spiritual authority of the bishop of Rome. The scandals of the tenth century had been atoned for by the virtues of Leo IX and Hildebrand; amid the oscillations and struggles of the twelfth century the power of the papacy had grown until, in Innocent III, it claimed to overspread the earth. Kings and emperors held the stirrup and kissed the feet of the white-robed Servant of the Servants of God. The papacy was now the highest reach of human ambition; the finest minds of the time prepared themselves in rigorous schools of theology and law for a place in the hierarchy of the Church; and those who rose to the top were men of intelligence and courage, who were not appalled by the task of governing a continent. Their individual deaths hardly disturbed the pursuit of the policies formed by them and their councils; what Gregory VII left unfinished Innocent III completed; and Innocent IV and Alexander IV carried to a victorious end the struggle that Innocent III and Gregory IX had fought against Imperial encirclement of the papacy.

In theory the authority of the pope was derived from his succession to the power conferred upon the apostles by Christ; in this sense the government of the Church was a theocracy—a government of the people, through religion, by the earthly vicars of God. In another sense the Church was a democracy: every man in Christendom except the mentally or physically defective, the convicted criminal, the excommunicate and the slave was eligible to the priesthood and the papacy. As in every system, the rich had superior opportunities to prepare themselves for the long hierarchical climb; but career was open to all, and talent, not ancestry, chiefly determined success. Hundreds of bishops, and several popes, came from the ranks of the poor.[117] This flow of fresh blood into the hierarchy from every rank continually nourished the intelligence of the clergy, and "was for ages the only practical recognition of the equality of man." *

In 1059, as we have seen, the right to select the pope was confined to "cardinal bishops" stationed near Rome. These seven cardinals were gradually increased, by papal appointment from various nations, to a Sacred College of seventy members, who were marked off by their red caps and purple robes, and constituted a new rank in the hierarchy, second only to the pope himself.

Aided by such men, and by a large staff of ecclesiastics and other officials constituting the papal Curia or executive and judicial court, the pope governed a spiritual empire which in the thirteenth century was at the height of its curve. He alone could summon a general council of the bishops, and their legislation had no force except when confirmed by his decree. He was free to interpret, revise, and extend the canon law of the Church, and to grant dispensations from its rules. He was the final court of appeals from the decisions

---

* James Westfall Thompson, *Economic and Social History of the Middle Ages*, N. Y., 1928, p. 601. Cf. Voltaire: "The Roman Church has always had the advantage of giving that to merit which in other governments is given only to birth" (*Essay on the Manners and Morals of Europe*, in *Works*, N. Y., 1927, XIII b, 30). This, said Hitler, "is the origin of the incredibly vigorous power that inhabits this age-old institution. This gigantic host of clerical dignitaries, by uninterruptedly supplementing itself from the lowest layers of the nations, preserves not only its instinctive bond with the people's world of sentiment, but it also assures itself of a sum of energy and active force which in such a form will forever be present only in the broad masses of the people" (*Mein Kampf*, N. Y., 1939, p. 643).

of episcopal courts. He alone could absolve from certain grave sins, or issue major indulgences, or canonize a saint. After 1059 all bishops had to swear obedience to him, and submit to supervision of their affairs by legates of the pope. Islands like Sardinia and Sicily, nations like England, Hungary, and Spain, acknowledged him as their feudal lord, and sent him tribute. Through bishops, priests, and monks his eyes and hands could be on every part of his realm; these men constituted a service of intelligence and administration with which no state could compete. Gradually, subtly, the rule of Rome was restored over Europe by the astonishing power of the word.

VII. THE PAPACY SUPREME: 1085–1294

The conflict between Church and state over lay investitures did not die with Gregory VII and the apparent triumph of the Empire; it continued for a generation through several pontificates, and reached a compromise in the Concordat of Worms (1122) between Pope Calixtus II and the Emperor Henry V. Henry surrendered to the Church "all investiture by ring and staff," and agreed that elections of bishops and abbots "shall be conducted canonically"—i.e., be made by the affected clergy or monks—"and shall be free from all interference" and simony. Calixtus conceded that in Germany the elections of bishops or abbots holding lands from the crown should be held in the presence of the king; that in disputed elections the king might decide between the contenders after consulting with the bishops of the province; and that an abbot or bishop holding lands from the king should render to him all feudal obligations due from vassal to suzerain.[118] Similar agreements had already been signed for England and France. Each side claimed the victory. The Church had made substantial progress toward autonomy, but the feudal nexus continued to give the kings a predominant voice in the choice of bishops everywhere in Europe.[119]

In 1130 the college of cardinals divided into factions; one chose Innocent II, the other Anacletus II. Anacletus, though of the noble family of the Pierleoni, had had a Jewish grandfather, a convert to Christianity; his opponents called him "Judaeo-pontifex"; and St. Bernard, who on other occasions was friendly to the Jews, wrote to the Emperor Lothaire II that "to the shame of Christ a man of Jewish origin was come to occupy the chair of St. Peter"—forgetting Peter's origin. The greater part of the clergy, and all but one of Europe's kings, upheld Innocent. The populace of Europe amused itself with slanders charging Anacletus with incest, and with plundering Christian churches to enrich his Jewish friends; but the people of Rome supported him till his death (1138). It was probably the story of Anacletus that led to the fourteenth-century legend of Andreas "the Jewish Pope." [119a]

Hadrian IV (1154–9) exemplified again the ecclesiastical *carrière ouverte aux talents*. Born in England of lowly parentage, and coming as a beggar to a monastery, Nicholas Breakspear raised himself by pure ability to be abbot, cardinal, and pope. He bestowed Ireland upon Henry II of England, compelled Barbarossa to kiss his feet, and almost maneuvered the great Emperor into conceding the right of the popes to dispose of royal thrones. When Hadrian died a majority of cardinals chose Alexander III (1159–81), a minority chose Victor IV. Barbarossa, thinking to restore the power once held by German emperors over the papacy, invited both men to lay their claims before him; Alexander refused, Victor agreed; and at the Synod of Pavia (1160) Barbarossa recognized Victor as Pope. Alexander excommunicated Frederick, released the Emperor's subjects from civil obedience, and helped revolt in Lombardy. The victory of the Lombard League at Legnano (1176) humbled Frederick. He made his peace with Alexander at Venice, and once more kissed papal feet. The same pontiff compelled Henry II of England to repair barefoot to the tomb of Becket, and there receive discipline from the canons of Canterbury. It was Alexander's long struggle and complete victory that made straight the way for one of the greatest popes.

Innocent III was born at Anagni, near Rome, in 1161. As Lotario dei Conti, son of the count of Segni, he had all the advantages of aristocratic birth and cultured rearing. He studied philosophy and theology at Paris, canon and civil law at Bologna. Back in Rome, by his mastery of both diplomacy and doctrine, and his influential connections, he advanced rapidly on the ecclesiastical ladder; at thirty he was a cardinal deacon; and at thirty-seven, though still not a priest, he was unanimously chosen pope (1198). He was ordained on one day, and consecrated on the next. It was his good fortune that the Emperor Henry VI, who had acquired control of South Italy and Sicily, had died in 1197, leaving the throne to the three-year-old Frederick II. Innocent seized the opportunity vigorously: deposed the German prefect in Rome, ousted the German feudatories from Spoleto and Perugia, received the submission of Tuscany, re-established the rule of the papacy in the Papal States, was recognized by Henry's widow as overlord of the Two Sicilies, and consented to be the guardian of her son. In ten months Innocent had made himself master of Italy.

He had, on the existing evidence, the best mind of his time. In his early thirties he had written four works of theology; they were learned and eloquent, but they are lost in the glare of his political fame. His pronouncements as Pope were characterized by a clarity and logic of thought, a fitness and pungency of phrase, that could have made him a brilliant Aquinas or an orthodox Abélard. Despite his small stature he derived a commanding presence from his keen eyes and stern dark face. He was not without humor; he sang well, and composed poetry; he had a tender side, and could be kindly, patient, and personally tolerant. But in doctrine and morals he allowed no deviation from the dogmas or ethics of the Church. The world of Christian faith and hope was the empire that he had been named to protect; and like any king he would guard his realm with the sword when the word did not suffice. Born to riches, he lived in philosophic simplicity; in an age of universal venality he remained incorruptible;[120] at once after his consecration he forbade the officials of his Curia to charge for their services. He liked to see the wealth of the world enrich Peter's See, but he administered the papal funds with a reasonably honest hand. He was a consummate diplomat, and moderately shared in the reluctant unmorality of that distinguished trade.[121] As if eleven centuries had fallen away, he was a Roman emperor, Stoic rather than Christian, and never doubting his right to rule the world.

With so many strong popes in the fresh memory of Rome, it was natural that Innocent should base his policies upon a belief in the sanctity and high mission of his office. He carefully maintained the pomp and majesty of papal ceremony, and never stooped in public from imperial dignity. Sincerely believing himself the heir to the powers then generally conceded to have been given by the Son of God to the apostles and the Church, he could hardly recognize any authority as equal to his own. "The Lord left to Peter," he said, "the government not only of all the Church, but of the whole world." [122] He did not claim supreme power in earthly or purely secular affairs, except in the Papal States;[123] but he insisted that where the spiritual conflicted with the secular power the spiritual power should be held as superior to the secular as the sun is to the moon. He shared the ideal of Gregory VII—that all governments should accept a place in a world state of which the pope should be the head, with paramount authority over all matters of justice, morality, and faith; and for a time he almost realized that dream.

In 1204, through the conquest of Constantinople by the Crusaders, he achieved one part of his plans: the Greek Church submitted to the Bishop of Rome, and Innocent could speak with joy of "the seamless garment of Christ." He brought Serbia and even distant Armenia under the dominion of the Roman See. Gradually he secured control over ecclesiastical appointments, and made the powerful episcopacy the organ and servant of the papacy. Through an astonishing succession of vital conflicts he reduced the potentates of Europe to an unprecedented recognition of his sovereignty. His policies were least effective in Italy: he failed in repeated efforts to end the wars of the Italian city-states; and in Rome his political enemies made life so unsafe for him that for a time he had to shun his capital. King Sverre of Norway (1184–1202) successfully resisted him despite excommunication and interdict.[124] Philip II of France ignored his command to make peace with England, but yielded to the Pope's insistence that he take back his discarded wife. Alfonso IX of Leon was persuaded to put away Berengaria, whom he had married within the forbidden degrees of kinship. Portugal, Aragon, Hungary, and Bulgaria acknowledged themselves as feudal fiefs of the papacy, and sent it tribute yearly. When King John rejected Innocent's appointment of Langton as archbishop of Canterbury, the Pope drove him by interdict and shrewd diplomacy to add England to the list of papal fiefs. Innocent extended his power in Germany by supporting Otto IV against Philip of Swabia, then Philip against Otto, then Otto against Frederick II, then Frederick against Otto, in each case exacting concessions to the papacy as the price of his favor, and freeing the Papal States from the threat of encirclement. He reminded the emperors that it was a pope who had "translated" the *imperium* or imperial power from the Greeks to the Franks; that Charlemagne had been made Emperor only by papal anointment and coronation; and that what the popes had given they could take away. A Byzantine visitor to Rome described Innocent as "the successor not of Peter but of Constantine." [125]

He repelled all secular efforts to tax the Christian clergy without papal consent. He provided papal funds for necessitous priests, and labored to improve the education of the clergy. He raised the social status of the clergy by defining the Church not as all Christian believers but as all the Christian clergy. He condemned the episcopal or monastic absorption of parochial tithes at the expense of the parish priest.[126] To reform monastic laxity he ordered the regular surveillance and visitation of monasteries and convents. His legislation reduced to order the complex relations of clergy and laity, priest and bishop, bishop and pope. He developed the papal Curia to an efficient court of counsel, administration, and judgment; it became now the most competent governing body of its time, and its methods and terminology helped to form the art and technique of diplomacy. Innocent himself was probably the best lawyer of the age, capable of finding legal support, in logic and precedent, for every decision that he made. Lawyers and learned men frequented the "consistory" where he presided over the cardinals as a superior ecclesiastical court, to profit from his discussions and decisions on points of civil or canon law. Some called him *Pater iuris*, Father of the Law; [127] others, in fond humor, called him Solomon III.[128]

In his final triumph as legislator and Pope, he presided in 1215 over the Fourth Lateran Council, held in the church of St. John's Lateran in Rome. To this twelfth ecumenical council came 1500 abbots, bishops, archbishops, and other prelates, and plenipotentiaries from all the important nations of a united Christendom. The Pope's opening address was a bold admission and challenge: "The corruption of the people has its chief source in the clergy. From this arise the evils of Christendom: faith perishes, religion is defaced ... justice is trodden under foot, heretics multiply, schismatics are emboldened, the faithless grow strong, the Saracens triumph." [129] The assembled power and intellect of the Church here allowed itself to be completely dominated by one man. His judgments became the Council's decrees. It allowed him to redefine the basic dogmas of the Church; now for the first time the doctrine of transubstantiation was officially defined. It accepted his decrees requiring that a distinctive badge be worn by non-Christians in Christian lands. It responded enthusiastically to his call for a war against the Albigensian heretics. But it also followed his lead in recognizing the shortcomings of the Church. It denounced the peddling of fraudulent relics. It severely censured the "indiscreet and superfluous indulgences which some prelates . . . are not afraid to grant, whereby the Keys of the Church are made contemptible, and the satisfaction of penance is deprived of its force." [130] It attempted a far-reaching reform of monastic life. It denounced clerical drunkenness, immorality, and clandestine marriage, and passed vigorous measures against them; but it condemned the Albigensian claim that all sexual intercourse is sinful. In its attendance, scope, and effects the Fourth Lateran Council was the most important assembly of the Church since the Council of Nicaea.

From that apex of his career Innocent declined rapidly to an early death. He had given himself so unremittingly to the administration and enlargement of his office that at fifty-five he was exhausted. "I have no leisure," he mourned, "to meditate on supramundane things. Scarce can I breathe. So much must I live for others that almost I am a stranger to myself." [131] Perhaps in his last year he could look back upon his work and judge it more objectively than in the heat of strife. The crusades that he had organized for the reconquest of Palestine had failed; the one that would succeed after his death was the ferocious extermination of the Albigensians in southern France. He had won the admiration of his contemporaries, but not, like Gregory I or Leo IX, their affection. Some churchmen complained that he was too much the king, too little the priest; St. Lutgardis thought he could only by a narrow margin escape hell; [132] and the Church herself, though proud of his genius and grateful for his labors, withheld from him that canonization which she had conferred upon lesser and more scrupulous men.

But we must not refuse him the credit of having brought the Church to her greatest height, and close to the realization of her dream of a moral world-state. He was the ablest statesman of his age. He pursued his aims with vision, devotion, flexible persistence, and unbelievable energy. When he died (1216) the Church had reached a height of organization, splendor, repute, and power which she had never known before, and would only rarely and briefly know again.

Honorius III (1216–27) does not rank high in the cruel annals of history, because he was too gentle to carry on with vigor the war between Empire and papacy. Gregory IX (1227–41), though eighty when made Pope, waged that war with almost fanatical tenacity; fought Frederick II so successfully as to postpone the Renaissance for a hundred years; and organized the Inquisition. Yet he too was a man of unquestionable sincerity and heroic devotion, who defended what seemed to him the most precious possession of mankind —its Christ-begotten faith. He could not have been a hard man who, as cardinal, had protected and wisely guided the possibly heretical Francis. Innocent IV (1243–54) destroyed Frederick II, and sanctioned the use of torture by the Inquisition.[133] He was a good patron of philosophy, aided the universities, and founded schools of law. Alexander IV (1254–61) was a man of peace, kindly, merciful, and just, who "astounded the world by his freedom from despotism"; [134] he deprecated the martial qualities of his predecessors,[135] preferred piety to politics, and "died of a broken heart," said a Franciscan chronicler, "considering daily the terrible and increasing strife among Christians." [136] Clement IV (1265–8) returned to war, organized the defeat of Manfred, and ruined the Hohenstaufen dynasty and Imperial Germany. The recapture of Constantinople by the Greeks threatened to end the accord between the Greek and the Roman Church; but Gregory X (1271–6) earned the gratitude of Michael Palaeologus by discountenancing the ambition of Charles of Anjou to conquer Byzantium; the restored Greek Emperor submitted the Eastern Church to Rome; and the papacy was again supreme.

VIII. THE FINANCES OF THE CHURCH

A Church that was actually a European superstate, dealing with the worship, morals, education, marriages, wars, crusades, deaths, and wills of the population of half a continent, sharing actively in the administration of secular affairs, and raising the most expensive structures in medieval history, could sustain its functions only through exploiting a hundred sources of revenue.

The widest stream of income was the tithe: after Charlemagne all secular lands in Latin Christendom were required by state law to pay a tenth of their gross produce or income, in kind or money, to the local church. After the tenth century every parish had to remit a part of its tithes to the bishop of the diocese. Under the influence of feudal ideas the tithes of a parish could be enfeoffed, mortgaged, bequeathed, or sold like any other property or revenue, so that by the twelfth century a financial web had been woven in which the local church and its priest were rather the collectors than the consumers of its tithes. The priest was expected to "curse for his tithes," as the English put it—to excommunicate those who shirked or falsified their returns; for men were as reluctant then to pay tithes to the Church, whose functions they considered vital to their salvation, as men are now to pay taxes to the state. We hear of occasional revolts of the tithepayers: in Reggio Emilia in 1280, says Fra Salimbene, the citizens, defying excommunication and interdict, promised one another "that none should pledge the clergy any tithe . . . nor sit at meat with them . . . nor give them eat or drink"—an excommunication in reverse; and the bishop was compelled to compromise.[137]

The basic revenue of the Church was from her own lands. These she had received through gift or bequest, through purchase or defaulted mortgage, or through reclamation of waste lands by monastic or other ecclesiastic groups. In the feudal system each owner or tenant was expected to leave something to the Church at death; those who did not were suspected of heresy, and might be refused burial in consecrated ground.[138] Since only a few of the laity could write, a priest was usually called in to draft the wills; Pope Alexander III decreed in 1170 that no one could make a valid will except in presence of a priest; any secular notary who drew up a will except under these conditions was to be excommunicated; [139] and the Church had exclusive jurisdiction over the probate of wills. Gifts or legacies to the Church were held to be the most dependable means of telescoping the pains of purgatory. Many bequests to the Church, especially before the year 1000, began with the words *adventante mundi vespero*—"since the evening of the world is near." [140] Some owners, as we have seen, gave their property to the Church *in precarium* as disability insurance: the Church provided an annuity, and care in sickness and old age, to the donor, and received the property free of lien at his death.[141] Some monasteries, by "confraternities," gave their benefactors a share in the merits or purgatorial deductions earned by the prayers and good works of the monks.[142] Crusaders not only sold lands to the Church at low prices to raise cash, but they received loans from church bodies on the security of pledged property, which was in many cases forfeited by default. Some persons, dying without natural heirs, left their whole estate to the Church; the Countess Matilda of Tuscany tried to bequeath to the Church almost a fourth of Italy.

As the property of the Church was inalienable, and, before 1200, was normally free from secular taxation,[143] it grew from century to century. It was not unusual for a cathedral, a monastery, or a nunnery to own several thousand manors, including a dozen towns or even a great city or two.[144] The bishop of Langres owned the whole county; the abbey of St. Martin of Tours ruled over 20,000 serfs; the bishop of Bologna held 2000 manors; so did the abbey of Lorsch; the abbey of Las Huelgas, in Spain, held sixty-four townships.[145] In Castile, about 1200, the Church owned a quarter of the soil; in England a fifth; in Germany a third; in Livonia one half;[146] these, however, are loose and uncertain estimates. Such accumulations became the envy and target of the state. Charles Martel confiscated church property to finance his wars; Louis the Pious legislated against bequests that disinherited the children of the testator in favor of the Church; [147] Henry II of Germany stripped many monasteries of their lands, saying that monks were vowed to poverty; and several English statutes of mortmain put restrictions on the deeding of property to "corporations"—meaning ecclesiastical bodies. Edward I levied from the English Church in 1291 a tenth of its property, and in 1294 a half of its annual revenue. Philip II began, St. Louis continued, Philip IV established, the taxation of ecclesiastical property in France. As industry and commerce developed, and money multiplied and prices rose, the income of abbeys and bishoprics, derived largely from feudal dues once fixed at a low-price level and now hard to raise, proved inadequate not only for luxury but even for maintenance.[148] By 1270 the majority of French cathedrals and abbeys were heavily in debt; they had borrowed from the bankers at high interest rates to meet the exactions of the kings; hence, in part, the decline of architectural activity in France at the end of the thirteenth century.

The popes added to the impoverishment of bishoprics by taxing their property and revenues first to finance the Crusades, later to pay the mounting expenses of the papal see. New sources of central income became necessary as the papacy widened the area and complexity of its functions. Innocent III (1199) directed all bishops to send to the See of Peter yearly a fortieth of their revenue. A *cens* or tax was levied upon all monasteries, convents, and churches that came directly under papal protection. "An annate" —theoretically the whole, actually half, the first year's revenue of a newly elected bishop—was required by the popes as a fee for confirming his appointment; and large sums were expected from recipients of the archiepiscopal pallium. All Christian households were asked to send an annual penny (some 90 cents) to the Roman See as "Peter's Pence." Normally fees were charged for litigation brought to the papal court. The popes claimed the power to dispense in certain cases from canon law, as in permitting consanguineous marriage where some good political end seemed to justify the deviation; and fees were charged for legal processes involved in such dispensations. Considerable sums came to the popes from the recipients of papal indulgences, and from pilgrims to Rome. It has been calculated that the total income of the papal see about 1250 was greater than the combined revenues of all the secular sovereigns of Europe.[149] From England in 1252 the papacy received a sum thrice the revenue of the crown.[150]

The wealth of the Church, however proportionate to the extent of its functions, was the chief source of heresy in this age. Arnold of Brescia proclaimed that any priest or monk who died possessing property would surely go to hell.[151] The Bogomiles, the Waldenses, the Paterines, the Cathari made headway by denouncing the wealth of the followers of Christ. A favorite satire in the thirteenth century was the "Gospel According to Marks of Silver," which began: "In those days the Pope said to the Romans: 'When the Son of Man shall come to the seat of our majesty say first of all, "Friend, wherefore art Thou come hither?" And if He give you naught, cast Him forth into outer darkness.' " [152] Throughout the literature of the time—in the *fabliaux*, the *chansons de geste*, the *Roman de la Rose*, the poems of the wandering scholars, the troubadours, Dante, even in the monastic chroniclers, we find complaints of ecclesiastical avarice or wealth.[153] Matthew Paris, an English monk, denounced the venality of English and Roman prelates "living daintily on the patrimony of Christ"; [154] Hubert de Romans, head of the Dominican order, wrote of "pardoners corrupting with bribes the prelates of the ecclesiastical courts"; [155] Petrus Cantor, a priest, told of priests who sold Masses or Vespers; [156] Becket, Archbishop of Canterbury, declaimed against the papal chancery as bought and sold, and quoted Henry II as boasting that he had the whole college of cardinals in his pay.[157] Charges of corruption have been made against every government in history; they are nearly always partly true, and partly exaggerated from startling instances; but at times they rise to a revolutionary resentment. The same parishioners who built cathedrals to Mary with their pennies could protest angrily against the collective propensities of the Church, and occasionally they murdered a pertinacious priest.[158]

The Church herself joined in this criticism of clerical money-grubbing, and made many efforts to control the acquisitiveness and luxury of her personnel. Hundreds of clergymen, from St. Peter Damian, St. Bernard, St. Francis, and Cardinal de Vitry down to simple monks, labored to mitigate these natural abuses; [159] it is chiefly from the writings of such ecclesiastical reformers that our knowledge of the abuses is derived. A dozen monastic orders devoted themselves to preaching reform by their good example. Pope Alexander III and the Lateran Council of 1179 condemned the exaction of fees for administering baptism or extreme unction, or performing a marriage; and Gregory X called the Ecumenical Council of Lyons in 1274 specifically to take measures for the reform of the Church. The popes themselves, in this age, showed no taste for luxury, and earned their keep by arduous devotion to their exhausting tasks. It is the tragedy of things spiritual that they languish if unorganized, and are contaminated by the material needs of their organization.

CHAPTER XXVIII

The Early Inquisition

1000-1300

I. THE ALBIGENSIAN HERESY

ANTICLERICALISM rose to a flood at the end of the twelfth century. There were, in the Age of Faith, recesses of religious mysticism and sentiment that escaped and resented organized sacerdotal Christianity. Moving perhaps with returning Crusaders, new waves of Oriental mysticism flowed into the West. From Persia, through Asia Minor and the Balkans, came echoes of Manichean dualism and Mazdakian communism; from Islam a hostility to images, an obscure fatalism, and distaste for priests; and from the failure of the Crusades a secret doubt as to the divine origin and support of the Christian Church. The Paulicians, driven westward by Byzantine persecution, carried through the Balkans into Italy and Provence their scorn of images, sacraments, and the clergy; they divided the cosmos into a spiritual world created by God and a material world created by Satan; and they identified Satan with the Yahveh of the Old Testament. The Bogomiles (i.e., Friends of God) took form and name in Bulgaria, and spread especially in Bosnia; they were attacked by fire and sword at various times in the thirteenth century, defended themselves tenaciously, and finally (1463) surrendered not to Christianity but to Islam.

About the year 1000 a sect appeared in Toulouse and Orléans which denied the reality of miracles, the regenerative virtue of baptism, the presence of Christ in the Eucharist, and the efficacy of prayers to the saints. They were ignored for a time, then condemned; and thirteen of their number were burned at the stake in 1023. Similar heresies developed, and led to uprisings, at Cambrai and Liége (1025), Goslar (1052), Soissons (1114), Cologne (1146), etc. Berthold of Regensburg reckoned 150 heretical sects in the thirteenth century.[1] Some were harmless groups who gathered to read the Bible to one another in the vernacular without a priest, and to put their own interpretation upon its disputed passages. Several, like the Humiliati in Italy, the Béguines and Beghards in the Low Countries, were orthodox in everything except their embarrassing insistence that priests should live in poverty. The Franciscan movement arose as such a sect, and narrowly escaped being classed as heretical.

The Waldenses did not escape. About 1170 Peter Waldo, a rich merchant of Lyons, engaged some scholars to translate the Bible into the *langue d'oc* of south France. He studied the translation zealously, and concluded that Christians should live like the apostles—without individual property. He gave part of his wealth to his wife, distributed the remainder among the poor, and began to preach evangelical poverty. He gathered about him a small group, the "Poor Men of Lyons," who dressed like monks, lived in chastity, went barefoot or in sandals, and pooled their earnings communistically.[2] For a time the clergy made no objection, and allowed them to read and sing in the churches.[3] But when Peter thrust his sickle into another man's harvest in too literal fulfillment of the Gospel, the archbishop of Lyons sharply reminded him that only bishops were allowed to preach. Peter went to Rome (1179), and asked Alexander III for a preaching license. It was granted, on condition of consent and supervision by the local clergy. Peter resumed his preaching, apparently without such local consent. His followers became devotees of the Bible, and learned large sections of it by heart. Gradually the movement took on an antisacerdotal tinge, rejected all priesthood, denied the validity of sacraments administered by a sinful priest, and attributed to every believer in a state of sanctity the power to forgive sins. Some members repudiated indulgences, purgatory, transubstantiation, and prayer to the saints; one group preached that "all things should be in common";[4] another identified the Church with the scarlet woman of the Apocalypse.[5] The sect was condemned in 1184. One part of it, the "Poor Catholics," was received into the Church in 1206 by Innocent III; the majority persisted in heresy, and spread through France into Spain and Germany. Probably to check their increase, a Council of Toulouse in 1229 decreed that no lay folk should possess scriptural books except the Psalter and the Hours (which were chiefly psalms); nor should they read these except in Latin, for no vernacular translation had yet been examined and guaranteed by the Church.[6] In the suppression of the Albigenses thousands of Waldenses went to the stake. Peter himself died in Bohemia in 1217, apparently by a natural death.

By the middle of the twelfth century the towns of Western Europe were honeycombed with heretical sects; "the cities," said a bishop in 1190, "are filled with these false prophets";[7] Milan alone had seventeen new religions. The leading heretics there were the Patarines—named apparently from Pataria, a poor quarter of the town. The movement seems to have begun as a protest against the rich; it was turned to anticlericalism, denounced the simony, wealth, marriage, and concubinage of the clergy, and proposed, in the words of one leader, that "the wealth of the clergy be impounded, their property put up at auction; if they resist, let their houses be given up to pillage, and let them and their bastards be hounded out of the city."[8] Similar anticlerical parties rose in Viterbo, Orvieto, Verona, Ferrara, Parma, Piacenza, Rimini....[9] At times they dominated the popular assemblies, captured city governments, and taxed the clergy to pay for civic enterprises.[10] Innocent III instructed his legate in Lombardy to exact an oath from all municipal officials that they would not appoint or admit heretics to office. In 1237 a Milanese mob, "blaspheming and reviling," polluted several churches with "unmentionable filth." [11]

The most powerful of the heretical sects was variously named Cathari, from the Greek for "pure"; Bulgari, from their Balkan provenance (whence the abusive term *bugger*); and Albigenses, from the French town of Albi, where they were especially numerous. Montpellier, Narbonne, and Marseille were the first French centers of the heresy, perhaps through contact with Moslems and Jews, and through frequentation by merchants from heretical centers in Bosnia, Bulgaria, and Italy. Merchants spread the movement to Toulouse, Orléans, Soissons, Arras, and Reims, but Languedoc and Provence remained its strongholds. There French medieval civilization had reached its height; the great religions mingled in urbane amity, women were imperiously beautiful, morals were loose, troubadours spread gay ideas, and, as in Frederick's Italy, the Renaissance was ready to begin. Southern France was at that time (1200) composed of practically independent principalities, tenuously bound in theoretical allegiance to the king of France. In this region the counts of Toulouse were the greatest lords, possessing territories more extensive than those directly owned by the king. The doctrines and practices of the Cathari were in part a return to primitive Christian beliefs and ways, partly a vague memory of the Arian heresy that had prevailed in southern France under the Visigoths, partly a product of Manichean and other Oriental ideas. They had a black-robed clergy of priests and bishops called *perfecti*, who at their ordination vowed to leave parents, mate, and children, to devote themselves "to God and the Gospel . . . never to touch a woman, never to kill an animal, never to eat meat, eggs, or dairy food, nor anything but fish and vegetables." *·The "believers" (*credentes*) were followers who promised to take these vows later; they were allowed meanwhile to eat meat and marry, but they were required to renounce the Catholic Church, to advance toward the "perfect" life, and to greet any of the *perfecti* with a triple and reverent genuflection.

The theology of the Cathari divided the cosmos Manicheanly into Good, God, Spirit, Heaven; and Evil, Satan, Matter, the material universe. Satan, not God, created the visible world. All matter was accounted evil, including the cross on which Christ died, and the consecrated Host of the Eucharist; Christ spoke only figuratively when He said of the bread, "This is my body." [13] All flesh was matter, and all contact with it was impurity; all sexual congress was sinful; the sin of Adam and Eve was coitus.[14] Opponents describe the Albigenses as rejecting the sacraments, the Mass, the veneration of images, the Trinity, and the Virgin Birth; Christ was an angel, but not one

---

* From a report by the inquisitor Sacchoni.[12] We know the doctrines and practices of the Cathari only from their enemies; their own literature was lost or destroyed.

with God. They repudiated (we are told) the institution of private property, and aspired to an equality of goods.[15] They made the Sermon on the Mount the essence of their ethics. They were taught to love their enemies, to care for the sick and the poor, never to swear, always to keep the peace; force was never moral, even against infidels; capital punishment was a capital crime; one should quietly trust that in the end God would triumph over evil, without using evil means.[16] There was no hell or purgatory in this theology; every soul would be saved, if only after many purifying transmigrations. To attain heaven one had to die in a state of purity; for this it was necessary to receive from a Catharist priest the *consolamentum*, a last sacrament which completely cleansed the soul of sin. Cathari believers (like some early Christians in the case of baptism) postponed this sacrament to what they judged to be their final illness. Those who recovered ran a risk of acquiring new impurity and dying without the *consolamentum*; hence it was a great misfortune to recover after receiving it; and it is charged that the Albigensian priests, to avert this calamity, persuaded many a recovering patient to starve himself into paradise. Sometimes, we are assured, they made matters certain by suffocating a patient with his consent.[17]

The Church might have allowed this sect to die of its own suicide had not the Cathari engaged in active criticism of the Church. They denied that the Church was the Church of Christ; St. Peter had never come to Rome, had never founded the papacy; the popes were successors to the emperors, not to the apostles. Christ had no place to lay His head, but the pope lived in a palace; Christ was propertyless and penniless, but Christian prelates were rich; surely, said the Cathari, these lordly archbishops and bishops, these worldly priests, these fat monks, were the Pharisees of old returned to life! The Roman Church, they were sure, was the Whore of Babylon, the clergy were a Synagogue of Satan, the pope was Antichrist.[18] They denounced the preachers of crusades as murderers.[19] Many of them laughed at indulgences and relics. One group, it is alleged, made an image of the Virgin, ugly, one-eyed, and deformed, pretended to work miracles with it, secured wide credence for the imposture, and then revealed the hoax.[20] Many views of the Cathari were spread on the wings of song by troubadours who resented the ethics of Christ without quite adopting those of the new sect; all the leading troubadours except two were considered to be on the side of the Albigensians; these troubadours made fun of pilgrims, confession, holy water, the cross; they called the churches "dens of thieves," and Catholic priests seemed to them "traitors, liars, and hypocrites." [21]

For some time the Cathari received a broad toleration from the ecclesiastics and the secular powers of southern France. Apparently the people were allowed to choose freely between the old religion and the new.[22] Public debates were held between Catholic and Catharist theologians; one such took place at Carcassonne in the presence of a papal legate and King Pedro II of Aragon

(1204). In 1167 various branches of the Cathari held a council of their clergy, attended by representatives from several countries; it discussed and regulated Catharist doctrine, discipline, and administration, and adjourned without having been disturbed.[23] Moreover, the nobility found it desirable to weaken the Church in Languedoc; the Church was rich, and owned much land; the nobles, relatively poor, began to seize Church property. In 1171 Roger II, Viscount of Béziers, sacked an abbey, threw the bishop of Albi into prison, and set a heretic to guard him. When the monks of Allet chose an abbot unsatisfactory to the Viscount, he burned the monastery and jailed the abbot; when the latter died the merry Viscount installed his corpse in the pulpit and persuaded the monks to choose a pleasing substitute. Raymond Roger, Count of Foix, drove abbot and monks from the abbey of Pamiers; his horses ate oats from the altar; his soldiers used the arms and legs of the crucifixes as pestles to grind grain, and practiced their markmanship upon the image of Christ. Count Raymond VI of Toulouse destroyed several churches, persecuted the monks of Moissac, and was excommunicated (1196). But excommunication had become a trifle to the nobles of southern France. Many of them openly professed, or liberally protected, the Catharist heresy.[24]

Innocent III, coming to the papacy in 1198, saw in these developments a threat to both Church and state. He recognized some excuse for criticism of the Church, but he felt that he could hardly remain idle when the great ecclesiastical organization for which he had such lofty plans and hopes, and which seemed to him the chief bulwark against human violence, social chaos, and royal iniquity, was attacked in its very foundations, robbed of its possessions and dignity, and mocked with blasphemous travesties. The state too had committed sins and cherished corruption and unworthy officials, but only fools wished to destroy it. How could any continuing social order be built on the principles that forbade parentage and counseled suicide? Could any economy prosper on the idolatry of poverty and without the incentives of property? Could the relations of the sexes, and the rearing of children, be rescued from a wild disorder except by some such institution as marriage? Catharism seemed to Innocent a mess of nonsense, made poisonous by the simplicity of the people. What was the sense of a crusade against infidels in Palestine, when these Albigensian infidels were multiplying in the heart of Christendom?

Two months after his accession Innocent wrote to the archbishop of Auch in Gascony:

> The little boat of St. Peter is beaten by many storms and tossed about on the sea. But it grieves me most of all that . . . there are now arising, more unrestrainedly and injuriously than ever before, ministers of diabolical error who are ensnaring the souls of the simple. With their superstitions and false inventions they are perverting the meaning of the Holy Scriptures and trying to destroy the unity of the

Catholic Church. Since . . . this pestilential error is growing in Gas-cony and the neighboring territories, we wish you and your fellow bishops to resist it with all your might. . . . We give you a strict com-mand that, by whatever means you can, you destroy all these heresies, and repel from your diocese all who are polluted by them. . . . If neces-sary, you may cause the princes and people to suppress them with the sword.[25]

The archbishop of Auch, a man indulgent to others as well as to himself, seems to have taken no action on this letter; and the archbishop of Narbonne and the bishop of Béziers resisted the papal legates that Innocent sent to enforce his decrees. About this time six noble ladies, led by the sister of the Count of Foix, were converted to Catharism in a public ceremony attended by many of the nobility. Innocent replaced his unsuccessful legates with a more resolute agent, Arnaud, head of the Cistercian monks (1204); gave him extraordinary powers to make inquisition throughout France, and commis-sioned him to offer a plenary indulgence to the king and nobles of France for aid in suppressing the Catharist heresy. To Philip Augustus, in return for such aid, the Pope offered the lands of all who should fail to join in a crusade against the Albigensians.[26] Philip demurred; he had just conquered Nor-mandy, and wanted time for digestion. Raymond VI of Toulouse agreed to use persuasion on the heretics, but refused to join a war against them. Innocent excommunicated him; he promised to comply, was absolved, and proved negligent again. "How can we do it?" asked a knight who had been com-manded by a papal legate to expel the Cathari from their lands. "We have been brought up with these people, we have kindred among them, and we see them living righteously." [27] St. Dominic entered the scene from Spain, preached peaceably against the heretics, and made converts to orthodoxy by the holiness of his life.[28] Perhaps the problem could have been met by such means, aided by clerical reform, had not Pierre de Castelnau, a papal legate, been slain by a knight who was thereafter protected by Raymond.[29] Inno-cent, who had borne with patience the frustration of his efforts against the heresy for almost ten years, now resorted to extreme measures. He excom-municated Raymond and all his abettors; laid under interdict all lands subject to them, and offered these lands to any Christian who could seize them. He summoned Christians from all countries to a crusade against the Albigensians and their protectors. Philip Augustus allowed many barons of his realm to enlist, and contingents came from Germany and Italy. To all participants the same plenary indulgence was promised as to those who took the cross for Palestine. Raymond asked forgiveness, did public penance (being scourged, half naked, in the church of St. Gilles), was absolved again, and joined the holy war (1209).

Most of the population of Languedoc, nobles and commoners alike, re-sisted the crusaders, seeing in the attack of northern barons and soldiers of fortune an attempt to seize their lands under cover of religious zeal; even the orthodox Christians of the south fought the invasion from the north.[30] When the crusaders approached Béziers they offered to spare it the horrors of war if it would surrender all heretics listed by its bishop; the city leaders refused, saying they would rather stand siege till they should be reduced to eating their children. The crusaders scaled the walls, captured the town, and slew 20,000 men, women, and children in indiscriminate massacre; even those who had sought asylum in the church.[31] Caesarius of Heisterbach, a Cistercian monk writing twenty years after, is our only authority for the story that when Arnaud, the papal legate, was asked should Catholics be spared, he answered, "Kill them all, for God knows His own";[32] perhaps he feared that all the defeated would profess orthodoxy for the occasion. Béziers having been burned to the ground, the crusaders, led by Raymond, advanced to attack the fortress of Carcassonne, where Raymond's nephew, Count Roger of Béziers, made a final stand. The fortress was taken, and Roger died of dysentery.

The bravest leader in this siege was Simon de Montfort. Born in France about 1170, he was the elder son of the lord of Montfort, near Paris; he became Earl of Leicester through his English mother. Like many men of that swashbuckling age, he was able to combine great piety with great wars; he heard Mass every day, was famous for his chastity, and had served with honor in Palestine. With his small army of 4500 men, and urged on by the papal legate, he now assaulted town after town, overcame all resistance, and gave the population a choice between swearing allegiance to the Roman faith or suffering death as heretics. Thousands swore, hundreds preferred death.[33] For four years Simon continued his campaigns, devastating nearly all the territory of Count Raymond except Toulouse. In 1215 Toulouse itself surrendered to him; Count Raymond was deposed by a council of prelates at Montpellier, and Simon succeeded to his title and most of his lands.

Innocent III did not quite approve of these proceedings. He was shocked to find that the crusaders had appropriated the holdings of men never guilty of heresy, and had robbed and murdered like savage buccaneers.[34] Taking mercy on Raymond, he assigned him an annuity, and took under the care of the Church a portion of his lands in trust for Raymond's son. Raymond VII, coming of age, recaptured Toulouse; Simon died in a second siege of the city (1218); the crusade was suspended now that Innocent had died; and such Albigensian devotees as had survived came forth to practice and preach again under the lenient rule of the new Count of Toulouse.

In 1223 Louis VIII of France offered to depose Raymond VII, and to crush out all heresy in Raymond's territory, if Honorius III would allow him to add the region to the royal domain. We do not know the Pope's reply. But a new crusade was begun, and Louis was on the verge of victory when he died at Montpensier (1226). Seizing the opportunity to make peace with Blanche of Castile, regent for Louis IX, Raymond offered the hand of his daughter Jeanne to Louis' brother Alphonse, with the reversion of Raymond's lands to Jeanne and her husband at Raymond's death. Blanche, harassed by rebellious nobles, accepted, and Pope Gregory IX approved on Raymond's pledge to suppress all heresy. A treaty of peace was signed at Paris in 1229, and the Albigensian wars came to an end after thirty years of strife and devastation. Orthodoxy triumphed, toleration ceased; and the Council of Narbonne (1229) forbade the possession of any part of the Bible by laymen.[35] Feudalism spread, municipal liberty declined, the gay age of the troubadours passed away, in southern France. In 1271 Jeanne and Alphonse, who had inherited Raymond's possessions, died without issue, and the spacious county of Toulouse fell to Louis IX and the French crown. Central France now had free commercial outlets on the Mediterranean, and France had taken a great step toward unity. This, and the Inquisition, were the chief results of the Albigensian crusades.

II. THE BACKGROUND OF THE INQUISITION

The Old Testament laid down a simple code for dealing with heretics: they were to be carefully examined; and if three reputable witnesses testified to their having "gone and served other gods," the heretics were to be led out from the city and "stoned with stones till they die" (Deut. xvii, 25).

> If there arise among you a prophet, or a dreamer of dreams . . . saying, Let us go after other gods . . . that prophet, or that dreamer of dreams, shall be put to death. . . . If thy brother . . . or thy son, or thy daughter, or the wife of thy bosom, or thy friend which is as thine own soul, entice thee secretly, saying, Let us go and serve other gods . . . thou shalt not consent unto him, nor hearken unto him; neither shalt thine eye pity him, neither shalt thou . . . conceal him; but thou shalt surely kill him (Deut. xiii, 1-9). . . . Thou shalt not suffer a witch to live (Exod. xxii, 18).

According to the Gospel of St. John (xv, 6), Jesus accepted this tradition: "If anyone abide not in me he shall be cast forth as a branch, and shall wither; and they shall gather him up, and cast him into the fire, and he burneth." Medieval Jewish communities retained the Biblical law of heresy in theory, but rarely practiced it. Maimonides adopted it without reserve.[36]

The laws of the Greeks made *asebeia*—failure to worship the gods of the orthodox Hellenic pantheon—a capital crime; it was by such a law that Socrates was put to death. In classic Rome, where the gods were allied with the state in close harmony, heresy and blasphemy were classed with treason, and were punishable with death. Where no accuser could be found to denounce an offender, the Roman judge summoned the suspect and made an *inquisitio*, or inquiry, into the case; from this procedure the medieval Inquisition took its form and name. The Eastern emperors, applying Roman law in the Byzantine world, inflicted the death penalty upon Manicheans and other heretics. During the Dark Ages in the West, when Christianity was seldom challenged by its own children, tolerance increased, and Leo IX held that excommunication should be the only punishment for heresy.[37] In the twelfth century, as heresy spread, some ecclesiastics argued that the excommunication of heretics by the Church should be followed with their banishment or imprisonment by the state.[38] The revival of Roman law at Bologna in the twelfth century provided terms, methods, and stimulus for a religious inquisition; and the canon law of heresy was copied word for word from the fifth law of the title *De haereticis* in the Justinian Code.[39] Finally, in the thirteenth century, the Church took over the law of its greatest enemy, Frederick II, that heresy should be punished with death.

It was a general assumption of Christians—even of many heretics—that the Church had been established by the Son of God. On this assumption any attack upon the Catholic faith was an offense against God Himself; the contumacious heretic could only be viewed as an agent of Satan, sent to undo the work of Christ; and any man or government that tolerated heresy was serving Lucifer. Feeling herself an inseparable part of the moral and political government of Europe, the Church looked upon heresy precisely as the state looked upon treason: it was an attack upon the foundations of social order. "The civil law," said Innocent III, "punishes traitors with confiscation of their property, and death. . . . All the more, then, should we excommunicate, and confiscate the property of, those who are traitors to the faith of Jesus Christ; for it is an infinitely greater sin to offend the divine majesty than to attack the majesty of the sovereign." [40] To ecclesiastical statesmen like Innocent the heretic seemed worse than a Moslem or a Jew; these lived either outside of Christendom, or by an orderly—and equally severe—law within it; the alien enemy was a soldier in open war; the heretic was a traitor within, who undermined the unity of a Christendom engaged in a gigantic conflict with Islam. Furthermore, said the theologians, if every man may interpret the Bible according to his own light (however dim), and make his own individual brand of Christianity, the religion that held up the frail moral code of Europe would soon be shattered into a hundred creeds, and lose its efficacy as a social cement binding natively savage men into a society and a civilization.

Whether because it shared these views without formulating them, or because simple souls naturally fear the different or the strange, or because men enjoy releasing, in the anonymity of the crowd, instincts normally suppressed by individual responsibility, the people themselves, except in southern France and northern Italy, were the most enthusiastic persecutors; "the mob lynched heretics long before the Church began to persecute." [41] The orthodox population complained that the Church was too lenient with heretics.[42] Sometimes it "snatched sectaries from the hands of protecting priests." [43] "In this country," wrote a priest of northern France to Innocent III, "the piety of the people is so great that they are always ready to send to the stake not only avowed heretics, but those merely suspected of heresy." [44] In 1114 the bishop of Soissons imprisoned some heretics; while he was away the populace, "fearing that the clergy might be too lenient," broke into the jail, dragged forth the heretics, and burned them at the stake.[45] In 1144 at Liége the mob insisted on burning some heretics whom Bishop Adalbero still hoped to convert.[46] When Pierre de Bruys said, "The priests lie when they pretend to make the body of Christ" (in the Eucharist),[47] and burned a pile of crosses on Good Friday, the people killed him there and then.[48]

The state, with some reluctance, joined in persecuting heretics because it feared that government would be impossible without the aid of a Church inculcating a unified religious belief. Moreover, it suspected religious heresy to be a cloak for political radicalism, and was not always wrong.[49] Material considerations may have played a part, for religious or political heresy threatened the possessions of Church and state. The public opinion of the upper classes—again excepting Languedoc—demanded the extirpation of heresy at any cost.[50] Henry VI of Germany (1194) ordered severe punishment of heretics, and the confiscation of their property; and similar edicts were issued by Otto IV (1210), Louis VIII of France (1226), Florence (1227), and Milan (1228). The most rigorous code of suppression was enacted by Frederick II in 1220–39. Heretics condemned by the Church were to be delivered to the "secular arm"—the local authorities—and burned to death. If they recanted they were to be let off with imprisonment for life. All their property was to be confiscated, their heirs were to be disinherited, their children were to remain ineligible to any position of emolument or dignity unless they atoned for their parents' sin by denouncing other heretics. The houses of heretics were to be destroyed and never rebuilt.[51] The gentle Louis IX placed similar laws among the statutes of France. Indeed it was the kings who disputed with the people the distinction of inaugurating the persecution of heresy. King Robert of France had thirteen heretics burned at Orléans in 1022; this is the first known case of capital punishment of heresy since the secular execution of Priscillian in 385. In 1051 Henry III of Germany hanged several Manicheans or Cathari at Goslar over the protests of Bishop Wazo of Liége, who argued that excommunication was enough.[52] In 1183 Count Philip of Flanders, in collaboration with the archbishop of Reims, "sent to the stake a great many nobles, clerics, knights, peasants, young girls, married women, and widows, whose property they confiscated and shared between them." [53]

Normally, before the thirteenth century, inquisition into heresy was left to the bishops. They were hardly inquisitors; they waited for public rumor or clamor to point out the heretics. Summoning them, they found it difficult to elicit confessions by inquiry; loath to use torture, they resorted to trial by ordeal, apparently in the sincere belief that God would work miracles to protect the innocent. St. Bernard approved of this expedient, and an episcopal council at Reims (1157) prescribed it as regular procedure in trials for heresy; but Innocent III forbade it. In 1185 Pope Lucius III, dissatisfied with the negligence of the bishops in pursuing heresy, ordered them to visit their parishes at least once a year, to arrest all suspects, to reckon as guilty any who would not swear full loyalty to the Church (the Cathari refused to take any oaths), and to hand over such recalcitrants to the secular arm. Papal legates were empowered to depose bishops negligent in stamping out heresy.[54] Innocent III, in 1215, required all civil authorities, on pain of being themselves indicted for heresy, to swear publicly "to exterminate, from the lands subject to their obedience, all heretics who have been marked out by the Church for *animadversio debita*—"due punishment." Any prince who neglected this duty was to be deposed, and the pope would release his subjects from their allegiance.[55] "Due punishment" was as yet only banishment and confiscation of goods.[56]

When Gregory IX mounted the papal throne (1227), he found that despite popular, governmental, and episcopal prosecutions, heresy was growing; all the Balkans, most of Italy, much of France were so turbulent with heresy that the Church, so soon after Innocent's splendid power, seemed doomed to division and disintegration. As the aged pontiff saw the matter, the Church, simultaneously fighting Frederick and heresy, was engaged in a struggle for survival, and was warranted in adopting the morals and measures of a state of war. Shocked at learning that Bishop Filippo Paternon, whose diocese extended from Pisa to Arezzo, had been converted to Catharism, Gregory appointed a board of inquisitors, headed by a Dominican monk, to sit in Florence and bring the heretics to judgment (1227). This, in effect, was the beginning of the papal inquisition, though formally the inquisitors were to be subject to the local bishop. In 1231 Gregory adopted into the law of the Church Frederick's legislation of 1224; henceforth Church and state agreed that impenitent heresy was treason, and should be punished with death. The Inquisition was now officially established under the control of the popes.

III. THE INQUISITORS

After 1227 Gregory and his successors sent out an increasing number of special *inquisitores* to pursue heresy. He favored for this task the members of the new mendicant orders, partly because the simplicity and devotion of their lives would counteract the scandals of ecclesiastical luxury, and partly because he could not depend upon the bishops; however, no inquisitor was to condemn a heretic to serious punishment without episcopal consent. So many Dominicans were employed in this work that they were nicknamed *Domini canes*—the (hunting) "dogs of the Lord." [57] Most of them were men of strict morals, but few had the quality of mercy. They thought of themselves not as judges impartially weighing evidence, but as warriors pursuing the enemies of Christ. Some were careful and conscientious men like Bernard Gui; some were sadists like "Robert the Dominican," a converted Patarine heretic, who in one day in 1239 sent 180 prisoners to the stake, including a bishop who, in his judgment, had given heretics too much freedom. Gregory suspended Robert from office, and imprisoned him for life.[58]

The jurisdiction of the inquisitors extended only to Christians; Jews and Moslems were not summoned unless they were relapsed converts.[59] The Dominicans made special efforts to convert Jews, but only by peaceful means. When, in 1256, some Jews were accused of ritual murder, Dominican and Franciscan monks risked their own lives to save them from the mob.[60] The purpose and scope of the Inquisition are best expressed by a bull of Nicholas III (1280):

> We hereby excommunicate and anathematize all heretics—Cathari, Patarines, Poor Men of Lyons . . . and all others, by whatever name they may be called. When condemned by the Church they shall be given over to the secular judge to be punished. . . . If any, after being seized, repent and wish to do penance, they shall be imprisoned for life. . . . All who receive, defend, or aid heretics shall be excommunicated. If anyone remains under excommunication a year and a day, he shall be proscribed. . . . If those who are suspected of heresy cannot prove their innocence, they shall be excommunicated. If they remain under the ban of excommunication a year, they shall be condemned as heretics. They shall have no right of appeal. . . . Whoever grants them Christian burial shall be excommunicated until he makes proper satisfaction. He shall not be absolved until he has with his own hands dug up their bodies and cast them forth. . . . We prohibit all laymen to discuss matters of the Catholic faith; if anyone does so he shall be excommunicated. Whoever knows of heretics, or of those who hold secret meetings, or of those who do not conform in all respects to the orthodox faith, shall make it known to his confessor, or to someone else who will bring it to the knowledge of the bishop or the inquisitor. If he does not do so he shall be excommunicated. Heretics and all who receive, support, or aid them, and all their children to the second generation, shall not be admitted to an ecclesiastical office. . . . We now deprive all such of their benefices forever.[61]

Inquisitorial procedure might begin with the summary arrest of all heretics, sometimes also of all suspects; or the visiting inquisitors might summon the entire adult population of a locality for a preliminary examination. During an initial "time of grace," about thirty days, those who confessed heresy and repented were let off with brief imprisonment or some work of piety or charity.[62] Heretics who did not now confess, but were detected in this initial inquiry, or by the spies of the Inquisition,[63] or elsewise, were cited before the inquisitorial court. Normally this court was composed of twelve men chosen by the local secular ruler from a list of nominees presented to him by the bishop and the inquisitors; two notaries and several "servitors" were added. If the accused took this second chance to confess they received punishments varying with the degree of their adjudged offense; if they denied their guilt they were imprisoned. Accused persons might be tried in their absence, or after their death. Two condemnatory witnesses were required. Confessed heretics were accepted as witnesses against others; wives and children were allowed to testify against, but not for, husbands and fathers.[64] All the accused in a locality were, on demand, allowed to see a combined list of all accusers, without any specification as to which had accused whom; it was feared that individual confrontations would lead to the killing of accusers by friends of the accused; and "in fact," says Lea, "a number of witnesses were slain on simple suspicion." [65] Usually the accused man was asked to name his enemies, and any evidence against him by such men was rejected.[66] False accusers were severely punished.[67] Before 1300 the accused was not allowed to have legal aid.[68] After 1254 the inquisitors were required by papal decree to submit the evidence not only to the bishop but also to men of high repute in the locality, and to decide in agreement with their votes.[69] Sometimes a board of experts (*periti*) was called in to pass on the evidence. In general the inquisitors were instructed that it was better to let the guilty escape than to condemn the innocent, and that they must have either clear proof or a confession.

Roman law had permitted the eliciting of confessions by torture. It was not used in the episcopal courts, nor in the first twenty years of the papal inquisition; but Innocent IV (1252) authorized it where the judges were convinced of the accused man's guilt, and later pontiffs condoned its use.[70] The popes advised that torture should be a last resort, should be applied only once, and should be kept "this side of loss of limb and danger of death." The inquisitors interpreted "only once" as meaning only once for each examination; sometimes they interrupted torture to resume examination, and then felt free to torture anew. Torture was in several cases used to force witnesses to testify, or to induce a confessing heretic to name other heretics.[71] It took the form of flogging, burning, the rack, or solitary imprisonment in dark and narrow dungeons. The feet of the accused might be slowly roasted over burning coals; or he might be bound upon a triangular frame, and have his arms and legs pulled by cords wound on a windlass. Sometimes the diet of the imprisoned man was restricted to weaken his body and will and render him susceptible to such psychological torture as alternate promises of mercy or threats of death.[72] Confessions elicited under torture were little respected by the inquisitorial court, but this difficulty was met by having the accused confirm, three hours later, the admissions he had made under torture; if he refused, the torture could be resumed. In 1286 the officials of Carcassonne sent to Philip IV of France and Pope Nicholas IV a letter of complaint alleging the severity of the tortures used by the inquisitor Jean Galand. Some of Jean's prisoners were left for long periods in complete darkness and solitude; some were so manacled that they had to sit in their own filth, and could only lie on their backs on the cold earth.[73] Some men had been so drawn on the rack that they had lost the use of their arms and legs; some had died under torture.[74] Philip denounced these barbarities, and Pope Clement V (1312) endeavored to moderate the use of torture by inquisitors; but his cautions were soon ignored.[75]

Prisoners who had refused two opportunities to confess and were later convicted, and those who had relapsed into heresy after recanting, were imprisoned for life, or were put to death. Life imprisonment might be mitigated with certain freedom of movement, visitation, and games; or it might be enhanced with fasting or chains.[76] Confiscation of property was an added penalty of conviction after resistance. Usually a part of the confiscated goods went to the secular ruler of the province, part to the Church; in Italy one third was given to the informer; in France the crown took all. These considerations stimulated individuals and the state to join in the hunt, and led to trials of the dead; at any time the possessions of innocent persons might be seized on the charge that the testator had died in heresy; this was one of many abuses that popes vainly denounced.[77] The bishop of Rodez boasted that he had made 100,000 sols in a single campaign against the heretics of his diocese.[78]

Periodically the inquisitors, in a fearful ceremony (*sermo generalis*), announced convictions and penalties. The penitents were placed on a stage in the center of a church, their confessions were read, and they were asked to confirm them, and to pronounce a formula abjuring heresy. The celebrant inquisitor then absolved the penitents from excommunication, and announced the various sentences. Those who were to be "relaxed," or abandoned to the secular arm, were allowed another day for conversion; those who confessed and repented, even at the foot of the stake, were given life imprisonment; the obdurate were burned to death in the public square. In Spain this entire procedure of *sermo generalis* and execution was termed an act of faith, *auto-da-fé*, for it was intended to strengthen the orthodoxy of the people and to reaffirm the faith of the Church. The Church never pronounced a sentence of death; her old motto was *ecclesia abhorret a sanguine* —"the Church shrinks from blood"; clerics were forbidden to shed blood. So, in turning over to the secular arm those whom she had condemned, the Church confined herself to asking the state authorities to inflict the "due penalty," with a caution to avoid "all bloodshed and all danger of death." After Gregory IX it was agreed by both Church and state that the caution should not be taken literally, but that the condemned were to be put to death without shedding of blood—i.e., by burning at the stake.[79]

The number of those sentenced to death by the official Inquisition was smaller than historians once believed.[80] Bernard de Caux, a zealous inquisitor, left behind him a long register of cases tried by him; not one of these was "relaxed." [81] In seventeen years as an inquisitor Bernard Gui condemned 930 heretics, forty-five of them to death.[82] At a *sermo generalis* in Toulouse in 1310 twenty persons were ordered to go on pilgrimage, sixty-five were condemned to life imprisonment, eighteen to death. In an auto-da-fé of 1312 fifty-one were sent on pilgrimage, eighty-six received various terms of imprisonment, five were turned over to the secular arm.[83] The worst tragedies of the Inquisition were concealed in the dungeons rather than brought to light at the stake.

IV. RESULTS

The medieval Inquisition achieved its immediate purposes. It stamped out Catharism in France, reduced the Waldenses to a few scattered zealots, restored south Italy to orthodoxy, and postponed by three centuries the dismemberment of Western Christianity. France lost to Italy the cultural leadership of Europe; but the French monarchy, strengthened by the acquisition of Languedoc, grew powerful enough to subdue the papacy under Boniface VIII, and to imprison it under Clement V.

In Spain the Inquisition played a minor role before 1300. Raymond of Peñafort, Dominican confessor to James I of Aragon, persuaded him to admit the Inquisition in 1232. Perhaps to check inquisitorial zeal a statute of 1233 made the state the chief beneficiary of confiscations for heresy; in later centuries, however, this would prove a heady stimulus to monarchs who found that inquisition and acquisition were near allied.

In northern Italy heretics continued to exist in great number. The orthodox majority were too indifferent to join actively in the hunt; and independent dictators like Ezzelino at Vicenza and Pallavicino at Cremona and Milan clandestinely or openly protected heretics. In Florence the monk Ruggieri organized a military order of orthodox nobles to support the Inquisition; the Patarines fought bloody battles with them in the streets, and were defeated (1245); thereafter Florentine heresy hid its head. In 1252 the inquisitor Fra Piero da Verona was assassinated by heretics at Milan; and his canonization as Peter Martyr did more to check heresy in north Italy than all the rigors of the inquisitors. The papacy organized crusades against Ezzelino and Pallavicino; the one was overthrown in 1259, the other in 1268. The triumph of the Church in Italy was, on the surface, complete.

In England the Inquisition never took hold. Henry II, anxious to prove his orthodoxy amid his controversy with Becket, scourged and branded twenty-nine heretics at Oxford (1166); [84] for the rest there was little heresy in England before Wyclif. In Germany the Inquisition flourished with brief madness, and then died away. In 1212 Bishop Henry of Strasbourg burned eighty heretics in one day. Most of them were Waldenses; their leader, Priest John, proclaimed their disbelief in indulgences, purgatory, and sacerdotal celibacy, and held that ecclesiastics should own no property. In 1227 Gregory IX made Conrad, a priest of Marburg, head of the Inquisition in Germany, and commissioned him not only to exterminate heresy but to reform the clergy, whose immorality was denounced by the Pope as the chief cause of waning faith. Conrad approached both tasks with outstanding cruelty. He gave all indicted heretics a simple choice: to confess and be punished, or to deny and be burned at the stake. When he applied like energy to reforming the clergy, orthodox and heretics joined to oppose him; he was killed by the friends of his victims (1233); and the German bishops took over the Inquisition and domesticated it to a juster procedure. Many sects, some heretical, some mystical, survived in Bohemia and Germany, and prepared the way for Huss and Luther.

In judging the Inquisition we must see it against the background of a time accustomed to brutality. Perhaps it can be better understood by our age, which has killed more people in war, and snuffed out more innocent lives without due process of law, than all the wars and persecutions between Caesar and Napoleon. Intolerance is the natural concomitant of strong faith; tolerance grows only when faith loses certainty; certainty is murderous. Plato sanctioned intolerance in his *Laws*; the Reformers sanctioned it in the sixteenth century; and some critics of the Inquisition defend its methods when practiced by modern states. The methods of the inquisitors, including torture, were adopted into the law codes of many governments; and perhaps our contemporary secret torture of suspects finds its model in the Inquisition even more than in Roman law. Compared with the persecution of heresy in Europe from 1227 to 1492, the persecution of Christians by Romans in the first three centuries after Christ was a mild and humane procedure. Making every allowance required of an historian and permitted to a Christian, we must rank the Inquisition, along with the wars and persecutions of our time, as among the darkest blots on the record of mankind, revealing a ferocity unknown in any beast.

CHAPTER XXIX

Monks and Friars

1095-1300

I. THE MONASTIC LIFE

IT may be that the Church was saved not by the tortures of the Inquisition but by the rise of new monastic orders that took out of the mouths of heretics the gospel of evangelical poverty, and for a century gave to the older monastic orders, and to the secular clergy, a cleansing example of sincerity.

The monasteries had multiplied during the Dark Ages, reaching a peak in the troubled nadir of the tenth century, and then declining in number as secular order and prosperity grew. In France, about 1100, there were 543; about 1250 there were 287;[1] possibly this loss in the number of abbeys was compensated by a rise in their average membership, but very few monasteries had a hundred monks.[2] It was still a custom in the thirteenth century for pious or burdened parents to commit children of seven years or older to monasteries as *oblates*—"offered up" to God; St. Thomas Aquinas began his monastic career so. The Benedictine order considered the vows taken for an oblate by his parents as irrevocable;[3] St. Bernard and the new orders held that the oblate, on reaching maturity, might without reproach return to the world.[4] Generally an adult monk required a papal dispensation if he wished, without sin, to renounce his vows.

Before 1098 most Western monasteries followed, with variable fidelity, some form of the Benedictine rule. A year of novitiate was prescribed, during which the candidate might freely withdraw. One knight drew back, says the monk Caesarius of Heisterbach, "on the cowardly plea that he feared the vermin of the [monastic] garment; for our woolen clothing harbors much vermin."[5] Prayer occupied some four hours of the monk's day; meals were brief, and usually vegetarian; the remainder of the day was given to labor, reading, teaching, hospital work, charity, and rest. Caesarius tells how his monastery, in the famine of 1197, gave as many as 1500 "doles" of food in a day, and "kept alive till harvest time all the poor who came to us."[6] In the same crisis a Cistercian abbey in Westphalia slaughtered all its flocks and herds, and pawned its books and sacred vessels, to feed the poor.[7] Through their own labor and that of their serfs, the monks built abbeys, churches, and cathedrals, farmed great manors, subdued marshes and jungles to tillage, practiced a hundred handicrafts, and brewed excellent wines and ales. Though the monastery seemed to take many good and able men from the world to bury them in a selfish sanctity, it trained thousands of them in mental and moral discipline, and then returned them to the world to serve as councilors and administrators to bishops, popes, and kings.*

In the course of time the growing wealth of the communities overflowed into the monasteries, and the generosity of the people financed the occasional luxury of the monks. The abbey of St. Riquier was not among the richest; yet it had 117 vassals, owned 2500 houses in the town where it was placed, and received from its tenants yearly 10,000 chickens, 10,000 capons, 75,000 eggs . . . and a money rent individually reasonable, cumulatively great.[8] Much richer were the monasteries of Monte Cassino, Cluny, Fulda, St. Gall, St. Denis. Abbots like Suger of St. Denis, Peter the Venerable of Cluny, or even Samson of Bury St. Edmund's, were mighty lords controlling immense material wealth and social or political power. Suger, after feeding his monks and building a majestic cathedral, had enough resources left to half-finance a crusade.[9] It was probably of Suger that St. Bernard wrote: "I lie if I have not seen an abbot riding with a train of sixty horses and more"; [10] but Suger was prime minister, and had to clothe himself in pomp to impress the populace; he himself lived with austere simplicity in a humble cell, observing all the rules of his order so far as his public duties would allow. Peter the Venerable was a good man, but he failed, despite repeated efforts, to check the progress of the Cluniac monasteries—once the leaders of reform—toward a corporate wealth that enabled the monks, while owning nothing, to live in a degenerative idleness.

Morals fall as riches rise, and nature will out according to men's means. In any large group certain individuals will be found whose instincts are stronger than their vows. While the majority of monks remained reasonably loyal to their rule, a minority took an easier view toward the world and the flesh. In many cases the abbot had been appointed by some lord or king, usually from a rank accustomed to comfort; such abbots were above monastic rules; they enjoyed hunting, hawking, tournaments, and politics; and their example infected the monks. Giraldus Cambrensis paints a merry picture of the abbot of Evesham: "None was safe from his lust"; the neighborhood reckoned his offspring at eighteen; finally he had to be deposed.[11] Worldly abbots, fat and rich and powerful, became a target of public humor and literary diatribe. The most merciless and incredible satire in medieval literature is a descrip-

---

* Said a great scholar not usually tender to the faults of the Church: "The vulgar charge frequently made that medieval monks were gluttonous, wasteful, extravagant, and profligate is belied by the hundreds of cartularies, or inventories, which have been preserved, and which show care, intelligence, and honesty in management. The enormous economic betterment of medieval Europe which the monks achieved proves them as a whole to have been intelligent landlords and agriculturalists."—Thompson, *Economic and Social History of the Middle Ages*, 630. "The most perfect and efficacious works of Christianity," said the skeptical Renan, "were those executed by the monastic orders."—*Marc Aurèle*, Paris, n.d., 627.

tion of an abbot by Walter Map.[12] Some cloisters were known for their fine food and wines. We should not grudge the monks a little good cheer, and we can understand how weary they were of vegetables, how they longed for meat; we can sympathize with their occasional gossiping, quarreling, and sleeping at Mass.[13]

The monks, in vowing celibacy, had underestimated the power of a sexual instinct repeatedly stirred by secular example and sights. Caesarius of Heisterbach tells a story, often repeated in the Middle Ages, of an abbot and a young monk riding out together. The youth saw women for the first time. "What are they?" he asked. "They be demons," said the abbot. "I thought," said the monk, "that they were the fairest things that ever I saw." [14] Said the ascetic Peter Damian, nearing the end of a saintly but acerbic life:

> I, who am now an old man, may safely look upon the seared and wrinkled visage of a blear-eyed crone. Yet from sight of the more comely and adorned I guard my eyes like boys from fire. Alas, my wretched heart!—which cannot hold scriptural mysteries read through a hundred times, and will not lose the memory of a form seen but once.[15]

To some monks virtue seemed a contest for their souls between woman and Christ; their denunciation of woman was an effort to deaden themselves to her charms; their pious dreams were sometimes softened with the dews of desire; and their saintly visions often borrowed the terms of human love.[16] Ovid was a welcome friend in some monasteries, and not least thumbed were his manuals of the amorous art.[17] The sculptures of certain cathedrals, the carvings of their furniture, even the paintings in some missals, portrayed riotous monks and nuns—pigs dressed as monks, monastic robes bulging over erect phalli, nuns sporting with devils.[18] A relief on the Portal of the Judgment at Reims shows a devil dragging condemned men to hell; among them is a mitered bishop. Medieval ecclesiastics—perhaps seculars envying regulars —allowed such caricatures to remain in place; modern churchmen thought it better to have most of them removed. The Church herself was the severest critic of her sinning members; a noble succession of ecclesiastical reformers labored to bring monks and abbots back to the ideals of Christ.

II. ST. BERNARD

At the end of the eleventh century, simultaneously with the purification of the papacy and the fervor of the First Crusade, a movement of self-reform swept through Christendom, immensely improved the secular clergy, and founded new monastic orders dedicated to the full rigor of the Augustinian or Benedictine rule. At an unknown date before 1039 St. John Gualbertus [19] established the order of Vallombrosa in the "shady valley" of that name in

Italy, and inaugurated in it the institution of lay brothers later developed by the mendicant orders. The Roman Synod of 1059 exhorted canons—clergymen sharing the labors and revenues of a cathedral—to live in community and hold all their property in common, like the apostles. Some were reluctant, and remained "secular canons"; many responded, adopted a monastic rule that they ascribed to St. Augustine, and formed semimonastic communities collectively known as Augustinian or Austin Canons.* In 1084 St. Bruno of Cologne, having declined the archbishopric of Reims, founded the Carthusian order by establishing a monastery at a desolate spot named Chartreuse, in the Alps near Grenoble; other pious men, sick of worldly strife and clerical laxity, formed similar Carthusian units in secluded places. Each monk worked, ate, and slept in his own separate cell, lived on bread and milk, wore garments of horsehair, and practiced almost perpetual silence. Three times a week they came together for Mass, vespers, and midnight prayers; and on Sundays and holydays they indulged themselves in conversation and a common meal. Of all the monastic orders this was the most austere, and has kept most faithfully, through eight centuries, to its original rule.

In 1098 Robert of Molesmes, tired of trying to reform the various Benedictine monasteries of which he had been prior, built a new monastic house at a wild point called Cîteaux near Dijon; and as Chartreuse named the Carthusians, so Cîteaux named the Cistercian monks. The third abbot of Cîteaux, Stephen Harding of Dorsetshire, reorganized and expanded the monastery, opened branches of it, and drew up the *Carta caritatis*, or Charter of Love, to insure the peaceful federal co-operation of the Cistercian houses with Cîteaux. The Benedictine rule was restored in full severity: absolute poverty was essential, all flesh food was to be avoided, learning was to be discouraged, verse-making was forbidden, and all splendor of religious vestment, vessel, or building was to be shunned. Every physically able monk was to join in manual labor in gardens and workshops that would make the monastery independent of the outside world, and give no excuse for any monk to leave the grounds. The Cistercians outshone all other groups, monastic or secular, in agricultural energy and skill; they set up new centers of their order in unsettled regions, subdued marshes, jungles, and forests to cultivation, and played a leading part in colonizing eastern Germany, and in repairing the damage that William the Conqueror had done in northern England. In this magnificent labor of civilization the Cistercian monks were aided by lay brothers—*conversi*—vowed to celibacy, silence, and illiteracy,[20] and working as farmers or servants in return for shelter, clothing, and food.[21]

These austerities frightened potential novices; the little band grew slowly, and the new order might have died in infancy had not fresh ardor come to it in the person of St. Bernard. Born near Dijon (1091) of a knightly family,

---

* Not to be confused with the Augustinian or Austin Friars founded by anchorites in Tuscany in 1256.

he became a shy and pious youth, loving solitude. Finding the secular world an uncomfortable place, he determined to enter a monastery. But, as if desiring companionship in solitude, he made effective propaganda among his relatives and friends to enter Cîteaux with him; mothers and nubile girls, we are told, trembled at his approach, fearing that he would lure their sons or lovers into chastity. Despite their tears and charms he succeeded; and when he was admitted to Cîteaux (1113) he brought with him a band of twenty-nine candidates, including brothers, an uncle, and friends. Later he persuaded his mother and sister to become nuns, and his father a monk, on the promise that "unless thou do penance thou shalt burn forever . . . and send forth smoke and stench." [22]

Stephen Harding came presently to such admiration for Bernard's piety and energy that he sent him forth (1115) as abbot, with twelve other monks, to found a new Cistercian house. Bernard chose a heavily wooded spot, ninety miles from Cîteaux, known as *Clara vallis*, Bright Valley, Clairvaux. There was no habitation there, and no human life. The initial task of the fraternal band was to build with their own hands their first "monastery"—a wooden building containing under one roof a chapel, a refectory, and a dormitory loft reached by a ladder; the beds were bins strewn with leaves; the windows were no larger than a man's head; the floor was the earth. Diet was vegetarian except for an occasional fish; no white bread, no spices, little wine; these monks eager for heaven ate like philosophers courting longevity. The monks prepared their own meals, each serving as cook in turn. By the rule that Bernard drew up, the monastery could not buy property; it could own only what was given it; he hoped that it would never have more land than could be worked by the monks' own hands and simple tools. In that quiet valley Bernard and his growing fellowship labored in silence and content, free from the "storm of the world," clearing the forest, planting and reaping, making their own furniture, and coming together at the canonical hours to sing, without an organ, the psalms and hymns of the day. "The more attentively I watch them," said William of St. Thierry, "the more I believe that they are perfect followers of Christ . . . a little less than angels, but much more than men." [23] The news of this Christian peace and self-containment spread, and before Bernard's death there were 700 monks at Clairvaux. They must have been happy there, for nearly all who were sent from that communistic enclave to serve as abbots, bishops, and councilors longed to return; and Bernard himself, offered the highest dignities in the Church, and going to many lands at her bidding, always yearned to get back to his cell at Clairvaux, "that my eyes may be closed by the hands of my children, and that my body may be laid at Clairvaux side by side with the bodies of the poor." [24]

He was a man of moderate intellect, of strong conviction, of immense force and unity of character. He cared nothing for science or philosophy. The mind of man, he felt, was too infinitesimal a portion of the universe to sit in judgment upon it or pretend to understand it. He marveled at the silly pride of philosophers prating about the nature, origin, and destiny of the cosmos. He was shocked by Abélard's proposal to submit faith to reason, and he fought that rationalism as a blasphemous impudence. Instead of trying to understand the universe he preferred to walk unquestioning and grateful in the miracle of revelation. He accepted the Bible as God's word, for otherwise, it seemed to him, life would be a desert of dark uncertainty. The more he preached that childlike faith the more surely he felt it to be the Way. When one of his monks, in terror, confessed to him that he could not believe in the power of the priest to change the bread of the Eucharist into the body and blood of Christ, Bernard did not reprove him; he bade him receive the sacrament nevertheless; "go and communicate with *my* faith"; and we are assured that Bernard's faith overflowed into the doubter and saved his soul.[25] Bernard could hate and pursue, almost to the death, heretics like Abélard or Arnold of Brescia, who weakened a Church which, with all her faults, seemed to him the very vehicle of Christ; and he could love with almost the tenderness of the Virgin whom he worshiped so fervently. Seeing a thief on the way to the gallows, he begged the count of Champagne for him, promising that he would subject the man to a harder penance than a moment's death.[26] He preached to kings and popes, but more contentedly to the peasants and shepherds of his valley; he was lenient with their faults, converted them by his example, and earned their mute love for the faith and love he gave them. He carried his piety to an exhausting asceticism; he fasted so much that his superior at Cîteaux had to command him to eat; and for thirty-eight years he lived in one cramped cell at Clairvaux, with a bed of straw and no seat but a cut in the wall.[27] All the comforts and goods of the world seemed to him as nothing compared with the thought and promise of Christ. He wrote in this mood several hymns of unassuming simplicity and touching tenderness:

Iesu dulcis memoria,
dans vera cordi gaudia,
sed super mel et omnia
eius dulcis praesentia.
    Nil canitur suavius,
    auditur nil iocundius,
    nil cogitatur dulcius
    quam Iesu Dei filius.
Iesu spes poenitentibus,
quam pius es petentibus,
quam bonus es quaerentibus,
sed quid invenientibus? [28]

Jesus sweet in memory,
Giving the heart true joy,
Yea, beyond honey and all things,
Sweet is His presence.
    Nothing sung is lovelier,
    Nothing heard is pleasanter,
    Nothing thought is sweeter
    Than Jesus the Son of God.
Jesus hope of the penitent,
How gentle Thou art to suppliants!
How good to those seeking Thee!
What must Thou be to those finding
    Thee?

Despite his flair for graceful speech he cared little for any but spiritual beauty. He covered his eyes lest they take too sensual a delight from the lakes of Switzerland.[29] His abbey was bare of all ornament except the crucified Christ. He berated Cluny for spending so much on the architecture and adornment of its abbeys. "The church," he said, "is resplendent in its walls and wholly lacking in its poor. It gilds its stones and leaves its children naked. With the silver of the wretched it charms the eyes of the rich." [30] He complained that the great abbey of St. Denis was crowded with proud and armored knights instead of simple worshipers; he called it "a garrison, a school of Satan, a den of thieves." [31] Suger, humbly moved by these strictures, reformed the customs of his church and his monks, and lived to earn Bernard's praise.

The monastic reform that radiated from Clairvaux, and the improvement of the hierarchy through the elevation of Bernard's monks to bishoprics and archbishoprics, were but a part of the influence which this astonishing man, who asked nothing but bread, wielded on all ranks in his half century. Henry of France, brother of the king, came to visit him; Bernard spoke to him; on that day Henry became a monk, and washed the dishes at Clairvaux.[32] Through his sermons—themselves so eloquent and sensuous as to verge on poetry—he moved all who heard him; through his letters—masterpieces of passionate pleading—he influenced councils, bishops, popes, kings; through personal contacts he molded the policies of Church and state. He refused to be more than an abbot, but he made and unmade popes, and no pontiff was heard with greater respect or reverence. He left his cell on a dozen errands of high diplomacy, usually at the call of the Church. When contending groups chose Anacletus II and Innocent II as rival popes (1130), Bernard supported Innocent; when Anacletus captured Rome Bernard entered Italy, and by the pure power of his personality and his speech roused the Lombard cities for Innocent; the crowds, drunk with his oratory and his sanctity, kissed his feet and tore his garments to pieces as sacred relics for their posterity. The sick came to him at Milan, and epileptics, paralytics, and other ailing faithful announced that they had been cured by his touch. On his return to Clairvaux from his diplomatic triumphs the peasants would come in from the fields, and the shepherds down from the hills, to ask his blessing; and receiving it they would return to their toil uplifted and content.

When Bernard died in 1153 the number of Cistercian houses had risen from 30 in 1134 (the year of Stephen Harding's death) to 343. The fame of his sanctity and his power brought many converts to the new order; by 1300 it had 60,000 monks in 693 monasteries. Other monastic orders took form in the twelfth century. About 1100 Robert of Arbrissol founded the order of Fontevrault in Anjou; in 1120 St. Norbert gave up a rich inheritance to establish the Premonstratensian order of Canons Regular at Prémontré near

Laon; in 1131 St. Gilbert constituted the English order of Sempringham—the Gilbertines—on the model of Fontevrault. About 1150 some Palestinian anchorites adopted the eremitical rule of St. Basil, and spread throughout Palestine; when the Moslems captured the Holy Land these "Carmelites" migrated to Cyprus, Sicily, France, and England. In 1198 Innocent III approved the articles of the order of Trinitarians, and dedicated it to the ransoming of Christians captured by Saracens. These new orders were a saving and uplifting leaven in the Christian Church.

The burst of monastic reform climaxed by Bernard died down as the twelfth century advanced. The younger orders kept their arduous rules with reasonable fidelity; but not many men could be found, in that dynamic period, to bear so strict a regimen. In time the Cistercians—even at Bernard's Clairvaux—became rich through hopeful gifts; endowments for "pittances" enabled the monks to add meat to their diet, and plenty of wine; [33] they delegated all manual labor to lay brothers; four years after Bernard's death they bought a supply of Saracen slaves; [34] they developed a large and profitable trade in the products of their socialistic industry, and aroused guild animosity through their exemption from transportation tolls. [35] The decline of faith as the Crusades failed reduced the number of novices, and disturbed the morale of all the monastic orders. But the old ideal of living like the apostles in a propertyless communism did not die; the conviction that the true Christian must shun wealth and power, and be a man of unflinching peace, lingered in thousands of souls. At the opening of the thirteenth century a man appeared, in the Umbrian hills of Italy, who brought these old ideals to vigor again by such a life of simplicity, purity, piety, and love that men wondered had Christ been born again.

III. ST. FRANCIS *

Giovanni de Bernadone was born in 1182 in Assisi, son of Ser Pietro de Bernadone, a wealthy merchant who did much business with Provence. There Pietro had fallen in love with a French girl, Pica, and he had brought her back to Assisi as his wife. When he returned from another trip to Provence, and found that a son had been born to him, he changed the child's name to Francesco, Francis, apparently as a tribute to Pica. The boy grew up in one of the loveliest regions of Italy, and never lost his affection for the Umbrian landscape and sky. He learned Italian and French from his parents, and Latin from the parish priest; he had no further formal schooling, but

---

* The literature on Francis is partly history, partly legend. As the legends are among the masterpieces of medieval literature, some of them are included in the following pages, with a warning in each instance. Most of the *Fioretti* ("Little Flowers of St. Francis") and the *Speculum perfectionis* ("Mirror of Perfection") are legend; and quotations from these writings are to be so construed.

soon entered his father's business. He disappointed Ser Pietro by showing more facility in spending money than in making it. He was the richest youth in town, and the most generous; friends flocked about him, ate and drank with him, and sang with him the songs of the troubadours; Francis wore, now and then, a parti-colored minstrel's suit.[36] He was a good-looking boy, with black eyes and hair and kindly face, and a melodious voice. His early biographers protest that he had no relations with the other sex, and, indeed, knew only two women by sight;[37] but this surely does Francis some injustice. Possibly, in those formative years, he heard from his father about the Albigensian and Waldensian heretics of southern France, and their new-old gospel of evangelical poverty.

In 1202 he fought in the Assisian army against Perugia, was made prisoner, and spent a year in meditative captivity. In 1204 he joined as a volunteer the army of Pope Innocent III. At Spoleto, lying in bed with a fever, he thought he heard a voice asking him: "Why do you desert the Lord for the servant, the Prince for his vassal?" "Lord," he asked, "what do you wish me to do?" The voice answered, "Go back to your home; there it shall be told you what you are to do."[38] He left the army and returned to Assisi. Now he showed ever less interest in his father's business, ever more in religion. Near Assisi was a poor chapel of St. Damian. Praying there in February, 1207, Francis thought he heard Christ speak to him from the altar, accepting his life and soul as an oblation. From that moment he felt himself dedicated to a new life. He gave the chapel priest all the money he had with him, and went home. One day he met a leper, and turned away in revulsion. Rebuking himself for unfaithfulness to Christ, he went back, emptied his purse into the leper's hand, and kissed the hand; this act, he tells us, marked an era in his spiritual life.[39] Thereafter he frequently visited the dwellings of the lepers, and brought them alms.

Shortly after this experience he spent several days in or near the chapel, apparently eating little; when he appeared again in Assisi he was so thin, haggard, and pale, and his clothes so tattered, his mind so bewildered, that the urchins in the public square cried out, *Pazzo! Pazzo!*—"A madman! A madman!" There his father found him, called him a half-wit, dragged him home, and locked him in a closet. Freed by his mother, Francis hurried back to the chapel. The angry father overtook him, upbraided him for making his family a public jest, reproached him for making so little return on the money spent in his rearing, and bade him leave the town. Francis had sold his personal belongings to support the chapel; he handed the proceeds to his father, who accepted them; but he would not recognize the authority of his father to command one who now belonged to Christ. Summoned before the tribunal of the bishop in the Piazza Santa Maria Maggiore, he presented himself humbly, while a crowd looked on in a scene made memorable by Giotto's brush. The bishop took him at his word, and bade him give up all his property. Francis retired to a room in the episcopal palace, and soon reappeared stark naked; he laid his bundled clothing and a few remaining coins before the bishop, and said: "Until this time I have called Pietro Bernadone my father, but now I desire to serve God. That is why I return to him this money . . . as well as my clothing, and all that I have had from him; for henceforth I desire to say nothing else than 'Our Father, Who art in heaven.'" [40] Bernadone carried off the clothing, while the bishop covered the shivering Francis with his mantle. Francis returned to St. Damian's, made himself a hermit's robe, begged his food from door to door, and with his hands began to rebuild the crumbling chapel. Several of the townspeople came to aid him, and they sang together as they worked.

In February, 1209, as he was hearing Mass, he was struck by the words which the priest read from the instructions of Jesus to the apostles:

> And as ye go, preach, saying, "The kingdom of heaven is at hand." Heal the sick, cleanse the lepers, raise the dead, cast out devils. Freely ye have received, freely give. Provide neither gold nor silver nor brass in your purses, nor scrip for your journey, neither two coats, neither shoes, nor a staff. (Matt. x, 7-10.)

It seemed to Francis that Christ Himself was speaking, and directly to him. He resolved to obey those words literally—to preach the kingdom of heaven, and possess nothing. He would go back across the 1200 years that had obscured the figure of Christ, and would rebuild his life on that divine exemplar.

So, that spring, braving all ridicule, he stood in the squares of Assisi and nearby towns and preached the gospel of poverty and Christ. Revolted by the unscrupulous pursuit of wealth that marked the age, and shocked by the splendor and luxury of some clergymen, he denounced money itself as a devil and a curse, bade his followers despise it as dung,[41] and called upon men and women to sell all that they had, and give to the poor. Small audiences listened to him in wonder and admiration, but most men passed him by as a fool in Christ. The good bishop of Assisi protested, "Your way of living without owning anything seems to me very harsh and difficult"; to which Francis replied, "My lord, if we possessed property we should need arms to defend it." [42] Some hearts were moved; twelve men offered to follow his doctrine and his way; he welcomed them, and gave them the above-quoted words of Christ as their commission and their rule. They made themselves brown robes, and built themselves cabins of branches and boughs. Daily they and Francis, rejecting the old monastic isolation, went forth, barefoot and penniless, to preach. Sometimes they would be absent for several days, and sleep in haylofts, or leper hospitals, or under the porch of a church. When they returned, Francis would wash their feet and give them food.

They greeted one another, and all whom they met on the road, with the ancient Oriental salutation: "The Lord give thee peace." They were not yet named Franciscans. They called themselves *Fratres minores*, Friars Minor, or Minorites; friars as meaning brothers rather than priests, minor as being the least of Christ's servants, and never wielding, but always under, superior authority; they were to hold themselves subordinate to even the lowliest priest, and to kiss the hand of any priest they met. Very few of them, in this first generation of the order, were ordained; Francis himself was never more than deacon. In their own little community they served one another, and did manual work; and no idler was long tolerated in the group. Intellectual study was discouraged; Francis saw no advantage in secular knowledge except for the accumulation of wealth or the pursuit of power; "my brethren who are led by desire of learning will find their hands empty in the day of tribulation." [43] He scorned historians, who perform no great deed themselves, but receive honors for recording the great deeds of others.[44] Anticipating Goethe's dictum that knowledge that does not lead to action is vain and poisonous, Francis said, *Tantum homo habet de scientia, quantum operatur* —"A man has only so much knowledge as he puts to work." [45] No friar was to own a book, not even a psalter. In preaching they were to use song as well as speech; they might even, said Francis, imitate the *jongleurs*, and become *ioculatores Dei*, gleemen of God.[46]

Sometimes the friars were derided, beaten, or robbed of almost their last garment. Francis bade them offer no resistance. In many cases the miscreants, astonished at what seemed a superhuman indifference to pride and property, begged forgiveness and restored their thefts.[47] We do not know if the following specimen of the *Little Flowers of St. Francis* is history or legend, but it portrays the ecstatic piety that runs through all that we hear of the saint:

> One winter's day as Francis was going from Perugia, suffering sorely from the bitter cold, he said: "Friar Leo, although the Friars Minor give good examples of holiness and edification, nevertheless write and note down diligently that perfect joy is not to be found therein." And Francis went his way a little farther, and said: "O Friar Leo, even though the Friars Minor gave sight to the blind, made the crooked straight, cast out devils, made the deaf to hear and the lame to walk . . . and raised to life those who had lain four days in the grave —write: perfect joy is never found there." And he journeyed on a little while, and cried aloud: "O Friar Leo, if the Friar Minor knew all tongues and sciences and all the Scriptures, so that he could foretell and reveal not only future things but even the secrets of the conscience and the soul—write: perfect joy is not there." . . . Yet a little farther he went, and cried again aloud: "O Friar Leo, although the Friar Minor were skilled to preach so well that he should convert all infidels to Christ—write: not there is perfect joy." And when this

fashion of talk had continued for two miles, Friar Leo asked: . . . "Father, prithee in God's name tell me where is perfect joy to be found?" And Francis answered him: "When we are come to St. Mary of the Angels" [then the Franciscan chapel in Assisi], "wet through with rain, frozen with cold, foul with mire, and tormented with hunger, and when we knock at the door, and the doorkeeper comes in a rage and says, 'Who are you?' and we say, 'We are two of your friars,' and he answers, 'You lie, you are rather two knaves who go about deceiving the world and stealing the alms of the poor. Begone!' and he opens not to us, and makes us stay outside hungry and cold all night in the rain and snow; then, if we endure patiently such cruelty . . . without complaint or mourning, and believe humbly and charitably that it is God who made the doorkeeper rail against us—O Friar Leo, write: there is perfect joy! And if we persevere in our knocking; and he issues forth, and angrily drives us away, abusing us and smiting us on the cheek, saying, 'Go hence, you vile thieves!'—if this we suffer patiently with love and gladness, write, O Friar Leo: this is perfect joy! And if, constrained by hunger and by cold, we knock once more and pray with many tears that he open to us for the love of God, and he . . . issues forth with a big knotted stick and seizes us by our cowls and flings us on the ground, and rolls us in the snow, bruising every bone in our bodies with that heavy club; if we, thinking on the agony of the blessed Christ, endure all these things patiently and joyously for love of Him—write, O Friar Leo, that here and in this is found perfect joy." [48]

The remembrance of his early life of indulgence gave him a haunting sense of sin; and if we may believe the *Little Flowers* he sometimes wondered whether God would ever forgive him. A touching story tells how, in the early days of the order, when they could find no breviary from which to read the divine office, Francis extemporized a litany of contrition, and bade Brother Leo repeat after him words accusing Francis of sin. Leo at each sentence tried to repeat the accusation, but found himself saying, instead, "The mercy of God is infinite." [49] On another occasion, just convalescing from quartan fever, Francis had himself dragged naked before the people in the market place of Assisi, and commanded a friar to throw a full dish of ashes into his face; and to the crowd he said: "You believe me to be a holy man, but I confess to God and you that I have in this my infirmity eaten meat and broth made with meat." [50] The people were all the more convinced of his sanctity. They told how a young friar had seen Christ and the Virgin conversing with him; they attributed many miracles to him, and brought their sick and "possessed" to him to be healed. His charity became a legend. He could not bear to see others poorer than himself; he so often gave to the passing poor the garments from his back that his disciples found it hard to keep him clothed. Once, says the probably legendary *Mirror of Perfection*,[51] when he was returning from Siena he came across a poor man on the way, and said to a fellow monk: "We ought to return this mantle to its owner. For we received it only as a loan until we should come upon one poorer than ourselves. . . . It would be counted to us as a theft if we should not give it to him who is more needy."

His love overflowed from men to animals, to plants, even to inanimate things. The *Mirror of Perfection*, unverified, ascribes to him a kind of rehearsal for his later Canticle of the Sun:

In the morning, when the sun rises, every man ought to praise God, who created it for our use. . . . When it becomes night, every man ought to give praise on account of Brother Fire, by which our eyes are then enlightened; for we be all, as it were, blind; and the Lord by these two, our brothers, doth enlighten our eyes.

He so admired fire that he hesitated to extinguish a candle; the fire might object to being put out. He felt a sensitive kinship with every living thing. He wished to "supplicate the Emperor" (Frederick II, a great hunter of birds) "to tell him, for the love of God and me, to make a special law that no man should take or kill our sisters the larks, nor do them any harm; likewise that all the podestas or mayors of the towns, and the lords of castles and villages, should require men every year on Christmas Day to throw grain outside the cities and castles, that our sisters the larks, and other birds, may have something to eat." [52] Meeting a youth who had snared some turtle doves and was taking them to market, Francis persuaded the boy to give them to him; the saints built nests for them, "that ye may be fruitful and multiply"; they obeyed abundantly, and lived near the monastery in happy friendship with the monks, occasionally snatching food from the table at which these were eating.[53] A score of legends embroidered this theme. One told how Francis preached to "my little sisters the birds" on the road between Cannora and Bevagna; and "those that were on the trees flew down to hear him, and stood still the while St. Francis made an end of his sermon."

My little sisters the birds, much are ye beholden to God your Creator, and always and in every place ye ought to praise Him for that He hath given you a double and triple vesture. He hath given you freedom to go into any place. . . . Moreover ye sow not, neither do ye reap, and God feedeth you and giveth you the rivers and the fountains for your drink; He giveth you the mountains and the valleys for your refuge, and the tall trees wherein to build your nests; and for as much as ye can neither spin nor sew, God clotheth you and your children. . . . Therefore beware, little sisters mine, of the sin of ingratitude, but ever strive to praise God.[54]

We are assured by Friars James and Masseo that the birds bowed in reverence to Francis, and would not depart until he had blessed them. The *Fioretti* or

Little Flowers from which this story comes are an Italian amplification of a Latin *Actus Beati Francisci* (1323); they belong less to factual history than to literature; but there they rank among the most engaging compositions of the Age of Faith.

Having been advised that he needed papal permission to establish a religious order, Francis and his twelve disciples went to Rome in 1210, and laid their request and their rule before Innocent III. The great Pope gently counseled them to defer formal organization of a new order until time should test the practicability of the rule. "My dear children," he said, "your life appears to me too severe. I see indeed that your fervor is great ... but I ought to consider those who will come after you, lest your mode of life be beyond their strength." [55] Francis persisted, and the Pope finally yielded—incarnate strength to incarnate faith. The friars took the tonsure, submitted themselves to the hierarchy, and received from the Benedictines of Mt. Subasio, near Assisi, the chapel of St. Mary of the Angels, so small—some ten feet long— that it came to be called Portiuncula—"little portion." The friars built themselves huts around the chapel, and these huts formed the first monastery of the First Order of St. Francis.

Now not only did new members join the order, but, to the joy of the saint, a wealthy girl of eighteen, Clara dei Sciffi, asked his permission to form a Second Order of St. Francis, for women (1212). Leaving her home, she vowed herself to poverty, chastity, and obedience, and became the abbess of a Franciscan convent built around the chapel of St. Damian. In 1221 a Third Order of St. Francis—the Tertiaries—was formed among laymen who, while not bound to the full Franciscan rule, wished to obey that rule as far as possible while living in the "world," and to help the First and Second Orders with their labor and charity.

The ever more numerous Franciscans now (1211) brought their gospel to the towns of Umbria, and later to the other provinces of Italy. They uttered no heresy, but preached little theology; nor did they ask of their hearers the chastity, poverty, and obedience to which they themselves were vowed. "Fear and honor God," they said, "praise and bless Him. . . . Repent . . . for you know that we shall soon die. . . . Abstain from evil, persevere in the good." Italy had heard such words before, but seldom from men of such evident sincerity. Crowds came to their preaching; and one Umbrian village, learning of Francis' approach, went out *en masse* to greet him with flowers, banners, and song.[56] At Siena he found the city in civil war; his preaching brought both factions to his feet, and at his urging they ended their strife for a while.[57] It was on these missionary tours in Italy that he contracted the malaria which was to bring him to an early death.

Nevertheless, encouraged by his Italian success, and knowing little of Islam, Francis resolved to go to Syria and convert the Moslems, even the sultan. In 1212 he sailed from an Italian port, but a storm cast his ship upon the

Dalmatian coast, and he was forced to return to Italy; legend, however, tells how "St. Francis converted the soldan of Babylon." [58] In the same year, says a story probably also mythical, he went to Spain to convert the Moors; but on arrival he fell so ill that his disciples had to bring him back to Assisi. Another questionable narrative takes him to Egypt; he passed unharmed, we are told, into the Moslem army that was resisting the Crusaders at Damietta; he offered to go through fire if the sultan would promise to lead his troops into the Christian faith in case Francis emerged unscathed; the sultan refused, but had the saint escorted safely to the Christian camp. Horrified by the fury with which the soldiers of Christ massacred the Moslem population at the capture of Damietta,[59] Francis returned to Italy a sick and saddened man. To his chilling malaria, it is said, he added in Egypt an eye infection that would in later years almost destroy his sight.

During these long absences of the saint his followers multiplied faster than was good for his rule. His fame brought recruits who took the vows without due reflection; some came to regret their haste; and many complained that the rule was too severe. Francis made reluctant concessions. Doubtless, too, the expansion of the order, which had divided itself into several houses scattered through Umbria, made such demands upon him for administrative skill and tact as his mystic absorption could hardly meet. Once, we are told, when one monk spoke evil of another, Francis commanded him to eat a lump of ass's dung so that his tongue should not relish evil any more; the monk obeyed, but his fellows were more shocked by the punishment than by the offense.[60] In 1220 Francis resigned his leadership, bade his followers elect another minister-general, and thereafter counted himself a simple monk. A year later, however, disturbed by further relaxations of the original (1210) rule, he drew up a new rule—his famous "Testament"—aiming to restore full observance of the vow of poverty, and forbidding the monks to move from their huts at the Portiuncula to the more salubrious quarters built for them by the townspeople. He submitted this rule to Honorius III, who turned it over to a committee of prelates for revision; when it came from their hands it made a dozen obeisances to Francis, and as many relaxations of the rule. The predictions of Innocent III had been verified.

Reluctantly but humbly obedient, Francis now gave himself to a life of mostly solitary contemplation, asceticism, and prayer. The intensity of his devotion and his imagination occasionally brought him visions of Christ, or Mary, or the apostles. In 1224, with three disciples, he left Assisi, and rode across hill and plain to a hermitage on Mt. Verna, near Chiusi. He secluded himself in a lonely hut beyond a deep ravine, allowed none but Brother Leo to visit him, and bade him come only twice a day, and not to come if he received no answer to his call of approach. On September 14, 1224, the Feast of the Exaltation of the Holy Cross, after a long fast and a night spent in vigil and prayer, Francis thought he saw a seraph coming down from the sky, bearing an image of the crucified Christ. When the vision faded he felt strange pains, and discovered fleshy excrescences on the palms and backs of his hands, on the soles and tops of his feet, and on his body, resembling in place and color the wounds—*stigmata*—presumably made by the nails that were believed to have bound the extremities of Jesus to the cross, and by the lance that had pierced His side.*

Francis returned to the hermitage, and to Assisi. A year after the appearance of the stigmata he began to lose his sight. On a visit to St. Clara's nunnery he was struck completely blind. Clara nursed him back to sight, and kept him at St. Damian's for a month. There one day in 1224, perhaps in the joy of convalescence, he composed, in Italian poetic prose, his "Canticle of the Sun": [62]

> Most High, Omnipotent, Good Lord.
> Thine be the praise, the glory, the honor, and all benediction;
> to Thee alone, Most High, they are due,
>   and no man is worthy to mention Thee.
>
> Be Thou praised, my Lord, with all Thy creatures,
>   above all Brother Sun,
>   who gives the day and lightens us therewith.
>
> And he is beautiful and radiant with great splendor;
>   of Thee, Most High, he bears similitude.
>
> Be Thou praised, my Lord, of Sister Moon and the stars;
>   in the heaven hast Thou formed them, clear and precious
>   and comely.
>
> Be Thou praised, my Lord, of Brother Wind,
>   and of the air, and the cloud, and of fair and of all weather,
>   by the which Thou givest to Thy creatures sustenance.
>
> Be Thou praised, my Lord, of Sister Water,
>   which is much useful and humble and precious and pure.
>
> Be Thou praised, my Lord, of Brother Fire,
>   by which Thou hast lightened the night,
>   and he is beautiful and joyful and robust and strong.
>
> Be Thou praised, my Lord, of our Sister Mother Earth,
>   which sustains and hath us in rule,
>   and produces divers fruits with colored flowers and herbs.

---

* It has been suggested that these swellings could have been due to malignant malaria, which, in the absence of modern treatment, has been known to produce purple hemorrhages of blood in the skin.[61]

> Be Thou praised, my Lord, of those who pardon for Thy love
>   and endure sickness and tribulations.
>
> Blessed are they who will endure it in peace,
>   for by Thee, Most High, they shall be crowned.

In 1225 some physicians at Rieti, having to no good effect anointed his eyes with "the urine of a virgin boy," resorted to drawing a rod of white-hot iron across his forehead. Francis, we are told, appealed to "Brother Fire: you are beautiful above all creatures; be favorable to me in this hour; you know how much I have always loved you"; he said later that he had felt no pain. He recovered enough sight to set forth on another preaching tour. He soon broke down under the hardships of travel; malaria and dropsy crippled him, and he was taken back to Assisi.

Despite his protestations he was put to bed in the episcopal palace. He asked the doctor to tell him the truth, and was told that he could barely survive the autumn. He astonished everyone by beginning to sing. Then, it is said, he added a stanza to his Canticle of the Sun:

> Be praised, Lord, for our Sister Bodily Death, from whom
>   no man can escape.
> Alas for them who die in mortal sin;
>   Blessed are they who are found in Thy holy will,
>   for the second death will not work them harm.[63]

It is said that in these last days he repented of his asceticism, as having "offended his brother the body." [64] When the bishop was called away Francis persuaded the monks to remove him to Portiuncula. There he dictated his will, at once modest and commanding: he bade his followers be content with "poor and abandoned churches," and not to accept habitations out of harmony with their vows of poverty; to surrender to the bishop any heretic or recreant monk in the order; and never to change the rule.[65]

He died October 3, 1226, in the forty-fifth year of his age, singing a psalm. Two years later the Church named him a saint. Two other leaders dominated that dynamic age: Innocent III and Frederick II. Innocent raised the Church to its greatest height, from which in a century it fell. Frederick raised the Empire to its greatest height, from which in a decade it fell. Francis exaggerated the virtues of poverty and ignorance, but he reinvigorated Christianity by bringing back into it the spirit of Christ. Today only scholars know of the Pope and the Emperor, but the simple saint reaches into the hearts of millions of men.

The order that he had founded numbered at his death some 5000 members, and had spread into Hungary, Germany, England, France, and Spain. It proved the bulwark of the Church in winning northern Italy from heresy back to Catholicism. Its gospel of poverty and illiteracy could be accepted by only a small minority; Europe insisted on traversing the exciting parabola of wealth, science, philosophy, and doubt. Meanwhile even the modified rule that Francis had so unwillingly accepted was further relaxed (1230); men could not be expected to stay long, and in needed number, on the heights of the almost delirious asceticism that had shortened Francis' life. With a milder rule the Friars Minor grew by 1280 to 200,000 monks in 8000 monasteries. They became great preachers, and by their example led the secular clergy to take up the custom of preaching, heretofore confined to bishops. They produced saints like St. Bernardino of Siena and St. Anthony of Padua, scientists like Roger Bacon, philosophers like Duns Scotus, teachers like Alexander of Hales. Some became agents of the Inquisition; some rose to be bishops, archbishops, popes; many undertook dangerous missionary enterprises in distant and alien lands. Gifts poured in from the pious; some leaders, like Brother Elias, learned to like luxury; and though Francis had forbidden rich churches, Elias raised to his memory the imposing basilica that still crowns the hill of Assisi. The paintings of Cimabue and Giotto there were the first products of an immense and enduring influence of St. Francis, his history and his legend, on Italian art.

Many Minorites protested against the relaxation of Francis' rule. As "Spirituals" or "Zealots" they lived in hermitages or small convents in the Apennines, while the great majority of Franciscans preferred spacious monasteries. The Spirituals argued that Christ and His apostles had possessed no property; St. Bonaventura agreed; Pope Nicholas III approved the proposition in 1279; Pope John XXII pronounced it false in 1323; and thereafter those Spirituals who persisted in preaching it were suppressed as heretics. A century after the death of Francis his most loyal followers were burned at the stake by the Inquisition.

IV. ST. DOMINIC

It is unjust to Dominic that his name should suggest the Inquisition. He was not its founder, nor was he responsible for its terrors; his own activity was to convert by example and preaching. He was of sterner stuff than Francis, but revered him as the saintlier saint; and Francis loved him in return. Essentially their work was the same: each organized a great order of men devoted not to self-salvation in solitude but to missionary work among Christians and infidels. Each took from the heretics their most persuasive weapons—the praise of poverty and the practice of preaching. Together they saved the Church.

Domingo de Guzman was born at Calaruega in Castile (1170). Brought up by an uncle priest, he was one of thousands who in those days took Christianity to heart. When famine struck Palencia he is said to have sold all his goods, even his precious books, to feed the poor. He became an Augustinian canon regular in the cathedral of Osma, and in 1201 accompanied his bishop on a mission to Toulouse, then a center of the Albigensian heresy. Their very host was an Albigensian; it may be a legend that Dominic converted him overnight. Inspired by the advice of the bishop and the example of some heretics, Dominic adopted the life of voluntary poverty, went about barefoot, and strove peaceably to bring the people back to the Church. At Montpellier he met three papal legates—Arnold, Raoul, and Peter of Castelnau. He was shocked by their rich dress and luxury, and attributed to this their confessed failure to make headway against the heretics. He rebuked them with the boldness of a Hebrew prophet: "It is not by the display of power and pomp, nor by cavalcades of retainers and richly houseled palfreys, nor by gorgeous apparel, that the heretics win proselytes; it is by zealous preaching, by apostolic humility, by austerity, by holiness." [66] The shamed legates, we are told, dismissed their equipage and shed their shoes.

For ten years (1205–16) Dominic remained in Languedoc, preaching zealously. The only mention of him in connection with physical persecution tells how, at a burning of heretics, he saved one from the flames.[67] Some of his order proudly called him, after his death, *Persecutor haereticorum*—not necessarily the persecutor but the pursuer of heretics. He gathered about him a group of fellow preachers, and their effectiveness was such that Pope Honorius III (1216) recognized the Friars Preachers as a new order, and approved the rule drawn up for it by Dominic. Making his headquarters at Rome, Dominic gathered recruits, taught them, inspired them with his almost fanatical zeal, and sent them out through Europe as far east as Kiev, and into foreign lands, to convert Christendom and heathendom to Christianity. At the first general chapter of the Dominicans at Bologna in 1220, Dominic persuaded his followers to adopt by unanimous vote the rule of absolute poverty. There, a year later, he died.

Like the Franciscans, the Dominicans spread everywhere as wandering, mendicant friars. Matthew Paris describes them in the England of 1240:

> Very sparing in food and raiment, possessing neither gold nor silver nor anything of their own, they went through cities, towns, and villages, preaching the Gospel . . . living together by tens or sevens . . . thinking not of the morrow, nor keeping anything for the next morning. . . . Whatsoever was left over from their table of the alms given them, this they gave forthwith to the poor. They went shod only with the Gospel, they slept in their clothes on mats, and laid stones for pillows under their heads.[68]

They took an active, and not always a gentle, part in the work of the Inquisition. They were employed by the popes in high posts and diplomatic missions. They entered the universities and produced the two giants of Scholastic philosophy, Albertus Magnus and Thomas Aquinas; it was they who saved the Church from Aristotle by transforming him into a Christian. Together with the Franciscans, the Carmelites, and the Austin Friars they revolutionized the monastic life by mingling with the common people in daily ministrations, and raised monasticism in the thirteenth century to a power and beauty which it had never attained before.

A large perspective of monastic history does not bear out the exaggerations of moralists nor the caricatures of satirists. Many cases of monastic misconduct can be cited; they draw attention precisely because they are exceptional; and which of us is so saintly that he may demand an untarnished record from any class of men? The monks who remained faithful to their vows—who lived in obscure poverty, chastity, and piety—eluded both gossip and history; virtue makes no news, and bores both readers and historians. We hear of "sumptuous edifices" possessed by Franciscan monks as early as 1249, and in 1271 Roger Bacon, whose hyperboles often forfeited him a hearing, informed the pope that "the new orders are now horribly fallen from their original dignity." [69] But this is hardly the picture that we get from Fra Salimbene's candid and intimate *Chronicle* (1288?). Here a Franciscan monk takes us behind the scenes and into the daily career of his order. There are peccadilloes here and there, and some quarrels and jealousy; but over all that arduously inhibited life hovers an atmosphere of modesty, simplicity, brotherliness, and peace. [70] If, occasionally, a woman enters this story, she merely brings a touch of grace and tenderness into narrow and lonely lives. Hear a sample of Fra Salimbene's guileless chatter:

> There was a certain youth in the convent of Bologna who was called Brother Guido. He was wont to snore so mightily in his sleep that no man could rest in the same house with him, wherefore he was set to sleep in a shed among the wood and straw; yet even so the brethren could not escape him, for the sound of that accursed rumbling echoed throughout the whole convent. So all the priests and discreet brethren gathered together . . . and it was decreed by a formal sentence that he should be sent back to his mother, who had deceived the order, since she knew all this of her son before he was received among us. Yet was he not sent back forthwith, which was the Lord's doing. . . . For Brother Nicholas, considering within himself that the boy was to be cast out through a defect of nature, and without guilt of his own, called the lad daily about the hour of dawn to come and serve him at Mass; and at the end of the Mass the boy would kneel at his bidding behind the altar, hoping to receive some grace of him. Then would Brother Nicholas touch the boy's face and nose with his hands, desiring, by God's gifts, to bestow on him the boon of health. In brief, the boy was suddenly and wholly healed, without further discomfort to the brethren. Thenceforth he slept in peace and quiet, like any dormouse. [71]

V. THE NUNS

As early as the time of St. Paul it had been the custom, in Christian communities, for widows and other lonely or devout women to give some oi all of their days and their property to charitable work. In the fourth centuiy some women, emulating monks, left the world and lived the life of religious in solitude or in communities, under vows of poverty, chastity, and obedience. About 530 St. Benedict's twin sister Scholastica established a nunnery near Monte Cassino under his guidance and rule. From that time Benedictine convents spread through Europe, and Benedictine nuns became almost as numerous as Benedictine monks. The Cistercian Order opened its first convent in 1125, its most famous one, Port Royal, in 1204; by 1300 there were 700 Cistercian nunneries in Europe.[72] In these older orders most of the nuns came from the upper classes,[73] and nunneries were too often the repository of women for whom their male relations had no room or taste. In 458 the Emperor Majorian had to forbid parents to rid themselves of supernumerary daughters by compelling them to enter a convent.[74] Entry into Benedictine nunneries usually required a dowry, though the Church prohibited any but voluntary offerings.[75] Hence a prioress, like Chaucer's, could be a woman of proud breeding and large responsibilities, administering a spacious domain as the source of her convent's revenues. In those days a nun was usually called not Sister but Madame.

St. Francis revolutionized conventual as well as monastic institutions. When Santa Clara came to him in 1212, and expressed her wish to found for women such an order as he had founded for men, he overlooked canonical regulations and, though himself only a deacon, received her vows, accepted her into the Franciscan Order, and commissioned her to organize the Poor Clares. Innocent III, with his usual ability to forgive infractions of the letter by the spirit, confirmed the commission (1216). Santa Clara gathered about her some pious women who lived in communal poverty, wove and spun, nursed the sick, and distributed charity. Legends formed around her almost as fondly as around Francis himself. Once, we are told, a pope

> went to her convent to hear her discourse of divine and celestial things. ... Santa Clara had the table laid, and set loaves of bread thereon that the Holy Father might bless them. ... Santa Clara knelt down with great reverence, and besought him to be pleased to bless the bread. ... The Holy Father answered: "Sister Clare, most faithful one, I desire that thou shouldst bless this bread, and make over it the sign of the most holy cross of Christ, to which thou hast completely devoted thyself." And Santa Clara said: "Most Holy Father, forgive me, but I should merit great reproof if, in the presence of the Vicar of Christ, I, who am a poor, vile woman, should presume to give such benedic-

tion." And the Pope answered: "To the end that this be not imputed to thy presumption but to the merit of obedience, I command thee, by holy obedience, that thou . . . bless this bread in the name of God." And then Santa Clara, even as a true daughter of obedience, devoutly blessed the bread with the sign of the most holy cross. Marvelous to tell! forthwith on all those loaves the sign of the cross appeared figured most beautifully. And the Holy Father, when he saw this miracle, partook of the bread and departed, thanking God and leaving his blessing with Santa Clara.[76]

She died in 1253, and was canonized soon afterward. Franciscan monks in divers localities organized similar groups of *Clarissi*, or Poor Clares. The other mendicant orders—Dominicans, Augustinians, Carmelites—also established a "second order" of nuns; and by 1300 Europe had as many nuns as monks. In Germany the nunneries tended to be havens of intense mysticism; in France and England they were often the refuge of noble ladies "converted" from the world, or deserted, disappointed, or bereaved. The *Ancren Riwle*—i.e., the Rule of the Anchorites—reveals the mood expected of English nuns in the thirteenth century. It may have been written by Bishop Poore probably for a convent at Tarrant in Dorsetshire. It is darkened with much talk of sin and hell, and some blasphemous abuse of the female body;[77] but a tone of fine sincerity redeems it, and it is among the oldest and noblest specimens of English prose.[78]

It would be a simple matter to gather, from ten centuries, some fascinating instances of conventual immorality. A number of nuns had been cloistered against their wills,[79] and found it uncomfortable to be saints. Archbishop Theodore of Canterbury and Bishop Egbert of York deemed it necessary to forbid the seduction of nuns by abbots, priests, and bishops.[80] Bishop Ivo of Chartres (1035–1115) reported that the nuns of St. Fara's Convent were practicing prostitution; Abélard (1079–1142) gave a similar picture of some French convents of his time; Pope Innocent III described the convent of St. Agatha as a brothel that infected the whole surrounding country with its evil life and repute.[81] Bishop Rigaud of Rouen (1249) gave a generally favorable report of the religious groups in his diocese, but told of one nunnery in which, out of thirty-three nuns and three lay sisters, eight were guilty, or suspected, of fornication, and "the prioress is drunk almost any night."[82] Boniface VIII (1300) tried to improve conventual discipline by decreeing strict claustration, or seclusion from the world; but the decree could not be enforced.[83] At one nunnery in the diocese of Lincoln, when the bishop came to deposit this papal bull, the nuns threw it at his head, and vowed they would never obey it;[84] such isolation had probably not been in their vows. The prioress in Chaucer's *Tales* had no business there, for the Church had forbidden nuns to go on pilgrimage.[85]

If history had been as careful to note instances of obedience to conventual rules as to record infractions, we should probably be able to counter each sinful lapse with a thousand examples of fidelity. In many cases the rules were inhumanly severe, and merited violation. Carthusian and Cistercian nuns were required to keep silence except when speech was indispensable—a command sorely uncongenial to the gentle sex. Usually the nuns attended to their own needs of cleaning, cooking, washing, sewing; they made clothing for monks and the poor, linen for the altar, vestments for the priest; they wove and embroidered hangings and tapestries, and depicted on them, with nimble fingers and patient souls, half the history of the world. They copied and illuminated manuscripts; they received children to board, and taught them letters, hygiene, and domestic arts; for centuries they provided the only higher education open to girls. Many of them served as nurses in hospitals. They rose at midnight for prayers, and again before dawn, and recited the canonical hours. Many days were fast days, on which they ate no food till the evening meal.

Let us hope that these hard rules were sometimes infringed. If we look back upon the nineteen centuries of Christianity, with all their heroes, kings, and saints, we shall find it difficult to list many men who came so close to Christian perfection as the nuns. Their lives of quiet devotion and cheerful ministration have made many generations blessed. When all the sins of history are weighed in the balance, the virtues of these women will tip the scale against them, and redeem our race.

VI. THE MYSTICS

Many such women could be saints because they felt divinity closer to them than hands and feet. The medieval imagination was so stimulated by all the forces of word, picture, statue, ceremony, even by the color and quantity of light, that supersensory visions came readily, and the believing soul felt itself breaking through the bounds of nature to the supernatural. The human mind itself, in all the mystery of its power, seemed a supernatural and unearthly thing, surely akin to—a blurred image and infinitesimal fraction of—the Mind behind and in the matter of the world; so the top of the mind might touch the foot of the throne of God. In the ambitious humility of the mystic the hope burned that a soul unburdened of sin and uplifted with prayer might rise on the wings of grace to the Beatific Vision and a divine companionship. That vision could never be attained through sensation, reason, science, or philosophy, which were bound to time, the many, and the earth, and could never reach to the core and power and oneness of the universe. The problem of the mystic was to cleanse the soul as an internal organ of spiritual perception, to wash away from it all stain of selfish individuality and illusory multiplicity, to widen its reach and love to the uttermost inclusion, and then to see, with clear and disembodied sight, the cosmic, eternal, and divine, and thereby to return, as from a long exile, to union with the God from Whom birth had meant a penal severance. Had not Christ promised that the pure in heart would see God?

Mystics, therefore, appeared in every age, every religion, and every land. Greek Christianity abounded in them despite the Hellenic legacy of reason. St. Augustine was a mystic fountain for the West; his *Confessions* constituted a return of the soul from created things to God; seldom had any mortal so long conversed with the Deity. St. Anselm the statesman, St. Bernard the organizer, upheld the mystical approach against the rationalism of Roscelin and Abélard. When William of Champeaux was driven from Paris by the logic of Abélard, he founded in a suburb (1108) the Augustinian abbey of St. Victor as a school of theology; and his successors there, Hugh and Richard, ignoring the perilous adventure of young philosophy, based religion not on argument but on the mystical experience of the divine presence. Hugh (d. 1141) saw supernatural sacramental symbols in every phase of creation; Richard (d. 1173) rejected logic and learning, preferred the "heart" to the "head" *à la* Pascal, and described with learned logic the mystical rise of the soul to God.

The passion of Italy kindled mysticism into a gospel of revolution. Joachim of Flora—Giovanni dei Gioacchini di Fiori—a noble of Calabria, developed a longing to see Palestine. Impressed on the way by the misery of the people, he dismissed his retinue and continued as a humble pilgrim. Legend tells how he passed an entire Lent in an old well on Mt. Tabor; how, on Easter Sunday, a great splendor appeared to him, and filled him with such divine light that he understood at once all the Scriptures, all the future and the past. Returning to Calabria, he became a Cistercian monk and priest, thirsted for austerity, and retired to a hermitage. Disciples gathered, and he formed them into a new Order of Flora, whose rule of poverty and prayer was approved by Celestine III. In 1200 he sent to Innocent III a series of works which he had written, he said, under divine inspiration, but which, nevertheless, he submitted for papal censorship. Two years later he died.

His writings were based on the Augustinian theory—widely accepted in orthodox circles—that a symbolic concordance existed between the events of the Old Testament and the history of Christendom from the birth of Christ to the establishment of the Kingdom of Heaven on earth. Joachim divided the history of man into three stages: the first, under the rule of God the Father, ended at the Nativity; the second, ruled by the Son, would last, according to apocalyptic calculations, 1260 years; the third, under the Holy Ghost, would be preceded by a time of troubles, of war and poverty and ecclesiastical corruption, and would be ushered in by the rise of a new monastic order which would cleanse the Church, and would realize a world-wide utopia of peace, justice, and happiness.[86]

Thousands of Christians, including men high in the Church, accepted

Joachim's claim to divine inspiration, and looked hopefully to 1260 as the year of the Second Advent. The Spiritual Franciscans, confident that theirs was the new Order, took courage from Joachim's teachings; and when they were outlawed by the Church they carried on their propaganda through writings published under his name. In 1254 an edition of Joachim's main works appeared under the title of *The Everlasting Gospel*, with a commentary proclaiming that a pope tainted with simony would mark the close of the Second Age, and that in the Third Age the need of sacraments and priests would be ended by the reign of universal love. The book was condemned by the Church; its presumptive author, a Franciscan monk Gherardo da Borgo, was imprisoned for life; but its circulation secretly continued, and deeply affected mystical and heretical thought in Italy and France from St. Francis to Dante—who placed Joachim in paradise.

Perhaps in excited expectation of the coming Kingdom, a mania of religious penitence flared up around Perugia in 1259, and swept through northern Italy. Thousands of penitents of every age and class marched in disorderly procession, dressed only in loincloths, weeping, praying God for mercy, and scourging themselves with leather thongs. Thieves and usurers fell in, and restored their illegal gains; murderers, catching the contagion of repentance, knelt before their victims' kin and begged to be slain; prisoners were released, exiles were recalled, enmities were healed. The movement spread through Germany into Bohemia; and for a time it seemed that a new and mystical faith, ignoring the Church, would inundate Europe. But in a little while the nature of man reasserted itself; new enmities developed, sinning and murder were renewed; and the Flagellant craze disappeared into the psychic recesses from which it had emerged.[87]

The mystic flame burned less fitfully in Flanders. A priest of Liége, Lambert le Bégue (i.e., the stutterer), established in 1184 on the Meuse a house for women who, without taking monastic vows, wished to live together in small semi-communistic groups, supporting themselves by weaving wool and making lace. Similar *maisons-Dieu*, or houses of God, were established for men. The men called themselves Beghards, the women Beguines. These communities, like the Waldenses, condemned the Church for owning property, and themselves practiced a voluntary poverty. A similar sect, the Brethren of the Free Spirit, appeared about 1262 in Augsburg, and developed in the cities along the Rhine. Both movements claimed a mystical inspiration which absolved them from ecclesiastical control, even from state or moral law.[88] State and Church combined to suppress them; they went underground, emerged repeatedly under new names, and contributed to the origin and fervor of the Anabaptists and other radical sects in the Reformation.

Germany became the favorite land of mysticism in the West. Hildegarde of Bingen (1099–1179), the "Sibyl of the Rhine," lived all but eight of her eighty-two years as a Benedictine nun, and ended as abbess of a convent on the Rupertsberg. She was an unusual mixture of administrator and visionary, pietist and radical, poet and scientist, physician and saint. She corresponded with popes and kings, always in a tone of inspired authority, and in Latin prose of masculine power. She published several books of visions (*Scivias*), for which she claimed the collaboration of the Deity; the clergy were chagrined to hear it, for these revelations were highly critical of the wealth and corruption of the Church. Said Hildegarde, in accents of eternal hope:

> Divine justice shall have its hour . . . the judgments of God are about to be accomplished; the Empire and the Papacy, sunk into impiety, shall crumble away together. . . . But upon their ruins shall appear a new nation. . . . The heathen, the Jews, the worldly and the unbelieving, shall be converted together; springtime and peace shall reign over a regenerated world, and the angels will return with confidence to dwell among men.[89]

A century later Elizabeth of Thuringia (1207-31) aroused Hungary with her brief life of ascetic sanctity. Daughter of King Andrew, she was married at thirteen to a German prince, was a mother at fourteen, a widow at twenty. Her brother-in-law despoiled her and drove her away penniless. She became a wandering pietist, devoted to the poor; she housed leprous women and washed their wounds. She too had heavenly visions, but she gave them no publicity, and claimed no supernatural powers. Meeting the fiery inquisitor Conrad of Marburg, she was morbidly fascinated by his merciless devotion to orthodoxy; she became his obedient slave; he beat her for the slightest deviation from his concept of sanctity; she submitted humbly, inflicted additional austerities upon herself, and died of them at twenty-four.[90] Her reputation for saintliness was so great that at her funeral half-mad devotees cut off her hair, ears, and nipples as sacred relics.[91] Another Elizabeth entered the Benedictine nunnery of Schonau, near Bingen, at the age of twelve (1141), and lived there till her death in 1165. Bodily infirmities and extreme asceticism generated trances, in which she received heavenly revelations from various dead saints, nearly all anticlerical. "The Lord's vine has withered," her guardian angel told her; "the head of the Church is ill, and her members are dead. . . . Kings of the earth! the cry of your iniquity has risen even to me." [92]

Toward the end of this period the mystic tide ran high in Germany. Meister Eckhart, born about 1260, would come to his ripe doctrine in 1326, to his trial and death in 1327. His pupils Suso and Tauler would continue his mystic pantheism; and from that tradition of unecclesiastical piety would flow one source of the Reformation.

Usually the Church bore patiently with the mystics in her fold. She did not tolerate serious doctrinal deviations from the official line, or the anarchic individualism of some religious sects; but she admitted the claim of the mystics to a direct approach to God, and listened with good humor to saintly denunciations of her human faults. Many clergymen, even high dignitaries, sympathized with the critics, recognized the shortcomings of the Church, and wished that they too could lay down the contaminating tools and tasks of world politics and enjoy the security and peace of monasteries fed by the piety of the people and protected by the power of the Church. Perhaps it was such patient ecclesiastics who kept Christianity steady amid the delirious revelations that periodically threatened the medieval mind. As we read the mystics of the twelfth and thirteenth centuries it dawns upon us that ortho-doxy was often a barrier to contagious superstitions, and that in one aspect the Church was belief—as the state was force—organized from chaos into order to keep men sane.

VII. THE TRAGIC POPE

When Gregory X came to the papacy in 1271 the Church was again at the summit of her power. He was a Christian as well as a pope: a man of peace and amity, seeking justice rather than victory. Hoping to regain Palestine by one united effort, he persuaded Venice, Genoa, and Bologna to end their wars; he secured the election of Rudolf of Hapsburg as Emperor, but soothed with courtesy and kindness the defeated candidates; and he reconciled Guelf and Ghibelline in factious Florence and Siena, saying to his Guelf supporters: "Your enemies are Ghibellines, but they are also men, citizens, and Chris-tians." [93] He summoned the prelates of the Church to the Council of Lyons (1274); 1570 leading churchmen came; every great state sent a representa-tive; the Greek emperor sent the heads of the Greek Church to reaffirm its submission to the Roman See; Latin and Greek churchmen sang together a *Te Deum* of joy. Bishops were invited to list the abuses that needed reform in the Church; they responded with startling candor;[94] and legislation was passed to mitigate these evils. All Europe was magnificently united for a mighty effort against the Saracens. But on the way back to Rome Gregory died (1276). His successors were too busy with Italian politics to carry out his plans.

Nevertheless when Boniface VIII was chosen pope in 1294 the papacy was still the strongest government in Europe, the best organized, the best admin-istered, the richest in revenue. It was the misfortune of the Church that at this juncture, nearing the end of a virile and progressive century, the mightiest throne in Christendom should have fallen to a man whose love of the Church, and sincerity of purpose, were equaled by his imperfect morals, his personal pride, and his tactless will to power. He was not without charm: he loved learning, and rivaled Innocent III in legal training and wide culture; he founded the University of Rome, and restored and extended the Vatican Library; he gave commissions to Giotto and Arnolfo di Cambio, and helped finance the amazing façade of Orvieto Cathedral.

He had prepared his own elevation by persuading the saintly but incom-

petent Celestine V to resign after a pontificate of five months—an unprecedented act that surrounded Boniface with ill will from the start. To scotch
all plans for a restoration, he ordered the eighty-year-old Celestine to be kept
in detention in Rome; Celestine escaped, was captured, escaped again, wandered for weeks through Apulia, reached the Adriatic, attempted a crossing
to Dalmatia, was wrecked, was cast ashore in Italy, and was brought before
Boniface. He was condemned by the Pope to imprisonment in a narrow cell
at Ferentino; and there, ten months later, he died (1296).[95]

The temper of the new Pope was sharpened by a succession of diplomatic
defeats and costly victories. He tried to dissuade Frederick of Aragon from
accepting the throne of Sicily; when Frederick persisted Boniface excommunicated him, and laid an interdict upon the island (1296). Neither King
nor people paid any heed to these censures;[96] and in the end Boniface recognized Frederick. To prepare for a crusade he ordered Venice and Genoa to
sign a truce; they continued their war for three years more, and rejected his
intervention in making peace. Failing to secure a favorable order in Florence,
he placed the city under interdict, and invited Charles of Valois to enter and
pacify Italy (1300). Charles accomplished nothing, but won the hatred of the
Florentines for himself and the Pope. Seeking peace in his own Papal States,
Boniface had attempted to settle a quarrel among the members of the powerful Colonna family; Pietro and Jacopo Colonna, both cardinals, repudiated
his suggestions; he deposed and excommunicated them (1297); whereupon
the rebellious nobles affixed to the doors of Roman churches, and laid upon
the altar of St. Peter's, a manifesto appealing from the Pope to a general council. Boniface repeated the excommunication, extended it to five other rebels,
ordered their property confiscated, invaded the Colonna domain with papal
troops, captured its fortresses, razed Palestrina to the ground, and had salt
strewn over its ruins. The rebels surrendered, were forgiven, revolted again,
were again beaten by the warrior Pope, fled from the Papal States, and
planned revenge.

Amid these Italian tribulations Boniface was suddenly confronted by a
major crisis in France. Philip IV, resolved to unify his realm, had seized the
English province of Gascony; Edward I had declared war (1294); now, to
finance their struggle, both kings decided to tax the property and personnel
of the Church. The popes had permitted such taxation for crusades, but never
for a purely secular war. The French clergy had recognized their duty of
contributing to the defense of the state that protected their possessions, but
they feared that if the power of the state to tax were unchecked, it would be a
power to destroy. Philip had already reduced the role of the clergy in France;
he had removed them from the manorial and royal courts, and from their old
posts in the administration of the government and in the council of the king.
Disturbed by this trend, the Cistercian Order refused to send Philip the fifth
of their revenues which he had asked for the war with England, and its head

addressed an appeal to the Pope. Boniface had to move carefully, for France had long been the chief support of the papacy in the struggle with Germany and the Empire; but he felt that the economic basis of the power and freedom of the Church would soon be lost if she could be shorn of her revenues by state taxation of Church property without papal consent. In February, 1296, he issued one of the most famous bulls in ecclesiastical history. Its first words, *Clericis laicos*, gave it a name, its first sentence made an unwise admission, and its tone recalled the papal bolts of Gregory VII:

> Antiquity reports that laymen are exceedingly hostile to the clergy; and our experience certainly shows this to be true at present. . . . With the counsel of our brethren, and by our apostolic authority, we decree that if any clergy . . . shall pay to laymen . . . any part of their income or possessions . . . without the permission of the pope, they shall incur excommunication. . . . And we also decree that all persons of whatever power or rank, who shall demand or receive such taxes, or shall seize or cause to be seized, the property of churches or of the clergy . . . shall incur excommunication.[97]

Philip for his part was convinced that the great wealth of the Church in France should share in the costs of the state. He countered the papal bull by prohibiting the export of gold, silver, precious stones, or food, and by forbidding foreign merchants or emissaries to remain in France. These measures blocked a main source of papal revenue, and banished from France the papal agents who were raising funds for a crusade in the East. In the bull *Ineffabilis amor* (September, 1296) Boniface retreated; he sanctioned voluntary contributions from the clergy for the necessary defense of the state, and conceded the right of the King to be the judge of such a necessity. Philip rescinded his retaliatory ordinances; he and Edward accepted Boniface—not as pope but as a private person—as arbitrator of their dispute; Boniface decided most of the issues in Philip's favor; England yielded for the moment; and the three warriors enjoyed a passing peace.

Perhaps to replenish the papal treasury after the decline of receipts from England and France, perhaps to finance a war for the recovery of Sicily as a papal fief, and another war to extend the Papal States into Tuscany,[98] Boniface proclaimed 1300 as a jubilee year. The plan was a complete success. Rome had never in its history seen such crowds before; now, apparently for the first time, traffic rules were enforced to govern the movement of the people.[99] Boniface and his aides managed the affair well; food was brought in abundantly and was sold at moderate prices papally controlled. It was an advantage for the Pope that the great sums so collected were not earmarked for any special purpose, but could be used according to his judgment. Despite half victories and severe defeats, Boniface was now at the crest of his curve.

In the meantime, however, the Colonna exiles were entertaining Philip with tales of the Pope's greed, injustice, and private heresies. A quarrel arose between Philip's aides and a papal legate, Bernard Saisset; the legate was arrested on a charge of inciting to insurrection; he was tried by the royal court, convicted, and committed to the custody of the archbishop of Narbonne (1301). Boniface, shocked by this summary treatment of his legate, demanded Saisset's immediate release, and instructed the French clergy to suspend payment of ecclesiastical revenues to the state. In the bull *Ausculta fili* ("Listen, son"; December, 1301) he appealed to Philip to listen modestly to the Vicar of Christ as the spiritual monarch over all the kings of the earth; he protested against the trial of a churchman before a civil court, and the continued use of ecclesiastical funds for secular purposes; and he announced that he would summon the bishops and abbots of France to take measures "for the preservation of the liberties of the Church, the reformation of the kingdom, and the amendment of the King." [100] When this bull was presented to Philip, the count of Artois snatched it from the hands of the Pope's emissary and flung it into the fire; and a copy destined for publication by the French clergy was suppressed. Passion was inflamed on both sides by the circulation of two spurious documents, one allegedly from Boniface to Philip demanding obedience even in temporal affairs, the other from Philip to Boniface informing "thy very great fatuity that in temporal things we are subject to no one"; and these forgeries were widely accepted as genuine.[101]

On February 11, 1302, the bull *Ausculta fili* was officially burned at Paris before the King and a great multitude. To forestall the ecclesiastical council proposed by Boniface, Philip summoned the three estates of his realm to meet at Paris in April. At this first States-General in French history all three classes —nobles, clergy, and commons—wrote separately to Rome in defense of the King and his temporal power. Some forty-five French prelates, despite Philip's prohibition, and the confiscation of their property, attended the council at Rome in October, 1302. From that council issued the bull *Unam sanctam*, which made arrestingly specific the claims of the papacy. There is, said the bull, but one true Church, outside of which there is no salvation; there is but one body of Christ, with one head, not two; that head is Christ and His representative, the Roman pope. There are two swords or powers— the spiritual and the temporal; the first is borne by the Church; the second is borne for the Church by the king, but under the will and sufferance of the priest. The spiritual power is above the temporal, and has the right to instruct it regarding its highest end, and to judge it when it does evil. "We declare and define and pronounce," concluded the bull, "that it is necessary for salvation that all men should be subject to the Roman pontiff." [102]

Philip replied by calling two assemblies (March and June, 1303), which drew up a formal indictment of Boniface as a tyrant, sorcerer, murderer, embezzler, adulterer, sodomite, simoniac, idolator, and infidel,[103] and demanded his deposition by a general council of the Church. The King commissioned William of Nogaret, his chief legist, to go to Rome and notify the Pope of the King's appeal to a general council. Boniface, then in the papal palace at Anagni, declared that only the pope could call a general council, and prepared a decree excommunicating Philip and laying an interdict upon France. Before he could issue it William of Nogaret and Sciarra Colonna, heading a band of 2000 mercenaries, burst into the palace, presented Philip's message of notification, and demanded the Pope's resignation (September 7, 1303). Boniface refused. A tradition "of considerable trustworthiness" [104] says that Sciarra struck the Pontiff in the face, and would have killed him had not Nogaret intervened. Boniface was seventy-five years old, physically weak, but still defiant. For three days he was kept a prisoner in his palace, while the mercenaries plundered it. Then the people of Anagni, reinforced by 400 horsemen from the Orsini clan, scattered the mercenaries and freed the Pope. Apparently his jailers had given him no food in the three days; for standing in the market place he begged: "If there be any good woman who would give me an alms of wine and bread, I would bestow upon her God's blessing and mine." The Orsini led him to Rome and the Vatican. There he fell into a violent fever; and in a few days he died (October 11, 1303).

His successor, Benedict XI (1303-4), excommunicated Nogaret, Sciarra Colonna, and thirteen others whom he had seen breaking into the palace at Anagni. A month later Benedict died at Perugia, apparently poisoned by Italian Ghibellines.[105] Philip agreed to support Bertrand de Got, Archbishop of Bordeaux, for the papacy if he would adopt a conciliatory policy, absolve those who had been excommunicated for the attack upon Boniface, allow an annual income tax of ten per cent to be levied upon the French clergy for five years, restore the Colonnas to their offices and property, and condemn the memory of Boniface.[106] We do not know how far Bertrand consented. He was chosen Pope, and took the name of Clement V (1305). The cardinals warned him that his life would be unsafe in Rome; and after some hesitation, and perhaps a pointed suggestion from Philip, Clement removed the papal seat to Avignon, on the east bank of the Rhone just outside the southeastern boundary of France (1309). So began the sixty-eight years of the "Babylonian Captivity" of the popes. The papacy had freed itself from Germany, and surrendered to France.

Clement, against his weak will, became the humiliated tool of the insatiable Philip. He absolved the King, restored the Colonna family, withdrew the bull *Clericis laicos*, allowed the spoliation of the Templars, and finally (1310) consented to a post-mortem trial of Boniface by an ecclesiastical consistory at Groseau, near Avignon. In the preliminary examinations held before the Pope and his commissioners, six ecclesiastics testified to having heard Boniface, a year before his pontificate, remark that all supposedly divine laws were inventions of men to keep the common people in good behavior through fear of hell; that it was "fatuous" to believe that God was at once one and three, or that a virgin had borne a child, or that God had become a man, or that bread could be changed into the body of Christ, or that there was a future life. "So I believe and so I hold, as doth every educated man. The vulgar hold otherwise. We must speak as the vulgar do, and think and believe with the few." So these six quoted Boniface, and three of them, later re-examined, repeated their testimony. The Prior of St. Giles at San Gemino reported that Boniface, as Cardinal Gaetani, had denied the resurrection of either body or soul; and several other ecclesiastics confirmed this testimony. One ecclesiastic quoted Boniface as saying, of the consecrated Host, "It is mere paste." Men formerly belonging to the household of Boniface accused him of repeated sexual sins, natural and unnatural; others accused the supposed skeptic of attempting magical communication with the "powers of darkness." [107]

Before the actual trial could be held, Clement persuaded Philip to leave the question of Boniface's guilt to the coming ecumenical Council of Vienne. When that Council met (1311), three cardinals appeared before it and testified to the orthodoxy and morality of the dead Pope; two knights, as challengers, threw down their gauntlets to maintain his innocence by wager of battle; no one accepted the challenge; and the Council declared the matter closed.

VIII. RETROSPECT

The testimony against Boniface, true or false, reveals the undercurrent of skepticism that was preparing to end the Age of Faith. Likewise the blow—physical or political—given Boniface VIII at Anagni marks in one sense the beginning of "modern times": it was the victory of nationalism against super-nationalism, of the state against the Church, of the power of the sword over the magic of the word. The papacy had been weakened by its struggle against the Hohenstaufens, and by the failure of the Crusades. France and England had been strengthened by the collapse of the Empire, and France had been enriched by acquiring Languedoc with the help of the Church. Perhaps the popular support given to Philip IV against Boniface VIII reflected public resentment of the excesses of the Inquisition and the Albigensian Crusade. Some of Nogaret's ancestors, it was said, had been burned by the inquisitors.[108] Boniface had not realized, in undertaking so many conflicts, that the weapons of the papacy had been blunted by overuse. Industry and commerce had generated a class less pious than the peasantry; life and thought were becoming secularized; the laity was coming into its own. For seventy years now the state would absorb the Church.

Looking back over the panorama of Latin Christianity, we are impressed, above all, by the relative unanimity of religious faith among diverse peoples, and the overspreading hierarchy and power of the Roman Church, giving to Western Europe—non-Slavic, non-Byzantine Europe—a unity of mind and morals such as it has never known again. Nowhere else in history has an organization wielded so profound an influence over so many men for so long a time. The authority of the Roman Republic and Empire over its immense realm endured from Pompey to Alaric, 480 years; that of the Mongol Empire or the British Empire, some 200 years; but the Roman Catholic Church was the dominant force in Europe from the death of Charlemagne (814) to the death of Boniface VIII (1303)—489 years. Her organization and administration do not appear to have been as competent as that of the Roman Empire, nor was her personnel as capable or cultured as the men who governed the provinces and cities for the Caesars; but the Church inherited a barbarous bedlam, and had to find a laborious way back to order and education. Even so her clergy were the best instructed men of the age, and it was they who provided the only education available in Western Europe during the five centuries of her supremacy. Her courts offered the justest justice of their time. Her papal Curia, sometimes venal, sometimes incorruptible, constituted in some degree a world court for the arbitration of international disputes and the limitation of war; and though that court was always too Italian, the Italians were the best trained minds of those centuries, and any man could rise to membership in that court from any rank and nation in Latin Christendom.

Despite the chicanery usually accompanying collective human power, it was good that above the states and kings of Europe there should be an authority that could call them to account and moderate their strife. If any world state was to be, what could seem fitter than that its seat should be the throne of Peter, whence men, however limited, could see with a continental eye and from the background of centuries? What decisions would be more peaceably accepted, or could be more easily enforced, than those of a pontiff revered as the Vicar of God by nearly all the population of Western Europe? When Louis IX left on crusade in 1248, Henry III of England made extreme demands upon France, and prepared to invade; Pope Innocent IV threatened England with interdict should Henry persist; and Henry refrained. The power of the Church, said the skeptical Hume, was a rampart of refuge against the tyranny and injustice of kings.[109] The Church might have realized the high conception of Gregory VII—might have made her moral power supreme over the physical forces of the states—had she used her influence only for spiritual and moral purposes, and never for material ends. When Urban II united Christendom against the Turks the dream of Gregory was almost realized; but when Innocent III, Gregory IX, Alexander IV, and Boniface VIII gave the holy name of crusade to their wars against the Albigensians, Frederick II, and the Colonnas, the great ideal broke to pieces in papal hands stained with Christian blood.

Where the Church was not threatened she responded with considerable tolerance for diverse, even heretical, views. We shall find an unexpected freedom of thought among the philosophers of the twelfth and thirteenth centuries, even among professors at universities chartered and supervised by the Church. All that she asked was that such discussions should be confined and intelligible only to the educated, and should not take the form of revolutionary appeals to the people to abandon their creed or the Church.[110] "The Church," says her most industrious recent critic, "as it embraced the whole population, embraced also every type of mind, from the most superstitious to the most agnostic; and many of these unorthodox elements worked far more freely, under the cloak of outward conformity, than is generally supposed." [111]

All in all, the picture that we form of the medieval Latin Church is that of a complex organization doing its best, despite the human frailties of its adherents and its leaders, to establish moral and social order, and to spread an uplifting and consoling faith, amid the wreckage of an old civilization and the passions of an adolescent society. The sixth-century Church found Europe a flotsam of migratory barbarians, a babel of tongues and creeds, a chaos of unwritten and incalculable laws. She gave it a moral code buttressed with supernatural sanctions strong enough to check the unsocial impulses of violent men; she offered it monastic retreats for men, women, and classic manuscripts; she governed it with episcopal courts, educated it with schools and universities, and tamed the kings of the earth to moral responsibility and the tasks of peace. She brightened the lives of her children with poetry, drama, and song, and inspired them to raise the noblest works of art in history. Unable to establish a utopia of equality among unequally able men, she organized charity and hospitality, and in some measure protected the weak from the strong. She was, beyond question, the greatest civilizing force in medieval European history.

CHAPTER XXX

The Morals and Manners of Christendom

700-1300

I. THE CHRISTIAN ETHIC

MAN in the jungle or hunting stage had to be greedy—to seek food eagerly and gorge himself zealously—because, when food came, he could not be sure when it would come again. He had to be sexually sensitive, often promiscuous, because a high death rate compelled a high birth rate; every woman had to be made a mother whenever possible, and the function of the male was to be always in heat. He had to be pugnacious, ever ready to fight for food or mate. Vices were once virtues, indispensable to survival.

But when man found that the best means of survival, for individual as well as species, was social organization, he expanded the hunting pack into a system of social order in which the instincts once so useful in the hunting stage had to be checked at every turn to make society possible. Ethically every civilization is a balance and tension between the jungle instincts of men and the inhibitions of a moral code. The instincts without the inhibitions would end civilization; the inhibitions without the instincts would end life. The problem of morality is to adjust inhibitions to protect civilization without enfeebling life.

In the task of moderating human violence, promiscuity, and greed, certain instincts, chiefly social, took the lead, and provided a biological basis for civilization. Parental love, in beast and man, created the natural social order of the family, with its educative discipline and mutual aid. Parental authority, half a pain of love and half a joy of tyranny, transmitted a life-saving code of social conduct to the individualistic child. The organized force wielded by chieftain, baron, city, or state circumscribed and largely circumvented the unorganized force of individuals. Love of approval bent the ego to the will of the group. Custom and imitation guided the adolescent, now and then, into ways sanctioned by the trial-and-error experience of the race. Law frightened instinct with the specter of punishment. Conscience tamed youth with the detritus of an endless stream of prohibitions.

The Church believed that these natural or secular sources of morality could not suffice to control the impulses that preserve life in the jungle but destroy order in a society. Those impulses are too strong to be deterred by any human authority that cannot be everywhere at once with awesome police. A moral code bitterly uncongenial to the flesh must bear the seal of a supernatural origin if it is to be obeyed; it must carry a divine sanction and prestige that will be respected by the soul in the absence of any force, and in the most secret moments and coverts of life. Even parental authority, so vital to moral and social order, breaks down in the contest with primitive instincts unless it is buttressed by religious belief inculcated in the child. To serve and save a society, a religion must oppose to insistent instinct no disputable man-made directives, but the undebatable, categorical imperatives of God Himself. And those divine commandments (so sinful or savage is man) must be supported not only by praise and honor bestowed for obeying them, nor only by disgrace and penalties imposed for violating them, but also by the hope of heaven for unrequited virtue, and the fear of hell for unpunished sin. The commandments must come not from Moses but from God.

The biological theory of primitive instincts unfitting man for civilization was symbolized in Christian theology by the doctrine of original sin. Like the Hindu conception of karma, this was an attempt to explain apparently unmerited suffering: the good endured evil here because of some ancestral sin. In Christian theory the whole human race had been tainted by the sin of Adam and Eve. Said Gratian's *Decretum* (*c.* 1150), unofficially accepted by the Church as her teaching, "Every human being who is conceived by the coition of a man with a woman is born with original sin, subject to impiety and death, and therefore a child of wrath";[1] and only divine grace, and the atoning death of Christ, could save him from wickedness and damnation (only the gentle example of the martyred Christ could redeem man from violence, lust, and greed, and save him and his society from destruction). The preaching of this doctrine, combined with natural catastrophes that seemed unintelligible except as punishments for sin, gave many medieval Christians a sense of inborn impurity, depravity, and guilt, which colored much of their literature before 1200. Thereafter that sense of sin and fear of hell diminished till the Reformation, to reappear with fresh terror among the Puritans.

Gregory I and later theologians spoke of seven deadly sins—pride, avarice, envy, anger, lust, gluttony, and sloth; and opposed to them the seven cardinal virtues: four "natural" or pagan virtues praised by Pythagoras and Plato— wisdom, courage, justice, and temperance; and three "theological" virtues —faith, hope, and charity. But though accepting the pagan virtues, Christianity never assimilated them. It preferred faith to knowledge, patience to courage, love and mercy to justice, abstention and purity to temperance. It exalted humility, and ranked pride (so prominent in Aristotle's ideal man) as the deadliest of the Deadly Sins. It spoke occasionally of the rights of man, but it stressed rather the duties of man—to himself, his fellow man, his Church, and God. In preaching a "gentle Jesus meek and mild" the Church had no fear of making men effeminate; on the contrary, the men of medieval Latin Christendom were more masculine—because they met more hardships—than their modern beneficiaries and heirs. Theologies and philosophies, like men and states, are what they are because in their time and place they have to be.

II. PREMARITAL MORALITY

How far did medieval morality reflect or justify medieval ethical theory? Let us first look at the picture, with no thesis to prove.

The first moral incident of the Christian life was baptism: the child was solemnly inducted into the community and the Church, and was vicariously subjected to their laws. Every child received a "Christian name"—that is, usually, the name of some Christian saint. Surnames (i.e., added names) were of motley origin, and could go back through generations to kinship, occupation, place, a feature of body or character, even a bit of church ritual: Cicely Wilkinsdoughter, James Smith, Margaret Ferrywoman, Matthew Paris, Agnes Redhead, John Merriman, Robert Litany, Robert Benedicite or Benedict.[2]

Gregory the Great, like Rousseau, urged mothers to nurse their own infants;[3] most poor women did, most upper-class women did not.[4] Children were loved as now, but were beaten more. They were numerous, despite high infantile and adolescent mortality; they disciplined one another by their number, and became civilized by attrition. They learned a hundred arts of the country or the city from relatives and playmates, and grew rapidly in knowledge and wickedness. "Boys are taught evil as soon as they can babble," said Thomas of Celano in the thirteenth century; "and as they grow up they become steadily worse until they are Christians only in name"[5]—but moralists are bad historians. Boys reached the age of work at twelve, and legal maturity at sixteen.

Christian ethics followed, with adolescents, a policy of silence about sex: financial maturity—the ability to support a family—came later than biological maturity—the ability to reproduce; sexual education might aggravate the pains of continence in this interval; and the Church required premarital continence as an aid to conjugal fidelity, social order, and public health. Nevertheless, by the age of sixteen the medieval youth had probably sampled a variety of sexual experiences. Pederasty, which Christianity had effectively attacked in late antiquity, reappeared with the Crusades, the influx of Oriental ideas, and the unisexual isolation of monks and nuns.[6] In 1177 Henry, Abbot of Clairvaux, wrote of France that "ancient Sodom is springing up from her ashes."[7] Philip the Fair charged that homosexual practices were popular among the Templars. The Penitentials—ecclesiastical manuals prescribing penances for sins—mention the usual enormities, including bestiality;

an astonishing variety of beasts received such attentions.[8] Where amours of this sort were discovered they were punishable with the death of both participants; and the records of the English Parliament contain many cases of dogs, goats, cows, pigs, and geese being burned to death with their human paramours. Cases of incest were numerous.

Premarital and extramarital relations were apparently as widespread as at any time between antiquity and the twentieth century; the promiscuous nature of man overflowed the dikes of secular ecclesiastical legislation; and some women felt that abdominal gaiety could be atoned for by hebdomadal piety. Rape was common [9] despite the severest penalties. Knights who served highborn dames or damoiselles for a kiss or a touch of the hand might console themselves with the lady's maids; some ladies could not sleep with a good conscience until they had arranged this courtesy.[10] The Knight of La Tour-Landry mourned the prevalence of fornication among aristocratic youth; if we were to believe him, some men of his class fornicated in church, nay, "on the altar"; and he tells of "two queens which in Lent, on Holy Thursday . . . took their foul delight and pleasance within the church during divine service." [11] William of Malmesbury described the Norman nobility as "given over to gluttony and lechery," and exchanging concubines with one another [12] lest fidelity should dull the edge of husbandry. Illegitimate children littered Christendom, and gave a plot to a thousand tales. The heroes of several medieval sagas were bastards—Cuchulain, Arthur, Gawain, Roland, William the Conqueror, and many a knight in Froissart's *Chronicles*.

Prostitution adjusted itself to the times. Some women on pilgrimage, according to Bishop Boniface, earned their passage by selling themselves in the towns on their route.[13] Every army was followed with another army, as dangerous as the enemy. "The Crusaders," reports Albert of Aix, "had in their ranks a crowd of women wearing the habit of men; they traveled together without distinction of sex, trusting to the chances of a frightful promiscuity." [14] At the siege of Acre (1189), says the Arabic historian Emad-Eddin, "300 pretty Frenchwomen . . . arrived for the solace of the French soldiers . . . for these would not go into battle if they were deprived of women"; seeing which, the Moslem armies demanded similar inspiration.[15] In the first crusade of St. Louis, according to Joinville, his barons "set up their brothels about the royal tent." [16] The university students, particularly at Paris, developed urgent or imitative needs, and *filles* established centers of accommodation.[17]

Some towns—e.g., Toulouse, Avignon, Montpellier, Nuremberg—legalized prostitution under municipal supervision, on the ground that without such lupanars, *bordelli*, *Frauenhäuser*, good women could not venture safely into the streets.[18] St. Augustine had written: "If you do away with harlots the world will be convulsed with lust";[19] and St. Thomas Aquinas agreed.[20] London in the twelfth century had a row of "bordells" or "stews" near London

Bridge; originally licensed by the Bishop of Winchester, they were subsequently sanctioned by Parliament.[21] An act of Parliament in 1161 forbade the brothel keepers to have women suffering from the "perilous infirmity of burning"—the earliest known regulation against the spread of venereal disease.[22] Louis IX, in 1254, decreed the banishment of all prostitutes from France; the edict was enforced; soon a clandestine promiscuity replaced the former open traffic; the bourgeois gentlemen complained that it was well nigh impossible to guard the virtue of their wives and daughters from the solicitations of soldiers and students; at last criticism of the ordinance became so general that it was repealed (1256). The new decree specified those parts of Paris in which prostitutes might legally live and practice, regulated their dress and ornaments, and submitted them to supervision by a police magistrate popularly known as the *roi des ribauds*, or king of the bawds, beggars, and vagabonds.[23] Louis IX, dying, advised his son to renew the edict of expulsion; Philip did, with results much as before; the law remained in the statutes, but was not enforced.[24] In Rome, according to Bishop Durand II of Mende (1311), there were brothels near the Vatican, and the pope's marshals permitted them for a consideration.[25] The Church showed a humane spirit toward prostitutes; she maintained asylums for reformed women, and distributed among the poor the donations received from converted courtesans.[26]

III. MARRIAGE

Youth was brief, and marriage came early, in the Age of Faith. A child of seven could consent to a betrothal, and such engagements were sometimes made to facilitate the transfer or protection of property. Grace de Saleby, aged four, was married to a great noble who could preserve her rich estate; presently he died, and she was married at six to another lord; at eleven she was married to a third.[27] Such unions could be annulled at any time before the normal age of consummation, which in the girl was presumed to be twelve, in the boy fourteen.[28] The Church reckoned the consent of parents or guardian unnecessary for valid marriage if the parties were of age. She forbade the marriage of girls under fifteen, but allowed many exceptions; for in this matter the rights of property overruled the whims of love, and marriage was an incident in finance. The bridegroom presented gifts or money to the girl's parents, gave her a "morning gift," and pledged her a dower right in his estate; in England this was a life interest of the widow on one third of the husband's inheritance in land. The bride's family gave presents to the family of the groom, and assigned to her a dowry consisting of clothing, linen, utensils, and furniture, and sometimes of property. Engagement was an exchange of gages or pledges; the wedding itself was a pledge (Anglo-Saxon *weddian*, promise); the spouse was one who had re-spo-nded "I will."

State and Church alike accepted as valid marriage a consummated union accompanied by the exchange of a verbal pledge between the participants, without other ceremony legal or ecclesiastical.[29] The Church sought in this way to protect women from abandonment by seducers, and preferred such unions to fornication or concubinage; but after the twelfth century she denied validity to marriages contracted without ecclesiastical sanction; and after the Council of Trent (1563) she required the presence of a priest. Secular law welcomed the ecclesiastical regulation of marriage; Bracton (d. 1268) held a religious ceremony essential to valid matrimony. The Church raised marriage to a sacrament, and made it a sacred covenant between man, woman, and God. Gradually she spread her jurisdiction over every phase of marriage, from the duties of the nuptial bed to the last will and testament of the dying spouse. Her canon law drew up a long list of "impediments to matrimony." Each party must be free from any previous marriage bond, and from any vow of chastity. Marriage with an unbaptized person was forbidden; nevertheless there were many marriages between Christian and Jew.[30] Marriage between slaves, between slave and free, between orthodox Christian and heretic, even between the faithful and the excommunicate, was recognized as valid.[31] The parties must not be related within the fourth degree of kinship—i.e., must not have an identical ancestor within four generations; here the Church rejected Roman law and accepted the primitive exogamy that feared degeneration from inbreeding; perhaps also she deprecated the concentration of wealth through narrow family alliances. In rural villages such inbreeding was difficult to avoid, and the Church had to close her eyes to it, as to many another gap between reality and law.

After the marriage ceremony came the wedding procession—with blaring music and flaunting silk—from the church to the bridegroom's home. Festivities would there ensue through all the day and half the night. The marriage was not valid until consummated. Contraception was forbidden; Aquinas accounted it a crime second only to homicide;[32] nevertheless diverse means—mechanical, chemical, magical—were used to effect it, with chief reliance on *coitus interruptus*.[33] Drugs were peddled that would produce abortion, or sterility, or impotence, or sexual ardor; the penitential formulas of Rabanus Maurus decreed three years of penance for "her who mixes the semen of her husband with her food so that she may better receive his love." [34] Infanticide was rare. Christian charity established foundling hospitals in various cities from the sixth century onward. A council at Rouen, in the eighth century, invited women who had secretly borne children to deposit them at the door of the church, which would undertake to provide for them; such orphans were brought up as serfs on ecclesiastical properties. A law of Charlemagne decreed that exposed children should be the slaves of those who rescued and reared them. About 1190 a Montpellier monk founded the Fraternity of the Holy Ghost, dedicated to the protection and education of orphans.

Penalties for adultery were severe; Saxon law, for example, condemned the unfaithful wife at least to lose her nose and ears, and empowered her husband to kill her. Adultery was common notwithstanding;[35] least so in the middle classes, most in the nobility. Feudal masters seduced female serfs at the cost of a modest fine: he who "covered" a maid "without her thanks"—against her will—paid the court three shillings.[36] The eleventh century, said Freeman, "was a profligate age," and he marveled at the apparent marital fidelity of William the Conqueror,[37] who could not say as much for his father. "Medieval society," said the learned and judicious Thomas Wright, "was profoundly immoral and licentious." [38]

The Church allowed separation for adultery, apostasy, or grave cruelty; this was called *divortium*, but not in the sense of annulling the marriage. Such annulment was granted only when the marriage could be shown to have contravened one of the canonical impediments to matrimony. It is hardly probable that these were deliberately multiplied to provide grounds of divorce for those who could afford the substantial fees and costs required for an annulment. The Church used these impediments to meet with flexible judgment exceptional cases where divorce would promise an heir to a childless king, or would otherwise serve public policy or peace. Germanic law allowed divorce for adultery, sometimes even by mutual agreement.[39] The kings preferred the laws of their ancestors to the stricter law of the Church; and feudal lords and ladies, reverting to the ancient codes, sometimes divorced one another without ecclesiastical leave. Not till Innocent III refused divorce to Philip Augustus, the powerful King of France, was the Church strong enough, in authority and conscience, to hew bravely to her own decrees.

IV. WOMAN

The theories of churchmen were generally hostile to woman; some laws of the Church enhanced her subjection; many principles and practices of Christianity improved her status. To priests and theologians woman was still in these centuries what she had seemed to Chrysostom—"a necessary evil, a natural temptation, a desirable calamity, a domestic peril, a deadly fascination, a painted ill." [40] She was still the ubiquitous reincarnation of the Eve who had lost Eden for mankind, still the favored instrument of Satan in leading men to hell. St. Thomas Aquinas, usually the soul of kindness, but speaking with the limitations of a monk, placed her in some ways below the slave:

> The woman is subject to the man on account of the weakness of her nature, both of mind and of body.[41] . . . Man is the beginning of woman and her end, just as God is the beginning and end of every creature.[42] . . . Woman is in subjection according to the law of nature, but a slave is not.[43] . . . Children ought to love their father more than their mother.[44]

Canon law gave to the husband the duty of protecting his wife, and to the wife the duty of obeying her husband. Man, but not woman, was made in the image of God; "it is plain from this," argued the canonist, "that wives should be subject to their husbands, and should almost be servants." [45] Such passages have the ring of wistful wishing. On the other hand the Church enforced monogamy, insisted upon a single standard of morals for both sexes, honored woman in the worship of Mary, and defended woman's right to the inheritance of property.

Civil law was more hostile to her than canon law. Both codes permitted wife-beating,[46] and it was quite a forward step when, in the thirteenth century, the "Laws and Customs of Beauvais" bade a man beat his wife "only in reason." [47] Civil law ruled that the word of women could not be admitted in court, "because of their frailty";[48] it required only half as high a fine for an offense against a woman as for the same offense against a man; [49] it excluded even the most high-born ladies from representing their own estates in the Parliament of England or the Estates-General of France. Marriage gave the husband full authority over the use and usufruct of any property that his wife owned at marriage.[50] No woman could become a licensed physician.

Her economic life was as varied as the man's. She learned and practiced the wondrous unsung arts of the home: to bake bread and puddings and pies, cure meats, make soap and candles, cream and cheese; to brew beer and make home medicines from herbs; to spin and weave wool, and make linen from flax, and clothing for her family, and curtains and drapes, bedspreads and tapestries; to decorate her home and keep it as clean as the male inmates would allow; and to rear children. Outside the agricultural cottage she joined with strength and patience in the work of the farm: sowed and cultivated and reaped, fed chickens, milked cows, sheared sheep, helped to repair and paint and build. In the towns, at home or in the shop, she did most of the spinning and weaving for the textile guilds. It was a company of "silkwomen" that first established in England the arts of spinning, throwing, and weaving silk.[51] Most of the English guilds contained as many women as men, largely because craftsmen were permitted to employ their wives and daughters, and enlist them in the guilds. Several guilds, devoted to feminine manufactures, were composed wholly of women; there were fifteen such guilds at Paris at the end of the thirteenth century.[52] Women, however, rarely became masters in bisexual guilds, and they received lower wages than men for equal work. In the middle classes women displayed in raiment the wealth of their husbands, and took an exciting part in the religious feasts and social festivities of the towns. By sharing their husbands' responsibilities, and accepting with grace and restraint the grandiose or amorous professions of knights and troubadours, the ladies of the feudal aristocracy attained a status such as women had rarely reached before.

As usual, despite theology and law, the medieval woman found ways of annulling her disabilities with her charms. The literature of this period is rich in records of women who ruled their men.[53] In several respects woman was the acknowledged superior. Among the nobility she learned something of letters and art and refinement, while her letterless husband labored and fought. She could put on all the graces of an eighteenth-century *salonnière*, and swoon like a Richardson heroine; at the same time she rivaled man in lusty liberty of action and speech, exchanged risqué stories with him, and often took an unabashed initiative in love.[54] In all classes she moved with full freedom seldom chaperoned; she crowded the fairs and dominated the festivals; she joined in pilgrimages, and took part in the Crusades, not only as a solace but now and then as a soldier dressed in the panoply of war. Timid monks tried to persuade themselves of her inferiority, but knights fought for her favors, and poets professed themselves her slaves. Men talked of her as an obedient servant, and dreamed of her as a goddess. They prayed to Mary, but they would have been satisfied with Eleanor of Aquitaine.

Eleanor was but one of a score of great medieval women—Galla Placidia, Theodora, Irene, Anna Comnena, Matilda, Countess of Tuscany, Matilda, Queen of England, Blanche of Navarre, Blanche of Castile, Héloïse. . . . Eleanor's grandfather was a prince and a poet, William X of Aquitaine, patron and leader of the troubadours. To his court at Bordeaux came the best wits and graces and gallants of southwestern France; and in that court Eleanor was reared to be a queen to life and letters both. She absorbed all the culture and character of that free and sunny clime: vigor of body and poetry of motion, passion of temper and flesh, freedom of mind and manners and speech, lyric fantasies and sparkling *esprit*, a boundless love of love and war and every pleasure, even to the death. When she was fifteen (1137) the King of France offered her his hand, anxious to add her duchy of Aquitaine, and the great port of Bordeaux, to his revenues and his crown. She did not know that Louis VII was a man stolid and devout, gravely absorbed in affairs of state. She went to him gay and lovely and unscrupulous; he was not charmed by her extravagance, and did not care for the poets who followed her to Paris to reward her patronage with lauds and rhymes.

Hungry for a living romance, she resolved to accompany her husband to Palestine on the Second Crusade (1147). She and her attendant ladies donned male and martial costumes, sent their distaffs scornfully to stay-at-home knights, and rode off in the van of the army, flying bright banners and trailing troubadours.[55] Neglected or chided by the King, she allowed herself, at Antioch and elsewhere, a few amours; rumor gave her love now to her uncle Raymond of Poitiers, now to a handsome Saracen slave, now (said ignorant gossip) to the pious Saladin himself.[56] Louis bore these dalliances, and her keen tongue, patiently, but St. Bernard of Clairvaux, the watchdog of Christendom, denounced her to the world. In 1152, suspecting that the King would divorce her, she sued him for divorce on the ground that they were

related in the sixth degree. The Church smiled at the pretext, but granted
the divorce; and Eleanor returned to Bordeaux, resuming her title to Aquitaine. There a swarm of suitors courted her; she chose Henry Plantagenet,
heir to the throne of England; two years later he was Henry II, and Eleanor
was again a queen (1154)—"Queen of England," as she was to say, "by the
wrath of God."

To England she brought the tastes of the South; and she continued in
London to be the supreme lawgiver, patron, and idol of the trouvères and
troubadours. She was now old enough to bear fidelity, and Henry found no
scandal in her. But the tables were turned: Henry was eleven years her jun-
ior, quite her equal in temper and passion; soon he was spreading his love
among the ladies of the court; and Eleanor, who had once scorned a jealous
husband, fretted and fumed in jealousy. When Henry deposed her, she fled
from England, seeking the protection of Aquitaine; he had her pursued, arrested, imprisoned; and for sixteen years she languished in a confinement
that never broke her will. The troubadours roused the sentiment of Europe
against the King; his sons, at her behest, plotted to dethrone him, but he
fought them off until his death (1189). Richard Coeur de Lion succeeded
his father, released his mother, and made her regent of England while he
crusaded against Saladin. When her son John became king she retired to a
convent in France, and died there "through sorrow and anguish of mind,"
at the age of eighty-two. She had been "a bad wife, a bad mother, and a bad
queen"; [57] but who would think of her as belonging to a subject sex?

V. PUBLIC MORALITY

In every age the laws and moral precepts of the nations have struggled to
discourage the inveterate dishonesty of mankind. In the Middle Ages—not
demonstrably more nor less than in other epochs—men, good and bad, lied
to their children, mates, congregations, enemies, friends, governments, and
God. Medieval man had a special fondness for forging documents. He forged
apocryphal gospels, perhaps never intending them to be taken as more than
pretty stories; he forged decretals as weapons in ecclesiastical politics; loyal
monks forged charters to win royal grants for their monasteries;[58] Archbishop Lanfranc of Canterbury, according to the papal Curia, forged a
charter to prove the antiquity of his see;[59] schoolmasters forged charters to
endow some colleges at Cambridge with a false antiquity; and "pious frauds"
corrupted texts and invented a thousand edifying miracles. Bribery was general in education, trade, war, religion, government, law.[60] Schoolboys sent
pies to their examiners;[61] politicians paid for appointments to public office,
and collected the necessary sums from their friends;[62] witnesses could be
bribed to swear to anything; litigants gave presents to jurors and judges;[63]

in 1289 Edward I of England had to dismiss most of his judges and ministers for corruption.[64] The laws arranged for solemn oaths at every turn; men swore on the Scriptures or the most sacred relics; sometimes they were required to take an oath that they would keep the oath they were about to take;[65] yet perjury was so frequent that trial by combat was sometimes resorted to in the hope that God would identify the greater liar.[66]

Despite a thousand guild and municipal statutes and penalties, medieval craftsmen often deceived purchasers with shoddy products, false measures, and crafty substitutes. Some bakers stole small portions of dough under their customers' eyes by means of a trap door in the kneading board; cheap cloths were secretly put in the place of better cloths promised and paid for; inferior leather was "doctored" to look like the best;[67] stones were concealed in sacks of hay or wool sold by weight;[68] the meat packers of Norwich were accused of "buying measly pigs, and making from them sausages and puddings unfit for human bodies."[69] Berthold of Regensburg (c. 1220) described the different forms of cheating used in the various trades, and the tricks played upon country folk by merchants at the fairs.[70] Writers and preachers condemned the pursuit of wealth, but a medieval German proverb said, "All things obey money"; and some medieval moralists judged the lust for gain stronger than the urge of sex.[71] Knightly honor was often real in feudalism; but the thirteenth century was apparently as materialistic as any epoch in history. These examples of chicanery are drawn from a great area and time; though such instances were numerous they were presumably exceptional; they do not warrant any larger conclusion than that men were no better in the Age of Faith than in our age of doubt, and that in all ages law and morality have barely succeeded in maintaining social order against the innate individualism of men never intended by nature to be law-abiding citizens.

Most states made grave theft a capital crime, and the Church excommunicated brigands; even so, theft and robbery were common, from pickpockets in the streets to robber barons on the Rhine. Hungry mercenaries, fugitive criminals, ruined knights made roads unsafe; and city streets after dark saw many a brawl, robbery, rape, and murder.[72] Coroners' records from thirteenth-century Merrie England show "a proportion of manslaughters which would be considered scandalous in modern times";[73] murders were almost twice as numerous as deaths by accident; and the guilty were seldom caught.[74] The Church labored patiently to repress feudal wars, but her modest measure of success was won by diverting men and pugnacity to the Crusades, which were, in one aspect, imperialistic wars for territory and trade. Once at war, Christians were no gentler to the defeated, no more loyal to pledges and treaties, than the warriors of other faiths and times.

Cruelty and brutality were apparently more frequent in the Middle Ages than in any civilization before our own. The barbarians did not at once cease to be barbarians when they became Christians. Noble lords and ladies buffeted their servants, and one another. Criminal law was brutally severe, but failed to suppress brutality and crime. The wheel, the caldron of burning oil, the stake, burning alive, flaying, tearing the limbs apart with wild animals, were often used as penalties. Anglo-Saxon law punished a female slave convicted of theft by making each of eighty female slaves pay a fine, bring three faggots, and burn her to death.[75] In the wars of central Italy in the late thirteenth century, says the chronicle of the contemporary Italian monk Salimbene, prisoners were treated with a barbarity that in our youth would have been incredible:

> For some men's heads they bound with a cord and lever, and strained it with such force that their eyes started from their sockets and fell upon their cheeks; others they bound by the right or left thumb only, and thus lifted the whole weight of their bodies from the ground; others again they racked with yet more foul and horrible torments which I blush to relate; others . . . they would seat with hands bound behind their backs, and laid under their feet a pot of live coals . . . or they bound their hands and legs together round a spit (as a lamb is carried to the butcher), and kept them thus hanging all day long, without food or drink; or again, with a rough piece of wood they would rub and grate their shins until the bare bone appeared, which was a misery and sore pity even to behold.[76]

Medieval man bore suffering bravely, and perhaps with less sensitivity than the men of Western Europe would show today. In all classes men and women were hearty and sensual; their festivals were feasts of drinking, gambling, dancing, and sexual relaxation; their jokes were of a candor hardly rivaled today;[77] their speech was freer, their oaths vaster and more numerous.[78] Hardly a man in France, says Joinville, could open his mouth without mentioning the Devil.[79] The medieval stomach was stronger than ours, and bore without flinching the most Rabelaisian details; the nuns in Chaucer listen unperturbed to the scatology of the Miller's Tale; and the chronicle of the good monk Salimbene is at times untranslatably physical.[80] Taverns were numerous, and some, in modern style, supplied "tarts" with ale.[81] The Church tried to close the taverns on Sundays, with small success.[82] Occasional drunkenness was the prerogative of every class. A visitor to Lübeck found some patrician ladies in a wine cellar, drinking hard under their veils.[83] At Cologne there was a society that met to drink wine, and took for its motto, *Bibite cum hilaritate*; but it imposed upon its members strict rules for moderation in conduct and modesty in speech.[84]

The medieval man, like any other, was a thoroughly human mixture of lust and romance, humility and egotism, cruelty and tenderness, piety and greed. Those same men and women who drank and cursed so heartily were capable of touching kindnesses and a thousand charities. Cats and dogs were pets then as now; dogs were trained to lead the blind;[85] and knights developed an attachment for their horses, falcons, and dogs. The administration of charity reached new heights in the twelfth and thirteenth centuries. Individuals, guilds, governments, and the Church shared in relieving the unfortunate. Almsgiving was universal. Men hopeful of paradise left charitable bequests. Rich men dowered poor girls, fed scores of the poor daily, and hundreds on major festivals. At many baronial gates doles of food were distributed thrice weekly to all who asked.[86] Nearly every great lady felt it a social, if not a moral, necessity to share in the administration of charity. Roger Bacon, in the thirteenth century, advocated a state fund for the relief of poverty, sickness, and old age;[87] but most of this work was left to the Church. In one aspect the Church was a continent-wide organization for charitable aid. Gregory the Great, Charlemagne, and others required that one fourth of the tithes collected by any parish should be applied to succor the poor and the infirm;[88] it was so done for a time; but the expropriation of parish revenues by lay and ecclesiastical superiors disrupted this parochial administration in the twelfth century, and the work fell more than ever upon bishops, monks, nuns, and popes. All nuns but a few human sinners devoted themselves to education, nursing, and charity; their ever-widening ministrations are among the brightest and most heartening features of medieval and modern history. Monasteries, supplied by gifts and alms and ecclesiastical revenues, fed the poor, tended the sick, ransomed prisoners. Thousands of monks taught the young, cared for orphans, or served in hospitals. The great abbey of Cluny atoned for its wealth by an ample distribution of alms. The popes did what they could to help the poor of Rome, and continued in their own way the ancient imperial dole.

Despite all this charity, begging flourished. Hospitals and almshouses tried to provide food and lodging for all applicants; soon the gates were surrounded by the halt, the decrepit, the maimed, the blind, and ragged vagabonds who went from "spital to spital, prowling and poaching for lumps of bread and meat."[89] Mendicancy reached in medieval Christendom and Islam a scope and pertinacity unequaled today except in the poorest areas of the Far East.

VI. MEDIEVAL DRESS

Who were the people of medieval Europe? We cannot divide them into "races"; they were all of the "white race" except the Negro slaves. But what a baffling unclassifiable variety of men! Greeks of Byzantium and Hellas, the half-Greek Italians of southern Italy, the Greco-Moorish-Jewish population of Sicily, the Romans, Umbrians, Tuscans, Lombards, Genoese, Venetians of Italy—all so diverse that each at once betrayed his origin by dress and coiffure and speech; the Berbers, Arabs, Jews, and Christians of Spain; the Gascons, Provençals, Burgundians, Parisians, Normans, of France; the

Flemings, Walloons, and Dutch of the Lowlands; the Celtic, Anglian, Saxon, Danish, Norman stocks in England; the Celts of Wales, Ireland, and Scotland; the Norwegians, Swedes, and Danes; the hundred tribes of Germany; the Finns and Magyars and Bulgars; the Slavs of Poland, Bohemia, the Baltic States, the Balkans, and Russia: here was such a farrago of bloods and types and noses and beards and dress that no one description could fit their proud diversity.

The Germans, by a millennium of migrations and conquests, had made their type prevail in the upper classes of all Western Europe except central and southern Italy, and Spain. The blond type was so definitely admired in hair and eyes that St. Bernard struggled through an entire sermon to reconcile with this preference the "I am black but beautiful" of the Song of Songs. The ideal knight was to be tall and blond and bearded; the ideal woman in epic and romance was slender and graceful, with blue eyes and long blond or golden hair. The long hair of the Franks gave place, in the upper classes of the ninth century, to heads closely cropped in back, with only a cap of hair on the top; and beards disappeared among the European gentry in the twelfth century. The male peasantry, however, continued to wear long and unclean beards, and hair so ample that it was sometimes gathered in braids.[90] In England all classes kept long hair, and the male beaux of the thirteenth century dyed their hair, curled it with irons, and bound it with ribbons.[91] In the same land and century the married ladies tied up their hair in a net of golden thread, while highborn lasses let it fall down their backs, with sometimes a curl falling demurely over each shoulder upon the breast.[92]

The West Europeans of the Middle Ages were more abundantly and attractively dressed than before or since; and the men often excelled the women in splendor and color of costume. In the fifth century the loose toga and tunic of the Roman fought a losing war with the breeches and belt of the Gaul; the colder climate and military occupations of the North required tighter and thicker clothing than had been suggested by the warmth and ease of the South; and a revolution in dress followed the transfer of power across the Alps. The common man wore close-fitting pantaloons and tunic or blouse, both of leather or strong cloth; at the belt hung knife, purse, keys, sometimes the worker's tools; over the shoulders was flung a cloak or cape; on the head a cap or hat of wool or felt or skins; on the legs long stockings; and on the feet high leather shoes curled up at the toe to forestall stubbing. Toward the end of the Middle Ages the hose grew longer till they reached the hips and evolved into the uncomfortable trousers that modern man has substituted, as a perennial penance, for the hair shirt of the medieval saint. Nearly all garments were of wool except some of skin or leather among peasants or hunters; nearly all were spun, woven, cut, and sewed at home; but the rich had professional tailors, known in England as "scissors." Buttons, occasionally used in antiquity, were avoided before the thirteenth century, and then appeared as functionless ornaments; hence the phrase "not worth a button."[93] In the twelfth century the tight Germanic costume was overlaid in both sexes with a girdled gown.

The rich embellished these basic garments in a hundred fancy ways. Hems and necklines were trimmed with fur; silk, satin, or velvet replaced linen or wool when the weather allowed; a velvet cap covered the head, and shoes of colored cloth followed closely the form of the feet. The finest furs came from Russia; the choicest was ermine, made from white weasel; barons were known to mortgage their lands to buy ermine for their wives. The rich wore drawers of fine white linen; hose often colored, usually of wool, sometimes of silk; a shirt of white linen, with flaunty collar and cuffs; over this a tunic; and over all, in cold or rainy weather, a mantle or cape or *chaperon*—a cape with a cowl that could be drawn up over the head. Some caps were made with a flat square top; these *mortiers* or "mortar-boards" were affected in the later Middle Ages by lawyers and doctors, and survive in our college dignities. Dandies wore gloves in any weather, and (complained the monk Ordericus Vitalis) "swept the dusty ground with the prodigal trains of their mantles and robes."[94]

Jewelry was displayed by men not only on the person but on the clothing—cap, robe, shoes. Some garments were embroidered with sacred or profane texts in pearls;[95] some were trimmed with gold or silver lace, some wore cloth of gold. Kings had to distinguish themselves with extra finery: Edward the Confessor wore a robe resplendently embroidered with gold by his accomplished wife Edgitha, and Charles the Bold of Burgundy wore a robe of state so thickly inlaid with precious stones that it was valued at 200,000 ducats ($1,082,000). All but the poor wore rings; and every man of any account had a signet ring bearing his personal seal; a mark made with this seal was accepted as his personal signature.

Dress was an index of status or wealth; each class protested against the imitation of its raiment by the class below it; and sumptuary laws were vainly passed—as in France in 1294 and 1306—seeking to regulate a citizen's expenditure on wardrobe according to his fortune and his class. The retainers, or dependent knights, of a great lord wore, at formal functions, robes presented to them by him and dyed in his favorite or distinctive color; such robes were called livery (*livrée*) because the lord delivered them twice a year. Good medieval garments, however, were made to last a lifetime, and some were carefully bequeathed by will.

Wellborn ladies wore a long linen chemise; over this a fur-trimmed *pelisson* or robe reaching to the feet; over this a *bliaut* or blouse worn loose in dishabille, but tightly laced against the coming of company; for all fine ladies longed for slenderness. They might also wear jeweled girdles, a silken purse, and chamois-skin gloves. Often they wore flowers in their hair, or bound it with fillets of jeweled silk. Some ladies aroused the clergy, and doubtless worried their husbands, by wearing tall conical hats adorned with horns; at one time a woman without horns was subject to unbearable ridicule.[96] In the later Middle Ages high heels became the fashion. Moralists complained that women found frequent occasions to raise their robes an inch or two to show trim ankles and dainty shoes; female legs, however, were a private and costly revelation. Dante denounced the ladies of Florence for public décolleté that "showed the bosom and the breasts."[97] The dress of ladies at tournaments furnished an exciting topic for clergymen; and cardinals legislated on the length of women's robes. When the clergy decreed veils as vital to morality, the women "caused their veils to be made of fine muslin and silk inwoven with gold, wherein they showed ten times fairer than before, and drew beholders' eyes all the more to wantonness."[98] The monk Guyot of Provins complained that women used so much paint on their faces that none was left to color the icons in the churches; he warned them that when they wore false hair, or applied poultices of mashed beans and mares' milk to their faces to improve their complexion, they were adding centuries to their durance in purgatory.[99] Berthold of Regensburg, about 1220, berated women with vain eloquence:

> Ye women, ye have bowels of compassion, and ye go to church more readily than the men . . . and many of you would be saved but for this one snare: . . . in order that ye may compass men's praise ye spend all your labor on your garments. . . . Many of you pay as much to the seamstress as the cost of the cloth itself; it must have shields on the shoulders, it must be flounced and tucked all round the hem. It is not enough for you to show your pride in your very buttonholes; you must also send your feet to hell by special torments. . . . Ye busy yourselves with your veils: ye twitch them hither, ye twitch them thither; ye gild them here and there with gold thread, and spend thereon all your trouble. Ye will spend a good six months' work on a single veil, which is sinful great travail—and all that men may praise your dress: "Ah, God! how fair! Was ever so fair a garment?" "How, Brother Berthold" (you say), "we do it only for the goodman's sake, that he may gaze the less on other women." No, believe me, if thy goodman be a good man indeed he would far rather behold thy chaste conversation than thy outward adorning. . . . Ye men might put an end to this, and fight against it doughtily; first with good words; and if they are still obdurate step valiantly in . . . tear it from her head, even though four or ten hairs should come with it, and cast it into the fire! Do thus not thrice or four times only; and presently she will forbear.[100]

Sometimes the women took such preaching to heart, and—two centuries before Savonarola—cast their veils and ornaments into the fire.[101] Fortunately, such repentance was brief and rare.

VII. IN THE HOME

There was not much comfort in a medieval home. Windows were few, and seldom glazed; wooden shutters closed them against glare or cold. Heating was by one or more fireplaces; drafts came in from a hundred cracks in the walls, and made high-backed chairs a boon. In winter it was common to wear warm hats and furs indoors. Furniture was scanty but well made. Chairs were few, and usually had no backs; but sometimes they were elegantly carved, engraved with armorial bearings, and inlaid with precious stones. Most seats were cut into the masonry walls, or built upon chests in alcoves. Carpets were unusual before the thirteenth century. Italy and Spain had them; and when Eleanor of Castile went to England in 1254 as the bride of the future Edward I, her servants covered the floors of her apartment at Westminster with carpets after the Spanish custom—which then spread through England. Ordinary floors were strewn with rushes or straw, making some houses so malodorous that the parish priest refused to visit them. Walls might be hung with tapestries, partly as ornaments, partly to hinder drafts, partly to divide the great hall of the house into smaller rooms. Homes in Italy and Provence, still remembering Roman luxuries, were more comfortable and sanitary than those of the North. The homes of German bourgeois, in the thirteenth century, had water piped into the kitchen from wells.[102]

Cleanliness, in the Middle Ages, was not next to godliness. Early Christianity had denounced the Roman baths as wells of perversion and promiscuity, and its general disapproval of the body had put no premium on hygiene. The modern use of the handkerchief was unknown.[103] Cleanliness was next to money, and varied with income; the feudal lord and the rich bourgeois bathed with reasonable frequency, in large wooden tubs; and in the twelfth century the spread of wealth spread personal cleanliness. Many cities in Germany, France, and England had public baths in the thirteenth century; one student reckons that Parisians bathed more frequently in 1292 than in the twentieth century.[104] One result of the Crusades was the introduction into Europe of public steam baths in the Moslem style.[105] The Church frowned upon public baths as leading to immorality; and several of them justified her fears. Some towns provided public mineral baths.

Monasteries, feudal castles, and rich homes had latrines, emptying into cesspools, but most homes managed with outhouses; and in many cases one outhouse had to serve a dozen homes.[106] Pipes for carrying off waste were one of the sanitary reforms introduced into England under Edward I (1271–1307). In the thirteenth century the chamber pots of Paris were freely emptied from windows into the street, with only a warning cry of *Gar' l'eau!* —such contretemps were a cliché of comedies as late as Molière. Public comfort stations were a luxury; San Gimignano had some in 1255, but Florence as yet had none.[107] People eased themselves in courtyards, on stairways and balconies, even in the palace of the Louvre. After a pestilence in 1531 a decree ordered Parisian landlords to provide a latrine for every house, but this ordinance was much honored in the breach.[108]

The upper and middle classes washed before and after meals, for most eating was done with the fingers. There were but two regular meals daily, one at ten, another at four; but either repast might last several hours. In great houses the meal was announced by blasts on a hunting horn. The dinner board might be rude planks on trestles, or a great table strongly built of costly wood and admirably carved. Around it were stools or benches—in French, *bancs*, whence *banquet*. In some French homes ingenious machines raised or lowered into place, from a lower or upper story, a full table ready served, and made it disappear in a moment when the meal was finished.[109] Servants brought ewers of water to each diner, who washed the hands therein and wiped them on napkins which were then put away; in the thirteenth century no napkins were used during the meal, but the diner wiped his hands on the tablecloth.[110] The company sat in couples, gentleman and lady paired; usually each couple ate from one plate and drank from one cup.[111] Each person received a spoon; forks were known in the thirteenth century, but seldom provided; and the diner used his own knife. Cups, saucers, and plates were normally of wood;[112] but the feudal aristocracy and the rich *bourgeoisie* had dishes of earthenware or pewter, and some displayed dinner sets of silver, even, here and there, of gold.[113] Dishes of cut glass might be added, and a large silver vessel in the shape of a ship, containing various spices, and the knife and spoon of the host. Instead of a plate each couple received a large piece of bread, flat, round, and thick; upon this *tranchoir* the diner placed the meat and bread that he took with his fingers from the platters passed to him; when the meal was over the "trencher" was eaten by the diner, or given to the dogs and cats that swarmed around, or sent out to the neighboring poor. A great meal was completed with spices and sweets and a final round of wine.

Food was abundant, varied, and well prepared, except that lack of refrigeration soon made meats high, and put a premium on spices that could preserve or disguise. Some spices were imported from the Orient; but as these were costly, other spices were grown in domestic gardens—parsley, mustard, sage, savory, anise, garlic, dill. . . . Cookbooks were numerous and complex; in a great establishment the cook was a man of importance, bearing on his shoulders the dignity and reputation of the house. He was equipped with a gleaming armory of copper caldrons, kettles, and pans, and prided himself on serving dishes that would please the eye as well as the palate. Meat, poultry, and eggs were cheap,[114] though still dear enough to make most of the poor unwilling vegetarians.[115] Peasants flourished on coarse whole-grain bread of barley, oats, or rye, baked in their homes; city dwellers preferred white bread—baked by bakers—as a mark of caste. There were no potatoes, coffee, or tea; but nearly all meats and vegetables now used in Europe—including eels, frogs, and snails—were eaten by medieval man.[116] By the time of Charlemagne the European acclimatization of Asiatic fruits and nuts was almost complete; oranges, however, were still a rarity in the thirteenth century north of the Alps and the Pyrenees. The commonest meat was pork. Pigs ate the refuse in the streets, and people ate the pigs. It was widely believed that pork caused leprosy, but this did not lessen the taste for it; great sausages and black puddings were a medieval delight. Lordly hosts might have a whole roast pig or boar brought to the table, and carve it before their gaping guests; this was a delicacy almost as keenly relished as partridges, quails, thrushes, peacocks, and cranes. Fish was a staple food; herring was a main recourse of soldiers, sailors, and the poor. Dairy products were less used than today, but the cheese of Brie was already renowned.[117] Salads were unknown, and confections were rare. Sugar was still an import, and had not yet replaced honey for sweetening. Desserts were usually of fruits and nuts. Pastries were innumerable; and jolly bakers, quite unreproved, gave cakes and buns the most interesting shapes imaginable—*quaedam pudenda muliebra, aliae virilia*.[118] It seems incredible that there was no after-dinner smoking. Both sexes drank instead.

As unboiled water was seldom safe, all classes found substitutes for it in beer and wine. "Drinkwater" and "Boileau" were unusual names, indicating unusual tastes. Cider or perry was made from apples or pears, and provided cheap intoxicants for the peasantry. Drunkenness was a favorite vice of the Middle Ages, in all classes and sexes. Taverns were numerous, ale was cheap. Beer was the regular drink of the poor, even at breakfast. Monasteries and hospitals north of the Alps were normally allowed a gallon of ale or beer per person per day.[119] Many monasteries, castles, and rich homes had their own breweries, for in the northern countries beer was reckoned as second only to bread as a necessary of life. Among the well-to-do of all nations, and in all ranks of Latin Europe, wine was preferred. France produced the most famous wines, and proclaimed their glory in a thousand popular songs. At vintage time the peasants worked harder than usual, and were rewarded by good abbots with a moral holiday. A customal of the abbey of St. Peter in the Black Forest includes some tender clauses:

> When the peasants have unladen the wine, they shall be brought into the monastery, and shall have meat and drink in abundance. A great tub shall be set there and filled with wine . . . and each shall drink . . . and if they wax drunken and smite the cellarman or the cook, they shall pay no fine for this deed; and they shall drink so that two of them cannot beat the third to the wagon.[120]

After a banquet the host would usually offer entertainment by jugglers, tumblers, players, minstrels, or buffoons. Some manor houses had their own staff of such entertainers; some rich men kept jesters whose merry impudence and ribald humor could be vented without fear and without reproach. If the diners preferred to provide their own amusement they could tell stories, hear or make music, dance, flirt, play backgammon, chess, or parlor games; even barons and baronesses romped about in "forfeits" and "blind man's buff." Playing cards were still unknown. French laws of 1256 and 1291 forbade making, or playing with, dice, but gambling with dice was widespread nonetheless, and moralists told of fortunes and souls lost in the game. Gambling was not always forbidden by law; Siena provided booths for it in the public square.[121] Chess was prohibited by a council at Paris (1213) and by an edict of Louis IX (1254); no one paid much attention to these demurrers; the game became a consuming pastime among the aristocracy, and gave its name to the royal exchequer—a chequered table or chessboard on which the revenues of the state were reckoned.[122] In Dante's youth a Saracen player set all Florence agape by playing three games of chess at once against the best players of the city; he looked at one board and kept the plays on the other two in his head; of the three games he won two and tied the third.[123] The game of checkers was played in France as *dames*, in England as "draughts."

Dancing was condemned by preachers, and was practiced by nearly all persons except those dedicated to religion. St. Thomas Aquinas, with characteristic moderation, allowed dancing at weddings, or on the homecoming of a friend from abroad, or to celebrate some national victory; and the hearty saint went so far as to say that dancing, if kept decent, was a very healthy exercise.[124] Albertus Magnus showed a like liberality, but medieval moralists generally reprobated the dance as an invention of the Devil.[125] The Church frowned upon it as provocative of immorality;[126] the young blades of the Middle Ages did their best to justify her suspicions.[127] The French and Germans in particular were fond of the dance, and developed many folk dances to mark the festivals of the agricultural year, to celebrate victories, or to sustain public spirit in depression or plague. One of the *Carmina Burana* describes the dances of girls in the fields as among the sweetest pleasures of spring. When knighthood was conferred all the knights of the vicinity gathered in full armor and performed evolutions on horseback or on foot, while the populace danced around them to the accompaniment of martial music. Dancing could become an epidemic: in 1237 a band of German children danced all the way from Erfurt to Arnstadt; many died en route; and some survivors suffered to the end of their lives from St. Vitus' dance, or other nervous disorders.[128]

Most dancing took place by day and in the open air. Houses were poorly lit at night—by standing or hanging lamps with wick and oil, or a rushlight torch of mutton fat; and as fat and oils were expensive, very little work or reading was done after sunset. Soon after dark the guests dispersed, and the household retired. Bedrooms seldom sufficed; it was not uncommon to find an extra bed in the hall or reception room. The poor slept well on beds of straw, the rich slept poorly on perfumed pillows and feather mattresses. Lordly beds were overhung with mosquito netting or a canopy, and were mounted with the aid of stools. Several persons, of any age or sex, might sleep in the same room. In England and France all classes slept nude.[129]

VIII. SOCIETY AND SPORT

The general coarseness of medieval manners was smoothed by certain graces of feudal courtesy. Men shook hands on meeting, as a pledge of peace through unreadiness to draw a sword. Titles were innumerable, in a hundred grades of dignity; and by a charming custom each dignitary was addressed by his title and his Christian name, or the name of his estate. A code of manners was drawn up for polite society in any circumstance—at home, at the dance, on the street, at tournament, at court; ladies had to learn how to walk, curtsey, ride horseback, play, carry falcons gracefully on the wrist . . . ; all this, and a like code for men, constituted *courtoisie*, the manners of the court, courtesy. The thirteenth century saw the publication of many guides to etiquette.[130]

In traveling, one expected courtesies and hospitality from persons of his own class. The poor for charity, the rich for fee or gift, would be sheltered en route by convents or monasteries. As early as the eighth century monks established hospices in the passes of the Alps. Some monasteries had great guest-houses capable of sheltering 300 wayfarers, and stabling their horses.[131] Most travelers, however, put up at wayside inns; rates were low there, and a wench might be had at a reasonable rate, if one guarded his purse. Offered such comforts, many braved the dangers of travel—merchants, bankers, priests, diplomats, pilgrims, students, monks, tourists, tramps. The highways of the Middle Ages, however discouraging, were alive with curious and hopeful people who thought that they would be happier somewhere else.

Class distinctions were as sharp in amusement as in travel. The mighty and the lowly mingled now and then: when the king held a public assembly of his vassals, and distributed food to the crowd; when the aristocratic cavalry performed martial maneuvers; when some prince or princess, king or queen, entered the city in panoplied state, and masses lined the highway to feed on pageantry; or when a tournament or trial by combat was opened to the public eye. Planned spectacles were a vital part of medieval life; church processions, political parades, guild celebrations, filled the streets with banners, floats, wax saints, fat merchants, prancing knights, and military bands.

Traveling mummers staged short plays in the village or city square; minstrels sang and played and strummed romantic tales; acrobats tumbled and juggled, and men and women walked or danced on tightropes across mortal chasms; or two blindfolded men belabored each other with sticks; or a circus would come to town, exhibit strange animals and stranger men, and pit one animal against another in combat to the death.

Among the nobility hunting rivaled jousting as the royal sport. Game laws restricted the season to brief periods, and poaching laws kept game preserves for the aristocracy. The woods of Europe were still inhabited by beasts who had not yet acknowledged the victory of man in the war for the planet; medieval Paris, for example, was several times invaded by wolves. In one aspect the hunter was engaged in maintaining man's precarious ascendancy; in another he was adding to the food supply; and, not least, he was preparing himself for inevitable war by hardening body and spirit to danger, combat, and the shedding of blood. At the same time he made this, too, a pageant. Great olifants—hunting horns of ivory, sometimes chased with gold —rounded up the ladies and gentlemen and dogs: women sitting daintily side-saddle on prancing steeds; men in colorful attire and varied armament—bow and arrow, small ax, spear, and knife; greyhounds, staghounds, bloodhounds, boarhounds pulling on the leash. If the chase led across a peasant's fields, the baron, his vassals, and his guests were free to cross them at whatever cost to seeds and crops; and only reckless peasants would complain.[132] The French aristocracy organized hunting into a system, gave it the name of *chasse*, and developed for it a complex ritual and etiquette.

The ladies joined with especial flair in the most aristocratic game of all— falconry. Nearly all great estates had aviaries housing a variety of birds, of which the falcon was most prized. It was taught to perch on my lord or lady's wrist at any time; some piquant dames kept them so while hearing Mass. The Emperor Frederick II wrote an excellent book on falconry, running to 589 pages, and introduced into Europe from Islam the custom of controlling the nerves and curiosity of the bird by covering its head with a leather hood. Different varieties were trained to fly up and attack diverse birds, kill or wound them, and return to the hunter's wrist; there, lured and rewarded by a bit of meat, they allowed their feet to be snared in straps until fresh prey flew into view. A well-trained falcon was almost the finest gift that could be made to noble or king. The duke of Burgundy ransomed his son by sending twelve white hawks to the captor, Sultan Bajazet. The office of grand falconer of France was one of the highest and best paid in the kingdom.

Many another sport made tolerable the summer's heat and the winter's cold, and turned the passions and energies of youth to vital skills. Practically every lad learned to swim; and in the North all learned to skate. Horse racing was popular, especially in Italy. All classes practiced archery; but only the working classes had the leisure to fish. There were divers games of bowling, hockey, quoits, wrestling, boxing, tennis, football. . . . Tennis developed in France, probably from Moslem antecedents; the name was apparently derived from the *tenez!*—"play!"—with which a player announced his serve.[133] The sport became so popular in France and England that it was sometimes played before large crowds in theaters or the open air.[134] The Irish played hockey as early as our second century; and a Byzantine historian of the twelfth century gives a vivid description of a polo match played with cord-strung racquets as in lacrosse.[135] Football, says a horrified medieval chronicler, "is an abominable game wherein young people propel a huge ball not by throwing it into the air but by striking and rolling it along the ground, not with their hands but with their feet."[136] Apparently the game had come from China to Italy[137] to England, where it became so popular and violent in the thirteenth century that Edward II banned it as leading to breaches of the peace (1314).

Life was more social then than later; group activities stirred the monasteries, nunneries, universities, villages, guilds. Life was especially hilarious on Sundays and solemn holydays; then the peasant, the merchant, and the lord dressed their best, prayed the longest, drank the most.[138] On May Day the English raised Maypoles, lit bonfires, and danced around them in semi-conscious recollection of pagan fertility feasts. At Christmas time many towns and châteaux appointed a Lord of Misrule to organize pastimes and spectacles for the populace. Mummers in masks and beards and jolly garb went about performing street plays or pranks, or singing Christmas carols; houses and churches were decked with holly, ivy, "and whatsoever the season afforded to be green."[139] There were festivals for the agricultural seasons, for national or local triumphs, for saints, and for guilds; and rare was the man who on those occasions did not drink his fill. Merrie England had "scot-ales," or money-raising bazaars at which ale flowed fast but not free; the Church denounced these festivities in the thirteenth century, and adopted them in the fifteenth.[140]

Some festivals adapted the ceremonies of the Church to boisterous parodies that ranged from simple humor to scandalous satire. Beauvais, Sens, and other French towns through many years celebrated on January 14 a *fête de l'âne*, or Festival of the Ass: a pretty girl was placed on an ass, apparently to represent Mary on the Flight to Egypt; the ass was led into a church, was made to genuflect, was stationed beside the altar, and heard a Mass and hymns sung in its praise; and at the end both the priest and the congregation brayed thrice in honor of the animal that had saved the Mother of God from Herod, and borne Jesus into Jerusalem.[141] A dozen cities of France celebrated annually—usually on the Feast of the Circumcision—a *fête des fous*, or Feast of Fools. On that day the lower clergy were allowed to revenge themselves for their subordination to priest and bishop during the year by taking over the church and the ritual; they dressed themselves in feminine costumes, or in ecclesiastical vestments turned inside out; they chose one of their number to be *episcopus fatuorum* or fools' bishop; they chanted ribald hymns, ate sausages on the altar, played dice at its foot, burned old shoes in the censer, and preached hilarious sermons.[142] In the thirteenth and fourteenth centuries many towns in England, Germany, and France chose an *episcopus puerorum*, or boys' bishop, to lead his fellows in a good-humored imitation of ecclesiastical ceremonies.[143] The local clergy smiled on these popular buffooneries; the Church closed her eyes to them for a long time; but as they tended to ever greater irreverence and indecency she was forced to condemn them, and they finally disappeared in the sixteenth century.*

In general the Church was lenient with the lusty humor of the Age of Faith; she knew that men must have a moral holiday now and then, a moratorium on the unnatural moral restraints normally necessary to a civilized society. Some ultra-Puritans like St. John Chrysostom might cry out: "Christ is crucified, and yet you laugh!"—but there continued to be "cakes and ale," and wine ran hot in the mouth. St. Bernard was suspicious of mirth and beauty; but most churchmen in the thirteenth century were hearty livers who enjoyed their meat and drink with a good conscience, and took no offense at a well-turned joke or ankle. The Age of Faith was not so solemn after all; rather it was an age of abounding vitality and full-blooded merriment, and tender sentiment, and a simple joy in the blessings of the earth. On the back of a medieval vocabulary book some wistful student wrote a wish for all of us:

> And I wish that all times were April and May, and every month renew all fruits again, and every day fleur-de-lis and gillyflower and violets and roses wherever one goes, and woods in leaf and meadows green, and every lover should have his lass, and they to love each other with a sure heart and true, and to everyone his pleasure and a gay heart.[145]

IX. MORALITY AND RELIGION

Does the general picture of medieval Europe support the belief that religion makes for morality?

Our general impression suggests a wider gap between moral theory and practice in the Middle Ages than in other epochs of civilization. Medieval Christendom was apparently as rich as our own irreligious age in sensuality, violence, drunkenness, cruelty, coarseness, profanity, greed, robbery, dishonesty, and fraud. It seems to have outdone our time in the enslavement of individuals, but not to have rivaled it in the economic enslavement of colonial areas or defeated states. It surpassed us in the subjection of women;

---

* A boys' bishop, however, is still annually elected at Addlestone, Surrey, England.[144]

it hardly equaled us in immodesty, fornication, and adultery, or in the immensity and murderousness of war. Compared with the Roman Empire from Nerva to Aurelius, medieval Christendom was a moral setback; but much of the Empire had in Nerva's day enjoyed many centuries of civilization, while the Middle Ages, through most of their duration, represented a struggle between Christian morality and a virile barbarism that largely ignored the ethics of the religion whose theology it indifferently received. The barbarians would have called some of their vices virtues, as necessary to their time: their violence as the other side of courage, their sensuality as animal health, their coarse and direct speech, and their shameless talk about natural things, as no worse than the introverted prudery of our youth.

It would be an easy matter to condemn medieval Christendom from the mouths of its own moralists. St. Francis bemoaned the thirteenth century as "these times of superabundant malice and iniquity";[146] Innocent III, St. Bonaventura, Vincent of Beauvais, Dante considered the morals of that "wonderful century" to be dishearteningly gross; and Bishop Grosseteste, one of the most judicious prelates of the age, told the pope that "the Catholic population, as a body, was incorporate with the Devil."[147] Roger Bacon (1214?-94) judged his time with characteristic hyperbole:

> Never was so much ignorance. . . . Far more sins reign in these days than in any past age . . . boundless corruption . . . lechery . . . gluttony. . . . Yet we have baptism and the revelation of Christ . . . which men cannot really believe in or revere, or they would not allow themselves to be so corrupted. . . . Therefore many wise men believe that Antichrist is at hand, and the end of the world.[148]

Such passages, of course, are the exaggerations necessary to reformers, and could be matched in any age.

Apparently the fear of hell had less effect in raising the moral level than the fear of public opinion or the law has now—or had then; but the public opinion, and in a measure the law, had been formed by Christianity. Probably the moral chaos, born of half a millennium of invasion, war, and devastation, would have been far worse without the moderating effect of the Christian ethic. Our selection of instances in this chapter may have been unwittingly biased; at best they are fragmentary; statistics are lacking or unreliable; and history always leaves out the average man. There must have been, in medieval Christendom, thousands of good and simple people like Fra Salimbene's mother, whom he describes as "a humble lady and devout, fasting much, and gladly dispensing alms to the poor";[149] but how often do such women make the pages of history?

Christianity brought some moral retrogressions and some moral advances. The intellectual virtues naturally declined in the Age of Faith; intellectual conscience (fairness with the facts) and the search for truth were replaced by zeal and admiration for sanctity, and a sometimes unscrupulous piety; "pious frauds" of textual doctoring and documentary forgery seemed negligible venial sins. The civic virtues suffered from concentration on the afterlife, but more from the disintegration of the state; nevertheless there must have been some patriotism, however local, in the men and women who built so many cathedrals and some lordly town halls. Perhaps hypocrisy, so indispensable to civilization, increased in the Middle Ages as compared with the frank secularism of antiquity, or the unabashed corporate brutality of our time.

Against these and other debits many credits stand. Christianity struggled with heroic tenacity against an inundation of barbarism. It labored to diminish war and feud, trial by combat or ordeal; it extended the intervals of truce and peace, and sublimated something of feudal violence and pugnacity into devotion and chivalry. It suppressed the gladiatorial shows, denounced the enslavement of prisoners, forbade the enslavement of Christians, ransomed numberless captives, and encouraged—more than it practiced—the emancipation of serfs. It taught men a new respect for human life and work. It stopped infanticide, lessened abortion, and softened the penalties exacted by Roman and barbarian law. It steadfastly rejected the double standard in sexual morality. It immensely expanded the scope and operations of charity. It gave men peace of mind against the baffling riddles of the universe, though at the cost of discouraging science and philosophy. Finally, it taught men that patriotism unchecked by a higher loyalty is a tool of mass greed and crime. Over all the competing cities and petty states of Europe it established and maintained one moral law. Under its guidance, and at some necessary sacrifice of liberty, Europe achieved for a century that international morality for which it prays and struggles today—a law that shall raise states out of their jungle code, and free the energies of men for the battles and victories of peace.

CHAPTER XXXI

The Resurrection of the Arts

1095-1300

I. THE ESTHETIC AWAKENING

WHY is it that Western Europe, in the twelfth and thirteenth centuries, reached a climax of art comparable with Periclean Athens and Augustan Rome?

The Norse and Saracen raids had been beaten off, the Magyars had been tamed. The Crusades aroused a fever of creative energy, and brought back to Europe a thousand ideas and art forms from the Byzantine and Moslem East. The reopening of the Mediterranean, and the opening of the Atlantic to Christian commerce, the security and organization of trade along the rivers of France and Germany and on the northern seas, and the expansion of industry and finance, generated a wealth unknown since Constantine, new classes capable of affording art, and prosperous communes each resolved to build a finer cathedral than the last. The coffers of abbots, bishops, and popes were swelling with the tithes of the people, the gifts of the merchants, the grants of nobles and kings. The Iconoclasts had been defeated; art was no longer branded as idolatry; the Church, which once had feared it, found in it now a propitious medium for inculcating her faith and ideals among the letterless, and for stirring souls to a devotion that lifted spires like supplicating litanies to the sky. And the new religion of Mary, rising spontaneously from the hearts of the people, poured its love and trust of the Divine Mother into magnificent temples where thousands of her children might gather at once to do her homage and beg her aid. All these influences, and many more, came together to flood half a continent with profuse streams of unprecedented art.

The ancient techniques had here and there survived barbarian devastation and municipal decay. In the Eastern Empire the old skills were never lost; and it was above all from the Greek East and Byzantine Italy that artists and art themes now entered the life of the resurrected West. Charlemagne drew into his service Greek artists fleeing from Byzantine Iconoclasts; hence the art of Aachen married Byzantine delicacy and mysticism to German solidity and earthiness. The monk artists of Cluny, inaugurating in the tenth century a new era in Western architecture and adornment, began by copying Byzantine models. The school of monastic art developed at Monte Cassino

845

by Abbot Desiderius (1072) was taught by Greek teachers on Byzantine lines. When Honorius III (1218) wished to decorate San Paolo fuori le mura he sent to Venice for mosaicists; and those who came were steeped in the Byzantine tradition. Colonies of Byzantine artists could be found in a score of Western cities; and it was their style of painting that molded Duccio, Cimabue, and the early Giotto himself. Byzantine or Oriental motives—palmettes, acanthus leaves, animals within medallions—came to the West on textiles and ivories and in illuminated manuscripts, and lived hundreds of years in Romanesque ornament. Syrian, Anatolian, Persian forms of architecture—the vault, the dome, the tower-flanked façade, the composite column, the windows grouped by two or three under a binding arch—appeared again in the architecture of the West. History makes no leaps, and nothing is lost.

Just as the development of life requires variation as well as heredity, and the development of a society needs experimental innovation as well as stabilizing custom, so the development of art in Western Europe involved not only the continuity of a tradition in skills and forms, and the stimulation of Byzantine and Moslem examples, but also the repeated turning of the artist from the school to nature, from ideas to things, from the past to the present, from the imitation of models to the expression of self. There was a somber and static quality in Byzantine art, a fragile and feminine elegance in Arabic ornament, that could never represent the dynamic and masculine vitality of a rebarbarized and reinvigorated West. Nations that were rising out of the Dark Ages toward the noon of the thirteenth century preferred the noble grace of Giotto's women to the stiff Theodoras of Byzantine mosaics; and, laughing at the Semitic horror of images, they transformed mere decoration into the smiling angel of the Reims Cathedral, and the Golden Virgin of Amiens. The joy of life conquered the fear of death in Gothic art.

It was the monks who, as they preserved classic literature, maintained and disseminated Roman, Greek, and Oriental art techniques. Seeking self-containment, the monasteries trained their inmates to the decorative as well as the practical crafts. The abbey church required altar and chancel furniture, chalice and pyx, reliquaries and shrines, missal, candelabra, perhaps mosaics, murals, and icons to inform and inspire piety; these the monks for the most part fashioned with their own hands; indeed, the monastery itself was in many cases designed and built by them, as Monte Cassino rises by Benedictine labor today. Most monasteries included spacious workshops; at Chartres, for example, Bernard de Tiron founded a religious house and gathered into it, we are told, "craftsmen both in wood and iron, carvers and goldsmiths, painters and stonemasons . . . and others skilled in all manner of cunning work." [1] The illuminated manuscripts of the Middle Ages were almost all the work of monks; the finest textiles were produced by monks and nuns; the architects of the early Romanesque cathedrals were monks; [2] in

FIG. 16—*Cimabue: Madonna with Angels and St. Francis*
Cathedral of Assisi

FIG. 17—*Portrait of a Saint*
Book of Kells

FIG. 18—*Glass Painting, 12th Century*
Chartres Cathedral

FIG. 19—*Rose Window*
Strasbourg Cathedral

FIG. 20—*Notre Dame*
Paris

FIG. 21—*The Virgin of the Pillar*
Notre Dame, Paris

FIG. 22—*Gargoyle*
Notre Dame, Paris

FIG. 23–*Cathedral, West View*
Chartres

FIG. 25—"*The Visitation*"
North transept, Chartres Cathedral

FIG. 24—"*Modesty*"
North transept, Chartres Cathedral

the eleventh and early twelfth centuries the abbey of Cluny furnished most of the architects for Western Europe, and many of the painters and sculptors;[3] and in the thirteenth century the abbey of St. Denis was a thriving center of varied arts. Even the Cistercian monasteries, which in the days of the watchful Bernard had closed their doors to decoration, soon surrendered to the lure of form and the excitement of color, and began to build abbeys as ornate as Cluny or St. Denis. As the English cathedrals were usually monastic minsters, the regular or monastic clergy continued to the end of the thirteenth century to dominate ecclesiastical architecture in England.

But a monastery, however excellent as a school and refuge for the spirit, is condemned by its seclusion to be a repository of traditions rather than a theater of living experiment; it is better fitted to preserve than to create. Not until the widened demands of a richer laity nourished secular artists did medieval life find the exuberant expression, in unhackneyed forms, that brought Gothic art to fullness. First in Italy, most in France, least in England, the emancipated and specializing laymen of the twelfth century, grouped in guilds, took the arts from monastic teachers and hands, and built the great cathedrals.

II. THE ADORNMENT OF LIFE

Nevertheless it was a monk who wrote the most complete and revealing summary of medieval arts and crafts. Theophilus—"lover of God" in the monastery of Helmershausen near Paderborn—wrote, about 1190, a *Schedula diversarum artium*:

> Theophilus, a humble priest . . . addresses his words to all who wish, by the practical work of their hands, and by the pleasing meditation of what is new, to put aside . . . all sloth of mind and wandering of spirit. . . . [Here shall such men find] all that Greece possesses in the way of diverse colors and mixtures; all that Tuscany knows of the working of enamels . . . all that Arabia has to show of works ductile, fusible, or chased; all the many vases and sculptured gems and ivory that Italy adorns with gold; all that France prizes in costly variety of windows; all that is extolled in gold, silver, copper, or iron, or in subtle working of wood or stone.[4]

Here in a paragraph we see another side of the Age of Faith—men and women, and not least monks and nuns, seeking to satisfy the impulse to expression, taking pleasure in proportion, harmony, and form, and eager to make the useful beautiful. The medieval scene, however suffused with religion, is above all a picture of men and women working. And the first and basic purpose of their art is the adornment of their work, their bodies, and their homes. Thousands of woodworkers used knife, drill, gouge, chisel, and polishing materials to carve tables, chairs, benches, chests, caskets, cabinets, stairposts, wainscots, beds, cupboards, buffets, icons, altarpieces, choir stalls . . . with an incredible variety of forms and themes in high or low relief, and often with a mischievous humor that recognized no barrier between the sacred and the profane. On the misericords one might find figures of misers, gluttons, gossipers, grotesque beasts and birds with human heads. In Venice the wood carvers sometimes made frames more beautiful and costly than the pictures they enclosed. The Germans began in the twelfth century that remarkable wood sculpture which would become a major art in the sixteenth.*

The workers in metal rivaled the workers in wood. Iron was wrought into elegant gratings for windows, courtyards, and gates; for mighty hinges that spread across massive doors in a variety of floral designs (as on Notre Dame at Paris); for cathedral choir grilles as "strong as iron" and as delicate as lace. Iron or bronze or copper was fused or hammered into handsome vases, goblets, caldrons, ewers, candelabra, censers, caskets, and lamps; and bronze plates covered many cathedral doors. Armorers liked to add a touch of decoration to swords and scabbards, helmets, breastplates, and shields. The gorgeous bronze chandelier presented to the cathedral of Aachen by Frederick Barbarossa attested the ability of the German metalworkers; and the great bronze candlestick from Gloucester (c. 1100), now in the Victoria and Albert Museum, bears like testimony to English skill. The medieval fondness for making art of the simplest articles shows in the adornment of bolts, locks, and keys. Even weathervanes were carefully decorated with ornament that only a telescope could see.

The arts of the precious metals and stones flourished amid general poverty. The Merovingian kings had gold plate, and Charlemagne collected at Aachen a treasure of goldsmiths' work. The Church pardonably felt that if gold and silver brightened the tables of barons and bankers, they should also be used in the service of the King of Kings. Some altars were of chased silver, some of chased gold, as in the church of St. Ambrose at Milan, and the cathedrals of Pistoia and Basel. Gold was normal for the *ciborium* or pyx that held the consecrated Host, for the monstrance in which it was exposed to the veneration of the faithful, for the chalice that contained the sacramental wine, and for the reliquaries in which saintly relics were preserved; these vessels were in many cases more beautifully worked than the most costly prize cups of today. In Spain the goldsmiths made resplendent tabernacles to bear the Host in processions through the streets; in Paris the goldsmith Bonnard (1212) used 1544 ounces of silver, and 60 of gold, to make a shrine for the bones of St. Genevieve. We may judge the scope of the goldsmith's art from the seventy-nine chapters devoted to it by Theophilus. There we find that every medieval goldsmith was expected to be a Cellini—at once smelter, sculptor, enameler, jewel mounter, and inlay worker. Paris in the

---

* Cf. the twelfth-century *Crucifixion* in the Liebfrauenkirche of Halberstadt, or the thirteenth-century statue of James the Less in the Metropolitan Museum of Art, New York.

thirteenth century had a powerful guild of goldsmiths and jewelers; and Parisian jewel cutters had already a reputation for producing artificial gems.[5] The seals that rich men used to stamp the wax on their letters or envelopes were carefully designed and carved. Every prelate had an official ring; and every real or specious gentleman flaunted at least one ring on his hands. Those who cater to human vanity seldom starve.

Cameos—small reliefs on precious material—were popular among the rich. Henry III of England had a "great cameo" valued at £200 ($40,000); Baldwin II brought a still more celebrated cameo from Constantinople to house it at Paris in Sainte Chapelle. Ivory was painstakingly carved throughout the Middle Ages: combs, boxes, handles, drinking horns, icons, book covers, diptychs and triptychs, episcopal staffs and croziers, reliquaries, shrines. . . . Astonishingly close to perfection is a thirteenth-century ivory group in the Louvre depicting the Descent from the Cross. Towards the end of that century romance and humor gained upon piety, and delicate carvings of sometimes very delicate scenes appeared on mirror cases and toilet boxes designed for ladies who could not be pious all the time.

Ivory was one of many materials used for inlay, which the Italians called intarsia (from the Latin *interserere*, insert), and the French termed marquetry (*marquer*, to mark). Wood itself might be used as an inlay in other woods: a design was chiseled into a block of wood, and other woods were pressed and glued into the design. One of the more recondite medieval arts was niello (Latin *nigellus*, black)—inlaying an incised metal surface with a black paste composed of silver, copper, sulphur, and lead; when the inlay hardened, the surface was filed till the silver in the mixture shone. From this technique, in the fifteenth century, Finiguerra would develop copperplate engraving.

The ceramic arts matured again out of industrial pottery as the returning Crusaders aroused Europe from the Dark Ages. Cloisonné enamel entered the West from Byzantium in the eighth century. In the twelfth a plaque representing the Last Judgment * gave an excellent example of champlevé; i.e., the spaces between the lines of the design were hollowed out into a copper ground, and the depressions were filled with enamel paste. Limoges, in France, had made enameled wares since the third century; in the twelfth it was the chief center, in the West, of champlevé and cloisonné. In the thirteenth century Moorish potters in Christian Spain coated clay vessels with an opaque tin glaze or enamel as a base for painted decoration; in the fifteenth century Italian merchants imported such wares from Spain in Majorcan trading ships, and called the material majolica, changing *r* to *l* in their melodious way.

The art of glass, so nearly perfected in ancient Rome, returned to Venice from Egypt and Byzantium. As early as 1024 we hear of twelve *phiolarii*

---

* In the Victoria and Albert Museum.

there, whose products were so varied that the government took the industry under its protection, and voted the title "gentlemen" to glassmakers. In 1278 the glassworkers were removed to a special quarter on the island of Murano, partly for safety, partly for secrecy; strict laws were passed forbidding Venetian glassmakers to go abroad, or to reveal the esoteric techniques of their art. From that "foot of earth" the Venetians for four centuries dominated the art and industry of glass in the Western world. Enameling and gilding of glass were highly developed; Olivo de Venezia made textiles of glass; and Murano poured out glass mosaic, beads, phials, beakers, tableware, even glass mirrors, which in the thirteenth century began to replace mirrors of polished steel. France, England, and Germany also made glass in this period, but almost entirely for industrial use; the stained glass of the cathedrals was a brilliant exception.

Women have always received less credit in histories of art than they deserved. The adornment of the person and the home are precious elements in the art of life; and the work of women in dress design, interior decoration, embroidery, drapery, and tapestry has contributed more than most arts to that often unconscious pleasure which we derive from the intimate and silent presence of beautiful things. Delicate tissues deftly woven, and welcome to sight or touch, were highly prized in the Age of Faith; they clothed altars, relics, sacred vessels, priests, and men and women of high estate; and they themselves were wrapped in soft, thin paper which took from them its "tissue paper" name. In the thirteenth century France and England dethroned Constantinople as the chief producer of artistic embroidery; we hear of embroiderers' guilds in Paris in 1258; and Matthew Paris, under the year 1246, tells how Pope Innocent IV was struck by the gold-embroidered vestments of English prelates visiting Rome, and ordered such *opus anglicanum* for his copes and chasubles. Some ecclesiastical garments were so heavy with jewels, gold thread, and small enamel plaques that the priest so robed could hardly walk.[6] An American millionaire paid $60,000 for an ecclesiastical vestment known as the Cope of Ascoli.* The most famous of medieval embroideries was the "dalmatic of Charlemagne"; it was believed to be a product of Dalmatia, but was probably a Byzantine work of the twelfth century; it is now one of the most precious objects in the treasury of the Vatican.

In France and England embroidered hangings or tapestries took the place of paintings, especially in public buildings. Their full display was reserved for festal days; then they were hung under the arches of church bays, and in the streets, and on processional floats. Usually they were woven of wool and silk by the "tirewomen" or maids of feudal châteaux under the superintendence of the chatelaine; many were woven by nuns, some by monks. Tapestries made no pretense to rival the subtler qualities of painting; they were

---

* Learning that it had been stolen, he returned it to the Italian government, and contented himself with a medal for honesty.[7]

to be seen from some distance, and had to sacrifice nicety of line and shading to clarity of figure and brilliance and permanence of color. They commemorated an historical event or a famous legend, or cheered gloomy interiors with representations of landscapes, flowers, or the sea. Tapestries are mentioned as early as the tenth century in France, but the oldest extant full specimens hardly antedate the fourteenth. Florence in Italy, Chinchilla in Spain, Poitiers, Arras, and Lille in France, led the West in the art of tapestry and rugs. The world-renowned Bayeux tapestries were not strictly such, since their design was embroidered upon the surface instead of forming part of the weave. They derive their name from the cathedral of Bayeux that long housed them; tradition ascribed them to William the Conqueror's Queen Matilda and the ladies of her Norman court; but ungallant scholarship prefers an anonymous origin and a later date.[8] They rival the chronicles as an authority for the Norman Conquest. Upon a strip of brown linen nineteen inches wide and seventy-one yards long, sixty scenes show in procession the preparation for the invasion, the Norse vessels cleaving the Channel with high and figured prows, the wild battle of Hastings, the transfixing and death of Harold, the rout of the Anglo-Saxon troops, the triumph of blessed force. These tapestries are impressive examples of patient needlework, but they are not among the finer products of their kind. In 1803 Napoleon used them as propaganda to rouse the French to invade England;[9] but he neglected to secure the blessing of the gods.

III. PAINTING

1. Mosaic

The pictorial art in the Age of Faith took four principal forms: mosaic, miniatures, murals, and stained glass.

The mosaic art was now in its old age, but in the course of 2000 years it had learned many subtleties. To make the gold ground they loved so well, mosaicists wrapped gold leaf around glass cubes, covered the leaf with a thin film of glass to keep the gold from tarnishing, and then, to avoid surface glare, laid the gilded cubes in slightly uneven planes. The light was reflected at diverse angles from the cubes, and gave an almost living texture to the whole.

It was probably Byzantine artists who in the eleventh century covered the east apse and west wall of an old cathedral at Torcello—an island near Venice—with some of the most imposing mosaics in medieval history.[10] The mosaics of St. Mark's range over seven centuries in authorship and style. Doge Domenico Selvo commissioned the first interior mosaics in 1071, presumably using Byzantine artists; the mosaics of 1153 were still under Byzantine tutelage; not until 1450 were Italian artists predominant in the mosaic adornment of St. Mark's. The twelfth-century Ascension mosaic of the central cupola is a summit of the art, but it has a close rival in the Joseph mosaics of the vestibule dome. The marble mosaic of the pavement has survived through 700 years the tread of human feet.

At the other end of Italy Greek and Saracen workers united to produce the mosaic masterpieces of Norman Sicily—in the Capella Palatina and Martorana of Palermo, the monastery of Monreale, the cathedral of Cefalù (1148). The wars of the papacy in the thirteenth century may have retarded art in Rome; however, resplendent mosaics were made in that period for the churches of Santa Maria Maggiore, Santa Maria in Trastevere, St. John Lateran, and St. Paul Outside the Walls. An Italian, Andrea Tafi (1213–94), designed a mosaic for the Baptistery at Florence, but it was not up to the Greek work in Venice or Sicily. Suger's abbey at St. Denis (1150) had a magnificent mosaic floor, partly preserved in the Cluny Museum; and the pavement (c. 1268) of Westminster Abbey is an admirable mingling of mosaic shades. But the mosaic art never prospered north of the Alps; stained glass outshone it; and with the coming of Duccio, Cimabue, and Giotto, murals crowded it out even in Italy.

2. Miniatures

The illumination of manuscripts with miniature paintings and decoration in liquid silver and gold and colored inks continued to be a favorite art, gratefully adapted to monastic quiet and piety. Like so many phases of medieval activity, it reached its Western apogee in the thirteenth century; never again has it been so delicate, inventive, or profuse. The stiff figures and drapes, and hard greens and reds, of the eleventh century were gradually replaced with forms of grace and tenderness in richer hues on backgrounds of blue or gold; and the Virgin conquered the miniature even as she was capturing the cathedral.

During the Dark Ages many books were destroyed; those that remained were doubly precious, and constituted, so to speak, a thin life line of civilization in their text and art.[11] Psalters, gospels, sacramentaries, missals, breviaries, books of hours were cherished as the living vehicles of a divine revelation; no effort was too great for their fit adornment; one might reasonably spend a day on an initial, a week on a title page. Hartker, a monk of St. Gall, perhaps expecting the end of the world with the century, made a vow in 986 to remain within four walls the rest of his earthly life; he stayed in his tiny cell till he died fifteen years later; and there he illuminated—brightened with pictures and ornament—the Antiphonary of St. Gall.[12]

Perspective and modeling were now less ably practiced than in the Carolingian exuberance; the *enlumineur*, as the French called the miniaturist, sought depth and splendor of color, and a crowded fullness and vitality of representation, rather than the illusion of tridimensional space. Most frequently his subjects were taken from the Bible, or the apocryphal gospels, or the legends of the saints; but sometimes a herbal or a bestiary sought illustration, and he took delight in picturing real or imaginary plants and animals. Even in religious books the ecclesiastical rules for subject and treatment were less defined in the West than in the East, and the painter was allowed to range and frolic widely within his narrow room. Animal bodies with human heads, human bodies with animal heads, a monkey disguised as a monk, a monkey examining with proper medical gravity a phial of urine, a musician giving a concert by scraping together the jawbones of an ass—such were the topics that graced a *Book of the Hours of the Virgin*.[13] Other texts, sacred as well as profane, came to life with scenes of hunting, tournament, or war; one thirteenth-century psalter included in its pictures the inside of an Italian bank. The secular world, recovering from its terror of eternity, was invading the precincts of religion itself.

English monasteries were fertile in this peaceful art. The East Anglian school produced famous psalters: one treasured by the Brussels library, another ("Ormsby") at Oxford, a third ("St. Omer") in the British Museum. But the finest illumination of the age was French. The psalters painted for Louis IX inaugurate a style of centered composition, and division into framed medallions, obviously taken from the stained glass of the cathedrals. The Lowlands shared in this movement; the monks of Liége and Ghent attained in their miniatures something of the warm feeling and flowing grace of the sculptures at Amiens and Reims. Spain produced the greatest single chef-d'oeuvre of thirteenth-century illumination in a book of hymns to the Virgin—*Las cantigas del Rey Sabio* (*c.* 1280)—"The Canticles of [Alfonso X] the Wise King"; its 1226 miniatures suggest the labor and loyalty that medieval books might receive. Such books, of course, were works of calligraphic as well as pictorial art. Sometimes the same artist copied or composed and wrote the text, and painted the illumination. In several manuscripts one hesitates to decide which seems more beautiful—the decoration or the text. We paid a price for print.

3. *Murals*

It is difficult to tell how far the miniatures, in subject and design, influenced murals, panels, icons, ceramic painting, sculptural relief, and stained glass, and how far these influenced illumination. There was among these arts a free trade in themes and styles, a continuous interaction; and sometimes the same artist practiced them all. We do injustice to art and artist alike when we separate one art too sharply from the rest, or the arts from the life of their time; reality is always more integrated than our chronicles; and the historian disintegrates for convenience' sake the elements of a civilization whose components flowed as a united stream. We must try not to sever the artist from the cultural complex that reared and taught him, gave him traditions and topics—praised or tormented him, used him up, buried him, and—more often than not—forgot his name.

The Middle Ages, like any age of faith, discouraged individualism as insolent impiety, and bade the ego even of genius submerge itself in the work and current of its time. The Church, the state, the commune, the guild were the lasting realities; they were the artists; individuals were the hands of the group; and when the great cathedral took form its body and soul would stand for all the bodies and souls that its design and building and adornment had consecrated and consumed. So history has swallowed up nearly all the names of the men who painted the walls of medieval structures before the thirteenth century; and war, revolution, and the damp of time have almost swallowed up their work. Were the methods of the muralists to blame? They used the ancient processes of fresco and tempera—applying the colors to freshly plastered walls, or painting upon dry walls with colors made adhesive by some glutinous material. Both methods aimed at permanence, through permeation or cohesion; even so the colors tended to flake off in the course of years, so that very little remains of mural painting before the fourteenth century. Theophilus (1190) described the preparation of oil colors, but this technique lay undeveloped till the Renaissance.

The traditions of classic Roman painting were apparently snuffed out by the barbarian invasions and the ensuing centuries of poverty. When Italian mural painting revived it took its lead not from antiquity but from the half-Greek, half-Oriental methods of Byzantium. Early in the thirteenth century we find Greek painters working in Italy—Theophanes at Venice, Apollonius at Florence, Melormus at Siena. . . . The earliest signed panel pictures in the Italian art of this period bear Greek names. Such men brought with them Byzantine themes and styles—symbolic figures religio-mystical, making no claim to the representation of natural attitudes and scenes.

Gradually, as wealth and taste rose in thirteenth-century Italy, and the higher rewards of art drew better talents to their quest, Italian painters—Giunta Pisano at Pisa, Lapo at Pistoia, Guido at Siena, Pietro Cavallini at Assisi and Rome—began to abandon the dreamy Byzantine manner, and to infuse their painting with the color and passion of Italy. In the church of San Domenico at Siena Guido (1271) painted a Madonna whose "pure, sweet face" [14] left far behind it the frail and lifeless forms of the Byzantine painting of that age; this picture almost begins the Italian Renaissance.

A generation later Duccio di Buoninsegna (1273–1319) carried Siena to a kind of civic-esthetic frenzy with his *Maestà* or "Majesty" of the Virgin enthroned. The thriving citizens decided that the Divine Mother, their feudal queen, should have her picture painted on an imposing scale by the greatest artist available anywhere. They found it pleasant to choose their townsman Duccio. They promised him gold, gave him food and time, and watched every step of his work. When, after three years, it was complete (1311), and Duccio had added a touching signature—"Holy Mother of God, give Siena peace and Duccio life because he painted thee thus"—a procession of bishops, priests, monks, officials, and half the population of the city escorted the picture (fourteen feet long and seven wide) to the cathedral, amid the blare of trumpets and the ringing of bells. The work was still half Byzantine in style, aiming at religious expression rather than realistic portraiture; the Virgin's nose was too long and straight, her eyes too somber; but the surrounding figures had grace and character; and the scenes from the life of Mary and Christ, painted on the predellas and pinnacles, had a new and vivid charm. Altogether this was the greatest painting before Giotto.*

Meanwhile at Florence Giovanni Cimabue (1240?–1302) had inaugurated a dynasty of painters that would rule Italian art for almost three centuries. Born of a noble family, Giovanni doubtless saddened them by abandoning law for art. He was a proud spirit, apt to cast aside any of his works in which he or another had found a defect. While stemming, like Duccio, from the Italian-Byzantine school, he poured his pride and energy into his art to revolutionary effect; in him, more than in the greater artist Duccio, the Byzantine style was superseded, and a new path of advance was cleared. He bent and softened the hard lines of his predecessors, gave flesh to spirit, color and warmth to flesh, human tenderness to gods and saints; and by using bright reds, pinks, and blues for the drapery, he endowed his paintings with a life and brilliance unknown before him in medieval Italy. All this, however, we must accept on the testimony of his time; not one of the pictures attributed to him is unquestionably his; and the *Madonna and Child with Angels*, painted in tempera for the Rucellai Chapel of Santa Maria Novella in Florence, is more probably by Duccio.[15] A tradition disputed, but probably true, assigns to Cimabue a *Virgin and Child Between Four Angels* in the Lower Church of San Francesco at Assisi. This colossal fresco, usually dated 1296, and restored in the nineteenth century, is the first extant masterpiece in Italian painting. The figure of St. Francis is bravely realistic—a man frightened to emaciation by visions of Christ; and the four angels begin the Renaissance alliance of religious subjects with feminine beauty.

In the closing years of his life Cimabue was appointed *capomaestro* of mosaics at the cathedral of Pisa; and there, it is said, he designed for the apse a mosaic of *Christ in Glory Between the Virgin and St. John*. Vasari tells a pretty tale how Cimabue once found a shepherd lad of ten, called Giotto di Bondone, drawing a lamb on a slate with a piece of coal, and took him to

---

* The main picture is now in the Opera or Museum of the Siena Cathedral.

Florence as a pupil.[16] Certainly Giotto worked in Cimabue's studio, and occupied his master's house after Cimabue's death. So began the greatest line of painters in the history of art.

4. Stained Glass

Italy was a century ahead of the North in murals and mosaics, a century behind in architecture and stained glass. The art of painting glass had been known to antiquity, but chiefly in the form of glass mosaic. Gregory of Tours (538?–93) filled the windows of St. Martin's with glass "of varied colors"; and in the same century Paul the Silentiary remarked the splendor of sunlight as filtered through the variously colored windows of St. Sophia's at Constantinople. In these cases, so far as we know, there was no attempt at making pictures with the glass. But about 980 Archbishop Adalbero of Reims adorned his cathedral with windows "containing histories"; [17] and in 1052 the chronicle of St. Benignus described a "very ancient painted window," representing St. Paschasius, in a church at Dijon.[18] Here was historiated glass; but apparently the color was painted upon the glass, not fused into it. When Gothic architecture reduced the strain on walls and made space for larger windows, the abundant light thereby admitted into the church allowed—indeed, demanded—the coloring of the panes; and every stimulus was present to find a method of more permanently painting glass.

Stain-fused glass was probably an offshoot of the art of enameled glass. Theophilus described the new technique in 1190. A "cartoon" or design was laid upon a table, and was divided into small sections, each marked with a symbol of the desired color. Pieces of glass were cut, seldom more than an inch long or wide, to fit the sections of the cartoon. Each piece of glass was painted in the designated color with a pigment consisting of powdered glass mixed with varying metallic oxides—cobalt for blue, copper for red or green, manganese for purple. . . . The painted glass was then fired to fuse the enamel oxides with the glass; the cooled pieces were laid upon the design, and were soldered together with thin strips of lead. In viewing a window of such mosaic glass the eye hardly notices the leads, but makes of the parts a continuous colored surface. The artist was interested in color above all, and aimed at a fusion of color tones; he sought no realism, no perspective; he gave the queerest hues to the objects in his pictures—green camels, pink lions, blue-faced knights.[19] But he achieved the effect he aimed at: a brilliant and lasting picture, a softening and coloring of the light admitted to the church, and the instruction and exaltation of the worshiper.

The windows—even the great "roses"—were in most cases divided into panels, medallions, circles, lozenges, or squares, so that one window might show several scenes in a biography or theme. Old Testament prophets were pictured opposite their New Testament analogues or fulfillments; and the New Testament was amplified from the apocryphal gospels, whose picturesque fables were so dear to the medieval mind. Stories of the saints were even more frequent in the windows than episodes from the Bible; so the adventures of St. Eustace were narrated on the windows of Chartres, and again at Sens, Auxerre, Le Mans, and Tours. Events of profane history rarely appeared in stained glass.

Within a half century of its oldest known occurrence in France, stained glass reached perfection at Chartres. The windows of that cathedral served as models and goals for those at Sens, Laon, Bourges, and Rouen. Thence the art crossed to England, and inspired the glass of Canterbury and Lincoln; a treaty between France and England specified that one of the glass painters of Louis VII (1137–80) should be allowed to come to England.[20] In the thirteenth century the component parts of the pane were made larger, and the color lost something of the vibrating subtlety of the earlier work. Painting in grisaille—decorative tracery with thin lines of red or blue on a gray monochrome base—replaced, towards the end of that century, the color symphonies of the great cathedrals; the mullions themselves, in ever more complex designs, played a larger part in the picture; and though such window tracery became in its turn a lovely art, the skill of the glass painter declined. The splendor of stained glass had come with the Gothic cathedral; and when the Gothic glory faded, the ecstasy of color died away.

IV. SCULPTURE

Much Roman sculpture had been destroyed as loot by victorious barbarism, or as obscene idolatry by nascent Christianity; something had remained, especially in France, to excite the imagination of barbarism tamed and a Christian culture coming of age. In this art, as in others, the Eastern Roman Empire had preserved old models and skills, had overlaid them with Asiatic conventions and mysticism, and had redistributed to the West the seeds that had come to it from Rome. Greek carvers went to Germany after Theophano married Otto II (972); they went to Venice, Ravenna, Rome, Naples, Sicily, perhaps to Barcelona and Marseille. From such men, and from the Moslem artists of his *Regno*, the sculptors of Frederick II may have learned their trade. When barbarism became rich it could afford to wed beauty; when the Church became rich she took sculpture, like the other arts, into the service of her creed and ritual. That, after all, was the way the major arts had developed in Egypt and Asia, in Greece and Rome; great art is the child of a triumphant faith.

Like mural painting, mosaic, and stained glass, sculpture was conceived not as independent, but as one phase of an integrated art for which no language has a name—the adornment of worship. Primarily the sculptor's function was to beautify the house of God with statuary and reliefs; secondarily to make images or icons to inspire piety in the home; after that, if time and funds remained, he might carve the likeness of secular persons or adorn profane things. In church sculpture the preferred material was some lasting substance like stone, marble, alabaster, bronze; but for statuary the Church favored wood: such figures could be borne without agony by Christians marching in religious pageantry. Statues were painted, as in ancient religious art, and they were more often realistic than idealized. The worshiper was to feel the presence of the saint through the image; and so well was this end attained that the Christian, like the devotee of older faiths, expected miracles of the statue, and raised few doubts on hearing that the arm of an alabaster Christ had moved in benediction, or that the breast of a wooden Virgin had given milk.

Any study of medieval sculpture should begin with an act of contrition. A great part of that sculpture was destroyed in England by Puritan zealots— sometimes by act of Parliament; and in France by the Art Terror of the Revolution. In England the reaction was against what seemed to the new iconoclasts the pagan ornamentation of Christian shrines; in France it attacked the collections, effigies, and tombs of the hated aristocracy. All through these countries we find headless statues, broken noses, battered sarcophagi, smashed reliefs, shattered cornices and capitals; a fury of accumulated resentment against ecclesiastical or feudal tyranny vented itself at last in a Satanic demolition. As if enlisting in a conspiracy of ruin, time and its servant elements wore away surfaces, melted stone, effaced inscriptions, waged against the works of man a cold and silent war that never granted truce. And man himself, in a thousand campaigns, sought victory through competitive devastation. We know medieval sculpture only in its desolation.

We add misunderstanding to injury when we view its scattered members in museums. It was not meant to be seen in isolation; it was part of a theological theme and an architectural whole; and what might seem crude and ungainly in separation may have been skillfully suited to its context in stone. The cathedral statue was an element in a composition; it was adjusted to its place, and tended to follow, by elongation, the vertical lift of the cathedral lines: the legs were kept together, the arms were pressed to the body; sometimes a saint was thinned and stretched through all the length of a portal jamb. Less often a horizontal effect was stressed, and the figures over a door might be fattened and flattened as over the portal of Chartres, or a man or a beast might be crumpled into a capital like a Greek god cornered in a pediment. Gothic sculpture was fused in an unrivaled unity with the architecture it adorned.

This subordination of sculptural to structural line and aim especially marked the art of the twelfth century. The thirteenth witnessed an exuber-

ant rebellion of the sculptor, who now ventured out of formalism into realism, out of piety into humor and satire and the zest of earthy life. At Chartres, in the twelfth century, the figures are somber and stiff; at Reims, in the
thirteenth, they are caught in natural conversation or spontaneous action,
their features are individual, there is grace in their pose. Many figures on the
cathedrals of Chartres and Reims resemble the bearded peasants that still
meet us in French villages; the shepherd warming himself at the fire on the
west portal of Amiens might be in a Norman or Gaspé field today. No sculpture in history rivals the whimsical veracity of Gothic cathedral reliefs. At
Rouen, crowded into little quatrefoils, we find a meditative philosopher with
the head of a pig; a doctor, half man and half goose, studying another phial
of urine; a music teacher, half man and half rooster, giving a lesson on the
organ to a centaur; a man changed by a sorcerer into a dog, whose feet still
wear his boots.[21] Funny little figures crouch under the statues at Chartres,
Amiens, Reims. A capital in Strasbourg cathedral, since reformed, showed
the burial of Reynard the Fox: a boar and a goat carried his coffin, a wolf
bore the cross, a hare lighted the way with a taper, a bear sprinkled holy
water, a stag sang Mass, an ass chanted the funeral service from a book resting on the head of a cat.[22] In Beverley Minster a fox cowled like a monk
preaches from a pulpit to a congregation of pious geese.[23]

The cathedrals are, among other things, menageries in stone; almost all
animals known to man, and many known only to medieval fancy, find somewhere room in those tolerant immensities. At Laon sixteen bulls lower on the
cathedral towers; they represent, we are told, the mighty beasts that through
patient years transported the stone blocks from the quarries to the hilltop
church. One day, said a genial legend, an ox laboring upward fell in exhaustion; the load was precariously poised on a slope when a miraculous ox appeared, slipped into the harness, drew the cart to the summit, and then vanished into the supernatural air.[24] We smile at such fiction, and return to our
tales of sex and crime.

The cathedrals found place, too, for a botanical garden. Next to the Virgin, the angels, and the saints, what better ornament could there be for the
house of God than the plants, fruits, and flowers of the French or English or
German countryside? In Romanesque architecture (800–1200) the old
Roman floral motives persisted—acanthus leaves and the vine; in Gothic these
formalized motives yielded to an amazing profusion of indigenous plants,
carved into bases, capitals, spandrels, archivolts, cornices, columns, pulpits,
choirs, doorposts, stalls. . . . These forms are not conventional; they are often
individualized varieties locally loved, and rendered to the life; sometimes
they are composite plants, another play of Gothic imagination, but still fresh
with the feel of nature. Trees, branches, twigs, leaves, buds, flowers, fruit,
ferns, buttercups, plantains, watercress, celandine, rosebushes, strawberry
plants, thistle and sage, parsley and chicory, cabbage and celery—all are here,

falling from the never-emptied cornucopia of the cathedral; the intoxication of spring was in the heart of the sculptor, and guided the chisel into the stone. Not only spring; all the seasons of the year are in these carvings, all the toil and solace of sowing, reaping, and vintage are here; and in the whole history of sculpture there is nothing finer in its kind than the "Vintage Capital" in the cathedral of Reims.[25]

But this world of plants and flowers, birds and beasts, was ancillary to the main theme of medieval sculpture—the life and death of man. At Chartres, Laon, Lyons, Auxerre, Bourges, some preliminary reliefs tell the story of the creation. At Laon the Creator counts on His fingers the days left Him for His task; and in later scenes we see Him, tired with His cosmic toil, leaning on His staff, sitting down to rest, going to sleep; this is a god whom any peasant can understand. Other cathedral reliefs show the months of the year, each with its distinctive work and joy. Others show the occupations of man: peasants in the field or at the wine press; some guiding horses or oxen in breaking furrows or pulling carts; others shearing sheep or milking cows; and there are millers, carpenters, porters, merchants, artists, scholars, even a philosopher or two. The sculptor portrays abstractions through examples: Donatus is grammar, Cicero is oratory, Aristotle is dialectic, Ptolemy is astronomy. Philosophy sits with her head in the clouds, a book in her right hand, a scepter in her left; she is *Regina scientiarum*, Queen of the Sciences. Paired figures personify Faith and Idolatry, Hope and Despair, Charity and Avarice, Chastity and Lechery, Peace and Discord; a portal at Laon shows a combat of the Vices and the Virtues; and on the west front of Notre Dame at Paris a graceful figure with bandaged eyes represents the Synagogue, while opposite her is an even lovelier woman, with royal mantle and commanding air—the Church as the Bride of Christ. Christ Himself appears sometimes tender, sometimes terrible; taken down from the cross by His mother; rising from the tomb while near by, in symbol, a lion brings her cubs to life with a breath; or sternly judging the quick and the dead. That Last Judgment is everywhere in the sculpture and painting of the churches; man was never allowed to forget it; and here, too, only one intercessor could be relied upon to win forgiveness for his sins. So in the sculpture, as in the litanies, Mary took the leading place, the mother of infinite mercy, who would not let her Son take too literally those awful words about the many called, the few chosen.

There is a depth of feeling in this Gothic sculpture, a variety and energy of life, a sympathy with all the forms of the plant and animal world, a tenderness, gentleness, and grace, a miracle of stone revealing not flesh but the soul, that move and satisfy us when the bodily excellence of Greek statuary has lost—perhaps through our aging—something of its traditional lure. Beside the living figures of medieval faith the heavy gods of the Parthenon pediment seem cold and dead. Gothic sculpture is technically deficient; there is nothing in it that can match the perfection of the Parthenon frieze, or the handsome gods and sensuous goddesses of Praxiteles, or even the matrons and senators of the Ara Pacis at Rome; and doubtless those comely ephebi and pliant Aphrodites once meant the joy of healthy life and love. But the prejudices of our native creed, remembering its loveliness and forgetting its terror, bring us back again and again to the great cathedrals, and tip the scales to the *Beau Dieu* of Amiens, the Smiling Angel of Reims, and the Virgin of Chartres.

As the skill of the medieval sculptor grew, he aspired to free his art from architecture, and produce works that could please the increasingly secular taste of princes and prelates, nobles and *bourgeoisie*. In England the "marblers" of Purbeck, using the excellent material quarried in that Dorsetshire promontory, earned high repute in the thirteenth century for ready-made shafts and capitals, and for the recumbent effigies they carved on the sarcophagi of the affluent dead. About 1292 William Torel, a London goldsmith, cast in bronze the images of Henry III and his daughter-in-law Eleanor of Castile for their marble tombs in Westminster Abbey; these are as fine as any bronze work of the age. Remarkable schools of sculpture gathered in this period at Liége, Hildesheim, and Naumburg; and some unknown master, about 1240, made the strong and simple figures—with magnificent drapery— of Henry the Lion and his lioness in the cathedral of Brunswick. France led Europe in the quality of her Romanesque (twelfth-century) and Gothic (thirteenth-century) statuary; but most of it is integrated with her cathedrals, and is best studied there.

Sculpture in Italy was not so intimately bound up with architecture, the commune, and the guild as in France; and there, in the thirteenth century, we begin to get individual artists whose personality dominates their work and preserves their names. Niccolò Pisano embodied a diversity of influences fused into a unique synthesis. Born in Apulia about 1225, he enjoyed the stimulating air of Frederick II's regime; there, apparently, he studied the remains and restorations of classic art.[26] Moving to Pisa, he inherited the Romanesque tradition, and heard of the Gothic style then at its apex in France. When he carved a pulpit for Pisa's baptistery he took for his model a Roman sarcophagus of Hadrian's time. He was deeply moved by the firm but graceful lines of the classic forms; though his pulpit showed Romanesque and Gothic arches, most of its figures bore Roman features and dress; the face and robes of Mary in the panel of the Presentation were those of a Roman matron; and in one corner a nude athlete proclaimed the spirit of ancient Greece. Jealous of this masterpiece, Siena (1265) engaged Niccolò, his son Giovanni, and his pupil Arnolfo di Cambio to carve a still finer pulpit for the cathedral. They succeeded. Standing on columns with Gothic flowered capitals, this pulpit of white marble repeated the themes of the Pisan work, with a crowded panel of the Crucifixion. Here the Gothic influence won over the classical; but in the feminine figures that crowned the columns the antique mood found voice in the frank portrayal of rosy health. As if to underscore his classic sentiments, Niccolò chiseled upon the tomb of the ascetic St. Dominic at Bologna virile forms in pagan style, full of the joy of life. In 1271 he joined his son and Arnolfo to carve the marble font still standing in the public square of Perugia. He died seven years later, still relatively young; but in one lifetime he had made straight the way for Donatello and the rebirth of classic sculpture in the Renaissance.

His son Giovanni Pisano (c. 1240–c. 1320) rivaled him in influence, and surpassed him in technical skill. In 1271 Pisa commissioned Giovanni to build a cemetery fit for men who were then dividing the western Mediterranean with Genoa. Holy earth was brought from Mt. Calvary for the Campo Santo, or Sacred Field; around a grassy rectangle the artist raised graceful arches in mingled Romanesque and Gothic styles; masterpieces of sculpture were brought in to adorn the cloisters, and the Campo Santo remained a monument to Giovanni Pisano until the Second World War shattered half its arches into a neglected ruin.* When the Pisans were defeated by the Genoese (1284) they could no longer afford Giovanni; he went to Siena, and helped to design and execute the sculpture of the cathedral façade. In 1290 he chiseled some reliefs for the bizarre face of the Orvieto Cathedral. Thence he returned north to Pistoia, and carved for the church of Sant' Andrea a pulpit less virile than his father's at Pisa, but excelling it in naturalness and grace; this, indeed, is the loveliest product of Gothic sculpture in Italy.

The third member of this famous trio, Arnolfo di Cambio (c. 1232–c. 1300), continued the Gothic style under the patronage of the popes, several of whom had a French background. At Orvieto he shared in cutting the façade, and made a handsome sarcophagus for Cardinal de Braye. In 1296, with the multidextrous versatility of Renaissance artists, he designed, and began to execute, three of the glories of Florence: the cathedral of Santa Maria del Fiore, the church of Santa Croce, and the Palazzo Vecchio.

But with Arnolfo and these works we pass from sculpture to architecture. All the arts had now returned to life and health; the old skills were not only restored, but were breeding new ventures and techniques with almost reckless fertility. The arts were united as never before or since—in the same enterprise and the same man. Everything had been prepared for the culminating medieval art that would combine them all in perfect co-operation, and would give its name to a style and an age.

---

* The Campo Santo is being restored.

CHAPTER XXXII

The Gothic Flowering

1095-1300

I. THE CATHEDRAL

WHY did Western Europe build so many churches in the three centuries after 1000? What need was there, in a Europe with hardly a fifth of its present population, for temples so vast that they are now rarely filled even on the holiest days? How could an agricultural civilization afford to build such costly edifices, which a wealthy industrialism can barely maintain?

The population was small, but it believed; it was poor, but it gave. On holydays, or in pilgrimage churches, the worshipers were so numerous, said Suger of St. Denis, that "women were forced to run toward the altar on the heads of men as a pavement"; [1] the great abbot was raising funds to build his masterpiece, and could be forgiven a little exaggeration. In towns like Florence, Pisa, Chartres, York it was desirable on occasion to gather the entire population into one edifice. In populous monasteries the abbey church had to accommodate monks and nuns and laity. Relics had to be guarded in special shrines, with room for intimate devotion, and a spacious sanctuary was needed for major rituals. Side altars were required in abbeys and cathedrals whose many priests were expected to say Mass every day; a separate altar or chapel for each favored saint might incline his ear to petitioners; and Mary had to have a "Lady Chapel" if the whole cathedral was not hers.

The construction was financed largely by the accumulated funds of the episcopal see. In addition the bishop solicited gifts from kings, nobles, communes, guilds, parishes, and individuals. The communes were stirred to a wholesome rivalry, in which the cathedral became the symbol and challenge of their wealth and power. Indulgences were offered to those who contributed; relics were carried about the diocese to stimulate giving; and generosity might be prodded by an occasional miracle. [2] Competition for building funds was keen; bishops objected to collections made in their dioceses for undertakings in another; in some cases, however, bishops from many parts, even from foreign lands, sent aid to an enterprise, as at Chartres. Though some of these appeals verged on pressure, they hardly rivaled the intensity of the influences mobilized for the public financing of a modern war. The cathedral chapters exhausted their own funds, and almost bankrupted the French Church, in the Gothic ecstasy. The people themselves did not feel exploited when they contributed; they hardly missed the mite they individually gave; and for that mite they received, as a collective achievement and pride, a home for their worship, a meeting place for their community, a school of letters for their children, a school of arts and crafts for their guilds, and a Bible in stone whereby they might contemplate, in statue and picture, the story of their faith. The house of the people was the house of God.

Who designed the cathedrals? If architecture is the art of designing and beautifying a building and directing its construction, we must reject, for Gothic, the old view that the priests or monks were the architects. Their function was to formulate their needs, conceive a general plan, secure a location, and raise funds. Before 1050 it was usual for the clergy, especially the Cluniac monks, to design and superintend as well as to plan; but for the great cathedrals—all after 1050—it was found necessary to engage professional architects who, with rare exceptions, were neither monks nor priests. The architect would not receive that title till 1563; his medieval name was "master builder," sometimes "master mason"; and these terms reveal his origin. He began as an artisan physically engaged in the work that he directed. In the thirteenth century, as wealth permitted greater edifices and specialization, the master builder was one who—no longer sharing in the physical work —submitted designs and competitive estimates, accepted contracts, made ground plans and working drawings, procured materials, hired and paid artists and artisans, and supervised the construction from beginning to end. We know the names of many such architects after 1050—of 137 Gothic architects in medieval Spain alone. Some of them inscribed their names on their buildings, and a few wrote books about their craft. Villard de Honnecourt (c. 1250) left an album of architectural notes and sketches made on the travels that he undertook, in the practice of his profession, from Laon and Reims to Lausanne and Hungary.

The artists who did the more delicate work—who carved the figures and reliefs, or painted the windows or the walls, or decorated the altar or the choir—were not distinguished from the artisans by any special name; the artist was a master artisan, and every industry strove to be an art. Much of the work was distributed by contract among the guilds to which artists and artisans alike belonged. The unskilled labor was provided by serfs or hired migratory workers; and when time pressed, the government conscripted men —even skilled artisans—to complete the task.[3] Hours of labor were from sunrise to sunset in winter, from a little after sunrise to a little before sundown in summer, with time allowed for a substantial meal at noon. English architects, in 1275, received twelve pence ($12) a day, with traveling expenses and occasional gifts.

The ground plan of the cathedral was still essentially that of the Roman basilica: a longitudinal nave terminating in a sanctuary and an apse, and rising above and between two aisles to a roof supported by walls and colonnades. By a complex but fascinating evolution this simple basilica became first the Romanesque, and, then the Gothic, cathedral. The nave and aisles were cut by a transept—a transverse nave—giving the plan the figure of a Latin cross. The ground area was enlarged by rivalry or devotion until Notre Dame at Paris covered 63,000 square feet, Chartres or Reims 65,000, Amiens 70,000, Cologne 90,000, St. Peter's 100,000. The Christian church was almost always oriented—built with the head or apse pointing eastward—toward Jerusalem.

Hence the main portal was in the west façade, whose special decoration received the light of the setting sun. In the great cathedrals each portal was an archway with "recessed orders": i.e., the innermost arch was topped with a larger arch overlapping outward, and this again with a larger arch, until there might be as many as eight such overreaching layers or "orders," the whole forming an expanding shell. A similar "subordination of orders," or gradation of parts, enhanced the beauty of nave arches and window jambs. Each order or stone band of the compound arch could receive statuary or other sculptural ornament, so that the portal, above all in the west front, became a profuse chapter in the stone book of Christian lore.

The dignity of the west façade was heightened by flanking it with towers. Towers are as old as the records of history. In Romanesque and Gothic they were used not only to house bells, but to support the lateral pressure of the façade and the longitudinal pressure of the aisles. In Normandy and England a third tower had many windows, or was largely open at the base, and served as a "lantern" to give a natural light to the center of the church. Gothic architects, enamored of verticality, aimed to add a spire to every tower; funds or skill or spirit failed; some spires fell, as at Beauvais; Notre Dame, Amiens, and Reims received no spires, Chartres only two of its intended three, Laon one of five—and that was destroyed in the Revolution. As the spire pointed the landscapes of the North, so the campanile or bell tower dominated the cities of Italy. There they were usually separate from the church, like the Leaning Tower of Pisa, or Giotto's campanile at Florence. Possibly they took some hints from Moslem minarets; in turn they spread their style into Palestine and Syria; and they became the civic belfries of the northern towns.

Within the church the central aisle, if its flanking colonnades supported arches curving to meet across the ceiling vault, looked like the inner hull of an inverted ship, whence its name of nave. The full impression of its length was sometimes weakened, particularly in England, by a marble or iron grille, beautifully carved or cast, thrown across the nave to protect the sanctuary from lay intrusion during services. In the sanctuary were choir stalls, always works of art; two pulpits, sometimes called ambos from the Latin word for *both*; seats for the officiating priests; and the main altar, often displaying an adorned rear screen or reredos. Around the sanctuary, continuing the aisles into the apse, ran an ambulatory, designed to allow processions to make full circuit of the edifice. Beneath the altar some churches, as if recalling the burial chambers of the Roman catacombs, built a crypt to hold the relics of a patron saint, or the bones of the distinguished dead.

The central problem of Romanesque and Gothic architecture was how to support the roof. Early Romanesque churches had wooden ceilings, usually of well-seasoned oak; such timbers, if properly ventilated and yet guarded from damp, would last indefinitely; so the south transept of Winchester Cathedral still has its eleventh-century ceiling of wood. The disadvantage of such structures lay in the danger of fires, which, once ignited, were hard to reach. By the twelfth century nearly all major churches had ceilings of masonry. The weight of these roofs determined the evolution of medieval European architecture. Much of this weight had to be borne by the columns that flanked the nave. These had therefore to be strengthened or multiplied; and this was done by combining several columns into a cluster, or replacing them by massive piers of masonry. The column, cluster, or pier was crowned with a capital, perhaps also with an impost to provide a larger surface to bear the superincumbent weight. From each pier or column cluster rose a fan of masonry arches: a transverse arch thrown athwart the nave to the opposite pier; another transverse arch crossing over the aisle to a pier in the wall; two longitudinal arches to the next pier forward and the next to the rear; two diagonal arches connecting the pier with diagonally opposite piers across the nave; and perhaps two diagonal arches to diagonally opposite piers across the aisle. Usually each arch had its own individual support on the impost or capital of the pier. Better still, each might be continued in unbroken line to the ground to form a component of a column cluster or compound pier; the vertical effect so produced was among the fairest features of the Romanesque and Gothic styles. Each quadrangle of piers in nave or aisle constituted a "bay," from which the arches rose in graceful inward curvature to form a section of the vault. Externally this ceiling was covered by a gabled roof of wood, itself hidden and shielded by slate or tiles.

The vault became the crowning achievement of medieval architecture. The principle of the arch allowed a greater space to be spanned than had been practical with timbered ceiling or architrave. The nave could now be widened to harmonize with greater length; the widened nave required for proportion a greater height; this allowed the raising of the level at which the arches sprang inward from piers or walls; and this further prolongation of the direct shaft again enhanced the breath-taking verticality of the cathedral lines. The vault became a clearer harmony when its groins—the lines where the masonry arches met—were edged with "ribs" of brick or stone. These ribs in turn led to a major improvement in structure and style: the masons learned to begin the vault by erecting one rib at a time on an easily movable "centering" or wooden frame; they filled in with light masonry, one at a time, the triangles between each pair of ribs; this thin web of masonry was made concave, thereby shifting most of its weight to the ribs; and the ribs were made strong to channel the downward pressure to specific points—the piers of nave or wall. The groined and ribbed vault became the distinctive feature of medieval architecture at its height.

The problem of supporting the superstructure was further met by building the nave higher than the aisles; the roof of the aisle, with the outer wall, thus served as a buttress for the vault of the nave; and if the aisle itself was vaulted its ribbed arches would channel half their weight inward to counter the outward pressure of the central vault at the weakest points of the nave supports. At the same time, that part of the nave which rose beyond the roofs of the aisles became a clerestory or clearstory, whose unimpeded windows would illuminate the nave. The aisles themselves were usually divided into two or three stories, of which the uppermost constituted a gallery, and the second a triforium so called because the arched spaces by which it faced the nave were normally divided by two columns into "three doors." In Eastern churches the women were expected to worship there, leaving the nave to the men.

So, stage by stage, through ten or twenty or a hundred years, the cathedral rose, defying gravity to glorify God. When it was ready for use it was dedicated in a ceremonious ritual that brought together high prelates and dignitaries, pilgrims and sightseers, and all the townsfolk except the village atheist. Years more would be spent in finishing exterior and interior, and adding a thousand embellishments. For many centuries the people would read on its portals, windows, capitals, and walls the sculptured or painted history and legends of the faith—the story of the Creation, the Fall of Man and the Last Judgment, the lives of the prophets and patriarchs, the sufferings and miracles of the saints, the moral allegories of the animal world, the dogmas of the theologians, even the abstractions of the philosophers; all would be there, in a vast stone encyclopedia of Christianity. When he died, the good Christian would want to be buried near those walls, where demons would be loath to roam. Generation after generation would come to pray in the cathedral; generation after generation would file out from the church into the tombs. The gray cathedral would look upon their coming and their passing with the silent calm of stone, until, in the greatest death of all, the creed itself would die, and those sacred walls would be surrendered to omnivorous time, or be ravished to raise new temples to new gods.

II. CONTINENTAL ROMANESQUE: 1066–1200

We should misjudge the variety of Western architecture in the twelfth and thirteenth centuries if we allowed the foregoing sketch of cathedral structure to stand as valid for all Latin Christendom. In Venice the Byzantine influence continued; St. Mark's added ever new decorations, pinnacles, and spoils, but always in the manner of Constantinople crossed with that of Baghdad. Probably through Venice, perhaps through Genoa or Marseille, the Byzantine style of domes placed with pendentives upon a Greco-cruciform base entered France and appeared in the churches of St. Étienne and St. Front at Périgueux, and in the cathedrals of Cahors and Angoulême. In 1172, when Venice decided to restore and enlarge the Palace of the Doges, she took a medley of styles—Roman, Lombard, Byzantine, Arabic—and united them in a masterpiece that Villehardouin in 1202 thought *moult riche et biaux*, and which still remains the chief glory of the Grand Canal.

No definition of an architectural style has ever escaped exceptions; the works of man, like those of nature, resent generalizations, and flaunt their individuality in the face of every rule. Let us accept the round arch, thick walls and piers, narrow windows, attached buttresses or none, and predominantly horizontal lines, as characterizing Romanesque; and let us keep an open mind for deviations.

Almost a century after the foundation of its *duomo*, Pisa commissioned Diotisalvi to erect a baptistery across a square from the cathedral (1152). He adopted a circular plan, faced the structure with marble, disfigured it with blank arcades, encompassed it with colonnades, and crowned it with a dome that might have been perfect but for its conical cupola. Behind the cathedral Bonanno of Pisa and William of Innsbruck raised the Leaning Tower as a campanile (1174). It repeated the style of the cathedral façade— a series of superimposed Romanesque arcades, with the eighth story housing the bells. The Tower sank on the south side after three stages had been built upon a foundation only ten feet deep, and the architects tried to offset this by inclining the later stories toward the north. In a height of 179 feet the Tower now deviates 16½ feet from the perpendicular—an increase of one foot between 1828 and 1910.

Italian monks migrating into France, Germany, and England brought Romanesque fashions in their train. Perhaps because of them most French monasteries were Romanesque, so that in France Romanesque has the second name of the monastic style. The Benedictines of Cluny built a magnificent abbey there (1089–1131), with four side aisles, seven towers, and such an array of zoological sculpture as roused St. Bernard's ire.

> In the cloisters, under the eyes of the monks who read, what do these ridiculous monsters seek to do? What do these unclean monkeys

mean, these dragons, centaurs, tigers, and lions . . . these soldiers fighting, these hunting scenes? . . . What business here have these creatures
who are half beast and half man? . . . We can see here several bodies
under one head, and several heads on one body. Here we observe a
quadruped with the head of a serpent, there a fish with the head of a
quadruped; here an animal is a horse in front and a goat behind.[4]

The abbey of Cluny was destroyed in the *Jacqueries* of the Revolution, but
its architectural influence spread to its 2000 affiliated monasteries. Southern
France is still rich in Romanesque churches; the Roman tradition was strong
there in art as in law, and long resisted the "barbaric" Gothic that came down
from the North. Marble was rare in France, and the cathedrals atoned
for lack of external brilliance by a profusion of sculpture. Startling, in the
churches of southern France, is the expressionism of the statuary—the resolve
to convey a feeling instead of copying a scene; so the figure of St. Peter on
a portal of the abbey of Moissac (1150), with its tortured face and arachnid
legs, must have aimed not so much to accentuate structural lines as to impress and terrify the imagination. That the sculptors deliberately distorted
such figures appears from the minute realism of the foliage in the Moissac
capitals. The best of these French Romanesque façades is the west portal of
St. Trophime's at Arles (1152), crowded with animals and saints.

Spain raised a lordly Romanesque shrine in the church of Santiago de
Compostela (1078–1211), whose Portico de la Gloria contains the finest
Romanesque sculpture in Europe. Coimbra, soon to be the university city
of Portugal, built a handsome Romanesque cathedral in the twelfth century.
But it was in its more northern migrations that Romanesque reached its
apogee. The Île de France rejected it, but Normandy welcomed it; its rough
power accorded well with a people recently Viking and still buccaneers. As
early as 1048 the Benedictine monks of Jumièges, near Rouen, built an abbey
reputedly larger than any edifice that had been raised in Western Europe
since Constantine; the Middle Ages too were proud of size. It was half destroyed by the fanatics of the Revolution, but its surviving façade and towers preserve a bold and virile design. There, indeed, was formed the Norman
style of Romanesque, relying for its effect on mass and structural form
rather than on ornament.

In 1066 William the Conqueror, to expiate the sin of marrying Matilda of
Flanders, provided funds for a church of St. Étienne at Caen, known as the
Abbaye aux Hommes; and Matilda, perhaps with like motives, financed
there the church of La Trinité, known as the Abbaye aux Dames. About
1135, in a restoration of the Abbaye aux Hommes, each bay of the nave was
divided with an extra column on each side, bound with a transverse arch;
in this way the usual "quadripartite" became a "sexpartite" vault, a form
that proved popular throughout the twelfth century.

From France the Romanesque style passed into Flanders, raising a handsome cathedral at Tournai (1066); and from Flanders, France, and Italy it entered Germany. Mainz had begun its cathedral in 1009, Trier in 1016, Speyer in 1030; these were rebuilt before 1300, still in the rounded style. Cologne built in this period the church of St. Maria im Kapitol, famous for its interior, and the church of St. Maria, famous for its towers; both buildings were destroyed in the Second World War. The cathedral of Worms, dedicated in 1171 and restored in the nineteenth century, is still a monument of Rhenish Romanesque. These churches had an apse at each end, and cared little for sculptured façades; they adorned their exterior with colonnades, and buttressed the towers with slender turrets of very pleasing form. The non-German critic praises these Rhenish shrines with patriotic moderation, but they have a charming *gemütlich* beauty quite in harmony with the inviting loveliness of the Rhine.

III. THE NORMAN STYLE IN ENGLAND: 1066–1200

When Edward the Confessor came to the throne in 1042 he brought with him many friends and ideas from the Normandy in which he had spent his youth. Westminster Abbey began in his reign as a Norman church with round arches and heavy walls; that structure was buried under the Gothic abbey of 1245, but it inaugurated an architectural revolution. The rapid replacement of Saxon or Danish by Norman bishops ensured the triumph of the Norman style in England. The Conqueror and his successors lavished upon the bishops much of the wealth confiscated from Englishmen who had not appreciated conquest; the churches became instruments of mental pacification; soon the Norman English bishops matched the Norman English nobles in wealth; and cathedrals and castles multiplied as allies in the conquered land. "Nearly all tried to rival one another in sumptuous buildings in the Norman style," wrote William of Malmesbury; "for the nobles felt that day lost which they had not celebrated with some deed of magnificence."[5] Never had England seen such a frenzy of building.

Norman English architecture was a variation of the Romanesque theme. It followed French exemplars in supporting the roof by round arches on fat piers, and by heavy walls—though its ceilings were usually of wood; when the vault was of stone the walls were from eight to ten feet thick. It was largely monastic, and rose in out-of-the-way places rather than in cities. It used very little external statuary, fearing the effect of a damp climate, and even the capitals of the columns were simply or poorly carved; in sculpture England never caught up with the Continent. But not many towers could match the mighty structures that dominated the Norman castles, or guarded the façade—or covered the transept crossing—of the Norman church.

Hardly any ecclesiastical architecture in England is still purely Romanesque. Most cathedrals underwent a Gothic lifting of arch and vault in the thirteenth century, and only the basic Norman form remains. In 1067 fire destroyed the old cathedral of Canterbury; Lanfranc rebuilt it (1070-7) along the lines of his former Abbaye aux Hommes at Caen; nothing survives of Lanfranc's cathedral except a few patches of masonry where Becket fell. In 1096-1110 the priors Ernulf and Conrad built a new choir and crypt; they kept the round arch, but channeled the strains to points supported by external buttresses. The transition to Gothic had begun.

York Minster,* built in 1075 on a Norman plan, disappeared in 1291 under a Gothic edifice. Lincoln Cathedral, originally Norman (1075), was rebuilt in Gothic after the earthquake of 1185; but the two great towers and sumptuously carved portals of the west façade survive from the Norman church, and reveal the skill and power of the older style. At Winchester the transepts and crypt remain of the Norman cathedral of 1081-1103. Bishop Walkelin built it to receive the flow of pilgrims to the tomb of St. Swithin.† Walkelin appealed to his cousin the Conqueror for timber to roof the enormous nave; William agreed to let him take from Hempage Forest as much wood as he could cut in three days; Walkelin's flock cut down and carried off the entire forest in seventy-two hours. When the cathedral was finished nearly all the abbots and bishops of England attended its consecration; we may readily imagine the competitive stimulus aroused by such an enormous edifice.

Some echo of the scope of Norman building comes down to us when we note that St. Alban's Abbey was begun in 1075, Ely Cathedral in 1081, Rochester in 1083, Worcester in 1084, Old St. Paul's in 1087, Gloucester in 1089, Durham in 1093, Norwich in 1096, Chichester in 1100, Tewkesbury in 1103, Exeter in 1112, Peterborough in 1116, Romsey Abbey in 1120, Fountains Abbey in 1140, St. David's, in Wales, in 1176. These are not names, they are masterpieces; shame bows us at leaving them after a few hours, or dismissing them in a line. All but one were later rebuilt or reclothed in Gothic. Durham is still predominantly Norman, and remains the most impressive Romanesque structure in Europe.

Durham is a little mining town of some 20,000 souls. At a turn of the river Wear a rocky promontory rises; on that strategic elevation stands the gigantic mass of the cathedral, "half church of God, half castle against the Scots."[6] Monks from the island of Lindisfarne, fleeing from Danish raiders, built a stone church there in 995. In 1093 its second Norman bishop, William of St. Carilef, demolished this building, and with incredible courage and

---

* The word *minster*, an abbreviation of *monastery*, should properly be used only for an abbey church; but custom has congealed the phrase "York Minster," though that cathedral was never monastic.

† A ninth-century bishop of Winchester. Legend said that rain had delayed for forty days the transference of his body in 971 to the shrine prepared for it; hence the popular adage that rain on St. Swithin's day (July 15) presages forty days of rain.

mysterious wealth raised the present edifice. The work continued till 1195, so that the cathedral represents the aspiration and labor of a hundred years. The lofty nave is Norman, with a double arcade of round arches resting on uncarved capitals and stout piers. The vault of Durham introduced to England two vital innovations: the groins were ribbed, helping to localize pressures; and the transverse arches were pointed, while the diagonals were round. If the transverse arches had been round, their crowns would not have reached the same height as the diagonals, which are longer, and the apex of the vault would have been a disturbingly uneven line. By lifting the crowns of the transverse arches to a point, they could be made to reach the desired height. This structural consideration, and no esthetic aim, apparently fathered the most prominent feature of the Gothic style.

In 1175 Bishop Pudsey added at the west end of Durham Cathedral an attractive porch or narthex, which for some unknown reason received the name of *galilee*. Here—where lies the tomb of the Venerable Bede—the arches are round, but the slender columns approach the Gothic form. Early in the thirteenth century the vault of the choir collapsed; in rebuilding it the architects supported the nave arcade with flying buttresses hidden in the triforium. In 1240–70 a Chapel of the Nine Altars was added to hold the remains of St. Cuthbert; and in that shrine the arches were pointed, and the transition to Gothic was complete.

IV. THE EVOLUTION OF GOTHIC

Gothic architecture might be defined as a localization and balancing of structural strains, emphasizing vertical lines, ribbed vaults, and pointed forms. It evolved through the solution of mechanical problems set by ecclesiastical needs and artistic aspiration. Fear of fire led to vaults of stone or brick; heavier ceilings necessitated thick walls and clumsy piers; the ubiquity of downward pressure limited window space, the thick walls shadowed the narrow windows, and the interior was left too dark for northern climes. The invention of the ribbed vault lessened the ceiling weight, allowing slenderer columns and localized strains; the concentration and balancing of pressures gave the building stability without heaviness; the localization of support through buttresses allowed longer windows in thinner walls; the windows offered inviting scope for the already existing art of stained glass; and the stone frames surmounting compound windows aroused the new art of pierced design or tracery. The arches of the vault became pointed to allow arches of uneven length to reach their crowns at an even height; and other arches, and window forms, became pointed to harmonize with the arches of the vault. Better ways of bearing pressure permitted higher naves; the towers and spires and pointed arches emphasized verticality of line, and produced the soaring flight and buoyant grace of the Gothic style. All these together made the Gothic cathedral the supreme achievement and expression of the soul of man.

But it is presumptuous to concentrate a century of architectural evolution into a paragraph. Some steps in the development invite calmer scrutiny. The problem of reconciling light grace with stable strength was better solved by Gothic than by any architecture before our time; and we do not know how long our own bold challenges to gravity will escape the leveling jealousy of the earth. Neither did the Gothic architect always succeed; Chartres is still without a crack, but the choir of Beauvais Cathedral crumbled twelve years after it was built. The essential feature of the Gothic style was the functional rib: the transverse and diagonal arch ribs rising from each bay of the nave united to form a light and graceful web upon which a thin vault of masonry could rest. Each bay of the nave became a structural unit, bearing the weight and thrusts brought down by the arches rising from its piers, and supported by counter pressures from the corresponding bays of the aisles, and by outer buttresses applied to the walls at the inward springing of each transverse arch.

The buttress was an old device. Many pre-Gothic churches had pillars of masonry externally added at points of special strain. A flying buttress, however, carries a thrust or strain over open space to a base support and to the ground. Some Norman cathedrals used half arches in the triforium to prop up the arches of the nave; but such internal buttresses reached the nave wall at too low a point, and gave no strength to the clerestory where the explosive pressure of the vault was most intense. To apply support at this high point it was necessary to take the buttress out of its hiding place. let it rise from the solid ground and throw it through open space over the aisle roof to directly sustain the clerestory wall. The earliest known use of such an external flying buttress was in the cathedral of Noyon about 1150.[7] By the end of that century it had become a favorite device. It had serious faults: sometimes it gave the impression of a structural skeleton, a scaffolding negligently unremoved, or the makeshift afterthought of a designer whose building sagged; "the cathedral had crutches," said Michelet. The Renaissance would reject the flying buttress as an unsightly obstruction, and would support by other means such burdens as St. Peter's dome. The Gothic architect thought differently; he liked to expose the lines and mechanisms of his art; he developed a fondness for buttresses, and perhaps multiplied them beyond need; he compounded them, so that they would give support at two or more points, or to one another; he beautified their stabilizing piers with pinnacles; and sometimes, as at Reims, he proved that at least one angel could stand on the point of a pinnacle.

The balancing of strains was far more vital to Gothic than the ogive or pointed arch, but this became the outward and visible sign of an inward grace. The pointed arch was a very old form. At Diarbekr in Turkey it appears on a Roman colonnade of uncertain date. The earliest dated example is at Qasr-ibn-Wardan in Syria in 561.[8] The form is found in the Dome of the Rock and the Mosque of el-Aqsa at Jerusalem in the seventh century; on a Nilometer in Egypt in 861; in the Mosque of Ibn Tulun at Cairo in 879; it was in frequent use among Persians, Arabs, Copts, and Moors before its first appearance in Western Europe in the second half of the eleventh century.[9] It may have come to Southern France from Moslem Spain or through pilgrims returning from the East; or it may have arisen spontaneously in the West to meet mechanical problems in architectural design. It should be noted, however, that the problem of bringing arches of uneven length to an even crown could be solved without the ogive by "stilting" the shorter arches, i.e., raising their point of inward springing from pier or wall. This, too, had an esthetic effect, as emphasizing vertical lines; and the device was widely adopted, seldom as a substitute for the pointed arch, often as a helpful accompaniment. The ogive solved a further problem: since the aisles were narrower than the nave, an aisle bay had more length than width, and the crowns of its transverse arches would fall far short of those of its diagonals, unless the transverse arches were either pointed, or stilted so high as to prevent their harmonious inward movement with the diagonals. The ogive offered a similar solution for the difficult task of vaulting with arches of even crown the ambulatory of the apse, where the outer wall was longer than the inner, and each bay formed a trapezoid whose vault could not be forgivably designed without the pointed arch. That this was not at first chosen for its grace appears from the large number of buildings in which it was used to meet these problems, while the round arch continued to be used in windows and portals. Gradually the vertical lift of the ogive, and perhaps a desire for harmonized form, gave the pointed arch the victory. The ninety years of struggle between the round and the pointed arch—from the appearance of the ogive in the Romanesque cathedral of Durham (1104) to the final building of Chartres (1194)—constitute, in French Gothic, the period of the transition style.

The application of the pointed arch to windows created new problems, new solutions, and new charms. The channeling of strains through ribs from vault to piers, and from piers to specific points supported by buttresses, ended the need for thick walls. The space between each point of support and the next bore relatively little pressure; the wall there could be thinned, could even be removed. So large an opening could not be safely fitted with a single pane of glass. The space was therefore divided into two or more pointed windows (lancets), surmounted by an arch of stone; in effect the outer wall, like that of the nave, became a series of arches, an arcade. The four-pointed "shield" of masonry left between the upper ends of the paired and pointed windows and the top of the enclosing stone arch made an ugly blank, and cried out for decoration. About 1170 the architects of France responded with plate tracery; i.e., they pierced this shield in such a way as to leave stone bars or mullions in ornamental designs—circular, cusped, or lobed; and they filled the interstices, as well as the windows, with stained glass. In the thirteenth century the sculptors cut away more and more of the stone, and inserted into the opening little bars of stone carved into cusps or other forms. This bar tracery took on ever more complex paterns, whose predominating lines gave names to styles and periods of Gothic architecture: lancet, geometrical, curvilinear, perpendicular, and flamboyant. Similar processes applied to wall surfaces over the portals produced the great "rose windows," whose radiating tracery generated the term *rayonnant* for the style that began at Notre Dame in 1230 and reached perfection in Reims and Sainte Chapelle. In the Gothic cathedral only the soaring articulation of the vault transcends the beauty of the "rose."

Stone tracery, in the large sense of any piercing of stone in a decorative design, passed from the walls to other parts of the Gothic cathedral—the buttress pinnacles, the gables above the portals, the soffits and spandrels of arches, the triforium arcade, the sanctuary screen, the pulpit and reredos; for the Gothic sculptor, in the joy of his art, could scarcely touch a surface without adorning it. He crowded façades and cornices and towers with apostles, devils, and saints, with the saved and the damned; he cut his fancy into capitals, corbels, moldings, lintels, frets, and jambs; he laughed in stone with the whimsical or terrifying animals that he invented as gargoyles ("little throats") to carry staining rain away from the walls or channel it into the ground through buttresses. Never elsewhere have wealth and skill, piety and lusty humor combined to provide such a feast of ornament as revels in the Gothic cathedral. Undeniably the decoration was sometimes too profuse, the tracery was carried to a fragile excess, the statues and capitals must have been too gaudy with the paint that time has cleansed away. But these are the signs of a vital exuberance, to which almost any fault can be forgiven. Wandering in these jungles and gardens of stone, it dawns upon us that Gothic art, despite its heaven-pointing lines and spires, was an art that loved the earth. Amid these saints proclaiming the vanity of vanities and the terror of the Judgment soon to come, we perceive the unseen but omnipresent medieval artisan, proud of his skill, joyful in his strength, laughing at theologies and philosophies, and drinking with relish, and to the last drop, the bubbling, brimming, lethal cup of life.

V. FRENCH GOTHIC: 1133–1300

Why did the Gothic revolution begin and culminate in France?

The Gothic style was not a virgin birth. A hundred traditions joined in a fertilizing flow: Roman basilicas, arches, vaults, and clerestories; Byzantine themes of ornament; Armenian, Syrian, Persian, Egyptian, Arabic ogives, groined vaults, and clustered piers; Moorish motifs and arabesques; Lombard ribbed vaults and façade towers; the Germanic flair for the humorous and grotesque. . . . But why did these streams of influence converge in France? Italy, as in wealth and heritage the favored country of Western Europe, might have led the Gothic flowering, but she was the prisoner of her classic inheritance. Italy excepted, France was in the twelfth century the richest, and most advanced, nation of the West. She above all others had manned and financed the Crusades, and profited from their cultural stimulus; she led Europe in education, literature, and philosophy; and her craftsmen were conceded to be the best this side of Byzantium. By the time of Philip Augustus (1180–1223) the royal power had triumphed over feudal disunity, and the affluence, power, and intellectual life of France were congregating in the king's own domain—that île de France loosely definable as the region of the middle Seine. Along the Seine, Oise, Marne, and Aisne a fruitful commerce moved, leaving behind it a wealth that turned to stone in cathedrals at Paris, St. Denis, Senlis, Mantes, Noyon, Sòissons, Laon, Amiens, and Reims. The manure of money had prepared the soil for the growth of art.

The first masterpiece of the transition style was the magnificent abbey church of St. Denis, in the Paris suburb of that name. It was the work of one of the most complete and successful personalities in French history. Suger (1081?–1151), Benedictine abbot and regent of France, was a man of refined tastes, who, while living simply, thought it no sin to love beautiful things and to gather them for the adornment of his church. "If the ancient law," he replied to St. Bernard's criticisms, "ordained that cups of gold should be used for libations, and to receive the blood of rams . . . how much rather should we devote gold, precious stones, and the rarest of materials to vessels designed to hold the blood of Our Lord?" [10] So he tells us proudly of the beauty and cost of the gold and silver, the jewels and enamels, the mosaics and stained windows, the rich vestments and vessels, which he gathered or had made for his church. In 1133 he brought together artists and artisans "from all lands" to raise and adorn a new home for France's patron St. Denis, and to house the tombs of the kings of France; he persuaded King Louis VII and the court to contribute the necessary funds; "following our example," he says, "they took the rings from their fingers" to pay for his costly designs.[11] We picture him rising early to superintend the construction, from the felling of the trees that he chose for timbers to the installation of the stained glass whose subjects he had selected and whose inscriptions he had composed. When he dedicated his edifice in 1144 twenty bishops officiated; the King, two queens, and hundreds of knights attended; and Suger might well have felt that he had won a crown more glorious than any king's.

Of his church only parts remain in the present edifice: the west front, two bays of the nave, the chapels of the ambulatory, and the crypt; most of the interior is a reconstruction by Pierre de Montereau between 1231 and 1281. The crypt is Romanesque; the west façade mingles round and pointed arches; its sculptures, mostly from Suger's time, include a hundred figures, many well individualized, and all centering about one of the best conceptions of Christ the Judge in the whole sweep of medieval art.

Twelve years after Suger's death Bishop Maurice de Sully paid him the compliment of bettering his instruction, and Notre Dame de Paris rose on an island in the Seine. Its chronology suggests the immensity of the task: the choir and transepts were built in 1163–82; the nave in 1182–96, the westernmost bays and the towers in 1218–23; the cathedral was finished in 1235. In the original design the triforium was to be Romanesque, but in the completion the whole structure adopted the Gothic style. The west front is unusually horizontal for a Gothic cathedral, but that is because the spires that were meant to top the towers were never built; perhaps for that reason there is a firm and simple dignity in this façade that has led able students to rank it as "the noblest architectural conception of man." [12] The rose windows of Our Lady of Paris are masterpieces of bar tracery and coloring; but they were not meant to be described by words. The sculptures, though injured by time and revolution, represent the finest work in that art between the age of Constantine and the building of Reims Cathedral. In the tympanum over the main portal the Last Judgment is carved with greater calm than in most later renderings of that ubiquitous theme; the Christ is a figure of quiet majesty; and the angel at His right is one of the triumphs of Gothic sculpture. Better still is *La Vierge du trumeau*—the Virgin of the Pillar—on the north portal: here is a new delicacy of treatment, finish of surface, naturalness of drapery; a new ease and grace of stance, with the weight on one foot and the body thereby freed from stiff verticality; in this lovely figure Gothic sculpture almost declared its independence from architecture, and produced a masterpiece quite capable of being taken from its context and standing triumphantly alone. In Notre Dame at Paris the transition was ended, and Gothic came of age.

The story of Chartres illuminates the medieval scene and character. It was a small town fifty-five miles southwest of Paris, just outside the royal domain, a market for the plain of Beauce, the "granary of France." But the Virgin was said to have visited the place in person; the pious lame or blind or sick or bereaved made it a goal of pilgrimage; some were healed or comforted at her shrine; Chartres became a Lourdes. Furthermore, its Bishop Fulbert, a man mingled of goodness, intellect, and faith, made it in the eleventh century a shrine of higher education, *alma mater* to some of the most brilliant figures in early Scholastic philosophy. When Fulbert's ninth-century cathedral burned down in 1020 he set himself at once to rebuild it, and lived long enough to see it finished. This, in turn, was destroyed by fire in 1134. Bishop Theodoric made the construction of a new cathedral a veritable crusade; he aroused such devotion to the task, financial and physical, that in 1144, according to the eye-witness account of Abbot Haimon of Normandy,

> kings, princes, mighty men of the world, puffed up with honors and riches, men and women of noble birth, bound bridles upon their proud and swollen necks, and submitted themselves to wagons which, after the fashion of brute beasts, they dragged with loads of wine, corn, oil, lime, stones, beams, and other things necessary to sustain life or build churches. . . . Moreover, as they draw the wagons we may see this miracle, that although sometimes a thousand men and women . . . are bound in the traces . . . yet they go forward in such silence that no voice, no murmur, is heard. . . . When they pause on the way no words are heard but confessions of guilt, with supplication and pure prayer. . . . The priests preach peace, hatred is soothed, discord is driven away, debts are forgiven, unity is restored.[13]

This cathedral of Bishop Theodoric had hardly been completed (1180) when, in 1194, fire gutted the nave, brought vault and walls to the ground, and left, as scarred survivors, only the subterranean crypt and the west façade with its two towers and spires. We are told that every house in the town was destroyed in that awful conflagration, whose traces are visible on the cathedral today. The discouraged people for a time lost faith in the Virgin, and wished to abandon the town. But the indomitable papal legate Melior told them that the calamity had been sent by God to punish their sins; he commanded them to rebuild their church and their homes; the clergy of the diocese contributed nearly all their income for three years; new miracles were reported of the Virgin of Chartres; faith was rekindled; multitudes came again, as in 1144, to help the paid workers pull the carts and set the stones; funds were contributed by every cathedral in Europe;[14] and by 1224 toil and hope completed the cathedral that makes Chartres again a goal of pilgrimage.

The unknown architect had planned to top with towers not merely the flanks of the west front but also the transept portals and the apse. Only the two façade towers were built. *Le Clocher vieux*—the Old Bell-Tower (1145–70)—rose with its spire to 351 feet at the south end of the façade; it is simple and unadorned, and wins the preference of professional architects.[15] Its northern mate—*Le Clocher neuf*—twice lost its wooden spire by fire; the spire was rebuilt in stone (1506–12) by Jean le Texier in flamboyant Gothic style of crowded and delicate ornament; Fergusson thought it "the most beautifully designed spire on the continent of Europe";[16] but it is generally agreed that so ornate a spire mars the unity of an austere façade.[17]

The fame of Chartres rests on its sculpture and its glass. In this palace of the Virgin live 10,000 carved or pictured personages—men, women, chil-

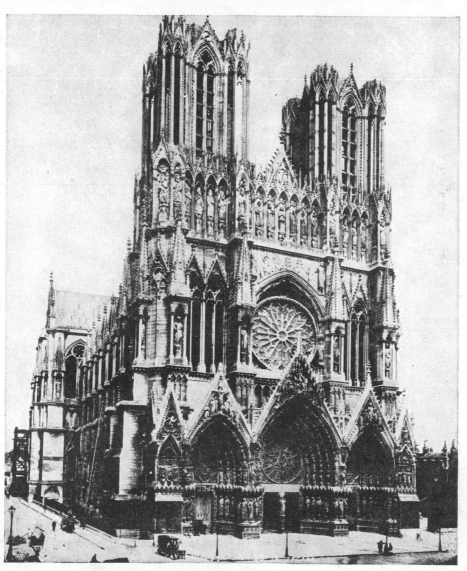

FIG. 26—*Cathedral*
Rheims

FIG. 27—*St. Nicaise Between Two Angels*
Rheims Cathedral

FIG. 28—"*The Annunciation and Visitation*"
Rheims Cathedral

FIG. 29—*Wrought Iron Grille*
Abbey of Ourscamp

FIG. 30—*Cathedral*
Canterbury

FIG. 31—*Hôtel de Ville*
Ypres

FIG. 32—*Cathedral*
Salisbury

FIG. 33—*Cathedral Interior*
Durham

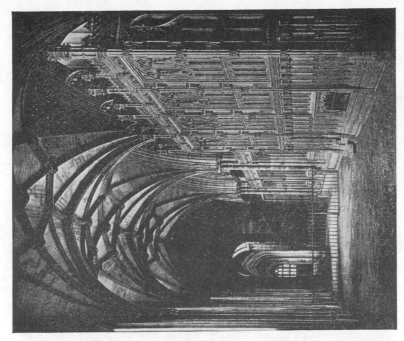

FIG. 34—*Cathedral Interior*
Winchester

FIG. 35—*Westminster Abbey*
London

FIG. 36—*Cathedral*
Strasbourg

Fig. 37—"*The Church*"
Strasbourg Cathedral

Fig. 38—"*The Synagogue*"
Strasbourg Cathedral

FIG. 39—*Saint Elizabeth*
Detail from "The Visitation"
Bamberg Cathedral

FIG. 40—*Mary*
Detail from "The Visitation,"
Bamberg Cathedral

FIG. 41—*Ekkehard and His Wife Uta*
Naumburg Cathedral

Fig. 42—*Rose Façade*
Orvieto Cathedral

FIG. 43—*Façade*
Siena Cathedral

FIG. 44—*Pulpit of Pisano*
Siena Cathedral

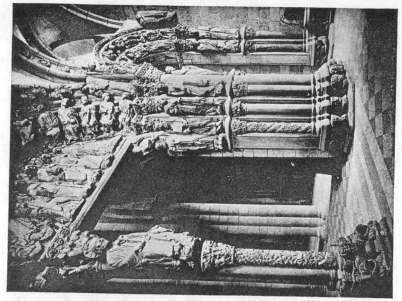

Fig. 46—*Cathedral Interior*
Santiago di Compostela

Fig. 45—*Rear View of Cathedral*
Salamanca

dren, saints, devils, angels, and the Persons of the Trinity. There are 2000 statues in the portals alone; [18] additional statues stand against columns in the interior; visitors who climb the 312 steps to the roof are astonished to see carefully carved life-size figures where none but the vigorous curious can ever notice them. Over the central portal is a splendid Christ, not, as in later façades, sternly judging the dead, but seated in calm majesty amid a happy throng, His hand held out as if to bless the entering worshipers. Attached to the recessed "orders" of the portal arch are nineteen prophets, kings, and queens; they are slender and stiff as befits their station as literally pillars of the church; many are crude and unfinished, perhaps injured or worn; but some of the faces have the philosophic depth, the gentle repose, or the maiden grace, that were to be perfected at Reims.

The transept façades and porches are the fairest in Europe. Each has three portals, flanked and separated by beautifully carved columns and jambs, and almost covered with statues every one of which is so individualized that several have received names from the folk of Chartres. The south porch centers its 783 figures around Christ enthroned on His judgment seat. Here Notre Dame de Chartres is subordinated to her Son; but in compensation she is endowed, as in Albertus Magnus, with all the sciences and philosophy, and in her service, on this portal, appear the Seven Liberal Arts—Pythagoras as Music, Aristotle as Dialectic, Cicero as Rhetoric, Euclid as Geometry, Nicomachus as Arithmetic, Priscian as Grammar, Ptolemy as Astronomy. St. Louis, in the words of his charter of 1259, caused the north porch to be completed "by reason of his particular devotion to the church of Our Lady of Chartres, and for the saving of his soul and the souls of his forefathers." [19] In 1793 the French Revolutionary Assembly defeated by a narrow margin a motion to destroy the statues of Chartres Cathedral in the name of philosophy and the Republic; "philosophy" compromised by chopping off some of the hands.[20] This north porch belongs to the Virgin, and tells her story with reverent affection. The statues here stand out in the round, as fully matured sculpture; the drapery is as graceful and natural as in any Greek carving; the figure of Modesty is French girlhood at its best, where modesty gives to beauty a double power; there is nothing finer in all the history of sculpture. "These statues," said Henry Adams, "are the Aeginetan marbles of French art." [21]

As one enters the cathedral, four impressions mingle: the simple lines of the nave and vault, hardly comparable in size or beauty with the nave of Amiens or Winchester; the ornate choir screen, begun in 1514 by the flamboyant Jean le Texier; the peaceful figure of Christ on a pillar of the south transept, and, suffusing all with soft color, the unequaled stained glass. Here, in 174 windows, are 3884 figures from legend and history, ranging from cobblers to kings. It is medieval France seen through the richest colors ever developed—dark reds, soft blues, emerald greens, saffron, yellow, brown, white; here above all is the glory of Chartres. We must not look to these windows for realistic portraiture; the figures are ungainly, sometimes absurd; Adam's head, in the medallion of the Expulsion from Eden, is painfully askew, and the bilateral charms of Eve could hardly divert the worshiper to concupiscence. It seemed to these artists enough that the pictures told a story while the colors fused in the viewer's vision, and in their mingling painted the cathedral air. Excellent in design is the window of the Prodigal Son; famous for color and line the window of the symbolic Tree of Jesse; but better than all the rest is *Notre Dame de la belle verrière*—"Our Lady of the Beautiful Window." Tradition holds that this lovely panel was rescued from the fire of 1194.[22]

Standing at the crossing of transept and nave, one may see the major roses of Chartres. In the main façade the central rose spans forty-four feet, almost as wide as the nave that it surveys; some have called it the finest work in glass known to history.[23] Flooding the north transept is the "Rose of France," given by Louis IX and Blanche of Castile, and dedicated to the Virgin; facing it across the church is the "Rose of Dreux," in the south transept façade, given by Blanche's enemy, Pierre Mauclerc of Dreux, and opposing Mary's Son to Blanche's Mother of God. Thirty-five lesser roses and twelve still smaller roselets complete the roster of Chartres' circular glass. The modern spirit, too hurried and nervous to achieve patient and placid perfection, stands in wonder before works that must be ascribed not to the genius of singular individuals, but to the spirit and industry of a people, a community, an epoch, and a faith.

We have taken Chartres as typifying mature or *rayonnant* Gothic, and we must not indulge in similar tarrying over Reims, Amiens, and Beauvais. But who could pass hurriedly by the west front of Reims? If the original spires still rose from the towers, that façade would be the noblest work of man. Astonishing are the unity and harmony of style and parts in a structure raised by six generations. The cathedral finished by Hincmar in 841 was burned down in 1210; on the first anniversary of that fire a new cathedral was begun, designed by Robert de Coucy and Jean d'Orbais to be fit for the crowning of France's kings. After forty years of labor, funds ran out; the work was stopped (1251), and the great church was not completed till 1427. A fire in 1480 destroyed the spires; the savings of the cathedral were used up in repairing the main structure, and the spires were not rebuilt. In the First World War shells smashed several buttresses, and tore huge gaps in roof and vault; the outer roof was destroyed by fire, and many statues were ruined. Other figures have been mutilated by fanatics, or by the erosion of centuries. History is a duel between art and time.

The sculptures of Reims, like its façade, mark the acme of Gothic art. Some are archaically crude; those in the central doorway are unsurpassed; and at various points on the portals, the pinnacles, the interior, we come upon figures that have almost the finish of Periclean statuary. Some, like the Virgin in the pillar of the central portal, are perhaps too graceful, and suggest a weakening of Gothic force; but the Virgin of the Purification at the left of the same portal, and the Virigin of the Visitation at the right, are among those achievements, of conception and execution, before which tongue and pen are stilled. More renowned, but not so near perfection, are the smiling angels in the Annunciation group of this façade. How different those joyous faces are from the St. Paul of the north portal!—itself one of the most powerful portraits ever carved in stone.

The sculptures of Amiens Cathedral excel those of Reims in elegance and finish, but fall short of them in dignity of conception and depth of revelation. Here on the western porch is the famous *Beau Dieu*, a little formal and lifeless after the living figures of Reims; here also is St. Firmin, no frightened ascetic but a firm, calm man, who never doubted right would triumph; and here is a Virgin holding her child in her arms with all the absorbed tenderness of young motherhood. On the south portal the *Vierge dorée*, the Golden Virgin, smiles as she watches her child playing with a ball; she is a bit prettified, but too gracious to deserve Ruskin's ungallant epithet, the "soubrette of Picardy." Pleasant it is to see how the Gothic sculptors, after a century of serving theology, discovered men and women, and carved the joy of life on church façades. The Church, which also had learned to enjoy the earth, winked at the discovery, but thought it wise to have a Last Judgment on the main façade.

Amiens Cathedral was built in 1220–88 by a succession of architects— Robert de Luzarches, Thomas de Cormont, and his son Regnault. The towers were not completed till 1402. The interior is the most successful of Gothic naves; it rises to a vault 140 feet high, and seems rather to be drawing the church upward than to be bearing a weight. Continuous shafts from ground to vault bind the three-storied arcades of the nave into a majestic unity; the vaulting of the apse is a triumph of harmonious design over baffling irregularities; and the heart stands still at first sight of the clerestory windows and the roses of transepts and façade. But the nave seems too narrow for its height, the walls too frail for the roof; an element of insecurity enters into the awe aroused by this buoyant stone.

In Beauvais Cathedral this vaulting ambition of Gothic overleaped itself and reached its fated fall. The magnificence of Amiens stirred the citizens of Beauvais to jealousy. In 1227 they began to build, and vowed to raise the vault of their shrine thirteen feet higher than Amiens'. They brought the choir to the promised height; but hardly had they roofed it when it fell. In 1272 a recuperating generation built the choir again as high as before, and in 1284 it fell again. Once more they built the choir, this time to 157 feet from the ground; then their funds ran out, and they left the church for two centuries without transepts or nave. In 1500, when France had at last recovered from the Hundred Years' War, the gigantic transepts were begun; and in 1552—to top the spire of St. Peter's in Rome—a lantern tower was raised over the transept cross to a height of 500 feet. In 1573 this tower collapsed, and brought down with it large sections of the transepts and the choir. The brave Beauvaisois at last compromised: they repaired the choir to its precarious pitch, but never added a nave. Beauvais Cathedral is therefore all head and no body; externally two rich transept façades and an apse engulfed in buttresses; internally a cavernous choir aglow with magnificent stained glass. If, ran an old French saying, one could combine the choir of Beauvais with the nave of Amiens, the façade of Reims, and the spires of Chartres, one would have a perfect Gothic cathedral.

In later ages men would look back to that thirteenth century and wonder what fountain of wealth and faith had poured out such glory upon the earth. For no man can know what France accomplished in that century—besides her universities, her poets, her philosophers, and her Crusades—unless he stands in person before one after another of the Gothic audacities that can here be only names: Notre Dame and Chartres and Reims and Amiens and Beauvais; Bourges (1195–1390) with its vast nave and four aisles and famed glass and lovely sculptured Angel with the Scales; Mont St. Michel with its marvel of a monastery (*La Merveille*, 1204–50) set in a fortress towering on an island rock off the coast of Normandy; Coutances (1208–1386) with its noble spires; Rouen (1201–1500) with its ornate *Portail des libraires*; and Sainte Chapelle in Paris—a "jewel box" of Gothic glass built (1245–8) by Pierre de Montereau as a chapel adjunct to the palace of St. Louis, to house the relics that the King had purchased from the East. It is good to remember, in ages of destruction, that men, when they will, can build as once they built in France.

VI. ENGLISH GOTHIC: 1175–1280

From Chartres and the Île de France the Gothic style swept into the French provinces, and crossed frontiers into England, Sweden, Germany, Spain, at last into Italy. French architects and craftsmen accepted foreign commissions, and everywhere the new art was called *opus Francigenum*—work born in France. England welcomed it because she was in the twelfth century half French; the Channel was but a river between two sides of a British realm that included half of France; and of that realm Rouen was the cultural capital. English Gothic derived from Normandy rather than from the Île de France, and kept in a Gothic frame the Norman massiveness. The transition from Romanesque to Gothic was almost simultaneous in England and France; about the same time that the pointed arch was being used at St. Denis (1140) it was appearing in Durham and Gloucester cathedrals, at

Fountains Abbey and Malmesbury.[24] Henry III (1216–72) admired every-thing French, envied the architectural glory of St. Louis' reign, and taxed his people into poverty to rebuild Westminster Abbey, and to pay the school of artists—builders, sculptors, painters, illuminators, goldsmiths—whom he gathered near his court to execute his plans.

Of the three periods into which English Gothic falls—Early English (1175–1280), Decorated (1280–1380), and Perpendicular (1380–1450)—we confine ourselves here to the first. The long and pointed form of Early English windows and arches gave the style another name—Lancet. Façades and portals were simpler than in France; Lincoln and Rochester had some sculptures, Wells many more; but these were exceptional, and could not be compared, in quality or quantity, with the portal statuary of Chartres, Amiens, or Reims. Towers were massive rather than tall; but the steeples of Salisbury, Norwich, and Lichfield show what the English builder could do when he preferred elegance and height to dignity and mass. Interior eleva-tion likewise failed to lure the architects of England; sometimes they tried it, as at Westminster and Salisbury; but more often they allowed the vault to lie oppressively low, as at Gloucester and Exeter. The great length of English cathedrals discouraged the effort to attain proportionate height; Winchester is 556 feet long, Ely 517, Canterbury 514, Westminster Abbey 511; Amiens is 435, Reims 430, even Milan only 475. But Winchester's in-ternal height was but 78 feet, Canterbury's 80, Lincoln's 82, Westminster's 103, while Amiens rose to 140 feet.

The east end of the English Gothic church retained the square apse of the Anglo-Saxon style, ignoring the convenient French development of the polygonal or semicircular apse. In many cases the east end was expanded into a Lady Chapel for the special worship of the Virgin; but the adoration of Mary never reached in England the enthusiasm that marked it in France. Often in England the chapter house of the cathedral canons, and the palace of the bishop, were attached to the church and constituted with it the "ca-thedral close," usually surrounded by a wall. In the Gothic monasteries of England and Scotland—as at Fountains, Dryburgh, Melrose, Tintern—the spread of dormitories, refectories, abbey, and cloistered walks formed in one enclosure an impressive artistic whole.

The essential principle of Gothic architecture—the balancing and channel-ing of pressures to reduce ungainly massiveness of support—seems never to have won full acceptance in England. The old Romanesque thickness of wall was only slightly moderated in English Gothic, even when, as at Salisbury, the design did not have to adapt itself to a Romanesque base. English archi-tects, like the Italian, were repelled by the flying buttress; they adopted it here and there, but halfheartedly; they felt that the supports of a building should be contained in the structure itself, and not in excrescences. Perhaps they were right; and though their cathedrals lack the feminine grace of the French chef-d'oeuvres, they have a firm and masculine power that reaches beyond the beautiful to the sublime.

Four years after the murder of Becket at Canterbury, the choir of the cathedral burned down (1174). The people of the town beat their heads against the walls in anger and bewilderment that the Almighty had permitted such disaster to a shrine that had already become a goal of religious pilgrimage.[25] The monks entrusted the work of rebuilding the choir to William of Sens, a French architect who had made a name for himself with the cathedral that he had built for his city. William worked at Canterbury from 1175 to 1178; a fall from a scaffolding disabled him, and the undertaking was carried on by William the Englishman, a man "small in body," says the monk Gervase, "but in workmanship of many kinds acute and honest." [26] Much of the Romanesque cathedral of 1096 remained; round arches survived amid the generally Gothic renovation; but the old wooden ceiling of the choir was replaced by a ribbed vault of stone, the columns were lengthened to a graceful height, the capitals were exquisitely carved, and the windows were filled with brilliant stained glass. Gathered in its cathedral close, and yet towering over its quaint and lovely town, Canterbury Cathedral is today one of the most inspiring sights of the earth.

Its example, seen by countless prelates and pilgrims, spread the Gothic style through Britain. In 1177 Peterborough fronted the west transept of its cathedral with a splendid Gothic portico. In 1189 Bishop Hugh de Lacy built the handsome retrochoir of Winchester Cathedral. In 1186 an earthquake rent Lincoln Cathedral from top to base; six years later Bishop Hugh began its reconstruction on a Gothic design by Geoffrey de Noyers; the noble Grosseteste finished it about 1240. It stands on a hill overlooking a typically beautiful English countryside. Seldom has sublimity of mass been so well reconciled with delicacy of detail. The three great towers, the broad façade with its sculptured portal and complex arcades, the lordly nave, seemingly light despite its mass and span, the graceful shafts and carving of the piers, the rose windows, the palmlike vaulting of the chapter house, the magnificent arches of the cloisters—these would have made Lincoln Cathedral a credit to mankind even had there been no "Angel Choir." In 1239 an old Norman tower fell and crushed Bishop Hugh's choir; a new choir rose in 1256–80 in the nascent Decorated style, ornate but exquisite; legend ascribed its name to the angels who were said to have built it, since no human hands could have compassed such perfection; but probably the name came from the smiling angel musicians sculptured on the spandrels of the triforium. On the south portal of this choir English sculptors almost rivaled the carvings of Reims and Amiens. Four statues there, beheaded and otherwise mutilated by the Puritans, can bear such comparison; one representing the Synagogue and another representing the Church are the finest English statuary of the thirteenth century. A great scientist, Sir William Osler, thought this Angel Choir the fairest of all products of human art.[27]

In 1220 Bishop Poore engaged Elias de Derham to design and build Salisbury Cathedral. It rose to completion in the unusually short space of twenty-five years; it is Early English throughout, and breaks the rule that English cathedrals mingle several styles. The unity of design, the harmony of mass and line, the simple majesty of the transept tower and spire, the grace of the vault in the Lady Chapel, and the lovely windows of the chapter house redeem the squat heaviness of the nave piers and the oppressive shallowness of the vault. Ely Cathedral still has a wooden ceiling, but not unpleasing; there is a warm and living quality in wood that never comes to architecture in stone. To Ely's fine Norman nave the Gothic architects added a pretty west porch, or galilee (c. 1205); a presbytery with handsome column clusters of Purbeck marble; and, in fourteenth-century Decorated Gothic, a Lady Chapel, a choir, and, over the transept crossing, a gorgeous lantern tower—the "Ely Octagon." Wells Cathedral (1174–91) was one of the earliest examples of English Gothic; its nave was not too well designed; but the west front added (1220–42) by Bishop Jocelyn "narrowly escaped being the most beautiful in England." [28] In the niches of this façade were 340 statues; 106 are missing, victims of Puritanism, vandalism, and time; those that remain constitute the largest collection of figure sculpture in Britain. We cannot say as much for their quality.

The culminating achievement of Early English Gothic was Westminster Abbey. Henry III, who had made Edward the Confessor his patron saint, felt that the Norman church built by Edward (1050) was unworthy to house Edward's bones; he ordered his artists to replace it with a Gothic edifice in the French style; and for this purpose he raised by taxation £750,-000, which we may diffidently equate at $90,000,000 today. The work began in 1245, and continued till Henry's death in 1272. The design followed Reims and Amiens, even to admitting the Continental polygonal apse. The sculptures of the north porch, portraying the Last Judgment, were influenced by those of Amiens' west front. In the spandrels of the transept triforium are remarkable reliefs of angels; one angel in the south transept offers to the centuries a tender, gracious face rivaling the cherubim of Reims. Over the doorway of the chapter house are two figures representing the Annunciation, and showing the Virgin in a charming gesture of modest deprecation. Even finer are the early royal tombs in the Abbey, and, best of all, that of Henry III himself—an ideally handsome and well-proportioned improvement upon the stout and stunted King. The crimes of a score of rulers are in those splendid tombs forgotten, and half redeemed by the English genius that lies buried under the stones of this sovereign sepulcher.

VII. GERMAN GOTHIC: 1200–1300

Flanders imported Gothic from France at an early date. St. Gudule's, proud on its hill in Brussels, was begun in 1220; its chief glory is its stained glass. St. Bavon's, at Ghent, built a Gothic choir in 1274; and St. Rombaut's, at Mechlin, surveyed the countryside from huge towers never finished but still too ornate. Flanders was more interested in textiles than in theology; its characteristic architecture was civic; and its earliest Gothic triumphs were the cloth halls at Ypres, Bruges, and Ghent. That of Ypres (1200–1304) was the most majestic: a 450-feet-long façade of three-storied arcades, with colonnaded corner pinnacles and stately central tower; it was reduced to ruins in the First World War. The Cloth Hall of Bruges (1284f) still dominates its square with a superb and world-famous belfry. These fine buildings, and those of Ghent (1325f), suggest the prosperity and just pride of the Flemish guilds, and constitute some part of the charm of these now quiet and pleasant towns.

As Gothic spread eastward into Holland and Germany it encountered increasing resistance. In general the grace of the Gothic style did not accord with the sturdy force of the Teutonic frame and mind; Romanesque was more congenial, and Germany clung to it till the thirteenth century. The great cathedral of Bamberg (1185–1237) is transitional: the windows are small and round-arched, and there are no flying buttresses; but the vault is in ribbed and pointed form. Here at the outset of German Gothic we find a remarkable development of sculpture: at first imitating the French, but soon advancing to a style of splendid naturalism and power; indeed, the figure of the Synagogue on the Bamberg church is more satisfying than the similar figure at Reims.[29] The Elizabeth and Mary in the choir are far from replicas of like subjects in France; Elizabeth has the face and form of a togaed Roman senator, and Mary is a woman of physical substance and vigor, such as Germany has always loved.

Almost every German cathedral surviving from this period contains outstanding statuary. The best is in the cathedral of Naumburg (c. 1250). In the west choir is a series of twelve statues portraying local dignitaries with a ruthless realism that suggests that the artists were underpaid; as if in atonement, the portrait of Uta, the margrave's wife, is a wistful German's conception of an ideal woman. A frieze on the screen of the choir shows Judas taking money to betray Christ; the figures are crowded together in bold composition, but without damage to their individuality; Judas is represented with some sympathy, and the Pharisees are powerful personalities. This is the masterpiece of German sculpture in the thirteenth century.

In 1248 Conrad of Hochstaden, Archbishop of Cologne, laid the foundation stone of the most famous and least German of German cathedrals. The work progressed slowly in the chaos that followed the death of Frederick II; the cathedral was not consecrated till 1322; much of it dates from the four-teenth century; the elegant spires, complex with crockets and open-work tracery, were built in 1880 from fifteenth-century designs. Modeled on Amiens, Cologne followed French style and methods closely. The lines of the façade are too straight and hard, but the tall, slender pillars of the nave, the brilliant windows, and the fourteen statues on the piers of the choir make an attractive interior, almost miraculously spared by the Second World War.

The cathedral of Strasbourg is more satisfying. There, as at Cologne, proximity to France made a French style seem no more foreign than it would seem in Strasbourg today (1949). The exterior is French grace, the interior is German force. The cathedral is approached through a picturesque conges-tion of gabled houses. Statues adorn the façade, but are outshone by a rose window of great compass and splendor. The single tower at one corner of the front gives the structure a crippled look. But the combination of dignity and decoration is here perfectly successful; we come to understand Goethe's description of this façade as "frozen music," though we should use a warmer phrase. "Brought up as I was," Goethe wrote, "to looking upon Gothic architecture with contempt, I despised it; but when I went inside I was struck with wonder, and I felt the attraction of its beauty." [30] The stained glass here is very old, perhaps older than any in France. The sculptures of the south transept portal (1230–40) are of rare excellence. The tympanum over the door is a deep relief of the Virgin's death; the apostles gathered at her bed-side are inadequately individualized; but the figure of Christ is well con-ceived and skillfully carved. Rising alongside this portal are two pre-eminent statues: one representing the Church—a buxom German queen; the other a slim and graceful figure, blindfold but beautiful, symbolizing the Syna-gogue; remove the bandage, and the Synagogue would win the argument. The French Revolutionary Convention, in 1793, ordered the destruction of the cathedral's statues to transform it into a "Temple of Reason"; a natural-ist known to us merely as Hermann rescued the figures of Church and Syna-gogue by concealing them in his botanical garden, and saved the tympanum reliefs by covering them with a board bearing a French inscription: *Liberté, Égalité, Fraternité.*[31]

VIII. ITALIAN GOTHIC: 1200–1300

Medieval Italians called Gothic *lo stile Tedesco*; and Renaissance Italians, equally mistaken about its origin, invented the name Gothic for it, on the ground that only the transalpine barbarians could have developed so ex-travagant an art. The decorative exuberance and exalted audacity of the style offended the classic and long-chastened tastes of the Italian soul. If Italy at last adopted Gothic, it was with a reluctance verging on contempt; and only after she had transformed it to her own needs and mood could she produce not only the exotic brilliance of Milan Cathedral, but the strange Byzantine-Romanesque Gothic of Orvieto and Siena, Assisi and Florence. Her soil and her ruins alike abounded in marble, with which she could face her shrines in slabs of many tints; but how could she carve a marble façade into the complex portals of the freestone North? She did not need the enormous windows by which the chill and cloudy North invited light and warmth; she preferred the small windows that made her cathedrals cool sanctuaries against the sun; she thought thick walls, even iron braces, no uglier than stilted buttresses. Not needing pinnacles or pointed arches as devices of support, she used them as ornaments, and never quite appropriated the constructive logic of the Gothic style.

In the North that style had been, before 1300, almost entirely ecclesiastical; and the few exceptions were in such commercial cities as Ypres, Bruges, and Ghent. In northern and Central Italy, even richer than the Lowlands in manufacturing and trade, civic architecture played a prominent role in the Gothic development. Town halls, city walls, gates, and towers, feudal castles and merchant palaces took on Gothic form or ornament. Perugia began its Palazzo del Municipio in 1281, Siena its Palazzo Pubblico in 1289, Bologna its Palazzo Comunale in 1290, Florence its unique and graceful Palazzo Vecchio in 1298—all in Tuscan Gothic style.

At Assisi in 1228 Brother Elias, to accommodate his numerous Franciscan monks and the swelling crowd of pilgrims to St. Francis' tomb, ordered the erection of the spacious convent and church of San Francesco—the first Gothic church in Italy. The commission was given to a German master builder whom the Italians named Iacopo d'Alemannia; perhaps it was for this reason that Gothic was known in Italy as "the German style." Iacopo built a Lower Church in Romanesque groined-vault style, and upon this an Upper Church with traceried windows and ribbed and pointed vault. The churches and the convent make an imposing mass, not quite as interesting as the remarkable frescoes by Cimabue, Giotto, and Giotto's pupils, or the tourists and worshipers who daily flock from a hundred towns to the shrine of Italy's favorite and least-heeded saint.

Siena is still a medieval city: a public square with government buildings, open market stands, and modest adjoining shops that make no effort to attract the eye. From this center a dozen alleys pick their shady, hazardous way between dark and ancient tenements hardly ten feet apart, filled with a kindly and volatile people to whom water is a luxury rarer and more dangerous than wine. On a hill behind the tenements rises La Metropolitana—the cathedral of the city—in an unpleasant striation of black and white marble. Begun in 1229, it was completed in 1348. In 1380, from plans left by Giovanni Pisano, a new and gorgeous façade was added, all of red, black, or white marble, with three Romanesque portals flanked by jambs of splendid carving and surmounted by gables of crocketed design; a vast rose window filtered the setting sun; arcades and colonnades running along the front presented a parade of statuary; pinnacles and towers of white marble softened the corners; and in the high pediment a vast mosaic showed the Virgin Mother floating up to paradise. The Italian architect was interested in a bright and colorful surface; not, like the French, in the subtle play of light and shade upon recessed portal orders and deeply sculptured façades. There are no buttresses here; the choir is topped with a Byzantine dome; the weight is borne by thick walls and by round arches of gigantic span rising from clustered columns of marble to a vault of round and pointed ribs. Here is a Tuscan Gothic still predominantly Romanesque, all the world apart from the heavy miracles of Amiens and Cologne. Within is the white marble pulpit of Niccolò and Giovanni Pisano, a bronze Baptist by Donatello (1457), frescoes by Pinturicchio, an altar by Baldassare Peruzzi (1532), richly carved choir stalls by Bartolomeo Neroni (1567); so an Italian church could grow from century to century through the never-ending stream of Italian genius.

While Siena's cathedral and campanile were taking form, a miracle reported from the village of Bolsena had architectural results. A priest who had doubted the doctrine of transubstantiation was convinced by seeing blood on the consecrated Host. In commemoration of this marvel, Pope Urban IV not only instituted the Feast of Corpus Christi (1264), but ordered the erection of a cathedral at neighboring Orvieto. Arnolfo di Cambio and Lorenzo Maetani designed it, engaged forty architects, sculptors, and painters from Siena and Florence, and worked on it from 1290 to its completion in 1330. The façade followed the style of Siena's, but with finer finish of execution and better proportion and symmetry; it is a vast painting in marble, whose every element is itself a painstaking masterpiece. Incredibly detailed and yet precise reliefs on the broad pilasters between the portals tell again the story of creation, the life of Christ, the Redemption, and the Last Judgment; one of these reliefs, the Visitation, has already the perfection of Renaissance sculpture. Delicately carved colonnades divide the three stages of the lofty façade, and shelter a population of prophets, apostles, Fathers, and saints; a rose window dubiously ascribed to Orcagna (1359) centers the whole complex composition; and above it a dazzling mosaic (now removed) portrayed the Coronation of the Virgin. The strangely striated interior is a simple basilican arcade under a low wooden ceiling; the light is poor, and one can hardly do justice to the frescoes by Fra Angelico, Benozzo Gozzoli, and Luca Signorelli.

But it was in opulent Florence that the fury of building which swept through Italy in the thirteenth century worked its greatest marvels. In 1294 Arnolfo di Cambio began the church of Santa Croce; he retained the traditional basilican plan without transepts and with flat wooden ceiling, but he adopted the pointed arch for the windows, the nave arcade, and the marble façade. The beauty of the church consisted less in its architecture than in the wealth of sculptures and frescoes within, showing all the skill of a maturing Italian art. In 1298 Arnolfo refaced the baptistery with that tasteless alternation of black and white marble layers which disfigures so many works of the Tuscan style by crushing the vertical elevation under a plethora of horizontal lines. But the proud spirit of the age—another cockcrow of the Renaissance—can be heard in the edict (1294) by which the Signoria commissioned Arnolfo to build the great cathedral:

> Whereas it is sovereign prudence on the part of a people of high origin to proceed in its affairs in such wise that the wisdom and magnanimity of its proceedings may shine forth in its visible works, it is ordered that Arnolfo, master architect of our commune, shall prepare models or designs for the restoration of [the cathedral of] Santa Maria Reparata, with the most exalted and the most prodigal magnificence, in order that the industry and power of men may never create or undertake anything whatsoever more vast and more beautiful; in accordance with that which our wisest citizens have declared and counseled in public session and in secret conclave—that no hand be laid upon the works of the commune without the intention of making them correspond to the noble soul which is composed of the souls of all its citizens united in one will.[32]

As doubtless this expansive proclamation was intended to do, it stimulated public giving. The guilds of the city joined in financing the enterprise; and when, later on, other guilds proved slack, the wool guild took over the entire cost, contributing as high as 51,500 gold lire ($9,270,000) a year.[33] Accordingly, Arnolfo laid out dimensions on a grandiose scale. The stone vault was to be 150 feet high, equal to Beauvais'; the nave 260 by 55; and the weight was to be borne by thick walls, iron braces, and pointed nave arches remarkable for their small number—four—and their enormous sixty-five-foot span and ninety-foot height. Arnolfo died in 1301; the work went on, with considerable alteration of plans, under Giotto, Andrea Pisano, Brunelleschi, and others; and the ugly pile, renamed Santa Maria de Fiore, was not consecrated till 1436. It is a structure immense and bizarre, which spanned six centuries in building, covered 84,000 square feet, and proved inadequate for Savonarola's audience.

IX. SPANISH GOTHIC: 1091–1300

As the monks of France had brought Romanesque architecture to Spain in the eleventh century, so in the twelfth they carried Gothic over the Pyrenees. In the picturesque little town of Ávila the cathedral of San Salvador

(1091f) inaugurated the transition with round arches, a Gothic portal, and, in the apse, elegant columns rising to pointed ribs in the vault. At Salamanca piety preserved the old transitional cathedral of the twelfth century beside the new one of the sixteenth; the two together form one of the most imposing architectural ensembles in Spain. At Tarragona difficulties of finance prolonged the building of the *seo* or episcopal see from 1089 to 1375; the simple solidity of the older elements forms a fit background for the Gothic and Moorish decoration; and the cloisters—Romanesque colonnades under a Gothic vault—are among the most beautiful productions of medieval art.

Tarragona is distinctly Spanish; Burgos, Toledo, and Leon are progressively more French. The marriage of Blanche of Castile to Louis VIII of France (1200) widened the road of intercourse already opened by migratory monks. It was her nephew, Fernando III of Castile, who laid the first stone of Burgos Cathedral in 1221; it was an unknown French architect who designed the structure; a German of Cologne—Juan de Colonia—who raised the spires (1442); a Burgundian, Felipé de Borgoña, who rebuilt the great lantern over the transept cross (1539–43); at last his pupil, the Spaniard Juan de Vallejo, completed the edifice in 1567. The ornate traceried spires, the open towers that uphold them, and the sculptured arcade give to the west front of Santa Maria la Mayor a dignity and splendor that one cannot soon forget. Originally all this stone façade was painted; the colors have long since worn away; we can only try to imagine the resplendent mass that here once rivaled the sun.

The same Fernando III provided the funds for the still more magnificent cathedral of Toledo. Few inland cities have a more scenic site—nestling in a bend of the Tagus River, and hidden by protective hills; none would guess from its present poverty that once Visigothic kings, then Moorish emirs, then the Christian monarchs of Leon and Castile made it their capital. Begun in 1227, the cathedral rose in slow installments, and was hardly finished by 1493. Only one tower was executed on the original plan; it is half Moorish in the style of the Giralda at Seville, and almost as elegant. The other tower was capped in the seventeenth century with a dome designed by Toledo's most famous citizen, Domingo Teotocópuli—El Greco. The interior, 395 feet long and 178 feet wide, is a five-aisled maze of tall piers, ornate chapels, ascetic stone saints, iron grilles, and 750 windows of stained glass. All the energy of the Spanish character, all the gloom and passion of Spanish piety, all the elegance of Spanish manners, and something of the Moslem's flair for ornament find form and voice in this immense cathedral.

It is a proverb in Spain that "Toledo has the richest of our cathedrals, Oviedo the holiest, Salamanca the strongest, Leon the most beautiful." [34] Begun by Bishop Manrique in 1205, the cathedral of Leon was financed by small contributions rewarded with indulgences, and was completed in 1303. It adopted the French Gothic plan of building a cathedral chiefly of windows; and its stained glass ranks high among the masterpieces of that art. It may be true that the ground plan is taken from Reims, the west front from Chartres, the south portal from Burgos; the result is a charming cento of the French cathedrals—with finished towers and spires.

Many other shrines rose to celebrate the reconquest of Spain for Christianity—at Zamora in 1174, Tudela in 1188, Lerida in 1203, Palma in 1229, Valencia in 1262, Barcelona in 1298. But, excepting Leon, we should hardly describe the Spanish cathedrals of this period as Gothic. They avoided large windows and flying buttresses; they rested their weight on heavy walls and piers; instead of arch ribs running from base to ceiling, the piers themselves rose almost to the vault; and these tall columns, rising like stone giants in the caverns of immense naves, give to Spanish cathedral interiors a dark grandeur that subdues the soul with terror, while Northern Gothic lifts it up with light. Portals and windows, in Spanish Gothic, often kept the Romanesque arch; amid the Gothic ornament the decoration by diverse layers and patterns of colored brick preserved a Moorish element; and the Byzantine influence survived in domes and half domes rising with pendentive modulations from a polygonal base. It was from these varied constituents that Spain evolved a unique style for some of the finest cathedrals in Europe.

Not the least notable achievements of medieval architecture were the castles and fortresses of the countryside, and the walls and gates of the towns. The walls of Ávila still stand to prove the medieval sense of form; and such gates as the Puerto del Sol in Toledo typically married beauty to use. From memories of the Roman *castellum*, and perhaps from observation of Moslem forts,[35] the Crusaders built in the Near East mighty fortresses like that of Kerak (1121), superior in both mass and form to anything of their kind in that warlike age. Hungary, the bastion of Europe against the Mongols, raised magnificent castle-fortresses in the thirteenth century. The art flowed west, and left in Italy such masterpieces of military art as the fortress-tower of Volterra, and in France the thirteenth-century castles of Coucy and Pierrefonds, and the famous Château Gaillard that Richard Coeur de Lion constructed (1197) on returning from Palestine. Castles in Spain were no figments of fancy, but powerful masses of masonry that kept back the Moors and gave a name to Castile. When Alfonso VI of Castile (1073–1108) captured Segovia from the Moslems he built there a castle-fortress on the plan of the Alcazar of Toledo. In Italy castles rose as urban citadels for nobles; the towns of Tuscany and Lombardy still bristle with them; San Gimignano alone had thirteen before the Second World War. As early as the tenth century, at Châteaudun, France began to build the châteaux that in the Renaissance period were to form a lordly feature of her art. The technique of erecting stone castles passed into England with the Norman favorites of Edward the Confessor; it was advanced by the offensive and defensive measures of William the Conqueror, under whose iron hand the Tower of London, Windsor Castle, and Durham Castle took their earliest forms. From France, again, castle-building migrated to Germany, where it became a passion with lawless barons, warrior kings, and conquering saints. The monstrous *Schloss* of Königsberg, built (1257) as a fortress from which the Teutonic Knights might rule a hostile population, was a proper victim of the Second World War.

X. CONSIDERATIONS

Gothic architecture was the supreme achievement of the medieval soul. The men who dared to suspend those vaults on a few stilts of stone studied and expressed their science with greater thoroughness and effect than any medieval philosopher in any *summa*, and the lines and harmonies of Notre Dame make a greater poem than *The Divine Comedy*. Comparison of Gothic with classic architecture cannot be made in gross but demands specification. No one city in medieval Europe rivaled the architectural product of either Athens or Rome, and no Gothic shrine has the pure beauty of the Parthenon; but neither has any classic structure known to us the complex sublimity of the Reims façade, or the uplifting inspiration of Amiens' vault. The restraint and repose of the classic style expressed the rationality and moderation that Greece preached to effervescent Greece; the romantic ecstasy of French Gothic, the somber immensity of Burgos or Toledo, unwittingly symbolized the tenderness and longing of the medieval spirit, the terror and myth and mystery of a religious faith. Classical architecture and philosophy were sciences of stability; the architraves that bound the columns of the Parthenon were the *meden agan* of the Delphic inscription, laying a heavy hand upon exaltation, counseling steadiness, and almost forcing men's thoughts back to this life and earth. The spirit of the North was properly called Gothic, for it inherited the restless audacity of the conquering barbarians; it passed insatiate from victory to victory, and finally, with flying buttress and soaring arch, laid siege to the sky. But it was also a Christian spirit, appealing to heaven for the peace that barbarism had alienated from the earth. Out of those contradictory motives came the greatest triumph of form over matter in all the history of art.

Why did Gothic architecture decline? Partly because every style, like an emotion, exhausts itself by complete expression, and invites reaction or change. The development of Gothic into Perpendicular in England, Flamboyant in France, left the form no future except exaggeration and decay. The collapse of the Crusades, the decline of religious belief, the diversion of funds from Mary to Mammon, from Church to state, broke the spirit of the Gothic age. The taxation of the clergy, after Louis IX, depleted the cathedral treasuries. The communes and the guilds that had shared in the glory and the costs lost their independence, their wealth, and their pride. The Black Death and the Hundred Years' War exhausted both France and England. Not only did new construction diminish in the fourteenth century, but most of the great cathedrals begun in the twelfth and thirteenth were left unfinished. Finally the rediscovery of classic civilization by the humanists, and the revival of classical architecture in Italy, where it had never died, superseded Gothic with a new exuberance. From the sixteenth to the nineteenth century Renaissance architecture dominated Western Europe, even through baroque and rococo. When, in its turn, the classic mood paled away, the Romantic movement of the early nineteenth century re-created the Middle Ages in idealizing imagination, and Gothic architecture returned. The struggle between the classic and the Gothic styles still rages in our churches and schools, our marts and capitals, while a new and indigenous architecture, bolder even than Gothic, rides the sky.

Medieval man thought that truth had been revealed to him, so that he was spared from its wild pursuit; the reckless energy that we give to seeking it was turned in those days to the creation of beauty; and amid poverty, epidemics, famines, and wars men found time and spirit to make beautiful a thousand varieties of objects, from initials to cathedrals. Breathless before some medieval manuscript, humble before Notre Dame, feeling the far vision of Winchester's nave, we forget the superstition and squalor, the petty wars and monstrous crimes, of the Age of Faith; we marvel again at the patience, taste, and devotion of our medieval ancestors; and we thank a million forgotten men for redeeming the blood of history with the sacrament of art.

CHAPTER XXXIII

Medieval Music

326-1300

I. THE MUSIC OF THE CHURCH

WE have done the cathedral injustice. It was not the cold and empty tomb that the visitor enters today. It functioned. Its worshipers found in it not only a work of art but the consoling, strengthening presence of Mary and her Son. It received the monks or canons who many times each day stood in the choir stalls and sang the canonical Hours. It heard the importunate litanies of congregations seeking divine mercy and aid. Its nave and aisles guided the processions that carried before the people the image of the Virgin or the body and blood of their God. Its great spaces echoed solemnly with the music of the Mass. And the music was as vital as the church edifice itself, more deeply stirring than all the glory of glass or stone. Many a stoic soul, doubtful of the creed, was melted by the music, and fell on his knees before the mystery that no words could speak.

The evolution of medieval music concurred remarkably with the development of architectural styles. As the early churches passed in the seventh century from the ancient domed or basilican forms to a simple masculine Romanesque, and in the thirteenth century to Gothic complexity, elevation, and ornament, so Christian music kept till Gregory I (540–604) the ancient monodic airs of Greece and the Near East, passed in the seventh century to Gregorian or plain chant, and flowered in the thirteenth century into polyphonic audacities rivaling the balanced strains of a Gothic cathedral.

The barbarian invasions in the West, and the resurgence of Orientalism in the Near East, combined to break the tradition of Greek musical notation through letters placed above the words; but the four Greek "modes"—Dorian, Phrygian, Lydian, Mixolydian—survived, and begot by division the *octoechos*, or "eight manners" of musical composition—contemplative, restrained, grave, solemn, cheerful, joyful, spirited, or ecstatic. The Greek language persisted for three centuries after Christ in the church music of the West, and still remains in the *Kyrie eleison*. Byzantine music took form under St. Basil, mated Greek and Syrian chants, reached its height in the hymns of Romanus (*c.* 495) and Sergius (*c.* 620), and made its greatest conquest in Russia.

Some early Christians opposed the use of music in religion, but it soon appeared that a religion without music could not survive in competition with creeds that touched man's sensitivity to song. The priest learned to sing the Mass, and inherited some of the melodies of the Hebrew cantor. Deacons and acolytes were taught to chant responses; some were technically trained in a *schola lectorum*, which under Pope Celestine I (422–32) became a *schola cantorum*. Such trained singers formed great choirs; that of St. Sophia's had 25 cantors and 111 "lectors," mostly boys.[1] Congregational singing spread from East to West; the men alternated with the women in antiphonal song, and joined with them in the Alleluia. The psalms they sang were thought to echo or imitate on earth the hymns of praise sung before God by the angels and saints in paradise. St. Ambrose, despite the apostolic counsel that women should be silent in church, introduced antiphonal singing to his diocese; "psalms are sweet for every age, and becoming to either sex," said this wise administrator; "they create a great bond of unity when all the people raise their voices in one choir." [2] Augustine wept when he heard the Milan congregation singing Ambrose's hymns, and verified St. Basil's dictum that the listener who surrenders to the pleasure of music will be drawn to religious emotion and piety.[3] The "Ambrosian chant" is still used in Milan churches today.

A tradition universally accepted in the Middle Ages, and now, after long doubts, generally received,[4] ascribes to Gregory the Great and his aides a reform and canonical determination of Roman Catholic music, resulting in the establishment of the "Gregorian chant" as the official music of the Church for six centuries. Hellenistic and Byzantine strains combined with Hebrew melodies of Temple or synagogue to mold this Roman or plain chant. It was monodic—one song—music; no matter how many voices participated, they all sang the same note, though women and boys often sang an octave higher than the men. It was simple music for voices of modest range; now and then it allowed a more complex "melisma"—a melodious wordless embellishment of a note or phrase. It was a free and continuous rhythm, not divided into regular meter or measures of time.

Before the eleventh century the only musical notation used by the Gregorian chant consisted of small signs derived from the Greek accent marks, and placed over the words to be sung. These "neumes" (airs, breaths) indicated a rise or fall of tone, but not the degree of rise or fall, nor the duration of the note; such matters had to be learned by oral transmission and the memorizing of an enormous body of liturgical song. No instrumental accompaniment was allowed. Despite these limitations—perhaps because of them—Gregorian chant became the most impressive feature of the Christian ritual. The modern ear, accustomed to complex harmony, finds these old chants monotonous and thin; they carry on a Greek, Syrian, Hebrew, Arab tradition of monody which only the Oriental ear can appreciate today. Even so, the chants sung in a Roman Catholic cathedral during Holy Week reach to the heart with a directness and weird power withheld from music whose complications divert the ear instead of moving the soul.

Gregorian chant spread through Western Europe like another conversion to Christianity. Milan rejected it, as it likewise resisted papal authority; and southern Spain long preserved its "Mozarabic" chant, formed by Christians under Moslem rule, and still used in a part of Toledo Cathedral. Charlemagne, who loved unity like a ruler, replaced the Gallican with the Gregorian chant in Gaul, and established schools of Roman church music at Metz and Soissons. The Germans, however, with throats formed by climate and needs quite different from the Italian, had trouble with the more delicate strains of the chant. Said John the Deacon: "Their coarse voices, which roar like thunder, cannot execute soft modulations, because their throats are hoarse with too much drinking." [5]

Perhaps the Germans deprecated the *fioritura* that from the eighth century forward embellished the Gregorian chant with "tropes" and "sequences." The trope or turn began as a composition of words for a melisma, making this easier to remember. Later it became an interpolation of words and music into a Gregorian chant, as when the priest sang not *Kyrie eleison* but *Kyrie (fons pietatis, a quo bona cuncta procedunt) eleison*. The Church permitted such embellishments, but never accepted them into the official liturgy. Bored monks amused themselves by composing or singing such interpolations, until there were so many tropes that books known as "tropers" were published to teach or preserve the favored ones. The music of the ecclesiastical drama grew out of such tropes. Sequences were tropes designed to follow the Alleluia of the Mass. The custom had grown of prolonging the final vowel of this word in a long melody known as a *iubilus* or chant of joy; in the eighth century various texts were written for these inserted melodies. The composition of tropes and sequences became a highly developed art, and gradually changed Gregorian chant into an ornate form uncongenial to its original spirit and "plain" intent.* This evolution ended the purity and dominance of Gregorian chant in that same twelfth century which saw the transition from Romanesque to Gothic in the architecture of the West.

The multiplication of complex compositions demanded for their transmission a better notation than that which plain chant had used. In the tenth century Odo, Abbot of Cluny, and Notker Balbulus, a monk of St. Gall, resurrected the Greek device of naming notes by letters. In the eleventh century an anonymous writer described the use of the first seven capitals of the Latin

---

* Only five sequences have been admitted by the Church into her liturgy: *Victimae paschali laudes*, by Wipo; *Veni Sancte Spiritus*, ascribed to Innocent III; *Lauda Sion*, by Thomas Aquinas; *Stabat Mater*, by Iacopone da Todi; and *Dies irae*, by Thomas of Celano.

alphabet for the first octave of a scale, the corresponding lower-case Latin letters for the second octave, and Greek letters for the third.[6] About 1040 Guido of Arezzo, a monk of Pomposa (near Ferrara), gave their present strange names to the first six notes of the scale by taking the first syllables of each half-line of a hymn to John the Baptist:

> *Ut* queant laxis *re*sonare *f*loris
> *Mi*ra gestorum *f*amuli tuorum,
> *Sol*ve polluti *la*bii reatum.

This "solmization," or naming of the musical tones by the syllables *ut* (or *do*), *re*, *mi*, *fa*, *sol*, *la*, became part of the inexorable heritage of Western youth.

More vital was Guido's development of a musical staff. About 1000 the practice had arisen of using a red line to indicate the note now represented by F; later a second line, yellow or green, was added to represent C. Guido, or someone shortly before him, extended these lines to make a staff of four lines, to which later teachers added a fifth. With this new staff and the *ut*, *re*, *mi*, wrote Guido, his choir boys could learn in a few days what formerly had taken them many weeks. It was a simple but epochal advance, which earned for Guido the title of *inventor musicae*, and a splendid statue still to be seen in Arezzo's public square. The results were revolutionary. Singers were free from the task of memorizing the whole musical liturgy; music could be more readily composed, transmitted, and preserved; the performer could now read music at sight and hear it with the eye; and the composer, no longer bound to keep close to traditional melodies lest singers refuse to memorize his work, could venture upon a thousand experiments. Most important of all, he could now write polyphonic music, in which two or more voices could simultaneously sing or play different but harmonizing strains.

We owe to our medieval forebears still another invention that made modern music possible. Tones could now be determined by dots placed on or between the lines of the staff, but these signs gave no hint as to how long a note was to be held. Some system for measuring and denoting the duration of each note was indispensable to the development of contrapuntal music—the simultaneous and harmonious procedure of two or more independent melodies. Perhaps some knowledge had seeped up from Spain of Arab treatises by al-Kindi, al-Farabi, Avicenna, and other Moslems who had dealt with measured music or mensural notation.[7] At some time in the eleventh century [8] Franco of Cologne, a priest mathematician, wrote a treatise *Ars cantus mensurabilis*, in which he gathered up the suggestions of earlier theory and practice, and laid down essentially our present system for indicating the duration of musical notes. A square-headed *virga* or rod, formerly used as a neume, was chosen to represent a long note; another neume, the *punctum* or point, was enlarged into a lozenge to represent a short note; these signs were in time altered; tails were added; by trial and error, through a hundred absurdities, our simple mensural notation was evolved.

These vital developments opened a wide door to polyphonic music. Such music had been written before Franco, but crudely. Toward the close of the ninth century we find a musical practice called "organizing"—the singing of concords by concurring voices. Little is heard of it again till the end of the tenth century, when we find the names *organum* and *symphonia* applied to such compositions for two voices. The *organum* was a liturgical piece, in which an old monodic strain was carried or "held" by the tenor (who was therefore so named), while another voice added a harmonizing melody. A variant of this form, the *conductus*, gave the tenor a new or popular tune, and conducted another voice in a concurrent air. In the eleventh century the composers took a step as bold in its way as the Gothic balancing of thrusts: they wrote harmonies in which the "conducted" voice did not slavishly accompany the tenor in the rise or fall of the melody, but ventured upon other harmonies through notes not necessarily moving in a parallel line with the *cantus firmus* of the tenor. This declaration of independence became almost a rebellion when the second voice accompanied the ascending melody of the tenor with a descending movement. This harmony by contrast, and fluent resolution of momentary discords, became a passion with composers, almost a law; so, about 1100, John Cotton wrote: "If the main voice is ascending, the accompanying part shall descend." [9] Finally, in the *motet* (apparently a diminutive from the French *mot*, a word or phrase), three, four, five, even six different voices were made to sing in a complex weave of individual melodies whose diverse but concordant strains crossed and merged in a vertical-horizontal web of harmony as subtle and graceful as the converging arches of a Gothic vault. By the thirteenth century this *Ars antiqua* of polyphony had built the foundations of modern musical composition.

In that exciting century the enthusiasm for music rivaled the interest in architecture and philosophy. The Church looked askance upon polyphony; she distrusted the religious effect of music becoming a lure and end in itself; John of Salisbury, bishop and philosopher, called a halt to complexity of composition; Bishop Guillaume Durand branded the motet as "disorganized music"; Roger Bacon, a rebel in science, deplored the vanishing of the stately Gregorian chant. The Council of Lyons (1274) denounced the new music; and Pope John XXII (1324) issued a papal condemnation of *discantus*, or polyphony, on the ground that the innovating composers "chop up the melodies . . . so that these rush around ceaselessly, intoxicating the ear without quieting it, and disturbing devotion instead of evoking it." [10] But the revolution continued. In one citadel of the Church—Notre Dame de Paris—the choirmaster Leoninus, about 1180, composed the finest *organa* of his time; and his successor Perotinus was guilty of compositions for three or four voices. Polyphony, like Gothic, spread from France to England and Spain.

Giraldus Cambrensis (1146?–1220) reported two-part singing in Iceland, and said of his native Wales what one might say of it today:

> In their songs they do not utter the tunes uniformly . . . but manifoldly—in many manners and many notes; so that in a multitude of singers, such as it is the custom of this people to bring together, as many songs are to be heard as there are singers to be seen, and a various diversity of parts, finally coming together in one consonance and organic melody.[11]

In the end the Church bowed to the infallibility of the *Zeitgeist*, accepted polyphony, made it a powerful servant of the faith, and prepared it for its Renaissance victories.

II. THE MUSIC OF THE PEOPLE

The impulse to rhythm expressed itself in a hundred forms of secular music and dance. The Church had her reasons for fearing this instinct uncontrolled; it allied itself naturally with love, the great rival of religion as a source of song; and the hearty earthiness of the medieval mind, when the priest was out of sight, inclined it to a freedom, sometimes an obscenity, of text that shocked the clergy, and provoked councils to vain decrees. The goliards, or wandering scholars, found or composed music for their paeans to woman and wine, and their scandalous parodies of sacred ritual; manuscripts circulated containing solemn music for the hilarious words of the *Missa de potatoribus*—the Mass of the Topers—and the *Officium ribaldorum*—a Prayer Book for Roisterers.[12] Love songs were as popular as today. Some were as tender as a nymph's orisons; some were seduction dialogues with delicate accompaniments. And of course there were war songs, calculated to forge unity through vocal unison, or to anesthetize the pursuit of glory with hypnotic rhythm. Some music was folk song, composed by anonymous genius, and appropriated—perhaps transformed—by the people. Other popular music was the product of professional skill using all the arts of polyphony learned in the liturgy of the Church. In England a favorite and complex form was the roundel, in which one voice began a melody, a second began the same or a harmonizing melody when the first had reached an agreed point, a third chimed in after the second was on its way, and so on, until as many as six voices might be running the rounds in a lively contrapuntal fugue.

Almost the oldest roundel known is the famous "Sumer is i-cumen in," probably composed by a Reading monk about 1240. Its six-part complexity shows polyphony already at home among the people. The words still live with the spirit of a century in which all medieval civilization was coming to flower:

Sumer is i-cumen in;	Summer is a-coming in,
Llude sing cuccu!	Loudly sing cuckoo!
Groweth sed and bloweth med	Groweth seed and bloweth mead,
And springth the wude nu:	And blossoms the woodland now:
Sing cuccu!	Sing cuckoo!
Awe bleteth after lomb,	Ewe bleateth after lamb,
Lhouth after calve cu;	Loweth after calf the cow;
Bulluc sterteth, bucke verteth:	Bullock leapeth, buck turns off;
Murie sing cuccu!	Merry sing cuckoo!
Cuccu, cuccu, wel singes thu cuccu;	Cuckoo, cuckoo, well singest thou
Ne swik thu naver nu;	cuckoo;
Sing cuccu nu, sing cuccu,	Cease thou not, never now;
Sing cuccu, sing cuccu, nu!	Sing cuckoo now, sing cuckoo,
	Sing cuckoo, sing cuckoo, now!

Such a song must have been congenial to the minstrels or jongleurs who wandered from town to town, from court to court, even from land to land; we hear of minstrels from Constantinople singing in France, of English glee-men singing in Spain. A performance by minstrels was a usual part of any formal festivity; so Edward I of England engaged 426 singers for the wedding of his daughter Margaret.[13] Such minstrel groups often sang part songs, sometimes of bizarre complexity. Usually the songs were composed—words and music—by troubadours in France, *trovatori* in Italy, minnesingers in Germany. Most medieval poetry before the thirteenth century was written to be sung; "a poem without music," said the troubadour Folquet, "is a mill without water." [14] Of 2600 troubadour songs extant, we have the music of 264, usually in the form of neumes and ligatures on a four- or five-line staff. The bards of Ireland and Wales probably played instruments, and sang.

In the manuscripts that preserve the *Cantigas* or canticles collected by Alfonso X of Castile several illustrations show musicians in Arab dress performing on Arab instruments; the pattern of many of the songs is Arabic; [15] possibly the music, as well as the early themes and poetic forms, of the troubadours was derived from Moorish songs and melodies passing through Christian Spain into Southern France.[16] Returning Crusaders may have brought Arab musical forms from the East; it is to be noted that the troubadours appear about 1100, contemporary with the First Crusade.

Startling is the variety of medieval musical instruments. Percussion instruments—bells, cymbals, timbrels, the triangle, the bombulum, the drum; string instruments—lyre, cithera, harp, psaltery, noble, organistrum, lute, guitar, vielle, viola, monochord, gigue; wind instruments—pipe, flute, hautboy, bagpipe, clarion, flageolet, trumpet, horn, organ: these are a selection out of hundreds; everything was there for hand or finger, foot or bow. Some of them had survived from Greece, some had come, in form and name, from Islam, like the rebec, lute, and guitar; many were precious examples of medieval artistry in metal, ivory, or wood. The usual instrument of the minstrel was the vielle, a short violin played with an archer's curved-back bow. Before the eighth century most organs were hydraulic; but Jerome in the fourth century described a pneumatic organ; [17] and Bede (673–735) wrote of organs with "brass pipes filled with air from bellows, and uttering a grand and most sweet melody." [18] St. Dunstan (c. 925–88) was accused of sorcery when he built an Aeolian harp that played when placed against a crack in the wall.[19] In Winchester Cathedral, about 950, an organ was installed having twenty-six bellows, forty-two bellows-blowers, and four hundred pipes; the keys were so Gargantuan that the organist had to strike them with fists protected by thickly padded gloves.[20] Milan had an organ whose pipes were of silver; Venice had one with pipes of gold.[21]

All notion of medieval hell-stricken gloom vanishes before a collection of medieval musical instruments. What remains is again the picture of a people at least as happy as ourselves, full of the bounce and lust of life, and no more oppressed with fear of the end of the world than we with doubts whether civilization will be destroyed before we can complete its history.

CHAPTER XXXIV

The Transmission of Knowledge

1000–1300

I. THE RISE OF THE VERNACULARS

AS the Church had preserved in some measure that political unity of western Europe that the Roman Empire had achieved, so her ritual, her sermons, and her schools maintained a Roman heritage now lost—an international language intelligible to all the literate population of Italy, Spain, France, England, Scandinavia, the Lowlands, Germany, Poland, Hungary, and the western Balkans. Educated men in these countries used Latin for correspondence, business records, diplomacy, law, government, science, philosophy, and nearly all literature before the thirteenth century. They spoke Latin as a living language, which almost daily developed a new word or phrase to denote the new or changing realities or ideas of their lives. They wrote their love letters in Latin, from the simplest billets-doux to the classic epistles of Héloïse and Abélard. A book was written not for a nation but for the continent; it needed no translation, and passed from country to country with a speed and freedom unknown today. Students went from one university to another with no thought of linguistic embarrassments; scholars could lecture in the same language at Bologna, Salamanca, Paris, Oxford, Uppsala, and Cologne. They did not hesitate to import new words into Latin, sometimes to the horror of the Petrarcan-Ciceronian ear; so Magna Carta ruled that no freeman should be *dissaisiatus* or *imprisonatus*. Such words make us wince, but they kept Latin alive. Many modern English terms—for instance *instance, substantive, essence, entity*—descended from medieval additions to the Latin tongue.

Nevertheless the disruption of international intercourse by the collapse of Rome, the introverting poverty of the Dark Ages, the decay of roads and the decline of commerce, developed in speech those variations which segregation soon expands. Even in its heyday Latin had suffered national modifications from diversities of climate and oral physiology. In its very homeland the old language had been changed. The abdication of literature had left the field to the vocabulary and sentence structure of the common man, which had always been different from those of the poets and orators. The influx of Germans, Gauls, Greeks, and Asiatics into Italy brought a multiformity of pronunciation; and the natural laziness of tongue and mind sloughed off the precise inflections and terminations of careful speech. *H* became silent in late Latin; *V*, classically pronounced like the English *W*, acquired the sound of the English *V*; *N* before *S* dropped away—*mensa* (table) was pronounced *mesa*; the diphthongs *Æ* and *Œ*, classically pronounced like the English *I* and *OI*, were now like long English *A* or French *E*. As final consonants were slurred and forgotten (*portus, porto, porte*; *rex, re, roi*; *coelum, cielo, ciel*), case endings had to be replaced by prepositions, conjugational endings by auxiliary verbs. The old demonstrative pronouns *ille* and *illa* became definite articles—*il, el, lo, le, la*; and the Latin *unus* (one) was shortened to form the indefinite article *un*. As declensions disappeared, it sometimes became difficult to tell whether a noun was the subject before, or the object after, the predicate. Viewing this continuous process of change over twenty centuries, we may think of Latin as the still living and literary language of Italy, France, and Spain, no more transformed from the speech of Cicero than his from that of Romulus, or ours from Chaucer's.

Spain had begun to speak Latin as early as 200 B.C.; by Cicero's time its dialect had diverged so far from the usage of Rome that Cicero was shocked by what seemed to him the barbarisms of Corduba. Contact with Iberian dialects softened the Latin consonants in Spain: *T* into *D*, *P* into *B*, *K* into *G*; *totum* into *todo*, *operam* into *obra*, *ecclesia* into *iglesia*. French also softened the Latin consonants, and while often keeping them in writing, frequently dropped them in speech: *tout, oeuvre, église, est*. The oath taken at Strasbourg in 842 by Louis the German and Charles the Bald was sworn in two languages—German and French *—a French still so Latin that it was called *lingua romana*; not till the tenth century was it sufficiently distinct to receive the name *lingua gallica*. The *lingua romana* in turn divided into what France called two languages: the *langue d'oc* of France south of the Loire, and the *langue d'oïl* of northern France. It was a medieval custom to differentiate dialects by their way of saying *yes*: South France said it with *oc* from the Latin *hoc*, this; the North used *oïl*, a fusion of the Latin *hoc ille*, this-that. Southeastern France had a dialect of the *langue d'oc* called Provençal; it became a polished literary language in the hands of the troubadours, and was almost snuffed out by the Albigensian Crusades.

Italy formed her vernacular more slowly than Spain or France. Latin was her native speech; the clergy, who spoke Latin, were especially numerous in Italy; and the continuity of her culture and her schools kept the language from changing so freely as in lands with broken traditions. As late as 1230

---

* The first three lines will indicate how slowly French and German evolved: "Pro Deo amur et pro Christian poblo et nostro commun salvament, dist di in avant, in quant Deus savir et podir me dunat."

"In Gedes minna ind in these Christianes folches ind unser bedhero gealtnissi, fon thesemo dage frammordes, so fram so mir Got gewizci indi madh furgibit."

English translation: "For the love of God, and for the Christian people and our common salvation, from this day forth, as God may give me wisdom and strength." [1]

St. Anthony of Padua preached to the common people in Latin; however, a Latin sermon delivered at Padua in 1189 by a visiting prelate had to be translated by the local bishop into the popular tongue.[2] Italian hardly existed as a language at the beginning of the thirteenth century; there were merely some fourteen dialects continued and variously corrupted from the ancient Latin of the market place, each barely intelligible to the rest, and cherishing its differences with passionate atomism; sometimes different quarters of the same city, as at Bologna, had distinct dialects. The predecessors of Dante had to create a language as well as a literature. The poet, in a pleasant fancy, thought that the Tuscan troubadours chose Italian as their medium because they wrote of love, and the ladies they addressed might not understand Latin.[3] Even so, about 1300, he hesitated between Latin and the Tuscan dialect as the language of *The Divine Comedy*. By the narrow margin of this choice he escaped oblivion.

While Latin was dividing reproductively into the Romance languages, Old German was splitting into Middle German, Frisian, Dutch, Flemish, English, Danish, Swedish, Norwegian, and Icelandic. "Old German" is merely a convenient phrase to cover the many dialects that exercised their tribal or provincial sovereignty in Germany before 1050: Flemish, Dutch, Westphalian, Eastphalian, Alemannic, Bavarian, Franconian, Thuringian, Saxon, Silesian. . . . Old German passed into Middle German (1050–1500) partly through the influx of new words with the coming of Christianity. Monks from Ireland, England, France, and Italy labored to invent terms to translate Latin. Sometimes they appropriated Latin words bodily into German—*Kaiser, Prinz, Legende*. This was legitimate thievery; tragic, however, was the influence of Latin sentence structure—keeping the verb to the end—in changing the once simple syntax of the German people into the stiff, inverted, and breath-taking periods of the later German style.[4] Perhaps the finest German was the Middle High German written by the great poets of the thirteenth century—Walter von der Vogelweide, Hartmann von Aue, Gottfried of Strasbourg, Wolfram von Eschenbach. Never again, except in Heine and the young Goethe, was German so simple, flexible, direct, clear.

The Teutonic speech of the Angles, Saxons, and Jutes went with them to England in the fifth century, and laid the foundations of the English language—gave it almost all its short and racy words. French flooded the land with the Normans, and ruled the court, the courts, and the aristocracy from 1066 to 1362, while Latin continued to preside over religion and education, and (till 1731) remained *de rigueur* in official documents. Thousands of French words entered into English, above all in costume, cookery, and law; half the terminology of English law is French.[5] For three centuries the literatures of France and England were one; and as late as Chaucer (1340–1400) the spirit and language of English letters were half French. After the loss of her French possessions England was thrown back upon herself, and the

Anglo-Saxon elements in English speech triumphed. When the French domination passed, the English language had been immeasurably enriched. By adding French and Latin to its German base, English could triply express any one of a thousand ideas (*kingly*, *royal*, *regal*; *twofold*, *double*, *duplex*; *daily*, *journal*, *diurnal*, . . .); to this it owes its wealth of discriminating synonyms and verbal nuances. He who should know the history of words would know all history.

II. THE WORLD OF BOOKS

How were these diverse languages written? After the fall of Rome in 476 the conquering barbarians adopted the Latin alphabet, and wrote it with a "cursive" or running hand that bound the letters together and gave most of them a curved form instead of the straight lines that had been found convenient in writing upon hard surfaces like stone or wood. The Church preferred in those centuries a "majuscule," or large-letter writing, to facilitate the reading of missals and books of hours. When the copyists of Charlemagne's time preserved Latin literature by making many copies of the classics, they saved costly parchment by adopting a "minuscule," or small-letter writing; they agreed on set forms for the letters, and created the "set minuscule" lettering that became for four centuries the usual medium of medieval books. In the twelfth century, as if in accord with the exuberant decoration then developing in Gothic architecture, the letters acquired flourishes, hairlines, and hooks, and became the "Gothic" lettering that prevailed in Europe till the Renaissance, and in Germany till our time. Very few medieval manuscripts were punctuated; this breath-guiding device, known to the Hellenistic Greeks, had been lost in the barbarian upheaval; it reappeared in the thirteenth century, but was not generally adopted till printing established it in the fifteenth century. Printing was in some measure prepared as early as 1147 by the use of woodcuts, in Rhenish monasteries, for printing initial letters or patterns upon textiles.[6] Divers forms of shorthand were practiced, much inferior to the "Tironian notes" developed by Cicero's slave.

Writing was upon parchment, papyrus, vellum, or paper, with quill or reed pens using black or colored inks. Papyrus disappeared from common use in Europe after the Islamic conquest of Egypt. Vellum, prepared from the skin of young lambs, was expensive, and was reserved for luxurious manuscripts. Parchment, made from coarse sheepskin, was the usual medium of medieval writing. Till the twelfth century paper was a costly import from Islam; but in 1190 paper mills were set up in Germany and France, and in the thirteenth century Europe began to make paper from linen.

Many parchments were scraped to erase an old manuscript and receive a second composition ("palimpsest"). Old works were lost by such erasures, by misplacement of manuscripts, by war and pillage, by fire or decay. Huns sacked monastic libraries in Bavaria, Northmen in France, Saracens in Italy.

Many Greek classics perished in the plunder of Constantinople in 1204. The Church had at first discountenanced the reading of the pagan classics; in nearly every century some fearful voice—Gregory I, Isidore of Seville, Peter Damian—was raised against them; Theophilus, Archbishop of Alexandria, destroyed all pagan manuscripts that he could find; and Greek priests, according to Demetrius Chalcondylas,[7] persuaded Greek emperors to burn the works of the Greek erotic poets, including Sappho and Anacreon. But in those same centuries there were many ecclesiastics who cherished a fondness for the old pagans, and saw to it that their works were preserved. In some cases, to disarm censure, they read the most Christian sentiments into pagan poetry, and by genial allegory turned even Ovid's amatory art into moral verse. An abundant heritage of classical literature was preserved by monastic copyists.[8] Tired monks were told that God would forgive one of their sins for every line they copied; Ordericus Vitalis informs us that one monk escaped hell by the margin of a single letter.[9] Second only to the monks as copyists were private or professional scribes, who were engaged by rich men, or by booksellers, or by monasteries. Their labor was wearisome, and evoked from them strange requests on the final page:

Explicit hoc totum;	This completes the whole;
Pro Christo da mihi potum.	For Christ's sake give me a drink.[10]

Another scribe thought he deserved more, and wrote, as his colophon: *Detur pro penna scriptori pulchra puella*—"For the [work of the] pen let the writer receive a beautiful girl." [11]

The medieval Church exercised no regular censorship over the publication of books. If a book proved both heretical and influential, like Abélard's on the Trinity, it would be denounced by a Church council. But books were then too few to be a prime peril to orthodoxy. Even the Bible was rare outside of monasteries; a year was required to copy it, a year's income of a parish priest to buy it; few clergymen had a full copy.[12] The New Testament, and special books of the Old, had a wider circulation. Bibles of great size, magnificently decorated, were produced in the twelfth century; they could be handled only on a reading desk, usually in a monastic library, and might be chained to the desk for better preservation. The Church took fright when she found that the Waldensians and Albigensians were making and disseminating their own translations of scriptural books; and a Church council at Narbonne (1227), as we have seen, forbade laymen to possess any portion of the Scriptures.[13] But in general, before the fourteenth century, the Church was not opposed to Bible reading on the part of the laity. She did not encourage it, for she distrusted popular interpretations of scriptural mysteries.

The size of a book and its pages was determined by the size of the available skins, each of which was folded to make a "folio." After the fifth century books were no longer issued in rolls as in antiquity;* the skins were cut in rectangular sizes to make four ("quarto"), eight ("octavo"), twelve ("duodecimo"), or sixteen ("sextodecimo") sheets to a folio. Some sextodecimos, written in a "fine Italian hand," crowded long works into small compass to fit into the pocket or be a convenient manual. The binding might be of heavy parchment, cloth, leather, or board. Leather covers might be decorated by "blind tooling"—i.e., stamping uncolored designs into them with hot metal dies. Moslem artists settled in Venice introduced into Europe the technique of filling in such depressed parts with gold tints. Wood covers might be decorated with enamel or carved ivory, or inlaid with gold, silver, or gems. St. Jerome rebuked the Romans: "Your books are carved with precious stones, and Christ died naked!"[14] Few modern volumes rival the sumptuous bindings of medieval books.

Even simple books were a luxury. An ordinary volume cost between $160 and $200 in the currency of the United States of America in 1949.[15] Bernard of Chartres, a leader in the twelfth-century revival of the ancient classics, left a library of only twenty-four volumes. Italy was richer than France, and its famous jurist, the elder Accursius, collected sixty-three books. We hear of a great Bible being sold for ten talents—at least $10,000; of a missal exchanged for a vineyard; of two volumes of Priscian, the fifth-century grammarian, being paid for with a house and lot.[16] The cost of books delayed the rise of a booksellers' trade till the twelfth century; then the university towns engaged men as *stationarii* and *librarii* to organize corps of copyists to transcribe books for teachers and students; and these men sold copies to all who cared to pay. They seem never to have dreamed of paying a live author. If a man insisted on writing a new book, he had to pay its costs, or find a king or lord or magnate to grace his palm for a dedication or a laud. He could not advertise his book except by word of mouth. He could not publish it—make it public—except by getting it used in a school, or having it recited before whatever audience he could collect. So Gerald of Wales, on returning from Ireland in 1200, read his *Topography* of that country before an assemblage at Oxford.

The cost of books, and the dearth of funds for schools, produced a degree of illiteracy which would have seemed shameful to ancient Greece or Rome. North of the Alps, before 1100, literacy was almost confined to "clerics"— clergymen, accountants, scribes, governmental officials, and professional men. In the twelfth century the business classes must have been literate, for they kept elaborate accounts. In a household a book was a precious thing. Usually it was read aloud to several listeners; many later rules of punctuation and style were determined by convenience for oral reading. Books were

---

* Many government records continued to be written on rolls; such "pipe rolls" were used in England from 1131 to 1833. The keeper of these archives was "Master of the Rolls."

carefully exchanged from family to family, monastery to monastery, country to country.

Libraries, though small, were numerous. St. Benedict had ruled that every Benedictine monastery should have a library. Carthusian and Cistercian houses, despite St. Bernard's aversion to learning, became sedulous collectors of books. Many cathedrals—Toledo, Barcelona, Bamberg, Hildesheim—had substantial libraries; Canterbury had 5000 books in 1300. But this was exceptional;[17] most libraries had less than a hundred; Cluny, one of the best, had 570 volumes.[18] Manfred, King of the Sicilies, had a valuable collection, which passed to the papacy and became the nucleus of the Greek collections in the Vatican. The papal library began with Pope Damasus (366–84); its precious manuscripts and archives were mostly lost in the turmoil of the thirteenth century; the present Vatican Library dates from the fifteenth century. The universities—or, rather, their college halls—began to have libraries in the twelfth century. St. Louis founded the library of Sainte Chapelle in Paris, and enriched it with books copied for him from a hundred monasteries. Many libraries, like those of Notre Dame, St. Germain des Près, and the Sorbonne, were open to responsible students, and volumes might be taken out on adequate security. The student of today can hardly appreciate the literary wealth that city and college libraries lay freely at his feet.

There were, here and there, private libraries. Even in the darkness of the tenth century we find Gerbert collecting books with true bibliophile passion. Some other churchmen, like John of Salisbury, had their own collections, and a few nobles had small libraries in their châteaux. Frederick Barbarossa and Frederick II had considerable collections. Henry of Aragon, lord of Villena in Spain, gathered a great library, which was publicly burned on the charge that he had intercourse with the Devil.[19] About 1200 Daniel of Morley brought to England from Spain "a precious multitude of books."[20] In the twelfth century Europe discovered the wealth of Spain in books; scholars descended upon Toledo, Cordova, and Seville; and a flood of new learning poured up over the Pyrenees to revolutionize the intellectual life of the adolescent North.

III. THE TRANSLATORS

Medieval Europe, partly united by a common language, was still divided into Latin and Greek halves, mutually hostile and ignorant. The Latin heritage, except of law, was forgotten in the Greek East; the Greek heritage, except in the Sicilies, was forgotten in the West. Part of the Greek heritage was hidden beyond the walls of Christendom—in Moslem Jerusalem, Alexandria, Cairo, Tunis, Sicily, and Spain. As for the vast and distant world of India, China, and Japan, long rich in literature, philosophy, and art, Christians, before the thirteenth century, knew almost nothing.

Some of the work of linking the diverse cultures was performed by the Jews, who moved among them like fertilizing subterranean streams. As more and more Jews migrated from Moslem realms into Christendom, and lost knowledge of Arabic, their scholars found it desirable to translate Arabic works (many written by Jews) into the only language generally understood by the savants of the scattered race—Hebrew. So Joseph Kimchi (*c*. 1105–*c*. 1170), at Narbonne, translated the Jewish philosopher Bahya's *Guide to the Duties of the Heart*. Joseph was the father of brilliant sons; but even more important, as translators, were the progeny of Judah ben Saul ibn Tibbon (*c*. 1120–*c*. 1190). He too, like Kimchi, had moved from Moslem Spain to southern France; and though he was one of the most successful physicians of his time, he found energy to translate into Hebrew the Judeo-Arabic works of Saadia Gaon, Ibn Gabirol, and Jehuda Halevi. His son Samuel (*c*. 1150–*c*. 1232) stirred the Jewish world by translating into Hebrew Maimonides' *Guide to the Perplexed*. Samuel's son Moses ibn Tibbon translated from the Arabic Euclid's *Elements*, Avicenna's smaller *Canon*, al-Razi's *Antidotary*, three works of Maimonides, and Averroës' shorter commentaries on Aristotle. Samuel's grandson Jacob ibn Tibbon, besides leading the fight for Maimonides in Montpellier, and earning fame as an astronomer, translated several Arabic treatises into Hebrew, and some into Latin. Samuel's daughter married a still more famous scholar, Jacob Anatoli. Born in Marseille about 1194, Jacob was invited by Frederick II to teach Hebrew at the University of Naples; there he translated into Hebrew the larger commentaries of Averroës, profoundly affecting Jewish philosophy. A like stimulus was given to Hebrew medicine through the translation of al-Razi's *Kitab al-Mansuri* by the physician and philosopher Shem Tob at Marseille (1264).

Many Hebrew translations from the Arabic were rendered into Latin; so a Hebrew version of Avenzoar's *Taysir*, or *Aid to Health*, was turned into Latin at Padua (1280). Early in the thirteenth century a Jew translated the entire Old Testament directly and literally into Latin. The devious routes of cultural migration are exemplified by the *Fables of Bidpai*, which were translated into English from a Spanish translation of a Latin translation of a Hebrew translation of an Arabic translation of a Pahlavi translation of the supposedly original Sanskrit.[21]

The main stream whereby the riches of Islamic thought were poured into the Christian West was by translation from Arabic into Latin. About 1060 Constantine the African translated into Latin al-Razi's *Liber Experimentorum*, the Arabic medical works of Isaac Judaeus, and Hunain's Arabic version of Hippocrates' *Aphorisms* and Galen's *Commentary*. At Toledo, soon after its conquest from the Moors, the enlightened and tolerant Archbishop Raymond (*c*. 1130) organized a corps of translators under Dominico Gundisalvi, and commissioned them to translate Arabic works of science and philosophy. Most of the translators were Jews who knew Arabic, Hebrew, and Spanish, sometimes also Latin. The busiest member of the group was a converted Jew, John of Spain (or "of Seville"), whose Arabic patronymic, ibn Daud (son of David), was remodeled by the Schoolmen into Avendeath. John translated a veritable library of Arabic and Jewish works by Avicenna, al-Ghazali, al-Farabi . . . and al-Khwarizmi; through this last work he introduced the Hindu-Arabic numerals to the West.[22] Almost as influential was his rendering of a pseudo-Aristotelian book of philosophy and occultism, the *Secretum Secretorum*, whose wide circulation is indicated by the survival of 200 manuscripts. Some of these translations were made directly from Arabic into Latin; some were made into Castilian and then translated into Latin by Gundisalvi. In this way the two scholars transformed Ibn Gabirol's *Mekor Hayim* into that *Fons Vitae*, or *Fountain of Life*, which made "Avicebron" into one of the most famous philosophers in the Scholastic ken.

Minor tributaries fed the Arabic-Latin current. Adelard of Bath, having learned Arabic in Antioch, Tarsus, and Toledo, made from an Arabic version the first Latin rendering of Euclid (1120), and introduced Moslem trigonometry to the West by translating the astronomical tables of al-Khwarizmi (1126).[23] In 1141 Peter the Venerable, Abbot of Cluny, with the aid of three Christian scholars and an Arab, turned the Koran into Latin. Moslem alchemy and chemistry entered the Latin world through a translation of an Arabic text by Robert of Chester in 1144. A year later an Italian, Plato of Tivoli, translated the epochal treatise *Hibbur ha-meshihah* of the Jewish mathematician Abraham bar Hiyya.

The greatest of the translators was Gerard of Cremona. Arriving in Toledo about 1165, he was impressed by the wealth of Arabic literature in science and philosophy. He resolved to translate the best of it into Latin, and spent the remaining nine years of his life in the task. He learned Arabic, and apparently had the help of a native Christian and a Jew;[24] it seems incredible that he should have made his seventy-one translations unaided. To him the West owed Latin versions of Arabic versions of Aristotle's *Posterior Analytics, On the Heavens and the Earth, On Generation and Corruption*, and *Meteorology*; several commentaries by Alexander of Aphrodisias; Euclid's *Elements* and *Data*; Archimedes' *On the Measurement of the Circle*; Apollonius of Perga's *Conics*; eleven works ascribed to Galen; several works of Greek astronomy; four volumes of Greco-Arabic physics; eleven books of Arabic medicine, including the largest works of al-Razi and Avicenna; al-Farabi *On the Syllogism*; three works by al-Kindi, and two by Isaac Israeli; fourteen works of Arabic mathematics and astronomy; three sets of astronomical tables; and seven Arabic works on geomancy and astrology. No other man in history has ever done so much to enrich one culture with another. We can only compare Gerard's industry with that of Hunain ibn Ishaq and al-Mamun's "House of Wisdom," which in the ninth century had poured Greek science and philosophy into an Arabic mold.

Next to Spain as donor in this transfusion of culture was the Norman kingdom of the Sicilies. Soon after their conquest of the island (1091) the Norman rulers employed translators to turn into Latin the Arabic or Greek works on mathematics and astronomy then current in Palermo. Frederick II, at Foggia, carried on the work, and partly for that purpose brought to his court one of the strangest and most active minds of the early thirteenth century. Michael Scot derived his cognomen from his native Scotland. We find him at Toledo in 1217, in Bologna in 1220, in Rome in 1224–7, thereafter at Foggia or Naples. His first important translation was al-Bitruji's *Spherics*, a critique of Ptolemy. Fascinated by discovering the scope and freedom of Aristotle's thought, Scot translated into Latin, from Arabic versions, the *History of Animals*, including *On the Parts of Animals* and *On the Generation of Animals*; and an unverified tradition ascribed to him translations of the *Metaphysics*, the *Physics*, *On the Soul*, *On the Heavens*, perhaps also the *Ethics*. Michael's versions of Aristotle reached Albertus Magnus and Roger Bacon, and stirred the development of science in the thirteenth century. Charles of Anjou continued the royal patronage of translators in southern Italy; the Jewish savant Moses of Salerno worked for him, and it was probably Charles who financed the Latin translation (1274) of al-Razi's medical leviathan, the *Liber Continens*, by the Jewish scholar Faraj ben Salim of Girgenti.

All the Latin translations, so far mentioned, of Greek science and philosophy were made from Arabic versions—sometimes from Arabic versions of Syriac versions—of the already obscure originals. They were not as inaccurate as Roger Bacon charged, but there was clearly need of more direct renderings. Among the earliest such versions were those made of Aristotle's *Topics*, *Elenchi*, and *Posterior Analytics* by James, known to us only as "a clerk of Venice," at some time before 1128. In 1154 Eugene "the Emir" of Palermo translated the *Optics* of Ptolemy; and in 1160 he shared in a Latin translation of the *Almagest* directly from the Greek. Meanwhile Aristippus of Catania had translated (c. 1156) *The Lives of the Philosophers* by Diogenes Laërtius, and the *Meno* and *Phaedo* of Plato. The capture of Constantinople by the Crusaders had less result in translations than might have been expected; we hear only of a partial version of Aristotle's *Metaphysics* (1209). A fallow interval ensued; then, about 1260, William of Moerbeke, Flemish Archbishop of Corinth, began, probably with aides, a series of direct translations from the Greek whose number and importance rank him only next to Gerard of Cremona among the heroes of cultural transmission. It was partly at the request of his friend and fellow Dominican Thomas Aquinas that he translated so many of Aristotle's works: the *History of Animals*, *On the Generation of Animals*, *Politics*, and *Rhetoric*, and completed or revised earlier direct versions of the *Metaphysics*, the *Meteorology*, and *On the Soul*. For St. Thomas he translated several Greek commentaries on Aristotle or Plato. For good measure he added versions of Hippocrates' *Prognostics*, Galen *On Foods*, and divers works in physics by Hero of Alexandria and Archimedes. Perhaps we owe to him also a translation—formerly ascribed to Robert Grosseteste—of Aristotle's *Ethics*. These translations provided part of the material from which St. Thomas built his magistral *Summa Theologica*. By 1280 Aristotle had been almost completely transmitted to the Western mind.

The effects of all these translations upon Latin Europe were revolutionary. The influx of texts from Islam and Greece profoundly stirred the reawakening world of scholarship, compelled new developments in grammar and philology, enlarged the curriculum of the schools, and shared in the astonishing growth of universities in the twelfth and thirteenth centuries. It was merely an incident that, through the inability of the translators to find Latin equivalents, many Arabic words were now introduced into the languages of Europe. It was more important that algebra, the zero, and the decimal system entered the Christian West through these versions; that the theory and practice of medicine were powerfully advanced by the translation of the Greek, Latin, Arabic, and Jewish masters; and that the importation of Greek and Arabic astronomy compelled an expansion of theology, and a reconception of deity, prefacing the greater change that would follow Copernicus. The frequent references of Roger Bacon to Averroës, Avicenna, and "Alfarabius" give one measure of the new influence and stimulation; "philosophy," said Bacon, "has come down to us from the Arabs"; [25] and we shall see that Thomas Aquinas was led to write his *Summas* to halt the threatened liquidation of Christian theology by Arabic interpretations of Aristotle. Islam had now repaid to Europe the learning that it had borrowed through Syria from Greece. And as that learning had aroused the great age of Arabic science and philosophy, so now it would excite the European mind to inquiry and speculation, would force it to build the intellectual cathedral of Scholastic philosophy, and would crack stone after stone of that majestic edifice to bring the collapse of the medieval system in the fourteenth century, and the beginnings of modern philosophy in the ardor of the Renaissance.

IV. THE SCHOOLS

The transmission of culture from generation to generation was undertaken by the family, the Church, and the school. Moral education was stressed in the Middle Ages at the expense of intellectual enlightenment, as intellectual education is today stressed at the expense of moral discipline. In England it was not unusual, in the middle and upper classes, to send a boy of seven or so to be brought up for a time in another home, partly to cement family friendships, partly to offset the laxity of parental love.[26] The splendid school system of the Roman Empire had decayed in the tumult of invasion and the depopulation of the towns. When the tidal wave of migration subsided in the sixth century a few lay schools survived in Italy; the rest were mostly schools for training converts and prospective priests. For some time (500–800) the Church gave all her attention to moral training, and did not reckon the transmission of secular knowledge as one of her functions. But under the prodding of Charlemagne cathedrals, monasteries, parish churches, and convents opened schools for the general education of boys and girls.

At first the monastic schools bore nearly all this burden. A *schola interior* provided instruction for novices or oblates, and a *schola exterior* offered education to boys, apparently without charge.[27] In Germany these monastic schools survived the disorders of the ninth century, and shared productively in the Ottonian Renaissance; in the ninth and tenth centuries Germany led France in the graces of the mind. In France the disintegration of the Carolingian house, and the raids of the Northmen, struck cruel blows at the monastic schools. The palace school that Charlemagne had established at the Frank court did not long outlive Charles the Bald (d. 877). The French episcopacy grew stronger as the kings grew weaker; when the Norse raids subsided the bishops and secular clergy were richer than the abbots and the monasteries; and while the monastic schools declined in the tenth century, cathedral schools rose at Paris, Chartres, Orléans, Tours, Laon, Reims, Liége, and Cologne. When the good and great Fulbert died at Chartres, Bishop Ivo (1040?–1116) maintained the standards and renown of its cathedral school in classical studies; and this fine tradition was carried on by Ivo's successor Bernard of Chartres, whom John of Salisbury, in the twelfth century, described as "in *modern* times the most astounding spring of letters in Gaul."[28] In England the cathedral school of York was famous even before it gave Alcuin to Charlemagne. The school of Canterbury became almost a university, with an abundant library, and no less a man as secretary than the aforesaid John of Salisbury, one of the sanest scholars and philosophers of the Middle Ages. In such schools those students who were preparing for the priesthood were apparently supported by cathedral funds, while others paid a modest fee. The Third Lateran Council (1179) decreed that "in order that the opportunity of reading and making progress may not be taken away from poor children . . . let some sufficient benefice be assigned in every cathedral church for a master who shall teach gratis the clerks of the same church, and poor scholars."[29] The Fourth Lateran Council (1215) required the establishment of a chair of grammar in every cathedral of the Christian world, and instructed each archbishop to maintain also chairs of philosophy and canon law.[30] The decretals of Pope Gregory IX (1227–41) directed every parish church to organize a school of elementary instruction; and recent researches indicate that such parochial schools—chiefly devoted to religious instruction—were common throughout Christendom.[31]

What proportion of the adolescent population went to school? Of girls apparently only the well-to-do. Most convents maintained schools for girls, like that which at Argenteuil gave such excellent classical training to Héloïse (c. 1110); but these schools probably reached only a modest percentage of girls. Some cathedral schools admitted girls; Abélard speaks of the "women of noble birth" who attended his school at Notre Dame in Paris in 1114.[32] Boys had a better chance, but it was presumably difficult for the son of a serf to get an education;[33] however, we hear of serfs who managed to get sons into Oxford.[34] Much that is now taught in schools was then learned at home or through apprenticeship in shops; certainly the spread and excellence of medieval art suggest wide opportunities for training in arts and crafts. One calculation reckons the number of boys in elementary schools in England in 1530 at 26,000 in an estimated population of 5,000,000—about one thirtieth of the proportion in 1931;[35] but a recent study concludes that "the thirteenth century made a closer approach to popular and social education than the sixteenth."[36]

Normally the cathedral school was directed by a canon of the cathedral chapter, variously called *archiscola*, *scolarius*, or *scholasticus*. The teachers were clerks in minor orders. All instruction was in Latin. Discipline was severe; flogging was considered as necessary in education as hell in religion; Winchester School greeted its students with a frank hexameter: *Aut disce aut discede; manet sors tertia caedi*—"Learn or depart; a third alternative is to be flogged."[37] The curriculum began with the "trivium"—grammar, rhetoric, logic—and passed on to the "quadrivium"—arithmetic, geometry, music, astronomy; these were the "seven liberal arts." These terms did not then bear quite their modern meaning. Trivium, of course, meant three ways. Liberal arts were those that Aristotle had defined as the proper subjects for freemen who sought not practical skills (which were left to apprentices) but intellectual and moral excellence.[38] Varro (116–27 B.C.) had written *Nine Books of Disciplines*, listing nine studies as constituting the Greco-Roman curriculum; Martianus Capella, a North African scholar of the fifth century A.D., in a widely used pedagogical allegory *On the Marriage of Philology and Mercury*, had barred medicine and architecture as too practical; and the famous seven remained. "Grammar" was not the dull study that loses the soul of a language in studying its bones; it was the art of writing (*grapho, gramma*); Cassiodorus defined it as such study of great poetry and oratory as would enable one to write with correctness and elegance. In medieval schools it began with the Psalms, passed to other books of the Bible, then to the Latin Fathers, then to the Latin classics—Cicero, Virgil, Horace, Statius, Ovid. Rhetoric continued to mean the art of speaking, but again included considerable study of literature. Logic seems a rather advanced subject for the trivium, but perhaps it was good that students should learn to reason as early as they loved to argue.

The economic revolution brought some changes in the educational scene. Cities that lived by commerce and industry felt a need for employees with practical training; and against much ecclesiastical opposition they established secular schools in which lay teachers gave instruction in return for fees paid by the parents of the pupils. In 1300 the fee for a year in a private grammar school in Oxford was four or five pence ($4.50). Villani in 1283 reckoned 9000 boys and girls in the church schools of Florence, 1100 in six "abacus" schools that prepared them for a business career, and 575 pupils in secondary schools. Secular schools appeared in Flanders in the twelfth century; by the second half of the thirteenth the movement had spread to Lübeck and the Baltic cities. In 1292 we hear of a schoolmistress keeping a private school in Paris; soon she was one of many.[39] The secularization of education was on its way.

V. UNIVERSITIES OF THE SOUTH

Secular schools were especially numerous in Italy; teachers there were usually laymen, not clerics as beyond the Alps. In general the spirit and culture of Italy were less ecclesiastical than elsewhere; indeed, about the year 970, one Vilgardus organized at Ravenna a movement for the restoration of paganism.[40] There were, of course, many cathedral schools; those of Milan, Pavia, Aosta, and Parma were particularly competent, as we may judge from such graduates as Lanfranc and Anselm; and Monte Cassino under Desiderius was almost a university. The survival of municipal institutions, the successful resistance of the Lombard cities to Barbarossa (1176), and the rising demand for legal and commercial knowledge worked together to give Italy the honor of establishing the first medieval university.

In 1925 the University of Pavia celebrated the eleven hundredth anniversary of its foundation by Lothair I. Probably this was a school of law rather than a university; it was not till 1361 that it received its charter as a *studium generale*—the medieval name for a university uniting diverse faculties. It was one of many schools that from the ninth century onward revived the study of Roman law: Rome, Ravenna, and Orléans in the ninth century, Milan, Narbonne, and Lyons in the tenth, Verona, Mantua, and Angers in the eleventh. Bologna was apparently the first of the West European cities to enlarge its school into a *studium generale*. In 1076, says the chronicler Odofredus, a "certain master Pepo began by his own authority to lecture on the laws . . . at Bologna, and he was a man of the greatest renown."[41] Other teachers joined him; and by the time of Irnerius the Bologna school of law was by common consent the best in Europe.

Irnerius began to teach law at Bologna in 1088. Whether his studies of Roman law convinced him of the historical and practical arguments for the supremacy of the imperial over the ecclesiastical power, or whether the rewards of imperial service attracted him, he turned from the Guelf to the Ghibelline side, and interpreted the revived jurisprudence to favor imperial claims. Appreciative emperors contributed funds to the school, and a swarm of German students came down to Bologna. Irnerius composed a volume of glosses, or comments, on the *Corpus iuris* of Justinian, and applied scientific method to the organization of law. The *Summa codicis Irnerii*, compiled by him or from his lectures, is a masterpiece of exposition and argument.

With Irnerius began the golden age of medieval jurisprudence. Men from every country in Latin Europe came to Bologna to learn the rejuvenated science of the law. Irnerius' pupil Gratian applied the new methods to ecclesiastical legislation, and published the first code of canon law (1139). After Irnerius the "Four Doctors"—Bulgarus, Martinus, Iacobus, and Hugo—in a series of famous glosses, applied the Justinian Code to the legal problems of the twelfth century, and secured the adoption of Roman law in an ever-widening sphere. Early in the thirteenth century the elder Accursius (1185?–1260), the greatest of the "glossators," summed up their work and his own in a *Glossa ordinaria*, which became the standard authority by which kings and communes broke the sway of feudal law, and fought the power of the popes. The papacy did what it could to halt this exhumation of a code that made religion a function and servant of the state; but the new study fed and expressed the bold rationalism and secularization of the twelfth and thirteenth centuries, and raised a proliferating class of lawyers who labored to reduce the role of the Church in government, and to extend the authority of the state. St. Bernard complained that the courts of Europe rang with the laws of Justinian and no longer heard the laws of God.[42] The spread of the new jurisprudence was as strong a stimulus as the Arabic and Greek translations in generating that respect and passion for reason which was to beget and bedevil Scholasticism.

We do not know when a school of arts—i.e., the seven liberal arts—arose in Bologna, nor when was founded its celebrated school of medicine. So far as we know, the only connection among the three schools was in the fact that the graduates of any of them received their degrees from the archdeacon of Bologna. The professors organized themselves into a *collegium* or guild. About 1215 the students, in whatever faculty, associated themselves into two groups: a *universitas citramontanorum* or union of students from south of the Alps, and a *universitas ultramontanorum* or union of students from beyond the Alps. From the beginning of the thirteenth century there were women students in these "universities," and in the fourteenth century there were women professors on the Bologna faculties.[43]

The student guilds, originated to provide mutual protection and self-government, came in the thirteenth century to exercise extraordinary power over the teaching staffs. By organized boycotts of unsatisfactory teachers, the students could end the pedagogical career of any man at Bologna. In many cases the salaries of the professors were paid by the student "universities," and the professors were compelled to swear obedience to the "rectors" of the "universities"—i.e., to the head officers of the student guilds.[44] A teacher desiring leave of absence, even for a day, was obliged to obtain permission from his pupils through their rectors, and he was expressly forbidden to "create holidays at his pleasure."[45] Regulations established by the student guilds determined at what minute the teacher should begin his lecture, when he should end it, and what penalties he should pay for deviations from these rules. If he overtalked his hour the students were instructed by the guild statutes to leave. Other guild regulations fined a teacher for skipping a chapter or decretal in his exposition of the laws, and determined how much of the course was to be given to each part of the texts. At the outset of each academic year the professor was required to deposit ten pounds with a Bologna bank; from this sum the fines laid upon him by the rectors were deducted; and the remainder was refunded to him at the close of the year on instruction from the rectors. Committees of students were appointed to observe the conduct of each teacher, and report irregularities or deficiencies to the rectors.[46] If these arrangements seem to the modern student unusually sensible, it should be remembered that the law students at Bologna were men between seventeen and forty years of age, old enough to provide their own discipline; that they came to study, not to play; that the professor was not the employee of trustees, but a free-lance lecturer whom the students in effect engaged to instruct them. The teacher's salary at Bologna consisted of fees paid him by his students and fixed by agreement with them. This system of payment was changed toward the end of the thirteenth century when Italian cities eager to have universities of their own offered municipal salaries to certain Bolognese professors; the city of Bologna thereupon (1289) promised to pay two professors an annual stipend; but the choice of professors was still left to the students. Gradually the number of these municipal *salaria* increased; and in the fourteenth century the selection of professors passed, with their payment, to the city. When Bologna became part of the Papal States in 1506 the appointment of the teachers became a function of the ecclesiastical authorities.

In the thirteenth century, however, the University of Bologna, and in less degree the other universities of Italy, were marked by a lay spirit, almost an anticlericalism, hardly to be found in other centers of European education. Whereas in these others the chief faculty was theology, there was at Bologna no theological faculty at all before 1364; theology there was replaced by canon law. Even rhetoric took the form of law, and the art of writing became—at Bologna, Paris, Orléans, Montpellier, Tours . . .—the *ars dictaminis* or *ars notaria*, the art of writing legal, business, or official documents; and special degrees were given in this art.[47] It was a common saying that the most realistic education obtainable was to be had in Bologna; a favorite story told how a Parisian pedagogue unlearned at Bologna what he had taught at Paris, and then came back to Paris and untaught it.[48] In the twelfth century Bologna led the movement of the European mind; in the thirteenth it allowed its teaching to stiffen into a stagnant scholasticism of law; the Accursian gloss became a sacred and almost unchangeable text, impeding the progressive adaptation of law to the flux of life. The spirit of inquiry fled to freer fields.

Italy broke out into universities in the twelfth and thirteenth centuries. Some of them were spawned by Bologna through the emigration of professors or students; so in 1182 Pillius left to set up a school in Modena; in 1188 Iacobus de Mandra went to Reggio Emilia and brought his pupils with him; in 1204 another migration, probably from Bologna, established a *studium generale*, or union of several faculties, at Vicenza; in 1215 Roffredus left the University of Bologna to open a law school at Arezzo; in 1222 a large secession of teachers and students from Bologna expanded an old school at Padua. Faculties of medicine and the arts were added to this school of law at Padua; Venice sent her students there, and contributed to the professorial salaries paid by the city; and in the fourteenth century Padua became one of the most vigorous centers of European thought. In 1224 Frederick II founded the University of Naples to keep the students of South Italy from flocking north. Perhaps for like reasons, as well as to train men for ecclesiastical diplomacy, Innocent IV established the University of the Court of Rome (1244), which followed the papal court in its migration, even to Avignon. In 1303 Boniface VIII founded the University of Rome, which rose to glory under Nicholas V and Leo X, and won the name of Sapienza under Paul III. Siena inaugurated its municipal university in 1246, Piacenza in 1248. By the end of the thirteenth century schools of law and the arts, and sometimes schools of medicine too, were to be found in every major city of Italy.

The universities of Spain were unique in being founded and chartered by the kings, serving them, and submitting to governmental control. Castile developed a royal university at Palencia (1208), later at Valladolid (1304); Leon had one at Salamanca (1227), the Baleares at Palma (1280), Catalonia at Lerida (1300). Despite this royal connection the Spanish universities accepted ecclesiastical supervision and funds, and some, like Palencia, grew out of cathedral schools. The University of Salamanca was richly endowed in the thirteenth century by San Fernando and Alfonso the Wise, and soon stood on an equal footing of fame and learning with Bologna and Paris. Most of these institutions gave instruction in Latin, mathematics, astronomy, theology, and law; some in medicine, Hebrew, or Greek. A School of Oriental Studies was opened at Toledo in 1250 by Dominican monks to teach Arabic and Hebrew; good work must have been done there, for one of its graduates, Raymond Martin (c. 1260), showed familiarity with all major philosophers and theologians of Islam. Arabic studies were prominent also at the University of Seville, founded by Alfonso the Wise in 1254. At Lisbon, in 1290, the poet-king Diniz gave a university to Portugal.

VI. UNIVERSITIES OF FRANCE

The unquestioned leader of the European mind, in the medieval meridian of the twelfth and thirteenth centuries, was France. Its cathedral schools had from the early eleventh century achieved international renown. If these schools flowered into a great university at Paris, rather than at Chartres, Laon, or Reims, it was probably because the thriving commerce of the Seine,

and the business of a capital, had brought to the city the wealth that lures
the intellect and finances science, philosophy, and art.

The first known master of the cathedral school of Notre Dame was
William of Champeaux (1070?–1121); it was his lectures, given in the cloisters of Notre Dame, that stirred up the intellectual movement out of which
the University of Paris grew. When (*c.* 1103) Abélard came out of Brittany,
slew William with a syllogism, and began the most famous lectures in French
history, students flocked to hear him. The schools of Paris swelled their
ranks, and masters multiplied. A master (*magister*), in the educational world
of twelfth-century Paris, was a man licensed to teach by the chancellor of
the Cathedral of Notre Dame. The University of Paris rose by now un-
traceable steps from the church schools of the city, and derived its first unity
from this single source of pedagogical licensing. Normally the license was
given gratis to anyone who had been for an adequate period the pupil of
an authorized master, and whose application was approved by that master.
It was one of the charges made against Abélard that he had set himself up
as a teacher without having served such an approved apprenticeship.

This conception of the teaching art in terms of master and apprentice
shared in the idea and origin of the university. As the masters multiplied,
they naturally formed a guild. The word *universitas* had for centuries been
applied to any collectivity, including guilds. In 1214 Matthew Paris described a "fellowship of the elect masters" at Paris as an institution of long
standing. We may assume, but cannot prove, that the "university" took form
toward 1170, rather as a guild of teachers than as a union of faculties. About
1210 a bull of Innocent III—himself a graduate of Paris—recognized and approved the written statutes of this teachers' guild; and another bull of the
same Pope empowered the guild to choose a proctor to represent it at the
papal court.

By the middle of the thirteenth century the Parisian masters were divided
into four faculties or powers: theology, canon law, medicine, and "arts." In
contrast with Bologna, civil law had, after 1219, no place in the University
of Paris; the curriculum began with the seven arts, advanced to philosophy,
and culminated in theology. The arts students (who were called *artistae*,
art-ists) corresponded to our "undergraduates." As they constituted by far
the greatest part of the academic population in Paris, they divided, probably
for mutual aid, sociability, and discipline, into four "nations" according to
their place of birth (*natio*) or origin: "France" (i.e., the narrow realm directly subject to the French king), Picardy, Normandy, and England. Students from southern France, Italy, and Spain were taken into the French
"nation," students from the Low Countries into "Picardy," students from
central and eastern Europe into "England." So many students came from
Germany that that country was delayed in establishing its own universities
until 1347. Each "nation" was governed by a *procurator* or proctor, each

faculty by a *decanus* or dean. The students—and perhaps also the masters—in the faculty of arts chose a rector as their head; gradually his functions widened until by 1255 he had become the rector of the university.

We hear of no special university buildings. Apparently, in the twelfth century, the lectures were given in the cloisters of Notre Dame, St. Genevieve, St. Victor, or other ecclesiastic structures; but in the thirteenth century we find teachers hiring private rooms for their classes. The masters, who came to be called also *professores*, proclaimers, were tonsured clerics, who, before the fifteenth century, lost their position if they married. Teaching was by lectures, largely for the reason that not every student could afford to buy all the texts to be studied, and could not always secure copies from the libraries. The students sat on pavement or floor, and took many notes. The burden on their memories was so severe that many mnemonic devices were contrived, usually in the form of verses pregnant with meaning and repulsive in form. University regulations forbade the teacher to read his lecture; he was required to speak extempore; he was even forbidden to "drawl."[49] Students graciously warned newcomers not to pay for a course until they had attended three lectures. William of Conches, in the twelfth century, complained that teachers gave easy courses to gain popularity, students, and fees; and that the elective system by which each student had a wide choice among teachers and subjects was lowering the standard of education.[50]

The teaching was occasionally enlivened by public disputations among the masters, advanced students, and distinguished visitors. Usually the discussion followed a set form, the *scholastica disputatio*: the question was stated; a negative answer was given, and was defended by scriptural and patristic quotations, and by reasoning in the form of objections; a positive answer followed, defended by quotations from the Bible and the Fathers of the Church, and by reasoned replies to the objections. This *scholastica·disputatio* determined the finished form of the Scholastic philosophy in St. Thomas Aquinas. In addition to such formal *quaestiones disputatae* there were informal discussions called *quodlibeta*—"whatever you please"—where the disputants took up any question that might be propounded at the moment. These looser debates also created a literary form, as in the minor writings of St. Thomas. Such debates, formal or informal, sharpened the medieval mind, and gave scope for much freedom of thought and speech; in some men, however, they tended to promote a cleverness that could prove anything, or a logorrhea that piled mountains of argument on trivial points.

Most of the students lived in *hospicia* or guesthouses hired by organized student groups. Sometimes a hospital would board poor students at a nominal fee; so the Hôtel-Dieu, adjoining Notre Dame, set aside a room for "poor clerks." In 1180 Jocius of London bought this apartment, and thereafter shared with the hospital in providing lodging and meals for eighteen students in it. By 1231 this group of students had taken larger quarters, but they still called themselves the *Collège des dix-huit*—the College of Eighteen. Other *hospicia* or residence halls were established by monastic orders, or churches, or philanthropists, with endowments (*bursae*) or annuities that reduced the cost of living for the student. In 1257 Robert de Sorbon, chaplain to St. Louis, endowed the "House of Sorbonne" for sixteen theological students; additional benefactions from Louis and others provided more accommodations, and raised the number of scholarships to thirty-six; out of this "house" grew the College of the Sorbonne.* Further "colleges"—*collegia* in the old sense of associations—were founded after 1300; masters came to live in them, served as tutors, heard recitations, and "read" texts with the students. In the fifteenth century the masters gave courses in the residence halls; such courses increased in number, courses given outside decreased, and the college became a hall of education as well as a student dwelling place. A similar evolution of the college out of the *hospicium* occurred at Oxford, Montpellier, and Toulouse. The university began as an association of teachers dealing with associations of students, and became an association of faculties and colleges.

Among the residence halls at Paris were two designed for student members or novices of the Dominican or the Franciscan Order. The Dominicans had from their inception stressed education as a means of combating heresy; they established their own system of schools, of which the Dominican *studium generale* at Cologne was the most renowned; and they had similar institutions at Bologna and Oxford. Many friars became masters, and taught in the halls of their orders. In 1232 Alexander of Hales, one of the ablest teachers in Paris, joined the Franciscans, and continued his public courses in their Convent of the Cordeliers. Year by year the number of friars lecturing at Paris increased, and their nonmonastic audiences grew. The secular masters mourned that they were left sitting at their desks "like lonely sparrows on the housetops"; to which the friars replied that the secular masters ate and drank too much, and became lazy and dull.[51] In 1253 a student was killed in a street brawl; the city authorities arrested several students, and ignored their right and demand to be tried by the University masters or the bishop; the masters, in protest, ordered a cessation of lectures. Two Dominican teachers and one Franciscan, all members of the masters' association, refused to obey the order to cease talk; the association suspended them from membership; they appealed to Alexander IV, who (1255) ordered the university of masters to readmit them. To avoid compliance, the masters disbanded; the Pope excommunicated them; students and populace attacked the friars in the streets. After six years of controversy a compromise was reached: the

---

* In the sixteenth century the Sorbonne became the theological faculty of the University; in 1792 it was closed by the Revolution; it was restored by Napoleon, and is now the seat of public courses in science and letters at the University of Paris.

reorganized masters admitted the monastic masters, who pledged full obedience to "university" statutes thereafter; but the faculty of arts permanently excluded all monks from membership. The University of Paris, once a favorite of the popes, became hostile to the papacy, supported the kings against the pontiffs, and formed in later days the center of the "Gallican" movement that sought to separate the French Church from Rome.

No educational institution since Aristotle has rivaled the influence of the University of Paris. For three centuries it drew to itself not only the largest number of students, but the greatest dynasty of intellectually distinguished men. Abélard, John of Salisbury, Albertus Magnus, Siger of Brabant, Thomas Aquinas, Bonaventura, Roger Bacon, Duns Scotus, William of Occam—these are almost the history of philosophy from 1100 to 1400. There must have been great teachers at Paris to produce these greater ones, and an atmosphere of mental exhilaration that comes only to the peaks of human history. Furthermore, through those centuries, the University of Paris was a power in both Church and state. It was an influential organ of opinion; in the fourteenth century a hotbed of free speculation; in the fifteenth a citadel of orthodoxy and conservatism. It cannot be said to have played "no mean role" in the condemnation of Joan of Arc.

Other universities shared in giving France the cultural leadership of Europe. Orléans had had a school of law as far back as the ninth century; in the twelfth it rivaled Chartres as a center of classical and literary studies; in the thirteenth it was second only to Bologna in the teaching of civil and canon law. Hardly less famous was the school of law at Angers, which in 1432 became one of the major universities of France. Toulouse owed its university to its heresies: in 1229 Gregory IX compelled Count Raymond to pledge himself to pay the salaries of fourteen professors—in theology, canon law, and the arts—who should be sent from Paris to Toulouse to combat the Albigensian heresy by their influence on Aquitanian youth.

The most renowned of the French universities outside of Paris was at Montpellier. Situated on the Mediterranean halfway between Marseille and Spain, that city enjoyed a stirring mixture of French, Greek, Spanish, and Jewish blood and culture, with a sprinkling of Italian merchants, and some remnants of the Moorish colony that had once held the town. Commerce was active there. Whether through the influence of Salernian or Arabic or Jewish medicine, Montpellier, at an unknown date, established a school of medicine that soon outshone Salerno; schools of law, theology, and the "arts" were added; and though these colleges were independent, their propinquity and co-operation earned for Montpellier a high repute. The university declined in the fourteenth century, but the school of medicine revived in the Renaissance; and in 1537 one François Rabelais gave there, in Greek, a course of lectures on Hippocrates.

VII. UNIVERSITIES OF ENGLAND

Oxford, like the equivalently named Bosporus, developed as a cattle crossing; the Thames narrowed and grew shallow at that point; a fortress was built there in 912, a market formed, and Kings Cnut and Harold held gemots there long before the University arose. Presumably there were schools at Oxford in Cnut's days, but we hear of no cathedral school. About 1117 we find mention of a "master at Oxenford." In 1133 Robert Pullen, a theologian, came from Paris and lectured at Oxford on theology.[52] By steps now lost to history, the schools of Oxford became in the twelfth century a *studium generale* or university—"no man can say when."[53] In 1209, according to a contemporary estimate, there were 3000 students and teachers at Oxford.[54] As at Paris there were four faculties: arts, theology, medicine, and canon law. In England the teaching of civil law escaped the universities, and lodged at the Inns of Court in London. Lincoln's Inn, Gray's Inn, the Inner and the Middle Temple were the fourteenth-century descendants of the homes or chambers in which judges and teachers of the law, in the twelfth and thirteenth centuries, received students as apprentices.

At Oxford, as at Paris and Cambridge, the colleges began as endowed residence halls for poor students. At an early date they became also lecture halls; masters dwelt in them with the students; and by the end of the thirteenth century the *aulae* or halls had become the physical and pedagogical constituents of the University. About 1260 Sir John de Balliol of Scotland (father of the Scotch king of 1292), as penance for an unknown crime, established at Oxford a "House of Balliol" to maintain, by a grant of eight pence ($8) a week, certain poor scholars called *socii*, "fellows." Three years later Walter de Merton founded and endowed the "House of the Scholars of Merton," first at Malden, soon at Oxford, to care for as many students as its income could support. These revenues were repeatedly doubled by the rise of land values, so that Archbishop Peckham in 1284 complained that the "poor scholars" were receiving additional allowances for "delicate living."[55] In general the English colleges grew wealthy not only by fellowship grants and other gifts, but through the rise in the value of the estates with which they were endowed. About 1280 a bequest by William of Durham, Archbishop of Rouen, established University Hall, now University College; the modest beginnings of these famous colleges is shown in the terms of foundation, which provided for four masters and such scholars as might care to board with them. The masters chose one of their number as "senior fellow" to manage the hall; in time he or his successors appropriated those titles of "master" or "principal" by which the heads of the English colleges are known today. The University of Oxford in the thirteenth century was the association of these colleges under a "university" or guild of masters, themselves governed by regents and a chancellor of their own choosing, who in turn was subject to the bishop of Lincoln and the king.

By 1300 Oxford ranked next to Paris as a center of intellectual activity and influence. Its most famous graduate was Roger Bacon; other Franciscan monks, including Adam Marsh, Thomas of York, John Peckham, formed with him there a distinguished group of learned men. Their leader and inspiration, Robert Grosseteste (1175?–1253), was the finest figure in the life of Oxford in the thirteenth century. He studied law, medicine, and natural science there, graduated in 1179, took his divinity degree in 1189, and soon afterward was chosen "Master of the Oxford Schools"—the earlier form of the title of chancellor. In 1235, while still remaining head of Oxford, he became Bishop of Lincoln, and superintended the completion of the great cathedral. He energetically promoted the study of Greek and of Aristotle, and shared in the heroic effort of the thirteenth-century mind to reconcile Aristotle's philosophy with the Christian faith. He wrote commentaries on Aristotle's *Physics* and *Posterior Analytics*, summarized the science of his time in a *Compendium Scientiarum*, and worked for a reform of the calendar. He understood the principles of the microscope and the telescope, and opened many paths for Roger Bacon in mathematics and physics; it was probably he who acquainted Bacon with the magnifying property of the lens.[56] Many ideas that we ascribe to Bacon—on perspective, the rainbow, tides, the calendar, the desirability of experiment—were apparently suggested to him by Grosseteste; above all, the notion that all science must be based upon mathematics, since all force, in its passage through space, follows geometrical forms and rules.[57] He wrote French poetry and a treatise on husbandry, and was a lawyer and a physician as well as a theologian and a scientist. He encouraged the study of Hebrew with a view to converting the Jews; meanwhile he behaved toward them in an anomalously Christian way, and protected them as well as he could from the sadism of the mob. He was an active social reformer, always loyal to the Church, but daring to lay before Pope Innocent IV (1250) a written memorial in which he ascribed the shortcomings of the Church to the practices of the Papal Curia.[58] At Oxford he established the first "chest" to make gratuitous loans to scholars.[59] He was the first of a thousand brilliant minds whose achievements created the magnificent prestige of Oxford in the educational and intellectual world.

Today Oxford is a manufacturing center as well as a university, and makes automobiles as well as dons. But Cambridge is still a city of colleges, a medieval jewel brightened with modern wealth and British good taste; everything in it pertains to its colleges, and the medieval peace of mind survives in this loveliest of university towns. Apparently its intellectual eminence must be dated from a murder at Oxford. In 1209 a woman was killed there by a student; the townspeople raided a residence hall, and hanged two or three students. The university—i.e., the association of masters—suspended operations in protest against the action of the townsfolk; and, if we may believe the usually trustworthy Matthew Paris, 3000 students, and presumably many masters, left Oxford. A large number of them, we are told, went to Cambridge and set up halls and faculties; this is the first mention we have of anything higher there than an elementary school. A second migration— of Parisian students in 1228—swelled the ranks of the student body. Monks mendicant or Benedictine came and established colleges. In 1281 the Bishop of Ely organized the first secular college in Cambridge—St. Peter's College, now Peterhouse. The fourteenth, fifteenth, and sixteenth centuries saw the foundation and embellishment of additional colleges, some of them among the masterpieces of medieval architecture. All of them together, embraced by the quiet winding Cam, constitute with their campuses one of the fairest works of man.

VIII. STUDENT LIFE

The medieval student might be of any age. He might be a curate, a prior, an abbot, a merchant, a married man; he might be a lad of thirteen, troubled with the sudden dignity of his years. He went to Bologna, Orléans, or Montpellier to become a lawyer or a physician; to other universities he went in some cases to prepare for governmental service, usually to make a career in the Church. He encountered no entrance examinations; the only requirements were a knowledge of Latin, and ability to pay a modest fee to each master whose course he took. If he was poor he might be helped by a scholarship, or by his village, his friends, his church, or his bishop. There were thousands of such cases.[60] Abbot Samson, hero of Jocelyn's *Chronicle* and Carlyle's *Past and Present*, owed his education to a poor priest who sold holy water to keep Samson in fees.[61] A student traveling to or from a university usually received free transportation, and free food and lodging at monasteries on the way.[62]

Arriving at Oxford, Paris, or Bologna, he would find himself one of a large crowd of happy, embarrassed, and eager students riding on a wave of intellectual enthusiasm that made philosophy—with a dash of heresy—as exciting as war, and a debate as fascinating as a tournament. At Paris he would have found, in 1300, some 7000 students, at Bologna 6000, at Oxford 3000;* in general the universities of Paris, Oxford, and Bologna had more students in

---

* These are the conservative estimates of Rashdall.[63] The jurist Odofredus, writing about 1250, reckoned the students in Bologna in 1200 at 10,000. Rabanus Gauma, a Nestorian monk, put the number of students at Paris in 1287 at 30,000. Fitzralph, Archbishop of Armagh, calculated, about 1360, that there had once been 30,000 students at Oxford; about 1380 Wyclif doubled this estimate; in 1450 Bishop Gascoigne, who had been Chancellor of Oxford, returned to 30,000.[64] These estimates are evidently guesswork and exaggeration; but we cannot prove them false.

the thirteenth century than later, probably because they had less competition. The newcomer would be received by his "nation," and might be guided into living quarters—perhaps with some poor family; if he had the right connections he might get a bed and share a room in one of the *hospicia* or residence halls, where his expenses would be light. In 1374 a student at Oxford paid 104 shillings ($1040) a year for bed and board, twenty ($200) for tuition, forty for clothes.[65]

No specific academic dress was enjoined upon him; however, he was requested to button his robe and not go shoeless unless his robe reached to his heels.[66] For distinction masters wore a *cappa*—a red or purple cope with miniver border and hood; sometimes they covered the head with a square biretta, topped with a tuft instead of a tassel. The student at Paris had the status and ecclesiastical immunities of a cleric: he was exempt from military service, state taxation, or secular trial; he was expected—not always compelled—to take the tonsure; if he married he could continue as a student, but he lost his clerical privileges, and could not take a degree. A judicious promiscuity, however, involved no such penalties. The monk Jacques de Vitry, about 1230, described the Parisian students as

> more dissolute than the people. They counted fornication no sin. Prostitutes dragged passing clerics to brothels almost by force, and openly through the streets; if the clerics refused to enter, the whores called them sodomites. . . . That abominable vice [sodomy] so filled the city that it was held a sign of honor if a man kept one or more concubines. In one and the same house there were classrooms above and a brothel beneath; upstairs masters lectured, downstairs courtesans carried on their base services; in the same house the debates of philosophers could be heard with the quarrels of courtesans and pimps.[67]

This has all the earmarks of righteous exaggeration; we may only conclude that at Paris *cleric* and *saint* were not synonyms.* Jacques goes on to tell how each national group among the students had favorite adjectives for the other groups: the English were heavy drinkers and had tails; the French were proud and effeminate; the Germans were *furibundi* (blusterers) and "obscene in their cups"; the Flemish were fat and greedy and "soft as butter"; and all of them, "through such backbiting, often passed from words to blows."[69] At Paris the students were crowded at first into the island holding Notre Dame; this was the original Latin Quarter, so called because the students were required to speak Latin even in non-scholastic converse—a rule often breached. Even when the *quartier latin* was extended to include the west end of the suburb south of the Seine, the students were too numerous to be easily policed. Altercations were frequent between student and student, student and master, student and townsman, secular and monk. At Oxford

---

* But cf. Rashdall: "There is only too much evidence that de Vitry's picture of the scholastic life of his age, if exaggerated, is not fundamentally untruthful."[68]

the bell of St. Mary's summoned the students, and the bell of St. Martin's called the burghers, to do battle in an intermittent war between gown and town. One riot in Oxford (1298) cost £3,000 ($150,000) in damage to property.[70] A Paris official (1269) issued a proclamation against scholars who "by day and night atrociously wound and slay many, carry off women, ravish virgins, break into houses," and commit "over and over again robberies and many other enormities."[71] Oxford boys may have been less given to lechery than the pupils of Paris, but homicides were frequent there, and executions were rare. If the murderer left town he was seldom pursued; and an Oxford man considered it sufficient punishment for an Oxford murderer to be compelled to go to Cambridge.[72]

As water was hardly safe to drink, and neither tea nor coffee nor tobacco had yet reached Europe, the students reconciled themselves with wine and beer to Aristotle and heatless rooms. One of the main reasons for organizing a "university" of students was to celebrate religious or academic festivals with conspicuously virile drinking. Every step in the scholastic year was a "jocund advent" to be graced with wine. Students in many cases provided such refreshments for their examiners; and the "nations" usually consumed in the taverns whatever remained in their treasuries at the end of the scholastic year. Dicing was an added solace; some students earned excommunication by playing dice on the altars of Notre Dame.[73] In their more orderly moments the students amused themselves with dogs, hawks, music, dancing, chess, telling stories, and hazing newcomers. Such fledglings were styled *bejauni*—yellow-bills; they were bullied and hoaxed, and were made to provide a feast for their lords of a year's advantage. Discipline relied largely on rules established by each hall of residence; violations were punished with fines or by "sconces"—whereby an offending student was mulcted in gallons of wine, to be corporately consumed. Flogging, though frequent in grammar schools, is not mentioned in university discipline till the fifteenth century. For the rest the university authorities required every student at the beginning of each year to take a solemn oath to obey all regulations. Among the required oaths at Paris was one pledging the student not to take vengeance on examiners who failed to pass him.[74] The students swore in haste and sinned at leisure. Perjury was prevalent; hell had no terrors for young theologians.

Nevertheless the students found time for lectures. There were sluggards among them; some who preferred leisure to fame favored the courses in canon law, whose sessions began at the third hour and allowed them to complete their sleep.[75] As the third hour was nine A.M., it is apparent that most classes met soon after dawn, probably at seven. At the beginning of the thirteenth century the school season lasted eleven months; by the end of the fourteenth century the "long vacation," originating in the need for youthful hands at harvest time, ran from June 28 to August 25 or September 15. At

Oxford and Paris only a few days were left free at Christmas and Easter; at Bologna, whose students were of greater age and means, and perhaps more distant provenance, ten days were allowed at Christmas, fourteen at Easter, twenty-one for the carnival preceding Lent.

There were seemingly no examinations during the scholastic course. There were recitations and disputations, and incompetent students might be weeded out en route. Toward the middle of the thirteenth century the custom arose of requiring the student, after five years of resident study, to pass a preliminary examination by a committee of his nation. This involved first a private test—a *responsio* to questions; second, a public disputation in which the candidate defended one or more theses against challengers, and concluded with a summation of the results (*determinatio*). Those who passed these preliminary trials were called *baccalarii*, bachelors, and were allowed to serve a master as assistant teacher or "cursory" lecturer. The bachelor might continue his resident studies for three years more; then, if his master thought him fit for the ordeal, he was presented to examiners appointed by the chancellor. Masters were expected not to present clearly unprepared candidates unless these were rich in money or dignity; in such cases the public examination was adjusted to the candidate's capacity, or it might be dispensed with altogether.[76] Qualities of character were included as subjects for examination; moral offenses committed during his four or seven years at the university might then block the candidate's access to a degree, for the degree attested moral fitness as well as intellectual preparation. Of seventeen failures at the examination of forty-three candidates in Vienna in 1449, all were for moral, none for intellectual, deficiency.

If the student passed this public and final examination he became a master or "doctor," and automatically received an ecclesiastically sanctioned license to teach anywhere in Christendom. As a bachelor he had taught with uncovered head; now he was crowned with a biretta, received a kiss and a blessing from his master, and, seated in the magisterial chair, gave an inaugural lecture or held an inaugural disputation; this was his *inceptio*—called at Cambridge his "commencement" as a master. It was essential to such graduation that he should entertain all or a large number of the masters of the university at a banquet, and make presents to them. By these and other ceremonies he was received into the magisterial guild.

It is comforting to observe that medieval education had defects as troublesome as the educational systems of today. Only a small proportion of matriculants survived the five years required for the baccalaureate. The assumption of all the defined doctrines of the Church as binding on belief put the mind to rest instead of to work. The search for arguments to prove these beliefs, the citing of scriptural or patristic support for them, the interpretation of Aristotle to harmonize with them, trained intellectual subtlety rather than intellectual conscience. We may forgive these faults more readily if we consider that any way of life develops a similar dogmatism about the assumptions on which it rests. So today we leave men free to question the religious, but not the political, faith of their fathers; and political heresy is punished by social ostracism as theological heresy was punished by excommunication in the Age of Faith; now that the policeman labors to take the place of God, it becomes more dangerous to question the state than to doubt the Church. No system smiles upon the challenging of its axioms.

The transmission of knowledge and the training of appreciation are obviously more widespread, and seem more abundant, than in the Middle Ages; but we should not readily say the same for the education of character. Practical ability was not lacking in the medieval graduate; the universities sent forth a considerable number of able administrators, lawyers who made the French monarchy, philosophers who led Christianity out upon the high seas of reason, popes who dared to think in European terms. The universities sharpened the intellect of Western man, created a language for philosophy, made learning respectable, and ended the mental adolescence of the triumphant barbarians.

While so many other achievements of the Middle Ages crumble before the juggernaut of time, the universities, bequeathed to us by the Age of Faith in all the elements of their organization, adjust themselves to inescapable change, moult their old skins to live new lives, and wait for us to wed them to government.

CHAPTER XXXV

Abélard

1079-1142

I. DIVINE PHILOSOPHY

LET us give a separate chapter to Abélard. Not merely as a philosopher, nor as one of the creators of the University of Paris, nor as a flame that set the mind of Latin Europe afire in the twelfth century; but as, with Héloïse, part and personification of the morals and literature and highest fascination of their time.

He was born in Brittany, near Nantes, in the village of Le Pallet. His father, known to us only as Bérenger, was the seigneur of a modest estate, and could afford to give his three sons and one daughter a liberal education. Pierre (we do not know the origin of his surname Abélard) was the oldest, and could claim the rights of primogeniture; but he felt so lively an interest in studies and ideas that, on growing up, he surrendered to his brothers his claim and share in the family property, and set out to woo philosophy wherever a philosophic battle raged, or some famous teacher taught. It meant much for his career that one of his first masters was Jean Roscelin (c. 1050– c. 1120), a rebel who prefigured Abélard by drawing down upon his head the condemnation of the Church.

The controversy that Roscelin had aroused stemmed from what seemed the most harmless problem of the driest logic—the objective existence of "universals." In Greek and medieval philosophy a universal was a general idea denoting a class of objects (book, stone, planet, man, mankind, the French people, the Catholic Church), actions (cruelty, justice), or qualities (beauty, truth). Plato, seeing the transitoriness of individual organisms and things, had suggested that the universal is more lasting, therefore more real, than any member of the class it describes: beauty more real than Phryne, justice more real than Aristides, man more real than Socrates; this is what the Middle Ages meant by "realism." Aristotle had countered that the universal is merely an idea formed by the mind to represent a class of like objects; the class itself exists, he thought, only as its constituent members. In our time men have debated whether there is a "group mind" apart from the desires, ideas, and feelings of the individuals composing the group; and Hume argued that the individual "mind" itself is only an abstract name for the series and collection of sensations, ideas, and volitions in an organism. The Greeks did

931

not take the problem too much to heart; and one of the last pagan philoso-phers—Porphyry (c. 232–c. 304) of Syria and Rome—merely phrased it without offering a solution. But to the Middle Ages the question was vital. The Church claimed to be a spiritual entity additional to the sum of her in-dividual adherents; the whole, she felt, had qualities and powers beyond those of its parts; she could not admit that she was an abstraction, and that the endless ideas and relations suggested by the term "the Church" were nothing but ideas and feelings in her constituent members; she was the living "bride of Christ." Worse yet: if only individual persons, things, actions, and ideas existed, what became of the Trinity? Was the unity of the three Per-sons a mere abstraction; were they three separate gods? We must place our-selves in his theological environment to understand the fate of Roscelin.

We know his views only through the reports of his opponents. We are told that he considered universals or general ideas to be mere words (voces), mere winds of the voice (flatus vocis); individual objects and persons exist; all else is names (nomina). Genera and species and qualities have no inde-pendent existence; man does not exist, only men; color exists only in the form of colored things. The Church would doubtless have let Roscelin alone had he not applied this "nominalism" to the Trinity. God, he is reported to have said, is a word applied to the three Persons of the Trinity, just as man is ap-plied to many men; but all that really exists is the three Persons—in effect, three gods. This was to admit the polytheism of which Islam implicitly ac-cused Christianity five times a day from a thousand minarets. The Church could not allow such teaching in one who was a canon of the cathedral at Compiègne. Roscelin was summoned before an episcopal synod at Soissons (1092), and was given a choice between retraction and excommunication. He retracted. He fled to England, attacked clerical concubinage there,[1] re-turned to France, and taught at Tours and Loches. It was probably at Loches that Abélard sat impatiently at his feet.[2] Abélard rejected nominalism, but it was for doubts about the Trinity that he was twice condemned. It deserves also to be noted that the twelfth century called realism "the ancient doc-trine," and gave to its opponents the name of moderni—moderns.[3]

The Church was ably defended by Anselm (1033–1109) in several works that seem to have deeply moved Abélard, if only to opposition. Anselm came of a patrician family in Italy; he was made Abbot of Bec in Normandy in 1078; under his rule, as under that of Lanfranc, Bec became one of the major schools of learning in the West. As perhaps ideally described by his fellow monk Eadmer in a loving biography, Anselm was a gentle ascetic who wished only to meditate and pray, and reluctantly emerged from his cell to govern the monastery and its school. To such a man, whose faith was his life, doubt was impossible; faith must come long before understanding; and how could any finite mind expect ever to understand God? "I do not seek to un-derstand in order to believe," he said, following Augustine, "I believe in order to understand." But his pupils asked for arguments for use against infidels; he himself considered it "negligent if, after we are confirmed in our faith, we should not aim to understand what we have believed"; [4] he accepted the motto *fides quaerens intellectum*—faith in quest of understanding; and in a series of immensely influential works he inaugurated Scholastic philosophy by attempting a rational defense of the Christian faith.

In a little treatise, *Monologion*, he argued for the objective existence of universals: our notions of goodness, justice, and truth are relative, and have meaning only by comparison with some absolute goodness, justice, and truth; unless this Absolute exists we have no certain standards of judgment, and our science and our morality alike are baseless and void; God—objective goodness, justice, and truth—is this saving Absolute, the necessary assumption of our lives. As if to carry this realism to the utmost, Anselm proceeded in his *Proslogion* (c. 1074) to his famous ontological proof of the existence of God: God is the most perfect being that we can conceive; but if He were merely an idea in our heads He would lack one element of perfection—namely, existence: therefore God, the most perfect being, exists. A modest monk, Gaunilo, signing himself *Insipiens* (Fool), wrote to Anselm, protesting that we cannot pass so magically from conception to existence, and that an equally valid argument would prove the existence of a perfect island; and Thomas Aquinas agreed with Gaunilo.[5] In another brilliant but unconvincing tract—*Cur Deus homo?*—Anselm sought some rational ground for the fundamental Christian belief that God had become man. Why was this incarnation necessary? An opinion defended by Ambrose, Pope Leo I, and several Fathers of the Church [6] held that by eating the forbidden fruit Adam and Eve had sold themselves and all their progeny to the Devil, and that only the death of God become man could ransom humanity from Satan and hell. Anselm proposed a subtler argument: the disobedience of our first parents was an infinite offense, because it sinned against an infinite being, and disturbed the moral order of the world; only an infinite atonement could balance and wipe out that infinite offense; only an infinite being could offer such infinite atonement; God became man to restore the moral balance of the world.

The realism of Anselm was developed by one of Roscelin's pupils, William of Champeaux (1070?–1121). In 1103 William began to teach dialectics in the cathedral school of Notre Dame at Paris. If we may believe Abélard, who was too good a warrior to be a good historian, William out-Platoed Plato, and held not only that universals are objectively real, but that the individual is an incidental modification of the generic reality, and exists solely by participating in the universal; so humanity is the real being, which enters into, and thereby gives existence to, Socrates. Moreover (William is reported to have taught) the whole universal is present in every individual of its class; all humanity is in Socrates, in Alexander.

To William's school Abélard came after much scholarly wandering (1103?), aged twenty-four or twenty-five. He had a fine figure, a proud carriage, good looks,[7] an imposing breadth of brow; and the vivacity of his spirit gave life and charm to his manners and speech. He could compose songs and sing them; his lusty humor shook the cobwebs in the dialectical halls; he was a gay and joyous youth who had discovered at the same time Paris and philosophy. His defects were those of his qualities: he was conceited, boastful, insolent, self-centered; and in the exhilaration of his conscious talent he rode with young thoughtlessness over the dogmas and sensibilities of his masters and his time. He was drunk with the "dear delight" of philosophy; this famous lover loved dialectic more than he loved Héloïse.

He was amused by the exaggerated realism of his teacher, and challenged him in open class. All humanity present in Socrates? Then, when all humanity is in Alexander, Socrates (included in all humanity) must be present in Alexander. Presumably William had meant that all the essential elements of humanity are present in each human being; we have not received William's side of the argument. In any case Abélard would have none of it. To William's realism, and to Roscelin's nominalism, he opposed what came to be called conceptualism. The class (man, stone) physically exists only in the form of its constituent members (men, stones); qualities (whiteness, goodness, truth) exist only in the objects, actions, or ideas that they qualify. But the class and the quality are not mere names; they are concepts formed by our minds from elements or features observed to be common to a group of individuals, objects, actions, or ideas. These common elements are real, though they appear only in individual forms. The concepts by which we think of these common elements—the generic or universal ideas by which we think of classes of like objects—are not "winds of voice," but the most useful and indispensable instruments of thought; without them science and philosophy would be impossible.

Abélard remained with William, he tells us, "for some time." Then he himself began to teach, first at Melun, later at Corbeil, the one forty, the other twenty-five, miles from Paris. Some criticized him for setting up his own shop after too brief an apprenticeship, but a goodly number of students followed him, relishing his quick mind and tongue. Meanwhile William became a monk at St. Victor, and "by request" continued his lectures there. To him, after a "grievous illness," Abélard returned as a pupil; apparently there was more meat on the bones of William's philosophy than a hasty reading of Abélard's brief autobiography suggests. But soon their old debates were resumed; Abélard (in Abélard's report) forced William to modify his realism, and William's prestige waned. His successor and appointee at Notre Dame now (1109?) offered to yield his place to Abélard; William refused consent. Abélard resumed lecturing at Melun, then on Mont Ste.-Geneviève, just outside Paris. Between him and William, and between their students, a war of logic ran its wordy course for years; and Abélard, despite his rejection of nominalism, became the leader and hero of the *moderni*, the ardent young rebels of the "modern" school.

While he was so embattled, his father and mother entered religious orders, presumably as a viaticum, and Abélard had to return to Le Pallet to bid them Godspeed, and perhaps to settle some problems of property. In 1115, after a term of studying theology at Laon, Abélard returned to Paris, and, apparently without opposition, established his school, or lecture course, in those very cloisters of Notre Dame where he had squatted as a student some twelve years before. He became a canon of the cathedral,[8] though not yet a priest, and might look forward to ecclesiastical dignities if he could hold his tongue. But it was a hard condition. He had studied literature as well as philosophy, and was a master of lucid and graceful exposition; like any Frenchman he acknowledged a moral obligation to be clear; and he was not afraid to let some humor lighten the burden of his speech. Students came from a dozen countries to hear him; his classes were so large that they brought him considerable money as well as international fame.[9] A letter written to him a few years later by the Abbé Foulques bears witness:

> Rome sent you her children to instruct. . . . Neither distance nor mountains nor valleys nor roads infested with brigands prevented the youth of the world from coming to you. Young Englishmen crowded to your classes across a dangerous sea; all quarters of Spain, Flanders, Germany sent you pupils; and they were never tired of praising the power of your mind. I say nothing of all the inhabitants of Paris, and the most distant parts of France, which were also thirsty for your teaching, almost as if no science existed which could not be learned from you.[10]

From that height and splendor of success and renown why should he not move on to a bishopric (as William had done), then to an archbishopric? Why not to the papacy?

II. HÉLOÏSE

Up to this time (1117?), he doth protest, he had maintained "the utmost continence," and "had diligently refrained from all excesses." [11] But in the maiden Héloïse, niece of the cathedral canon Fulbert, there was a comeliness of person, and a flair for learning, which aroused the sensitivity of his manhood and the admiration of his mind. During those hectic years when Abélard and William fought the universal war, Héloïse had grown from infancy to girlhood as an orphan of whose parentage no certain trace remains. Her uncle sent her for many years to a convent at Argenteuil; there, falling in love with the books in the little library, she became the brightest pupil the nuns had ever had. When Fulbert learned that she could converse in Latin as readily as in French, and was even studying Hebrew,[12] he took new pride in her, and brought her to live with him in his home near the cathedral.

She was sixteen when Abélard came into her life (1117). Presumably she had heard of him long since; she must have seen the hundreds of students who crowded the cloisters and lecture rooms to hear him; perhaps, so intellectually eager, she had gone openly or furtively to see and hear the idol and paragon of the scholars of Paris. We can imagine her modest trepidation when Fulbert told her that Abélard was to live with them and be her tutor. The philosopher himself gives the frankest explanation of how it had come about:

> It was this young girl whom I . . . determined to unite with myself in the bonds of love. And indeed the thing seemed to me very easy to be done. So distinguished was my name, and I possessed such advantages of youth and comeliness, that no matter what woman I might favor with my love, I dreaded rejection of none. . . . Thus, utterly aflame with passion for this maiden, I sought to discover means whereby I might have daily and familiar speech with her, thereby the more easily to win her consent. For this purpose I persuaded the girl's uncle . . . to take me into his household . . . in return for the payment of a small sum. . . . He was a man keen in avarice, and . . . believed that his niece would vastly benefit from my teaching. . . . The man's simplicity was nothing short of astounding; I should not have been more surprised if he had entrusted a tender lamb to the care of a ravenous wolf. . . .
>
> Why should I say more? We were united, first in the dwelling that sheltered our love, and then in the hearts that burned within us. Under the pretext of study we spent our hours in the happiness of love. . . . Our kisses outnumbered our reasoned words; our hands sought less the book than each other's bosoms; love drew our eyes together.[13]

What had begun with his simple physical desire graduated through Héloïse's delicacy into "a tenderness surpassing in sweetness the most fragrant balm." It was a new experience for him, and wooed him quite from philosophy; he borrowed passion from his lectures for his love, and left them anomalously dull. His students mourned the dialectician, but welcomed the lover; they were delighted to learn that even Socrates could sin; they consoled themselves for lost jousts of argument by singing the love songs that he now composed; and Héloïse from her windows could hear on their lips the boisterous echo of his enchantment.[14]

Not long afterward she announced to him that she was with child. Secretly by night he stole her from her uncle's house, and sent her to his sister's home in Brittany.[15] Half from fear and half from pity, he offered to the infuriated uncle to marry Héloïse provided Fulbert would let him keep the marriage secret. The canon agreed, and after his classes had adjourned Abé-lard went to Brittany to fetch a tender but unwilling bride. Their son, Astro-labe, was three days old when he arrived. Héloïse long refused to marry him. The reforms of Leo IX and Gregory VII, a generation back, had barred mar-ried men from the priesthood unless the wife became a nun; she was not ready to contemplate such a surrender of her mate and her child; she pro-posed to remain his mistress, on the ground that such a relationship, kept judiciously secret, would not, like marriage, close his road to advancement in the Church.[16] A long passage in Abélard's *History of My Calamities* (vii) ascribes to Héloïse at this point a learned array of authorities and instances against the marriage of philosophers, and an eloquent plea against "robbing the Church of so shining a light": "Remember that Socrates was wedded, and with how sordid a case he first purged that stain on philosophy, that thereafter other men might be more prudent." "It would be far sweeter for her," he reports her as saying, "to be called my mistress than to be known as my wife; nay, this would be more honorable for me as well." [17] He persuaded her by promising that the marriage would be known only to an intimate few.

They left Astrolabe with the sister, returned to Paris, and were married in the presence of Fulbert. To keep the marriage secret Abélard went back to his bachelor lodgings, and Héloïse lived again with her uncle; the lovers saw each other now only rarely and clandestinely. But Fulbert, anxious to redeem his prestige, and overruling his promise to Abélard, divulged the marriage. Héloïse denied it, and Fulbert "visited her repeatedly with pun-ishments." Abélard again stole her away; this time he sent her, much against her will, to the convent at Argenteuil, and bade her don the garb of a nun, but not to take the vows or the veil. When Fulbert and his kinsmen heard of this, says Abélard,

> they were convinced that now I had completely played them false, and had rid myself forever of Héloïse by forcing her to become a nun. Violently incensed, they laid a plot against me; and one night, while . . . I was asleep in a secret room in my lodgings, they broke in with the help of one of my servants whom they had bribed. There they had vengeance upon me with a most cruel and shameful punish-ment . . . for they cut off those parts of my body whereby I had done that which was the cause of their sorrow. This done, they fled; but two of them were captured, and suffered the loss of their eyes and their genitals.[18]

His enemies could not have chosen a subtler revenge. It did not immedi-ately disgrace him; all Paris, including the clergy, sympathized with him; [19] his students flocked to comfort him. Fulbert shrank into hiding and oblivion, and the bishop confiscated his property. But Abélard realized that he was ruined, and that "the tale of this amazing outrage would spread to the very ends of the earth." He could no longer think of ecclesiastical preferment.

He felt that his fair fame had been "utterly blotted out," and that he would be a butt of jokes for generations to come. He felt a certain unpoetic justice in his fall: he had been maimed in the flesh that had sinned, and had been betrayed by the man whom he had betrayed. He bade Héloïse take the veil, and he himself, at St. Denis, took the vows of a monk.

III. THE RATIONALIST

A year later (1120), at the urging of his students and his abbot, he resumed his lecturing, in a "cell" of the Benedictine priory of Maisoncelle. Presumably we have the substance of his lecture courses in his books. These, however, were composed in hectic installments, and hardly allow dating; they were revised in his final years, when his spirit was quite broken, and there is no telling how much youthful fire was quenched by the flow of time. Four minor logical works circle about the problem of universals; we need not disturb their rest. The *Dialectica*, however, is a 375-page treatise on logic in the Aristotelian sense: a rational analysis of the parts of speech, the categories of thought (substance, quantity, place, position, time, relation, quality, possession, action, "passion"), the forms of propositions, and the rules of reasoning; the renascent mind of Western Europe had to clarify these basic ideas for itself like a child learning to read. Dialectic was the major interest of philosophy in Abélard's time, partly because the new philosophy stemmed from Aristotle through Boethius and Porphyry, and only the logical treatises of Aristotle (and not all of these) were known to this first generation of Scholastic philosophy. So the *Dialectica* is not a fascinating book; yet even in its formal pages we hear a shot or two in the first skirmishes of a Two Hundred Years' War between faith and reason. How can we, in an age already doubtful of the intellect, recapture the glow of a time that was just discovering "this great mystery of knowledge"? [20] Truth cannot be contrary to truth, Abélard pleads; the truths of Scripture must agree with the findings of reason, else the God who gave us both would be deluding us with one or the other.[21]

Perhaps in his early period—before his tragedy—he wrote his *Dialogue Between a Philosopher, a Jew, and a Christian*. "In a vision of the night," he says, three men came to him as a famous teacher, and asked his judgment on their dispute. All three believe in one God; two accept the Hebrew Scriptures; the philosopher rejects these, and proposes to base life and morality on reason and natural law. How absurd, argues the philosopher, to cling to the beliefs of our childhood, to share the superstitions of the crowd, and to condemn to hell those who do not accept these puerilities! [22] He ends unphilosophically by calling Jews fools, and Christians lunatics. The Jew replies that men could not live without laws; that God, like a good king, gave man a code of conduct; and that the precepts of the Pentateuch sustained the courage and morality of the Jews through centuries of dispersion and tragedy. The philosopher asks, How, then, did your patriarchs live so nobly, long before Moses and his laws?—and how can you believe in a revelation that promised you earthly prosperity, and yet has allowed you to suffer such poverty and desolation? The Christian accepts much that the philosopher and the Jew have said, but he argues that Christianity developed and perfected the natural law of the one and the Mosaic law of the other; Christianity raised higher than ever before the moral ideals of mankind. Neither philosophy nor scriptural Judaism offered man eternal happiness; Christianity gives harassed man such a hope, and is therefore infinitely precious. This unfinished dialogue is an amazing product for a cathedral canon in the Paris of 1120.

A like freedom of discussion found another medium in Abélard's most famous work, *Sic et non—Yes and No* (1120?). The earliest known mention of it is in a letter from William of St. Thierry to St. Bernard (1140), describing it as a suspicious book secretly circulating among the pupils and partisans of Abélard.[23] Thereafter it disappeared from history until 1836, when the manuscript was discovered by Victor Cousin in a library at Avranches. Its very form must have made the mitered grieve. After a pious introduction it divided into 157 questions, including the most basic dogmas of the faith; under each question two sets of quotations were ranged in opposite columns; one set supported the affirmative, the other the negative; and each set quoted from the Bible, the Fathers of the Church, the pagan classics, even from Ovid's *Art of Loving (Ars amandi)*. The book may have been intended as an armory of references for scholastic disputation; but the introduction, purposely or not, impugned the authority of the Fathers by showing them in contradiction of one another, even of themselves. Abélard did not question the authority of the Bible; but he argued that its language was meant for unlettered people, and must be interpreted by reason; that the sacred text had sometimes been corrupted by interpolation or careless copying; and that where scriptural or patristic passages contradicted one another, reason must attempt their reconciliation. Anticipating the "Cartesian doubt" by 400 years, he wrote in the same prologue: "The first key to wisdom is assiduous and frequent questioning. . . . For by doubting we come to inquiry, and by inquiry we arrive at the truth." [24] He points out that Jesus Himself, facing the doctors in the Temple, plied them with questions. The first debate in the book is almost a declaration of independence for philosophy: "That faith should be founded in human reason, and the contrary." He quotes Ambrose, Augustine, and Gregory I as defending faith, and cites Hilary, Jerome, and Augustine to the effect that it is good to be able to prove one's faith by reason. While repeatedly affirming his orthodoxy, Abélard opens up for debate such problems as Divine Providence vs. free will, the existence of sin and evil in a world created by a good and omnipotent God, and the possibility that God is not omnipotent. His free reasoning about such questions must have shaken the faith of youthful students enamored of debate. Nevertheless this method of education by the freest discussion became, probably through Abélard's example,[25] the regular procedure at French universities and in philosophical or theological writing; we shall find St. Thomas adopting it without fear and without reproach. In the very birth of Scholasticism rationalism found a place.

If the *Sic et non* offended only a few because its circulation was limited, Abélard's attempt to apply reason to the mystery of the Trinity could not so narrowly confine its influence and alarm, for it was the subject of his lectures in 1120, and of his book *On the Divine Unity and Trinity*. He wrote this, he says,

> for my students, because they were always seeking for rational and philosophical explanations, asking rather for reasons they could understand than for mere words, saying that it was futile to utter words which the intellect could not possibly follow, that nothing could be believed unless it could first be understood, and that it was absurd for anyone to preach to others a thing which neither he himself, nor those whom he sought to teach, could comprehend.[26]

This book, he tells us, "became exceedingly popular," and people marveled at his subtlety. He pointed out that the unity of God was the one point agreed upon by the greatest religions and the greatest philosophers. In the one God we may view His power as the First Person, His wisdom as the Second, His grace, charity, and love as the Third; these are phases or modalities of the Divine Essence; but all the works of God suppose and unite at once His power, His wisdom, and His love.[27] Many theologians felt that this was a permissible analogy; the bishop of Paris rejected the appeal of the now aged and orthodox Roscelin to indict Abélard for heresy; and Bishop Geoffroy of Chartres defended Abélard through all the fury that now fell upon the reckless philosopher. But in Reims two teachers—Alberic and Lotulphe—who had quarreled with Abélard at Laon in 1113, stirred up the archbishop to summon him to come to Soissons with his book on the Trinity, and defend himself against charges of heresy. When Abélard appeared at Soissons (1121) he found that the populace had been roused against him, and "came near to stoning me . . . in the belief that I had preached the existence of three gods." [28] The Bishop of Chartres demanded that Abélard be heard by the council in his own defense; Alberic and others objected, on the ground that Abélard was irresistible in persuasion and argument. The council condemned him unheard, compelled him to cast his book into a fire, and bade the abbot of St. Médard to confine him in that monastery for a year. But shortly thereafter a papal legate freed him, and sent him back to St. Denis.

After a turbulent year with the unruly monks there, Abélard secured permission from the new abbot, the great Suger, to build himself a hermitage in a lonely spot halfway between Fontainebleau and Troyes (1122). There, with a companion in minor orders, he raised with reeds and stalks a little oratory or place of prayer, which he called by the name of the Holy Trinity. When students heard that he was free to teach again they came to him and made themselves into an impromptu school; they built huts in the wilderness, slept on rushes and straw, and lived on "coarse bread and the herbs of the field." [29] Here was a thirst for knowledge that would soon make and crowd universities; now, indeed, the Dark Ages were a nightmare almost forgotten. In return for his lectures the students tilled the field, raised buildings, and built him a new oratory of timber and stone, which he called the Paraclete, as if to say that the affection of his disciples had come like a holy spirit into his life just when he had fled from human society to solitude and despair.

The three years that he spent there were as happy as any that he could now know. Probably the lectures that he gave to those eager students are preserved and reshaped in two books, one called *Theologia christiana*, the other simply *Theologia*. Their doctrine was orthodox, but an age still a stranger to most of Greek philosophy was a bit shocked to find in them so many laudatory references to pagan thinkers, and a suggestion that Plato too had in some degree enjoyed divine inspiration.[30] He could not believe that all these wonderful pre-Christian minds had missed salvation; [31] God, he insisted, gives His love to all peoples, Jews and heathen included.[32] Abélard impenitently returned to the defense of reason in theology, and argued that heretics should be restrained by reason rather than by force.[33] Those who recommend faith without understanding are in many cases seeking to cover up their inability to teach the faith intelligibly: [34] here was a barb that must have pierced some skins! In attempting a rationale of Christianity Abélard might seem to have dared no more than what Alexander of Hales, Albertus Magnus, and Thomas Aquinas would essay after him; but whereas even the brave Thomas would leave the Trinity, and the creation in time, to a faith beyond or above reason, Abélard sought to embrace the most mystic doctrines of the Church within the grasp of reason.

The audacity of the enterprise, and the sharpness of his reviving wit, brought him new enemies. Probably referring to Bernard of Clairvaux, and Norbert, founder of the Premonstratensian Order, he writes:

> Certain new apostles in whom the world put great faith ran hither and yon . . . shamelessly slandering me in every way they could, so that in time they succeeded in drawing down upon my head the scorn of many having authority. . . . God is my witness that whensoever I learned that a new assemblage of the clergy was convened, I believed that it was done for the express purpose of my condemnation.[35]

Perhaps to silence such criticism he abandoned his teaching, and accepted an invitation to be the abbot of the monastery of St. Gildas in Brittany (1125?); more likely the politic Suger had arranged the transfer in the hope of quieting the storm. It was at once a promotion and an imprisonment. The philosopher found himself amid a "barbarous" and "unintelligible" population, among monks "vile and untamable," who openly lived with concubines.[36] Resenting his reforms, the monks put poison in the chalice from which he drank at Mass; this failing, they bribed his servant to poison his food; another monk ate the food and "straightway fell dead";[37] but Abélard is our sole authority here. He fought this battle bravely enough, for, with some interruptions, he remained in this lonely post for eleven years.

IV. THE LETTERS OF HÉLOÏSE

He had an interlude of moderate happiness when Suger decided to use for other purposes than a nunnery the house at Argenteuil. Since her separation from Abélard Héloïse had so devoted herself there to her duties as a nun that she had been made prioress, and had won "such favor in the eyes of all . . . that the bishops loved her as a daughter, the abbots as a sister, and the laity as a mother." Learning that Héloïse and her nuns were looking for new quarters, Abélard offered them the oratory and buildings of "the Paraclete." He went in person to help establish them there, and frequently visited them to preach to them and the villagers who had settled near by. Gossip murmured "that I, who of old could scarcely endure to be parted from her whom I loved, was still swayed by the delights of earthly lust."[38]

It was during his troubled abbacy at St. Gildas that he composed his autobiography—*Historia calamitatum mearum* (1133?). We do not know its motive; it assumed the guise of an essay in consolation offered to a plaintive friend, "so that, in comparing your sorrows with mine, you may discover that yours are in truth naught"; but apparently it was intended for the world, as both a moral confession and a theological defense. An old but unverifiable tradition says that a copy of it came to Héloïse, and that she wrote this astonishing reply:

> To her master, nay father, to her husband, nay brother: his handmaid, nay daughter, his spouse, nay sister: to Abélard, Héloïse. Your letter written to a friend for his comfort, beloved, was lately brought to me by chance. . . . Which things I deem that no one can read or hear with dry eyes, for they renewed in fuller measure my griefs. . . . In His name Who still protects thee . . . in the name of Christ, as His handmaids and thine, we beseech thee to deign to inform us by frequent letters of those shipwrecks in which thou still art tossed, that thou mayest have us, at least, who alone have remained to thee as partners in thy grief or joy. . . .

Thou knowest, dearest—all men know—what I have lost in thee. . . . Obeying thy command, I changed both my habit and my heart, that I might show thee to be the possessor of both my body and my mind. . . . Not for the pledge of matrimony, nor for any dowry, did I look. . . . And if the name of wife appears more sacred and valid, sweeter to me is ever the word friend, or, if thou be not ashamed, concubine or whore. . . . I call God to witness, if Augustus, ruling over the whole world, were to deem me worthy of the honor of marriage, and to confirm the whole world to me, to be ruled by me forever, dearer to me and of greater dignity would it seem to be called thy strumpet than his empress. . . .

For who among kings or philosophers could equal thee in fame? What kingdom or city or village did not burn to see thee? Who, I ask, did not hasten to gaze upon thee when thou appearedst in public? . . . What wife, what maiden did not yearn for thee in thine absence, nor burn in thy presence? What queen or powerful lady did not envy me my joys and my bed? . . .

Tell me one thing only if thou canst: why, after our conversion [to the religious life], which thou alone didst decree, I am fallen into such neglect and oblivion with thee that I am neither refreshed by thy speech and presence, nor comforted by a letter in thine absence. Tell me one thing only, if thou canst, or let me tell thee what I feel, nay, what all suspect: concupiscence joined thee to me rather than affection. . . . When, therefore, what thou hadst desired ceased, all that thou hadst exhibited at the same time failed. This, most beloved, is not mine only but the conjecture of all. . . . Would that it seemed thus to me only, and thy love found others to excuse it, by whom my grief might be a little quieted.

Attend, I beseech thee, to what I ask. . . . While I am cheated of thy presence, at least by written words—whereof thou hast abundance—present the sweetness of thine image. . . . I deserved more from thee, having done all things for thee . . . I, who as a girl was allured to the asperity of monastic conversion . . . not by religious devotion, but by thy command alone. . . . No reward for this may I expect from God, for the love of Whom it is well known that I did not anything. . . .

And so in His name to Whom thou hast offered thyself, before God I beseech thee that in whatsoever way thou canst thou restore to me thy presence by writing to me some word of comfort. . . . Farewell, my all.[39]

Abélard was physiologically incapacitated from responding to such passion in kind. The reply that tradition assigns to him is a reminder of religious vows: "To Héloïse his dearly beloved sister in Christ, Abélard her brother in the same." He counsels her to accept their misfortunes humbly, as a cleansing and saving punishment from God. He asks for her prayers, bids her assuage her grief with the hope of their reunion in heaven, and begs her to bury him, when he is dead, in the grounds of the Paraclete. Her second letter repeats her fond impieties: "I have ever feared to offend thee rather than God, I seek to please thee more than Him. . . . See how unhappy a life I must lead, if I endure all these things in vain, having no hope of reward in the future. For a long time thou, like many others, hast been deceived by my simulation, so as to mistake hypocrisy for religion." [40] He answers that Christ, not he, truly loved her: "My love was concupiscence, not love; I satisfied my wretched desires in thee, and this was all that I loved. . . . Weep for thy Saviour, not for thy seducer; for thy Redeemer, not for thy defiler." [41] And he composes a touching prayer which he asks her to recite for him. Her third letter shows her resigned to the earthly death of his love; she asked him now only for a new rule by which she and her nuns might live properly the religious life. He complied, and drew up for them a kindly moderate code. He wrote sermons for their edification, and sent these compositions to Héloïse over a tender signature: "Farewell in the Lord to His servant, once dear to me in the world, now most dear in Christ." In his own broken heart he still loved her.

Are these famous letters genuine? The difficulties leap to the eye. The first letter of Héloïse purports to follow upon his *Historia calamitatum*, which records several visits of Abélard to Héloïse at the Paraclete; yet she complains that he has ignored her. Possibly the *Historia* was issued in installments, and only the earlier parts preceded the letter. The bold carnality of certain passages seems incredible in a woman whose religious devotion through fourteen years had already earned her the high and general regard which we find attested by Peter the Venerable as well as by Abélard. There are artifices of rhetoric in these letters, and pedantic quotations from the classics and the Fathers, which would hardly occur to a mind sincerely feeling love or piety or remorse. The oldest manuscripts of the letters date from the thirteenth century. Jean de Meung appears to have translated them from Latin into French in 1285. [42] We may provisionally conclude that they are among the most brilliant forgeries in history, unreliable in fact, but an imperishable part of the romantic literature of France. [43]

V. THE CONDEMNED

We do not know when or how Abélard escaped from the dignities and trials of his abbacy. We find John of Salisbury reporting that in 1136 he had attended Abélard's lectures on Mont Ste.-Geneviève. Nor do we know by what license he had resumed his teaching; perhaps he had asked none. It may be that some flouting of Church discipline set ecclesiastics against him, and by a devious route led to his final fall.

If emasculation had unmanned him there is no sign of it in the works that have transmitted to us the substance of his teaching. It is difficult to find explicit heresy in them, but easy to discover passages that must have made churchmen fret. In a book of moral philosophy entitled *Scito te ipsum* (*Know Thyself*) he argued that sin lies not in the act but in the intention; no act—not even killing—is sinful in itself. So a mother, having too little clothing to warm her babe, pressed it against her bosom and unwittingly suffocated it; she killed the thing she loved, and was properly punished by the law to make other women more careful; but in the eyes of God she was sinless. Furthermore, that there should be sin, the agent must violate his own moral conscience, not merely that of others. Hence the killing of Christian martyrs was not a sin in Romans who felt such persecution necessary to the preservation of their state or of a religion which seemed to them true. Nay, "those even who persecuted Christ or His followers, whom they considered it their duty to persecute, are said to have sinned in action; but they would have committed a graver fault if, contrary to their conscience, they had spared them."[44] All this might be logical as well as irritating; but on such a theory the whole doctrine of sin as a violation of God's law threatened to go up in a haze of casuistry about intentions; who but a few Pauls would admit that he had acted against his own conscience? Of the sixteen excerpts for which Abélard was condemned in 1141, six were taken from this book.

What disturbed the Church more than any specific heresy in Abélard was his assumption that there were no mysteries in the faith, that all dogmas should be capable of rational explanation. Was he not so drunk with the lees of logic that he had dared to connect it with the Logos, the Word of God, as a science almost divine?[45] Granted that this seductive teacher arrived by unorthodox methods at orthodox conclusions; how many immature minds, infected by him with the logic-chopping germ, must have been, by his specious pros and cons, unsettled on the way! If he had been the only one of his kind he might have been left untouched, in the hope that he would not take too long to die. But he had hundreds of eager followers; and there were other teachers—William of Conches, Gilbert de la Porrée, Bérenger of Tours—who were also summoning the faith to trial by reason. How long, on this procedure, could the Church maintain that unity and fervor of religious belief on which the moral and social order of Europe seemed to rest? Already one of Abélard's pupils, Arnold of Brescia, was fomenting revolution in Italy.

Probably it was considerations like these that finally brought St. Bernard into open war with Abélard. The eager watchdog of the faith scented the wolf at the flock, and led the pack to the hunt. He had long looked with distrust upon the prowling, invading, audacious intellect; to seek knowledge except as ministering to sanctity seemed to him plain paganism; to attempt to explain the sacred mysteries by reason was impiety and folly; and the same rationalism that began by explaining those mysteries would end by desecrating them. The saint was not truculent; when (1139) William of St. Thierry, a monk of Reims, called his attention to the dangers in Abélard's teaching, and begged him to denounce the philosopher, he put the monk off and did nothing. Abélard himself precipitated matters by writing to the archbishop of Sens, asking that at the coming church council there he should be given an opportunity to defend himself against the charges of heresy that were being circulated about him. The archbishop agreed, not unwilling to have his see become the cynosure of the Christian world; and to ensure a good fight he invited Bernard to attend. Bernard refused, saying that in the dialectical game he would be "a mere child" against an Abélard trained in logic through forty years. But he wrote to several bishops, urging them to attend and defend the faith:

> Peter Abélard is trying to make void the merit of Christian faith when he deems himself able by human reason to comprehend God altogether. He ascends to the heavens and descends even to the abyss; nothing may hide from him! . . . Not content to see things through a glass darkly, he must behold all things face to face. . . . He savors of Arius when he speaks of the Trinity, of Pelagius when he speaks of grace, of Nestorius when he speaks of the person of Christ. . . . The faith of the righteous believes, it does not dispute. But this man has no mind to believe what his reason has not previously argued.[46]

Bernard's allies, pleading their own weakness, prevailed upon him to attend. When Abélard arrived at Sens (June, 1140) he found the public mood, as at Soissons nineteen years before, so set against him by the mere presence and hostility of Bernard that he hardly dared appear in the streets. The archbishop realized his dream; for a week Sens seemed the center of the world; the king of France was present with his ceremonious court; scores of church dignitaries were on hand; and Bernard, crippled with rheumatism and stern with sanctity, overawed all. Some of these prelates had felt the sting, in person or collectively, of Abélard's attacks upon the shortcomings of the clergy, the immorality of priests and monks, the sale of indulgences, the invention of bogus miracles. Convinced that the judgment of the council would condemn him, Abélard appeared at its first session, announced that he would accept none but the Pope as his judge, and left the assembly and the town. The council was not sure, after this appeal from it, that it could legally try Abélard; Bernard reassured it; and it proceeded to condemn sixteen propositions from Abélard's books, including his definition of sin, and his theory of the Trinity as the power, wisdom, and love of the one God.

Almost penniless, Abélard set out for Rome to lay his case before the Pope. Age and infirmity retarded him. Reaching the monastery of Cluny in Burgundy, he was received with compassion and solicitude by Peter the Venerable, and rested there a few days. Meanwhile Innocent II issued a decree confirming the sentence of the council, imposing perpetual silence upon Abélard, and ordering his confinement in a monastery. Abélard wished nevertheless to continue his pilgrimage; Peter dissuaded him, saying that the Pope would never decide against Bernard. Weary to physical and spiritual exhaustion, Abélard yielded. He became a monk at Cluny, and hid himself in the obscurity of its walls and its ritual. He edified his fellow monks by his piety, his silence, and his prayers. He wrote to Héloïse—whom he never saw again—a touching profession of faith in the teachings of the Church. He composed, probably for her, some of the most beautiful hymns in medieval literature. One "Plaint" ascribed to him is formally a Lament of David for Jonathan, but any reader will catch tender overtones in it:

Vel confossus pariter	If I might lie in one same grave with thee,
morerer feliciter	Happily would I die,
cum, quid amor faciat,	Since of all gifts that earthly love can give
maius hoc non habeat,	No greater boon know I.
et me post te vivere	That I should live when thou art cold and dead
mori sit assidue;	Would be unceasing death;
nec ad vitam anima	Nor in my wraith would half a soul suffice
satis sit dimidia. . . .	To life, or half a breath.
Do quietem fidibus;	I let the harp lie still.
vellem ut et planctibus	Would that I might
sic possum et fletibus	So still my tears and plaints!
Laesis pulsu manibus,	My hands are sore with striking,
raucis planctu vocibus,	Sore my throat
deficit et spiritus.[47]	With grief. My spirit faints.

Soon thereafter he fell ill, and his kindly Abbot sent him to the priory of St. Marcel near Châlons for a change of air. There, on April 21, 1142, he died, aged sixty-three. He was buried in the priory chapel; but Héloïse reminded Peter the Venerable that Abélard had asked to be interred at the Paraclete. The good Abbot brought the body to her himself, tried to comfort her by speaking of her dead lover as the Socrates, Plato, and Aristotle of his time, and left with her a letter rich in Christian tenderness:

> Thus, dear and venerable sister in God, him to whom you were united, after your tie in the flesh, by the better and stronger bond of divine love, and with whom . . . you have served the Lord, him the Lord now takes in your stead, or as another you, and warms in His bosom; and for the day of His coming, when shall sound the voice of the archangel and the trumpet descending from heaven, He keeps him to restore him to you by His grace.[48]

She joined her dead lover in 1164, having lived to equal his age, and almost his fame. She was buried beside him in the gardens of the Paraclete. That oratory was destroyed in the Revolution, and the graves were disturbed and perhaps confused. What were reasonably believed to be the remains of Abélard and Héloïse were transferred to Père Lachaise Cemetery in Paris in 1817. There, even till our time, men and women might be seen, on a summer Sunday, bringing flowers to adorn the tomb.

CHAPTER XXXVI

The Adventure of Reason

1120-1308

I. THE SCHOOL OF CHARTRES

HOW shall we explain the remarkable outburst of philosophy that began with Anselm, Roscelin, and Abélard, and culminated in Albertus Magnus and St. Thomas Aquinas? As usual, many causes conspired. The Greek East had never surrendered its classical heritage; the ancient philosophers were studied in every century in Constantinople, Antioch, and Alexandria; men like Michael Psellus, Nicephorus Blemydes (1197?–1272), George Pachymeres (1242?–1310), and the Syrian Bar-Hebraeus (1226?–82) knew the works of Plato and Aristotle at first hand; and Greek teachers and manuscripts gradually entered the West. Even there some fragments of the Hellenic legacy had survived the barbarian storm; most of Aristotle's *Organon* of logic remained; and of Plato the *Meno* and the *Timaeus*, whose vision of Er had colored Christian imaginations of hell. The successive waves of translations from the Arabic and the Greek in the twelfth and thirteenth centuries brought to the West the revelation and challenge of Greek and Moslem philosophies so different from the Christian that they threatened to sweep away the whole theology of Christendom unless Christianity could construct a counterphilosophy. But these influences would hardly have produced a Christian philosophy if the West had continued poor. What brought these factors to effect was the growth of wealth through the agricultural conquest of the Continent, the expansion of commerce and industry, the services and accumulations of finance. This economic revival collaborated with the liberation of the communes, the rise of the universities, the rebirth of Latin literature and Roman law, the codification of canon law, the glory of Gothic, the flowering of romance, the "gay science" of the troubadours, the awakening of science, and the resurrection of philosophy, to constitute the "Renaissance of the twelfth century."

From wealth came leisure, study, schools; *scholê* at first meant leisure. A *scholasticus* was a director or professor of a school; the "Scholastic philosophy" was the philosophy taught in the medieval secondary schools or in the universities that for the most part grew out of them. The "Scholastic method" was the form of philosophical argument and exposition used in such schools. In the twelfth century, barring Abélard's classes in or near

Paris, Chartres was the most active and famous of these schools. There philosophy was combined with literature, and the graduates managed to write of abstruse problems with the clarity and grace that became an honorable tradition in France. Plato, who also had made philosophy intelligible, was a favorite there, and the quarrel between realists and nominalists was mediated by identifying the "real" universals with the Platonic Ideas, or creative archetypes, in the mind of God. Under Bernard of Chartres (c. 1117) and his brother Theodoric (c. 1140) the school of Chartres reached the height of its influence. Three of its graduates dominated the philosophical scene in Western Europe in the half century after Abélard: William of Conches, Gilbert de la Porrée, and John of Salisbury.

The widening of the Scholastic ken is startlingly revealed in William of Conches (1080?-1154). Here was a man who knew the works of Hippocrates, Lucretius, Hunain ibn Ishaq, Constantine the African, even Democritus.[1] He was fascinated by the atomic theory; all the works of nature, he concluded, originate in combinations of atoms; and this is true even of the highest vital processes of the human body.[2] The soul is a union of the vital principle of the individual with the cosmic soul or vital principle of the world.[3] Following Abélard into a dangerous mystery, William writes: "There is in the Godhead power, wisdom, and will, which the saints call three persons." [4] He takes with a large grain of allegory the story that Eve was created from Adam's rib. He answers vigorously a certain Cornificius and other "Cornificians" who condemned science and philosophy on the ground that simple faith sufficed.

> Because they know not the forces of nature, and in order that they may have comrades in their ignorance, they suffer not that others should search out anything, and would have us believe like rustics and ask no reason.... But we say that in all things a reason must be sought; if reason fails, we must confide the matter ... to the Holy Ghost and faith....[5] [They say] "We do not know how this is, but we know that God can do it." You poor fools! God can make a cow out of a tree, but has He ever done so? Therefore show some reason why a thing is so, or cease to hold that it is so. . . .[6] *Rejoicing not in the many but in the probity of the few, we toil for truth alone.*[7]

This was too strong for the stomach of William of St. Thierry; the zealous monk who had set St. Bernard to hound Abélard hastened to denounce this new rationalist to the watchful abbot of Clairvaux. William of Conches retracted his heresies, agreed that Eve had been made from Adam's rib,[8] abandoned philosophy as an enterprise in which the profit was not commensurate with the risk, became tutor to Henry Plantagenet of England, and retired from history.

Gilbert de la Porrée (1070-1154) managed the dangerous business more successfully. He studied and taught at Chartres and Paris, became Bishop of

Poitiers, and wrote a *Liber sex principiorium,* or *Book of Six Principles,* which remained for many centuries a standard text in logic. But his *Commentary on Boethius* suggested that the nature of God was so far beyond human understanding that all statements about it must be taken as mere analogies, and so stressed the unity of God as to make the Trinity seem but a figure of speech.[9] In 1148, though he was now seventy-two, he was charged with heresy by St. Bernard; he stood trial at Auxerre, baffled his opponents with subtle distinctions, and went home uncondemned. A year later he was tried again, consented to burn certain passages torn from his books, but again returned a free man to his diocese. When it was suggested that he should discuss his views with Bernard he refused, saying that the saint was too inexpert a theologian to understand him.[10] Gilbert, said John of Salisbury, "was so ripe in liberal culture as to be surpassed by no one." [11]

John might have spoken so for himself, since of all the Scholastic philosophers he possessed the widest culture, the most urbane spirit, the most elegant pen. Born at Salisbury about 1117, he studied under Abélard at Mont Ste.-Geneviève, under William of Conches at Chartres, under Gilbert de la Porrée at Paris. In 1149 he returned to England, and served as secretary to two archbishops of Canterbury, Theobald and Thomas à Becket. He undertook for them various diplomatic missions, visited Italy six times, and stayed at the papal court eight years. He shared Becket's exile in France, and saw him killed in his cathedral. He became bishop of Chartres in 1176, and died in 1180. It was a full and varied career, in which John learned to check logic with life, and to take metaphysics with the modesty of an atom judging the cosmos. Revisiting the schools in his later years, he was amused to find them still debating nominalism vs. realism.

> One never gets away from this question. The world has grown old discussing it, and it has taken more time than the Caesars consumed in conquering and governing the world. . . . From whatever point a discussion starts, it is always led back and attached to that. It is the madness of Rufus about Naevia: "He thinks of nothing else, talks of nothing else; and if Naevia did not exist, Rufus would be dumb." [12]

John himself settled the question simply: the universal is a mental concept conveniently uniting the common qualities of individual beings; John, rather than Abélard, proposed "conceptualism."

In the best Latin since Alcuin's letters, he composed a history of Greek and Roman philosophy—an astonishing evidence of the widening medieval horizon; a *Metalogicon* which lightened logic with autobiography; and a *Polycraticus* (1159) whimsically subtitled *De nugis curialium et vestigiis philosophorum*—"On the Follies of Courtiers and the Vestiges of Philosophers." This is the first important essay in political philosophy in the literature of Christendom. It exposes the errors and vices of contemporary governments, delineates an ideal state, and describes the ideal man. "Today," he consoles us, "everything is bought openly, unless this is prevented by the modesty of the seller. The unclean fire of avarice threatens even the sacred altars. . . . Not even the legates of the Apostolic See keep their hands pure from gifts, but at times rage through the provinces in bacchanalian frenzy."[13] If we may believe his account (already quoted), he told Pope Hadrian IV that the Church shared liberally in the corruption of the times; to which the Pope in effect replied that men will be men however gowned. And John adds, wisely: "In every office of God's household [the Church], while some fall behind, others are added to do their work. Among deacons, archdeacons, bishops, and legates I have seen some who labored with such earnestness in the harvest of the Lord that from the merits of their faith and virtue it could be seen that the vineyard of the Father had been rightly placed under their care."[14] Civil government, he thinks, is far more corrupt than the clergy; and it is good that the Church, for the protection of the people, should exercise a moral jurisdiction over all the kings and states of the earth.[15]

The most famous passages in the *Polycraticus* concern tyrannicide:

> If princes have departed little by little from the true way, even so it is not well to overthrow them utterly at once, but rather to rebuke injustice with patient reproof until finally it becomes obvious that they are obstinate in their evil-doing. . . . But if the power of the ruler opposes the divine commandments, and wishes to make me share in its war against God, then with unrestrained voice I answer that God must be preferred before any man on earth. . . . To kill a tyrant is not merely lawful, but right and just.[16]

This was an unusually excitable outburst for John, and in a later passage of the same volume he added, "provided that the slayer is not bound by fealty to the tyrant." [17] It was a saving clause, for every ruler exacted an oath of fealty from his subjects. In the fifteenth century Jean Petit defended the assassination of Louis of Orléans by quoting the *Polycraticus*; but the Council of Constance condemned Petit on the ground that even the king may not condemn an accused person without summons and trial.

We "moderns" cannot always agree with the *moderni* to whom John belonged in the twelfth century; he talks now and then what seems to us to be nonsense; but even his nonsense is couched in a style of such tolerance and grace as we shall hardly find again before Erasmus. John too was a humanist, loving life more than eternity, loving beauty and kindness more than the dogmas of any faith, and quoting the ancient classics with more relish than the sacred page. He made a long list of *dubitabilia*—"things about which a wise man may doubt"—and included the nature and origin of the soul, the creation of the world, the relation of God's foresight to man's free will. But he was too clever to commit himself to heresy. He moved among the controversies of his time with diplomatic immunity and charm. He thought of philosophy not as a form of war but as a balm of peace: *philosophia moderatrix omnium*—philosophy was to be a moderating influence in all things; and "he who has by philosophy reached *caritas*, a charitable kindliness, has attained to philosophy's true end."[18]

II. ARISTOTLE IN PARIS

Toward 1150 one of Abélard's pupils, Peter Lombard, published a book which was at once a compilation of Abélard's thought purified of heresy, and a beginning of the formal Scholastic philosophy. Peter, like Anselm, Arnold of Brescia, Bonaventura, and Thomas Aquinas, was an Italian who came to France for advanced work in theology and philosophy. He liked Abélard, and called the *Sic et non* his breviary; but also he wanted to be a bishop. His *Sententiarum libri IV*, or *Four Books of Opinions*, applied and chastened the method of the *Sic et non*: he drew up under each question of theology an array of Biblical and Patristic quotations for and against; but this Peter labored conscientiously to resolve all contradictions into orthodox conclusions. He was made bishop of Paris, and his book became for four centuries so favorite a text in theological courses that Roger Bacon reproved it for having displaced the Bible itself. More than 4000 theologians, including Albert and Thomas, are said to have written commentaries on the *Sentences*.

As the Lombard's book upheld the authority of the Scriptures and the Church against the claims of the individual reason, it stayed for half a century the advance of rationalism. But in that half century a strange event transformed theology. As the translation of Aristotle's scientific and metaphysical works into Arabic had in the ninth century compelled Moslem thinkers to seek a reconciliation between Islamic doctrine and Greek philosophy; and as the impingement of Aristotle upon the Hebrew mind in Spain was in this twelfth century driving Ibn Daud and Maimonides to seek a harmony between Judaism and Hellenic thought; so the arrival of Aristotle's works in Latin dress in the Europe of 1150–1250 impelled Catholic theologians to attempt a synthesis of Greek metaphysics and Christian theology. And as Aristotle seemed immune to scriptural authority, the theologians were forced to use the language and weapons of reason. How the Greek philosopher would have smiled to see so many world-shaking faiths pay homage to his thought!

But we must not exaggerate the influence of Greek thinkers in stimulating the efflorescence of philosophy in this period. The spread of education, the vitality of discussion and intellectual life in the schools and universities of the twelfth century, the stimulus of such men as Roscelin, William of Champeaux, Abélard, William of Conches, and John of Salisbury, the enlargement of horizons by the Crusades, the increasing acquaintance with Islamic life and thought in East and West—all these could have produced an Aquinas even if Aristotle had remained unknown; indeed the industry of Aquinas was due not to love of Aristotle but to fear of Averroës. Already in the twelfth century the Arabic and Jewish philosophers were influencing Christian thought in Spain. Al-Kindi, al-Farabi, al-Ghazali, Avicenna, Ibn Gabirol, Averroës, and Maimonides entered Latin Europe by the same doors that admitted Plato and Aristotle, Hippocrates and Galen, Euclid and Ptolemy.

Such an invasion by alien thought was a mental shock of the first order to the immature West. We need not wonder that it was met at first with an attempt at repression or delay; we must marvel rather at the astonishing feat of adaptation by which the old-new knowledge was absorbed into the new faith. The initial impact of Aristotle's *Physics* and *Metaphysics*, and of Averroës' commentaries, which reached Paris in the first decade of the thirteenth century, shook the orthodoxy of many students; and some scholars, like Amalric of Bène and David of Dinant, were moved to attack such basic doctrines of Christianity as creation, miracles, and personal immortality. The Church suspected that the seeping of Arabic-Greek thought into south France had loosened orthodoxy among the educated classes, and had weakened their will to control the Albigensian heresy. In 1210 a Church council at Paris condemned Amalric and David, and forbade the reading of Aristotle's "metaphysics and natural philosophy," or of "comments"— commentaries—thereon. As the prohibition was repeated by a papal legate in 1215 we may assume that the decree of 1210 had stimulated the reading of these otherwise forbidding works. The Fourth Council of the Lateran allowed the teaching of Aristotle's works on logic and ethics, but proscribed the rest. In 1231 Gregory IX gave absolution to masters and scholars who had disobeyed these edicts, but he renewed the edicts "provisionally, until the books of the Philosopher had been examined and expurgated." The three Parisian masters appointed to attend to this fumigation of Aristotle seem to have abandoned the task. The prohibitions were not long enforced, for in 1255 the *Physics, Metaphysics*, and other works of Aristotle were required reading at the University of Paris.[19] In 1263 Urban IV restored the prohibitions; but apparently Thomas Aquinas assured him that Aristotle could be sterilized, and Urban did not press his vetoes. In 1366 the legates of Urban V at Paris required a thorough study of the works of Aristotle by all candidates for the arts degree.[20]

The dilemma presented to Latin Christendom in the first quarter of the thirteenth century constituted a major crisis in the history of the faith. The rage for the new philosophy was an intellectual fever that could hardly be controlled. The Church abandoned the effort; instead, she deployed her forces to surround and absorb the invaders. Her loyal monks studied this amazing Greek who had upset three religions. The Franciscans, though they preferred Augustine to Aristotle, welcomed Alexander of Hales, who made the first attempt to harmonize "the Philosopher" with Christianity. The Dominicans gave every encouragement to Albertus Magnus and Thomas Aquinas in the same enterprise; and when these three men had finished their work it seemed that Aristotle had been made safe for Christianity.

III. THE FREETHINKERS

To understand Scholasticism as no vain accumulation of dull abstractions, we must see the thirteenth century not as the unchallenged field of the great Scholastics, but as a battleground on which, for seventy years, skeptics, materialists, pantheists, and atheists contested with the theologians of the Church for possession of the European mind.

We have noted the presence of unbelief in a small minority of the European population. Contact with Islam through the Crusades and the translations extended this minority in the thirteenth century. The discovery that another great religion existed, and had produced fine men like Saladin and al-Kamil, philosophers like Avicenna and Averroës, was in itself a disturbing revelation; comparative religion does religion no good. Alfonso the Wise (1252–84) reported a common disbelief in immortality among the Christians of Spain;[21] perhaps Averroism had trickled down to the people. In southern France there were in the thirteenth century rationalists who argued that God, after creating the world, had left its operation to natural law; miracles, they held, were impossible; no prayer could change the behavior of the elements; and the origin of new species was due not to special creation but to natural development.[22] At Paris some freethinkers—even some priests—denied transubstantiation;[23] and at Oxford a teacher complained that "there is no idolatry like that of the sacrament of the altar."[24] Alain of Lille (1114–1203) remarks that "many false Christians of our time say there is no resurrection, since the soul perishes with the body"; they quoted Epicurus and Lucretius, adopted atomism, and concluded that the best thing to do is to enjoy life here on earth.[25]

The urban industrialism of Flanders seems to have promoted unbelief. At the beginning of the thirteenth century we find David of Dinant, and near its end Siger of Brabant, leading a strongly skeptical movement. David (c. 1200) taught philosophy at Paris, and entertained Innocent III with his subtle disputations.[26] He played with a materialistic pantheism in which God, mind, and pure matter (matter before receiving form) all became one in a new trinity.[27] His book, *Quaternuli*, now lost, was condemned and burned by the Council of Paris in 1210. The same synod denounced the pantheism of another Parisian professor, Amalric of Bène, who had argued that God and the creation are one. Amalric was compelled to retract, and died, we are told, of mortification (1207).[28] The Council had his bones exhumed, and burned them in a Paris square as a hint to his many followers. They persisted nevertheless, and enlarged his views to a denial of heaven and hell and the power of the sacraments. Ten of these Amalricians were burned at the stake (1210).[29]

Free thought flourished in the southern Italy of Frederick II, where St. Thomas grew up. Cardinal Ubaldini, friend of Frederick, openly professed materialism.[30] In northern Italy the industrial workers, the business classes, the lawyers, and the professors indulged in a measure of skepticism. The Bolognese faculty was notoriously indifferent to religion; the medical schools there and elsewhere were centers of doubt; and an adage arose that *ubi tres medici, duo athei*—"where there are three physicians two of them are atheists."[31] About 1240 Averroism became almost a fashion among the educated laity of Italy.[32] Thousands accepted the Averroistic doctrines that natural law rules the world without any interference by God; that the world is coeternal with God; that there is only one immortal soul, the "active intellect" of the cosmos, of which the individual soul is a transitory phase or form; and that heaven and hell are tales invented to coax or terrify the populace into decency.[33] To appease the Inquisition, some Averroists advanced the doctrine of twofold truth: a proposition, they argued, might seem true in philosophy or according to natural reason, and yet be false according to Scripture and the Christian faith; they professed at the same time to believe according to faith what they doubted according to reason. Such a theory denied the basic assumption of Scholasticism—the possibility of reconciling reason and faith.

Towards the end of the thirteenth, and throughout the fourteenth and fifteenth centuries, the University of Padua was a turbulent center of Averroism. Peter of Abano (*c.* 1250–1316), professor of medicine at Paris and then of philosophy at Padua, wrote in 1303 a book, *Conciliator controversiarum*, designed to harmonize medical and philosophical theory. He earned a place in the history of science by teaching that the brain is the source of the nerves, and the heart of the vessels, and by measuring the year with remarkable accuracy as 365 days, six hours, and four minutes.[34] Convinced of astrology, he reduced almost all causation to the power and movement of the stars, and practically eliminated God from the government of the world.[35] Inquisitors accused him of heresy, but Marquis Azzo d'Este and Pope Honorius IV were among his patients, and protected him. He was accused again in 1315, and this time escaped trial by dying a natural death. The inquisitors condemned his corpse to be burned at the stake, but his friends so well concealed his remains that the judgment had to be executed in effigy.[36]

When Thomas Aquinas went from Italy to Paris he discovered that Averroism had long since captured a part of the faculty. In 1240 William of

Auvergne noted that "many men" at the University "swallow these [Averroistic] conclusions without investigation"; and in 1252 Thomas found Averroism flourishing among the University youth.[37] Perhaps alarmed by Thomas' report, Pope Alexander IV (1256) charged Albertus Magnus to write a treatise *On the Unity of the Intellect Against Averroës*. When Thomas taught at Paris (1252–61, 1269–72) the Averroistic movement was at its height; its leader in France, Siger of Brabant, taught in the University from 1266 to 1276. For a generation Averroism and Catholicism made Paris their battlefield.

Siger (1235?–?1281), a secular priest,[38] was a man of learning: even the surviving fragments of his works quote al-Kindi, al-Farabi, al-Ghazali, Avicenna, Avempace, Avicebron, Averroës, and Maimonides. In a series of commentaries on Aristotle, and in a controversial tract *Against Those Famous Men in Philosophy, Albert and Thomas*, Siger argued that Albert and Thomas falsely—Averroës justly—interpreted the Philosopher.[39] He concluded with Averroës that the world is eternal, that natural law is invariable, and that only the soul of the species survives the individual's death. God, said Siger, is the final, not the efficient, cause of things—He is the goal, not the cause, of creation. Led like Vico and Nietzsche by the fascination of logic, Siger played with the dismal doctrine of eternal recurrence: since (he argued) all earthly events are ultimately determined by stellar combinations, and the number of these possible combinations is finite, each combination must be exactly repeated again and again in an infinity of time, and must bring in its train the same effects as before; "the same species" will return, "the same opinions, laws, religions."[40] Siger was careful to add: "We say this according to the opinion of the Philosopher, but without affirming that it is true."[41] To all his heresies he appended a similar caution. He did not profess the doctrine of two truths; he taught certain conclusions as, in his judgment, following from Aristotle and reason; when these conclusions contradicted the Christian creed he affirmed his belief in the dogmas of the Church, and applied only to them, not to philosophy, the label of truth.[42]

That Siger had a large following at the University is evident from his candidacy for the rectorship (1271), though it failed. Nothing could better prove the strength of the Averroistic movement in Paris than its repeated denunciation by the Bishop of Paris, Étienne Tempier. In 1269 he condemned as heresies thirteen propositions taught by certain professors in the University:

> That there is only one intellect in all men. . . . That the world is eternal. . . . That there never was a first man. . . . That the soul is corrupted with the corruption of the body. . . . That the will of man wills and chooses from necessity. . . . That God does not know individual events. . . . That human actions are not ruled by Divine Providence.[43]

Apparently the Averroists continued to teach as before, for in 1277 the Bishop issued a list of 219 propositions which he officially condemned as heresies. These, according to the Bishop, were doctrines taught by Siger, or Boethius of Dacia, or Roger Bacon, or other Parisian professors, including St. Thomas himself. The 219 included those condemned in 1269, and others of which the following are samples:

> That creation is impossible. . . . That a body once corrupted [in death] cannot rise again as the same body. . . . That a future resurrection should not be believed by a philosopher, since it cannot be investigated by reason. . . . That the words of theologians are founded on fables. . . . That nothing is added to our knowledge by theology. . . . That the Christian religion impedes learning. . . . That happiness is obtained in this life, not in another. . . . That the wise men of the earth are philosophers alone. . . . That there is no more excellent condition than to have leisure for philosophy.[44]

In October, 1277, Siger was condemned by the Inquisition. He passed his last years in Italy as a prisoner of the Roman Curia, and was murdered at Orvieto by a half-mad assassin.[45]

IV. THE DEVELOPMENT OF SCHOLASTICISM

To meet this frontal attack upon Christianity it was not enough to condemn the heretical propositions. Youth had tasted the strong wine of philosophy; could it be won back by reason? As the *mutakallimun* had defended Mohammedanism from the Mutazilites, so now Franciscan and Dominican theologians, and secular prelates like William of Auvergne and Henry of Ghent, came to the defense of Christianity and the Church.

The defense divided itself into two main camps: the mystic-Platonic, mostly Franciscans; and the intellectual-Aristotelian, mostly Dominicans. Benedictines like Hugh and Richard of St. Victor felt that the best defense of religion lay in man's direct consciousness of a spiritual reality deeper than all intellectual fathoming. "Rigorists" like Peter of Blois and Stephen of Tournai argued that philosophy should not discuss the problems of theology, or, if it did, it should speak and behave as a modest servant of theology —*ancilla theologiae*.[46] It should be noted that this view was held by only a sector of the Scholastic front.[47]

A few Franciscans, like Alexander of Hales (1170?–1245), adopted the intellectual approach, and sought to defend Christianity in philosophical and Aristotelian terms. But most Franciscans distrusted philosophy; they felt that the adventure of reason, whatever strength and glory it might bring to the Church for a time, might later elude control, and lead men so far from faith as to leave Christianity weak and helpless in an unbelieving and unmoral world. They preferred Plato to Aristotle, Bernard to Abélard, Augustine to Aquinas. They defined the soul, with Plato, as an independent spirit inhabiting, and thwarted by, the body, and they were shocked to hear Thomas accepting Aristotle's definition of the soul as the "substantial form" of the body. They found in Plato a theory of impersonal immortality quite useless for checking the bestial impulses of men. Following Augustine, they ranked will above intellect in both God and man, and aimed at the good rather than the true. In their hierarchy of values the mystic came closer than the philosopher to the secret essence and significance of life.

This Platonic-Augustinian division of the Scholastic army dominated orthodox theology in the first half of the thirteenth century. Its ablest exponent was the saintly Bonaventura—a gentle spirit who persecuted heresy, a mystic writing philosophy, a scholar who deprecated learning, a lifelong friend and opponent of Thomas Aquinas, a defender and exemplar of evangelical poverty under whose ministry the Franciscan Order made great gains in corporate wealth. Born in Tuscany in 1221, Giovanni di Fidanza came for some unknown reason to be called Bonaventura—Good Luck. He nearly died of a childhood malady; his mother prayed to St. Francis for his recovery; Giovanni thereafter felt that he owed his life to the saint. Entering the Order, he was sent to Paris to study under Alexander of Hales. In 1248 he began to teach theology in the University; in 1257, still a youth of thirty-six, he was chosen minister-general of the Franciscans. He did his best to reform the laxity of the Order, but was too genial to succeed. He himself lived in ascetic simplicity. When messengers came to announce that he had been made a cardinal they found him washing dishes. A year later (1274) he died of overwork.

His books were well written, clear, and concise. He pretended to be a mere compiler, but he infused order, fervor, and a disarming modesty into every subject that he touched. His *Breviloquium* was an admirable summary of Christian theology; his *Soliloquium* and *Itinerarium mentis in Deum* (Journey of the Mind to God) were jewels of mystic piety. True knowledge comes not through perception of the material world by the senses, but through intuition of the spiritual world by the soul. While loving St. Thomas, Bonaventura frowned upon the reading of philosophy, and freely criticized some of Aquinas' conclusions. He reminded the Dominicans that Aristotle was a heathen, whose authority must not be ranked with that of the Fathers; and he asked could the philosophy of Aristotle explain a moment's movements of a star?[48] God is not a philosophical conclusion but a living presence; it is better to feel Him than to define Him. The good is higher than the true, and simple virtue surpasses all the sciences. One day, we are told, Brother Egidio, overwhelmed by Bonaventura's learning, said to him: "Alas! what shall we ignorant and simple ones do to merit the favor of God?" "My brother," replied Bonaventura, "you know very well that it suffices to love the Lord." "Do you then believe," asked Egidio, "that a simple woman might please him as well as a master in theology?" When the theologian answered in the affirmative, Egidio rushed into the street and cried out to a beggar woman: "Rejoice, for if you love God, you may have a higher place in the Kingdom of Heaven than Brother Bonaventura!"[49]

Obviously it is a mistake to think of "the" Scholastic philosophy as a dreary unanimity of opinion and approach. There were a hundred Scholastic philosophies. The same university faculty might harbor a Thomas honoring reason, a Bonaventura deprecating it, a William of Auvergne (1180–1249) following Ibn Gabirol into voluntarism, a Siger teaching Averroism. The divergences and conflicts within orthodoxy were almost as intense as between faith and unbelief. A Franciscan bishop, John Peckham, would denounce Aquinas as sternly as Thomas denounced Siger and Averroës; and Albertus Magnus, in an unsaintly moment, wrote: "There are ignorant men who would fight by every means the employment of philosophy; and particularly the Franciscans—brutish beasts who blaspheme that which they do not know." [50]

Albert loved knowledge, and admired Aristotle this side of heresy. It was he who first among the Scholastics surveyed all the major works of the Philosopher, and undertook to interpret them in Christian terms. He was born at Lauingen, Swabia, about 1201, son of the rich count of Bollstädt. He studied at Padua, joined the Dominican Order, and taught in Dominican schools at Hildesheim, Freiburg, Ratisbon, Strasbourg, Cologne (1228–45), and Paris (1245–8). Despite his preference for the scholastic life he was made Provincial of his Order for Germany, and Bishop of Ratisbon (1260). Tradition claims that he walked barefoot on all his journeys.[51] In 1262 he was allowed to retire to a cloister at Cologne. He left its peace when he was seventy-six (1277) to defend the doctrine and memory of his dead pupil Thomas Aquinas at Paris. He succeeded, returned to his monastery, and died at seventy-nine. His devoted life, unassuming character, and vast intellectual interests show medieval monasticism at its best.

Only the quiet routine of his monastic years, and the massive diligence of German scholarship, can explain how a man who spent so much of his time in teaching and administration could write essays on almost every phase of science, and substantial treatises on every branch of philosophy and theology.* Few men in history have written so much, or borrowed so much, or so frankly acknowledged their debts. Albert bases his works almost title

---

* Albert's major works in philosophy and theology: I. Logic: *Philosophia rationalis*; *De praedicabilibus*; *De praedicamentis*; *De sex principiis*; *Perihermenias* (i.e., *De interpretatione*); *Analytica priora*; *Analytica posteriora*; *Topica*; *Libri elenchorum*. II. Metaphysics: *De unitate intellectus contra Averroistas*; *Metaphysica*; *De fato*. III. Psychology: *De anima*, *De sensu et sensato*, *De memoria et reminiscentia*; *De intellectu et intelligibili*; *De potentiis animae*. IV. Ethica. V. Politica. VI. Theology: *Summa de creaturis*; *Summa theologiae*; *Commentarium in Sententias Petri Lombardi*; *Commentarium de divinis nominibus*. The first five treatises here listed fill twenty-one volumes of Albert's works, which are still incompletely published.

for title on Aristotle; he uses Averroës' commentaries to interpret the Philosopher; but he corrects both of them manfully when they differ from Christian theology. He draws on the Moslem thinkers to such an extent that his works are an important source for our knowledge of Arabic philosophy. He cites Avicenna on every other page, and occasionally Maimonides' *Guide to the Perplexed*. He recognizes Aristotle as the highest authority in science and philosophy, Augustine in theology, the Scriptures in everything. His immense mound of discourse is poorly organized, and never becomes a consistent system of thought; he defends a doctrine in one place, attacks it in another, sometimes in the same treatise; he had no time to resolve his contradictions. He was too good a man, too pious a soul, to be an objective thinker; he was capable of following a commentary on Aristotle with a long treatise in twelve "books" *In Praise of the Blessed Virgin Mary*, in which he argued that Mary had a perfect knowledge of grammar, rhetoric, logic, arithmetic, geometry, music, and astronomy.

What, then, was his achievement? Above all, as we shall see, he contributed substantially to the scientific research and theory of his time. In philosophy he "gave Aristotle to the Latins"—which was all that he aimed to do; he promoted the use of Aristotle in the teaching of philosophy; he accumulated the storehouse of pagan, Arabic, Jewish, and Christian thought and argument from which his famous pupil drew for a more lucid and orderly synthesis. Perhaps without Albert, Thomas would have been impossible.

V. THOMAS AQUINAS

Like Albert, Thomas came of lordly stock, and gave up riches to win eternity. His father, Count Landulf of Aquino, belonged to the German nobility, was a nephew of Barbarossa, and was among the highest figures at the Apulian court of the impious Frederick II. His mother was descended from the Norman princes of Sicily. Though born in Italy, Thomas was on both sides of northern origin, essentially Teutonic; he had no Italian grace or deviltry in him, but grew to heavy German proportions, with large head, broad face, and blond hair, and a quiet content in intellectual industry. His friends called him "the great dumb ox of Sicily."[52]

He was born in 1225 in his father's castle at Roccasecca, three miles from Aquino, and halfway between Naples and Rome. The abbey of Monte Cassino was near by, and there Thomas received his early schooling. At fourteen he began five years of study at the University of Naples. Michael Scot was there, translating Averroës into Latin; Jacob Anatoli was there, translating Averroës into Hebrew; Peter of Ireland, one of Thomas' teachers, was an enthusiastic Aristotelian; the University was a hotbed of Greek, Arabic, and Hebrew influences impinging upon Christian thought. Thomas' brothers took to poetry; one, Rainaldo, became a page and falconer at Frederick's court, and begged Thomas to join him there. Piero delle Vigne and Frederick himself seconded the invitation. Instead of accepting, Thomas entered the Dominican Order (1244). Soon thereafter he was sent to Paris to study theology; at the outset of his journey he was kidnaped by two of his brothers at their mother's urging; he was taken to the Roccasecca castle, and was kept under watch there for a year.[53] Every means was used to shake his vocation; a story, probably a legend, tells how a pretty young woman was introduced into his chamber in the hope of seducing him back to life, and how, with a flaming brand snatched from the hearth, he drove her from the room, and burned the sign of the cross into the door.[54] His firm piety won his mother to his purposes; she helped him to escape; and his sister Marotta, after many talks with him, became a Benedictine nun.

At Paris he had Albert the Great as one of his teachers (1245). When Albert was transferred to Cologne Thomas followed him, and continued to study with him there till 1252. At times Thomas seemed dull, but Albert defended him, and prophesied his greatness.[55] He returned to Paris to teach as a bachelor in theology; and now, following in his master's steps, he began a long series of works presenting Aristotle's philosophy in Christian dress. In 1259 he left Paris to teach at the *studium* maintained by the papal court now in Anagni, now in Orvieto, now in Viterbo. At the papal court he met William of Moerbeke, and asked him to make Latin translations of Aristotle directly from the Greek.

Meanwhile Siger of Brabant was leading an Averroistic revolution at the University of Paris. Thomas was sent up to meet this challenge. Reaching Paris, he brought the war into the enemy's camp with a tract *On the Unity of the Intellect Against the Averroists* (1270). He concluded it with unusual fire:

> Behold our refutation of these errors. It is based not on documents of faith but on the reasons and statements of the philosophers themselves. If, then, there be anyone who, boastfully taking pride in his supposed wisdom, wishes to challenge what we have written, let him not do it in some corner, nor before children who are powerless to decide on such difficult matters. Let him reply openly if he dare. He shall find me here confronting him, and not only my negligible self, but many another whose study is truth. We shall do battle with his errors, and bring a cure to his ignorance.[56]

It was a complex issue, for Thomas, in this his second period of teaching at Paris, had not only to combat Averroism, but also to meet the attacks of fellow monks who distrusted reason, and who rejected Thomas' claim that Aristotle could be harmonized with Christianity. John Peckham, successor to Bonaventura in the Franciscan chair of philosophy at Paris, upbraided Thomas for sullying Christian theology with the philosophy of a pagan.

Thomas—Peckham later reported—stood his ground, but answered "with great mildness and humility."[57] Perhaps it was those three years of controversy that undermined his vitality.

In 1272 he was called back to Italy at the request of Charles of Anjou to reorganize the University of Naples. In his final years he ceased writing, whether through weariness or through disillusionment with dialectics and argument. When a friend urged him to complete his *Summa theologica* he said: "I cannot; such things have been revealed to me that what I have written seems but straw."[58] In 1274 Gregory X summoned him to attend the Council of Lyons. He set out on the long mule ride through Italy; but on the way between Naples and Rome he grew weak, and took to his bed in the Cistercian monastery of Fossanuova in the Campagna. There, in 1274, still but forty-nine, he died.

When he was canonized witnesses testified that he "was soft-spoken, easy in conversation, cheerful and bland of countenance... generous in conduct, most patient, most prudent; radiant with charity and gentle piety; wondrous compassionate to the poor."[59] He was so completely captured by piety and study that these filled every thought and moment of his waking day. He attended all the hours of prayer, said one Mass or heard two each morning, read and wrote, preached and taught, and prayed. Before a sermon or a lecture, before sitting down to study or compose, he prayed; and his fellow monks thought that "he owed his knowledge less to the effort of the mind than to the virtue of his prayer."[60] On the margin of his manuscripts we find, every now and then, pious invocations like *Ave Maria!* [61] He became so absorbed in the religious and intellectual life that he hardly noticed what happened about him. In the refectory his plate could be removed and replaced without his being aware of it; but apparently his appetite was excellent. Invited to join other clergymen at dinner with Louis IX, he lost himself in meditation during the meal; suddenly he struck the table with his fist and exclaimed: "That is the decisive argument against the Manicheans!" His prior reproved him: "You are sitting at the table of the King of France"; but Louis, with royal courtesy, bade an attendant bring writing materials to the victorious monk.[62] Nevertheless the absorbed saint could write with good sense on many matters of practical life. People remarked how he could adjust his sermons either to the studious minds of his fellow monks, or to the simple intellects of common folk. He had no airs, made no demands upon life, sought no honors, refused promotion to ecclesiastical office. His writings span the universe, but contain not one immodest word. He faces in them every argument against his faith, and answers with courtesy and calm.

Improving upon the custom of his time, he made explicit acknowledgments of his intellectual borrowings. He quotes Avicenna, al-Ghazali, Averroës, Isaac Israeli, Ibn Gabirol, and Maimonides; obviously no student can understand the Scholastic philosophy of the thirteenth century without considering its Moslem and Jewish antecedents. Thomas does not share William of Auvergne's affection for "Avicebron," but he has a high respect for "Rabbi Moyses," as he calls Moses ben Maimon. He follows Maimonides in holding that reason and religion can be harmonized, but also in placing certain mysteries of the faith beyond the grasp of reason; and he cites the argument for this exclusion as given in the *Guide to the Perplexed.*[63] He agrees with Maimonides that the human intellect can prove God's existence, but can never rise to a knowledge of His attributes; and he follows Maimonides closely in discussing the eternity of the universe.[64]* In logic and metaphysics he takes Aristotle as his guide, and quotes him on almost every page; but he does not hesitate to differ from him wherever the Philosopher strays from Christian doctrine. Having admitted that the Trinity, the Incarnation, the Redemption, and the Last Judgment cannot be proved by reason, he proceeds on all other points to accept reason with a fullness and readiness that shocked the followers of Augustine. He was a mystic in so far as he acknowledged the suprarationality of certain Christian dogmas, and shared the mystic longing for union with God; but he was an "intellectualist" in the sense that he preferred the intellect to the "heart" as an organ for arriving at truth. He saw that Europe was bound for an Age of Reason, and he thought that a Christian philosopher should meet the new mood on its own ground. He prefaced his reasonings with Scriptural and Patristic authorities, but he said, with pithy candor: *Locus ab auctoritate est infirmissimus*—"the argument from authority is the weakest."[66] "The study of philosophy," he wrote, "does not aim merely to find out what others have thought, but what the truth of the matter is."[67] His writings rival those of Aristotle in the sustained effort of their logic.

Seldom in history has one mind reduced so large an area of thought to order and clarity. We shall find no fascination in Thomas' style; it is simple and direct, concise and precise, with not a word of padding or flourish; but we miss in it the vigor, imagination, passion, and poetry of Augustine. Thomas thought it out of place to be brilliant in philosophy. When he wished he could equal the poets at their own game. The most perfect works of his pen are the hymns and prayers that he composed for the Feast of Corpus Christi. Among them is the stately sequence *Lauda Sion salvatorem*, which preaches the Real Presence in sonorous verse. In the Lauds is a hymn beginning with a line from Ambrose—*Verbum supernum prodiens*—and ending with two stanzas—*O salutaris hostia*—regularly sung at the Benediction of the Sacrament. And in the Vespers is one of the great hymns of all time, a moving mixture of theology and poetry:

---

* "If," says the learned Gilson, "Maimonides had not been moved by Averroës to a special notion of immortality, we might say that Maimonides and Thomas agreed on all important points."[65] It is a slight exaggeration, unless we rank the Trinity, the Incarnation, and the Atonement as unimportant elements of the Christian faith.

Pange, lingua, gloriosi	Sing, O tongue, the mystery
corporis mysterium	of the body glorious,
sanguinisque pretiosi,	and of blood beyond all price,
quem in mundi pretium	which, in ransom of the world,
fructus ventris generosi,	fruit of womb most bountiful,
rex effudit gentium.	all the peoples' King poured forth.
Nobis datus, nobis natus	Given to us and born for us
ex intacta virgine,	from an untouched maid,
et in mundo conversatus,	and, sojourning on the planet,
sparso verbi semine,	spreading seed of Word made flesh,
sui moras incolatus	as a dweller with us lowly,
miro clausit ordine.	wondrously He closed His stay.
In supremae nocte cenae	In the night of the Last Supper,
recumbens cum fratribus,	with apostles while reclining,
observata lege plene	all the ancient law observing
cibis in legalibus,	in the food by law prescribed,
cibum turbae duodenae	food He gives to twelve assembled,
se dat suis manibus.	gives Himself with His own hands.
Verbum caro panem verum	Word made flesh converts true bread
verbo carnem efficit,	with a word into His flesh;
fitque sanguis Christi merum,	wine becomes the blood of Christ,
et, si sensus deficit,	and if sense should fail to see,
ad firmandum cor sincerum	let the pure in heart be strengthened
sola fides sufficit.	by an act of faith alone.
Tantum ergo sacramentum	Therefore such great sacrament
veneremur·cernui,	venerate we on our knees;
et antiquum documentum	let the ancient liturgy
novo cedat ritui;	yield its place to this new rite;
praestet fides supplementum	let our faith redeem the failure
sensuum defectui.	of our darkened sense.
Genitori genitoque	To Begetter and Begotten
laus et iubilatio	praise and joyful song,
salus, honor, virtus quoque	salutation, honor, power,
sit et benedictio;	blessings manifold;
procedenti ab utroque	and to Him from both proceeding
compar sit laudatio.*	let our equal praise be told.

Thomas wrote almost as much as Albert, in a life little more than half as long. He composed commentaries on the *Sentences* of Peter Lombard, on the Gospels, Isaiah, Job, Paul; on Plato's *Timaeus*, on Boethius and Pseudo-

---

* The final stanzas are also sung in the Benediction of the Sacrament; and the entire hymn is used as the processional on Holy Thursday.

Dionysius; on Aristotle's *Organon, Of Heaven and Earth, Of Generation and Corruption, Meteorology, Physics, Metaphysics, On the Soul, Politics, Ethics; quaestiones disputatae—On Truth, On Power, On Evil, On the Mind, On Virtues*, etc.; *quodlibeta* discussing points raised at random in university sessions; treatises *On the Principles of Nature, On Being and Essence, On the Rule of Princes, On the Occult Operations of Nature, On the Unity of the Intellect*, etc.; a four-volume *Summa de veritate catholicae fidei contra Gentiles* (1258–60), a twenty-one-volume *Summa theologica* (1267–73), and a *Compendium theologiae* (1271–3). Thomas' published writings fill 10,000 double-column folio pages.

The *Summa contra Gentiles*, or *Summary of the Catholic Faith Against the Pagans*, was prepared at the urging of Raymond of Peñafort, General of the Dominican Order, to aid in the conversion of Moslems and Jews in Spain. Therefore Thomas in this work argues almost entirely from reason, though remarking sadly that "this is deficient in the things of God."[68] He abandons here the Scholastic method of disputation, and presents his material in almost modern style, occasionally with more acerbity than befitted him whom posterity would call *doctor angelicus* and *seraphicus*. Christianity must be divine, he thinks, because it conquered Rome and Europe despite its unwelcome preaching against the pleasures of the world and the flesh; Islam conquered by preaching pleasure and by force of arms.[69] In Part IV he frankly admits that the cardinal dogmas of Christianity cannot be proved by reason, and require faith in the divine revelation of the Hebrew and Christian Scriptures.

Thomas' most extensive work, the *Summa theologica*, is addressed to Christians; it is an attempt to expound and to defend—from Scripture, the Fathers, and reason—the whole body of Catholic doctrine in philosophy and theology.* "We shall try," says the Prologue, "to follow the things that pertain to sacred doctrine with such brevity and lucidity as the subject matter allows." We may smile at this twenty-one-volume brevity, but it is there; this *Summa* is immense, but not verbose; its size is merely the result of its scope. For within this treatise on theology are full treatises on metaphysics, psychology, ethics, and law; thirty-eight treatises, 631 questions or topics, 10,000 objections or replies. The orderliness of argument within each question is admirable, but the structure of the *Summa* has received more praise than its due. It cannot compare with the Euclidean organization of Spinoza's *Ethics*, or the concatenation of Spencer's *Synthetic Philosophy*. The treatise on psychology (Part I, QQ. 75-94) is introduced between a discussion of the six days of creation and a study of man in the state of original innocence. The form is more interesting than the structure. Essentially it continues, and perfects, the method of Abélard as developed by Peter

---

* The *Summa* to and including Part III, Question 90, is by Thomas; the remainder may be by Reginald of Piperno, his companion and editor.

Lombard: statement of the question, arguments for the negative, objections to the affirmative, arguments for the affirmative from the Bible, from the Fathers, and from reason, and answers to objections. The method occasionally wastes time by putting up a straw man to beat down; but in many cases the debate is vital and real. It is a mark of Thomas that he states the case against his own view with startling candor and force; in this way the *Summa* is a summary of heresy as well as a monument of dogma, and might be used as an arsenal of doubt. We may not always be satisfied with the answers, but we can never complain that the Devil has had an incompetent advocate.

VI. THE THOMIST PHILOSOPHY

1. Logic

What is knowledge? Is it a divine light infused into man by God, without which it would be impossible? Thomas parts company at the very outset from Augustine, the mystics, the intuitionists: knowledge is a natural product, derived from the external corporeal senses and the internal sense called consciousness of the self. It is an extremely limited knowledge, for up to our time no scientist yet knows the essence of a fly; [70] but within its limits knowledge is trustworthy, and we need not fret over the possibility that the external world is a delusion. Thomas accepts the Scholastic definition of truth as *adequatio rei et intellectus*—the equivalence of the thought with the thing. [71] Since the intellect draws all its natural knowledge from the senses, [72] its direct knowledge of things outside itself is limited to bodies—to the "sensible" or sensory world. It cannot directly know the super-sensible, meta-physical world—the minds within bodies, or God in His creation; but it may by analogy derive from sense experience an indirect knowledge of other minds, and likewise of God. [73] Of a third realm, the supernatural—the world in which God lives—the mind of man can have no knowledge except through divine revelation. We may by natural understanding know that God exists and is one, because His existence and unity shine forth in the wonders and organization of the world; but we cannot by unaided intellect know His essence, or the Trinity. Even the knowledge of the angels is limited, for else they would be God.

The very limitations of knowledge indicate the existence of a supernatural world. God reveals that world to us in the Scriptures. Just as it would be folly for the peasant to consider the theories of a philosopher false because he cannot understand them, so it is foolish for man to reject God's revelation on the ground that it seems at some points to contradict man's natural knowledge. We may be confident that if our knowledge were complete there would be no contradiction between revelation and philosophy. It is wrong to say that a proposition can be false in philosophy and true in faith; all truth comes from God and is one. Nevertheless it is desirable to distinguish what we understand through reason and what we believe by faith; [74] the fields of philosophy and ideology are distinct. It is permissible for scholars to discuss among themselves objections to the faith, but "it is not expedient for simple people to hear what unbelievers have to say against the faith," for simple minds are not equipped to answer.[75] Scholars and philosophers, as well as peasants, must bow to the decisions of the Church; "we must be directed by her in all things"; [76] for she is the divinely appointed repository of divine wisdom. To the pope belongs the "authority to decide matters of faith finally, so that they may be held by all with unshaken belief." [77] The alternative is intellectual, moral, and social chaos.

2. Metaphysics

The metaphysics of Thomas is a complex of difficult definitions and subtle distinctions, on which his theology is to rest.

1. In created things essence and existence are different. Essence is that which is necessary to the conception of a thing; existence is the act of being. The essence of a triangle—that it is three straight lines enclosing a space—is the same whether the triangle exists or is merely conceived. But in God essence and existence are one; for His essence is that He is the First Cause, the underlying power (or, as Spinoza would say, *sub-stantia*) of all things; by definition He must exist in order that anything else should be.

2. God exists in reality; He is the Being of all beings, their upholding cause. All other beings exist by analogy, by limited participation in the reality of God.

3. All created beings are both active and passive—i.e., they act and are acted upon. Also, they are a mixture of being and becoming: they possess certain qualities, and may lose some of these and acquire others—water may be warmed. Thomas denotes this susceptibility to external action or internal change by the term *potentia*—possibility. God alone has no *potentia* or possibility; He cannot be acted upon, cannot change; He is *actus purus*, pure activity; pure actuality; He is already everything that He can be. Below God all entities can be ranged in a descending scale according to their greater "possibility" of being acted upon and determined from without. So man is superior to woman because "the father is the active principle, while the mother is a passive and material principle; she supplies the formless matter of the body, which receives its form through the formative power that is in the semen of the father." [78]

4. All corporeal beings are composed of matter and form; but here (as in Aristotle) form means not figure but inherent energizing, characterizing principle. When a form or vital principle constitutes the essence of a being, it is a substantial or essential form; so the rational soul—i.e., a life-giving force capable of thought—is the substantial form of the human body, and God is the substantial form of the world.

5. All realities are either substance or accident: either they are separate entities, like a stone or a man; or they exist only as qualities in something else, like whiteness or density. God is pure substance, as the only completely self-existent reality.

6. All substances are individuals; nothing but individuals exists except in idea; the notion that individuality is a delusion is a delusion.

7. In beings composed of matter and form, the principle or source of individuation—i.e., of the multiplicity of individuals in a species or class—is matter.

Throughout the species the form or vital principle is essentially the same; in each individual this principle uses, appropriates, gives shape to, a certain quantity and figure of matter; and this *materia signata quantitate*, or matter marked off by quantity, is the principle of individuation—not of individuality but of separate identity.

3. *Theology*

God, not man, is the center and theme of Thomas' philosophy. "The highest knowledge we can have of God in this life," he writes, "is to know that He is above all that we can think concerning Him." [79] He rejects Anselm's ontological argument,[80] but he comes close to it in identifying God's existence with His essence. God is Being itself: "I am Who am."

His existence, says Thomas, can be proved by natural reason. (1) All motions are caused by previous motions, and so on either to a Prime Mover unmoved, or to an "infinite regress," which is inconceivable. (2) The series of causes likewise requires a First Cause. (3) The contingent, which may but need not be, depends upon the necessary, which must be; the possible depends upon the actual; this series drives us back to a necessary being who is pure actuality. (4) Things are good, true, noble in various degrees; there must be a perfectly good, true, and noble source and norm of these imperfect virtues. (5) There are thousands of evidences of order in the world; even inanimate objects move in an orderly way; how could this be unless some intelligent power exists who created them? * [81]

Aside from the existence of God, Thomas is almost an agnostic in natural theology. "We cannot know what God is, but only what He is not" [82]—not movable, multiple, mutable, temporal. Why should infinitesimal minds expect to know more about the Infinite? It is hard for us to conceive an immaterial spirit, said Thomas (anticipating Bergson), because the intellect is dependent upon the senses, and all our external experience is of material things; consequently "incorporeal things, of which there are no images, are known to us by comparison with sensible bodies, of which there are images." [83] We can know God (as Maimonides taught) only by analogy, reasoning from ourselves and our experience to Him; so if there is in men goodness, love, truth, intelligence, power, freedom, or any other excellence, these must be also in man's Creator, and in such greater degree in Him as corresponds to the proportion between infinity and ourselves. We apply the masculine pronouns to God, but only for convenience; in God and the angels there is no sex. God is one because by definition He is existence itself, and the unified operation of the world reveals one mind and law. That there are three Persons in this divine unity is a mystery beyond reason, to be held in trusting faith.

Nor can we know whether the world was created in time, and therefore out of nothing, or whether, as Aristotle and Averroës thought, it is eternal. The arguments offered by the theologians for creation in time are weak, and should be rejected "lest the Catholic faith should seem to be founded on empty reason-

---

* (1), (2), and (5) are from Aristotle through Albert; (3) from Maimonides; (4) from Anselm.

ings." [84] Thomas concludes that we must believe on faith in a creation in time; but he adds that the question has little meaning, since time had no existence before creation; without change, without matter in motion, there is no time. He struggles manfully to explain how God could pass from noncreation to creation without suffering change. The act of creation, he says, is eternal, but it included in its willing the determination of the time for its effect to appear [85]—a nimble dodge for a heavy man.

The angels constitute the highest grade of creation. They are incorporeal intelligences, incorruptible and immortal. They serve as ministers of God in the government of the world; the heavenly bodies are moved and guided by them; [86] every man has an angel appointed to guard him, and the archangels have the care of multitudes of men. Being immaterial, they can travel from one extremity of space to another without traversing the space between. Thomas writes ninety-three pages on the hierarchy, movements, love, knowledge, will, speech, and habits of the angels—the most farfetched part of his far-flung *Summa*, and the most irrefutable.

As there are angels, so there are demons, little devils doing Satan's will. They are no mere imaginings of the common mind; they are real, and do endless harm. They may cause impotence by arousing in a man a repulsion for a woman.[87] They make possible various forms of magic; so a demon may lie under a man, receive his semen, carry it swiftly through space, cohabit with a woman, and impregnate her with the seed of the absent man.[88] Demons can enable magicians to foretell such events as do not depend upon man's free will. They can communicate information to men by impressions on the imagination, or by appearing visibly or speaking audibly. Or they may co-operate with witches, and help them to hurt children through the evil eye.[89]

Like nearly all his contemporaries, and most of ours, Thomas allowed considerable truth to astrology.

> The movements of bodies here below . . . must be referred to the movements of the heavenly bodies as their cause. . . . That astrologers not infrequently forecast the truth by observing the stars may be explained in two ways. First, because a great number of men follow their bodily passions, so that their actions are for the most part disposed in accordance with the inclination of the heavenly bodies; while there are few—namely, the wise alone—who moderate these inclinations by their reason. . . . Secondly, because of the interference of demons.[90]

However, "human actions are not subject to the action of heavenly bodies save accidentally and indirectly"; [91] a large area is left to human freedom.

4. Psychology

Thomas considers carefully the philosophical problems of psychology, and his pages on these topics are among the best in his synthesis. He begins with an organic, as against a mechanical, conception of organisms: a machine is composed of externally added parts; an organism makes its own parts, and moves itself by its own internal force.[92] This internal formative power is the soul. Thomas expresses the idea in Aristotelian terms: the soul is the "substantial form" of the body—i.e., it is the vital principle and energy that gives existence and form to an organism. "The soul is the primary principle of our nourishment, sensation, movement, and understanding." [93] There are three grades of soul: the vegetative—the power to grow; the sensitive—the power to feel; the rational—the power to reason. All life has the first, only animals and men have the second, only men have the third. But the higher organisms, in their corporeal and individual development, pass through the stages in which the lower organisms remain; "the higher a form is in the scale of being . . . the more intermediate forms must be passed through before the perfect form is reached"[94]—an adumbration of the nineteenth-century theory of "recapitulation," that the embryo of man passes through the stages by which the species developed.

Whereas Plato, Augustine, and the Franciscans thought of the soul as a prisoner within the body, and identified the man with the soul alone, Thomas boldly accepts the Aristotelian view, and defines man—even personality—as a composite of body and soul, matter and form.[95] The soul, or life-giving, form-creating inner energy, is indivisibly in every part of the body.[96] It is bound up with the body in a thousand ways. As vegetable soul it depends upon food; as sensitive soul it depends upon sensation; as rational soul it needs the images produced by, or compounded from, sensation. Even intellectual ability and moral perceptions depend upon a body reasonably sound; a thick skin usually implies an insensitive soul.[97] Dreams, passions, mental diseases, temperament, have a physiological basis.[98] At times Thomas speaks as if body and soul were one unified reality, the inward energy and outward form of an indivisible whole. Nevertheless it seemed obvious to him that the rational soul—abstracting, generalizing, reasoning, charting the universe—is an incorporeal reality. Try as we will, and despite our tendency to think of all things in material terms, we can find nothing material in consciousness; it is a reality all the world unlike anything physical or spatial. This rational soul must be classed as spiritual, as something infused into us by that God Who is the psychical force behind all physical phenomena. Only an immaterial power could form a universal idea, or leap backward and forward in time, or conceive with equal ease the great and the small.[99] The mind can be conscious of itself; but it is impossible to conceive a material entity as conscious of itself.

Therefore it is reasonable to believe that this spiritual force in us survives the death of the body. But the soul so separated is not a personality; it cannot feel or will or think; it is a helpless ghost that cannot function without its flesh.[100] Only when it is reunited, through the resurrection of the body, with the corporeal frame of which it was the inward life, will it constitute with that body an individual and deathless personality. It was because Averroës and his followers lacked faith in the resurrection of the body that they were driven to the theory that only the "active intellect," or soul of the cosmos or species, is immortal. Thomas deploys all the resources of his dialectic to refute this theory. To him this conflict with Averroës over immortality was the vital issue of the century, beside which such mere shiftings of boundaries and titles as physical battles brought were a trivial lunacy.

The soul, says Thomas, has five faculties or powers: vegetative, by which it feeds, grows, and reproduces; sensitive, by which it receives sensations from the external world; appetitive, by which it desires and wills; locomotive, by which it initiates motions; and intellectual, by which it thinks.[101] All knowledge originates in the senses, but the sensations do not fall upon an empty surface or *tabula rasa*; they are received by a complex structure, the *sensus communis*, or common sensory center, which co-ordinates sensations or perceptions into ideas. Thomas agrees with Aristotle and Locke that "there is nothing in the intellect that was not first in the senses"; but he adds, like Leibniz and Kant, "except the intellect itself" —an organized capacity to organize sensations into thought, at last into those universals and abstract ideas which are the tools of reason and, on this earth, the exclusive prerogative of man.

Will or appetition is the faculty by which the soul or vital force moves toward that which the intellect conceives as good. Thomas, following Aristotle, defines the good as "that which is desirable."[102] Beauty is a form of the good; it is that which pleases when seen. Why does it please? Through the proportion and harmony of parts in an organized whole. Intellect is subject to will in so far as desire can determine the direction of thought; but will is subject to the intellect in so far as our desires are determined by the way we conceive things, by the opinions we (usually imitating others) have of them; "the good as understood moves the will." Freedom lies not really in the will, which "is necessarily moved" by the understanding of the matter as presented by the intellect,[103] but in the judgment (*arbitrium*); therefore freedom varies directly with knowledge, reason, wisdom, with the capacity of the intellect to present a true picture of the situation to the will; only the wise are really free.[104] Intelligence is not only the best and highest, it is also the most powerful, of the faculties of the soul. "Of all human pursuits the pursuit of wisdom is the most perfect, the most sublime, the most profitable, the most delightful."[105] "The proper operation of man is to understand."[106]

5. Ethics

The proper end of man, therefore, is in this life the acquisition of truth, and in the afterlife to see this Truth in God. For assuming, with Aristotle, that what man seeks is happiness, where shall he best find it? Not in bodily pleasures, nor in honors, nor in wealth, nor in power, nor even in actions of moral virtue, though all of these may give delight. Let us grant, too, that "perfect disposition of the body is necessary . . . for perfect happiness."[107] But none of these goods can compare with the quiet, pervasive, continuing happiness of understanding. Perhaps remembering Virgil's *Felix qui potuit rerum cognoscere causas*—"happy he who has been able to know the causes of things"—Thomas believes that the highest achievement and satisfaction of the soul—the natural culmination of its peculiar rationality—would be this, "that on it should be inscribed the total order of the universe and its causes." [108] The peace that passeth understanding comes from understanding.

But even this supreme mundane bliss would leave man not quite content, still unfulfilled. Vaguely he knows that "perfect and true happiness cannot be had in this life." There is that in him which undiscourageably longs for a happiness and an understanding that shall be secure from mortal vicissitude and change. Other appetites may find their peace in intermediate goods, but the mind of the full man will not rest except it come to that sum and summit of truth which is God.[109] In God alone is the supreme good, both as the source of all other goods, and as the cause of all other causes, the truth of all truths. The final goal of man is the Beatific Vision—the vision that gives bliss.

Consequently all ethics is the art and science of preparing man to attain this culminating and everlasting happiness. Moral goodness, virtue, may be defined as conduct conducive to the true end of man, which is to see God. Man naturally inclines to the good—the desirable; but what he judges to be good is not always morally good. Through Eve's false judgment of the good, man disobeyed God, and now bears in every generation the taint of that first sin.* If at this point one asks why a God who foresees all should have created a man and a woman destined to such curiosity, and a race destined to such heritable guilt, Thomas answers that it is metaphysically impossible for any creature to be perfect, and that man's freedom to sin is the price he must pay for his freedom of choice. Without that freedom of will man would be an automaton not beyond but below good and evil, having no greater dignity than a machine.

Steeped in the doctrine of original sin, steeped in Aristotle, steeped in monastic isolation and terror of the other sex, it was almost fated that Thomas should think ill of woman, and speak of her with masculine innocence. He follows the climactic egotism of Aristotle in supposing that nature, like a medieval patriarch, always wishes to produce a male, and that woman is something defective and accidental (*deficiens et occasionatum*); she is a male gone awry (*mas occasionatum*); probably she is the result of some weakness in the father's generative power, or of some external factor, like a damp south wind.[111] Relying on Aristotelian and contemporary biology, Thomas supposed that woman contributed only passive matter to the offspring, while the man contributed active form; woman is the triumph of matter over form. Consequently she is the weaker vessel in body, mind, and will. She is to man as the senses are to reason. In her the sexual appetite predominates, while man is the expression of the more stable element. Both man and woman are made in the image of God, but man more especially so. Man is the principle and end of woman, as God is the principle and end of the universe. She needs man in everything; he needs her only for procreation. Man can accomplish all tasks better than woman—even the care of the home.[112] She is unfitted to fill any vital position in Church or state. She is a part of man, literally a rib.[113] She should look upon man as her natural master, should accept his guidance and sub-

---

* Thomas, not foreseeing that the Church would decide in favor of the Immaculate Conception of the Virgin—i.e., her freedom from the taint of original sin—thought that Mary too had been "conceived in sin"; he added, with tardy gallantry, that she was "sanctified before her birth from the womb." [110]

mit to his corrections and discipline. In this she will find her fulfillment and her happiness.

As to evil, Thomas labors to prove that metaphysically it does not exist. *Malum est non ens*, evil is no positive entity; every reality, as such, is good; [114] evil is merely the absence or privation of some quality or power that a being ought naturally to have. So it is no evil for a man to lack wings, but an evil for him to lack hands; yet to lack hands is no evil for a bird. Everything as created by God is good, but even God could not communicate His infinite perfection to created things. God permits certain evils in order to attain good ends or to prevent greater evils, just "as human governments . . . rightly tolerate certain evils"—like prostitution—"lest . . . greater evils be incurred." [115]

Sin is an act of free choice violating the order of reason, which is also the order of the universe. The order of reason is the proper adjustment of means to ends. In man's case it is the adjustment of conduct to win eternal happiness. God gives us the freedom to do wrong, but He also gives us, by a divine infusion, a sense of right and wrong. This innate conscience is absolute, and must be obeyed at all costs. If the Church commands something against a man's conscience he must disobey. If his conscience tells him that faith in Christ is an evil thing, he must abhor that faith.[116]

Normally conscience inclines us not only to the natural virtues of justice, prudence, temperance, and fortitude, but also to the theological virtues of faith, hope, and charity. These last three constitute the distinguishing morality and glory of Christianity. Faith is a moral obligation, since human reason is limited. Man must believe on faith not only those dogmas of the Church that are above reason, but those too that can be known through reason. Since error in matters of faith may lead many to hell, tolerance should not be shown to unbelief except to avoid a greater evil; so "the Church at times has tolerated the rites even of heretics and pagans, when unbelievers were very numerous." [117] Unbelievers should never be allowed to acquire dominion or authority over believers.[118] Tolerance may especially be shown to Jews, since their rites prefigured those of Christianity, and so "bear witness to the faith." [119] Unbaptized Jews should never be forced to accept Christianity.[120] But heretics—those who have abandoned faith in the doctrines of the Church—may properly be coerced.[121] No one should be considered a heretic unless he persists in his error after it has been pointed out to him by ecclesiastical authority. Those who abjure their heresy may be admitted to penance, and even restored to their former dignities; if, however, they relapse into heresy "they are admitted to penance, but are not delivered from the pain of death." [122]

6. Politics

Thomas wrote thrice on political philosophy: in his commentary on Aristotle's *Politics*, in the *Summa theologica*, and in a brief treatise *De regimine principum* —*On the Rule of Princes*.* A first impression is that Thomas merely repeats Aris-

---

* Of this only Book I, and Chapters 1-4 of Book II, are by Thomas; the remainder is by Ptolemy of Lucca.

totle; as we read on we are astonished at the amount of original and incisive thought contained in his work.

Social organization is a tool that man developed as a substitute for physiological organs of acquisition and defense. Society and the state exist for the individual, not he for them. Sovereignty comes from God, but is vested in the people. The people, however, are too numerous, scattered, fickle, and uninformed to exercise this sovereign power directly or wisely; hence they delegate their sovereignty to a prince or other leader. This grant of power by the people is always revocable, and "the prince holds the power of legislating only so far as he represents the will of the people." [123]

The sovereign power of the people may be delegated to many, to a few, or to one. Democracy, aristocracy, and monarchy may all be good if the laws are good and well administered. In general a constitutional monarchy is best, as giving unity, continuity, and stability; "a multitude," as Homer said, "is better governed by one than by several." [124] The prince or king, however, should be chosen by the people from any free rank of the population.[125] If the monarch becomes a tyrant he should be overthrown by the orderly action of the people.[126] He must always remain the servant, not the master, of the law.

Law is threefold: natural, as in the "natural laws" of the universe; divine, as revealed in the Bible; human or positive, as in the legislation of states. The third was made necessary by the passions of men and the development of the state. So the Fathers believed that private property was opposed to natural and divine law, and was the result of the sinfulness of man. Thomas does not admit that property is unnatural. He considers the arguments of the communists of his time, and answers like Aristotle that when everybody owns everything nobody takes care of anything.[127] But private property is a public trust. "Man ought to possess external things not as his own but as common, so that he is ready to communicate them to others in their need." [128] For a man to desire or pursue wealth beyond his need for maintaining his station in life is sinful covetousness.[129] "Whatever some people possess in superabundance is due by natural law to the purpose of succoring the poor"; and "if there is no other remedy it is lawful for a man to succor his own need by means of another's property, by taking it either openly or secretly." [130]

Thomas was not the man to make economics a dismal science by divorcing it from morality. He believed in the right of the community to regulate agriculture, industry, and trade, to control usury, even to establish a "just price" for services and goods. He looked with suspicious eye upon the art of buying cheap and selling dear. He condemned outright all speculative trading, all attempts to make gain by skillful use of market fluctuations.[131] He opposed lending at interest, but saw no sin in borrowing "for a good end" from a professional moneylender.[132]

He did not rise above his time on the question of slavery. Sophists, Stoics, and Roman legists had taught that by "nature" all men are free; the Church Fathers had agreed, and had explained slavery, like property, as a result of the sinfulness acquired by man through Adam's Fall. Aristotle, friend of the mighty, had justified slavery as produced by the natural inequality of men. Thomas tried to reconcile these views: in the state of innocence there was no slavery; but since the Fall it has been found useful to subject simple men to wise men; those who have strong bodies but weak minds are intended by nature to be bondmen.[133] The slave, however, belongs to his master only in body, not in soul; the slave is not obliged to give sexual intercourse to the master; and all the precepts of Christian morality must be applied in the treatment of the slave.

7. Religion

As economic and political problems are ultimately moral, it seems just to Thomas that religion should be ranked above politics and industry, and that the state should submit, in matters of morals, to supervision and guidance by the Church. Authority is nobler, the higher its end; the kings of the earth, guiding men to earthly bliss, should be subject to the pope, who guides men to everlasting happiness. The state should remain supreme in secular affairs; but even in such matters the pope has the right to intervene if rulers violate the rules of morality, or do avoidable injury to their peoples. So the pope may punish a bad king, or absolve subjects from their oath of allegiance. Moreover, the state must protect religion, support the Church, and enforce her decrees.[134]

The supreme function of the Church is to lead men to salvation. Man is a citizen not alone of this earthly state but of a spiritual kingdom infinitely greater than any state. The supreme facts of history are that man committed an infinite crime by disobeying God, thereby meriting infinite punishment; and that God the Son, by becoming man and suffering ignominy and death, created a redeeming store of grace by which man can be saved despite original sin. God gives of this grace to whom He will; we cannot fathom the reasons of His choice; but "nobody has been so insane as to say that merit is the cause of divine predestination." [135] The terrible doctrine of Paul and Augustine recurs in the gentle Thomas:

> It is fitting that God should predestine men. For all things are subject to His Providence. . . . As men are ordained to eternal life through the Providence of God, it likewise is part of that Providence to permit some to fall away from that end; this is called reprobation. . . . As predestination includes the will to confer grace and glory, so also reprobation includes the will to permit a person to fall into sin, and to impose the punishment of damnation on account of that sin. . . . "He chose us in Him before the foundation of the world." [136]

Thomas struggles to reconcile divine predestination with human freedom, and to explain why a man whose fate is already sealed should strive to virtue, how prayer can move an unchangeable God, or what the function of the Church can be in a society whose individuals have already been sorted out into the saved and the damned. He answers that God has merely foreseen how each man would freely choose. Presumably all pagans are among the damned except possibly a few to whom God vouchsafed a special and personal revelation.* [137]

---

* The oft-quoted passage about the blessed in heaven enhancing their bliss by observing the sufferings of the damned occurs in the *Summa*'s Supplement (xcvii, 7), and is to be discredited not to Thomas but to Reginald of Piperno.[138]

The chief happiness of the saved will consist in seeing God. Not that they will understand Him; only infinity can understand infinity; nevertheless, by an infusion of divine grace, the blessed will see the essence of God.[139] The whole creation, having proceeded from God, flows back to Him; the human soul, gift of His bounty, never rests until it rejoins its source. Thus the divine cycle of creation and return is completed, and Thomas' philosophy ends, as it began, with God.

8. The Reception of Thomism

It was received by most of his contemporaries as a monstrous accumulation of pagan reasonings fatal to the Christian faith. The Franciscans, who sought God by Augustine's mystic road of love, were shocked by Thomas' "intellectualism," his exaltation of intellect above will, of understanding above love. Many wondered how so coldly negative and remote a God as the *Actus Purus* of the *Summa* could be prayed to, how Jesus could be part of such an abstraction, what St. Francis would have said of—or to—such a God. To make body and soul one unity seemed to put out of court the incorruptible immortality of the soul; to make matter and form one unity was, despite Thomas' denials, to fall into the Averroistic theory of the eternity of the world; to make matter, not form, the principle of individuation seemed to leave the soul undifferentiated, and to fall into the Averroistic theory of the unity and impersonal immortality of the soul. Worst of all, the triumph of Aristotle over Augustine in the Thomist philosophy seemed to the Franciscans the victory of paganism over Christianity. Were there not already, in the University of Paris, teachers and students who put Aristotle above the Gospels?

Just as orthodox Islam, at the end of the twelfth century, denounced and banished the Aristotelian Averroës, and orthodox Judaism, at the beginning of the thirteenth century, burned the books of the Aristotelian Maimonides, so in the third quarter of that century Christian orthodoxy defended itself against the Aristotelian Thomas. In 1277, at the prompting of Pope John XXI, the bishop of Paris issued a decree branding 219 propositions as heresies. Among these were three expressly charged "against Brother Thomas": that angels have no body, and constitute each of them a separate species; that matter is the principle of individuation; and that God cannot multiply individuals in a species without matter. Anyone holding these doctrines, said the bishop, was *ipso facto* excommunicated. A few days after this decree Robert Kilwardby, a leading Dominican, persuaded the masters of the University of Oxford to denounce various Thomistic doctrines, including the unity of soul and body in man.

Thomas was now three years dead, and could not defend himself; but his old teacher Albert rushed from Cologne to Paris, and persuaded the Dominicans of France to stand by their fellow friar. A Franciscan, William de la Mare, joined the fray with a tract called *Correctorium fratris Thomae*, setting Thomas right on 118 points; and another Franciscan, John Peckham, Archbishop of Canterbury, officially condemned Thomism, and urged a return to Bonaventura and St. Francis. Dante entered the lists by making a modified Thomism the doctrinal framework of *The Divine Comedy*, and choosing Thomas to guide him on the stairway to the highest heaven. After half a hundred years' war the Dominicans convinced Pope John XXII that Thomas had been a saint; and his canonization (1323) gave the victory to Thomism. Thereafter the mystics found in the *Summa*[140] the deepest and clearest exposition of the mystic-contemplative life. At the Council of Trent (1545–63) the *Summa theologica* was placed upon the altar together with the Bible and the Decretals.[141] Ignatius Loyola imposed upon the Jesuit Order the obligation to teach Thomism. In 1879 Pope Leo XIII, and in 1921 Pope Benedict XV, while not pronouncing the works of St. Thomas free from all error, made them the official philosophy of the Catholic Church; and in all Roman Catholic colleges that philosophy is taught today. Thomism, though it has some critics among Catholic theologians, has won new defenders in our time, and now rivals Platonism and Aristotelianism as one of the most enduring and influential bodies of philosophical thought.

It is a simple matter for one who stands on the shoulders of the last 700 years to point out in the work of Aquinas those elements that have ill borne the test of time. It is both a defect and a credit that he relied so much on Aristotle: to that degree he lacked originality, and showed a courage that cleared new paths for the medieval mind. Carefully securing direct and accurate translations, Thomas knew Aristotle's philosophical (not the scientific) works more thoroughly than any other medieval thinker except Averroës. He was willing to learn from Moslems and Jews, and treated their philosophers with a self-confident respect. There is a heavy ballast of nonsense in his system, as in all philosophies that do not agree with our own; it is strange that so modest a man should have written at such length on how the angels know, and what man was before the Fall, and what the human race would have been except for Eve's intelligent curiosity. Perhaps we err in thinking of him as a philosopher; he himself honestly called his work theology; he made no pretense to follow reason wherever it should lead him; he confessed to starting with his conclusions; and though most philosophers do this, most denounce it as treason to philosophy. He covered a wider range than any thinker except Spencer has dared to do again; and to every field he brought the light of clarity, and a quiet temper that shunned exaggeration and sought a moderate mean. *Sapientis est ordinare*, he said—"the wise man creates order."[142] He did not succeed in reconciling Aristotle and Christianity, but in the effort he won an epochal victory for reason. He had led reason as a captive into the citadel of faith; but in his triumph he had brought the Age of Faith to an end.

VII. THE SUCCESSORS

The historian always oversimplifies, and hastily selects a manageable minority of facts and faces out of a crowd of souls and events whose multitudinous complexity he can never quite embrace or comprehend. We must not think of Scholasticism as an abstraction purged of a thousand individual peculiarities, but as a lazy name for the hundreds of conflicting philosophical and theological theories taught in the medieval schools from Anselm in the eleventh century to Occam in the fourteenth. The historian is miserably subject to the brevity of time and human patience, and must dishonor with a line men who were immortal for a day, but now lie hidden between the peaks of history.

One of the strangest figures of the many-sided thirteenth century was Ramon Lull—Raymond Lully (1232?–1315). Born in Palma of a wealthy Catalan family, he found his way to the court of James II at Barcelona, enjoyed a riotous youth, and slowly narrowed his amours to monogamy. Suddenly, at the age of thirty, he renounced the world, the flesh, and the Devil to devote his polymorphous energy to mysticism, occultism, philanthropy, evangelism, and the pursuit of martyrdom. He studied Arabic, founded a college of Arabic studies in Majorca, and petitioned the Council of Vienne (1311) to set up schools of Oriental languages and literature to prepare men for missionary work among Saracens and Jews. The Council established five such schools—at Rome, Bologna, Paris, Oxford, and Salamanca—with chairs of Hebrew, Chaldaic, and Arabic. Perhaps Lully learned Hebrew, for he became an intimate student of the Cabala.

His 150 works defy classification. In youth he founded Catalan literature with several volumes of love poetry. He composed in Arabic, and then translated into Catalan, his *Libre de contemplacio en Deu*, or *Book of Contemplation on God*—no mere mystic revery but a million-word encyclopedia of theology (1272). Two years later, as if with another self, he wrote a manual of chivalric war—*Libre del orde de cavalyeria*; and almost at the same time a handbook of education—*Liber doctrinae puerilis*. He tried his hand at philosophical dialogue, and published three such works, presenting Moslem, Jewish, Greek Christian, Roman Christian, and Tatar points of view with astonishing tolerance, fairness, and kindliness. About 1283 he composed a long religious romance, *Blanquerna*, which patient experts have pronounced "one of the masterpieces of the Christian Middle Ages." [143] At Rome in 1295 he issued another encyclopedia, the *Arbre de sciencia*, or *Tree of Science*, stating 4000 questions in sixteen sciences, and giving confident replies. During a stay in Paris (1309–11) he fought the lingering Averroism there with some minor theological works, which he signed, with unwonted accuracy, *Phantasticus*. Throughout his long life he poured forth so many volumes on science and philosophy that even to list them would empty the pen.

Amid all these interests he was fascinated by an idea that has captured brilliant minds in our own time—that all the formulas and processes of logic could be reduced to mathematical or symbolical form. The *ars magna*, or "great art" of logic, said Raymond, consists in writing the basic concepts of human thought on movable squares, and then combining these in various positions not only to reduce all the ideas of philosophy to equations and diagrams, but to prove, by mathematical equivalence, the truths of Christianity. Raymond had the gentleness of some lunatics, and hoped to convert Mohammedans to Christianity by the persuasive manipulations of his *ars*. The Church applauded his confidence, but frowned upon his proposal to reduce all faith to reason, and to put the Trinity and the Incarnation into his logical machine.[144]

In 1292, resolved to balance the loss of Palestine to the Saracens by peaceably converting Moslem Africa, Raymond crossed to Tunis, and secretly organized there a tiny colony of Christians. In 1307, on one of his missionary trips to Tunisia, he was arrested and brought before the chief judge of Bougie. The judge arranged a public disputation between Raymond and some Moslem divines; Raymond, says his biographer, won the argument, and was thrown into jail. Some Christian merchants contrived his rescue, and brought him back to Europe. But in 1314, apparently longing for martyrdom, he crossed again to Bougie, preached Christianity openly, and was stoned to death by a Moslem mob (1315).

To pass from Raymond Lully to John Duns Scotus is like emerging from *Carmen* into the *Well-Tempered Clavichord*. John's middle and last names came from his birth (1266?) at Duns in Berwickshire (?). He was sent at eleven to a Franciscan monastery at Dumfries; four years later he entered the Order. He studied at Oxford and Paris, and then taught at Oxford, Paris, and Cologne. Then, still a youth of forty-two, he died (1308), leaving behind him a multiplicity of writings, chiefly on metaphysics, distinguished by such obscurity and subtlety as would hardly appear again in philosophy before the coming of another Scot. And indeed the function of Duns Scotus was very much like that of Kant five centuries later—to argue that the doctrines of religion must be defended by their practical-moral necessity rather than their logical cogency. The Franciscans, willing to jettison philosophy to save Augustine from Dominican Thomas, made their young *Doctor Subtilis* their champion, and followed his lead, alive and dead, through generations of philosophical war.

This Duns was one of the keenest minds in medieval history. Having studied mathematics and other sciences, and feeling the influence of Grosseteste and Roger Bacon at Oxford, he formed a severe notion of what constituted proof; and applying that test to the philosophy of Thomas, he ended, almost in its honeymoon, the rash marriage of theology with philoso-phy. Despite his clear understanding of the inductive method, Duns argued —precisely contrary to Francis Bacon—that all inductive or a posteriori proof—from effect to cause—is uncertain; that the only real proof is deduc-tive and a priori—to show that certain effects must follow from the essential nature of the cause. For example, to prove the existence of God, we must first study metaphysics—i.e., study "being as being," and by strict logic ar-rive at the essential qualities of the world. In the realm of essences there must be one which is the source of all the rest, the *Primus*; this *First Being* is God. Duns agrees with Thomas that God is *Actus Purus*, but he interprets the phrase not as Pure Actuality but as Pure Activity. God is primarily will rather than intellect. He is the cause of all causes, and is eternal. But that is all that we can know of Him by reason. That He is a God of Mercy, that He is Three in One, that He created the world in time, that He watches over all by Providence—these and practically all the doctrines of the Christian faith are *credibilia*; they should be believed on the authority of the Scriptures and the Church, but they cannot be demonstrated by reason. Indeed, the mo-ment we begin to reason about God we run into baffling contradictions (the Kantian "antinomies of pure reason"). If God is omnipotent He is the cause of all defects, including all evil; and secondary causes, including the human will, are illusory. In view of these ruinous conclusions, and because of the necessity of religious belief for our moral life (Kant's "practical reason"), it is wiser to abandon the Thomistic attempt to prove theology by philoso-phy, and to accept the dogmas of the faith on the authority of the Bible and the Church.[145] We cannot know God, but we can love Him, and that is better than knowing.[146]

In psychology Duns is a "realist" after his own subtle fashion: universals are objectively real in the sense that those identical features, which the mind abstracts from similar objects to form a general idea, must be in the objects, else how could we perceive and abstract them? He agrees with Thomas that all natural knowledge is derived from sensation. For the rest he differs from him all along the psychologic line. The principle of individuation is not mat-ter but form, and form only in the strict sense of thisness (*haecceitas*)—the peculiar qualities and distinguishing marks of the individual person or thing. The faculties of the soul are not distinct from one another, nor from the soul itself. The basic faculty of the soul is not understanding but will; it is the will that determines to what sensations or purposes the intellect is to at-tend; only the will (*voluntas*), not the judgment (*arbitrium*), is free. Thomas' argument that our hunger for continuance and for perfect happi-ness proves the immortality of the soul proves too much, for it could be applied to any beast in the field. We cannot prove personal immortality; we must simply believe.[147]

As the Franciscans had claimed to see in Thomas the victory of Aristotle over the Gospels, so the Dominicans might have seen in Duns the triumph of Arabic over Christian philosophy: his metaphysic is Avicenna's, his cosmology is Ibn Gabirol's. But the tragic and basic fact in Scotus is his abandonment of the attempt to prove the basic Christian doctrines by reason. His followers carried the matter further, and removed one after another of the articles of faith from the sphere of reason, and so multiplied his distinctions and subtleties that in England a "Dunsman" came to mean a hairsplitting fool, a dull sophist, a dunce. Those who had learned to love philosophy refused to be subordinated to theologians who rejected philosophy; the two studies quarreled and parted; and the rejection of reason by faith issued in the rejection of faith by reason. So ended, for the Age of Faith, the brave adventure.

Scholasticism was a Greek tragedy, whose nemesis lurked in its essence. The attempt to establish the faith by reason implicitly acknowledged the authority of reason; the admission, by Duns Scotus and others, that the faith could not be established by reason shattered Scholasticism, and so weakened the faith that in the fourteenth century revolt broke out all along the doctrinal and ecclesiastical line. Aristotle's philosophy was a Greek gift to Latin Christendom, a Trojan horse concealing a thousand hostile elements. These seeds of the Renaissance and the Enlightenment were not only "the revenge of paganism" over Christianity, they were also the unwitting revenge of Islam; invaded in Palestine, and driven from nearly all of Spain, the Moslems transmitted their science and philosophy to Western Europe, and it proved to be a disintegrating force; it was Avicenna and Averroës, as well as Aristotle, who infected Christianity with the germs of rationalism.

But no perspective can dim the splendor of the Scholastic enterprise. It was an undertaking as bold and rash as youth, and had youth's faults of overconfidence and love of argument; it was the voice of a new adolescent Europe that had rediscovered the exciting game of reason. Despite heresy-hunting councils and inquisitors, Scholasticism enjoyed and displayed, during the two centuries of its exaltation, a freedom of inquiry, thought, and teaching hardly surpassed in the universities of Europe today. With the help of the jurists of the twelfth and thirteenth centuries it sharpened the Western mind by forging the tools and terms of logic, and by such subtle reasoning as nothing in pagan philosophy could excel. Certainly this facility in argument ran to excess, and generated the disputatious verbosity and "scholastic" hairsplitting against which not only Roger and Francis Bacon, but the Middle Ages themselves, rebelled.* Yet the good of the inheritance far outweighed the bad. "Logic, ethics, and metaphysics," said Condorcet, "owe

---

* Giraldus Cambrensis tells of a youth who, at his father's painful expense, studied philosophy for five years at Paris, and, returning home, proved to his father, by remorseless logic, that the six eggs on the table were twelve; whereupon the father ate the six eggs that he could see, and left the others for his son.[148]

to Scholasticism a precision unknown to the ancients themselves"; and "it is to the Schoolmen," said Sir William Hamilton, "that the vulgar languages are indebted for what precision and analytical subtlety they possess." [149] The peculiar quality of the French mind—its love of logic, its clarity, its finesse—was in large measure formed by the heyday of logic in the schools of medieval France.[150]

Scholasticism, which in the seventeenth century was to be an obstacle to the development of the European mind, was in the twelfth and thirteenth centuries a revolutionary advance, or restoration, in human thought. "Modern" thought begins with the rationalism of Abélard, reaches its first peak in the clarity and enterprise of Thomas Aquinas, sustains a passing defeat in Duns Scotus, rises again with Occam, captures the papacy in Leo X, captures Christianity in Erasmus, laughs in Rabelais, smiles in Montaigne, runs riot in Voltaire, triumphs sardonically in Hume, and mourns its victory in Anatole France. It was the medieval dash into reason that founded that brilliant and reckless dynasty.

CHAPTER XXXVII

Christian Science

1095-1300

I. THE MAGICAL ENVIRONMENT

THE Romans at their Imperial height had valued applied science, but had almost forgotten the pure science of the Greeks. Already in the *Natural History* of the elder Pliny we find supposedly medieval superstitions on every other page. The indifference of the Romans co-operated with that of the Christians to almost dry up the stream of science long before the barbarian invasions littered the routes of cultural transmission with the debris of a ruined society. What remained of Greek science in Europe was buried in the libraries of Constantinople, and that remnant suffered in the sack of 1204. Greek science migrated through Syria into Islam in the ninth century, and stirred Moslem thought to one of the most remarkable cultural awakenings in history, while Christian Europe struggled to lift itself out of barbarism and superstition.

Science and philosophy, in the medieval West, had to grow up in such an atmosphere of myth, legend, miracle, omens, demons, prodigies, magic, astrology, divination, and sorcery as comes only in ages of chaos and fear. All these had existed in the pagan world, and exist today, but tempered by a civilized humor and enlightenment. They were strong in the Semitic world, and triumphed after Averroës and Maimonides. In Western Europe, from the sixth to the eleventh century, they broke the dikes of culture, and overwhelmed the medieval mind in an ocean of occultism and credulity. The greatest, most learned men shared in this credulity: Augustine thought that the pagan gods still existed as demons, and that fauns and satyrs were real;[1] Abélard thought that demons can work magic through their intimate acquaintance with the secrets of nature;[2] Alfonso the Wise accepted magic, and sanctioned divination by the stars;[3] how, then, should lesser men doubt?

A multitude of mysterious and supernatural beings had descended into Christianity from pagan antiquity, and were still coming into it from Germany, Scandinavia, and Ireland as trolls, elves, giants, fairies, goblins, gnomes, ogres, banshees, mysterious dragons, blood-sucking vampires; and new superstitions were always entering Europe from the East. Dead men walked the air as ghosts; men who had sold themselves to the Devil roamed woods and fields as werewolves; the souls of children dead before baptism

984

haunted the marshes as will-o'-the-wisps. When St. Edmund Rich saw a flight of black crows he recognized them at once as a flock of devils come to fetch the soul of a local usurer.[4] When a demon is exorcised from a man, said many a medieval story, a big black fly—sometimes a dog—could be seen issuing from his mouth.[5] The population of devils never declined.

A hundred objects—herbs, stones, amulets, rings, gems—were worn for their magic power to ward off devils and bring good luck. The horseshoe was lucky because it had the shape of the crescent moon, which had once been a goddess. Sailors, at the mercy of the elements, and peasants, subject to all the whims of earth and sky, saw the supernatural at every turn, and lived in a vital medium of superstitions. The attribution of magic powers to certain numbers came down from Pythagoras through the Christian Fathers: three, the number of the Trinity, was the holiest number, and stood for the soul; four represented the body; seven, their sum, symbolized the complete man; hence a predilection for seven—ages of man, planets, sacraments, cardinal virtues, deadly sins. A sneeze at the wrong time was a bad omen, and had better be disarmed with a "God bless you" in any case. Philters could be used to create or destroy love. Conception could be avoided by spitting thrice into the mouth of a frog, or holding a jasper pebble in the hand during coitus.[6] The enlightened Agobard, Archbishop of Lyons in the ninth century, complained that "things of such absurdity are believed by Christians as no one ever aforetime could induce the heathen to believe." [7]

The Church struggled against the paganism of superstition, condemned many beliefs and practices, and punished them with a gradation of penances. She denounced black magic—resort to demons to obtain power over events; but it flourished in a thousand secret places. Its practitioners circulated privately a *Liber perditionis*, or *Book of Damnation*, giving the names, habitats, and special powers of the major demons.[8] Nearly everybody believed in some magical means of turning the power of supernatural beings to a desired end. John of Salisbury tells of magic used by a deacon, a priest, and an archbishop.[9] The simplest form was by incantation; a formula was recited, usually several times; by such formulas a miscarriage might be averted, a sickness healed, an enemy put out of the way. Probably the majority of Christians considered the sign of the cross, the Lord's Prayer, and the Ave Maria as magic incantations, and used holy water and the sacraments as magic rites bringing miraculous effects.

Belief in witchcraft was next to universal. The Penitential Book of the bishop of Exeter condemned women "who profess to be able to change men's minds by sorcery and enchantments, as from hate to love or from love to hate, or to bewitch or steal men's goods," or who "profess to ride on certain nights and on certain beasts with a host of demons in women's shape, and to be enrolled in the company of such" [10]—the "Witches' Sabbath" that became notorious in the fourteenth century. A simple witchery consisted in making a wax model of an intended victim, piercing it with needles, and pronouncing formulas of cursing; a minister of Philip IV was accused of hiring a witch to do this to an image of the King. Some women were believed able to injure or kill by a look of their "evil eye." Berthold of Regensburg thought that more women than men would go to hell because so many women practiced witchcraft—"spells for getting a husband, spells for the marriage, spells before the child is born, spells before the christening . . . it is a marvel that men lose not their wits for the monstrous witchcrafts that women practice on them." [11] Visigothic law accused witches of invoking demons, sacrificing to devils, causing storms, etc., and ordered that those convicted of such offenses should have their heads shaved and receive two hundred stripes.[12] The laws of Cnut in England recognized the possibility of slaying a person by magic means. The Church was at first lenient with these popular beliefs, looking upon them as pagan survivals that would die out; on the contrary they grew and spread; and in 1298 the Inquisition began its campaign to suppress witchcraft by burning women at the stake. Many theologians sincerely believed that certain women were in league with demons, and that the faithful must be protected from their spells. Caesarius of Heisterbach assures us that in his time many men entered into pacts with devils; [13] and it is alleged that such practitioners of black magic so disdained the Church that they travestied her rites by worshiping Satan in a Black Mass.[14] Thousands of sick or timid people believed themselves to be possessed by devils. The prayers, formulas, and ceremonies of exorcism used by the Church may have been intended as psychological medicine to calm superstitious minds.

Medieval medicine was in some measure a branch of theology and ritual. Augustine thought that the diseases of mankind were caused by demons, and Luther agreed with him; it seemed logical, therefore, to cure illness with prayer, and epidemics by religious processions or building churches. So Santa Maria della Salute at Venice was raised to check a plague, and the prayers of St. Gerbold, Bishop of Bayeux, cured that city of an epidemic of dysentery.[15] Good physicians welcomed the aid of religious faith in effecting cures; they recommended prayer, and the wearing of amulets.[16] As far back as Edward the Confessor we find English rulers blessing rings for the cure of epilepsy.[17] Kings, having been consecrated by religious touch, felt that they might cure by imposition of hands. Persons suffering from scrofula were supposed to be especially amenable to the royal touch; hence the name "king's evil" for that ailment. St. Louis labored assiduously with such impositions; and Philip of Valois is said to have "touched" 1,500 persons at one sitting.[18]

There were magical means to knowledge as well as to health. Most of the old pagan methods for divining the future or seeing the absent flourished throughout the Middle Ages despite repeated condemnation by the Church. Thomas à Becket, wishing to advise Henry II about a contemplated invasion of Brittany, consulted an aruspex, who foretold the future by watching the flight of birds, and a chiromancer, who predicted by studying the lines of the hand.[19] This art of palmistry claimed divine sanction from a verse in Exodus (xiii, 9): "It shall be for a sign unto thee upon thine hand." Other prophets tried to foretell events by observing the movements of the winds (aëromancy) or the waters (hydromancy), or the smoke rising from a fire (pyromancy). Some, imitating the Moslems, marked points at random upon the earth (or upon any writing material), connected the points with lines, and told fortunes from the geometrical figures so formed (geomancy). Some, it was alleged, learned the future from the evoked dead (necromancy); Albertus Grotus, at the request of Frederick Barbarossa, evoked (we are told) the spirit of the Emperor's wife.[20] Some consulted prophetic books, like those purporting to contain the predictions of the Sibyls, or Merlin, or Solomon. Some opened the Bible at random (*sortes sanctorum*) or the *Aeneid* (*sortes vergilianae*), and told the future from the first verse seen. The gravest medieval historians nearly always found (like Livy) that important events had been directly or symbolically foretold by portents, visions, prophecies, or dreams. There were heaps of books—e.g., one by Arnold of Villanova—offering the latest scientific interpretation of dreams (oneiromancy)—not much sillier than those which famous scientists have written in the twentieth century. Nearly all these modes of divination or clairvoyance had been practiced in antiquity, and are practiced today.

But our time, despite some effort, has not yet equaled the Age of Faith— in Islam, Judaism, or Christendom—in belief that the future is decipherably written in the stars. If the climate of the earth, and the growth of plants, could be so clearly-influenced by the heavenly bodies, why should not these affect—nay, determine—the growth, nature, illnesses, periods, fertility, epidemics, revolutions, and destinies of men or states? So nearly every medieval mind believed. A professional astrologer could be found in the household of almost every prince or king. Doctors bled their patients, as many farmers still plant their seeds, according to phases of the moon. Most universities gave courses in astrology, meaning by it the science of the stars; astronomy was included in astrology, and progressed largely through astrologic interest and aims. Sanguine students professed to have found predictable regularities in the effects of celestial bodies on the earth. Persons born under the ascendancy of Saturn would be cold, cheerless, saturnine; those born under Jupiter, temperate and jovial; under Mars, ardent and martial; under Venus, tender and fruitful; under Mercury, inconstant, mercurial; under a high moon, melancholy almost to the point of lunacy. Genethlialogy predicted the entire life of the individual from the position of the constellations at his birth. To draw a proper horoscope, therefore, one had to *observe the hour*, take the precise moment of birth, the precise position of the stars. Astronomic tables were compiled chiefly to aid the drawing of such horoscopes.

Certain names stand out in this period as pundits of the occult. Peter of Abano almost reduced philosophy to astrology; and Arnold of Villanova, a famous physician, had a predilection for magic. Cecco d'Ascoli (1257?–1327), who taught astrology at the University of Bologna, boasted that he could read a man's thoughts, or tell what he concealed in his hand, by knowing the date of his birth. To illustrate his views he cast the horoscope of Christ, and showed how the constellations at the Nativity had made the crucifixion inevitable. He was condemned by the Inquisition (1324), abjured, was spared on condition of silence, went to Florence, practiced astrology for numerous clients, and was burned at the stake for denying the freedom of the will (1327). Many sincere students—Constantine the African, Gerbert, Albertus Magnus, Roger Bacon, Vincent of Beauvais—were accused of magic, and of relations with devils, because the people could not believe that their knowledge had been obtained by natural means. Michael Scot earned the suspicion by writing famous treatises on the occult: a *Liber introductorius* on astrology; a *Physiognomia* on the correlation of qualities of character with peculiarities of body; and two texts of alchemy. Michael condemned magic, but enjoyed writing about it. He listed twenty-eight methods of divination, and seems to have believed in all of them.[21] Unlike most of his contemporaries he made careful observations, and some experiments; on the other hand he suggested that carrying a jasper or topaz would help a man to preserve continence.[22] He was clever enough to keep on good terms with both Frederick II and the popes; but the inexorable Dante consigned him to hell.

The Church and the Inquisition were part of the environment of European science in the thirteenth century. The universities for the most part operated under ecclesiastical authority and supervision. The Church, however, allowed considerable latitude of doctrine to professors, and in many cases encouraged scientific pursuits. William of Auvergne, Bishop of Paris (d. 1249), promoted scientific investigation, and ridiculed those who were ready to see the direct action of God in any unusual event. Bishop Grosseteste of Lincoln was so advanced in the study of mathematics, optics, and experimental science that Roger Bacon ranked him with Aristotle. The Dominican and Franciscan Orders made no known objection to the scientific studies of Albertus Magnus or Roger Bacon. St. Bernard and some other zealots discouraged the pursuit of science, but this view was not adopted by the Church.[23] She found it hard to reconcile herself to the dissection of human cadavers, for it was among her basic doctrines that man was made in the image of God and that the body, as well as the soul, would rise from the grave; and this reluctance was fully shared by the Moslems and the Jews,[24] and by the people at large.[25]

Guido of Vigevano in 1345 spoke of dissection as "forbidden by the Church"; [26] but we find no ecclesiastical prohibition before the bull *De sepulturis* of Boniface VIII in 1300; and this merely forbade the cutting up of corpses and the boiling away of their flesh in order to send the sterilized bones of dead Crusaders back to their relatives for burial at home.[27] This may have been misinterpreted as forbidding post-mortem dissection, but we find the Italian surgeon Mondino boiling and dissecting corpses about 1320, without any known ecclesiastical protest.[28]

If the achievements of medieval science in the West should seem meager in the following summary, let us remember that it grew in a hostile environment of superstition and magic, in an age that drew the best minds into law and theology, and at a time when nearly all men believed that the major problems of cosmic and human origin, nature, and destiny had been solved. Nevertheless, after 1150, as wealth and leisure grew, and translations began to pour in from Islam, the mind of Western Europe was aroused from its torpor, curiosity flared into eagerness, men began to discuss the brave old world of the unfettered Greeks, and within a century all Latin Europe was astir with science and philosophy.

II. THE MATHEMATICAL REVOLUTION

The first great name in the science of this period is Leonardo Fibonacci of Pisa.

Sumerian mathematics, born of forgotten parentage, had descended through Babylonia to Greece; Egyptian geometry, still visible in the pyramids, had passed, perhaps through Crete and Rhodes, to Ionia and Greece; Greek mathematics had gone to India in the wake of Alexander, and had played a part in the Hindu development that culminated in Brahmagupta (588?–660); about 775, translations were made of Hindu mathematicians, and soon afterward of Greek mathematicians, into Arabic; about 830 the Hindu numerals entered Eastern Islam; about 1000 Gerbert brought them to France; in the eleventh and twelfth centuries Greek, Arabic, and Hebrew mathematics streamed into Western Europe through Spain and Sicily, and came with Italian merchants to Venice and Genoa, Amalfi and Pisa. Transmission is to civilization what reproduction is to life.

Another line of transmission appeared in the sixth century B.C. in the form of the Chinese abacus (Greek *abax*, a board), an instrument for counting by transferring little bamboo rods from one group to another; its descendant, the *suanpan*, is still used by the Chinese. In the fifth century B.C., says Herodotus, the Egyptians reckoned with pebbles, "bringing the hand from right to left"; the Greeks proceeded contrariwise. The Romans used several forms of the abacus; in one form the counters slid in grooves; they were made of stone, metal, or colored glass, and were called *calculi*, little stones.[29] Boethius, about 525, mentioned the abacus as enabling one to count by tens; but this invitation to a decimal system was ignored. The merchants of Italy used the abacus, but wrote the results in clumsy Roman numerals.

Leonardo Fibonacci was born at Pisa in 1180. His father was manager of a Pisan trade agency in Algeria; Leonardo in adolescence joined him there, and was taught by a Moslem master. He traveled in Egypt, Syria, Greece, and Sicily, studied the methods of the merchants, and learned to reckon, he tells us, "by a marvelous method through the nine figures of the Indians";[30] here at the outset of their European career the new numerals were properly called Hindu, and what is now a bore and chore of our childhood was then a wonder and delight. Perhaps Leonardo learned Greek as well as Arabic; in any case we find him well acquainted with the mathematics of Archimedes, Euclid, Hero, and Diophantus. In 1202 he published his *Liber abaci*; it was the first thorough European exposition of the Hindu numerals, the zero, and the decimal system by a Christian author, and it marked the rebirth of mathematics in Latin Christendom. The same work introduced Arabic algebra to Western Europe, and made a minor revolution in that science by occasionally using letters, instead of numbers, to generalize and abbreviate equations.[31] In his *Practica geometriae* (1220) Leonardo, for the first time in Christendom so far as we know, applied algebra to the treatment of geometrical theorems. In two smaller works of the year 1225 he made original contributions to the solution of equations of the first and second degree. In that year Frederick II presided at Pisa over a mathematical tournament in which different problems were set by John of Palermo and solved by Fibonacci.

Despite his epoch-making work, the new method of calculation was long resisted by the merchants of Europe; many of them preferred to finger the abacus and write the results with Roman numerals; as late as 1299 the abacists of Florence had a law passed against the use of the "new-fangled figures." [32] Only a few mathematicians realized that the new symbols, the zero, and the decimal alignment of units, tens, hundreds ... opened the way to such developments of mathematics as were almost impossible with the old letter numerals of Greeks, Romans, and Jews. Not till the sixteenth century did the Hindu numerals finally replace the Roman; in England and America the duodecimal system of reckoning survives in many fields; 10 has not finally won its thousand-year-long war against 12.

Mathematics in the Middle Ages had three purposes: the service of mechanics, the keeping of business accounts, and the charting of the skies. Mathematics, physics, and astronomy were closely allied, and those who wrote on one of them usually contributed to the others as well. So John of Holywood (in Yorkshire), known to the Latin world as Joannes de Sacrobosco, studied at Oxford, taught at Paris, wrote a *Tractatus de sphaera—Treatise on the (Earthly) Sphere—*and an exposition of the new mathematics, *Algorismus vulgaris—Mathematics for the Millions* (c. 1230). *Algorismus*, a corruption of the name al-Khwarizmi, was the Latin term for an arithmetical system using the Hindu numerals. John credited the "Arabs" with the invention of this system, and was partly responsible for the misnomer "Arabic numerals." [33] Robert of Chester, about 1149, in adapting the astronomical tables of al-Battani and al-Zarqali, brought Arabic trigonometry to England, and introduced the word *sinus* (bay, sine) into the new science.

Interest in astronomy was maintained by the needs of navigation and the passion for astrology. The immense authority of the oft-translated *Almagest* petrified the astronomy of Christian Europe into the Ptolemaic theory of eccentrics and epicycles, with the earth at the hub of the world; alert minds like Albertus Magnus, Thomas Aquinas, and Roger Bacon felt the force of the criticisms that the Moorish astronomer al-Bitruji had aimed at this system in the twelfth century; but no satisfactory alternative to Ptolemy's celestial mechanics was found before Copernicus. Christian astronomers in the thirteenth century pictured the planets as revolving about the earth; the fixed stars, snared in a crystal firmament, and steered by divine intelligences, revolved as a regimented host around the earth; the center and summit of the universe was that same man whom the theologians described as a miserable worm tainted with sin and mostly doomed to hell. The suggestion offered by Heracleides Ponticus, four centuries before Christ, that the apparent daily motion of the heavens was due to the axial rotation of the earth, was discussed by Semitic astronomers in the thirteenth century, but was quite forgotten in Christendom. Another notion of Heracleides, that Mercury and Venus revolve about the sun, had been handed down by Macrobius and Martianus Capella; John Scotus Erigena had seized upon it in the eighth century, and had extended it to Mars and Jupiter; the heliocentric system was on the verge of victory; [34] but these brilliant hypotheses were among the casualties of the Dark Ages, and the earth held the center of the stage till 1521. All astronomers, however, agreed that the earth is a sphere. [35]

The astronomical instruments and tables of the West were imported from Islam, or were modeled on Islamic originals. In 1091 Walcher of Lorraine, later Prior of Malvern Abbey, observed lunar eclipses in Italy with an astrolabe; this is the earliest known case of observational astronomy in the Christian West; but even two centuries later (c. 1296) William of St. Cloud had to remind astronomers, by precept and example, that the science grew best on observation rather than on reading or philosophy. The best contribution to Christian astronomy in this period was the Alfonsine Tables of celestial movements, prepared for Alfonso the Wise by two Spanish Jews.

The accumulation of astronomic data revealed the imperfections of the calendar established by Julius Caesar (46 B.C.) from the work of Sosigenes, which made the year too long by eleven minutes and fourteen seconds; and the increasing intercourse of astronomers, merchants, and historians across frontiers exposed the inconvenience of conflicting calendars. Al-Biruni had made a useful study of the rival systems of dividing time and dating events (c. 1000); Aaron ben Meshullam and Abraham bar Hiyya furthered the study in 1106 and 1122; and Robert Grosseteste and Roger Bacon followed with constructive proposals in the thir-

teenth century. The *Computus* (*c.* 1232) of Grosseteste—a set of tables for calculating astronomic events and movable dates (e.g., Easter)—was the first step toward the Gregorian calendar (1582) that guides and confuses us today.

III. THE EARTH AND ITS LIFE

The least progressive medieval science was geology. The earth was the chosen
home of Christ, and the shell of hell, and weather was the whim of God. Moslem,
Jew, and Christian alike covered mineralogy with superstition, and composed
"lapidaries" on the magical powers of stones. Marbod, Bishop of Rennes (1035–
1123), wrote in Latin verse a popular *Liber lapidum*, describing the occult qualities of sixty precious stones; a sapphire held in the hand during prayer, said this
erudite bishop, would secure a more favorable answer from God.[36] An opal
folded in a bay leaf rendered its holder invisible; an amethyst made him immune
to intoxication; a diamond made him invincible.[37]

The same eager curiosity that spawned superstitions upon the minerals of the
earth sent medieval men wandering over Europe and the East, and slowly enriched geography. Giraldus Cambrensis—Gerald of Wales (1147–1223)—roamed
over many lands and topics, mastered many tongues but not his own, accompanied Prince John to Ireland, lived there two years, toured Wales to preach the
Third Crusade, and wrote four vivacious books on the two countries. He weighed
down his pages with bias and miracles, but lightened them with vivid accounts
of persons and places, and lively gossip of the trivial things that make the color
of a character or an age. He was sure that his works would immortalize him,[38]
but he underestimated the forgetfulness of time.

He was one of thousands who in the twelfth and thirteenth centuries made a
pilgrimage to the East. Maps and routes were drawn to guide them, and geography benefited. In 1107–11 Sigurd Jorsalafare, King of Norway, sailed as a
crusader with sixty ships via England, Spain, and Sicily to Palestine; after fighting
Moslems at every opportunity he led his lessened band to Constantinople, and
thence overland through the Balkans, Germany, and Denmark to Norway; the
story of this adventurous journey forms one of the great Scandinavian sagas. In
1270 Lanzarotte Malocello rediscovered the Canary Islands, which had been
known to antiquity. About 1290 Ugolino and Vadino Vivaldo, acording to an unverified tradition, set out from Genoa in two galleys to sail around Africa to India;
all hands, it appears, were lost. A famous hoax took the form of a letter from a
mythical "Prester John" (*c.* 1150), who told of his dominions in Central Asia, and
gave a fantastic geography of the Orient. Despite the Crusades, few Christians
believed in the antipodes; St. Augustine considered it "incredible that a people
inhabits the antipodes, where the sun rises when it sets with us, and where men
walk with their feet toward ours." [39] An Irish monk, St. Fergil, had suggested,
about 748, the possibility of "another world and other men under the earth"; [40]
Albertus Magnus and Roger Bacon accepted the idea, but it remained the daring
concept of a few until Magellan circumnavigated the globe.

The chief contributions to European knowledge of the Far East were made by two Franciscan monks. In April 1245 Giovanni de Piano Carpini, sixty-five and fat, was sent by Innocent IV to the Mongol court at Karakorum. Giovanni and his companion suffered in the enterprise every hardship this side of death. They traveled for fifteen months, changing horses four times a day. Pledged by the Franciscan rule to eat no meat, they almost starved among nomads who had hardly any other food to give them. Giovanni's mission failed, but after his return to Europe he compiled an account of his journey which is a classic in the literature of geography—clear, impersonal, matter-of-fact, without a word of self or complaint. In 1253 Louis IX sent William of Rubruquis (Wilhelm van Ruysbroeck) to the Great Khan to renew the Pope's suggestion of an alliance; William brought back a stern invitation to submit France to the Mongol power;[41] and all that came of the expedition was William's excellent account of Mongol manners and history. Here, for the first time, European geography learned the sources of the Don and the Volga, the position of Lake Balkhash, the cult of the Dalai Lama, the settlements of Nestorian Christians in China, and the distinction of Mongols from Tatars.

The most famous and successful of medieval European travelers in the Far East were the Polo family of Venetian merchants. Andrea Polo had three sons—Marco the elder, Niccolò, and Maffeo—all engaged in Byzantine trade, and living in Constantinople. About 1260 Niccolò and Maffeo moved to Bokhara, where they remained three years. Thence they traveled in the train of a Tatar embassy to the court of Kublai Khan at Shangtu. Kublai sent them back as emissaries to Pope Clement IV; they took three years to reach Venice, and by that time Clement was dead. In 1271 they started back to China, and Niccolò took with him his boy Marco the younger, then seventeen. For three and a half years they traveled across Asia via Balkh, the Pamir plateau, Kashgar, Khotan, Lop Nor, the Gobi Desert, and Tangut; when they reached Shangtu Marco was almost twenty-one. Kublai took a fancy to him, gave him important posts and missions, and kept the three Poli in China for seventeen years. Then they sailed back, through three years, via Java, Sumatra, Singapore, Ceylon, and the Persian Gulf, overland to Trebizond, and by boat to Constantinople and Venice, where, as all the world knows, no one would believe the tales "Marco Millions" told of the "gorgeous East." Fighting for Venice in 1298, Marco was captured, and was kept for a year in a Genoese jail; there he dictated his narrative to a fellow prisoner. Nearly every element in the once incredible story has been verified by later exploration. Marco gave the first description of a trip across all Asia; the first European glimpse of Japan; the first good account of Pekin, Java, Sumatra, Siam, Burma, Ceylon, the Zanzibar coast, Madagascar, and Abyssinia. The book was a revelation of the East to the West. It helped to open new routes to commerce, ideas, and arts, and shared in molding the geography that in-spired Columbus to sail westward to the East.

As the orbit of commerce and travel widened, the science of cartography crept laboriously back toward the level it had reached in Augustus' days. Navigators prepared *portolani*—guides to the ports of trade, with maps, charts, itineraries, and descriptions of the various harbors; in the hands of the Pisans and Genoese these *portolani* reached a high degree of accuracy. The *mappae mundi* drawn by the monks of this period are by comparison schematic and incomprehensible.

Stimulated by the zoological treatises of Aristotle and the botanical classic of Theophrastus, the awakening mind of the West struggled to graduate from legend and Pliny to a science of animals and plants. Nearly everyone believed that minute organisms, including worms and flies, were spontane-ously generated from dust, slime, and putrefaction. "Bestiaries" had almost replaced zoology; since monks did almost all the writing, the animal world was considered largely in theological terms, as a storehouse of edifying sym-bolism; and additional creatures were invented in playful fancy or pious need. Said Bishop Honorius of Autun in the twelfth century:

> The unicorn is a very fierce beast with only one horn. To capture it
> a virgin maid is placed in the field. The unicorn approaches her, and
> resting in her lap, is so taken. By the beast Christ is figured; by the
> horn his insuperable strength. . . . Resting in the womb of a virgin, he
> was taken by the hunters—i.e., Christ was found in the form of a man
> by those who loved him.[42]

The most scientific work of medieval biology was Frederick II's *De arte venandi cum avibus*, a 589-page treatise on "the art of hunting with birds." It was based partly on Greek and Moslem manuscripts, but largely on direct observation and experiment; Frederick himself was an expert falconer. His description of bird anatomy contains a great number of original contribu-tions; his analysis of the flight and migration of birds, his experiments on the artificial incubation of eggs and the operations of vultures show a scientific spirit unique in his age.[43] Frederick illustrated his text with hundreds of drawings of birds, perhaps from his own hand—drawings "true to life down to the tiniest details." [44] The menagerie that he collected was not, as most contemporaries thought, a whim of bizarre display, but a laboratory for the direct study of animal behavior. This Alexander was his own Aristotle.

IV. MATTER AND ENERGY

Physics and chemistry did better than geology and biology; their laws and marvels have always harmonized better than a "Nature red in tooth and claw" with a theistic view of the world. Their vitality is suggested near the outset of this period by the efforts of Oliver of Malmesbury to make an airplane; in 1065 his contraption was ready, he soared in it from a high place, and was killed.[45]

The science of mechanics produced in the thirteenth century a remarkable figure, a Dominican monk who anticipated several basic conceptions of Isaac Newton. Jordanus Nemorarius became the second General of the Dominican Order in 1222; that such a man could do such brilliant work in science bears witness—if Albert and Thomas were not enough—to the intellectual eagerness of the Preaching Friars. In three mathematical treatises rivaling those of Fibonacci in courage and influence, he accepted the Hindu numerals, and advanced algebra by regularly using letters instead of figures for his general formulas. His *Elementa super demonstrationem ponderis* studied the component of gravity along a trajectory, and laid down a principle now known as the axiom of Jordanus: that which can raise a certain weight to a certain height can raise a weight K times heavier to a height K times less. Another treatise, *De ratione ponderis* (perhaps by a pupil), analyzed the notion of statical moment—the product of a force into its lever arm—and anticipated modern ideas in the mechanics of the lever and the inclined plane.[46] A third treatise, ascribed to "the school of Jordanus," gave tentative expression to the theory of virtual displacements—a principle developed by Leonardo da Vinci, Descartes, and John Bernoulli, and finally formulated by J. Willard Gibbs in the nineteenth century.

The progress of mechanics slowly affected invention. In 1271 Robert of England clearly stated the theory of the pendulum clock. In 1288 we hear of a great clock in a tower at Westminster, and, about the same time, of similar giants in churches on the Continent; but there is no certain indication that these were fully mechanical. The first clear mention of a clock operated by pulleys, weights, and gears is dated 1320.[47]

The most successful branch of physics in this period was optics. The Arabic treatises of al-Haitham, translated into Latin, opened almost a new world to the West. In an essay on the rainbow Robert Grosseteste, about 1230, wrote of a

> third branch of perspective . . . untouched and unknown among us until the present time . . . [which] shows us how to make things very far off seem very close at hand, and how to make large objects which are near seem tiny, and how to make distant objects appear as large as we choose.

These marvels, he adds, can be achieved through breaking up "the visual ray" by passing it through several transparent objects or lenses of varying structure. These ideas fascinated his pupil Roger Bacon. Another Franciscan monk, John Peckham, probably also a pupil of Grosseteste at Oxford, dealt with reflection, refraction, and the structure of the eye in a treatise *Perspectiva communis*; when we recall that Peckham became Archbishop of Canterbury we perceive again an unsuspected *entente* between science and the medieval Church.

One result of these studies in optics was the invention of spectacles. Magnifying glasses had been known to Greek antiquity,[48] but the construction of such glasses to focus properly when near the eye seems to have awaited research in the geometry of refraction. A Chinese document of uncertain date between 1260 and 1300 speaks of glasses called *ai tai*, which enabled old people to read fine script. A Dominican friar, preaching at Piacenza in 1305, remarked: "It is not twenty years since there was discovered the art of making eyeglasses [*occhiali*], which enable one to see well. . . . I myself have spoken to the man who first discovered and made them." A letter dated 1289 says: "I am so heavy with years that without the glasses called *okiali*, recently invented, I should not be able to read or write." The invention is usually credited to Salvino d'Amarto, whose tombstone, dated 1317, read: "the inventor of spectacles." In 1305 a Montpellier physician announced that he had prepared an eyewash that made spectacles superfluous.[49]

The attractive power of the magnet had also been known to the Greeks. Its power to indicate direction was apparently discovered by the Chinese in the first century of our era. Chinese tradition ascribes to Moslems, about 1093, the earliest use of the magnetic needle in guiding navigation. Such use was probably widespread among Moslem and Christian mariners by the end of the twelfth century. The oldest Christian reference to it is in 1205, the oldest Moslem reference is in 1282;[50] but perhaps those who had long known the precious secret had been in no haste to publish it. Moreover, mariners who used it were suspected of magic, and some sailors refused to sail with a captain who kept such a demonic instrument.[51] The first known description of a pivoted floating compass occurs in an *Epistola de magnete* by Petrus Peregrinus in 1269. This Peter the Pilgrim recorded many experiments, advocated the experimental method, and expounded the operation of the magnet in attracting iron, magnetizing other objects, and finding the north. He tried also to construct a perpetual motion machine operated by self-regenerating magnets.[52]

Chemistry advanced largely through alchemical research. From the tenth century onward Arabic texts in this field were translated into Latin, and soon the West steamed with alchemy, even in monasteries. Brother Elias, successor to St. Francis, edited a work on alchemy for Frederick II; another Franciscan, Grosseteste, wrote in favor of the possibility of transmuting metals; and one of the most famous of medieval books, the *Liber de causis*, presented alchemy and astrology in a work foisted upon Aristotle. Several European kings employed alchemists in the hope of rescuing their treasuries by changing cheap metals into gold.[53] Other zealots continued the search for the elixir of life and the philosopher's stone. In 1307 the Church condemned alchemy as a diabolical art, but its practice continued. Perhaps to escape ecclesiastical censure several authors of the twelfth or thirteenth century attributed their works on alchemy to the Moslem "Gebir."

Medical experience with drugs added to chemical knowledge, and industrial operations almost compelled experiment or discovery. The brewing of beer, the manufacture of dyes, pottery, enamels, glass, glue, lacquer, ink, and cosmetics contributed to the science of chemistry. Peter of St. Omer, about 1270, composed a *Liber de coloribus faciendis*, containing recipes for the various pigments used in painting; one recipe described the making of oil colors by mixing the pigment with linseed oil.[54] About 1150 a treatise known as the *Magister Salernus*—presumably a product of the Salerno school of medicine—mentioned the distillation of alcohol; this is the first clear reference to that now universal operation. The grape-producing countries distilled wine, and called the result *aqua vitae, eau de vie*, water of life; the North, with less grapes and bitterer cold, found it cheaper to distill grain. The Celtic term *uisqebeatha*, which was shortened into *whisky*, also meant "water of life." [55] Distillation had been known long before to Moslem alchemists; but the discovery of alcohol—and, in the thirteenth century, of mineral acids—vastly enlarged chemical knowledge and industry.

Almost as important in its effects as the distillation of alcohol was the discovery of gunpowder. The old Chinese claim to priority here is now challenged; and there is no clear mention of the substance in Arabic manuscripts before 1300.[56] The earliest known notice of the explosive is in a *Liber ignium ad comburendos hostes*, or *Book of Fires for Burning Enemies*, written by Marcus Graecus, about 1270. After describing Greek fire and phosphorescence Mark the Greek gave a recipe for making gunpowder: reduce to a fine powder, separately, one pound of live sulphur, two pounds of charcoal from the lime or willow tree, and six pounds of saltpeter (potassium nitrate); then mix them.[57] There is no record of any military use of gunpowder before the fourteenth century.

V. THE REVIVAL OF MEDICINE

Poverty always mingles myth with medicine, for myth is free and science is dear. The basic picture of medieval medicine is the mother with her little store of household remedies; old women wise in herbs and plasters and magic charms; herbalists peddling curative plants, infallible drugs, and miraculous pills; midwives ready to sever new life from old in the ridiculous ignominy of birth; quacks ready to cure or kill for a pittance; monks with a heritage of monastic medicine; nuns quietly comforting the sick with ministration or prayer; and, here and there, for those who could afford them, trained physicians practicing more or less scientific medicine. Monstrous drugs and fabulous formulas flourished; and just as certain stones held in the hand were by some believed to ward off conception, so—even in medical Salerno—some women and men ate asses' dung to promote fertility.[58]

Until 1139 some members of the clergy practiced medicine, and what hos-
pitalization could be had was usually to be found in monastic or conventual
infirmaries. The monks played an honorable role in preserving the medical
heritage, and led the way in the cultivation of medicinal plants; and perhaps
they knew what they were doing in mingling miracle with medicine. Even
nuns might be skilled in healing. Hildegarde, the mystic Abbess of Bingen,
wrote a book of clinical medicine—*Causae et curae* (*c.* 1150)—and a book of
Subtilitates, marred here and there with magic formulas, but rich in medical
lore. The retirement of old men or women into monasteries or convents may
have been motivated in part by a desire for continuous medical attendance.
As lay medicine developed, and the love of gain infected monastic healing,
the Church (1130, 1339, 1663) progressively forbade the public practice of
medicine by the clergy; and by 1200 the ancient art was almost completely
secular.

Scientific medicine survived the Dark Ages in the West chiefly through
Jewish physicians, who circulated Greco-Arabic medical knowledge in
Christendom; through the Byzantine culture of southern Italy; and through
translations of Greek and Arabic medical treatises into Latin. Probably the
School of Salerno was best situated and prepared to take advantage of these
influences; Greek, Latin, Moslem, and Jewish physicians taught or studied
there; and till the twelfth century it remained the leading medical institution
in Latin Europe. Women studied nursing and obstetrics at Salerno; [59] *mu-
lieres Salernitanae* were probably midwives trained in the school. One of the
most famous Salernitan products was an obstetrical treatise of the early
twelfth century, entitled *Trotulae curandarum aegritudinum muliebrum—
Trotula on the Cure of Diseases of Women*; in the generally accepted theory
Trotula was a midwife of Salerno.[60] Several important treatises, covering
nearly all branches of medicine, have reached us from the School of Salerno.
One, by Archimatheus, prescribes the proper bedside manner: the physician
must always regard the patient's condition as grave, so that a fatal end may
not disgrace him, and a cure may add another marvel to his fame; he should
not flirt with the patient's wife, daughter, or maidservant; and even if no
medicine is necessary he should prescribe some harmless concoction, lest the
patient think the treatment not worth the fee, and lest nature should seem to
have healed the patient without the physician's aid.[61]

The School of Salerno gave way to the University of Naples after 1268,
and little is heard of it thereafter. By that time its graduates had spread Salernitan medicine through Europe. Good schools of medicine existed in the
thirteenth century at Bologna, Padua, Ferrara, Perugia, Siena, Rome, Montpellier, Paris, and Oxford. In these schools the three main medical traditions
of the Middle Ages—Greek, Arabic, and Judaic—were merged and absorbed,
and the entire medical heritage was reformulated to become the basis of
modern medicine. Ancient methods of diagnosis by auscultation and uri-

nalysis retained (and retain) their popularity, so that in some places the urinal became the emblem or signboard of the medical profession.[62] Ancient methods of treatment by purgation and bloodletting continued, and in England the physician was a "leech." Hot baths were a favorite prescription; patients traveled to "take the waters" of mineral springs. Diet was minutely prescribed in nearly every illness.[63] But drugs abounded. Almost every element was used as a cure, from seaweed (rich in iodine), which Roger of Salerno recommended for goiter in 1180, to gold, which was imbibed to "comfort sore limbs" [64]—apparently our fashionable treatment for arthritis. Practically every animal organ found some therapeutic use in the medieval pharmacopeia—the horns of deer, the blood of dragons, the bile of vipers, the semen of frogs; and animal excrement was occasionally prescribed.[65] The most popular of all drugs was *theriacum*, a weird mixture composed of some fifty-seven substances, of which the chief was the flesh of poisonous snakes. Many drugs were imported from Islam, and kept their Arabic names.

As the supply of trained physicians increased, governments began to regulate medical practice. Roger II of Sicily, probably influenced by old Moslem precedents, restricted the practice of medicine to persons licensed by the state. Frederick II (1224) required for such practice a license from the School of Salerno. To obtain it the student had to survive a three-year course in *scientia logicalis*—presumably meaning natural science and philosophy; he had then to study medicine at the school for five years, pass two examinations, and practice for a year under the supervision of an experienced physician.[66]

Every city of any importance paid physicians to treat the poor without charge.[67] Some cities had a measure of socialized medicine. In Christian Spain of the thirteenth century a physician was hired by the municipality to care for a specified part of the population; he made periodically a medical examination of each person in his territory, and gave each one advice according to his findings; he treated the poor in a public hospital, and was obliged to visit every sick person three times a month; all without charge, except that for any visit above three in any month he was allowed to ask a fee. For these services the physician was exempted from taxes, and received an annual salary of twenty pounds,[68] equivalent to some $4000 today.*

As licensed physicians were not numerous in thirteenth-century Christian Europe, they earned good fees, and had a high social status. Some amassed considerable fortunes; some became art collectors; several won an international reputation. Petrus Hispanus—Peter of Lisbon and Compostela—migrated to Paris and then to Siena, wrote the most popular medieval handbook of medicine (*Thesaurus pauperum—Treasure of the Poor*) and the best medieval discussion of psychology (*De anima*), became Pope John XXI in

---

* In the laws of Visigothic Spain the physician was not entitled to a fee if his patient died.[69]

1276, and was crushed to death by a falling ceiling in 1277. The most famous Christian physician of this period was Arnold of Villanova (*c.* 1235–1311). Born near Valencia, he learned Arabic, Hebrew, and Greek, studied medicine at Naples, taught it or natural philosophy at Paris, Montpellier, Barcelona, Rome, and wrote a great number of works on medicine, chemistry, astrology, magic, theology, wine making, and the interpretation of dreams. Made physician to James II of Aragon, he repeatedly warned the King that unless he protected the poor against the rich he would go to hell.[70] James loved him nevertheless, and sent him on many diplomatic missions. Shocked by the misery and exploitation that he saw in many countries, he became a follower of the mystic Joachim of Flora, and declared, in letters to princes and prelates, that the wickedness of the mighty and the luxury of the clergy heralded the destruction of the world. He was accused of magic and heresy, and was charged with having alchemically produced ingots of gold for King Robert of Naples. He was condemned by an ecclesiastical court, but was released from prison by Boniface VIII. He successfully treated the old Pope for kidney stones, and received from him a castle at Anagni. He warned Boniface that unless the Church should be thoroughly reformed the divine wrath would soon descend upon her; soon thereafter Boniface suffered famous indignities at Anagni, and died in despair. The Inquisition continued to pursue Arnold, but kings and popes protected him for their ailments' sake, and he died by drowning on a mission from James II to Clement V.[71]

Surgery in this period fought a two-front war against the barbers on one side and general practitioners on the other. For a long time the barbers had given enemas, pulled teeth, treated wounds, and let blood. Surgeons who had received formal medical training protested against the tonsorial performance of such ministrations, but the law defended the barbers throughout the Middle Ages. In Prussia till the time of Frederick the Great it remained one of the duties of the army surgeon to shave the officers.[72] Partly through this overlapping of functions, the surgeons were considered inferior to the physicians in science and society; they were looked upon as simple technicians obeying the directions of the doctor, who usually, before the thirteenth century, disdained to practice surgery himself.[73] Surgeons were further discouraged by fear of imprisonment or death if their procedures failed; only the bravest undertook dangerous operations; and most surgeons, before such an enterprise, required a written guarantee that no harm would come to them in case of failure.[74]

Nevertheless surgery advanced more rapidly in this period than any other branch of medicine, partly because it was forced to deal with conditions rather .than theories, partly through plentiful opportunity to treat the wounds of soldiers. Roger of Salerno, about 1170, published his *Practica chirurgiae*, the earliest surgical treatise in the Christian West; for three centuries it remained a classic text. In 1238 Frederick II ordered that a corpse should be dissected in every five-year period at Salerno; [75] such dissection of cadavers was practiced regularly in Italy after 1275.[76] In 1286 a Cremona physician opened a corpse to study the cause of a current pestilence; this is the first known case of a post-mortem examination. In 1266 Teodorico Borgognoni, Bishop of Cervia, began a long struggle of Italian medicine against the Arabic notion that suppuration must first be encouraged in the treatment of wounds; his discussion of aseptic treatment is a classic of medieval medicine. Guglielmo Salicetti—William of Saliceto (1210–77)—professor of medicine at Bologna, made notable improvements in his *Chirurgia* (1275); it associated surgical diagnosis with a knowledge of internal medicine, used careful clinical records, showed how to suture divided nerves, and advocated the knife—as allowing better healing, and leaving less scar—in preference to the cautery so popular with Moslem practitioners. In a general treatise—*Summa conservationis et curationis*—William ascribed chancre and bubo to intercourse with an infected courtesan, gave a classical description of dropsy as due to hardening and narrowing of the kidneys, and offered excellent advice on hygiene and diet for every age of life.

His pupils Henri de Mondeville (1260?–1320) and Guido Lanfranchi (d. 1315) brought the medical lore of Bologna to France. Like Teodorico, de Mondeville improved asepsis by advocating a return to Hippocrates' method of maintaining simple cleanliness in a wound. Lanfranchi, exiled from Milan in 1290, went to Lyons and Paris, and wrote a *Chirurgia magna* which became the recognized text of surgery at the University of Paris. He laid down a principle that rescued surgery from barberism: "No one can be a good physician if he is ignorant of surgery; and no one can properly perform operations if he does not know medicine." [77] Lanfranchi was the first to use neurotomy for tetanus, and intubation of the esophagus, and gave the first surgical description of concussion of the brain. His chapter on injuries of the head is one of the peaks in the history of medicine.

Surgical sleeping draughts are mentioned by Origen (185–254) and Bishop Hilary of Poitiers (c. 353). The usual method of anesthesia in medieval Christendom was by inhaling, and probably drinking, a mixture based on mandragora (mandrake), and generally containing also opium, hemlock, and mulberry juice; mention of this "soporific sponge" occurs from the ninth century onward.[78] Local anesthesia was induced by a poultice soaked in a similar solution. The patient was awakened by applying fennel juice to his nostrils. Surgical instruments had as yet made no progress since the Greeks. Obstetrics had fallen behind the practice of Soranus (c. A.D. 100) and Paul of Aegina (c. A.D. 640). Caesarean section was discussed in the literature, but apparently not practiced. Embryotomy—mutilation of the foetus for removal from the womb—was in many cases performed because the obstetrician rarely understood version. Delivery was accomplished in specially designed chairs.[79]

Hospitals were now advanced far beyond anything known in antiquity. The Greeks had had *asklepieia*, religious institutions for the treatment of the sick; the Romans had maintained hospitals for their soldiers; but it was Christian charity that gave the institution a wide development. In 369 St. Basil founded at Caesarea in Cappadocia an institution called after him the *Basilias*, with several buildings for patients, nurses, physicians, workshops, and schools. St. Ephraim opened a hospital at Edessa in 375; others rose throughout the Greek East, and in specialized variety. The Byzantine Greeks had *nosocomia* for the sick, *brephotrophia* for foundlings, *orphanotrophia* for orphans, *ptochia* for the poor, *xenodochia* for poor or infirm pilgrims, and *gerontochia* for the old. The first hospital in Latin Christendom was founded by Fabiola at Rome about 400. Many monasteries provided small hospitals, and several orders of monks—Hospitalers, Templars, Antonines, Alexians— and nuns arose to care for the sick. Innocent III organized at Rome in 1204 the hospital of Santo Spirito, and under his inspiration similar institutions were set up throughout Europe; Germany alone had, in the thirteenth century, over a hundred such "hospitals of the Holy Spirit." In France the hospitals served the poor and old and the pilgrim, as well as the sick; like the monastic centers they offered *hospital*ity. About 1260 Louis IX established at Paris an asylum, *Les Quinze-vingt*; originally a retreat for the blind, it became a hospital for eye diseases, and is now one of the most important medical centers in Paris. The first English hospital known to history (not necessarily the first) was established at Canterbury in 1084. Usually the service in these hospitals was provided free for those who could not pay, and (except in monastic hospitals) the attendants were nuns. The apparently cumbersome costume of these "angels and ministers of grace" took form in the thirteenth century, probably to protect them from communicable disease; hence, perhaps, the shearing of the hair and the covering of the head.[80]

Two special diseases evoked special defenses. "St. Anthony's fire" was a skin ailment—perhaps erysipelas—so severe that an order of monks, the Congregation of the Antonines, was founded about 1095 to treat its victims. Leper hospitals are mentioned by Gregory of Tours (*c.* 560); the Order of St. Lazarus was organized to serve in these *leprosaria*. Eight diseases were regarded as contagious: bubonic plague, tuberculosis, epilepsy, scabies, erysipelas, anthrax, trachoma, and leprosy. A victim of any of these was forbidden to enter a city except under segregation; or to engage in selling food or drink. The leper was required to give warning of his approach by horn or bell. Usually his disease expressed itself in purulent eruptions on face and body. It was only mildly contagious, but probably medieval authorities feared that it could be spread by coitus. Possibly the term was used to include what would now be diagnosed as syphilis; but there is no certain reference to syphilis before the fifteenth century.[81] No special provision seems to have been made for the care of the insane before the fifteenth century.

The Middle Ages, too poor to be clean or properly fed, suffered more than any other known period from epidemics. The "Yellow Plague" devastated Ireland in 550 and 664, killing, we are unreliably informed, two thirds of the population.[82] Similar pestilences struck Wales in the sixth century, England in the seventh. A malady known to the French as *mal des ardents*—which was described as burning out the intestines—swept through France and Germany in 994, 1043, 1089, and 1130. Plagues of "leprosy" and scurvy may have come from returning Crusaders. The *plica polonica*, a disease of the hair, was apparently brought to Poland by the Mongol invasion of 1287. The harassed population ascribed these epidemics to famines, droughts, swarms of insects, astral influences, poisoning of wells by Jews, or the wrath of God; the likelier causes were the crowded condition of the small walled towns, poor sanitation and hygiene, and a consequent lack of defense against infections carried by returning soldiers, pilgrims, or students.[83] We have no mortality statistics for the Middle Ages, but it is probable that not more than half of those born reached maturity. The fertility of women labors to atone for the stupidity of men and the bravery of generals.

Public sanitation improved in the thirteenth century, but never in the Middle Ages did it regain its excellence under Imperial Rome. Most cities and wards appointed officials to care for the streets,[84] but their work was primitive. Moslem visitors to Christian towns complained—as Christian visitors now to Moslem towns—of the filth and smell of the "infidel cities."[85] At Cambridge, now so beautiful and clean, sewage and offal ran along open gutters in the streets, and "gave out an abominable stench, so ... that many masters and scholars fell sick thereof."[86] In the thirteenth century some cities had aqueducts, sewers, and public latrines; in most cities rain was relied upon to carry away refuse; the pollution of wells made typhoid cases numerous; and the water used for baking and brewing was usually—north of the Alps—drawn from the same streams that received the sewage of the towns.[87] Italy was more advanced, largely through its Roman legacy, and through the enlightened legislation of Frederick II for refuse disposal; but malarial infection from surrounding swamps made Rome unhealthy, killed many dignitaries and visitors, and occasionally saved the city from hostile armies that succumbed to fever amid their victories.

VI. ALBERTUS MAGNUS: 1193–1280

Three men stand out in this period as devotees of science: Adelard of Bath, Albert the Great, and Roger Bacon.

Adelard, after studying in many Moslem countries, returned to England and wrote (*c.* 1130) a long dialogue, *Quaestiones naturales*, covering many sciences. It begins Platonically by describing Adelard's reunion with his friends. He asks about the state of affairs in England; he is told that the kings make war, judges take bribes, prelates drink too much, all promises are broken, all friends are envious. He accepts this as a genial summary of the natural and unchangeable condition of things, and proposes to forget it. His nephew inquires what has Adelard learned among the Moslems? He expresses a general preference for Arabic as against Christian science; they challenge him; and his replies constitute an interesting selection from all the sciences of the age. He inveighs against the bondage of tradition and authority. "I learned from my Arabian masters under the leading of reason; you, however, captivated by . . . authority, follow your halter. For what else should authority be called than a halter?" Those who are now counted as authorities gained their reputation by following reason, not authority. "Therefore," he tells his nephew, "if you want to hear anything more from me, give and take reason. . . . Nothing is surer than reason . . . nothing is falser than the senses."[88] Though Adelard relies too confidently on deductive reasoning, he gives some interesting replies. Asked how the earth is upheld in space, he answers that the center and the bottom are the same. How far would a stone fall if dropped into a hole bored through the center of the earth to the other side?—he answers, Only to the center of the earth. He states clearly the indestructibility of matter, and argues that universal continuity makes a vacuum impossible. All in all, Adelard is a brilliant proof of the awakening intellect in Christian Europe in the twelfth century. He was enthusiastic about the possibilities of science, and proudly calls his age—the age of Abélard—*modernus*,[89] the climax of all history.

Albertus Magnus had a little less of the scientific spirit than Adelard, but so cosmic a curiosity that the very immensity of his product won him the name Great. His scientific, like his philosophical, works took mostly the form of commentaries on the corresponding treatises of Aristotle, but they contain now and then fresh breaths of original observation; amid a cloud of quotations from Greek, Arabic, and Jewish authors he finds some opportunities to look at nature in the first person. He visited laboratories and mines, studied diverse metals, examined the fauna and flora of his native Germany, noted displacements of land by sea, sea by land, and explained thereby the fossil shells in rocks. Too much of a philosopher to be a thorough scientist, he allowed a priori theories to color his vision, as when he claimed to have seen horsehairs in water change into worms. But, like Adelard, he rejected the explanation of natural phenomena in terms of the will of God; God acts through natural causes, and man must seek Him there.

His notion of experiment was obscured by his confidence in Aristotle. A famous passage in Book X of his *De vegetabilibus* stirs us with the words *Experimentum solum certificat*, which seems to say that "only experiment gives certainty." But the word *experimentum* had then a broader meaning than now; it meant *experience* rather than *experiment*, as appears from the context of the passage: "All that is here set down is the result of our own experience, or has been borrowed from authors whom we know to have written what their personal experience has confirmed; for in these matters *experimentum solum certificat*." Even so, it was a wholesome advance. Albert laughs at such mythical creatures as the harpies or the griffin, and the animal legends of a then popular book, the *Physiologus*, and he notes that "philosophers tell many lies."[90] Sometimes, not often, he performed experiments, as when he and his associates proved that a beheaded cicada continued for a while to sing. But he trusted Pliny's authority with saintly innocence, and believed too simply the tales told him by such notorious liars as hunters and fishermen.[91]

He yielded to his times in accepting astrology and divination. He attributes marvelous powers to gems and stones, and claims to have seen with his own eyes a sapphire that cured ulcers. He thinks, like undoubting Thomas, that magic is real, and is due to demons. Dreams sometimes foretell events. In corporeal matters "the stars are in truth rulers of the world"; the conjunctions of the planets probably explain "great accidents and great prodigies"; and comets may signify wars and the death of kings. "There is in man a double spring of action—nature, and the will; the nature is ruled by the stars, the will is free; but unless the will resists it is swept along by nature." He believes that competent astrologers may in considerable measure prophesy the events of a man's life, or the issue of an enterprise, from the position of the stars. He accepts, with certain reserves, the alchemic (today the nuclear physicist) theory of the transmutation of elements.[92]

His best scientific work was in botany. He was the first botanist since Theophrastus (so far as we know) to consider plants for their own sake instead of for their use in agriculture or medicine. He classified plants, described their color, odor, parts, and fruit, studied their feeling, sleep, sex, and germination, and ventured an essay on husbandry. Humboldt was surprised to find in Albert's *De vegetabilibus* "exceedingly acute remarks on the organic structure and physiology of plants."[93] His enormous work *De animalibus* is largely a paraphrase of Aristotle, but here, too, we find original observation. Albert tells of "sailing the North Sea for the sake of research [*experimenti causa*], and landing on islands and sandy shores to collect" objects for study.[94] He compared similar organs in animals and man.[95]

From the vantage point of our hindsight these works contain many mistakes; viewed against the intellectual background of their time they are among the major achievements of the medieval mind. Albert was recognized in his own lifetime as the greatest teacher of his age, and he lived long enough to be quoted as an authority by men like Peter of Spain and Vincent of Beauvais, who both died before him. He could not rival Averroës or Maimonides or Thomas in keenness of judgment or philosophic grasp; but he was the greatest naturalist of his time.

VII. ROGER BACON: c. 1214-92

The most famous of medieval scientists was born in Somerset about 1214. We know that he lived till 1292, and that in 1267 he called himself an old man.[96] He studied at Oxford under Grosseteste, and caught from the great polymath a fascination for science; already in that circle of Oxford Franciscans the English spirit of empiricism and utilitarianism was taking form. He went to Paris about 1240, but did not find there the stimulation that Oxford had given him; he marveled that so few Parisian professors knew any learned language besides Latin, that they gave so little time to science, and so much to logical and metaphysical disputes that seemed to Bacon criminally useless for life. He "majored" in medicine, and began to write a treatise on the relief of old age. To get data he visited Italy, studied Greek in Magna Graecia, and there became acquainted with some works of Moslem medicine. In 1251 he returned to Oxford, and joined the teaching staff. He wrote in 1267 that in the preceding twenty years he had spent "more than £2000 in the purchase of secret books and instruments," and in training young men in languages and mathematics.[97] He engaged Jews to teach him and his students Hebrew, and to help him read the Old Testament in the original. About 1253 he entered the Franciscan Order, but he seems never to have become a priest.

Sick of the metaphysics of the schools, Bacon gave himself with passion to mathematics, natural science, and philology. We must not think of him as a lone originator, a scientific voice crying out in the scholastic wilderness. In every field he was indebted to his predecessors, and his originality was the forceful summation of a long development. Alexander Neckham, Bartholomew the Englishman, Robert Grosseteste, and Adam Marsh had established a scientific tradition at Oxford; Bacon inherited it, and proclaimed it to the world. He acknowledged his indebtedness, and gave his predecessors unmeasured praise. He recognized also his debt—and the debt of Christendom—to Islamic science and philosophy, and through these to the Greeks, and suggested that the "heathen" savants of Greece and Islam had also, in their own fashion, been inspired and guided by God.[98] He had a high regard for Isaac Israeli, Ibn Gabirol, and other Hebrew thinkers, and had the courage to say a good word for the Jews who lived in Palestine at the time of the crucifixion of Christ.[99] He learned avidly not only from learned men, but from any man whose practical knowledge in handicraft or husbandry could augment his store. He writes with unwonted humility:

> It is certain that never, before God is seen face to face, shall a man know anything with final certainty. . . . For no one is so learned in nature that he knows all . . . the nature and properties of a single fly. . . . And since, in comparison with what a man knows, those things of

which he is ignorant are infinite, and beyond comparison greater and more beautiful, he is out of his mind who extols himself in regard to his own knowledge. . . . The wiser men are, the more humbly they are disposed to receive the instruction of another, nor do they disdain the simplicity of the teacher, but behave humbly toward peasants, old women, and children, since many things are known to the simple and unlearned which escape the notice of the wise. . . . I have learned more important truths from men of humble station than from all the famous doctors. Let no man, therefore, boast of his wisdom.[100]

He labored with such fervor and haste that in 1256 his health broke down; he retired from university life, and for ten years we lose track of him. Probably in this period he composed some of his minor works—*De speculis comburentibus* (*On Burning Glasses*), *De mirabili potestate artis et naturae* (*On the Marvelous Power of Invention and Nature*), and *Computus naturalium* (*Computation of Natural Events*). Now also he planned his "Principal Work"—*Scriptum principale*, a one-man encyclopedia to be in four volumes: (1) grammar and logic; (2) mathematics, astronomy, and music; (3) natural science—optics, geography, astrology, alchemy, agriculture, medicine, and experimental science; and (4) metaphysics and morals.

He had written some scattered portions when what seemed a stroke of good fortune interrupted his program. In February, 1265, Guy Foulques, Archbishop of Narbonne, became Pope Clement IV, and carried into the papacy something of the liberal spirit that had developed in southern France from the mingling of peoples and creeds. In June he wrote to Bacon bidding him send a "fair copy" of his works, "secretly and without delay," and "notwithstanding the prohibition of any prelate, or any constitution of thy Order." [101] Bacon set himself feverishly (as may be seen from the passion of his style) to finish his encyclopedia; then, in 1267, fearing that Clement might die or lose interest before its completion, he put it aside, and composed in twelve months—or put together from his manuscripts—the preliminary treatise which we known as the *Opus maius*, or *Larger Work*. Suspecting that even this would prove too long for a busy Pope, he wrote a synopsis of it, an *Opus minus*, or *Smaller Work*. Early in 1268 he sent these two manuscripts to Clement, with an essay *De multiplicatione specierum* (*On the Multiplication of Vision*). Worried lest these be lost in transit, he composed still another summary of his ideas, an *Opus tertium*, and sent it to Clement by special messenger, together with a lens with which, he suggested, the Pope might himself make experiments. Clement died in November, 1268. So far as we know, no word of acknowledgment from him or his successors ever reached the eager philosopher.

The *Opus maius*, therefore, is now for us literally his "major work," though in his intention it was but a prelude. It is substantial enough. Its 800 pages are divided into seven treatises: (1) on ignorance and error; (2) the relations between philosophy and theology; (3) the study of foreign languages; (4) the usefulness of mathematics; (5) perspective and optics; (6) experimental science; (7) moral philosophy. The book contains its due quota of nonsense, and many digressions, and too many extensive quotations from other authors; but it is written with vigor, directness, and sincerity, and is more readable today than any other work of medieval science or philosophy. Its excited disorder, its adulation of the papacy, its anxious professions of orthodoxy, its reduction of science and philosophy to the role of servants to theology, are understandable in a book of such scope and subject, written in hasty summary, and designed to win papal support for scientific education and research. For Roger, like Francis, Bacon felt that the advancement of learning would need the aid and money of prelates and magnates for books, instruments, records, laboratories, experiments, and personnel.

As if anticipating the "idols" denounced by his namesake three centuries later, Roger begins by listing four causes of human error: the "example of frail and unworthy authority, long-established custom, the sense of the ignorant crowd, and the hiding of one's ignorance under the show of wisdom."[102] He takes care to add that he is "in no way speaking of that solid and sure authority which ... has been bestowed upon the Church." He regrets the readiness of his time to consider a proposition proved if it can be found in Aristotle, and declares that if he had the power he would burn all the books of the Philosopher as a fountain of error and a stream of ignorance;[103] after which he quotes Aristotle on every second page.

"After the four causes of error have been banished to the lower regions," he writes at the outset of Part II, "I wish to show that there is one wisdom which is perfect, and that this is contained in the Scriptures." If the Greek philosophers enjoyed a sort of secondary inspiration, it was because they read the books of the prophets and patriarchs.[104] Bacon apparently accepts the Biblical story with simple faith, and wonders why God no longer allows men to live 600 years.[105] He believes in the approaching advent of Christ and end of the world. He pleads for science as revealing the Creator in the creation, and as enabling Christians to convert heathens immune to Scripture. So "the human mind can be influenced to accept the truth of the Virgin Birth, because certain animals in a state of virginity conceive and bear young, as for example vultures and apes, as Ambrose states in the *Hexaemeron*. Moreover, mares in many regions conceive by virtue of the winds alone, when they desire the male, as Pliny states"[106]—unlucky instances of trust in authority.

In Part III Bacon labors to teach the Pope Hebrew. The study of languages is necessary to theology, philosophy, and science, for no translation conveys the precise sense of the Scriptures or the heathen philosophers. In the *Opus minus* Bacon gives a remarkably learned account of the various translations of the Bible, and shows an intimate acquaintance with the Hebrew and Greek texts. He proposes that the Pope appoint a committee of scholars learned in Hebrew, Greek, and Latin to revise the Vulgate, and that this revised version—and no longer the *Sentences* of Peter Lombard—be made the main study in theology. He urges the establishment of university professorships in Hebrew, Greek, Arabic, and Chaldean. He denounces the use of force in converting non-Christians, and asks how the Church can deal with Greek, Armenian, Syrian, Chaldean Christians except through their own languages. In this field Bacon labored as well as preached; he was the first scholar in Western Christendom to complete a Greek grammar for Latin use, and the first Christian to compose a Hebrew grammar. He claimed ability to write Greek and Hebrew, and seems also to have studied Arabic.[107]

When Bacon reaches the subject of mathematics his pages become eloquent with enthusiasm, then recondite with theorems. "Next to languages I hold mathematics necessary." He makes his usual obeisance to theology: mathematics "should aid us in ascertaining the position of paradise and hell," promote our knowledge of Biblical geography and sacred chronology, and enable the Church to correct the calendar;[108] and observe, he says, how "the first proposition of Euclid"—constructing an equilateral triangle on a given line—helps us to "perceive that if the person of God the Father be granted, a Trinity of equal persons presents itself."[109] From this sublimity he proceeds to a remarkable anticipation of modern mathematical physics, by insisting that though science must use experiment as its method, it does not become fully scientific until it can reduce its conclusions to mathematical form. All nonspiritual phenomena are the product of matter and force; all forces act uniformly and regularly, and may consequently be expressed by lines and figures; "it is necessary to verify the matter by demonstrations set forth in geometrical lines"; ultimately all natural science is mathematics.[110]

But though mathematics is the result, experiment must be the means and test of science. Whereas the Scholastic philosophers from Abélard to Thomas had put their trust in logic, and had made Aristotle almost a member of the Trinity, veritably a holy ghost, Bacon formulates a scientific revolution in terms of mathematics and experiment. The most rigorous conclusions of logic leave us uncertain until they are confirmed by experience; only a burn really convinces us that fire burns. "He who wishes to rejoice without doubt with regard to the truths underlying phenomena must know how to devote himself to experiment."[111] At times he seems to think of *experimentum* not as a method of research but as a final mode of proof through putting ideas—reached by experience or reasoning—to test by constructing on their basis things of practical utility.[112] More clearly than Francis Bacon, he perceives and declares that in natural science experiment is the only proof. He did not pretend that this idea was new; Aristotle, Hero, Galen, Ptolemy, the Moslems, Adelard, Petrus Hispanus, Robert Grosseteste, Albertus Magnus, and others had made or lauded experiments. Roger Bacon made the implicit explicit, and planted the flag of science firmly on the conquered ground.

Except in optics and calendar reform, Roger, like Francis, Bacon made only negligible contributions to science itself; they were philosophers of science rather than scientists. Continuing the work of Grosseteste and others, Roger concluded that the Julian calendar exaggerated the length of the solar year by one day every 125 years—the most accurate computation theretofore made—and that the calendar, in 1267, was ten days ahead of the sun. He proposed that a day be dropped from the Julian calendar every 125 years. Almost as brilliant were the hundred pages on geography in Part IV of the *Opus maius*. Bacon talked eagerly with William of Rubruquis on the return of his fellow Franciscan from the Orient, learned much from him about the Orient, and was impressed by William's account of the unnumbered millions who had never heard of Christianity. Starting from statements in Aristotle and Seneca, he remarked that "the sea between the end of Spain on the west and the beginning of India on the east is navigable in a very few days if the wind is favorable."[113] This passage, copied in the *Imago mundi* (1480) of Cardinal Pierre d'Ailly, was cited by Columbus in a letter to Ferdinand and Isabella in 1498 as one of the suggestions that had inspired his voyage of 1492.[114]

Bacon's work in physics is a vision of modern inventions, colored now and then with the popular ideas of his time. Here, in literal translation, are the famous passages in which he leaps from the thirteenth to the twentieth century:

> A fifth part of experimental science concerns the fabrication of instruments of wonderfully excellent usefulness, such as machines for flying, or for moving in vehicles without animals and yet with incomparable speed, or of navigating without oarsmen more swiftly than would be thought possible through the hands of men. For these things have been done in our day, lest anyone should ridicule them or be astonished. And this part teaches how to make instruments by which incredible weights can be raised or lowered without difficulty or labor. . . .[115] Flying machines can be made, and a man sitting in the middle of the machine may revolve some ingenious device by which artificial wings may beat the air in the manner of a flying bird. . . . Also machines can be made for walking in the sea and the rivers, even to the bottom, without danger.[116]

A passage in the *Opus maius* (vi, 12) has been interpreted as referring to gunpowder:

> Important arts have been discovered against foes of the state, so that without a sword or any weapon requiring physical contact they could destroy all who offer resistance. . . . From the force of the salt called

saltpeter so horrible a sound is produced at the bursting of so small a
thing, namely, a small piece of parchment, that . . . it exceeds the roar
of sharp thunder, and the flash exceeds the greatest brilliancy of the
lightning accompanying the thunder.

In a possibly interpolated passage of the *Opus tertium* Bacon adds that certain toys, "crackers," are already in use, containing a mixture of saltpeter
(41.2%), charcoal (29.4%), and sulphur (29.4%);[117] and he suggests that
the explosive power of the powder can be increased by enclosing it in solid
material. He does not claim to have invented gunpowder; he was merely one
of the first to study its chemistry and foresee its possibilities.

The best work of Bacon is Part V of the *Opus maius*, "On Perspectival
Science," and in the supplementary treatise *On the Multiplication of Vision*.
This brilliant essay on optics stemmed from Grosseteste's work on the rainbow, from Witelo's adaptation of al-Haitham, and from the tradition of
optical studies mounting through Avicenna, al-Kindi, and Ptolemy to Euclid (300 B.C.), who had ingeniously applied geometry to the movements
of light. Is light an emanation of particles from the object seen, or is it a
movement of some medium between the object and the eye? Bacon believed
that every physical thing radiates force in all directions, and that these rays
may penetrate solid objects:

> No substance is so dense as altogether to prevent rays from pass-
> ing. Matter is common to all things, and thus there is no substance on
> which the actions involved in the passage of a ray may not produce
> a change. . . . Rays of heat and sound penetrate through the walls of
> a vessel of gold or brass. It is said by Boethius that a lynx's eye will
> pierce thick walls.[118]

We are not so sure of the lynx, but otherwise we must applaud the bold
fancy of the philosopher, "of imagination all compact." Experimenting with
lenses and mirrors, Bacon sought to formulate the laws of refraction, reflection, magnification, and microscopy. Recalling the power of a convex lens
to concentrate many rays of the sun at one burning point, and to spread the
rays beyond that point to form a magnified image, he wrote:

> We can so shape transparent bodies [lenses], and arrange them in
> such a way with respect to our sight and the objects of vision, that the
> rays will be refracted and bent in any direction we desire; and under
> any angle we wish we shall see the object near or at a distance. Thus
> from an incredible distance we might read the smallest letters, and
> number grains of dust or sand. . . . Thus a small army might appear
> very large and . . . close at hand. . . . So also we might cause the sun,
> moon, and stars in appearance to descend here below, . . . and many
> similar phenomena, so that the mind of a man ignorant of the truth
> could not endure them. . . .[119] The heavens might be portrayed in all

their length and breadth on a corporeal figure moving with their diurnal motion; *and this would be worth a whole kingdom to a wise man.* . . . An infinite number of other marvels could be set forth.[120]

These are brilliant passages. Almost every element in their theory can be found before Bacon, and above all in al-Haitham; but here the material was brought together in a practical and revolutionary vision that in time transformed the world. It was these passages that led Leonard Digges (d. *c.* 1571) to formulate the theory on which the telescope was invented.[121]

But what if the progress of physical science gives man more power without improving his purposes? Perhaps the profoundest of Bacon's insights is his anticipation of a problem that has become clear only in our time. In the concluding treatise of the *Opus maius* he expresses the conviction that man cannot be saved by science alone.

> All these foregoing sciences are speculative. There is, indeed, in every science a practical side. . . . But only of moral philosophy can it be said that it is . . . essentially practical, for it deals with human conduct, with virtue and vice, with happiness and misery. . . . All other sciences are of no account except as they help forward right action. In this sense "practical" sciences, such as experiment, chemistry (*alkimia*), and the rest, are seen to be speculative in reference to the operations with which moral or political science is concerned. This science of morality is the mistress of every department of philosophy.[122]

Bacon's final word is not for science but for religion; only by a morality supported by religion can man save himself. But which religion should it be? He tells of the parliament of religions—Buddhist, Mohammedan, Christian—which William of Rubruquis reported to have been held at Karakorum at the suggestion and under the presidency of Mangu Khan.[123] He compares the three religions, and concludes in favor of Christianity, but with no merely theological conception of its function in the world. He felt that the papacy, despite Grosseteste's criticisms, was the moral bond of a Europe that without it would be a chaos of clashing faiths and arms; and he aspired to strengthen the Church with science, languages, and philosophy for her better spiritual government of the world.[124] He ended his book as he had begun it, with a warm profession of fidelity to the Church, and concluded with a glorification of the Eucharist—as if to say that unless man seeks periodical communion with his highest ideal he will be lost in the conflagration of the world.

Perhaps the failure of the popes to respond in any way to Bacon's program and appeals darkened his spirit and embittered his pen. In 1271 he published an unfinished *Compendium studii philosophiae*, which contributed little to philosophy, but much to the *odium theologicum* that was disordering the schools. He settled summarily the subsiding debate between realism and nominalism: "a universal is nothing but the similarity of several individuals," and "one individual has more reality than all universals put together."[125] He adopted Augustine's doctrine of *rationes seminales*, and arrived at a view in which the efforts of all things to better themselves engendered a long series of developments.[126] He accepted the Aristotelian notion of an Active Intellect or Cosmic Intelligence "flowing into our minds and illuminating them," and came dangerously near to Averroistic pantheism.[127]

But what shocked his time was not his philosophical ideas so much as his attacks upon his rivals and the morals of the age. In the *Compendium philosophiae* almost every phase of thirteenth-century life felt his lash: the disorder of the papal court, the degeneration of the monastic orders, the ignorance of the clergy, the dullness of sermons, the misconduct of students, the sins of the universities, the windy verbiage of the philosophers. In a *Tractatus de erroribus medicorum* he listed "thirty-six great and radical defects" in the medical theory and practice of his time. In 1271 he wrote a passage that may incline us to take with better grace the shortcomings of our age:

> More sins reign in these days than in any past age . . . the Holy See is torn by the deceit and fraud of unjust men. . . . Pride reigns, covetousness burns, envy gnaws upon all; the whole Curia is disgraced with lechery, and gluttony is lord of all. . . . If this be so in the Head, what then is done among the members? Let us see the prelates, how they run after money, neglect the care of souls, promote their nephews and other carnal friends, and crafty lawyers who ruin all by their counsel. . . . Let us consider the Religious Orders; I exclude none from what I say; see how far they are fallen, one and all, from their right state; and the new Orders [the Friars] are already horribly decayed from their original dignity. The whole clergy is intent upon pride, lechery, and avarice; and wheresoever clerks [students] are gathered together . . . they scandalize the laity with their wars and quarrels and other vices. Princes and barons and knights oppress one another, and trouble their subjects with infinite wars and exactions. . . . The people, harassed by their princes, hate them, and keep no fealty save under compulsion; corrupted by the evil example of their betters, they oppress and circumvent and defraud one another, as we see everywhere with our eyes; and they are utterly given over to lechery and gluttony, and are more debased than tongue can tell. Of merchants and craftsmen there is no question, since fraud and deceit and guile reign beyond all measure in their words and deeds. . . . The ancient philosophers, though without that quickening grace which makes men worthy of eternal life, lived beyond all comparison better than we, both in decency and in contempt of the world with all its delights and riches and

honors, as all men may read in the works of Aristotle, Seneca, Tully,
Avicenna, al-Farabi, Plato, Socrates, and others; and so it was that they
attained to the secrets of wisdom and found out all knowledge. But we
Christians have discovered nothing worthy of those philosophers, nor
can we even understand their wisdom; which ignorance of ours
springs from this cause, that our morals are worse than theirs. . . .
There is no doubt whatever among wise men but that the Church
must be purged.[128]

He was not impressed by his contemporaries in philosophy; not one of them,
he wrote to Clement IV, could in ten years write such a book as the *Opus
maius*; their tomes seemed to Bacon a mass of voluminous superfluity and
"ineffable falsity";[129] and the whole structure of their thought rested upon
a Bible and an Aristotle mistranslated and misunderstood.[130] He ridiculed
Thomas' long discussion of the habits, powers, intelligence, and movements
of the angels.[131]

Such an exaggerated indictment of European life, morals, and thought in
a brilliant century must have left Bacon alone against the world. Nevertheless there is no evidence that his Order or the Church persecuted him, or
interfered with his freedom of thought or utterance, before 1277—i.e., six
years after the issuance of the above Jeremiad. But in that year John of Vercelli, head of the Dominicans, and Jerome of Ascoli, head of the Franciscans,
conferred to allay certain quarrels that had arisen between the two orders.
They agreed that the friars of each order should abstain from criticizing the
other, and that "any friar who was found by word or deed to have offended
a friar of the other order should receive from his provincial such punishment as ought to satisfy the offended brother."[132] Shortly thereafter Jerome,
according to the fourteenth-century Franciscan *Chronicle of the XXIV
Generals of the Order*, "acting on the advice of many friars, condemned
and reprobated the teaching of Friar Roger Bacon, master of sacred theology, as containing some suspected novelties, on account of which the same
Roger was condemned to prison."[133] We have no further knowledge of the
matter. Whether the "novelties" were heresies, or reflected a suspicion that
he dabbled in magic, or covered up a decision to silence a critic offensive to
Dominicans and Franciscans alike, we cannot say. Nor do we know how
severe were the conditions of Bacon's imprisonment, nor how long it lasted.
We are told that in 1292 certain prisoners condemned in 1277 were freed.
Presumably Bacon was released then or before, for in 1292 he published a
Compendium studii theologiae. Thereafter we have only an entry in an old
chronicle: "The noble doctor Roger Bacon was buried at the Grey Friars"
(the Franciscan church) "in Oxford in the year 1292."[134]

He had little influence on his time. He was remembered chiefly as a man
of many marvels, a magician and conjurer; it was as such that he was presented in a play by Robert Greene 300 years after his death. It is hard to

say how much Francis Bacon (1561–1626) owed to him; we can only note that the second Bacon, like the first, rejected Aristotelian logic and Scholastic method, questioned authority, custom, and other "idols" of traditional thought, praised science, listed its expected inventions, charted its program, stressed its practical utility, and sought financial aid for scientific research. Slowly, from that sixteenth century, Roger Bacon's fame grew, until he became a legend—the supposed inventor of gunpowder, the heroic freethinker, the lifelong victim of religious persecution, the great initiator of modern thought. Today the pendulum returns. Historians point out that he had only a confused idea of experiment; that he did little experimenting himself; that in theology he was more orthodox than the pope; that his pages were peppered with superstitions, magic, misquotations, false charges, and legends taken for history.

It is true. It is also true that though he made few experiments he helped to state their principle and to prepare their coming; and that his protestations of orthodoxy may have been the diplomacy of a man seeking papal support for suspected sciences. His errors were the infection of his time or the haste of a spirit too eager to take all knowledge for its province; his self-praise was the balm of genius ignored; his denunciations the wrath of a frustrated Titan helplessly witnessing the submergence of his noblest dreams in an ocean of ignorance. His attack on authority in philosophy and science opened the way to wider and freer thought; his emphasis on the mathematical basis and goal of science was half a millennium ahead of his age; his warning against subordinating morality to science is a lesson for tomorrow. With all its faults and sins, his *Opus maius* deserves its name as a work greater than any other in all the literature of its amazing century.

VIII. THE ENCYCLOPEDISTS

Intermediate between science and philosophy were the reckless polymaths who sought to give order and unity to the expanding knowledge of their period, to bring science and art, industry and government, philosophy and religion, literature and history into an orderly whole that might provide a base for wisdom. The thirteenth century excelled in encyclopedias, and in *summae* that were all-encompassing syntheses. The more modest encyclopedists limited themselves to summarizing natural science. Alexander Neckam, Abbot of Cirencester (*c.* 1200), and Thomas of Cantimpré, a French Dominican (*c.* 1244), wrote popular surveys of science under the title of *The Nature of Things*; and Bartholomew of England, a Franciscan, sent forth a chatty volume *On the Properties of Things* (*c.* 1240). About 1266 Brunetto Latini, a Florentine notary exiled for his Guelf politics, and living for some years in France, wrote in the *langue d'oïl Li livres dou tresor* (*The Treasure*

Books), a brief encyclopedia of science, morals, history, and government. It proved so permanently popular that Napoleon thought of having a revised edition published by the state, half a century after the world-shaking *Grande Encyclopédie* of Diderot. All these works of the thirteenth century mingled theology with science, and superstition with observation; they breathed the air of their time; and we should be chagrined if we could foresee how our own omniscience will be viewed seven centuries hence.

The most famous encyclopedia of the Christian Middle Ages was the *Speculum maius* of Vincent of Beauvais (*c*. 1200–*c*. 1264). He joined the Dominican Order, became tutor to Louis IX and his sons, was given charge of the King's library, and undertook, with several aides, the task of reducing to digestible form the knowledge that encompassed him. He called his encyclopedia *Imago mundi, Image of the World*, presenting the universe as a mirror that reflected the divine intelligence and plan. It was a gigantic compilation, equal to forty sizable modern tomes. Vincent, with copyists and shears, completed three parts—*Speculum naturale, Speculum doctrinale, Speculum historiale*; the heirs of the task added, about 1310, a *Speculum morale*, largely "cribbed" from Thomas' *Summa*. Vincent himself was a modest and gentle soul. "I do not know even a single science," he said; he disclaimed all originality, and merely proposed to gather excerpts from 450 authors, Greek, Latin, or Arabic. He transmitted Pliny's errors faithfully, accepted all the marvels of astrology, and filled his pages with the occult qualities of plants and stones. Nevertheless the wonder and beauty of nature shine out now and then through his paste, and he himself feels them as no mere bookworm could:

> I confess, sinner as I am, with mind befouled in flesh, that I am moved with spiritual sweetness toward the Creator and Ruler of this world, and honor Him with greater veneration, when I behold the magnitude and beauty ... of His creation. For the mind, lifting itself from the dunghill of its affections, and rising, as it is able, into the light of speculation, sees as from a height the greatness of the universe containing in itself infinite places filled with the diverse orders of creatures.[135]

The outburst of scientific activity in the thirteenth century rivals the magnitude of its philosophies, and the variety and splendor of a literature ranging from the troubadours to Dante. Like the great *summae* and *The Divine Comedy*, the science of this age suffered from too great certainty, from a failure to examine its assumptions, and from an indiscriminate mingling of knowledge with faith. But the little bark of science, riding an occult sea, made substantial progress even in an age of faith. In Adelard, Grosseteste, Albert, Arnold of Villanova, William of Saliceto, Henri de Mondeville, Lanfranchi, Bacon, Peter the Pilgrim, and Peter of Spain, fresh observation and timid experiment began to break down the authority of Aristotle, Pliny, and Galen; a zest for exploration and enterprise filled the sails of the adventurers; and already at the beginning of the wonderful century Alexander Neckam expressed the new devotion well: "Science is acquired," he wrote, "at great expense, by frequent vigils, by great expenditure of time, by sedulous diligence of labor, by vehement application of mind." [136]

But at the end of Alexander's book the medieval mood spoke again, at its best, with timeless tenderness:

> Perchance, O book, you will survive this Alexander, and worms will eat me before the bookworm gnaws you. . . . You are the mirror of my soul, the interpreter of my meditations . . . the true witness of my conscience, the sweet comforter of my grief. . . . To you as faithful depositary I have confided my heart's secrets; . . . in you I read myself. You will come into the hands of some pious reader who will deign to pray for me. Then indeed, little book, you will profit your master; then you will recompense your Alexander by a most grateful interchange. I do not begrudge my labor. There will come the devotion of a pious reader who will now let you repose in his lap, now move you to his breast, sometimes place you as a sweet pillow beneath his head; sometimes, gently closing you, he will fervently pray for me to Lord Jesus Christ, Who with Father and Holy Spirit lives and reigns God through infinite cycles of ages. Amen.[137]

CHAPTER XXXVIII

The Age of Romance

1100-1300

I. THE LATIN REVIVAL

EVERY age is an age of romance, for men cannot live by bread alone, and imagination is the staff of life. Perhaps the twelfth and thirteenth centuries in Europe were slightly more romantic than most periods. Besides inheriting all the mystic creatures of Europe's faery lore, they accepted the Christian epic in all the beauty and terror of its vision, they made an art and religion of love and war, they saw the Crusades, they imported a thousand tales and wonders from the East. In any case they wrote the longest romances known to history.

The growth of wealth and leisure and laic literacy, the rise of towns and the middle class, the development of universities, the exaltation of woman in religion and chivalry—all furthered the literary flowering. As schools multiplied, Cicero, Virgil, Horace, Ovid, Livy, Sallust, Lucan, Seneca, Statius, Juvenal, Quintilian, Suetonius, Apuleius, Sidonius, even the ribald Martial and Petronius, brightened with their art and exotic world many a pedagogic or monastic retreat, perhaps, here and there, some palace bower. From Jerome to Alcuin to Héloïse and Hildebert Christian souls stole minutes from their Hours to chant the *Aeneid*'s music silently. The University of Orléans particularly cherished the classics of pagan Rome, and a horrified puritan complained that it was the old gods, not Christ or Mary, that were worshiped there. The twelfth century was almost "the Age of Ovid"; he dethroned then the Virgil whom Alcuin had made the poet laureate of Charlemagne's court, and monks and ladies and "wandering scholars" alike read with delight the *Metamorphoses*, the *Heroides*, and the *Art of Love*. We can forgive many a benedictine carouse to the monks who preserved these damned souls so lovingly, and taught them so devotedly to the reluctant, then grateful, young.

From such classic studies a medieval Latin arose whose diversity and interest are among the most pleasant surprises of literary exploration. St. Bernard, who thought so poorly of intellectual accomplishments, wrote letters of loving tenderness, vituperative eloquence, and masterly Latin. The sermons of Peter Damian, Bernard, Abélard, and Berthold of Regensburg kept Latin a language of living power.

The monastic chroniclers wrote terrible Latin, but they made no claim to offer esthetic thrills. They recorded first of all the growth and history of their own abbeys—the elections, buildings, and deaths of abbots, the miracles and quarrels of the monks; they added notes on the eclipses, comets, droughts, floods, famines, plagues, and portents of their time; and some of them expanded to include national, even international, events. Few scrutinized their sources critically, or inquired into causes; most of them were carelessly inaccurate, and added a cipher or two to bring dead statistics to life; all dealt in miracles, and showed an amiable credulity. So the French chroniclers assumed that France had been settled by noble Trojans, and that Charlemagne had conquered Spain and captured Jerusalem. The *Gesta Francorum* (*c.* 1100) attempted a relatively honest account of the First Crusade, but the *Gesta Romanorum* (*c.* 1280) provided frankly fictional history for Chaucer, Shakespeare, and a thousand romancers. Geoffrey of Monmouth (*c.* 1100–54) made his *Historia Britonum* a kind of national mythology, in which poets found the legends of King Lear and Arthur, Merlin, Lancelot, Tristram, Perceval, and the Holy Grail. Still living literature, however, are the gossipy and guileless chronicles of Jocelyn of Bury St. Edmunds (*c.* 1200) and Fra Salimbene of Parma (*c.* 1280).

About 1208 Saxo Lange, posthumously named Saxo Grammaticus, dedicated to Archbishop Absalon of Lund his *Gesta Danorum* or *Deeds of the Danes*, a bit bombastic, incredibly credulous,[1] but a vivid narrative nevertheless, with more continuity than in most contemporary chronicles of the West. In Book III we learn of Amleth, Prince of Jutland, whose uncle killed the king and married the queen. Amleth, says Saxo, "chose to feign dullness and an utter lack of wits. This cunning course ensured his safety." The courtiers of the fratricide king tested Amleth by putting a pretty woman in his way; he accepted her embraces, but won her love and fidelity. They tried him with cunning questions, but "he mingled craft and candor in such wise that there was nothing to betoken the truth." From such bones Shakespeare made a man.

Five Latin historians in these centuries rose from chronicles to history, even when keeping the chronicle form. William of Malmesbury (*c.* 1090–1143) arranged the matter of his *Gesta pontificum* and *Gesta regum Anglorum* to give a connected and lively story, trustworthy and fair, of British prelates and kings. Ordericus Vitalis (*c.* 1075–1143), born in Shrewsbury, was sent as an oblate at the age of ten to the monastery of St. Evroul in Normandy; there he lived the remainder of his sixty-eight years, never seeing his parents again. Eighteen of these years he spent on the five volumes of his *Historia ecclesiastica*, only stopping, we are told, on the coldest winter days, when his fingers were too numb to write. It is remarkable that a mind so limited in space should have spoken so well of varied affairs, secular as well as ecclesiastical, with asides on the history of letters and manners and everyday life. Bishop Otto of Freising (*c.* 1114–58), in *De duabus civitatibus* (*On the Two Cities*), narrated the history of religion and the secular world from Adam to 1146, and began a proud biography of his nephew Frederick Barbarossa, but died while his hero was in mid-career. William of Tyre (*c.* 1130–90), a Frenchman born in Palestine, became chancellor to Baldwin IV of Jerusalem, and then Archbishop of Tyre; learned French, Latin, Greek, Arabic, and some Hebrew; and wrote in good Latin our most reliable source for the history of the earlier Crusades—*Historia rerum in partibus transmarinis gestarum* (*History of Events Overseas*). He sought natural explanations for all events; and his fairness in depicting the characters of Nur-ud-din and Saladin had much to do with the favorable opinion that Christian Europe formed of those infidel gentlemen. Matthew Paris (*c.* 1200–1259) was a monk of St. Albans. As historiographer to his abbey, and later to King Henry III, he composed his lively *Chronica maiora*, covering the major events of European history between 1235 and 1259. He wrote with clarity, accuracy, and unexpected partialities; he condemned the "avarice that has alienated the people from the pope," and favored Frederick II against the papacy. He crowded his pages with miracles, and told the story of the Wandering Jew (*anno* 1228), but he frankly recorded the skepticism with which Londoners viewed the transference of some drops of Christ's blood to Westminster Abbey (1247). He drew for his book several maps of England, the best of the period, and may himself have made the drawings that illustrate his work. We admire his industry and learning; but his sketch of Mohammed (*anno* 1236) is an astonishing revelation of how ignorant an educated Christian could be of Islamic history.

The greatest historians of this age were two Frenchmen writing in their own language, and sharing with the troubadours and trouvères the honor of making French a literary tongue. Geoffroy de Villehardouin (*c.* 1150–*c.* 1218) was a noble and a warrior, of little formal education; but precisely because he knew not the tricks of rhetoric taught in the schools, he dictated his *Conquête de Constantinople* (1207) in a French whose simple directness and matter-of-fact precision made his book a classic of historiography. Not that he was impartial; he played too intimate a role in the Fourth Crusade to see that picturesque treachery with an objective eye; but he was there, and saw and felt events with an immediacy that gave his book a living quality half immune to time. Almost a century later Jean Sire de Joinville, Seneschal of Champagne, after serving Louis IX on crusade and in France, wrote, when he was eighty-five, his *Histoire de St. Louis* (1309). We are grateful to him for describing, with artless sincerity, the human beings of history, and for lingering on illuminating customs and anecdotes; through him we feel the tang of the time as not even in Villehardouin. We are with him when he leaves his castle after pawning nearly all his possessions to go on crusade; he did not dare look back, he says, lest his heart should melt at sight of the wife and children whom he might never see again. He had not the subtle and crafty mind of Villehardouin, but he had common sense, and saw the clay in his saint. When Louis wished him to go a second time on crusade he refused, foreseeing the hopelessness of the enterprise. And when the pious King asked him, "Which would you choose—to be a leper or to have committed a mortal sin?"

> I, who never lied to him, answered that I would rather have committed thirty mortal sins than be a leper. When the monks had departed he called me to him alone, and made me sit at his feet, and said: "How came you to say that?" ... And I told him that I said it again. And he replied: "You spoke hastily and foolishly. For you should know that there is no leprosy so hideous as being in mortal sin." ... He asked me if I washed the feet of the poor on Holy Thursday. "Sire," said I, "it would make me sick! The feet of these *villeins* will I not wash." "In truth," said the King, "that was ill said, for you should never disdain what God did for our teaching. So I pray you, for the love of God first, and then for love of me, that you accustom yourself to wash the feet of the poor." [2]

Not all Lives of the Saints were as honest as this. The sense of history, and the intellectual conscience, were so poorly developed in medieval minds that the writers of these edifying narratives seem to have felt that much good and little harm could come if their readers accepted the accounts as true. Probably in most cases the authors received the spreading tales from others, and believed what they wrote. If we take the Lives of the Saints simply as stories we shall find them full of interest and charm. Consider how St. Christopher got his name. He was a giant of Canaan, eighteen feet tall. He entered the service of a king because he had heard that this was the most powerful man in the world. One day the king crossed himself at mention of the Devil; Christopher concluded that the Devil was more powerful than the king, and thereupon he entered the Devil's service. But at sight of a cross on the roadside the Devil took flight; and Christopher, reasoning that Jesus must be stronger than Satan, dedicated himself to Christ. He found it hard to observe the Christian fasts, there was so much of him to feed, and his great tongue tripped over the simplest prayers. A saintly hermit placed him on the bank of a ford whose swift waters annually drowned many who tried to cross it; Christopher took the wayfarers on his back and carried them dry and safe to the other shore. One day he bore a child across the stream; he asked why it was so heavy, and the child replied that it carried the weight of the world; safely across, the child thanked him, said, "I am Jesus Christ," and disappeared; and Christopher's staff, which he had stuck in the sand, suddenly blossomed with flowers.[3] And who was Britain's St. George? Near Silenum, in Libya, a dragon annually received as food a living youth or maiden, chosen by lot, as the price of not poisoning the village with his breath. Once the lot fell to the virgin daughter of the king. When the fated day arrived she walked to the pond where the dragon stayed. There St. George saw her, and asked why she wept. "Young man," she said, "I believe that you have a great and noble heart, but hasten to leave me." He refused, and induced her to answer his question. "Fear nothing," he told her, "for I will help you in the name of Jesus Christ." At that moment the monster emerged from the water. George made the sign of the cross, recommended himself to Christ, charged, and plunged his lance into the beast. Then he bade the maiden throw her girdle around the neck of the wounded dragon; she did, and the beast, yielding like any gallant to so potent a charm, followed her docilely forever afterward. These and other pretty tales were gathered, about 1290, into a famous book by Iacopo de Voragine, Archbishop of Genoa; for each day in the year he told the story of its appointed saint; and he called his book *Legenda sanctorum—Readings about the Saints*. Iacopo's collection became a favorite with medieval readers, who called it *Legenda aurea*, the *Golden Legend*. The Church counseled a certain suspension of belief in regard to some of these stories,[4] but the people loved and accepted them all, and perhaps were not more deceived about life than the simple folk who absorb the popular fiction of our day.

The glory of medieval Latin was its verse. Much of it was poetry in form only, for all varieties of didactic material—history, legend, mathematics, logic, theology, medicine—were given rhythm and rhyme as mnemonic aids. And there were epics of small moment and great length, like Walter of Châtillon's *Alexandreis* (1176), which seem to us now as dull as *Paradise Lost*. There were also poetical disputations—between body and soul, death and man, mercy and truth, rustic and cleric, man and woman, wine and water, wine and beer, rose and violet, the poor student and the well-fed priest, even between Helen and Ganymede as to the rival merits of heterosexual and homosexual love.[5] Nothing human was alien to medieval poetry.

The classic reliance on vowel quantity as the measure of meter was abandoned from the fifth century onward, and medieval Latin verse, rising out of popular feeling rather than from learned art, achieved a new poetry based on accent, rhythm, and rhyme. Such forms had existed among the Romans before Greek meters came to them, and had clandestinely survived a thousand years of the classic style. Classic forms—hexameter, elegiac, Sapphic—remained throughout the Middle Ages, but the Latin world had tired of them; they seemed unattuned to the moods of piety, tenderness, delicacy, and prayer that Christianity had spread. Simpler rhythms came, short lines of iambic feet that could convey almost any emotion from the beating of the heart to the tread of soldiers marching on to war.

Whence rhyme came to Western Christendom no one knows and many guess. It had been used in a few pagan poems, as by Ennius, Cicero, Apuleius; occasionally in Hebrew and Syriac poetry; sporadically in Latin poetry of the fifth century; abundantly in Arabic verse as early as the sixth century. Possibly the Moslem passion for rhymes affected the Christians who touched Islam; the surfeit of rhymes, medial and terminal, in medieval Latin verse recalls a like excess in Arabic poetry. In any case the new forms begot an entire new corpus of Latin poetry, utterly unlike the classic types, astonishing in abundance, and of unsuspected excellence. Here, for example, is Peter Damian (1007–72), the ascetic reformer, likening the call of Christ to the call of a lover to a maid:

Quis est hic qui pulsat ad ostium?	Who is this that knocks at my door?
noctis rumperis somnium?	Would you shatter my night's dream?
Me vocat: "O virginum pulcherimma,	He calls me: "O loveliest of maidens,
soror, coniux, gemma splendidissima.	Sister, mate, gem most resplendent!
Cito, surgens aperi, dulcissima.	Quick! rise! open, most sweet!
Ego sum summi regis filius,	I am the son of the highest king,
primus et novissimus;	His first and youngest son,
qui de caelis in has veni tenebras,	Who from heaven has come to this darkness
liberare captivorum animas:	To free the souls of captives;
passus mortem et multas iniurias."	Death have I suffered, and many injuries."
Mox ego dereliqui lectulum,	Quickly I left my couch,
cucurri ad pessulum:	Ran to the threshold,
ut dilecto tota domus pateat,	That to the beloved all the house might lie open,
et mens mea plenissime videat	And my soul might in fullest see
quem videre maxime desiderat.	Him whom it most longs to see.
At ille iam inde transierat;	But he so soon had passed by,
ostium reliquerat.	Had left my door.
Quid ergo, miserrima, quid facerem?	What then, miserable me, should I do?
Lacrymando sum secuta iuvenem	Weeping I followed after the youth
manus cuius plasmaverunt hominem....	Whose hands formed man.

To Peter Damian poetry was an incident; to Hildebert of Lavardin (1055?–1133), Archbishop of Tours, it was a passion that fought his faith for his soul. Probably from the Bérenger of Tours who had studied under Fulbert at Chartres he imbibed a love for the Latin classics. After many tribulations he journeyed to Rome, not sure which he sought more—papal benediction or a sight of the scenes endeared to him by his reading. He was touched by the grandeur and decay of the old capital, and expressed his feelings in classic elegiac form:

> Par tibi, Roma, nihil, cum sis prope tota ruina;
> quam magni fueris integra fracta doces.
> Longa tuos fastus aetas destruxit, et arces
> Caesaris et superum templa palude iacent.
> Ille labor, labor ille ruit quem dirus Araxes
> et stantem tremuit et cecidisse dolet. . . .
> Non tamen annorum series, non flamma, nec ensis
> ad plenum potuit hoc abolere decus.*

Here for a moment a medieval poet used the Latin language as nobly as Virgil himself. But once a Christian, always a Christian. Hildebert found more comfort in Jesus and Mary than in Jupiter and Minerva; and in a later poem he impeccably dismissed the ancient shrines:

> Gratior haec iactura mihi successibus illis;
> maior sum pauper divite, stante iacens.
> Plus aquilis vexilla crucis, plus Caesare Petrus,
> plus cinctis ducibus vulgus inerme dedit.
> Stans domui terras, infernum diruta pulso;
> corpora stans, animas fracta iacensque rego.
> Tunc miserae plebi, modo principibus tenebrarum
> impero; tunc urbes, nunc mea regna polus.†

Not since Fortunatus had any Latin penned such poetry.

II. WINE, WOMAN, AND SONG

Our knowledge of the pagan or skeptical aspects of medieval life is naturally fragmentary; the past has not transmitted itself to us impartially, except in our blood. We must all the more admire the liberality of spirit—or the fellowship of enjoyment—that led the monastery of Benediktbeuern (in Upper Bavaria) to preserve the manuscript which reached print in 1847 as *Carmina Burana* (*Beuern Poems*), and is now our main source for the poetry of the "wandering scholars." ‡ These were not tramps; some were footloose monks straying from their monasteries, some were clerics out of a job, most were students en route, often by foot, between home and university, or from one university to another. Many students stopped at taverns on the way;

* "Equal to you, O Rome! there is nothing, even when you are almost a ruin; how great you were when whole, broken you teach us. Long time has destroyed your pride, and the citadels of Caesar sink in the marshes with the temples of the gods. That work, that mighty work lies low which the dire barbarian trembled to see standing and mourns to see fallen. . . . But no lapse of years, no fire, no sword can all destroy this glory."

† (Rome speaks:) "Sweeter to me this defeat than those victories; greater am I poor than when rich, greater prone than standing; more than the eagles has the standard of the cross given me, more Peter than Caesar, more a weaponless crowd than commanders girt with arms. Standing I mastered nations; ruined I strike the depths of the earth; standing I ruled bodies, broken and prostrate I rule souls. Then I commanded a miserable populace, now the princes of darkness; then cities were my realm, now the sky."

‡ Another source is a manuscript in the Harleian Library, written before 1264, and published by Thomas Wright in 1841 as *Latin Poems Commonly Attributed to Walter Mapes*.

some sampled wines and women, and learned unscheduled lore. Some composed songs, sang them, sold them; some abandoned hope of an ecclesiastical career, and lived from pen to mouth by dedicating their poetic powers to bishops or lords. They labored chiefly in France and western Germany, but as they wrote in Latin their poems achieved an international currency. They pretended to have an organization—the *Ordo vagorum*, or guild of wanderers; and they invented as its founder and patron saint a mythical Rabelaisian personage whom they called Golias. As early as the tenth century Archbishop Walter of Sens fulminated against the scandalous "family of Golias"; and as late as 1227 a Church council condemned the "Goliardi" for singing parodies on the most sacred songs of the liturgy.[6] "They go about in public naked," said the Council of Salzburg in 1281; "they lie in bake ovens, frequent taverns, games, harlots, earn their bread by their vices, and cling with obstinacy to their sect."[7]

We know only a few of these Goliardic poets individually. One was Hugh or Hugo Primas, a canon at Orléans about 1140, "a vile fellow, deformed of visage," says a rival scribe,[8] but famed "through many provinces" for his ready wit and verse; dying of unbought poetry, and flinging angry satires at the ecclesiastical rich; a man of great erudition and little shame, writing coarse indecencies in hexameters almost as chaste as Hildebert's. Still more renowned was one whose name is lost, but whom his admirers called Archipoeta, the Archpoet (*c.* 1161), a German knight who preferred wine and ink to sword and blood, and lived fitfully on the occasional charity of Rainald von Dassel, archbishop-elect of Cologne and ambassador of Barbarossa at Pavia. Rainald tried to reform him, but the poet begged off with one of the most famous of medieval poems—the "Confession of Goliath"—whose final stanza became a favorite drinking song in German universities.

1. Seething over inwardly
     With fierce indignation,
   In my bitterness of soul
     Hear my declaration.
   I am of one element,
     Levity my matter,
   Like enough a withered leaf
     For the winds to scatter.

2. Never yet could I endure
     Soberness and sadness.
   Jests I love, and sweeter than
     Honey find I gladness.
   Whatsoever Venus bids
     Is a joy excelling;
   Never in an evil heart
     Did she make her dwelling.

3. Down the broad way do I go,
     Young and unregretting;
   Wrap me in my vices up,
     Virtue all forgetting.
   Greedier for all delight
     Than heaven to enter in,
   Since the soul in me is dead,
     Better save the skin.

4. Pardon pray you, good my lord,
     Master of discretion,
   But this death I die is sweet,
     Most delicious poison.
   Wounded to the quick am I
     By a young girl's beauty;
   She's beyond my touching? Well,
     Can't the mind do duty?

5. Sit you down amid the fire,
      Will the fire not burn you?
   Come to Pavia; will you
      Just as chaste return you?
   Pavia, where beauty draws
      Youth with fingertips,
   Youth entangled in her eyes,
      Ravished with her lips.

6. Let you bring Hippolytus,
      In Pavia dine him;
   Never more Hippolytus
      Will the morning find him.
   In Pavia not a road
      But leads to Venery,
   Nor among its crowding towers
      One to chastity.

7. Meum est propositum
      in taberna mori,
   ut sint vina proxima
      morientis ori.
   Tunc cantabunt laetius
      angelorum chori:
   "Sit deus propitius
      huic potatori!"

7. For on this my heart is set:
      When the hour is nigh me,
   Let me in the tavern die,
      With a tankard by me,
   While the angels, looking down,
      Joyously sing o'er me:
   Deus sit propitius
      *Huic potatori.** [9]

The *Carmina Burana* range over all the themes of youth: spring, love, boasts of seductions achieved, delicate obscenities, tender lyrics of love un-returned, a student's song counseling a moratorium on studies and a holiday with love (*omittamus studia, dulce est desipere*).... In one song a girl inter-rupts a scholar's labor with *Quid tu facis, domine? Veni mecum ludere* ("What are you doing, master? Come and play with me"); another sings the faithlessness of woman; another, the grief of the betrayed and forsaken lass whose horizontal growth brings down parental blows. Many chant the joys of drinking or gambling; some attack the wealth of the Church ("The Gos-pel According to the Silver Mark"); some parody the noblest hymns, like Thomas' *Lauda Sion*; one is a Whitmanesque song of the open road.[10] Many are doggerel, some are masterpieces of lyrical craftsmanship. Here is a lover's idyl of ideal death:

> When she recklessly
> Gave herself wholly unto Love and me,
> Beauty in heaven afar
> Laughed from her joyous star.
> Too great desire hath overwhelmed me;
>   My heart's not great enough
> For this huge joy that overmastered me,
>   What time my love
> Made in her arms another man of me,
> And all the gathered honey of her lips
> Drained in one yielded kiss.
> Again, again I dream the freedom given
>   Of her soft breast;

---

* "May God be propitious to this toper!"

> And so am come, another god, to heaven
>   Among the rest;
> Yea, and serene would govern gods and men
> If I might find again
>   My hand upon her breast.[11]

Most of the love poetry in the *Carmina* is frankly sensual; there are moments of tenderness and grace, but they are brief preludes. We might have guessed that by the side of the hymns of the Church there would sooner or later be hymns to Venus; woman, the devoted supporter of religion, is the chief rival of the gods. The Church listened patiently enough to these chants of love and wine. But in 1281 a council decreed that any cleric (therefore any student) who composed or sang licentious or impious songs should lose his clerical rank and privileges. Such wandering students as thereafter remained loyal to Golias sank to the level of jongleurs, and fell out of literature into ribald doggerel. By 1250 the day of the goliards was over. But as they had inherited a pagan current running beneath the Christian centuries, so their mood and poetry secretly survived to enter the Renaissance.

Latin poetry itself almost died with the goliards. The thirteenth century turned the best minds to philosophy; the classics retreated to a minor place in the university curriculum; and the almost Augustan grace of Hildebert and John of Salisbury had no heirs. When the thirteenth century ended, and Dante chose Italian for his medium, the vernacular languages became literature. Even drama, child and servant of the Church, put off its Latin dress, and spoke the peoples' tongues.

III. THE REBIRTH OF DRAMA

The classic drama had died before the Middle Ages began, for it had degenerated into mime and farce, and had been replaced by hippodrome spectacles. The plays of Seneca and Hroswitha were literary exercises, which apparently never reached the stage. Two lines of active continuity remained: the mimetic rituals of agricultural festivals, and the farces played by wandering minstrels and clowns in castle hall or village square.[12]

But in the Middle Ages, as in ancient Greece, the main fountainhead of drama was in religious liturgy. The Mass itself was a dramatic spectacle; the sanctuary was a sacred stage; the celebrants wore symbolic costumes; priest and acolytes engaged in dialogue; and the antiphonal responses of priest and choir, and of choir to choir, suggested precisely that same evolution of drama from dialogue that had generated the sacred Dionysian play. In the ceremonies of certain holydays the dramatic element was explicitly developed. At Christmas, in some religious rites of the eleventh century, men dressed as shepherds entered the church, were greeted with "glad tidings" by a choirboy "angel," and worshiped a wax or plaster babe in a manger; from an eastern door three "kings" entered, and were guided to the manger by a star pulled along a wire.[13] On the 28th of December certain churches represented the "slaughter of the innocents": boy choristers marched up nave and aisles, fell as if murdered by Herod, rose, and walked up into the sanctuary as a symbol of mounting into heaven.[14] On Good Friday many churches removed the crucifix from the altar, and carried it to a receptacle representing the Holy Sepulcher, from which on Easter morning it was solemnly restored to the altar in token of resurrection.[15] As far back as 380 the story of Christ's Passion had been written as a Euripidean drama by Gregory Nazianzen, Patriarch of Constantinople; [16] and from that time to this the Passion Play has kept its hold upon Christian peoples. The first such play recorded as having been performed was presented at Siena about 1200; probably there had been many such representations long before.

As the Church used architecture, sculpture, painting, and music to impress upon the faithful the central scenes and ideas of the Christian epic, so she appealed to the imagination, and intensified the piety, of the people by developing in increasing splendor and detail the dramatic implications of the greater feasts. The "tropes," or amplifying texts added for musical elaboration to the liturgy, were sometimes turned into little plays. So an "Easter trope" in a tenth-century manuscript at St. Gall assigns this dialogue to parts of a choir divided to represent angels and the three Marys:

> *Angels*: Whom seek ye in the tomb, O servants of Christ?
> *Marys:* We seek Christ that was crucified, O heavenly host.
> *Angels*: He is not here; He is risen, as He foretold. Go, and announce that He is risen.
> *United chorus*: Alleluia, the Lord has risen.[17]

Gradually, from the twelfth century onward, the religious spectacles grew too complex for representation within doors. A platform was set up outside the church, and the *ludus* or play was performed by actors chosen from the people and trained to memorize an extended script. The oldest extant example of this form is a twelfth-century *Representation of Adam*, written in French with Latin "rubrics" in red ink as directions to the players.

Adam and Eve, dressed in white tunics, are shown playing in an Eden represented by shrubs and flowers in front of the church. Devils appear, in those red tights that have clung to them ever since in the theater; they run through the audience, twisting their bodies and making horrible grimaces. They offer the forbidden fruit to Adam, who refuses it, then to Eve, who takes it; and Eve persuades Adam. So convicted of a desire for knowledge, Adam and Eve are fettered with irons and are dragged off by the devils to hell—a hole in the ground, from which comes an infernal noise of rejoicing. In a second act Cain prepares to murder Abel. "Abel," he announces, "you are a dead man."

Abel: "Why am I a dead man?" Cain: "Do you wish to hear why I want to kill you? . . . I will tell you. Because you ingratiate yourself too much with God." Cain flings himself upon Abel, and beats him to death. But the author is merciful: "Abel," reads the rubric, "shall have a saucepan beneath his clothes." [18]

Such Biblical *ludi* were later called "mysteries," from the Latin *ministerium* in the sense of an action; this was also the meaning of *drama*. When the story was post-Biblical it was called a *miraculum* or miracle play, and usually turned on some marvelous deed of the Virgin or the saints. Hilarius, a pupil of Abélard, composed several such short plays (*c.* 1125), in a mixture of Latin and French. By the middle of the thirteenth century the vernacular languages were the regular medium of such "miracles"; humor, increasingly broad, played a rising role in them; and their subjects became more and more secular.

Meanwhile the farce had made its own development toward drama. The evolution is exemplified in two short plays that have come down to us from the pen of an Arras hunchback, Adam de la Halle (*c.* 1260). One of them, *Li jus Adam*—the Play of Adam—is about the author himself. He had planned to be a priest, but fell in love with sweet Marie. "It was a beautiful and clear summer day, mild and green, with delightful song of birds. In the high woods near the brook . . . I caught sight of her who is now my wife, and who now seems pale and yellow to me. . . . My hunger for her is satisfied." He tells her so with peasant directness, and plans to go to Paris and the university. Into this marital scene, with more rhyme than reason, the author introduces a physician, a madman, a monk begging alms and promising miracles, and a troop of fairies singing songs, like a ballet projected by main force into a modern opera. Adam offends one of the fairies, who lays upon him the curse of never leaving his wife. From such nonsense there is a line of continuous development to Bernard Shaw.

As secularization proceeded, the performances moved from the church grounds to the market place or some other square in the town. There were no theaters. For the few performances to be given—usually on some summer festival—a temporary stage was erected, with benches for the people and gaily decorated booths for nobilities. Surrounding houses might be used as background and "properties." In religious plays the actors were young clerics; in secular plays they were town "mummers" or wandering jongleurs; women rarely took part. As the plays strayed farther from the church in scene and theme, they tended toward buffoonery and obscenity, and the Church, which had given birth to the serious drama, found herself forced to condemn the village *ludi* as immoral. So Bishop Grosseteste of Lincoln classed the plays, even the "miracles," along with drinking bouts and the Feast of Fools, as performances that no Christian should attend; and by such edicts as his (1236-44) the actors who took part were automatically excommunicated. St. Thomas was more lenient, and ruled that the profession of *histrio* had been ordained for the solace of humanity, and that an actor who practiced it becomingly might, by God's mercy, escape hell.[19]

IV. EPICS AND SAGAS

The secularization of literature went hand in hand with the rise of the national languages. By and large, by the twelfth century, only clerics could understand Latin, and writers who wished to reach a lay audience were compelled to use the vernacular tongues. As social order grew, the reading audience widened, and national literatures rose to meet its demand. French literature began in the eleventh century, German in the twelfth, English, Spanish, and Italian in the thirteenth.

The natural early form of these indigenous literatures was the popular song. The song was drawn out into the ballad; and the ballad, by proliferation or agglutination, swelled into such minor epics as *Beowulf*, the *Chanson de Roland*, the *Nibelungenlied*, and the *Cid*. The *Chanson* was probably put together about 1130 from ballads of the ninth or tenth century. In 4000 simple, flowing iambic lines it tells the story of Roland's death at Roncesvalles. Charlemagne, having "conquered" Moorish Spain, turns back with his army toward France; the traitorous Ganelon reveals their route to the enemy; and Roland volunteers to lead the dangerous rear guard. In a narrow winding gorge of the Pyrenees a horde of Basques pours down from the cliffs upon Roland's little force. His friend Olivier begs him to sound his great horn as a call to Charlemagne for aid, but Roland proudly refuses to ask for help. He and Olivier and Archbishop Turpin lead their troops in a desperate resistance, and they fight till nearly all are dead. Olivier, blinded by blood flowing from mortal wounds in his head, mistakes Roland for an enemy, and strikes him. Roland's helmet is split from crown to nosepiece, but saves him.

> At this blow Roland looks at him,
> Asks him gently and softly:
> "Sir comrade, do you this in earnest?
> I am that Roland who loves you so well.
> In no wise have you sent me defiance."
> Says Olivier: "Now I hear you speak;
> I do not see you. God see and save you!
> Struck you have I. Forgive it to me!"
> Roland replies: "I have no injury.
> I forgive you here and before God."
> At this word one to the other bows;
> And with such love they part.[20]

Roland at last blows his oliphant, blows till the blood bursts from his temples. Charlemagne hears, and turns back to the rescue, "his white beard flying in the wind." But the way is long; "high are the mountains, vast and dark; deep are the valleys, swift the streams." Meanwhile Roland mourns over the corpse of Olivier, and says to it: "Sir comrade, we have been together through many days and many years. You never did me evil, nor I to you. Life is all pain if you are dead." The Archbishop, also dying, begs Roland to save himself by flight; Roland refuses, and continues to fight till the attackers flee; but he too is mortally wounded. With his last strength he breaks his jeweled sword Durendal against a stone, lest it fall into heathen hands. Now "Count Roland lay under a pine tree, his face turned toward Spain. . . . Many memories came upon him then; he thought of the lands he had conquered, of sweet France, and his family, and Charles, who had brought him up, and he wept." He held up his glove to God as a sign of loyal vassalage. Charles, arriving, finds him dead. No translation can catch the simple but knightly dignity of the original, and none but one reared to love France and honor her can feel to the full the power and sentiment of this, the national epic that every French child learns, almost with its prayers.

About 1160 an unknown poet, romantically idealizing the character and exploits of Ruy or Rodrigo Diaz (d. 1099), gave a national epic to Spain in the *Poema del Cid*. Here too the theme is the struggle of Christian knights against the Spanish Moors, the exaltation of feudal courage, honor, and magnanimity, the glory of war rather than the servitude of love. So Rodrigo, banished by an ungrateful king, leaves his wife and children in a nunnery, and vows never to live with them again until he has won five battles. He goes to fight the Moors, and the first half of the poem resounds with Homeric victories. Between battles the Cid robs Jews, scatters alms among the poor, feeds a leper, eats from the same dish with him, sleeps in the same bed, and discovers him to be Lazarus, whom Christ raised from the dead. This, of course, is not the Cid of history, but it does no greater injury to fact than the *Chanson* with its idealization of Charlemagne. The *Cid* became a heady stimulant to Spanish thought and pride; hundreds of ballads were composed about its hero, and a hundred histories more or less historical. There are few things in the world so unpopular as truth, and the backbone of men and states is a concatenation of romance.

No one has yet explained why little Iceland, harassed by the elements and isolated by the sea, should have produced in this period a literature of scope and brilliance quite out of proportion to its place and size. Two circumstances helped: a rich store of orally transmitted historical traditions, dear to any segregated group; and a habit of reading—or being read to—which was favored by long winter nights. Already in the twelfth century there were many private libraries in the island, in addition to those in the monasteries. When writing became a familiar accomplishment, laymen as well as priests put this racial lore, once the property of scalds, into literary form.

By a rare anomaly the leading writer of thirteenth-century Iceland was also its richest man, and twice the president of the republic—the "speaker of the law." Snorri Sturluson (1178–1241) loved life more than letters; he traveled widely, engaged vigorously in politics and feuds, and was murdered by his son-in-law at sixty-two. His *Heimskringla—The Round World*—told Norse history and legend with a spare and brief simplicity natural to a man of action. His *Edda Snorra Sturlusonar*, or Prose Edda, gave a summary of Biblical history, a synopsis of Norse mythology, an essay on poetic meters, a treatise on the art of poetry, and a unique explanation of the art's urological origin. Two warring groups of gods made peace by spitting into a jar; from this spittle was formed a demigod, Kvasir, who taught men wisdom like Prometheus. Kvasir was slain by dwarfs, who mixed his blood with wine and produced a nectar that conferred the gift of song on all who drank of it. The great god Odin found his way to where the dwarfs had stored this poetic wine, drank it all up, and flew to heaven. But some of the pent-up liquid escaped from him by a means rarely used in public fountains; this divine stream fell in an inspiring spray upon the earth; and those who were bedewed by it imbibed the gift of poesy.[21] It was a learned man's nonsense, quite as rational as history.

The literature of Iceland in this period is astonishingly rich, and still alive with interest, vivacity, humor, and a poetic charm that pervades its prose. Hundreds of sagas were written, some brief, some as long as a novel, some historical, most of them mingling history and myth. In general they were civilized memories of a barbarous age, compact of honor and violence, complicated with litigation, and mitigated with love. The Ynglinga sagas of Snorri repeatedly tell of Norse knights who burned one another, or themselves, in their halls or cups. The most fertile of these legends was the *Volsungasaga*. Its stories had an early form in the Elder or Poetic Edda; they have their latest form in Wagner's *Ring of the Nibelungs*.

A Volsung was any descendant of Waels, a Norse king, who was great-grandson of Odin and grandfather to Sigurd (Siegfried). In the *Nibelungenlied* the Nibelungs are Burgundian kings; in the *Volsungasaga* they are a race of dwarfs guarding in the Rhine a gold treasure and ring which are infinitely precious but bring a curse and misfortune to all who possess them. Sigurd slays Fafnir the dragon guardian of the hoard, and captures it. On his wanderings he comes to a fire-encircled hill, on which the Valkyrie (an Odin-descended demigoddess) Brunhild sleeps; this is one form of the Sleeping Beauty tale. Sigurd is ravished by her beauty, and she is ravished; they plight their troth; and then—as is the way of men in many medieval romances—he leaves her and resumes his travels. At the court of Giuki, a Rhine king, he finds the princess Gudrun. Her mother gives him an enchanted drink, which enables him to forget Brunhild and marry Gudrun. Gunnar, son of Giuki, marries Brunhild, and brings her to the court. Resenting Sigurd's amnesia, she has him killed; then in remorse she mounts his funeral pyre, slays herself with his sword, and is consumed with him.

The most modern in form of these Icelandic sagas is *The Story of Burnt Njal* (*c.* 1220). The characters are sharply defined by their deeds and words rather than by description; the tale is well constructed, and moves with inherent fatality through stirring events to the central catastrophe—the burning of Njal's house, with himself and his wife Bergthora and his sons, by an armed band of enemies led by one Flosi, and bent on blood vengeance against Njal's sons.

> Then Flosi . . . called out to Njal, and said,
> "I will offer thee, master Njal, leave to go out, for it is unworthy that thou shouldst burn indoors."
> "I will not go out," said Njal, "for I am an old man, and little fitted to avenge my sons, but I will not live in shame."
> Then Flosi said to Bergthora, "Come thou out, housewife, for I will for no sake burn thee indoors."
> "I was given away to Njal young," said Bergthora, "and I have promised him this, that we would both share the same fate."
> After that they both went back into the house.
> "What counsel shall we now take?" said Bergthora.
> "We will go to our bed," said Njal, "and lay us down; I have long been eager for rest."
> Then she said to the boy Thord, Kari's son, "Thee will I take out, and thou shalt not burn in here."
> "Thou hast promised me this, grandmother," said the boy, "that we should never part so long as I wished to be with thee; but methinks it is much better to die with thee and Njal than to live after you."
> Then she bore the boy to her bed, and . . . put him between herself and Njal. Then they signed themselves and the boy with the cross, and gave over their souls into God's hand; and that was the last word men heard them utter.[22]

The age of the migrations (300–600) had deposited in the confused memory of peoples and minstrels a thousand stories of social chaos, barbaric courage, and murderous love. Some of these tales were carried to Norway and Iceland, and produced the *Volsungasaga*; many, with kindred names and themes, lived and multiplied in Germany in the form of legends, ballads, and sagas. At an unknown time in the twelfth century an unknown German, uniting and transforming such materials, composed the *Nibelungenlied*, or *Song of the Nibelungs*. Its form is a concatenation of rhyming couplets in

Middle High German; its narrative is a brew of primitive passions and pagan moods.

Sometime in the fourth century King Gunther and his two brothers ruled Burgundy from their castle at Worms on the Rhine; and with them dwelt their young sister Kriemhild—"in no land was any fairer." In those days King Siegmund governed the Lowlands, and enfeoffed his son Siegfried (Sigurd) with a rich estate near Xanten, also on the Rhine. Hearing of Kriemhild's loveliness, Siegfried invited himself to Gunther's court, made himself welcome there, lived there for a year, but never saw Kriemhild, though she, looking from her high window upon the youths tilting in the courtyard, loved him from the first. Siegfried surpassed all in jousts, and fought bravely for the Burgundians in their wars. When Gunther celebrated a victorious peace he bade the ladies join the feast.

> Many a noble maiden adorned herself with care, and the youths longed exceedingly to find favor in their eyes, and had not taken a rich King's land in lieu thereof. . . . And lo, Kriemhild appeared, like the dawn from out the dark clouds; and he that had borne her so long in his heart was no more aweary. . . . And Siegfried joyed and sorrowed, for he said in his heart, "How should I woo such as thee? Surely it was a vain dream; yet I were liefer dead than a stranger to thee". . . . Her color was kindled when she saw before her the high-minded man, and she said, "Welcome, Sir Siegfried, noble knight and good." His courage rose at her words; and graceful as beseemed a knight he bowed himself before her and thanked her. And love that is mighty constrained them, and they yearned with their eyes in secret.

Gunther, unmarried, hears of the Icelandic queen Brunhild; but she, he is informed, can be won only by one who excels her in three trials of strength; and if he fails in any, he forfeits his head. Siegfried agrees to help Gunther win Brunhild if the King will give him Kriemhild to wife. They cross the sea with the speed and ease of romance; Siegfried, made invisible by a magic cape, helps Gunther meet the tests; and Gunther brings the reluctant Brunhild home as his bride. Eighty-six damsels help Kriemhild prepare rich garments for her. In a double marriage of great pomp Gunther weds Brunhild, and Siegfried is joined to Kriemhild.

But Brunhild, seeing Siegfried, feels that he, not Gunther, was meant to be her mate. When Gunther goes in to her on their marriage night she repulses him, ties him in a knot, and hangs him up on the wall. Gunther, released, begs Siegfried's aid; the hero, on the next night, disguises himself as Gunther, and lies beside Brunhild, while Gunther, hidden in the darkened room, hears all and sees nothing. Brunhild throws Siegfried out of bed, and engages him in a bone-crunching, head-cracking combat quite without rules. "Alas," he says to himself amid the fight, "if I lose my life by the hand of a woman, all wives evermore will make light of their husbands." Brunhild is finally overcome, and promises to be a wife; Siegfried retires unseen, bearing away her girdle and her ring; and Gunther takes his place beside the exhausted queen. Siegfried makes a present of the girdle and ring to

Kriemhild. He brings her to his father, who crowns him King of the Lowlands. Using his Nibelungen wealth, Siegfried clothes his wife and her maidens more richly than ever women were robed before.

Some time later Kriemhild visits Brunhild at Worms; Brunhild, jealous of Kriemhild's finery, reminds her that Siegfried is Gunther's vassal. Kriemhild retorts by showing her the girdle and ring as proof that Siegfried, not Gunther, had overcome her. Hagen, gloomy half brother to Gunther, rouses him against Siegfried; they invite him to a hunt; and as he stoops over a brook to drink, Hagen pierces him with a spear. Kriemhild, seeing her hero dead, "lay senseless in a swoon all that day and night." She inherits the Nibelung treasure as Siegfried's widow, but Hagen persuades Gunther to take it from her. Gunther, his brothers, and Hagen bury it in the Rhine, and take oath never to reveal its hiding place.

For thirteen years Kriemhild broods over vengeance upon Hagen and her brothers, but finds no opportunity. Then she accepts the marriage proposal of the widowed Etzel (Attila), King of the Huns, and goes to Vienna to live as his queen. "So famed was Etzel's rule that the boldest knights, Christian or heathen, drew ceaselessly to his court. . . . One saw there what one never sees now— Christian and heathen together. Howso diverse their beliefs, the King gave with such free hand that all had plenty." There Kriemhild "ruled virtuously" for thirteen years, seeming to forgo vengeance. Indeed she asks Etzel to invite her brothers and Hagen to a feast; they accept despite Hagen's warning, but come with an armed retinue of yeomen and knights. While the royal brothers, Hagen, and the knights enjoy the hospitality of the Hun court in Etzel's hall, the yeomen outside are slain at Kriemhild's command. Hagen is told of it, and springs to arms; a terrible battle ensues in the hall between the Burgundians and the Huns (perhaps recalling their actual war of 437); with his first blow Hagen strikes off the head of Ortlieb, the five-year-old son of Kriemhild and Etzel, and he flings the head into Kriemhild's lap. When nearly all the Burgundians are dead Gernot, brother of Kriemhild and Gunther, asks Etzel to let the surviving visitors escape from the hall. The Hun knights wish it, Kriemhild forbids it, the slaughter goes on. Her youngest brother, Giselher, who was an innocent lad of five when Siegfried fell, appeals to her: "Fairest sister, how have I deserved death from the Huns? I was ever true to thee, nor did thee any hurt; I rode hither, dearest sister, for that I trusted to thy love. Needs must thou show mercy." She agrees to let them escape if they will deliver Hagen to her. "God in heaven forbid!" cries Gernot; "liefer would we all die than give one man for our ransom." Kriemhild draws the Huns from the building, locks the Burgundians in it, and has it set on fire. Maddened with heat and thirst, the Burgundians cry out in agony; Hagen bids them assuage their thirst with the blood of the slain; they do. Some emerge from the flaming and falling timbers; the battle continues in the courtyard until of the Burgundians only Gunther and Hagen remain alive. Dietrich the Goth fights and overcomes Hagen and brings him bound to Kriemhild. She asks Hagen where he has concealed the Nibelung treasure; he refuses to tell her as long as Gunther is alive; Gunther, also captive, is slain at his sister's bidding, and his head is brought to Hagen. But Hagen defies her: "Now none knows where the hoard is save God and I alone; that to thee, devil-woman, shall never more be known."

She seizes his sword and strikes him dead. Then Hildebrand the Goth, one of her warriors, surfeited with her blood lust, slays Kriemhild.

It is a terrible tale, as red with gore as any in literature or beneath. We do some injustice to it by taking its direst moments from their context of feasting, jousting, hunting, and womanly affairs; but this is the central and bitter theme—a gentle maiden changed by the experience of evil into a ferocious murderess. Strangely little of Christianity is left in the story; it is rather a Greek tragedy of nemesis, without the Greek reluctance to let violence come upon the stage. In this stream of crime almost all feudal virtues are submerged, even the honor of host to invited guest. Nothing could surpass the barbarism of such a tale, until our time.

V. THE TROUBADOURS

At the end of the eleventh century, when we should have expected all European letters to be colored by the religious enthusiasm of the Crusades, there developed in southern France a school of lyric poetry aristocratic, pagan, anticlerical, bearing the marks of Arab influence, and signalizing the triumph of woman over the chastisement laid upon her by the theory of the Fall. This style of verse moved from Toulouse to Paris to London with Eleanor of Aquitaine, captured the lion heart of her son Richard I, created the minnesingers of Germany, and molded the Italian *dolce stil nuovo* that led to Dante.

At the origin of the style stands Eleanor's grandfather, William IX, Count of Poitou and Duke of Aquitaine. This reckless blade found himself at eleven (1087) the practically independent ruler of southwestern France. He joined the First Crusade and sang its victory; but, like so many nobles in his heresy-infected lands, he had scant respect for the Church, and made gay mockery of her priests. An old Provençal biography describes him as "one of the most courteous men in the world, and a great deceiver of ladies; and he was a brave knight and had much to do with love affairs; and he knew well how to sing and make verses; and for a long time he roamed all through the land to deceive the ladies."[23] Though married, he carried off the beautiful viscountess of Châtellerault, and lived with her in open scandal. When the bold bald bishop of Angoulême bade him end his wicked ways he replied, "I will repudiate the viscountess as soon as your hair requires a comb." Excommunicated, he one day met the bishop of Poitiers. "Absolve me," he said, "or I will kill you." "Strike," answered the bishop, offering his neck. "No," said William; "I do not love you well enough to send you to paradise."[24] The Duke set a style of writing amorous poetry to noble dames. He suited the action to the word, led a short life and a merry one, and died at fifty-six (1137). He left to Eleanor his immense domain, and his taste for poetry and love.

She gathered poets about her at Toulouse, and willingly they sang for her and her court the beauty of women and the fever engendered by their charms. Bernard de Ventadour, whose poems seemed to Petrarch only slightly inferior to his own, began by praising the loveliness of the viscountess of Ventadour; she took him so seriously that her husband had to shut her up in his castle tower. Bernard, encouraged, turned to chant the splendor of Eleanor herself, and followed her to Rouen; when she preferred the love of two kings he emptied out his soul in a famous dirge. A generation later the troubadour Bertrand de Born became the bosom friend of Richard I, and his successful rival for the love of the most beautiful woman of her time, Dame Maenz of Martignac. Another troubadour, Peire Vidal (1167?–1215), accompanied Richard on crusade, returned intact, lived and rhymed in amours and poverty, and received at last an estate from Count Raymond VI of Toulouse.[25] We know the names of 446 other troubadours; but from these four we may judge their loose melodious tribe.

Some were musical vagabonds; most were minor nobles with a flair for song; four were kings—Richard I, Frederick II, Alfonso II, and Pedro III of Aragon. For a century (1150–1250) they dominated the literature of southern France, and molded the manners of an aristocracy emerging from rustic brutality into a chivalry that almost redeemed war with courtesy, and adultery with grace. The language of the troubadours was the *langue d'oc* or *roman* of southern France and northeastern Spain. Their name is a puzzle; *troubadour* is probably from the *roman* word *trobar*, to find or invent, as obviously the Italian *trovatore* is from *trovare*; but some would take it from the Arabic *tarraba*, to sing.[26] They called their art *gai saber* or *gaya ciencia*, "gay wisdom"; but they took it seriously enough to undergo a long period of training in poetry, music, and the forms and speech of gallantry; they dressed like the nobility, flaunted a mantle trimmed with gold embroidery and costly furs, rode often in knightly armor, entered the lists at tournaments, and fought with lance as well as pen for the ladies to whom they had pledged their lines, if not their lives. They wrote only for the aristocracy. Usually they composed music for their own lyrics, and hired minstrels to sing them at banquets or tournaments; but often they themselves would strum the lute and wring a passion through a song.

Probably the passion was a literary form; the burning longing, the celestial fulfillments, the tragic despair of the troubadours were poetic license and machinery; apparently the husbands took these ardors so, and had less sense of property than most males. Since marriage among the aristocracy was normally an incident in a transfer of property, romance had to come after marriage, as in French fiction; the amours of medieval literature are, with a few exceptions, tales of illicit love, from Francesca and Beatrice in the South to Isolde and Guinevere in the North. The general inaccessibility of the married lady generated the poetry of the troubadours; it is hard to romanticize desire fulfilled, and where there are no impediments there is no poetry. We hear of a few troubadours who received the ultimate favor from the ladies whom they had chosen for their lays, but this was a breach of literary etiquette; usually the poet had to sate his thirst with a kiss or a touch of the hand. Such restraint made for refinement; and in the thirteenth century the poetry of the troubadours—perhaps influenced by the worship of Mary—graduated from sensualism to an almost spiritual delicacy.

But they were seldom pious. Their resentment of chastity set them at odds with the Church. Several of them lampooned prelates, ridiculed hell,[27] defended the Albigensian heretics, and celebrated the victorious crusade of the impious Frederick where the saintly Louis had failed. Guillem Adémar approved one crusade, but only because it removed a husband from his path. Raimon Jorden preferred a night with his beloved to any promised transmundane paradise.[28]

Forms of composition seemed more important to the troubadours than commandments of morality. The *canzo* was a song of love; the *plante* was a dirge for a friend or lover lost to death; the *tenson* was a rhymed debate on a question of love, morality, or chivalry; the *sirvente* was a song of war, feud, or political attack; the *sixtine* was a complicated rhyme sequence of six stanzas, each of six lines, invented by Arnaud Daniel and much admired by Dante; the *pastourelle* was a dialogue between a troubadour and a shepherdess; the *aubade* or *alba*, a song of the dawn, usually warned lovers that the day would soon reveal them; the *serena* or *serenade* was an evening song; the *balada* was a narrative in verse. Here is an anonymous *aubade* partly spoken by a twelfth-century Juliet.

> In a garden where the white thorn spreads her leaves,
> My lady hath her love lain close beside her,
> Till the warden cries the dawn—ah, dawn that grieves!
> Ah God! ah God! that dawn should come so soon!
>
> "Please God that night, dear night, should never cease,
> Nor that my Love should parted be from me,
> Nor watch cry 'Dawn'—ah, dawn that slayeth peace!
> Ah God! ah God! that dawn should come so soon!
>
> "Fair friend and sweet, thy lips! Our lips again!
> Lo, in the meadow there the birds give song.
> Ours be the love, and jealousy's the pain!
> Ah God! ah God! that dawn should come so soon!
>
> "Of that sweet wind that comes from Far-Away
> Have I drunk deep of my Beloved's breath,
> Yea, of my Love's that is so dear and gay.
> Ah God! ah God! that dawn should come so soon!"

> Fair is this damsel and right courteous,
> And many watch her beauty's gracious way.
> Her heart toward love is nowise traitorous.
> Ah God! ah God! that dawn should come so soon! [29]

The troubadour movement in France came to an end amid the thirteenth century, partly through the increasing artificiality of its forms and sentiments, partly through the ruin of south France by the Albigensian Crusades. For in that troubled time many castles fell that had harbored troubadours; and when Toulouse itself suffered a double siege the knightly order in Aquitaine collapsed. Some singers fled to Spain, some to Italy. There in the second half of the thirteenth century the art of the love lyric was reborn, and Dante and Petrarch were scions of the troubadours. The gay science of their gallantry helped to mold the code of chivalry, and to turn the barbarians of northern Europe into gentlemen. Literature ever since has felt the influence of those subtle songs; and perhaps love now bears a finer fragrance from the incense of their praise.

VI. THE MINNESINGERS

The troubadour movement spread from France to southern Germany, and flourished there in the golden age of the Hohenstaufen emperors. The German poets were called *Minnesänger*, love singers, and their poetry coincided with the *Minnedienst* (love service) and *Frauendienst* (lady service) of contemporary chivalry. We know over 300 of these minnesingers by name, and have a plentiful legacy of their verse. Some of them belonged to the lower nobility; most of them were poor, and depended upon imperial or ducal patronage. Though they followed a strict law of rhythm and rhyme, many of them were illiterate, and dictated the words and music of their *Lieder*; to this day the German term for poetry—*Dichtung*—means dictation. Usually they let minstrels sing for them; sometimes they themselves sang. We hear of a great *Sängerkrieg*, or song contest, held at the Castle Wartburg in 1207; there, we are told, both Tannhäuser and Wolfram von Eschenbach took part.[30]* For a century the minnesingers helped to raise the status of woman in Germany, and the ladies of the aristocracy became the life and inspiration of a culture more refined than anything that Germany would know again till Schiller and Goethe.

Wolfram and Walther von der Vogelweide are classed as minnesingers because they wrote songs of love; but Wolfram and his *Parzival* may be better viewed under the heading of romance. Walther "of the Bird-Meadow" was born somewhere in the Tirol before 1170. Knight but poor, he made

---

* Tannhäuser, one of the later minnesingers, has been confused by legend with the knight Tannhäuser, who fled from Venusberg to Rome, and found a niche in opera.

matters worse by taking to poetry. We find him at twenty singing for his bread in the homes of the Viennese aristocracy. In those youthful years he wrote of love with a sensuous freedom frowned upon by his rivals. His *Unter den Linden* is treasured to this day in Germany:

Unter den linden,	Under the linden,
an der heide,	On the heather,
da unser sweier bette was;	For us two a bed there was;
du muget ir vinden	There could you see,
schone beide	Entwined together,
gebrochen bluomen under gras.	Broken flowers and bruised grass.
Vor dem valde in einem tal—	From a thicket in the dale—
tandaradei!—	Tandaradei!—
schone sanc diu nahtegal.	Sweetly sang the nightingale.
Ich kam gegangen	I sped thither
zuo der ouwe;	Through the glade;
do was min friedel komen e.	My love had reached the spot before.
Da wart ich empfangen,	There was I snared,
here frouwe!	Most happy maid!
Daz ich bin saelic iemer me.	For I am blessed evermore.
Kiste er mich? Wol tusend stunt;	Many a time he kissed me there—
tandaradei!	Tandaradei!
Sehet, wie rot mir ist der munt.	See my lips, how red they are!
Do het er gemachet	There he contrived
also riche	In joyful haste
von bluomen eine bettestat.	A bower of blossoms for us both.
Das wirt noch gelachet	That must be still
innecliche,	A fading jest
kum iemen an daz selbe pfat,	For those who take the selfsame path
bi den rosen er wol mac—	And see the spot where on that day—
tandaradei!—	Tandaradei!—
merken wa mir'z houbet lac.	My head among the roses lay.
Daz er bi mir laege,	How shamed were I
wesse ez iemen	If anyone
(nu en welle Got!) so schamte ich mich	(Now Heaven forfend!) had there been nigh.
wes er mit mir pflaege,	There we two lay,
niemer niemen	But that was known
bevinde daz wan er und ich	To none except my love and I,
unde ein kleinez vogellin—	And the little nightingale—
tandaradei!—	Tandaradei!—
daz mac wol getriuwe sin.[31]	Who, I know, will tell no tale.[32]

As he grew older his perception matured, and he began to see in woman charms and graces fairer than any budding flesh, and the rewards of unity in marriage seemed richer than the surface titillations of variety. "Happy the man, happy the woman, whose hearts are to each other true; their lives increase in price and worth; blessed their years, and all their days."[33] He deprecated the adulation with which his fellow warblers perfumed the ladies of the court; he proclaimed *wip* (*Weib*, woman) a higher title than *vrouwe* (*Frau*, lady); good women and good men were the real nobility. He thought "German ladies fair as God's angels; anyone who defames them lies in his teeth."[34]

In 1197 the Emperor Henry VI died, and Germany suffered a generation of chaos until Frederick II came of age. The aristocratic patronage of letters fell away, and Walther wandered from court to court, singing unhappily for his meals in competition with noisy jugglers and prideless clowns. An item in the expense account of Bishop Wolfger of Passau reads: "Five *solidi*, November 12, 1203, to Walther von der Vogelweide to buy himself a fur coat against the winter cold."[35] It was a doubly Christian act, for Walther was a zealous Ghibelline, tuned his lyre against the popes, denounced the shortcomings of the Church, and raged at the way in which German coins flew over the Alps to replenish Peter's Pence.[36] He was, however, a faithful Christian, and composed a mighty "Crusader's Hymn." But at times he could stand above the battle and see all men as brothers:

> Mankind arises from one virgin;
> We are alike both outward and within;
> Our mouths are sated with the selfsame fare;
> And when their bones into confusion fall,
> Say ye, who knew the living man by sight,
> Which is the villein now, and which the knight,
> That worms have gnawed their carcasses so bare?
> Christians, Jews, and heathens, serve they all,
> And God has all creation in His care.[37]

After a quarter century of wandering and poverty, Walther received from Frederick II an estate and an income (1221), and could spend in peace his remaining seven years. He mourned that he was too old and ill to go on crusade. He begged God to forgive him for not being able to love his enemies.[38] In a poetic testament he bequeathed his goods: "to the envious my ill luck; to the liars my sorrows; to false lovers my follies; to the ladies my heart's pain."[39] He was buried in Würzburg Cathedral, and near by a monument proclaims Germany's affection for the greatest poet of his age.

After him the minnesinger movement lost itself in extravaganzas, and shared in the disasters that shattered Germany after the fall of Frederick II. Ulrich von Lichtenstein (*c.* 1200–*c.* 1276) tells in his poetic autobiography, *Frauendienst*, how he was reared in all the sentiments of "lady service." He chose a lady as his goddess, had his harelip sewed up to mitigate her repulsion, and fought for her in tournament. When told of her surprise that he still had a finger which she thought he had lost in her honor, he cut off the offending member and sent it to her as tribute. He almost swooned with delight when fortune permitted him to drink the water in which she had washed her hands.[40] He received a letter from her, and carried it for weeks in his pocket before he found someone whom he could trust to read it for him secretly; for Ulrich could not read.[41] On promise of her favor he waited two days in beggar's clothing among the lepers at her gate; she admitted him; and finding him importunate, she had him lowered in a bed sheet from her window. All this time he had a wife and children.

The minnesinger movement ended with some dignity in Henrich von Meissen, whose songs in honor of women earned him the title *Frauenlob*, "women's praise." When he died at Mainz in 1317, the ladies of the city carried his bier with tuneful laments to bury him in the cathedral, and poured upon his coffin such abundance of wine that it flowed the full length of the church.[42] After him the art of song fell from the hands of the knights, and was taken up by the middle class; the romantic mood of the lady worshipers passed, and was succeeded in the fourteenth century by the robust joy and art of the meistersinger, announcing to Parnassus the ascent of the *bourgeoisie*.

VII. THE ROMANCES

But in romance the middle class had already captured the field. As aristocratic troubadours and *trovatori* wrote delicate lyrics for the ladies of southern France and Italy, so in northern France the poets of humble birth —known to the French as trouvères or inventors—brightened the evenings of the middle and upper classes with poetic tales of love and war.

The typical compositions of the trouvères were the *ballade*, the *lai*, the *chanson de geste*, and the *roman*. Some lovely examples of the *lai* have come down to us from one whom both England and France may claim as their first great poetess. Marie de France came from Brittany to live in England in the reign of Henry II (1154–89); at his suggestion she turned several Breton legends into verse, and with a delicacy of speech and sentiment not excelled by any troubadour. One of her lyrics craves room here, both for an unusual theme—the living beloved to her dead lover—and for an exquisite translation:

> Hath any loved you well down there,
>   Summer or winter through?
> Down there have you found any fair
>   Laid in the grave with you?
> Is death's long kiss a richer kiss

Than mine was wont to be—
  Or have you gone to some far bliss
    And quite forgotten me?

What soft enamoring of sleep
    Hath you in some soft way?
What charmèd death holds you with deep
    Strange lure by night and day?
A little space below the grass,
    Out of the sun and shade,
But worlds away from me, alas,
    Down there where you are laid. . . .

There you shall lie as you have lain,
    Though, in the world above,
Another live your life again,
    Loving again your love.
Is it not sweet beneath the palm?
    Is it not warm day, rife
With some long mystic golden calm
    Better than love and life?

The broad quaint odorous leaves like hands
    Weaving the fair day through,
Weave sleep no burnished bird withstands,
    While death weaves sleep for you.
And many a strange rich breathing sound
    Ravishes morn and noon;
And in that place you must have found
    Death a delicious swoon.

Hold me no longer for a word
    I used to say or sing;
Ah, long ago you must have heard
    So many a sweeter thing.
For rich earth must have reached your heart
    And turned the faith to flowers;
And warm wind stolen, part by part,
    Your soul through faithless hours.

And many a soft seed must have won
    Soil of some yielding thought,
To bring a bloom up to the sun
    That else had ne'er been brought;
And doubtless many a passionate hue
    Hath made that place more fair,
Making some passionate part of you
    Faithless to me down there.[43]

The *chanson de geste*, or song of deeds, probably arose as a concatenation of ballads or lays. Upon a core of history usually offered by the chronicles, the poet laid a web of fancied adventures, running in lines of ten or twelve syllables to such lengths as only Northern winter evenings could sustain. The *Chanson de Roland* was a lithe forerunner of this genre. The favorite hero of the French *chansons de geste* was Charlemagne. Great in history, the trouvères raised him to almost supernatural grandeur in their poetry; they converted his failure in Spain into a glorious conquest, and sent him off on triumphant expeditions to Constantinople and Jerusalem, his legendary white beard waving majesty. As *Beowulf* and the *Nibelungenlied* echoed the "heroic age" of the migrations, so the *chansons* reflected the feudal era in subject, morals, and mood; whatever their theme or scene or time, they moved in a feudal atmosphere to feudal motives and in feudal dress. Their constant subject was war, feudal or international or interfaith; and amid their rough alarums woman and love found only a minor place.

As social order improved, and the status of woman rose with the growth of wealth, war yielded to love as the major theme of the trouvères, and in the twelfth century the *chansons de geste* were succeeded by the *romans*. Woman mounted the throne of literature, and held it for centuries. The name *roman* meant at first any work written in that early French which, as a Roman legacy, was called *roman*. The romances were not called *romans* because they were romantic; rather certain sentiments came to be called romantic because they were found so abundantly in the French *romans*. The *Roman de la rose*, or *de Troie*, or *de Renard* merely meant the tale of a rose, or of Troy, or of a fox, in *roman* or early French. Since no literary form should be born without legitimate parents, we may derive the romances from the *chansons de geste* crossed with the troubadour sentiment of courtly love. Some of their material may have come from such Greek romances as the *Ethiopica* of Heliodorus. One Greek book, translated into Latin in the fourth century, had enormous influence—the fictitious biography of Alexander falsely ascribed to his official historian Callisthenes. Alexander stories became the most popular and prolific of all the "cycles" of medieval romance in Europe and the Greek-speaking East. The finest form of the tale in the West was the *Roman d'Alixandre* composed by the trouvères Lambert li Tors and Alexander of Bernay about 1200, and running to some 20,000 twelve-syllabled "Alexandrine" lines.

Richer in variety, tenderer in sentiment, was the cycle of romances—French, English, and German—stemming from the siege of Troy. Here the chief inspiration was not Homer but Virgil; the story of Dido was already a romance; and had not France and England, as well as Italy, been settled by Trojans fleeing from undeserved defeat? About 1184 a French trouvère, Benoît de Ste.-Maure, retold the *Roman de Troie* in 30,000 lines; it was translated into a dozen languages and was imitated in a dozen literatures. In

Germany Wolfram von Eschenbach wrote his *Büche von Troye*, of Iliadic size; in Italy Boccaccio took from Benoît the tale of Filostrato; in England Layamon's *Brut* (*c.* 1205) described in 32,000 lines the foundation of London by Brutus, the imaginary great-grandson of Aeneas; and from Benoît came Chaucer's Troilus and Criseyde, and Shakespeare's play.

The third great cycle of medieval romance was the Arthurian. We have seen reason to believe that Arthur was a British Christian noble who fought against the invading Saxons in the sixth century. Who was it that turned him and his knights into such delectable legends as only lovers of Malory have fully savored? Who created Gawaine, Galahad, Perceval, Merlin, Guinevere, Lancelot, Tristram, the Christian knightliness of the Round Table, and the mystic story of the Holy Grail? After a century of discussion no certain answer remains; inquiry is fatal to certainty. The oldest references to Arthur are in English chroniclers. Some elements of the legend appear in the *Chronicle* of Nennius (976); it was expanded in the *Historia Britonum* (1137) of Geoffrey of Monmouth; Geoffrey's account was put into French verse by Robert Wace, a trouvère of Jersey, in *Le Brut d'Angleterre* (1155); here first we find the Round Table. The oldest fragments of the legend are probably some Welsh tales now gathered in the *Mabinogion*; the oldest manuscripts of the developed story are French; Arthur's court and the Holy Grail are by common consent located in Wales and southwestern Britain. The earliest full presentation of the legend in prose is in an English manuscript doubtfully ascribed to an Oxford archdeacon, Walter Map (1137–96). The oldest verse form of the cycle is in the *romans* of Chrétien de Troyes (*c.* 1140–91).

Of Chrétien's life we know almost as little as of Arthur's. Early in his literary career he composed a *Tristan*, now lost. It reached the eyes of the Countess Marie de Champagne, daughter of Eleanor of Aquitaine, and apparently led her to hope that Chrétien might be the man to phrase "courtly love," and the highest ideals of chivalry, in the form of the *roman*. Marie invited him to be, so to speak, trouvère laureate at her court in Troyes. Under her patronage (1160–72) he composed four romances in rhyming couplets of eight-syllabled lines: *Erec et Enide*, *Cligès*, *Yvain*, and *Le Chevalier de la charrette* (*The Knight of the Wagon*)—no sublime title for the story of Lancelot the "perfect knight." In 1175, at the court of Philip, Count of Flanders, he began his *Conte del Graal*, or *Perceval le Gallois*, wrote 9000 lines, and left it to be finished to 60,000 lines by another hand. The atmosphere of these stories appears at the outset of *Erec*:

> One Easter Day King Arthur held court at Cardigan. Never was seen so rich a court; for many a good knight was there, hardy, bold, and brave, and rich ladies and damsels, gentle and fair daughters of kings. But before the court disbanded for the day the King told his knights that he wished on the morrow to hunt the White Stag, in

order to observe worthily the ancient custom. When my lord Gawain heard this he was sore displeased, and said: "Sire, you will derive neither thanks nor good will from this hunt. We all know long since what this custom of the White Stag is: whoever can kill the White Stag must kiss the fairest maiden of your court. . . . But of this there might come great ill; for there are here 500 damsels of high birth, . . . and there is none of them but has a bold and valiant knight who would be ready to contend, whether right or wrong, that she who is his lady is the fairest and gentlest of them all." "That I know full well," said the King; "yet will I not desist on that account. . . . Tomorrow we shall all go gaily to hunt the White Stag." [44]

And at the outset, too, the amusing exaggerations of romance: "Nature had used all her skill in forming Enid, and Nature had marveled more than 500 times how on this occasion she had succeeded in making so perfect a creature." In the Lancelot story we learn that "he who is a perfect lover is always obedient, and quickly and gladly does his mistress' pleasure. . . . Suffering is sweet to him; for Love, who guides and leads him on, assuages and relieves his pain."[45] But the Countess Marie had a flexible conception of love:

> If a knight found a damsel or lorn maid alone, and if he cared for his fair name, he would no more treat her with dishonor than he would cut his own throat. And if he assaulted her he would be disgraced forever in every court. But if, while she was under his escort, she should be won at arms by another who engaged him in battle, then this other knight might do with her what he pleased, without receiving shame or blame.[46]

Chrétien's verses are graceful but feeble, and their dull abundance soon surfeits our modern haste. He has the distinction of having written the first full and extant statement of the chivalric ideal, in his picture of a court where courtesy and honor, bravery and devoted love, seemed of more moment than Church or creed. In his final romance Chrétien proved true to his name, and raised the Arthurian cycle to a nobler pitch by adding to it the story of the Holy Grail.* Joseph of Arimathea, ran the tale, had caught some of the blood falling from the crucified Christ in the bowl from which Christ had drunk at the Last Supper; Joseph or his offspring had brought the bowl and the imperishable blood to Britain, where it was kept in a mysterious castle by an ailing imprisoned king; and only a knight perfectly pure in life and heart could find the Grail and free the king, by asking the cause of his illness. In Chrétien's story the Grail is sought by Perceval the Gaul; in the English form of the legend, by Galahad, the spotless son of the tarnished Lancelot; in both versions the finder carries it off to heaven. In Germany Wolfram

---

* *Grail* is uncertainly traced to a hypothetical *cratalis* derived from the Latin *crater*, cup.

von Eschenbach transformed Perceval into Parzival, and gave the tale its most famous medieval form.

Wolfram (*c.* 1165–*c.* 1220) was a Bavarian knight who risked his stomach on his verses, found patronage from the Landgrave Hermann of Thuringia, lived in the Castle Wartburg for twenty years, and wrote the outstanding poem of the thirteenth century. He must have dictated it, for we are assured that he never learned to read. He claimed to have derived his *Parzival* story not from Chrétien but from a Provençal poet named Kiot. We know of no such poet, nor of any other treatment of the legend between Chrétien's (1175) and Wolfram's (1205). Of the sixteen "books" in Wolfram's poem eleven seem based on Chrétien's *Conte del Graal.* The good Christians and fair knights of the Middle Ages felt no compulsion to acknowledge their literary debts. But the matter of the romances was felt to be common property; any man might forgivably borrow if he could improve. And Wolfram bettered Chrétien's tutelage.

Parzival is the son of a knight of Anjou by Queen Herzeleide (Sorrowful Heart), who is a granddaughter of Titurel—the first guardian of the Grail—and sister to Amfortas, its present ailing king. Shortly before she bears Parzival she learns that her husband has fallen in knightly combat before Alexandria. Resolved that Parzival shall not die so young, she brings him up in rural solitude, conceals from him his royal lineage, and keeps him ignorant of arms.

> Then full sore were her people grieved, for they held it an evil thing,
> And a training that ill beseemed the son of a mighty king.
> But his mother kept him hidden in the woodland valleys wild,
> Nor thought, in her love and sorrow, how she wronged the royal
>   child.
> No knightly weapon she gave him, save such as in childish play
> He wrought himself from the bushes that grew on his lonely way.
> A bow and arrows he made him, and with these, in thoughtless glee,
> He shot at the birds as they caroled o'erhead in the leafy tree.
> But when the feathered songster of the woods at his feet lay dead,
> In wonder and dumb amazement he bowed down his golden head,
> And in childish wrath and sorrow tore the locks of his sunny hair
> (For I know full well, of all earth's children was never a child so
>   fair). . . .
> Then he thought him well how the music, which his hand had forever
>   stilled,
> Had thrilled his soul with its sweetness, and his heart was with sorrow
>   filled.[47]

Parzival grows to manhood healthy and ignorant. One day he sees two knights on the road, admires their gleaming armor, thinks them gods, and falls on his knees before them. Informed that they are not gods but knights, he resolves to be as splendid as they. He leaves home to seek King Arthur, who makes men knights;

and his mother dies of grief at his going. On his way Parzival robs a sleeping duchess of a kiss, her girdle, and her ring; and the taint of this deed leaves him unclean for many years. He meets Ither the Red Knight, who sends by him a challenge to King Arthur. Presented to the King, Parzival asks permission to assume the challenge; he returns to Ither, slays him with beginner's luck, dons his armor, and rides off to seek adventure. At night he asks hospitality of Gurnemanz; the old baron takes a liking to him, teaches him the tricks of feudal combat, and gives him knightly counsel:

> Take pity on those in need; be kind, generous, and humble. The worthy man in need is ashamed to beg; anticipate his wants. . . . Yet be prudent, neither lavish nor miserly. . . . Do not ask too many questions, nor refuse to answer a question fitly asked. Observe and listen. . . . Spare him who yields, whatever wrong he has done you. . . . Be manly and gay. Hold women in respect and love; this increases a young man's honor. Be constant—that is manhood's part. Short his praise who betrays honest love.[48]

Parzival sallies forth again, rescues the besieged Kondwiramur, marries her, challenges her returning husband to combat, kills him, and leaves his wife in search of his mother. By chance he comes to the castle of the Grail. He is entertained by its guardian knights, sees the Grail (here a precious stone), and—remembering the good Gurnemanz' advice—asks no question about the magic Grail or the ailing king, whom he does not know to be his uncle. The next morning he finds the whole castle empty; he rides out, and the drawbridge rises behind him by unseen hands, as if forbidding his return. He rejoins Arthur's court; but amid his welcome there the seeress Kundry accuses him of ignorance and discourtesy in not having asked the cause of Amfortas' sickness. Parzival swears that he will find the Grail again.

But a mood of resentment darkens his life at this point. He feels that the disgrace that Kundry has laid upon him is unmerited; he perceives the abundance of injustice in the world, renounces and denounces God, and for four years visits no church, utters no prayer.[49] In those years he suffers a hundred misfortunes, ever seeking, never finding, the Grail. One day he stumbles upon the retreat of an anchorite, Trevrezent, who turns out to be his uncle; learns from him the story of the Grail, and how Amfortas' undying illness was due to leaving the guardianship of the Grail to serve an illicit love. The hermit wins Parzival back to Christian faith, and takes upon him the penalty of Parzival's sins. Humbled and chastened, cured of his ignorance and cleansed by his sufferings, Parzival resumes his quest of the Grail. The hermit reveals to Kundry that Parzival is Amfortas' nephew and heir; she finds him and announces that he has been chosen to succeed Amfortas as king and guardian of the Grail. Guided by her to the hidden castle, he asks Amfortas the cause of his illness, and at once the old king is healed. Parzival finds his wife Kondwiramur, who comes with him to be his queen. Lohengrin is their son.

As if to provide Wagner with another libretto, Gottfried of Strasbourg produced, about 1210, the most successful version of the Tristan story. It is an enthusiastic glorification of adultery and disloyalty, and dishonors the feudal as well as the Christian moral code.

Tristan, like Parzival, is born to a young mother, Blanchefleur, soon after she receives news that her prince husband has been killed in battle; she names the infant Tristan—sorrowful—and dies. The boy is reared and knighted by his uncle Mark, King of Cornwall. Grown up, he excels in tournaments, and kills the Irish challenger Morold; but in the combat he receives a poisoned wound, which the dying Morold tells him can be cured only by Ireland's queen Iseult. Disguised as Tantris, a harper, Tristan visits Ireland, is cured by the queen, and becomes the tutor of the queen's daughter, also named Iseult. Returning to Cornwall he tells Mark of the young Iseult's beauty and accomplishments, and Mark sends him back to woo her for him. Iseult is reluctant to leave her home; and discovering that Tristan is the slayer of her uncle Morold, she is inflamed with hatred for him. But the mother persuades her to go, and gives her maid Brangäne a love potion to administer to Iseult and Mark to arouse their love. The maid gives the potion by mistake to Iseult and Tristan, who soon fall into each other's arms. Dishonor multiplies; they agree to conceal their love; Iseult marries Mark, sleeps with Tristan, and plots to kill Brangäne as knowing too much. Mark is here (hardly in Malory) the only gentleman in the tale; he discovers the deception, tells Iseult and Tristan that they are too dear to him for revenge, and contents himself with exiling his nephew. In his wanderings Tristan meets a third Iseult, and falls in love with her, though he has sworn to be with Mark's queen "one heart, one troth, one body, one life." Here Gottfried leaves the tale unfinished, and all the ideals of chivalry shattered. The rest of the tale belongs to Malory and a later age.

In this astonishing generation—the first of the thirteenth century—Germany produced another poet who, with Walther, Wolfram, and Gottfried, made a quartet unequaled elsewhere in the literature of contemporary Christendom. Hartmann von Aue began by lamely following Chrétien in the poetic romances *Erec* and *Iwein*; but when he turned to the legends of his native Swabia he produced a minor masterpiece—*Der arme Heinrich* (*c.* 1205). "Poor Henry," like Job, is a rich man who at the height of his splendor is stricken with leprosy, which can only by cured (for medieval magic must have a say) when some pure maiden freely dies for him. Not expecting such a sacrifice, Henry abandons himself to lamentation and despair. But lo and behold, such a maiden appears, resolved to die that Heinrich may be healed. Her parents, thinking her decision God-inspired, give their incredible consent, and the girl bares her pretty bosom to the knife. But Heinrich suddenly becomes a man, calls a halt, refuses the sacrifice, stops his moaning, and accepts his pain as a divine visitation. Transformed in spirit by this new mood, his bodily ills rapidly disappear, and his rescuer becomes his wife. Hartmann redeemed the absurdity of the story with simple, flowing, unpretentious verse, and Germany treasured the poem until our unbelieving age.

A prettier tale was told, sometime in the first half of the thirteenth century, by an unknown Frenchman under the title *C'est d'Aucassin et*

Nicolette. Half romance, half laughing at romance, it was fittingly phrased now in poetry now in prose, with music noted in the poetic text.

Aucassin, son of the count of Beaucaire, falls in love with Nicolette, adoptive daughter of the viscount of Beaucaire. The count objects, desiring to marry his son into some feudal family that can bring him aid in war, and he bids his vassal viscount hide the girl. When Aucassin tries to see her the viscount counsels him to "leave Nicolette alone, or you will never see paradise." To which Aucassin answers in a literary correlate to the rising skepticism of the time.

> In paradise what have I to do? I care not to enter it, but only to have Nicolette.... For into paradise go none but such people as aged priests, old cripples, and the maimed, who all day and night cough before the altars.... With them have I nought to do. But to hell will I go. For to hell go the fine scholars, and the fair knights who are slain in the tourney or the great wars, and the stout archer, and the loyal man. With them will I go. And there go the fair and courteous ladies, who have friends—two or three—besides their wedded lord. And there pass the ... harpers and minstrels, and the kings of this world. With these will I go so only that I have Nicolette, my very sweet friend, by my side.[50]

Nicolette's father confines her to her room, and Aucassin's father imprisons him in a cellar, where the lad sings of a strange and charming cure:

> Nicolette, white lily-flower,
> Sweetest lady found in bower,
> Sweet as grape that brimmeth up
> Sweetness in the spicèd cup,
> On a day this chanced to you,
> Out of Limousin there drew
> One, a pilgrim, sore and dread,
> Lay in pain upon his bed,
> Tossed, and took with fear his breath,
> Very dolent, near to death.
> Then you entered, pure and white,
> Softly to the sick man's sight
> Raised the train that swept adown,
> Raised the ermine-bordered gown,
> Raised the smock, and bared to him
> Daintily each lovely limb.
> Then a wondrous thing befell,
> Straight he rose up sound and well,
> Left his bed, took cross in hand,
> Sought again his own dear land.
> Lily-flower, so white, so sweet,
> Fair the faring of thy feet,
> Fair thy laughter, fair thy speech,

> Fair our playing each with each.
> Sweet thy kisses, soft thy touch,
> All must love thee overmuch.[51]

Meanwhile the lily-flower makes a rope of her bed sheets, and lets herself down into the garden.

> Then she took her skirt in both hands . . . and kilted her lightly against the dew which lay thickly on the grass, and so she passed through the garden. Her hair was golden, with little love-locks; her eyes blue and laughing; her face most dainty to see, with lips more vermeil than ever rose or cherry in summer heat; her teeth white and small; her breasts so firm that they showed beneath her vesture like two rounded nuts. So frail was she about the girdle that your two hands could have spanned her; and the daisies that she brake with her feet in passing showed altogether black against her instep and her flesh, so white was the fair young maid.[52]

She finds her way to a barred window of Aucassin's cell, cuts a tress of her hair, slips it to him, and swears that her love is as great as his. Her father sends searchers for her; she flees into the woods, and lives with appreciative shepherds. After some time Aucassin's father, thinking her safely out of sight, frees him. Aucassin takes to the woods and hunts for her through half-comic vicissitudes. He finds her, sets her before him on his horse, "kissing her as they rode." To escape their pursuing parents they take ship across the Mediterranean; they come to a land where men give birth and wars are fought by jolly pummeling with fruit. They are captured by less amiable warriors, are separated for three years, but at last are made one again. The irate parents kindly die, and Aucassin and Nicolette become the Count and Countess of Beaucaire. There is nothing more exquisite in all the rich literature of France.

VIII. THE SATIRICAL REACTION

The humorous interludes of this story suggest that the French were beginning to feel a surfeit of romance. The most famous poem of the Middle Ages—far more widely known and read than *The Divine Comedy*—began as a romance and ended as one of the heartiest, bluntest satires in history. About 1237 Guillaume de Lorris, a young scholar of Orléans, composed an allegorical poem which was designed to enclose the whole art of courtly love, and to be, through its very abstractions, a model and summary of all amorous romance. We know nothing of William of the Loire except that he wrote the first 4266 lines of the *Roman de la rose*. He pictures himself wandering in a dream into a gorgeous Garden of Love, where every known flower blooms and all birds sing, and happy couples, personifying the joys and graces of the gallant life—Mirth, Gladness, Courtesy, Beauty . . . —dance under the presidency of the God of Love; here is a new religion, with a new conception of paradise, in which woman replaces God. Within this garden the dreamer sees a rose lovelier than all the beauty that surrounds it, but guarded by a thousand thorns. It is the symbol of the Beloved; and the hero's longing to reach and pluck it becomes an allegory of all the amorous campaigns ever waged by checked desire feeding imagination. No human being but the narrator enters the tale; all the other actors are personifications of the qualities of character to be found at any court where women are pursued by men: Fair-Seeming, Pride, Villainy, Shame, Wealth, Avarice, Envy, Sloth, Hypocrisy, Youth, Despair, even "New Thought"—which here means inconstancy. The marvel of it is that with these abstractions Guillaume managed to make interesting verse—perhaps because at any age and in any guise love is as interesting as the blood is warm.*

William died prematurely, leaving his poem unfinished; and for forty years the world had to wonder if the Lover, shot by Cupid and shivering with love, had ever done more than kiss the Rose. Then another Frenchman, Jean de Meung, took up the torch, and carried it to over 22,000 lines, in a poem as different from William's as Rabelais from Tennyson. The lapse of a generation had changed the mood; romance had talked itself out for a while; philosophy was casting the pall of reason over the poetry of faith; the Crusades had failed; the age of doubt and satire had begun. Some say that Jean wrote his boisterous continuation at the suggestion of the same King Philip IV who would send his skeptical lawyers to laugh in the face of the Pope. Jean Clopinel was born at Meung on the Loire about 1250, studied philosophy and literature at Paris, and became one of the most learned men of his time. We know not what imp of the perverse led him to put his learning, his anticlericalism, his contempt of woman and romance, into a continuation of the most romantic poem in all literature. In the same eight-syllabled lines and rhyming couplets as William's, but with a verve and vivacity all the world away from William's dreamy verse, Jean airs his views on all topics from the Creation to the Last Judgment, while his poor lover waits in the garden, all this time longing for the Rose. If Jean has any romance left in him it is Plato's fancy of a Golden Age in the past, when "no man called this or that his own, and lust and rapine were unknown"; when there were no feudal lords, no state, no laws; when men lived without eating flesh or fish or fowl, and "all shared earth's gift in common lot."[53] He is not a freethinker; he accepts the dogmas of the Church without winking an eye; but he dislikes "those stout and thriving blades, the begging friars, who cheat with lying words while drink and meat they batten on."[54] He cannot stomach hypocrites, and recommends garlic and onions to them to facilitate their

---

* Chaucer's translation—*The Romaunt of the Rose*—of the first half of William's poem is as fine as the original.

crocodile tears.[55] He admits that a "gracious woman's love" is life's best boon, but apparently he has not known it.[56] Perhaps he did not deserve it; satire never won fair maiden; and Jean, too schooled in Ovid, thought and taught more of using women than of loving them. Monogamy is absurd, he says; nature intended *toutes pour touz*—all women for all men. He makes a sated husband chide a primping wife:

> What comes of all this bravery?
> What benefit accrues to me
> From costly gowns and quaint-cut gear,
> Your flirting tricks and mincing cheer?
> What for these orphreys do I care
> With which you twist and bind your hair,
> Entwined with threads of gold? And why
> Must you have set in ivory
> Enameled mirrors, sprinkled o'er
> With golden circlets? . . . Why these gems
> Befitting kingly diadems?—
> Rubies and pearls, and sapphires fair,
> Which cause you to assume an air
> Of mad conceit? These costly stuffs,
> And plaited furbelows and ruffs,
> And cinctures to set off your waist,
> With pearls bedecked and richly chased?
> And wherefore, say, then, do you choose
> To fit your feet with gaudy shoes
> Except you have a lust to show
> Your shapely legs? By St. Thibaud,
> Ere yet three days are past I'll sell
> This trash, and trample you pell-mell! [57]

It is some consolation to learn that in the end the God of Love, at the head of his innumerable vassals, storms the tower where Danger, Shame, and Fear (the lady's hesitations) guard the Rose, and Welcome admits the Lover to the inner shrine, and lets him pluck the image of his dreams. But how can this long-deferred romantic termination wipe out 18,000 lines of peasant realism and goliardic ribaldry?

The three most widely read books in the Western Europe of the twelfth and thirteenth centuries were the *Romance of the Rose*, the *Golden Legend*, and *Reynard the Fox*. Reynard began his Latin career as Ysengrinus about 1150, and passed into various vernaculars as *Roman de Renart, Reynard the Fox, Reineke de Vos, Reinaert*, finally as Goethe's *Reinecke Fuchs*. Divers authors contributed some thirty merry tales to the cycle until it totaled 24,000 lines, nearly all devoted to satirizing feudal forms, royal courts, Christian ceremonies, and human frailties through animal analogies.

Renart the fox plays impish tricks on Noble the lion, king of the realm. He scents Noble's amour with Dame Harouge the leopardess, and by intrigues worthy of Talleyrand he persuades her to play mistress to himself. He propitiates Noble and other beasts by giving each a talisman that tells a husband of his wife's infidelities. Dreadful revelations ensue; the husbands beat their guilty wives, who flee for refuge to Renart, who gathers them into a harem. In one tale the animals engage in a tournament, in solemn knightly regalia and parade. In *La Mort Renart* the old fox is dying; Bernard the ass, archbishop of the court, comes to administer the sacraments to him with extreme unction and gravity. Renart confesses his sins, but stipulates that if he recovers his oath of reform is to be held null and void. To all appearances he dies, and the many beasts whom he has cuckolded, beaten, plucked, or cozened gather to mourn him with happy hypocrisy. The archbishop preaches a Rabelaisian sermon over the grave, and reproaches Renart for having considered "anything in season if you could get hold of it." But when holy water is sprinkled upon him Renart revives, catches Chantecler (who is swinging the censer) by the neck, and bolts into a thicket with his prey. To understand the Middle Ages one must never forget Renart.

The *Roman de Renart* was the greatest of the *fabliaux*. A *fabliau* was a fable of animals satirizing man, usually in octosyllabic verse running from thirty to a thousand lines. Some were as old as Aesop or older; some came from India through Islam. Mostly they lampooned women and priests, resenting the natural powers of the one class and the supernatural powers of the other; besides, ladies and priests had condemned the minstrels for reciting scandalous *fabliaux*. For the *fabliaux* were directed to strong stomachs; they appropriated the terminology of taverns and brothels, and gave meter to unmeasured pleasantries. But from their stews Chaucer, Boccaccio, Ariosto, La Fontaine, and a hundred other raconteurs brewed many a startling tale.

The rise of satire lowered the status of minstrelsy. The traveling singers derived their English name from the *ministeriales*, originally attendants in baronial courts, and their French name of jongleurs from the Latin *ioculator*, a purveyor of jokes. They filled the functions, and continued the lineage, of Greek rhapsodes, Roman mimes, Scandinavian scalds, Anglo-Saxon gleemen, and Welsh or Irish bards. In the twelfth-century heyday of the romances the minstrels took the place of printing, and kept their dignity by purveying stories occasionally worthy to be classed as literature. Harp or viol in hand, they recited lays, *dits* or *contes* (short stories), epics, legends of Mary or the saints, *chansons de geste*, *romans*, or *fabliaux*. In Lent, when they were not in demand, they attended, if they could, a *confrèrie* of minstrels and jongleurs like that which we know to have been held at Fécamp in Normandy about the year 1000; there they learned one another's tricks and airs, and the new tales or songs of trouvères and troubadours. Many of them were willing, if their recitations proved too much of an intellectual strain for their audiences, to entertain them with juggling, tumbling, contortions, and rope walking. When the trouvères went about reciting their own stories, and when the habit of reading spread and reduced the demand for reciters, the minstrel became more and more of a vaudevillian, so that the jongleur became a juggler; he tossed knives, pulled Punch and Judy puppets, or displayed the repertoire of trained bears, apes, horses, cocks, dogs, camels, and lions. Some of the minstrels turned *fabliaux* into farces, and acted them without skimping the obscenities. The Church more and more frowned upon them, and forbade the pious to listen to them, or the kings to feed them; and Bishop Honorius of Autun was of the opinion that no minstrel would be admitted to paradise.

The popularity of the jongleurs and the *fabliaux*, and the uproarious welcome with which the newly lettered classes, and the rebellious students of the universities, received Jean de Meung's epic of the *bourgeoisie*, marked the end of an age. Romance would continue, but it was challenged on every hand by satire, humor, and a realistic earthy mood that laughed at tales of chivalry long before Cervantes was born. For a century now satire would hold the stage, and would gnaw at the heart of faith until all the props and ribs of the medieval structure would crack and break, and leave the soul of man proud and tottering on the brink of reason.

CHAPTER XXXIX

Dante

1265-1321

I. THE ITALIAN TROUBADOURS

IT was at the Apulian court of Frederick II that Italian literature was born. Perhaps the Moslems in his retinue contributed some stimulus, for every literate Moslem versified. Some years before Frederick's death in 1250, Ciullo d'Alcamo (*c.* 1200) wrote a pretty "Dialogue Between Lover and Lady"; and Alcamo, in Sicily, was almost wholly a Moslem town. But a more decisive influence came from the troubadours of Provence, who sent their poems, or came in person, to the appreciative Frederick and his cultured aides. Frederick himself not only supported poetry, he wrote it, and in Italian. His prime minister, Piero delle Vigne, composed excellent sonnets, and may have invented that arduous form. Rinaldo d'Aquino (brother to St. Thomas), living at Frederick's court, Guido delle Colonne, a judge, and Iacopo da Lentino, a notary, in Frederick's *Regno*, were among the poets of this "Apulian Renaissance." A sonnet by Iacopo (*c.* 1233), a generation before Dante's birth, has already the delicacy of sentiment and finish of form of the poems in the *Vita Nuova*:

> I have it in my heart to serve God so
>   That into paradise I shall repair—
>   The holy place through the which everywhere
> I have heard say that joy and solace flow.
> Without my lady I were loath to go—
>   She who has the bright face and the bright hair;
>   Because if she were absent, I being there,
> My pleasure would be less than nought, I know.
> Look you, I say not this to such intent
>   As that I there would deal in any sin;
>   I only would behold her gracious mien,
>   And beautiful soft eyes, and lovely face,
> That so it should be my complete content
>   To see my lady joyful in her place.[1]

When Frederick's court traveled through Italy he took poets along with his menagerie, and they spread their influence into Latium, Tuscany, and Lombardy. His son Manfred continued his patronage of poetry, and wrote lyrics that Dante praised. Much of this "Sicilian" verse was translated into Tuscan, and shared in forming the school of poets that culminated in Dante. At the same time French troubadours, leaving a Languedoc harried by religious wars, found refuge in Italian courts, initiated Italian poets into the *gai saber*, taught Italian women to welcome verse eulogies, and persuaded Italian magnates to reward poetry even when addressed to their wives. Some early Tuscan poets carried their imitation of the French troubadours so far as to write in Provençal. Sordello (*c.* 1200–70), born near Virgil's Mantua, offended the terrible Ezzelino, fled to Provence, and wrote, in Provençal, poems of ethereal and fleshless love.

Out of this Platonic passion, by a strange marriage of metaphysics and poetry, came the *dolce stil nuovo*, or "sweet new style" of Tuscany. Instead of the frank sensuality which they found in the Provençal singers, the Italian poets preferred or pretended to love women as embodiments of pure and abstract beauty, or as symbols of divine wisdom or philosophy. This was a new note in an Italy that had known a hundred thousand poets of love. Perhaps the spirit of St. Francis moved these chaste pens, or the *Summa* of Thomas weighed upon them, or they felt the influence of Arabic mystics who saw only God in beauty, and wrote love poems to the deity.[2]

A bevy of learned singers constituted the new school. Guido Guinizelli (1230?–75) of Bologna, whom Dante saluted as his literary father,[3] rhymed the new philosophy of love in a famous *canzone* (the Provençal *canzo* or song) "Of the Gentle Heart," where he asked God's pardon for loving his lady so, on the plea that she seemed an embodiment of divinity. Lapa Gianni, Dino Frescobaldi, Guido Orlandi, Cino da Pistoia, spread the new style through northern Italy. It was brought to Florence by its finest pre-Dantean exponent, Guido Cavalcanti (*c.* 1258–1300), Dante's friend. By exception among these scholar poets, Guido was a noble, son-in-law of that Farinata degli Uberti who led the Ghibelline faction in Florence. He was an Averroistic freethinker, and played with doubts of immortality, even of God.[4] He took an active, violent part in politics, was exiled by Dante and the other priors in 1300, fell ill, was pardoned, and died in that same year. His proud, aristocratic mind was well fitted to mold sonnets of cold and classic grace:

> Beauty in woman; the high will's decree;
>   Fair knighthood armed for manly exercise;
>   The pleasant song of birds; love's soft replies;
> The strength of rapid ships upon the sea;
> The serene air when light begins to be;
>   The white snow, without wind, that falls and lies;
>   Fields of all flowers, the place where waters rise;
> Silver and gold; azure in jewelry:
> Weighed against these the sweet and quiet worth
>   Which my dear lady cherishes at heart

Might seem a little matter to be shown;
Being truly, over these, as much apart
As the whole heaven is greater than this earth.
All good to kindred creatures cleaveth soon.[5]

Dante learned much from Guido, imitated his *canzoni*, and perhaps owed to him the decision to write *The Divine Comedy* in Italian. "He desired," says Dante, "that I should always write to him in the vernacular speech, not in Latin."[6] In the course of the thirteenth century Dante's predecessors molded the new tongue from rude inadequacy to such melody of speech, such concentration and subtlety of phrase, as no other European vernacular could match; they created a language that Dante could call "illustrious, cardinal, courtly, and curial"[7]—fit for the highest dignities. Beside their sonnets the verses of the Provençaux were inharmonious, those of the trouvères and the minnesingers almost doggerel. Here poetry had become no rhyming rivulet of gay garrulity but a work of intense and compact art as painstakingly carved as the figures on the pulpits of Niccolò Pisano and his son. Partly a great man is great because those less than he have paved his way, have molded the mood of the time to his genius, have fashioned an instrument for his hands, and have given him a task already half done.

II. DANTE AND BEATRICE

In May 1265 Bella Alighieri presented to her husband, Alighiero Alighieri, a son whom they christened Durante Alighieri; probably they took no thought that the words meant *long-lasting wing-bearer*. Apparently the poet himself shortened his first name to Dante.[8] His family had a lengthy pedigree in Florence, but had slipped into poverty. The mother died in Dante's early years; Alighiero married again, and Dante grew up, perhaps unhappily, with a stepmother, a half brother, and two half sisters.[9] The father died when Dante was fifteen, leaving a heritage of debts.[10]

Of Dante's teachers he remembered most gratefully Brunetto Latini, who, returning from France, had shortened his French encyclopedia, *Tresor*, into an Italian *Tesoretto*; from him Dante learned *come l'uom s'eterna*—how man immortalizes himself.[11] Dante must have studied Virgil with especial delight; he speaks of the Mantuan's *bel stilo*; and what other student has so loved a classic as to follow its author through hell? Boccaccio tells of Dante being at Bologna in 1287. There or elsewhere the poet picked up so much of the sorry science and miraculous philosophy of his time that his poem became top-heavy with his erudition. He learned also to ride, hunt, fence, paint, and sing. How he earned his bread we do not know. In any case he was admitted to cultured circles, if only through his friendship with Cavalcanti. In that circle he found many poets.

The most famous of all love affairs began when both Dante and Beatrice were nine years old. According to Boccaccio the occasion was a May Day feast in the home of Folco Portinari, one of the leading citizens of Florence. Little "Bice" was Folco's daughter; that she was also Dante's Beatrice is probable,[12] but not close enough to certainty to calm the doubts of the meticulous. We know of this first meeting only through the idealized description written by Dante nine years later in the *Vita nuova*:

> Her dress on that day was of a most noble color, a subdued and goodly crimson, girdled and adorned in such sort as suited with her very tender age. At that moment I say most truly that the spirit of life, which hath its dwelling in the secretest chamber of the heart, began to tremble so violently that the least pulses of my body shook therewith; and in trembling it said these words: *Ecce deus fortior me, qui veniens dominabitur mihi* [Behold a deity stronger than I, who, coming, will rule me]. . . . From that time forward Love quite governed my soul.[13]

A lad nearing puberty is ripe for such a trembling; most of us have known it, and can look back upon "calf love" as one of the most spiritual experiences of our youth, a mysterious awakening of body and soul to life and sex and beauty and our individual incompleteness, and yet with no conscious hunger of body for body, but only a shy longing to be near the beloved, to serve her, and hear her speak, and watch her modest grace. Give the male soul such sensitivity as Dante's—a man of passion and imagination—and such a revelation and ripening might well remain a lifelong memory and stimulus. He tells us how he sought opportunities to see Beatrice, if only to gaze unseen upon her. Then he seems to have lost sight of her until, nine years later, when they were eighteen,

> it happened that the same wonderful lady appeared to me dressed all in pure white, between two gentle [i.e., highborn] ladies elder than she. And passing through a street, she turned her eyes thither where I stood sorely abashed; and by her unspeakable courtesy . . . she saluted me with so virtuous a bearing that I seemed then and there to behold the very limits of blessedness. . . . I parted thence as one intoxicated. . . . Then, for that I had myself in some sort the art of discoursing with rhyme, I resolved on making a sonnet.[14]

So, if we may believe his account, was born his sequence of sonnets and commentaries known as *La vita nuova*, *The New Life*. At intervals in the next nine years (1283–92) he composed the sonnets, and later added the prose. He sent one sonnet after another to Cavalcanti, who preserved them and now became his friend. The whole romance is in some measure a literary artifice. The poems are spoiled for our changed taste by their fanciful deification of Love in the manner of the troubadours, by the long scholastic dissertations that interpret them, and by a number mysticism of threes and nines; we must discount these infections of the time.

> Love saith concerning her: "How chanceth it
>   That flesh, which is of dust, should be thus pure?"
>   Then, gazing always, he makes oath: "For sure,
>   This is a creature of God till now unknown."
> She hath that paleness of the pearl that's fit
>   In a fair woman, so much and not more.
>   She is as high as nature and skill can soar;
>   Beauty is tried by her comparison.
> Whatever her sweet eyes are turned upon,
>   Spirits of love do issue thence in flame,
>   Which through their eyes who then may look on them
> Pierce to the heart's deep chamber every one.
> And in her smile Love's image you may see;
> Whence none can gaze upon her steadfastly.[15]

Some of the prose is more pleasing than the verse:

> When she appeared in any place it seemed to me, by the hope of her excellent salutation, that there was no man mine enemy any longer; and such warmth of charity came upon me that most certainly in that moment I would have pardoned whosoever had done me an injury. . . . She went along crowned and clothed with humility . . . and when she had gone it was said by many: "This is not a woman, but one of the beautiful angels of heaven" . . . I say, of very sooth, that she showed herself so very gentle that she bred in those who looked upon her a soothing quiet beyond any speech.[16]

There is no thought, in this possibly artificial infatuation, of marriage with Beatrice. In 1289 she wedded Simone de' Bardi, member of a rich banking firm. Dante took no notice of so superficial an incident, but continued to write poems about her, without mentioning her name. A year later Beatrice died, aged twenty-four, and the poet, for the first time naming her, mourned her in a quiet elegy:

> Beatrice is gone up into high heaven,
>   The kingdom where the angels are at peace,
>   And lives with them, and to her friends is dead.
> Not by the frost of winter was she driven
>   Away, like others, nor by summer heats;
>   But through a perfect gentleness instead.
>   For from the lamp of her meek lowlihead
> Such an exceeding glory went up hence
>   That it woke wonder in the Eternal Sire,
>   Until a sweet desire
> Entered Him for that lovely excellence,

> So that He bade her to Himself aspire,
> Counting this weary and most evil place
> Unworthy of a thing so full of grace.[17]

In another poem he pictured her surrounded with homage in paradise. "After writing this sonnet," he tells us,

> it was given unto me to behold a very wonderful vision, wherein I saw things which determined me that I would say nothing further of this blessed one until such time as I could discourse more worthily concerning her. And to this end I labor all I can, as she well knoweth. Wherefore, if it be His pleasure through Whom is the life of all things, that my life continue with me a few years, it is my hope that I shall yet write concerning her what hath not before been written of any woman. After the which may it seem good unto Him Who is the Master of Grace, that my spirit should go hence to behold the glory of its lady, to wit, of that blessed Beatrice who now gazeth continually on His countenance.

So, in the concluding words of his little book, he laid his sights for a greater one; and "from the first day that I saw her face in this life, until this vision" with which he ends the *Paradiso*, "the sequence of my song was never cut." [18] Rarely has any man, through all the tides and storms in his affairs, charted and kept so straight a course.

III. THE POET IN POLITICS

However, there were deviations. Some time after Beatrice' death Dante indulged himself in a series of light loves—"Pietra," "Pargoletta," "Lisetta," "or other vanity of such brief use." [19] To one lady, whom he names only *gentil donna*, he addressed love poems less ethereal than those to Beatrice. About 1291, aged twenty-six, he married Gemma Donati, a descendant of the oldest Florentine aristocracy. In ten years she gave him several children, variously reckoned at three, four, or seven.[20] Faithful to the troubadour code, he never mentioned his wife or his children in his poetry. It would have been indelicate. Marriage and romantic love were things apart.

Now, perhaps through Cavalcanti's aid, he entered politics. For reasons unknown to us he joined the Whites or *Bianchi*—the party of the upper middle class. He must have had ability, for as early as 1300 he was elected to the Priory or municipal council. During his brief incumbency the Blacks or *Neri*, led by Corso Donati, attempted a *coup d'état* to restore the old nobility to power. After suppressing this revolt the priors, Dante concurring, sought to promote peace by banishing the leaders of both parties—among them Donati, Dante's relative by marriage, and Cavalcanti, his friend. In 1301 Donati invaded Florence with a band of armed Blacks, deposed the priors, and captured the government. Early in 1302 Dante and fifteen other citizens were tried and convicted on various political charges, were exiled, and were sentenced to be burned to death if they should ever enter Florence again. Dante fled, and, hoping soon to return, left his family behind him. This exile, with confiscation of his property, condemned the poet to indigent wandering for nineteen years, embittered his spirit, and in some measure determined the mood and theme of *The Divine Comedy*. His fellow exiles, against Dante's advice, persuaded Arezzo, Bologna, and Pistoia to send against Florence an army of 10,000 men to restore them to power or their homes (1304). The attempt failed, and thereafter Dante followed an individual course, living with friends in Arezzo, Bologna, and Padua.

It was during the first decade of his exile that he gathered together some of the poems he had written to the *gentil donna*, and added to them a prose commentary transforming her into Dame Philosophy. The *Convivio* (*Banquet*, c. 1308) tells how, in the disappointments of love and life, Dante turned to philosophy for solace; what a divine revelation he found in the seductive study; and how he resolved to share his findings, in Italian, with those who could not read Latin. Apparently he had in mind to write a new *Summa* or *Tesoro*, in which each part would pretend to be a commentary on a poem about the beautiful lady; it was a remarkable scheme for redeeming the sensuous with the arid. The little book is a hodge-podge of weird science, farfetched allegories, and snatches of philosophy from Boethius and Cicero. We must mark it as a credit to Dante's intelligence that after completing three of fourteen intended commentaries he abandoned the book as a total loss.

He took on now the modest task of re-establishing the rule of the Holy Roman emperors in Italy. His experience had convinced him that the chaos and violence of politics in the Italian cities were due to an atomistic conception of freedom—each region, city, class, individual, and desire demanding anarchic liberty. Like Machiavelli two centuries later, he longed for some power that would co-ordinate individuals, classes, and cities into an orderly whole within which men might work and live in security and peace. That unifying power could come either from the pope or from the head of the Holy Roman Empire, to which northern Italy had long been subject in theory. But Dante had just been exiled by a party allied with the papacy; an uncertain tradition says that he had taken part in an unsuccessful embassy from Florence to Boniface VIII; and for a long time the popes had opposed the unification of Italy as a danger to their spiritual freedom as well as their temporal power. The only hope of order seemed to lie in the restoration of Imperial control, in a return to the majestic *pax Romana* of ancient Rome.

So, at a date unknown, Dante wrote his provocative treatise *De monarchia*. Writing in Latin as still the language of philosophy, Dante argued that since the appropriate function of man is intellectual activity, and since this can proceed only in peace, the ideal government would be a world state maintaining a stable order and uniform justice over all the earth. Such a state would be the proper image and correlate of the celestial order established throughout the universe by God. Imperial Rome had come nearest to being such an international state; God's approval of it was made manifest by His choosing to become man under Augustus; and Christ Himself had bidden men accept the political authority of the Caesars. Obviously the authority of the ancient Empire had not been derived from the Church. But the Holy Roman Empire was that older Empire revived. It is true that a pope crowned Charlemagne, and thereby appeared to make the Empire subordinate to the papacy; but the "usurpation of a right does not create a right; if it did, the same method could show the dependency of ecclesiastical authority on the Empire after the Emperor Otto restored Pope Leo and deposed Benedict." [21] The right of the Empire to govern was derived not from the Church but from the natural law that social order requires government; and since natural law is the will of God, the state derives its powers from God. It is indeed proper that the emperor should acknowledge the superior authority of the pope in matters of faith and morals; but this does not limit the sovereignty of the state in "the earthly sphere." [22]

The *De monarchia*, despite a scholastic mechanism of disputation no longer appetizing to the fashions of thought, was a powerful argument for "one world" of government and law. The manuscript was known only to a few during the author's lifetime. After his death it was more widely circulated, and was used as propaganda by the antipapal Louis the Bavarian. It was publicly burned by order of a papal legate in 1329, was placed on the papal Index of Forbidden Books in the sixteenth century, and was removed from that Index by Leo XIII in 1897.

According to Boccaccio,[23] Dante wrote the *De monarchia* "at the coming of Henry VI." In the year 1310 the King of Germany invaded Italy in the hope of re-establishing over all the peninsula except the Papal States that Imperial rule which had died with Frederick II. Dante welcomed him with excited hopes. In a "Letter to the Princes and Peoples of Italy" he called upon the Lombard cities to open their hearts and gates to the Luxembourg "Arrigo" who would deliver them from chaos and the pope. When Henry reached Milan Dante hastened thither and threw himself enthusiastically at the feet of the Emperor; all his dreams of a united Italy seemed near fulfillment. Florence, heedless of the poet, closed her gates against Henry, and Dante publicly addressed an angry letter *Scelestissimis Florentinis*—"to the most criminal Florentines" (March, 1311).

> Know ye not God hath ordained that the human race be under the rule of one emperor for the defense of justice, peace, and civilization, and that Italy has always been a prey to civil war whenever the Empire lapsed? You who transgress laws human and divine, you whom the

awful insatiability of avarice has led to be ready for any crimes—does not the terror of the second death harass you, that ye, first and alone . . . have raged against the glory of the Roman prince, the monarch of the earth and the ambassador of God? . . . Most foolish and insensate men! Ye shall succumb perforce to the Imperial Eagle! [24]

To Dante's dismay Henry took no action against Florence. In April the poet wrote to the Emperor like a Hebrew prophet warning kings:

We marvel what sluggishness delays you so long. . . . You waste the spring as well as the winter at Milan. . . . Florence (do you perchance know it not?) is the dire evil. . . . This is the viper . . . from her evaporating corruption she exhales an infectious smoke, and thence the neighboring flocks waste away. . . . Up, then, thou noble child of Jesse! [25]

Florence responded by declaring Dante forever excluded from amnesty and from Florence. Henry left Florence untouched, and passed via Genoa and Pisa to Rome and Siena, where he died (1313).

It was a crowning disaster for Dante. He had staked everything on Henry's victory, had burned all bridges to Florence behind him. He fled to Gubbio, and took refuge in the monastery of Santa Croce. There, apparently, he wrote much of *The Divine Comedy*.[26] But he had not yet had his fill of politics. In 1316 he was probably with Uguccione della Faggiuola at Lucca; in that year Uguccione defeated the Florentines at Montecatini; Florence recovered, and included Dante's two sons in a sentence of death—which was never carried out. Lucca revolted against Uguccione, and Dante was again homeless. Florence, in a mood of victorious generosity, and forgetting its forevers, offered amnesty and safe return to all exiles on condition that they pay a fine, walk through the streets in penitential garb, and submit to a brief imprisonment. A friend notified Dante of the proclamation. He replied in a famous letter:

To a Florentine friend: From your letter, which I received with due reverence and affection, I have learned with a grateful heart . . . how dear to your soul is my return to my country. Behold, then, the ordinance . . . that if I were willing to pay a certain amount of money, and suffer the stigma of oblation, I should be pardoned, and could return forthwith. . . .

Is this, then, the glorious recall wherewith Dante Alighieri is summoned back to his country after an exile patiently endured for almost fifteen years? . . . Far be it from a man who preaches justice . . . to pay his money to those inflicting injustice, as though they were his benefactors. This is not the way to return to my country. . . . If another way may be found . . . which does not derogate from the honor of Dante, that will I take with no lagging steps. But if Florence is not to be entered by such a path, then never will I enter. . . . What! Can I not look upon the face of the sun and the stars everywhere? Can I not under any sky contemplate the most precious truths? [27]

Probably toward the close of the year 1316 he accepted the invitation of Can Grande della Scala, ruler of Verona, to come and live as his guest. There, apparently, he finished—there he dedicated to Can Grande—the *Paradiso* of *The Divine Comedy* (1318). We may picture him at this period—aged fifty-one—as Boccaccio described him in the *Vita* of 1354: a man of medium height, "somewhat stooped," walking with grave and measured gait in somber dignity; dark hair and skin, long and pensive face, furrowed projecting brow, stern deep eyes, thin aquiline nose, tight lips, a pugnacious chin.[28] It was the face of a spirit once gentle, but hardened to bitterness by pain; the Dante of the *Vita nuova* could hardly have affected all the tenderness and sensibility there expressed; and something of those qualities appears in the pity with which he hears Francesca's tale. He was grim and austere as became a defeated exile; his tongue was sharpened by adversity; and he became imperious to cover his fall from power. He prided himself on his ancestry because he was poor. He despised the money-making *bourgeoisie* of Florence; he could not forgive Portinari for marrying Beatrice to a banker; and he took the only revenge open to him by placing usurers in one of the deepest pits of hell. He never forgot an injury or a slight, and there were few of his enemies who escaped damnation from his pen. He had less use than Solon for those who remained neutral in revolution or in war. The secret of his character was a flaming intensity. "Not by the grace of riches but by the grace of God I am what I am, and the zeal of His house hath eaten me up." [29]

He poured all his strength into his poem, and could not long survive its completion. In 1319 he left Verona and went to live with Count Guido da Polenta at Ravenna. He received an invitation from Bologna to come and be crowned poet laureate; he answered no in a Latin eclogue. In 1321 Guido sent him to Venice on a political mission, which failed; Dante returned with a fever caught from the marshes of the Veneto. He was too weak to fight it off, and it killed him on September 14, 1321, in the fifty-seventh year of his age. The Count planned to raise a handsome tomb above the poet's grave, but it was not done. The bas-relief that stands above the marble coffin today was carved by Pietro Lombardo in 1483. There, as all the world knows, Byron came and wept. Today the tomb lies almost unnoticed around the corner from Ravenna's busiest square; and its old and crippled custodian, for a few lire, will recite sonorous beauties from the poem that all men praise and few men read.

IV. *THE DIVINE COMEDY*

1. The Poem

Boccaccio relates that Dante began it in Latin hexameters, but changed to Italian to reach a broader audience. Perhaps the ardor of his feelings affected his choice; it seemed easier to be passionate in Italian than in a Latin so long associated with classic urbanity and restraint. In youth he had restricted Italian to the poetry of love; but now that his theme was the highest philosophy of human redemption through love he wondered dared he speak in the "vulgar" tongue. At some uncertain time he had begun—and then had left unfinished—a Latin essay *De vulgari eloquentia* (*On Vernacular Eloquence*), aspiring to win the learned to wider literary use of the vernacular; he had praised the compact majesty of Latin, but had expressed the hope that through the poetry of Frederick's *Regno* and the *stil nuovo* of the Lombard and Tuscan *trovatori* an Italian language might rise above its dialects to be (as the *Convivio* put it) "full of the sweetest and most exquisite beauty."[30] Even Dante's pride could hardly dream that his epic would not only make Italian a language fit for any enterprise of letters, but would raise it to such *dolce bellezza* as the world's literature has seldom known.

Never was a poem more painstakingly planned. A weakness for triads—as reflecting the Trinity—molded its form: there were to be three "canticles," each of thirty-three cantos, to correspond with the years of Christ's earthly life; an extra canto in the first canticle would make a neat round hundred; each canto was to be written in groups of three lines; and the second line of each group was to rhyme with the first and third of the next. Nothing could be more artificial; yet all art is artifice, though at its best concealed; and the *terza rima* or triple rhyme binds each stanza with its successor, and weaves them all into a continued song (*canto*), which in the original flows trippingly on the tongue, but in translation limps and halts on borrowed feet. Dante in advance condemned all translations of Dante: "Nothing that hath the harmony of musical connection can be transferred from its own tongue to another without shattering all its sweetness and harmony."[31] *

As number dictated the form, so allegory planned the tale. In his dedicatory epistle to Can Grande,[32] Dante explained the symbolism of his canticles. We might suspect this interpretation to be the afterthought of a poet who longed to be a philosopher; but the addiction of the Middle Ages to symbolism, the allegorical sculptures of the cathedrals, the allegorical frescoes of Giotto, Gaddi, and Raphael, and Dante's allegorical sublimations in the *Vita nuova* and the *Convivio* suggest that the poet really had in mind

---

* We should except Dante Gabriel Rossetti's translations of the *Vita nuova* and of Dante's predecessors.

the outlines of the scheme that he described in perhaps imaginary detail. The poem, he says, belongs to the genus philosophy, and its concern is morality. Like a theologian interpreting the Bible, he assigns three meanings to his words: the literal, the allegorical, and the mystical.

> The subject of this work according to the letter . . . is the state of souls after death. . . . But if the work be taken allegorically its subject is Man, in so far as by merit or demerit . . . he is exposed to the rewards or punishments of justice. . . . The aim of the whole and the part is to remove those living in this life from a state of misery, and to guide them to a state of happiness.

Otherwise expressed, the *Inferno* is man passing through sin, suffering, and despair; the *Purgatorio* is his cleansing through faith; the *Paradiso* is his redemption through divine revelation and unselfish love. Virgil, who guides Dante through hell and purgatory, stands for knowledge, reason, wisdom, which can lead us to the portals of happiness; only faith and love (Beatrice) can lead us in. In the epic of Dante's life his exile was his hell, his studies and his writings were his purgation, his hope and love were his redemption and his only bliss. It is perhaps because Dante takes his symbolism most seriously in the *Paradiso* that this canticle is the hardest to enjoy; for the Beatrice who was a heavenly vision in the *Vita nuova* becomes in Dante's vision of heaven a pompous abstraction—hardly a meet fate for such impeccable loveliness. Finally Dante explains to Can Grande why he calls his epic *Commedia* *— because the story passed from misery to happiness, and because "it is written in a careless and humble style, in the vulgar tongue, which even housewives speak." [33]

This painful comedy, "this book on which I have grown thin through all these years," [34] was the work and solace of his exile, and was finished only three years before his death. It summarized his life, his learning, his theology, his philosophy; if it had also embodied the humor and tenderness and full-blooded sensuality of the Middle Ages it might have been "a medieval synthesis." Into these hundred brief cantos Dante crowded the science that he had gathered from Brunetto Latini, and perhaps from Bologna; the astronomy, cosmology, geology, and chronology of an age too busy living to be learned. He accepted not only the mystic influences and fatalities of astrology, but all the cabalistic mythology that ascribed occult significance and powers to numbers and the alphabet. The number nine distinguishes Beatrice because its square root is the three made holy by the Trinity. There are nine circles in hell, nine levels in purgatory, nine spheres in paradise. By and large Dante adopts with awe and gratitude the philosophy and theology of Thomas Aquinas, but with no servile fidelity; St. Thomas would have winced at the arguments of the *De monarchia*, or the sight of popes in hell. Dante's concep-

---

* The adjective *Divina* was added by admirers in the seventeenth century.

tion of God as light and love (*l'amor che move il sole e l'altre stelle*—"the love that moves the sun and the other stars")[35] is Aristotle carried down through Arabic philosophy. He knows something of al-Farabi, Avicenna, al-Ghazali, Averroës; and though he assigns Averroës to limbo, he shocks orthodoxy by placing the Averroist heretic Siger de Brabant in heaven;[36] moreover he puts into the mouth of Thomas words of praise for the one man who had stirred the Seraphic Doctor to theological wrath. Yet Siger seems to have denied that personal immortality on which Dante's poem rests. History has exaggerated either the heterodoxy of Siger or the orthodoxy of Dante.

Recent studies have stressed Oriental, and especially Islamic, sources for Dante's ideas:[37] a Persian legend of Arda Viraf's ascension to heaven; the descriptions of hell in the Koran; the story of Mohammed's trip to heaven; the tour of heaven and hell in Abu-l-Ala al-Ma'arri's *Risalat al-Ghufran*; the *Futuhat* of Ibn Arabi. . . . In the *Risalat* al-Ma'arri pictures Iblis (Satan) bound and tortured in hell, and Christian and other "infidel" poets suffering there; at the gate of paradise the narrator is met by a houri or beautiful maiden, who has been appointed his guide.[38] In the *Futuhat* Ibn Arabi (who wrote love poems with pious allegorical interpretations) drew precise diagrams of the hereafter, described hell and heaven as exactly beneath and above Jerusalem, divided hell and heaven into nine levels, and pictured the circle of the Mystic Rose, and choirs of angels surrounding the Divine Light—all as in *The Divine Comedy*.[39] So far as we know, none of these Arabic writings had by Dante's time been translated into any language that he could read.

Apocalyptic literature describing tours or visions of heaven or hell abounded in Judaism and Christianity, not to speak of the sixth book of Virgil's *Aeneid*. An Irish legend told how St. Patrick had visited purgatory and hell, and had seen there tunics and sepulchers of fire, sinners hanging head downward, or devoured by serpents, or covered with ice.[40] In twelfth-century England a priest-trouvère, Adam de Ros, recounted in a substantial poem St. Paul's tour of hell under the guidance of the archangel Michael; made Michael expound the gradation of punishments for different degrees of sin; and showed Paul trembling like Dante before these horrors.[41] Joachim of Flora had told of his own descent into hell and ascent into heaven. There were hundreds of such visions and tales. With all this damning evidence it was hardly necessary for Dante to cross linguistic barriers into Islam in order to find models for his *Inferno*. Like any artist he fused existing material, transformed it from chaos to order, and set it on fire with his passionate imagination and his burning sincerity. He took the elements of his work wherever he could find them—in Thomas and the troubadours, in Peter Damian's fiery sermons on the pains of hell, in his brooding over Beatrice living and Beatrice dead, in his conflicts with politicians and popes; in the scraps of science that crossed his path; in the Christian theology of the Fall, the

Incarnation, sin and grace, and the Last Judgment; in the Plotinian-Augustinian conception of the graduated ascent of the soul to union with God; in Thomas' emphasis on the Beatific Vision as the final and only satisfying goal of man; and out of these he made the poem in which all the terror, hope, and pilgrimage of the medieval spirit found voice, symbol, and form.

2. Hell

Nel mezzo del cammin di nostra vita
Mi ritrovai per una selva oscura,
Che la diritta via era smarrita.

"Midway on the road of our life I found myself in a dark wood, whose direct way was blurred" and lost.[42] Wandering in this darkness, Dante meets Virgil, his "master and guide, from whom alone I took the beautiful style that has brought me honor." [43] Virgil tells him that the only safe exit from the wood is through hell and purgatory; but if Dante will accompany him through these, he will conduct him to the portals of paradise, "where a worthier than I must lead thee"; indeed, he adds, it is at Beatrice' command that he has come to the poet's aid.

They pass through an opening in the earth's surface to the gates of hell, inscribed with these bitter words:

Per me si va nella città dolente,
Per me si va nell' eterno dolore,
Per me si va tra la perduta gente.
Giustizia mosse il mio alto fattore;
Fecemi la divina potestate,
La somma sapienza e il primo amore.
Dinanzi a me non fur cose create,
Se non eterne, ed io eterno duro:
Lasciate ogni speranza, voi ch' entrate! [44]

"Through me one enters the sorrowful city; through me one enters into eternal pain; through me one enters among the lost race. Justice moved my high Maker; divine power made me, supreme wisdom, and primeval love. Before me were no things created except eternal ones; and I endure eternally. All hope abandon, ye who enter here!"

Hell is a subterranean funnel, reaching down to the center of the earth. Dante conceives it with a powerful, almost a sadistic, imagination: dark and frightening abysses between gigantic murky rocks; steaming, stinking marshes, torrents, lakes, and streams; storms of rain, snow, hail, and brands of fire; howling winds and petrifying cold; tortured bodies, grimacing faces, blood-stilling shrieks and groans. Nearest the top of this infernal funnel are those who were neither good nor bad, and those who were neutral;

ignoble irritations punish them; they are bitten by wasps and hornets, gnawed by worms, consumed with envy and remorse. The never neutral Dante scorns them, and makes Virgil say:

> Misericordia e giustizia gli sdegna:
> Non ragioniam di lor, ma guarda e passa— [45]

"Mercy and justice despise them. We do not speak of them, but look and pass on." The tourists come to the subterranean river Acheron, and are ferried over by old Charon, serving here since Homer's days. On the farther shore Dante finds himself in limbo, the first circle of hell, where stay the virtuous but unbaptized, including Virgil and all good heathen, and all good Jews except a few Old Testament heroes whom Christ, visiting limbo, released to heaven. Their only suffering is that they eternally desire a better fate, and know that they will never receive it. There in limbo, honored by all its denizens, are great pagan poets—Homer, Horace, Ovid, Lucan; they welcome Virgil, and make Dante the sixth of their tribe. Looking still higher, says Dante,

> Vidi il Maestro di color che sanno
> Seder tra filosofica famiglia—

"I saw the master of those who know, seated amid the philosophic family"— i.e., Aristotle, surrounded by Socrates, Plato, Democritus, Diogenes, Heraclitus, Anaxagoras, Empedocles, Thales, Zeno, Cicero, Seneca, Euclid, Ptolemy, Hippocrates, Galen, Avicenna, and Averroës "who made the great commentary." [46] Obviously, if Dante had had his way, all this noble company, including the Saracen infidels, would have graced paradise.

Virgil now leads him down into the second circle, where carnal sinners are ceaselessly tossed about by furious winds; here Dante sees Paris, Helen, Dido, Semiramis, Cleopatra, Tristan, and Paolo and Francesca. To end a family feud between the Polentas, lords of Ravenna, and the Malatestas, lords of Rimini, the lovely Francesca da Polenta was to wed the brave but deformed Gianciotto Malatesta. The rest of the story is uncertain; a favored version makes Paolo, the handsome brother of Gianciotto, pretend to be the suitor; to him Francesca pledged herself; but on the wedding day she found herself reluctantly marrying Gianciotto. Soon afterward she enjoyed for a moment Paolo's love; in that moment Gianciotto caught and slew them (c. 1265). Swaying in the wind as a fleshless wraith beside the ghost of her disembodied lover, Francesca da Rimini tells Dante her story:

> Nessun maggior dolore
> Che ricordarsi del tempo felice
> Nella miseria. . . .
> Noi leggevamo un giorno per diletto
> Di Lancelotto, come l'amor lo strinse:

Soli eravamo e senza alcun sospetto.
Per più fiate gli occhi ci sospinse
   Quella lettura, e scolorocci il viso:
   Ma solo un punto fu quel che ci vinse.
Quando leggemmo il disiato riso
   Esser baciato da cotante amante,
   Questi, che mai da me non fia diviso,
La bocca mi baciò tutto tremante.
   Galeotto fu il libro e chi lo scrisse:
   Quel giorno più non vi leggemmo avante.

No greater grief than to remember days
Of joy when misery is at hand. . . . One day
For our delight we read of Lancelot,
How him love thralled. Alone we were, and no
Suspicion near us. Ofttimes by that reading
Our eyes were drawn together, and the hue
Fled from our altered cheek. But at one point
Alone we fell. When of that smile we read,
The wishéd smile, so rapturously kissed
By one so deep in love, then he, who ne'er
From me shall separate, at once my lips
All trembling kissed. The book and writer both
Were love's purveyors. In its leaves that day
We read no more.[47]

    Dante faints with pity at this tale. He wakes to find himself in the third circle of hell, where those who were guilty of gluttony lie in mire under a continuous storm of snow, hail, and dirty water, while Cerberus barks over them and rends them piecemeal with threefold jaws. Virgil and Dante descend into the fourth circle, where Plutus is stationed; here the prodigal and the avaricious meet in conflict, rolling great weights against each other in a Sisyphean war. The poets follow the murky boiling river Styx down into the fifth circle; here those who sinned by wrath are covered with filth, and smite and tear themselves; and those who were sinfully slothful are submerged in the stagnant water of the Stygian lake, whose muddy surface bubbles with their gasps. The wanderers are conveyed across the lake by Phlegyas, and reach in the sixth circle the city of Dis or Lucifer, where heretics are roasted in flaming sepulchers. They descend into the seventh circle; there, under the presidency of the Minotaur, those who committed crimes of violence are perpetually near to drowning in a roaring river of blood; centaurs shoot them with arrows when their heads emerge. In one compartment of this circle are the suicides, including Piero delle Vigne; in another those who committed violence against God or nature or art stand with bare feet on hot sands, while flakes of fire fall upon their heads. Among the sodomites Dante meets his old teacher, Brunetto Latini—a tasteless doom for a guide, philosopher, and friend.

At the edge of the eighth circle a horrible monster appears, who bears the poets down into the pit of usurers. In the upper gulfs of this circle an ingenious diversity of unending pains falls upon seducers, flatterers, and simoniacs. The latter are fixed head downward in holes; only their legs protrude, and flames lick their feet caressingly. Among the simoniacs is Pope Nicholas III (1277–80), whose evil deeds, along with those of other popes, are bitterly denounced; and by a bold fancy Dante pictures Nicholas as mistaking him for Boniface VIII (d. 1303), whose arrival in hell is expected at any hour.[48] Soon, Nicholas predicts, Clement V (d. 1314) will also come. In the fourth gulf of the eighth circle are those who presumed to foretell the future; their heads are fixed face backward on their necks. From a bridge—"Malebolge" —over the fifth gulf they look down upon public peculators, who swim forever in a lake of boiling pitch. Hypocrites pass continually around the sixth gulf, wearing gilded cloaks of lead. Along the only pathway in that gulf lies Caiaphas, prostrate and crucified, so that all who pass must tread upon his flesh. In the seventh gulf robbers are tormented by venomous snakes; Dante recognizes here several Florentines. From an arch over the eighth gulf he sees flames consuming and reconsuming evil counselors; here is the wily Odysseus. In the ninth gulf scandalmongers and schismatics are torn limb from limb; here is Mohammed, described with appalling ferocity:

> As one I marked, torn from the chin throughout,
> Down to the hinder passage; 'twixt the legs
> Dangling his entrails hung; the midriff lay
> Open to view; and wretched ventricle
> That turns the englutted aliment to dross.
> Whilst eagerly I fixed on him my gaze,
> He eyed me, with his hands laid his breast bare,
> And cried: "Now mark how I do rip me; lo!
> And is Mohammed mangled. Before me
> Walks Ali weeping; from the chin his face
> Cleft to the forelock; and the others all,
> Whom here thou seest, while they live, did sow
> Scandal and schism, and therefore thus are rent.
> A friend is here behind, who with his sword
> Hacks us thus cruelly, slivering again
> Each of this ream when we have compassed round
> The dismal way; for first our gashes close
> Ere we repass him." [49]

In the tenth gulf of the eighth circle lie forgers, counterfeiters, and alchemists, moaning with varied ailments; a stench of sweat and pus fills the air, and the groans of the sufferers make a terrifying roar.

At last the poets reach the ninth and lowest circle of hell, which, strange to relate, is a vast well of ice. Here traitors are buried in the ice to their chins; tears of pain freeze into a "crystalline visor" over their faces. Count Ugolino della Gherardesca, who betrayed Pisa, is here eternally bound to Archbishop Ruggieri, who imprisoned him with his sons and grandsons and allowed them all to starve to death. Now Ugolino's head lies upon the Archbishop's, which it chews forever. At nadir, the center of the earth and the very bottom of the narrowing funnel of hell, the giant Lucifer lies buried to the waist in ice, flapping enormous wings from his shoulders, weeping icy tears of blood from the three faces that divide his head, and chewing a traitor in each of three jaws—Brutus, Cassius, and Judas.

Half the terrors of the medieval soul are gathered into this gory chronicle. As one reads its awful pages the gruesome horror mounts, until at last the cumulative effect is oppressive and overwhelming. Not all the sins and crimes of man from nebula to nebula could match the sadistic fury of this divine revenge. Dante's conception of hell is the crowning indecency of medieval theology. Classic antiquity had thought of a Hades or Avernus that received all the human dead into a subterranean and indiscriminate darkness; but it had not pictured that Tartarus as a place of torture. Centuries of barbarism, insecurity, and war had to intervene before man could defile his God with attributes of undying vengeance and inexhaustible cruelty.

With relief we learn at the end that Virgil and Dante have passed through the center of the earth, have inverted the direction of their heads and feet, and are moving upward toward the antipodes. With the time-disdaining swiftness of a dream the two poets traverse in two days the diameter of the earth. They emerge in the southern hemisphere on Easter morning, drink in the light of day, and stand at the foot of the terraced mountain which is purgatory.

3. Purgatory

The conception of purgatory is by comparison humane: man may by effort and pain, by hope and vision, cleanse himself of sin and selfishness, and mount step by step to understanding, love, and bliss. So Dante pictures purgatory as a mountainous cone divided into nine levels: an antepurgatory, seven terraces—one for the purgation of each of the Deadly Sins—and, at the summit, the Earthly Paradise. From each level the sinner moves with diminishing pain to a higher level; and at each ascent an angel chants one of the Beatitudes. In the lower stages there are stern punishments for sins shriven and forgiven but not yet atoned for with sufficient penalty; nevertheless, as against hell's bitter consciousness that suffering will never end, there is here the strengthening certainty that after finite punishment will come an eternity of happiness. A softer mood and a brightening light pervade these cantos, and reveal a Dante learning mildness from his pagan guide.

Virgil, with daubs of dew, washes from Dante's face the sweat and grime of hell. The sea surrounding the mountain shimmers under the rising sun, as the sin-darkened soul trembles with joy at the coming of divine grace. Here on the first level, in accord with Thomas' hope that some good heathen might be saved, Dante encounters Cato of Utica, the stern stiff Stoic who, rather than suffer Caesar's mercy, killed himself. Here, too, is Manfred, Frederick's son, who fought a pope but loved poetry. Virgil hurries Dante onward with oft quoted lines:

> Lascia dir le genti;
> Sta come torre ferma che non crolla
> Giammai la cima per soffiar de' venti—

"Let the people talk; stand like a firm tower, which never shakes its top for all the blowing of the winds." [50] Virgil is not at home in purgatory; he cannot answer Dante's questions as readily as in his wonted hell; he feels his lack, and shows at times an irritated wistfulness. He is comforted when they meet Sordello; the poet sons of Mantua fall into each other's arms, united by the Italian's affection for the city of his youth. Thereupon Dante breaks out into a bitter apostrophe to his country, summarizing his essay on the need of monarchy:

> Ah, slavish Italy! thou inn of grief!
> Vessel without a pilot in loud storm!
> Lady no longer of fair provinces,
> But brothel-house impure! This gentle spirit,
> Even from the pleasant sound of his dear land
> Was prompt to greet a fellow citizen
> With such glad cheer; while now thy living ones
> In thee abide not without war; and one
> Malicious gnaws another; ay, of those
> Whom the same wall and the same moat contain.
> Seek, wretched one, around thy seacoasts wide,
> Then homeward to thy bosom turn, and mark
> If any part of thee sweet peace enjoy.
> What boots it that for thee Justinian [Roman law revived]
> The bridle mend if empty be the saddle [without a king]? ...
> Ah, people, that devoted still should be
> And in the saddle let thy Caesar sit,
> If well thou markedst that which God commands! [51]

And as if to point his fondness for kings that can hold a steady rein, he tells how Sordello guides them, at the base of the purgatorial mount, to a lovely sunny valley, flower-strewn and fragrant, where dwell the Emperor Rudolf,

King Ottokar of Bohemia, Peter III of Aragon, Henry II of England, Philip III of France.

Conducted by Lucia (symbolizing the light of God's grace), Dante and Virgil are admitted by an angel to the first terrace of purgatory. Here the proud are punished by carrying on their bent backs each a massive stone; while reliefs on wall and pavement picture famous deeds of humility, and the dire results of pride. On the second terrace the envious, clad in sackcloth, have their eyes repeatedly sewn up with iron threads. On the third terrace anger, on the fourth sloth, on the fifth avarice, endure their appropriate penalties. Here Pope Hadrian V, once covetous of wealth, does penance peacefully, calm in the surety of ultimate salvation. In one of the many delightful episodes that brighten the *Purgatorio*, the Roman poet Statius appears, and greets the travelers with such joy as seldom moves a poet meeting another poet on the earth. Together the three mount to the sixth terrace, where the sin of gluttony is cleansed; trees dangle sweet-smelling fruit before the penitents, but withdraw them when hands reach out to grasp, while voices in the air recount historic feats of temperance. On the seventh and last terrace are those who sinned by incontinence, but were shriven before death; they are gently singed and purified by flames. Dante has a poet's sympathy for sins of the flesh, above all when committed by persons of artistic temperament, and therefore especially sensitive, imaginative, and precipitous. Here is Guido Guinizelli; Dante hails him as *pater in litteris*, and thanks him for "sweet songs which, as long as our language lasts, will make us love the very ink that traced them." [52]

An angel guides them through fire, by the last ascent, into the Earthly Paradise. Here Virgil bids him farewell:

> My ken
> No farther reaches. I with skill and art
> Thus far have drawn thee. Now thy pleasure take
> For guide.... Lo! the sun that darts
> His beam upon thy forehead, lo! the herb,
> The arborets and flowers, which of itself
> This land pours forth profuse. Till those bright eyes [of Beatrice]
> With gladness come, which, weeping, made me haste
> To succor thee, thou mayst or seat thee down,
> Or wander where thou wilt. Expect no more
> Sanction of warning voice or sign from me.
> Free of thine own arbitrament to choose,
> Discreet, judicious ... I invest thee then
> With crown and miter, sovereign o'er thyself. [53]

Virgil and Statius now behind instead of before him, Dante wanders through the woods and fields, and along the streams, of the Earthly Paradise, breathing the pleasant odor of its pure air, hearing from the trees the songs of "feathered choristers" chanting prime. A lady culling flowers stops her singing to explain to him why this fair country is deserted: it was once the Garden of Eden, but man's disobedience exiled him and mankind from its innocent delights. To this forfeited Paradise Beatrice descends from heaven, clothed in such blinding radiance that Dante can only feel her presence but not see it.

> Albeit my eyes discerned her not, there moved
> A hidden virtue from her, at whose touch
> The power of ancient love was strong within me.[54]

He turns to address his poet guide, but Virgil has returned to the limbo from which the summons of Beatrice had drawn him. Dante weeps, but Beatrice bids him mourn rather the sins of lust with which, after her death, he tarnished her image in his soul; indeed, she tells him, that dark wood, from which through Virgil she has rescued him, was the life of incontinence wherein, at the mid-point of his years, he had found himself lost, with the right road dimmed. Dante falls to the ground in shame, and confesses his sins. Celestial virgins come and intercede with the offended Beatrice, and beg her to reveal to him her second and spiritual beauty. Not that she has forgotten the first:

> Never didst thou spy,
> In art or nature, aught so passing sweet
> As were the limbs that in their beauteous frame
> Enclosed me, and are scattered now in dust.[55]

She relents, and shows her new celestial beauty; but the virgins warn Dante not to gaze upon her directly, but only to look at her feet. Beatrice leads him and Statius (who has completed, after twelve centuries, his term in purgatory) to a fountain from which issue two streams—Lethe (Forgetfulness) and Eunoë (Good Understanding). Dante drinks of Eunoë and is cleansed, and, now regenerate, is "made apt for mounting to the stars." [56]

It is not true that the *Inferno* is the only interesting part of *The Divine Comedy*. There are many arid didactic passages in the *Purgatorio*, and always a ballast of theology; but in this canticle the poem, freed from the horrors of damnation, mounts step by step in beauty and tenderness, cheers the ascent with nature's loveliness regained, and faces bravely the task of making the disembodied Beatrice beautiful. Through her again, as in his youth, Dante enters paradise.

4. Heaven

Dante's theology made his task harder. Had he allowed himself to picture paradise in Persian or Mohammedan style as a garden of physical as well as spiritual delights, his sensuous nature would have found abundant imagery.

But how can that "constitutional materialist," the human intellect, conceive a heaven of purely spiritual bliss? Moreover, Dante's philosophical development forbade him to represent God, or the angels and saints of heaven, in anthropomorphic terms; rather he visions them as forms and points of light; and the resultant abstractions lose in a luminous void the life and warmth of sinful flesh. But Catholic doctrine professed the resurrection of the body; and Dante, while struggling to be spiritual, endows some denizens of heaven with corporeal features and human speech. It is pleasant to learn that even in heaven Beatrice has beautiful feet.

His plan of paradise is worked out with impressive consistency, brilliant imagination, and bold detail. Following Ptolemaic astronomy, he thinks of the heavens as an expanding series of nine hollow crystal spheres revolving about the earth; these spheres are the "many mansions" of the "Father's house." In each sphere a planet and a multitude of stars are set like gems in a diadem. As they move, these celestial bodies, all endowed in gradation with divine intelligence, sing the joy of their blessedness and the praise of their Creator, and bathe the heavens in the music of the spheres. The stars, says Dante, are the saints of heaven, the souls of the saved; and according to the merits that they earned in life, so differently high is their station above the earth, so loftier is their happiness, so nearer are they to that empyrean which is above all the spheres, and holds the throne of God.

As if drawn by the light that radiates from Beatrice, Dante rises from the Earthly Paradise to the first circle of the heavens, which is that of the moon. There are the souls of those who by no fault of their own were forced to violate their religious vows. One such, Piccarda Donati, explains to Dante that though they are in the lowest circle of the heavens, and enjoy a degree of bliss less than that of the spirits above them, they are freed by the Divine Wisdom from all envy, longing, or discontent. For the essence of happiness lies in the joyful acceptance of the Divine Will: *la sua voluntate è nostra pace* —"His will is our peace." [57] This is the basic line of *The Divine Comedy*.

Subject to a celestial magnetism that draws all things to God, Dante rises with Beatrice to the second heaven, which is the sphere dominated by the planet Mercury. Here are those who on earth were absorbed in practical activity to good ends, but were more intent on worldly honor than on serving God. Justinian appears, and phrases in royal lines the historic functions of the Roman Empire and Roman law; through him Dante strikes another blow for one world under one law and king. Beatrice leads the poet to the third heaven, the circle of Venus, where the Provençal bard Folque foretells the tragedy of Boniface VIII. In the fourth heaven, whose orb is the sun, Dante finds the Christian philosophers—Boethius, Isidore of Seville, Bede, Peter Lombard, Gratian, Albertus Magnus, Thomas Aquinas, Bonaventura, and Siger de Brabant. In a gracious exchange Thomas the Dominican relates to Dante the life of St. Francis, and Bonaventura the Franciscan tells him the story of St. Dominic. Thomas, always a man and mind of some expanse, clogs the narrative with discourses on theological subtleties; and Dante is so anxious to be a philosopher that for several cantos he ceases to be a poet.

Beatrice leads him to the fifth heaven, that of Mars, where are the souls of warriors who died fighting for the true faith—Joshua, Judas Maccabaeus, Charlemagne, even Robert Guiscard, ravager of Rome. They are arranged as thousands of stars in the form of a dazzling cross and the figure of the Crucified; and every star in the luminous emblem joins in a celestial harmony. Ascending to the sixth heaven, that of Jupiter, Dante finds those who on earth administered justice equitably; here are David, Hezekiah, Constantine, Trajan—another pagan breaking into heaven. These living stars are arranged in the form of an eagle; they speak with one voice, discoursing to Dante on theology, and celebrating the praise of just kings.

Mounting what Beatrice figuratively calls the "stairway of the eternal palace," the poet and his guide reach the seventh heaven of delight, the planet Saturn and its attendant stars. At every ascent the beauty of Beatrice takes on new brilliance, as if enhanced by the rising splendor of each higher sphere. She dares not smile upon her lover, lest he be consumed to ashes in her radiance. This is the circle of monks who lived in piety and fidelity to their vows. Peter Damian is among them; Dante asks him how to reconcile man's freedom with God's foresight and consequent predestination; Peter replies that even the most enlightened souls in heaven, under God, cannot answer his question. St. Benedict appears, and mourns the corruption of his monks.

Now the poet floats upward from the circles of the planets to the eighth heaven, the zone of the fixed stars. From the constellation Gemini he looks down and sees the infinitesimal earth, "so pitiful of semblance that it moved my smiles." A moment of homesickness, even for that miserable planet, might have moved him then; but a glance from Beatrice tells him that this heaven of light and love, and not that scene of sin and strife, is his proper home.

Canto XXIII opens with one of Dante's characteristic similes:

> Even as the bird, who midst the leafy bower
> Has in her nest sat darkly through the night
> With her sweet brood, impatient to descry
> Their wishéd looks, and to bring home their food,
> In the fond quest unconscious of her toil;
> She, of the time prevenient, on the spray
> That overhangs their couch, with wakeful gaze
> Expects the sun, nor ever, till the dawn,
> Removeth from the east her eager ken—

So Beatrice fixes her eyes in one direction expectantly. Suddenly the heavens there shine with startling splendor. "Behold," cries Beatrice, "the triumphant hosts of Christ!"—souls new won for paradise. Dante looks, but sees only a light so full and strong that he is blinded, and cannot tell what passes by.

Beatrice bids him open his eyes; now, she says, he can endure her full radiance. She smiles upon him, and it is, he swears, an experience that can never be canceled from his memory. "Why doth my face enamor thee?" she asks, and bids him rather look at Christ and Mary and the apostles. He tries to make them out, but sees merely "legions of splendors, on whom burning rays shed lightnings from above"; while to his ears comes the music of the *Regina coeli*, sung by heavenly hosts.

Christ and Mary ascend, but the apostles remain behind, and Beatrice asks them to speak to Dante. Peter questions him about his faith, is pleased with his replies, and agrees with him that as long as Boniface is Pope the Apostolic See is vacant or defiled.[58] There is no mercy in Dante for Boniface.

The apostles vanish upward, and Dante mounts at last, with "her who hath imparadised my soul," into the ninth and highest heaven. Here in the empyrean there are no stars, only pure light, and the spiritual, incorporeal, uncaused, motionless source of all souls, bodies, causes, motions, light, and life— God. The poet struggles now to achieve the Beatific Vision; but all he sees is a point of light about which revolve nine circles of pure Intelligences—seraphim, cherubim, thrones, dominions, virtues, powers, principalities, archangels, and angels; through these, His agents and emissaries, the Almighty governs the world. But though Dante cannot perceive the Divine Essence, he beholds all the hosts of heaven forming themselves into a luminous rose, a marvel of shimmering lights and diverse hues expanding leaf by leaf into a gigantic flower.

Beatrice leaves her lover now, and takes her place in the rose. He sees her seated on her individual throne, and prays her still to help him; she smiles down upon him, and thereafter fixes her gaze upon the center of all light, but she sends St. Bernard to aid and comfort him. Bernard directs Dante's eyes to the Queen of Heaven; the poet looks, but discerns only a flaming luster surrounded by thousands of angels clothed in light. Bernard tells him that if he would obtain power to see the heavenly vision more clearly he must join with him in prayer to the Mother of God. The final canto opens with Bernard's melodious supplication:

> Vergine Madre, figlia del tuo Figlio,
> Umile ed alta più che creatura—

"Virgin Mother, daughter of thy Son, more humble and exalted than any creature." Bernard begs her of her grace to enable Dante's eyes to behold the Divine Majesty. Beatrice and many saints bend toward Mary with hands clasped in prayer. Mary looks for a moment benignly upon Dante, then turns her eyes upon the "Everlasting Light." Now, says the poet, "my vision, becoming pure, more and more entered the ray of that high light which in itself is Truth." What else he saw remains, he says, beyond all human speech and fantasy; but "in that abyss of radiance, clear and lofty, seemed, methought, three orbs of triple hue, combined in one." The majestic epic ends with Dante's gaze still fixed upon that radiance, drawn and impelled by "the Love that moves the sun and all the stars."

The Divine Comedy is the strangest and most difficult of all poems. No other, before yielding its treasures, makes such imperious demands. Its language is the most compact and concise this side of Horace and Tacitus; it gathers into a word or phrase contents and subtleties requiring a rich background and an alert intelligence for full apprehension; even the wearisome theological, psychological, astronomical disquisitions have here a pithy precision that only a Scholastic philosopher could rival or enjoy. Dante lived so intensely in his time that his poem almost breaks under the weight of contemporary allusions unintelligible today without a litter of notes obstructing the movement of the tale.

He loved to teach, and tried to pour into one poem nearly all that he had ever learned, with the result that the living verse lies abed with dead absurdities. He weakens the charm of Beatrice by making her the voice of his political loves and hates. He stops his story to denounce a hundred cities or groups or individuals, and at times his epic founders in a sea of vituperation. He adores Italy; but Bologna is full of panders and pimps,[59] Florence is the favorite product of Lucifer,[60] Pistoia is a den of beasts,[61] Genoa is "full of all corruption," [62] and as for Pisa, "A curse upon Pisa! May the Arno be dammed at its mouth, and drown all Pisa, man and mouse, beneath its raging waters!" [63] Dante thinks that "supreme wisdom and primal love" created hell. He promises to remove the ice for a moment from the eyes of Alberigo if the latter will tell his name and story; Alberigo does, and asks fulfillment—"reach hither now thy hand, open my eyes!"—but, says Dante, "I opened them not for him; to be rude to him was courtesy." [64] If a man so bitter could win a conducted tour through paradise we shall all be saved.

His poem is none the less the greatest of medieval Christian books, and one of the greatest of all time. The slow accumulation of its intensity through a hundred cantos is an experience that no thorough reader will ever forget. It is, as Carlyle said, the sincerest of poems; there is no pretense in it, no hypocrisy or false modesty, no sycophancy or cowardice; the most powerful men of the age, even a pope who claimed all power, are attacked with a force and fervor unparalleled in poetry. Above all there is here a flight and sustainment of imagination challenging Shakespeare's supremacy: vivid pictures of things never seen by gods or men; descriptions of nature that only an observant and sensitive spirit could achieve; and little narratives, like Francesca's or Ugolino's, that press great tragedies into narrow space with yet no vital matter missed. There is no humor in this man, but love was there till misfortune turned it into theology.

What Dante achieves at last is sublimity. We cannot find in his epic the

Mississippi of life and action that is the *Iliad,* nor the gentle drowsy stream of Virgil's verse, nor the universal understanding and forgiveness of Shakespeare; but here is grandeur, and a tortured, half-barbaric force that foreshadows Michelangelo. And because Dante loved order as well as liberty, and bound his passion and vision into form, he achieved a poem of such sculptured power that no man since has equaled it. Through the centuries that followed him Italy revered him as the liberator of her golden speech; Petrarch and Boccaccio and a hundred others were inspired by his battle and his art; and all Europe rang with the story of the proud exile who had gone to hell, and had returned, and had never smiled again.

Epilogue

IT is fitting that we should end our long and devious narrative with Dante; for in the century of his death those men appeared who would begin to destroy the majestic edifice of faith and hope in which he had lived: Wyclif and Huss would preface the Reformation; Giotto and Chrysoloras, Petrarch and Boccaccio would proclaim the Renaissance. In the history of man—so multiple is he and diverse—one mood may survive in some souls and places long after its successor or opposite has risen in other minds or states. In Europe the Age of Faith reached its last full flower in Dante; it suffered a vital wound from Occam's "razor" in the fourteenth century; but it lingered, ailing, till the advent of Bruno and Galileo, Descartes and Spinoza, Bacon and Hobbes; it may return if the Age of Reason achieves catastrophe. Great areas of the world remained under the sign and rule of faith while Western Europe sailed Reason's uncharted seas. The Middle Ages are a condition as well as a period: in Western Europe we should close them with Columbus; in Russia they continued till Peter the Great (d. 1725); in India till our time.

We are tempted to think of the Middle Ages as a fallow interval between the fall of the Roman Empire in the West (476) and the discovery of America; we must remind ourselves that the followers of Abélard called themselves *moderni*, and that the bishop of Exeter, in 1287, spoke of his century as *moderni tempores*, "modern times." [1] The boundary between "medieval" and "modern" is always advancing; and our age of coal and oil and sooty slums may some day be accounted medieval by an era of cleaner power and more gracious life. The Middle Ages were no mere interlude between one civilization and another; if we date them from Rome's acceptance of Christianity and the Council of Nicaea, A.D. 325, they included the final centuries of the classic culture, the ripening of Catholic Christianity into a full and rich civilization in the thirteenth century, and the breakup of that civilization into the opposed cultures of the Renaissance and the Reformation. The men of the Middle Ages were the victims of barbarism, then the conquerors of barbarism, then the creators of a new civilization. It would be unwise to look down with hybritic pride upon a period that produced so many great men and women, and raised from the ruins of barbarism the papacy, the European states, and the hard-won wealth of our medieval heritage.*

---

* The following recapitulation is mostly confined to medieval Christianity, and will not repeat the summary of Islamic civilization given at the conclusion of Book II.

That legacy included evil as well as good. We have not fully recovered from the Dark Ages: the insecurity that excites greed, the fear that fosters cruelty, the poverty that breeds filth and ignorance, the filth that generates disease, the ignorance that begets credulity, superstition, occultism—these still survive amongst us; and the dogmatism that festers into intolerance and Inquisitions only awaits opportunity or permission to oppress, kill, ravage, and destroy. In this sense modernity is a cloak put upon medievalism, which secretly remains; and in every generation civilization is the laborious product and precarious obligating privilege of an engulfed minority. The Inquisition left its evil mark on European society: it made torture a recognized part of legal procedure, and it drove men back from the adventure of reason into a fearful and stagnant conformity.

The preponderant bequest of the Age of Faith was religion: a Judaism absorbed till the eighteenth century in the Talmud; a Mohammedanism becalmed after the victory of the Koran over philosophy in the twelfth century; a Christianity divided between East and West, between North and South, and yet the most powerful and influential religion in the white man's history. The creed of the medieval Church is today (1950) cherished by 330,000,000 Roman, 128,000,000 Orthodox, Catholics; her liturgy still moves the soul after every argument has failed; and the work of the Church in education, charity, and the moral taming of barbaric man left to modernity a precious fund of social order and moral discipline. The papal dream of a united Europe faded in the strife of Empire and papacy; but every generation is stirred by a kindred vision of an international moral order superior to the jungle ethics of sovereign states.

When that papal dream broke, the nations of Europe took essentially the form that they retained till our century; and the principle of nationality prepared to write the political history of modern times. Meanwhile the medieval mind created great systems of civil and canon law, maritime and mercantile codes, charters of municipal freedom, the jury system and habeas corpus, and the Magna Carta of the aristocracy. Courts and curias prepared for states and Church modes and mechanisms of administration employed to this day. Representative government appeared in the Spanish Cortes, the Icelandic Althing, the French Estates-General, the English Parliament.

Greater still was the economic heritage. The Middle Ages conquered the wilderness, won the great war against forest, jungle, marsh, and sea, and yoked the soil to the will of man. Over most of Western Europe they ended slavery, and almost ended serfdom. They organized production into guilds that even now enter into the ideals of economists seeking a middle way between the irresponsible individual and the autocratic state. Tailors, cobblers, and dressmakers, until our own time, practiced their handicrafts in personal shops after the medieval fashion; their submission to large-scale production and capitalistic organization has occurred under our eyes. The great fairs that now and then gather men and goods in modern cities are a legacy of medieval trade; so are our efforts to check monopoly and regulate prices and wages; and nearly all the processes of modern banking were inherited from medieval finance. Even our fraternities and secret societies have medieval roots and rites.

Medieval morality was the heir of barbarism and the parent of chivalry. Our idea of the gentleman is a medieval creation; and the chivalric ideal, however removed from knightly practice, has survived as one of the noblest conceptions of the human spirit. Perhaps the worship of Mary brought new elements of tenderness into the behavior of European man. If later centuries advanced upon medieval morality, it was on a medieval foundation of family unity, moral education, and slowly spreading habits of honor and courtesy—much as the moral life of modern skeptics may be an afterglow of the Christian ethic absorbed in youth.

The intellectual legacy of the Middle Ages is poorer than our Hellenic inheritance, and is alloyed with a thousand occult perversions mostly stemming from antiquity. Even so it includes the modern languages, the universities, and the terminology of philosophy and science. Scholasticism was a training in logic rather than a lasting philosophical conquest, though it still dominates a thousand colleges. The assumptions of medieval faith hampered historiography; men thought they knew the origin and destiny of the world and man, and wove a web of myth that almost imprisoned history within the walls of monastic chronicles. It is not quite true that medieval historians had no notion of development or progress; the thirteenth century, like the nineteenth, was powerfully impressed by its own achievements. Nor were the Middle Ages as static as we once proudly supposed; distance immobilizes motion, assimilates differences, and freezes change; but change was as insistent then as now, in manners and dress, language and ideas, law and government, commerce and finance, literature and art. Medieval thinkers, however, did not attach as much importance as the modern thoughtless to progress in means unaccompanied by improvement in ends.

The scientific legacy of the Middle Ages is modest indeed; yet it includes the Hindu numerals, the decimal system, the conception of experimental science, substantial contributions to mathematics, geography, astronomy, and optics, the discovery of gunpowder, the invention of eyeglasses, the mariner's compass, the pendulum clock, and—apparently the most indispensable of all—the distillation of alcohol. Arabic and Jewish physicians advanced Greek medicine, and Christian pioneers emancipated surgery from the tonsorial arts. Half the hospitals of Europe are medieval foundations, or modern restorations of medieval establishments. Modern science has inherited the internationalism, and in part the international language, of medieval thought.

Next to moral discipline, the richest portion of our medieval heritage is in art. The Empire State Building is as sublime as Chartres Cathedral, and owes its grandeur to architecture alone—to the stability of its audacious height and the purity of its functional lines. But the union of sculpture, painting, poetry, and music with architecture in the life of a Gothic cathedral gives to Chartres, Amiens, Reims, and Notre Dame a scope and depth of sensuous and spiritual harmony, a wealth and diversity of content and ornament, that never lets our interest sleep, and more fully fills the soul. These portals, towers, and spires, these vaults that made a soaring counterpoint of stone, these statues, altars, fonts, and tombs so fondly carved, these windows that rivaled the rainbow and chastened the sun—one must forgive much to an age that loved so conscientiously the symbols of its faith and the work of its hands. It was for the cathedrals that polyphonic music was developed, and a musical notation and staff; and from the Church the modern drama was born.

The medieval heritage in literature, though it cannot vie in quality with that of Greece, may bear comparison with Rome's. Dante may stand beside Virgil, Petrarch beside Horace, the love poetry of the Arabs and the troubadours beside Ovid, Tibullus, and Propertius; the Arthurian romances are deeper and nobler than anything in the *Metamorphoses* or the *Heroides*, and as graceful; and the major medieval hymns top the finest lyrics of Roman poetry. The thirteenth century ranks with the age of Augustus or of Leo X. Rarely has any century seen so full and varied an intellectual or artistic flowering. A commercial expansion almost as vigorous as that which marked the close of the fifteenth century enlarged, enriched, and aroused the world; strong popes from Innocent III to Boniface VIII made the Church for a century the summit of European order and law; St. Francis dared to be a Christian; the mendicant orders restored the monastic ideal; great statesmen like Philip Augustus, St. Louis, Philip IV, Edward I, Frederick II, Alfonso X raised their states from custom to law, and their peoples to new medieval levels of civilization. Triumphing over the mystical tendencies of the twelfth century, the thirteenth sallied forth into philosophy and science with a zest and courage not surpassed by the Renaissance. In literature the "wonderful century" ran the gamut from Wolfram von Eschenbach's *Parzival* to the conception of *The Divine Comedy*. Nearly all elements of medieval civilization seemed in that century to reach unity, maturity, and culminating form.

We shall never do justice to the Middle Ages until we see the Italian Renaissance not as their repudiation but as their fulfillment. Columbus and Magellan continued the explorations already far advanced by the merchants and navigators of Venice, Genoa, Marseille, Barcelona, Lisbon, and Cadiz. The same spirit that had stirred the twelfth century gave pride and battle to the cities of Renaissance Italy. The same energy and vitality of character that marked Enrico Dandolo, Frederick II, and Gregory IX consumed the men of the Renaissance; the *condottieri* stemmed from Robert Guiscard, the "despots" from Ezzelino and Pallavicino; the painters walked in the paths opened by Cimabue and Duccio; and Palestrina mediated between Gregorian chant and Bach. Petrarch was the heir of Dante and the troubadours, Boccaccio was an Italian trouvère. Despite *Don Quixote* romance continued to flourish in Renaissance Europe, and Chrétien de Troyes came to perfection in Malory. The "revival of letters" had begun in the medieval schools; what distinguished the Renaissance was that it extended the revival from Latin to Greek classics, and rejected Gothic to revive Greek art. But Greek sculpture had already been accepted as a model by Niccolò Pisano in the thirteenth century; and when Chrysoloras brought the Greek language and classics to Italy (1393) the Middle Ages had still a century to run.

In Renaissance Italy, Spain, and France the same religion held sway that had built the cathedrals and composed the hymns, with only this difference, that the Italian Church, sharing richly in the culture of the time, gave to the Italian mind a freedom of thought born in the medieval universities, and predicated on the tacit understanding that philosophers and scientists would pursue their work without attempting to destroy the faith of the people.

So it was that Italy and France did not share in the Reformation; they moved from the Catholic culture of the thirteenth century to the humanism of the fifteenth and sixteenth, and thence to the Enlightenment of the seventeenth and eighteenth. It was this continuity, combined with pre-Columbian Mediterranean trade, that gave to the Latin peoples a temporary cultural advantage over northern nations more severely ravaged by religious wars. That continuity went back through the Middle Ages to classic Rome, and through southern Italy to classic Greece. Through Greek colonies in Sicily, Italy, and France, through the Roman conquest and Latinization of France and Spain, one magnificent thread of culture ran, from Sappho and Anacreon to Virgil and Horace, to Dante and Petrarch, to Rabelais and Montaigne, to Voltaire and Anatole France. In passing from the Age of Faith to the Renaissance we shall be advancing from the uncertain childhood to the lusty and exhilarating youth of a culture that married classic grace to barbaric strength, and transmitted to us, rejuvenated and enriched, that heritage of civilization to which we must always add, but which we must never let die.

THANK YOU AGAIN, FRIEND READER.

Bibliographical Guide

to editions referred to in the Notes

Books starred are recommended for further study.

ABBOTT, G. F., Israel in Egypt, London, 1907.
ABBOTT, NABIA, Two Queens of Baghdad, Univ. of Chicago Press, 1946.
*ABÉLARD, P., Historia Calamitatum, St. Paul, Minn., 1922.
     Ouvrages inédits, ed. V. Cousin, Paris, 1836.
ABRAHAMS, I., Chapters on Jewish Literature, Phila., 1899.
     Jewish Life in the Middle Ages, Phila., 1896.
ABU BEKR IBN TUFAIL, The History of Hayy ibn Yaqzan, tr. Ockley, N. Y., n.d.
ACKERMAN, PHYLLIS, Tapestry, the Mirror of Civilization, Oxford Univ. Press, 1933.
ADAMS, B., Law of Civilization and Decay, N. Y., 1921.
*ADAMS, H., Mont St. Michel and Chartres, Boston, 1926.
ADDISON, J. D., Arts and Crafts in the Middle Ages, Boston, 1908.
ALI, MAULANA MUHAMMAD, The Religion of Islam, Lahore, 1936.
ALI TABARI, The Book of Religion and Empire, N. Y., 1922.
AMEER ALI, SYED, The Spirit of Islam, Calcutta, 1900.
AMMIANUS MARCELLINUS, Works, Loeb Lib., 1935. 2v.
ANDRAE, TOR, Mohammed, tr. Menzel, N. Y., 1936.
ANGLO-SAXON CHRONICLE, tr. Ingram, Everyman Lib.
ANGLO-SAXON POETRY, ed. R. K. Gordon, Everyman Lib.
ARCHER, T. A., and KINGSFORD, C. L., The Crusades, N. Y., 1895.
*ARISTOTLE, Politics, tr. Ellis, Everyman Lib.
ARMSTRONG, SIR WALTER, Art in Great Britain and Ireland, London, 1919.
ARNOLD, M., Essays in Criticism, First Series, N. Y., n.d. Home Lib.
ARNOLD, SIR T. W., Painting in Islam, Oxford, 1928.
     The Preaching of Islam, N. Y., 1913.
     and GUILLAUME, A., The Legacy of Islam, Oxford, 1931.
ASHLEY, W. J., Introduction to English Economic History and Theory, N.Y., 1894f. 2v.
ASIN Y PALACIOS, M., Islam and the Divine Comedy, London, 1926.
ASSER OF ST. DAVID'S, Annals of the Reign of Alfred the Great, in Giles, J. A.
*AUCASSIN AND NICOLETTE, tr. Mason, Everyman Lib.
AUGUSTINE, ST., The City of God, tr. Healey, London, 1934.
*   Confessions, Loeb Lib. 2v.
     Letters, Loeb Lib.
AUSONIUS, Poems, Loeb Lib. 2v.
AVERROËS, A Decisive Discourse on . . . the Relation Between Religion and Philosophy, and An Exposition of the Methods of Argument Concerning the Doctrines of the Faith, Baroda, n.d.
AVICENNA, Canon Medicinae, Venice, 1608.

BACON, ROGER, Opus majus, tr. Burke, Univ. of Penn. Press, 1928. 2v.
BADER, G., Jewish Spiritual Heroes, N. Y., 1940. 3v.
BAEDEKER, K., Northern Italy, London, 1913.

AL-BALADHURI, ABU-L ABBAS AHMAD, Origins of the Islamic State; tr. Hitti, Columbia Univ. Press, 1916.
BARNES, H. E., Economic History of the Western World, N. Y., 1942.
      History of Western Civilization, N. Y., 1935. 2v.
BARON, S. W., Social and Religious History of the Jews. Columbia Univ. Press, 1937. 3v.
      ed., Essays on Maimonides, Columbia Univ. Press, 1941.
BEARD, MIRIAM, History of the Business Man, N. Y., 1938.
BEBEL, A., Woman under Socialism, N. Y., 1923.
BECKER, C. H., Christianity and Islam, London, 1909.
BEDE, VEN., Ecclesiastical History of England, ed. King, Loeb Lib.
BEER, M., Social Struggles in the Middle Ages, London, 1924.
BELLOC, H., Paris, N. Y., 1907.
BENJAMIN OF TUDELA, Travels; cf. Komroff, M., Contemporaries of Marco Polo.
BEVAN, E. R., and SINGER, C., The Legacy of Israel, Oxford, 1927.
BIEBER, M., History of the Greek and Roman Theater, Princeton Univ. Press, 1939.
AL-BIRUNI, Chronology of Ancient Nations, tr. Sachau, London, 1879.
      India, London, 1910. 2v.
BLOK, P. J., History of the People of the Netherlands, N. Y., 1898. 3v.
BOER, T. J. DE, History of Philosophy in Islam, London, 1903.
*BOETHIUS, Consolation of Philosophy, Loeb Lib.
BOISSIER, G., La fin du paganisme, Paris, 1913. 2v.
BOISSONNADE, P., Life and Work in Medieval Europe, N. Y., 1927.
BONAVENTURE, ST., Life of St. Francis, in Little Flowers of St. Francis, Everyman Lib.
BOND, FR., Gothic Architecture in England, London, 1906.
      Wood Carving in English Churches, London, 1910. 2v.
BOUCHIER, E. S., Life and Letters in Roman Africa, Oxford, 1913.
BREHAUT, E., An Encyclopedist of the Dark Ages, N. Y., 1912.
BRIDGES, J. H., Life and Work of Roger Bacon, London, 1914.
BRIFFAULT, R., The Mothers, N. Y., 1927. 3v.
BRIGHT, W., Age of the Fathers, N. Y., 1903. 2v.
BRITTAIN, A., Women of Early Christianity, Phila., 1907.
BROGLIE, DUC DE, St. Ambrose, London, 1899.
BROWN, P. HUME, History of Scotland, Cambridge Univ. Press, 1929. 3v.
BROWNE, E. G., Arabian Medicine, London, 1921.
      Literary History of Persia, Cambridge Univ. Press, 1929. 3v.
BROWNE, LEWIS, ed., The Wisdom of Israel, N. Y., 1945.
BRYCE, JAS., The Holy Roman Empire, N. Y., 1921.
BUKHSH, S. K., The Orient under the Caliphs, translated from A. Von Kremer's Kulturgeschichte des Orients, Calcutta, 1920.
      Studies: Indian and Islamic, London, 1927.
BULLETIN OF THE IRANIAN INSTITUTE, N. Y.
BURTON, SIR R. F., The Jew, the Gypsy, and El Islam, Chicago, 1898.
      Personal Narrative of a Pilgrimage to al-Madinah and Meccah, London, 1893. 2v.
BURY, J. B., History of the Eastern Roman Empire, London, 1912.
      History of the Later Roman Empire, London, 1923. 2v.
      Life of St. Patrick, London, 1905.

BUTLER, P., Women of Medieval France, Phila., 1908.

CALVERT, A. F., Cordova, London, 1907.
        Moorish Remains in Spain, N. Y., 1906.
        Seville, London, 1907.
CAMBRIDGE ANCIENT HISTORY, N. Y., 1924. 12v.
CAMBRIDGE MEDIEVAL HISTORY, N. Y., 1924f. 8v.
CAMPBELL, D., Arabian Medicine, London, 1926. 2v.
CAPES, W. W., University Life in Ancient Athens, N. Y., 1922.
CARLYLE, R. W., History of Medieval Political Theory in the West, Edinburgh,
        1928. 5v.
CARLYLE, TH., Past and Present, in Works, Collier ed., N. Y., 1901. 20v.
CARTER, T. F., The Invention of Printing in China, N. Y., 1925.
CASSIODORUS, Letters, ed. Hodgkin, London, 1886.
CASTIGLIONE, A., History of Medicine, N. Y., 1941.
CATHOLIC ENCYCLOPEDIA, N. Y., 1912. 16v.
CHAMBERS, E. K., The Medieval Stage, Oxford, 1903. 2v.
CHAPMAN, C. E., History of Spain, founded on the *Historia de España* of Rafael
        Altamira, N. Y., 1930.
CHARDIN, SIR J., Travels in Persia, London, 1927.
CHATEAUBRIAND, VICOMTE DE, The Genius of Christianity, Baltimore, n.d.
CLAPHAM, J. H., and POWER, EILEEN, Cambridge Economic History of Europe,
        Vol. I, Camb. Univ. Press, 1944.
CHRÉTIEN DE TROYES, Arthurian Romances, London, Everyman Lib.
CLAUDIAN, Poems, Loeb Lib. 2v.
CLAVIJO, GONZALEZ DE, Embassy to Tamberlane, 1403-6, N. Y., 1928.
CLAYTON, J., Pope Innocent III and His Times, Milwaukee, 1941.
COLLINGWOOD, R. G., and MYRES, J. L., Roman Britain, Oxford, 1937.
CONNICK, C. J., Adventures in Light and Color, N. Y., 1937.
COULTON, G. G., Chaucer and His England, London, 1921.
        Five Centuries of Religion, Camb. Univ. Press, 1923. 3v.
        From St. Francis to Dante: a tr. of the Chronicle of Salimbene,
           London, 1908.
        The Inquisition, N. Y., 1929.
        Inquisition and Liberty, London, 1938.
        Life in the Middle Ages, Camb. Univ. Press, 1930. 4v.
        Medieval Panorama, N. Y., 1944.
        The Medieval Scene, Camb. Univ. Press, 1930.
        The Medieval Village, Camb. Univ. Press, 1925.
        Social Life in Britain from the Conquest to the Reformation,
           Camb. Univ. Press, 1938.
CRAM, R. A., The Substance of Gothic, Boston, 1938.
CRESWELL, K. A., Early Muslim Architecture, Oxford, 1932. 2v.
CRONYN, G., The Fool of Venus: the Story of Peire Vidal, N. Y., 1934.
CRUMP, C. G., and JACOB, E. F., The Legacy of the Middle Ages, Oxford, 1926.
CUNNINGHAM, W., The Growth of English Industry and Commerce, Camb.
        Univ. Press, 1896.
CUTTS, E. L., St. Jerome, London, S.P.C.K., n.d.

DALTON, O. M., Byzantine Art and Archeology, Oxford, 1911.
DANTE, Eleven Letters, tr. Latham, Boston, 1891.

De Monarchia, tr. Henry, Boston, 1904.

Il Convito, tr. Sayer, London, 1887.

La Commedia, ed. Toynbee, London, 1900.

La Vita Nuova, tr. D. G. Rossetti, Portland, Me., 1898.

* The Vision of (The Divine Comedy), tr. Cary, Everyman Lib.

D'ARCY, M. C., Thomas Aquinas, London, 1930.

DASENT, G., tr., Story of Burnt Njal, Everyman Lib.

DAVIS, H. W. C., ed., Medieval England, Oxford, 1928.

DAVIS, WM. S., Life on a Medieval Barony, N. Y., 1923.

         and WEST, W. M., Readings in Ancient History, Boston, 1912.
         2v.

DAWSON, CHRISTOPHER, The Making of Europe, N. Y., 1932.

DAY, CLIVE, A History of Commerce, London, 1926.

DENNIS, G., Cities and Cemeteries of Etruria, Everyman Lib. 2v.

DE VAUX, BARON CARRA, Les penseurs de l'Islam, Paris, 1921. 5v.

DE WULF, M., History of Medieval Philosophy, London, 1925. 2v.
         Philosophy and Civilization in the Middle Ages, Princeton
         Univ. Press, 1922.

DHALLA, M. N., Zoroastrian Civilization, Oxford, 1922.

DIEHL, C., Byzantine Portraits, N. Y., 1926.
         Manuel d'art Byzantin, Paris, 1910.

DIESENDRUCK, LEVI, Maimonides and Thomas Aquinas, in N. Y. Public Library
         Pamphlets, v. 372.

DIEULAFOY, M., Art in Spain and Portugal, N. Y., 1913.

DILL, SIR S., Roman Society in Gaul in the Merovingian Age, London, 1926.
         Roman Society in the Last Century of the Western Empire, Lon-
         don, 1905.

DILLON, E., Glass, N. Y., 1907.

DIMAND, M. S., Handbook of Muhammadan Art, N. Y., 1944.

DOPSCH, A., Economic and Social Foundations of European Civilization, N. Y.,
         1937.

*DOUGHTY, CHAS. M., Travels in Arabia Deserta, N. Y., 1923. 2v.

DOZY, R., Spanish Islam, N. Y., 1913.

DRAPER, J. W., History of the Intellectual Development of Europe, N. Y., 1876.
         2v.

DRUCK, D., Yehuda Halevy, N. Y., 1941.

DUBNOW, S. M., History of the Jews in Russia and Poland, Phila., 1916. 3v.

DUCHAILLU, P., The Viking Age, N. Y., 1889. 2v.

DUCHESNE, L., Early History of the Christian Church, London, 1933. 3v.

DUDDEN, F. H., Gregory the Great, London, 1905. 2v.

DUHEM, P., Le système du monde, Paris, 1913. 5v.

EGINHARD, Life of Charlemagne, N. Y., 1880.

ENCYCLOPAEDIA BRITANNICA, 14th ed.

ERIGENA, JOHN SCOTUS, On the Division of Nature, Book I, Annapolis, Md.,
         1940.

EUNAPIUS, Lives of the Sophists, in Philostratus, Everyman Lib.

FARMER, H. G., History of Arabian Music, London, 1929.

FAURE, E., History of Art, N. Y., 1921. 4v. Vol. III: Medieval Art.

FENOLLOSA, E. F., Epochs of Chinese and Japanese Art, N. Y., 1921. 2v.

FERGUSSON, J., History of Architecture in All Countries, London, 1874. 2v.

FIEDLER, H. G., ed., Das Oxforder Buch Deutscher Dichtung, Oxford, 1936.

FIGGIS, J. N., Political Aspects of St. Augustine's City of God, London, 1921.

FINLAY, G., Greece under the Romans, Everyman Lib.
        History of Greece, Oxford, 1877. 7v.

FIRDOUSI, Epic of the Kings, retold by Helen Zimmern, N. Y., 1883.
        Shah Nameh, in Gottheil, R., Literature of Persia, N. Y., Vol. I.

FISHER, H. L., The Medieval Empire, London, 1898. 2v.

FOAKES-JACKSON, F., and LAKE, K., Beginnings of Christianity, London, 1920.
        3v.

FRANCKE, K., History of German Literature, N. Y., 1901.

FRANK, T., ed., Economic Survey of Ancient Rome, Baltimore, 1933f. 5v.

FRAZER, SIR J., Adonis, Attis, Osiris, London, 1907.
        The Magic Art, N. Y., 1935. 2v.

FREEMAN, E. A., Historical Essays, First Series, London, 1896.
        History of the Norman Conquest of England, London, 1870.
        4v.

FRENCH CLASSICS, ed. Perier, Paris, Librairie Hatier, n.d.

FRIEDLÄNDER, L., Roman Life and Manners under the Early Empire, London,
        n.d. 4v.

FUNK, F. X., Manual of Church History, London, 1910. 2v.

GABIROL, SOLOMON IBN, The Improvement of the Moral Qualities, tr. and introd.
        by Stephen S. Wise, N. Y., 1902.
        Selected Religious Poems, tr. Israel Zangwill, Phila.,
        1923.

GARDINER, E. N., Athletics of the Ancient World, Oxford, 1930.

GARDNER, ALICE, Julian, Philosopher and Emperor, N. Y., 1895.

GARRISON, F., History of Medicine, Phila., 1929.

GASQUET, A., CARDINAL, Monastic Life in the Middle Ages, London, 1922.

GEOFFREY OF MONMOUTH, British History, in Giles, Six Chronicles.

GEST, A. P., Roman Engineering, N. Y., 1930.

GESTA FRANCORUM, ed. Brehier, Paris, 1924.

AL-GHAZALI, ABU HAMID, The Alchemy of Happiness, tr. Field, London, 1910.
        Some Religious and Moral Teachings, tr. Nawab
        Ali, Baroda, 1920.

GIBBON, ED., Decline and Fall of the Roman Empire, Everyman Library. 6v.
        ed. J. B. Bury, London, 1900. 7v.

GILDAS, Works, in Giles, Six Chronicles.

GILES, J. A., Six Old English Chronicles, London, 1848.

GILSON, E., La philosophie au moyen âge, Paris, 1922. 2v.
        La philosophie au moyen âge, Paris. 1947.
        Philosophy of St. Bonaventure, N. Y., 1938.
        Reason and Revelation in the Middle Ages, N. Y., 1938.

GIRALDUS CAMBRENSIS, Itinerary through Wales, and Description of Wales,
        Everyman Lib.

GLOVER, T. R., Life and Letters in the Fourth Century, N. Y., 1924.

GORDON, R. K., ed., see Anglo-Saxon Poetry.

GOTTHEIL, R. J., ed., Literature of Persia, N. Y., 1900. 2v.

GRABMANN, M., Thomas Aquinas, N. Y., 1928.

GRAETZ, H., History of the Jews, tr. Bella Löwy, Phila., 1891f. 6v.

GREEN, J. R., Conquest of England, London, 1884.

The Making of England, London, 1882.
*   Short History of the English People, London, 1898. 3v.
GREGORY OF TOURS, History of the Franks, tr. Brehaut, N. Y., 1916.
GROUSSET, R., Civilizations of the East, London, 1931; Vol. I: The Near and
        Middle East.
GROVE's Dictionary of Music and Musicians, N. Y., 1928. 5v.
GRUNEBAUM, G. VON, Medieval Islam, Univ. of Chicago Press, 1946.
GRUNER, O. C., Treatise on the Canon of Medicine of Avicenna, London, 1930.
GUIBERT OF NOGENT, Autobiography, London, 1925.
GUIGNEBERT, C., Christianity Past and Present, N. Y., 1927.
GUILLAUME, A., The Traditions of Islam, Oxford, 1924.
GUIZOT, F., History of Civilization, London, 1898. 3v.
*   History of France, London, 1872. 8v.

HALEVI, J., Kitab al Khazari, tr. Hirschfeld, London, 1931.
        Selected Poems, tr. Nina Salaman, Phila., 1928.
HAMMERTON, J. A., ed., Universal History of the World, London, n.d. 8v.
HASKINS, C. H., The Normans in European History, Boston, 1915.
        The Renaissance of the Twelfth Century, Harvard Univ. Press,
        1928.
        Studies in Medieval Culture, Oxford, 1929.
HASTINGS, J., ed., Encyclopedia of Religion and Ethics, N. Y., 1928. 12v.
HAVERFIELD, F., The Roman Occupation of Britain, Oxford, 1924.
HAZLITT, W. C., The Venetian Republic, London, 1900. 2v.
HEADLAM, C., Story of Chartres, London, 1908.
        Story of Nuremberg, London, 1911.
HEARNSHAW, F., Social and Political Ideas of Some Great Medieval Thinkers,
        N. Y., 1923.
        Medieval Contributions to Modern Civilization, N. Y., 1922.
HEATH, SIR THOS., History of Greek Mathematics, Oxford, 1921. 2v.
HEBRAIC LITERATURE, translations from the Talmud, Midrashim, and Cabala,
        London, 1901.
HEBREW LITERATURE, ed. Epiphanius Wilson, N. Y., 1901.
HEFELE, C. J., History of the Christian Councils, Edinburgh, 1894. 5v.
HEITLAND, W., Agricola, Camb. Univ. Press, 1921.
HELL, Jos., The Arab Civilization, Camb. Univ. Press, 1926.
HIGHAM, T., and BOWRA, C., Oxford Book of Greek Verse, Oxford, 1930.
HIMES, N., Medical History of Contraception, Baltimore, 1936.
HITLER, A., Mein Kampf, N. Y., 1939.
HITTI, P. K., History of the Arabs, London, 1937.
HODGKIN, T., Italy and Her Invaders, Oxford, 1892. 7v.
        Charlemagne, N. Y., 1902.
HOLINSHED, Chronicle, Everyman Lib.
HOME, G., Roman London, London, 1926.
HOOVER, H., and GIBBONS, H. A., Conditions of a Lasting Peace, N. Y., 1939.
HOPKINS, C. EDWARD, The Share of Thomas Aquinas in the Growth of the
        Witchcraft Delusion, Univ. of Penn., 1940.
HORN, F. W., History of the Literature of the Scandinavian North, Chicago,
        1895.
HOUTSMA, M., ed., Encyclopedia of Islam, London, 1908–24.
HOWARD, C., Sex Worship, Chicago, 1909.

HULME, E. M., The Middle Ages, N. Y., 1938.
HUME, DAVID, History of England, N. Y., 1891. 6v.
HUME, MARTIN, The Spanish People, N. Y., 1911.
HURGRÖNJE, C., Mohammedanism, N. Y., 1916.
HUSIK, I., History of Medieval Jewish Philosophy, N. Y., 1930.
HYDE, DOUGLAS, Literary History of Ireland, London, 1899.

IACOPO DE VORAGINE, The Golden Legend, tr. Wm. Caxton, Cambridge Univ.
        Press, 1914.
IBN KHALDOUN, Les prolégomènes, tr. en français par M. de Slane, Paris, 1934.
        3v.
IBN KHALLIKAN, M., Biographical Dictionary, tr. M. de Slane, Paris, 1843. 2v.
INGE, W. R., Philosophy of Plotinus, London, 1929. 2v.
IRVING, W., Alhambra, N. Y., 1925.
        Life of Mahomet, Everyman Lib.

JACKSON, SIR T., Byzantine and Romanesque Architecture, Camb. Univ. Press,
        1920. 2v.
            Gothic Architecture in France, England, and Italy, Camb.
            Univ. Press, 1915. 2v.
JALAL UD-DIN RUMI, Selected Poems, ed. & tr. R. A. Nicholson, Camb. Univ.
        Press, 1898.
JAMES, B., Women of England, Phila., 1908.
JENKS, EDW., Law and Politics in the Middle Ages, N. Y., 1898.
JEROME, ST., Select Letters, tr. Wright, Loeb Lib.
*JOINVILLE, JEAN DE, Chronicle of the Crusade of St. Louis, Everyman Lib.
JORDANES, Gothic History, Princeton Univ. Press, 1915.
JÖRGENSEN, J., St. Francis of Assisi, N. Y., 1940.
JOSEPH BEN JOSHUA BEN MEIR, Chronicles, London, 1835. 2v.
JOYCE, P., Short History of Ireland, London, 1924.
JULIAN, Works, Loeb Lib. 3v.
JUSSERAND, J. J., English Wayfaring Life in the Middle Ages, London, 1891.
JUSTINIANI INSTITUTIONUM LIBRI QUATTUOR, ed. Moyle, Oxford Univ. Press,
        1888, 2v.

KANTOROWICZ, E., Frederick the Second, London, 1931.
KELLOGG, J. H., Rational Hydrotherapy, Battle Creek, Mich., 1928.
KER, W. P., Epic and Romance, London, 1897.
KIRSTEIN, L., Dance: a Short History, N. Y., 1935.
KLAUSNER, J., From Jesus to Paul, N. Y., 1943.
KLUCHEVSKY, V., History of Russia, London, 1912. 3v.
KOMROFF, M., Contemporaries of Marco Polo, N. Y., 1937.
KROEGER, A., The Minnesinger of Germany, N. Y., 1873.

LACROIX, PAUL, Arts of the Middle Ages, London, n.d.
            History of Prostitution, N. Y., 1931. 2v.
            Manners, Customs, and Dress during the Middle Ages, N. Y.,
            1876.
            Military and Religious Life in the Middle Ages, London, n.d.
            Science and Literature in the Middle Ages, London, n.d.
LANCIANI, R., Ancient Rome, Boston, 1889.

LANE, EDW., Arabian Society in the Middle Ages, London, 1883.
LANE-POOLE, S., Art of the Saracens in Egypt, London, 1886.
    Cairo, London, 1895.
    Saladin, London, 1920.
    Speeches and Table Talk of the Prophet Mohammad, London, 1882.
    Story of the Moors in Spain, N. Y., 1889.
    Studies in a Mosque, London, 1883.
LANG, P. H., Music in Western Civilization, N. Y., 1941. A model of scholarship and style.
LAVISSE, E., Histoire de France, Paris, 1900f. 18v.
LEA, H. C., Historical Sketch of Sacerdotal Celibacy, Boston, 1884.
    History of Auricular Confessions, Phila., 1886. 3v.
    History of the Inquisition in the Middle Ages, N. Y., 1888. 3v.
    History of the Inquisition in Spain, N. Y., 1906. 4v.
    Superstition and Force, Phila., 1892.
LECKY, W. E., History of European Morals, N. Y., 1926. 2v.
LESTRANGE, G., Baghdad during the Abbasid Caliphate, Oxford, 1924.
    Palestine under the Moslems, Boston, 1890.
LETHABY, W., Medieval Art, London, 1904.
LÖNNROT, E., Kalevala, Everyman Lib. 2v.
LITTLE, A. G., ed., Roger Bacon Essays, Oxford, 1914.
LITTLE FLOWERS OF ST. FRANCIS, Everyman Lib.
LORRIS, W., and JEAN CLOPINEL DE MEUNG, The Romance of the Rose, London, 1933. 3v.
LOT, F., The End of the Ancient World, N. Y., 1931.
LOUIS, PAUL, Ancient Rome at Work, N. Y., 1927.
LOWIE, R., Are We Civilized?, N. Y., 1929.
LÜTZOW, COUNT VON, Bohemia, an Historical Sketch, Everyman Lib.
LYRA GRAECA, ed. and tr. by J. M. Edmonds, Loeb Lib. 3v.

MABINOGION, tr. Lady Charlotte Guest, Everyman Lib.
MACDONALD, D. B., Aspects of Islam, N. Y., 1911.
    Development of Muslim Theology, Jurisprudence, and Constitutional Theory, N. Y., 1903.
    Religious Attitude and Life in Islam, Chicago, 1909.
MACLAURIN, C., Mere Mortals, N. Y., 1925. 2v.
MACROBII, Opera accedunt integra, London, 1694.
MAHAFFY, J. P., Old Greek Education, N. Y., n.d.
MAIMONIDES, Guide to the Perplexed, tr. Friedländer, London, 1885. 3v.
    Mishneh Torah, Book I, tr. Hyamson, N. Y., 1937.
MAINE, SIR H., Ancient Law, Everyman Lib.
MAITLAND, S. R., Dark Ages, London, 1890.
AL-MAKKARI, AHMED, History of the Mohammedan Dynasties in Spain, tr. de Gayangos, London, 1840. 2v.
MÂLE, É., L'art religieux du XIIIme siècle en France, Paris, 1902.
MALTER, H., Saadia Gaon, Phila., 1921.
MANTZIUS, K., History of Theatrical Art, London, 1903f. 6v.
MARCUS AURELIUS, Meditations, tr. Long, Boston, 1876.
MARCUS, J., The Jew in the Medieval World, Cincinnati, 1938.

MARGOLIOUTH, D. S., Cairo, Jerusalem, and Damascus, N. Y., 1907.
        Mohammed and the Rise of Islam, N. Y., 1905.
MARITAIN, J., The Angelic Doctor, N. Y., 1940.
AL-MASUDI, ABU-L HASAN, Meadows of Gold and Mines of Gems, tr. Sprenger,
        London, 1841.
MATTHEWS, B., Development of the Drama, N. Y., 1921.
MAVOR, J., Economic History of Russia, London, 1925. 2v.
MAY, SIR T., Democracy in Europe, London, 1877. 2v.
McCABE, J., Crises in the History of the Papacy, N. Y., 1916.
        Empresses of Constantinople, Boston, n.d.
        St. Augustine and His Age, N. Y., 1903.
        Story of Religious Controversy, Boston, 1929.
McKINNEY, H., and ANDERSON, W., Music in History, Cincinnati, 1940.
MICHELET, J. DE, History of France, N. Y., 1880. 2v.
MIGEON, G., Les arts musulmans, Paris, 1922. 2v.
MILMAN, H., History of Latin Christianity, N. Y., 1860. 8v.
MIRROR OF PERFECTION, in Little Flowers of St. Francis.
MOLMENTI, P., Venice, London, 1906. 6v.
MOMMSEN, TH., Provinces of the Roman Empire, N. Y., 1887. 2v.
MONROE, P., Source Book of the History of Education for the Greek and Roman
        Period, N. Y., 1932.
MONTALEMBERT, COUNT DE, The Monks of the West, Boston, n.d. 2v.
*MONTESQUIEU, CHAS. BARON DE, Spirit of Laws, N. Y., 1899. 2v.
MOORE, C. H., Development and Character of Gothic Architecture, London,
        1890.
MOORE, G. F., Judaism in the First Centuries of the Christian Era, Cambridge,
        Mass., 1932. 2v.
MOREY, CHAS., Medieval Art, N. Y., 1942.
MUIR, SIR W., The Caliphate, London, 1891.
        Life of Mohammed, Edinburgh, 1912.
MÜLLER-LYER, F., Evolution of Modern Marriage, N. Y., 1930.
MUMFORD, LEWIS, Technics and Civilization, N. Y., 1934.
MUNK, S., Mélanges de philosophie juive et arabe, Paris, 1859.
MUNRO, D. C., and SELLERY, G. C., Medieval Civilization, N. Y., 1926.
MURRAY, A. S., History of Greek Sculpture, London, 1890. 2v.

NENNIUS, History of the Britons, in Giles, Six Chronicles.
NEUMAN, A. A., The Jews in Spain, Phila., 1942. 2v.
*NEWMAN, LOUIS, and SPITZ, S., The Talmudic Anthology, N. Y., 1945.
NICHOLSON, R. A., Literary History of the Arabs, Camb. Univ. Press, 1930.
        The Mystics of Islam, Camb. Univ. Press, 1922.
        Studies in Islamic Mysticism, Camb. Univ. Press, 1921.
        Studies in Islamic Poetry, Camb. Univ. Press, 1921.
        Translations of Eastern Poetry and Prose, Camb. Univ.
        Press, 1922.
NICKERSON, H., The Inquisition, Boston, 1923.
NIETZSCHE, F., Beyond Good and Evil, N. Y., 1923.
NÖLDEKE, TH., Sketches from Eastern History, London, 1892.
NUN'S RULE, being the Ancren Riwle modernized, by Jas. Morton, London,
        1926.

Oesterley, W., and Box, G., Short Survey of the Literature of Rabbinical and Medieval Judaism, London, 1920.
Ogg, F., Source Book of Medieval History, N. Y., 1907.
O'Leary, DeLacy, Arabic Thought and Its Place in History, London, 1922.
Oman, C. W., The Byzantine Empire, London, 1892.
Oxford History of Music, Oxford, 1929f. 7v.

Paetow, L. J., Guide to the Study of Medieval History, N. Y., 1931.
Palmer, E. H., The Caliph Haroun Alraschid, N. Y., n.d.
Panofsky, Erwin, Abbot Suger, Princeton, 1948.
Paris, Matthew, English History from the Year 1235 to 1273, tr. Giles, London, 1852. 3v.
Paul the Deacon, History of the Longobards, tr. Foulke, Univ. of Penn., 1907.
Pauphilet, A., ed., Jeux et sapience du moyen âge, Paris, 1940.
Persian Art, Souvenir of the Exhibition at Burlington House, London, 1931.
Philby, H. St. John, A Pilgrim in Arabia, Golden Cockerel Press, n.d.
Pickthall, Marmaduke, The Meaning of the Glorious Koran, N. Y., 1930.
Pirenne, H., Economic and Social History of Medieval Europe, N. Y., n.d.
          History of Europe from the Invasions to the Sixteenth Century, N. Y., 1939.
          Medieval Cities, Princeton, 1939.
          Mohammed and Charlemagne, N. Y., 1930.
Pirenne, J., Les grands courants de l'histoire universelle, Neuchâtel, 1946. 3v.
Pliny the Elder, Natural History, London, 1855. 6v.
Plummer, C., Life and Times of Alfred the Great, Oxford, 1902.
Pokrovsky, M., History of Russia, N. Y., 1931.
Pollock, F., and Maitland, F., History of English Law before Edward I, Camb. Univ. Press, 1895. 2v.
*Polo, Marco, Travels, ed. Komroff, N. Y., 1926.
Poole, R. L., Illustrations of the History of Medieval Thought and Learning, N. Y., 1920.
Pope, A. U., Introduction to Persian Art, London, 1930.
          Iranian and Armenian Contributions to the Beginnings of Gothic Architecture, Bulletin of the Asia Institute, N. Y., 1946.
*   Masterpieces of Persian Art, N. Y., 1945.
          Survey of Persian Art, Oxford Univ. Press, 1938. 6v.
Porter, A. K., Medieval Architecture, N. Y., 1909. 2v.
Power, Eileen, Medieval People, Boston, 1924.
          and Power, Rhoda, Cities and Their Stories, Boston, 1927.
Prestage, E., Chivalry, N. Y., 1928.
Procopius, Anecdota, or Secret History, Loeb Lib.
          Buildings, Loeb Lib.
          History of the Wars, Loeb Lib. 5v.
Psellus, M., Chronographia, French tr. by Émile Renauld, Paris, n.d.

Quennell, M., Everyday Life in Roman Britain, N. Y., 1925.

Raby, F. J., History of Christian Latin Poetry in the Middle Ages, Oxford, 1927.
          History of Secular Latin Poetry in the Middle Ages, Oxford, 1934. 2v.
Rambaud, A., History of Russia, Boston, 1879. 3v.

RAPAPORT, S., Tales and Maxims from the Talmud, London, 1910.

RASHDALL, H., The Universities of Europe in the Middle Ages, Oxford, 1936, revised by F. M. Powicke and A. B. Emden. 3v.

RAWLINSON, G., The Seventh Great Oriental Monarchy, London, 1876.

REESE, G., Music in the Middle Ages, N. Y., 1940.

RÉMUSAT, C. DE, Abélard, Paris, 1845. 2v.

RENAN, E., Averroès et l'averroïsme, Paris, n.d.
    The Christian Church, London, n.d.
    Marc Aurèle, Paris, n.d.
    Poetry of the Celtic Races, in Harvard Classics, Vol. 38, N. Y., 1938.

RENARD, G., Guilds of the Middle Ages, London, 1918.

RICHARD, E., History of German Civilization, N. Y., 1911.

RICKARD, T., Man and Metals, N. Y., 1932. 2v.

RIEFSTAHL, R., The Parish-Watson Collection of Mohammedan Potteries, N. Y., 1922.

RIHANI, A., The Quatrains of Abu-l Ala, London, 1904.

RIVOIRA, G., Lombardic Architecture, London, 1910. 2v.
    Moslem Architecture, Oxford, 1918.

ROBERTSON, J. M., Short History of Free Thought, London, 1914. 2v.

ROBILLARD, M., Chartres, Grenoble, n.d.

ROGERS, J. E. T., Six Centuries of Work and Wages, N. Y., 1890.

ROSTOVTZEFF, M., History of the Ancient World, Oxford, 1928. Vol. II: Rome.
    Social and Economic History of the Roman Empire, Oxford, 1926.

ROTH, LEON, Spinoza, Descartes, and Maimonides, Oxford, 1924.

ROWBOTHAM, J., The Troubadours and Courts of Love, London, 1895.

RUSKIN, J., Stones of Venice, Everyman Lib. 3v.

RUSSELL, B., History of Western Philosophy, N. Y., 1945.

RUSSELL, C. E., Charlemagne, Boston, 1930.

SABATIER, P., Life of St. Francis of Assisi, N. Y., 1909.

SA'DI, The Gulistan, in Gottheil, R., Literature of Persia, Vol. II.
    The Rose Garden (Gulistan), tr. by L. Cranmer-Byng, London, 1919.

SALADIN, H., ET MIGEON, G., Manuel d'art musulman, Paris, 1907. 2v.

SALIBA, D., Étude sur la métaphysique d'Avicenne, Paris, 1926.

SALZMAN, L., English Industries of the Middle Ages, Oxford, 1923.

SANDYS, SIR J., Companion to Latin Studies, Cambridge, 1925.

SANGER, W., History of Prostitution, N. Y., 1910.

SARRE, F., Die Kunst des alten Persien, Berlin, 1925.

SARTON, G., Introduction to the History of Science, Baltimore, 1930f. 3v. in 5. A masterpiece of painstaking scholarship.

SAUNDERS, O. E., History of English Art in the Middle Ages, Oxford, 1932.

SAXO GRAMMATICUS, Danish History, London, n.d. 2v.

SCHECHTER, S., Studies in Judaism, N. Y., 1920. 3v.

SCHEVILL, F., Siena, N. Y., 1909.

SCHNEIDER, H., The History of World Civilization, N. Y., 1931. 2v.

SCHOENFELD, H., Women of the Teutonic Nations, Phila., 1908.

SCHOENHOF, J., History of Money and Prices, N. Y., 1896.

*SCOTT-MONCRIEFF, C. K., The Letters of Abélard and Héloïse, N. Y., 1926.

SEDGWICK, H. D., Italy in the Thirteenth Century, Boston, 1912. 2v.

SEEBOHM, F., The English Village Community, London, 1896.

SEIGNOBOS, C., The Feudal Regime, N. Y., 1902.

SHORT, E. H., The Painter in History, London, 1929.

SHOTWELL, J. T., and LOOMIS, L. R., The See of Peter, Columbia Univ. Press, 1927.

SIDONIUS APOLLINARIS, Poems and Letters, Loeb Lib. 2v.

SIGFUSSON, SAEMUND, The Elder Edda, London, 1907.

SIHLER, E. G., From Augustus to Augustine, Camb. Univ. Press, 1923.

SINGER, C., ed., Studies in the History and Method of Science, Oxford, 1917f. 2v.

SMITH, MARGARET, ed., The Persian Mystics: Attar, London, 1932.

SMITH, TOULMIN, English Gilds: the Original Ordinances, London, 1870.

SOCRATES, Ecclesiastical History, London, 1892.

SOZOMEN, Ecclesiastical History, London, 1855.

SPECULUM, A JOURNAL OF MEDIEVAL STUDIES, Cambridge, Mass.

SPENCER, H., Principles of Sociology, N. Y., 1910. 3v.

*SPENGLER, O., Decline of the West, N. Y., 1928. 2v.

STEPHENS, W. R., Hildebrand and His Times, London, 1914.

STERLING, M. B., The Story of Parzival, N. Y., 1911.

STEVENS, C. E., Sidonius Apollinaris, Oxford, 1933.

STREET, G. E., Gothic Architecture in Spain, London, 1869.

STRZYGOWSKI, J., Origin of Christian Church Art, Oxford, 1923.

STUBBS, WM., Constitutional History of England, Oxford, 1903. 3v.

STURLUSON, SNORRI, Heimskringla: The Norse Sagas, Everyman Lib.
　　　　　　　　Heimskringla: The Olaf Sagas, Everyman Lib.
　　　　　　　　The Younger Edda, in Sigfusson, S.

SUMNER, W. G., Folkways, Boston, 1906.

SYKES, SIR P., History of Persia, London, 1921. 2v.

SYMONDS, J. A., Studies of the Greek Poets, London, 1920.
　　　　　　　　Introduction to the Study of Dante, London, 1899.

AL-TABARI, Chronique, Fr. tr. by Zotenberg, Paris, 1867.

TAGORE, SIR R., Gitanjali, N. Y., 1928.

TAINE, H., Ancient Regime, N. Y., 1891.
　　　　　　Italy: Florence and Venice, N. Y., 1869.

TALMUD, Babylonian, Eng. tr., London, 1935f. 24v.

TARN, W., Hellenistic Civilization, London, 1927.

TAYLOR, H. O., The Classical Heritage of the Middle Ages, N. Y., 1911.
　　　　　　　　The Medieval Mind, London, 1927. 2v.

THATCHER, O., and MCNEAL, E., Source Book for Medieval History, N. Y., 1905.

THIERRY, A., History of the Conquest of England by the Normans, London, 1847. 2v.

THOMAS AQUINAS, ST., Summa contra Gentiles, London, 1924. 4v.
　　　　　　　　　　Summa theologica, tr. by Dominican Fathers, London, 1920. 22v.

THOMPSON, SIR E., Introduction to Greek and Latin Palaeography, Oxford, 1912.

THOMPSON, J. W., Economic and Social History of the Middle Ages, 300–1300, N. Y., 1928.
　　　　　　　　Economic and Social History of Europe in the Later Middle Ages, N. Y., 1931.
　　　　　　　　Feudal Germany, Chicago, 1928.
　　　　　　　　The Middle Ages, N. Y., 1931. 2v.

*THORNDIKE, LYNN, History of Magic and Experimental Science, N. Y., 1929f. A work of magnificent scholarship, which illuminates every subject that it touches.
* Short History of Civilization, N. Y., 1926.
TISDALL, W., Original Sources of the Qur'an.
TORNAY, S. C., Averroës' Doctrine of the Mind, Philadelphia Review, May, 1943.
*TOYNBEE, A. J., A Study of History, Oxford, 1935f. 6v.
TRAILL, H. D., Social England, N. Y., 1902. 6v.

UEBERWEG, F., History of Philosophy, N. Y., 1871. 2v.
USHER, A. P., History of Mechanical Inventions, N. Y., 1929.
AL-UTBI, ABUL-NASR, Memoirs of the Emir Sabaktagin and Mahmud of Ghazna, tr. Reynolds, London, 1858.

VACANDARD, E., The Inquisition, N. Y., 1908.
*VAN DOREN, MARK, An Anthology of World Poetry, N. Y., 1928. The best work of its kind.
VASARI, G., Lives of the Painters, Everyman Lib. 3v.
VASILIEV, A., History of the Byzantine Empire, Madison, Wis., 1929. 2v.
VERNADSKY, G., Kievan Russia, Yale Univ. Press, 1948.
VILLARI, P., The Two First Centuries of Florentine History, London, 1908.
*VILLEHARDOUIN, G. DE, Chronicle of the Fourth Crusade, Everyman Lib.
VINOGRADOFF, P., English Society in the Eleventh Century, Oxford, 1908.
VOLTAIRE, Essay on the Manners and Morals of Europe, in Works, Vol. XIII, N. Y., 1901.
VOSSLER, K., Medieval Culture: an Introduction to Dante and His Times, N. Y., 1929. 2v.

*WADDELL, HELEN, Medieval Latin Lyrics, N. Y., 1942.
* The Wandering Scholars, London, 1927.
* Peter Abélard, N. Y., 1933.
WAERN, C., Medieval Sicily, London, 1910.
WALKER TRUST REPORT, The Great Palace of the Byzantine Emperors, Oxford, 1947.
WALSH, J. J., The Popes and Science, N. Y., 1913.
The Thirteenth the Greatest of Centuries. Catholic Summer School Press, 1920.
WALTHER VON DER VOGELWEIDE, I Saw the World, tr. Colvin, London, 1938.
Songs and Sayings, tr. Betts, London, n.d.
WAXMAN, M., History of Jewish Literature, N. Y., 1930. 3v.
WEIGALL, A., The Paganism in Our Christianity, N. Y., 1928.
WEIR, T. H., Omar Khayyam the Poet, N. Y., 1926.
WELCH, ALICE, Of Six Medieval Women, London, 1913.
WEST, A. F., Alcuin, N. Y., 1916.
WESTERMARCK, E., Origin and Development of the Moral Ideas, London, 1917f. 2v.
Short History of Marriage, N. Y., 1926.
WHERRY, E. M., Commentary on the Qur'an, with Sale's tr. and notes, London, 1896. 4v.
WHITE, E. M., Woman in World History, London, n.d.

WICKSTEED, P. H., Dante and Aquinas, London, 1913.

WILLIAM OF MALMESBURY, Chronicle of the Kings of England, London, 1883.

WILLIAM OF TYRE, Godeffroy of Bologne, or the Siege and Conqueste of Jerusalem, tr. Caxton, London, 1893.

WILLOUGHBY, W. W., Social Justice, N. Y., 1900.

WINCKELMANN, J., History of Ancient Art, Boston, 1880. 2v.

WOLFRAM VON ESCHENBACH, Parzival, tr. Weston, London, 1894. 2v.

WRIGHT, TH., ed., The Book of the Knight of La Tour-Landry, London, 1868. A History of Domestic Manners and Sentiments in England during the Middle Ages, London, 1862.

YELLIN, D., and ABRAHAMS, I., Maimonides, Phila., 1903.

ZEITLIN, S., Maimonides, N. Y., 1935.

ZIMMERN, H., The Hansa Towns, N. Y., 1889.

Notes

Full titles of works referred to will be found in the Bibliography. Capital Roman numerals, except at the beginning of a note, indicate volumes, followed by page numbers; small Roman numerals indicate "books" (divisions of a text), followed by chapter or verse numbers.

CHAPTER I

1. Ammianus Marcellinus, xxi, 16.
2. Philostorgius, ii, 9, in Gibbon, *Decline and Fall of the Roman Empire*, II, 78.
3. Sozomen, *Ecclesiastical History*, ii, 3.
4. Lot, Ferdinand, *End of the Ancient World*, 71; Bury, J. B., *History of the Later Roman Empire*, I, 87.
5. *Cambridge Medieval History*, IV, 748.
6. Ibid., I, 593.
7. Munro and Sellery, *Medieval Civilization*, 87, says 30,000; Bury, op. cit., says 70,000.
8. Dudden, F. H., *Gregory the Great*, I, 129.
9. Duchesne, L., *Early History of the Christian Church*, II, 127.
10. Socrates, *Ecclesiastical History*, i, 37-8.
11. Ibid., ii, 7-11.
12. Boissier, G., *La Fin du paganisme*, I, 68; Duchesne, II, 250.
13. Boissier, op. cit., I, 82.
14. Eunapius, *Lives of the Sophists*, 487.
15. Capes, W. W., *University Life in Ancient Athens*, 66.
16. Boissier, I, 178.
17. Wright, W. C., Introd. to Eunapius, p. 333.
18. Cf. Inge, W. R., *Philosophy of Plotinus*, I, 11.
19. In Murray, A. S., *History of Greek Sculpture*, I, 100.
20. In Boissier, I, 96.
21. Ammianus, xxii, 5; Duchesne, II, 262.
22. Boissier, I, 102.
23. Socrates, iii, 1.
24. Julian, *Letter to the Athenians*, 278D-280C; Ammianus, xvi, 11-12.
25. Ammianus, xvi, 53; Duchesne, II, 199.
26. Ammianus, xviii, 1.
27. Ibid., xvi, 10.
28. Boissier, I, 107.
29. Ammianus, xxv, 4.
30. Julian, *Misopogon*, 338B.
31. Socrates, iii, 1; Ammianus, xxii, 4.
32. *Misopogon*, 340B.
33. Ammianus, xvi, 1.
34. Gardner, Alice, *Julian, Philosopher and Emperor*, 260.
35. Ammianus, xxii, 7.
36. Eunapius, 477.
37. Julian, Letter 441, in *Works*, III, 7.
38. Julian, *To Edicius*, 23, in *Works*, III.
39. Julian, *Against the Galileans*, 89A-94A, 106DE, 168B, 351D, 238A, 319D.
40. Julian, *To the Cynic Herakleios*, 205C.
41. Ibid., 217B.
42. Ibid., 237B.
43. Ammianus, xxii, 12.
44. Lucian, *Panegyric*, in Boissier, I, 140.
45. Julian, *Letter to a Priest*, 305B; *To Arsacius*.
46. Julian, *To the High Priest Theodorus*, 16.
47. *Letter to a Priest*, 290D.
48. Ammianus, xxii, 10.
49. Sozomen, v, 5, 18; Julian, *Works*, III, 41n.
50. In Boissier, I, 122.
51. Julian, Letter 10; Boissier, I, 127.
52. Julian, *Misopogon*, 368C.
53. Ammianus, xxii, 13.
54. Sozomen, vi, 2.
55. Ammianus, xxv, 3.
56. Milman, H. H., *History of Latin Christianity*, I, 112; Sihler, E. G., *From Augustus to Augustine*, 217.
57. Theodoret, iii, 28, in Lecky, W. E. H., *History of European Morals*, II, 261.
58. Duchesne, II, 268.

CHAPTER II

1. Dopsch, A., *Economic and Social Foundations of European Civilization*, 89.
2. William of Malmesbury, *Chronicle of the Kings of England*, i, 4.
3. Lea, H. C., *Superstition and Force*, 451.
4. Boissier, II, 180.
5. Rostovtzeff, M., *Social and Economic History of the Roman Empire*, 479.
6. Dill, S., *Roman Society in the Last Century of the Roman Empire*, 297.
7. Jordanes, *Gothic History*, #247.
8. In Thompson, J. W., *Economic and Social History of the Middle Ages*, 106.
9. Jordanes, #26f; Gibbon, III, 38.
10. Ammianus, xxxi, 13.
11. Socrates, iv, 31.
12. Broglie, Duc de, *St. Ambrose*, 120-4.
13. Gibbon, III, 168.
14. Bury, J. B., *History of the Later Roman Empire*, I, 129; Gibbon, III, 175.
15. Pirenne, H., *Medieval Cities*, 36.
16. Louis, Paul, *Ancient Rome at Work*, 231.

17. Boissier, I, 417; Dill, op. cit., 228, 272.
18. Salvianus, *De Gubernatione Dei*, v, 28, in Frank, T., *Economic Survey of Ancient Rome*, III, 260.
19. Boissier, II, 416.
20. Ibid.
21. Louis, Paul, 235.
22. In Hodgkin, T., *Italy and Her Invaders*, I, 423.
23. Cf. Augustine, Ep. 232.
24. Salvian, iv, 15; vii, *passim;* and excerpts in Heitland, W. E., *Agricola*, 423, Boissier, II, 410, 420, and Bury, *Later Roman Empire*, 307.
25. In Dill, 56.
26. Symmachus, Ep. vi, 42; ii, 46; in Dill, 150.
27. Friedländer, L., *Roman Life and Manners under the Early Empire*, II, 12.
28. Lot, 178; Dill, 58; Friedländer, II, 29.
29. Ammianus, xiv, 6.
30. Symmachus, Ep. iii, 43.
31. Ammianus, xxii, 10.
32. Ibid., xxi, 1; Thorndike, L., *History of Magic and Experimental Science*, I, 285.
33. Ammianus, xvi, 1.
34. Macrobius, *Opera accedunt integrae, Saturnalia, ad fin.*
35. Ibid., i, 11.
36. Claudian, *Poems*, "On the Consulate of Stilicho," iii, 130.
37. Voltaire, *Works*, XIII, 77.
38. Boissier, II, 180.
39. In Shotwell, J. T., and Loomis, R., *The See of Peter*, 675.
40. Symmachus, Ep. x, 3, in Boissier, II, 224.
41. In Boissier, II, 280.
42. Jordanes, 167f.
43. Procopius, *History of the Wars*, iii, 3.25.
44. Jordanes, #168.
45. Procopius, iii, 5.
46. Jordanes, #181.
47. Ibid., #254f.
48. Procopius, iii, 4.
49. Gibbon, III, 461; Sihler, 302.

CHAPTER III

1. Paul, I Cor. vii, 32.
2. Gibbon, II, 318; Lecky, *History of European Morals*, II, 49; Duchesne, II, 189.
3. Robertson, J. M., *Short History of Free Thought*, 242; Bury, *History of the Eastern Roman Empire*, 352f.
4. Hefele, C. J., *History of the Christian Councils*, III, 12.
5. Milman, I, 281f.
6. Davis, H. W. C., *Medieval England*, 128.
7. Ammianus, xxvii, 3.
8. Gibbon, II, 485n.
9. Ammianus, xxvii, 3; Duchesne, II, 364.
10. Cutts, E. L., *St. Jerome*, 30f.

11. Jerome, *Letters*, xxii, 30.
12. Ibid., xxxviii, 3; xxii, 13, 27.
13. Ep. cxvii, 7.
14. Ep. xxii, 14.
15. Ibid.
16. Ep. cvii, 3.
17. Ep. xxii, 21.
18. Ep. xxiii.
19. Adv. Jovin., i, 2.
20. Ep. xxii, 25.
21. Duchesne, III, 74.
22. Ibid., 446.
23. Cutts, 150.
24. Jerome, Ep. lx, 17.
25. Socrates, iv, 30.
26. Broglie, 10-13.
27. Augustine, *Confessions*, ix, 7.
28. In Davis, W. S., and West, W. M., *Readings in Ancient History*, II, 297.
29. Guizot, F., *History of Civilization*, I, 341.
30. Gregory of Tours, *History of the Franks*, 15.
31. Guizot, *History of Civilization*, II, 69.
32. Duchesne, II, 391.
33. Lecky, *Morals*, II, 107.
34. Cutts, 137.
35. Lecky, l.c.
36. Ibid., 210.
37. Ibid., 107, 158.
38. Boissier, II, 55.
39. Jerome, Ep. cxxv, 11.
40. Lecky, II, 115.
41. Ibid., 109.
42. Sozomen, vi, 33.
43. Lecky, II, 110; Nöldeke, Th., *Sketches from Eastern History*, 212f.
44. Lecky, II, 118.
45. Taylor, H. O., *Classical Heritage of the Middle Ages*, 78.
46. Ibid.; Glover, T. R., *Life and Letters in the Fourth Century*, 349.
47. In Gibbon, III, 75.
48. Socrates, vi, 3.
49. Bury, *Later Roman Empire*, I, 138-9.
50. Socrates, vi, 4-5.
51. In Clapham and Power, 116.
52. McCabe, J., *St. Augustine and His Age*, 228.
53. Ibid., 35.
54. Augustine, *Confessions*, ii, 3.
55. Ibid., vi, 3.
56. Augustine, *City of God*, ii, 14.
57. *Confessions*, v, 8.
58. Encylopaedia Britannica, II, 682.
59. McCabe, *Augustine*, 254.
60. Catholic Encyclopedia, II, 88; Augustine, *Letters*, introd., xvi-xviii.
61. Augustine, Ep. 86.
62. Ep. 93.
63. Ep. 173.
64. Ep. 204.

65. Eps. 103, 133.
66. *City of God*, v, 9; vi, 22, 27.
67. Sermon 289.
68. Sermon 165.
69. Duchesne, III, 143.
70. Sermon 131.
71. Ep. 181A.
72. Comment. in Joan. Evang., xxix, 6; Sermon 43.
73. In *Cambridge Medieval History*, I, 581.
74. *De Trinitate*, i, 1.
75. *De vera religione*, xxiv, 45.
76. Solil. i, 7.
77. *Confessions*, xiii, 16.
78. *City of God*, iv, 27.
80. *De libero arbitrio*, ii, 16.
81. *De Gen. ad litt.*, vii, 28; De Wulf, *History of Medieval Philosophy*, I, 118; Catholic Encyclopedia, II, 90.
82. In De Wulf, I, 117.
83. *Confessions*, Book xi.
84. *De Trin.*, x, 10.
85. Ibid., viii, 6; *Confessions*, x, 6.
86. *De bono conjugali*, x; Figgis, J. N., *Political Aspects of St. Augustine's City of God*, 76; Lea, H. C., *Sacerdotal Celibacy*, 47.
87. *Confessions*, x, 30.
88. Ibid., vii, 14; x, 6, 22; xiii, 9.
89. *City of God*, vi, 9.
90. Philippians, iii, 20; Ephesians, ii, 19.
91. Figgis, 46.
92. Marcus Aurelius, *Meditations*, iv, 19.
93. *City of God*, xv, 1.
94. Ibid., i, 34.
95. Ibid., xix, 7; xx, 9.
96. Boissier, II, 331.
97. Augustine, *Letters*, p. 38.
98. Comm. on Psalm cxxii.
99. Funk, F. X., *Manual of Church History*, I, 198.
100. Frazer, Sir J. G., *Adonis, Attis, Osiris*, 315.
101. Ibid., 306.
102. In Boissier, II, 118.
103. Renan, E., *Marc Aurèle*, 629.
104. Duchesne, III, 11.
105. Ibid., 16.
106. Lecky, *Morals*, II, 61.
107. Ibid., 72.
108. Ibid., 83.
109. Ibid., 81.
110. Fisher, H. L., *The Medieval Empire*, I, 14.
111. Guignebert, C., *Christianity Past and Present*, 151.
112. Ambrose, Ep. 2, in Boissier, II, 424.

CHAPTER IV

1. *Cambridge Ancient History*, XII, 287.
2. Haverfield, F., *The Roman Occupation of Britain*, 220; Home, G., *Roman Britain*, 104.
3. Quennell, M., *Everyday Life in Roman Britain*, 103.
4. Mommsen, Th., *Provinces of the Roman Empire*, I, 211.
5. Bede, *Ecclesiastical History*, v, 24.
6. Gildas, *Chronicle*, xxiii; *Anglo-Saxon Chronicle*, p. 25.
7. Bede, i, 15; *Anglo-Saxon Chronicle*, 26.
8. Collingwood, R. G., and Myres, J., *Roman Britain*, 320.
9. Geoffrey of Monmouth, *British History*, vii-xi.
10. William of Malmesbury, *Chronicle*, 11.
11. Collingwood, 324.
12. Joyce, P. W., *Short History of Ireland*, 123; Hyde, D., *Literary History of Ireland*, 77.
13. Hyde, 19.
14. Lecky, *Morals*, II, 253.
15. Joyce, 123.
16. Briffault, R., *The Mothers*, III, 230, quoting De Jubainville, *Le Droit du roi dans l'épopée irlandaise*, in *Révue archéologique*, XLIII, 332f.
17. Hyde, 71.
18. Ibid., 83.
19. From the seventh-century "Voyage of Brand," in Hyde, 96f.
20. Bede, i, 13; Bury, J. B., *Life of St. Patrick*, 54.
21. Duchesne, III, 425.
22. Bury, *Patrick*, 172.
23. Nennius, *History of the Britons*, 11, in Giles, *Six Old English Chronicles*, p. 410.
24. Bury, *Patrick*, 121.
25. Ausonius, *Poems, Commemoratio Professorum Burdigalensium*.
26. Waddell, H., *Medieval Latin Lyrics*, 32.
27. Ausonius, *Poems, Parentalia*, x.
28. Ibid., Ep. xxii, 23f.
29. Stevens, *Sidonius Apollinaris*, 68-9.
30. Guizot, *History of Civilization*, I, 343.
31. Dill, *Last Century*, 206.
32. Stevens, 134-8.
33. Ibid., 160f.
34. Sidonius Apollinaris, *Poems and Letters*, Ep. i, 2.
35. In Francke, K., *History of German Literature*, 10.
36. Sidonius in Lacroix, P., *Manners, Customs, and Dress*, 514.
37. Gibbon, IV, 65.
38. Gregory of Tours, viii, 9.
39. Lea, *Superstition and Force*, 318.
40. Sophocles, *Antigone*, 11, 264-7.
41. Gibbon, IV, 70.
42. Schoenfeld, Hermann, *Women of the*

Teutonic Nations, 41; Dill, *Roman Society in the Merovingian Age*, 47.
43. Salic law, xiv and xli, in Ogg, F., *Source Book of Medieval History*, 63-5.
44. Schoenfeld, 40.
45. Brittain, A., *Women of Early Christianity*, 203.
46. Lot, 397.
47. Gregory of Tours, ii, 37.
48. Ibid.
49. Id., ii, 40.
50. II, 43.
51. V, 132-6; vi, 165.
52. Dill, *Merovingian Age*, 279.
53. Gregory of Tours, vii, 178; x, 246.
54. Id., iv, 100.
55. Michelet, J., *History of France*, I, 107.
56. Gregory, introd., p. xxii.
57. Gregory, i, 5.
58. II, prologue.
59. Gregory, introd., p. xxiv.
60. Guizot, *History of Civilization*, I, 58.
61. Lecky, *Morals*, II, 204.
62. Isidore of Seville, *Etymologies*, in Brehaut, E., *An Encyclopedist of the Dark Ages*, 215.
63. Dieulafoy, M., *Art in Spain and Portugal*, 54.
64. Mahaffy, J. P., *Old Greek Education*, 52.
65. Thompson, J. W., *Economic History of the Middle Ages*, 120.
66. Cassiodorus, *Letters of, Variae*, ii, 27.
67. Procopius, v, 1.26.
68. This survives only as a crude abbreviation by Jordanes.
69. Milman, I, 433.
70. Ibid., 439.
71. In Cassiodorus, *Variae*, ii, 6; iii, 28.
72. Milman, I, 442.
73. Boethius, *Consolation of Philosophy*, ii, 3.
74. Ibid., 4.
75. Ibid., iii, 10.
76. Procopius, v, 1.

CHAPTER V

1. *Justiniani Institutionum libri quattuor*, Introd., I, 63.
2. Procopius, *Buildings*, i, 7.
3. Procopius, *Anecdota*, viii, 24.
4. John Malalas in Bury, *Later Roman Empire*, II, 24.
5. Procopius, *Anecdota*, xv, 11.
6. Id., *History of the Wars*, i, 24.
7. Id., *Buildings*, i, 11.
8. Dichl, C., *Byzantine Portraits*, 58.
9. Procopius, *Anecdota*, xi.
10. Ibid., ix, 50.
11. Bury, *Later Roman Empire*, II, 29.
12. Procopius, *Anecdota*, xvii, 5.
13. Diehl, *Portraits*, 70.

14. Bouchier, E., *Life and Letters in Roman Africa*, 107.
15. Procopius, *History of the Wars*, iv, 6.
16. Ibid., vii, 1.
17. Ibid., 5-8.
18. Lot, 267.
19. Gibbon, IV, 359.
20. Lot, 267.
21. *Justiniani Inst.*, Proemium.
22. Cod. I, xiv, 34.
23. Cod. IV, xliii, 21.
24. Cod. XI, xlviii, 21; lxix, 4.
25. Bury, *Later Roman Empire*, II, 406; Milman, I, 501.
26. Procopius, *History of the Wars*, vii, 32.
27. In Gibbon, V, 43.
28. Procopius, *Buildings*, i, 1.

CHAPTER VI

1. Frank, *Economic Survey of Ancient Rome*, IV, 152.
2. Rostovtzeff, M., *History of the Ancient World*, II, 353-4.
3. Procopius, *History*, viii, 17.
4. Lopez, R. S., in *Speculum*, XX, i, 3, 7, 19.
5. Ibid., 10-12.
6. Novella 122 in Bury, *Later Roman Empire*, II, 356.
7. Dalton, O. M., *Byzantine Art*, 50.
8. Bury, 357.
9. Diehl, C., *Manuel d'art Byzantin*, 248.
10. Procopius, *Anecdota*, xvii, 24.
11. Himes, N., *Medical History of Contraception*, 92-6.
12. Boissier, *La fin du paganisme*, I, 168.
13. Gibbon, I, 382.
14. Schneider, H., *History of World Civilization*, II, 640.
15. Castiglione, A., *History of Medicine*, 252; Garrison, F. H., *History of Medicine*, 123.
16. Thorndike, L., *History of Magic and Experimental Science*, I, 147.
17. O'Leary, D., *Arabic Thought*, 53.
18. Himes, 95.
19. Thorndike, I, 584.
20. Augustine, *Confessions*, vii, 6.
21. Heath, Sir T., *History of Greek Mathematics*, II, 528.
22. Socrates, vii, 15.
23. Lecky, *Morals*, II, 315.
24. Bury, *Later Roman Empire*, I, 217.
25. Duchesne, III, 210.
26. Socrates, vii, 15.
27. Gregory Nazianzen, *Panegyric on St. Basil*, in Monroe, P., *Source Book of the History of Education for the Greek and Roman Period*, 305.
28. Bury, *Later Roman Empire*, I, 377.
29. Diehl, *Manuel*, 218.
30. Higham and Bowra, *Oxford Book of Greek Verse*, 654.

31. Ibid., 665.
32. Socrates, vii, 48.
33. Procopius, *History*, viii, 32; v, 3.
34. Winckelmann, J., *History of Ancient Art*, I, 360-1; Finlay, G., *Greece under the Romans*, 195.
35. Strzygowski, J., *Origin of Christian Church Art*, 4-6.
36. Procopius, *Buildings*, i, 10.
37. Ibid., i, 1.
38. Ibid.
39. Ibid., i, 3.
40. Dalton, 258.
41. Lot, 143.
42. Diehl, *Manuel*, 249; Dalton, 579; Lot, 146.
43. Boethius, ix.

CHAPTER VII

1. Ammianus, xxii, 6.
2. Ibid.
3. Dhalla, M. N., *Zoroastrian Civilization*, 371.
4. Rawlinson, G., *Seventh Great Oriental Monarchy*, 29.
5. Procopius, *Persian War*, ix, 19.
6. Bury, *Later Roman Empire*, I, 92.
7. Ammianus, xxiii, 6.
8. Talmud, Berachoth, 8b.
9. Dhalla, 301f.
10. Ameer Ali, *Spirit of Islam*, 188.
11. Macrobius, *Saturnalia*, vii, 1.
12. Gottheil, R. J., *Literature of Persia*, I, 159.
13. Firdousi, *Epic of the Kings*, retold by Helen Zimmern, 191; Sykes, Sir P., *History of Persia*, I, 466.
14. Gottheil, I, 166.
15. Dhalla, 377.
16. Ibid., 305.
17. Browne, E. G., *Literary History of Persia*, I, 107.
18. Sarton, G., *Introd. to the History of Science*, I, 435.
19. Browne, E. G., *Arabian Medicine*, 23.
20. Dhalla, 354.
21. Ibid., 362.
22. Ibid., 274; Bury, *Later Roman Empire*, I, 91.
23. Rawlinson, G., *Seventh Great Oriental Monarchy*, 636.
24. Bright, W., *Age of the Fathers*, I, 202.
25. Sykes, I, 414.
26. Lowie, R. H., *Are We Civilized?*, 37.
27. Pope, A. U., *Survey of Persian Art*, I, 755.
28. Dhalla, 356.
29. Pope, 761.
30. Baron, S. W., *Social and Religious History of the Jews*, I, 256.
31. Ammianus, xxiii, 6.
32. Pope, 716.

33. Browne, *Literary History*, I, 127.
34. Ibn Khaldun, *Prolégomènes*, I, 80. Rawlinson, 61, attributes this saying to Ardashir I.
35. Eunapius, #466.
36. *Cambridge Ancient History*, XII, 112.
37. Sykes, I, 403.
38. Rawlinson, 141.
39. Browne, *Literary History*, I, 171. Sykes, I, 449, places this massacre in the early years of Khosru I.
40. Pope, 755.
41. Procopius, *History of the Wars*, ii, 9.
42. Nöldeke, Th., *Geschichte der Perser . . . aus Tabari*, 160, in De Vaux, *Les Penseurs de l'Islam*, I, 92.
43. Rawlinson, 446.
44. Sykes, I, 460.
45. Procopius, *History*, i, 26.
46. Mommsen, *Provinces*, II, 47.
47. Graetz, H., *History of the Jews*, III, 18.
48. Sykes, I, 480f.
49. Pope, 524.
50. Creswell, K. A., *Early Muslim Architecture*, I, 101.
51. Dieulafoy, *Art in Spain*, 13.
52. Ibid.; Pope, A. U., *Iranian and Armenian Contributions to the Beginnings of Gothic Architecture*, 130.
53. Theophylactus Simocatta in Rivoira, G. T., *Moslem Architecture*, 114. Herzfeld thought the Ctesiphon palace the work of Shapur I.
54. Gottheil, I, 167.
55. Arnold, Sir T., *Painting in Islam*, 62.
56. Pope, *Survey*, I, 717; Dieulafoy, 21.
57. Ackerman, P., in *Bulletin of the Iranian Institute*, Dec., 1946, p. 42.
58. Pope, A. U., *Introd. to Persian Art*, 144, 168.
59. Sykes, I, 465.
60. Pope, A. U., *Masterpieces of Persian Art*, 182.
61. Pope, *Introd.*, 64.
62. Fenollosa, E., *Epochs of Chinese and Japanese Art*, I, 21.
63. Riefstahl, R. M., *The Parish-Watson Collection of Mohammedan Potteries*, p. viii; Pope, *Survey*, I, 779; Lot, 141.
64. Sir Percy Sykes in Hammerton, J. A., *Universal History of the World*, IV, 2318.
65. Examples in Sarre, F., *Die Kunst des alten Persien*, 143.
66. Pope, *Introd.*, 100.
67. Pope, *Survey*, I, 775.
68. Dhalla, 273.
69. Sykes, I, 490.
70. Browne, *Literary History*, I, 194.
71. Sykes, I, 490.
72. Ibid., 498.

CHAPTER VIII

1. Burton, Sir R. F., ed., *Thousand Nights and a Night*, I, vii.
2. Hell, J., *The Arab Civilization*, 7; Dawson, Christopher, *The Making of Europe*, 136.
3. Encyclopaedia Britannica, II, 184.
4. Doughty, Chas., *Travels in Arabia Deserta*, I, xx.
5. Margoliouth, D. S., *Mohammed and the Rise of Islam*, 29; Nöldeke, *Sketches*, 7.
6. Burton, R. F., *Personal Narrative of a Pilgrimage to al-Medinah and Meccah*, II, 93.
7. Blunt, Lady A. and Sir W. S., *The Seven Golden Odes of Pagan Arabia*, 43.
8. Ibid.
9. Koran, ix, 98; tr. and ed. Pickthall, *The Meaning of the Glorious Koran*. Pickthall's numbering of the verses differs occasionally from that of other translations.
10. Sale, G., in Wherry, E. M., *Commentary on the Qur'an*, with Sale's tr., I, 43.
11. Herodotus, iii, 8.
12. Ali Tabari, *Book of Religion and Empire*, Prologue, ix; Margoliouth, *Mohammed*, 59; Muir, Sir W., *Life of Mohammed*, 512.
13. Browne, E. G., *Literary History of Persia*, I, 261.
14. al-Tabari, Abu Jafar Muhammad, *Chronique*, Part III, ch. xlvi, p. 202.
15. Pickthall, p. 2.
16. Browne, *Literary History*, I, 247.
17. Tisdall, W. S., *Original Sources of the Koran*, 264, quoting Ibn Ishaq; Lane-Poole, S., *Speeches and Table Talk of the Prophet Mohammed*, xxiv.
18. Nicholson, R. A., *Translations of Eastern Poetry and Prose*, 38-40. Cf. Koran, xcvi.
19. Muir, *Life*, 51.
20. Koran, xliii, 3; lvi, 76; lxxxv, 22.
21. II, 91.
22. Lxxxvii, 6.
23. Ali, Maulana Muhammad, *The Religion of Islam*, 174.
24. Macdonald, D. B., *Religious Attitude and Life in Islam*, 42.
25. Margoliouth, *Mohammed*, 45.
26. Dozy, R., *Spanish Islam*, 15.
27. Hell, 19.
28. Sale in Wherry, I, 80.
29. al-Baladhuri, Abu-l Abas, *Origins of the Islamic State*, i, 1.
30. Ameer Ali, Syed, *Spirit of Islam*, 54.
31. Muir, *Life*, 214, 234.
32. Ibid., 236.
33. Ibid., 238, quoting traditions.
34. Ibid.
35. Andrae, Tor, *Mohammed*, 206; Muir,

245f, quoting Ibn Hisham and al-Tabari.
36. Ameer Ali, *Spirit of Islam*, 58f.
37. Muir, 252f.
38. al-Baladhuri, i, 2.
39. Ibid., i, 4.
40. Ameer Ali, 94.
41. Andrae, 238.
42. Koran, ii, 100; Macdonald, D. B., *Development of Muslim Theology, Jurisprudence, and Constitutional Theory*, 69.
43. Koran, xli, 6.
44. XXXIII, 37.
45. Andrae, 267.
46. Koran, xxxiii, 51.
47. Muir, 77, 244.
48. Koran, xxxiii, 51.
49. Muir, 201.
50. Bukhsh, S. K., *Studies, Indian and Islamic*, 6.
51. Muir, 511.
52. Lane-Poole, *Speeches*, xxx.
53. Ameer Ali, *Spirit of Islam*, 110.
54. Bukhsh, *Studies*, 6.
55. Irving, W., *Life of Mahomet*, 238.
56. Margoliouth, 105; Irving, 231.
57. Koran, xxxi, 19.
58. Sa'di, *Gulistan*, ii, 29.
59. Margoliouth, 458.
60. Gibbon, V, 254.
61. Margoliouth, 466.

CHAPTER IX

1. E.g., sura lv.
2. Lane-Poole, *Speeches*, 180.
3. Koran, xliv, 53; xxxv, 33.
4. XLVII, 15, lxxvi, 14-15.
5. LV, 56-8, lxxviii, 33; xxxvii, 48.
6. LVI, 17; lxxvii, 19.
7. Margoliouth, 69.
8. Koran, xvii, 35; Lane-Poole, 157.
9. Ibid., 158.
10. Ali, Maulana M., *Religion of Islam*, 587.
11. Lane-Poole, 161, 163.
12. Ibid., 162.
13. Ibid.
14. Ali, Maulana, 390.
15. Koran, lv, 10; iv, 31-2.
16. Ali, Maulana, 655.
17. Koran, xxxiii, 53.
18. Ali, 602.
19. Koran, ii, 232; Ali, 632.
20. Ibid., 684.
21. Pickthall, p. 594n.
22. Lane-Poole, 161.
23. Koran, xxxi, 14; xlvi, 15.
24. Ameer Ali, 183.
25. Lane-Poole, 167.
26. Quoted in Muir, *Life*, 520.
27. Lane-Poole, 159.
28. Ibid.
29. Sale in Wherry, I, 122.

30. E.g., Deut. xviii, 15-18; Hag. ii, 7; Song of Songs, ii, 3, xxi, 7; John xvi, 12-13.
31. Talmud, Pirke Aboth, ii, 18.
32. Nöldeke, *Sketches*, 44.
33. Cf. Koran, v, 35 with Talmud, Sanh., ii, 5; Koran, ii, 183 with Ber., i, 2; and Nöldeke, 31.
34. Lane-Poole, xl.
35. Bevan, E. R., *Legacy of Israel*, 147; Hitti, P. K., *History of the Arabs*, 125.
36. Baron, S. W., *Social and Religious History of the Jews*, I, 335-7.
37. Hurgronje, C. S., *Mohammedanism*, 65

CHAPTER X

1. *Cambridge Medieval History*, II, 331.
2. Burton, *Personal Narrative*, I, 149.
3. Finlay, G., *Greece under the Romans*, 367.
4. Muir, Sir W., *The Caliphate*, 56.
5. Ibid., 57.
6. Ibid., 198.
7. Hitti, 176.
8. Gibbon, V, 296.
9. Macdonald, *Development of Muslim Theology*, 23.
10. Hitti, 197.
11. Sykes, Sir P., *History of Persia*, I, 538.
12. Hell, J., 59-60.
13. Muir, *Caliphate*, 376; Hitti, 222.
14. Dozy, 161; Hitti, 227.
15. Muir, *Caliphate*, 428-37; Hitti, 285.
16. Nöldeke, 132.
17. Sa'di, *Gulistan*, i, 3.
18. Burton, Sir R. F., *The Thousand Nights and a Night*, I, 186.
19. Palmer, E. H., *The Caliph Haroun Alraschid*, 30, 78.
20. Arnold, Sir T. W., *Painting in Islam*, 16.
21. Abbott, Nabia, *Two Queens of Baghdad*, 183.
22. Muir, *Caliphate*, 482.
23. Palmer, 221.
24. Ibid., 35; Abbott, 113.
25. Palmer, 81f.
26. Ibn Khaldun, *Les Prolégomènes*, I, 26.
27. Hitti, 300.
28. Eginhard, *Life of Charlemagne*, xvi, 3.
29. Palmer, 121.
30. Nicholson, R. A., *Translations of Eastern Poetry and Prose*, 64.
31. Utbi, Abul-Nasr Muhammad, *Historical Memoirs of the Emir Sabaktagin and Mahmud of Ghazni*, ch. 50, p. 466.
32. Saladin, H., et Migeon, G., *Manuel d'art musulman*, I, 441.

CHAPTER XI

1. Lestrange, G., *Palestine under the Moslems*, quoting Masudi, ii, 438.
2. Hitti, 351.
3. Milman, H. H., *History of Latin Christianity*, III, 65n.
4. Lane, E. W., *Arabian Society in the Middle Ages*, 117.
5. Usher, A. P., *History of Mechanical Inventions*, 128-9.
6. De Vaux, Baron Carra, *Les Penseurs d'Islam*, I, 8.
7. Barnes, H. E., *Economic History of the Western World*, 111.
8. Renard, G., *Life and Work in Prehistoric Times*, 113.
9. Hitti, 344.
10. Thompson, J. W., *Economic and Social History of the Middle Ages*, 373.
11. Ibn Khaldun, *Les Prolégomènes*, 416.
12. Hitti, 348.
13. Muir, *Caliphate*, 501.
14. Hitti, 344.
15. Hurgronje, 128.
16. Browne, E. G., *Literary History*, I, 323.
17. Ibid., 318.
18. Dawson, 158.
19. Browne, I, 323; Muir, *Caliphate*, 510.
20. Nöldeke, 146-75.
21. Arnold, *Painting in Islam*, 104.
22. Guillaume, A., *The Traditions of Islam*, 13.
23. Ibid., 134-8; Becker, C. H., *Christianity and Islam*, 62.
24. Guillaume, 47-52, 77.
25. Margoliouth, *Mohammed*, 80.
26. Guillaume, 80.
27. Sykes, I, 521.
28. Andrae, 101.
29. Sale in Wherry, I, 172.
30. Ali, Maulana, 730.
31. Philby, H., *A Pilgrim in Arabia*, 40.
32. Doughty, I, 59.
33. Burton, *Pilgrimage*, I, 325.
34. Ali, Maulana, 522.
35. Burton, *Pilgrimage*, II, 63; Sale in Wherry, I, 185.
36. Graetz, H., *History of the Jews*, III, 87; Hitti, 234.
37. Lestrange, *Palestine*, 212; Arnold, Sir T., and Guillaume, A., *The Legacy of Islam*, 81.
38. Baron, S. W., *History*, I, 319.
39. Guillaume, 132.
40. Catholic Encyclopedia, VIII, 459.
41. Becker, 32.
42. Hitti, 685; Sarton, G., *Introduction to the History of Science*, Vol. II, Part I, 80.
43. Westermarck, E., *Origin and Development of the Moral Ideas*, II, 476.
44. Kremer, A. von, *Kulturgeschichte des Orients unter den Khalifen*, 52.
45. Abbott, 98.
46. Lane, E. W., *Arabian Society*, 219-20.

47. Bukhsh, S. K., *Studies*, 83.
48. Hitti, 239.
49. Ali, Maulana, 390.
50. Lane-Poole, S., *Saladin*, 247.
51. Macdonald, D. B., *Aspects of Islam*, 294; Ameer Ali, *Spirit of Islam*, 362.
52. Müller-Lyer, F., *Evolution of Modern Marriage*, 42.
53. Lane-Poole, *Saladin*, 217.
54. Ibid., 251; Sumner, W. G., *Folkways*, 353.
55. Lane, E. W., *Arabian Society*, 221.
56. Ibid., 223.
57. Hitti, 342.
58. Bukhsh, *Studies*, 88.
59. Abbott, 137, 149.
60. Bukhsh, 84.
61. al-Ghazzali, Abu Hamid, *Kimiya'e Saadat*, tr. as *The Alchemy of Happiness* by C. Field, 93.
62. Himes, N. E., *Medical History of Contraception*, 136.
63. Lane-Poole, *Saladin*, 415.
64. Guillaume, *Traditions*, 115.
65. Westermarck, *Moral Ideas*, I, 94.
66. Sale in Wherry, I, 168.
67. Hitti, 338.
68. De Vaux, II, 272f; Chardin, Sir J., *Travels in Persia*, 198.
69. Muir, *Caliphate*, 374.
70. Ibid., 519.
71. Lane, *Saladin*, 285.
72. Bury, J. B., *History of the Eastern Roman Empire*, 236.
73. Hurgronje, 98.
74. Macdonald, *Muslim Theology*, 84; Guillaume, 69; Burton, *Personal Narrative*, I, 148, 167.
75. Arnold and Guillaume, *Legacy*, 305.
76. Macdonald, *Theology*, 66.
77. Muir, *Caliphate*, 170.
78. Lestrange, *Palestine*, 24.
79. Hitti, 236f.
80. In Lestrange, 120.
81. Ibid., 342.
82. Ibid., 301.
83. Ibid., 295-301, 342, 348, 353, 361, 377.
84. Ibid., 265.
85. Ibid., 237.
86. Creswell, K. A. C., *Early Muslim Architecture*, I, 137; Rivoira, G. T., *Moslem Architecture*, 110.
87. Yaqub, ii, 587, in Lestrange, 262.
88. Lane, *Saladin*, 184.
89. Ameer Ali, *Spirit of Islam*, 339.
90. Baron, I, 320.
91. Abulfeda, in Rowbotham, J. F., *The Troubadours and the Courts of Love*, 16n.
92. Lestrange, G., *Baghdad during the Abbasid Caliphate*, 253.

93. Lane, E. W., *Arabian Society*, 203.
94. Lane-Poole, S., *Studies in a Mosque*, 185.

CHAPTER XII

1. In Ameer Ali, *Spirit of Islam*, 331.
2. Lane, *Saladin*, 86.
3. Lane-Poole, S., *Cairo*, 183.
4. Hitti, 409.
5. Macdonald, *Aspects of Islam*, 289, 301.
6. Bukhsh, *Studies*, 195.
7. Carter, T. F., *The Invention of Printing in China*, introduction and p. 85; Thompson, Sir E. M., *Introduction to Greek and Latin Palaeography*, 34; Barnes, *Economic History*, 113.
8. Bukhsh, 49-50.
9. Ibid., 197.
10. Gibbon, V, 411.
11. Browne, *Literary History*, I, 275.
12. Pope, *Masterpieces of Persian Art*, 151.
13. Sarton, I, 662.
14. Gibbon, V, 298.
15. al-Tabari, *Chronique*, i, 1.
16. Ibid., i, 17.
17. Ibid., i, 118.
18. Sarton, I, 637.
19. De Vaux, I, 78.
20. Ibn Khaldun, I, 78.
21. Sarton, I, 530.
22. Arnold and Guillaume, *Legacy*, 385.
23. Sarton, I, 602.
24. Bukhsh, 168.
25. De Vaux, II, 76.
26. Ibid., 78.
27. al-Biruni, Abu Rayhan Muhammad, *Chronology of Ancient Nations*, introd., xiii.
28. al-Biruni, *India*, I, 3.
29. In Boer, T. J. de, *History of Philosophy in Islam*, 146.
30. De Vaux, II, 217; Arnold and Guillaume, 395.
31. al-Biruni, *India*, I, 198.
32. Bukhsh, 181.
33. Sarton, I, 707.
34. Ibid., 693.
35. Lane, *Arabian Society*, 54n.
36. Ibn Khaldun, III, 250-5.
37. Thompson, J. W., *Economic and Social History*, 358.
38. Grunebaum, G. von, *Medieval Islam*, 331.
39. Ameer Ali, *Spirit of Islam*, 392.
40. Kellogg, J. H., *Rational Hydrotherapy*, 1928, 24.
41. Ibid.
42. Lane, *Arabian Society*, 56.
43. Garrison, F., *History of Medicine*, 1929, 137.
44. Arnold and Guillaume, 336.
45. Bukhsh, 197.
46. Hitti, 364.

47. Ibid.
48. Campbell, D., *Arabian Medicine*, 66f.
49. Sarton, I, 609.
50. Ibn Khallikan, Muhammad, *Biographical Dictionary*, I, 440.
51. Ibid., 443.
52. In Draper, J. W., *History of the Intellectual Development of Europe*, I, 411.
53. John, i, 1-3.
54. Bukhsh, 59.
55. Boer, 101; Arnold and Guillaume, 255.
56. Aristotle, *De Anima*, iii, 5.
57. Macdonald, *Muslim Theology*, 150.
58. Barhebraeus in Grunebaum, 182; Hitti, 353; Muir, *Caliphate*, 521.
59. In Ameer Ali, *Spirit of Islam*, 408.
60. Dawson, 155.
61. Ibn Khallikan, III, 308.
62. O'Leary, DeL., *Arabic Thought and Its Place in History*, 153.
63. Ueberweg, F., *History of Philosophy*, I, 412.
64. De Vaux, IV, 12-18.
65. Boer, 123.
66. Ibid., 81f.
67. Husik, I., *History of Medieval Jewish Philosophy*, xxxix.
68. Salibu, D., *Étude sur la metaphysique d'Avicenne*, 21.
69. Ibid., 106, 114, 121, 151; Hastings, *Encyclopedia of Religion and Ethics*, XI, 275-6; Boer, 136.
70. Salibu, 170; Gruner, O. C., *Treatise on the Canon of Medicine of Avicenna*, introd., p. 9.
71. Boer, 138-42.
72. Salibu, 208.
73. In Ameer Ali, 395.
74. Boer, 144.
75. al-Baladhuri, i, 6; Bacon, Roger, *Opus Maius*, tr. R. B. Burke, Vol. I, p. 15.
76. Salibu, 27.
77. Arnold and Guillaume, 311.
78. *Avicennae Canon Medicinae*, p. 118.
79. In Nicholson, R. A., *Mystics of Islam*, 7.
80. Ibn Khaldun, III, 106.
81. Browne, *Literary History*, I, 426.
82. In Hitti, 435.
83. Nicholson, R. A., *Studies in Islamic Mysticism*, 4-5.
84. Macdonald, *Religious Attitude*, 169-71; Nicholson, *Studies in Mysticism*, 78.
85. Ibid., 25.
86. Arnold and Guillaume, 219.
87. Hitti, 438.
88. Browne, II, 261.
89. Nicholson, *Studies in Mysticism*, 6-21.
90. Id., *Translations of Eastern Poetry*, 98-100.
91. In Browne, II, 265.
92. Nicholson, *Mysticism*, 28-31, 38.
93. Browne, I, 404; Dawson, 158.
94. Hitti, 443.
95. Browne, I, 404.
96. al-Masudi, Abu-l Hasan, *Meadows of Gold*, French tr., IV, 89.
97. Lane-Poole, *Cairo*, 154.
98. Nicholson, *Studies in Islamic Poetry*, 48.
99. Id., *Translations*, 33.
100. Nicholson, R. A., *Literary History of the Arabs*, 295; Ibn Khallikan, I, 393.
101. De Vaux, IV, 252.
102. Browne, I, 369.
103. Nicholson, *Islamic Poetry*, 133-7.
104. Rihani, A. F., *The Quatrains of Abu'l 'Ala* (al-Ma'arri), vii.
105. Nicholson, *Literary History*, 319.
106. Id., *Islamic Poetry*, 148.
107. Ibid., 102, 145; Rihani, 120.
108. Nicholson, *Islamic Poetry*, 108-10.
109. Ibid., 191-2.
110. Ibid., 121.
111. Id., *Translations*, 102.
112. Id., *Islamic Poetry*, 150.
113. Ibid., 160.
114. Ibid., 161-5.
115. Id., *Translations*, 102.
116. Id., *Islamic Poetry*, 119.
117. Ibid., 127.
118. Id., *Translations*, 102.
119. Id., *Islamic Poetry*, 140.
120. In Browne, II, 120.
121. In Firdousi, *The Epic of Kings*, retold by Helen Zimmern, 4.
122. Firdousi, *The Shah Nameh*, in Gottheil, R. J., ed., *The Literature of Persia*, I, 54.
123. Ibid., 156, tr. Jas. Atkinson. Matthew Arnold has retold the story in *Sohrab and Rustum*.
124. In Pope, *Survey of Persian Art*, II, 975.
125. Cf. "The Nazarene Broker's Story" in Burton, *Thousand Nights and a Night*, I, 270.
126. Pope, *Survey*, II, 1439.
127. Lane-Poole, *Saladin*, 29.
128. Lane, *Arabian Society*, 54-61.
129. Pope, II, 927; Hell, 109.
130. Creswell, I, 329.
131. In Lane, *Arabian Society*, 58.
132. Pope, II, 975.
133. Pope, IV, 317-28.
134. Pope, Arthur U., *Introduction to Persian Art*, 200.
135. Arnold and Guillaume, 117.
136. Pope, II, 1447.
137. Fenollosa, E. F., *Epochs of Chinese and Japanese Art*, I, 21; Pope, *Survey*, I, 2.
138. Pope, II, 1468.
139. Guillaume, 128.
140. Encyclopaedia Britannica, XV, 654.
141. Ibid.; Hitti, 420.
142. Arnold, *Painting in Islam*, 85.
143. Ibid., 21.

144. Lane, *Arabian Society*, 117.
145. Ibid., 15.
146. Hitti, 274.
147. Farmer, H. G., in Arnold and Guillaume, 358.
148. Sa'di, *Gulistan*, ii, 26.
149. In Arnold and Guillaume, 359.
150. Farmer in Arnold and Guillaume, 367.
151. Ibid., 372.
152. Ibid., 361; Farmer, H. G., *History of Arabian Music*, 154.
153. Farmer in Arnold and G., 359.
154. Hitti, 214.
155. Farmer, 31.
156. Ibid., 112.
157. Ibid., 60-4; Lane-Poole, *Cairo*, 156.
158. Farmer, 120.
159. Ibid., 124.
160. Lane, *Arabian Society*, 172-6.

CHAPTER XIII

1. Gibbon, V, 344.
2. Sarton, I, 466; II (ii), 599.
3. Ueberweg, I, 409.
4. Tarn, W. W., *Hellenistic Civilization*, 217; Sarton, I, 466.
5. Gibbon, V, 346.
6. Munro, D. C., and Sellery, G. C., *Medieval Civilization*, 170.
7. Lane-Poole, *Cairo*, 65.
8. Browne, II, 223.
9. Hitti, 625.
10. Browne, II, 223; Margoliouth, D. S., *Cairo, Jerusalem, and Damascus*, 46.
11. Nöldeke, 3.
12. Hitti, 626.
13. Arnold and Guillaume, 163.
14. Pope, Arthur U., *Iranian and Armenian Contributions to the Beginnings of Gothic Architecture*, 237.
15. Lane, *Arabian Society*, 54f.
16. Lane-Poole, *Cairo*, 44, 60.
17. Pope, II, 1488.
18. Arnold and Guillaume, 116.
19. Dimand, M. S., *Handbook of Muhammadan Art*, 255; Arnold, *Painting in Islam*, 127.
20. Margoliouth, *Cairo*, 69.
21. Arnold and Guillaume, 333.
22. Arnold, Sir T. W., *The Preaching of Islam*, 102.
23. Pirenne, Henri, *Mohammed and Charlemagne*, 160f.
24. Hitti, 605.
25. Waern, Cecilia, *Medieval Sicily*, 20.
26. Arnold and Guillaume, 241.
27. Waern, 25.
28. Calvert, A. F., *Moorish Remains in Spain*, 239.
29. al-Maqqari, Ahmed ibn Muhammad, *History of the Mohammedan Dynasties in Spain*, ii, 146.

30. Ibid., vi, 6.
31. Ibid.
32. Dozy, 458-65.
33. Maqqari, vii, 1.
34. Dozy, 516.
35. Ibid., 522; Calvert, A. F., *Seville*, 11.
37. Lane-Poole, S., *Story of the Moors in Spain*, 43.
38. Dozy, 633, 689.
39. Cf. Maqqari, vi, 3.
40. Dozy, 234.
41. Gibbon, V, 376.
42. Chapman, C. E., *History of Spain*, 50.
43. Ibid., 41; Dozy, 236; Lane-Poole, *Moors*, 50.
44. Chapman, 41.
45. Clapham, J. H., and Power, E., *Cambridge Economic History of Europe*, 136; Barnes, *Economic History*, 114.
46. Clapham, 354-5; Thompson, J. W., *Economic and Social History*, 547.
48. *Cambridge Medieval History*, III, 432.
49. Pirenne, Jacques, *Les grands courants de l'histoire universelle*, II, 117.
50. Ibid., 19.
51. Arnold, *Preaching*, 134; Dozy, 235.
52. Chapman, 49, 58.
53. Dozy, 268.
54. Ibid.
55. Arnold, *Preaching*, 144.
56. Dozy, 235; Lane-Poole, *Moors*, 47.
57. Rivoira, *Moslem Architecture*, 240.
58. Dozy, 278.
59. Ibid., 286.
60. Arnold, *Preaching*, 141.
61. Dozy, 534.
62. Maqqari, iii, 1.
63. Thompson, J. W., *Economic and Social History*, 549.
64. Maqqari, iii, 2.
65. Ibid., iii, 1.
66. Calvert, *Moorish Remains*, 189.
67. Calvert, A. F., *Cordova*, 107.
68. Maqqari, Vol. II, 139-200.
69. Dozy, 455; Chapman, 50.
70. Pirenne, J., II, 20.
71. Maqqari, II, 3.
72. In Dozy, 576.
73. Sarton, I, 713.
74. Dozy, 281.
75. Maqqari, vii, 1.
76. Arnold and Guillaume, 186.
77. Dozy, 326.
78. Ibid.
79. Tr. by Dulcie Smith in Van Doren, Mark, *Anthology of World Poetry*, 99.

CHAPTER XIV

1. Browne, II, 176.
2. Ibid., 177; Gibbon, V, 17.
3. Browne, II, 190.
4. Marco Polo, *Travels*, i, 24.

5. Ameer Ali, *Spirit of Islam*, 313.
6. Hitti, 446.
7. Thompson, J. W., *Economic and Social History*, 391; Arnold, *Preaching*, 96.
8. William of Tripoli in Lane-Poole, *Cairo*, 84.
9. Hitti, 679.
10. Adams, Brooks, *Law of Civilization and Decay*, 128.
11. In Lane-Poole, *Cairo*, 27.
12. Irving, W., *The Alhambra*, 47.
13. Lane-Poole, *Moors*, 225.
14. Pope, *Introduction*, 30; Pope, *Survey*, II, 1043.
15. Cf. Migeon, G., *Les arts musulmans*, II, 11.
16. Fry, Roger, in *Persian Art: Souvenir of the Exhibition of Persian Art at Burlington House*, xix.
17. Dillon, E., *Glass*, 165.
18. Lane, *Arabian Society*, 200.
19. Pope, *Masterpieces*, 65.
20. Dimand, *Handbook*, 280.
21. *Time* Magazine, Jan. 23, 1939.
22. Arnold, *Painting*, 127.
23. *N. Y. Times Book Review*, May 19, 1940, p. 2.
24. Bukhsh, 96.
25. Nicholson, *Translations*, 116.
26. Ibn Khaldun, III, 438.
27. Ibid., 426.
28. Browne, II, 375.
29. Ibid., 392.
30. Sarton, I, 759.
31. Ibid., II (i), 8.
32. Ibid., I, 760.
33. Browne, II, 246.
34. Nicholson, *Islamic Poetry*, 4-5.
35. Weir, T. H., *Omar Khayyam the Poet*, 21.
36. Nicholson, *Islamic Mysticism*, 1.
37. Browne, II, 108.
38. Ibid., 256.
39. Heron-Allen, Edw., in Houtsma, M., ed., *Encyclopedia of Islam*, III (ii), 988.
40. Weir, 16; Nicholson, *Islamic Poetry*, 5.
41. Browne, II, 249.
42. Quatrain cxv of the Bodleian MS. in Weir, 36.
43. Weir, 71.
44. In Browne, II, 247.
45. Smith, Margaret, ed., *The Persian Mystics: Attar*, 20-7.
46. Jalal ud-Din Rumi, *Selected Poems from the Divani Shamsi Tabriz*, ed. and tr. by R. A. Nicholson, 107.
47. Ibid., 71.
48. Ibid., 47.
49. Sarton, II (ii), 872.
50. Browne, II, 521.
51. Sa'di, *Rose Garden*, 12.
52. Sa'di, *Gulistan*, ii, 7.

53. Ibid., iii, 19.
54. In Browne, II, 530.
55. *Gulistan*, ii, 30.
56. Bustan in Grousset, R., *The Civilizations of the East, Vol. l: The Near and Middle East*, 272.
57. *Gulistan*, i, 12.
58. I, 3.
59. II, 27.
60. II, 40.
61. IV, 7.
62. V, 5.
63. V, 4.
64. VII, 2.
65. VII, 4.
66. VIII, 31.
67. VIII, 38.
68. I, 4.
69. V, 8.
70. III, 11.
71. Browne, II, 534.
72. Grunebaum, 39.
73. Sarton, II (i), 12.
74. Ibid., 216.
75. Ibid., 27; II (ii), 632.
76. Ibid., II (i), 31.
77. Margoliouth, *Cairo*, 220.
78. Sarton, II (ii), 1014.
79. Ibid., II (i), 51; II (ii), 663.
80. Ibid., II (i), 424.
81. Hitti, 686.
82. Sarton, II (i), 232.
83. Garrison, 136.
84. Lestrange, *Baghdad*, 104.
85. Garrison, 136; Hell, 117; Lane-Poole, *Cairo*, 34; Margoliouth, *Cairo*, 124-9; Hitti, 677.
86. Baron, S., ed., *Essays on Maimonides*, 112.
87. al-Ghazzali, *Some Religious and Moral Teachings*, 138.
88. al-Ghazzali, *Destruction of Philosophy*, 155f.
89. Macdonald, *Muslim Theology*, 239.
90. Asin y Palacios, Miguel, *Islam and the Divine Comedy*, 273-5.
91. In Sa'di, *Gulistan*, ii, 25.
92. Muir, *Caliphate*, 146.
93. Arnold, *Painting*, 54.
94. Becker, 31.
95. Boer, 175; Duhem, P., *Le système du monde*, IV, 522, 526; Macdonald, *Muslim Theology*, 250.
96. Abu Bekr ibn Tufail, *History of Hayy ibn Yaqzan*, 68.
97. Ibid., 99, 139.
97. In Renan, E., *Averroès et l'averroïsme*, 16.
99. Sarton, II (i), 305.
100. Averroës, *Exposition of the Methods of Argument Concerning the Doctrines of the Faith*, 230.

101. Id., *A Decisive Discourse on the Relation between Religion and Philosophy*, 52.
102. Id., *Exposition*, 190; *Discourse*, 50-1; Gilson, E., *Reason and Revelation in the Middle Ages*, 40f.
103. Averroës, *Exposition*, 193.
104. Sarton, II (i), 358.
105. Averroës, *Discourse*, 14.
106. Commentary on Aristotle's *Metaphysics*, xii, in Renan, 108.
107. Commentary on Aristotle's *Physics*, viii, in Renan, 112; Duhem, IV, 549.
108. De Vaux, IV, 70.
109. Commentary on Aristotle's *De Anima*, bk. iii, in Renan, 122; Duhem, IV, 573.
110. *Destruction of the Destruction*, in Renan, 137n.
111. In Renan, 143.
112. Ibid., 146.
113. Arnold and Guillaume, 277-9; Tornay, S. C., *Averroës' Doctrine of the Mind, Philosophical Review*, May, 1943, 282n.; De Vaux, IV, 71; Duhem, IV, 566.
114. Bacon, R., *Opus maius*, i, 6; De Vaux, IV, 87.
115. Renan, 32.
116. In Browne, II, 440.
117. Ibid., 439.
118. Pope, *Survey*, II, 1542.
119. Lestrange, *Baghdad*, 350; Browne, II, 460.
120. Cf. Arnold, *Painting*, 99.
121. Pope, *Survey*, II, 1044.
122. Burton, *Personal Narrative*, 90-2.
123. Arnold and Guillaume, 169.
124. Encyclopaedia Britannica, XVIII, 339.
125. Arnold and Guillaume, 121; Pope, *Introduction*, 241; Encyclopaedia Britannica, XV, 657.
126. Dennis, Geo., *Cities and Cemeteries of Etruria*, I, 37.
127. Browne, II, 432.
128. Arnold and Guillaume, 93.

CHAPTER XV

1. Abbott, G. F., *Israel in Egypt*, 43.
2. Baron, S., *Social and Religious History of the Jews*, I, 266; Graetz, H., *History of the Jews*, II, 566.
3. Socrates, *Ecclesiastical History*, iii, 20; Julian, *Works*, III, 51.
4. Abbott, 45.
5. Ammianus Marcellinus, *Works*, xxiii, 1.
6. Jerome, *Commentary on Isaiah*, vi, 11-13, in Baron, I, 261.
7. Baron, I, 255.
8. Baeder, Gershom, *Jewish Spiritual Heroes*, III, 46.
9. Talmud, Yebamoth, 37b.
10. Friedländer, L., *Roman Life and Manners under the Early Empire*, III, 173.
11. Gregory of Tours, *History of the Franks*, 1916, viii, 1.
12. References to the Mishna will be by tractate, chapter, and section; to the (Babylonian) Gemara by tractate and folio sheet.
13. Baba Kama, 60b.
14. Megilla, 16b.
15. Tanhuma, ed. Buber, Yitro, sect. 7, in Moore, G. F., *Judaism in the First Centuries of the Christian Era*, II, 242.
16. Menachoth, 99b.
17. Pesikta Rabbati, 10, 4, in Newman, L., and Spitz, S., *Talmudic Anthology*, 300.
18. Chagiga, 10a.
19. Examples in Moore, I, 259.
20. Berachoth, 6b.
21. Aboda Zara, 3b; Newman, 31.
22. Chagiga, 3b.
23. Succah, 52b.
24. Barachoth, 6a.
25. Aboda Zara, 3b.
26. Mechilta, 65a, on Exod. xix, 18.
27. From Deut. vi, 4.
28. Shebuoth, 77b.
29. Erubin, 18a.
30. Bereshit Rabbah on Gen. xxiii, 9.
31. Berachoth, 6a.
32. Aboda Zara, 5a.
33. Sifre on Deut. 32.
34. Shebuoth, 55a.
35. Midrash Mishle, 28, in Newman, 90.
36. Genesis Rabbah, xlviii, 8.
37. Baba Metzia, 58b.
38. Berachoth, 34a.
39. Ketuboth, 111a.
40. Wayyikra Rabbah, 34, in Newman, 108.
41. Bereshit Rabbah, 44, 1, in Newman, 292.
42. Quoted in Cohen, A., *Everyman's Talmud*, 89.
43. Aboda Zara, 20b.
44. Kiddushin, 66d.
45. Shebuoth, 41a.
46. In Cohen, A., 258.
47. Leviticus xxi, 2-5.
48. Yebamoth, 48b.
49. Ketuboth, 27; Cohen, A., 257.
50. Pesachim, 113a.
51. Shebuoth, 152.
52. Pesachim, 49b.
53. Exod. xxiii, 19; xxiv, 26; Deut. xiv, 21.
54. Nidda, 17.
55. Yoma, 75.
56. Shebuoth, 33.
57. Ibid., 152a.
58. Baba Bathra, 58b.
59. Pesachim, 109a.
60. Berachoth, 55a, 60b.
61. Taanith, 11a.
62. Pesachim, 108.
63. Exod. xii, 13.

64. Megilla on Esther, 7b, in Moore, II, 51.
65. In Oesterley, W. O., and Box, G. H., *Short Survey of the Literature of Rabbinical and Medieval Judaism*, 149.
66. Kiddushin, 31a; Isaiah vi, 1.
67. Baba Bathra, 8b; Baron, I, 277-8.
68. Berachoth, 10a.
69. Gen. i, 28; Kiddushin, 29b.
70. Genesis Rabbah, lxxi, 6.
71. Yebamoth, 12b; Himes, N. E., *Medical History of Contraception*, 72.
72. Baba Bathra, 21.
73. Exodus Rabbah, i, 1.
74. Harris, M. H., ed., *Hebraic Literature: Translations from the Talmud, Midrashim, and Kabbala*, 336.
75. Baba Bathra, 9a.
76. Ketuboth, 50a, 67.
77. Taanith, 22.
78. Ibid., 20b.
79. Graetz, II, 486, 545.
80. Baba Bathra, 9.
81. Gittin, 70a.
82. Chagiga, 16a.
83. Berachoth, 61a.
84. Kiddushin, 29b.
85. Sota, 44a.
86. Taanith, lv, 8.
87. Yebamoth, 63a.
88. Ibid., 65a, 44a.
89. Pesikta Rabbati, 25, 2, in Newman, 3.
90. Berachoth, xxiv, 1.
91. Kiddushin, 4.
92. Yebamoth, xlv, 1; 64b.
93. Gittin, lx, 10.
94. Ketuboth, vii, 6.
95. Cohen, A., 179.
96. Ketuboth, 77a; Neuman, A. A., *The Jews in Spain*, Philadelphia, 1942, II, 59.
97. Yebamoth, xix, in Baeder, III, 66.
98. Gittin, 90b.
99. Kiddushin, 80b.
100. Nidda, 45.
101. Kiddushin, 49b.
102. Yoma, 83b.
103. Mikvaoth, 9b, in Cohen, A., 170.
104. Hai Gaon in Newman, 540.
105. Yebamoth, 88b.
106. Ketuboth, 47b.
107. Shebuoth, 30b.
108. Erubin, 41b.
109. Baeder, III, 15.
110. Bereshit Rabbah, xvii, 7.
111. Harris, M. H., *Hebraic Literature*, 340.
112. Pirke Aboth, iv, 1.
113. Ibid., iv, 3.
114. Ibid., i, 17.
115. Ibid., iii, 17.
116. Shemot Rabbah, xxv, 16, in Newman, 397.
117. Menachoth 29b, in Moore, II, 187.
118. Renan, E., *Origins of Christianity: The Christian Church*, 131; Baron, I, 305-6.

CHAPTER XVI

1. Graetz, III, 308.
2. Abrahams, Israel, *Jewish Life in the Middle Ages*, 219.
3. Benjamin of Tudela, *Travels*, in Komroff, M., ed., *Contemporaries of Marco Polo*, 290.
4. Graetz, III, 90. Others date the Gaonate from 589; cf. Oesterley and Box, 209.
5. Graetz, III, 133.
6. Ibid., 148.
7. Druck, D., *Yehuda Halevy*, 66.
8. Baron, I, 353.
9. Husik, I., *History of Medieval Jewish Philosophy*, 35, 42f.
10. Malter, H., *Saadia Gaon*, 279, 291.
11. Benjamin of Tudela, in Komroff, 310.
12. Baron, I, 318.
13. Friedländer, III, 181.
14. Dill, Sir S., *Roman Society in Gaul in the Merovingian Age*, 246.
15. Graetz, III, 143, 161, 241, 389.
16. Benj. of Tudela, in Komroff, 260.
17. Ibid., 257.
18. Ameer Ali, Syed, *The Spirit of Islam*, 260.
19. Druck, 26.
20. Dozy, R., *Spanish Islam*, 597f.
21. Abbott, G. F., 71.
22. Abrahams, *Jewish Life*, 366.
23. Dozy, 721.
24. Graetz, III, 617.
25. Neuman, A., *Jews in Spain*, I, 5.
26. Ibid., 164.
27. Ibid., II, 184.
28. Ibid., II, 221; Graetz, III, 281.
29. Neuman, II, 221.
30. Graetz, III, 360f.
31. Baron, II, 37; Graetz, III, 506.
32. Neuman, II, 149.
33. Ibid., 247.
34. Abrahams, *Jewish Life*, 67.
35. Sholom Asch in Browne, Lewis, ed., *The Wisdom of Israel*, 698.
36. Baba Kama, 113a.
37. Pirke Aboth, iii, 2.
38. Baron, II, 17.
39. Ibid., 26.
40. Ibid.
41. Bracton, *De Legibus*, vi, 51, in Baron, II, 24.
42. Pollock, F., and Maitland, F. W., *History of English Law before Edward I*, I, 455.
43. *Cambridge Medieval History*, VII, 643.
44. Rickard, T. A., *Man and Metals*, II, 602.
45. Abrahams, *Jewish Life*, 241.
46. Rapaport, S., *Tales and Maxims from the Talmud*, 147.

47. Graetz, III, 229.
48. Arnold, Sir T., and Guillaume, A., *The Legacy of Islam*, 102.
49. Pirenne, H., *Medieval Cities*, 258.
50. Baron, II, 8f.
51. Jewish Encyclopedia, IV, 379.
52. Deut. xxiii, 20.
53. Baba Metzia, v, 1-2, 11.
54. Abrahams, *Jewish Life*, 110.
55. Baron, II, 120.
56. Pirenne, H., *Economic and Social History of Medieval Europe*, 134.
57. *Cambridge Medieval History*, VII, 644.
58. Ibid., 646.
59. Neuman, A., I, 202; Lacroix, P., *Manners, Customs, and Dress during the Middle Ages*, 451.
60. Coulton, G. G., *Medieval Panorama*, 352.
61. Abbott, *Israel*, 113.
62. Lacroix, *Manners*, 451.
63. Ashley, W. J., *Introduction to English Economic History and Theory*, 202.
64. Abbott, 117.
65. Pollock and Maitland, 451.
66. *Cambridge Medieval History*, VI, 226.
67. Abbott, 122.
68. Husik, 508.
69. Abbott, 125; Graetz, III, 588.
70. Abbott, 135; Lacroix, *Manners*, 445.
71. In Foakes-Jackson, F., and Lake, K., *Beginnings of Christianity*, I, 76.
72. Baba Bathra, 90.
73. Baba Metzia, iv, 3.
74. Baron, I, 277-8; II, 108.
75. Baron, II, 99.
76. Moore, II, 174-5.
77. Abrahams, *Jewish Life*, 141, 319, 326, 335; Baron, II, 99.
78. Coulton, *Panorama*, 357.
79. Abrahams, 277.
80. Ibid., 281.
81. Burton, Sir R. F., *The Jew, the Gypsy, and El Islam*, 128; Baron, II, 169.
82. Abrahams, 331.
83. Baba Kama, 113b.
84. Abrahams, 106.
85. Ibid., 104.
86. Ibid., 90.
87. Baron, II, 112.
88. Abrahams, 166.
89. Kiddushin, 41a; Neuman, II, 21.
90. Ibid.
91. Moore, II, 22.
92. Abrahams, 117.
94. Burton, *The Jew*, 43.
95. White, E. M., *Woman in World History*, 176.
96. Abrahams, 155.
97. Brittain, A., *Women of Early Christianity*, 10.
98. White, 189.

99. Neuman, II, 63.
100. White, 185.
101. Marcus, J., *The Jew in the Medieval World*, 313.
102. Abrahams, 32.
103. Neuman, II, 153.
104. Baron, I, 288; II, 97.
105. Abrahams, 126.
106. Brittain, 12.
107. Moore, I, 316.
108. Maimonides, *Mishneh Torah*, Book I, tr. Moses, Hyamson, 63a.
109. In Waxman, M., *History of Jewish Literature*, I, 214.
110. Jewish Encyclopedia, IX, 122.
111. *Oxford History of Music*, introd. volume, 60.
112. Jewish Encyclopedia, III, 453.
112a. In Zeitlin, S., *Maimonides*, 44.
113. Baron, II, 83.
114. Lacroix, *Manners*, 439.
115. Baron, II, 35.
116. Abrahams, 411; Moore, II, 74.
117. Deut. vii, 3; Nehemiah xiii, 25.
118. Klausner, J., *From Jesus to Paul*, 515.
119. Baron, II, 55.
120. Gittin, 61.
121. Abrahams, 413-4.
122. Ibid., 418.
123. Ibid., 424; Baron, II, 40.
124. Baron, II, 36.
125. Abbott, 93.
126. Coulton, *Panorama*, 352.
127. Ibid.
128. Graetz, IV, 33.
129. Gregory I, Epistle ii, 6, in Dudden, F. H., *Gregory the Great*, II, 154.
130. Ep. xiii, 15, in Dudden, II, 155.
131. Belloc, H., *Paris*, 170.
132. Graetz, III, 421.
133. Coulton, *Panorama*, 352.
134. Thatcher, O. J., and McNeal, E. H., *Source Book of Medieval History*, 212.
135. Lea, H. C., *History of the Inquisition in the Middle Ages*, II, 63.
136. Graetz, III, 563.
137. Ibid., 583.
138. Marcus, 151.
139. Baron, II, 85.
140. Abbott, 51; Jewish Encyclopedia, III, 453.
141. *Camb. Med. H.*, VII, 624; Jewish Encyclopedia, IX, 368.
142. Graetz, III, 299.
143. Ibid., 300.
144. Ibid., 301f; *Cambridge Medieval History*, V, 275f; VII, 641.
145. Graetz, III, 350; Abbott, 88.
146. Jewish Encyclopedia, IV, 379.
147. Graetz, III, 356.
148. *Cambridge Medieval History*, VII, 642.

149. Graetz, IV, 35; Jewish Encyclopedia, IX, 358.
150. Abbott, 124.
151. Coulton, *Panorama*, 359.
152. Cunningham, W., *Growth of English Industry and Commerce*, 204.
153. Jewish Encyclopedia, IV, 379.
154. Lacroix, *Manners*, 439; Coulton, 352.
155. Graetz, III, 642; Abbott, 130.
156. Abbott, 131.
157. Ibid., 68.
158. Lacroix, *Manners*, 447.
159. Abbott, 68.
160. Montesquieu, C. Baron de, *The Spirit of Laws*, I, xii, 5.
161. Joseph ben Joshua ben Meir, *Chronicles*, I, 197.
162. Marcus, 24.
163. Graetz, III, 570.
164. Villehardouin, G. de, *Chronicles of the Crusades*, 148.
165. Abbott, 113.
166. *Cambridge Medieval History*, VII, 641.

CHAPTER XVII

1. Abrahams, *Jewish Life*, 210.
2. Sarton, G., *Introduction to the History of Science*, II(i), 295.
3. Abrahams, I., *Chapters on Jewish Literature*, 116.
4. Waxman, I, 226.
5. Graetz, III, 269.
6. Gabirol, S. ibn, *Selected Religious Poems*, tr. Israel Zangwill, 52.
7. Ibid., 30.
8. Abrahams, *Literature*, 109.
9. Abrahams, *Jewish Life*, 163.
10. In Wilson, E., ed., *Hebrew Literature*, 383.
11. Sarton, II(i), 188.
12. Halevi, J., *Selected Poems*, tr. Nina Salaman, 58.
13. Abbott, 72.
14. Druck, 97.
15. Ibid., 94.
16. Wilson, *Hebrew Literature*, 365-6.
17. Novella 146 in Burton, *The Jew*, 105.
18. Graetz, III, 573.
19. Sarton, II(ii), 557.
20. Schechter, S., *Studies in Judaism*, I, 107.
21. Graetz, III, 604.
22. Sarton, II(i), 145.
23. *N. Y. Times*, June 2, 1937.
24. Sarton, II(i), 145.
25. Cf. Komroff, M., *The Contemporaries of Marco Polo*.
26. Husik, 24.
27. Munk, S., *Mélanges de philosophie juive et arabe*, 153.
28. Marcus, 312.
29. Cf. Gabirol, S. ibn, *Improvement of the Moral Qualities*, tr. Stephen Wise, 4, 27.
30. Gabirol, *Fons Vitae*, i, 3, in Munk, 6.
31. Halevi, J., *Kitab al-Khazari*, tr. H. Hirschfeld, i, 116.
32. Ibid., III, 5, 7.
33. Husik, 215.
34. Yellin, D., and Abrahams, I., *Maimonides*, 11; Zeitlin, *Maimonides*, 1.
35. Ueberweg, F., *History of Philosophy*, I, 427.
36. Zeitlin, *Maimonides*, 5.
37. "Letter of Consolation" in Yellin, 46.
38. Zeitlin, 178.
39. Arnold, Sir T., *Preaching of Islam*, 421.
40. Baron, S., ed., *Essays on Maimonides*, 290.
41. Maimonides, Aphorisms, in Thorndike, L., *History of Magic and Experimental Science*, I, 176.
42. Zeitlin, 172.
43. In Baron, *Essays*, 288.
44. Zeitlin, 174.
45. Baron, *Essays*, 284.
46. Maimonides, *Mishneh Torah*, Introd., 4b.
47. Zeitlin, 214.
48. *Mishneh Torah*, Introd., 16, 3a.
49. In Baron, *Essays*, 117.
50. Maimonides, *Guide to the Perplexed*, tr. M. Friedländer, III, xli.
51. Ibid., III, 35, in Baron, *Essays*, 139.
52. *Guide*, III, xxxvii, xli; Deut. xxiii, 17; Exod. xxii, 1; xxxi, 15.
53. *Mishneh Torah*, 40b.
54. Ibid., 59a.
55. Ibid., 54a.
56. Ibid., 53a.
57. Ibid., 53ab.
58. Ibid., 52b.
59. In Baron, *Essays*, 110.
60. Zeitlin, 132.
61. *Guide*, I, Introd.
62. Ibid., II, xix; III, xiv.
63. II, Pt. II, Introd. and Prop. xx.
64. Ibid., xxxvi-xlvi.
65. III, xxii.
66. II, xviif.
67. II, xxx.
68. III, x, xii.
69. III, lxx.
70. Zeitlin, 151.
71. Ibid., 103; Baron, *Essays*, 143.
72. *Guide*, II, Pt. II, Introd.
73. Baron, *Essays*, 119-21; Zeitlin, 209.
74. Marcus, 307-9.
75. Spinoza, *Tractatus Theologico-Politicus*, xv, 4.
76. Roth, L., *Spinoza, Descartes, and Maimonides*, 66; Baron, *Essays*, 7.
77. Husik, 302; Graetz, IV, 23.
78. Ibid., III, 631.

79. Neuman, A., II, 122.
80. Ibid., 118; Graetz, IV, 29-41.
81. Jewish Encyclopedia, III, 457, 479.
82. Sarton, II(i), 366.
83. Graetz, IV, 21.
84. Baron, *History*, II, 136.
85. Ibid., 142.
86. Abrahams, *Jewish Life*, 143, 157, 193.
87. In Marcus, 314.

CHAPTER XVIII

1. Thompson, J. W., *Economic and Social History*, 173.
2. Gibbon, IV, 504.
3. *Cambridge Medieval History*, II, 289.
4. Ibid., IV, 6; Gibbon, V, 142.
5. In Diehl, *Manuel*, 335.
6. *Cambridge Medieval History*, IV, 115f.
7. Voltaire, *Works*, XIII, 190.
8. Diehl, *Portraits*, 159; Bury, *Eastern Roman Empire*, 169.
9. McCabe, J., *Empresses of Constantinople*, 174.
10. *Cambridge Medieval History*, IV, 108; Diehl, *Portraits*, 264.
11. Boissonnade, P., *Life and Work in Medieval Europe*, 56.
12. *Cambridge Medieval History*, IV, 750.
13. Diehl, *Portraits*, 236.
14. *Cambridge Medieval History*, IV, 745.
15. Komroff, *Contemporaries of Marco Polo*, 266.
16. *Cambridge Medieval History*, IV, 760.
17. Ibid.
18. Clapham and Power, 212.
19. Diehl, *Portraits*, 153; Gibbon, V, 458; Brittain, *Women of Early Christianity*, 318.
20. Lopez, R. S., in *Speculum*, Vol. XX, No. 1, pp. 17-18; Boissonnade, 46-7; *Cambridge Medieval History*, IV, 761.
21. Boissonnade, 50.
22. Ibid., 51.
23. Castiglione, 254.
24. Bury, *Eastern Roman Empire*, 436; Grunebaum, *Medieval Islam*, 54.
25. Psellus, *Chronographia*, vi, 46.
26. Ibid., v, 25-37.
27. Diehl, *Manuel*, 405.
28. Luitprand in Grunebaum, 29.
29. Cf. Walker Trust Report, *The Great Palace of the Byzantine Emperors*, plates 24-37 and 57.
30. The judgment of Kondakof in Diehl, *Manuel*, 580.
31. Diehl, 590.
32. Ibid., 381.
33. Finlay, *Greece under the Romans*, 21.
34. Thompson, J. W., *Feudal Germany*, 458.
35. Kluchevsky, V. O., *History of Russia*, I, 46; Thompson, *Feudal Germany*, 456.
36. Pokrovsky, M. N., *History of Russia*, 11; Fustel de Coulanges questioned this —cf. Dopsch, 26.
37. *Cambridge Medieval History*, IV, 186.
38. Mavor, J., *Economic History of Russia*, I, 15.
39. Kluchevsky, I, 88.
40. Rambaud, A., *History of Russia*, I, 84.

CHAPTER XIX

1. Paul the Deacon, *History of the Longobards*, i, 9.
2. Bury, *Later Roman Empire*, II, 299.
3. Munro and Sellery, 538.
4. Dante, *Eleven Letters*, 135.
5. Note by W. D. Foulke in Paul the Deacon, 309.
6. Voltaire, *Works*, XIII, 80.
7. Molmenti, P., *Venice*, I, I, 212-4.
8. *Cambridge Medieval History*, III, 170.
9. Pirenne, *Medieval Cities*, 110.
10. Ruskin, *Stones of Venice*, II, 55.
11. Lanciani, R., *Ancient Rome*, 57.
12. Ibid., 275.
13. Castiglione, 301.
14. Dozy, *Spanish Islam*, 440.
15. Coulton, G. G., *Five Centuries of Religion*, I, 174.
16. Hume, M., *The Spanish People*, 129; *Spain*, 191; Encyclopaedia Britannica, V, 699.
17. In Guizot, *History of France*, I, 171.
18. Ibid., 168.
19. Pirenne, *Cities*, 243; Voltaire, XIII, 131.
20. Freeman, E. A., *Historical Essays*, First Series, 179.
21. *Cambridge Medieval History*, II, 613.
22. Guizot, *France*, I, 229f; Guizot, *History of Civilization*, II, 193-6.
23. Pollock and Maitland, I, 117; Barnes, H. E., *History of Western Civilization*, I, 775.
24. Lea, *Superstition and Force*, 469.
25. Guizot, *Civilization*, II, 225f.
26. Capitulary of Charlemagne, year 803, #3, in Guizot, *Civilization*, II, 222.
27. In Pirenne, *Cities*, 166.
28. Ibid., 58; *Cambridge Medieval History*, II, 665; Rickard, *Man and Metals*, II, 510.
29. *Cambridge Medieval History*, II, 657.
30. Letter of Alcuin in William of Malmesbury, i, 3, p. 66.
31. Eginhard, *Life of Charlemagne*, 61.
32. Hodgkin, T., *Life of Charlemagne*, 312.
33. West, A. F., *Alcuin*, 55.
34. Eginhard, p. 14.
35. Ibid., 62.
36. Ibid., 64.
37. Capitulary of 802 in Bebel, A., *Woman under Socialism*, 60.
38. Eginhard, 33.
39. Bury, *Eastern Empire*, 318.

40. Eginhard, 56-8.
41. Raby, F. J., *History of Secular Latin Poetry in the Middle Ages*, I, 190.
42. Eginhard, 52.
43. Ibid., 48; Russell, C. E., *Charlemagne*, 262.
44. Guizot, *France*, I, 241.
45. Morey, C. R., *Medieval Art*, 207.
46. Ibid., 191.
47. Davis, *Medieval England*, 266.
48. Guizot, *Civilization*, II, 375.
49. Erigena, J. S., *De divisione naturae*, i, 69.
50. In Guizot, *Civilization*, II, 383.
51. Erigena, #517.
52. Ibid., #443.
53. #518.
54. #896.
55. #919-26, 937-40.
56. #861.
57. Poole, R. L., *Illustrations of the History of Medieval Thought*, 61.
58. Guizot, *Civilization*, II, 388.
59. William of Malmesbury, ii, 4.
60. Guizot, *France*, I, 303.
61. Ibid., 311.
62. Ibid., 329.
63. Ibid., 336.

CHAPTER XX

1. Asser, *Alfred the Great*, 51.
2. Asser, 66, 78, 85.
3. Alfred, Preface to tr. of Gregory I's *Cura pastoralis*, in Ogg, *Source Book of Medieval History*, 191.
4. Voltaire, *Works*, XIII, 176.
5. Boissonnade, *Life and Work in Medieval Europe*, 83.
6. Green, J. R., *Conquest of England*, 135, 329, 359-60.
7. Stubbs, W., *Constitutional History of England*, I, 146, 157.
8. Hume, D., *History of England*, I, 181.
9. Pollock and Maitland, II, 450.
10. William of Malmesbury in Coulton, G. G., *Social Life in Britain*, 20; Green, J. R., *Making of England*, 192.
11. Traill, H. D., *Social England*, I, 204.
12. Hume, D., *History of England*, I, 188.
13. Briffault, R., *The Mothers*, II, 419.
14. William of Malmesbury, i, 4.
15. Ibid., i, 2.
16. Ibid., ii, 5.
17. Bede, v, 24.
18. Ibid., i, 15.
19. Ibid., Introd., xvi.
20. Gordon, R. K., *Anglo-Saxon Poetry*, 81-2.
21. In Ker, W. P., *Epic and Romance*, 63.
22. *Beowulf*, xxxvii and xliii, in Gordon, *Anglo-Saxon Poetry*, 60, 70.
23. Bede, iv, 23.

24. Plummer, *Life and Times of Alfred the Great*, 14.
25. In Addison, J., *Arts and Crafts in the Middle Ages*, 4.
26. Aldhelme (c. 709) in Addison, 199.
27. Bede, iv, 18.
28. Freeman, E. A., *Norman Conquest*, II, 298.
29. William of Malmesbury, iii, 238; Ordericus Vitalis, *Historia Ecclesiastica*, 492A; Freeman, *Norman Conquest*, II, 244.
30. Guizot, *France*, I, 345; Freeman, *Norman Conquest*, III, 320.
31. *Mabinogion*, 1f.
32. Hyde, *Literary History of Ireland*, 233.
33. Joyce, *Short History of Ireland*, 39-46.
34. Thompson, J. W., *Economic History*, 148.
35. Boissonnade, 78.
36. Joyce, 80.
37. Ibid., 163.
38. Ibid., 155, 158.
39. Hyde, 222.
40. Ibid., 239.
41. Ibid., 279f.
42. Thompson, Sir E. M., *Introd. to Greek and Latin Palaeography*, 374.
43. Joyce, 189-92.
44. Keating in Hyde, 488.
45. Horn, F. W., *Literature of the Scandinavian North*, 13; *Cambridge Medieval History*, II, 481.
46. Sturluson, S., *Heimskringla*, Harald the Fairhaired, ch. 3.
47. Ibid., Haakon the Good, ch. 23.
48. Ibid., Olaf Tryggvesson, ch. 7.
49. Ibid., ch. 92.
50. Ibid., ch. 87.
51. Ibid., St. Olaf, ch. 56, 131.
52. Ibid., ch. 74.
53. Ibid., Appendix to Olaf Tryggvesson's Saga; Encyclopaedia Britannica, art. Columbus.
54. *Beowulf*, xxxv.
55. Sturluson, Son of Magnus, ch. 33; DuChaillu, P., *The Viking Age*, II, 370, 379.
56. Saxo Grammaticus, *Danish History*, I, 23.
57. Hastings, *Encyclopedia*, III, 499c.
58. DuChaillu, II, 1.
59. Haskins, *Normans in European History*, 36.
60. DuChaillu, I, 486.
61. Saxo, 25.
62. Thompson, J. W., *The Middle Ages*, I, 327.
63. Sturluson, Magnus the Good, ch. 16.
64. Sigfusson, Saemund, *The Elder Edda*, 22-56.
65. Ibid., 23.
66. 59.

67. 66.
68. 14.
69. 84.
70. 102.
71. 81.
72. 65.
73. 73.
74. 121.
75. 58.
76. 55-6.
77. 36.
78. 68.
79. Horn, *Literature of the Scandinavian North*, 41.
80. Faereyinga Saga in Ker, *Epic and Romance*, 236.
81. Sturluson, Olaf Tryggvesson's Saga, ch. 9.
82. Sturluson, Ynglinga Saga, ch. 6, and note; Hodgkin, *Charlemagne*, 154; Saxo, 44.
83. Milman, III, 216. Milman persuasively defends the credibility of this account, which German historians deny.
84. *Cambridge Medieval History*, 270.
85. West, *Alcuin*, 127.
86. Raby, F. J. E., *History of Christian Latin Poetry in the Middle Ages*, 183.
87. Welch, Alice K., *Of Six Medieval Women*, 5.
88. Addison, *Arts and Crafts*, 16.

CHAPTER XXI

1. *Cambridge Medieval History*, I, 536.
2. In Russell, B., *History of Western Philosophy*, 379.
3. Rule of St. Benedict, ch. 3, in Ogg, 87.
4. Ch. 2.
5. Ch. 53.
6. Dudden, I, 111.
7. In Maitland, S. R., *Dark Ages*, 196-8.
8. In Dudden, I, 58.
9. Ibid., 289.
10. Bede, ii, 1.
11. Gregory of Tours, 227.
12. Dudden, I, 245.
13. Thompson, J. W., *Middle Ages*, I, 178.
14. Dudden, II, 156; McCabe, J., *Story of Religious Controversy*, 307.
15. Bede, ii, 1.
16. Ibid., 198.
17. Gregory I, Ep. xiii, 45, in Dudden, I, 278.
18. In Abélard, *Ouvrages inédits, Quaestio*, 1a.
19. Gregory I, *Magna Moralia*, in Dudden, II, 313.
20. *Dialogues*, iv, 7, in Dudden, I, 330.
21. Dudden, II, 434f.
22. Ibid., 38.
23. Thompson, J. W., *Middle Ages*, I, 178.
24. Voltaire, *Works*, XIII, 90.

25. *Cambridge Medieval History*, II, 690.
26. Funk, I, 287; *Cambridge Medieval History*, V, 710.
27. In Milman, III, 25.
28. Gibbon, IV, 82.
29. Sarton, I, 555.
30. Poole, R. L., *Illustrations*, 20.
31. Taylor, H. O., *Medieval Mind*, I, 136.
32. Dudden, I, 86.
33. Ibid.
34. Montalembert, Comte de, *Monks of the West*, I, 553.
35. Guizot, *Civilization*, II, 113-9; Toynbee, A. J., *Study of History*, II, 331.
36. Waddell, H., *Wandering Scholars*, 34.
37. Bede, i, 17.
38. William of Malmesbury, i, 2.
39. Bede, i, 30.
40. Bede, Letter to Egbert.
41. Green, *Making of England*, 413.
42. Gibbon, V, 534.
43. Coulton, *Five Centuries of Religion*, I, 222.
44. Ibid., 352.
45. *Cambridge Medieval History*, V, 662.
46. Ibid., III, 67.
47. Milman, III, 111.
48. *Cambridge Medieval History*, III, 455.
49. Milman, III, 160; McCabe, *Crises in the History of the Papacy*, 128f.
50. Ibid., 131, quoting the *Liber Pontificalis*.
51. Milman, III, 171; *Cambridge Medieval History*, III, 455.
52. Milman, III, 178.
53. Ibid., 185f.
54. Sandys, Sir John, *Companion to Latin Studies*, 847.
55. Vincent of Beauvais, *Spec. Hist.*, in Milman, III, 221.
56. Thorndike, *Magic and Experimental Science*, I, 704.
57. *Cambridge Medieval History*, III, 199.
58. Hulme, E. M., *Middle Ages*, 339; Coulton, G. G., *Life in the Middle Ages*, I, 1; Sarton, I, 734.
59. Funk, I, 262.
60. Stephens, W. R. W., *Hildebrand*, 14; Milman, III, 220; McCabe, *Crises*, 140.
61. *Cambridge Medieval History*, 510.
62. Guizot, *France*, I, 160.
63. Porter, A. K., *Medieval Architecture*, II, 2.
64. Ibid.
65. Carlyle, R. W., *History of Medieval Political Theory in the West*, IV, 52.
66. Coulton, *Five Centuries of Religion*, IV, 187.
67. Coulton, *From St. Francis to Dante*, a tr. of *The Chronicle of Salimbene*, 286.
68. *Cambridge Medieval History*, V, 9-10.
69. Catholic Encyclopedia, I, 156.

70. *Cambridge Medieval History*, V, 12.
71. Lea, *Sacerdotal Celibacy*, 210.
72. Lecky, *Morals*, II, 237.
73. Lea, *History of Auricular Confessions*, I, 46.
74. Letter to Egbert in Bede, p. 4.
75. Catholic Encyclopedia, III, 486.
76. *Cambridge Medieval History*, IV, 268.
77. Ibid., 272.
78. Lea, *Sacerdotal Celibacy*, 194, 223; Thompson, *Social and Economic History*, 662.
79. Lea, *Celibacy*, 226.
80. Bryce, Jas., *Holy Roman Empire*, 158.
81. *Cambridge Medieval History*, V, 99.
82. Thompson, *Social and Economic History*, 663.
83. Taylor, *Medieval Mind*, II, 55.
84. Letter of Gregory VII to William I of England, 1080, in Bryce, 160.
85. Catholic Encyclopedia, X, 871c.
86. Figgis, *Political Aspects of St. Augustine's City of God*, 88.
87. Catholic Encyclopedia, X, 871c.
88. Carlyle, R. W., *Medieval Political Theory*, IV, 64.
89. Stephens, *Hildebrand*, 116.
90. Thatcher and McNeal, 159.
91. *Cambridge Medieval History*, V, 74f.

CHAPTER XXII

1. Lot, *End of the Ancient World*, 125.
2. Dopsch, 283.
3. Seebohm, F., *English Village Community*, 126f, 179.
4. Seignobos, C., *Feudal Regime*, 34; Barnes, *Economic History*, 139.
5. Clapham and Power, 237-8.
6. Letters, iv, 2.
7. Coulton, G. G., *Medieval Village*, 151.
8. McCabe, *Story of Religious Controversy*, 325.
9. Thompson, *Social and Economic History*, 679.
10. Coulton, *Medieval Village*, 492.
11. Coulton, *Medieval Panorama*, 322.
12. Thomas Aquinas, *Summa Theologica*, I IIae, xciv, 5.
13. Decree of Fourth Council of Orléans, in Dopsch, 250.
14. Lecky, *Morals*, II, 70; Sarton, II(ii), 799; but cf. Catholic Encyclopedia, XIV, 38.
15. Ashley, *Introd. to English Economic History*, II, 276.
16. Coulton, *Medieval Village*, 59.
17. Westermarck, E., *Short History of Marriage*, 14; Coulton, *Medieval Village*, 80.
18. Seignobos, 14; Coulton, *Medieval Village*, 464.
19. Bebel, 57.

20. *Cambridge Medieval History*, VII, 721.
21. Coulton, *Life in the Middle Ages*, III, 123-5.
21a. *Cambridge Medieval History*, VII, 722.
22. Seignobos, 21.
23. Coulton, *Medieval Village*, 65.
24. Cram, R. A., *Substance of Gothic*, 181.
25. Lynn White, Jr., in *Speculum*, Apr. 1940, p. 151.
26. Taine, H., *Ancient Regime*, 9; Carlyle, T., *Past and Present*, 55f.
27. Barnes, *Economic History*, 145.
28. *Cambridge Medieval History*, VII, 741.
29. Coulton, *Medieval Village*, 311-18.
30. Ibid., 21, 243.
31. Coulton, *Panorama*, 92.
32. *Speculum*, Apr. 1940, 154.
33. Ibid., 155.
34. Chateaubriand, Vicomte de, *The Genius of Christianity*, iv, 1.4.
35. Coulton, *Medieval Village*, 119.
36. Lacroix, Paul, *Military and Religious Life in the Middle Ages*, 165.
37. Hitti, *History of the Arabs*, 663; Arnold, *Legacy of Islam*, 131.
38. Lacroix, Paul, *Science and Literature in the Middle Ages*, 299f.
39. Beaumanoir in Seignobos, 55.
40. Coulton, *Panorama*, 50.
41. Voltaire, *Works*, XIII, 131.
42. Thompson, *Feudal Germany*, 301.
43. Carlyle, R. W., *Medieval Political Theory*, 463.
44. Pollock and Maitland, II, 242.
45. Maine, Sir H., *Ancient Law*, 135.
46. Coulton, *Medieval Village*, 528.
47. Jenks, E., *Law and Politics in the Middle Ages*, 23.
48. Coulton, *Medieval Village*, 187.
49. Lea, *Superstition and Force*, 286, 297, 314.
50. Coulton, *Panorama*, 379.
51. Lea, *Superstition*, 178.
52. Ibid., 140f, 179.
53. Seignobos, 79.
54. Lea, *Superstition*, 129.
55. Sumner, W. G., *Folkways*, 522.
56. Barnes, *Western Civilization*, I, 798.
57. Seignobos, 81.
58. Coulton, *Medieval Village*, 248.
59. Lacroix, *Military Life*, 49.
60. Davis, W. S., *Life on a Medieval Barony*, 176.
61. Coulton, *From St. Francis to Dante*, 20.
62. Seignobos, 74.
63. Coulton, *Chaucer and His England*, 199.
64. Coulton, *Panorama*, 247.
65. Prestage, E., *Chivalry*, 72.
66. *Speculum*, Apr. 1930, 189.
67. Thorndike, *Magic and Science*, II, 31.
68. Hoover, H., and Gibbons, H. A., *Conditions of a Lasting Peace*, 29.

69. Prestage, 75.
70. Coulton, *Panorama*, 239.
71. Traill, I, 379.
72. In Briffault, *Mothers*, III, 383, 394-5.
73. Bebel, 63.
74. Prestage, 9.
75. Rowbotham, 283.
76. Prestage, 98.
77. Davis, *Life on a Medieval Barony*, 77.
78. Vossler, K., *Medieval Culture*, I, 299; Taylor, *Medieval Mind*, II, 562.
79. Miss Amy Kelly in *Speculum*, Jan. 1937, 5.
80. Rowbotham, 224, 235.
81. Ibid., 249.
82. Ibid., 245.
83. In Vossler, I, 323.

CHAPTER XXIII

1. Thompson, *Middle Ages*, I, 565.
2. LeStrange, *Palestine under the Moslems*, 202.
3. Coulton, *Panorama*, 327.
4. Lacroix, *Military and Religious Life*, 108.
5. Ogg, 282-8.
6. William of Malmesbury, 358.
7. *Chanson de Roland*, ll. 848f, in French Classics, Paris, n.d., Lib. Hatier.
8. Munro, D. C., in *N. Y. Herald Tribune*, Apr. 26, 1931.
9. Thompson, *Social and Economic History*, 389.
10. Guizot, *France*, I, 384.
11. Lacroix, P., *History of Prostitution*, 904.
12. Guizot, *France*, 388.
13. *Cambridge Medieval History*, IV, 334.
14. Gibbon, VI, 72.
15. *Gesta Francorum*, app.
16. Thompson, *Social and Economic History*, 396.
17. Gibbon, VI, 75.
18. William of Tyre, *Siege of Jerusalem*, ch. clxi.
19. In Taylor, *Medieval Mind*, I, 551.
20. Albertus Aquens in Milman, IV, 38n.
21. Thompson, *Economic History*, 397.
22. Archer and Kingsford, *Crusades*, 171.
23. Milman, IV, 251.
24. William of Tyre, xxi, 7.
25. Archer, 176.
26. Muir, *Caliphate*, 578.
27. Guizot, *France*, 427f; *Cambridge Medieval History*, V, 307.
28. Adams, B., *Law of Civilization and Decay*, 94.
29. In Munro and Sellery, 275f.
30. Lane-Poole, *Saladin*, 175.
31. Ibid., 205f.
32. 232.
33. 246.
34. De Vaux, Carra, *Penseurs d'Islam*, I, 26.

35. Guizot, *France*, 439f; Gibbon, VI, 119.
36. Lane-Poole, *Saladin*, 307.
37. Ibid., 351f.
38. 357.
39. Ibid.
40. De Vaux, I, 27.
41. Lane-Poole, *Saladin*, 367.
42. Giraldus Cambrensis, *Itinerary through Wales*, i, 3.
43. Adams, *Civilization and Decay*, 133.
44. Gibbon, ed. Bury, VI, 528.
45. Villehardouin, Introd., xvii.
46. Adams, *Civilization and Decay*, 130.
47. Gibbon, VI, 100.
48. Oman, C. W. C., *Byzantine Empire*, 280-2.
49. Robert of Clari in Villehardouin, Introd., xxiv.
50. Villehardouin, 31.
51. Jackson, Sir T. C., *Byzantine and Romanesque Architecture*, I, 101.
52. Diehl, *Manuel*, 635.
53. Dalton, *Byzantine Art*, 538.
54. Gibbon, VI, 171.
55. Beard, Miriam, *History of the Business Man*, 109.
56. Encyclopaedia Britannica, VI, 788; MacLaurin, C., *Mere Mortals*, II, 215f.
57. Kantorowicz, E., *Frederick II*, 185f.
58. Villehardouin, 177.
59. Ibid., 220.
60. 320.
61. Day, Clive, *History of Commerce*, 88.
62. Hitti, 346.
63. Guizot, *Civilization*, I, 534.
64. Lea, *Auricular Confession*, III, 152.
65. *Speculum*, Oct. 1938, 391.
66. In Gibbon, VI, I, 25n.
67. *Speculum*, Oct. 1938, 403.
68. Hitti, 665.
69. Arnold, *Legacy of Islam*, 60.

CHAPTER XXIV

1. Day, *Commerce*, 57; Pirenne, *Medieval Cities*, 87.
2. Boissonnade, 173.
3. Thompson, *Economic History*, 577.
4. *Speculum*, Apr. 1940, 145.
5. Boissonnade, 173.
6. Coulton, *Panorama*, 325.
7. Ibid., 322.
8. Beard, 79.
9. Zimmern, H., *The Hansa Towns*, 183.
10. Ibid., 95.
11. Ibid., 152, 200.
12. Thompson, J. W., *Economic and Social History of Europe in the Later Middle Ages*, 451.
13. Id., *Economic and Social History of the Middle Ages*, 581.
14. *Cambridge Medieval History*, VI, 478.
15. Gest, A. P., *Roman Engineering*, 142.

16. Haskins, C. H., *Studies in Medieval Culture*, 101.
17. Usher, *History of Inventions*, 125.
18. Thompson, *Later Middle Ages*, 504.
19. Hitti, 667.
20. Rickard, *Man and Metals*, II, 561.
21. Salzman, L. F., *English Industries of the Middle Ages*, 1.
22. Rickard, II, 595.
23. Ibid., 615.
24. *Cambridge Medieval History*, VI, 500.
25. Renard, G., *Guilds in the Middle Ages*, 24.
26. Pirenne, H., *Economic and Social History of Medieval Europe*, 211.
27. Thompson, J. W., *Later Middle Ages*, 5.
28. Boissonnade, 187.
29. Ibid., 186.
30. Pirenne, H., *Economic History*, 113.
31. *Anglo-Saxon Chronicle*, 198.
32. Schoenhof, J., *History of Money and Prices*, 98.
33. Jusserand, J. J., *English Wayfaring Life in the Middle Ages*, 192.
34. Boissonnade, 221.
35. Coulton, *Panorama*, 285.
36. Id., *Five Centuries of Religion*, V, 282.
37. Pirenne, *Economic History*, 120.
38. Coulton, *Panorama*, 343.
39. Boissonnade, 167.
40. Pirenne, 128.
41. Pirenne, *Cities*, 223.
42. Matthew Paris, *Historia maior*, 1235, I, p. 2.
43. Ashley, *English Economic History and Theory*, I, 201.
44. Pirenne, *Economic History*, 130.
45. Ibid., 135.
46. Thompson, *Economic History of the Middle Ages*, 15.
47. Ibid.
48. Id., *Later Middle Ages*, 449; Day, 93.
49. Schoenhof, 63.
50. Ibid., 57; Thompson, *Later Middle Ages*, 432.
51. Adams, *Law of Civilization*, 167.
52. Lacroix, *Manners, Customs, and Dress*, 272.
53. Davis, *Medieval England*, 376.
54. Zimmern, *Hansa*, 165; Thompson, *Later Middle Ages*, 449.
55. Molmenti, *Venice*, Part I, Vol. I, 149; Thompson, *Later Middle Ages*, 420, 452; Crump, C. G., *Legacy of the Middle Ages*, 441.
56. Thompson, *Economic History of the Middle Ages*, 246; *Later Middle Ages*, 449-50.
57. Aristotle, *Politics*, i, 10.
58. Luke vi, 34.
59. In Ashley, *English Economic History and Theory*, I, 126.
60. Ibid., 128.
61. Ibid.
62. 158.
63. 149.
64. 411.
65. Coulton, G. G., *Medieval Scene*, 146.
66. Ashley, I, 149, 157.
67. Ibid., II, 405.
68. Pirenne, *Economic History*, 137.
69. Thompson, *Economic History of the Middle Ages*, 638.
70. Coulton, *Medieval Village*, 284.
71. Pirenne, *Economic History*, 129.
72. Ashley, I, 198.
73. *Cambridge Medieval History*, VI, 491.
74. Thomas Aquinas, *Summa Theologica*, II IIae, lxxviii, 2.
75. Ashley, I, 196; Coulton, *Panorama*, 336.
76. Boissonnade, 166.
77. Ashley, I, 203.
78. Abbott, G. F., *Israel in Egypt*, 112.
79. Baron, S., *Social and Religious History of the Jews*, II, 16.
80. Rivoira, G., *Lombardic Architecture*, I, 108.
81. Dopsch, 338.
82. *Cambridge Medieval History*, VI, 484.
83. Thompson, *Economic History of the Middle Ages*, 792.
84. Lethaby, W., *Medieval Art*, 145.
85. Richard, E., *History of German Civilization*, 195; Lacroix, *Manners*, 271.
86. Saunders, O. E., *History of English Art in the Middle Ages*, 85.
87. Thompson, *Economic History of the Middle Ages*, 493.
88. Id., *Later Middle Ages*, 196.
89. Day, 47.
90. Coulton, *Medieval Scene*, 92.
91. Walsh, J. J., *Thirteenth the Greatest of Centuries*, 437.
92. Barnes, *Economic History*, 184; Renard, *Guilds*, 37.
93. Ashley, I, 81.
94. Addison, J., *Arts and Crafts*, 2.
95. Power, Eileen, and Power, R., *Cities and Their Stories*, 74.
96. Bebel, 59.
97. Villari, P., *Two First Centuries of Florentine History*, 35.
98. Guibert of Nogent, *Autobiography*, 6-bis, 7-9.
99. Pirenne, H., *History of Europe*, 276.
100. Boissonnade, 207; Renard, *Guilds*, 62; Coulton, *Panorama*, 293; Schevill, *Siena*, 68.
101. Barnes, *Economic History*, 162-3.
102. Day, 51.
103. Headlam, C., *Story of Nuremberg*, 152.
104. Salzman, 335.
105. Pirenne, *Economic History*, 213.

106. Coulton, *Chaucer*, 128; *Medieval Village*, 329.
107. Boissonnade, 237.
108. Pirenne, *Cities*, 75.
109. Barnes, *Economic History*, 163.
110. Clapham and Power, 337.
111. Ibid.
112. Matthew Paris, I, 11, 42, 48, 156, 164, etc.
113. Coulton, *Panorama*, 456.
114. Porter, *Medieval Architecture*, II, 149.
115. Thompson, *Economic History of the Middle Ages*, 801.
116. Guizot, *France*, I, 614.
117. Beard, 85.
118. In Zimmern, *Hansa*, 49.
119. Coulton, *Social Life in Britain*, 101; Schoenhof, 125.
120. Rogers, J. E. T., *Six Centuries of Work and Wages*, 92; Jusserand, 99; Schoenhof 119.
121. Rogers, 73; Renard, 16.
122. Matthew Paris, 1251; Milman, VI, 57f; Lea, H. C., *History of the Inquisition in the Middle Ages*, I, 270.
123. Munro and Sellery, 468.
124. Pirenne, *Economic History*, 203.
125. Ashley, I, 82.
126. Ralph Higben's *Chronicle*, viii, 145, in Coulton, *Social Life*, 356.
127. Beard, 145.

CHAPTER XXV

1. Benjamin of Tudela in Komroff, *Contemporaries*, 265; Diehl, *Manuel*, 390.
2. *Cambridge Medieval History*, IV, 760.
3. Vasiliev, A. A., *History of the Byzantine Empire*, II, 151.
4. Matt. Paris, *Chronica maiora*, v, 38; *Historia minor*, iii, 38-9, in *Cambridge Medieval History*, IV, 493.
5. Vasiliev, II, 237, 241.
6. Finlay, G., *History of Greece*, III, 372.
7. Kluchevsky, I, 185; Pokrovsky, 78.
8. Rambaud, I, 96.
9. Vernadsky, G., *Kievan Russia*, 93-5.
10. Rambaud, I, 129; Kluchevsky, I, 323.
11. Vasiliev, II, 237.
12. Rambaud, I, 154.
13. Affirmed by Karamsin, denied by Soloviev, cf. Rambaud, I, 169.
14. Rambaud, I, 172.
15. Morey, *Medieval Art*, 158f.
16. *Cambridge Medieval History*, VI, 468.
17. Lönnrot, E., *Kalevala*, I, vii.
18. Rambaud. I, 144.
19. Lützow, *Bohemia*, 44.
20. *Cambridge Medieval History*, V, 348.
21. Richard, *German Civilization*, 186; Thompson, *Feudal Germany*, 161.
22. Richard, 186.
23. Carlyle, R. W., *Medieval Political Theory*, V, 88; III, 89.
24. Freeman, *Norman Conquest*, II, 181.
25. *Anglo-Saxon Chronicle*, 168.
26. Ibid., 163.
27. Voltaire, *Works*, XIII, 274.
28. Hume, D., *History of England*, I, 504.
29. Davis, *Medieval England*, 355; Milman, IV, 298, 302.
30. Stubbs, *Constitutional History*, I, 309; Freeman, *Norman Conquest*, IV, 430.
31. Ibid., 714.
32. Vinogradoff, P., *English Society in the Eleventh Century*, 472; Coulton, *Medieval Village*, 11.
33. Stubbs, I, 330.
34. Encyclopaedia Britannica, XI, 432.
35. Cf. *Anglo-Saxon Chronicle*, 206-8.
36. Coulton, *Life*, III, 5-7; *Panorama*, 229.
37. Pollock and Maitland, I, 104; Freeman, *Historical Essays*, 2d Series, 114.
38. Text in Rowbotham, 62.
39. Coulton, *Panorama*, 231.
40. Hume, D., I, 478.
41. Holinshed, *Chronicle*, 18.
42. Ogg, 304-10.
43. Jenks, 35.
44. Pollock and Maitland, I, 138.
45. Encyclopaedia Britannica, VIII, 9a.
46. Draper, *Intellectual Development of Europe*, II, 81.
47. Pollock and Maitland, I, 465; II, 398.
48. Coulton, *Panorama*, 379.
49. Home, *Roman London*, 118.
50. *Speculum*, Jan. 1937, 20.
51. Coulton, *Panorama*, 297.
52. Joyce, *Ireland*, 246-8; Hume, I, 356. Cardinal Gasquet (*Monastic Life in the M. Ages*, 169) argues unconvincingly against the authenticity of this bull.
53. In Coulton, *Panorama*, 66.
54. Brown, P. H., *History of Scotland*, I, 88.
55. Thierry, A., *Conquest of England by the Normans*, I, 21.
56. Blok, P. J., *History of . . . the Netherlands*, I, 230.
57. May, Sir T., *Democracy in Europe*, I, 338-9.
58. Encyclopaedia Britannica, XXI, 912c.
59. Guizot, *France*, I, 524.
60. Ibid., 312.
61. 522.
62. Belloc, *Paris*, 154.
63. Adams, H., *Mont St. Michel and Chartres*, 177.
64. Joinville, *Chronicle*, 153.
65. Lacroix, *Manners*, 32.
66. In Munro and Sellery, 520.
67. Joinville, 308.
68. *Cambridge Medieval History*, VI, 347.
69. Joinville, 139.
70. Taylor, H. O., *Medieval Mind*, I, 365.
71. *Cambridge Medieval History*, VI, 349.
72. Joinville, 149.

73. Ibid., 310; Guizot, *France*, I, 556; Munro and Sellery, 496.
74. Joinville, 316.
75. Munro and Sellery, 498.
76. Joinville, 148.
77. Munro and Sellery, 493, 500.
78. Guizot, *France*, I, 543.
79. Joinville, 150.
80. Guizot, *Civilization*, I, 184; Lacroix, *Manners*, 234.
81. Coulton, *From St. Francis*, 140.
82. Guizot, *France*, I, 452.
83. Thompson, *Economic History of the Middle Ages*, 44; Porter, *Medieval Architecture*, II, 264.
84. Thompson, 40.
85. Ibid., 22.
86. Hearnshaw, F., *Medieval Contributions to Modern Civilization*, 67; Encyclopaedia Britannica, X, 702b; Hearnshaw, *Social and Political Ideas of Some Great Medieval Thinkers*, 145, 157, 163.
87. *Cambridge Medieval History*, VI, 409.
88. Thompson, 349.
89. Chapman, C. E., *History of Spain*, 90; Carlyle, R. W., *Political Theory*, V, 134.
90. *Cambridge Medieval History*, VII, 695-702.
91. Pirenne, J., *Les grands courants*, II, 157.
92. Lea, H. C., *History of the Inquisition in Spain*, I, 58.
93. Sterling, M. B., *Story of Parzival*, 20f.
94. Milman, V, 61.

CHAPTER XXVI

1. In Waern, *Sicily*, 36.
2. *Cambridge Medieval History*, VI, 131.
3. Sarton, II(1), 119.
4. In Waern, 50f.
5. Bryce, 292.
6. Catholic Encyclopedia, I, 749a.
7. Hazlitt, W. C., *Venetian Republic*, I, 190f.
8. Molmenti, I(1), 82.
9. Ibid., 84.
10. 145.
11. Thompson, *Economic History of the Later Middle Ages*, 11.
12. Beard, 107.
13. Ruskin, *Stones of Venice*, I, 8.
14. Beard, 102-5.
15. Dante, *Eleven Letters*, 160, letter of March 1314 to Guido da Polenta.
16. Molmenti, I(2), 49, 53.
17. Ibid., 9, 13-15; Sedgwick, H. D., *Italy in the Thirteenth Century*, II, 200.
18. Molmenti, I(2), 139, 154, 157.
19. Molmenti, I(1), 204.
20. Beard, 146.
21. Coulton, *From St. Francis*, 215.
22. Ibid.

23. Thompson, *Economic History of the Middle Ages*, 421.
24. Sedgwick, I, 175.
25. Thompson, 441; *Cambridge Medieval History*, V, 230.
26. Kantorowicz, 26.
27. Ibid., 30.
28. *Cambridge Medieval History*, VI, 137.
29. Kantorowicz, 204.
30. Ibid., 219.
31. 282.
32. 310.
33. *Cambridge Medieval History*, VI, 150.
34. Kantorowicz, 288.
35. Ibid., 529.
36. Pirenne, J., *Grands courants*, II, 114; Kantorowicz, 311.
37. Ibid., 307.
38. 355.
39. 195.
40. Matt. Paris, 1238, 157.
41. Ibid.
42. Sedgwick, I, 133; Kantorowicz, 308.
43. Ibid., 251.
44. 343.
45. 460.
46. 615.
47. 624-32.
48. Nietzsche, F., *Beyond Good and Evil*, #200.
49. Kantorowicz, 611.
50. Sedgwick, I, 440; Kantorowicz, 332.
51. Ibid., 292.
52. Milman, VI, 240f.
53. Renard, 24; *Cambridge Medieval History*, VI, 496.
54. Thompson, *Later Middle Ages*, 259.
55. Beard, 140.
56. Thompson, *Economic History of the Middle Ages*, 471.
57. Villari, *First Centuries of Florentine History*, 178.
58. Ibid., 221.
59. 498.

CHAPTER XXVII

1. In Coulton, *Social Life*, 15.
2. Thomas Aquinas, *Summa Theologica*, I, lxiv, 4.
3. In Coulton, *Five Centuries of Religion*, I, 60.
4. Ibid., 31.
5. Gregory I, *Dialogues*, iv, 30, 35, in Lecky, *Morals*, II, 220.
6. Ibid., 221.
7. Westermarck, *Moral Ideas*, I, 723; Coulton, *Five Centuries*, I, 71.
8. Thomas Aquinas, *Summa Theologica*, Supplement, xcvii, 5, 7.
9. Lea, *Inquisition in Middle Ages*, III, 384.
10. Ibid., 385.
11. Coulton, *Five Centuries*, I, 40.

12. Gregory I, *Dialogues*, i, 4, in Dudden, II, 367.
13. Coulton, *Five Centuries*, I, 445-9; II, 665.
14. Coulton, *Panorama*, 416.
15. Id., *Social Life*, 337.
16. Westermarck, *Moral Ideas*, I, 722.
17. Coulton, *Panorama*, 416.
18. *Cambridge Medieval History*, VII, 635.
19. Coulton, *Inquisition and Liberty*, 19.
20. Id., *Panorama*, 417.
21. Id., *Medieval Village*, 241.
22. Thomas Aquinas, *Summa Theologica*, I, xxiii, 7.
23. Coulton, *Life*, I, 54.
24. Lecky, *Morals*, II, 220.
25. In Coulton, *Inquisition and Liberty*, 18.
26. Lea, *Auricular Confession*, III, 322.
27. Dudden, II, 427.
28. Renan, E., *Poetry of the Celtic Races*, 177.
29. Coulton, *Five Centuries*, I, 75.
30. Id., *Inquisition and Liberty*, 2.
31. John of Salisbury, *Metalogicus*, vii, 2.
32. In Munro and Sellery, 489.
33. Giraldus Cambrensis, *Gemma Ecclesiastica*, ii, 24, in Robertson, J. M., *Short History of Free Thought*, II, 311.
34. Ibid., i, 51, in Robertson, II, 311.
35. Lea, *Inquisition in Middle Ages*, III, 558.
36. Coulton, *Social Life*, 218; *Five Centuries*, I, 71.
37. Vincent of Beauvais, *Speculum Morale*, ii, 3.6; ii, 1.11.
38. Coulton, *Five Centuries*, I, 31.
39. Coulton, *The Inquisition*, 62.
40. Quoted by Berthold of Regensburg in Coulton, *Five Centuries*, I, 72.
41. *Aucassin et Nicolette*, line 22.
42. Coulton, *Panorama*, 17.
43. Id., *Five Centuries*, I, 303.
44. Reese, G., *Music in the Middle Ages*, 110.
45. Wright, Th., *The Book of the Knight of La Tour-Landry*, prologue, and ch. 35, 174.
46. Coulton, *Village*, 254.
47. Raby, *Christian Latin Poetry*, 358.
48. Durand, *Rationale divinorum officiorum*, in Raby, 357.
49. Raby, 356.
50. Giraldus Cambrensis, *Itinerary*, i, 2.
51. Vincent of Beauvais, *Speculum Historiale*, vi, 99, in Coulton, *Life*, i, 1.
52. Caesar of Heisterbach, ii, 170.
53. Ibid.
54. Milman, III, 242.
55. Coulton, *Five Centuries*, I, 300.
56. Moore, *Judaism*, II, 4.
57. Catholic Encyclopedia, I, 634.
58. Voltaire, *Works*, XIII, 136.
59. In Spengler, O., *Decline of the West*, II, 295.
60. Voltaire, III, 137.
61. Lea, *Auricular Confession*, II, 443.
62. Ibid., III, 285.
63. Catholic Encyclopedia, VII, 787.
64. *Cambridge Medieval History*, VI, 678; Funk, I, 379.
65. Adams, B., *Law of Civilization and Decay*, 64.
66. Lanfranc, *De corpore et sanguine Domini*, in *Cambridge Medieval History*, VI, 678.
66a. Lacroix, *Military*, 454.
67. Matt. vi, 7.
68. Encyclopaedia Britannica, VI, 795.
69. Montalembert, I, 57.
70. Male, E., *L'art religieux du XIIIe siècle en France*, 309-11.
71. Coulton, *Panorama*, 107.
72. Coulton, *Life*, I, 168.
73. Addison, *Arts*, 65.
74. Coulton, *Five Centuries*, IV, 94.
75. Haskins, *Renaissance of Twelfth Century*, 235.
76. Jusserand, 327.
77. Ibid.
78. Coulton, *Five Centuries*, IV, 106.
79. Clavijo, G. de, *Embassy to Tamerlane*, 7, 63, 81.
80. Coulton, *Five Centuries*, V, 105.
81. Ibid., IV, 120.
82. V, 99.
83. Coulton, *Five*, IV, 98.
84. Ibid., 116.
85. 111.
86. Haskins, *Renaissance*, 235.
87. Coulton, *Five Centuries*, IV, 121.
88. Funk, J, 297.
89. Howard, C., *Sex Worship*, 78-93; Coulton, *Life*, IV, 209-10.
90. Davis, *Medieval England*, 202; Frazer, Sir J., *Magic Art*, II, 370.
91. Weigall, A., *The Paganism in Our Christianity*, 131.
92. Adams, H., *Mont St. Michel*, 91.
93. Coulton, *From St. Francis*, 119.
94. In Adams, H., 262.
95. Ibid., 93, 254.
96. 259.
97. 258.
98. Funk, I, 296.
99. Catholic Encyclopedia, IX, 791d.
100. Julian Ribera in Thorndike, *Short History of Civilization*, 350.
101. For tr. of *Dies irae* cf. Van Doren, M., *Anthology*, 460.
102. Gibbon, VI, 494f.
103. Renard, 42; Brentano in Smith, T., *English Guilds*, lxxxv.
104. Thompson, *Economic History of the*

Middle Ages, 674; Barnes, *Economic History,* 164.
105. Catholic Encyclopedia, V, 679.
106. Villari, 161.
107. Coulton, *Five Centuries,* IV, 333; *Medieval Village,* 294.
108. Ibid.
109. Maine, *Ancient Law,* 132.
110. Coulton, *Panorama,* 172, 293; *From St. Francis,* 293; Lea, *Sacerdotal Celibacy,* 283; Matthew Paris, I, 83.
111. Davis, *Medieval England,* 28.
112. Coulton, *Panorama,* 137, 154.
113. Id., *Medieval Village,* 295.
114. Ibid., 303; id., *Panorama,* 197, 204; *Social Life,* 213; *Life,* III, 39.
115. Lecky, *Morals,* II, 335.
116. Coulton, *Panorama,* 129.
117. Lea, *Inquisition in Middle Ages,* I, 3.
118. Thatcher, 165-6.
119. *Cambridge Medieval History,* VI, 543.
119a. Jewish Encyclopedia, I, 550.
120. Lea, op. cit., I, 13.
121. *Cambridge Medieval History,* VI, 8.
122. Ibid., 3; Taylor, *Medieval Mind,* II, 303.
123. Carlyle, R. W., *Political Theory,* V, 157, 182.
124. Ibid., 162.
125. Encyclopaedia Britannica, II, 370a.
126. Clayton, J., *Pope Innocent III,* 181.
127. Walsh, J., *Thirteenth Century,* 370.
128. *Cambridge Medieval History,* VI, 2.
129. In Lea, *Inquisition in Middle Ages,* I, 129.
130. *Cambridge Medieval History,* VI, 694.
131. Encyclopaedia Britannica, XII, 370b.
132. Coulton, *From St. Francis,* 275.
133. Funk, I, 358.
134. Coulton, *From St. Francis,* 277.
135. *Cambridge Medieval History,* VI, 120.
136. Luke Wadding in Coulton, *From St. Francis,* 277.
137. Ibid., 225.
138. Coulton, *Panorama,* 165.
139. Thompson, *Economic History of the Middle Ages,* 688.
140. Voltaire, XIII, 130.
141. Clapham and Power, 189.
142. Lea, *Auricular Confession,* III, 17.
143. Taylor, *Medieval Mind,* II, 303; Thompson, *Economic Middle Ages,* 689.
144. Id., *Feudal Germany,* 19.
145. Boissonnade, 82, 243.
146. Ibid., Lacroix, *Manners,* 12.
147. Fisher, H. L., *Medieval Empire,* II, 64.
148. Thompson, *Economic History of the Middle Ages,* 692.
149. Ibid., 691.
150. Id., *Later Middle Ages,* 12.
151. Funk, I, 355.
152. Lea, *Inquisition in Middle Ages,* III, 624.
153. Lavisse, E., *Histoire de France,* III, 318.

154. Matthew Paris, I, 50.
155. Coulton, *Five Centuries,* IV, 522.
156. Coulton, *Life,* I, 36.
157. Milman, V, 139.
158. Porter, *Medieval Architecture,* II, 164; Coulton, *Social Life,* 215.
159. Cf. Lea, *Inquisition in Middle Ages,* I, 21-30, for many instances of ecclesiastical self-reform.

CHAPTER XXVIII

1. Coulton, *From St. Francis,* 12.
2. Beer, M., *Social Struggles in the Middle Ages,* 135, 177.
3. Luchaire in Munro and Sellery, 438.
4. Ibid.; Beer, 133.
5. Encyclopaedia Britannica, XXIII, 288b.
6. Coulton, *Panorama,* 463.
7. Vacandard, *Inquisition,* 70.
8. Thompson, *Economic History of the Middle Ages,* 662.
9. *Cambridge Medieval History,* VI, 21.
10. Sabatier, *Life of St. Francis,* 43.
11. Matthew Paris, I, 66.
12. Vacandard, 83.
13. Ibid., 74.
14. 91.
15. Luchaire, 444.
16. Vacandard, 77; Beer, 129-31.
17. Coulton, *Inquisition and Liberty,* 79; Vacandard, 97; Luchaire, 441.
18. Coulton, *Inquisition and Liberty,* 70; Vacandard, 73; Morey, *Medieval Art,* 255.
19. Vacandard, 77.
20. Lea, *Inquisition in Middle Ages,* I, 103.
21. Rowbotham, 293.
22. Luchaire, 434.
23. Ibid., 436.
24. Lea, I, 120, 133.
25. Thatcher, 209.
26. Lea, I, 139.
27. Ibid., 141.
28. Ibid.
29. 146.
30. 153.
31. 154.
32. Guizot, *France,* I, 507; Coulton, *Life,* I, 68.
33. Lea, I, 162.
34. Thompson, *Economic History of the Middle Ages,* 490.
35. Lea, 554.
36. Maimonides, *Guide to the Perplexed,* III, introd., xli.
37. Vacandard, 48.
38. Ibid.
39. 63.
40. 68.
41. Sumner, *Folkways,* 238.
42. Catholic Encyclopedia, VIII, 28c.
43. Lea, 237.

44. Vacandard, 63.
45. Coulton, *Inquisition and Liberty*, 49.
46. Vacandard, 37.
47. Lea, 69.
48. Nickerson, H., *Inquisition*, 61.
49. Thompson, *Economic History of the Middle Ages*, 689; Jusserand, 280.
50. Lea, 318.
51. Ibid., 321.
52. Coulton, *Inquisition and Liberty*, 49.
53. Catholic Encyclopedia, VIII, 29a; Vacandard, 52.
54. Ibid., 119.
55. Coulton, *Inquisition*, 59; *Inquisition and Liberty*, 66.
56. Vacandard, 61.
57. Sarton, II(2), 546.
58. Vacandard, 183.
59. Ibid., 163.
60. Davis, *Medieval England*, 406.
61. Thatcher, 309.
62. Lea, 371; Vacandard, 190.
63. Lea, 381.
64. Ibid., 436.
65. 317.
66. Catholic Encyclopedia, VIII, 31d.
67. Lea, 441.
68. Catholic Encyclopedia, VIII, 31c.
69. Lea, 441.
70. Catholic Encyclopedia, VIII, 32b.
71. Ibid., 32d.
72. Ibid.
73. Coulton, *Inquisition*, 86.
74. Vacandard, 183.
75. Lea, II, 97.
76. Catholic Encyclopedia, VIII, 33d.
77. *Cambridge Medieval History*, VI, 723; Vacandard, 203.
78. Thompson, *Economic History of the Middle Ages*, 689.
79. Vacandard, 144, 178.
80. Lea, I, 549.
81. Ibid., 550.
82. *Cambridge Medieval History*, VI, 723; Vacandard, 196; Lea, I, 551.
83. Ibid., 393.
84. 113.

CHAPTER XXIX

1. Thompson, *Economic History of the Middle Ages*, 603.
2. Coulton, *Five Centuries*, IV. 15.
3. Gilson, E., *Philosophy of St. Bonaventure*, 31.
4. Coulton, *Life*, IV, 98.
5. In Coulton, *From Francis*, 70.
6. Coulton, *Life*, IV, 238.
7. Lea, I, 35.
8. Thompson, *Economic History of the Middle Ages*, 604.
9. Milman, IV, 259.
10. Coulton, *Life*, IV, 155.

11. Coulton, *Five Centuries*, IV, 96, 367-77.
12. In Coulton, *Life*, IV, 199.
13. Caesar of Heisterbach, i, 249, in Coulton, *Five Centuries*, I, 377; Jocelyn's *Chronicle*, in Carlyle, Th., *Past and Present*, p. 72.
14. Waddell, H., *Wandering Scholars*, 210.
15. Taylor, *Medieval Mind*, I, 268.
16. Ibid., 430.
17. Coulton, *Five Centuries*, I, 183.
18. Lacroix, Paul, *History of Prostitution*, 692.
19. Cf. Longfellow's "Golden Legend."
20. *Cambridge Medieval History*, V, 675.
21. Thompson, *Economic History of the Middle Ages*, 612.
22. Étienne de Bourbon, *Anecdotes*, in Coulton, *Five Centuries*, I, 79.
23. Ogg, 258.
24. Coulton, *Five Centuries*, I, 308.
25. Ibid., IV, 165.
26. I, 304.
27. Munro and Sellery, 410.
28. In Gilson, É., *La philosophie au moyen âge*, I, 92.
29. W. B. Yeats, Introd. to Tagore, R., *Gitanjali*, xviii.
30. Munro and Sellery, 412.
31. Ibid.
32. Coulton, *Five Centuries*, I, 305.
33. Ibid., 391.
34. 336.
35. 387.
36. Jörgensen, *St. Francis*, 12.
37. In Sabatier, 149.
38. Jörgensen, 21.
39. Sabatier, 26; Bonaventure, *Life of St. Francis*, ch. 1.
40. Sabatier, 59f.
41. *Mirror of Perfection*, ch. 14.
42. *Tres Socii*, 35, in Sabatier, 74.
43. *Mirror*, ch. 69.
44. Ibid., ch. 11.
45. Ibid.
46. Coulton, *Panorama*, 529.
47. *Tres Socii*, 38-41.
48. *Little Flowers of St. Francis*, ch. 8.
49. Ibid., ch. 9.
50. *Mirror*, ch. 61.
51. Ibid., chs. 29-35.
52. Ibid., ch. 114.
53. *Little Flowers*, ch. 22.
54. Ch. 16.
55. Sabatier, 97.
56. Arnold, M., *Essays in Criticism*, First Series, 155.
57. *Little Flowers*, ch. 11.
58. Ch. 24.
59. Sabatier, 229.
60. Ibid., 227.
61. Dr. E. F. Hartung in *Time*, Mar. 11, 1935.

62. *Mirror*, ch. 116.
63. Ch. 120.
64. Faure, É., *Medieval Art*, 398.
65. Text of the will in Sabatier, 337.
66. Milman, V, 242.
67. *Cambridge Medieval History*, VI, 737f.
68. Matt. Paris, ii, 443, in Coulton, *Five Centuries*, IV, 170.
69. Ibid., 388.
70. Coulton, *From Francis*, 101-2.
71. Ibid.
72. Funk, I, 370.
73. Crump, 413.
74. Lea, *Sacerdotal Celibacy*, 105.
75. Power, E., *Medieval People*, 64.
76. *Little Flowers*, ch. 33.
77. E.g., *Nun's Rule* (Ancren Riwle), 105, 185.
78. Cf. pp. 294-6.
79. Montalembert, II, 703.
80. Ibid.
81. Lea, *Celibacy*, 264.
82. Taylor, *Medieval Mind*, I, 492.
83. Coulton, *Panorama*, 622.
84. Power, *Medieval People*, 80.
85. Ibid.
86. Lea, *Inquisition in Middle Ages*, III, 10-17.
87. Lea, I, 272.
88. *Cambridge Medieval History*, VII, 789.
89. Sabatier, 52.
90. Lea, II, 326.
91. Coulton, *Life*, III, 54; Kantorowicz, 419.
92. Sabatier, 52; Taylor, *Medieval Mind*, I, 460.
93. Milman, VI, 123.
94. Coulton, *Life*, I, 205.
95. Catholic Encyclopedia, II, 662d.
96. Ibid., 663.
97. Thatcher, 311.
98. *Cambridge Medieval History*, VII, 7-8.
99. Milman, VI, 282; Coulton, *Panorama*, 212.
100. Guizot, *France*, I, 591.
101. Catholic Encyclopedia, II, 666c.
102. Ibid., 667c; Ogg, 383-8.
103. Adams, B., *Law of Civilization and Decay*, 173; Draper, *Intellectual Development*, II, 83.
104. Guizot, *France*, I, 596.
105. *Cambridge Medieval History*, VII, 18.
106. Guizot, 601; Draper, II, 86.
107. Milman, VI, 494f.
108. Lea, II, 58.
109. Hume, *England*, I, 511.
110. Coulton, *Five Centuries*, IV, 118.
111. Coulton, *From Francis*, 150.

CHAPTER XXX

1. In Coulton, *Five Centuries*, I, 176.
2. Id., *Medieval Village*, 103.
3. Bede, i, 27.

4. Coulton, *Life*, IV, 160n.
5. In Coulton, *From Francis*, 18.
6. Benvenuta da Imola in Coulton, *From Francis*, 416; Lacroix, *Prostitution*, I, 694.
7. Ibid., 695.
8. 700.
9. 697.
10. II, 908.
11. Wright, ed., *Book of the Knight of La Tour-Landry*, Prologue and ch. 35.
12. In Briffault, *Mothers*, III, 417.
13. Lecky, *Morals*, II, 152.
14. Lacroix, *Prostitution*, II, 904.
15. Ibid., 905.
16. 904.
17. I, 721.
18. II, 869; Sumner, *Folkways*, 529; Bebel, 61; Garrison, *History of Medicine*, 192; Sanger, Wm., *History of Prostitution*, 98.
19. St. Augustine, *De ordine*, ii, 4.
20. Thomas Aquinas, *Summa Theologica*, II IIae, x, 11.
21. Encyclopaedia Britannica, XVIII, 598a.
22. Ibid.
23. Lacroix, *Prostitution*, I, 733-42.
24. Ibid., II, 751; Sanger, 95.
25. Coulton, *Panorama*, 172.
26. Lecky, *Morals*, II, 218.
27. Power, E., *Medieval People*, 118.
28. Pollock and Maitland, II, 387.
29. Coulton, *Panorama*, 634.
30. Bevan, E., and Singer, C., *Legacy of Israel*, 102.
31. Crump, 346.
32. Thomas Aquinas, *Summa contra Gentiles*, iii, 122.
33. Himes, *Contraception*, 160f.
34. Lacroix, *Prostitution*, I, 699.
35. Coulton, *Medieval Village*, 404.
36. Schoenfeld, H., *Women of the Teutonic Nations*, 122.
37. Freeman, *Norman Conquest*, II, 166.
38. Wright, Th., *History of Domestic Manners and Sentiments*, 275.
39. Pollock and Maitland, II, 390; Crump, 297; Butler, P., *Women of Medieval France*, 30.
40. St. John Chrysostom in James, B., *Women of England*, 108.
41. Thomas Aquinas, *Summa Theologica*, Supplement, lxxxi, 3.
42. Ibid., I, xciii, 4.
43. Supplement, xxxix, 3.
44. II IIae, xxvi, 10.
45. In Coulton, *Panorama*, 614, quoting Gratian, *Decretum*, II, xxxiii, 5.
46. Coulton, *Life*, III, 114; *Five Centuries*, I, 174.
47. Id., *Chaucer's England*, 212.
48. Id., *Panorama*, 618.

49. Schoenfeld, 41.
50. Davis, *Life on a Medieval Barony*, 102.
51. James, *Women of England*, 182.
52. Renard, 20.
53. Cf. James, 116.
54. Wright, T., *Domestic Manners*, 273-4.
55. Butler, *Women of France*, 104.
56. Adams, H., *Mont St. Michel*, 211.
57. Butler, 123.
58. Tout, T. F., *Medieval Forgers*, in Coulton, *Five Centuries*, IV, 310.
59. Haskins, *Renaissance*, 89.
60. Exs. in Coulton, *Chaucer's England*, 200; *Five Centuries*, I, 251.
61. Lacroix, *Manners*, 41.
62. Coulton, *Medieval Village*, 72, 344.
63. Id., *Panorama*, 74, 369.
64. Encyclopaedia Britannica, VIII, 8d.
65. Coulton, *Inquisition*, 47.
66. Hume, I, 185.
67. Salzman, 309.
68. Ashley, II, 73.
69. Coulton, *Chaucer*, 131.
70. Coulton, *Life*, III, 57f.
71. Id., *Medieval Village*, 30.
72. Thompson, *Economic History of the Middle Ages*, 571; Porter, *Medieval Architecture*, II, 159.
73. Coulton, *Panorama*, 377.
74. Ibid.
75. Lea, *Inquisition in Middle Ages*, I, 234-5.
76. Coulton, *From Francis*, 218.
77. Sumner, 472; Jusserand, 212; Boissonnade, 262.
78. Coulton, *Social Life*, 395.
79. Joinville, 309.
80. Cf. Coulton, *From Francis*, app. C.
81. Jusserand, 132f.
82. Davis, *Medieval England*, 425.
83. Zimmern, *Hansa*, 111.
84. Ibid.
85. Coulton, *Social Life*, 371, 425.
86. Ashley, II, 328.
87. Bacon, R., *Opus maius*, ed. Bridges, II, 251.
88. Ashley, II, 307.
89. Ibid., 323.
90. Davis, *Life on a Medieval Barony*, 95.
91. Traill, I, 484.
92. James, *Women*, 208.
93. *Speculum*, Apr. 1940, 148; Encyclopaedia Britannica, IV, 470.
94. In Adams, H., 202.
95. Friedländer, *Roman Manners*, II, 183.
96. Butler, *Women*, 147.
97. Dante, *Purgatorio*, xxiii, 102.
98. Coulton, *From Francis*, 271.
99. Davis, *Life on a Medieval Barony*, 96.
100. In Coulton, *Life*, III, 64.
101. Crump, 431.
102. Beard, 69.
103. Coulton, *Life*, IV, 173.

104. *Speculum*, Apr. 1928, 198.
105. Sarton, II(1), 96.
106. *Speculum*, Jan. 1934, 306.
107. Ibid.
108. Lowie, *Are We Civilized?*, 75.
109. Lacroix, *Manners*, 176.
110. Butler, *Women*, 150.
111. Giraldus Cambrensis, *Description of Wales*, i, 10.
112. Salzman, 171.
113. Lacroix, P., *Arts of the Middle Ages*, 13.
114. Rogers, *Six Centuries*, 46.
115. Sedgwick, *Italy*, II, 197.
116. Power, *Medieval People*, 103.
117. Thompson, *Economic History of the Middle Ages*, 595.
118. Müller-Lyer, *Marriage*, 56.
119. Coulton, *Panorama*, 313; Addison, *Arts*, 272.
120. Coulton, *Medieval Village*, 27.
121. Schevill, *Siena*, 349.
122. Haskins, *Studies in Medieval Culture*, 122.
123. Sedgwick, II, 206.
124. Coulton, *Panorama*, 96.
125. Power, E., *Medieval People*, 76.
126. Lacroix, *Manners*, 239; Coulton, *Medieval Village*, 559.
127. Coulton, *Panorama*, 96.
128. Kirstein, L., *Dance*, 88.
129. Wright, Th., *Domestic Manners*, 257.
130. Walsh, J., *Thirteenth Century*, 452.
131. Davis, *Medieval England*, 372.
132. Davis, *Life on a Medieval Barony*, 64.
133. Encyclopaedia Britannica, XIII, 791c.
134. Lacroix, *Manners*, 233.
135. Gardiner, E. N., *Athletics of the Ancient World*, 237.
136. Coulton, *Panorama*, 83.
137. Gardiner, 238.
138. Coulton, *Panorama*, 95.
139. Coulton, *Social Life*, 392.
140. Id., *Chaucer*, 278.
141. Chambers, E. K., *The Medieval Stage*, I, 287; Maitland, *Dark Ages*, 174; Lacroix, *Science and Literature in the Middle Ages*, 240
142. Ibid.; Chambers, I, 323; Coulton, *Panorama*, 606.
143. Chambers, I, 343.
144. *Time*, Dec. 31, 1945.
145. Waddell, *Wandering Scholars*, 200.
146. Coulton, *From Francis*, 56.
147. Ibid., 55.
148. 57.
149. 13.

CHAPTER XXXI

1. Jackson, Sir T., *Byzantine and Romanesque Architecture*, 94.
2. Id., *Gothic Architecture*, I, 59.
3. Spencer, H., *Principles of Sociology*,

III, 291; Coulton, *Life*, IV, 169.
4. Theophilus, *Schedula diversarum artium*, Introd., in Dillon, *Glass*, 126.
5. Addison, *Arts*, 86, 59.
6. Ibid., 186.
7. Walsh, *Thirteenth Century*, 115.
8. Saunders, *English Art in the Middle Ages*, 65.
9. Ackerman, Phyllis, *Tapestry*, 42f.
10. Ruskin, *Stones of Venice*, I, ch. 2.
11. Morey, 195.
12. Short, E. H., *The Painter in History*, 75.
13. Mâle, *L'art religieux du XIIIe siècle*, 80.
14. Taine, H., *Italy: Florence and Venice*, 49.
15. Encyclopaedia Britannica, V, 706d.
16. Vasari, *Lives*, I, 66.
17. Morey, 267.
18. Lacroix, *Arts*, 251f.
19. Adams, H., *Mont St. Michel*, 137.
20. Saunders, 105.
21. Mâle, 78.
22. Bond, F., *Wood Carvings in English Churches*, I, 167.
23. Ibid.
24. Mâle, 74.
25. S. Reinach in Walsh, *Thirteenth Century*, 106.
26. Kantorowicz, 535; Morey, 314; Sedgwick, II, 225.

CHAPTER XXXII

1. Pope, A. U., *Iranian and Armenian Contributions to the Beginnings of Gothic Architecture*, 127.
2. Porter, II, 170.
3. *Speculum*, Jan. 1927, 23.
4. Mâle, 66; Morey, 234.
5. William of Malmesbury, v, 3.
6. Encyclopaedia Britannica, VII, 763.
7. Cram, *Substance of Gothic*, 119.
8. Pope, *Contributions*, 137.
9. Bond, F., *Gothic Architecture in England*, 263; Pirenne, J., *Grands courants*, II, 135; Porter, II, 63.
10. Addison, *Arts*, 201.
11. Panofsky, I., *Abbot Suger*.
12. Cram, 144.
13. Coulton, *Life*, II, 18; Porter, I, 151f.
14. Headlam, C., *Story of Chartres*, 140.
15. Jackson, *Gothic Architecture*, I, 96.
16. Ferguson, J., *History of Architecture*, I, 540.
17. Adams, H., 66.
18. Headlam, *Chartres*, 229.
19. Ibid., 208.
20. Ibid.
21. Adams, H., 76.
22. Connick, C. J., *Adventures in Light and Color*, 10.
23. Robillard, M., *Chartres*, 54.
24. Faure, *Medieval Art*, 348; Bond, *Gothic*

Architecture in England, 33; Moore, C. H., *Development of Gothic Architecture*, 124.
25. Jackson, *Gothic Architecture*, I, 189.
26. Ibid.
27. Walsh, *Thirteenth Century*, 108.
28. Armstrong, Sir W., *Art in Great Britain*, 46.
29. Morey, 293. Germany was closed to mere scholars during the composition of these pages, which must therefore speak of German architecture and sculpture at second hand, or from vague memories of visits in 1912 and 1932.
30. De Wulf, *Medieval Philosophy*, I, 3.
31. Morey, 297.
32. In Taine, *Italy: Florence*, 89.
33. Beard, 143.
34. Street, G., *Gothic Architecture in Spain*, 106.
35. Arnold, *Legacy of Islam*, 168; Dieulafoy, *Art in Spain*, 147.

CHAPTER XXXIII

1. Lang, P. H., *Music in Western Civilization*, 51.
2. Ibid., 43.
3. Reese, *Music in the Middle Ages*, 63.
4. Ibid., 20f; *Oxford History of Music*, introductory volume, 137.
5. Lang, 71.
6. Grove, *Dictionary of Music*, s.v. Notation.
7. Arnold, *Legacy of Islam*, 17; Sarton, II (1), 25, 406.
8. The date and identity of Franco are disputed; cf. Grove, s.v. Franco of Cologne.
9. Lang, 130.
10. Ibid., 139.
11. Giraldus Cambrensis, *Description of Wales*, i, 8.
12. Lang, 97.
13. Jusserand, 196.
14. Reese, 206.
15. Ibid., 246.
16. So argues, with considerable scholarship, Julian Ribera in *La musica de las cantigas*; cf. McKinney, H. D., and Anderson, W. R., *Music in History*, 181. Beck, Gennrich, and Reese prefer to derive the name and songs of the troubadours from the trope; cf. Reese, 218.
17. Lacroix, *Arts*, 203.
18. Addison, *Arts*, 110.
19. Reese, 123.
20. Rowbotham, 6; Lacroix, *Arts*, 205.
21. Ibid., 204.

CHAPTER XXXIV

1. In Ogg, 145.
2. Vossler, K., *Medieval Culture*, I, 5.

3. Dante, *La Vita Nuova*, xxv.
4. Munro and Sellery, 330.
5. Cf. Pollock and Maitland, I, 57.
6. Mumford, L., *Technics and Civilization*, 438; Encyclopaedia Britannica, XXI, 1006a.
7. *Lyra Graeca*, III, 679, app. by J. M. Edmonds.
8. Munro and Sellery, 282; Haskins, *Renaissance*, 16; id., *Normans*, 236.
9. Haskins, *Renaissance*, 72.
10. Thorndike in *Speculum*, Apr. 1937, 268.
11. Haskins, *Renaissance*, 72.
12. Coulton, *Panorama*, 683.
13. Lea, *Inquisition in Middle Ages*, I, 554.
14. Lacroix, *Arts*, 472.
15. Walsh, *Thirteenth Century*, 156.
16. Coulton, *Medieval Scene*, 124; *Panorama*, 576; Haskins, *Renaissance*, 71.
17. Encyclopaedia Britannica, XIV, 3.
18. Haskins, *Renaissance*, 43.
19. Calvert, *Moorish Remains in Spain*, 426.
20. Haskins, *Studies in Medieval Culture*, 100.
21. Bevna, *Legacy of Israel*, 230.
22. Ibid., 211.
23. Sarton, II(1), 125.
24. Arnold, *Legacy of Islam*, 347.
25. Ibid., 244.
26. Wright, *Domestic Manners*, 271.
27. De Wulf, *Medieval Philosophy*, I, 61; West, *Alcuin*, 57.
28. John of Salisbury, *Metalogicus*, i, 24, in Poole, *Illustrations*, 98.
29. Thorndike in *Speculum*, Oct. 1940, 401.
30. Walsh, *Thirteenth Century*, 28.
31. Thorndike, l.c.; Rashdall, *Universities of Europe in the Middle Ages*, III, 350; Crump, *Legacy of the Middle Ages*, 262-3.
32. Abélard, *Historia Calamitatum*, Introd. by R. A. Cram, p. v.
33. Coulton, *Medieval Village*, 254.
34. Jusserand, 279.
35. Coulton, *Panorama*, 388.
36. Thorndike, *Speculum*, Oct. 1940, 408.
37. Rashdall, *Universities*, III, 370.
38. Aristotle, *Politics*, viii, 1.
39. Crump, 266.
40. Rashdall, I, 93.
41. Ibid., 113.
42. Lea, *Inquisition in the Middle Ages*, I, 59.
43. Walsh, *Thirteenth Century*, 33; Baedeker, K., *Northern Italy*, 471.
44. Rashdall, I, 149-67.
45. Ibid., 196.
46. 196-7.
47. Paetow, L. J., *Guide to the Study of Medieval History*, 448.
48. Haskins, *Renaissance*, 396.
49. Rashdall, I, 445.
50. Thorndike, *Magic*, II, 53.
51. *Cambridge Medieval History*, VI, 746.
52. Encyclopaedia Britannica, XI, 995.
53. Rashdall, III, 29n.
54. Ibid., 33.
55. 199.
56. 246n; Sarton, II(2), 584.
57. Davis, *Medieval England*, 398.
58. Encyclopaedia Britannica, X, 9006b.
59. Ashley, I, 203.
60. Munro and Sellery, 350; Walsh, *Thirteenth Century*, 65.
61. Waddell, *Wandering Scholars*, 171.
62. Walsh, 65.
63. Rashdall, IV, 325-36.
64. Ibid.
65. Coulton, *Social Life*, 95.
66. Rashdall, III, 386.
67. Ibid., 439.
68. 441.
69. 440.
70. 96n.
71. 431.
72. 432; Coulton, *Life*, III, 73.
73. Rashdall, III, 439.
74. Castiglione, 328.
75. Munro and Sellery, 350.
76. Rashdall, I, 466-70.

CHAPTER XXXV

1. V. Cousin in Abélard, *Ouvrages inédits*, xcix.
2. Gilson, É., *La philosophie au moyen âge*, ed. 1947, 238.
3. De Wulf, *Medieval Philosophy*, I, 103.
4. Ibid., 46.
5. Thomas Aquinas, *Summa Theologica*, I, i, 1.
6. Ueberweg, *History of Philosophy*, I, 386.
7. Abélard, *Historia Calamitatum*, ch. 6.
8. Rémusat, C. de, *Abélard*, I, 39.
9. Abélard, *Calamitatum*, ch. 5.
10. Gilson, *La philosophie au moyen âge*, ed. 1922, I, 89.
11. Abélard, *Calamitatum*, ch. 5.
12. Rémusat, I, 30n.
13. Abélard, ch. 16.
14. Rémusat, I, 54.
15. Abélard, ch. 6. He does not say that he accompanied her.
16. Ibid., ch. 7; Lea, *Celibacy*, 269.
17. Abélard, ch. 7.
18. Ibid.
19. Poole, *Illustrations*, 125.
20. Abélard, *Dialectica*, introd. to Part IV, in *Ouvrages inédits*.
21. Ibid.
22. In Rémusat, II, 534-5.
23. *Ouvrages inédits*, p. clxxxvii.
24. Abélard, *Sic et non*, in *Ouvrages*, p. 16.
25. De Wulf, *Medieval Philosophy*, I, 201.

26. Abélard, *Calamitatum*, ch. 9.
27. Rémusat, I, 77.
28. Abélard, *Calamitatum*, ch. 9.
29. Ch. 11.
30. Rémusat, II, 197.
31. Ibid., 196; Gilson, *La philosophie au moyen âge*, ed. 1947, p. 291.
32. Ueberweg, I, 387.
33. Rémusat, II, 203.
34. Ibid., 205.
35. Abélard, *Calamitatum*, ch. 12.
36. Ch. 13.
37. Ch. 15.
38. Ch. 14.
39. In Scott-Moncrieff, *Letters of Abélard and Héloïse*, 53-6.
40. Ibid., p. 82.
41. P. 103.
42. Butler, *Women*, 68.
43. Prof. Paetow considered the "letters of Héloïse . . . the vain imaginings of a very vain man."—*Speculum*, Apr. 1927, 227. Prof. Gilson concludes in favor of their general authenticity; cf. his *Héloïse et Abélard*, Paris, 1938, and *Speculum*, July 1939, 394.
44. Abélard, *Scito te ipsum*, xiii-xiv, in Rémusat, II, 466.
45. Abélard, Ep. xiii, in *Cambridge Medieval History*, V, 798.
46. St. Bernard, Eps. 191 and 338, in Taylor, *Medieval Mind*, I, 417, and II, 385; Adams, H., 313; Ueberweg, 396.
47. Raby, *Christian Latin Poetry*, 321.
48. Rémusat, I, 260.

CHAPTER XXXVI

1. Duhem, *Système du monde*, III, 88.
2. De Wulf, *History of Medieval Philosophy*, I, 154.
3. Poole, *Illustrations*, 151.
4. Ibid., 185.
5. 108.
6. Thorndike, *Magic*, II, 58.
7. Ibid., 50; italics mine.
8. Ibid., 58.
9. Poole, 158.
10. Taylor, *Medieval Mind*, II, 402.
11. In Poole, *Illustrations*, 164.
12. In Adams, H., 292.
13. John of Salisbury, *Polycraticus*, v, 16; vi, 24; vii, 17.
14. V, 16.
15. IV, 3.
16. V, 6; vi, 6, 12, 25; iii, 15.
17. VIII, 20.
18. VII, 11.
19. Munro and Sellery, 460; Sarton, II(2), 860; De Wulf, *History of Medieval Philosophy*, I, 248.
20. Ibid.
21. Robertson, J. M., *History of Free Thought*, I, 325.
22. Lea, *Inquisition in Middle Ages*, I, 99.
23. Coulton, *Five Centuries*, I, 345.
24. Id., *Medieval Scene*, 111.
25. De Wulf, I, 189.
26. Lea, II, 319.
27. Gilson, *La philosophie au moyen âge*, ed. 1947, 384.
28. Rashdall, I, 354.
29. Lea, II, 320-3.
30. Renan, *Averroès*, 288.
31. Coulton, *Panorama*, 449.
32. Rashdall, I, 264.
33. De Wulf, II, 97.
34. Hearnshaw, *Medieval Contributions to Modern Civilization*, 145.
35. Lea, III, 440.
36. Castiglione, 330.
37. Coulton, *Panorama*, 461.
38. Gilson, *La philosophie*, ed. 1947, 564.
39. De Wulf, II, 96, 103.
40. In Gilson, ed. 1947, 564.
41. Ibid., 565.
42. 562.
43. 558; Renan, *Averroès*, 268.
44. Ibid., 273-5; Gilson, ed. 1947, 559.
45. *Cambridge Medieval History*, V, 822.
46. De Wulf, I, 144.
47. Id., *Philosophy and Civilization in the Middle Ages*, 51.
48. Gilson, *Philosophy of St. Bonaventure*, 8.
49. Sabatier, 41.
50. Gilson, *La philosophie*, ed. 1922, II, 9.
51. Sarton, II(2), 938; Taylor, *Medieval Mind*, II, 451.
52. Maritain, J., *The Angelic Doctor*, 32.
53. Ibid., 29.
54. 31; D'Arcy, *Thomas Aquinas*, 35.
55. Ibid., 51.
56. 46.
57. Grabmann, M., *Thomas Aquinas*, 32.
58. Wicksteed, P. H., *Dante and Aquinas*, 93; D'Arcy, 47.
59. Maritain, 45.
60. D'Arcy, 52.
61. De Wulf, *Philosophy and Civilization*, 166.
62. Maritain, 40.
63. Bevan, *Legacy of Israel*, 267.
64. Diesendruck, Z., *Maimonides and Thomas Aquinas*, 5.
65. Gilson, *La philosophie*, ed. 1922, I, 114.
66. In Sarton, II(2), 915.
67. Thomas Aquinas, *De caelo et mundo*, lect. 22, in Grabmann, 44.
68. Id., *Summa contra Gentiles*, i, 2.
69. Ibid.
70. Id., *Comm. on Aristotle's Metaphysics*, 333.
71. Id., *Summa Theologica*, I, xvi, 8.

72. Id., *Summa contra Gentiles*, i, 12.
73. Ibid., i, 3.
74. Id., *Summa Theologica*, II IIae, i, 5.
75. Ibid., II IIae, x, 7.
76. Id., *Quodlibeta*, II, *a*, 7, in Grabmann, 50.
77. Id., *Summa Theologica*, II IIae, i, 10.
78. Ibid., xxvi, 10.
79. Id., *De veritate*, ii, 10.
80. Id., *Summa contra Gentiles*, i, 11.
81. Id., *Summa Theologica*, I, ii, 3; *Summa contra Gentiles*, i, 16.
82. Ibid., i, 3; i, 30.
83. Id., *Summa Theologica*, I, lxxxiv, 7.
84. Id., *Summa contra Gentiles*, ii, 38.
85. Ibid., 35.
86. Ibid., iii, 23.
87. Id., *Quodlibeta*, xi, 4.
88. Id., *Comm. on II Sent.*, VIII, vi, 4, in Hopkins, C. E., *Share of Thomas Aquinas in . . . the Witchcraft Delusion*, 78.
89. Thomas Aquinas, *Summa Theologica*, I, cxvii, 3.
90. Ibid., lcxv, 3; xcv, 5.
91. Ibid., 4.
92. Id., *Comm. on Aristotle's Metaphysics*, 146, 157.
93. Id., *Summa Theologica*, I, lxxvi, 1.
94. In Walsh, *Thirteenth Century*, 444.
95. Thomas Aquinas, *Summa Theologica*, I, lxxv, 4.
96. Id., *Summa contra Gentiles*, ii, 72.
97. D'Arcy, 147.
98. Thomas Aquinas, *Comm. on Aristotle's Metaphysics*, 179.
99. Id., *Summa contra Gentiles*, ii, 49.
100. Id., *De anima*, iii, 7.
101. Id., *Summa Theologica*, I, lxxviii, 1-4.
102. Ibid., I, v, 6.
103. De Wulf, *History of Medieval Philosophy*, II, 25.
104. Thomas Aquinas, *De veritate*, xxiv, 1.
105. Id., *Summa contra Gentiles*, i, 1.
106. Id., *Summa Theologica*, I, lxxvi, 1.
107. Ibid., I IIae, iv, 6.
108. Id., *De veritate*, ii, 2.
109. Id., *Summa contra Gentiles*, iii, 27-31.
110. Id., *Summa Theologica*, II IIae, xiv, 3; xxvii, 1; xxxi, 4.
111. Id., *Comm. on Aristotle's Metaphysics*, 207; *Summa Theologica*, I, xcii, 1; xcix, 2; cxv, 3.
112. Ibid.
113. Ibid., I, xcii, 3.
114. Ibid., I, v, 3.
115. Ibid., II IIae, x, 11.
116. Ibid., II IIae, civ, 1; I IIae, xix, 5; *De veritate*, xvii, 5; *on IV Sent.*, 38.
117. Id., *Summa Theologica*, II IIae, x, 11.
118. Ibid., 10.
119. Ibid., 11.
120. Ibid., 8.
121. Ibid.

122. Ibid., II IIae, xi, 4.
123. Ibid., I IIae, xcvii, 3.
124. Ibid., I, ciii, 3.
125. Ibid., I IIae, cv, 1; cvii, 1.
126. Id., *De regimine principum*, i, 6.
127. Id., *Summa Theologica*, II IIae, lxvi, 2.
128. Ibid.
129. Ibid., II IIae, cxviii, 1.
130. Ibid., II IIae, lxvi, 7.
131. Ibid., II IIae, lxxvii, 4.
132. Ibid., II IIae, lxxviii, 1-4.
133. Ibid., I IIae, xcii, 1; cv, 1; II IIae, lvii, 3; lxx, 3.
134. Ibid., I IIae, vii, 1f; *Comm. on II Sent.*, xliv; *Summa contra Gentiles*, iv, 76; Hearnshaw, *Social and Political Ideas*, 102.
135. Thomas Aquinas, *Summa Theologica*, I, xxiii, 5.
136. Ibid., I, xxiii, 1, 3; *Summa contra Gentiles*, iii, 163, quoting Paul, Ephesians, i, 4.
137. Wicksteed, 266.
138. Gilson, *Bonaventure*, 7.
139. Thomas Aquinas, *Summa Theologica*, I, xii, 1, 7-8.
140. Ibid., II IIae, clxxix-clxxxii.
141. Sarton, II(2), 916.
142. Thomas Aquinas, *Summa contra Gentiles*, i, 1.
143. Sarton, II(2), 906.
144. Gilson, *Reason and Revelation*, 30.
145. Id., *La philosophie*, ed. 1947, 606.
146. De Wulf, *Medieval Philosophy*, II, 85.
147. Ibid., 84; Gilson, 603.
148. Quoted in Mill, J. S., *System of Logic*, pref.
149. Waddell, *Wandering Scholars*, 113.
150. Gilson, *La philosophie*, ed. 1922, I, 154.

CHAPTER XXXVII

1. James, *Women*, 120.
2. Thorndike, *Magic*, II, 8.
3. Ibid., 814.
4. Coulton, *Panorama*, 105.
5. Coulton, *Five Centuries*, I, 251.
6. Himes, 161.
7. Coulton, *Panorama*, 106.
8. Kantorowicz, 354.
9. Thorndike, *Magic*, II, 169.
10. Coulton, *Life*, I, 33.
11. Id., *Panorama*, 115.
12. Milman, I, 542.
13. Lea, *Inquisition in Middle Ages*, III, 424.
14. Hastings, *Encyclopedia of Religion and Ethics*, III, 421a.
15. Pauphilet, A., *Jeux et sapience du moyen âge*, 317n.
16. Coulton, *Social Life*, 526.
17. Singer, Chas., *Studies in the History and Method of Science*, I, 165.
18. Castiglione, 385.

19. Thorndike, *Magic*, II, 167.
20. Lacroix, *Science and Literature*, 208.
21. Thorndike, II, 319.
22. Ibid., 328.
23. 689, 949.
24. Sarton II(2), 1082.
25. Walsh, *The Popes and Science*, 52.
26. Sarton, II(2), 1082.
27. Cf. text in Walsh, *Popes*, app.
28. Ibid., 31, 43.
29. Pliny, *Natural History*, xxxvi, 26, 67.
30. Thorndike, II, 237.
31. Sarton, II(2), 611.
32. Thorndike, II, 449.
33. Sarton, II(2), 617.
34. Singer, *Studies*, II, 105.
35. Ibid., I, 18.
36. Thorndike, I, 775.
37. Addison, *Arts*, 78.
38. Giraldus Cambrensis, *Itinerary*, 6.
39. Augustine, *City of God*, xvi, 9.
40. Sarton, I, 516.
41. Joinville, 258.
42. Raby, *Christian Latin Poetry*, 356.
43. Sarton II(2), 575.
44. Kantorowicz, 360.
45. Mumford, 22.
46. Sarton, II(1), 21.
47. *Speculum*, Apr. 1941, 242.
48. Sarton, II(2), 1024.
49. Ibid.; Singer, II, 398.
50. Arnold, *Legacy of Islam*, 97.
51. Kantorowicz, 354.
52. Sarton, II(2), 1030.
53. Willoughby, W., *Social Justice*, 14.
54. Sarton, II(2), 1041.
55. Ibid., 1098.
56. 1037.
57. 1038-9.
58. Thorndike, I, 740.
59. Garrison, 148.
60. Sarton, II(1), 81, 242.
61. Garrison, 175.
62. Ibid., 181.
63. Castiglione, 381.
64. Bartholomaeus Anglicus, xlv, 4, in Coulton, *Social Life*, 502.
65. Castiglione, 384.
66. Kantorowicz, 356.
67. Lacroix, *Science*, 149.
68. Thorndike in *Speculum*, Apr. 1928, 194; Neuman, *Jews in Spain*, II, 110.
69. Garrison, 170.
70. Lea, *Inquisition in Middle Ages*, III, 52.
71. Ibid., 52-7.
72. Garrison, 144, 172.
73. Lacroix, *Science*, 154.
74. Garrison, 144.
75. Coulton, *Panorama*, 448.
76. Sarton, II(1), 72.
77. In Castiglione, 337.
78. Garrison, 153.

79. Castiglione, 388.
80. Walsh, *Thirteenth Century*, 345.
81. Sarton, II(1), 84.
82. Joyce, *Ireland*, 151.
83. Garrison, 186.
84. *Speculum*, Jan. 1937, 19.
85. Munro and Sellery, 266.
86. In Coulton, *Panorama*, 304.
87. Jackson, *Byzantine and Romanesque Architecture*, I, 142; Barnes, *Economic History*, 165.
88. Thorndike, II, 28f.
89. Ibid., 25.
90. 538.
91. Ibid.
92. 526, 551, 566, 568, 583.
93. Walsh, *Thirteenth Century*, 48.
94. Albertus Magnus, *De animalibus*, iv, 3, in Sarton, II(2), 938.
95. Sarton, II(1), 72.
96. Bacon, *Opus tertium*, ch. 17.
97. Id., *Opus maius*, I, xi.
98. Bridges, J. H., *Life and Work of Roger Bacon*, 125.
99. Bacon, *Opus tertium*, Brewer ed., p. 28.
100. Id., *Opus maius*, i, 10.
101. In Little, A. G., *Roger Bacon Essays*, 10.
102. *Opus maius*, i, 1.
103. *Compendium studii philosophiae*, ed. Brewer, p. 469.
104. *Opus maius*, ii, 12.
105. Ibid.
106. VII, 1.
107. Little, 117; Sarton, II(2), 805, 961.
108. *Opus tertium*, ch. 29.
109. *Opus maius*, iv, 16.
110. Ibid., iv, 4; *De coelestibus*, in Little, 15.
111. *Opus maius*, vi, 1.
112. Thorndike, II, 650.
113. *Opus maius*, iv, 4.
114. Bridges, 36; Little, 180.
115. Sloane MS., folio 83b, 1-2, in Little, 178.
116. *De secretis operibus artis et naturae*, ch. iv, in Little, 178.
117. Little, 321; En. Br., XI, 3.
118. In Bridges, 93.
119. *Opus maius*, v, 4.
120. *De secretis operibus*, in Singer, II, 397.
121. Singer, II, 132.
122. *Opus maius*, vii, *ad initium*.
123. Bridges, 387.
124. Ibid., 127.
125. 52.
126. De Wulf, *Med. Philosophy*, II, 139.
127. *Opus maius*, ii, 5.
128. *Compendium philosophiae*, in Coulton, *Life*, II, 55f.
129. *Opus tertium*, in Taylor, *Medieval Mind*, II, 523.
130. Ibid. in Coulton, *Five Centuries*, I, 135.
131. Taylor, II, 530.

132. Little, 26.
133. Ibid.
134. 28.
135. Taylor, II, 347.
136. Thorndike, II, 196.
137. Ibid., 203.

CHAPTER XXXVIII

1. Cf. Saxo Grammaticus, 89.
2. Joinville, 140.
3. Iacopo de Voragine, *Golden Legend*, pp. 48-56.
4. Mâle, 320.
5. Raby, *Secular Latin Poetry*, II, 289.
6. Haskins, *Renaissance*, 177.
7. Waddell, *Wandering Scholars*, 188.
8. In Raby, op. cit., 171.
9. Tr. by Helen Waddell in *Medieval Latin Lyrics*, 171.
10. In Van Doren, M., *Anthology of World Poetry*, 454.
11. In Waddell, op. cit., 278.
12. Bieber, M., *History of the Greek and Roman Theater*, 423.
13. Chambers, *Medieval Stage*, II, 44; Matthews, B., *Development of the Drama*, 115.
14. Mantzius, *History of Theatrical Art*, II, 5.
15. Matthews, 114.
16. Symonds, J. A., *Studies of the Greek Poets*, 310.
17. Raby, *Christian Latin Poetry*, 219.
18. Mantzius, II, 10f.
19. Thomas Aquinas, *Summa Theologica*, II IIae, clxviii, 3.
20. *Chanson de Roland*, ll. 1989-2009.
21. Sturluson, *Prose Edda*, #72, in Sigfusson.
22. Dasent, G., *Story of Burnt Njal*, 237-58.
23. In Butler, *Women*, 101.
24. *Cambridge Medieval History*, III, 128.
25. Cf. an excellent fictionalized biography of Peire Vidal in Cronyn, G., *The Fool of Venus*.
26. Arnold, *Legacy of Islam*, 17.
27. Lecky, *Morals*, II, 232.
28. *Speculum*, Oct. 1938, 380-7.
29. Tr. by Ezra Pound in Van Doren, 660.
30. Reese, *Medieval Music*, 232.
31. Fiedler, *Das Oxforder Buch Deutscher Dichtung*, 5.
32. Walther von der Vogelweide, *I Saw the World*, 41.
33. In Taylor, *Medieval Mind*, II, 56.
34. Walther von der Vogelweide, *Songs and Sayings*, 33.
35. Walther von der Vogelweide, *I Saw the World*, 16.
36. Taylor, II, 62.
37. Walther von der Vogelweide, *I Saw the World*, 69.

38. Walther von der Vogelweide, *Songs and Sayings*, 22.
39. Taylor, II, 58.
40. Prestage, *Chivalry*, 100; Coulton, *Life*, III, 77; Francke, *German Literature*, 111.
41. Kroeger, A. E., *The Minnesinger of Germany*, 4.
42. Schoenfeld, *Women of the Teutonic Nations*, 162.
43. Tr. by Arthur O'Shaughnessy in Van Doren, 663.
44. Chrétien de Troyes, *Arthurian Romances*, 1.
45. Ibid., 318, 309.
46. 287.
47. Wolfram von Eschenbach, *Parzival*, I, 67.
48. In Taylor, II, 8.
49. Wolfram, I, 188; vi, 937.
50. *Aucassin et Nicolette*, 6.
51. Ibid., 12. French text in Pauphilet, 444.
52. *Aucassin*, 13.
53. William of Lorris and Jean Clopinel de Meung, *Romance of the Rose*, ll. 8767f, 8858.
54. Lines 8511f.
55. 7849.
56. 1685.
57. 9267-70, 9725-47.

CHAPTER XXXIX

1. Tr. by D. G. Rossetti.
2. Asin y Palacios, *Islam and the Divine Comedy*, 271f.
3. Dante, *Purgatorio*, xxvi, 91f.
4. Sedgwick, *Italy*, II, 277.
5. Tr. by D. G. Rossetti.
6. Vossler, II, 152.
7. In Sedgwick, II, 291.
8. Cf. *Purgatorio*, xxx, 55.
9. Sedgwick, II, 283.
10. Vossler, I, 323.
11. Dante, *Inferno*, xv, 85.
12. Vossler, I, 164.
13. Dante, *La Vita Nuova*, ii, tr. Rossetti.
14. Ibid., iii.
15. xix.
16. xxvi.
17. xxxii.
18. *Paradiso*, xxx, 28.
19. Id., *Purgatorio*, xxxi, 60.
20. Symonds, *Dante*, 55.
21. Dante, *De monarchia*, iii, 11.
22. Ibid., 16.
23. *De monarchia*, pref., xxxiii.
24. Dante, *Eleven Letters*, vi.
25. Ep. vii.
26. Symonds, *Dante*, 79.
27. Ep. x.
28. Symonds, *Dante*, 92.
29. Letter to the Italian Cardinals (1314).

30. Dante, *Il Convito*, x, 5.
31. Ibid., vii, 4.
32. The authenticity of this letter has been unconvincingly questioned by Vossler, I, 76.
33. Dante, *Eleven Letters*, p. 197.
34. In Coulton, *Panorama*, 208.
35. Dante, *Paradiso*, end.
36. Ibid., x, 137f.
37. Cf. Blochet, *Sources orientales de la Divine Comédie*, Paris, 1901, and Asin y Palacios, *La escatologia musulmana en la Divina Comedia*, Madrid, 1919, translated as *Islam and the Divine Comedy*.
38. Asin y Palacios, 55-61.
39. Ibid., 171-3, 276-7.
40. Ibid., 232.
41. Rowbotham, 130.
42. Dante, *Inferno*, i, 1-3.
43. Ibid., i, 86.
44. Ibid., iii, 1-9.
45. Ibid., iii, 50.

46. Ibid., iv, 131-43.
47. Ibid., v, 121-42; tr. Cary.
48. Ibid., xix, 53.
49. Ibid., xxviii, 22-42; tr. Cary.
50. Id., *Purgatorio*, v, 13.
51. Ibid., vi, 76-93.
52. Ibid., xxvi, 112.
53. Ibid., xxvii, end.
54. Ibid., xxx, 37-9.
55. Ibid., xxxi, 49-51.
56. Ibid., end.
57. Id., *Paradiso*, iii, 85.
58. Ibid., xxvii, 22-8.
59. Id., *Inferno*, xviii, 57-63.
60. Id., *Paradiso*, ix, 127.
61. Id., *Inferno*, xxiv, 125.
62. Ibid., xxxiii, 152.
63. Ibid., xxxiii, 80-4.
64. Ibid., xxxiii, 148.

EPILOGUE

1. Coulton, *Medieval Village*, 290.

Index

The main reference to an item is italicized. The articles
a, the, al, and *el* are ignored in alphabetization.

About the Authors

WILL DURANT was born in North Adams, Massachusetts, in 1885. He was educated in the Catholic parochial schools there and in Kearny, New Jersey, and thereafter in St. Peter's (Jesuit) College, Jersey City, New Jersey, and Columbia University, New York. For a summer he served as a cub reporter on the New York *Journal*, in 1907, but finding the work too strenuous for his temperament, he settled down at Seton Hall College, South Orange, New Jersey, to teach Latin, French, English, and geometry (1907–11). He entered the seminary at Seton Hall in 1909, but withdrew in 1911 for reasons which he has described in his book *Transition*. He passed from this quiet seminary to the most radical circles in New York, and became (1911–13) the teacher of the Ferrer Modern School, an experiment in libertarian education. In 1912 he toured Europe at the invitation and expense of Alden Freeman, who had befriended him and now undertook to broaden his borders.

Returning to the Ferrer School, he fell in love with one of his pupils, resigned his position, and married her (1913). For four years he took graduate work at Columbia University, specializing in biology under Morgan and Calkins and in philosophy under Woodbridge and Dewey. He received the doctorate in philosophy in 1917, and taught philosophy at Columbia University for one year. In 1914, in a Presbyterian church in New York, he began those lectures on history, literature, and philosophy which, continuing twice weekly for thirteen years, provided the initial material for his later works.

The unexpected success of *The Story of Philosophy* (1926) enabled him to retire from teaching in 1927. Thenceforth, except for some incidental essays, Mr. and Mrs. Durant gave nearly all their working hours (eight to fourteen daily) to *The Story of Civilization*. To better prepare themselves they toured Europe in 1927, went around the world in 1930 to study Egypt, the Near East, India, China, and Japan, and toured the globe again in 1932 to visit Japan, Manchuria, Siberia, Russia, and Poland. These travels provided the background for *Our Oriental Heritage* (1935) as the first volume in *The Story of Civilization*. Several further visits to Europe prepared for Volume II, *The Life of Greece* (1939) and Volume III, *Caesar and Christ* (1944). In 1948, six months in Turkey, Iraq, Iran, Egypt, and Europe provided perspective for Volume IV, *The Age of Faith* (1950). In 1951 Mr. and Mrs. Durant returned to Italy to add to a lifetime of gleanings for Volume V, *The Renaissance* (1953); and in 1954 further studies in Italy, Switzerland, Germany, France, and England opened new vistas for Volume VI, *The Reformation* (1957).

Mrs. Durant's share in the preparation of these volumes became more and more substantial with each year, until in the case of Volume VII, *The Age of Reason Begins* (1961), it was so pervasive that justice required the union of both names on the title page. The name Ariel was first applied to his wife by Mr. Durant in his novel *Transition* (1927) and in his *Mansions of Philosophy* (1929) —now reissued as *The Pleasures of Philosophy*.

With the publication of Volume X, *Rousseau and Revolution*, the Durants have concluded over four decades of work.

KINGDOM OF
NORWAY

Oslo
Tönsberg

KING

Aberdeen

NORTH

Viborg
Calma

SEA
KINGDOM

Perth

Edinburgh
Berwick

Glasgow

IRELAND

KINGDOM OF SCOTLAND

Carlisle
Durham

JUTLAND

OF DENMARK

Lund

York

Rügen

ATLANTIC

ANGLO-NORMAN
COLONIES & EARLDOMS

Limerick

Dublin

Hamburg

Wexford

Leicester

Bremen

Utrecht

Brunswick

Stettin

KINGDOM OF ENGLAND

Northampton

Oxford

Milford

Gloucester

Bruges

Cologne

Rhine R.

HOLY

Posen

KIN

OCEAN

Exeter
KING
Southampton

Winchester
Canterbury

London

Ghent

Rouen

Trier

Mainz

KINGDOM OF GERMAN

Boulogne

Elbe R.

Prague

Reims

Metz

Nuremberg

ENGLISH CHANNEL

PARIS
FRANCE

Clairvaux

Speyer

Ratisbon

Orléans

Strasbourg

Tours

Vézelay

Vienna

Loire R.

Poitiers

Bourges

Basel

Constance

Salzburg

Augsburg

Danube R.

Bordeaux

Clermont

Lyon

Limoges

Geneva

ROMAN

Drave R.

SLAV

Santiago de
Compostela

Oviedo

Pamplona

K. OF

Milan

Turin

Pavia

Trent

Verona

CROATIA

Oporto

León

Burgos

K. OF
NAVARRE

Toulouse

Avignon

Po R.

Alessandria

Venice

BO

Coimbra

CASTILE

Duero R.

K. OF PORTUGAL

Valladolid

Salamanca

LEÓN

KINGDOM

Tudela

Saragossa

K. OF
ARAGON

Narbonne

Arles

Marseille

Genoa

Ravenna

ADRIATIC

Zara

Sp

Pisa

Florence

Ancona

Lisbon

Tagus R.

Toledo

Cuenca

Valencia

Barcelona

Tarragona

CORSICA

EMPIRE

APULIA

Rome

Guadiana R.

Calatrava

DOMINION

Córdoba

Guadalquivir R.

Murcia

SARDINIA

O.F. PETER

NORMAN KINGDOM
OF THE TWO SICILIES

Naples

Seville

Cadiz

Granada

Balearic Is.

Salerno

Palermo

Tar

Algeciras

Gibraltar

Tangier

Tenes

Algiers

M E D I T E R
R A N

CALABRIA

Reggio

Messina

Syracuse

Fez

Oran

OF THE ALMOHADS

Bona

Setif

Tunis

MALTA

Morocco

Kairwan

Gabes

Tripoli

Sirt